Eleventh Edition

STRATEGIC MANAGEMENT and BUSINESS POLICY

CONCEPTS AND CASES

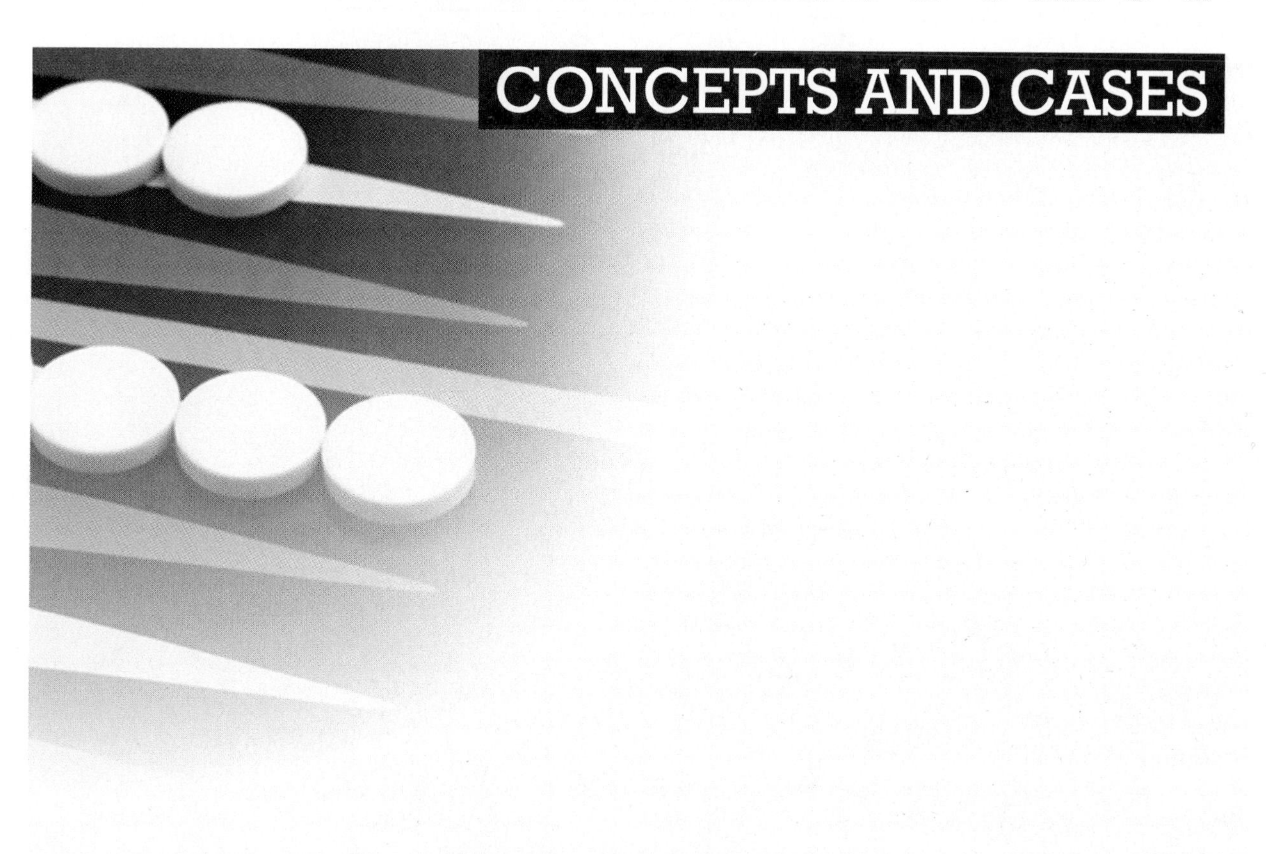

Eleventh Edition

STRATEGIC MANAGEMENT and BUSINESS POLICY

CONCEPTS AND CASES

Thomas L. Wheelen
Wheelen Strategic Audits

J. David Hunger
Iowa State University
St. John's University (MN)

Upper Saddle River, NJ 07458

Library of Congress Cataloging-in-Publication Data
Wheelen, Thomas L.
Strategic management and business policy : Concepts and cases / Thomas L. Wheelen, J. David Hunger. — Eleventh ed.
p. cm.
Includes bibliographical references.
ISBN-13: 978-0-13-232346-8
ISBN-10: 0-13-232346-X
1. Strategic planning. 2. Strategic planning—Case studies. I. Hunger, J. David, 1941- II. Title.
HD30.28.W43 2008
658.4'012—dc22 2007019734

Editor-in-Chief: David Parker
Acquisitions Editor: Bob Horan
Product Development Manager: Ashley Santora
Project Manager, Editorial: Claudia Fernandes
Assistant Editor: Denise Vaughn
Editorial Assistant: Kristin Varina
Media Project Manager: Ashley Lulling
Marketing Manager: Jodi Bassett
Marketing Assistant: Ian Gold
Associate Managing Editor: Renata Butera
Permissions Project Manager: Charles Morris
Senior Operations Supervisor: Arnold Vila
Operations Specialist: Michelle Klein
Art Director: Pat Smythe
Interior Design: Karen Quigley
Cover Design: Karen Quigley
Cover Illustration/Photo: Corbis/Jupiter
Composition: Aptara, Inc.
Full-Service Project Management: Aptara, Inc.
Printer/Binder: Courier/Kendallville
Typeface: 10/12 pt. Times Roman

Credits and acknowledgments borrowed from other sources and reproduced, with permission, in this textbook appear on appropriate page within text.

Pearson Education LTD.
Pearson Education Singapore, Pte. Ltd
Pearson Education, Canada, Ltd
Pearson Education–Japan
Pearson Education Australia PTY, Limited
Pearson Education North Asia Ltd
Pearson Educación de Mexico, S.A. de C.V.
Pearson Education Malaysia, Pte. Ltd.

10 9 8 7 6 5 4 3 2 1
ISBN-13: 978-0-13-232346-8
ISBN-10: 0-13-232346-X

Dedicated to

Kathy, Richard, and Tom

Betty, Kari and Jeff, Maddie and Megan, Suzi and Nick, Summer and Kacey, Lori and Dave, Merry and Dylan, and to Smokey the dog: Those for whom this book was written; and to Elizabeth Carey and Jackson S. Hunger—without whom there would be no book.

Special Dedication: *Thomas Wheelen expresses his admiration and indebtedness to* ***Dr. Harry Page,*** *Professor Emeritus of George Washington University. Dr. Page was a military leader, an excellent academic professor and administrator, a successful consultant and book author, and a true gentleman. Dr. Page was Tom Wheelen's dissertation chairman. Tom was his case grader for three years while in GW's doctoral program. Harry was an excellent role model for doctoral students. Tom ranks Harry among the top two or three men that he has had the honor to know.*

This book is also dedicated to the following Prentice Hall sales representatives who work so hard to promote this book:

KEVIN AARON
DAVID ALEVY
GEORGE ALEXANDRIS
TARA ALGEO
KAY ALLEN
HECTOR AMAYA
PETER ANCONA
LAUREN ANDERSON
KATHY APOGEE
DAVID ARMSTRONG
RACHAEL AVERY
LINDA BABAT
NICK BAKER
BRAD BALABAN
HAL BALMER
ALICE BARR
SHERRY BARTEL
JESSICA BARTELT
JOHN BARTIZAL
KELLY BELL
KEITH BELLOFF
CATHY BENNETT
BILL BEVILLE
JOAN BLASCO-PAUL
JODI BOLOGNESE
JENNIFER BOYLE
CHARLENE BREWSTER
JULIE BROICH
JEANNE BRONSON
JARED BRUECKNER
ROSARIO BURGA-PINEYRUA
RUTH CARDIFF
MEREDITH CHANDLER
BEVERLY CHANNING
TARYLL CONNOLLY
DONNA CONROY
GEORGE COOK
CANDACE COONEY
JONATHAN COTTRELL
CYNDI CRIMMINS
KASEY CROCKETT
AMANDA CROTTS
DAN CURRIER
ERIN DAVIS
SHEILA DAVITT
SCOTT DAY
CHRISTOPHER DELANEY
IAN DESROSIERS
GEORGE DEVENNEY
WENDY DiLEONARDO
DANA DODGE
KATE DOLDER
BARBARA DONLON
AMY DUNKELBERGER
MATTHEW EARLY
TRISH EICHHOLD
CHRISTINE ELLINGTON
SUE FACKERT
TREY FEIGLE
DENNIS FERNANDES
MARY FERNANDEZ
KATIE FITCH
RACHEL FLANNERY
LINDSEY FLEISCHHAUER
CANDAS FLETCHER
JULIA FORD
BRAD FORRESTER
EVELYN FORTE
MARK GAFFNEY
JOSIE GALL
JESSICA GAMPER
AMBER GARDNER
ERIN GARDNER
CHERYL GEHRLICH
SYBIL GERAUD
CODY GILES
CHIP GILLIKIN
GINA GIMELLI
CAROLYN GOGOLIN
KERI GOLDBERG
ERIC GONZALES
LARRY GRANEC
JAY GUTHRIE
LOIS HAIGH
GREG HAITH
SANDI HAKANSON
GINNY HARBOLD
PAUL HARROLD
PHOENIX HARVEY
CARTER HASEGAWA
SARA HAUGEN
THOMAS HAYWARD
JESSICA HECTOR
JENNIFER HEILBRUNN
CHRISTINE HENRY
KATHERINE HEPBURN
LYNN HICKS
JULIE HILDEBRAND
DAUNNE HINGLE
KATIE HINKLE
KENT HUGHES
CHRISTINE HUMENIUK
CATHERINE HUTCHINSON
ANDREA IORIO
HEATHER JACKSON
MAIREAD JACOBY
PAM JEFFRIES
BETH JOHNSON
TOM JOHNSON
DAVID JURMAN
CHERYL KABB
KIMBERLY KANDEL
SUSAN KAPFF
GIA KAUL
LAUREN KEIBLER
ROCK KENDZIOR
MOLLY KETCHERSIDE
KIMBERLY KIEHLER
WALT KIRBY
EMILY KNIGHT

MARY-JO KOVACH
GREG KRAMP
EMILY KREIDER
MICHAEL KRISANDA
NICOLE KUNZMANN
DAVID KURZAWA
NILA LABORIEL
DAN LaCHAPELLE
GINA LaMANTIA
REBECCA LEIDY
APRIL LEMONS
ANDREA LINN
TRICIA LISCIO
JONATHAN LONGINO
DAVID LOPEZ
CARY LUNA
KELLY MANN
LAURA MANN
KIMBERLY MANZI
LISA MARCH
PATRICIA MARTINEZ
DEEDEE MARTINSON
SUSAN MATOS
CARRIE MATTAINI
BROOK MATTHEWS
JACK MAYLEBEN
KAREN McFADYEN
BRIAN McGARRY
IRENE McGUINNESS
RYAN McHENRY
KATE McKAIN
RAY MEDINA
MATT MESAROS
ANDREA MESSINEO
LAURA MIDDLETON
MAREN MILLER
CHRIS MILLIKAN
WHITNEY MONAHAN
KATE MOORE
JULIE MOREL
KATIE MORGAN
WYATT MORRIS
JENNIFER MOYERS
EARL MURPHY
BETSY NIXON
TOM NIXON
KIM NORBUTA
BRIAN NORMOYLE
CELESTE NOSSITER
DEBBIE OGILIVE
KATIE O'NEILL
SUE PALMER
TINA PANAGIOTOU
MATTHEW PASTIER
TONI PAYNE
MIKE PERMAN
CARRIE PIZZUTI
DAVID PLOSKONKA
BELEN POLTORAK
JIM PORTER HAMANN
JILL PROMESSO
STACEY PROPPS
JULIE RESLER
MARY RHODES
TELVIS RICH
TORIAN RICHARDSON
DAVID RINGLER
DAN ROBERTSON
CHRIS ROGERS
TESSA ROHDE
MICHAEL ROSEMAN
DOROTHY ROSENE
KELLY ROSS
RICH ROWE
GARY SACHECK
SUSAN SCHAUM
KRISTEN SCHMITT
CORRINA SCHULTZ
SCOTT SHAFER
KRISTINA SHUBEL
COLLETTE SIEVER
LEA SILVERMAN
PHYLLIS SIMON
ANGIE SMAJSTRLA
ROSS SMANIA
ELIZABETH SMITH
JANELL SMITH
KARA SMITH
KATE SPENCE
JEFF SPENCER
MATTHEW SPIEGEL
BEN STEPHEN
ANGELA STONE
BETH STONER
SUSAN STOUDT-SMITH
CINDY SULLIVAN
DAN SULLIVAN
LORI SULLIVAN
STEPHANIE SURFUS
KARIN SWANSON
LORI SYPHER
CHRISTINA TATE
DAVID THEISEN
SARAH THOMAS
NICHOLE THOMPSON
AMANDA TILLEY
FRANK TIMONEY
EMILY TRUMBOLD
JULIE TURLEY
HUNTER WAGNER
BALLARD WARD
MARY FRANCES WEATHERLY
LIZ WEIR
SHANNON WEIR
ERIC WEISS
DANIEL WELLS
TIFFANY WENDT
KIMBERLY WERNER
MARK WHEELER
LIZ WILDES
ERIN WILLIAMS
MONICA WOLFF
CRAIG WORTMANN
CINDY YATES
GEORGE YOUNG
SHARON YOUNG
ANDREW ZORICH

Brief Contents

PART ONE Introduction to Strategic Management and Business Policy 1

Chapter 1 Basic Concepts in Strategic Management 1

Chapter 2 Corporate Governance 34

Chapter 3 Ethics and Social Responsibility in Strategic Management 55

PART TWO Scanning the Environment 71

Chapter 4 Environmental Scanning and Industry Analysis 71

Chapter 5 Internal Scanning: Organizational Analysis 104

PART THREE Strategy Formulation 137

Chapter 6 Strategy Formulation: Situation Analysis and Business Strategy 137

Chapter 7 Strategy Formulation: Corporate Strategy 163

Chapter 8 Strategy Formulation: Functional Strategy and Strategic Choice 188

PART FOUR Strategy Implementation and Control 213

Chapter 9 Strategy Implementation: Organizing for Action 213

Chapter 10 Strategy Implementation: Staffing and Directing 238

Chapter 11 Evaluation and Control 261

PART FIVE Other Strategic Issues 291

Chapter 12 Strategic Issues in Managing Technology and Innovation 291

Chapter 13 Strategic Issues in Entrepreneurial Ventures and Small Businesses 316

Chapter 14 Strategic Issues in Not-For-Profit Organizations 338

PART SIX Introduction to Case Analysis 353

Chapter 15 Suggestions for Case Analysis 353

PART SEVEN Cases in Strategic Management 1-1

Contents

Preface xxix

PART ONE Introduction to Strategic Management and Business Policy 1

Chapter 1 Basic Concepts in Strategic Management 1

1.1 The Study of Strategic Management 3

Phases of Strategic Management 3

Benefits of Strategic Management 5

1.2 Globalization and Electronic Commerce: Challenges to Strategic Management 6

Impact of Globalization 6

Global Issue: Regional Trade Associations Replace National Trade Barriers 7

Electronic Commerce 7

1.3 Theories of Organizational Adaptation 8

1.4 Creating a Learning Organization 9

1.5 Basic Model of Strategic Management 10

Environmental Scanning 10

Strategy Formulation 12

Strategy Highlight 1.1: Do You Have a Good Mission Statement? 13

Strategy Implementation 16

Evaluation and Control 17

Feedback/Learning Process 18

1.6 Initiation of Strategy: Triggering Events 18

Strategy Highlight 1.2: Triggering Event at Sun Microsystems 19

1.7 Strategic Decision Making 20

What Makes a Decision Strategic? 20

Mintzberg's Modes of Strategic Decision Making 20

Strategic Decision-Making Process: Aid to Better Decisions 21

1.8 The Strategic Audit: Aid to Strategic Decision Making 23

1.9 Conclusion 24

Appendix 1.A Strategic Audit of a Corporation 26

Chapter 2 Corporate Governance 34

2.1 Role of the Board of Directors 36

Responsibilities of the Board 36

Members of a Board of Directors 39

Strategy Highlight 2.1: Agency Theory Versus Stewardship Theory in Corporate Governance 41

Global Issue: POSCO Adds an International Director 42

Nomination and Election of Board Members 44

Organization of the Board 44

Impact of the Sarbanes-Oxley Act on U.S. Corporate Governance 46

Trends in Corporate Governance 47

2.2 The Role of Top Management 48

Responsibilities of Top Management 48

Strategy Highlight 2.2: CEO Hubris at Disney? 51

2.3 Conclusion 52

Chapter 3 Ethics and Social Responsibility in Strategic Management 55

3.1 Social Responsibilities of Strategic Decision Makers 56

Responsibilities of a Business Firm 57

Corporate Stakeholders 59

3.2 Ethical Decision Making 61

Strategy Highlight 3.1: The Johnson & Johnson Credo 62

Some Reasons for Unethical Behavior 62

Strategy Highlight 3.2: Unethical Practices at Enron and WorldCom Exposed by Whistle-Blowers 63

Global Issue: How Rule-Based and Relationship-Based Governance Systems Affect Ethical Behavior 64

Encouraging Ethical Behavior 66

3.3 Conclusion 68

PART ENDING VIDEO CASE: Newbury Comics, Inc. 70

PART TWO Scanning the Environment 71

Chapter 4 Environmental Scanning and Industry Analysis 71

4.1 Environmental Scanning 73

Identifying External Environmental Variables 73

Global Issue: Identifying Potential Markets in Developing Nations 79

Identifying External Strategic Factors 81

4.2 Industry Analysis: Analyzing the Task Environment 82

Porter's Approach to Industry Analysis 82

Industry Evolution 86

Categorizing International Industries 87

International Risk Assessment 87

Strategic Groups 88

Strategic Types 88
Hypercompetition 89
Strategy Highlight 4.1: Microsoft in a Hypercompetitive Industry 90
Using Key Success Factors to Create an Industry Matrix 91
4.3 Competitive Intelligence 92
Sources of Competitive Intelligence 93
Strategy Highlight 4.2: Evaluating Competitive Intelligence 94
Monitoring Competitors for Strategic Planning 94
4.4 Forecasting 95
Danger of Assumptions 95
Using Forecasting Techniques 96
4.5 The Strategic Audit: A Checklist for Environmental Scanning 97
4.6 Synthesis of External Factors—EFAS 97
4.7 Conclusion 99
Appendix 4.A Competitive Analysis Techniques 101

Chapter 5 Internal Scanning: Organizational Analysis 104
5.1 A Resource-Based Approach to Organizational Analysis 106
Core and Distinctive Competencies 106
Using Resources to Gain Competitive Advantage 107
Determining the Sustainability of an Advantage 108
5.2 Business Models 110
5.3 Value-Chain Analysis 111
Industry Value-Chain Analysis 112
Corporate Value-Chain Analysis 113
5.4 Scanning Functional Resources and Capabilities 114
Basic Organizational Structures 114
Corporate Culture: The Company Way 116
Global Issue: Managing Corporate Culture for Global Competitive Advantage: ABB Versus Matsushita 117
Strategic Marketing Issues 117
Strategic Financial Issues 119
Strategic Research and Development (R&D) Issues 120
Strategy Highlight 5.1: A Problem of Technology Transfer at Xerox Corporation 121
Strategic Operations Issues 123
Strategic Human Resource Management (HRM) Issues 125
Strategic Information Systems/Technology Issues 127

5.5 The Strategic Audit: A Checklist for Organizational Analysis 129

5.6 Synthesis of Internal Factors 129

5.7 Conclusion 131

PART ENDING VIDEO CASE: Newbury Comics, Inc. 134

PART THREE Strategy Formulation 137

Chapter 6 Strategy Formulation: Situation Analysis and Business Strategy 137

6.1 Situational Analysis: SWOT Analysis 138

Generating a Strategic Factors Analysis Summary (SFAS) Matrix 139

Finding a Propitious Niche 142

Global Issue: SAB Defends Its Propitious Niche 143

6.2 Review of Mission and Objectives 143

6.3 Generating Alternative Strategies by Using a TOWS Matrix 144

6.4 Business Strategies 145

Porter's Competitive Strategies 145

Strategy Highlight 6.1: Grim Reaper Uses Focused Differentiation Strategy 149

Cooperative Strategies 156

6.5 Conclusion 161

Chapter 7 Strategy Formulation: Corporate Strategy 163

7.1 Corporate Strategy 164

7.2 Directional Strategy 165

Growth Strategies 165

Strategy Highlight 7.1: Transaction Cost Economics Analyzes Vertical Growth Strategy 168

Strategy Highlight 7.2: Screening Criteria for Concentric Diversification 171

International Entry Options 171

Global Issue: Wal-Mart Looks to International Markets for Growth 172

Controversies in Directional Growth Strategies 174

Stability Strategies 175

Retrenchment Strategies 176

Strategy Highlight 7.3: Turnaround Strategy at IBM 177

7.3 Portfolio Analysis 179

BCG Growth-Share Matrix 179

GE Business Screen 181

Advantages and Limitations of Portfolio Analysis 182

7.4 Corporate Parenting 183

Developing a Corporate Parenting Strategy 184

Horizontal Strategy and Multipoint Competition 185

7.5 Conclusion 185

Chapter 8 Strategy Formulation: Functional Strategy and Strategic Choice 188

8.1 Functional Strategy 189

Marketing Strategy 190

Financial Strategy 191

Research and Development (R&D) Strategy 192

Operations Strategy 193

Global Issue: International Differences Alter Whirlpool's Operations Strategy 194

Purchasing Strategy 195

Logistics Strategy 196

Strategy Highlight 8.1: Staples Uses Internet to Replenish Inventory from 3M 197

Human Resource Management (HRM) Strategy 197

Information Technology Strategy 198

8.2 The Sourcing Decision: Location of Functions 198

8.3 Strategies to Avoid 201

8.4 Strategic Choice: Selecting of the Best Strategy 201

Constructing Corporate Scenarios 202

Process of Strategic Choice 207

8.5 Developing Policies 208

8.6 Conclusion 209

PART ENDING VIDEO CASE: Newbury Comics, Inc. 212

PART FOUR Strategy Implementation and Control 213

Chapter 9 Strategy Implementation: Organizing for Action 213

9.1 Strategy Implementation 214

9.2 Who Implements Strategy? 215

9.3 What Must Be Done? 216

Developing Programs, Budgets, and Procedures 216

Achieving Synergy 218

9.4 How Is Strategy to Be Implemented? Organizing for Action 219

Structure Follows Strategy 219

Stages of Corporate Development 220

Strategy Highlight 9.1: The Founder of the Modem Blocks Transition to Stage II 224

Organizational Life Cycle 224

Advanced Types of Organizational Structures 226

Reengineering and Strategy Implementation 229

Six Sigma 230

Designing Jobs to Implement Strategy 231

Strategy Highlight 9.2: Designing Jobs with the Job Characteristics Model 232

9.5 International Issues in Strategy Implementation 232

Global Issue: Multiple Headquarters: A Sixth Stage of International Development? 234

9.6 Conclusion 236

Chapter 10 Strategy Implementation: Staffing and Directing 238

10.1 Staffing 240

Staffing Follows Strategy 240

Selection and Management Development 243

Strategy Highlight 10.1: How Hewlett-Packard Identifies Potential Executives 244

Problems in Retrenchment 245

International Issues in Staffing 246

10.2 Leading 248

Managing Corporate Culture 248

Strategy Highlight 10.2: Admiral Assimilates Maytag's Culture 252

Action Planning 253

Management By Objectives 254

Total Quality Management 255

International Considerations in Leading 256

Global Issue: Cultural Differences Create Implementation Problems in Merger 258

10.3 Conclusion 258

Chapter 11 Evaluation and Control 261

11.1 Evaluation and Control in Strategic Management 263

11.2 Measuring Performance 263

Appropriate Measures 263

Types of Controls 265

Activity-Based Costing 266

Enterprise Risk Management 267

Primary Measures of Corporate Performance 267

Strategy Highlight 11.1: Eyeballs and MUUs: Questionable Performance Measures 269

Primary Measures of Divisional and Functional Performance 273

International Measurement Issues 276

Global Issue: Piracy: 15%–20% of China's Goods Are Counterfeit 277

11.3 Strategic Information Systems 278
Enterprise Resource Planning (ERP) 278
Divisional and Functional IS Support 279
11.42 Problems in Measuring Performance 279
Short-Term Orientation 279
Goal Displacement 280
11.5 Guidelines for Proper Control 282
Strategy Highlight 11.2: Some Rules of Thumb in Strategy 282
11.6 Strategic Incentive Management 283
11.7 Conclusion 285
PART ENDING VIDEO CASE: Newbury Comics, Inc. 288

PART FIVE Other Strategic Issues 291

Chapter 12 Strategic Issues in Managing Technology and Innovation 291
12.1 The Role of Management 293
Strategy Highlight 12.1: Examples of Innovation Emphasis in Mission Statements 294
12.2 Environmental Scanning 295
External Scanning 295
Internal Scanning 298
12.3 Strategy Formulation 299
Product Versus Process R&D 299
Technology Sourcing 300
Importance of Technological Competence 302
Global Issue: Use of Intellectual Property at Huawei Technologies 302
Categories of Innovation 303
Product Portfolio 305
12.4 Strategy Implementation 305
Developing an Innovative Entrepreneurial Culture 305
Organizing for Innovation: Corporate Entrepreneurship 306
Strategy Highlight 12.2: How Not to Develop an Innovative Organization 309
12.5 Evaluation and Control 309
Evaluation and Control Techniques 309
Evaluation and Control Measures 311
12.6 Conclusion 312

Chapter 13 Strategic Issues in Entrepreneurial Ventures and Small Businesses 316
13.1 Importance of Small Business and Entrepreneurial Ventures 317

Global Issue: Entrepreneurship: Some Countries Are More Supportive Than Others 318

Definition of Small-Business Firms and Entrepreneurial Ventures 319

The Entrepreneur as a Strategist 319

13.2 Use of Strategic Planning and Strategic Management 319

Degree of Formality 320

Usefulness of the Strategic Management Model 320

Usefulness of the Strategic Decision-Making Process 320

13.3 Issues in Corporate Governance 324

Boards of Directors and Advisory Boards 324

Impact of the Sarbanes-Oxley Act 324

13.4 Issues in Environmental Scanning and Strategy Formulation 325

Sources of Innovation 326

Factors Affecting a New Venture's Success 327

Strategy Highlight 13.1: Suggestions for Locating an Opportunity and Formulating a Business Strategy 329

13.5 Issues in Strategy Implementation 330

Substages of Small Business Development 330

Transfer of Power and Wealth in Family Businesses 332

13.6 Issues in Evaluation and Control 334

13.7 Conclusion 335

Chapter 14 Strategic Issues in Not-For-Profit Organizations 338

14.1 Why Not-For-Profit? 340

Global Issue: Which Is Best for Society: Business or Not-For-Profit? 341

Importance of Revenue Source 341

Sources of Not-For-Profit Revenue 342

Patterns of Influence on Strategic Decision Making 343

Usefulness of Strategic Management Concepts and Techniques 343

14.2 Impact of Constraints on Strategic Management 344

Impact on Strategy Formulation 345

Impact of Strategy Implementation 346

Impact on Evaluation and Control 346

14.3 Not-for-Profit Strategies 347

Strategic Piggybacking 348

Strategy Highlight 14.1: Resources Needed for Successful Strategic Piggybacking 349

Mergers 349

Strategic Alliances 349

14.4 Conclusion 350

PART SIX Introduction to Case Analysis 353

Chapter 15 Suggestions for Case Analysis 353

15.1 The Case Method 355

15.2 Researching the Case Situation 355

15.3 Financial Analysis: A Place to Begin 356

Analyzing Financial Statements 356

Global Issue: Financial Statements of Multinational Corporations: Not Always What They Seem 359

Common-Size Statements 359

Z-Value, Index of Sustainable Growth, and Free Cash Flow 360

Useful Economic Measures 360

15.4 Format for Case Analysis: The Strategic Audit 361

15.5 Conclusion 363

Appendix 15.A Resources for Case Research 365

Appendix 15.B Suggested Case Analysis Methodology Using the Strategic Audit 368

Appendix 15.C Example of a Student-Written Strategic Audit 371

Endnotes 376

PART SEVEN Cases in Strategic Management 1-1

SECTION A Corporate Governance, Social Responsibility, and Executive Leadership

case 1 The Recalcitrant Director at Byte Products, Inc.: Corporate Legality Versus Corporate Responsibility 1-9

(Contributors: Dan R. Dalton, Richard A. Cosier, and Cathy A. Enz)

A plant location decision forces a confrontation between the board of directors and the CEO regarding an issue in social responsibility and ethics.

case 2 The Wallace Group 2-1

(Contributor: Laurence J. Stybel)

Managers question the strategic direction of the company and how it is being managed by its founder and CEO. Company growth has resulted not only in disorganization and confusion among employees, but in poorer overall performance. How should the board deal with the founder of the company?

case 3 The Boeing Company's Board of Directors Fires the CEO 3-1

(Contributors: Kathryn E. Wheelen, Richard D. Wheelen, Thomas L. Wheelen II, and Thomas L. Wheelen)

new and exclusive

On February 25, 2005, Boeing's Chairman of the Board Lewis Platt was informed of a romantic affair between Boeing's President and Chief Executive Officer, Harry Stonecipher, and a female executive. What action should the board take?

SECTION B **Ethics and Social Responsibility**

case 4 The Audit 4-1

(Contributors: Gamewell D. Gantt, George A. Johnson and John A. Kilpatrick)

A questionable accounting practice by the company being audited puts a new CPA in a difficult position. Although the practice is clearly wrong, she is being pressured by her manager to ignore it because it is common in the industry.

case 5 Everyone Does It 5-1

(Contributors: Steven M. Cox and Shawana P. Johnson)

new

When Jim Willis, Marketing VP learns that the launch date for the company's new satellite will be late by at least a year, he is told by the company's president to continue using the earlier published date for the launch. When Jim protests that the use of an incorrect date to market contracts was unethical, he is told that spacecraft are never launched on time and that it is common industry practice to list unrealistic launch dates. If a realistic date was used, no one would contract with the company.

SECTION C **International Issues in Strategic Management**

case 6 GlaxoSmithKline's Retaliation Against Cross-Border Sales of Prescription Drugs 6-1

(Contributors: Sara Smith Shull and Rebecca J. Morris)

Double-digit increases in costs for health care and pharmaceutical drugs were driving a number of people in the United States to purchase cheaper drugs from Canadian pharmacies via the Internet. In response, GlaxoSmithKline, the second-largest pharmaceutical firm in the world, stopped supplying Canadian drug wholesalers that were exporting drugs to the United States. Portrayed as a powerful, mean-spirited company more concerned with profits than with the health and well-being of its consumers, the company struggled to repair its public image in both Canada and the United States.

case 7 Starbucks' International Operations 7-1

(Contributors: Sanjib Dutta and K. Subhadra)

The growing saturation of the U.S. market in coffee houses was driving Starbucks to look outside North America for continued growth. This presented a dilemma. Even though Starbucks' North American coffee houses continued to be profitable, the firm's international operations were losing money. Analysts felt that the company should rethink its entry strategy for international markets.

case 8 Turkcell: The Only Turk on Wall Street 8-1

(Contributor: Sue Greenfeld)

Having more than 60% of the Turkish market for mobile phones, Turkcell was the only Turkish company listed on the New York Stock Exchange. With three additional Turkish competitors entering the market and an onerous 66% tax burden, management wondered how it should position the company for success in the coming years. What strategies will enable Turkcell to become one of the largest mobile communications operators in Europe?

case 9 Guajilote Cooperativo Forestal, Honduras 9-1

(Contributors: Nathan Nebbe and J. David Hunger)

exclusive

This forestry cooperative has the right to harvest, transport, and sell fallen mahogany trees in La Muralla National Park of Honduras. Although the cooperative has been successful thus far, it was facing some serious issues: low prices for its product, illegal logging, deforestation by poor farmers, and possible world trade restrictions on the sale of mahogany.

SECTION D General Issues in Strategic Management

INDUSTRY ONE: INFORMATION TECHNOLOGY

case 10 Apple Computer and Steve P. Jobs (2006): Pixar Animation and Walt Disney Company 10-1

(Contributors: Moustafa H. Abedelsamad, Hitesh (John) Adhia, David B. Croll, Alan N. Hoffman, Charles E. Michaels Jr., and Thomas L. Wheelen)

new and exclusive

Apple, the first company to mass-market a personal computer, had been the darling of Wall Street in the 1980s, but by the mid-1990s, the company was in serious difficulty. After being expelled from the company in 1985, Steve Jobs returned as CEO in 1997 to reenergize the firm. The introduction of the iPod in 2001 catapulted Apple back into the spotlight. How can Apple continue its success and avoid becoming just another niche company? How dependent is the company on Steve Jobs?

case 11 McAfee 2005: Antivirus and Antispyware 11-1

(Contributors: Bethany Sweesy and Alan N. Hoffman)

new

Founded as McAfee Associates in 1989 to market anti-virus software, McAfee had successfully competed against market leader Symantec to become a major provider of computer security software. Microsoft's announcement that it was entering the security business rocked the industry. What strategy should McAfee pursue to continue as a market leader in the computer security industry?

INDUSTRY TWO: INTERNET COMPANIES

case 12 eBay, Inc. 12-1

(Contributors: Darrin Kuykendall, Vineet Walia, and Alan N. Hoffman)

By 2002, eBay had successfully captured the lion's share of the American online auction market and was attempting to do the same globally. Meg Whitman, its CEO, was considering multiple strategic alternatives with the goal of becoming the "World's Online Marketplace." In their emphasis on growth, management was aware that they needed to take care not to dilute brand value or company image, but instead to focus on leveraging the firm's core competencies.

case 13 Amazon.com: An E-Commerce Retailer 13-1

(Contributors: Patrick Collins, Robert J. Mockler, and Marc Gartenfeld)

Initially an online bookstore, Amazon.com successfully expanded to become the world's premier online retailer. Although it earned its first operating profit in 2002, the company still lost $150 million that year. Amazon was meeting its goals of increasing market share, greater product offerings, and overall sales growth, but was under growing pressure to produce consistent profits and prove that its business model worked financially over the long term.

case 14 Google: An Internet Search Service Company 14-1

(Contributors: Joseph Teye-Kofi, Robert J. Mockler, and Marc Gartenfeld)

new

Google, an online company that provided a reliable Internet search engine, was founded in 1998 by two Stanford Ph.D. students. Google soon replaced Yahoo as the market leader in Internet search engines. The issue by 2005 was how to develop an effective differentiating enterprise-wide strategy, especially for the company's internet search segment.

case 15 AOL Time Warner, Inc.—A Bad Idea from the Start? 15-1

(Contributors: Vineet Walia, Irene Hagenbuch Sanjana, Stacey Foster, and Alan N. Hoffman)

The $183 billion acquisition of Time Warner by the Internet provider American Online (AOL) in 2001 was criticized as one of worst mergers of all time. Even though revenues increased for the combined company in 2001 and 2002, both operating and net income dropped significantly. The stock price fell from $64.75 in 2001 to $9.90 in 2003. Management was examining various turnaround strategies to make the company profitable once again.

INDUSTRY THREE: RECREATION AND TRANSPORTATION

case 16 Harley-Davidson, Inc., 2006: The Building of a Second Century 16-1

(Contributors: Patricia A. Ryan and Thomas L. Wheelen)

new and exclusive

Harley-Davidson is a modern success story of a company that turned itself around by emphasizing quality manufacturing and image marketing. Encouraged by the high market demand for Harley's motorcycles in the 1980s and 1990s, competitors increasingly challenged Harley's dominant position. Meanwhile, Harley's sales were slowing as the Baby Boomers, the firm's target market, continued to age.

case 17 JetBlue Airways' Success Story 17-1

(Contributors: Sanjib Dutta and Shirisha Regani)

JetBlue Airways in 2003 was a three-year-old no-frills low-cost American airline modeled on Southwest Airlines. It earned profits when most in the industry were posting losses and facing bankruptcy. The company cut costs, but also added services, such as a personal television set and a comfortable leather seat for every passenger. Even though JetBlue focused on a market niche with little competition, analysts wondered if the company's success could be maintained as the company grew.

case 18 Carnival Corporation & plc (2006): Twelve Distinct Brands Serving Seven Continents 18-1

(Contributors: Michael J. Keefe, John K. Ross III, Bill J. Middlebrook, and Thomas L. Wheelen)

new and exclusive

With its "fun ships," Carnival Cruises changed the way people think of ocean cruises. The cruise has become more important than the destination. Through acquisition, Carnival expanded its product line to encompass an entire range of industry offerings. How can Carnival continue to grow in the industry it now dominates?

INDUSTRY FOUR: MASS MERCHANDISING

case 19 Wal-Mart Stores, Inc.: Under Attack (2006) 19-1

(Contributors: James W. Camerius and J. David Hunger)

new and exclusive

Wal-Mart's low prices, wide selection, and courteous service generated high sales and profits, but its stores tended to drive local stores out of business. The union contended that Wal-Mart underpaid its workers and offered them substandard benefits. Wal-Mart's hard stance with suppliers was portrayed by others as an abuse of power. Management faced lawsuits alleging discrimination against women and underage workers operating dangerous machinery. The company had become a lightning rod for any and all criticism against big business. What should management do?

case 20 The Home Depot, Inc. (2006): Executive Leadership 20-1

(Contributors: J. David Hunger and Thomas L. Wheelen)

new and exclusive

Home Depot is the world's largest home improvement retailer. CEO Bob Nardelli was hired from GE to replace the founders and to increase sales to the professional market. Nardelli's aggressive management style contrasted with the company's supportive corporate culture to generate conflict and employee turnover. With sales at an all-time high and solid earnings per share, why was the financial community downgrading Home Depot stock and why were the shareholders so upset?

INDUSTRY FIVE: SPECIALTY RETAILERS

case 21 Gap Inc.: A Specialty Apparel Retailer 21-1

(Contributors: Joanna Tochowicz, Robert J. Mockler, and Marc Gartenfeld)

Composed of Banana Republic, Gap, and Old Navy retail divisions, Gap, Inc., in September 2002 reported its 28th straight month of sales declines in stores open at least one year and a net loss for the year. New product lines in the Gap stores were no longer appealing to regular customers and failed to attract new ones. Overexpansion resulted in higher operating costs and in lower sales per individual store. What should management do to turn around the Gap division and thus return the company to profitability?

case 22 Tiffany & Co.: A Specialty Fine Jewelry Retailer 22-1

(Contributors: Marcia Chan, Robert J. Mockler, and Marc Gartenfeld)

Tiffany was a retailer, designer, manufacturer, and distributor of luxury goods and specialty fine jewelry. It was known for luxury brand quality, craftsmanship, and value jewelry, but faced a number of strong competitors. Even though the company had almost twice as many stores (82) outside the United States than it did within the United States (44), its international stores produced less than 42% of overall net sales. How could the company increase its international sales and thus boost its overall sales and profits?

INDUSTRY SIX: ENTREPRENEURIAL VENTURES

case 23 Oprah Winfrey—The Story of an Entrepreneur 23-1

(Contributors: A. Mukund and A. Neela Radhika)

One of the world's most well-known media personalities, Oprah Winfrey headed Forbes' *list of highest-paid entertainers. Not content with acting and hosting* The Oprah Winfrey Show, *Winfrey founded her own movie studio, Harpo Productions, to produce feature films and to publish her own magazine in partnership with Hearst Magazines. Despite being owner of a huge business empire, Winfrey could not read a balance sheet and tended to make sudden decisions on the basis of "gut feel."*

case 24 Inner-City Paint Corporation (Revised) 24-1

(Contributors: Donald F. Kuratko and Norman J. Gierlasinski)

Inner-City Paint Corporation makes paint for sale to contractors in the Chicago area. The founder's lack of management knowledge is creating difficulties for the firm, and the firm is in financial difficulty. Unless something is done soon, it may go out of business.

INDUSTRY SEVEN: MANUFACTURING

case 25 Hasbro, Inc. 25-1

(Contributors: Kristina Fogg, Robert J. Mockler, and Marc Gartenfeld)

new

Hasbro was the second-largest toy maker in the United States after Mattel, but was facing difficulty in 2005. Revenue in the U.S. toy industry had fallen from $318.9 million a year earlier to $263 million in 2005. Major retail outlets, such as Toys R' Us and FAO Schwarz, were in bankruptcy. Hasbro, the maker of Monopoly, GI Joe, My Little Pony, and Transformers, needed to develop an effective strategy if it was to survive and prosper against aggressive competition in a changing industry.

case 26 The Haier Group: U.S. Expansion 26-1

(Contributors: YongJun Lu, Robert J. Mockler, and Marc Gartenfeld)

new

Already a market leader in China, Haier was rapidly expanding into Europe and the Americas. The Chinese company faced a number of long-term decisions needed to build an American presence. The main problem for Haier was how to differentiate itself from General Electric, Whirlpool, Maytag, and Electrolux in major appliances and from Sony, Panasonic, Philips, and LG in electronics to achieve a winning competitive advantage.

case 27 Invacare Corporation, 2004 27-1

(Contributors: Walter E. Greene and Jeff Totten)

new

Invacare had grown from a minor player in home medical equipment to the world's largest manufacturer of home medical equipment, such as wheelchairs, respiratory equipment, hospital-type beds, and motorized scooters. Although the company was well positioned to take advantage of an aging population's growing need for health care, government regulations were making things difficult. The challenge for Invacare's executive team was to decide how to deal with restrictive government regulations and an increasingly competitive industry.

case 28 The Carey Plant 28-1

(Contributors: Thomas L. Wheelen and J. David Hunger)

exclusive

The Carey Plant had been a profitable manufacturer of quality machine parts until being acquired by the Gardner Company. Since its acquisition, the plant has been plagued by labor problems, increasing costs, leveling sales, and decreasing profits. Gardner Company's top management is attempting to improve the plant's performance and better integrate its activities with those of the corporation by selecting a new person to manage the plant.

INDUSTRY EIGHT: BEVERAGE/FOOD

case 29 Hershey Foods Company: Board of Directors and Stakeholders Conflict over Sale 29-1

(Contributor: Cynthia Clark Williams)

new

The CEO of the Hershey Trust Company (HTC), which owned 77% voting control of the Hershey Foods Company, was facing one of the most challenging decisions of his 25-year career as a trust officer: whether or not to recommend to his board that the American chocolate-making icon be sold. Hershey Foods' profit margins had been steadily declining against strong competition from competitors Nestle and Mars, but the firm's new CEOs had introduced a turnaround strategy.

case 30 Panera Bread Company: Rising Fortunes? 30-1

(Contributors: Ted Repetti and Joyce P. Vincelette)

exclusive

Panera Bread was a successful bakery-café known for its quality soups and sandwiches. Even though Panera's revenues and net earnings were rising rapidly, new unit expansion (419 new stores over three years) had fueled this growth. The growth rate of average annualized unit volumes and year-to-year comparable sales had actually dropped from 9.1% and 12.0%, respectively, in 2000 to only 0.2% and 0.5% in 2003. Growth was slowing. Management was now looking for new growth strategies.

case 31 Whole Foods Market (2005): Will There Be Enough Organic Food to Satisfy a Growing Demand? 31-1

(Contributors: Patricia Harasta and Alan N. Hoffman)

new

Whole Foods Market was the world's leading retailer of natural and organic foods, with 172 stores in North America and the United Kingdom. The supply of natural and organic foods was not keeping up with steadily increasing demand and could become a serious problem for the company. As the industry attracted more competitors, new prime locations were becoming harder to find. Whole Foods' CEO was uncertain about how to meet the company's aggressive growth targets.

case 32 Church & Dwight Builds a Corporate Portfolio 32-1

(Contributor: Roy A. Cook)

new

Church & Dwight, the maker of Arm & Hammer baking soda, has used line extension to successfully market multiple consumer products based on sodium bicarbonate. Searching for a new growth strategy, the firm has turned to acquisitions. Can management successfully achieve a balancing act based on finding growth through expanded uses of sodium bicarbonate while assimilating a divergent group of consumer products into an expanding international footprint?

SECTION E **Issues in Not-For-Profit Organizations**

case 33 A.W.A.R.E. 33-1

(Contributors: John K. Ross, III and Eric G. Kirby)

A.W.A.R.E is a not-for-profit therapeutic horseback riding organization in San Marcos, Texas. Increasing expenses and declining revenues create a cash flow problem. With the Executive Director retiring for health reasons, the board has to decide what must be done to save the organization.

SECTION F Mini-Cases

case 34 Intel Corporation 34-1

(Contributor: J. David Hunger)

new and exclusive

Although more than 80% of the world's personal computers and servers used its microprocessors, Intel was facing strong competition from AMD in a maturing market. Sales growth was slowing. Profits were expected to rise only 5% in 2006 compared to 40% annual growth previously. The new CEO decided to reinvent Intel to avoid a fate of eventual decline.

case 35 AirTran Holdings, Inc. 35-1

(Contributor: Maryanne M. Rouse)

AirTran (known as ValuJet before a disastrous crash in the Everglades) was the second largest low-fare scheduled airline (after Southwest) in the United States in terms of departures and along with Southwest the only U.S. airline to post a profit in 2004. The company's labor costs as a percentage of sales were the lowest in the industry. Will AirTran continue to be successful in this highly competitive industry?

case 36 Boise Cascade/OfficeMax 36-1

(Contributor: Maryanne M. Rouse)

Boise Cascade, an integrated manufacturer and distributor of paper, packaging, and wood products, purchased OfficeMax, third-largest office supplies catalog retailer (after Staples and Office Depot), in 2003. Soon thereafter, Boise announced that it was selling its land, plants, headquarters location, and even its name to an equity investment firm. On completion of the sale in 2004, the company assumed the name of OfficeMax. Can this manufacturer become a successful retailer?

case 37 Dell, Inc. 37-1

(Contributor: J. David Hunger)

new and exclusive

Dell was the largest PC vendor in the world, but its chief advantages—direct marketing and power over suppliers—were losing their punch. The percentage of 2005 PC sales via the phone and Internet fell in the United States as the sales through U.S. retail stores rose—a channel in which Dell was absent. By 2006, the once torrid-growth in PC sales had slowed to about 5% a year. How should Dell adjust to its changing environment?

case 38 Six Flags, Inc.: The 2006 Business Turnaround 38-1

(Contributor: Patricia A. Ryan)

new and exclusive

Known for its fast roller coasters and adventure rides, Six Flags had successfully built a group of regional theme and water parks in the United States. Nevertheless, the company had not turned a profit since 1998. Long-term debt had increased to 61% of total assets by 2005. New management was implementing a retrenchment strategy, but industry analysts were unsure if this would be enough to save the company.

case 39 H.J. Heinz Company 39-1

(Contributor: Maryanne M. Rouse)

Heinz, a manufacturer and marketer of processed food products, pursued global growth via market penetration and acquisitions. Unfortunately, its modest sales growth was primarily from its acquisitions. Now that the firm had divested a number of lines of businesses and brands to Del Monte Foods, analysts wondered how a 20% smaller Heinz would grow its sales and profits in this very competitive industry.

case 40 Lowe's Companies, Inc. 40-1

(Contributor: Maryanne M. Rouse)

As the second-largest U.S. "big box" home improvement retailer (behind Home Depot), Lowe's competed in a highly fragmented industry. The company had grown with the increase in home ownership and had no plans to expand internationally. With more than 1,000 stores in 2004, Lowe's intended to increase its U.S. presence with 150 store openings per year in 2005 and 2006. Were there limits to Lowe's current growth strategy?

case 41 Nike, Inc. 41-1

(Contributor: Maryanne M. Rouse)

Nike was the largest maker of athletic footwear and apparel in the world with a U.S. market share exceeding 40%. Because almost all its products were manufactured by 700 independent contractors (99% of which were in Southeast Asia), Nike was a target of activists opposing manufacturing practices in developing nations. Although industry sales growth in athletic footwear was slowing, Nike refused to change its product mix in 2002 to suit Foot Locker, the dominant global footwear retailer. Was it time for Nike to change its strategy and practices?

case 42 Outback Steakhouse, Inc. 42-1

(Contributor: Maryanne M. Rouse)

With 1,185 restaurants in 50 states and 21 foreign countries, OSI was one of the largest casual dining restaurant companies in the world. In addition to Outback Steakhouse, the company was composed of Carrabba's Italian Grill, Fleming's Prime Steakhouse & Wine Bar, Bonefish Grill, Roy's, Lee Roy Selmon's, Cheeseburger in Paradise, and Paul Lee's Chinese Kitchen. Analysts wonder how long OSI could continue to grow by adding new types of restaurants to its portfolio.

case 43 Movie Gallery, Inc. 43-1

(Contributor: J. David Hunger)

new and exclusive

Movie Gallery was the second largest North American video retail rental company, specializing in the rental and sale of movies and video games through its Movie Gallery and Hollywood Entertainment stores. Growing through acquisitions, the company was heavily in debt. The recent rise of online video rental services, such as Netflix, was cutting into retail store revenues and reducing the company's cash flow. With just $135 million in cash at the end of 2005, Movie Gallery's management found itself facing possible bankruptcy.

Additional Mini-Cases Available on the Companion Web Site at *www. prenhall.com/wheelen*

web case 1 Eli Lilly & Company 1-1

(Contributor: Maryanne M. Rouse)

A leading pharmaceutical company, Eli Lilly produced a wide variety of ethical drugs and animal health products. Despite an array of new products, the company's profits declined after the firm lost patent protection for Prozac. The FDA found quality problems at several of the company's manufacturing sites, resulting in a delay of new product approvals. How should Lilly position itself in a very complex industry?

web case 2 Tech Data Corporation 2-1

(Contributor: Maryanne M. Rouse)

Tech Data, a distributor of information technology and logistics management, had rapidly grown through acquisition to become the second-largest global IT distributor. Sales and profits had been declining, however, since 2001. As computers become more like a commodity, the increasing emphasis on direct distribution by manufacturers threatened wholesale distributors such as Tech Data.

web case 3 Stryker Corporation 3-1

(Contributor: Maryanne M. Rouse)

Stryker was a leading maker of specialty medical and surgical products, a market expected to show strong sales growth. Stryker marketed its products directly to hospitals and physicians in the United States and 100 other countries. Given the decline in the number of hospitals due to consolidation and cost containment efforts by government programs and health care insurers, the industry expected continued downward pressure on prices. How could Stryker effectively deal with these developments to continue its growth?

web case 4 Sykes Enterprises 4-1

(Contributor: Maryanne M. Rouse)

Sykes provided outsourced customer relationship management services worldwide in a highly competitive, fragmented industry. Like its customers, Sykes had recently been closing its call centers in America and moving to Asia in order to reduce costs. Small towns felt betrayed by the firm's decision to leave—especially after they had provided financial incentives to attract the firm. Nevertheless, declining revenue and net income caused the company's stock to drop to an all-time low.

web case 5 Pfizer, Inc. 5-1

(Contributor: Maryanne M. Rouse)

With its acquisition in 2000 of rival pharmaceutical firm Warner-Lambert for its Lipitor prescription drug, Pfizer had become the world's largest ethical pharmaceutical company in terms of sales. Already the leading company in the United States, Pfizer's purchase of Pharmacia in 2002 moved Pfizer from fourth to first place in Europe. Will large size hurt or help the company's future growth and profitability in an industry facing increasing scrutiny?

web case 6 Williams-Sonoma 6-1

(Contributor: Maryanne M. Rouse)

Williams-Sonoma was a specialty retailer of home products. Following a related diversification growth strategy, the company operated 415 Williams-Sonoma, Pottery Barn, and Hold Everything retail stores throughout North America. Its direct sales segment included six retail catalogs and three e-commerce sites. The company must deal with increasing competition in this fragmented industry characterized by low entry barriers.

web case 7 Tyson Foods, Inc. 7-1

(Contributor: Maryanne M. Rouse)

Tyson produced and distributed beef, chicken, and pork products in the United States. It acquired IBP, a major competitor, but had been the subject of lawsuits by its employees and the EPA. How should management deal with its poor public relations and position the company to gain and sustain competitive advantage in an industry characterized by increasing consolidation and intense competition?

web case 8 Southwest Airlines Company 8-1

(Contributor: Maryanne M. Rouse)

The fourth largest U.S. airline in terms of passengers carried and second largest in scheduled domestic departures, Southwest was the only domestic airline to remain profitable in 2001. Emphasizing high-frequency, short-haul, point-to-point, and low-fare service, the airline had the lowest cost per available seat mile flown of any U.S. major passenger carrier. Can Southwest continue to be successful as competitors increasingly imitate its competitive strategy?

Preface

Welcome to the 11th edition of *Strategic Management and Business Policy*! The chapters are the same as those in the 10th edition, but the cases are different. We completely revised five of your favorite cases and added 10 brand-new ones for a total of **15 new full-length cases**. This book contains a broad-based review of strategic management research and cases of well-known and not-so-well known companies dealing with complicated strategic issues. Enjoy!

How This Book Is Different from Other Strategy Textbooks

This book contains a **Strategic Management Model** that runs through the first 11 chapters and is made operational through the **Strategic Audit**, a complete case analysis methodology. The Strategic Audit provides a professional framework for case analysis in terms of external and internal factors and takes the student through the generation of strategic alternatives and implementation programs.

To help the student synthesize the many factors in a complex strategy case, we developed three useful techniques:

- **External Factor Analysis (EFAS) Table in Chapter 4**
  This reduces the external Opportunities and Threats to the 8 to 10 most important external factors facing management.
- **Internal Factor Analysis (IFAS) Table in Chapter 5**
  This reduces the internal Strengths and Weaknesses to the 8 to 10 most important internal factors facing management.
- **Strategic Factor Analysis Summary (SFAS) Matrix in Chapter 6**
  This condenses the 16 to 20 factors generated in the EFAS and IFAS Tables into the 8 to 10 most important (strategic) factors facing the company. These strategic factors become the basis for generating alternatives and a recommendation for the company's future direction.

Suggestions for Case Analysis are provided in **Appendix 15.B (end of Chapter 15)** and contain step-by-step procedures for how to use the Strategic Audit in analyzing a case. This appendix includes an example of a student-written Strategic Audit. Thousands of students around the world have applied this methodology to case analysis with great success. ***The Case Instructor's Manual*** contains examples of student-written Strategic Audits for each of the comprehensive strategy cases.

Features New to This Eleventh Edition

NEW CASES: BOTH FULL-LENGTH AND MINI-LENGTH

Fifteen full-length cases and four mini-cases are new to this edition for a total of 19 new cases. Together with 18 full-length and 6 mini-cases cases carried forward from past editions, this edition contains a total of 43 cases.

New Full-Length Cases

Fifteen full-length cases are new to this edition. Ten of them are brand-new cases. Five of them are newly revised versions of favorites from the 10th edition. Of the 33 full-length cases appearing in this book, nine are exclusive and do not appear in other books.

- Two of the new cases deal with corporate governance (**Boeing**) and ethics (**Everyone Does It**).
- Three of the new cases are in information technology (**Apple** and **McAfee**) and the Internet (**Google**).
- Two new cases are in transportation and leisure (**Harley-Davidson** and **Carnival Cruise**).
- Two new cases are of well-known mass merchandisers (**Wal-Mart** and **Home Depot**) that have been having some recent difficulties.
- Three new manufacturing cases deal with products ranging from toys (**Hasbro**) to major appliances (**Haier**) and wheelchairs (**Invacare**).
- Three new cases come from the food industry (**Hershey**, **Whole Foods**, and **Church & Dwight**).

New Mini-cases

Four of the 10 mini-cases are new. They can be quickly read for class discussion or used as Internet research assignments for students to update. The new mini-cases deal with companies in a wide range of industries from computers (**Intel** and **Dell**) to entertainment (**Movie Gallery** and **Six Flags**). Of the 10 mini-cases appearing in this edition, four are exclusive and do not appear in other books. In addition to the four new mini-cases are six carried forward from the 10th edition: AirTran, Office Max, H. J. Heinz, Lowe's, Nike, and Outback Steakhouse.

(Additional mini-cases are provided on the Internet at www.prenhall.com/wheelen. They include Eli Lilly, Tech Data, Stryker Corporation, Sykes Enterprises, Pfizer, Williams-Sonoma, Tyson Foods, and Southwest Airlines.)

Time-Tested Features

This edition contains many of the same features and content that helped make previous editions successful. Some of the features are the following:

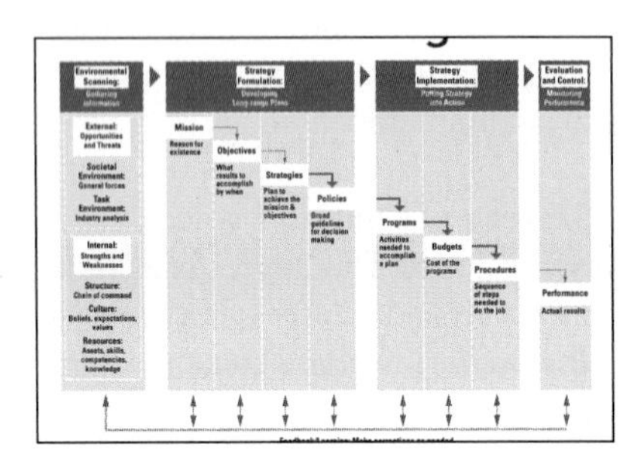

- A **strategic management model** runs throughout the first 11 chapters as a unifying concept. (Explained in ***Chapter 1***) ◀

- The **strategic audit**, a way to operationalize the strategic decision-making process, serves as a checklist in case analysis. (***Chapter 1***) ▶

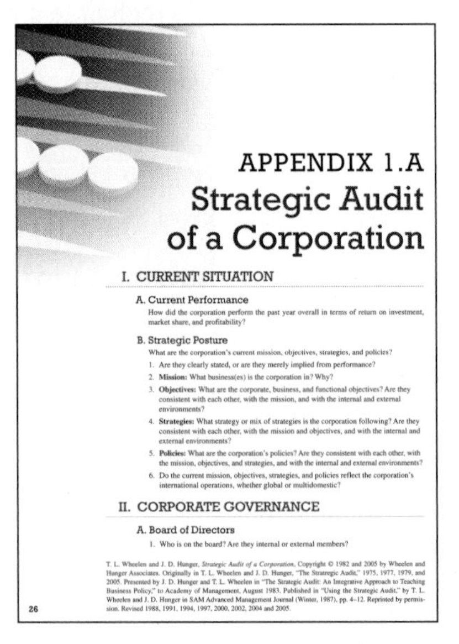

APPENDIX 1.A
Strategic Audit of a Corporation

I. CURRENT SITUATION

A. Current Performance

How did the corporation perform the past year overall in terms of return on investment, market share, and profitability?

B. Strategic Posture

What are the corporation's current mission, objectives, strategies, and policies?

1. Are they clearly stated, or are they merely implied from performance?
2. **Mission:** What business(es) is the corporation in? Why?
3. **Objectives:** What are the corporate, business, and functional objectives? Are they consistent with each other, with the mission, and with the internal and external environments?
4. **Strategies:** What strategy or mix of strategies is the corporation following? Are they consistent with each other, with the mission and objectives, and with the internal and external environments?
5. **Policies:** What are the corporation's policies? Are they consistent with each other, with the mission, objectives, and strategies, and with the internal and external environments?
6. Do the current mission, objectives, strategies, and policies reflect the corporation's international operations, whether global or multidomestic?

II. CORPORATE GOVERNANCE

A. Board of Directors

1. Who is on the board? Are they internal or external members?

T. L. Wheelen and J. D. Hunger, *Strategic Audit of a Corporation*, Copyright © 1982 and 2005 by Wheelen and Hunger Associates. Originally in T. L. Wheelen and J. D. Hunger, "The Stratregic Audit," 1975, 1977, 1979, and 2005. Presented by J. D. Hunger and T. L. Wheelen in "The Strategic Audit: An Integrative Approach to Teaching Business Policy," to Academy of Management, August 1983. Published in "Using the Strategic Audit," by T. L. Wheelen and J. D. Hunger in SAM Advanced Management Journal (Winter, 1987), pp. 4–12. Reprinted by permission. Revised 1988, 1991, 1994, 1997, 2000, 2002, 2004 and 2005.

26

- **Corporate governance** is examined in terms of the roles, responsibilities, and interactions of top management and the board of directors and includes the impact of the Sarbanes-Oxley Act. (***Chapter 2***) ▶

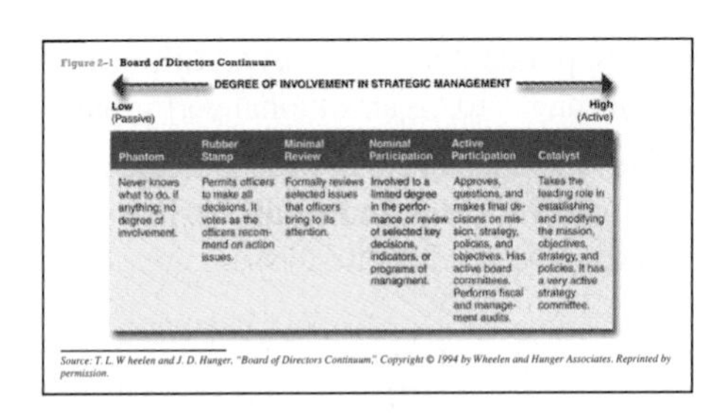

Figure 2–1 **Board of Directors Continuum**

DEGREE OF INVOLVEMENT IN STRATEGIC MANAGEMENT

Low (Passive) ← → High (Active)

Phantom	Rubber Stamp	Minimal Review	Nominal Participation	Active Participation	Catalyst
Never knows what to do, if anything; no degree of involvement.	Permits officers to make all decisions. It votes as the officers recommend on action issues.	Formally reviews selected issues that officers bring to its attention.	Involved to a limited degree in the performance or review of selected key decisions, indicators, or programs of managment.	Approves, questions, and makes final decisions on mission, strategy, policies, and objectives. Has active board committees. Performs fiscal and management audits.	Takes the leading role in establishing and modifying the mission, objectives, strategy, and policies. It has a very active strategy committee.

Source: T. L. W heelen and J. D. Hunger, "Board of Directors Continuum," Copyright © 1994 by Wheelen and Hunger Associates. Reprinted by permission.

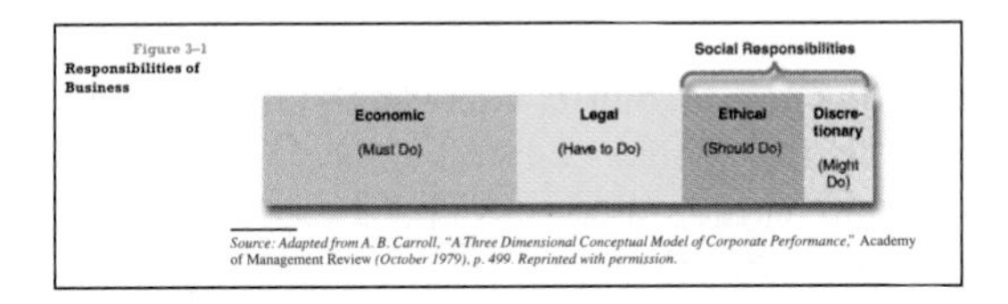

Source: Adapted from A. B. Carroll, "A Three Dimensional Conceptual Model of Corporate Performance," Academy of Management Review (October 1979), p. 499. Reprinted with permission.

- **Social responsibility and managerial ethics** are examined in detail in terms of how they affect strategic decision making. They include the process of stakeholder analysis and the concept of social capital. (***Chapter 3***) ◀

- Equal emphasis is placed on **environmental scanning** of the societal environment as well as on the task environment. Topics include forecasting and Miles and Snow's typology in addition to competitive intelligence techniques and Porter's industry analysis. (***Chapter 4***) ▶

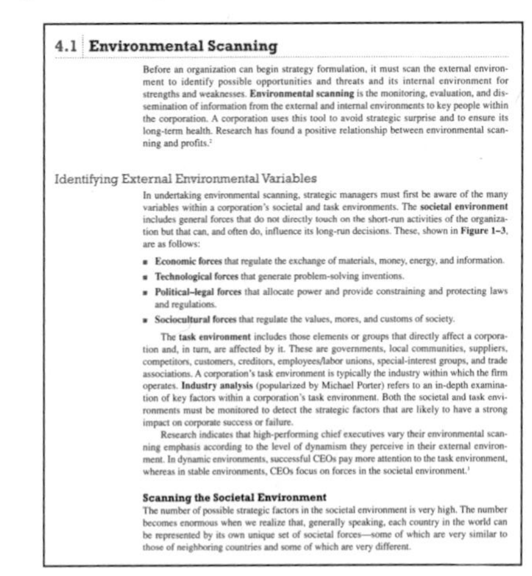

4.1 Environmental Scanning

Before an organization can begin strategy formulation, it must scan the external environment to identify possible opportunities and threats and its internal environment for strengths and weaknesses. **Environmental scanning** is the monitoring, evaluation, and dissemination of information from the external and internal environments to key people within the corporation. A corporation uses this tool to avoid strategic surprise and to ensure its long-term health. Research has found a positive relationship between environmental scanning and profits.[2]

Identifying External Environmental Variables

In undertaking environmental scanning, strategic managers must first be aware of the many variables within a corporation's societal and task environments. The **societal environment** includes general forces that do not directly touch on the short-run activities of the organization but that can, and often do, influence its long-run decisions. These, shown in **Figure 1–3**, are as follows:

- **Economic forces** that regulate the exchange of materials, money, energy, and information.
- **Technological forces** that generate problem-solving inventions.
- **Political–legal forces** that allocate power and provide constraining and protecting laws and regulations.
- **Sociocultural forces** that regulate the values, mores, and customs of society.

The **task environment** includes those elements or groups that directly affect a corporation and, in turn, are affected by it. These are governments, local communities, suppliers, competitors, customers, creditors, employees/labor unions, special-interest groups, and trade associations. A corporation's task environment is typically the industry within which the firm operates. **Industry analysis** (popularized by Michael Porter) refers to an in-depth examination of key factors within a corporation's task environment. Both the societal and task environments must be monitored to detect the strategic factors that are likely to have a strong impact on corporate success or failure.

Research indicates that high-performing chief executives vary their environmental scanning emphasis according to the level of dynamism they perceive in their external environment. In dynamic environments, successful CEOs pay more attention to the task environment, whereas in stable environments, CEOs focus on forces in the societal environment.[3]

Scanning the Societal Environment

The number of possible strategic factors in the societal environment is very high. The number becomes enormous when we realize that, generally speaking, each country in the world can be represented by its own unique set of societal forces—some of which are very similar to those of neighboring countries and some of which are very different.

- **Core and distinctive competencies** are examined within the framework of the resource-based view of the firm. (***Chapter 5***)
- **Organizational analysis** includes material on business models, supply chain management, and corporate reputation. (***Chapter 5***)
- Internal and external strategic factors are emphasized through the use of specially-designed **EFAS, IFAS**, and **SFAS tables**. (***Chapters 4, 5, and 6***)
- **Functional strategies** are examined in light of **outsourcing.** (***Chapter 8***)

- Two chapters deal with issues in **strategy implementation**, such as organizational and job design plus strategy-manager fit, action planning, corporate culture, and international strategic alliances. (***Chapters 9 and 10***) ◀

- A separate chapter on **evaluation and control** explains the importance of measurement and incentives to organizational performance. (***Chapter 11***)
- Special chapters deal with strategic issues in **managing technology and innovation**, **entrepreneurial ventures and small businesses**, and **not-for-profit organizations**. (***Chapters 12, 13, and 14***, respectively) These issues are often ignored by other strategy textbooks.

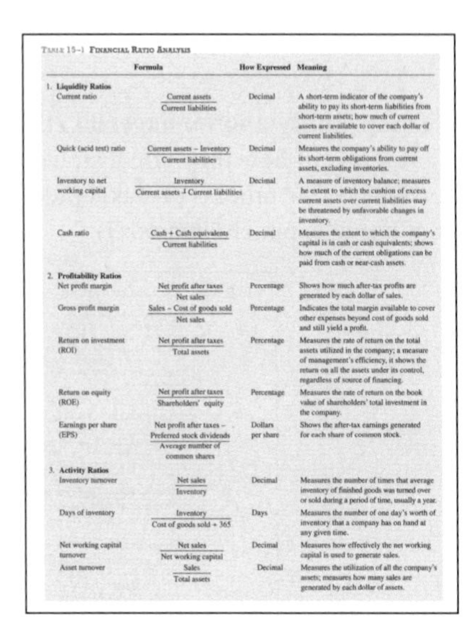

TABLE 15–1 FINANCIAL RATIO ANALYSIS

	Formula	How Expressed	Meaning
1. Liquidity Ratios			
Current ratio	$\frac{\text{Current assets}}{\text{Current liabilities}}$	Decimal	A short-term indicator of the company's ability to pay its short-term liabilities from short-term assets; how much of current assets are available to cover each dollar of current liabilities.
Quick (acid test) ratio	$\frac{\text{Current assets} - \text{Inventory}}{\text{Current liabilities}}$	Decimal	Measures the company's ability to pay off its short-term obligations from current assets, excluding inventories.
Inventory to net working capital	$\frac{\text{Inventory}}{\text{Current assets} - \text{Current liabilities}}$	Decimal	A measure of inventory balance; measures he extent to which the cushion of excess current assets over current liabilities may be threatened by unfavorable changes in inventory.
Cash ratio	$\frac{\text{Cash} + \text{Cash equivalents}}{\text{Current liabilities}}$	Decimal	Measures the extent to which the company's capital is in cash or cash equivalents; shows how much of the current obligations can be paid from cash or near-cash assets.
2. Profitability Ratios			
Net profit margin	$\frac{\text{Net profit after taxes}}{\text{Net sales}}$	Percentage	Shows how much after-tax profits are generated by each dollar of sales.
Gross profit margin	$\frac{\text{Sales} - \text{Cost of goods sold}}{\text{Net sales}}$	Percentage	Indicates the total margin available to cover other expenses beyond cost of goods sold and still yield a profit.
Return on investment (ROI)	$\frac{\text{Net profit after taxes}}{\text{Total assets}}$	Percentage	Measures the rate of return on the total assets utilized in the company; a measure of management's efficiency, it shows the return on all the assets under its control, regardless of source of financing.
Return on equity (ROE)	$\frac{\text{Net profit after taxes}}{\text{Shareholders' equity}}$	Percentage	Measures the rate of return on the book value of shareholders' total investment in the company.
Earnings per share (EPS)	$\frac{\text{Net profit after taxes} - \text{Preferred stock dividends}}{\text{Average number of common shares}}$	Dollars per share	Shows the after-tax earnings generated for each share of common stock.
3. Activity Ratios			
Inventory turnover	$\frac{\text{Net sales}}{\text{Inventory}}$	Decimal	Measures the number of times that average inventory of finished goods was turned over or sold during a period of time, usually a year.
Days of inventory	$\frac{\text{Inventory}}{\text{Cost of goods sold} \div 365}$	Days	Measures the number of one day's worth of inventory that a company has on hand at any given time.
Net working capital turnover	$\frac{\text{Net sales}}{\text{Net working capital}}$	Decimal	Measures how effectively the net working capital is used to generate sales.
Asset turnover	$\frac{\text{Sales}}{\text{Total assets}}$	Decimal	Measures the utilization of all the company's assets; measures how many sales are generated by each dollar of assets.

- **Suggestions for in-depth case analysis** provide a complete listing of financial ratios, recommendations for oral and written analysis, and ideas for further research. (***Chapter 15***)

Figure 15–1 **Strategic Audit Worksheet**

Strategic Audit Heading	Analysis (+) Factors	Analysis (–) Factors	Comments
I. Current Situation			
A. Past Corporate Performance Indexes			
B. Strategic Posture: Current Mission, Current Objectives, Current Strategies, Current Policies			
SWOT Analysis Begins:			
II. Corporate Governance			
A. Board of Directors			
B. Top Management			
III. External Environment (EFAS): Opportunities and Threats (SWOT)			
A. Societal Environment			
B. Task Environment (Industry Analysis)			
IV. Internal Environment (IFAS): Strengths and Weaknesses (SWOT)			
A. Corporate Structure			
B. Corporate Culture			
C. Corporate Resources			
1. Marketing			
2. Finance			
3. Research and Development			
4. Operations and Logistics			
5. Human Resources			
6. Information Systems			
V. Analysis of Strategic Factors (SFAS)			
A. Key Internal and External Strategic Factors (SWOT)			
B. Review of Mission and Objectives			
SWOT Analysis Ends. Recommendation Begins:			
VI. Alternatives and Recommendations			
A. Strategic Alternatives—pros and cons			
B. Recommended Strategy			
VII. Implementation			
VIII. Evaluation and Control			

Note: See the complete Strategic Audit on pages 26–33. It lists the pages in the book that discuss each of the eight headings.

Source: T. L. Wheelen and J. D. Hunger, "Strategic Audit Worksheet." Copyright © 1985, 1986, 1987, 1988, 1989, and 2005 by T. L. Wheelen. Copyright © 1989 and 2005 by Wheelen and Hunger Associates. Revised 1991, 1994, and 1997. Reprined by permission. Additional copies available for classroom use in Part D of *Case Instructors Manual* and on the Prentice Hall Web site (www.prenhall.com/wheelen).

362

- The **Strategic Audit Worksheet** is based on the time-tested strategic audit and is designed to help students organize and structure daily case preparation in a brief period of time. The worksheet works exceedingly well for checking the level of daily student case preparation—especially for open class discussions of cases. (***Chapter 15***)

Strategic Practice Exercise

Levi Strauss & Company, the California gold rush outfitter whose trademark blue jeans have been an American clothing staple for generations, had fallen on hard times by 2004 and needed a change in strategic direction. At the end of 2003, the company had undergone seven straight years of declining sales after its sales peaked in 1996 at $7.1 billion. Although the company earned $311 million in operating profits in 2003 on $4 billion in revenues, it posted a record $349 million in net losses, largely due to non-cash charges for accounting purposes. The firm's global workforce had shrunk from more than 37,000 in 1996 to around 12,000. According to Walter Loeb, a retail analyst, "There was a time when Levi's was the fashion garment of the day. The exclusivity of the Levi's brand is no longer as important to customers."

Management responded to the decline by moving its manufacturing plants offshore and by introducing a new line of discount jeans. In the early 1980s, the company had 63 manufacturing plants in the United States. Beset by strong competition in the 1990s, the company had hoped to cut costs and invigorate sales by steadily shifting production to overseas contractors. On January 8, 2004, the company closed its San Antonio, Texas, plant, its last U.S. plant. Levi's continued to base its headquarters staff, designers, and sales employees in the United States. According to company spokesperson Jeff Beckman, the company's identity would also stay in the United States. "We're still an American brand, but we're also a brand and a company whose products have been adopted by consumers around the world. We have to operate as a global company," said Beckman.

In July 2003, the company introduced its new line of Signature jeans at Wal-Mart, priced at $21 to $23 a pair. The company had traditionally sold its products in department stores, where prices ranged from $35 for the 501 jeans to $44 for 599 Giant Fit baggy jeans. In 2004, management was considering selling its $1 billion Dockers casual-pants unit in order to reduce its $2.2 billion debt and to refocus on the jeans business.[a]

1. What is Levi's problem?
2. What do you think of its actions to completely outsource its manufacturing overseas and to introduce a new low-priced line of jeans in discount stores?
3. Should it sell its Dockers unit?
4. What would you recommend to Levi's top management to boost company sales and profits?

- An **experiential exercise** focusing on the material covered in each chapter helps the reader to apply strategic concepts to an actual situation.

- A list of **key terms** and the pages in which they are discussed enable the reader to keep track of important concepts as they are introduced in each chapter.
- A **glossary** of key terms and definitions helps the student to find and learn the important terms in the field. This is the only strategy book with this feature.
- **Learning objectives** begin each chapter.
- **Strategy Bits** end each chapter with some interesting statistics.
- **Timely, well-researched, and class-tested cases** deal with interesting companies and industries. Many of the cases are about well-known, publicly held corporations—ideal subjects for further research by students wishing to "update" the cases.

Both the text and the cases have been class-tested in strategy courses and revised based on feedback from students and instructors. The first 11 chapters are organized around a strategic management model that begins each chapter and provides a structure for both content and case analysis. We emphasize those concepts that have proven to be most useful in understanding strategic decision making and in conducting case analysis. Our goal was to make the text as comprehensive as possible without getting bogged down in any one area. Endnote references are provided for those who wish to learn more about any particular topic. All cases are about actual organizations. The firms range in size from large, established multinationals to small, entrepreneurial ventures and cover a broad variety of issues. As an aid to case analysis, we propose the strategic audit as an analytical technique.

Supplements

Supplemental materials are available to the instructor from the publisher. These include a *Concepts Instructor's Manual with Test Bank*; a *Case Instructor's Manual;* an *Instructor's Resource CD-ROM* containing testing software and PowerPoint files; videos; a book-specific web site; and black-and-white transparency acetates (upon demand).

INSTRUCTOR'S MANUALS

Two comprehensive Instructor's Manuals have been carefully constructed to accompany this book. The first one accompanies the concepts chapters; the second one accompanies the cases.

Concepts Instructor's Manual

To aid in discussing the 15 chapters dealing with strategic management concepts, the *Concepts Instructor's Manual* includes:

1. *Suggestions for Teaching Strategic Management*—discusses various teaching methods and includes suggested course syllabi.
2. *Chapter Notes*—includes summaries of each chapter, suggested answers to discussion questions, suggestions for using end of chapter cases/exercises, plus additional discussion questions (with answers) and lecture modules.
3. *Test questions*—contains more than 50 questions for each of the 15 chapters, for a total of more than 700 questions from which to choose. Questions include true/false, multiple choice, and essay.

Case Instructor's Manual

To aid in case method teaching, the *Case Instructor's Manual* includes detailed suggestions for use, teaching objectives, and examples of student analyses for each of the 33 full-sized cases. This is the most comprehensive Instructor's Manual available in strategic management. A standardized format is provided for each case:

1. Case Abstract
2. Case Issues and Subjects
3. Steps Covered in the Strategic Decision-making Process
4. Case Objectives
5. Suggested Classroom Approaches
6. Discussion Questions
7. Case Author's Teaching Note
8. Student-written Strategic Audit or Paper
9. EFAS, IFAS, SFAS Exhibits
10. Financial Analysis—ratios and common-size income statements
11. Student Strategic Audit Worksheet.

INSTRUCTOR'S RESOURCE CD-ROM

The *Instructor's Resource CD-ROM* contains tools to facilitate the instructor's lectures and examinations. These include PowerPoint Electronic Transparency Masters, containing figures and tables from the text. The instructor may customize these presentations and can present individual slides for student handouts. The CD also contains a computerized test bank of all the questions listed in the *Concepts Instructor's Manual*. Both Instructor's Manuals are included in the *Instructor's Resource CD-ROM*, as well as the video case notes for Newbury Comics.

VIDEO: NEWBURY COMICS

This video features part-ending segments shot at Newbury Comics, an exciting and current popular-culture retail chain. After beginning life as a store buying and selling used CDs, Newbury Comics has been expanding its product line and locations. Segments address key issues such as the company's basic model, mission and vision, and decision-making models. Accompanying case information can be found at the end of the parts in the concepts and full-volume text, and a video guide is included in the *Concepts Instructor's Manual*.

POWERPOINT SLIDES

PowerPoint slides, provided in a comprehensive package of text outlines and figures corresponding to the text, are designed to aid the educator and supplement in-class lectures. The PowerPoint slides can be found as ppt files on the Instructor's CD, as well as on the text web site, located at *www.prenhall.com/wheelen*.

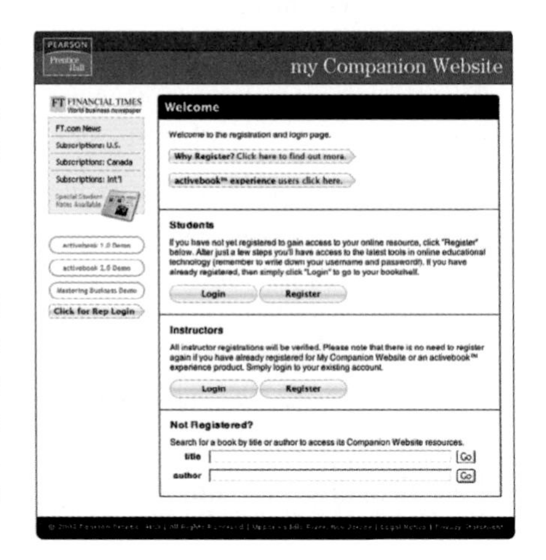

COMPANION WEBSITE

The new Companion Website provides professors with a customized course. It features an online study guide for students that includes multiple choice, true/false, and essay questions. Instructors may download files from both Instructor's Manuals, PowerPoint slides, and test bank files from the Instructor's Resource Center link at the Companion Website. The site also includes additional min-cases for use in class. Point your browser to *www.prenhall.com/wheelen*.

Acknowledgments

We thank the many people at Prentice Hall who helped to make this edition possible. We thank our editor, David Parker. We are especially grateful to David's project manager, Claudia Fernandes, who managed to keep everything on an even keel. We also thank Renata Butera and Kelly Ricci who took the book through the production process.

We are also very grateful to Kathy Wheelen for her first-rate administrative support of the cases and *Case Instructor's Manual*. We are especially thankful to the many students who tried out the cases we chose to include in this book. Their comments helped us find any flaws in the cases before the book went to the printer.

In addition, we express our appreciation to Dr. Labh Hira, Dean, and Dr. Thomas Chacko, Management Department Chair, of Iowa State University's College of Business and to John Hasselberg, Management Department Chair of St. John's University, for their support and provision of the resources so necessary to produce a textbook. The University of South Florida provided no support for this book. Both of us acknowledge our debt to Dr. William Shenkir and Dr. Frank S. Kaulback, former Deans of the McIntire School of Commerce of the University of Virginia for the provision of a work climate most supportive to the original development of this book.

We offer a special thanks to the hundreds of case authors who have provided us with excellent cases for the 11 editions of this book. We consider many of these case authors to be our friends. A special thanks to you!! The adage is true: The path to greatness is through others.

We especially thank Mary Anne Rouse, an outstanding classroom teacher and case author. A true professional, Mary Anne believed in turning her students into lifelong learners. On her own, she wrote 24 mini-cases for our 9th, 10th, and 11th editions. Retired in 2005, she and her husband look forward to many years of new and exciting adventures.

Last, to the many strategy instructors and students who have moaned to us about their problems with the strategy course: we have tried to respond to your problems and concerns as best we could by providing a comprehensive yet usable text coupled with recent and complex cases. To you, the people who work hard in the strategy trenches, we acknowledge our debt. This book is yours.

T. L. W.
Tampa, Florida

J. D. H.
St. Joseph, Minnesota

About the Contributors

Moustafa H. Abdelsamad, D.B.A. (Geroge Washington University), is Dean of the College of Business at Texas A&M University—Corpus Christi. He previously served as Dean of the College of Business and Industry at University of Massachsetts—Dartmouth and as Professor of Finance and Associate Dean of Graduate Studies in Business at Virginia Commonthwealth University. He is Editor-in-Chief of SAM *Advanced Management Journal* and International President of the Society of Advancement of Management. He is author of *A Guide to Capital Expenditure Analysis* and two chapters in the *Dow Jones–Irwin Capital Budgeting Handbook.* He is the author and coauthor of numerous articles in various publications.

Hitesh (John) P. Adhia, CPA, B.A., and M.S. (University of South Florida), is the President and Chief Investment Officer of Adhia Investment Advisors, Inc. (the "Firm"). Mr. Adhia is a CPA and has been in the finance industry since 1982. Mr. Adhia is the founder and Investment Manager for the Adhia Twenty Fund, the Adhia Health Care Fund, the Adhia Short Term Advantage Fund, the Adhia Arbitrage Fund, and the Adhia Derivative Fund. Prior to forming Adhia Investment Advisors, Mr. Adhia owned a Tampa-based public accounting practice and also served as Acting CFO and Independent Advisor to the Well Care Group of Companies. Mr. Adhia has more than 20 years of experience in managing fixed income strategies.

James W. Camerius, M.S. (University of North Dakota), is Professor of Marketing at Northern Michigan University. He has served as President of the Society for Case Research, Marketing Track Chair of the North American Case Research Association, and Workshop and Colloquium Director of the World Association for Case Method Research. He is a research grant recipient of the Walker L. Cisler College of Business at Northern Michigan University and also a 1995 recipient of the Distinguished Faculty Award of the Michigan Association of Governing Boards of State Universities. His cases appear in more than 90 management, marketing, and retailing textbooks in addition to *Annual Advances in Business Cases,* a publication of the Society for Case Research. His studies of corporate situations include Kmart Corporation; Tanner Companies, Inc.; Mary Kay Cosmetics, Inc.; Sasco Products,Inc.; The Fuller Brush Company; Wal-Mart Stores, Inc.; Longberger Marketing, Inc.; Encyclopaedia Britannica International; RWC, Inc.; and several others. His writings include several studies of the case method of instruction. He is an award and grant recipient of the Direct Selling Educational Foundation, Washington, D.C., and is listed in *Who's Who in the World, America, Midwest, American Education, and Finance and Industry.*

Marcia Chan is a Graduate Research Assistant at the Tobin School of Business at Saint Johns.

Richard A. Cosier, Ph.D. (University of Iowa), is Dean and Leeds Professor of Management at Purdue University. He formerly was Dean and Fred B. Brown Chair at the University of Oklahoma and was Associate Dean for Academics and Professor of Business Administration at Indiana University. He served as Chairperson of the Department of Management at Indiana University for seven years prior to assuming his current positions. He was formerly a Planning Engineer with Western Electric Company and Instructor of Management and Quantitative Methods at the University of Notre Dame. Dr. Coiser is interested in researching the managerial decision-making process, organization responses to external forces, and participative management. He has published in *Behavior Science, Academy of Management Journal, Academy of Management Review, Organizational Behavior and Human Performance, Management Science, Strategic Management Journal, Business Horizons, Decisions Sciences, Personnel Pyschology, Journal of Creative Behavior, International Journal of Management, The Business Quarterly, Public Administration Quarterly, Human Relations,* and other journals. In addition, Dr. Coiser has presented numerous papers at professional meetings and has coauthored a management text. He has been active in many executive development programs and has acted as management-education consultant for several organizations. Dr. Coiser is the recipient of teaching Excellence Awards in the M.B.A. Program at Indiana and a Richard D. Irwin Fellowship. He belongs to the Institute of Management, Sigma Iota Epsilon, and the Decision Sciences Institute.

Patrick Collins is a Graduate Research Assistant at the Tobin School of Business at St. John's University.

Roy A. Cook, D.B.A. (Mississippi State University), is Associate Dean of the School of Business Administration and Professor of Management, Fort Lewis College, Durango, Colorado. He has written a best-selling textbook, *Tourism: The Business of Travel,* now in its second edition, and has two forthcoming textbooks: *Cases and Experiential Exercises in Human Resource Management* and *Guide to Business Etiquette.* He has authored numerous articles, cases, and papers based on his extensive experience in the hospitality industry and research interests in the areas of strategy, small business management, human resource management, and communication. Dr. Cook is the Director of Colorado's Center for Tourism Research, was Editor of *Annual Advances in Business Cases,* and also serves on the editorial boards of the *Business Case Journal,* the *Journal of Business Strategies,* and the *Journal of Teaching and Tourism.* He is member of the Academy of Management, Society for Case Research (past President), and the International Society of Travel and Tourism Educators. Dr. Cook teaches courses in strategic management, small business management, tourism and resort management, and human resource management.

David B. Croll, Ph.D. (Pennsylvania State University) is Professor of Emeritus of Accounting at the McIntire School of Commerce, the University of Virginia. He was Visiting Associate Professor at the Graduate Business School, the University of Michigan. He is on the editorial board of *SAM Advanced Management Journal.* He has published in the *Accounting Review* and the *Case Research Journal.* His cases appear in 12 accounting and management textbooks.

Steven M. Cox, Ph.D. (University of Nebraska) is an Associate Professor of Marketing, McColl School of Business, Queens University of Charlotte. He has a 25-year career in executive level marketing and sales positions with AT&T, GE, and several satellite imaging companies. He owns and manages LSI, a geographic information system company. He currently serves as a case reviewer for the *Business Case Journal* and the *Southeast Case Research Journal.*

Dan R. Dalton, Ph.D. (University of California, Irvine), is the Dean of the Graduate School of Business, Indiana University, and Harold A. Polipl Chair of Strategic Management. He was formerly with General Telephone & Electronics for 13 years. Widely published in business and psychology periodicals, his articles have appeared in the *Academy of Management Journal,* the *Journal of Applied Psychology, Personnel Psychology, Academy of Management Review,* and *Strategic Management Journal.*

Sanjib Dutta is a Faculty Member at the ICFAI Center for Management Research (ICMR), Hyderabad and Consulting Editor for *Effective Executive*, a monthly management magazine from ICFAI Publications. He holds an M.B.A. degree from the University of Ljubljana, Slovenia. He has six years of experience in research activities related to case study development. He teaches strategic management at the ICFAI Business School, Hyderabad.

Cathy A. Enz, Ph.D. (Ohio State University), is the Lewis G. Schaeneman Jr. Professor of Innovation and Dynamic Management at Cornell University's School of Hotel Administration, where she is also the Executive Director of the Center for Hospitality Research. Her doctoral degree is in organization theory and behavior. Professor Enz has written numerous articles, cases, and books on corporate culture, value sharing, change management, and strategic human resource management effects on performance. Professor Enz consults extensively in the service sector and serves on the Board of Directors for two hospitality-related organizations.

Kristina Fogg is a Graduate Research Assistant at the Tobin School of Business at St. John's.

Marc Gartenfeld, B.S./M.B.A. (St. John's University), is the Associate Director of The Strategic Management Research Group and the Center for Case Development and Use. He has coauthored more than 75 books, monographs, instructor's guides, case studies, journal articles, conference presentations, and table topic papers in the areas of multinational strategic management, e-business, expert knowledge-based systems, entrepreneurship, and application service providers. One of his coauthored papers won a "Distinguished Paper Award" and various case studies won national and international awards. He is also the recipient of the 2001 Teaching Excellence Award and Professor of the Year Award, both from the Tobin College of Business, St. John's University.

Gamewell D. Gantt, J.D., CPA, is Professor of Accounting and Management in the College of Business at Idaho State University in Pocatello, Idaho, where he teaches a variety of legal studies courses. He is past President of the Rocky Mountain Academy of Legal Studies in Business and a past Chair of the Idaho Endowment Investment Fund Board. His published articles and papers have appeared in journals including *Midwest Law Review, Business Law Review, Copyright World,* and *Intellectual Property World.* His published cases have appeared in several textbooks and in *Annual Advances in Business Cases.*

Norman J. Gierlasinski, D.B.A., CPA, CFE, CIA, is Professor of Accounting at Central Washington University. He served as Chairman of the Small Business Division of the Midwest Business Administration Association. He has authored and coauthored cases for professional associations and the Harvard Case Study Series. He has authored various articles in professional journals as well as serving as a contributing author for textbooks and as a consultant to many organizations. He has also served as a reviewer for various publications.

Sue Greenfeld, D.B.A. (University of Southern California), is a Professor of Management and Associate Dean for Student Affairs in the College of Business Administration, California State University, San Bernardino. She is a two-time recipient of a Fulbright Senior Fellowship, teaching at the National Chengchi University in Taipei, Taiwan, and at the Marmara University in Istanbul, Turkey. She has written numerous cases on business policy and strategic issues and has served on the editorial board of the *Case Research Journal.*

Walter E. Greene, Ph.D. (University of Arkansas), PHR (SHRM lifetime award); College Management Certificate, 1967 University of Nebraska, Omaha; M.S. University of North Dakota, 1967 (Industrial Management); and B.S. University of Maryland, 1959 (Military Science—Logistics). He is the Owner and President of Greene and Associates, which offers consulting services to small businesses in Management and Human Resource Management. In 1994, Dr. Greene was awarded a "Fellowship" by SW Small Business Institute Association. Dr. Greene is a member of BGS (Business Honor Society), AIDS (American Decision Sciences Honor Society), and DNA (Marketing Transportation Honor Society). He received numerous nominations for outstanding teaching and service awards during his 38 years as a college professor (1967–2004). In addition to classroom lecturing, Dr. Greene has used various teaching methods such as teaching distant learning classes, WebCT (computer assisted learning),

PowerPoint presentations, videos, and other innovated teaching methods. Prior to entering the teaching profession, Dr. Greene was a retired USAF Commission Officer, seeing service in the U.S. Army of Occupation of Germany, WWII. Captain Greene was on active duty during both the Korean War and the SE Asian conflicts, and held the highest possible security clearances through top secret, cryptographic, and EWO clearances. In addition, Dr. Greene has over six dozen refereed teaching cases published in over four dozen textbooks in: Marketing Management, Strategic Management, International Business, Marketing Strategy, Small Business, and Retail Marketing. His case "Invacare" was translated into French for an International MBA competition in Canada. Dr. Greene has over three dozen refereed articles in such journals as: *The Review of Business, Journal of World Business, Journal of Management Systems, The Journal of Big Bend Studies, International Journal of Manpower, The Journal of Services in Marketing, Southwest Journal of Business & Economics, The Journal of Business & Entrepreneurship. International Journal of Commerce and Management,* and *The International Journal of Case Studies and Research.*

Irene Hagenbuch-Sanjana B.S. (Bently College), is currently working as an Operations Specialist for Warburg Dillon Read in Stamford, Connecticut. Among her various roles at Warburg Dillon Read, Irene has spent time with Precious Metals, Domestic Equities, and Fixed Income Groups. Some of her responsibilities have included the reduction of settlement risk through operational controls, new product development, design and testing, and general project management. Irene is an avid skier and runner. In her spare time, she enjoys foreign travel.

Patricia Harasta, M.B.A. (Bentley McCallum Graduate School of Business) is Director of Quality Assurance at CA (formerly Computer Associates). She manages a distributed team responsible for new development and maintenance QA activities for products that provide management of applications such as SAP, Microsoft Exchange, Lotus Domino, WebSphere, WebLogic, MQ, and web servers.

Stacey D. (Foster) Hedman, B.A. (St. Michael's College), M.A. in Business Administration in International Business (Bentley College), is a Strategic Marketing Manager at Textron Systems, Wilmington, MA. She has worked as a Senior Consultant for Competitive Intelligence firms Fuld & Company, Cambridge, MA, and Fletcher/CSI, Williston, VT.

Alan N. Hoffman, D.B.A. (Indiana University), is an Associate Professor of Management and M.B.A. Director, Bentley College, Waltham, Massachusetts, and was formerly Assistant Professor of Business Environment and Policy at the University of Connecticut. He is co-author of *The Strategic Management Casebook and Skill-Builder*, with Hugh O'Neill. Publications have appeared in the *Academy of Management Journal*, *Human Relations*, the *Journal of Business Research*, *Business Horizons,* and the *Journal of Business Ethics*. His cases appear in more than 20 strategy textbooks. He is coauthor of the following strategic management cases: "Harley-Davidson: The Eagle Soars Alone," "The Boston YWCA: 1991," "Ryka Inc.: The Athletic Shoe with a 'Soul,'" "Liz Claiborne: Troubled Times for the Women's Retail Giant," "Snapple Beverage," "NTN Communications: The Future is Now!," "Ben & Jerry's Homemade, Yo! I'm Your CEO," "Cisco Systems," "Sun Microsystems," "Chipcom, Inc," "Palm Computing," "Handspring Inc.," "AOL/Time Warner," and "eBay, Inc."

J. David Hunger, Ph.D. (Ohio State University), is Strategic Management Scholar in Residence, St. John's University, Collegeville, Minnesota, and Professor Emeritus, Iowa State University, Ames, Iowa. He previously taught at George Mason University, the University of Virginia, and Baldwin-Wallace College. He has served as Academic Director of the Pappajohn Center for Entrepreneurship at Iowa State University. He previously worked in brand management at Procter & Gamble Company, Cincinnati, Ohio, and as a selling supervisor at Lazarus Department Store in Columbus, Ohio. He served to the rank of Captain in U.S. Army Military Intelligence during the Vietnam War. He has been active as consultant and trainer to many business corporations, as well as to state and federal government agencies. His articles and cases have appeared in the *Academy of Management Journal, International Journal of Management, Human Resource Management, Journal of Business Strategies, Case Research Journal, Business Case Journal, Handbook of Business Strategy, Journal of Management Case Studies, Annual Advances in Business Cases, Journal of Retail Banking, SAM Advanced Management Journal,* and the *Journal of Management*, among others.

Dr. Hunger is a past President of the North American Case Research Association (NACRA), Society for Case Research (SCR), and the ISU Press Board of Directors. He also served as Vice President of the U.S. Association for Small Business and Entrepreneurship (USASBE). He has served on the editorial review boards of the *Case Research Journal, Business Case Journal, SAM Advanced Management Journal, Journal of Business Strategies,* and the *Journal of Business Research*. He currently serves on the board of directors of the North American Management Society and on the Advisory Council of MBAA International. He is coauthor with Thomas Wheelen of *Strategic Management and Business Policy, Essentials of Strategic Management, Cases in Strategic Management and Business Policy, Strategic Management Cases (PIC: Preferred Individualized Cases), Concepts in Strategic Management and Business Policy*, and the monograph, *An Assessment of Undergraduate Business Education in the United States*. The eighth edition of *Strategic Management and Business Policy* received the 1999 McGuffey Award for Excellence and Longevity from the Text and Academic Authors Association. Dr. Hunger received the Best Case Award given by the McGraw-Hill Publishing Company and the Society for Case Research in 1991 for Outstanding Case Development. He also received the Distinguished Paper Award in 1988 given by Richard D. Irwin, Business Publications, Inc., and the Midwest Management Society. He is listed in various editions of *Who's Who*, including *Who's Who in the United States* and *Who's Who in the World*. He was also recognized in 1999 by the Iowa State University College of Business with its Innovation in Teaching Award and was made a Fellow of the Text and Academic Authors Association in 2001.

George A. Johnson, Ph.D., is Professor of Management and Director of the Idaho State University M.B.A. program. He has published in the fields of management education, ethics, project management, and simulation. He is also active in developing and publishing case material for educational purposes. His industry experience includes several years as a Project Manager in the development and procurement of aircraft systems.

Shawana P. Johnson is at the University of Nebraska.

Michael J. Keeffe, Ph.D. (University of Arkansas), is Associate Professor of Management at Southwest Texas State University. He has served as Chair of the Department of Management and Marketing, Co-Director of AACSB—International Accreditation at SWT, authored numerous cases in the field of strategic management, published in several journals, and served as an independent consultant since 1982. He currently teaches and conducts research in the fields of strategic management and human resource management.

John A. Kilpatrick, Ph.D. (University of Iowa), is Professor of Management and International Business, Idaho State University. He has taught in the areas of business and business ethics for over 25 years. He served as Co-Chair of the management track of the Institute for Behavioral and Applied Management from its inception and continues as a board member for that organization. He is author of *The Labor Content of American Foreign Trade* and coauthor of *Issues in International Business*. His cases have appeared in a number of organizational behavior and strategy texts and casebooks and in *Annual Advances in Business Cases*.

Eric G. Kirby, Ph.D. (University of Kentucky), is Assistant Professor of Strategic Management at Southwest Texas State University. He previously held joint appointments on the faculties of the College of Business Administration and Medicine at Texas Tech University. He has received numerous awards for his research in the areas of health care administration and sport management. He has published more than a dozen articles in scholarly journals and presented many more at academic conferences. Most of his research examines how businesses understand and respond to their external environment. Prior to becoming an academic, he was a building contractor, technical writer, and information system manager. He can be contacted online at *www.EricKirby.com.*

Donald F. Kuratko, is the Jack M. Gill Chair of Entrepreneurship, Professor of Entrepreneurship, and Executive Director of the Johnson Center for Entrepreneurship & Innovation at The Kelley School of Business, Indiana University–Bloomington. Dr. Kuratko is considered a preeminent scholar and national leader in the field of entrepreneurship. He has published more than 150 articles on aspects of entrepreneurship, new venture development, and corporate entrepreneurship. His work has been published in journals such as *Strategic Management Journal, Academy of Management Executive, Journal of Business Venturing, Entrepreneurship Theory & Practice, Journal of Small Business Management, Journal of Small Business Strategy, Family Business Review,* and *Advanced Management Journal.* Dr. Kuratko has authored 20 books, including the leading entrepreneurship book in American universities today, *Entrepreneurship: Theory, Process, Practice*, 7th ed. (South-Western/Thomson Publishers, 2007), as well as *Strategic Entrepreneurial Growth,* 2nd ed. (South-Western/Thomson Publishers, 2004*), Corporate Entrepreneurship* (South-Western/Thomson Publishers, 2007), and *Effective Small Business Management*, 7th ed. (Wiley & Sons Publishers, 2001). In addition, Dr. Kuratko has been consultant on Corporate Entrepreneurship and Entrepreneurial Strategies to a number of major corporations such as Anthem Blue Cross/Blue Shield, AT&T, United Technologies, Ameritech, The Associated Group (Acordia), Union Carbide Corporation, ServiceMaster, and TruServ.

Under his leadership, Indiana University's Entrepreneurship Program has recently been ranked 4th in the nation by *Entrepreneur* magazine, 11th in Graduate Business Schools for Entrepreneurship by *U.S. News & World Report*, 4th in Graduate Business Schools (Public Institutions) for Entrepreneurship by *U.S. News & World Report,* and one of the Top 5 Entrepreneurial Business Schools by the *Princeton Review* as reported in *Forbes* magazine. Before coming to Indiana University he was the Stoops Distinguished Professor of Entrepreneurship and Founding Director of the Entrepreneurship Program at Ball State University. In addition, he was the Executive Director of The Midwest Entrepreneurial Education Center. Dr. Kuratko was the first professor ever to be named a Distinguished Professor for the College of Business at Ball State University and held that position for 15 years. The Entrepreneurship Program that Dr. Kuratko developed at Ball State University continually earned national rankings including top 20 in *Business Week* and *Success* magazines; top 10 business schools for entrepreneurship research (*Journal of Management*); top 4 in *U.S. News & World Report's* elite ranking (including the number 1 public university for entrepreneurship); and the number 1 Regional Entrepreneurship Program in *Entrepreneur* magazine.

Dr. Kuratko's honors include earning the Ball State University College of Business Teaching Award for 15 consecutive years, as well as being the only professor in the history of Ball State University to achieve all four of the university's major lifetime awards: Outstanding Young Faculty (1987); Outstanding Teaching Award (1990); Outstanding Faculty Award (1996); and Outstanding Researcher Award (1999). He was also honored as the Entrepreneur of the Year for the state of Indiana and was inducted into the Institute of American Entrepreneurs Hall of Fame (1990). He has been honored with The George Washington Medal of Honor; the Leavey Foundation Award for Excellence in Private Enterprise; the NFIB Entrepreneurship Excellence Award; and the National Model Innovative Pedagogy Award for Entrepreneurship. In addition, Dr. Kuratko was named the National Outstanding Entrepreneurship Educator (by the U.S. Association for Small Business and Entrepreneurship) and he was selected one of the Top Three Entrepreneurship Professors in the U.S. by the Kauffman Foundation, Ernst & Young, *Inc.* magazine, and Merrill Lynch. He received the Thomas W. Binford Memorial Award for Outstanding

Contribution to Entrepreneurial Development from the Indiana Health Industry Forum. Dr. Kuratko has been named a 21st Century Entrepreneurship Research Fellow by the National Consortium of Entrepreneurship Centers, as well as the U.S. Association for Small Business & Entrepreneurship Scholar for Corporate Entrepreneurship in 2003. Finally, he has been honored by his peers in *Entrepreneur* magazine as one of the Top Two Entrepreneurship Program Directors in the nation for three consecutive years, including the number 1 Entrepreneurship Program Director in 2003.

Darrin Kuykendall, M.B.A., M.S.F.P., is a consultant for PriceWaterhouse Coopers in Boston. He is also a professional licensed realtor in the state of Massachusetts. He received his Information Age M.B.A. and Master's in Financial Planning from the McCallum Graduate School of Business at Bentley University. Bentley is the first business university that is distinguished by grooming knowledge professionals for today's information- and technology-driven business world. He also holds a B.S.B.A. in Marketing and International Communications from Robert Morris University, located in Pittsburgh, Pennsylvania. He has also served in the U.S. Army National Guard in financial and administrative roles. He is a member of NAR—National Association of Realtors, MAR—Massachusetts Association of Realtors and NBMBAA—National Black M.B.A. Association. In addition, he owns and operates his own firm, Khamelian International, LLC—a diversified portfolio firm positioned to engage in ventures in real estate investment, marketing consulting, and investment management.

YongJun Lu is a Graduate Research Assistant at the Tobin School of Business at St. John's.

Bill J. Middlebrook, Ph.D. (University of North Texas), is Professor of Management at Southwest Texas State University. He has served as Acting Chair of the Department of Management and Marketing, published in numerous journals, served as a consultant in industry, and is currently teaching and researching in the fields of Strategic Management and Human Resources.

Charles E. Michaels, Jr., Ph.D. (University of South Florida), is Associate Professor of Management. He has served on the review board for *SAM Advanced Management Journal* and has authored articles appearing in the *Journal of Applied Psychology, Journal of Retail Banking,* and *Journal of Occupational Psychology,* as well as papers in the fields of business management and industrial psychology. He has developed a research and teaching interest in international business.

Robert J. Mockler, Ph.D. (Columbia, 1961), B.A. and M.B.A. (Harvard, 1954, 1959), is the Joseph F. Adams Professor of Management at St. John's University's Graduate School of Business. He is the director of the Strategic Management Research Group and its Centers of Knowledge-Based Systems for Business (one of the largest databases of prototype expert systems for management decision making in the United States), Case Study Development and Use Program (the third largest case study development program in the United States), and Cross-Cultural Management. He has authored, coauthored, or edited more than 50 books and monographs, some 230 case studies, more than 70 articles, more than 50 book chapters, and more than 200 presentations covering such areas as strategic management, case study development and use, competitive market analysis, new venture management, multinational planning, business ethics, management decision making, modeling of cognitive and behavioral management processes, contingency theory, business process reengineering, computer information systems, group decision support systems for management, expert knowledge-based systems, and innovative teaching. His first articles on strategic management and situational decision theory were published in *Harvard Business Review* in 1970 and 1971. His first book on strategic management was published in 1969 (Prentice Hall). His books include three on expert systems and computer information systems development in 1992 (Macmillan); five on strategic management, information systems, and case study development and use in 1993 and 1994 (Addison-Wesley, Simon and Schuster, The Planning Forum); and four on multinational strategic management in 1997, 1998, 1999, and 2003 (John Wiley & Sons, Quorum Books, Haworth Press, and Strategic Management Research Group Publishing). Three of his books have been translated into Chinese and published in China, two into Romanian and published in Romania, one into Greek and published in Greece, and one into Russian and published in Russia. He has lectured, consulted and taught worldwide in (China—Xian, Beijing, and Shanghai; Russia—Moscow and St. Petersburg; Finland; Japan; England; Poland; Germany; Brazil; Argentina; Costa Rica; Ireland; Italy; Taiwan; Philippines; India; Egypt; Mexico; Canada; and Romania), received national awards for innovative teaching (Decision Sciences Institute), been a Fulbright Scholar, and taught M.B.A. courses in Rome, Milan, Latin America, and Beijing, and won numerous other awards for his work. He also successfully started, ran and eventually sold his own multimillion-dollar business ventures. He has developed and published more than 120 presentations, case studies, and articles with other faculty at St. John's University. In addition, more than 80 joint publications have been done with professors of other domestic and overseas universities.

Rebecca J. Morris, Ph.D. (University of Nebraska at Lincoln), is Associate Professor of Management, University of Nebraska at Omaha. She has published cases in the *Case Research Journal* and the *Business Case Journal*. Her cases have appeared in a number of strategic management, international management, and business ethics textbooks. Dr. Morris is an active member of the North American Case Research Association (NACRA) and the Society for Case Research (SCR). She is currently serving as President-Elect of NACRA and on the Editorial Review Board for the *Journal of Business Strategies*. In 2004, Dr. Morris received the University of Nebraska at Omaha Excellence in Teaching Award. She is currently teaching and conducting case research in the fields of strategic management and international management.

A. Mukund, is a former Faculty Member at the ICFAI Center for Management Research.

Nathan Nebbe, M.B.A. and M.A. (Iowa State University), has significant interests in the indigenous peoples of the Americas. With an undergraduate degree in Animal Ecology, he served as a Peace Corps Volunteer in Honduras, where he worked at the Honduran national forestry school ESNAACIFORE (Escuela National de Ciencias Forestales). After the Peace Corps, Nathan worked for a year on a recycling project for the town of Ignacio and the Southern Ute Indian Tribe in southwestern Colorado. Following his experience in Colorado, Nathan returned to Iowa State University, where he obtained his M.B.A. followed by an M.A. in Anthropology. He is currently studying how globalization of the Chilean forestry industry is affecting the culture of the indigenous Mapuche people of south central Chile.

A. Neela Radhika is a former Faculty Associate at the ICFAI Center for Management Research.

Shirisha Regani is a Faculty Associate at the ICFAI Center for Management Research.

Ted Repetti, B.S. (The College of New Jersey), is currently a valuation analyst at Management Planning, Inc., in Princeton. Management Planning renders financial advice to corporations, and specializes in the valuation of closely held corporations.

John K. Ross, III, Ph.D. (University of North Texas), is Associate Professor of Management at Southwest Texas State University. He has served as SBI Director, Associate Dean, Chair of the Department of Management and Marketing, published in numerous journals, and is currently teaching and researching in the fields of strategic management and human resource.

Maryanne M. Rouse, CPA, M.B.A. (University of South Florida), B.A. in English, Romance Languages, and Political Science (Syracuse University), is a Certified Public Accountant (Florida). She joined the faculty of the College of Business Administration at the University of South Florida in 1971. She served as the College's Assistant Dean from 1974 to 1976 and as Director of Executive Education and Management Development from 1981 to

1994. She returned in 2005. Ms. Rouse's current teaching assignments include Strategic Management, the undergraduate capstone course, Measuring Organization Performance in the Graduate Leadership Program, Integrative Business Applications II in the M.B.A., and Managerial Accounting in the Executive M.B.A. and the M.B.A. Program for Physicians. She has also taught in the USF/EDC French executive M.B.A. Program in Paris. The recipient of a number of M.B.A. teaching awards, including "MVP" by the Physicians M.B.A. class and Outstanding Professor for the executive M.B.A., she is a frequent program speaker and continuing education faculty member. A consultant in strategic planning and accounting in several industries including the not-for-profit sector and health care, she served as one of four international accreditation fellows for the Accreditation Commission for Education in Health Services Administration (ACEHSA). Maryanne is a member of the Board of Directors and Vice Chair of the Tampa Economic Development Corporation, and CDC, serves on the board of the University's Small Business Development Center, and chairs the college's Undergraduate Programs Committee.

Patricia A. Ryan, Ph.D. (University of South Florida), is an Associate Professor of Finance, Colorado State University. She currently serves on the Board of the Midwest Finance Association and is the Associate Editor of the *Business Case Journal*. Her research interests lie in corporate finance, specifically initial public offerings, capital budgeting, and case writing. She has published in the *Journal of Business and Management*, the *Business Case Journal*, *Educational and Psychological Measurement*, the *Journal of Research in Finance*, the *Journal of Financial and Strategic Decisions*, and the *Journal of Accounting and Finance Research*. Her research has been cited in the *Wall Street Journal*, *CFO Magazine*, and *Investment Dealers Digest*.

Sara Smith Shull, Pharm.D. (University of Nebraska Medical Center), M.B.A. (University of Nebraska at Omaha), is a Drug Policy and Economics Pharmacist Specialist at the Nebraska Health Systems. In 2003, Sara received the Outstanding Student-Authored Case Award at the North American Case Research Association for her case on GlaxoSmithKline. She was further recognized for this achievement with the M.B.A. Business Case Student Research Award at the University of Nebraska at Omaha in 2004. She received the Jack Hill Award for academic excellence in the M.B.A. program at the University of Nebraska at Omaha in 2003. Sara's primary research and clinical interests include pharmacoeconomics, outcomes research, and the implementation of cost-effective programs.

Laurence J. Stybel, Ed.D (Harvard University), is Cofounder of Stybel Peabody Lincolnshire, a Boston-based management consulting firm devoted to enhancing career effectiveness of executives who report to boards of directors. Services include search, outplacement, outplacement avoidance, and valued executive career consulting. Stybel Peabody Lincolnshire was voted "Best Outplacement Firm" by the readers of *Massachusetts Lawyers Weekly*. Its programs are the only ones officially endorsed by the Massachusetts Hospital Association and the Financial Executives Institute. He serves on the Board of Directors of the New England Chapter of the National Association of Corporate Directors and the Boston Human Resources Association. His home page can be found at *www.stybelpeabody.com*. The "Your Career" department of the home page contains downloadable back issues of his monthly *Boston Business Journal* column, "Your Career."

K. Subhadra is a former Faculty Associate at the ICFAI Center for Management Research.

Bethany Sweesy, M.B.A., is a 2005 graduate of McCallum School of Business, Bentley College. She has received several awards including *The National Dean's List 2002/2003*, *The 2004 Wall Street Journal Student Achievement Award,* and a research assistantship position at Bentley College. She has worked as a writer and editor in both financial services and medical devices. Currently, she is studying cardiac rhythm management at Arrhythmia Technologies Institute.

Joseph Teye-Kofi is a Graduate Research Assistant at the Tobin School of Business at St. John's.

Joanna Tochowicz is a Graduate Research Assistant at the Tobin School of Business at St. John's.

Jeffrey W. Totten, D.B.A., (Louisiana Tech University); PCM, M.B.A., and B.S. (Northwestern State University) is an Assistant Professor of Marketing at McNeese State University in Lake Charles, Louisiana. Jeff especially enjoys teaching marketing research, and has taught several other marketing courses, including principles, retailing, personal selling, and promotion strategy. His research interests include fast food nutrition, students' use and perceptions of mobile phones and body art, case research and writing, and students' perceptions of personal selling as a career choice. He has published in *Services Marketing Quarterly, International Journal of Consumer Studies, Journal of Healthcare Marketing,* and *Marketing Intelligence & Planning,* among others.

Joyce P. Vincelette, D.B.A. (Indiana University), is Professor of Management at The College of New Jersey. She was previously a faculty member at the University of South Florida. She has authored and coauthored various articles, chapters, and cases that have appeared in management journals and strategic management texts and casebooks. She is also active as a consultant and trainer for a number of local and national business organizations as well as for a variety of not-for-profit and government agencies. She currently teaches and conducts research in the fields of strategic management and leadership.

Vineet Walia is a Graduate Research Assistant at the Tobin School of Business at St. John's.

Kathryn E. Wheelen, B.A., L.M.T. (University of Tampa), has worked as an Administrative Assistant for case and textbook development with the Thomas L. Wheelen Company (circa 1879). She is the owner of Kathryn E. Wheelen Inc. and works as a ESE Language Arts Teacher at Dorothy Thomas, Tampa, Florida.

Richard D. Wheelen, B.S. (University of South Florida), has worked as a case research assistant. He is currently practicing in the field of health care and he currently lives in Everett, Washington.

Thomas L. Wheelen II, B.A. (Boston College), has worked as a case research assistant. He is currently working and living in Boulder, Colorado.

Thomas L. Wheelen, D.B.A. (George Washington University), M.B.A. (Babson College, 1961); Boston College, B.S. cum laude (1957); has been Visiting Professor; Trinity College, University of Dublin (Fall 1999); Professor of Strategic Management, University of South Florida (1983–present); at the University of Virginia McIntire School of Commerce, Ralph A. Beeton Professor of Free Enterprise (1981–1985); Professor (1981–1974); Associate Professor (1971–1974); and Assistant Professor (1968–1971); Visiting Professor, University of Arizona (1980–1979) and Northeastern University (Summer 1979, 1977, and 1975). His academic, industry, and military experience includes, at the University of Virginia College of Continuing Education; Coordinator for Business Education (1978–1983, 1971–1976)—approve all undergraduate courses offered at seven Regional Centers and approved faculty; Liaison Faculty and Consultant to the National Academy of the FBI Academy (1972–1983); and developing, selling, and conducting more than 200 seminars for local, state, and national governments and companies for McIntire School of Commerce and Continuing Education. At General Electric Company, he held various management positions (1961–1965), and he served in the U.S. Navy Supply Corps as assistant supply officer aboard a nuclear support tender (1957–1960). His publications include the monograph, "An Assessment of Undergraduate Business Education in the United States" (with J. D. Hunger), 1980; as well as 60 books, 14 of which have been translated into eight languages (Arabic, Bahasa, Indonesian, Chinese, Chinese Simplified, Greek, Italian, Japanese, Portuguese, and Thai). With J. D. Hunger, he has coauthored five current books: *Strategic Management and*

Business Policy, 10th Edition (2006); *Cases in Strategic Management and Business Policy,* 10th Edition (2006); *Concepts in Strategic Management and Business Policy,* 10th Edition (2006); *Strategic Management and Business Policy,* 10th Edition; International Edition (2006); and *Essentials of Strategic Management,* 3rd Edition (2003). Dr. Wheelen served as co-editor, Developments in Information Systems (1974) and Collective Bargaining in the Public Sector (1977) and was Co-developer of Software—STrategic Financial ANalyzer (ST. FAN) (1993, 1990, 1989—various versions). He has authored more than 40 articles that have appeared in such journals as the *Journal of Management, Business Quarterly, Personnel Journal, SAM Advanced Management Journal, Journal of Retailing, International Journal of Management,* and the *Handbook of Business Strategy*. He has written about 280 cases appearing in more than 83 text and case books, as well as the *Business Case Journal, Journal of Management Case Studies, International Journal of Case Studies and Research,* and *Case Research Journal*. His awards include Fellow, the Society for Advancement of Management in 2002, Fellow, North American Case Research Association 2000; Fellow, Text and Academic Authors Association, 2000; the 1999 Phil Carroll Advancement of Management Award in Strategic Management from the Society for Advancement of Management; the 1999 McGuffey Award for Excellence and Longevity for *Strategic Management and Business Policy,* 6th Edition, from the Text and Academic Authors Association; the 1996/97 Teaching Incentive Program Award for teaching undergraduate strategic management; a Fulbright, 1996–97, to Ireland, that he had to turn down; Endowed Chair, Ralph A. Beeton Professor, at University of Virginia (1981–1985); Sesquicentennial Associateship research grant from the Center for Advanced Studies at the University of Virginia, 1979–80; Small Business Administration (Small Business Institute) supervised undergraduate team that won District, Regional III, and Honorable Mention Awards; and awards for two articles. Dr. Wheelen currently serves on the Board of Directors of Adhia Mutual Fund, Society for Advancement of Management, and on the Editorial Board and the Associate Editor of *SAM Advanced Management Journal*. He served on the Board of Directors of Lazer Surgical Software, Inc., and Southern Management Association and on the Editorial Boards of the *Journal of Management* and *Journal of Management Case Studies, Journal of Retail Banking, Case Research Journal,* and *Business Case Journal*. He was Vice President of Strategic Management for the Society for the Advancement of Management, and President of the North American Case Research Association. Dr. Wheelen is a member of the Academy of Management, Beta Gamma Sigma, Southern Management Association, North American Case Research Association, Society for Advancement of Management, Society for Case Research, Strategic Management Association, and World Association for Case Method Research and Application. He has been listed in *Who's Who in Finance and Industry, Who's Who in the South and Southwest,* and *Who's Who in American Education*.

Cynthia Clark Williams, Ph.D., is an assistant professor of management and serves as the assistant director of the doctoral programs at Bentley College. She holds a Ph.D. from the honors program at Boston University and an M.A. from Northwestern University. Her research interests focus on various topics including corporate disclosures, governance, management strategy, and organizational ethics. Prior to joining Bentley, she was a member of the faculty at Merrimack College and Boston University following a career in the securities industry. She is a member of the Academy of Management, the International Association of Business & Society, the Society for Business Ethics, and the North American Case Research Association. She is a reviewer for several journals and has presented numerous papers at conferences in both the United States and Europe. Recent published work has appeared in *Business & Society, The Case Research Journal, Investor Relations Quarterly,* and *Public Relations Review.*

Eleventh Edition

STRATEGIC MANAGEMENT and BUSINESS POLICY

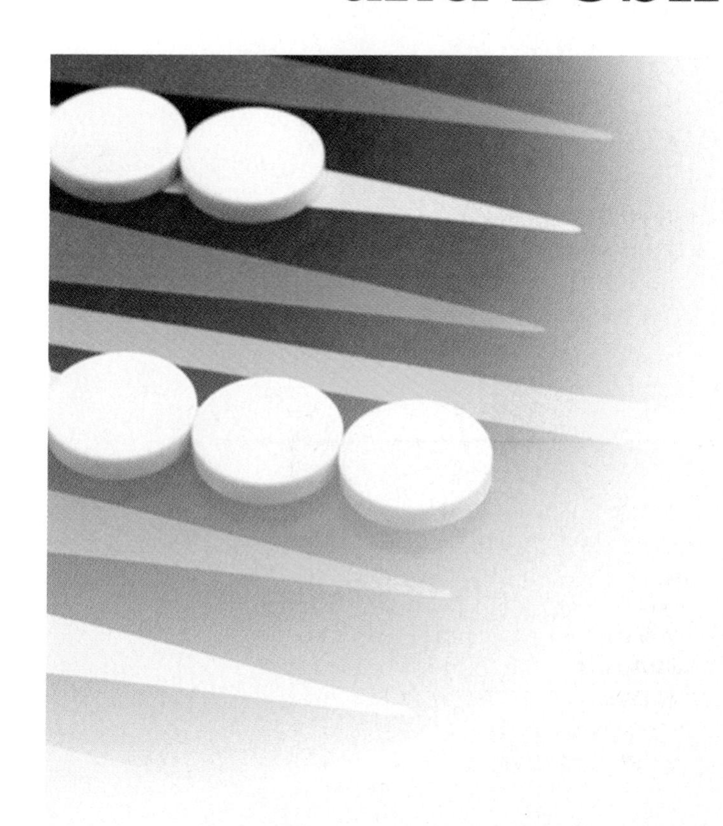

PART ONE

Introduction to Strategic Management and Business Policy

CHAPTER 1

Basic Concepts of Strategic Management

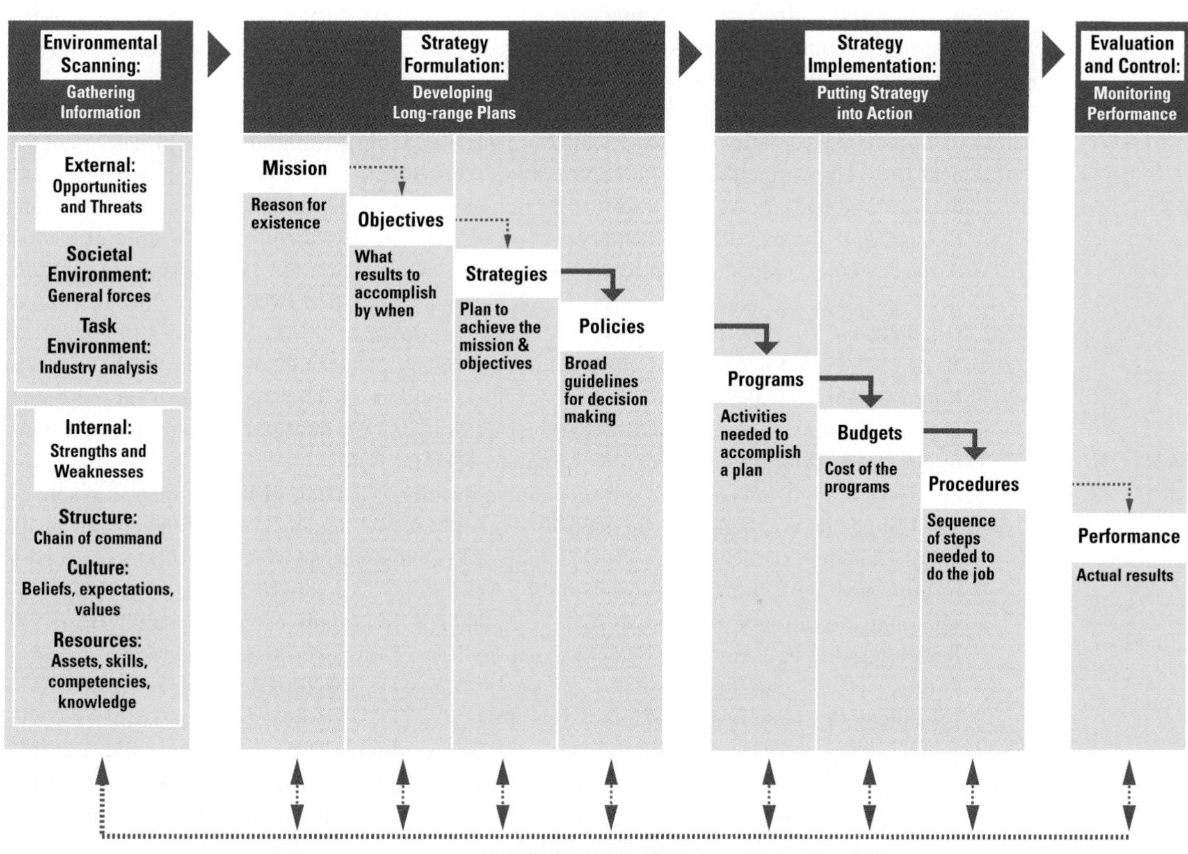

Learning Objectives

After reading this chapter, you should be able to:

- Understand the benefits of strategic management
- Explain how globalization and electronic commerce influence strategic management
- Understand the basic model of strategic management
- Identify some common triggering events that act as stimuli for strategic change
- Understand strategic decision-making modes
- Use the strategic audit as a method of analyzing corporate functions and activities

How does a company become successful and stay successful? Certainly not by playing it safe and following the traditional ways of doing business! This was the dilemma facing The Boeing Company, the well-known U.S.-based manufacturer of commercial and military aircraft, in 2004. Long the leader of the global airframe manufacturing industry, Boeing had been slowly losing market share since the 1990s to the European-based Airbus Industrie—a division of the European Aeronautic & Space Company (EADS). In December 2001, the EADS board of directors had committed the corporation to an objective it had never before achieved—taking from Boeing the leadership of the commercial aviation industry by building the largest commercial jet plane in the world, the Airbus 380. The A380 would carry 481 passengers in a normal multiple-class seating configuration compared to the 416 passengers carried by Boeing's 747-400 in a similar seating configuration. The A380 would not only fly 621 miles further than the 747, but it would cost airlines 15%–20% less per passenger to operate. With orders for 50 A380 aircraft in hand, the EADS board announced that the new plane would be ready for delivery during 2006. The proposed A380 program decimated the sales of Boeing's jumbo jet. Since 2000, airlines had ordered only 10 passenger Boeing 747s.

Boeing was clearly a company in difficulty in 2003. Distracted by the 1996 acquisitions of McDonnell Douglas and Rockwell Aerospace, Boeing's top management had spent the next few years strengthening the corporation's historically weak position in aerospace and defense and had allowed its traditional competency in commercial aviation to deteriorate. Boeing, once the manufacturing marvel of the world, was now spending 10%–20% more than Airbus to build a plane. The prices it asked for its planes were thus also higher. As a result, Boeing's estimated market share of the commercial market slid from nearly 70% in 1996 to less than half that by the end of 2003. Airbus claimed to have delivered 300 aircraft to Boeing's 285 and to have won 56% of the 396 orders placed by airlines in 2003—quite an improvement from 1994, when Airbus controlled only one-fifth of the market! This was quite an accomplishment, given that the A380 was so large that the modifications needed to accommodate it at airports would cost $80 million to $100 million.

Even though defense sales now accounted for more than half of the company's revenues, CEO Stonecifer realized that he needed to quickly act to regain Boeing's leadership of the commercial part of the industry. In December 2003, the board approved the strategic decision to promote a new commercial airplane, the Boeing 787, for sale to airlines. The 787 was a midrange aircraft, not a jumbo jet like the A380. The 787 would carry between 220 and 250 passengers but consume 20% less fuel and be 10% cheaper to operate than its competitor, Airbus' current midrange plane, the smaller wide-body A330-200. It was to be made from a graphite/epoxy resin instead of aluminum. It was planned to fly faster, higher, farther, cleaner, more quietly, and more efficiently than any other medium-sized jet. This was the first time since approving the 777 jet in 1990 that the company had launched an all-new plane program. Development costs were estimated at $8 billion over five years. Depending on the results of these sales efforts, the board would decide sometime during 2004 to either begin or cancel the 787 construction program. If the program was approved, the planes could be delivered in 2008—two years after the delivery of the A380.

The Boeing 787 decision was based on a completely different set of assumptions from those used by the EADS board to approve the A380. EADS' top management believed that the commercial market wanted even larger jumbo jets to travel long international routes. Airports in Asia, the Middle East, and Europe were becoming heavily congested. In these locations, the "hub-and-spoke" method of creating major airline hubs was flourishing. Using larger planes was a way of dealing with that congestion by flying more passengers per plane out of these hubs. EADS' management believed that over the next 20 years, airlines and freight carriers would need a minimum of 1,500 more aircraft at least as big as the B747. EADS' management had concluded that the key to controlling the future commercial market was by using larger, more expensive planes. The A380 was a very large bet on that future scenario. The A380 program would cost EADS almost $13 million before the first plane was delivered.

In contrast, Boeing's management believed in a very different future scenario. Noting the success of Southwest and JetBlue, among other airlines in North America, it concluded that no more than 320 extra-large planes would be sold in the future as the airline industry moved away from hub-and-spoke networks toward more direct flights between smaller airports. The fragmentation of the airline industry, with its emphasis on competing through lower costs, was the primary rationale for Boeing's fuel-efficient 787. A secondary reason was to deal with increasing passenger complaints about shrinking legroom and seat room on current planes flown by cost-conscious airlines. The 787 was designed with larger windows, seats, lavatories, and overhead bins. The plane was being designed in both short- and long-range versions. Boeing's management predicted a market for 2,000 to 3,000 such planes. Additional support for the midrange plane came from some industry analysts who predicted that the huge A380 would give new meaning to the term "cattle class." To reach necessary economies of scale, the A380 would likely devote a large portion of both of its decks to economy class, with passengers sitting three or four across, the same configuration as most of Boeing's 747s. "What's in it for me to sit on an airplane with 500 other people, wait for my bags with 500 other people, and check in with 500 other people?" asked Continental Airlines' chief, Gordon Bethune.

Which vision of the future was correct? The long-term fortunes of both Boeing and Airbus depended on two very different strategic decisions, based on two very different assessments of the market. If Airbus was correct, the market would continue to demand ever-larger airplanes. If Boeing was correct, the current wave of jumbo jets had crested, and a new wave of fuel-saving midrange jets would soon replace them. Which company's strategy had the best chance of succeeding?[1]

1.1 The Study of Strategic Management

Strategic management is that set of managerial decisions and actions that determines the long-run performance of a corporation. It includes environmental scanning (both external and internal), strategy formulation (strategic or long-range planning), strategy implementation, and evaluation and control. The study of strategic management, therefore, emphasizes the monitoring and evaluating of external opportunities and threats in light of a corporation's strengths and weaknesses. Originally called business policy, strategic management incorporates such topics as strategic planning, environmental scanning, and industry analysis.

Phases of Strategic Management

Many of the concepts and techniques that deal with strategic management have been developed and used successfully by business corporations such as General Electric and the Boston Consulting Group. Over time, business practitioners and academic researchers have expanded and refined these concepts. Initially, strategic management was of most use to large corporations operating in multiple industries. Increasing risks of error, costly mistakes, and even economic ruin are causing today's professional managers in all organizations to take strategic management seriously in order to keep their companies competitive in an increasingly volatile environment.

As managers attempt to better deal with their changing world, a firm generally evolves through the following four **phases of strategic management**[2]:

Phase 1—Basic financial planning: Managers initiate serious planning when they are requested to propose the following year's budget. Projects are proposed on the basis of very little analysis, with most information coming from within the firm. The sales force usually provides the small amount of environmental information. Such simplistic operational planning only pretends to be strategic management, yet it is quite time-consuming. Normal company activities are often suspended for weeks while managers try to cram ideas into the proposed budget. The time horizon is usually one year.

Phase 2—Forecast-based planning: As annual budgets become less useful at stimulating long-term planning, managers attempt to propose five-year plans. At this point, they consider projects that may take more than one year. In addition to internal information, managers gather any available environmental data—usually on an ad hoc basis—and extrapolate current trends five years into the future. This phase is also time-consuming, often involving a full month of managerial activity to make sure all the proposed budgets fit together. The process gets very political as managers compete for larger shares of funds. Endless meetings take place to evaluate proposals and justify assumptions. The time horizon is usually three to five years.

Phase 3—Externally oriented (strategic) planning: Frustrated with highly political yet ineffectual five-year plans, top management takes control of the planning process by initiating strategic planning. The company seeks to increase its responsiveness to changing markets and competition by thinking strategically. Planning is taken out of the hands of lower-level managers and concentrated in a planning staff whose task is to develop strategic plans for the corporation. Consultants often provide the sophisticated and innovative techniques that the planning staff uses to gather information and forecast future trends. Ex-military experts develop competitive intelligence units. Upper-level managers meet once a year at a resort "retreat" led by key members of the planning staff to evaluate and update the current strategic plan. Such top-down planning emphasizes formal strategy formulation and leaves the implementation issues to lower management levels. Top management typically develops five-year plans with help from consultants but minimal input from lower levels.

Phase 4—Strategic management: Realizing that even the best strategic plans are worthless without the input and commitment of lower-level managers, top management forms planning groups of managers and key employees at many levels, from various departments and workgroups. They develop and integrate a series of strategic plans aimed at achieving the company's primary objectives. Strategic plans at this point detail the implementation, evaluation, and control issues. Rather than attempting to perfectly forecast the future, the plans emphasize probable scenarios and contingency strategies. The sophisticated annual five-year strategic plan is replaced with strategic thinking at all levels of the organization throughout the year. Strategic information, previously available only centrally to top management, is available via local area networks and intranets to people throughout the organization. Instead of a large centralized planning staff, internal and external planning consultants are available to help guide group strategy discussions. Although top management may still initiate the strategic planning process, the resulting strategies may come from anywhere in the organization. Planning is typically interactive across levels and is no longer top down. People at all levels are now involved.

General Electric, one of the pioneers of strategic planning, led the transition from strategic planning to strategic management during the 1980s.[3] By the 1990s, most other corporations around the world had begun the conversion to strategic management.

Benefits of Strategic Management

Research has revealed that organizations that engage in strategic management generally outperform those that do not.[4] The attainment of an appropriate match, or "fit," between an organization's environment and its strategy, structure, and processes has positive effects on the organization's performance.[5] For example, studies of the impact of deregulation on the U.S. railroad and trucking industries found that companies that changed their strategies and structures as their environment changed outperformed companies that did not change.[6]

A survey of nearly 50 corporations in a variety of countries and industries found the three most highly rated benefits of strategic management to be:

- Clearer sense of strategic vision for the firm
- Sharper focus on what is strategically important
- Improved understanding of a rapidly changing environment[7]

To be effective, however, strategic management need not always be a formal process. It can begin with a few simple questions:

1. Where is the organization now? (Not where do we hope it is!)
2. If no changes are made, where will the organization be in 1 year? 2 years? 5 years? 10 years? Are the answers acceptable?
3. If the answers are not acceptable, what specific actions should management undertake? What are the risks and payoffs involved?

In 2003, Bain & Company's annual Management Tools Survey of senior executives at 708 companies on five continents revealed the most popular management tools to be strategic planning (used by 89% of firms) and developing mission and vision statements (used by 84%)—essential parts of strategic management.[8] Research into the planning practices of companies in the oil industry concludes that the real value of modern strategic planning is more in the *strategic thinking* and *organizational learning* that is part of a future-oriented planning process than in any resulting written strategic plan.[9] Small companies, in particular, may plan informally and irregularly. Nevertheless, studies of small and medium-sized businesses reveal that the greater the level of planning intensity, as measured by the presence of a formal strategic plan, the greater the level of financial performance, especially when measured in terms of sales increases.[10]

Planning the strategy of large, multidivisional corporations can be complex and time-consuming. It often takes slightly more than a year for a large company to move from situation assessment to a final decision agreement. For example, strategic plans in the global oil industry tend to cover four to five years. The planning horizon for oil exploration is even longer—up to 15 years.[11] Because of the relatively large number of people affected by a strategic decision in a large firm, a formalized, more sophisticated system is needed to ensure that strategic planning leads to successful performance. Otherwise, top management becomes isolated from developments in the business units, and lower-level managers lose sight of the corporate mission and objectives.

1.2 Globalization and Electronic Commerce: Challenges to Strategic Management

Not too long ago, a business corporation could be successful by focusing only on making and selling goods and services within its national boundaries. International considerations were minimal. Profits earned from exporting products to foreign lands were considered frosting on the cake but not really essential to corporate success. During the 1960s, for example, most U.S. companies organized themselves around a number of product divisions that made and sold goods only in the United States. All manufacturing and sales outside the United States were typically managed through one international division. An international assignment was usually considered a message that the person was no longer promotable and should be looking for another job.

Similarly, until the mid-1990s, a business firm could be very successful without using the Internet for anything more than as a public relations web site. Most business was done through a sales force and a network of distributors, with the eventual sale to the consumer being made through retail outlets. Few executives used personal computers, let alone surfed the World Wide Web. The Internet may have been useful for research, but until recently it was not seriously viewed as a means to actually conduct normal business transactions.

Impact of Globalization

Today, everything has changed. **Globalization**, the internationalization of markets and corporations, has changed the way modern corporations do business. To reach the economies of scale necessary to achieve the low costs, and thus the low prices, needed to be competitive, companies are now thinking of a global (worldwide) market instead of a national market. Nike and Reebok, for example, manufacture their athletic shoes in various countries throughout Asia for sale on every continent. Like Nike and Reebok, many other companies in North America and Western Europe are outsourcing their manufacturing, software development, or customer service to companies in China, Eastern Europe, or India. Instead of using one international division to manage everything outside the home country, large corporations are now using matrix structures in which product units are interwoven with country or regional units. International assignments are now considered key for anyone interested in reaching top management.

As more industries become global, strategic management is becoming an increasingly important way to keep track of international developments and position a company for long-term competitive advantage. For example, General Electric moved a major research and development lab for its medical systems division from Japan to China in order to learn more about developing new products for developing economies. According to Wilbur Chung, a Wharton professor, "Whatever China develops is rolled out to the rest of the world. China may have a lower GDP per-capita than developed countries, but the Chinese have a strong sense of how products should be designed for their market."[12]

The formation of regional trade associations and agreements, such as the European Union, NAFTA, Mercosur, CAFTA, and ASEAN, is changing how international business is being conducted. See the GLOBAL ISSUE feature to learn how regional trade associations are forcing corporations to establish a manufacturing presence wherever they wish to market goods or else face significant tariffs. These associations have led to the increasing harmonization of standards so that products can more easily be sold and moved across national boundaries. International considerations have led to the strategic alliance between British Airways and American Airlines and to the merger between Daimler-Benz and Chrysler Corporation, among others.

GLOBAL ISSUE

Regional Trade Associations Replace National Trade Barriers

The **European Union (EU)** is the most significant trade association in the world. The goal of the EU is the complete economic integration of its 25 member countries so that goods made in one part of Europe can move freely, without ever stopping for a customs inspection. The EU includes Austria, Belgium, Denmark, Finland, France, Germany, Greece, Ireland, Italy, Luxembourg, The Netherlands, Portugal, Spain, Sweden, the United Kingdom plus the 10 countries admitted in 2004: Czech Republic, Estonia, Hungary, Latvia, Lithuania, Poland, Slovakia, Slovenia, Cyprus, and Malta. Romania and Bulgaria hope to join in 2007. Others, including Croatia, Macedonia, and Turkey, have either recently applied or are in the process of applying. One currency, the euro, is being used throughout the region as members integrate their monetary systems. The steady elimination of barriers to free trade is providing the impetus for a series of mergers, acquisitions, and joint ventures among business corporations. The requirement of at least 60% local content to avoid tariffs has forced many U.S. and Asian companies to abandon exporting in favor of having a strong local presence in Europe.

Canada, the United States, and Mexico are affiliated economically under the **North American Free Trade Agreement (NAFTA)**. The goal of NAFTA is improved trade among the three member countries rather than complete economic integration. Launched in 1994, the agreement requires all three members to remove all tariffs among themselves over 15 years, but they are allowed to have their own tariff arrangements with nonmember countries. Cars and trucks must have 62.5% North American content to qualify for duty-free status. Transportation restrictions and other regulations are being significantly reduced. Some Asian and European corporations are locating operations in one of the NAFTA countries to obtain access to the entire North American region. Vicente Fox, the President of Mexico, proposed that NAFTA become more like the European Union in that both people and goods should have unlimited access across borders from Mexico to Canada. A number of corporations, such as Sweden's Electrolux, are building manufacturing facilities in Mexico to take advantage of the country's lower wages and easy access to U.S. and Canadian markets.

South American countries are also working to harmonize their trading relationships with each other and to form trade associations. The establishment of the **Mercosur** (**Mercosul**, in Portuguese) free-trade area among Argentina, Brazil, Uruguay, and Paraguay means that a manufacturing presence within these countries is becoming essential to avoid tariffs for nonmember countries. Claiming to be NAFTA's southern counterpart, Mercosur has extended free-trade agreements to Bolivia and Venezuela. With Chile and Argentina cooperating to build a tunnel through the Andes to connect the two countries, it is likely that Chile may also form an economic relationship with Mercosur.

In 2004, the five Central American countries of El Salvador, Guatemala, Honduras, Nicaragua, and Costa Rica, and the Dominican Republic, plus the United States signed the **Central American Free Trade Agreement (CAFTA)**. Previously, Central American textile manufacturers had to pay import duties of 18%–28% to sell their clothes in the United States unless they bought their raw material from U.S. companies. Under CAFTA, members can buy raw material from anywhere, and their exports are duty free. In addition, CAFTA eliminates import duties on 80% of all U.S. consumer and industrial goods exported to CAFTA countries and all duties on many U.S. farm exports. The agreement awaits ratification by the U.S. Congress before going into effect.

Asia has yet no comparable regional trade association to match the potential economic power of either NAFTA or the EU. Japan, South Korea, China, and India generally operate as independent economic powers. Nevertheless, the **Association of Southeast Asian Nations (ASEAN)**—composed of Brunei Darussalam, Indonesia, Malaysia, Philippines, Singapore, Thailand, Laos, Myanmar, Cambodia, and Vietnam—is attempting to link its members into a borderless economic zone. Increasingly referred to as ASEAN+3, it now includes China, Japan, and South Korea in its annual summit meetings. The ASEAN nations negotiated linkage of the ASEAN Free Trade Area (AFTA) with the existing free trade area of Australia and New Zealand. With the EU extending eastward and NAFTA extending southward to someday connect with CAFTA and Mercosur, pressure is already building on the independent Asian nations to form an expanded version of ASEAN.

Electronic Commerce

Electronic commerce refers to the use of the Internet to conduct business transactions. The Internet is reshaping the global marketplace, and it will continue to do so for many more years. Not only is the Internet changing the way customers, suppliers, and companies interact, it is changing the way companies work internally. Since its introduction, it has profoundly affected the basis of competition in many industries. Instead of the traditional focus on product features and costs, the Internet is shifting the basis for competition to a more strategic level in which the traditional value chain of an industry is drastically altered. A report by AMR Research indicated that industry leaders are in the process of moving 60%–100% of their business-to-business (B2B) transactions to the Internet. The net B2B marketplace includes (a) trading exchange platforms such as VerticalNet and i2 Technologies' TradeMatrix, which support trading communities in multiple markets; (b) industry-sponsored exchanges, such as the one being built by major automakers; and (c) net market makers, such as e-Steel, NECX, and BuildPoint, which focus on a specific industry's value chain or business processes to mediate multiple transactions among businesses.

The Internet either causes or accelerates seven current world-wide trends[13]:

1. The Internet is forcing companies to transform themselves. The concept of electronically networking customers, suppliers, and partners is now a reality.
2. New channels are changing market access and branding, causing the *disintermediation* (breaking down) of traditional distribution channels. By working directly with customers, companies are able to avoid the usual distributors—thus forming closer relationships with the end-users, improving service, and reducing costs.
3. The balance of power is shifting to the consumer. Now having unlimited access to information on the Internet, customers are much more demanding than their "non-wired" predecessors.
4. Competition is changing. New technology-driven firms plus older traditional competitors are exploiting the Internet to become more innovative and efficient.
5. The pace of business is increasing drastically. Planning horizons, information needs, and customer/supplier expectations are reflecting the immediacy of the Internet. Because of this turbulent environment, time is compressed into "dog years," in which one year feels like seven years.
6. The Internet is pushing corporations out of their traditional boundaries. The traditional separation between suppliers, manufacturers, and customers is becoming blurred with the development and expansion of extranets, in which cooperating firms have access to each other's internal operating plans and processes. For example, Lockheed Martin, the aerospace company, has an extranet that links Lockheed to Boeing, a project partner, and to the U.S. Department of Defense, a key customer.
7. Knowledge is becoming a key asset and a source of competitive advantage. For example, traditional accounting assets, such as cash and equipment, accounted for about 80% of the total market value of the Standard & Poor 500 firms in 1982, but they accounted for only about 25% in 2002. The remainder of the market value is composed of *intangible assets*, primarily powerful brands as well as intellectual capital, such as key relationships, proprietary processes, and skilled employees.[14]

1.3 Theories of Organizational Adaptation

Globalization and electronic commerce present real challenges to the strategic management of business corporations. How can any one company keep track of all the changing technological, economic, political–legal, and sociocultural trends around the world and make the necessary adjustments? This is not an easy task. Various theories have been proposed to account for how organizations obtain fit with their environment. The theory of **population ecology**, for example, proposes that once an organization is successfully established in a particular environmental niche, it is unable to adapt to changing conditions. Inertia prevents the organization from changing. The company is thus replaced (is bought out or goes bankrupt) by other organizations more suited to the new environment. Although it is popular in sociology, research fails to support the arguments of population ecology.[15] **Institution theory**, in contrast, proposes that organizations can and do adapt to changing conditions by imitating other successful organizations. To its credit, many examples can be found of companies that have adapted to changing circumstances by imitating an admired firm's strategies and management techniques.[16] The theory does not, however, explain how or by whom successful new strategies are developed in the first place. The **strategic choice perspective** goes one step further by proposing that not only do organizations adapt to a changing environment, they also have the opportunity and power to reshape their environment. This perspective is supported by research indicating that the decisions of a firm's management have at least as great an impact on firm performance as overall industry factors.[17] Because of its emphasis on managers making rational strategic decisions, the strategic choice perspective is the dominant one taken in strategic management. Its argument that adaptation is a dynamic process fits with the view of **organizational learning theory**, which says that an organization adjusts defensively to a changing environment and uses knowledge offensively to improve the fit between itself and its environment. This perspective expands the strategic choice perspective to include people at all levels becoming involved in providing input into strategic decisions.[18]

In agreement with the concepts of organizational learning theory, an increasing number of companies are realizing that they must shift from a vertically organized, top-down type of organization to a more horizontally managed, interactive organization. They are attempting to adapt more quickly to changing conditions by becoming "learning organizations."

1.4 Creating a Learning Organization

Strategic management has now evolved to the point that its primary value is in helping an organization operate successfully in a dynamic, complex environment. Inland Steel Company, for example, uses strategic planning as a tool to drive organizational change. Managers at all levels are expected to continually analyze the changing steel industry in order to create or modify strategic plans throughout the year.[19] To be competitive in dynamic environments, corporations are becoming less bureaucratic and more flexible. In stable environments such as those that existed in years past, a competitive strategy simply involved defining a competitive position and then defending it. As it takes less and less time for one product or technology to replace another, companies are finding that there is no such thing as a permanent competitive advantage. Many agree with Richard D'Aveni, who says in his book *Hypercompetition* that any sustainable competitive advantage lies not in doggedly following a centrally managed five-year plan but in stringing together a series of strategic short-term thrusts (as Intel does by cutting into the sales of its own offerings with periodic introductions of new products).[20] This means that corporations must develop *strategic flexibility*—the ability to shift from one dominant strategy to another.[21]

Strategic flexibility demands a long-term commitment to the development and nurturing of critical resources. It also demands that the company become a **learning organization**—an organization skilled at creating, acquiring, and transferring knowledge and at modifying its behavior to reflect new knowledge and insights. Organizational learning is a critical component of competitiveness in a dynamic environment. It is particularly important to innovation and new product development.[22] For example, Hewlett-Packard uses an extensive network of informal committees to transfer knowledge among its cross-functional teams and to help spread new sources of knowledge quickly.[23] Learning organizations are skilled at four main activities:

- Solving problems systematically
- Experimenting with new approaches

- Learning from their own experiences and past history as well as from the experiences of others
- Transferring knowledge quickly and efficiently throughout the organization[24]

Business historian Alfred Chandler proposes that high-technology industries are defined by "paths of learning" in which organizational strengths derive from learned capabilities.[25] According to Chandler, companies spring from an individual entrepreneur's knowledge, which then evolves into organizational knowledge. This organizational knowledge is composed of three basic strengths: technical skills, mainly in research; functional knowledge, such as production and marketing; and managerial expertise. This knowledge leads to new businesses where the company can succeed and creates an entry barrier to new competitors. Chandler points out that once a corporation has built its learning base to the point where it has become a core company in its industry, entrepreneurial startups are rarely able to successfully enter. Thus, organizational knowledge becomes a competitive advantage.

Strategic management is essential for learning organizations to avoid stagnation through continuous self-examination and experimentation. People at all levels, not just top management, participate in strategic management—helping to scan the environment for critical information, suggesting changes to strategies and programs to take advantage of environmental shifts, and working with others to continuously improve work methods, procedures, and evaluation techniques. For example, Motorola developed an action learning format in which people from marketing, product development, and manufacturing meet to argue and reach agreement about the needs of the market, the best new product, and the schedules of each group producing it. This action learning approach overcame the problems that arose previously when the three departments met and formally agreed on plans but continued with their work as if nothing had happened.[26] Research indicates that involving more people in the strategy process results in people not only viewing the process more positively but also acting in ways that make the process more effective.[27]

Organizations that are willing to experiment and are able to learn from their experiences are more successful than those that do not.[28] For example, in a study of U.S. manufacturers of diagnostic imaging equipment, the most successful firms were those that improved products sold in the United States by incorporating some of what they had learned from their manufacturing and sales experiences in other nations. The less successful firms used the foreign operations primarily as sales outlets, not as important sources of technical knowledge.[29]

1.5 Basic Model of Strategic Management

Strategic management consists of four basic elements:

- **Environmental scanning**
- **Strategy formulation**
- **Strategy implementation**
- **Evaluation and control**

Figure 1–1 illustrates how these four elements interact; **Figure 1–2** expands each of these elements and serves as the model for this book.[30] The terms used in **Figure 1–2** are explained on the following pages.

Environmental Scanning

Environmental scanning is the monitoring, evaluating, and disseminating of information from the external and internal environments to key people within the corporation. Its purpose is to identify **strategic factors**—external and internal elements that will determine the future of the corporation. The simplest way to conduct environmental scanning is through **SWOT**

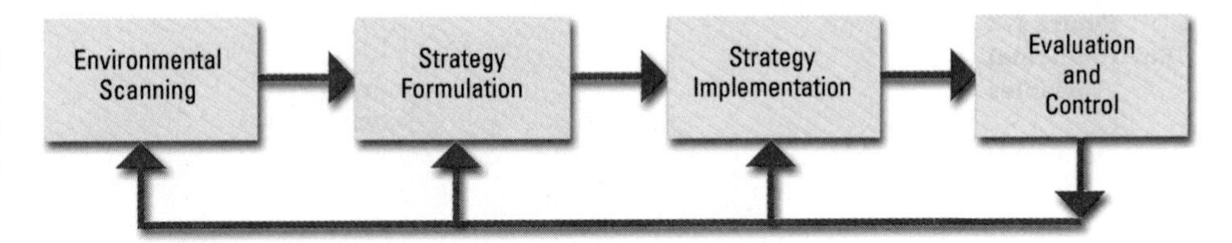

Figure 1–1 **Basic Elements of the Strategic Management Process**

Analysis. SWOT is an acronym used to describe the particular strengths, weaknesses, opportunities, and threats that are strategic factors for a specific company. The **external environment** consists of variables (opportunities and threats) that are outside the organization and not typically within the short-run control of top management. These variables form the context within which the corporation exists. **Figure 1–3** depicts key environmental variables. They may be general forces and trends within the overall societal environment or specific factors that operate within an organization's specific task environment—often called its *industry*. (These external variables are defined and discussed in more detail in **Chapter 4**.)

The **internal environment** of a corporation consists of variables (Strengths and Weaknesses) that are within the organization itself and are not usually within the short-run control of top management. These variables form the context in which work is done. They include the corporation's structure, culture, and resources. Key strengths form a set of core

Figure 1–2 **Strategic Management Model**

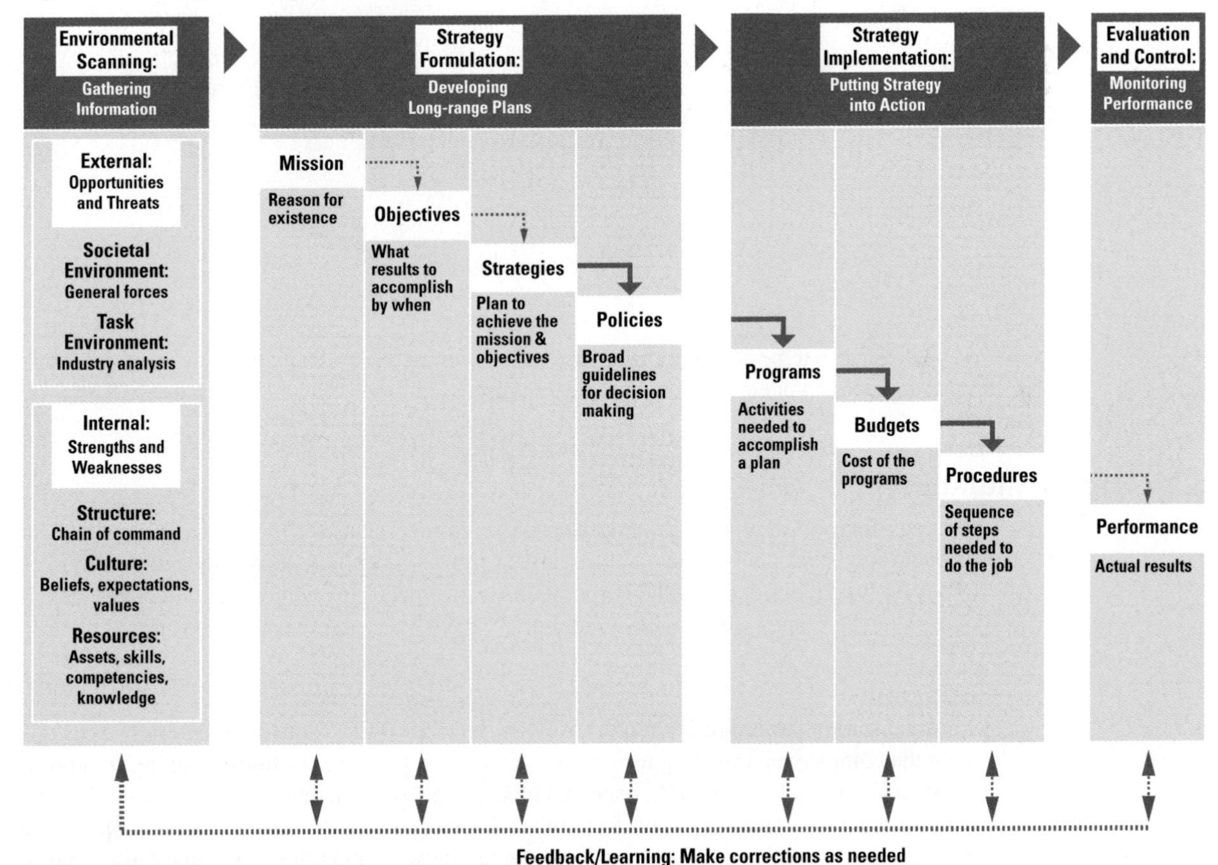

Source: T. L. Wheelen, "Strategic Management Model," adapted from "Concepts of Management," presented to Society for Advancement of Management (SAM), International Meeting, Richmond, VA, 1981. Copyright © 1981 by T. L. Wheelen and SAM. Copyright © 1982, 1985, 1988, and 2005 by T. L. Wheelen and J. D. Hunger. Revised 1989, 1995, 1998, 2000, and 2005. Reprinted by permission.

Figure 1–3
Environmental Variables

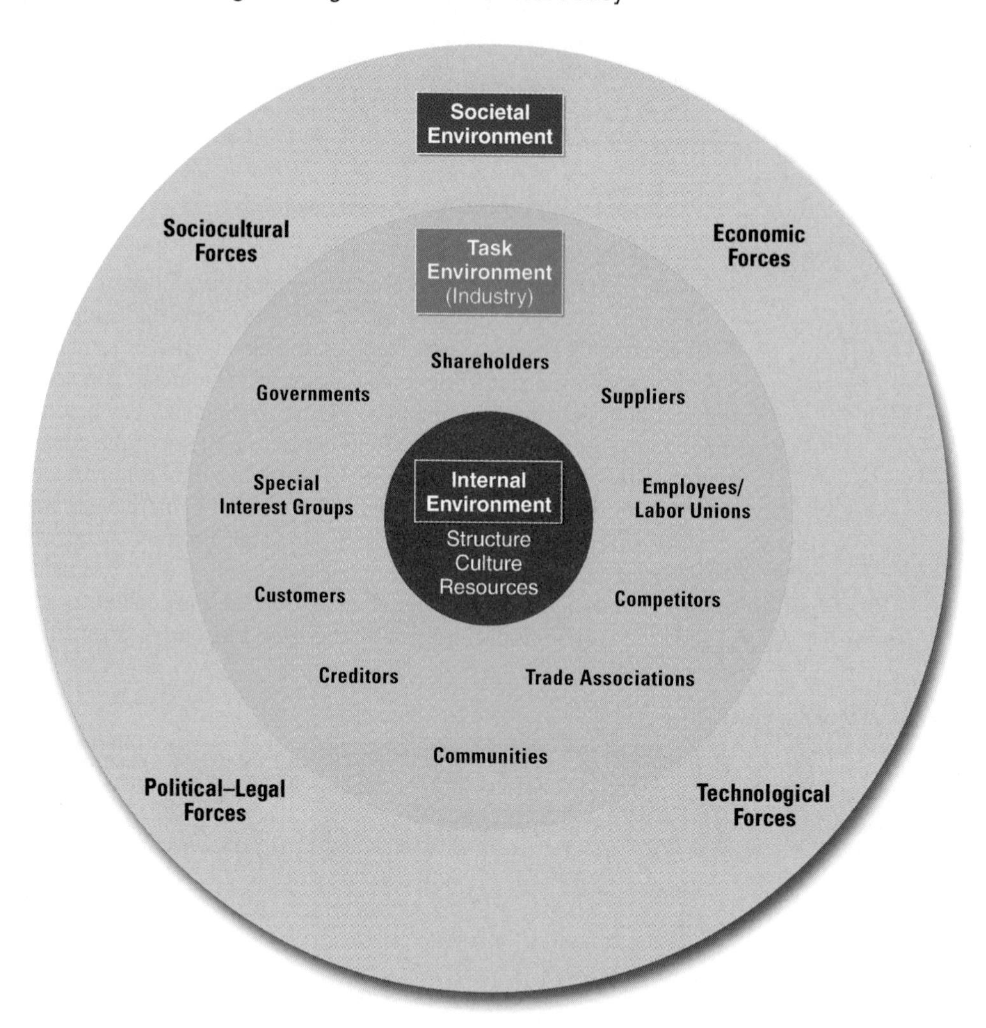

competencies that the corporation can use to gain competitive advantage. (These internal variables and core competencies are defined and discussed in more detail in **Chapter 5**.)

Strategy Formulation

Strategy formulation is the development of long-range plans for the effective management of environmental opportunities and threats, in light of corporate strengths and weaknesses (SWOT). It includes defining the corporate mission, specifying achievable objectives, developing strategies, and setting policy guidelines.

Mission

An organization's **mission** is the purpose or reason for the organization's existence. It tells what the company is providing to society—either a service such as housecleaning or a product such as automobiles. A well-conceived mission statement defines the fundamental, unique purpose that sets a company apart from other firms of its type and identifies the scope of the company's operations in terms of products (including services) offered and markets served. It may also include the firm's values and philosophy about how it does business and treats its employees. It puts into words not only what the company is now but what it wants to become—management's strategic vision of the firm's future. The mission statement promotes a sense of shared expectations in employees and communicates a public image to important stakeholder groups in the company's task environment. Some people like to consider vision and mission as two different concepts: A *mission statement* describes what the organization is now; a *vision statement* describes what the organization would like to become. We prefer to combine these ideas into a single mission statement.[31] Some companies prefer to list their values and philosophy of doing business in a separate publication called a *values statement*. For a listing of the many things that could go into a mission statement, see **STRATEGY HIGHLIGHT 1.1**.

One example of a mission statement is that of Maytag Corporation:

> *To improve the quality of home life by designing, building, marketing, and servicing the best appliances in the world.*

Another classic example is that etched in bronze at Newport News Shipbuilding, unchanged since its founding in 1886:

> *We shall build good ships here—at a profit if we can—at a loss if we must—but always good ships.*[32]

A mission may be defined narrowly or broadly in scope. An example of a *broad* mission statement is that used by many corporations: "Serve the best interests of shareowners, customers, and employees." A broadly defined mission statement such as this keeps the company from restricting itself to one field or product line, but it fails to clearly identify either what it makes or which products/markets it plans to emphasize. Because this broad statement is so general, a *narrow* mission statement, such as the preceding one by Maytag, which emphasizes appliances, is generally more useful. A narrow mission very clearly states the organization's primary busi-

STRATEGY HIGHLIGHT 1.1

Do You Have a Good Mission Statement?

Andrew Campbell, a director of the Ashridge Strategic Management Centre and a long-time contributor to *Long Range Planning*, proposes a means for evaluating a mission statement. Arguing that mission statements can be more than just an expression of a company's purpose and ambition, he suggests that they can also be a company flag to rally around, a signpost for all stakeholders, a guide to behavior, and a celebration of a company's culture. For a company trying to achieve all of the above, evaluate its mission statement using the following 10-question test. Score each question 0 for no, 1 for somewhat, or 2 for yes. According to Campbell, a score of over 15 is exceptional, and a score of less than 10 suggests that more work needs to be done.

1. Does the statement describe an inspiring purpose that avoids playing to the selfish interests of the stakeholders?
2. Does the statement describe the company's responsibility to its stakeholders?
3. Does the statement define a business domain and explain why it is attractive?
4. Does the statement describe the strategic positioning that the company prefers in a way that helps to identify the sort of competitive advantage it will look for?
5. Does the statement identify values that link with the organization's purpose and act as beliefs with which employees can feel proud?
6. Do the values resonate with and reinforce the organization's strategy?
7. Does the statement describe important behavior standards that serve as beacons of the strategy and the values?
8. Are the behavior standards described in a way that enables individual employees to judge whether they are behaving correctly?
9. Does the statement give a portrait of the company, capturing the culture of the organization?
10. Is the statement easy to read?

Source: Reprinted from *Long Range Planning*, Vol. 30, No. 6, 1997, Campbell, "Mission Statements," pp. 931–932. Copyright © 1997 with permission of Elsevier.

ness, but it may limit the scope of the firm's activities in terms of the product or service offered, the technology used, and the market served. Research indicates that a narrow mission statement may be best in a turbulent industry because it keeps the firm focused on what it does best; a broad mission statement may be best in a stable environment that lacks growth opportunities.[33]

Objectives

Objectives are the end results of planned activity. They should be stated as *action verbs* and tell what is to be accomplished by when and quantified if possible. The achievement of corporate objectives should result in the fulfillment of a corporation's mission. In effect, this is what society gives back to the corporation when the corporation does a good job of fulfilling its mission. For example, by providing society with office supplies of every kind for home and work at better quality, price, and location than its competitors, Staples has become one of the most successful retailers in the United States. Even though the office supplies market is maturing, Staples' management established the twin objectives of doubling sales to $20 billion from 2003 to 2008 while boosting net income more than 20% annually.[34]

The term *goal* is often used interchangeably with the term *objective*. In this book, we prefer to differentiate the two terms. In contrast to an objective, we consider a **goal** as an open-ended statement of what one wants to accomplish, with no quantification of what is to be achieved and no time criteria for completion. For example, a simple statement of "increased profitability" is thus a goal, not an objective, because it does not state how much profit the firm wants to make or when. A good objective should be action oriented and begin with the word *to*. An example of an objective is "to increase the firm's profitability in 2007 by 10% over 2006."

Some of the areas in which a corporation might establish its goals and objectives are:

- Profitability (net profits)
- Efficiency (low costs, etc.)
- Growth (increase in total assets, sales, etc.)
- Shareholder wealth (dividends plus stock price appreciation)
- Utilization of resources (ROE or ROI)
- Reputation (being considered a "top" firm)
- Contributions to employees (employment security, wages, diversity)
- Contributions to society (taxes paid, participation in charities, provision of a needed product or service)
- Market leadership (market share)
- Technological leadership (innovations, creativity)
- Survival (avoiding bankruptcy)
- Personal needs of top management (using the firm for personal purposes, such as providing jobs for relatives)

Strategies

A **strategy** of a corporation forms a comprehensive master plan that states how the corporation will achieve its mission and objectives. It maximizes competitive advantage and minimizes competitive disadvantage. For example, even though Staples is a major competitor in office supplies retailing, it is not likely to achieve its challenging growth objective of doubling sales within five years without making a major change in strategy. The North American and European markets for office supplies have been growing only 2% faster than their economies. Staples CEO Ronald Sargent decided to think "outside the box" by reducing new store openings and instead emphasizing delivering office supplies from warehouses directly to businesses. Sargent believed that the delivery business could equal revenue from Staples store sales.[35]

The typical business firm usually considers three types of strategy: corporate, business, and functional.

1. **Corporate strategy** describes a company's overall direction in terms of its general attitude toward growth and the management of its various businesses and product lines. Corporate strategies typically fit within the three main categories of stability, growth, and retrenchment. Staples, for example, was following a corporate strategy of growth by diversifying from its base in retailing into the delivery business.
2. **Business strategy** usually occurs at the business unit or product level, and it emphasizes improvement of the competitive position of a corporation's products or services in the specific industry or market segment served by that business unit. Business strategies are grouped into two overall categories, *competitive* and *cooperative* strategies. For example, Staples has used a competitive strategy to differentiate its retail stores from its competitors by adding services to its stores, such as copying, UPS shipping, and hiring mobile technicians who can fix computers and install networks. British Airways has followed a cooperative strategy by forming an alliance with American Airlines in order to provide global service. Cooperative strategy may thus be used to support a competitive strategy. Intel, a manufacturer of computer microprocessors, uses its alliance (cooperative strategy) with Microsoft to differentiate itself (competitive strategy) from AMD, its primary competitor.
3. **Functional strategy** is the approach taken by a functional area to achieve corporate and business unit objectives and strategies by maximizing resource productivity. It is concerned with developing and nurturing a distinctive competence to provide a company or business unit with a competitive advantage. Examples of research and development (R&D) functional strategies are technological followership (imitation of the products of other companies) and technological leadership (pioneering of an innovation). For years, Magic Chef had been a successful appliance maker by spending little on R&D but by quickly imitating the innovations of other competitors. This has helped the company to keep its costs lower than those of its competitors and consequently to compete with lower prices. In terms of marketing functional strategies, Procter & Gamble (P&G) is a master of marketing "pull"—the process of spending huge amounts on advertising in order to create customer demand. This supports P&G's competitive strategy of differentiating its products from those of its competitors.

Business firms use all three types of strategy simultaneously. A **hierarchy of strategy** is a grouping of strategy types by level in the organization. Hierarchy of strategy is a nesting of one strategy within another so that they complement and support one another. (See **Figure 1–4**.) Functional strategies support business strategies, which, in turn, support the corporate strategy(ies).

Just as many firms often have no formally stated objectives, many firms have unstated, incremental, or intuitive strategies that have never been articulated or analyzed. Often the only way to spot a corporation's implicit strategies is to look not at what management says but at what it does. Implicit strategies can be derived from corporate policies, programs approved (and disapproved), and authorized budgets. Programs and divisions favored by budget increases and staffed by managers who are considered to be on the fast promotion track reveal where the corporation is putting its money and its energy.

Policies

A **policy** is a broad guideline for decision making that links the formulation of a strategy with its implementation. Companies use policies to make sure that employees throughout the firm make decisions and take actions that support the corporation's mission, objectives, and strategies. For example, when Cisco decided on a strategy of growth through acquisitions, it estab-

Figure 1–4 **Hierarchy of Strategy**

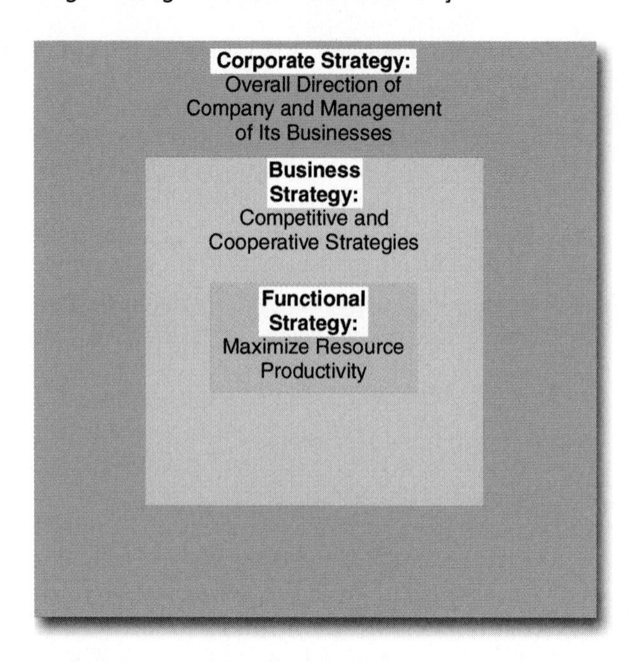

lished a policy to consider only companies with no more than 75 employees, 75% of whom were engineers.[36] Consider the following company policies:

- **Maytag Company:** Maytag will not approve any cost-reduction proposal if it reduces product quality in any way. (This policy supports Maytag's competitive strategy in which Maytag brands compete on quality rather than on price.)
- **3M:** 3M says researchers should spend 15% of their time working on something other than their primary project. (This supports 3M's strong product development strategy.)
- **Intel:** Intel cannibalizes its own product line (undercuts the sales of its current products) with better products before a competitor does so. (This supports Intel's objective of market leadership.)
- **General Electric:** GE must be number one or two wherever it competes. (This supports GE's objective to be number one in market capitalization.)
- **Southwest Airlines:** Southwest offers no meals or reserved seating on airplanes. (This supports Southwest's competitive strategy of having the lowest costs in the industry.)

Policies like these provide clear guidance to managers throughout the organization. (Strategy formulation is discussed in greater detail in **Chapters 6, 7**, and **8**.)

Strategy Implementation

Strategy implementation is a process by which strategies and policies are put into action through the development of programs, budgets, and procedures. This process might involve changes within the overall culture, structure, and/or management system of the entire organization. Except when such drastic corporatewide changes are needed, however, the implementation of strategy is typically conducted by middle and lower-level managers, with review by top management. Sometimes referred to as *operational planning*, strategy implementation often involves day-to-day decisions in resource allocation.

Programs

A **program** is a statement of the activities or steps needed to accomplish a single-use plan. It makes a strategy action oriented. It may involve restructuring the corporation, changing the company's internal culture, or beginning a new research effort. For example, Boeing's strategy to regain industry leadership with its proposed 787 airplane meant that the company had to increase its manufacturing efficiency in order to keep the price low. To significantly cut costs, management decided to implement a series of programs:

- Outsource approximately 70% of manufacturing.
- Reduce final assembly time to 3 days (compared to 20 for its 737 plane) by having suppliers build completed plane sections.
- Use new, lightweight composite materials in place of aluminum to reduce inspection time.
- Resolve poor relations with labor unions caused by downsizing and outsourcing.

Another example is discount retailer Dollar General's programs to double the amount of space in the company's distribution centers in order to reduce the number of truck deliveries and to redesign its stores to provide wider aisles and a brighter, cleaner appearance.[37]

Budgets

A **budget** is a statement of a corporation's programs in terms of dollars. Used in planning and control, a budget lists the detailed cost of each program. Many corporations demand a certain percentage return on investment, often called a "hurdle rate," before management will approve a new program. This ensures that the new program will significantly add to the corporation's profit performance and thus build shareholder value. The budget thus not only serves as a detailed plan of the new strategy in action, it also specifies through pro forma financial statements the expected impact on the firm's financial future.

For example, General Motors budgeted $4.3 billion during 2000 through 2004 to update and expand its Cadillac line of automobiles. With this money, the company was able to increase the number of models from five to nine and to offer more powerful engines, sportier handling, and edgier styling. The company reversed its declining market share by appealing to a younger market. (The average Cadillac buyer was 67 years old in 2000.[38]) Another example is the $8 billion budget that General Electric established to invest in new jet engine technology for regional-jet airplanes. Management decided that an anticipated growth in regional jets should be the company's target market. The program paid off in 2003 when GE won a $3 billion contract to provide jet engines for China's new fleet of 500 regional jets in time for the 2008 Beijing Olympics.[39]

Procedures

Procedures, sometimes termed Standard Operating Procedures (SOP), are a system of sequential steps or techniques that describe in detail how a particular task or job is to be done. They typically detail the various activities that must be carried out in order to complete the corporation's program. For example, when the home improvement retailer Home Depot noted that sales were lagging because its stores were full of clogged aisles, long checkout times, and too few sales people, management changed its procedures for restocking shelves and pricing the products. Instead of requiring its employees to do these activities at the same time they were working with customers, management moved these activities to when the stores were closed at night. Employees were then able to focus on increasing customer sales during the day. In order to repair poor labor relations, Boeing's CEO agreed to allow the machinists' union a greater voice in specifying manufacturing procedures. (Strategy implementation is discussed in more detail in **Chapters 9** and **10**.)

Evaluation and Control

Evaluation and control is a process in which corporate activities and performance results are monitored so that actual performance can be compared with desired performance. Managers at all levels use the resulting information to take corrective action and resolve problems.

Although evaluation and control is the final major element of strategic management, it can also pinpoint weaknesses in previously implemented strategic plans and thus stimulate the entire process to begin again.

Performance is the end result of activities.[40] It includes the actual outcomes of the strategic management process. The practice of strategic management is justified in terms of its ability to improve an organization's performance, typically measured in terms of profits and return on investment. For evaluation and control to be effective, managers must obtain clear, prompt, and unbiased information from the people below them in the corporation's hierarchy. Using this information, managers compare what is actually happening with what was originally planned in the formulation stage.

For example, when the Legend (renamed Lenovo) Group of China decided to diversify out of personal computers to increase its revenues from $3 to $10 billion over a five-year period, it monitored, among other things, the sales of its personal computers. When management noted that the Chinese market share of its PCs had dropped from 30% to 27% over three years, it realized that its strategy was flawed.

The evaluation and control of performance completes the strategic management model. Based on performance results, management may need to make adjustments in its strategy formulation, in implementation, or in both. (Evaluation and control is discussed in more detail in **Chapter 11**.)

Feedback/Learning Process

Note that the strategic management model depicted in **Figure 1–2** includes a feedback/learning process. Arrows are drawn coming out of each part of the model and taking information to each of the previous parts of the model. As a firm or business unit develops strategies, programs, and the like, it often must go back to revise or correct decisions made earlier in the process. For example, poor performance (as measured in evaluation and control) usually indicates that something has gone wrong with either strategy formulation or implementation. It could also mean that a key variable, such as a new competitor, was ignored during environmental scanning and assessment. In the case of the Legend (Lenovo) Group, falling market share in PCs meant that its diversification strategy was not performing as expected. According to Legend's Chairman Liu Chuanzhi: "In view of these developments, this year [2004] Legend carried out a thorough and careful review of our plans in the past three years. We have decided to retreat from diversification and refocus on the PC business."[41]

1.6 Initiation of Strategy: Triggering Events

After much research, Henry Mintzberg discovered that strategy formulation is typically not a regular, continuous process: "It is most often an irregular, discontinuous process, proceeding in fits and starts. There are periods of stability in strategy development, but also there are periods of flux, of groping, of piecemeal change, and of global change."[42] This view of strategy formulation as an irregular process can be explained by the very human tendency to continue on a particular course of action until something goes wrong or a person is forced to question his or her actions. This period of strategic drift may result from inertia on the part of the organization, or it may reflect management's belief that the current strategy is still appropriate and needs only some fine-tuning.

Most large organizations tend to follow a particular strategic orientation for about 15 to 20 years before making a significant change in direction. This phenomenon, called **punctuated equilibrium**, describes corporations as evolving through relatively long periods of stability (equilibrium periods) punctuated by relatively short bursts of fundamental change (revolutionary periods).[43] After this rather long period of fine-tuning an existing strategy, some sort of shock to the system is needed to motivate management to seriously reassess the corporation's situation.

A **triggering event** is something that acts as a stimulus for a change in strategy. Some possible triggering events are[44]:

- **New CEO:** By asking a series of embarrassing questions, a new CEO cuts through the veil of complacency and forces people to question the very reason for the corporation's existence.
- **External intervention:** A firm's bank suddenly refuses to approve a new loan or suddenly demands payment in full on an old one. A customer complains about a serious product defect.
- **Threat of a change in ownership:** Another firm may initiate a takeover by buying a company's common stock.
- **Performance gap:** A **performance gap** exists when performance does not meet expectations. Sales and profits either are no longer increasing or may even be falling.
- **Strategic inflection point:** Coined by Andy Grove, past-CEO of Intel Corporation, a strategic inflection point is what happens to a business when a major change takes place due to the introduction of new technologies, a different regulatory environment, a change in customers' values, or a change in what customers prefer.[45]

Sun Microsystems is an example of one company in which a triggering event forced management to radically rethink what it was doing. See **STRATEGY HIGHLIGHT 1.2** to learn how one phone call to Sun's president stimulated a change in strategy at Sun.

STRATEGY HIGHLIGHT 1.2

Triggering Event at Sun Microsystems

Sun Microsystems President Edward Zander received a personal phone call directly from Margaret Whitman, CEO of eBay, Inc., an Internet auction firm. After a string of small computer crashes, eBay had just suffered a 22-hour outage of its web site. Whitman called Zander to report that there was a bug in Sun's top-of-the-line server and that Sun had better fix it immediately or else lose eBay's business. A series of around-the-clock meetings at Sun revealed that the problem was that Sun's customers had no idea of how to maintain a $1 million-plus computer. eBay had failed to provide sufficient air conditioning to keep the machine cool. Even though Sun had issued a software patch to fix a problem many months earlier, eBay had neglected to install it. The list went on and on. Sun soon realized that the problem was bigger than just eBay. More than 40% of the servers that manage most web sites were made by Sun. As more firms were expanding their business to include the Internet, this market for Sun's servers was expected to boom. Nevertheless, many of these firms were too new and small to have the proper technology infrastructure. "It suddenly hit me," said Zander. "How many future eBays are buying their first computer from us this very minute?" According to Scott McNealy, CEO of Sun, "That's when we realized that it wasn't eBay's fault. It was our fault."

Since that realization, Sun's management team has been rebuilding the company to make its servers as reliable as the telephone system. In a drastic strategic change, management decided to expand beyond simply selling servers to providing many of the technologies required to make Web servers completely reliable. It now provides storage products, e-business software, and consultants who not only supply the hardware but work directly with the customers to ensure that the servers are operated properly. Just as high-tech mainframe managers used to say that "No one gets fired for choosing IBM," Zander aims to have the same said of Sun Microsystems. "I want to be the safe bet for companies that need the most innovative technology," added Sun's president.

Source: Summarized from P. Burrows, "Sun's Bid to Rule the Web," *Business Week E.Biz* (July 24, 2000), pp. EB 31–42.

1.7 Strategic Decision Making

The distinguishing characteristic of strategic management is its emphasis on strategic decision making. As organizations grow larger and more complex, with more uncertain environments, decisions become increasingly complicated and difficult to make. In agreement with the strategic choice perspective mentioned earlier, this book proposes a strategic decision-making framework that can help people make these decisions, regardless of their level and function in a corporation.

What Makes a Decision Strategic?

Unlike many other decisions, **strategic decisions** deal with the long-run future of an entire organization and have three characteristics:

1. **Rare:** Strategic decisions are unusual and typically have no precedent to follow.
2. **Consequential:** Strategic decisions commit substantial resources and demand a great deal of commitment from people at all levels.
3. **Directive:** Strategic decisions set precedents for lesser decisions and future actions throughout an organization.[46]

One example of a strategic decision was that made by Zippo Manufacturing, the maker of the Zippo cigarette lighter. The lighter's distinctive click, its windproof design, and its lifetime guarantee made it a favorite of smokers around the world. It was also popular with a worldwide community of Zippo "tricksters"—people who use Zippos not to light cigarettes but to perform sleight of hand. Realizing that tobacco products were a declining industry, in 2003 Zippo's management established the twin objectives of not only doubling current sales of $140 million but also deriving half the company's revenue from products unrelated to tobacco by 2010. The company began to think of itself as "selling flame" and no longer limiting itself to products that light tobacco. As a result, Zippo introduced a line of multipurpose lighters for candles, grills, and fireplaces. It also purchased the knifemaker Case Cutlery. Executives initiated discussions with manufacturers of grills, torches, space heaters, and fireplaces, among other fire-related products, for a series of Zippo-branded patio products. Management's decision to diversify was clearly a strategic one.[47]

Mintzberg's Modes of Strategic Decision Making

Some strategic decisions are made in a flash by one person (often an entrepreneur or a powerful chief executive officer) who has a brilliant insight and is quickly able to convince others to adopt his or her idea. Other strategic decisions seem to develop out of a series of small incremental choices that over time push an organization more in one direction than another. According to Mintzberg, the three most typical approaches, or modes, of strategic decision making are entrepreneurial, adaptive, and planning (a fourth mode, logical incrementalism, was added later by Quinn)[48]:

- **Entrepreneurial mode.** Strategy is made by one powerful individual. The focus is on opportunities; problems are secondary. Strategy is guided by the founder's own vision of direction and is exemplified by large, bold decisions. The dominant goal is growth of the corporation. Amazon.com, founded by Jeff Bezos, is an example of this mode of strategic decision making. The company reflected Bezos' vision of using the Internet to market books and more. Although Amazon's clear growth strategy was certainly an advantage of the entrepreneurial mode, Bezos' eccentric management style made it difficult to retain senior executives.[49]

- **Adaptive mode.** Sometimes referred to as "muddling through," this decision-making mode is characterized by reactive solutions to existing problems rather than a proactive search for new opportunities. Much bargaining goes on concerning priorities of objectives. Strategy is fragmented and is developed to move a corporation forward incrementally. This mode is typical of most universities, many large hospitals, a large number of governmental agencies, and a surprising number of large corporations. Encyclopaedia Britannica, Inc., operated successfully for many years in this mode, but it continued to rely on the door-to-door selling of its prestigious books long after dual-career couples made that marketing approach obsolete. Only after it was acquired in 1996 did the company change its door-to-door sales to television advertising and Internet marketing. The company now charges libraries and individual subscribers for complete access to Britannica.com and offers CD-ROMs in addition to a small number of its 32-volume print set.[50]
- **Planning mode.** This decision-making mode involves the systematic gathering of appropriate information for situation analysis, the generation of feasible alternative strategies, and the rational selection of the most appropriate strategy. It includes both the proactive search for new opportunities and the reactive solution of existing problems. IBM under CEO Louis Gerstner is an example of planning mode. When Gerstner accepted the position of CEO in 1993, he realized that IBM was in serious difficulty. Mainframe computers, the company's primary product line, were suffering a rapid decline in both sales and market share. One of Gerstner's first actions was to convene a two-day meeting on corporate strategy with senior executives. An in-depth analysis of IBM's product line revealed that the only part of the company that was growing was services, but it was a relatively small segment and not very profitable. Rather than focus on making and selling its own computer hardware, IBM made the strategic decision to invest in services that integrated information technology. IBM thus decided to provide a complete set of services, from building systems to defining architecture to actually running and managing the computers for the customer—regardless of who made the products. Because it was no longer important that the company be completely vertically integrated, it sold off its DRAM and disk-drive businesses and exited software application development. Since making this strategic decision in 1993, 80% of IBM's revenue growth has come from services.[51]
- **Logical incrementalism.** A fourth decision-making mode, which can be viewed as a synthesis of the planning, adaptive, and, to a lesser extent, the entrepreneurial modes. In this mode, top management has a reasonably clear idea of the corporation's mission and objectives, but, in its development of strategies, it chooses to use "an interactive process in which the organization probes the future, experiments and learns from a series of partial (incremental) commitments rather than through global formulations of total strategies."[52] Thus, although the mission and objectives are set, the strategy is allowed to emerge out of debate, discussion, and experimentation. This approach appears to be useful when the environment is changing rapidly and when it is important to build consensus and develop needed resources before committing an entire corporation to a specific strategy. In his analysis of the petroleum industry, Grant described strategic planning in this industry as "planned emergence." Corporate headquarters established the mission and objectives but allowed the business units to propose strategies to achieve them.[53]

Strategic Decision-Making Process: Aid to Better Decisions

Good arguments can be made for using either the entrepreneurial or adaptive modes (or logical incrementalism) in certain situations. This book proposes, however, that in most situations the planning mode, which includes the basic elements of the strategic management process, is a more rational and thus better way of making strategic decisions. Research indicates that the planning mode is not only more analytical and less political than are the other modes, but it is also more appropriate for dealing with complex, changing environments.[54] We therefore pro-

Figure 1–5
Strategic Decision-Making Process

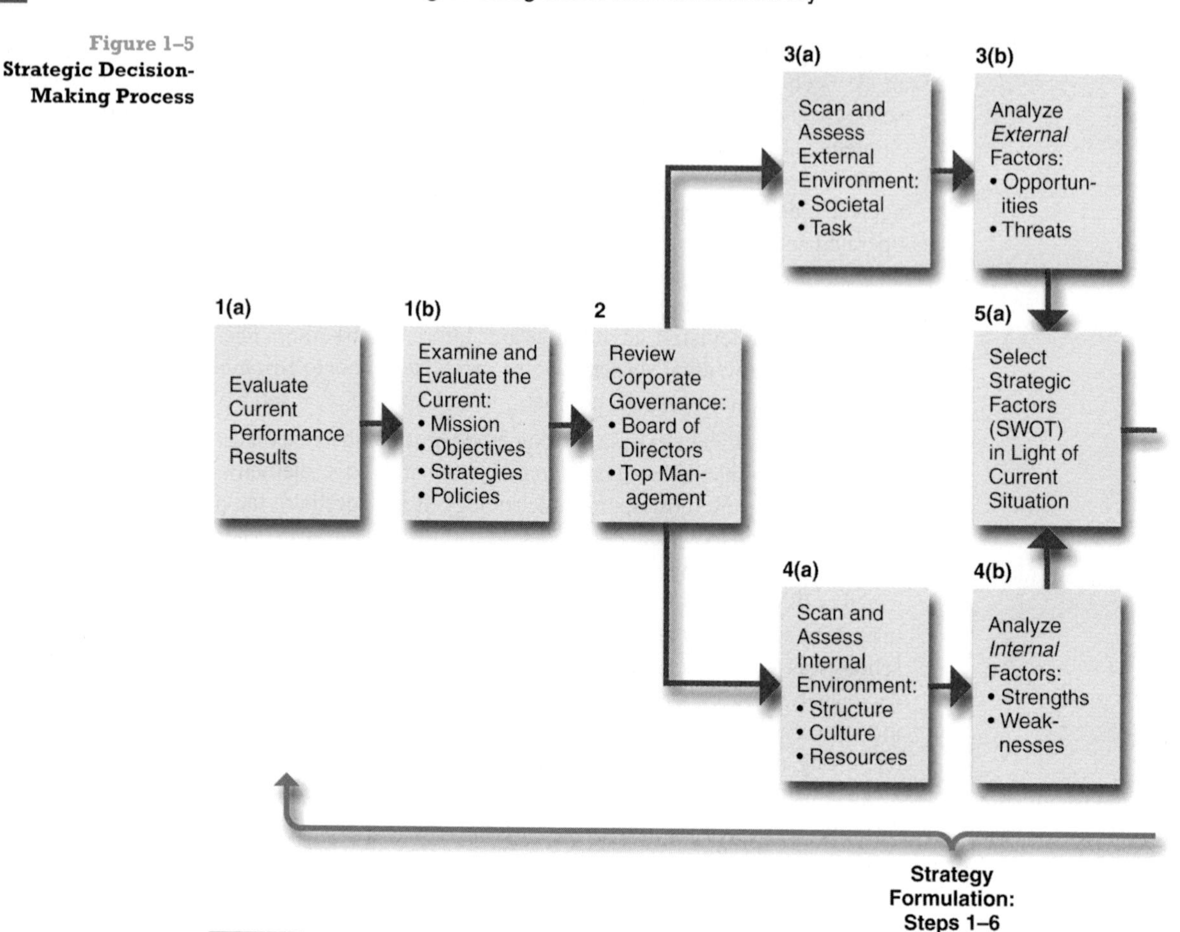

Source: T. L. Wheelen and J. D. Hunger, "Strategic Decision-Making Process." Copyright © 1994 and 1997 by Wheelen and Hunger Associates. Reprinted by permission.

pose the following eight-step **strategic decision-making process** to improve the making of strategic decisions (see **Figure 1–5**):

1. **Evaluate current performance results** in terms of (a) return on investment, profitability, and so forth, and (b) the current mission, objectives, strategies, and policies.
2. **Review corporate governance**—that is, the performance of the firm's board of directors and top management.
3. **Scan and assess the external environment** to determine the strategic factors that pose Opportunities and Threats.
4. **Scan and assess the internal corporate environment** to determine the strategic factors that are Strengths (especially core competencies) and Weaknesses.
5. **Analyze strategic (SWOT) factors** to (a) pinpoint problem areas and (b) review and revise the corporate mission and objectives, as necessary.
6. **Generate, evaluate, and select the best alternative strategy** in light of the analysis conducted in step 5.
7. **Implement selected strategies** via programs, budgets, and procedures.
8. **Evaluate implemented strategies** via feedback systems and the control of activities to ensure their minimum deviation from plans.

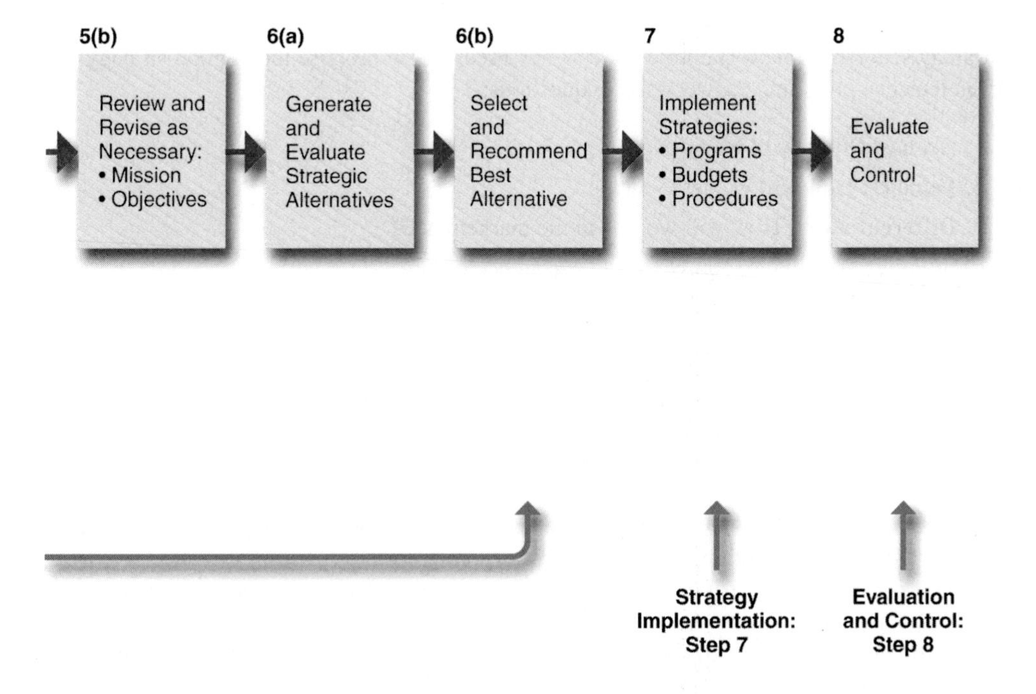

This rational approach to strategic decision making has been used successfully by corporations such as Warner-Lambert, Target, General Electric, IBM, Avon Products, Bechtel Group, Inc., and Taisei Corporation.

1.8 The Strategic Audit: Aid to Strategic Decision Making

The strategic decision-making process is put into action through a technique known as the strategic audit. A **strategic audit** provides a checklist of questions, by area or issue, that enables a systematic analysis to be made of various corporate functions and activities. (See **Appendix 1.A** at the end of this chapter.) Note that the numbered primary headings in the audit are the same as the numbered blocks in the strategic decision-making process in **Figure 1–5**. Beginning with an evaluation of current performance, the audit continues with environmental scanning, strategy formulation, and strategy implementation. It concludes with evaluation and control. A strategic audit is a type of management audit and is extremely useful as a diagnostic tool to pinpoint corporatewide problem areas and to highlight organizational strengths and weaknesses.[55] A strategic audit can help determine why a certain area is creating problems for a corporation and help generate solutions to the problem.

A strategic audit is not an all-inclusive list, but it presents many of the critical questions needed for a detailed strategic analysis of any business corporation. Some questions or even some areas might be inappropriate for a particular company; in other cases, the questions may be insufficient for a complete analysis. However, each question in a particular area of a strategic audit can be broken down into an additional series of subquestions. A company can develop these subquestions when they are needed for a complete strategic analysis of the company.

1.9 Conclusion

Strategy scholars Donald Hambrick and James Fredrickson propose that a good strategy has five elements, providing answers to five questions:

1. **Arenas:** Where will we be active?
2. **Vehicles:** How will we get there?
3. **Differentiators:** How will we win in the marketplace?
4. **Staging:** What will be our speed and sequence of moves?
5. **Economic logic:** How will we obtain our returns?[56]

This chapter introduces you to a well-accepted model of strategic management (**Figure 1–2**) in which environmental scanning leads to strategy formulation, strategy implementation, and evaluation and control. It further shows how that model can be put into action through the strategic decision-making process (**Figure 1–5**) and a strategic audit (**Appendix 1.A**). As pointed out by Hambrick and Fredrickson, "a strategy consists of an integrated set of choices."[57] The questions "Where will we be active?" and "How will we get there?" are dealt with by a company's mission, objectives, and corporate strategy. The question "How will we win in the marketplace?" is the concern of business strategy. The question "What will be our speed and sequence of moves?" is answered not only by business tactics but also by functional strategy and by implemented programs, budgets, and procedures. The question "How will we obtain our returns?" is the primary emphasis of the evaluation and control element of the strategic management model. Each of these questions and topics is dealt with in greater detail in the chapters to come. Welcome to the study of strategic management!

Strategy Bits

- From 1993 to 2002, U.S. trade with Canada and Mexico increased from 25% to 33% of total U.S. international trade.
- Average Gross Domestic Product (GDP) per person in the 10 countries joining the European Union in 2004 is only 46% of that of the original 15 member countries.
- Indonesia and Brazil have the fourth and fifth largest populations in the world after China (first), India (second), and the United States (third).[58]

Discussion Questions

1. Why has strategic management become so important to today's corporations?
2. How does strategic management typically evolve in a corporation?
3. What is a learning organization? Is this approach to strategic management better than the more traditional top-down approach in which strategic planning is primarily done by top management?
4. Why are strategic decisions different from other kinds of decisions?
5. When is the planning mode of strategic decision making superior to the entrepreneurial and adaptive modes?

Strategic Practice Exercises

Mission statements vary widely from one company to another. Why is one mission statement better than another? Using Campbell's questions in **STRATEGY HIGHLIGHT 1.1** as a starting point, develop criteria for evaluating any mission statement. Then do one or both of the following exercises:

1. Evaluate the following mission statement of Celestial Seasonings. How many points would Campbell give it?

   Our mission is to grow and dominate the U.S. specialty tea market by exceeding consumer expectations with the best tasting, 100% natural hot and iced teas, packaged with Celestial art and philosophy, creating the most valued tea experience. Through leadership, innovation, focus, and teamwork, we are dedicated to continuously improving value to our consumers, customers, employees, and stakeholders with a quality-first organization.[59]

2. Using the Internet, find the mission statements of three different organizations, which can be business or not-for-profit. (Hint: Check annual reports and 10-K forms. They can often be found via a link on a company's Web page or through Hoovers.com.) Which mission statement is best? Why?

Key Terms

adaptive mode (p. 21)
Association of Southeast Asian Nations (ASEAN) (p. 7)
budget (p. 17)
business strategy (p. 15)
Central American Free Trade Agreement (CAFTA) (p. 7)
corporate strategy (p. 15)
electronic commerce (p. 7)
entrepreneurial mode (p. 20)
environmental scanning (p. 10)
European Union (EU) (p. 7)
evaluation and control (p. 17)
external environment (p. 11)
functional strategy (p. 15)
globalization (p. 6)
goal (p. 14)
hierarchy of strategy (p. 15)
institution theory (p. 9)
internal environment (p. 11)
learning organization (p. 9)
logical incrementalism (p. 21)
mission (p. 12)
Mercosur/Mercosul (p. 7)
North American Free Trade Agreement (NAFTA) (p. 7)
objective (p. 14)
organizational learning theory (p. 9)
performance (p. 18)
performance gap (p. 19)
phases of strategic management (p. 4)
planning mode (p. 21)
policy (p. 15)
population ecology (p. 8)
procedures (p. 17)
program (p. 16)
punctuated equilibrium (p. 18)
strategic audit (p. 23)
strategic choice perspective (p. 9)
strategic decision-making process (p. 22)
strategic decisions (p. 20)
strategic factors (p. 10)
strategic management (p. 3)
strategy (p. 14)
strategy formulation (p. 12)
strategy implementation (p. 16)
SWOT analysis (p. 11)
triggering event (p. 19)

APPENDIX 1.A
Strategic Audit of a Corporation

I. CURRENT SITUATION

A. Current Performance

How did the corporation perform the past year overall in terms of return on investment, market share, and profitability?

B. Strategic Posture

What are the corporation's current mission, objectives, strategies, and policies?

1. Are they clearly stated, or are they merely implied from performance?
2. **Mission:** What business(es) is the corporation in? Why?
3. **Objectives:** What are the corporate, business, and functional objectives? Are they consistent with each other, with the mission, and with the internal and external environments?
4. **Strategies:** What strategy or mix of strategies is the corporation following? Are they consistent with each other, with the mission and objectives, and with the internal and external environments?
5. **Policies:** What are the corporation's policies? Are they consistent with each other, with the mission, objectives, and strategies, and with the internal and external environments?
6. Do the current mission, objectives, strategies, and policies reflect the corporation's international operations, whether global or multidomestic?

II. CORPORATE GOVERNANCE

A. Board of Directors

1. Who is on the board? Are they internal or external members?

Source: T. L. Wheelen and J. D. Hunger, *Strategic Audit of a Corporation*, Copyright © 1982 and 2005 by Wheelen and Hunger Associates. Originally in T. L. Wheelen and J. D. Hunger, "The Strategic Audit," 1975, 1977, 1979, and 2005. Presented by J. D. Hunger and T. L. Wheelen in "The Strategic Audit: An Integrative Approach to Teaching Business Policy," to Academy of Management, August 1983. Published in "Using the Strategic Audit," by T. L. Wheelen and J. D. Hunger in *SAM Advanced Management Journal* (Winter, 1987), pp. 4–12. Reprinted by permission. Revised 1988, 1991, 1994, 1997, 2000, 2002, 2004 and 2005.

2. Do they own significant shares of stock?
3. Is the stock privately held or publicly traded? Are there different classes of stock with different voting rights?
4. What do the board members contribute to the corporation in terms of knowledge, skills, background, and connections? If the corporation has international operations, do board members have international experience?
5. How long have members served on the board?
6. What is their level of involvement in strategic management? Do they merely rubber-stamp top management's proposals, or do they actively participate and suggest future directions?

B. Top Management

1. What person or group constitutes top management?
2. What are top management's chief characteristics in terms of knowledge, skills, background, and style? If the corporation has international operations, does top management have international experience? Are executives from acquired companies considered part of the top management team?
3. Has top management been responsible for the corporation's performance over the past few years? How many managers have been in their current position for less than three years? Were they promoted internally or externally hired?
4. Has top management established a systematic approach to strategic management?
5. What is top management's level of involvement in the strategic management process?
6. How well does top management interact with lower-level managers and with the board of directors?
7. Are strategic decisions made ethically, in a socially responsible manner?
8. What role do stock options play in executive compensation?
9. Is top management sufficiently skilled to cope with likely future challenges?

III. EXTERNAL ENVIRONMENT: OPPORTUNITIES AND THREATS (SW**OT**)

A. Societal Environment

1. What general environmental forces are currently affecting both the corporation and the industries in which it competes? Which present current or future threats? Opportunities? (Refer to **Table 4–1**)
   a. Economic
   b. Technological
   c. Political–legal
   d. Sociocultural
2. Are these forces different in other regions of the world?

B. Task Environment

1. What forces drive industry competition? Are these forces the same globally, or do they vary from country to country? Rate each force as **high, medium,** or **low.**
   a. Threat of new entrants
   b. Bargaining power of buyers

c. Threat of substitute products or services
d. Bargaining power of suppliers
e. Rivalry among competing firms
f. Relative power of unions, governments, special interest groups, etc.

2. What key factors in the immediate environment (that is, customers, competitors, suppliers, creditors, labor unions, governments, trade associations, interest groups, local communities, and shareholders) are currently affecting the corporation? Which are current or future Threats? Opportunities?

C. Summary of External Factors *(List in the EFAS Table 4–5, p. 97)*

Which of these forces are the most important to the corporation and to the industries in which it competes at the present time? Which will be important in the future?

IV. INTERNAL ENVIRONMENT: STRENGTHS AND WEAKNESSES (**SW**OT)

A. Corporate Structure

1. How is the corporation structured at present?
   a. Is the decision-making authority centralized around one group or decentralized to many units?
   b. Is the corporation organized on the basis of functions, projects, geography, or some combination of these?
2. Is the structure clearly understood by everyone in the corporation?
3. Is the present structure consistent with current corporate objectives, strategies, policies, and programs, as well as with the firm's international operations?
4. In what ways does this structure compare with those of similar corporations?

B. Corporate Culture

1. Is there a well-defined or emerging culture composed of shared beliefs, expectations, and values?
2. Is the culture consistent with the current objectives, strategies, policies, and programs?
3. What is the culture's position on important issues facing the corporation (that is, on productivity, quality of performance, adaptability to changing conditions, and internationalization)?
4. Is the culture compatible with the employees' diversity of backgrounds?
5. Does the company take into consideration the values of the culture of each nation in which the firm operates?

C. Corporate Resources

1. **Marketing**
   a. What are the corporation's current marketing objectives, strategies, policies, and programs?
      i. Are they clearly stated or merely implied from performance and/or budgets?
      ii. Are they consistent with the corporation's mission, objectives, strategies, and policies and with internal and external environments?

b. How well is the corporation performing in terms of analysis of market position and marketing mix (that is, product, price, place, and promotion) in both domestic and international markets? What percentage of sales comes from foreign operations? Where are current products in the product life cycle?
    i. What trends emerge from this analysis?
    ii. What impact have these trends had on past performance and how might these trends affect future performance?
    iii. Does this analysis support the corporation's past and pending strategic decisions?
    iv. Does marketing provide the company with a competitive advantage?
c. How well does the corporation's marketing performance compare with that of similar corporations?
d. Are marketing managers using accepted marketing concepts and techniques to evaluate and improve product performance? (Consider product life cycle, market segmentation, market research, and product portfolios.)
e. Does marketing adjust to the conditions in each country in which it operates?
f. What is the role of the marketing manager in the strategic management process?

2. **Finance**
    a. What are the corporation's current financial objectives, strategies, policies, and programs?
        i. Are they clearly stated or merely implied from performance and/or budgets?
        ii. Are they consistent with the corporation's mission, objectives, strategies, and policies and with internal and external environments?
    b. How well is the corporation performing in terms of financial analysis? (Consider ratio analysis, common size statements, and capitalization structure.) How balanced, in terms of cash flow, is the company's portfolio of products and businesses?
        i. What trends emerge from this analysis?
        ii. Are there any significant differences when statements are calculated in constant versus reported dollars?
        iii. What impact have these trends had on past performance and how might these trends affect future performance?
        iv. Does this analysis support the corporation's past and pending strategic decisions?
        v. Does finance provide the company with a competitive advantage?
    c. How well does the corporation's financial performance compare with that of similar corporations?
    d. Are financial managers using accepted financial concepts and techniques to evaluate and improve current corporate and divisional performance? (Consider financial leverage, capital budgeting, ratio analysis, and managing foreign currencies.)
    e. Does finance adjust to the conditions in each country in which the company operates?
    f. What is the role of the financial manager in the strategic management process?

3. **Research and Development (R&D)**
    a. What are the corporation's current R&D objectives, strategies, policies, and programs?
        i. Are they clearly stated or merely implied from performance or budgets?
        ii. Are they consistent with the corporation's mission, objectives, strategies, and policies and with internal and external environments?
        iii. What is the role of technology in corporate performance?
        iv. Is the mix of basic, applied, and engineering research appropriate, given the corporate mission and strategies?
        v. Does R&D provide the company with a competitive advantage?

b. What return is the corporation receiving from its investment in R&D?
c. Is the corporation competent in technology transfer? Does it use concurrent engineering and cross-functional work teams in product and process design?
d. What role does technological discontinuity play in the company's products?
e. How well does the corporation's investment in R&D compare with the investments of similar corporations? How much R&D is being outsourced?
f. Does R&D adjust to the conditions in each country in which the company operates?
g. What is the role of the R&D manager in the strategic management process?

4. **Operations and Logistics**
   a. What are the corporation's current manufacturing/service objectives, strategies, policies, and programs?
      i. Are they clearly stated or merely implied from performance or budgets?
      ii. Are they consistent with the corporation's mission, objectives, strategies, and policies and with internal and external environments?
   b. What are the type and extent of operations capabilities of the corporation? How much is done domestically versus internationally? Is the amount of outsourcing appropriate to be competitive? Is purchasing being handled appropriately?
      i. If the corporation is product oriented, consider plant facilities, type of manufacturing system (continuous mass production, intermittent job shop, or flexible manufacturing), age and type of equipment, degree and role of automation and/or robots, plant capacities and utilization, productivity ratings, and availability and type of transportation.
      ii. If the corporation is service oriented, consider service facilities (hospital, theater, or school buildings), type of operations systems (continuous service over time to same clientele or intermittent service over time to varied clientele), age and type of supporting equipment, degree and role of automation and use of mass communication devices (diagnostic machinery, videotape machines), facility capacities and utilization rates, efficiency ratings of professional and service personnel, and availability and type of transportation to bring service staff and clientele together.
   c. Are manufacturing or service facilities vulnerable to natural disasters, local or national strikes, reduction or limitation of resources from suppliers, substantial cost increases of materials, or nationalization by governments?
   d. Is there an appropriate mix of people and machines (in manufacturing firms) or of support staff and professionals (in service firms)?
   e. How well does the corporation perform relative to the competition? Is it balancing inventory costs (warehousing) with logistical costs (just-in-time)? Consider costs per unit of labor, material, and overhead; downtime; inventory control management and scheduling of service staff; production ratings; facility utilization percentages; and number of clients successfully treated by category (if service firm) or percentage of orders shipped on time (if product firm).
      i. What trends emerge from this analysis?
      ii. What impact have these trends had on past performance and how might these trends affect future performance?
      iii. Does this analysis support the corporation's past and pending strategic decisions?
      iv. Does operations provide the company with a competitive advantage?
   f. Are operations managers using appropriate concepts and techniques to evaluate and improve current performance? Consider cost systems, quality control and reliability systems, inventory control management, personnel scheduling, total quality management (TQM), learning curves, safety programs, and engineering programs that can improve efficiency of manufacturing or of service.

g. Does operations adjust to the conditions in each country in which it has facilities?
h. What is the role of outsourcing in the company's strategy for operations?
i. What is the role of the operations manager in the strategic management process?

5. **Human Resources Management (HRM)**
   a. What are the corporation's current HRM objectives, strategies, policies, and programs?
      i. Are they clearly stated or merely implied from performance and/or budgets?
      ii. Are they consistent with the corporation's mission, objectives, strategies, and policies and with internal and external environments?
   b. How well is the corporation's HRM performing in terms of improving the fit between the individual employee and the job? Consider turnover, grievances, strikes, layoffs, employee training, and quality of work life.
      i. What trends emerge from this analysis?
      ii. What impact have these trends had on past performance and how might these trends affect future performance?
      iii. Does this analysis support the corporation's past and pending strategic decisions?
      iv. Does HRM provide the company with a competitive advantage?
   c. How does this corporation's HRM performance compare with that of similar corporations?
   d. Are HRM managers using appropriate concepts and techniques to evaluate and improve corporate performance? Consider the job analysis program, performance appraisal system, up-to-date job descriptions, training and development programs, attitude surveys, job design programs, quality of relationships with unions, and use of autonomous work teams.
   e. How well is the company managing the diversity of its workforce? What is the company's record on human rights?
   f. Does HRM adjust to the conditions in each country in which the company operates? Does the company have a code of conduct for HRM in developing nations? Are employees receiving international assignments to prepare them for managerial positions?
   g. What is the role of the HRM manager in the strategic management process?

6. **Information Systems (IS)**
   a. What are the corporation's current IS objectives, strategies, policies, and programs?
      i. Are they clearly stated or merely implied from performance and/or budgets?
      ii. Are they consistent with the corporation's mission, objectives, strategies, and policies and with internal and external environments?
   b. How well is the corporation's IS performing in terms of providing a useful database, automating routine clerical operations, assisting managers in making routine decisions, and providing information necessary for strategic decisions?
      i. What trends emerge from this analysis?
      ii. What impact have these trends had on past performance and how might these trends affect future performance?
      iii. Does this analysis support the corporation's past and pending strategic decisions?
      iv. Does IS provide the company with a competitive advantage?
   c. How does this corporation's IS performance and stage of development compare with that of similar corporations? Is it appropriately using the Internet, intranet, and extranets?
   d. Are IS managers using appropriate concepts and techniques to evaluate and improve corporate performance? Do they know how to build and manage a com-

plex database, establish web sites with firewalls, conduct system analyses, and implement interactive decision-support systems?

e. Does the company have a global IS and Internet presence? Does it have difficulty getting data across national boundaries?

f. What is the role of the IS manager in the strategic management process?

D. Summary of Internal Factors *(List in the IFAS Table 5–2, p. 130)*

Which of these factors are core competencies? Which, if any, are distinctive competencies? Which of these factors are the most important to the corporation and to the industries in which it competes at the present time? Which might be important in the future? Which functions or activities are candidates for outsourcing?

V. ANALYSIS OF STRATEGIC FACTORS (SWOT)

A. Situational Analysis *(List in the SFAS Matrix, Figure 6–1, p. 141)*

Of the external (EFAS) and internal (IFAS) factors listed in III.C and IV.D, which are the strategic (most important) factors that strongly affect the corporation's present and future performance?

B. Review of Mission and Objectives

1. Are the current mission and objectives appropriate in light of the key strategic factors and problems?
2. Should the mission and objectives be changed? If so, how?
3. If they are changed, what will be the effects on the firm?

VI. STRATEGIC ALTERNATIVES AND RECOMMENDED STRATEGY

A. Strategic Alternatives *(See the TOWS Matrix, Figure 6–2, p. 144)*

1. Can the current or revised objectives be met through more careful implementation of those strategies presently in use (for example, fine-tuning the strategies)?
2. What are the major feasible alternative strategies available to the corporation? What are the pros and cons of each? Can corporate scenarios be developed and agreed upon? (Alternatives must fit societal environment, industry, and company for the next three to five years.)
   a. Consider *stability*, *growth*, and *retrenchment* as corporate strategies.
   b. Consider *cost leadership* and *differentiation* as business strategies.
   c. Consider any functional strategic alternatives that might be needed for reinforcement of an important corporate or business strategic alternative.

B. Recommended Strategy

1. Specify which of the strategic alternatives you are recommending for the corporate, business, and functional levels of the corporation. Do you recommend different business or functional strategies for different units of the corporation?
2. Justify your recommendation in terms of its ability to resolve both long- and short-term problems and effectively deal with the strategic factors.

3. What policies should be developed or revised to guide effective implementation?
4. What is the impact of your recommended strategy on the company's core and distinctive competencies?

VII. IMPLEMENTATION

A. What kinds of programs (for example, restructuring the corporation or instituting TQM) should be developed to implement the recommended strategy?

1. Who should develop these programs?
2. Who should be in charge of these programs?

B. Are the programs financially feasible? Can pro forma budgets be developed and agreed upon? Are priorities and timetables appropriate to individual programs?

C. Will new standard operating procedures need to be developed?

VIII. EVALUATION AND CONTROL

A. Is the current information system capable of providing sufficient feedback on implementation activities and performance? Can it measure strategic factors?

1. Can performance results be pinpointed by area, unit, project, or function?
2. Is the information timely?
3. Is the corporation using benchmarking to evaluate its functions and activities?

B. Are adequate control measures in place to ensure conformance with the recommended strategic plan?

1. Are appropriate standards and measures being used?
2. Are reward systems capable of recognizing and rewarding good performance?

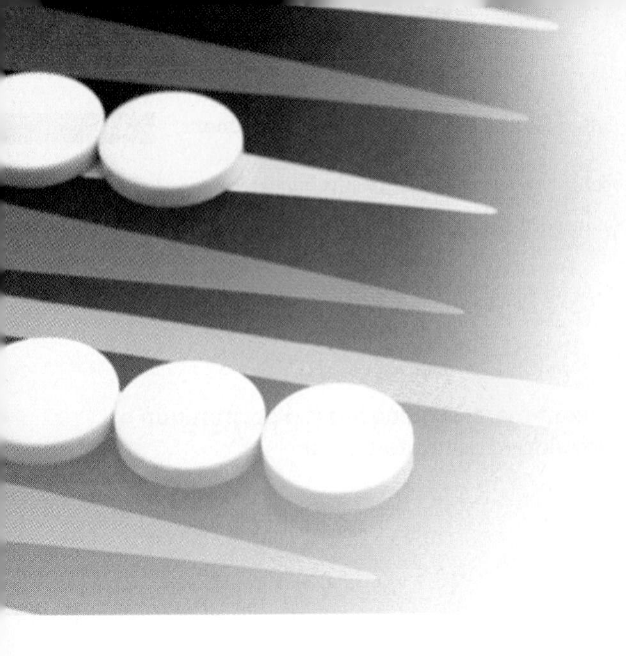

CHAPTER 2 Corporate Governance

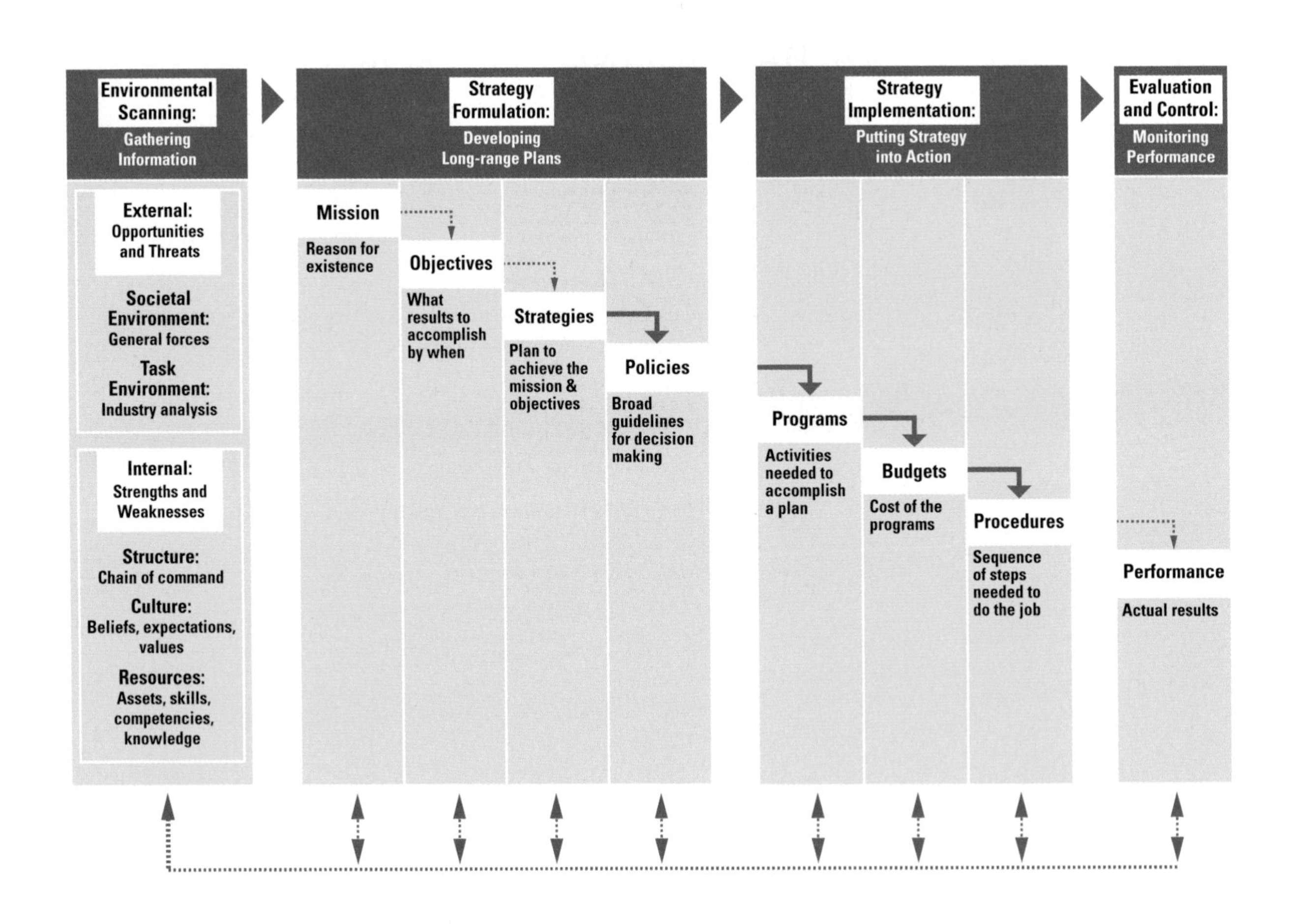

Learning Objectives

After reading this chapter, you should be able to:

- Describe the role and responsibilities of the board of directors in corporate governance
- Understand how the composition of a board can affect its operation
- Describe the impact of the Sarbanes-Oxley Act on corporate governance in the United States
- Discuss trends in corporate governance
- Explain how executive leadership is an important part of strategic management

TYCO INTERNATIONAL LTD. IS A DIVERSIFIED MANUFACTURING AND SERVICE COMPANY that operates in more than 100 countries and has annual revenues of over $36 billion. Taking over as CEO in 1992, Dennis Kozlowski transformed Tyco from an obscure U.S. manufacturer into the world's largest provider of undersea telecommunications systems, fire protection systems, and electronic security services. In doing so, Kozlowski treated Tyco as his own personal empire, lavishing hundreds of millions of dollars in unauthorized loans and exorbitant gifts on himself and his top managers. Even though his annual compensation jumped from $8.8 million in 1996 to $136.1 million in 1999, Kozlowski regularly took from the company loans worth hundreds of millions of dollars. Among his purchases were a $2.1 million birthday celebration for his wife plus a $6,000 shower curtain and a $15,000 dog umbrella stand for his $16.8 million New York apartment. By operating without a second in command and by handpicking top managers who were "smart, poor, and want-to-be-rich," he kept personal control of the corporation. He handpicked members of the board of directors and filtered all information, such as internal audits, that went to the board. Without board approval, Kozlowski gave $56 million in bonuses to 51 Tyco employees to effectively cancel loans they had earlier taken from the company.

In the wake of the Enron scandal, the U.S. Securities and Exchange Commission (SEC), the Internal Revenue Service, and the State of New Hampshire began investigating Tyco for accounting irregularities and its CPA firm for failing to report the questionable practices. Kozlowski resigned as CEO just before being indicted on tax evasion. Subsequent investigation revealed why the board of directors had been so silent during this period of top management excess. Of the company's 10 directors, 3 were Tyco executives who had serious conflicts of interest. Even though board member Joshua Berman had been serving as a Tyco executive since 1997, the company continued to pay millions of dollars in legal fees to his former law firm. John Fort, the Tyco executive who was named the company's interim CEO upon Kozlowski's resignation, had been an investor in a buyout fund that made an $810 million purchase of Tyco operations in 1999, while Fort served as a board member. Tyco's Chief Financial Officer, Mark Swartz, also served as a board member when he received $6.5 million in loans from the company.

In addition, the non-management, or "outside," directors had such deep ties to the company that it raised questions about the board's ability to oversee management. For example, Michael Ashcroft had previously worked for the company until 1997. Another board member, Stephen Foss, leased an airplane to Tyco. The lead director, Frank Walsh, Jr., received $20 million for his services in helping to arrange Tyco's disastrous 2001 acquisition of the commercial-finance company CIT Group.

In the first six months of 2002, the actions, inactions, and reversals of actions by the Tyco board cost stockholders about $88 billion in lost shareholder value, three times the $33 billion in equity losses at Enron and almost twice the equity losses at WorldCom. Tyco agreed to pay $5 million to the State of New Hampshire to reimburse shareholders and the public who had been hurt by the financial misconduct of its former officers. After pleading guilty of securities fraud, lead director Frank Walsh agreed to pay $22.5 million in fines and restitution to settle civil and criminal charges. In addition, Tyco's auditing firm was investigated for its failure to identify accounting irregularities. According to Lyn Turner, former Chief Accountant for the SEC, $41 million of a $96 million loan forgiveness scheme was charged to the balance sheet for "accrued federal income tax." Said Turner, "I can't understand how they missed that one."[1]

2.1 Role of the Board of Directors

A **corporation** is a mechanism established to allow different parties to contribute capital, expertise, and labor for their mutual benefit. The investor/shareholder participates in the profits of the enterprise without taking responsibility for the operations. Management runs the company without being responsible for personally providing the funds. To make this possible, laws have been passed that give shareholders limited liability and, correspondingly, limited involvement in a corporation's activities. That involvement does include, however, the right to elect directors who have a legal duty to represent the shareholders and protect their interests. As representatives of the shareholders, directors have both the authority and the responsibility to establish basic corporate policies and to ensure that they are followed.[2]

The board of directors, therefore, has an obligation to approve all decisions that might affect the long-run performance of the corporation. This means that the corporation is fundamentally governed by the board of directors overseeing top management, with the concurrence of the shareholder. The term **corporate governance** refers to the relationship among these three groups in determining the direction and performance of the corporation.[3]

Over the past decade, shareholders and various interest groups have seriously questioned the role of the board of directors in corporations. They are concerned that inside board members may use their position to feather their own nests and that outside board members often lack sufficient knowledge, involvement, and enthusiasm to do an adequate job of monitoring and providing guidance to top management. Instances of widespread corruption and questionable accounting practices at Enron, Global Crossing, WorldCom, Tyco, and Qwest, among others, seem to justify their concerns. Tyco's board, for example, seemed more interested in keeping CEO Kozlowski happy than in safeguarding shareholder interests. The very passivity of the board (in addition to questionable financial dealings) was one reason why the Kozlowski-era directors were forced to resign in 2003.[4]

The general public has not only become more aware and more critical of many boards' apparent lack of responsibility for corporate activities, it has begun to push government to demand accountability. As a result, the board as a rubber stamp of the CEO or as a bastion of the "old-boy" selection system is being replaced by more active, more professional boards.

Responsibilities of the Board

Laws and standards defining the responsibilities of boards of directors vary from country to country. For example, board members in Ontario, Canada, face more than 100 provincial and federal laws governing director liability. The United States, however, has no clear national standards or federal laws. Specific requirements of directors vary, depending on the state in which the corporate charter is issued. There is, nevertheless, a developing worldwide consensus concerning the major responsibilities of a board. Interviews with 200 directors from eight countries (Canada, France, Germany, Finland, Switzerland, the Netherlands, the United Kingdom, and Venezuela) revealed strong agreement on the following five **board of director responsibilities**, listed in order of importance:

1. Setting corporate strategy, overall direction, mission, or vision
2. Hiring and firing the CEO and top management
3. Controlling, monitoring, or supervising top management

4. Reviewing and approving the use of resources
5. Caring for shareholder interests[5]

These results are in agreement with a recent survey by the National Association of Corporate Directors, in which CEOs reported that the four most important issues boards should address are corporate performance, CEO succession, strategic planning, and corporate governance.[6] Directors in the United States must make certain, in addition to the duties just listed, that the corporation is managed in accordance with the laws of the state in which it is incorporated. Because more than half of all publicly traded companies in the United States are incorporated in the state of Delaware, this state's laws and rulings have more impact than do those of any other state.[7] Directors must also ensure management's adherence to laws and regulations, such as those dealing with the issuance of securities, insider trading, and other conflict-of-interest situations. They must also be aware of the needs and demands of constituent groups so that they can achieve a judicious balance among the interests of these diverse groups while ensuring the continued functioning of the corporation.

In a legal sense, the board is required to direct the affairs of the corporation but not to manage them. It is charged by law to act with **due care**. If a director or the board as a whole fails to act with due care and, as a result, the corporation is in some way harmed, the careless director or directors can be held personally liable for the harm done. This is no small concern, given that one survey of outside directors revealed that more than 40% had been named as part of lawsuits against corporations.[8] For example, board members of Equitable Life in Britain were sued for up to $5.4 billion for failure to question the CEO's reckless policies.[9] For this reason, the percentage of U.S. boards purchasing directors' and officers' liability insurance had increased to 84% by 2003.[10]

Role of the Board in Strategic Management

How does a board of directors fulfill these many responsibilities? The **role of the board of directors in strategic management** is to carry out three basic tasks:

- **Monitor:** By acting through its committees, a board can keep abreast of developments inside and outside the corporation, bringing to management's attention developments it might have overlooked. A board should at least carry out this task.
- **Evaluate and influence:** A board can examine management's proposals, decisions, and actions; agree or disagree with them; give advice and offer suggestions; and outline alternatives. More active boards perform this task in addition to monitoring.
- **Initiate and determine:** A board can delineate a corporation's mission and specify strategic options to its management. Only the most active boards take on this task in addition to the two previous ones.

Board of Directors Continuum

A board of directors is involved in strategic management to the extent that it carries out the three tasks of monitoring, evaluating and influencing, and initiating and determining. The **board of directors continuum** shown in **Figure 2–1** shows the possible degree of involvement (from low to high) in the strategic management process. Boards can range from being phantom boards with no real involvement to catalyst boards with a very high degree of involvement.[11] Research suggests that active board involvement in strategic management is positively related to a corporation's financial performance and its credit rating.[12]

Highly involved boards tend to be very active. They take their tasks of monitoring, evaluating, influencing, initiating, and determining very seriously; they provide advice when necessary and keep management alert. As depicted in **Figure 2–1**, their heavy involvement in the strategic management process places them in the active participation or even catalyst positions. For example, in a survey of directors of large U.S. corporations conducted by Korn/Ferry

Figure 2–1 **Board of Directors Continuum**

DEGREE OF INVOLVEMENT IN STRATEGIC MANAGEMENT

Low (Passive) ←→ **High** (Active)

Phantom	Rubber Stamp	Minimal Review	Nominal Participation	Active Participation	Catalyst
Never knows what to do, if anything; no degree of involvement.	Permits officers to make all decisions. It votes as the officers recommend on action issues.	Formally reviews selected issues that officers bring to its attention.	Involved to a limited degree in the performance or review of selected key decisions, indicators, or programs of managment.	Approves, questions, and makes final decisions on mission, strategy, policies, and objectives. Has active board committees. Performs fiscal and management audits.	Takes the leading role in establishing and modifying the mission, objectives, strategy, and policies. It has a very active strategy committee.

Source: T. L. Wheelen and J. D. Hunger, "Board of Directors Continuum," Copyright © 1994 by Wheelen and Hunger Associates. Reprinted by permission.

International, more than 60% indicated that they were deeply involved in the strategy-setting process. In the same survey, 54% of the respondents indicated that their boards participate in an annual retreat or special planning session to discuss company strategy. Nevertheless, only slightly more than 32% of the boards help develop the strategy. More than two-thirds of the boards review strategy only after it has first been developed by management. Another 1% admit playing no role at all in strategy.[13] This and other studies suggest that most large publicly owned corporations have boards that operate at some point between nominal and active participation. Nevertheless, the percentage of U.S. companies surveyed by Korn/Ferry International that have written corporate governance guidelines rose from 71% in 2002 to 88% in 2003.[14] Seventy-four percent now have periodic board meetings devoted primarily to the review of overall company strategy.[15] Some corporations with actively participating boards are Target, Medtronic, Best Western, Service Corporation International, Bank of Montreal, Mead Corporation, Rolm and Haas, Whirlpool, 3M, Apria Healthcare, General Electric, Pfizer, and Texas Instruments.[16] Target, a corporate governance leader, has a board that each year sets three top priorities, such as strategic direction, capital allocation, and succession planning. Each of these priority topics is placed at the top of the agenda for at least one meeting. Target's board also devotes one meeting a year to setting the strategic direction for each major operating division.[17]

As a board becomes less involved in the affairs of the corporation, it moves farther to the left on the continuum (see **Figure 2–1**). On the far left are passive phantom or rubber-stamp boards that typically never initiate or determine strategy (like Tyco) unless a crisis occurs. In these situations, the CEO also serves as Chairman of the Board, personally nominates all directors, and works to keep board members under his or her control by giving them the "mushroom treatment"—throw manure on them and keep them in the dark!

Generally, the smaller the corporation, the less active is its board of directors. In an entrepreneurial venture, for example, the privately held corporation may be 100% owned by the founders—who also manage the company. In this case, there is no need for an active board to protect the interests of the owner–manager shareholders—the interests of the owners and the managers are identical. In this instance, a board is really unnecessary and only meets to satisfy legal requirements. If stock is sold to outsiders to finance growth, however, the board becomes more active. Key investors want seats on the board so they can oversee their investment. To the extent that they still control most of the stock, however, the founders dominate the board. Friends, family members, and key shareholders usually become members, but the board acts primarily as a rubber stamp for any proposals put forward by the owner–managers. In this type of company, the founder tends to be both CEO and chairman of the board, and the board includes few people who are not affiliated with the firm or family.[18] This cozy relationship between the board and management should change, however, when the corporation goes public and stock is more widely dispersed. The founders, who are still acting as management, may sometimes make decisions that conflict with the needs of the other shareholders (especially if the founders own less than 50% of the common stock). In this instance, problems could occur if the board fails to become more active in terms of its roles and responsibilities.

Members of a Board of Directors

The boards of most publicly owned corporations are composed of both inside and outside directors. **Inside directors** (sometimes called management directors) are typically officers or executives employed by the corporation. **Outside directors** (sometimes called non-management directors) may be executives of other firms but are not employees of the board's corporation. Although there is yet no clear evidence indicating that a high proportion of outsiders on a board results in improved financial performance, as measured by return on equity,[19] there is a trend in the United States to increase the number of outsiders on boards. The typical large U.S. Fortune 1000 corporation has an average of 11 directors, 2 of whom are insiders.[20] Even though outsiders account for slightly over 80% of the board members in these large U.S. corporations (approximately the same as in Canada), they account for only about 42% of board membership in small U.S. companies.[21] Boards in the UK typically have 5 inside and 5 outside directors, whereas in France boards usually consist of 3 insiders and 8 outsiders. Japanese boards, in contrast, contain 2 outsiders and 12 insiders.[22] A survey of 1,376 *privately held* U.S. companies reveals that the average board consists of 4 members, but only 19% contain any outsiders.[23]

People who favor a high proportion of outsiders state that outside directors are less biased and more likely to evaluate management's performance objectively than are inside directors. This is the main reason why the U.S. Securities and Exchange Commission (SEC) in 2003 required that a majority of directors on the board be independent outsiders. The SEC also required that all listed companies staff their audit, compensation, and nominating/corporate governance committees entirely with independent, outside members. This view is in agreement with **agency theory**, which states that problems arise in corporations because the agents (top management) are not willing to bear responsibility for their decisions unless they own a substantial amount of stock in the corporation. The theory suggests that a majority of a board needs to be from outside the firm so that top management is prevented from acting selfishly to the detriment of the shareholders. For example, proponents of agency theory argue that management-controlled firms select less risky strategies with quick payoffs in order to keep their jobs. This view is supported by research revealing that manager-controlled firms are more likely to go into debt to diversify into unrelated markets (thus quickly boosting sales and assets)—resulting in poorer long-term performance—than owner-controlled firms.[24] Boards with a larger proportion of outside directors tend to favor growth through international expansion and innovative venturing activities than do boards with a smaller proportion of outsiders.[25] Outsiders tend to be more objective and critical of corporate activities. For example, research reveals that the likelihood of a firm engaging in illegal behavior or being sued declines with the addition of outsiders on the board.[26] Research on *privately owned* family businesses has found that boards with a larger number of outsiders tended to have better corporate governance than did boards with fewer outsiders.[27]

In contrast, those who prefer inside over outside directors contend that outside directors are less effective than are insiders because the outsiders are less likely to have the necessary interest, availability, or competency. **Stewardship theory** proposes that, because of their long tenure with the corporation, insiders (senior executives) tend to identify with the corporation and its success. Rather than use the firm for their own ends, these executives are thus most interested in guaranteeing the continued life and success of the corporation. (See **STRATEGY HIGHLIGHT 2.1** for a discussion of Agency Theory contrasted with Stewardship Theory.) Excluding all insiders but the CEO reduces the opportunity for outside directors to see potential successors in action or to obtain alternate points of view of management decisions. Outside directors may sometimes serve on so many boards that they spread their time and interest too thin to actively fulfill their responsibilities. The average board member of a U.S. Fortune 500 firm serves on three boards. Research indicates that firm performance decreases as the number of directorships held by the average board member increases.[28] Only 10% of surveyed U.S. boards limit the number of directorships a board member may hold in other corporations.[29]

Those who question the value of having more outside board members point out that the term *outsider* is too simplistic because some outsiders are not truly objective and should be considered more as insiders than as outsiders. For example, there can be:

1. **Affiliated directors** who, though not really employed by the corporation, handle the legal or insurance work for the company or are important suppliers (thus dependent on the current management for a key part of their business). These outsiders face a conflict of interest and are not likely to be objective. The number of affiliated directors on Tyco's board was one of the reasons why the board was so strongly criticized. As a result of recent actions by the U.S. Congress, Securities and Exchange Commission, New York Stock Exchange, and NASDAQ, affiliated directors are being banned from corporate boardrooms. U.S. boards can no longer include representatives of major suppliers or customers or even professional organizations that might do business with the firm, even though these people could provide valuable knowledge and expertise.[30] The New York Stock Exchange decided in 2004 that anyone paid by the company during the previous three years could not be classified as an independent outside director.[31]
2. **Retired executive directors** who used to work for the company, such as the past CEO (who is partly responsible for much of the corporation's current strategy and who probably groomed the current CEO as his or her replacement). Many boards of large firms keep the firm's recently retired CEO on the board for a year or two after retirement as a courtesy, especially if he or she performed well as the CEO. It is almost certain, however, that this person will not be able to objectively evaluate the corporation's performance. Nevertheless, a survey by the Conference Board found that only 14% of U.S. boards surveyed require the former CEO to leave the board upon retirement.[32]
3. **Family directors** who are descendants of the founder and own significant blocks of stock (with personal agendas based on a family relationship with the current CEO). The Schlitz Brewing Company, for example, was unable to complete its turnaround strategy with a non-family CEO because family members serving on the board wanted their money out of the company, forcing it to be sold.[33]

The majority of outside directors are active or retired CEOs and COOs of other corporations. Others are major investors/shareholders, academicians, attorneys, consultants, former government officials, and bankers. Given that approximately 60% of the outstanding stock in the largest U.S. and UK corporations is now owned by institutional investors, such as mutual funds and pension plans, these investors are taking an increasingly active role in board membership and activities.[34] For example, TIAA-CREF's Corporate Governance team monitors governance practices of the 4,000 companies in which it invests its pension funds through its Corporate Assessment Program. If its analysis of a company reveals problems, TIAA-CREF first sends letters stating its concerns, followed up by visits, and it finally sponsors a share-

STRATEGY HIGHLIGHT 2.1

Agency Theory Versus Stewardship Theory in Corporate Governance

Managers of large, modern publicly held corporations are typically not the owners. In fact, most of today's top managers own only nominal amounts of stock in the corporation they manage. The real owners (shareholders) elect boards of directors who hire managers as their agents to run the firm's day-to-day activities. Once hired, how trustworthy are these executives? Do they put themselves or the firm first?

Agency Theory. As suggested in the classic study by Berle and Means, top managers are, in effect, "hired hands" who may very likely be more interested in their personal welfare than that of the shareholders. For example, management might emphasize strategies, such as acquisitions, that increase the size of the firm (to become more powerful and to demand increased pay and benefits) or that diversify the firm into unrelated businesses (to reduce short-term risk and to allow them to put less effort into a core product line that may be facing difficulty) but that result in a reduction of dividends and/or stock price.

Agency theory is concerned with analyzing and resolving two problems that occur in relationships between principals (owners/shareholders) and their agents (top management):

1. The agency problem that arises when (a) the desires or objectives of the owners and the agents conflict or (b) it is difficult or expensive for the owners to verify what the agent is actually doing. One example is when top management is more interested in raising its own salary than in increasing stock dividends.
2. The risk-sharing problem that arises when the owners and agents have different attitudes toward risk. Executives may not select risky strategies because they fear losing their jobs if the strategy fails.

According to agency theory, the likelihood that these problems will occur increases when stock is widely held (that is, when no one shareholder owns more than a small percentage of the total common stock), when the board of directors is composed of people who know little of the company or who are personal friends of top management, and when a high percentage of board members are inside (management) directors.

To better align the interests of the agents with those of the owners and to increase the corporation's overall performance, agency theory suggests that top management have a significant degree of ownership in the firm and/or have a strong financial stake in its long-term performance. In support of this argument, research indicates a positive relationship between corporate performance and the amount of stock owned by directors.

Stewardship Theory. In contrast, stewardship theory suggests that executives tend to be more motivated to act in the best interests of the corporation than in their own self-interests. Whereas agency theory focuses on extrinsic rewards that serve the lower-level needs, such as pay and security, stewardship theory focuses on the higher-order needs, such as achievement and self-actualization. Stewardship theory argues that senior executives over time tend to view the corporation as an extension of themselves. Rather than use the firm for their own ends, these executives are most interested in guaranteeing the continued life and success of the corporation. The relationship between the board and top management is thus one of principal and steward, not principal and agent ("hired hand"). Stewardship theory notes that in a widely held corporation, the shareholder is free to sell her or his stock at any time. A diversified investor may care little about risk at the company level—preferring management to assume extraordinary risk so long as the return is adequate. Because executives in a firm cannot easily leave their jobs when in difficulty, they are more interested in a merely satisfactory return and put heavy emphasis on the firm's continued survival. Thus, stewardship theory argues that in many instances top management may care more about a company's long-term success than do more short-term–oriented shareholders.

For more information about agency theory and stewardship theory, see A. A. Berle and G. C. Means, *The Modern Corporation and Private Property* (New York: Macmillan, 1936); J. H. Davis, F. D. Schoorman, and L. Donaldson, "Toward a Stewardship Theory of Management," *Academy of Management Review* (January 1997), pp. 20–47; P. J. Lane, A. A. Cannella, Jr., and M. H. Lubatkin, "Agency Problems as Antecedents to Unrelated Mergers and Diversification: Amihud and Lev Reconsidered," *Strategic Management Journal* (June 1998), pp. 555–578; M. L. Hayward and D. C. Hambrick, "Explaining the Premiums Paid for Large Acquisitions: Evidence of CEO Hubris," *Administrative Science Quarterly* (March 1997), pp. 103–127.

holder resolution in opposition to management's actions.[35] Institutional investors are also powerful in many other countries. In Germany, bankers are represented on almost every board—primarily because they own large blocks of stock in German corporations. In Denmark, Sweden, Belgium, and Italy, however, investment companies assume this role. For example, the investment company Investor AB casts 42.5% of the Electrolux AB shareholder votes, thus guaranteeing itself positions on the Electrolux board.

Boards of directors have been working to increase the number of women and minorities serving on boards. Korn/Ferry International reports that of the Fortune 1000 largest U.S. firms, 80% had at least one woman director in 2003 (compared to 74% in 2000) for a total of 13.6% of all U.S. directors. In contrast, generally one-half of the boards in Australia, Canada, Japan, Norway, South Africa, Spain, and the United Kingdom included a female director. Korn/Ferry's survey also revealed that 75% of the U.S. boards had at least one ethnic minority in 2003 (African-American, 47%; Latino, 19%; Asian, 10%) as director compared to 65% in 2000.[36]

The globalization of business is having an impact on board membership. By 2003, according to the Spencer Stuart executive recruiting firm, 33% of U.S. boards had an international director, an increase of more than 50% over the previous five years.[37] Europe was the most "globalized" region of the world, with most companies reporting one or more non-national directors.[38] Asian and Latin American boards were still predominantly staffed by nationals, primarily because of travel requirements.[39] See the **Global Issue** feature to learn about a South Korean firm's addition of a non-Korean director.

Outside directors serving on the boards of large Fortune 1000 U.S. corporations annually earned on average $46,640. Most of the companies (71%) paid their outside directors an annual retainer plus a fee for every meeting attended. Almost 90% of these large U.S. corporations included stock options or grants in their compensation to board members.[40] Directors serving on the boards of small companies usually received much less compensation (around $10,000). One study found directors of a sample of large U.S. firms to hold on average 3% of their corporations' outstanding stock.[41]

The vast majority of inside directors are the chief executive officer and either the chief operating officer (if not also the CEO) or the chief financial officer. Presidents or vice presidents of key operating divisions or functional units sometimes serve on the board. Few, if any, inside directors receive any extra compensation for assuming this extra duty. Very rarely does a U.S. board include any lower-level operating employees.

Codetermination: Should Employees Serve on Boards?

Codetermination, the inclusion of a corporation's workers on its board, began only recently in the United States. Corporations such as Chrysler, Northwest Airlines, United Airlines (UAL), and Wheeling-Pittsburgh Steel have added representatives from employee associa-

GLOBAL ISSUE

POSCO Adds an International Director

In an attempt to make Korean businesses more attractive to foreign investors, the South Korean government recommended that companies listed on the stock exchange introduce a two-tiered structure. One structure was to consist entirely of non-executive (outside) directors. One of the few companies to immediately adopt this new system of governance was Pohang Iron & Steel Company, Ltd. (POSCO), the world's largest steelmaker. POSCO was listed on the New York Stock Exchange and had significant operations in the United States, plus a joint venture with U.S. Steel. According to Youn-Gil Ro, Corporate Information Team Manager, "We needed professional advice on international business practices as well as American practices."

Among the eight outside directors added to the board was Samuel Chevalier, an international financier from the United States. Chevalier previously sat on boards in Hong Kong and Brazil and had no problem traveling long distances to attend board meetings. In order to overcome language problems, Youn-Gil Ro explained, "There are simultaneous interpretations during the meetings, and agendas and other materials are written in English as well as Korean."

Source: Summarized from *Globalizing the Board of Directors: Trends and Strategies* (New York: Conference Board, 1999), p. 16. Reprinted by permission of the The Conference Board.

tions to their boards as part of union agreements or Employee Stock Ownership Plans (ESOPs). For example, United Airlines workers traded 15% in pay cuts for 55% of the company (through an ESOP) and 3 of the firm's 12 board seats. In this instance, workers represent themselves on the board not so much as employees but primarily as owners. At Chrysler, however, the United Auto Workers union obtained a temporary seat on the board as part of a union contract agreement in exchange for changes in work rules and reductions in benefits. This was at a time when Chrysler was facing bankruptcy in the late 1970s. In situations like this, when a director represents an internal stakeholder, critics raise the issue of conflict of interest. Can a member of the board, who is privy to confidential managerial information, function, for example, as a union leader whose primary duty is to fight for the best benefits for his or her members? Although the movement to place employees on the boards of directors of U.S. companies shows little likelihood of increasing (except through employee stock ownership), the European experience reveals an increasing acceptance of worker participation (without ownership) on corporate boards.

Germany pioneered codetermination during the 1950s with a two-tiered system: (1) a supervisory board elected by shareholders and employees to approve or decide corporate strategy and policy and (2) a management board (composed primarily of top management) appointed by the supervisory board to manage the company's activities. Most other Western European countries have either passed similar codetermination legislation (as in Sweden, Denmark, Norway, and Austria) or use worker councils to work closely with management (as in Belgium, Luxembourg, France, Italy, Ireland, and the Netherlands).

Interlocking Directorates

CEOs often nominate chief executives (as well as board members) from other firms to membership on their own boards in order to create an interlocking directorate. A *direct* **interlocking directorate** occurs when two firms share a director or when an executive of one firm sits on the board of a second firm. An *indirect* interlock occurs when two corporations have directors who also serve on the board of a third firm, such as a bank.

Although the Clayton Act and the Banking Act of 1933 prohibit interlocking directorates by U.S. companies competing in the same industry, interlocking continues to occur in almost all corporations, especially large ones. Interlocking occurs because large firms have a large impact on other corporations, and these other corporations, in turn, have some control over the firm's inputs and marketplace. For example, most large corporations in the United States, Japan, and Germany are interlocked either directly or indirectly with financial institutions.[42] Interlocking directorates are useful for gaining both inside information about an uncertain environment and objective expertise about potential strategies and tactics.[43] For example, Kleiner Perkins, a high-tech venture capital firm, not only has seats on the boards of the companies in which it invests, but it also has executives (which Kleiner Perkins hired) from one entrepreneurial venture who serve as directors on others. Kleiner Perkins refers to its network of interlocked firms as its *keiretsu*.[44] Family-owned corporations, however, are less likely to have interlocking directorates than are corporations with highly dispersed stock ownership, probably because family-owned corporations do not like to dilute their corporate control by adding outsiders to boardroom discussions.

There is some concern, however, when the chairs of separate corporations serve on each other's boards. Twenty-two such pairs of corporate chairs (who typically also served as their firm's CEO) existed in 2003. In one instance, the three chairs of Anheuser-Busch, SBC Communications, and Emerson Electric served on all three of the boards. Typically a CEO sits on only one board in addition to his or her own—down from two additional boards five years ago. Although such interlocks may provide valuable information, they are increasingly frowned upon because of the possibility of collusion.[45] Nevertheless, evidence indicates that well-interlocked corporations are better able to survive in a highly competitive environment.[46]

Nomination and Election of Board Members

Traditionally the CEO of a corporation decided whom to invite to board membership and merely asked the shareholders for approval in the annual proxy statement. All nominees were usually elected. There are some dangers, however, in allowing the CEO free rein in nominating directors. The CEO might select only board members who, in the CEO's opinion, will not disturb the company's policies and functioning. Given that the average length of service of a U.S. board member is for three 3-year terms (but can range up to 20 years for some boards), CEO-friendly, passive boards are likely to result. This is especially likely given that only 7% of surveyed directors indicated that their company had term limits for board members. (However, 60% of U.S. boards have a mandatory retirement around age 70.[47]) Research reveals that boards rated as least effective by the Corporate Library, a corporate governance research firm, tend to have members serving longer (an average of 9.7 years) than boards rated as most effective (7.5 years).[48] Directors selected by the CEO often feel that they should go along with any proposal the CEO makes. Thus board members find themselves accountable to the very management they are charged to oversee. Because this is likely to happen, more boards are using a nominating committee to nominate new outside board members for the shareholders to elect. Eighty-seven percent of large U.S. corporations now use nominating committees to identify potential directors. This practice is far less common in Europe, where only 60% of boards use nominating committees.[49]

Virtually every corporation whose directors serve terms of more than one year divides the board into classes and staggers elections so that only a portion of the board stands for election each year. This is called a **staggered board**. Sixty-three percent of U.S. boards currently have staggered boards.[50] Arguments in favor of this practice are that it provides continuity by reducing the chance of an abrupt turnover in its membership and that it reduces the likelihood of electing people unfriendly to management (who might be interested in a hostile takeover) through cumulative voting. An argument against staggered boards is that they make it more difficult for concerned shareholders to curb a CEO's power—especially when that CEO is also Chairman of the Board. An increasing number of shareholder resolutions to replace staggered boards with annual elections of all board members are currently being passed at annual meetings.

A survey of directors of U.S. corporations revealed the following criteria in a good director:

- Is willing to challenge management when necessary (95%)
- Has special expertise important to the company (67%)
- Is available outside meetings to advise management (57%)
- Has expertise on global business issues (41%)
- Understands the firm's key technologies and processes (39%)
- Brings external contacts that are potentially valuable to the firm (33%)
- Has detailed knowledge of the firm's industry (31%)
- Has high visibility in his or her field (31%)
- Is accomplished at representing the firm to stakeholders (18%)[51]

Organization of the Board

The size of a board in the United States is determined by the corporation's charter and its bylaws, in compliance with state laws. Although some states require a minimum number of board members, most corporations have quite a bit of discretion in determining board size. The average large, publicly held U.S. firm has around 11 directors on its board. The average small/medium-size privately held company has approximately 7 to 8 members. Privately owned family businesses usually have only 4 board members. The average size of boards elsewhere is Japan, 14; Non-Japan Asia, 9; Germany, 16; UK, 10; and France, 11.[52]

Seventy-nine percent of the top executives of U.S. publicly held corporations hold the dual designation of chairman and CEO. (Only 5% of the firms in the UK have a combined chairman/CEO.[53]) The combined chair/CEO position is being increasingly criticized because of the potential for conflict of interest. The CEO is supposed to concentrate on strategy, planning, external relations, and responsibility to the board. The Chairman's responsibility is to ensure that the board and its committees perform their functions as stated in the board's charter. Further, the chairman schedules board meetings and presides over the annual shareholders' meeting. Critics of having one person in the two offices ask how the board can properly oversee top management if the Chairman is also a part of top management. For this reason, the Chairman and CEO roles are separated by law in Germany, the Netherlands, and Finland. A similar law has been considered in the United Kingdom and Australia. Although research is mixed regarding the impact of the combined Chair/CEO position on overall corporate financial performance, firm stock price and credit ratings both respond negatively to announcements of CEOs also assuming the Chair position.[54]

Many of those who prefer that the Chairman and CEO positions be combined agree that the outside directors should elect a **lead director**. This person is consulted by the Chairman/CEO regarding board affairs and coordinates the annual evaluation of the CEO.[55] The lead director position is very popular in the United Kingdom, where it originated. Of those U.S. companies combining the Chairman and CEO positions, 62% had a lead director in 2003, up from only 32% in 2002.[56] This is one way to give the board more power without undermining the power of the Chairman/CEO. The lead director becomes increasingly important because 87% of U.S. boards in 2003 (compared to only 41% in 2002) held executive sessions without the CEO being present.[57] Nevertheless, there are many ways in which an unscrupulous Chairman/CEO such as Dennis Kozlowski at Tyco can guarantee a director's loyalty. For example, Frank Walsh, the lead director of Tyco's board, was secretly paid $20 million (by Kozlowski and CFO Swartz) in exchange for his help in arranging an acquisition.[58] Research indicates that an increase in board independence often results in higher levels of CEO ingratiation behavior aimed at persuading directors to support CEO proposals. Long-tenured directors who support the CEO may use social pressure to persuade a new board member to conform to the group.[59] For example, more than half of the 16 board members at Walt Disney Productions had personal ties to CEO Michael Eisner or to the company—a big reason why Disney's board has been so strongly criticized. Even in those situations when the board has a nominating committee composed only of outsiders, the committee often obtains the CEO's approval for each new board candidate.[60]

The most effective boards accomplish much of their work through committees. Although they do not usually have legal duties, most committees are granted full power to act with the authority of the board between board meetings. Typical standing committees (in order of prevalence) are the audit (100%), compensation (99%), nominating (87%), stock options (85%), corporate governance (72%), and executive (52%) committees.[61] The executive committee is usually composed of two inside and two outside directors located nearby who can meet between board meetings to attend to matters that must be settled quickly. This committee acts as an extension of the board and, consequently, may have almost unrestricted authority in certain areas.[62] Although only the audit committee was 100% staffed by outsiders in 2003, this may soon become the rule for U.S. boards, given the recent requirements by the New York Stock Exchange and the SEC. Although each board committee typically meets four to five times annually, the average audit committee met seven times during 2003.[63]

Impact of the Sarbanes-Oxley Act on U.S. Corporate Governance

In response to the many corporate scandals uncovered since 2000, the U.S. Congress passed the **Sarbanes-Oxley Act** in June 2002. This act was designed to protect shareholders from the excesses and failed oversight that characterized failures at Enron, Tyco, WorldCom, Adelphia Communications, Qwest, and Global Crossing, among other prominent firms. Several key elements of Sarbanes-Oxley were designed to formalize greater board independence and oversight. For example, the act requires that all directors serving on the audit committee be independent of the firm and receive no fees other than for services of the director. In addition, boards may no longer grant loans to corporate officers (one of the problems at Tyco). The act has also established formal procedures for individuals (known as "whistle-blowers") to report incidents of questionable accounting or auditing. Firms are prohibited from retaliating against anyone reporting wrongdoing. Both the CEO and CFO must certify the corporation's financial information. The act bans auditors from providing both external and internal audit services to the same company. It also requires that a firm identify whether it has a "financial expert" serving on the audit committee who is independent from management.

Improving Governance

In implementing the Sarbanes-Oxley Act, the U.S. Securities and Exchange Commission (SEC) required in 2003 that a company disclose whether it has adopted a code of ethics that applies to the CEO and to the company's principal financial officer. Among other things, the SEC requires that the audit, nominating, and compensation committees be staffed *entirely* by outside directors. The New York Stock Exchange reinforced the mandates of Sarbanes-Oxley by requiring that companies have a Nominating/Governance Committee composed entirely of independent outside directors. Similarly, NASDAQ rules require that nominations for new directors be made by either a nominating committee of independent outsiders or by a majority of independent outside directors.[64]

Partially in response to Sarbanes-Oxley, a recent survey of directors of *Fortune 1000* U.S. companies by Mercer Delta Consulting and the University of Southern California revealed that 60% of directors spent more time on board matters in 2003 than the previous year, with 85% spending more time on their company's accounts, 83% more on governance practices, and 52% on monitoring financial performance.[65] Newly elected outside directors with financial management experience increased to 10% of all outside directors in 2003 from only 1% of outsiders in 1998.[66] Fifty-seven percent of *Fortune 1000* U.S. boards required in 2003 that directors own stock in the corporation—an increase from 51% the previous year.[67]

Evaluating Governance

To help investors evaluate a firm's corporate governance, a number of independent rating services, such as Standard & Poor's (S&P), Moody's, The Corporate Library, Institutional Shareholder Services (ISS), and Governance Metrics International (GMI), have established criteria for good governance. *Business Week* annually publishes a list of the best and worst boards of U.S. corporations. Whereas rating service firms like S&P, Moody's, and The Corporate Library use a wide mix of research data and criteria to evaluate companies, ISS and GMI have been criticized because they primarily use public records to score firms, using simple checklists.[68] In contrast, the S&P Corporate Governance Scoring System researches four major issues:

- Ownership Structure and Influence
- Financial Stakeholder Rights and Relations
- Financial Transparency and Information Disclosure
- Board Structure and Processes

Although the S&P scoring system is proprietary and confidential, independent research using generally accepted measures of S&P's four issues revealed that moving from the poorest- to the best-governed categories nearly doubled a firm's likelihood of receiving an investment-grade credit rating.[69]

An increasing number of boards are evaluating not only the performance of the CEO but also the performance of the board in total and that of individual directors. Korn/Ferry International reported that 82% of boards in 2003 had a formal process to evaluate CEO performance compared to 67% a year earlier. Regular formal evaluations of the full board were conducted in 2003 by 65% (37% in 2002) of U.S. boards compared to 37% of European boards and 41% of Asian boards. Individual directors were formally evaluated in 2003 by 29% of American boards compared to 41% of Asian boards, 52% of UK boards, 23% of French boards, and only 1% of German boards.[70]

Avoiding Governance Improvements

A number of corporations are concerned that various requirements to improve corporate governance will constrain top management's ability to effectively manage the company. For example, more U.S. public corporations have gone private in the years since the passage of Sarbanes-Oxley than before its passage. Other companies use multiple classes of stock to keep outsiders from having sufficient voting power to change the company. Insiders, usually the company's founders, get stock with extra votes, while others get second-class stock with fewer votes. For example, Brian Roberts, CEO of Comcast, owns "superstock" that represents only 0.4% of outstanding common stock but guarantees him one-third of the voting stock. The Investor Responsibility Research Center reports that 11.3% of the companies it monitored in 2004 had multiple classes, up from 7.5% in 1990.[71]

Another approach to sidestepping new governance requirements is being used by corporations such as Google, Infasource Services, Orbitz, and W&T Offshore. If a corporation in which an individual group or another company controls more than 50% of the voting shares decides to become a "controlled company," the firm is then exempt from requirements by the New York Stock Exchange and NASDAQ that a majority of the board and all members of key board committees be independent outsiders. According to governance authority Jay Lorsch, this will result in a situation in which "the majority shareholders can walk all over the minority."[72]

Trends in Corporate Governance

The role of the board of directors in the strategic management of a corporation is likely to be more active in the future. Although neither the composition of boards nor the board leadership structure has been consistently linked to firm financial performance, better governance does lead to higher credit ratings and stock prices. A McKinsey survey reveals that investors are willing to pay 16% more for a corporation's stock if it is known to have good corporate governance. The investors explained that they would pay more because, in their opinion (1) good governance leads to better performance over time, (2) good governance reduces the risk of the company getting into trouble, and (3) governance is a major strategic issue.[73]

Some of today's **trends in governance** (particularly prevalent in the United States and the United Kingdom) that are likely to continue include the following[74]:

- Boards are getting more involved not only in reviewing and evaluating company strategy but also in shaping it.
- Companies involved in class-action lawsuits by shareholders are making concessions in corporate governance as part of the settlements. For example, as part of its recent settlement, Sprint agreed to add a lead director, to elect directors annually, and to have only independent outsiders serve on key board committees.[75]

- Institutional investors, such as pension funds, mutual funds, and insurance companies, are becoming active on boards and are putting increasing pressure on top management to improve corporate performance. This trend is supported by a 2004 SEC requirement that a mutual fund must publicly disclose the proxy votes cast at company board meetings in its portfolio. This reduces the tendency for mutual funds to rubber-stamp management proposals.[76]
- Shareholders are demanding that directors and top managers own more than token amounts of stock in a corporation. Research indicates that when compensation committee members are significant shareholders, they tend to offer the CEO less salary but with a higher incentive component than do compensation committee members who own little to no stock.[77]
- Non-affiliated outside (non-management) directors are increasing their numbers and power in publicly held corporations as CEOs loosen their grip on boards. Outside members are taking charge of annual CEO evaluations. Except for the executive, finance, and investment committees, board committees are moving toward complete outsider composition. An increasing number of boards will be evaluating not only overall board performance but also that of individual directors.
- Boards are getting smaller—partially because of the reduction in the number of insiders but also because boards desire new directors to have specialized knowledge and expertise instead of general experience.
- Boards continue to take more control of board functions by either splitting the combined chair/CEO into two separate positions or establishing a lead outside director position.
- As corporations become more global, they are increasingly looking for board members with international experience.
- Instead of merely being able to vote for or against directors nominated by the board's nominating committee, shareholders may be allowed to nominate board members. Supported by the AFL-CIO, a more open nominating process would enable shareholders to vote out directors who ignore shareholder interests.[78]
- Society, in the form of special interest groups, increasingly expects boards of directors to balance the economic goal of profitability with the social needs of society. Issues dealing with workforce diversity and the environment are now reaching the board level.

2.2 The Role of Top Management

The top management function is usually conducted by the CEO of the corporation in coordination with the Chief Operating Officer (COO) or president, executive vice president, and vice presidents of divisions and functional areas. Even though strategic management involves everyone in the organization, the board of directors holds top management primarily responsible for the strategic management of a firm.[79]

Responsibilities of Top Management

Top management responsibilities, especially those of the CEO, involve getting things accomplished through and with others in order to meet the corporate objectives. Top management's job is thus multidimensional and is oriented toward the welfare of the total organization. Specific top management tasks vary from firm to firm and are developed from an analysis of the mission, objectives, strategies, and key activities of the corporation. Tasks are typically divided among the members of the top management team. A diversity of skills can thus be very important. Research indicates that top management teams with a diversity of functional and educational backgrounds and length of time with the company tend to be significantly related to improvements in corporate market share and profitability.[80] In addition, highly diverse teams with some international experience tend to emphasize international growth strategies and strategic innovation, especially in uncertain environments, to boost financial performance.[81] The CEO, with the support of the rest of the top management team, must successfully handle two primary responsibilities that are crucial to the effective strategic management of the corporation: (1) provide executive leadership and a strategic vision and (2) manage the strategic planning process.

Executive Leadership and Strategic Vision

Executive leadership is the directing of activities toward the accomplishment of corporate objectives. Executive leadership is important because it sets the tone for the entire corporation. A **strategic vision** is a description of what the company is capable of becoming. It is often communicated in the company's mission and vision statements (as described in **Chapter 1**). People in an organization want to have a sense of mission, but only top management is in the position to specify and communicate this strategic vision to the general workforce. Top management's enthusiasm (or lack of it) about the corporation tends to be contagious. The importance of executive leadership is illustrated by Steve Reinemund, CEO of PepsiCo: "A leader's job is to define overall direction and motivate others to get there."[82]

Successful CEOs are noted for having a clear strategic vision, a strong passion for their company, and an ability to communicate with others. They are often perceived to be dynamic and charismatic leaders—which is especially important for high firm performance and investor confidence in uncertain environments.[83] They have many of the characteristics of **transformational leaders**—that is, leaders who provide change and movement in an organization by providing a vision for that change.[84] For instance, the positive attitude characterizing many well-known industrial leaders—such as Bill Gates at Microsoft, Anita Roddick at The Body Shop, Ted Turner at CNN, Steve Jobs at Apple Computer, Herb Kelleher at Southwest Airlines, and Louis Gerstner at IBM—has energized their respective corporations. These transformational leaders are able to command respect and to influence strategy formulation and implementation because they tend to have three key characteristics:

1. **The CEO articulates a strategic vision for the corporation:** The CEO envisions the company not as it currently is but as it can become. The new perspective that the CEO's vision brings to activities and conflicts gives renewed meaning to everyone's work and enables employees to see beyond the details of their own jobs to the functioning of the total corporation. Louis Gerstner proposed a new vision for IBM when he proposed that the company change its business model from computer hardware to services: "If customers were going to look to an integrator to help them envision, design, and build end-to-end solutions, then the companies playing that role would exert tremendous influence over the full range of technology decisions—from architecture and applications to hardware and software choices."[85] In a recent survey of 1,500 senior executives from 20 different countries, when asked the most important behavioral trait a CEO must have, 98% responded that the CEO must convey "a strong sense of vision."[86]
2. **The CEO presents a role for others to identify with and to follow:** The leader sets an example in terms of behavior, dress, and actions. The CEO's attitudes and values concerning the corporation's purpose and activities are clear-cut and constantly communicated in words and deeds. For example, when design engineers at General Motors had

problems with monitor resolution using the Windows operating system, Steve Ballmer, CEO of Microsoft, personally crawled under conference room tables to plug in PC monitors and diagnose the problem.[87] People know what to expect and have trust in their CEO. Research indicates that businesses in which the general manager has the trust of the employees have higher sales and profits with lower turnover than do businesses in which there is a lesser amount of trust.[88]

3. **The CEO communicates high performance standards and also shows confidence in the followers' abilities to meet these standards:** No leader ever improved performance by setting easily attainable goals that provided no challenge. Communicating high expectations to others can often lead to high performance.[89] The CEO must be willing to follow through by coaching people. As a result, employees view their work as very important and thus motivating.[90] Ivan Seidenberg, chief executive of Verizon Communications, was closely involved in deciding Verizon's strategic direction, and he showed his faith in his people by letting his key managers handle important projects and represent the company in public forums. "All of these people could be CEOs in their own right. They are warriors and they are on a mission," explained Steidenberg. Grateful for his faith in them, his managers were fiercely loyal both to him and the company.[91]

The negative side of confident executive leaders is that their very confidence may lead to *hubris*, in which their confidence blinds them to information that is contrary to a decided course of action. For example, overconfident CEOs tend to charge ahead with mergers and acquisitions even though they are aware that most acquisitions destroy shareholder value. Research by Tate and Malmendier found that "overconfident CEOs are more likely to conduct mergers than rational CEOs at any point in time . . . . Overconfident CEOs view their company as undervalued by outside investors who are less optimistic about the prospects of the firm." Overconfident CEOs were most likely to make acquisitions when they could avoid selling new stock to finance them, and they were more likely to do deals that diversified their firm's lines of businesses.[92] For an example of a once-excellent CEO who became overconfident, see **Strategy Highlight 2.2**.

Managing the Strategic Planning Process

As business corporations adopt more of the characteristics of the learning organization, strategic planning initiatives can come from any part of an organization. A survey of 90 U.S. global corporations revealed that, in 90% of the firms, strategies were first proposed in the subsidiaries and sent to headquarters for approval.[93] However, unless top management encourages and supports the planning process, strategic management is not likely to result. In most corporations, top management must initiate and manage the strategic planning process. It may do so by first asking business units and functional areas to propose strategic plans for themselves, or it may begin by drafting an overall corporate plan within which the units can then build their own plans. Research suggests that bottom-up strategic planning may be most appropriate in multidivisional corporations operating in relatively stable environments but that top-down strategic planning may be most appropriate for firms operating in turbulent environments.[94] Other organizations engage in concurrent strategic planning in which all the organization's units draft plans for themselves after they have been provided with the organization's overall mission and objectives.

Regardless of the approach taken, the typical board of directors expects top management to manage the overall strategic planning process so that the plans of all the units and functional areas fit together into an overall corporate plan. Top management's job therefore includes the tasks of evaluating unit plans and providing feedback. To do this, it may require each unit to justify its proposed objectives, strategies, and programs in terms of how well they satisfy the organization's overall objectives in light of available resources.[95]

STRATEGY HIGHLIGHT 2.2

CEO Hubris at Disney?

When Michael Eisner was recruited from Paramount Pictures by Roy Disney (nephew of the late Walt Disney) and Stanley Gold in 1984, he worked quickly to put the faltering company back on its feet. Earnings per share had fallen from $4.16 in 1980 to $2.73 when Eisner took over. With Roy Disney's support and the help of his friend Frank Wells (previously Vice Chair of Warner Brothers) as President and COO, Eisner revitalized the failing animation division. The unit soon churned out successful films such as *The Little Mermaid*, *The Lion King*, *Aladdin*, and *Beauty and the Beast*. He expanded the theme park business and opened 681 new Disney stores full of merchandise. Eisner succeeded not only because he was an excellent manager but also because of his passion and enthusiasm for Disney values. He even took Walt's place as the emcee of Disney's television programs.

Following the death of his colleague Frank Wells, Eisner became even more like the late Walt Disney—increasingly autocratic. His tendency to micromanage the company drove away top executives such as Jeffrey Katzenberg and other studio heads. Taking advantage of Disney's growth in sales and profits, Eisner bought Miramax Films and the Anaheim Ducks hockey team, followed by the acquisition of Capital Cities/ABC in the early 1990s. Because the success of the company drove the stock price up significantly, Eisner's stock options were worth over $650 million when he cashed them in 1998–2000.

Over time, Eisner manipulated the board of directors to make sure that it supported his decisions. Although the board included few people with any knowledge of corporate finance, Eisner nominated to the board his personal lawyer, his architect, and the principal of the elementary school attended by his sons. He enabled his good friend Michael Ovitz to collect $140 million when he left the company after 15 months as its president. According to the Delaware Supreme Court, the board's willingness to follow Eisner's recommendation in giving Ovitz the largest payout allowed by his contract "[pushed] the envelope of judicial respect for the business judgment of directors in making compensation decisions." In 2003, the board chose not to re-nominate Andrea Van de Kamp as a board member because of her criticism of Eisner's decisions. The board reclassified Stanley Gold as an insider, thus forcing him to resign as chair of the powerful Governance and Nominating Committee. Critics wondered why Eisner's long-time critic was suddenly an insider when other board members who had closer financial or family ties to the company were deemed independent outsiders. For these and other reasons, the Walt Disney Company twice led *Business Week's* annual list of worst boards of directors.

From its peak in 1997, Disney's performance continued to slump. Although revenue grew 4% from 1997 to 2004, operating profits fell 7% a year, and earnings per share stagnated. Analysts criticized Eisner for paying too much for acquisitions. Ratings at ABC continued to fall, as did theme parks' profit margins. Because the company refused to agree to a change in its distribution contract with Steve Jobs' Pixar, the maker of *Toy Story* and *Finding Nemo*, the contract was not renewed. Critics explained that Eisner was unable to work with Jobs because both men were supremely confident (some said arrogant) that their own judgment was correct—regardless of what others said. Harvey Weinstein of Miramax studios also indicated that he wanted out of his partnership with the Disney Company. Meanwhile, Disney's own animation unit was faltering and unable to match Pixar's new computer technology and creativity. Roy Disney and Stanley Gold left the board in 2003 in protest over Eisner's leadership. Early in 2004 Disney was the target of a takeover attempt by Comcast, a cable firm.

At its March 3, 2004, shareholders meeting, 45% of the votes withheld support for Eisner in his post as Disney chairman. Leading the fight were the pension funds of CALPERS and the Ohio Public Employees Retirement System. Soon thereafter, the Disney board announced that it was splitting the positions of CEO and Chairman of the Board. Eisner kept his title as CEO, but the Chairman's position went to George Mitchell, former Maine senator and a supporter of Eisner. According to California State Controller Steve Westly, "Major shareholders intend to keep pressure on Disney's audit committee, its compensation committee, and the management."

On September 10, 2004, 62-year-old Michael Eisner announced that he would step down as Disney CEO in late 2006. Critics responded that Eisner needed to be replaced sooner and that the board needed to be significantly strengthened. Roy Disney considered proposing a minority slate of board nominations for 2005 if the SEC changed the rules to allow investors to place their own candidates on the official ballot.

Sources: C. B. Shrader and J. D. Hunger, "Walt Disney Productions—1984," in T. L. Wheelen and J. D. Hunger, *Strategic Management and Business Policy*, 2nd edition (Reading, MA: Addison-Wesley Publishing, 1986), pp. 419–458; D. Lieberman, "Disney Tries to Work Magic with New Board Lineup," *USA Today* (March 3, 2003), pp. B1–B2; "The One Time Lion King," *Economist* (September 18, 2004), p. 70; R. Grover and T. Lowry, "Now It's Time to Say Goodbye," *Business Week* (March 15, 2004), pp. 31–32; "Finding Another Nemo," *Economist* (February 7, 2004), p. 64; R. Grover and A. Borrus, "Can Michael Eisner Hold the Fort?" *Business Week* (March 22, 2004), p. 96; M. McCarthy, "Disney Strips Chairmanship from Eisner," *USA Today* (March 4, 2004), pp. 1B–2B; K. Maney, "Who Can Save a Disney in Distress?" *USA Today* (March 3, 2004), p. 3B; R. Grover, "Eisner's Goofy Timetable," *Business Week* (September 27, 2004), p. 50.

Many large organizations have a **strategic planning staff** charged with supporting both top management and the business units in the strategic planning process. This planning staff typically consists of fewer than 10 people, headed by a senior vice president or director of corporate planning. The staff's major responsibilities are to:

1. Identify and analyze companywide strategic issues and suggest corporate strategic alternatives to top management.
2. Work as facilitators with business units to guide them through the strategic planning process.

2.3 Conclusion

Who determines a corporation's performance? According to the popular press, the chief executive officer seems to be personally responsible for a company's success or failure. When a company is in trouble, one of the first alternatives usually presented is to fire the CEO. That was certainly the case at the Walt Disney Company under Michael Eisner. He was first viewed as a transformational leader who saved the company in the 1980s. By 2003, he was perceived to be the primary reason for the company's poor performance. The truth is not this simple.

According to research by Margarethe Wiersema, firing the CEO rarely solves a corporation's problems. In a study of CEO turnover caused by dismissals and retirements in the 500 largest public U.S. companies, 71% of the departures were involuntary. In those firms in which the CEO was fired or asked to resign and replaced by another, Wiersema found *no* significant improvement in the company's operating earnings or stock price. She couldn't find a single measure suggesting that CEO dismissal had a positive effect on corporate performance! Wiersema placed the blame for the poor results squarely on the shoulders of the boards of directors. Boards typically lack an in-depth understanding of the business and consequently rely too heavily on executive search firms that know even less about the business. According to Wiersema, boards that successfully managed the executive succession process had three things in common:

- The board set the criteria for candidate selection based on the strategic needs of the company.
- The board set realistic performance expectations rather than demanding a quick fix to please the investment community.
- The board developed a deep understanding of the business and provided strong strategic oversight of top management, including thoughtful annual reviews of CEO performance.[96]

As noted at the beginning of this chapter, corporate governance involves not just the CEO or the board of directors. It involves the combined active participation of the board, top management, and shareholders. One positive result of the many corporate scandals during 2001–2004 is the increased interest in governance. Institutional investors are no longer content to be passive shareholders. Thanks to new regulations, boards of directors are taking their responsibilities more seriously and including more independent outsiders on key oversight committees. Top managers are beginning to understand the value of working with boards as partners, not just as adversaries or as people to be manipulated. Although there will always be passive shareholders, rubber-stamp boards, and dominating CEOs, the simple truth is that good corporate governance means better strategic management.

Strategy Bits

- The frequency of CEO turnover has increased 53% since 1995.
- The average tenure of a U.S. *Fortune 500* CEO dropped from 9.5 years in 1995 to 7.3 years in 2002.[97]
- The average total compensation for a board member of a *Fortune 500* company approached $500,000 in 2005, up 14% from 2004.[98]

Discussion Questions

1. When does a corporation need a board of directors?
2. Who should and should not serve on a board of directors? What about environmentalists or union leaders?
3. Should a CEO be allowed to serve on another company's board of directors?
4. What would be the result if the only insider on a corporation's board were the CEO?
5. Should all CEOs be transformational leaders? Would you like to work for a transformational leader?

Strategic Practice Exercises

A. Think of the **best manager** for whom you have ever worked. What was it about that person that made him or her such a good boss? Consider the following statements as they pertain to that person. **Fill in the blank *in front of each* statement with one of the following values:**

STRONGLY AGREE = 5; AGREE = 4; NEUTRAL = 3;
DISAGREE = 2; STRONGLY DISAGREE = 1.

1.___ I respect him/her personally and want to act in a way that merits his/her respect and admiration. ___

2.___ I respect his/her competence about things with which he/she is more experienced than I. ___

3.___ He/she can give special help to those who cooperate with him/her. ___

4.___ He/she can apply pressure on those who cooperate with him/her. ___

5.___ He/she has a legitimate right, considering his/her position, to expect that his/her suggestions will be carried out. ___

6.___ I defer to his/her judgment in areas with which he/she is more familiar than I. ___

7.___ He/she can make things difficult for me if I fail to follow his/her advice. ___

8.___ Because of his/her job title and rank, I am obligated to follow his/her suggestions. ___

9.___ I can personally benefit by cooperating with him/her. ___

10.___ Following his/her advice results in better decisions. ___

11.___ I cooperate with him/her because I have high regard for him/her as an individual. ___

12.___ He/she can penalize those who do not follow his/her suggestions. ___

13.___ I feel I have to cooperate with him/her. ___

14.___ I cooperate with him/her because I wish to be identified with him/her. ___

15.___ Cooperating with him/her can positively affect my performance. ___

Source: Questionnaire developed by J. D. Hunger from the article "Influence and Information: An Exploratory Investigation of the Boundary Role Person's Basis of Power" by Robert Spekman, *Academy of Management Journal*, March 1979. Copyright © 2004 by J. David Hunger.

B. Now think of the **worst manager** for whom you have ever worked. What was it about that person that made him or her such a poor boss? Consider the statements above as they pertain to that person. **Place a number *after each statement* with one of the values from 5 = strongly agree to 1 = strongly disagree.**

C. Add the values you marked for the best manager within each of the five categories of power below. Then do the same for the values you marked for the worst manager.

BEST MANAGER

Reward	Coercive	Legitimate	Referent	Expert
3.	4.	5.	1.	2.
9.	7.	8.	11.	6.
15.	12.	13.	14.	10.
Total	Total	Total	Total	Total

WORST MANAGER

Reward	Coercive	Legitimate	Referent	Expert
3.	4.	5.	1.	2.
9.	7.	8.	11.	6.
15.	12.	13.	14.	10.
Total	Total	Total	Total	Total

D. Consider the differences between how you rated your best and your worst manager. How different are the two profiles? In many cases, the best manager's profile tends to be similar to that of transformational leaders in that the best manager tends to score highest on referent, followed by expert and reward, power—especially when compared to the worst manager's profile. The worst manager often scores highest on coercive and legitimate power, followed by reward power. The results of this survey may help you to answer the fifth discussion question for this chapter.

Key Terms

affiliated director (p. 40)
agency theory (p. 39)
board of directors continuum (p. 37)
board of director responsibilities (p. 36)
codetermination (p. 42)
corporate governance (p. 36)
corporation (p. 36)
due care (p. 37)
executive leadership (p. 49)
family director (p. 40)
inside director (p. 39)
interlocking directorate (p. 43)
lead director (p. 45)
outside director (p. 39)
retired executive director (p. 40)
role of the board of directors in strategic management (p. 37)
Sarbanes-Oxley Act (p. 46)
staggered board (p. 44)
stewardship theory (p. 40)
strategic planning staff (p. 52)
strategic vision (p. 49)
top management responsibilities (p. 48)
transformational leader (p. 49)
trend in governance (p. 47)

CHAPTER 3
Ethics and Social Responsibility in Strategic Management

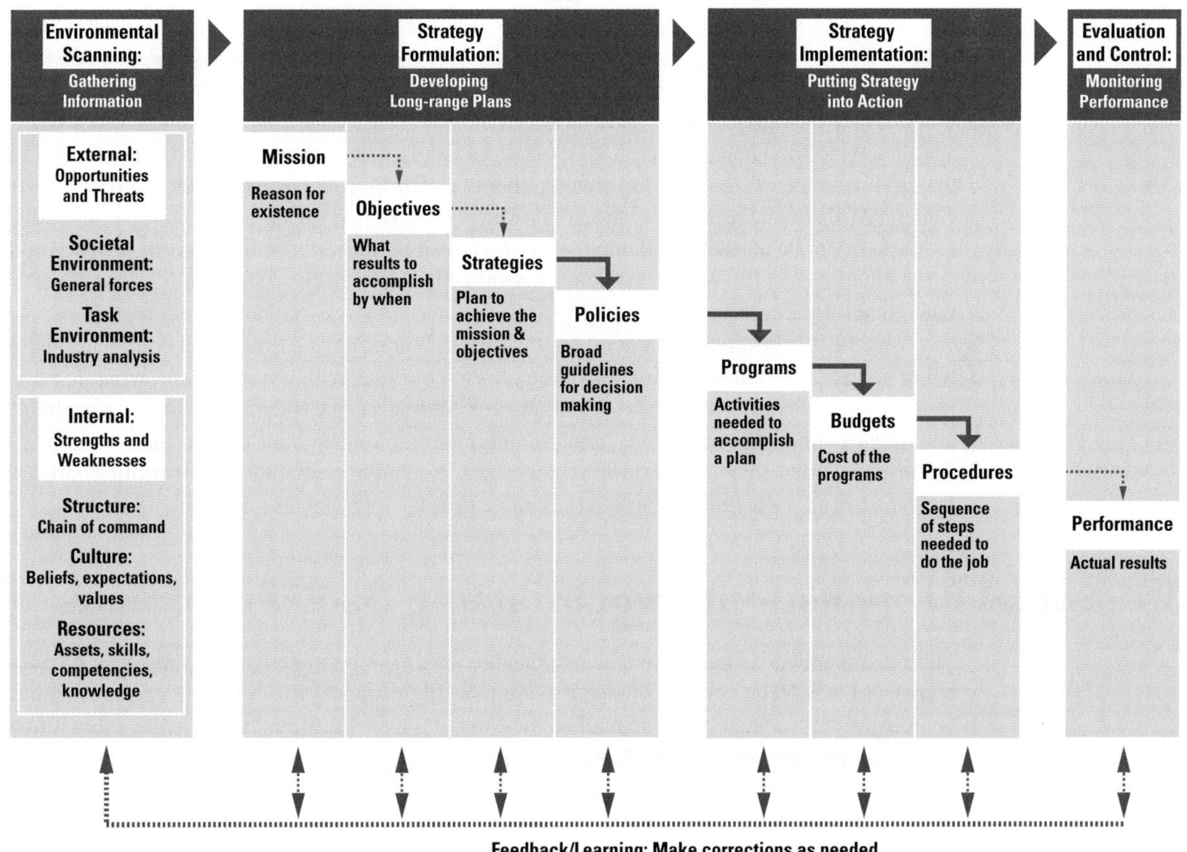

Learning Objectives

After reading this chapter, you should be able to:

- Compare and contrast Friedman's traditional view with Carroll's contemporary view of social responsibility
- Understand the relationship between social responsibility and corporate performance
- Be able to conduct a stakeholder analysis
- Explain why people may act unethically
- Describe different views of ethics according to the utilitarian, individual rights, and justice approaches

ONLY A FEW MILES FROM THE GLEAMING SKYSCRAPERS OF PROSPEROUS MINNEAPOLIS WAS a neighborhood littered with shattered glass from stolen cars and derelict houses used by drug lords. During the 1990s, the Hawthorne neighborhood became a no-man's-land where gun battles terrified local residents and raised the per capita murder rate 70% higher than that of New York.

Executives at General Mills became concerned when the murder rate reached a record high in 1996. The company's headquarters was located just five miles away from Hawthorne, then the city's most violent neighborhood. Working with law enforcement, politicians, community leaders, and residents, General Mills spent $2.5 million and donated thousands of employee hours to help clean up Hawthorne. Crack houses were demolished to make way for a new elementary school. Dilapidated houses in the neighborhood's core were rebuilt. General Mills provided grants to help people buy Hawthorne's houses. By 2003, homicides were down 32% and robberies had declined 56% in Hawthorne.

This story was nothing new for General Mills, a company listed in *Business Week's* 2003 list of most generous corporate philanthropists. In 2002 alone, the company donated $65 million out of revenues of $10.5 billion to causes ranging from education and the arts to social services. Every day, the company ships three truckloads of Cheerios, Wheaties, and other packaged goods to food banks throughout the nation. Community performance is even reflected in the performance reviews of top management. According to Christina Shea, president of General Mills Foundation, "We take as innovative approach to giving back to our communities as we do in our business." For joining with a nonprofit organization and a minority-owned food company to create 150 inner-city jobs, General Mills received *Business Ethics*' annual corporate citizenship award.[1]

Was this the best use of General Mills' time and money? At a time when companies were being pressured to cut costs and outsource jobs to countries with cheaper labor, what do business corporations owe their local communities? Should business firms give away shareholders' money, support social causes, and ask employees to donate their time to the community? Critics argue that this sort of thing is done best by government and not-for-profit charities. Isn't the primary goal of business to maximize profits, not to be a social worker?

3.1 Social Responsibilities of Strategic Decision Makers

Should strategic decision makers be responsible only to shareholders, or do they have broader responsibilities? The concept of **social responsibility** proposes that a private corporation has responsibilities to society that extend beyond making a profit. Strategic decisions often affect more than just the corporation. A decision to retrench by closing some plants and discontinuing product lines, for example, affects not only the firm's workforce but also the communities where the plants are located and the customers with no other source for the discontinued product. Decisions to outsource manufacturing, software development, or customer service to contractors in other countries are likely to have a significant impact on more than just company profits. Such decisions can cause many to question the appropriateness of certain missions, objectives, and strategies of business corporations. Managers must be able to deal with these conflicting interests in an ethical manner to formulate a viable strategic plan.

Responsibilities of a Business Firm

What are the responsibilities of a business firm and how many of them must be fulfilled? Milton Friedman and Archie Carroll offer two contrasting views of the responsibilities of business firms to society.

Friedman's Traditional View of Business Responsibility

Urging a return to a laissez-faire worldwide economy with a minimum of government regulation, Milton Friedman argues against the concept of social responsibility. A business person who acts "responsibly" by cutting the price of the firm's product to prevent inflation, or by making expenditures to reduce pollution, or by hiring the hard-core unemployed, according to Friedman, is spending the shareholder's money for a general social interest. Even if the business person has shareholder permission or encouragement to do so, he or she is still acting from motives other than economic and may, in the long run, harm the very society the firm is trying to help. By taking on the burden of these social costs, the business becomes less efficient—either prices go up to pay for the increased costs or investment in new activities and research is postponed. These results negatively affect—perhaps fatally—the long-term efficiency of a business. Friedman thus referred to the social responsibility of business as a "fundamentally subversive doctrine" and stated:

> *There is one and only one social responsibility of business—to use its resources and engage in activities designed to increase its profits so long as it stays within the rules of the game, which is to say, engages in open and free competition without deception or fraud.*[2]

Following Friedman's reasoning, the management of General Mills was clearly guilty of misusing corporate assets and negatively affecting shareholder wealth. The millions spent in social services could have been invested in new product development or given back as dividends to the shareholders. Instead of General Mills' management acting on its own, shareholders could have decided which charities to support.

Carroll's Four Responsibilities of Business

Friedman's contention that the primary goal of business is profit maximization is only one side of an ongoing debate regarding corporate social responsibility (CSR). According to William J. Byron, Distinguished Professor of Ethics at Georgetown University and past-President of Catholic University of America, profits are merely a means to an end, not an end in itself. Just as a person needs food to survive and grow, so does a business corporation need profits to survive and grow. "Maximizing profits is like maximizing food." Thus, contends Byron, maximization of profits cannot be the primary obligation of business.[3]

As shown in **Figure 3–1**, Archie Carroll proposes that the managers of business organizations have four responsibilities: economic, legal, ethical, and discretionary.[4]

1. **Economic** responsibilities of a business organization's management are to produce goods and services of value to society so that the firm may repay its creditors and shareholders.
2. **Legal** responsibilities are defined by governments in laws that management is expected to obey. For example, U.S. business firms are required to hire and promote people based on their credentials rather than to discriminate on non-job-related characteristics such as race, gender, or religion.

Figure 3–1
Responsibilities of Business

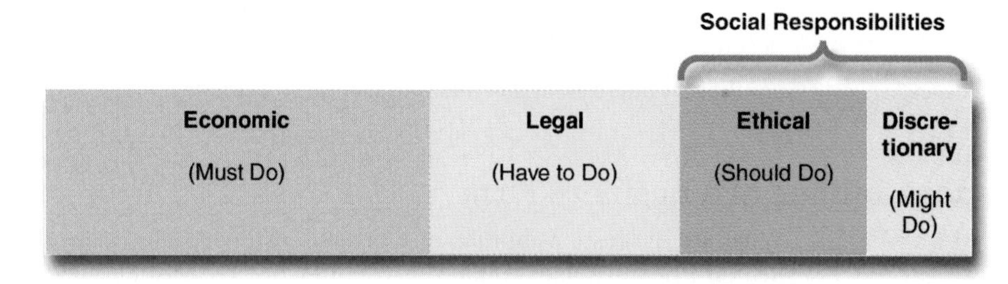

Source: Adapted from A. B. Carroll, "A Three Dimensional Conceptual Model of Corporate Performance," Academy of Management Review *(October 1979), p. 499. Reprinted with permission.*

3. **Ethical** responsibilities of an organization's management are to follow the generally held beliefs about behavior in society. For example, society generally expects firms to work with the employees and the community in planning for layoffs, even though no law may require this. The affected people can get very upset if an organization's management fails to act according to generally prevailing ethical values.
4. **Discretionary** responsibilities are the purely voluntary obligations a corporation assumes. Examples are philanthropic contributions, training the hard-core unemployed, and providing day-care centers. The difference between ethical and discretionary responsibilities is that few people expect an organization to fulfill discretionary responsibilities, whereas many expect an organization to fulfill ethical ones.[5]

Carroll lists these four responsibilities *in order of priority*. A business firm must first make a profit to satisfy its economic responsibilities. To continue in existence, the firm must follow the laws, thus fulfilling its legal responsibilities. There is evidence that companies found guilty of violating laws have lower profits and sales growth after conviction.[6] To this point Carroll and Friedman are in agreement. Carroll, however, goes further by arguing that business managers have responsibilities beyond economic and legal ones.

Having satisfied the two basic responsibilities, according to Carroll, a firm should look to fulfilling its social responsibilities. Social responsibility, therefore, includes both ethical and discretionary, but not economic and legal, responsibilities. A firm can fulfill its ethical responsibilities by taking actions that society tends to value but has not yet put into law. When ethical responsibilities are satisfied, a firm can focus on discretionary responsibilities—purely voluntary actions that society has not yet decided are important. For example, when Cisco Systems decided to dismiss 6,000 full-time employees, it provided a novel severance package. Those employees who agreed to work for a local nonprofit organization for a year would receive one-third of their salaries plus benefits and stock options and be the first to be rehired. Nonprofits were delighted to hire such highly qualified people, and Cisco was able to maintain its talent pool for when it could hire once again.[7]

The discretionary responsibilities of today may become the ethical responsibilities of tomorrow. The provision of day-care facilities is, for example, moving rapidly from being a discretionary to an ethical responsibility. Carroll suggests that to the extent that business corporations fail to acknowledge discretionary or ethical responsibilities, society, through government, will act, making them legal responsibilities. Government may do this, moreover, without regard to an organization's economic responsibilities. As a result, the organization may have greater difficulty in earning a profit than it would have if it had voluntarily assumed some ethical and discretionary responsibilities.

Both Friedman and Carroll argue their positions based on the impact of socially responsible actions on a firm's profits. Friedman says that socially responsible actions hurt a firm's efficiency. Carroll proposes that a lack of social responsibility results in increased government regulations, which reduce a firm's efficiency.

Empirical research now indicates that socially responsible actions may have a positive effect on a firm's financial performance. Although a number of studies in the past have found no significant relationship,[8] an increasing number are finding a positive relationship.[9] A recent in-depth analysis by Margolis and Walsh of 127 studies found that "there is a positive association and very little evidence of a negative association between a company's social performance and its financial performance."[10] Another meta-analysis of 52 studies on social responsibility and performance reached this same conclusion.[11]

According to Porter and Kramer, "social and economic goals are not inherently conflicting, but integrally connected."[12] Being known as a socially responsible firm may provide a company with **social capital**, the goodwill of key stakeholders, that can be used for competitive advantage.[13] Target, for example, tries to attract socially concerned younger consumers by offering brands from companies that can boost ethical track records and community involvement.[14] A survey of more than 700 global companies by the Conference Board reported that 60% of the managers stated that citizenship activities had led to (1) goodwill that opened doors in local communities and (2) an enhanced reputation with consumers.[15] Another survey of 140 U.S. firms revealed that being more socially responsible resulted not only in competitive advantages but also in cost savings.[16] For example, companies that take the lead in being environmentally friendly, such as by using recycled materials, preempt attacks from environmental groups and enhance their corporate image. Programs to reduce pollution, for example, can actually reduce waste and maximize resource productivity. One study that examined 70 ecological initiatives taken by 43 companies found the average payback period to be 18 months.[17] Other examples of benefits received from being socially responsible are:

- Their environmental concerns may enable them to charge premium prices and gain brand loyalty (for example, Ben & Jerry's Ice Cream).
- Their trustworthiness may help them generate enduring relationships with suppliers and distributors without requiring them to spend a lot of time and money policing contracts (for example, Maytag).
- They can attract outstanding employees who prefer working for a responsible firm (for example, Procter & Gamble).
- They are more likely to be welcomed into a foreign country (for example, Levi Strauss).
- They can utilize the goodwill of public officials for support in difficult times. (For example, Minnesota supported Dayton Hudson's (now Target) fight to avoid being acquired by Dart Industries of Maryland.)
- They are more likely to attract capital infusions from investors who view reputable companies as desirable long-term investments (for example, 3M).[18]

Corporate Stakeholders

The concept that business must be socially responsible sounds appealing until we ask, "Responsible to whom?" A corporation's task environment includes a large number of groups with interest in a business organization's activities. These groups are referred to as **corporate stakeholders** because they affect or are affected by the achievement of the firm's objectives.[19] Should a corporation be responsible only to some of these groups, or does business have an equal responsibility to all of them? Does a company have any responsibility to the employees of suppliers (especially in other countries) to ensure that they are treated fairly and have safe working conditions?

A survey of the U.S. general public by Harris Poll revealed that 95% of the respondents felt that U.S. corporations owe something to their workers and the communities in which they operate and that they should sometimes sacrifice some profit for the sake of making things better for their workers and communities. People were concerned that business executives seemed to be more interested in making profits and boosting their own pay than they were in the safety and quality of the products made by their companies.[20] These negative feelings receive some support from a study which revealed that the CEOs at the 50 U.S. companies that outsourced the greatest number of jobs received a greater increase in pay (up 46%) from 2002 to 2003 than did the CEOs of 365 U.S. firms overall (only a 9% increase).[21]

In any one strategic decision, the interests of one stakeholder group can conflict with those of another. For example, a business firm's decision to use only recycled materials in its manufacturing process may have a positive effect on environmental groups but a negative effect on shareholder dividends. In another example, Maytag Corporation's top management decided to move refrigerator production from Galesburg, Illinois, to a lower-wage location in Mexico. On the one hand, shareholders were generally pleased with the decision because it would lower costs. On the other hand, officials and local union people were very unhappy at the loss of jobs when the Galesburg plant closed. Which group's interests should have priority?

Stakeholder Analysis

Stakeholder analysis is the identification and evaluation of corporate stakeholders. This can be done in a three-step process.

The *first step* in stakeholder analysis is to identify **primary stakeholders**, those who have a direct connection with the corporation and who have sufficient bargaining power to directly affect corporate activities. Primary stakeholders are directly affected by the corporation and usually include customers, employees, suppliers, shareholders, and creditors.

But who exactly are a firm's customers or employees and what do they want? This is not always a simple exercise. For example, Intel's customers were clearly computer manufacturers because that's to whom Intel sold its electronic chips. When a math professor found a small flaw in Intel's Pentium microprocessor in 1994, computer users demanded that Intel replace the defective chips. At first Intel refused to do so because it hadn't sold PCs to these individuals. According to then-CEO Andy Grove, "I got irritated and angry because of user demands that we take back a device we didn't sell." Intel wanted the PC users to follow the supply chain and complain to the firms from whom they had bought the computers. Gradually Grove was persuaded that Intel had a direct duty to these consumers. "Although we didn't sell to these individuals directly, we marketed to them. . . . It took me a while to understand this," explained Grove. In the end, Intel paid $450 million to replace the defective parts.[22]

Aside from the Intel example, business corporations usually know their primary stakeholders and what they want. The corporation systematically monitors these stakeholders because they are important to a firm's meeting its economic and legal responsibilities. Employees want a fair day's pay and fringe benefits. Customers want safe products and value for price paid. Shareholders want dividends and stock price appreciation. Suppliers want predictable orders and bills paid. Creditors want commitments to be met on time. In the normal course of affairs, the relationship between a firm and each of its primary stakeholders is regulated by written or verbal agreements and laws. Once a problem is identified, negotiation takes place based on costs and benefits to each party. (Government is not usually considered a primary stakeholder because laws apply to all in a category and usually cannot be negotiated.)

The *second step* in stakeholder analysis is to identify the **secondary stakeholders**—those who have only an indirect stake in the corporation but who are also affected by corporate activities. These usually include nongovernmental organizations (NGOs, such as Greenpeace), activists, local communities, trade associations, competitors, and governments. Because the corporation's relationship with each of these stakeholders is usually not covered by any written or verbal agreement, there is room for misunderstanding. As in the case of NGOs and activists, there actually may be no relationship until a problem develops—usually brought up by the stakeholder. In the normal course of events, these stakeholders do not affect the corporation's ability to meet its economic or legal responsibilities. Aside from competitors, these secondary stakeholders are not usually monitored by the corporation in any systematic fashion. As a result, relationships are usually based on a set of questionable assumptions about each other's needs and wants. Although these stakeholders may not directly affect a firm's short-term profitability, their actions could determine a corporation's reputation and thus its long-term performance. A number of companies, such as Nike, have been strongly criticized for purchasing their supplies from contractors (usually in developing nations) with unsafe manufacturing plants and "sweatshop" working conditions.

The *third step* in stakeholder analysis is to estimate the effect on each stakeholder group from any particular strategic decision. Because the primary decision criteria are typically economic, this is the point where secondary stakeholders may be ignored or discounted as unimportant. For a firm to fulfill its ethical or discretionary responsibilities, it must seriously consider the needs and wants of its secondary stakeholders in any strategic decision. For example, how much will specific stakeholder groups lose or gain? What other alternatives do they have to replace what may be lost?

Stakeholder Input

Once stakeholder impacts have been identified, managers should decide whether stakeholder input should be invited into the discussion of the strategic alternatives. A group is more likely to accept or even help implement a decision if it has some input into which alternative is chosen and how it is to be implemented. In the case of Maytag's decision to close its Galesburg, Illinois, refrigerator production, the community was not a part of the decision. Nevertheless, management decided to inform the local community of its decision three years in advance of the closing instead of the 60 days required by law. Although the announcement created negative attention, it gave the Galesburg employees and townspeople more time to adjust to the eventual closing.

Given the wide range of interests and concerns present in any organization's task environment, one or more groups, at any one time, probably will be dissatisfied with an organization's activities—even if management is trying to be socially responsible. A company may have some stakeholders of which it is only marginally aware. For example, McDonald's is known for its environmentally sound practices, its willingness to hire and train disabled workers, and its charitable donations. Nevertheless, the film documentary *Super Size Me* criticized the health benefits of eating McDonald's fast food and contributed to falling sales. Therefore, before making a strategic decision, strategic managers should consider how each alternative will affect various stakeholder groups. What seems at first to be the best decision because it appears to be the most profitable may actually result in the worst set of consequences to the corporation. One example of a company that does its best to consider its responsibilities to its primary and secondary stakeholders when making strategic decisions is Johnson & Johnson. See **STRATEGY HIGHLIGHT 3.1** for the J&J credo.

3.2 Ethical Decision Making

Some people joke that there is no such thing as "business ethics." They call it an oxymoron—a concept that combines opposite or contradictory ideas. Unfortunately, there is some truth to this sarcastic comment. For example, a survey by the Ethics Resource Center of 1,324 employees of 747 U.S. companies found that 48% of employees surveyed said that they had engaged in one or more unethical and/or illegal actions during the past year. The most common questionable behaviors involved cutting corners on quality (16%), covering up incidents (14%), abusing or lying about sick days (11%), and lying to or deceiving customers (9%).

STRATEGY HIGHLIGHT 3.1

The Johnson & Johnson Credo

We believe our first responsibility is to the doctors, nurses, and patients, to mothers and fathers and all others who use our products and services. In meeting their needs everything we do must be of high quality. We must constantly strive to reduce our costs in order to maintain reasonable prices. Customers' orders must be serviced promptly and accurately. Our suppliers and distributors must have an opportunity to make a fair profit.

We are responsible to our employees, the men and women who work with us throughout the world. Everyone must be considered as an individual. We must respect their dignity and recognize their merit. They must have a sense of security in their jobs. Compensation must be fair and adequate, and working conditions clean, orderly, and safe. We must be mindful of ways to help our employees fulfill their family responsibilities. Employees must feel free to make suggestions and complaints. There must be equal opportunity for employment, development, and advancement for those qualified. We must provide competent management, and their actions must be just and ethical.

We are responsible to the communities where we live and work and to the world community as well. We must be good citizens—support good works and charities and bear our fair share of taxes. We must encourage civic improvements and better health and education. We must maintain in good order the property we are privileged to use, protecting the environment and natural resources.

Our final responsibility is to our stockholders. Business must make a sound profit. We must experiment with new ideas. Research must be carried on, innovative programs developed, and mistakes paid for. New equipment must be purchased, new facilities provided, and new products launched. Reserves must be created for adverse times. When we operate according to these principles, the stockholders should realize a fair return.

Source: Johnson & Johnson Company web site (*www.jnj.com*), September 28, 2004. Reprinted by permission of Johnson & Johnson.

Some 56% of workers reported pressure to act unethically or illegally on the job.[23] In another survey, 53% of employees in corporations of all sizes admitted that they would be willing to misrepresent corporate financial statements if asked to do so by a superior.[24] A survey of 141 chief financial executives revealed that 17% had been pressured by their CEOs over a five-year period to misrepresent the company's financial results. Five percent admitted that they had succumbed to the request.[25]

In the past 10 years, there have been massive write-downs and restatements of profits caused by misclassification of expenses as capital expenditures. Top executives have appropriated corporate assets for personal gain. Illegal advantage has been given to large stakeholders in mutual funds to the financial disadvantage of smaller investors. Executive compensation has been perceived as being exorbitant and out of line with corporate performance. Stock dividends have been given to management without any improvement in corporate performance. It should be no surprise that in a recent survey of the U.S. general public, 70% of the respondents stated that they distrust business executives.[26] See **STRATEGY HIGHLIGHT 3.2** for examples of unethical practices at Enron and WorldCom.

Some Reasons for Unethical Behavior

Why are business people perceived to be acting unethically? It may be that the involved people are not even aware that they are doing something questionable. There is no worldwide standard of conduct for business people. This is especially important given that at least 22% of revenues of U.S. corporations come from other countries.[27] Cultural norms and values vary between countries and even between different geographic regions and ethnic groups within a country. For example, what is considered in one country to be a bribe to expedite service is sometimes considered in another country to be normal business practice. Some of these dif-

STRATEGY HIGHLIGHT 3.2

Unethical Practices at Enron and WorldCom Exposed by Whistle-Blowers

Corporate scandals at Enron, WorldCom, and Tyco, among other international companies, have caused people around the world to seriously question the ethics of business executives. Enron, in particular, has become infamous for the questionable actions of its top executives in the form of (1) off-balance sheet partnerships used to hide the company's deteriorating finances, (2) revenue from long-term contracts being recorded in the first year instead of being spread over multiple years, (3) financial reports being falsified to inflate executive bonuses, and (4) manipulation of the electricity market—leading to a California energy crisis. Only Sherron Watkins, an Enron accountant, was willing to speak out regarding the questionable nature of these practices. In a now-famous memo to then-CEO Kenneth Lay, Watkins warned:

> *I realize that we have had a lot of smart people looking at this and a lot of accountants including AA & Co. [Arthur Anderson] have blessed the accounting treatment. None of that will protect Enron if these transactions are ever disclosed in the bright light of day.*

At WorldCom, Cynthia Cooper, an internal auditor, noted that some of the company's capital expenditures should have been listed on the second-quarter financial statements as expenses. When she mentioned this to both WorldCom's controller and its chief financial officer, she was told to stop what she was doing and to delay the audit until the third quarter (when expensing the transactions would not be noticed). Instead, Cooper informed the board of directors' audit committee. Two weeks later, WorldCom announced that it was reducing earnings by $3.9 billion, the largest restatement in history.

Sources: G. Colvin, "Wonder Women of Whistleblowers," *Fortune* (August 12, 2002), p. 56; W. Zellner, "The Deadly Sins of Enron," *Business Week* (October 14, 2002), pp. 26–28; M. J. Mandel, "And the Enron Award Goes to . . . Enron," *Business Week* (May 20, 2002), p. 46.

ferences may derive from whether a country's governance system is rule based or relationship based. Relationship-based countries tend to be less transparent and have a higher degree of corruption than do rule-based countries.[28] See the GLOBAL ISSUE feature for an explanation of country governance systems and how they may affect business practices.

Another possible reason for what is often perceived to be unethical behavior lies in differences in values between business people and key stakeholders. Some business people may believe profit maximization is the key goal of their firm, whereas concerned interest groups may have other priorities, such as the hiring of minorities and women or the safety of their neighborhoods. Of the six values measured by the Allport-Vernon-Lindzey Study of Values test (aesthetic, economic, political, religious, social, and theoretical), both U.S. and UK executives consistently score highest on economic and political values and lowest on social and religious ones. This is similar to the value profile of managers from Japan, Korea, India, and Australia, as well as those of U.S. business school students. U.S. Protestant ministers, in contrast, score highest on religious and social values and very low on economic values.[29]

This difference in values can make it difficult for one group of people to understand another's actions. For example, even though some people feel that the advertising of cigarettes (especially to youth) is unethical, the people managing tobacco companies respond that they are simply offering a product; "Let the buyer beware" is a traditional saying in free-market capitalism. They argue that customers in a free-market democracy have the right to choose how they spend their money and live their lives. Social progressives may contend that business people working in tobacco, alcoholic beverages, and gambling industries are acting unethically by making and advertising products with potentially dangerous and expensive side effects, such as cancer, alcoholism, and addiction. People working in these industries could respond by asking whether it is ethical for people who don't smoke, drink, or gamble to reject another person's right to do so.

GLOBAL ISSUE

How Rule-Based and Relationship-Based Governance Systems Affect Ethical Behavior

The developed nations of the world operate under governance systems quite different from those used by developing nations. The developed nations and the business firms within them follow well-recognized rules in their dealings and financial reporting. To the extent that a country's rules force business corporations to publicly disclose in-depth information about the company to potential shareholders and others, that country's financial and legal system is said to be **transparent**. Transparency is said to simplify transactions and reduce the temptation to behave illegally or unethically. Finland, the United Kingdom, Hong Kong, the United States, and Australia have very transparent business climates. The Kurtzman Group, a consulting firm, developed an *opacity index* that measures the risks associated with unclear legal systems, regulations, economic policies, corporate governance standards, and corruption in 48 countries. The countries with the most opaque/least transparent ratings are Indonesia, Venezuela, China, Nigeria, India, Egypt, and Russia.

Developing nations tend to have **relationship-based governance**. Transactions are based on personal and implicit agreements, not on formal contracts enforceable by a court. Information about a business is largely local and private—thus cannot be easily verified by a third party. In contrast, **rule-based governance** relies on publicly verifiable information—the type of information that is typically not available in a developing country. The rule-based system has an infrastructure, based on accounting, auditing, ratings systems, legal cases, and codes, to provide and monitor this information. If present in a developing nation, the infrastructure is not very sophisticated. This is why investing in a developing country is very risky. The relationship-based system in a developing nation is inherently nontransparent due to the local and nonverifiable nature of its information. A business person needs to develop and nurture a wide network of personal relationships. *What* you know is less important than *who* you know.

The investment in time and money needed to build the necessary relationships to conduct business in a developing nation creates a high entry barrier for any newcomers to an industry. Thus, key industries in developing nations tend to be controlled by a small number of companies, usually privately owned, family-controlled conglomerates. Because public information is unreliable and insufficient for decisions, strategic decisions may depend more on a CEO playing golf with the prime minister than with questionable market share data. In a relationship-based system, the culture of the country (and the founder's family) strongly affects corporate culture and business ethics. What is "fair" depends on whether one is a family member, a close friend, a neighbor, or a stranger. Because behavior tends to be less controlled by laws and agreed-upon standards than by tradition, businesspeople from a rule-based developed nation perceive the relationship-based system in a developing nation to be less ethical and more corrupt. According to Larry Smeltzer, ethics professor at Arizona State University, "The lack of openness and predictable business standards drives companies away. . . . Why would you want to do business in, say Libya, where you don't know the rules?"

Sources: S. Li, S. H. Park, and S. Li, "The Great Leap Forward: The Transition from Relation-Based Governance to Rule-Based Governance," *Organizational Dynamics*, Vol. 33, No. 1 (2003), pp. 63–78; M. Davids, "Global Standards, Local Problems," *Journal of Business Strategy* (January/February 1999), pp. 38–43; "The Opacity Index," *Economist* (September 18, 2004), p. 106.

Seventy percent of executives representing 111 diverse national and multinational corporations reported that they bend the rules to attain their objectives.[30] The three most common reasons given were:

- Organizational performance required it—74%
- Rules were ambiguous or out of date—70%
- Pressure from others and everyone does it—47%

The financial community's emphasis on short-term earnings performance is a significant pressure for executives to "manage" quarterly earnings. For example, a company achieving its forecasted quarterly earnings figure signals to the investment community that its strategy and operations are proceeding as planned. Failing to meet its target signals that the company is in trouble—thus causing the stock price to fall and shareholders to become worried. The company's exceeding its forecast in the fourth quarter of 2005 would raise analysts' expectations unrealistically high for the fourth quarter of 2006. Research by Degeorge and Patel involving more than 100,000 quarterly earnings reports revealed that a preponderance (82%) of reported earnings *exactly* matched analysts' expectations or exceeded them by only 1%. The disparity between the number of earnings reports that missed estimates by a penny and the number that exceeded them by a penny suggests that executives who risked falling short of forecasts "borrowed" earnings from future quarters.[31]

In explaining why executives at Enron engaged in unethical and illegal actions, former Enron Vice President Sherron Watkins used the "frogs in boiling water" analogy. If, for example, one were to toss a frog into a pan of boiling water, the frog would quickly jump out. It might be burned, but the frog would survive. However, if one put a frog in a pan of cold water and turned up the heat very slowly, the frog would not sense the increasing heat until it was too lethargic to jump out and would be boiled. According to Watkins:

> *Enron's accounting moved from creative to aggressive, to fraudulent, like the pot of water moving from cool to lukewarm to boiling; those involved with the creative transactions soon found themselves working on the aggressive transactions and were finally in the uncomfortable situation of working on fraudulent deals.*[32]

Moral Relativism

Some people justify their seemingly unethical positions by arguing that there is no one absolute code of ethics and that morality is relative. Simply put, **moral relativism** claims that morality is relative to some personal, social, or cultural standard and that there is no method for deciding whether one decision is better than another.

Adherents of moral relativism may believe that all moral decisions are deeply personal and that individuals have the right to run their own lives; each person should be allowed to interpret situations and act on his or her own moral values. They may also argue that social roles carry with them certain obligations to those roles only. A manager in charge of a department, for example, must put aside his or her personal beliefs and do instead what the role requires—that is, act in the best interests of the department. They could also argue that a decision is legitimate if it is common practice, regardless of other considerations ("everyone's doing it"). Some propose that morality itself is relative to a particular culture, society, or community. People should therefore understand the practices of other countries but not judge them. If the citizens of another country share certain norms and customs, what right does an outsider have to criticize them?

Although these arguments make some sense, moral relativism could enable a person to justify almost any sort of decision or action, so long as it is not declared illegal.

Kohlberg's Levels of Moral Development

Another reason some business people might be seen as unethical is that they may have no well-developed personal sense of ethics. A person's ethical behavior is affected by his or her level of moral development, certain personality variables, and such situational factors as the job itself, the supervisor, and the organizational culture.[33] Kohlberg proposes that a person progresses through three **levels of moral development**.[34] Similar in some ways to Maslow's hierarchy of needs, in Kohlberg's system, the individual moves from total self-centeredness to a concern for universal values. Kohlberg's three levels are as follows:

1. **The preconventional level:** This level is characterized by a concern for self. Small children and others who have not progressed beyond this stage evaluate behaviors on the basis of personal interest—avoiding punishment or quid pro quo.
2. **The conventional level:** This level is characterized by considerations of society's laws and norms. Actions are justified by an external code of conduct.

3. **The principled level:** This level is characterized by a person's adherence to an internal moral code. An individual at this level looks beyond norms or laws to find universal values or principles.

Kohlberg places most people in the conventional level, with fewer than 20% of U.S. adults in the principled level of development.[35]

Encouraging Ethical Behavior

Following Carroll's work, if businesspeople do not act ethically, government will be forced to pass laws regulating their actions—and usually increasing their costs. For self-interest, if for no other reason, managers should be more ethical in their decision making. One way to do that is by encouraging codes of ethics. Another is by providing guidelines for ethical behavior.

Codes of Ethics

A **code of ethics** specifies how an organization expects its employees to behave while on the job. Developing a code of ethics can be a useful way to promote ethical behavior, especially for people who are operating at Kohlberg's conventional level of moral development. Such codes are currently being used by more than half of U.S. corporations. A code of ethics (1) clarifies company expectations of employee conduct in various situations and (2) makes clear that the company expects its people to recognize the ethical dimensions in decisions and actions.[36]

Various studies indicate that an increasing number of companies are developing codes of ethics and implementing ethics training workshops and seminars. However, research also indicates that when faced with a question of ethics, managers tend to ignore codes of ethics and try to solve dilemmas on their own.[37] To combat this tendency, the management of a company that wants to improve its employees' ethical behavior should not only develop a comprehensive code of ethics but also communicate the code in its training programs, in its performance appraisal system, in policies and procedures, and through its own actions. It may even include key values in its values and mission statements (as discussed in **Chapter 1**). According to a 2004 survey of CEOs by the Business Roundtable Institute for Corporate Ethics, 74% of CEOs confirmed that their companies had made changes within the previous two years in how they handled or reported ethics issues. Specific changes reported were:

- Enhanced internal reporting and communications—33%
- Ethics hotlines—17%
- Improved compliance procedures—12%
- Greater oversight by the board of directors—10%[38]

A company's executives may also want to establish and enforce a code of ethical behavior for those companies with which it does business—especially if it outsources its manufacturing to a company in another country. For example, Reebok International has developed a set of production standards for the manufacturers that supply the company with its athletic shoes on a contract basis. In response to a report commissioned by Reebok (at a cost of $50,000) that found health and safety problems at two subcontractor plants in Indonesia, the two suppliers were forced to spend $500,000 in factory improvements in order to keep Reebok's business.[39]

Guidelines for Ethical Behavior

Ethics is defined as the consensually accepted standards of behavior for an occupation, a trade, or a profession. **Morality**, in contrast, is the precepts of personal behavior based on religious or philosophical grounds. **Law** refers to formal codes that permit or forbid certain behaviors and may or may not enforce ethics or morality.[40] Given these definitions, how do we arrive at a comprehensive statement of ethics to use in making decisions in a specific occupation, trade, or profession? A starting point for such a code of ethics is to consider the three basic approaches to ethical behavior[41]:

1. **Utilitarian Approach:** The **utilitarian approach** proposes that actions and plans should be judged by their consequences. People should therefore behave in a way that will produce the greatest benefit to society and produce the least harm or the lowest cost. A problem with this approach is the difficulty in recognizing all the benefits and costs of any particular decision. Research reveals that only the stakeholders who have the most *power* (ability to affect the company), *legitimacy* (legal or moral claim on company resources), and *urgency* (demand for immediate attention) are given priority by CEOs.[42] It is therefore likely that only the most obvious stakeholders will be considered, while others are ignored.
2. **Individual Rights Approach:** The **individual rights approach** proposes that human beings have certain fundamental rights that should be respected in all decisions. A particular decision or behavior should be avoided if it interferes with the rights of others. A problem with this approach is in defining "fundamental rights." The U.S. Constitution includes a Bill of Rights that may or may not be accepted throughout the world. The approach can also encourage selfish behavior when a person defines a personal need or want as a "right."
3. **Justice Approach:** The **justice approach** proposes that decision makers be equitable, fair, and impartial in the distribution of costs and benefits to individuals and groups. It follows the principles of *distributive justice* (people who are similar on relevant dimensions such as job seniority should be treated in the same way) and *fairness* (liberty should be equal for all persons). The justice approach can also include the concepts of *retributive justice* (punishment should be proportional to the offense) and *compensatory justice* (wrongs should be compensated in proportion to the offense). Affirmative action issues such as reverse discrimination are examples of conflicts between distributive and compensatory justice.

Cavanagh proposes that we solve ethical problems by asking the following three questions regarding an act or a decision:

1. **Utility:** Does it optimize the satisfactions of all stakeholders?
2. **Rights:** Does it respect the rights of the individuals involved?
3. **Justice:** Is it consistent with the canons of justice?

For example, is padding an expense account ethical? Using the utility criterion, this action increases the company's costs and thus does not optimize benefits for shareholders or customers. Using the rights approach, a person has no right to the money (otherwise, we wouldn't call it "padding"). Using the justice criterion, salary and commissions constitute ordinary compensation, but expense accounts only compensate a person for expenses incurred in doing his or her job—expenses that the person would not normally incur except in doing the job.[43]

Another approach to resolving ethical dilemmas is by applying the logic of the philosopher Immanuel Kant. Kant presents two principles (called **categorical imperatives**) to guide our actions:

1. A person's action is ethical only if that person is willing for that same action to be taken by everyone who is in a similar situation. This is same as the *Golden Rule*: Treat others as you would like them to treat you. For example, padding an expense account would be considered ethical if the person were also willing for everyone else to do the same if they

were the boss. Because it is very doubtful that any manager would be pleased with expense account padding, the action must be considered unethical.

2. A person should never treat another human being simply as a means but always as an end. This means that an action is morally wrong for a person if that person uses others merely as means for advancing his or her own interests. To be moral, the act should not restrict other people's actions so that they are disadvantaged in some way.[44]

3.3 Conclusion

In his book *Defining Moments*, Joseph Badaracco states that most ethics problems deal with "right versus right" problems in which neither choice is wrong. These are what he calls "dirty hands problems" in which a person has to deal with very specific situations that are covered only vaguely in corporate credos or mission statements. For example, many mission statements endorse fairness but fail to define the term. At the personal level, *fairness* could mean playing by the rules of the game, following basic morality, treating everyone alike and not playing favorites, treating others as you would want to be treated, being sensitive to individual needs, providing equal opportunity for everyone, or creating a level playing field for the disadvantaged. According to Badaracco, codes of ethics are not always helpful because they tend to emphasize problems of misconduct and wrongdoing, not a choice between two acceptable alternatives, such as keeping an inefficient plant operating for the good of the community or closing the plant and relocating to a more efficient location to lower costs.[45]

This chapter provides a framework for understanding the social responsibilities of a business corporation. Following Carroll, it proposes that a manager should consider not only the economic and legal responsibilities of a firm but also its ethical and discretionary responsibilities. It also provides a method for making ethical choices, whether they are right versus right or some combination of right and wrong. It is important to consider Cavanaugh's questions, using the three approaches of utilitarian, rights, and justice, plus Kant's categorical imperatives when making a strategic decision. A corporation should try to move from Kohlberg's conventional to a principled level of ethical development. If nothing else, the frameworks should contribute to well-reasoned strategic decisions that a person can defend when interviewed by hostile media or questioned in a court room.

Strategy Bits

- In a survey of 192 U.S. companies, 92% monitored employees' use of e-mail and the Internet.
- Of the surveyed companies, 26% monitored their employees' electronic activities all the time.
- Almost none of the companies surveyed had checks in place to protect employees' privacy or to ensure that such monitoring was not abused.[46]

Discussion Questions

1. What is the relationship between corporate governance and social responsibility?
2. What is your opinion of Reebok's having production standards of human rights for its suppliers? What would Milton Friedman say? Contrast his view with Archie Carroll's view.
3. Does a company have to act selflessly to be considered socially responsible? For example, when building a

new plant, a corporation voluntarily invested in additional equipment that enabled it to reduce its pollution emissions beyond any current laws. Knowing that it would be very expensive for its competitors to do the same, the firm lobbied the government to make pollution regulations more restrictive on the entire industry. Is this company socially responsible? Were its managers acting ethically?

4. Are people living in a relationship-based governance system likely to be unethical in business dealings?
5. Given that people rarely use a company's code of ethics to guide their decision making, what good are the codes?

Strategic Practice Exercise

It is 1982. Zombie Savings and Loan is in trouble. This is a time when many savings and loans (S&Ls) are in financial difficulty. Zombie holds many 30-year mortgages at low fixed interest rates in its loan portfolio. Interest rates have risen significantly, and the Deregulation Act of 1980 has given Zombie and other S&Ls the right to make business loans and hold up to 20% of its assets as such. Because interest rates in general have risen, but the rate that Zombie receives on its old mortgages has not, Zombie must now pay out higher interest rates to its deposit customers or see them leave, and it has negative cash flow until rates fall below the rates in its mortgage portfolio or Zombie itself fails.

In present value terms, Zombie is insolvent, but the accounting rules of the time do not require marking assets to market, so Zombie is allowed to continue to operate and is faced with two choices: It can wait and hope interest rates fall before it is declared insolvent and is closed down, or it can raise fresh (insured) deposits and make risky loans that have high interest rates. Risky loans promise high payoffs (if they are repaid), but the probability of loss to Zombie and being closed later with greater loss to the Federal Savings & Loan Insurance Corporation (FSLIC) is high. Zombie stays in business if its gamble pays off, and it loses no more than it has already lost if the gamble does not pay off. Indeed, if not closed, Zombie will raise increasingly greater new deposits and make more risky loans until it either wins or is shut down by the regulators.

Waiting for lower interest rates and accepting early closure if they do not arrive is certainly in the best interest of the FSLIC and of the tax payers, but the manager of Zombie has more immediate responsibilities, such as employees' jobs, mortgage customers, depositors, the local neighborhood, and his or her job. As a typical S&L, Zombie's depositors are its shareholders and vote according to how much money they have in savings accounts with Zombie. If Zombie closes, depositors may lose some, but not all, of their money, because their deposits are insured by the FSLIC. There is no other provider of home mortgages in the immediate area. What should the manager do?

Source: Adapted from D. W. Swanton, "Teaching Students the Nature of Moral Hazard: An Ethical Component for Finance Classes," paper presented to the annual meeting of the *Academy of Finance*, Chicago (March 13, 2003). Reprinted with permission.

Key Terms

categorical imperative (p. 67)
code of ethics (p. 66)
corporate stakeholders (p. 59)
ethics (p. 66)
individual rights approach (p. 67)
justice approach (p. 67)
law (p. 66)
levels of moral development (p. 65)
moral relativism (p. 65)
morality (p. 66)
primary stakeholder (p. 60)
relationship-based governance (p. 64)
rule-based governance (p. 64)
secondary stakeholder (p. 60)
social capital (p. 59)
social responsibility (p. 56)
stakeholder analysis (p. 60)
transparent (p. 64)
utilitarian approach (p. 67)

PART ENDING VIDEO CASE PART ONE

Newbury Comics, Inc.

STRATEGY BASICS

Newbury Comics was founded in 1978 by MIT roommates, Mike Dreese and John Brusger. With $2,000 and a comic book collection they converted a Newbury Street studio apartment in Boston's trendy Back Bay into the second organized comic book shop in the area. In 1979, Newbury Comics began selling punk and new wave music and quickly became the region's leading specialist in alternative music. By 1982, with a second store open in Harvard Square, the company's revenues were being generated mostly from cutting-edge music and rock-related merchandise.

Newbury Comics consists of 22 stores spanning the New England region and is known to be the place to shop for everything from the best of the underground/independent music scene to major label superstars. The chain also stocks a wide variety of non-music related items such as T-shirts, Dr. (doc) Martens shoes, posters, jewelry, cosmetics, books, magazines, and other trendy items.

The video features Cofounders Mike Dreese and John Brusger, as well as Jan Johannet, Manager of one of the New Hampshire stores, talking about the entrepreneurial beginning of Newbury Comics. They point out that the company wants its customers and its employees to "have a good time" in the store. Newbury Comics hires good people who like working in the store. The company attracts creative people because it is different from other retailers. Mike Dreese thinks of the company as expanding out of a comic book retailer into a lifestyle store emphasizing popular culture. He wants Newbury Comics to dominate its product categories and to be the retailer customers seek out in order to obtain what they want. He refers to an expression used throughout the company: "If you can't dominate it, don't do it." He wants the company to grow by looking for "incredible opportunities" (elephant hunting). This approach seems to work at Newbury Comics. The company sustained an annual growth rate of about 80% over the past 7 years resulting in 1,000% overall growth.

With some input from others at corporate headquarters, Mike Dreese develops the overall plan for the company by looking at where he would like the company to be in 3, 5, or 10 years. He analyzes the external environment in terms of competition, trends, and customer preferences. John Brusger then puts Mike's plan into action. The company identifies product growth areas by conducting dozens of experiments each month to learn what the customer wants.

Concepts Illustrated in the Video

- The Learning Organization
- Theories of Organizational Adaptation
- Model of Strategic Management
- Modes of Strategic Decision Making
- Strategic Decision Making Process
- Executive Leadership
- Strategic Vision

Study Questions

1. How is Newbury Comics an example of a learning organization?
2. What is the process of strategic management at Newbury Comics? Who is involved in each part?
3. What do you think might be the company's (a) current mission/vision, (b) objectives, (c) strategies, and (d) policies? Give an example of each from the video.
4. What theory of organizational adaptation is being followed by Mike Dreese?
5. Newbury Comics illustrates what mode of strategic decision making? Is it appropriate?

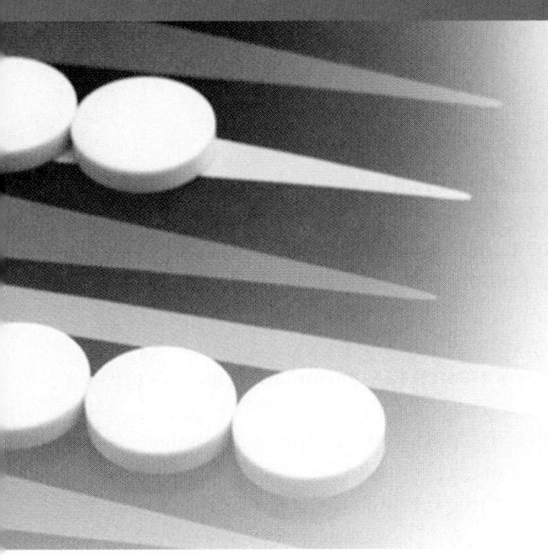

CHAPTER 4
Environmental Scanning and Industry Analysis

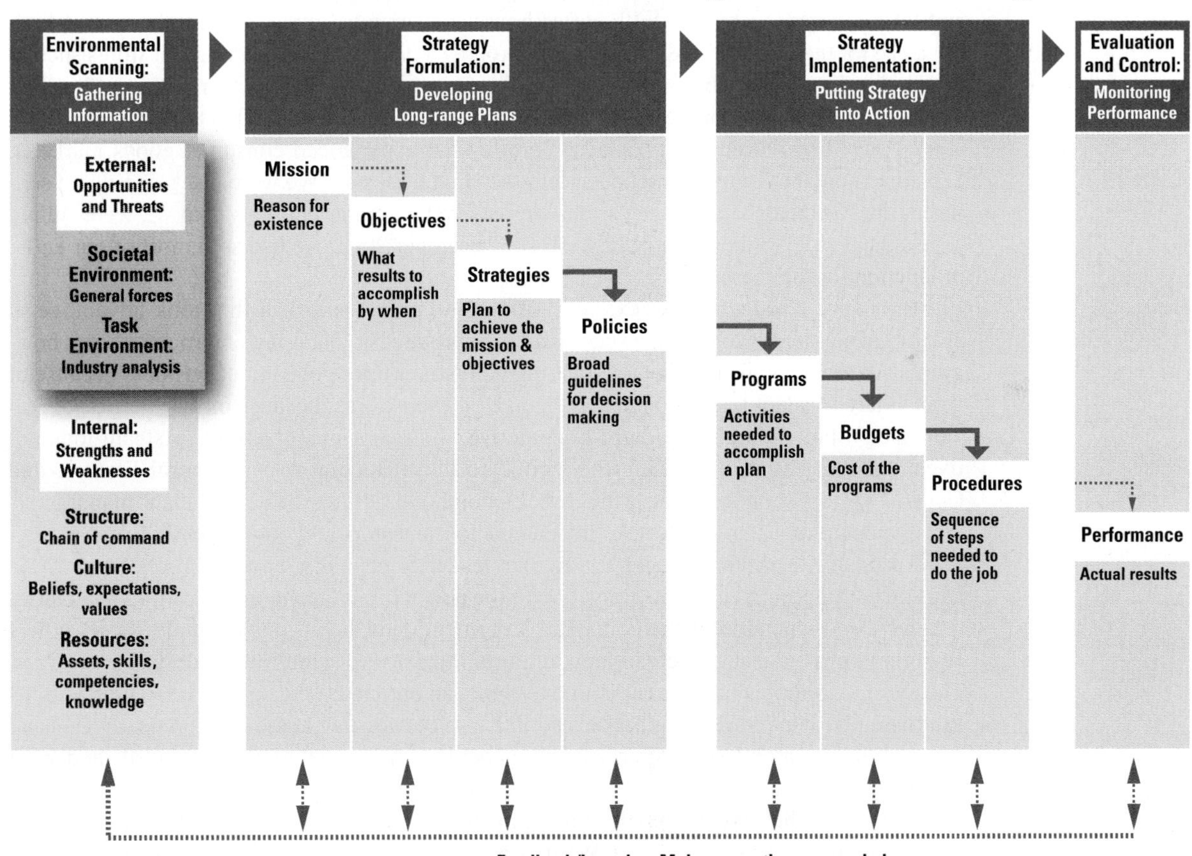

Learning Objectives

After reading this chapter, you should be able to:

- Recognize aspects of an organization's environment that can influence its long-term decisions
- Identify the aspects of an organization's environment that are most strategically important
- Conduct an industry analysis to understand the competitive forces that influence the intensity of rivalry within an industry
- Understand how industry maturity affects industry competitive forces
- Categorize international industries based on their pressures for coordination and local responsiveness
- Construct strategic group maps to assess the competitive positions of firms in an industry
- Identify key success factors and develop an industry matrix
- Use publicly available information to conduct competitive intelligence
- Know how to develop an industry scenario
- Construct an EFAS Table that summarizes external environmental factors

ROD SPRULES INVENTED JAVA-LOGS TO TAKE ADVANTAGE OF TWO INTERSECTING ENVIRON-mental trends—the increasing interest in recycling and the rapid growth of retail coffee houses throughout North America. The Java-Log is a fireplace log made primarily from recycled coffee grounds. It is different from traditional firewood in that it burns with a hotter, brighter flame, emits less carbon dioxide, and is made from a waste product. Sprules first learned of the high heat capacity of coffee grounds while working on a heated cold weather suit for his former employer. With coffee houses becoming popular, Sprules thought of finding a use for the used coffee grounds being produced daily in huge quantities at stores such as Starbucks. Together with his wife, Joanne Johnson, and business partner, Marcel Sbrollini, Sprules formed Robustion Products, Inc., in St. Laurent, Quebec, in 2000 to manufacture and market Java-Logs throughout Canada. Sbrollini, an experienced consumer goods marketer, explained how the company expanded into the United States: "We were just planning on selling in the Northeast United States, but we received so much publicity that we were selling across the entire Northeast and Midwest. By December 2003, we had sold most of our entire production for the season."[1]

Robustion Products is an example of an entrepreneurial firm that took advantage of environmental trends to create a successful new product. A changing environment can, however, also hurt a company. Many pioneering companies have gone out of business because of their failure to adapt to environmental change or, even worse, because of their failure to create change. For example, Baldwin Locomotive, the major manufacturer of steam locomotives, was very slow in making the switch to diesel locomotives. General Electric and General Motors soon dominated the diesel locomotive business. The dominant manufacturers of vacuum tubes failed to make the change to transistors and consequently lost that market. Eastman Kodak, the pioneer and market leader of chemical-based film photography, is currently struggling to make its transition to the newer digital technology. Failure to adapt is, however, only one side of the coin. The aforementioned Java-Logs example shows how a changing environment can create new opportunities at the same time it destroys old ones. The lesson is simple: To be successful over time, an organization needs to be in tune with its external environment. There must be a strategic fit between what the environment wants and what the corporation has to offer, as well as between what the corporation needs and what the environment can provide.

Current predictions are that the environment for all organizations will become even more uncertain with every passing year. What is **environmental uncertainty**? It is the *degree of complexity* plus the *degree of change* existing in an organization's external environment. As more and more markets become global, the number of factors a company must consider in any decision become huge and much more complex. With new technologies being discovered every year, markets change—and products must change with them.

On the one hand, environmental uncertainty is a threat to strategic managers because it hampers their ability to develop long-range plans and to make strategic decisions to keep the corporation in equilibrium with its external environment. On the other hand, environmental uncertainty is an opportunity because it creates a new playing field in which creativity and innovation can play a major part in strategic decisions.

4.1 Environmental Scanning

Before an organization can begin strategy formulation, it must scan the external environment to identify possible opportunities and threats and its internal environment for strengths and weaknesses. **Environmental scanning** is the monitoring, evaluation, and dissemination of information from the external and internal environments to key people within the corporation. A corporation uses this tool to avoid strategic surprise and to ensure its long-term health. Research has found a positive relationship between environmental scanning and profits.[2]

Identifying External Environmental Variables

In undertaking environmental scanning, strategic managers must first be aware of the many variables within a corporation's societal and task environments. The **societal environment** includes general forces that do not directly touch on the short-run activities of the organization but that can, and often do, influence its long-run decisions. These, shown in **Figure 1–3**, are as follows:

- **Economic forces** that regulate the exchange of materials, money, energy, and information.
- **Technological forces** that generate problem-solving inventions.
- **Political–legal forces** that allocate power and provide constraining and protecting laws and regulations.
- **Sociocultural forces** that regulate the values, mores, and customs of society.

The **task environment** includes those elements or groups that directly affect a corporation and, in turn, are affected by it. These are governments, local communities, suppliers, competitors, customers, creditors, employees/labor unions, special-interest groups, and trade associations. A corporation's task environment is typically the industry within which the firm operates. **Industry analysis** (popularized by Michael Porter) refers to an in-depth examination of key factors within a corporation's task environment. Both the societal and task environments must be monitored to detect the strategic factors that are likely to have a strong impact on corporate success or failure.

Research indicates that high-performing chief executives vary their environmental scanning emphasis according to the level of dynamism they perceive in their external environment. In dynamic environments, successful CEOs pay more attention to the task environment, whereas in stable environments, CEOs focus on forces in the societal environment.[3]

Scanning the Societal Environment

The number of possible strategic factors in the societal environment is very high. The number becomes enormous when we realize that, generally speaking, each country in the world can be represented by its own unique set of societal forces—some of which are very similar to those of neighboring countries and some of which are very different.

For example, even though Korea and China share Asia's Pacific Rim area with Thailand, Taiwan, and Hong Kong (sharing many similar cultural values), they have very different views about the role of business in society. It is generally believed in Korea and China (and to a lesser extent in Japan) that the role of business is primarily to contribute to national development; however, in Hong Kong, Taiwan, and Thailand (and to a lesser extent in the Philippines, Indonesia, Singapore, and Malaysia), the role of business is primarily to make profits for the shareholders.[4] Such differences may translate into different trade regulations and varying difficulty in the **repatriation of profits** (the transfer of profits from a foreign subsidiary to a corporation's headquarters) from one group of Pacific Rim countries to another.

Monitoring Societal Trends. As shown in **Table 4–1**, large corporations categorize the societal environment in any one geographic region into four areas and focus their scanning in each area on trends that have corporatewide relevance. Obviously, trends in any one area may be very important to the firms in one industry but of lesser importance to firms in other industries.

Trends in the *economic* part of the societal environment can have an obvious impact on business activity. For example, an increase in interest rates means fewer sales of major home appliances. Why? A rising interest rate tends to be reflected in higher mortgage rates. Because higher mortgage rates increase the cost of buying a house, the demand for new and used houses tends to fall. Because most major home appliances are sold when people change houses, a reduction in house sales soon translates into a decline in sales of refrigerators, stoves, and dishwashers and reduced profits for everyone in the appliance industry.

The economic development of China and India is having a major impact on the rest of the world. By 2004, China had become the fourth-largest industrial producer in the world after the United States, Japan, and Germany. With India graduating more English-speaking scien-

TABLE 4–1 SOME IMPORTANT VARIABLES IN THE SOCIETAL ENVIRONMENT

Economic	Technological	Political–Legal	Sociocultural
GDP trends	Total government spending for R&D	Antitrust regulations	Lifestyle changes
Interest rates	Total industry spending for R&D	Environmental protection laws	Career expectations
Money supply	Focus of technological efforts	Tax laws	Consumer activism
Inflation rates	Patent protection	Special incentives	Rate of family formation
Unemployment levels	New products	Foreign trade regulations	Growth rate of population
Wage/price controls	New developments in technology transfer from lab to marketplace	Attitudes toward foreign companies	Age distribution of population
Devaluation/revaluation	Productivity improvements through automation	Laws on hiring and promotion	Regional shifts in population
Energy availability and cost	Internet availability	Stability of government	Life expectancies
Disposable and discretionary income	Telecommunication infrastructure	Outsourcing regulation	Birthrates
Currency markets	Computer hacking activity	Foreign "sweat shops"	Pension plans
			Health care
			Level of education

tists, engineers, and technicians than all other nations combined, it has become the primary location for the outsourcing of services, computer software, and telecommunications.[5]

Changes in the *technological* part of the societal environment can also have a great impact on multiple industries. Improvements in computer microprocessors have not only led to the widespread use of home computers but also to better automobile engine performance in terms of power and fuel economy through the use of microprocessors to monitor fuel injection. Digital technology allows movies and music to be available instantly over the Internet or through cable service, but it also means falling fortunes for video rental shops such as Blockbuster and CD stores such as Tower Records. Computer viruses developed by hackers create havoc in the information systems of corporations worldwide. Researchers at George Washington University have identified a number of breakthrough developments in technology that are already having a significant impact on many industries:

- **Portable Information Devices and Electronic Networking:** Combining the computing power of the personal computer, the networking of the Internet, the images of the television, and the convenience of the telephone, these appliances will soon be used by a majority of the population of industrialized nations to make phone calls, send e-mail, and transmit documents and other data. Even now, homes, autos, and offices are being connected (via wires and wirelessly) into intelligent networks that interact with one another. The traditional stand-alone desktop computer may soon join the manual typewriter as a historical curiosity.
- **Fuel Cells and Alternative Energy Sources:** The use of wind, geothermal, hydroelectric, solar, biomass, and other alternative energy sources should increase from the present level of 10% to about 30% by 2010. Once used exclusively to power spacecraft, fuel cells offer the prospect of pollution-free electrical power. Fuel cells chemically combine hydrogen and oxygen to produce electricity, with water as a byproduct. Although it will take a number of years before fuel cells replace gas-powered engines or vast power-generation plants, this technology is already providing an alternative source of power for large buildings.
- **Precision Farming:** The computerized management of crops to suit variations in land characteristics will make farming more efficient. Farm equipment dealers, such as Case and John Deere, add this equipment to tractors for an additional $6,000 or so. It enables farmers to reduce costs, increase yields, and decrease environmental impact. The old system of small, low-tech farming is becoming less viable as large corporate farms increase crop yields on limited farmland for a growing population.
- **Virtual Personal Assistants:** Very smart computer programs that monitor e-mail, faxes, and phone calls will be able to take over routine tasks, such as writing a letter, retrieving a file, making a phone call, or screening requests. Acting like a secretary, a person's virtual assistant could substitute for a person at meetings or in dealing with routine actions.
- **Genetically Altered Organisms:** A convergence of biotechnology and agriculture is creating a new field of life sciences. Plant seeds can be genetically modified to produce more needed vitamins or to be less attractive to pests and more able to survive. Animals (including people) could be similarly modified for desirable characteristics and to eliminate genetic disabilities and diseases.
- **Smart, Mobile Robots:** Robot development has been limited by a lack of sensory devices and sophisticated artificial intelligence systems. Improvements in these areas mean that robots will be created to perform more sophisticated factory work, run errands, do household chores, and assist the disabled.[6]

Trends in the *political–legal* part of the societal environment have a significant impact not only on the level of competition within an industry but also on which strategies might be

TABLE 4–2 CURRENT U.S. GENERATIONS

Generation	Born	Age in 2005	Number
WW II/ Silent Generation	1932–1945	60–73	32 million
Baby Boomers	1946–1964	41–59	77 million
Generation X	1965–1977	28–40	45 million
Generation Y	1978–1994	11–27	70 million

Source: Developed from data listed in D. Parkinson, *Voices of Experience: Mature Workers in the Future Workforce* (New York: The Conference Board, 2002), p. 19.

successful.[7] For example, periods of strict enforcement of U.S. antitrust laws directly affect corporate growth strategy. As large companies find it more difficult to acquire another firm in the same or a related industry, they are typically driven to diversify into unrelated industries.[8] High levels of taxation and constraining labor laws in Western European countries stimulate companies to find better locations elsewhere. For example, France's statutory 35-hour work week led companies such as Robert Bosch, a German maker of car parts, to consider moving manufacturing to low-cost locations in Eastern Europe.[9]

Demographic trends are part of the *sociocultural* aspect of the societal environment. The demographic bulge in the U.S. population caused by the baby boom in the 1950s continues to affect market demand in many industries. This group of 77 million people in their 40s and 50s is the largest age group in all developed countries, especially in Europe. (See **Table 4–2.**) Although the median age in the United States will rise from 35 in 2000 to 40 by 2050, it will increase from 40 to 47 during the same time period in Germany, and it will increase up to 50 in Italy as soon as 2025.[10] With its low birthrate, Japan's population is expected to fall from 127.6 million in 2004 to around 100 million by 2050.[11] Companies with an eye on the future can find many opportunities to offer products and services to the growing number of "woofies" (well-off old folks)—defined as people over 50 with money to spend.[12] These people are very likely to purchase recreational vehicles (RVs), take ocean cruises, and enjoy leisure sports such as boating, fishing, and bowling, in addition to needing financial services and health care. Anticipating the needs of seniors for prescription drugs is one reason the Walgreen Company is opening a new corner pharmacy every 19 hours![13]

This trend can mean increasing sales for firms such as Winnebago (RVs), Carnival Cruise Lines, and Brunswick (sports equipment), among others. For example, the U.S. motor home industry sold more units in 2004 than it had in any year since 1978.[14] To attract older customers, retailers will need to place seats in their larger stores so aging shoppers can rest. Washrooms need to be more accessible. Signs need to be larger. Restaurants need to raise the level of lighting so people can read their menus. Home appliances need simpler and larger controls. Automobiles need larger door openings and more comfortable seats. Zimmer Holdings, an innovative manufacturer of artificial joints, is looking forward to its market growing rapidly over the next 20 years. According to J. Raymond Elliot, chair and CEO of Zimmer, "It's simple math. Our best years are still in front of us."[15]

Eight current sociocultural trends in the United States are transforming North America and the rest of the world:

1. **Increasing environmental awareness:** Recycling and conservation are becoming more than slogans. Busch Gardens, for example, has eliminated the use of disposable styrofoam trays in favor of washing and reusing plastic trays.
2. **Growing health consciousness:** Concerns about personal health fuel the trend toward physical fitness and healthier living. As a result, sales growth is slowing at fast-food

"burgers and fries" retailers such as McDonald's. Changing public tastes away from sugar-laden processed foods forced Interstate Bakeries, the maker of Twinkies and Wonder Bread, to declare bankruptcy in 2004. The European Union forbade the importation of genetically altered grain ("Frankenfood") because of possible side effects. The spread of AIDS to more than 40 million people worldwide adds even further impetus to the health movement.

3. **Expanding seniors market:** As their numbers increase, people over age 55 will become an even more important market. Already some companies are segmenting the senior population into Young Matures, Older Matures, and the Elderly—each having a different set of attitudes and interests. The desire for companionship by people whose children are grown is causing the pet care industry to grow 4.5% annually, and it is expected to reach about $36 billion in the United States by 2007.[16]
4. **Impact of the Generation Y boomlet:** Born between 1978 and 1994 to the baby boom and X generations, this cohort is almost as large as the baby boom generation. In 1957, the peak year of the postwar boom, 4.3 million babies were born. In 1990, there were 4.2 million births in Generation Y's peak year. By 2000, they were overcrowding elementary and high schools and entering college in numbers not seen since the baby boomers. Now in its teens and early 20s, this cohort is expected to have a strong impact on future products and services.
5. **Declining mass market:** Niche markets are defining the marketers' environment. People want products and services that are adapted more to their personal needs. For example, Estée Lauder's "All Skin" and Maybelline's "Shades of You" lines of cosmetic products are specifically made for African-American women. "Mass customization"—the making and marketing of products tailored to a person's requirements (for example, Dell and Gateway computers)—is replacing the mass production and marketing of the same product in some markets. Only 10% of the 6,200 magazines sold in the United States in 2004 were aimed at the mass market, down from 30% in the 1970s.[17]
6. **Changing pace and location of life:** Instant communication via e-mail, cell phones, and overnight mail enhances efficiency, but it also puts more pressure on people. Merging the personal computer with the communication and entertainment industries through telephone lines, satellite dishes, and cable television increases consumers' choices and allows workers to leave overcrowded urban areas for small towns and telecommute via personal computers and modems.
7. **Changing household composition:** Single-person households, especially those of single women with children, could soon become the most common household type in the United States. Married-couple households slipped from nearly 80% in the 1950s to 50.7% of all households in 2002.[18] A typical family household is no longer the same as it was once portrayed in *The Brady Bunch* in the 1970s or even *The Cosby Show* in the 1980s.
8. **Increasing diversity of workforce and markets:** Between now and 2050, minorities will account for nearly 90% of population growth in the United States. Over time, group percentages of the total U.S. population are expected to change as follows: Non-Hispanic Whites—from 90% in 1950 to 74% in 1995 to 53% by 2050; Hispanic Whites—from 9% in 1995 to 22% in 2050; Blacks—from 13% in 1995 to 15% in 2050; Asians—from 4% in 1995 to 9% in 2050; Native Americans—1%, with slight increase.[19] The number of Mexican immigrants residing illegally in the United States increased from 2.04 million in 1990 to 4.81 million in 2000.[20] Traditional minority groups are increasing their numbers in the workforce and are being identified as desirable target markets. For example, Sears, Roebuck transformed 97 of its stores in October 2004 into "multicultural stores" containing fashions for Hispanic, African-American, and Asian shoppers.[21]

International Societal Considerations. Each country or group of countries in which a company operates presents a unique societal environment with a different set of economic, technological, political–legal, and sociocultural variables for the company to face. International societal environments vary so widely that a corporation's internal environment and strategic management process must be very flexible. Cultural trends in Germany, for example, have resulted in the inclusion of worker representatives in corporate strategic planning. Because Islamic law (*sharia*) forbids interest (*riba*), loans of capital in Islamic countries must be arranged on the basis of profit-sharing instead of interest rates.[22] Differences in societal environments strongly affect the ways in which a **multinational corporation (MNC)**, a company with significant assets and activities in multiple countries, conducts its marketing, financial, manufacturing, and other functional activities. For example, the existence of regional associations such as the European Union, NAFTA in North America, Mercosur in South America, and ASEAN in Asia has a significant impact on the competitive rules of the game both for MNCs operating within and for MNCs wanting to enter these areas.

To account for the many differences among societal environments from one country to another, consider **Table 4–3**. It includes a list of economic, technological, political–legal, and sociocultural variables for any particular country or region. For example, an important economic variable for any firm investing in a foreign country is currency convertibility. Without convertibility, a company operating in Russia cannot convert its profits from rubles to dollars. In terms of sociocultural variables, many Asian cultures (especially China) are less concerned with the values of human rights than are European and North American cultures. Some Asians actually contend that U.S. companies are trying to impose Western human rights requirements on them in an attempt to make Asian products less competitive by raising their costs.[23]

Before planning its strategy for a particular international location, a company must scan the particular country environment(s) in question for opportunities and threats, and it must

TABLE 4–3 SOME IMPORTANT VARIABLES IN INTERNATIONAL SOCIETAL ENVIRONMENTS

Economic	Technological	Political–Legal	Sociocultural
Economic development	Regulations on technology transfer	Form of government	Customs, norms, values
Per capita income	Energy availability/cost	Political ideology	Language
Climate	Natural resource availability	Tax laws	Demographics
GDP trends	Transportation network	Stability of government	Life expectancies
Monetary and fiscal policies	Skill level of workforce	Government attitude toward foreign companies	Social institutions
Unemployment levels	Patent-trademark protection	Regulations on foreign ownership of assets	Status symbols
Currency convertibility	Internet availability	Strength of opposition groups	Lifestyle
Wage levels	Telecommunication infrastructure	Trade regulations	Religious beliefs
Nature of competition	Computer hacking technology	Protectionist sentiment	Attitudes toward foreigners
Membership in regional economic associations, e.g., EU, NAFTA, ASEAN		Foreign policies	Literacy level
Membership in World Trade Organization (WTO)		Terrorist activity	Human rights
Outsourcing capability		Legal system	Environmentalism
			"Sweat shops'
			Pension plans
			Health care

compare those with its own organizational strengths and weaknesses. For example, to operate successfully in a global industry such as automobiles, tires, electronics, or watches, a company must be prepared to establish a significant presence in the three developed areas of the world known collectively as the **Triad**. This term, coined by the Japanese management expert Kenichi Ohmae, refers to the three developed markets of Japan, North America, and Western Europe, which now form a single market with common needs.[24] Focusing on the Triad is essential for an MNC pursuing success in a global industry, according to Ohmae, because close to 90% of all high–value-added, high-technology manufactured goods are produced and consumed in North America, Western Europe, and Japan. Ideally, a company should have a significant presence in each of these regions so that it can develop, produce, and market its products simultaneously in all three areas. Otherwise, it will lose competitive advantage to Triad-oriented MNCs. No longer can an MNC develop and market a new product in one part of the world before it exports it to other developed countries.

Focusing only on the developed nations, however, causes a corporation to miss important market opportunities in the developing nations of the world. Although those nations may not have developed to the point that they have significant demand for a broad spectrum of products, they may very likely be on the threshold of rapid growth in the demand for specific products. This would be the ideal time for a company to enter this market—before competition is established. The key is to be able to identify the "trigger point" when demand for a particular product or service is ready to boom. See the GLOBAL ISSUE boxed highlight for an in-depth explanation of a technique to identify the optimum time to enter a particular market in a developing nation.

GLOBAL ISSUE

Identifying Potential Markets in Developing Nations

Research by the Deloitte & Touche Consulting Group reveals that the demand for a specific product increases exponentially at certain points in a country's development. Identifying this trigger point of demand is thus critical to entering emerging markets at the best time. A **trigger point** is the time when enough people have enough money to buy what a company has to sell but before competition is established. This can be determined by using the concept of **purchasing power parity (PPP)**, which measures the cost in dollars of the U.S.-produced equivalent volume of goods that an economy produces.

PPP offers an estimate of the material wealth a nation can purchase, rather than the financial wealth it creates, as is typically measured by Gross Domestic Product (GDP). As a result, restating a nation's GDP in PPP terms reveals much greater spending power than market exchange rates would suggest. For example, a shoe shine costing $5 to $10 in New York City can be purchased for 50¢ in Mexico City. Consequently, the people of Mexico City can enjoy the same standard of living (with respect to shoe shines) as people in New York City with only 5% to 10% of the money. Correcting for PPP restates all Mexican shoe shines at their U.S. purchase value of $5. If one million shoe shines were purchased in Mexico last year, using the PPP model would effectively increase the Mexican GDP by $5 million to $10 million. Using PPP, China becomes the world's second-largest economy after the United States, followed by Japan, India, and Germany.

A trigger point identifies when demand for a particular product is about to rapidly increase in a country. Identifying a trigger point can be a very useful technique for determining when to enter a new market in a developing nation. Trigger points vary for different products. For example, an apparent trigger point for long-distance telephone services is at $7,500 in GDP per capita—a point when demand for telecommunications services increases rapidly. Once national wealth surpasses $15,000 per capita, demand increases at a much slower rate with further increases in wealth. The trigger point for life insurance is around $8,000 in GDP per capita. At this point, the demand for life insurance increases between 200% and 300% above those countries with GDP per capita below the trigger point.

Source: D. Fraser and M. Raynor, "The Power of Parity," *Forecast* (May/June, 1996), pp. 8–12; "A Survey of the World Economy: The Dragon and the Eagle," Special Insert, *Economist* (October 2, 2004), p. 8; "The Big Mac Index: Food for Thought," *Economist* (May 29, 2004), pp. 71–72.

Creating a Scanning System How can anyone monitor and keep track of all the trends and factors in the worldwide societal environment? With the existence of the Internet, it is now possible to scan the entire world. Nevertheless, the vast amount of raw data makes scanning for information similar to drinking from a fire hose. It is a daunting task for even a large corporation with many resources. To deal with this problem, in 2002 IBM created a tool called *WebFountain* to help a company analyze the vast amounts of environmental data available on the Internet. WebFountain is an advanced information discovery system designed to help extract trends, detect patterns, and find relationships within vast amounts of raw data. For example, IBM sought to learn whether there was a trend toward more positive discussions about e-business. Within a week, the company had data that experts within the company used to replace their hunches with valid conclusions. The company uses WebFountain to:

- Locate negative publicity or investor discontent
- Track general trends
- Learn competitive information
- Identify emerging competitive threats
- Unravel consumer attitudes[25]

Scanning the Task Environment

As shown in **Figure 4–1**, a corporation's scanning of the environment includes analyses of all the relevant elements in the task environment. These analyses take the form of individual reports written by various people in different parts of the firm. At Procter & Gamble (P&G), for example, people from each of the brand management teams work with key people from the sales and market research departments to research and write a "competitive activity report" each quarter on each of the product categories in which P&G competes. People in purchasing also write similar reports concerning new developments in the industries that supply P&G. These and other reports are then summarized and transmitted up the corporate hierarchy for top management to use in strategic decision making. If a new development is reported regarding a particular product category, top management may then send memos asking people throughout the organization to watch for and

Figure 4–1
Scanning External Environment

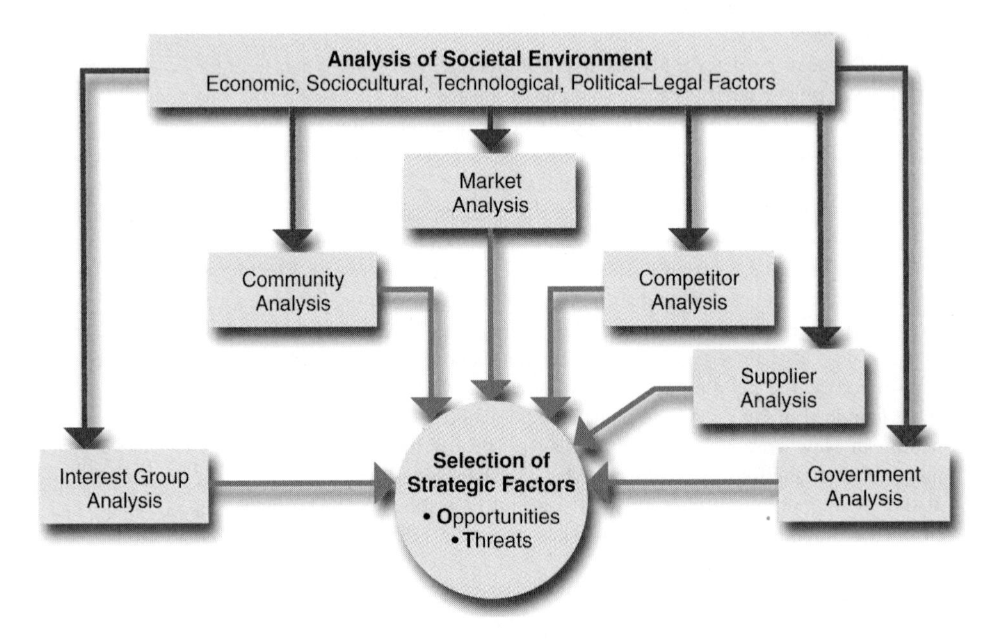

report on developments in related product areas. The many reports resulting from these scanning efforts, when boiled down to their essentials, act as a detailed list of external strategic factors.

Identifying External Strategic Factors

The origin of competitive advantage lay in the ability to identify and respond to environmental change well in advance of competition.[26] Although this seems obvious, why are some companies better able to adapt than others? One reason is because of differences in the ability of managers to recognize and understand external strategic issues and factors. For example, in a 2002 global survey conducted by the Fuld-Gilad-Herring Academy of Competitive Intelligence, two-thirds of 140 corporate strategists admitted that their firms had been surprised by as many as three high-impact events in the past five years. Moreover, 97% stated that their companies had no early warning system in place.[27]

No firm can successfully monitor all external factors. Choices must be made regarding which factors are important and which are not. Even though managers agree that strategic importance determines what variables are consistently tracked, they sometimes miss or choose to ignore crucial new developments.[28] Personal values and functional experiences of a corporation's managers as well as the success of current strategies are likely to bias both their perception of what is important to monitor in the external environment and their interpretations of what they perceive.[29]

This willingness to reject unfamiliar as well as negative information is called **strategic myopia.**[30] If a firm needs to change its strategy, it might not be gathering the appropriate external information to change strategies successfully. One way to identify and analyze developments in the external environment is to use the **issues priority matrix** (see **Figure 4–2**) as follows:

1. Identify a number of likely trends emerging in the societal and task environments. These are strategic environmental issues—important trends that, if they occur, determine what the industry or the world will look like in the near future.
2. Assess the probability of these trends actually occurring, from low to medium to high.
3. Attempt to ascertain the likely impact (from low to high) of each of these trends on the corporation being examined.

Figure 4–2
Issues Priority Matrix

Probable Impact on Corporation

Probability of Occurrence	High	Medium	Low
High	High Priority	High Priority	Medium Priority
Medium	High Priority	Medium Priority	Low Priority
Low	Medium Priority	Low Priority	Low Priority

Source: Reprinted from Long-Range Planning, *Vol. 17, No. 3, 1984, Campbell, "Foresight Activities in the U.S.A.: Time for a Re-Assessment?" pp. 46. Copyright © 1984 with permission from Elsevier.*

A corporation's **external strategic factors** are the key environmental trends that are judged to have both a medium to high probability of occurrence and a medium to high probability of impact on the corporation. The issues priority matrix can then be used to help managers decide which environmental trends should be merely scanned (low priority) and which should be monitored as strategic factors (high priority). Those environmental trends judged to be a corporation's strategic factors are then categorized as opportunities and threats and are included in strategy formulation.

4.2 Industry Analysis: Analyzing the Task Environment

An **industry** is a group of firms that produce a similar product or service, such as soft drinks or financial services. An examination of the important stakeholder groups, such as suppliers and customers, in a particular corporation's task environment is a part of industry analysis.

Porter's Approach to Industry Analysis

Michael Porter, an authority on competitive strategy, contends that a corporation is most concerned with the intensity of competition within its industry. The level of this intensity is determined by basic competitive forces, as depicted in **Figure 4–3**. "The collective strength of these forces," he contends, "determines the ultimate profit potential in the industry, where profit potential is measured in terms of long-run return on invested capital."[31] In carefully

Figure 4–3
Forces Driving Industry Competition

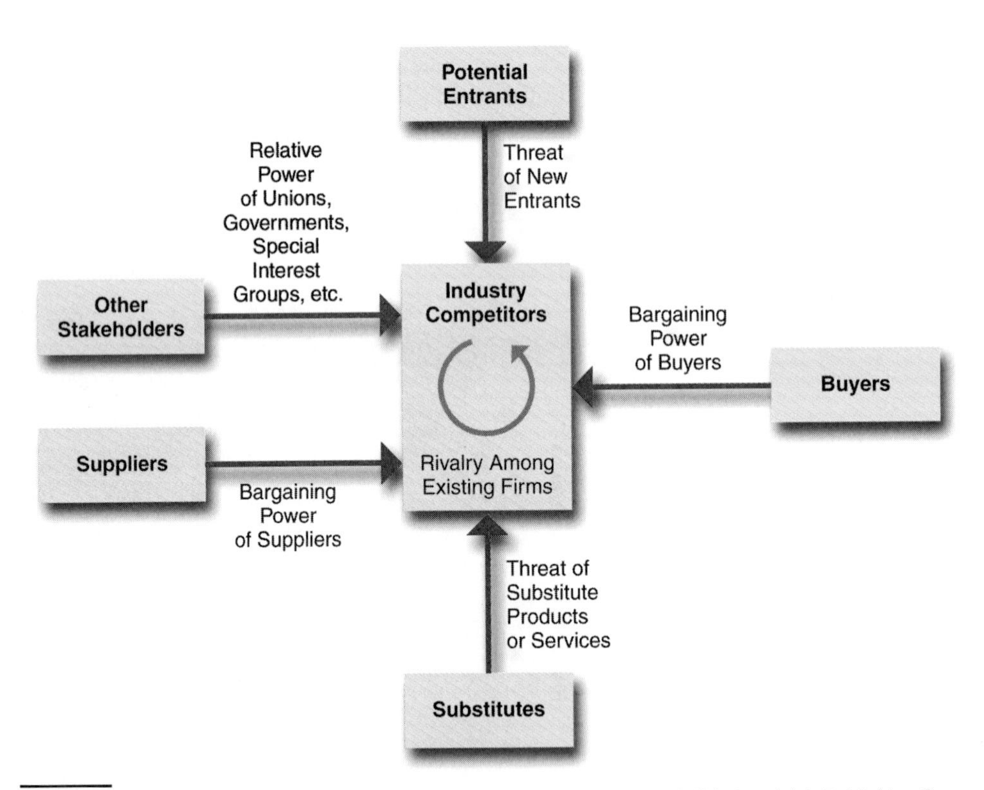

Source: Adapted with the permission of The Free Press, A Division of Simon & Schuster Adult Publishing Group, from COMPETITIVE STRATEGY: Techniques for Analyzing Industries and Competitors *by Michael Porter. Copyright © 1980, 1988 by The Free Press. All rights reserved.*

scanning its industry, a corporation must assess the importance to its success of each of the six forces: threat of new entrants, rivalry among existing firms, threat of substitute products or services, bargaining power of buyers, bargaining power of suppliers, and relative power of other stakeholders.[32] The stronger each of these forces, the more limited companies are in their ability to raise prices and earn greater profits. Although Porter mentions only five forces, a sixth—other stakeholders—is added here to reflect the power that governments, local communities, and other groups from the task environment wield over industry activities.

Using the model in **Figure 4–3**, a high force can be regarded as a threat because it is likely to reduce profits. A low force, in contrast, can be viewed as an opportunity because it may allow the company to earn greater profits. In the short run, these forces act as constraints on a company's activities. In the long run, however, it may be possible for a company, through its choice of strategy, to change the strength of one or more of the forces to the company's advantage. For example, Dell's early use of the Internet to market its computers was an effective way to negate the bargaining power of distributors in the PC industry.

A strategist can analyze any industry by rating each competitive force as high, medium, or low in strength. For example, the athletic shoe industry could be rated as follows: rivalry is high (Nike, Reebok, New Balance, and Adidas are strong competitors worldwide), threat of potential entrants is low (the industry has reached maturity/sales growth rate has slowed), threat of substitutes is low (other shoes don't provide support for sports activities), bargaining power of suppliers is medium but rising (suppliers in Asian countries are increasing in size and ability), bargaining power of buyers is medium but increasing (prices are falling; over half of consumers bought their sneakers on sale in 2002), and threat of other stakeholders is medium to high (government regulations and human rights concerns are growing). Based on current trends in each of these competitive forces, the industry's level of competitive intensity will continue to be high—meaning that sales increases and profit margins should continue to be modest for the industry as a whole.[33]

Threat of New Entrants

New entrants to an industry typically bring to it new capacity, a desire to gain market share, and substantial resources. They are, therefore, threats to an established corporation. The threat of entry depends on the presence of entry barriers and the reaction that can be expected from existing competitors. An **entry barrier** is an obstruction that makes it difficult for a company to enter an industry. For example, no new domestic automobile companies have been successfully established in the United States since the 1930s because of the high capital requirements to build production facilities and to develop a dealer distribution network. Some of the possible barriers to entry are:

- **Economies of Scale:** Scale economies in the production and sale of microprocessors, for example, gave Intel a significant cost advantage over any new rival.
- **Product Differentiation:** Corporations such as P&G and General Mills, which manufacture products such as Tide and Cheerios, create high entry barriers through their high levels of advertising and promotion.
- **Capital Requirements:** The need to invest huge financial resources in manufacturing facilities in order to produce large commercial airplanes creates a significant barrier to entry to any competitor for Boeing and Airbus.
- **Switching Costs:** Once a software program such as Excel or Word becomes established in an office, office managers are very reluctant to switch to a new program because of the high training costs.
- **Access to Distribution Channels:** Small entrepreneurs often have difficulty obtaining supermarket shelf space for their goods because large retailers charge for space on their

shelves and give priority to the established firms that can pay for the advertising needed to generate high customer demand.

- **Cost Disadvantages Independent of Size:** Once a new product earns sufficient market share to be accepted as the *standard* for that type of product, the maker has a key advantage. Microsoft's development of the first widely adopted operating system (MS-DOS) for the IBM-type personal computer gave it a significant competitive advantage over potential competitors. Its introduction of Windows helped to cement that advantage so that the Microsoft operating system is now on more than 90% of personal computers worldwide.
- **Government Policy:** Governments can limit entry into an industry through licensing requirements by restricting access to raw materials, such as oil-drilling sites in protected areas.

Rivalry Among Existing Firms

In most industries, corporations are mutually dependent. A competitive move by one firm can be expected to have a noticeable effect on its competitors and thus may cause retaliation or counterefforts. For example, the entry by mail order companies such as Dell and Gateway into a PC industry previously dominated by IBM, Apple, and Compaq increased the level of competitive activity to such an extent that any price reduction or new product introduction was quickly followed by similar moves from other PC makers. The same is true of prices in the U.S. airline industry. According to Porter, intense rivalry is related to the presence of several factors, including:

- **Number of Competitors:** When competitors are few and roughly equal in size, such as in the U.S. auto and major home appliance industries, they watch each other carefully to make sure that they match any move by another firm with an equal countermove.
- **Rate of Industry Growth:** Any slowing in passenger traffic tends to set off price wars in the airline industry because the only path to growth is to take sales away from a competitor.
- **Product or Service Characteristics:** A product can be very unique, with many qualities differentiating it from others of its kind, or it may be a **commodity**, a product whose characteristics are the same, regardless of who sells it. For example, most people choose a gas station based on location and pricing because they view gasoline as a commodity.
- **Amount of Fixed Costs:** Because airlines must fly their planes on a schedule, regardless of the number of paying passengers for any one flight, they offer cheap standby fares whenever a plane has empty seats.
- **Capacity:** If the only way a manufacturer can increase capacity is in a large increment by building a new plant (as in the paper industry), it will run that new plant at full capacity to keep its unit costs as low as possible—thus producing so much that the selling price falls throughout the industry.
- **Height of Exit Barriers: Exit barriers** keep a company from leaving an industry. The brewing industry, for example, has a low percentage of companies that voluntarily leave the industry because breweries are specialized assets with few uses except for making beer.
- **Diversity of Rivals:** Rivals that have very different ideas of how to compete are likely to cross paths often and unknowingly challenge each other's position. This happens often in the retail clothing industry when a number of retailers open outlets in the same location—thus taking sales away from each other. This is also likely to happen in some countries or regions when multinational corporations compete in an increasingly global economy.

Threat of Substitute Products or Services

A **substitute product** is a product that appears to be different but can satisfy the same need as another product. For example, e-mail is a substitute for the fax, Nutrasweet is a substitute for sugar, the Internet is a substitute for video stores, and bottled water is a substitute for a cola. According to Porter, "Substitutes limit the potential returns of an industry by placing a ceiling on the prices firms in the industry can profitably charge."[34] To the extent that switching costs are low, substitutes may have a strong effect on an industry. Tea can be considered a substitute for coffee. If the price of coffee goes up high enough, coffee drinkers will slowly begin switching to tea. The price of tea thus puts a price ceiling on the price of coffee. Sometimes a difficult task, the identification of possible substitute products or services means searching for products or services that can perform the same function, even though they have a different appearance and may not appear to be easily substitutable.

Bargaining Power of Buyers

Buyers affect an industry through their ability to force down prices, bargain for higher quality or more services, and play competitors against each other. A buyer or a group of buyers is powerful if some of the following factors hold true:

- A buyer purchases a large proportion of the seller's product or service (for example, oil filters purchased by a major auto maker).
- A buyer has the potential to integrate backward by producing the product itself (for example, a newspaper chain could make its own paper).
- Alternative suppliers are plentiful because the product is standard or undifferentiated (for example, motorists can choose among many gas stations).
- Changing suppliers costs very little (for example, office supplies are easy to find).
- The purchased product represents a high percentage of a buyer's costs, thus providing an incentive to shop around for a lower price (for example, gasoline purchased for resale by convenience stores makes up half their total costs).
- A buyer earns low profits and is thus very sensitive to costs and service differences (for example, grocery stores have very small margins).
- The purchased product is unimportant to the final quality or price of a buyer's products or services and thus can be easily substituted without affecting the final product adversely (for example, electric wire bought for use in lamps).

Bargaining Power of Suppliers

Suppliers can affect an industry through their ability to raise prices or reduce the quality of purchased goods and services. A supplier or supplier group is powerful if some of the following factors apply:

- The supplier industry is dominated by a few companies, but it sells to many (for example, the petroleum industry).
- Its product or service is unique and/or it has built up switching costs (for example, word processing software).
- Substitutes are not readily available (for example, electricity).
- Suppliers are able to integrate forward and compete directly with their present customers (for example, a microprocessor producer such as Intel can make PCs).
- A purchasing industry buys only a small portion of the supplier group's goods and services and is thus unimportant to the supplier (for example, sales of lawn mower tires are less important to the tire industry than are sales of auto tires).

Relative Power of Other Stakeholders

A sixth force should be added to Porter's list to include a variety of stakeholder groups from the task environment. Some of these groups are governments (if not explicitly included elsewhere), local communities, creditors (if not included with suppliers), trade associations, special-interest groups, unions (if not included with suppliers), shareholders, and complementors. According to Andy Grove, Chairman and past CEO of Intel, a **complementor** is a company (e.g., Microsoft) or an industry whose product works well with a firm's (e.g., Intel's) product and without which the product would lose much of its value.[35] An example of complementary industries is the tire and automobile industries. Key international stakeholders who determine many of the international trade regulations and standards are the World Trade Organization, the European Union, NAFTA, ASEAN, and Mercosur.

The importance of these stakeholders varies by industry. For example, environmental groups in Maine, Michigan, Oregon, and Iowa successfully fought to pass bills outlawing disposable bottles and cans, and thus deposits for most drink containers are now required. This effectively raised costs across the board, with the most impact on the marginal producers who could not internally absorb all these costs. The traditionally strong power of national unions in the U.S. auto and railroad industries has effectively raised costs throughout these industries but is of little importance in computer software.

Industry Evolution

Over time, most industries evolve through a series of stages from growth through maturity to eventual decline. The strength of each of the six forces mentioned earlier varies according to the stage of industry evolution. The industry life cycle is useful for explaining and predicting trends among the six forces that drive industry competition. For example, when an industry is new, people often buy the product, regardless of price, because it fulfills a unique need. This usually occurs in a **fragmented industry**—where no firm has large market share, and each firm serves only a small piece of the total market in competition with others (for example, cleaning services).[36] As new competitors enter the industry, prices drop as a result of competition. Companies use the experience curve (discussed in Chapter 5) and economies of scale to reduce costs faster than the competition. Companies integrate to reduce costs even further by acquiring their suppliers and distributors. Competitors try to differentiate their products from one another's in order to avoid the fierce price competition common to a maturing industry.

By the time an industry enters maturity, products tend to become more like commodities. This is now a **consolidated industry**—dominated by a few large firms, each of which struggles to differentiate its products from those of the competition. As buyers become more sophisticated over time, purchasing decisions are based on better information. Price becomes a dominant concern, given a minimum level of quality and features, and profit margins decline. The automobile, petroleum, and major home appliance industries are examples of mature, consolidated industries, each controlled by a few large competitors. In the case of the U.S. major home appliance industry, the industry changed from being a fragmented industry (pure competition) composed of hundreds of appliance manufacturers in the industry's early years to a consolidated industry (mature oligopoly) composed of four companies controlling over 98% of U.S. appliance sales. A similar consolidation is occurring now in European major home appliances.

As an industry moves through maturity toward possible decline, its products' growth rate of sales slows and may even begin to decrease. To the extent that exit barriers are low, firms begin converting their facilities to alternate uses or sell them to other firms. The industry tends to consolidate around fewer but larger competitors. The tobacco industry is an example of an industry currently in decline.

Categorizing International Industries

According to Porter, world industries vary on a continuum from multidomestic to global (see **Figure 4–4**).[37] **Multidomestic industries** are specific to each country or group of countries. This type of international industry is a collection of essentially domestic industries, such as retailing and insurance. The activities in a subsidiary of a multinational corporation (MNC) in this type of industry are essentially independent of the activities of the MNC's subsidiaries in other countries. Within each country, it has a manufacturing facility to produce goods for sale within that country. The MNC is thus able to tailor its products or services to the very specific needs of consumers in a particular country or group of countries having similar societal environments.

Global industries, in contrast, operate worldwide, with MNCs making only small adjustments for country-specific circumstances. In a global industry, an MNC's activities in one country are significantly affected by its activities in other countries. MNCs in global industries produce products or services in various locations throughout the world and sell them, making only minor adjustments for specific country requirements. Examples of global industries are commercial aircraft, television sets, semiconductors, copiers, automobiles, watches, and tires. The largest industrial corporations in the world in terms of sales revenue are, for the most part, MNCs operating in global industries.

The factors that tend to determine whether an industry will be primarily multidomestic or primarily global are:

1. *Pressure for coordination* within the MNCs operating in that industry
2. *Pressure for local responsiveness* on the part of individual country markets

To the extent that the pressure for coordination is strong and the pressure for local responsiveness is weak for MNCs within a particular industry, that industry will tend to become global. In contrast, when the pressure for local responsiveness is strong and the pressure for coordination is weak for multinational corporations in an industry, that industry will tend to be multidomestic. Between these two extremes lie a number of industries with varying characteristics of both multidomestic and global industries. The dynamic tension between these two factors is contained in the phrase "Think globally but act locally."

International Risk Assessment

Some firms, such as American Can Company and Mitsubishi Trading Company, develop elaborate information networks and computerized systems to evaluate and rank investment risks. Small companies can hire outside consultants such as Chicago's Associated Consultants International or Boston's Arthur D. Little, Inc., to provide political-risk assessments. Among the many systems that exist to assess political and economic risks are the Political System Stability Index, the Business Environment Risk Index, Business International's Country Assessment Service, the Economist Intelligence Unit, and Frost and Sullivan's World Political Risk Forecasts.[38] Business International provides subscribers with continuously

Figure 4–4
Continuum of International Industries

Multidomestic ⟷ Global

Multidomestic	Global
Industry in which companies tailor their products to the specific needs of consumers in a particular country. • Retailing • Insurance • Banking	Industry in which companies manufacture and sell the same products, with only minor adjustments made for individual countries around the world. • Automobiles • Tires • Television sets

updated information on conditions in 63 countries. Regardless of the source of data, a firm must develop its own method of assessing risk. It must decide on its most important risk factors and then assign weights to each.

Strategic Groups

A **strategic group** is a set of business units or firms that "pursue similar strategies with similar resources."[39] Categorizing firms in any one industry into a set of strategic groups is very useful as a way of better understanding the competitive environment.[40] Because a corporation's structure and culture tend to reflect the kinds of strategies it follows, companies or business units belonging to a particular strategic group within the same industry tend to be strong rivals and tend to be more similar to each other than to competitors in other strategic groups within the same industry.[41]

For example, although McDonald's and Olive Garden are a part of the same industry, the restaurant industry, they have different missions, objectives, and strategies, and thus they belong to different strategic groups. They generally have very little in common and pay little attention to each other when planning competitive actions. Burger King and Hardee's, however, have a great deal in common with McDonald's in terms of their similar strategy of producing a high volume of low-priced meals targeted for sale to the average family. Consequently, they are strong rivals and are organized to operate similarly.

Strategic groups in a particular industry can be mapped by plotting the market positions of industry competitors on a two-dimensional graph, using two strategic variables as the vertical and horizontal axes (see **Figure 4–5**):

1. Select two broad characteristics, such as price and menu, that differentiate the companies in an industry from one another.
2. Plot the firms, using these two characteristics as the dimensions.
3. Draw a circle around those companies that are closest to one another as one strategic group, varying the size of the circle in proportion to the group's share of total industry sales. (You could also name each strategic group in the restaurant industry with an identifying title, such as quick fast food or buffet-style service.)

Other dimensions, such as quality, service, location, or degree of vertical integration, could also be used in additional graphs of the restaurant industry to gain a better understanding of how the various firms in the industry compete. Keep in mind, however, that the two dimensions should not be highly correlated; otherwise, the circles on the map will simply lie along the diagonal, providing very little new information other than the obvious.

Strategic Types

In analyzing the level of competitive intensity within a particular industry or strategic group, it is useful to characterize the various competitors for predictive purposes. A **strategic type** is a category of firms based on a common strategic orientation and a combination of structure, culture, and processes consistent with that strategy. According to Miles and Snow, competing firms within a single industry can be categorized into one of four basic types on the basis of their general strategic orientation.[42] This distinction helps explain why companies facing similar situations behave differently and why they continue to do so over long periods of time. These general types have the following characteristics:

- **Defenders** are companies with limited product lines that *focus on improving the efficiency of their existing operations*. This cost orientation makes them unlikely to innovate in new areas. With its emphasis on efficiency, Lincoln Electric is an example of a defender.

Figure 4–5
Mapping Strategic Groups in the U.S. Restaurant Chain Industry

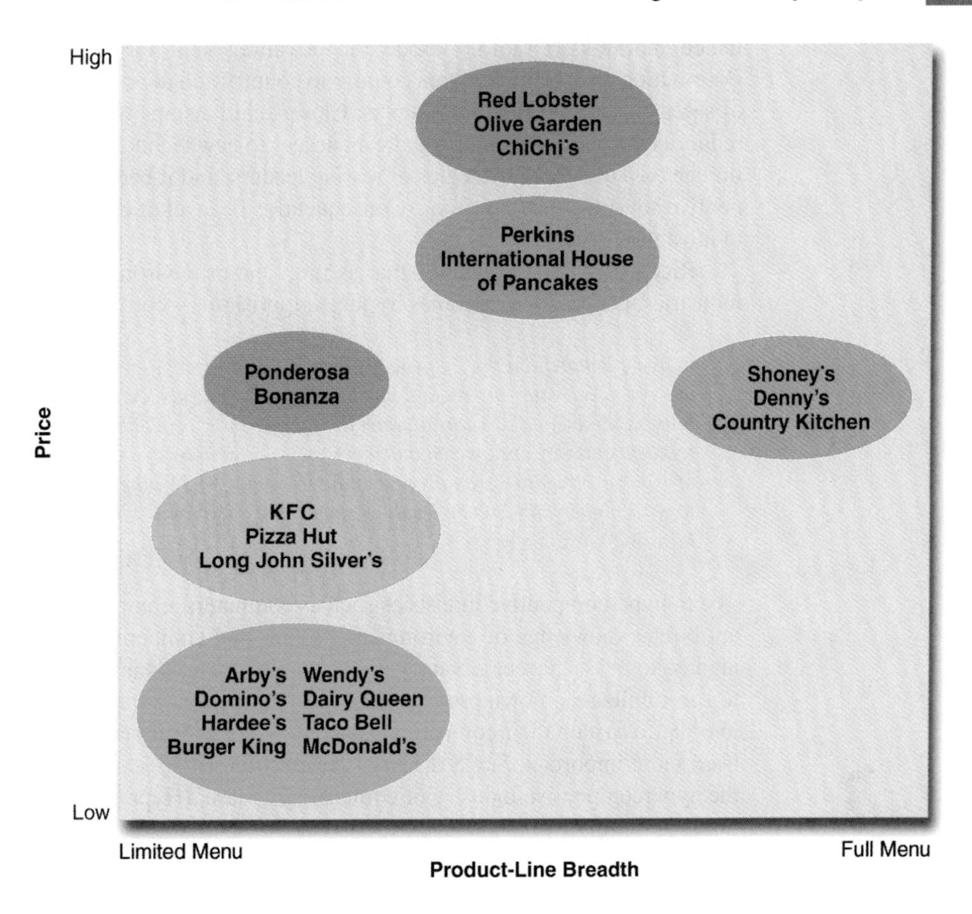

- **Prospectors** are companies with fairly broad product lines that *focus on product innovation and market opportunities*. This sales orientation makes them somewhat inefficient. They tend to emphasize creativity over efficiency. Rubbermaid's emphasis on new product development makes it an example of a prospector.
- **Analyzers** are corporations that *operate in at least two different product-market areas*, one stable and one variable. In the stable areas, efficiency is emphasized. In the variable areas, innovation is emphasized. Multidivisional firms, such as IBM and Procter & Gamble, which operate in multiple industries, tend to be analyzers.
- **Reactors** are corporations that *lack a consistent strategy–structure–culture relationship*. Their (often ineffective) responses to environmental pressures tend to be piecemeal strategic changes. Most major U.S. airlines have recently tended to be reactors—given the way they have been forced to respond to new entrants such as Southwest and JetBlue.

Dividing the competition into these four categories enables a strategic manager not only to monitor the effectiveness of certain strategic orientations but also to develop scenarios of future industry developments (discussed later in this chapter).

Hypercompetition

Most industries today are facing an ever-increasing level of environmental uncertainty. They are becoming more complex and more dynamic. Industries that used to be multidomestic are becoming global. New flexible, aggressive, innovative competitors are moving into established markets to rapidly erode the advantages of large previously dominant firms. Distribution channels vary from country to country and are being altered daily through the use of sophisticated information systems. Closer relationships with suppliers are being forged to reduce costs, increase quality, and gain access to new technology. Companies learn to quickly imitate the successful strategies of market leaders, and it becomes harder to sustain any competitive advantage for very long. Consequently, the level of competitive intensity is increasing in most industries.

Richard D'Aveni contends that as this type of environmental turbulence reaches more industries, competition becomes **hypercompetition**. According to D'Aveni:

> *In hypercompetition the frequency, boldness, and aggressiveness of dynamic movement by the players accelerates to create a condition of constant disequilibrium and change. Market stability is threatened by short product life cycles, short product design cycles, new technologies, frequent entry by unexpected outsiders, repositioning by incumbents, and tactical redefinitions of market boundaries as diverse industries merge. In other words, environments escalate toward higher and higher levels of uncertainty, dynamism, heterogeneity of the players and hostility.*[43]

In hypercompetitive industries such as computers, competitive advantage comes from an up-to-date knowledge of environmental trends and competitive activity coupled with a willingness to risk a current advantage for a possible new advantage. Companies must be willing to **cannibalize** their own products (that is, replace popular products before competitors do so) in order to sustain their competitive advantage. As a result, competitive intelligence has never been more important. See **STRATEGY HIGHLIGHT 4.1** to learn how Microsoft is operating in the hypercompetitive industry of computer software. (Hypercompetition is discussed in more detail in **Chapter 6**.)

STRATEGY HIGHLIGHT 4.1

Microsoft in a Hypercompetitive Industry

Microsoft is an aggressive firm operating in a hypercompetitive industry. It has used its dominance in operating systems (DOS and Windows) to move into a very strong position in application programs such as word processing and spreadsheets (Word and Excel). Even though Microsoft held 90% of the market for personal computer operating systems in 1992, it still invested millions in developing the next generation—Windows 95 and Windows NT. These were soon followed by Windows Me and XP. Instead of trying to protect its advantage in the profitable DOS operating system, Microsoft actively sought to replace DOS with various versions of Windows. Before hypercompetition, most experts argued against cannibalization of a company's own product line because it destroys a very profitable product instead of harvesting it like a "cash cow." According to this line of thought, a company would be better off defending its older products. New products would be introduced only if it could be proven that they would not take sales away from current products. Microsoft was one of the first companies to disprove this argument against cannibalization.

Bill Gates, Microsoft's co-founder, chair, and CEO, realized that if his company didn't replace its own DOS product line with a better product, someone else would (such as Linux or IBM's OS/2 Warp). He knew that success in the software industry depends not so much on company size as on moving aggressively to the next competitive advantage before a competitor does. "This is a hypercompetitive market," explained Gates. "Scale is not all positive in this business. Cleverness is the position in this business." By 2004, Microsoft still controlled over 90% of operating systems software and had achieved a dominant position in applications software as well.

Source: Adapted with permission of THE FREE PRESS, a Division of Simon & Schuster Adult Publishing Group, from HYPERCOMPETITION: Managing The Dynamics of Strategic Maneuvering by Richard D'Aveni.

Using Key Success Factors to Create an Industry Matrix

Within any industry there are usually certain variables—key success factors—that a company's management must understand in order to be successful. **Key success factors** are variables that can significantly affect the overall competitive positions of companies within any particular industry. They typically vary from industry to industry and are crucial to determining a company's ability to succeed within that industry. They are usually determined by the economic and technological characteristics of the industry and by the competitive weapons on which the firms in the industry have built their strategies.[44] For example, in the major home appliance industry, a firm must achieve low costs, typically by building large manufacturing facilities dedicated to making multiple versions of one type of appliance, such as washing machines. Because 60% of major home appliances in the U.S. are sold through "power retailers" such as Sears and Best Buy, a firm must have a strong presence in the mass merchandiser distribution channel. It must offer a full line of appliances and provide a just-in-time delivery system to keep store inventory and ordering costs to a minimum. Because the consumer expects reliability and durability in an appliance, a firm must have excellent process R&D. Any appliance manufacturer that is unable to deal successfully with these key success factors will not survive long in the U.S. market.

An **industry matrix** summarizes the key success factors within a particular industry. As shown in **Table 4–4**, the matrix gives a weight for each factor, based on how important that factor is for success within the industry. The matrix also specifies how well various competitors in the industry are responding to each factor. To generate an industry matrix using two industry competitors (called A and B), complete the following steps for the industry being analyzed:

1. In **Column 1 (*Key Success Factors*)**, list the 8 to 10 factors that appear to determine success in the industry.
2. In **Column 2 (*Weight*)**, assign a weight to each factor, from **1.0** (Most Important) to **0.0** (Not Important), based on that factor's probable impact on the overall industry's current and future success. **(All weights must sum to 1.0, regardless of the number of strategic factors.)**
3. In **Column 3 (*Company A Rating*)**, examine a particular company within the industry—for example, Company A. Assign a rating to each factor, from **5** (Outstanding) to **1** (Poor)

TABLE 4–4 INDUSTRY MATRIX

Key Success Factors	Weight	Company A Rating	Company A Weighted Score	Company B Rating	Company B Weighted Score
1	2	3	4	5	6
Total	1.00				

Source: T. L. Wheelen and J. D. Hunger, "Industry Matrix." Copyright © 1997, 2001, and 2005 by Wheelen and Hunger Associates. Reprinted with permission.

based on Company A's current response to that particular factor. Each rating is a judgment regarding how well that company is specifically dealing with each key success factor:

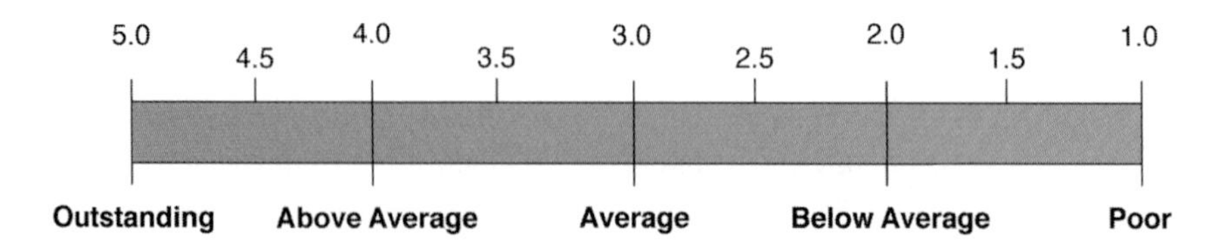

4. In **Column 4** (***Company A Weighted Score***), multiply the weight in **Column 2** for each factor by its rating in **Column 3** to obtain that factor's weighted score for Company A. This results in a weighted score for each key success factor, ranging from **5.0** (Outstanding) to **1.0** (Poor), with **3.0** as the average.
5. In **Column 5** (***Company B Rating***), examine a second company within the industry—in this case, Company B. Assign a rating to each key success factor, from **5.0** (Outstanding) to **1.0** (Poor), based on Company B's current response to each particular factor.
6. In **Column 6** (***Company B Weighted Score***), multiply the weight in **Column 2** for each factor by its rating in **Column 5** to obtain that factor's weighted score for Company B.
7. Finally, add the weighted scores for all the factors in **Columns 4 and 6** to determine the total weighted scores for companies A and B. **The total weighted score indicates how well each company is responding to current and expected key success factors in the industry's environment.** Check to ensure that the total weighted score truly reflects the company's current performance in terms of profitability and market share. The industry matrix can be expanded to include all the major competitors within an industry through the addition of two additional columns for each additional competitor.

4.3 Competitive Intelligence

Much external environmental scanning is done on an informal and individual basis. Information is obtained from a variety of sources—suppliers, customers, industry publications, employees, industry experts, industry conferences, and the Internet.[45] For example, scientists and engineers working in a firm's R&D lab can learn about new products and competitors' ideas at professional meetings; someone from the purchasing department, speaking with supplier–representatives' personnel, may also uncover valuable bits of information about a competitor. A study of product innovation found that 77% of all product innovations in scientific instruments and 67% in semiconductors and printed circuit boards were initiated by the customer in the form of inquiries and complaints.[46] In these industries, the sales force and service departments must be especially vigilant.

Competitive intelligence is a formal program of gathering information on a company's competitors. Often called *business intelligence*, it is one of the fastest growing fields within strategic management. According to P&G Chairman John Pepper, "I can't imagine a time in history when the competencies, skills, and knowledge of the men and women in competitive intelligence are more needed and more relevant to a company being able to design a winning strategy and act on it."[47] At General Mills, for example, all employees have been trained to recognize and tap sources of competitive information. Janitors no longer simply place orders with suppliers of cleaning materials; they also ask about relevant practices at competing firms! A survey of large U.S. corporations revealed that 78% of them reported competitive intelligence activities within their firms.[48] As mentioned earlier, IBM uses its WebFountain software to scan the Internet for a variety of data, including competitor information and emerging competitive threats. According to a survey of corporate information officers by Merrill Lynch, business intelligence software topped the list of corporate software spending plans in 2003.[49]

Sources of Competitive Intelligence

Most corporations use outside organizations to provide them with environmental data. Firms such as A. C. Nielsen Co. provide subscribers with bimonthly data on brand share, retail prices, percentages of stores stocking an item, and percentages of stock-out stores. Strategists can use this data to spot regional and national trends as well as to assess market share. Information on market conditions, government regulations, industry competitors, and new products can be bought from "information brokers" such as Market Research.com (Findex), LexisNexis (company and country analyses), and Finsbury Data Services. Company and industry profiles are generally available from the Hoover's web site, at www.hoovers.com. Many business corporations have established their own in-house libraries and computerized information systems to deal with the growing mass of available information.

The Internet has changed the way strategists engage in environmental scanning. It provides the quickest means to obtain data on almost any subject. Although the scope and quality of Internet information is increasing geometrically, it is also littered with "noise," misinformation, and utter nonsense. For example, a number of corporate web sites are sending unwanted guests to specially constructed bogus web sites![50] Unlike the library, the Internet lacks the tight bibliographic control standards that exist in the print world. There is no ISBN or Dewey Decimal System to identify, search, and retrieve a document. Many web documents lack the name of the author and the date of publication. A web page providing useful information may be accessible on the web one day and gone the next. Unhappy ex-employees, far-out environmentalists, and prank-prone hackers create "blog" web sites to attack and discredit otherwise reputable corporations. Rumors with no basis in fact are spread via chat rooms and personal web sites. This creates a serious problem for researchers. How can one evaluate the information found on the Internet? For a way to evaluate intelligence information, see **STRATEGY HIGHLIGHT 4.2**.

Some companies choose to use industrial espionage or other intelligence-gathering techniques to get their information straight from their competitors. According to a survey by the American Society for Industrial Security, PricewaterhouseCoopers, and the U.S. Chamber of Commerce, Fortune 1000 companies lost an estimated $59 billion in one year alone due to the theft of trade secrets.[51] By using current or former competitors' employees and private contractors, some firms attempt to steal trade secrets, technology, business plans, and pricing strategies. For example, Avon Products hired private investigators to retrieve from a public dumpster documents (some of them shredded) that Mary Kay Corporation had thrown away. Studies reveal that 32% of the trash typically found next to copy machines contains confidential company data, in addition to personal data (29%) and gossip (39%).[52] Even P&G, which defends itself like a fortress from information leaks, is vulnerable. A competitor was able to learn the precise launch date of a concentrated laundry detergent in Europe when one of its people visited the factory where machinery was being made. Simply asking a few questions about what a certain machine did, whom it was for, and when it would be delivered was all that was necessary.

To combat the increasing theft of company secrets, the U.S. government passed the Economic Espionage Act in 1996. The law makes it illegal (with fines up to $5 million and 10 years in jail) to steal any material that a business has taken "reasonable efforts" to keep secret and that derives its value from not being known.[53] The Society of Competitive Intelligence

STRATEGY HIGHLIGHT 4.2

Evaluating Competitive Intelligence

A basic rule in intelligence gathering is that before a piece of information can be used in any report or briefing, it must first be evaluated in two ways. First, the source of the information should be judged in terms of its truthfulness and reliability. How trustworthy is the source? How well can a researcher rely on it for truthful and correct information? One approach is to rank the reliability of the source on a scale of A (extremely reliable), B (reliable), C (unknown reliability), D (probably unreliable), or E (very questionable reliability). The reliability of a source can be judged on the basis of the author's credentials, the organization sponsoring the information, and past performance, among other factors. Second, the information or data should be judged in terms of its likelihood of being correct. The correctness of the data may be ranked on a scale of 1 (correct), 2 (probably correct), 3 (unknown), 4 (doubtful), or 5 (extremely doubtful). The correctness of a piece of data or information can be judged on the basis of its agreement with other bits of separately obtained information or with a general trend supported by previous data. For every piece of information found on the Internet, for example, it is important to list not only the URL of the web page but also the evaluation of the information from A1 (good information) to E5 (bad information). Information found through library research in sources such as Moody's Industrials, Standard & Poor's, or Value Line can generally be evaluated as having a reliability of A. The correctness of the data can still range anywhere from 1 to 5, but in most instances it is likely to be either 1 or 2, but probably no worse than 3 or 4. Web sites are quite different.

Web sites, such as those sponsored by the U.S. Securities and Exchange Commission (*www.sec.gov*) or Hoovers Online (*www.hoovers.com*) are extremely reliable. Company-sponsored web sites are generally reliable, but they are not the place to go for trade secrets, strategic plans, or proprietary information. For one thing, many firms think of their web sites primarily in terms of marketing and provide little data aside from product descriptions and distributors. Other companies provide their latest financial statements and links to other useful web sites. Nevertheless, some companies in very competitive industries may install software on their web site to ascertain a visitor's web address. Visitors from a competitor's domain name are thus screened before they are allowed to access certain web sites. They may not be allowed beyond the product information page, or they may be sent to a bogus web site containing misinformation. Cisco Systems, for example, uses its web site to send visitors from other high-tech firms to a special web page asking if they would like to apply for a job at Cisco.

Professionals (www.scip.org) urges strategists to stay within the law and to act ethically when searching for information. The society states that illegal activities are foolish because the vast majority of worthwhile competitive intelligence is available publicly via annual reports, web sites, and libraries. Unfortunately, a number of firms hire "kites," consultants with questionable reputations, who do what is necessary to get information when the selected methods do not meet SCIP ethical standards or are illegal. This allows the company that initiated the action to deny that it did anything wrong.[54]

Monitoring Competitors for Strategic Planning

The primary activity of a competitive intelligence unit is to monitor **competitors**—organizations that offer the same, similar, or substitutable products or services in the business area in which a particular company operates. To understand a competitor, it is important to answer the following 10 questions:

1. Why do your competitors exist? Do they exist to make profits or just to support another unit?
2. Where do they add customer value—higher quality, lower price, excellent credit terms, or better service?
3. Which of your customers are the competitors most interested in? Are they cherry-picking your best customers, picking the ones you don't want, or going after all of them?

4. What is their cost base and liquidity? How much cash do they have? How do they get their supplies?
5. Are they less exposed with their suppliers than your firm? Are their suppliers better than yours?
6. What do they intend to do in the future? Do they have a strategic plan to target your market segments? How committed are they to growth? Are there any succession issues?
7. How will their activity affect your strategies? Should you adjust your plans and operations?
8. How much better than your competitor do you need to be in order to win customers? Do either of you have a competitive advantage in the marketplace?
9. Will new competitors or new ways of doing things appear over the next few years? Who is a potential new entrant?
10. If you were a customer, would you choose your product over those offered by your competitors? What irritates your current customers? What competitors solve these particular customer complaints?[55]

To answer these and other questions, competitive intelligence professionals utilize a number of analytical techniques. In addition to the previously discussed SWOT analysis, Michael Porter's industry forces analysis, and strategic group analysis, some of these techniques are Porter's four corner exercise, Treacy and Wiersema's value disciplines, and Gilad's blind spot analysis. See **Appendix 4.A** for more information about these competitive analysis techniques.

Done right, competitive intelligence is a key input to strategic planning. Avnet, Inc., one of the world's largest distributors of electronic components, uses competitive intelligence in its growth by acquisition strategy. According to John Hovis, Avnet's senior vice president of corporate planning and investor relations:

> *Our competitive intelligence team has a significant responsibility in tracking all of the varied competitors, not just our direct competitors, but all the peripheral competitors that have a potential to impact our ability to create value. . . . One of the things we are about is finding new acquisition candidates, and our competitive intelligence unit is very much involved with our acquisition team, in helping to profile potential acquisition candidates.*[56]

4.4 Forecasting

Environmental scanning provides reasonably hard data on the present situation and current trends, but intuition and luck are needed to accurately predict whether these trends will continue. The resulting forecasts are, however, usually based on a set of assumptions that may or may not be valid.

Danger of Assumptions

Faulty underlying assumptions are the most frequent cause of forecasting errors. Nevertheless, many managers who formulate and implement strategic plans rarely consider that their success is based on a series of assumptions. Many long-range plans are simply based on projections of the current situation.

One example of what can happen when a corporate strategy rests on the very questionable assumption that the future will simply be an extension of the present is that of Tupperware, the company that originated air-tight, easy-to-use plastic food storage containers. Much of the company's success had been based on Tupperware parties in the 1950s, when housewives gathered in each other's homes to socialize and play games while the local Tupperware lady demonstrated and sold new products. Management assumed during the following decades that Tupperware parties would continue being an excellent distribution channel. Its faith in this assumption blinded it to information about America's changing lifestyle (toward two-career families and single-parent households) and its likely impact on sales. Even in the 1990s, when Tupperware executives realized that their extrapolated sales forecasts were no longer justified, they were unable to improve their forecasting techniques until they changed their assumption that the best way to sell Tupperware was at a Tupperware party. Consequently, Rubbermaid and other competitors, which chose to market their containers in grocery and discount stores, continued to grow at the expense of Tupperware.[57]

Useful Forecasting Techniques

Various techniques are used to forecast future situations. Each has proponents and critics. A study of nearly 500 of the world's largest corporations revealed trend extrapolation to be the most widely practiced form of forecasting—more than 70% use this technique either occasionally or frequently.[58] Simply stated, **extrapolation** is the extension of present trends into the future. It rests on the assumption that the world is reasonably consistent and changes slowly in the short run. Time-series methods are approaches of this type; they attempt to carry a series of historical events forward into the future. The basic problem with extrapolation is that a historical trend is based on a series of patterns or relationships among so many different variables that a change in any one can drastically alter the future direction of the trend. As a rule of thumb, the further back into the past you can find relevant data supporting the trend, the more confidence you can have in the prediction.

Brainstorming, expert opinion, and statistical modeling are also very popular forecasting techniques. **Brainstorming** is a nonquantitative approach that requires simply the presence of people with some knowledge of the situation to be predicted. The basic ground rule is to propose ideas without first mentally screening them. No criticism is allowed. Ideas tend to build on previous ideas until a consensus is reached. This is a good technique to use with operating managers who have more faith in "gut feel" than in more quantitative number-crunching techniques. **Expert opinion** is a nonquantitative technique in which experts in a particular area attempt to forecast likely developments. This type of forecast is based on the ability of a knowledgeable person(s) to construct probable future developments based on the interaction of key variables. One application is the **Delphi technique**, in which separated experts independently assess the likelihoods of specified events. These assessments are combined and sent back to each expert for fine-tuning until agreement is reached. **Statistical modeling** is a quantitative technique that attempts to discover causal or at least explanatory factors that link two or more time series together. Examples of statistical modeling are regression analysis and other econometric methods. Although very useful in the grasping of historic trends, statistical modeling, like trend extrapolation, is based on historical data. As the patterns of relationships change, the accuracy of the forecast deteriorates. Other forecasting techniques, such as *cross-impact analysis (CIA)* and *trend-impact analysis (TIA)*, have not established themselves successfully as regularly employed tools.[59]

Scenario writing appears to be the most widely used forecasting technique after trend extrapolation. Originated by Royal Dutch Shell, *scenarios* are focused descriptions of different likely futures presented in a narrative fashion. A scenario thus may be merely a written description of some future state, in terms of key variables and issues, or it may be generated in combination with other forecasting techniques.

An **industry scenario** is a forecasted description of a particular industry's likely future. Such a scenario is developed by analyzing the probable impact of future societal forces on key groups in a particular industry. The process may operate as follows[60]:

1. Examine possible shifts in the societal variables globally.
2. Identify uncertainties in each of the six forces of the task environment (that is, potential entrants, competitors, likely substitutes, buyers, suppliers, and other key stakeholders).
3. Make a range of plausible assumptions about future trends.
4. Combine assumptions about individual trends into internally consistent scenarios.
5. Analyze the industry situation that would prevail under each scenario.
6. Determine the sources of competitive advantage under each scenario.
7. Predict competitors' behavior under each scenario.
8. Select the scenarios that are either most likely to occur or most likely to have a strong impact on the future of the company. Use these scenarios in strategy formulation.

4.5 The Strategic Audit: A Checklist for Environmental Scanning

One way of scanning the environment to identify opportunities and threats is by using the Strategic Audit found in **Appendix 1.A** at the end of Chapter 1. The audit provides a checklist of questions by area of concern. For example, Part III of the audit examines the societal and task environments. It looks at the societal environment in terms of economic, technological, political-legal, and sociocultural forces. It also considers the task environment (industry) in terms of threat of new entrants, bargaining power of buyers and suppliers, threat of substitute products, rivalry among existing firms, and the relative power of other stakeholders.

4.6 Synthesis of External Factors—EFAS

After strategic managers have scanned the societal and task environments and identified a number of likely external factors for their particular corporation, they may want to refine their analysis of these factors by using a form such as that given in **Table 4–5**. Using an **EFAS (External Factors Analysis Summary) Table** is one way to organize the external factors into the generally accepted categories of opportunities and threats as well as to analyze how well a particular company's management (rating) is responding to these specific factors in light of the perceived importance (weight) of these factors to the company. To generate an EFAS Table for the company being analyzed, complete the following steps:

1. In **Column 1 (*External Factors*)**, list the 8 to 10 most important opportunities and threats facing the company.
2. In **Column 2 (*Weight*)**, assign a weight to each factor, from **1.0** (Most Important) to **0.0** (Not Important), based on that factor's probable impact on a particular company's current strategic position. The higher the weight, the more important is this factor to the current and future success of the company. **(All weights must sum to 1.0, regardless of the number of factors.)**
3. In **Column 3 (*Rating*)**, assign a rating to each factor, from **5.0** (Outstanding) to **1.0** (Poor), based on that particular company's specific response to that particular factor. Each rating

TABLE 4–5 EXTERNAL FACTOR ANALYSIS SUMMARY (EFAS TABLE): MAYTAG AS EXAMPLE

External Factors	Weight	Rating	Weighted Score	Comments
1	2	3	4	5
Opportunities				
• Economic integration of European Community	.20	4.1	.82	Acquisition of Hoover
• Demographics favor quality appliances	.10	5.0	.50	Maytag quality
• Economic development of Asia	.05	1.0	.05	Low Maytag presence
• Opening of Eastern Europe	.05	2.0	.10	Will take time
• Trend to "Super Stores"	.10	1.8	.18	Maytag weak in this channel
Threats				
• Increasing government regulations	.10	4.3	.43	Well positioned
• Strong U.S. competition	.10	4.0	.40	Well positioned
• Whirlpool and Electrolux strong globally	.15	3.0	.45	Hoover weak globally
• New product advances	.05	1.2	.06	Questionable
• Japanese appliance companies	.10	1.6	.16	Only Asian presence in Australia
Total Scores	1.00		3.15	

Notes:
1. List opportunities and threats (8–10) in Column 1.
2. Weight each factor from 1.0 (Most Important) to 0.0 (Not Important) in Column 2 based on that factor's probable impact on the company's strategic position. **The total weights must sum to 1.00.**
3. Rate each factor from 5.0 (Outstanding) to 1.0 (Poor) in Column 3 based on the company's response to that factor.
4. Multiply each factor's weight times its rating to obtain each factor's weighted score in Column 4.
5. Use Column 5 (comments) for rationale used for each factor.
6. Add the individual weighted scores to obtain the total weighted score for the company in Column 4. This tells how well the company is responding to the factors in its external environment.

Source: T. L. Wheelen and J. D. Hunger, "External Factors Analysis Summary (EFAS)." Copyright © 1987, 1988, 1989, 1990, and 2005 by T. L. Wheelen. Copyright © 1991, 2003, and 2005 by Wheelen and Hunger Associates. Reprinted by permission.

is a judgment regarding how well the company is currently dealing with each specific external factor.

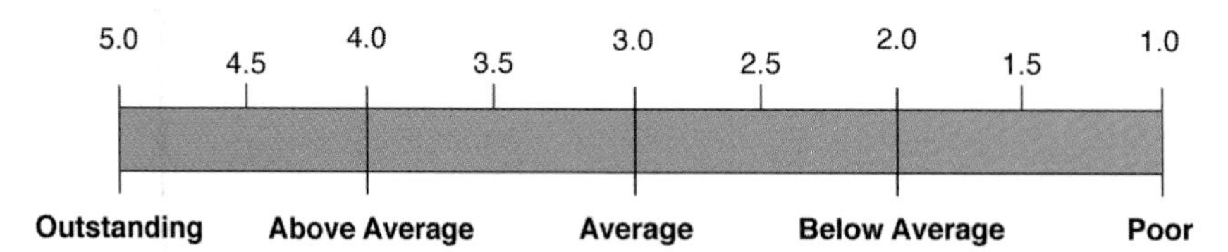

4. In **Column 4 (*Weighted Score*)**, multiply the weight in **Column 2** for each factor by its rating in Column 3 to obtain that factor's weighted score. This results in a weighted score for each factor ranging from **5.0** (Outstanding) to **1.0** (Poor), with **3.0** as average.
5. In **Column 5 (*Comments*)**, note why a particular factor was selected and how its weight and rating were estimated.
6. Finally, add the weighted scores for all the external factors in **Column 4** to determine the total weighted score for that particular company. ***The total weighted score* indicates how well a particular company is responding to current and expected factors in its external environment.** The score can be used to compare that firm to other firms in the industry. Check to ensure that the total weighted score truly reflects the company's current performance in terms of profitability and market share. ***The total weighted score for an average firm in an industry is always 3.0.***

As an example of this procedure, **Table 4–5** includes a number of external factors for Maytag Corporation, with corresponding weights, ratings, and weighted scores provided. This table is appropriate for 1995, before Maytag sold its European and Australian operations. Note that Maytag's total weight was 3.15, meaning that the corporation was slightly above average in the major home appliance industry at that time.

4.7 Conclusion

Wayne Gretzky was one of the most famous people ever to play professional ice hockey. He wasn't very fast. His shot was fairly weak. He was usually last in his team in strength training. He tended to operate in the back of his opponent's goal, anticipating where his team members would be long before they got there and fed them passes so unsuspected that he would often surprise his own team members. In an interview with *Time* magazine, Gretzky stated that the key to winning is *skating not to where the puck is but to where it is going to be.* "People talk about skating, puck handling and shooting, but the whole sport is angles and caroms, forgetting the straight direction the puck is going, calculating where it will be diverted, factoring in all the interruptions," explained Gretzky.[61]

Environmental scanning involves monitoring, collecting, and evaluating information in order to understand the current trends in the societal and task environments. The information is then used to forecast whether these trends will continue or whether others will take their place. What will an industry look like in 10 to 20 years? What kind of developments can we expect in the societal environment to affect the industry? Who will be the key competitors? Who is likely to fall by the wayside? We use this information to make certain assumptions about the future—assumptions that are then used in strategic planning. In many ways, success in the business world is like ice hockey: The key to winning is not to assume that your industry will continue as it is now but to assume that the industry will change and to make sure that your company will be in position to take advantage of that change.

Strategy Bits

How much richer is the average person in America versus China? Because prices tend to be lower in poor economies, a dollar of spending in China is worth more than a dollar in the United States. A better method is to use Purchasing Power Parity (PPP), which takes account of price differences. The Big Mac PPP is the exchange rate that would leave the burger in any country costing the same as in the United States. In 2005, what was the average price of a Big Mac in U.S. dollars?[62]

Brazil: $2.39
Britain: $3.44
Canada: $2.63
Czech Republic: $2.30
Egypt: $1.55
Euro area: $2.92
Hong Kong: $1.54
Japan: $2.34
Malaysia: $1.38
Mexico: $2.58
Russia: $1.48
Switzerland: $5.05
Turkey: $2.98
USA: $3.06

Discussion Questions

1. Discuss how a development in a corporation's societal environment can affect the corporation through its task environment.
2. According to Porter, what determines the level of competitive intensity in an industry?
3. According to Porter's discussion of industry analysis, is Pepsi Cola a substitute for Coca-Cola?
4. How can a decision maker identify strategic factors in a corporation's external international environment?
5. Compare and contrast trend extrapolation with the writing of scenarios as forecasting techniques.

Strategic Practice Exercise

How far should people in a business firm go in gathering competitive intelligence? Where do you draw the line?

Evaluate each of the following approaches that a person could use to gather information about competitors. For each approach, mark your feeling about its appropriateness:

1 (DEFINITELY NOT APPROPRIATE), 2 (PROBABLY NOT APPROPRIATE), 3 (UNDECIDED), 4 (PROBABLY APPROPRIATE), OR 5 (DEFINITELY APPROPRIATE)

The business firm should try to get useful information about competitors by:

1.___ Carefully studying trade journals
2.___ Wiretapping the telephones of competitors
3.___ Posing as a potential customer to competitors
4.___ Getting loyal customers to put out a phony "request for proposal," soliciting competitors' bids
5.___ Buying competitors' products and taking them apart
6.___ Hiring management consultants who have worked for competitors
7.___ Rewarding competitors' employees for useful "tips"
8.___ Questioning competitors' customers and/or suppliers
9.___ Buying and analyzing competitors' garbage
10.___ Advertising and interviewing for nonexistent jobs
11.___ Taking public tours of competitors' facilities
12.___ Releasing false information about the company in order to confuse competitors
13.___ Questioning competitors' technical people at trade shows and conferences
14.___ Hiring key people away from competitors
15.___ Analyzing competitors' labor union contracts
16.___ Having employees date persons who work for competitors
17.___ Studying aerial photographs of competitors' facilities

After marking each of the preceding approaches, compare your responses to those of other people in your class. For each approach, the people marking 4 or 5 should say why they thought this particular act would be appropriate. Those who marked 1 or 2 should then state why they thought this act would be inappropriate.

Go to the web site of the Society for Competitive Intelligence Professionals (www.scip.org). What does SCIP say about these approaches?

Source: Developed from W. A. Jones, Jr., and N. B. Bryan, Jr., "Business Ethics and Business Intelligence: An Empirical Study of Information-Gathering Alternatives," *International Journal of Management* (June 1995), pp. 204–208. For actual examples of some of these activities, see J. Kerstetter, P. Burrows, J. Greene, G. Smith, and M. Conlin, "The Dark Side of the Valley," *Business Week* (July 17, 2000), pp. 42–43.

Key Terms

brainstorming (p. 96)
cannibalize (p. 90)
commodity (p. 84)
competitive intelligence (p. 92)
competitor (p. 94)
complementor (p. 86)
consolidated industry (p. 86)
Delphi technique (p. 96)
EFAS Table (p. 97)
entry barrier (p. 83)
environmental scanning (p. 73)
environmental uncertainty (p. 72)
exit barrier (p. 84)
expert opinion (p. 96)
external strategic factor (p. 82)
extrapolation (p. 96)
fragmented industry (p. 86)
global industry (p. 87)
hypercompetition (p. 90)
industry (p. 82)
industry analysis (p. 73)
industry matrix (p. 91)
industry scenario (p. 96)
issues priority matrix (p. 81)
key success factor (p. 91)
multidomestic industry (p. 87)
multinational corporation (MNC) (p. 78)
new entrant (p. 83)
purchasing power parity (PPP)(p. 79)
repatriation of profits (p. 74)
scenario writing (p. 96)
societal environment (p. 73)
statistical modeling (p. 96)
strategic group (p. 88)
strategic myopia (p. 81)
strategic type (p. 88)
substitute product (p. 85)
task environment (p. 73)
Triad (p. 78)
trigger point (p. 79)

APPENDIX 4.A Competitive Analysis Techniques

Analytical techniques commonly used in competitive intelligence are *SWOT analysis*, *Porter's industry forces*, and *strategic group analysis* (also called *competitive cluster analysis*). In addition to these are Porter's *four-corner exercise*, Treacy and Wiersema's *value disciplines*, and Gilad's *blind spot analysis*. These can be used in a strategic war game in which people role-play different competitors and their possible future strategies.

Porter's four-corner exercise involves analyzing a specific competitor's future goals, assumptions, current strategies, and capabilities in order to compile a competitor's response profile. See **Figure 4–6**.

Figure 4–6 **Four-Corner Exercise: Porter's Components of Competitor Analysis**

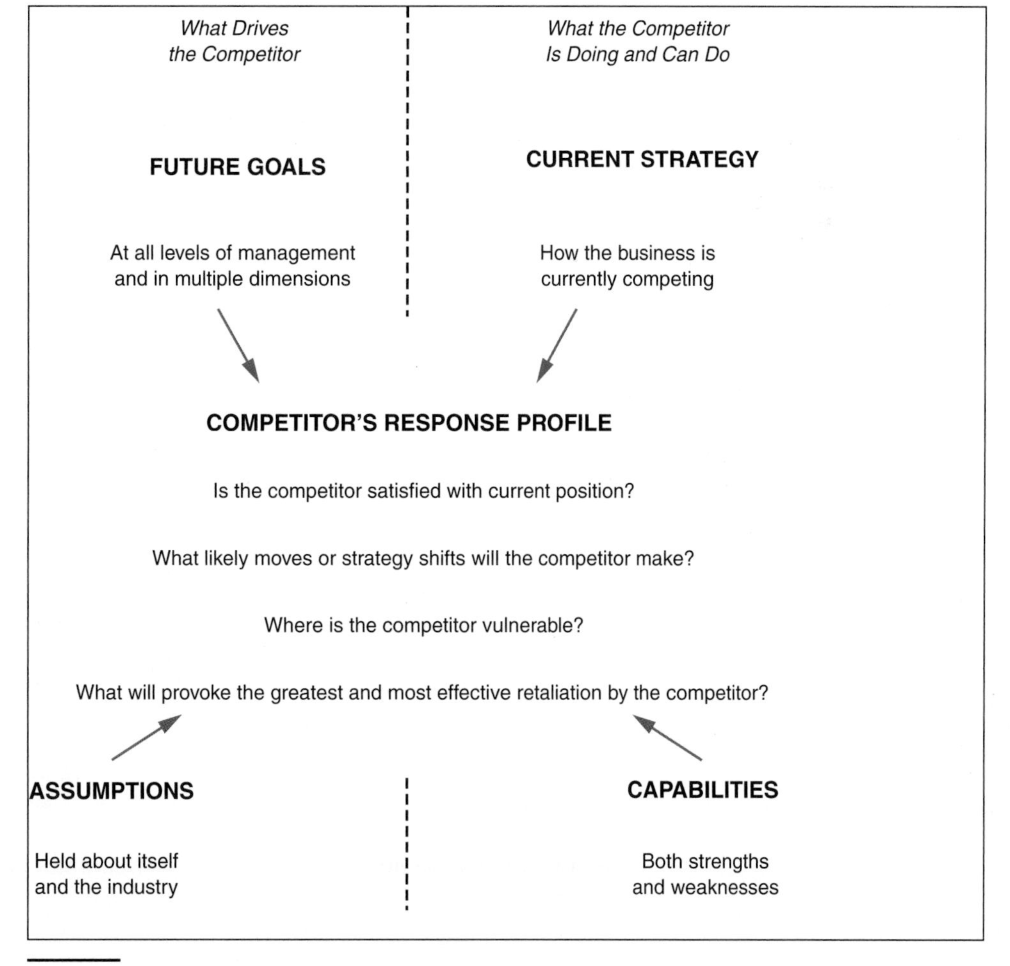

Source: Adapted with the permission of The Free Press, A Division of Simon & Schuster Adult Publishing Group, from COMPETITIVE STRATEGY: Techniques for Analyzing Industries and Competitors by Michael Porter.

Having knowledge of a competitor's goals allows predictions about how likely the competitor is to change strategy and respond to changing conditions. Identifying a competitor's assumptions about itself and the industry can reveal blind spots about how management perceives its environment. Considering a competitor's current strategy and how long it has been in place may indicate whether the company is likely to continue in its current direction. If a strategy is not stated explicitly, one should consider its actions and policies in order to note its implicit strategy. The last step is to objectively evaluate a competitor's capabilities in terms of strengths and weaknesses. The competitor's goals, assumptions, and current strategy influence the likelihood, timing, nature, and intensity of a competitor's reactions. Its strengths and weaknesses determine its ability to initiate or react to strategic moves and to deal with environmental changes.[63]

Treacy and Wiersema's value disciplines involves the evaluation of a competitor in terms of three dimensions: product leadership, operational excellence, and customer intimacy. (See **Figure 4–7**.) After analyzing 80 market-leading companies, Treacy and Wiersema noted that each of these firms developed a compelling and unmatched value proposition on one dimension but was able to maintain acceptable standards on the other two dimensions. *Operationally excellent* companies deliver a combination of quality, price, and ease of purchase that no other can match in their market. An example is Dell Computer, a master of operational excellence. A *product leader* consistently strives to provide its market with leading-edge products or new applications of existing products or services. Johnson & Johnson is an example of a product leader that finds new ideas, develops them quickly, and then looks for ways to

Figure 4–7
Value Discipline Triad

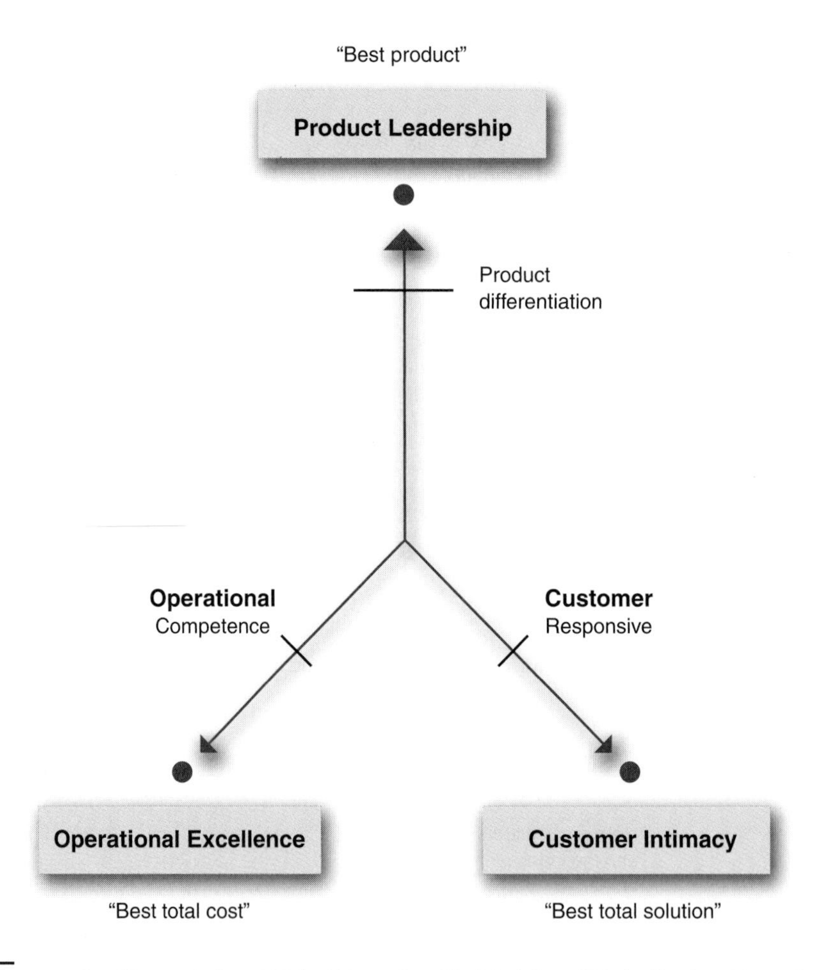

Source: Figure reprinted by permission of Michael Treacy from The Discipline of Market Leaders, *Figure 5, p. 45, by Michael Treacy and Fred Wiersema. Published by Addison-Wesley Publishing Company, Inc. Copyright © 1997 by Michael Treacy.*

improve them. A company that delivers value through *customer intimacy* bonds with its customers and develops high customer loyalty. IBM is an example of a company that pursues excellence in customer intimacy. IBM's current strategy is to provide a total information technology service to its customers so that customers can totally rely on IBM to take care of any information technology (IT) problems.[64] According to Wayne Rosenkrans, past president of SCIP, it is possible to mark a spot on each of the three value dimensions shown in Figure 4-7 for each competitor being analyzed. Then one can draw lines connecting each of the marks, resulting in a triangle that reveals that competitor's overall value proposition.[65]

Gilad's blind spot analysis is based on the premise that the assumptions held by decision makers regarding their own company and their industry may act as perceptual biases or blind spots. As a result, (1) the firm may not be aware of strategically important developments, (2) the firm may inaccurately perceive strategically important developments, or (3) even if the firm is aware of important developments, it may learn too slowly to allow for a timely response. It is important to gather sufficient information about a competitor and its executives to be able to list top management's assumptions about buyers' preferences, the nature of the supply chain, the industry's key success factors, barriers to entry, and the threat appeal of substitutes to customers. One should analyze the industry objectively without regard to these assumptions. Any gap between an objective industry analysis and a competitor's top management assumptions is a potential blind spot. One should include these blind spots when considering how this competitor might respond to environmental change.[66]

Rosenkrans suggests that an analyst should first use Porter's industry forces technique to develop the four-corner analysis. Then the analyst should use the four corner analysis to generate a strategic group (cluster) analysis. Finally, the analyst should include the three value dimensions to develop a blind spot analysis.

These techniques can be used to conduct a war game simulating the various competitors in the industry. Gather people from various functional areas in your own corporation and put them into teams identified as industry competitors. Each company team should perform a complete analysis of the competitor it is role-playing. Each company team first creates starting strategies for its company and presents it to the entire group. Each company team then creates counter-strategies and presents them to the entire group. After all the presentations are complete, the full group creates new strategic considerations to be included as items to monitor in future environmental scanning.[67]

Some competitive intelligence analysts take the war game approach one step further by creating an "invented" company that could appear in the future but does not exist today. A team brainstorms what type of strategy the invented competitor might employ. The strategy is often based on a new breakthrough product that is radically different from current offerings. Its goals, strategies, and competitive posture should be different from any currently being used in the industry. According to Liam Fahey, an authority on competitive intelligence, "the invented competitor is proving to be a spur to bold and innovative thinking."[68]

CHAPTER 5
Internal Scanning: Organizational Analysis

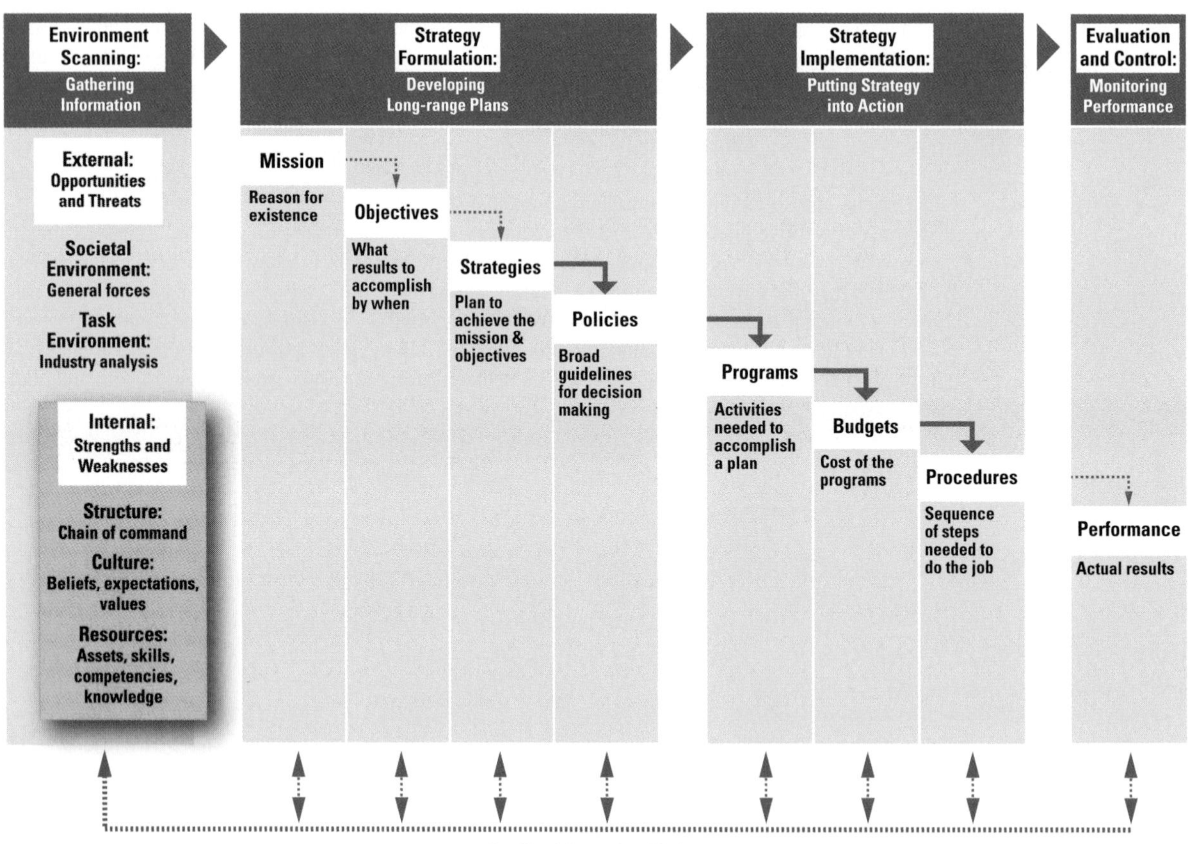

Learning Objectives

After reading this chapter, you should be able to:

- Apply the resource view of the firm to determine core and distinctive competencies
- Use the VRIO framework and the value chain to assess an organization's competitive advantage and how it can be sustained
- Understand a company's business model and how it could be imitated
- Assess a company's corporate culture and how it might affect a proposed strategy
- Scan functional resources to determine their fit with a firm's strategy
- Construct an IFAS Table that summarizes internal factors

ON AUGUST 12, 2004, HEWLETT-PACKARD COMPANY (HP) ANNOUNCED NOT ONLY THAT it had failed to meet its quarterly earnings estimates but also that it was lowering its earnings outlook for the remainder of the year. Its acquisition of Compaq was not growing the company's personal computer (PC) business as planned. At the same time, Dell Inc. announced not only that it achieved its profit targets but also that it would continue to do so in the coming quarters.[1] While other PC firms, such as HP and Gateway, were struggling to make money in the PC business, Dell continued to be "the little engine that could." Since 1995, Dell had gained 12.6 points of market share in desktops, laptops, and PC servers, to 16%—the same market share as HP and Compaq combined. IBM, the creator of the PC standard, divested its PC business and was now focusing on the selling of services and solutions instead of machines. Unhappy about the way Dell was taking large chunks out of the market for Windows servers, Oracle CEO Larry Ellison explained, "If you want to be in the PC business, you have to compete against Dell and that is very difficult."[2] What was the secret of Dell's success?

Dell's business model is simple: Dell machines are made to order and delivered directly to the customer. It has no distributors or retail stores. Dell's PCs have consistently been listed among the best PCs on the market by *PC World* and *PC Magazine*. Cash flow is never a problem. Customers pay Dell long before Dell pays its suppliers. The company holds virtually no parts inventory. As a result, Dell makes computers more quickly and cheaply than any other company.

Dell is the master of process engineering and value chain management. It spends only $440 million annually on R&D contrasted to $4 billion spent annually by HP, and it focuses all its spending on improving its manufacturing processes. It has many patents on its operations' methods. Instead of spending its money on new computer technology, Dell waits until a new technology becomes a standard. Founder and CEO Michael Dell explained that soon after a technology product arrives on the market, it is a high-priced, high-margin item that is made differently by each company. Over time, the technology standardizes—the way PCs standardized around Intel microprocessors and Microsoft operating systems. At a certain point between the development of the standard and its becoming a commodity, that technology is ripe for Dell. When the leaders are earning 40% or 50% profit margins, they are vulnerable to Dell making a profit on far smaller margins. Dell drives down costs further by perfecting its manufacturing processes and using its buying power to obtain cheaper parts. Its reduction of overhead expenses to only 9.6% of revenue means that Dell earns nearly $1 million in revenue per employee—three times the revenue per employee at IBM and almost twice HP's rate.[3] Explains Dell's President, Kevin Rollins: "Our business model excels in that transition."[4]

Given that the secret to Dell's success is well known and fairly simple, why doesn't someone else imitate its success? Explained Michael Dell, "If you look at a lot of truly great businesses, others can understand what they do, but they can't do it."[5] Gateway tried to follow the same business model as Dell but almost went bankrupt. Like Wal-Mart in retailing and Southwest in airlines, Dell has created a distinctive competency and used it to dominate the industry. So far, no other PC maker has been able to copy Dell's success.

5.1 A Resource-Based Approach to Organizational Analysis

Scanning and analyzing the external environment for opportunities and threats is not enough to provide an organization a competitive advantage. Analysts must also look within the corporation itself to identify **internal strategic factors**—critical *strengths* and *weaknesses* that are likely to determine whether a firm will be able to take advantage of opportunities while avoiding threats. This internal scanning, often referred to as **organizational analysis**, is concerned with identifying and developing an organization's resources and competencies.

Core and Distinctive Competencies

Resources are an organization's assets and are thus the basic building blocks of the organization. They include *physical assets*, such as plant, equipment, and location; *human assets*, in terms of the number of employees and their skills; and *organizational assets*, such as culture and reputation. **Capabilities** refer to a corporation's ability to exploit its resources. They consist of business processes and routines that manage the interaction among resources to turn inputs into outputs. For example, a company's marketing capability can be based on the interaction among its marketing specialists, information technology, and financial resources. A capability is functionally based and is resident in a particular function. Thus, there are marketing capabilities, manufacturing capabilities, and human resource management capabilities. A **competency** is a cross-functional integration and coordination of capabilities. For example, a competency in new product development in one division of a corporation may be the consequence of integrating management of information systems (MIS) capabilities, marketing capabilities, R&D capabilities, and production capabilities within the division. A **core competency** is a collection of competencies that crosses divisional boundaries, is widespread within the corporation, and is something that the corporation can do exceedingly well. Thus new product development is a core competency if it goes beyond one division.[6] For example, a core competency of Avon Products is its expertise in door-to-door selling. FedEx has a core competency in its application of information technology to all its operations. A company must continually reinvest in a core competency or risk its becoming a *core rigidity* or *deficiency*—that is, a strength that over time matures and may become a weakness.[7] Although it is typically not an asset in the accounting sense, a core competency is a very valuable resource—it does not "wear out" with use. In general, the more core competencies are used, the more refined they get, and the more valuable they become. When core competencies are superior to those of the competition, they are called **distinctive competencies**. For example, General Electric is well known for its distinctive competency in management development. Its executives are sought out by other companies hiring top managers.[8]

Barney, in his **VRIO framework** of analysis, proposes four questions to evaluate a firm's competencies:

1. **Value:** Does it provide customer value and competitive advantage?
2. **Rareness:** Do other competitors possess it?
3. **Imitability:** Is it costly for others to imitate?
4. **Organization:** Is the firm organized to exploit the resource?

If the answer to each of these questions is *yes* for a particular competency, it is considered to be a strength and thus a distinctive competence.[9]

It is important to evaluate the importance of a company's resources, capabilities, and competencies to ascertain whether they are internal strategic factors—that is, particular strengths and weaknesses that will help determine the future of the company. This can be done by comparing measures of these factors with measures of (1) the company's past performance, (2) the company's key competitors, and (3) the industry as a whole. To the extent that a resource (such as a firm's cash situation), capability, or competency is significantly different from the firm's own past, its key competitors, or the industry average, that resource is likely to be a strategic factor and should be considered in strategic decisions.

Even though a distinctive competency is certainly considered to be a corporation's key strength, a key strength may not always be a distinctive competency. As competitors attempt to imitate another company's competency (especially during hypercompetition), what was once a distinctive competency becomes a minimum requirement to compete in the industry.[10] Even though the competency may still be a core competency and thus a strength, it is no longer unique. For example, when Maytag Company alone made high-quality home appliances, this ability was a distinctive competency. As other appliance makers imitated Maytag's quality control and design processes, this continued to be a key strength (that is, a core competency) of Maytag, but it was less and less a distinctive competency.

Using Resources to Gain Competitive Advantage

Proposing that a company's sustained competitive advantage is primarily determined by its resource endowments, Grant proposes a five-step, resource-based approach to strategy analysis:

1. Identify and classify the firm's resources in terms of strengths and weaknesses.
2. Combine the firm's strengths into specific capabilities and core competencies.
3. Appraise the profit potential of these capabilities and competencies in terms of their potential for sustainable competitive advantage and the ability to harvest the profits resulting from their use. Are there any distinctive competencies?
4. Select the strategy that best exploits the firm's capabilities and competencies relative to external opportunities.
5. Identify resource gaps and invest in upgrading weaknesses.[11]

Where do these competencies come from? A corporation can gain access to a distinctive competency in four ways:

- It may be an asset endowment, such as a key patent, coming from the founding of the company. For example, Xerox grew on the basis of its original copying patent.
- It may be acquired from someone else. For example, Whirlpool bought a worldwide distribution system when it purchased Philips's appliance division.
- It may be shared with another business unit or alliance partner. For example, Apple Computer worked with a design firm to create the special appeal of its Apple II and Mac computers.
- It may be carefully built and accumulated over time within the company. For example, Honda carefully extended its expertise in small motor manufacturing from motorcycles to autos and lawnmowers.[12]

The desire to build or upgrade a core competency is one reason entrepreneurial and other fast-growing firms often tend to locate close to their competitors. They form **clusters**—geographic concentrations of interconnected companies and industries. Examples in the United States are computer technology in Silicon Valley in northern California; light aircraft in Wichita, Kansas; financial services in New York City; agricultural equipment in Iowa and Illinois; and home furniture in North Carolina. According to Michael Porter, clusters provide access to employees, suppliers, specialized information, and complementary products.[13] Being close to one's competitors makes it easier to measure and compare performance against rivals. Capabilities may thus be formed externally through a firm's network resources. An example is the presence of many venture capitalists located in Silicon Valley who provide financial support and assistance to high-tech startup firms in the region. Employees from competitive firms in these clusters often socialize. As a result, companies learn from each other while competing with each other. Interestingly, research reveals that companies with core competencies have little to gain from locating in a cluster with other firms and therefore do not do so. In contrast, firms with the weakest technologies, human resources, training programs, suppliers, and distributors are strongly motivated to cluster. They have little to lose and a lot to gain from locating close to their competitors.[14]

Determining the Sustainability of an Advantage

Just because a firm is able to use its resources, capabilities, and competencies to develop a competitive advantage does not mean it will be able to sustain it. Two characteristics determine the sustainability of a firm's distinctive competency(ies): durability and imitability.

Durability is the rate at which a firm's underlying resources, capabilities, or core competencies depreciate or become obsolete. New technology can make a company's core competency obsolete or irrelevant. For example, Intel's skills in using basic technology developed by others to manufacture and market quality microprocessors was a crucial capability until management realized that the firm had taken current technology as far as possible with the Pentium chip. Without basic R&D of its own, it would slowly lose its competitive advantage to others. It thus formed a strategic alliance with HP to gain access to a needed technology.

Imitability is the rate at which a firm's underlying resources, capabilities, or core competencies can be duplicated by others. To the extent that a firm's distinctive competency gives it competitive advantage in the marketplace, competitors will do what they can to learn and imitate that set of skills and capabilities. Competitors' efforts may range from **reverse engineering** (which involves taking apart a competitor's product in order to find out how it works), to hiring employees from the competitor, to outright patent infringement. A core competency can be easily imitated to the extent that it is transparent, transferable, and replicable:

- **Transparency** is the speed with which other firms can understand the relationship of resources and capabilities supporting a successful firm's strategy. For example, Gillette has always supported its dominance in the marketing of razors with excellent R&D. A competitor could never understand how the Sensor or Mach 3 razor was produced simply by taking one apart. Gillette's razor design is very difficult to copy, partially because the manufacturing equipment needed to produce it is so expensive and complicated.
- **Transferability** is the ability of competitors to gather the resources and capabilities necessary to support a competitive challenge. For example, it may be very difficult for a wine maker to duplicate a French winery's key resources of land and climate, especially if the imitator is located in Iowa.
- **Replicability** is the ability of competitors to use duplicated resources and capabilities to imitate the other firm's success. For example, even though many companies have tried to imitate Procter & Gamble's (P&G's) success with brand management by hiring brand managers away from P&G, they have often failed to duplicate P&G's success. The competitors have failed to identify less visible P&G coordination mechanisms or to realize that P&G's brand management style conflicted with the competitor's own corporate culture. Another example is Wal-Mart's sophisticated *cross-docking system*, which provides the company a substantial cost advantage by improving its ability to reduce shipping and handling cost. A truck arriving from a supplier transfers its goods not into Wal-Mart's ware-

house but into other trucks that move the goods directly to Wal-Mart's stores. While Wal-Mart has the same resources in terms of retail space, employee skills, and equipment as many other discount chains, it has the unique capability to manage its resources for maximum productivity.[15]

It is relatively easy to learn and imitate another company's core competency or capability if it comes from **explicit knowledge**—that is, knowledge that can be easily articulated and communicated. This is the type of knowledge that competitive intelligence activities can quickly identify and communicate. **Tacit knowledge**, in contrast, is knowledge that is *not* easily communicated because it is deeply rooted in employee experience or in a corporation's culture.[16] Tacit knowledge is more valuable and more likely to lead to a sustainable competitive advantage than is explicit knowledge because it is much harder for competitors to imitate.[17] As explained in a Michael Dell quote earlier in this chapter, "others can understand what they do, but they can't do it." The knowledge may be complex and combined with other types of knowledge in an unclear fashion such that even management cannot clearly explain the competency.[18] This can be a problem. Because P&G's successful approach to brand management is primarily composed of tacit knowledge, the firm's top management is very reluctant to make any significant modifications to it—fearing that they might destroy the very thing they would be trying to improve!

An organization's resources and capabilities can be placed on a continuum to the extent that they are durable and can't be imitated (that is, aren't transparent, transferable, or replicable) by another firm. This **continuum of sustainability** is depicted in **Figure 5–1**. At one extreme are slow-cycle resources, which are sustainable because they are shielded by patents, geography, strong brand names, or tacit knowledge. These resources and capabilities form distinctive competencies because they provide a sustainable competitive advantage. Gillette's razor technology is a good example of a product built around slow-cycle resources. The other extreme includes fast-cycle resources, which face the highest imitation pressures because they are based on a concept or technology that can be easily duplicated, such as Sony's Walkman. To the extent that a company has fast-cycle resources, the primary way it can compete successfully is through increased speed from lab to marketplace. Otherwise, it has no real sustainable competitive advantage.

With its low-cost position, good service, and reputation for quality PCs, Dell has successfully built a sustainable competitive advantage based on relatively slow-cycle patented manufacturing process resources—resources that are durable and can't be easily imitated because they lack transparency, transferability, and replicability.

Figure 5–1
Continuum of Resource Sustainability

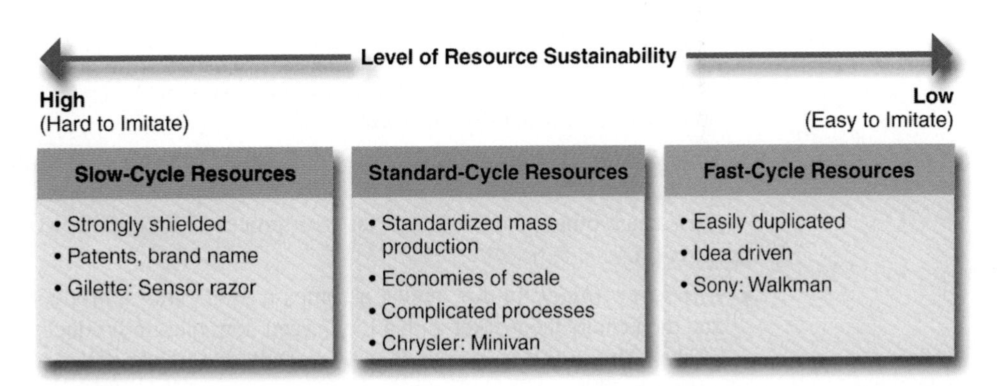

Source: Suggested by J. R. Williams, "How Sustainable Is Your Competitive Advantage?" California Management Review *(Spring 1992), p. 33.*

5.2 Business Models

When analyzing a company, it is helpful to learn what sort of business model it is following. This is especially important when analyzing Internet-based companies. A **business model** is a company's method for making money in the current business environment. It includes the key structural and operational characteristics of a firm—how it earns revenue and makes a profit. A business model is usually composed of five elements:

- Who it serves
- What it provides
- How it makes money
- How it differentiates and sustains competitive advantage
- How it provides its product/service[19]

The simplest business model is to provide a good or service that can be sold so that revenues exceed costs and expenses. Other models can be much more complicated. Some of the many possible business models are:

- ***Customer Solutions Model:*** IBM uses this model to make money not by selling IBM products but by selling its expertise to improve its customers' operations. This is a consulting model.
- ***Profit Pyramid Model:*** General Motors offers a full line of automobiles in order to close out any niches where a competitor might find a position. The key is to get customers to buy in at the low-priced, low-margin entry point (Saturn's basic sedans) and move them up to high-priced, high-margin products (SUVs and pickup trucks), where the company makes its money.
- ***Multi-Component System/Installed Base Model:*** Gillette invented this classic model to sell razors at break-even pricing in order to make money on higher-margin razor blades. HP does the same with printers and printer cartridges. The product is thus a system, not just one product, with one component providing most of the profits.
- ***Advertising Model:*** Similar to the multi-component system/installed base model, this model offers its basic product free in order to make money on advertising. Originating in the newspaper industry, this model is used heavily in commercial radio and television. This was a key model of the dot.com boom when web sites offered free services to users in order to expose them to the advertising that paid the bills. This model is analogous to Mary Poppins' "spoonful of sugar helps the medicine go down."
- ***Switchboard Model:*** In this model a firm acts as an intermediary to connect multiple sellers to multiple buyers. Financial planners juggle a wide range of products for sale to multiple customers with different needs.
- ***Time Model:*** Product R&D and speed are the keys to success in the time model. Being the first to market with a new innovation allows a pioneer such as Sony to earn high margins. Once others enter the market with process R&D and lower margins, it's time to move on.
- ***Efficiency Model:*** In this model, a company waits until a product becomes standardized and then enters the market with a low-priced, low-margin product that appeals to the mass market. This model is used by Wal-Mart, Dell, and Southwest.
- ***Blockbuster Model:*** In some industries, such as pharmaceuticals and motion picture studios, profitability is driven by a few key products. The focus is on high investment in a few products with high potential payoffs—especially if they can be protected by patents.

- ***Profit Multiplier Model:*** The idea of this model is to develop a concept that may or may not make money on its own but can spin off many profitable products. Walt Disney invented this concept by using cartoon characters to develop high-margin theme parks, merchandise, and licensing opportunities.
- ***Entrepreneurial Model:*** In this model, a company offers specialized products/services to market niches that are too small to be worthwhile to large competitors but have the potential to grow quickly. Small, local brew pubs have been very successful in a mature industry dominated by Anheuser-Busch. This model has been used by small high-tech firms that develop innovative prototypes in order to sell off the companies (without ever selling a product) to Microsoft or DuPont.
- ***De Facto Standard Model:*** In this model, a company offers products free or at a very low price in order to saturate the market and become the industry standard. Once users are locked in, the company offers higher-margin products using this standard. For example, Microsoft packaged Internet Explorer free with its Windows software in order to take market share from Netscape's web browser.[20]

In order to understand how some of these business models work, it is important to learn where on the value chain the company makes its money. Although a company might offer a large number of products and services, one product (such as HP's printers) might contribute most of the profits.

5.3 Value-Chain Analysis

A **value chain** is a linked set of value-creating activities that begin with basic raw materials coming from suppliers, move on to a series of value-added activities involved in producing and marketing a product or service, and end with distributors getting the final goods into the hands of the ultimate consumer. See **Figure 5–2** for an example of a typical value chain for a manufactured product. The focus of value-chain analysis is to examine the corporation in the context of the overall chain of value-creating activities, of which the firm may be only a small part.

Very few corporations include a product's entire value chain. Ford Motor Company did when it was managed by its founder, Henry Ford I. During the 1920s and 1930s, the company owned its own iron mines, ore-carrying ships, and a small rail line to bring ore to its mile-long River Rouge plant in Detroit. Visitors to the plant would walk along an elevated walkway, where they could watch iron ore being dumped from the rail cars into huge furnaces. The resulting steel was poured and rolled out onto a moving belt to be fabricated into auto frames and parts while the visitors watched in awe. As visitors walked along the walkway, they observed an automobile being built piece by piece. Reaching the end of the moving line, the finished automobile was driven out of the plant into a vast adjoining parking lot. Ford trucks would then load the cars for delivery to dealers. Although the Ford dealers were not employees of the company, they had almost no power in the arrangement. Dealerships were awarded by the company and taken away if a dealer was at all disloyal. Ford Motor Company at that

Figure 5–2
Typical Value Chain for a Manufactured Product

time was completely vertically integrated—that is, it controlled (usually by ownership) every stage of the value chain, from the iron mines to the retailers.

Industry Value-Chain Analysis

The value chains of most industries can be split into two segments: *upstream* and *downstream* segments. In the petroleum industry, for example, *upstream* refers to oil exploration, drilling, and moving of the crude oil to the refinery, and *downstream* refers to refining the oil plus transporting and marketing gasoline and refined oil to distributors and gas station retailers. Even though most large oil companies are completely integrated, they often vary in the amount of expertise they have at each part of the value chain. Amoco, for example, had strong expertise downstream in marketing and retailing. British Petroleum, in contrast, was more dominant in upstream activities like exploration. That's one reason the two companies merged to form BP Amoco.

An industry can be analyzed in terms of the profit margin available at any point along the value chain. For example, the U.S. auto industry's revenues and profits are divided among many value-chain activities, including manufacturing, new and used car sales, gasoline retailing, insurance, after-sales service and parts, and lease financing. From a revenue standpoint, auto manufacturers dominate the industry, accounting for almost 60% of total industry revenues. Profits, however, are a different matter. Auto leasing is the most profitable activity in the value chain, followed by insurance and auto loans. The core activities of manufacturing and distribution, however, earn significantly smaller shares of the total industry profits than they do of total revenues. For example, because auto sales have become marginally profitable, dealerships are now emphasizing service and repair. As a result of various differences along the industry value chain, manufacturers have moved aggressively into auto financing.[21] Ford, for example, generated $3.3 billion in profits from financial services in 2003 compared to a loss of $2 billion from automobiles, even though financing accounted for less than 16% of the company's revenues!

In analyzing the complete value chain of a product, note that even if a firm operates up and down the entire industry chain, it usually has an area of primary expertise where its primary activities lie. A company's **center of gravity** is the part of the chain that is most important to the company and the point where its greatest expertise and capabilities lie—its core competencies. According to Galbraith, a company's center of gravity is usually the point at which the company started. After a firm successfully establishes itself at this point by obtaining a competitive advantage, one of its first strategic moves is to move forward or backward along the value chain in order to reduce costs, guarantee access to key raw materials, or guarantee distribution.[22] This process, called *vertical integration*, is discussed in more detail in **Chapter 7**.

In the paper industry, for example, Weyerhaeuser's center of gravity is in the raw materials and primary manufacturing parts of the value chain, as shown in **Figure 5–2**. Weyerhaeuser's expertise is in lumbering and pulp mills, which is where the company started. It integrated forward by using its wood pulp to make paper and boxes, but its greatest capability still lay in getting the greatest return from its lumbering activities. In contrast, P&G is primarily a consumer products company that also owned timberland and operated pulp mills. Its expertise is in the product producer and marketer distributor parts of the **Figure 5–2** value chain. P&G purchased these assets to guarantee access to the large quantities of wood pulp it needed to expand its disposable diaper, toilet tissue, and napkin products. P&G's strongest capabilities have always been in the downstream activities of product development, marketing, and brand management. It has never been as efficient in upstream paper activities as Weyerhauser. It had no real distinctive competence on that part of the value chain. When paper supplies became more plentiful (and competition got rougher), P&G gladly sold its land

and mills to focus more on the part of the value chain where it could provide the greatest value at the lowest cost—creating and marketing innovative consumer products. As was the case with P&G's experience in the paper industry, it makes sense for a company to outsource any weak areas it may control internally on the industry value chain.

Corporate Value-Chain Analysis

Each corporation has its own internal value chain of activities. See **Figure 5–3** for an example of a corporate value chain. Porter proposes that a manufacturing firm's **primary activities** usually begin with inbound logistics (raw materials handling and warehousing), go through an operations process in which a product is manufactured, and continue on to outbound logistics (warehousing and distribution), to marketing and sales, and finally to service (installation, repair, and sale of parts). Several **support activities**, such as procurement (purchasing), technology development (R&D), human resource management, and firm infrastructure (accounting, finance, strategic planning), ensure that the primary value-chain activities operate effectively and efficiently. Each of a company's product lines has its own distinctive value chain. Because most corporations make several different products or services, an internal analysis of the firm involves analyzing a series of different value chains.

The systematic examination of individual value activities can lead to a better understanding of a corporation's strengths and weaknesses. According to Porter, "Differences among competitor value chains are a key source of competitive advantage."[23] Corporate value-chain analysis involves the following three steps:

1. ***Examine each product line's value chain in terms of the various activities involved in producing that product or service.*** Which activities can be considered strengths (core competencies) or weaknesses (core deficiencies)? Do any of the strengths provide competitive advantage, and can they thus be labeled distinctive competencies?
2. ***Examine the linkages within each product line's value chain.*** **Linkages** are the connections between the way one value activity (for example, marketing) is performed and the

Figure 5–3
A Corporation's Value Chain

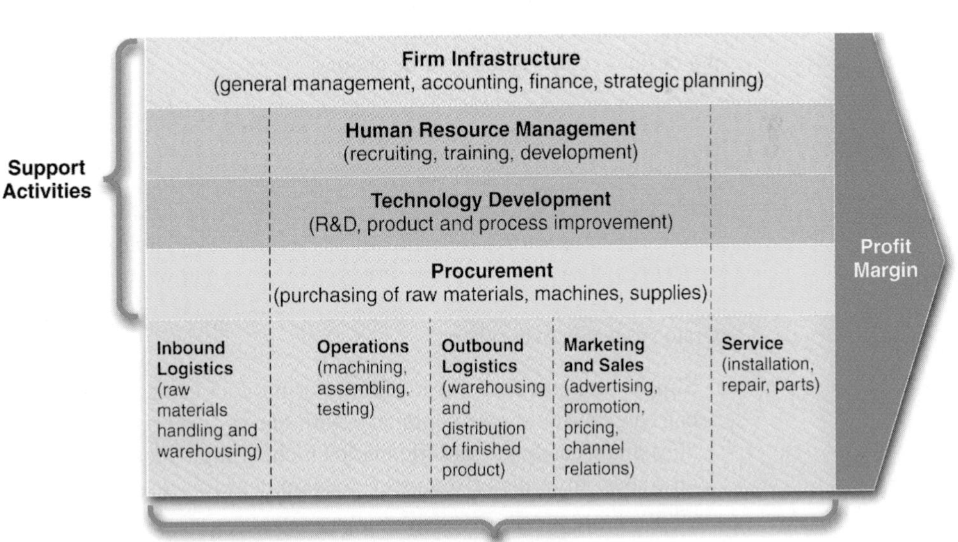

Source: Adapted with the permission of The Free Press, a Division of Simon & Schuster Adult Publishing Group, from COMPETITIVE ADVANTAGE: Creating and Sustaining Superior Performance *by Michael Porter. Copyright © 1985, 1988 by Michael E. Porter. All rights reserved.*

cost of performance of another activity (for example, quality control). In seeking ways for a corporation to gain competitive advantage in the marketplace, the same function can be performed in different ways with different results. For example, quality inspection of 100% of output by the workers themselves instead of the usual 10% by quality control inspectors might increase production costs, but that increase could be more than offset by the savings obtained from reducing the number of repair people needed to fix defective products and increasing the amount of salespeople's time devoted to selling instead of exchanging already-sold but defective products.

3. ***Examine the potential synergies among the value chains of different product lines or business units.*** Each value element, such as advertising or manufacturing, has an inherent economy of scale in which activities are conducted at their lowest possible cost per unit of output. If a particular product is not being produced at a high enough level to reach economies of scale in distribution, another product could be used to share the same distribution channel. This is an example of economies of scope, which result when the value chains of two separate products or services share activities, such as the same marketing channels or manufacturing facilities. For example, the cost of joint production of multiple products can be lower than the cost of separate production.

5.4 Scanning Functional Resources and Capabilities

The simplest way to begin an analysis of a corporation's value chain is by carefully examining its traditional functional areas for potential strengths and weaknesses. Functional resources and capabilities include not only the financial, physical, and human assets in each area but also the ability of the people in each area to formulate and implement the necessary functional objectives, strategies, and policies. These resources and capabilities include the knowledge of analytical concepts and procedural techniques common to each area as well as the ability of the people in each area to use them effectively. If used properly, these resources and capabilities serve as strengths to carry out value-added activities and support strategic decisions. In addition to the usual business functions of marketing, finance, R&D, operations, human resources, and information systems, we also discuss structure and culture as key parts of a business corporation's value chain.

Basic Organizational Structures

Although there is an almost infinite variety of structural forms, certain basic types predominate in modern complex organizations. **Figure 5–4** illustrates three basic **organizational structures**. The conglomerate structure is a variant of divisional structure and is thus not depicted as a fourth structure. Generally speaking, each structure tends to support some corporate strategies over others:

- **Simple structure** has no functional or product categories and is appropriate for a small, entrepreneur-dominated company with one or two product lines that operates in a reasonably small, easily identifiable market niche. Employees tend to be generalists and jacks-of-all-trades. In terms of stages of development (discussed in **Chapter 9**), this is a Stage I company.
- **Functional structure** is appropriate for a medium-sized firm with several product lines in one industry. Employees tend to be specialists in the business functions that are important to that industry, such as manufacturing, marketing, finance, and human resources. In terms of stages of development (discussed in **Chapter 9**), this is a Stage II company.

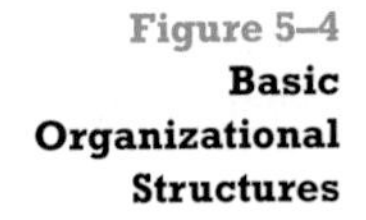
Figure 5–4
Basic Organizational Structures

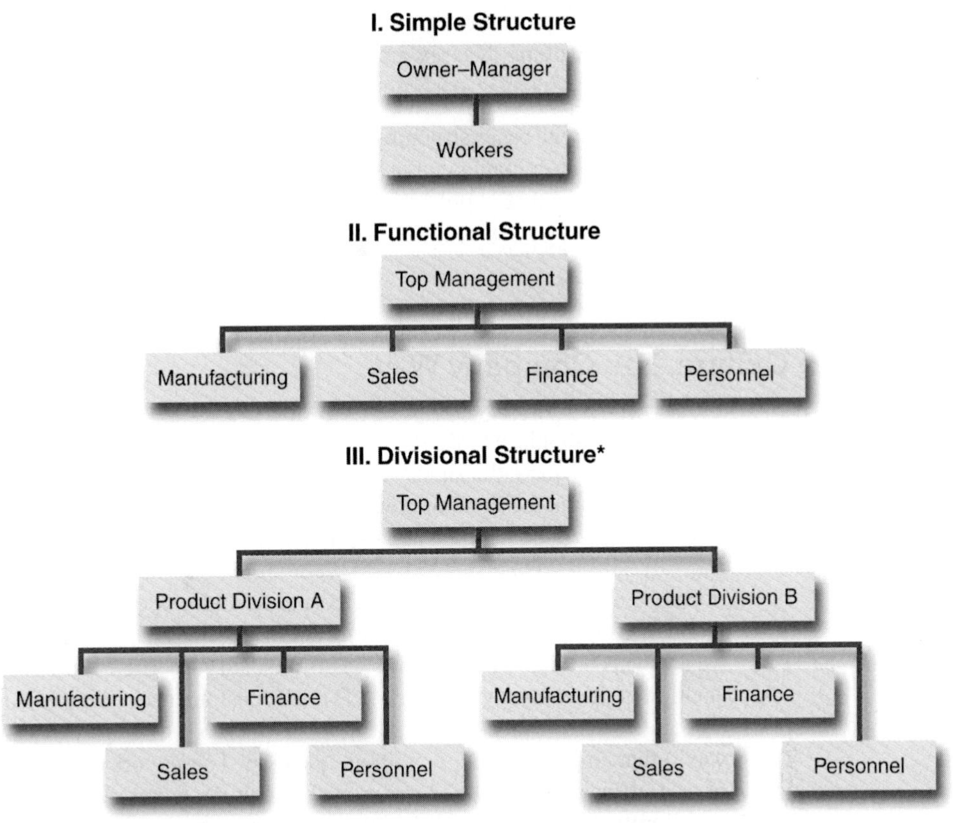

*Strategic Business Units and the conglomerate structure are variants of the divisional structure.

- **Divisional structure** is appropriate for a large corporation with many product lines in several related industries. Employees tend to be functional specialists organized according to product/market distinctions. General Motors, for example, groups its various auto lines into the separate divisions of Saturn, Chevrolet, Pontiac, Buick, and Cadillac. Management attempts to find some synergy among divisional activities through the use of committees and horizontal linkages. In terms of stages of development (discussed in **Chapter 9**), this is a Stage III company.
- **Strategic business units (SBUs)** are a modification of the divisional structure. SBUs are divisions or groups of divisions composed of independent product-market segments that are given primary responsibility and authority for the management of their own functional areas. An SBU may be of any size or level, but it must have (1) a unique mission, (2) identifiable competitors, (3) an external market focus, and (4) control of its business functions.[24] The idea is to decentralize on the basis of strategic elements rather than on the basis of size, product characteristics, or span of control and to create horizontal linkages among units previously kept separate. For example, rather than organize products on the basis of packaging technology, such as frozen foods, canned foods, and bagged foods, General Foods organized its products into SBUs on the basis of consumer-oriented menu segments: breakfast foods, beverages, main meals, desserts, and pet foods. In terms of stages of development (discussed in **Chapter 9**), this is also a Stage III company.
- **Conglomerate structure** is appropriate for a large corporation with many product lines in several unrelated industries. A variant of the divisional structure, the conglomerate structure (sometimes called a holding company) is typically an assemblage of legally independent firms (subsidiaries) operating under one corporate umbrella but controlled through

the subsidiaries' boards of directors. The unrelated nature of the subsidiaries prevents any attempt at gaining synergy among them. In terms of stages of development (discussed in **Chapter 9**), this is also a Stage III company.

If the current basic structure of a corporation does not easily support a strategy under consideration, top management must decide whether the proposed strategy is feasible or whether the structure should be changed to a more advanced structure, such as a matrix or network. (Advanced structural designs such as the matrix and network are discussed in **Chapter 9**.)

Corporate Culture: The Company Way

There is an oft-told story of a person new to a company asking an experienced co-worker what an employee should do when a customer calls. The old-timer responded: "There are three ways to do any job—the right way, the wrong way, and the company way. Around here, we always do things the company way." In most organizations, the "company way" is derived from the corporation's culture. **Corporate culture** is the collection of beliefs, expectations, and values learned and shared by a corporation's members and transmitted from one generation of employees to another. The corporate culture generally reflects the values of the founder(s) and the mission of the firm.[25] It gives a company a sense of identity: "This is who we are. This is what we do. This is what we stand for." The culture includes the dominant orientation of the company, such as R&D at HP, customer service at Nordstrom, or product quality at Maytag. It often includes a number of informal work rules (forming the "company way") that employees follow without question. These work practices over time become part of a company's unquestioned tradition. The culture, therefore, reflects the company's values

Corporate culture has two distinct attributes: intensity and integration.[26] **Cultural intensity** is the degree to which members of a unit accept the norms, values, or other culture content associated with the unit. This shows the culture's depth. Organizations with strong norms promoting a particular value, such as quality at Maytag, have intensive cultures, whereas new firms (or those in transition) have weaker, less intensive cultures. Employees in an intensive culture tend to exhibit consistent behavior—that is, they tend to act similarly over time. **Cultural integration** is the extent to which units throughout an organization share a common culture. This is the culture's breadth. Organizations with a pervasive dominant culture may be hierarchically controlled and power oriented, such as a military unit, and have highly integrated cultures. All employees tend to hold the same cultural values and norms. In contrast, a company that is structured into diverse units by functions or divisions usually exhibits some strong subcultures (for example, R&D versus manufacturing) and a less integrated corporate culture.

Corporate culture fulfills several important functions in an organization:

1. Conveys a sense of identity for employees.
2. Helps generate employee commitment to something greater than themselves.
3. Adds to the stability of the organization as a social system.
4. Serves as a frame of reference for employees to use to make sense of organizational activities and to use as a guide for appropriate behavior.[27]

Corporate culture shapes the behavior of people in a corporation. Because these cultures have a powerful influence on the behavior of people at all levels, they can strongly affect a corporation's ability to shift its strategic direction. A strong culture should not only promote survival, but it should also create the basis for a superior competitive position by increasing motivation and facilitating coordination and control.[28] For example, a culture emphasizing

GLOBAL ISSUE

Managing Corporate Culture for Global Competitive Advantage: ABB Versus Matsushita

Zurich-based ABB Asea Brown Boveri AG is a worldwide builder of power plants, electrical equipment, and industrial factories in 140 countries. By establishing one set of multicultural values throughout its global operations, ABB's management believes that the company will gain an advantage over its rivals Siemens AG of Germany, France's Alcatel-Alsthom NV, and the U.S.'s General Electric Company. ABB is a company with no geographic base. Instead, it has many "home" markets that can draw on expertise from around the globe. ABB created a set of 500 global managers who could adapt to local cultures while executing ABB's global strategies. These people are multilingual and move around each of ABB's 5,000 profit centers in 140 countries. Their assignment is to cut costs, improve efficiency, and integrate local businesses with the ABB worldview.

Few multinational corporations are as successful as ABB in getting global strategies to work with local operations. In agreement with the resource-based view of the firm, ABB Chair Percy Barnevik states, "Our strength comes from pulling together. . . . If you can make this work real well, then you get a competitive edge out of the organization which is very, very difficult to copy."

Contrast ABB's globally oriented corporate culture with the more Japanese-oriented parochial culture of Matsushita Electric Industrial Corporation of Japan (MEI). Operating under the brand names of Panasonic and Technic, MEI is the third-largest electrical company in the world. Konosuke Matsushita founded the company in 1918. His management philosophy led to the company's success but became institutionalized in the corporate culture—a culture that was more focused on Japanese values than on cross-cultural globalization. As a result, MEI's corporate culture does not adapt well to local conditions. Not only is MEI's top management *exclusively* Japanese, its subsidiary managers are *overwhelmingly* Japanese. The company's distrust of non-Japanese managers in the United States and some European countries results in a "rice-paper ceiling" that prevents non-Japanese people from being promoted into MEI subsidiaries' top management. Foreign employees are often confused by the corporate philosophy that has not been adapted to suit local realities. MEI's corporate culture perpetuates a cross-cultural divide that separates the Japanese from the non-Japanese managers, leaving the non-Japanese managers feeling frustrated and undervalued. This divide prevents the flow of knowledge and experience from regional operations to the headquarters and may hinder MEI's ability to compete globally.

Sources: Summarized from J. Guyon, "ABB Fuses Units with One Set of Values," *Wall Street Journal* (October 2, 1996), p. A15, and N. Holden, "Why Globalizing with a Conservative Corporate Culture Inhibits Localization of Management: The Telling Case of Matsushita Electric," *International Journal of Cross Cultural Management*, Vol. 1, No. 1 (2001), pp. 53–72.

constant renewal may help a company adapt to a changing, hypercompetitive environment.[29] To the extent that a corporation's distinctive competence is embedded in an organization's culture, it will be a form of tacit knowledge and very difficult for a competitor to imitate.[30] The GLOBAL ISSUE feature shows the differences between ABB Asea Brown Boveri AG and Matsushita Electric in terms of how they manage their corporate cultures in a global industry.

A change in mission, objectives, strategies, or policies is not likely to be successful if it is in opposition to the accepted culture of a firm. Foot-dragging and even sabotage may result, as employees fight to resist a radical change in corporate philosophy. As with structure, if an organization's culture is compatible with a new strategy, it is an internal strength. But if the corporate culture is not compatible with the proposed strategy, it is a serious weakness. Corporate culture is also important when considering an acquisition. The merging of two dissimilar cultures, if not handled wisely, can be a recipe for disaster.

Strategic Marketing Issues

The marketing manager is a company's primary link to the customer and the competition. The manager, therefore, must be especially concerned with the market position and marketing mix of the firm as well as with the overall reputation of the company and its brands.

Market Position and Segmentation

Market position deals with the question, "Who are our customers?" It refers to the selection of specific areas for marketing concentration and can be expressed in terms of market, product, and geographic locations. Through market research, corporations are able to practice **market segmentation** with various products or services so that managers can discover what niches to seek, which new types of products to develop, and how to ensure that a company's many products do not directly compete with one another.

Marketing Mix

Marketing mix refers to the particular combination of key variables under a corporation's control that can be used to affect demand and to gain competitive advantage. These variables are product, place, promotion, and price. Within each of these four variables are several subvariables, listed in **Table 5–1**, that should be analyzed in terms of their effects on divisional and corporate performance.

Product Life Cycle

One of the most useful concepts in marketing, insofar as strategic management is concerned, is the **product life cycle.** As depicted in **Figure 5–5**, the product life cycle is a graph showing time plotted against the monetary sales of a product as it moves from introduction through growth and maturity to decline. This concept enables a marketing manager to examine the marketing mix of a particular product or group of products in terms of its position in its life cycle.

Brand and Corporate Reputation

A **brand** is a name given to a company's product which identifies that item in the mind of the consumer. Over time and with proper advertising, a brand connotes various characteristics in the consumers' minds. For example, Maytag means quality home appliances. Disney stands for family entertainment. Ivory suggests "pure" soap. BMW means high-performance autos. A brand can thus be an important corporate resource. If done well, a brand name is connected to the product to such an extent that a brand may stand for an entire product category, such as Kleenex for facial tissue. The objective is for the customer to ask for the brand name (Coke or Pepsi) instead of the product category (cola). The world's 10 most valuable brands

TABLE 5–1 MARKETING MIX VARIABLES

Product	Place	Promotion	Price
Quality	Channels	Advertising	List price
Features	Coverage	Personal selling	Discounts
Options	Locations	Sales promotion	Allowances
Style	Inventory	Publicity	Payment periods
Brand name	Transport		Credit items
Packaging			
Sizes			
Services			
Warranties			
Returns			

Source: Philip Kotler, *MARKETING MANAGEMENT*, 11th edition © 2003, p. 16. Reprinted by Pearson Education, Inc., Upper Saddle River, NJ.

Figure 5–5
Product Life Cycle

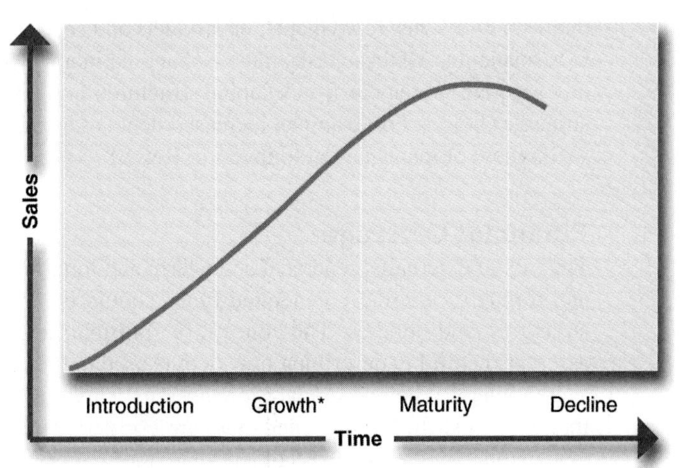

* The right end of the Growth stage is often called Competitive Turbulence because of price and distribution competition that shakes out the weaker competitors. For further information, see C. R. Wasson, *Dynamic Competitive Strategy and Product Life Cycles,* 3rd ed. (Austin, TX: Austin Press, 1978).

in 2004 were Coca-Cola, Microsoft, IBM, GE, Intel, Disney, McDonald's, Nokia, Toyota, and Marlboro, in that order. According to *Business Week*, the Coca-Cola brand is worth $67.4 billion.[31]

A **corporate brand** is a type of brand in which the company's name serves as the brand. Of the world's top 10 brands listed previously, all except Marlboro are corporate brands. The rest, such as Microsoft and IBM, are company names. The value of a corporate brand is that it typically stands for consumers' impressions of a company and can thus be extended onto products not currently offered—regardless of the company's actual expertise. For example, Caterpillar, a manufacturer of heavy earth-moving equipment, used consumer associations with the Caterpillar brand (*rugged*, *masculine*, *construction-related*) to market work boots. Thus, consumer impressions of a brand can suggest new product categories to enter even though a company may have no competencies in making or marketing that type of product or service.[32]

A **corporate reputation** is a widely held perception of a company by the general public. A good corporate reputation can be a strategic resource. It can serve in marketing as both a signal and an entry barrier. Reputation is especially important when the quality of a company's product or service is not directly observable and can be learned only through experience. For example, retail stores are willing to stock a new product from P&G or Anheuser-Busch because they know that both companies market only good-quality products that are highly advertised. Like tacit knowledge, reputation tends to be long lasting and hard for others to duplicate—thus providing sustainable competitive advantage.[33] Research reveals a positive relationship between corporate reputation and financial performance.[34]

Strategic Financial Issues

A financial manager must ascertain the best sources of funds, uses of funds, and control of funds. All strategic issues have financial implications. Cash must be raised from internal or external (local and global) sources and allocated for different uses. The flow of funds in the operations of an organization must be monitored. To the extent that a corporation is involved in international activities, currency fluctuations must be dealt with to ensure that profits aren't wiped out by the rise or fall of the dollar versus the yen, euro, or other currencies. Benefits in the form of returns, repayments, or products and services must be given to the sources of outside financing. All these tasks must be handled in a way that complements and supports overall corporate strategy. A firm's capital structure (amounts of debt and equity) can influence its strategic choices. For example, increased debt tends to increase risk aversion and decrease the willingness of management to invest in R&D.[35]

Financial Leverage

The mix of externally generated short-term and long-term funds in relationship to the amount and timing of internally generated funds should be appropriate to the corporate objectives, strategies, and policies. The concept of **financial leverage** (the ratio of total debt to total assets) is helpful in describing how debt is used to increase the earnings available to common shareholders. When a company finances its activities by sales of bonds or notes instead of through stock, the earnings per share are boosted: The interest paid on the debt reduces taxable income, but fewer shareholders share the profits than if the company had sold more stock to finance its activities. The debt, however, does raise the firm's break-even point above what it would have been if the firm had financed from internally generated funds only. High leverage may therefore be perceived as a corporate strength in times of prosperity and ever-increasing sales or as a weakness in times of recession and falling sales. This is because leverage acts to magnify the effect on earnings per share of an increase or decrease in monetary sales. Research indicates that greater leverage has a positive impact on performance for firms in stable environments but a negative impact for firms in dynamic environments.[36]

Capital Budgeting

Capital budgeting is the analyzing and ranking of possible investments in fixed assets such as land, buildings, and equipment in terms of the additional outlays and additional receipts that will result from each investment. A good finance department will be able to prepare such capital budgets and to rank them on the basis of some accepted criteria or hurdle rate (for example, years to pay back investment, rate of return, or time to break-even point) for the purpose of strategic decision making. Most firms have more than one hurdle rate and vary it as a function of the type of project being considered. Projects with high strategic significance, such as entering new markets or defending market share, often have low hurdle rates.[37]

Strategic Research and Development (R&D) Issues

An R&D manager is responsible for suggesting and implementing a company's technological strategy in light of its corporate objectives and policies. The manager's job, therefore, involves (1) choosing among alternative new technologies to use within the corporation, (2) developing methods of embodying the new technology in new products and processes, and (3) deploying resources so that the new technology can be successfully implemented.

R&D Intensity, Technological Competence, and Technology Transfer

A company must make available the resources necessary for effective research and development. A company's **R&D intensity** (that is, its spending on R&D as a percentage of sales revenue) is a principal means of gaining market share in global competition. The amount spent on R&D often varies by industry. For example, the U.S. computer software industry spends an average of 13.5% of its sales dollars for R&D, whereas the paper and forest products industry spends only 1.0%.[38] A good rule of thumb for R&D spending is that a corporation should spend at a "normal" rate for that particular industry, unless its strategic plan calls for unusual expenditures.

Simply spending money on R&D or new projects does not mean, however, that the money will produce useful results. For example, Pharmacia Upjohn spent more of its revenues on research than any other company in any industry (18%), but it was ranked low in innovation.[39] A company's R&D unit should be evaluated for **technological competence** in both the development and the use of innovative technology. Not only should the corporation make a consistent research effort (as measured by reasonably constant corporate expenditures that result in usable innovations), it should also be proficient in managing research personnel and integrating their innovations into its day-to-day operations. If a company is not proficient in **technology transfer**—the process of taking a new technology from the laboratory to the marketplace—it will not gain much advantage from new technological advances. For example, Xerox Corporation has been criticized for failing to take advantage of various innovations (such as the mouse and the graphical user interface for PCs) developed originally in its sophisticated Palo Alto Research Center. See **STRATEGY HIGHLIGHT 5.1** for a classic example of how Apple Computer's ability to imitate a core competency of Xerox gave it a competitive advantage (which was sustainable until Microsoft launched Windows 95).

R&D Mix

Basic R&D is conducted by scientists in well-equipped laboratories where the focus is on theoretical problem areas. The best indicators of a company's capability in this area are its patents and research publications. **Product R&D** concentrates on marketing and is concerned with product or product-packaging improvements. The best measurements of ability in this area are the number of successful new products introduced and the percentage of total sales and profits coming from products introduced within the past five years. **Engineering (or process) R&D** is concerned with engineering, concentrating on quality control and the development of design specifications and improved production equipment. A company's capability in this area can be measured by consistent reductions in unit manufacturing costs and by the number of product defects.

Most corporations have a mix of basic, product, and process R&D, and this mix varies by industry, company, and product line. The balance of these types of research is known as the **R&D mix** and should be appropriate to the strategy being considered and to each product's life cycle. For example, it is generally accepted that product R&D normally dominates the early stages of a product's life cycle (when the product's optimal form and features are still being

STRATEGY HIGHLIGHT 5.1

A Problem of Technology Transfer at Xerox Corporation

In the mid-1970s, Xerox Corporation's Palo Alto Research Center (PARC) had developed Alto, a new type of computer with some innovative features. Although Alto was supposed to serve as a research prototype, it became so popular among PARC personnel that some researchers began to develop Alto as a commercial product. Unfortunately, this put PARC into direct conflict with Xerox's product development group, which was at the same time developing a rival machine called the Star. Because the Star was in line with the company's expressed product development strategy, top management, which placed all its emphasis on the Star, ignored Alto.

In 1979, Steve Jobs, co-founder of Apple Computer, Inc., made a now-legendary tour of the normally very secretive PARC. Researchers gave Jobs a demonstration of the Alto. Unlike the computers that Apple was then building, Alto had the power of a minicomputer. Its user-friendly software generated crisp text and bright graphics. Jobs fell in love with the machine. He promptly asked Apple's engineers to duplicate the look and feel of Alto. The result was the Macintosh—a personal computer that soon revolutionized the industry.

Note: See the 1999 motion picture *The Pirates of Silicon Valley* for the fuller story of how Apple Computer imitated the features of the Alto and how Microsoft, in turn, imitated the "look and feel" of Apple's Macintosh.

debated), whereas process R&D becomes especially important in the later stages (when the product's design is solidified and the emphasis is on reducing costs and improving quality).

Impact of Technological Discontinuity on Strategy

An R&D manager must determine when to abandon present technology and when to develop or adopt new technology. Richard Foster of McKinsey and Company states that the displacement of one technology by another (**technological discontinuity**) is a frequent and strategically important phenomenon. Such a discontinuity occurs when a new technology cannot simply be used to enhance the current technology but actually substitutes for that technology to yield better performance. For each technology within a given field or industry, according to Foster, the plotting of product performance against research effort/expenditures on a graph results in an S-shaped curve. He describes the process depicted in **Figure 5–6**:

> *Early in the development of the technology a knowledge base is being built and progress requires a relatively large amount of effort. Later, progress comes more easily. And then, as the limits of that technology are approached, progress becomes slow and expensive. That is when R&D dollars should be allocated to technology with more potential. That is also—not so incidentally—when a competitor who has bet on a new technology can sweep away your business or topple an entire industry.*[40]

Computerized information technology is currently on the steep upward slope of its S-curve, in which relatively small increments in R&D effort result in significant improvement in performance. This is an example of Moore's Law, which states that silicon chips (microprocessors) double in complexity every 18 months.[41] The presence of a technological discontinuity in the world's steel industry during the 1960s explains why the large capital expenditures by U.S. steel companies failed to keep them competitive with the Japanese firms that adopted the new technologies. As Foster points out, "History has shown that as one technology nears the end of its S-curve, competitive leadership in a market generally changes hands."[42]

Figure 5–6 Technological Discontinuity

What the S-Curves Reveal

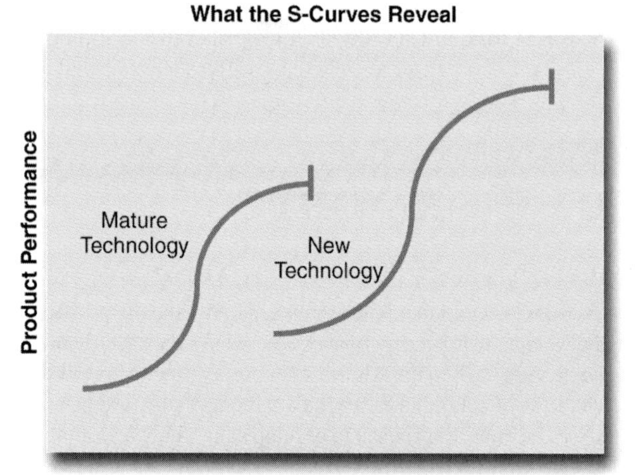

In the corporate planning process, it is generally assumed that incremental progress in technology will occur. But past developments in a given technology cannot be extrapolated into the future because every technology has its limits. The key to competitiveness is to determine when to shift resources to a technology that has more potential.

Source: From "Are You Investing in the Wrong Technology?" P. Pascarella, Industry Week, *July 25, 1983. Reprinted by permission of Penton Media, Inc.*

Christensen explains in *The Innovator's Dilemma* why this transition occurs when a "disruptive technology" enters an industry. In a study of computer disk drive manufacturers, he explains that established market leaders are typically reluctant to move in a timely manner to a new technology. This reluctance to switch technologies (even when the firm is aware of the new technology and may have even invented it!) is because the resource allocation process in most companies gives priority to those projects (typically based on the old technology) with the greatest likelihood of generating a good return on investment—those projects that appeal to the firm's current customers (whose products are also based on the characteristics of the old technology). For example, in the 1980s a disk drive manufacturer's customers (PC manufacturers) wanted a better, faster 5¼″ drive with greater capacity. These PC makers were not interested in the new 3½″ drives based on the new technology because (at that time) the smaller drives were slower and had less capacity. Smaller size was irrelevant because these companies primarily made desktop PCs that were designed to hold large drives.

New technology is generally riskier and of little appeal to the current customers of established firms. Products derived from the new technology are more expensive and do not meet the customers' requirements—requirements based on the old technology. New entrepreneurial firms are typically more interested in the new technology because it is one way to appeal to a developing market niche in a market currently dominated by established companies. Even though the new technology may be more expensive to develop, it offers performance improvements in areas that are attractive to this small niche but of no consequence to the customers of the established competitors.

This was the case with the entrepreneurial manufacturers of 3½″ disk drives. These smaller drives appealed to the PC makers who were trying to increase their small PC market share by offering laptop computers. Size and weight were more important to these customers than were capacity and speed. By the time the new technology was developed to the point that the 3½″ drive matched and even surpassed the 5¼″ drive in terms of speed and capacity (in addition to size and weight), it was too late for the established 5¼″ disk drive firms to switch to the new technology. Once their customers begin demanding smaller products using the new technology, the established firms were unable to respond quickly and lost their leadership position in the industry. They were able to remain in the industry (with a much reduced market share) only if they were able to utilize the new technology to be competitive in the new product line.[43]

Strategic Operations Issues

The primary task of an operations (manufacturing or service) manager is to develop and operate a system that will produce the required number of products or services, with a certain quality, at a given cost, within an allotted time. Many of the key concepts and techniques popularly used in manufacturing can be applied to service businesses.

In very general terms, manufacturing can be intermittent or continuous. In **intermittent systems** (job shops), an item is normally processed sequentially, but the work and sequence of the process vary. An example is an auto body repair shop. At each location, the tasks determine the details of processing and the time required for them. These job shops can be very labor intensive. For example, a job shop usually has little automated machinery and thus a small amount of fixed costs. It has a fairly low break-even point, but its variable cost line (composed of wages and costs of special parts) has a relatively steep slope. Because most of the costs associated with the product are variable (many employees earn piece-rate wages), a job shop's variable costs are higher than those of automated firms. Its advantage over other firms is that it can operate at low levels and still be profitable. After a job shop's sales reach the break-even point, however, the huge variable costs as a percentage of total costs keep the profit per unit at a relatively low level. In terms of strategy, such a firm should look for a niche in the marketplace for which it can produce and sell a reasonably small quantity of goods.

In contrast, **continuous systems** are those laid out as lines on which products can be continuously assembled or processed. An example is an automobile assembly line. A firm using continuous systems invests heavily in fixed investments such as automated processes and highly sophisticated machinery. Its labor force, relatively small but highly skilled, earns salaries rather than piece-rate wages. Consequently, this firm has a high amount of fixed costs. It also has a relatively high break-even point, but its variable cost line rises slowly. This is an example of **operating leverage**, the impact of a specific change in sales volume on net operating income. The advantage of high operating leverage is that once the firm reaches the break-even point, its profits rise faster than do those of less automated firms having lower operating leverage. Continuous systems reap benefits from economies of scale. In terms of strategy, such a firm needs to find a high-demand niche in the marketplace for which it can produce and sell a large quantity of goods. However, a firm with high operating leverage is likely to suffer huge losses during a recession. During an economic downturn, a firm with less automation and thus less leverage is more likely to survive comfortably because a drop in sales primarily affects variable costs. It is often easier to lay off labor than to sell off specialized plants and machines.

Experience Curve

A conceptual framework that many large corporations have used successfully is the experience curve (originally called the learning curve). The **experience curve** suggests that unit production costs decline by some fixed percentage (commonly 20%–30%) each time the total accumulated volume of production in units doubles. The actual percentage varies by industry and is based on many variables: the amount of time it takes a person to learn a new task, scale economies, product and process improvements, and lower raw materials costs, among others. For example, in an industry with an 85% experience curve, a corporation might expect a 15% reduction in unit costs for every doubling of volume. The total costs per unit can be expected to drop from $100 when the total production is 10 units, to $85 ($100 × 85%) when production increases to 20 units, and to $72.25 ($85 × 85%) when it reaches 40 units. Achieving these results often means investing in R&D and fixed assets; higher fixed costs and less flexibility thus result. Nevertheless, the manufacturing strategy is one of building capacity ahead of demand in order to achieve the lower unit costs that develop from the experience curve. On the basis of some future point on the experience curve, a corporation should price its product or service very low to preempt competition and increase market demand. The resulting high number of units sold and high market share should result in high profits, based on the low unit costs.

Management commonly uses the experience curve in estimating the production costs of (1) a product never before made with the present techniques and processes or (2) current products produced by newly introduced techniques or processes. The concept was first applied in the airframe industry and can be applied in the service industry as well. For example, a cleaning company can reduce its costs per employee by having its workers use the same equipment and techniques to clean many adjacent offices in one office building rather than just cleaning a few offices in multiple buildings. Although many firms have used experience curves extensively, an unquestioning acceptance of the industry norm (such as 80% for the airframe industry or 70% for integrated circuits) is very risky. The experience curve of an industry as a whole might not hold true for a particular company for a variety of reasons.

Flexible Manufacturing for Mass Customization

The use of large, continuous, mass-production facilities to take advantage of experience-curve economies has recently been criticized. The use of Computer-Assisted Design and Computer-Assisted Manufacturing (CAD/CAM) and robot technology means that learning times are shorter and products can be economically manufactured in small, customized batches in a process called **mass customization**—the low-cost production of individually customized goods and services.[44] **Economies of scope** (in which common parts of the manufacturing activities of various products are combined to gain economies even though small numbers of each product are made) replace **economies of scale** (in which unit costs are reduced by making large numbers of the same product) in flexible manufacturing. **Flexible manufacturing** permits the low-volume output of custom-tailored products at relatively low unit costs through economies of scope. It is thus possible to have the cost advantages of continuous systems with the customer-oriented advantages of intermittent systems.

Strategic Human Resource Management (HRM) Issues

The primary task of a manager of human resources is to improve the match between individuals and jobs. Research indicates that companies with good HRM practices have higher profits and a better survival rate than do firms without these practices.[45] A good HRM department should know how to use attitude surveys and other feedback devices to assess employees' satisfaction with their jobs and with the corporation as a whole. HRM managers should also use job analysis to obtain job description information about what each job needs to accomplish in terms of quality and quantity. Up-to-date job descriptions are essential not only for proper employee selection, appraisal, training, and development for wage and salary administration, as well as for labor negotiations, but also for summarizing the corporatewide human resources in terms of employee-skill categories. Just as a company must know the number, type, and quality of its manufacturing facilities, it must also know the kinds of people it employs and the skills they possess. The best strategies are meaningless if employees do not have the skills to carry them out or if jobs cannot be designed to accommodate the available workers. For example, HP uses employee profiles to ensure that it has the right mix of talents to implement its planned strategies.

Increasing Use of Teams

Management is beginning to realize that it must be more flexible in its utilization of employees in order for human resources to be a strength. Human resource managers, therefore, need to be knowledgeable about work options such as part-time work, job sharing, flex-time, extended leaves, and contract work, and especially about the proper use of teams. More than two-thirds of large U.S. companies are successfully using **autonomous (self-managing) work teams**, in which a group of people work together without a supervisor to plan, coordinate, and evaluate their own work.[46] Northern Telecom found productivity and quality to increase with work teams to such an extent that it was able to reduce the number of quality inspectors by 40%.[47]

As a way to move a product more quickly through its development stage, companies such as Motorola, Chrysler, NCR, Boeing, and General Electric are using **cross-functional work teams**. Instead of developing products in a series of steps—beginning with a request from sales, which leads to design, then to engineering and on to purchasing, and finally to manufacturing (and often resulting in a costly product rejected by the customer)—companies are tearing down the traditional walls separating the departments so that people from each discipline can get involved in projects early on. In a process called **concurrent engineering**, the once-isolated specialists now work side by side and compare notes constantly in an effort to design cost-effective products with features customers want. Taking this approach enabled Chrysler Corporation to reduce its product development cycle from 60 to 36 months.[48] For such cross-functional work teams to be successful, the groups must receive training and coaching. Otherwise, poorly implemented teams may worsen morale, create divisiveness, and raise the level of cynicism among workers.[49]

Virtual teams are groups of geographically and/or organizationally dispersed co-workers that are assembled using a combination of telecommunications and information technologies to accomplish an organizational task.[50] In the United States alone, more than half of companies that have more than 5,000 employees use virtual teams—involving around 8.4 million people.[51] Internet, intranet, and extranet systems are combining with other new technologies such as desktop videoconferencing and collaborative software to create a new workplace in which teams of workers are no longer restrained by geography, time, or organizational boundaries. As more companies outsource some of the activities previously conducted internally, the traditional organizational structure is being replaced by a series of virtual teams that rarely, if ever, meet face to face. Such teams may be established as temporary groups to accomplish a specific task or may be more permanent to address continuing issues such as strategic planning. Membership on these teams is often fluid, depending on the task to be accomplished. They may include not only employees from different functions within a company but also members of various stakeholder groups, such as suppliers, customers, and law or consulting firms. The use of virtual teams to replace traditional face-to-face work groups is being driven by five trends:

1. Flatter organizational structures with increasing cross-functional coordination needs
2. Turbulent environments requiring more interorganizational cooperation
3. Increasing employee autonomy and participation in decision making
4. Higher knowledge requirements derived from a greater emphasis on service
5. Increasing globalization of trade and corporate activity[52]

Union Relations and Temporary/Part-Time Workers

If a corporation is unionized, a good human resource manager should be able to work closely with the union. Even though union membership had dropped to only 13% of the U.S. workforce by 2003 compared to 24% in 1973, it still included 16 million people.[53] To save jobs, U.S. unions are increasingly willing to support new strategic initiatives and employee involvement programs. For example, United Steel Workers hired Ron Bloom, an investment banker, to propose a strategic plan to make Goodyear Tire & Rubber globally competitive in a way that would preserve as many jobs as possible. In a contract ratified in September 2003, the union gave up $1.15 billion in wage and benefit concessions over three years in return for a promise by Goodyear's top management to invest in 12 of its 14 U.S. factories, to limit imports from its factories in Brazil and Asia, and to maintain 85% of its 19,000-person workforce. The company also agreed to aggressively restructure the firm's $5 billion debt by 2007. According to Bloom, "We told Goodyear, 'We'll make you profitable, but you're going to adopt this strategy.'. . . We think the company should be a patient, long-term builder of value for the employees and shareholders."[54]

Outside the United States, the average proportion of unionized workers among major industrialized nations is around 50%. European unions tend to be militant, politically oriented, and much less interested in working with management to increase efficiency. Nationwide strikes can occur quickly. In contrast, Japanese unions are typically tied to individual companies and are usually supportive of management. These differences among countries have significant implications for the management of multinational corporations.

To increase flexibility, avoid layoffs, and reduce labor costs, corporations are using more temporary (also known as contingent) workers. Ninety percent of U.S. firms use temporary workers in some capacity; 43% use them in professional and technical functions.[55] Approximately 13% of those in the U.S. workforce are part-time workers. The percentage is even higher in some European countries, such as the Netherlands, where more than one-third of all employees work part time.[56] Labor unions are concerned that companies use temps to avoid hiring costlier unionized workers. At United Parcel Service, for example, 80% of the jobs created from 1993 to 1997 were staffed by part-timers, whose pay rates hadn't changed since 1982. Fully 10% of the company's 128,000 part-timers worked 30 hours or more per week but were still paid at a lower rate than were full-time employees.[57]

Quality of Work Life and Human Diversity

Human resource departments have found that to reduce employee dissatisfaction and unionization efforts (or, conversely, to improve employee satisfaction and existing union relations), they must consider the **quality of work life** in the design of jobs. Partially a reaction to the traditionally heavy emphasis on technical and economic factors in job design, quality of work life emphasizes improving the human dimension of work. A knowledgeable human resource manager, therefore, should be able to improve a corporation's quality of work life by (1) introducing participative problem solving, (2) restructuring work, (3) introducing innovative reward systems, and (4) improving the work environment. It is hoped that these improvements will lead to a more participative corporate culture and thus higher productivity and quality products. Ford Motor Company, for example, rebuilt and modernized its famous River Rouge plant by using flexible equipment and new processes. Employees work in teams and use Internet-connected PCs on the shop floor to share their concerns instantly with suppliers or product engineers. Workstations were redesigned to make them more ergonomic and reduce repetitive-strain injuries. "If you feel good while you're working, I think quality and productivity will increase, and Ford thinks that too, otherwise, they wouldn't do this," observed Jerry Sullivan, president of United Auto Workers Local 600.[58]

Human diversity refers to the mix in the workplace of people from different races, cultures, and backgrounds. Realizing that the demographics are changing toward an increasing percentage of minorities and women in the workforce, companies are now concerned with hiring and promoting people without regard to ethnic background. According to a study reported by *Fortune* magazine, companies that pursue diversity outperform the S&P 500.[59] In a survey of 131 leading European companies, 67.2% stated that a diverse workforce can provide competitive advantage.[60] A manager from Nestle stated, "To deliver products that meet the needs of individual consumers, we need people who respect other cultures, embrace diversity, and never discriminate on any basis."[61] Good human resource managers should be working to ensure that people are treated fairly on the job and are not harassed by prejudiced coworkers or managers. Otherwise, they may find themselves subject to lawsuits. Coca-Cola Company, for example, agreed to pay $192.5 million because of discrimination against African-American salaried employees in pay, promotions, and evaluations from 1995 to 2000. According to Chairman and CEO Douglas Daft, "Sometimes things happen in an unintentional manner. And I've made it clear that can't happen anymore."[62]

An organization's human resources may be the key to achieving a sustainable competitive advantage. Advances in technology are copied almost immediately by competitors around the world. However, people are not always willing to move to other companies in other countries. This means that the only long-term resource advantage remaining to corporations operating in industrialized nations may lie in the area of skilled human resources. Research reveals that competitive strategies are more successfully executed in companies with a high level of commitment to their employees than in firms with less commitment.[63]

Strategic Information Systems/Technology Issues

The primary task of a manager of information systems/technology is to design and manage the flow of information in an organization in ways that improve productivity and decision making. Information must be collected, stored, and synthesized in such a manner that it will answer important operating and strategic questions. A corporation's information system can be a strength or a weakness in multiple areas of strategic management. It can not only aid in environmental scanning and in controlling a company's many activities, it can also be used as a strategic weapon in gaining competitive advantage.

Impact on Performance

Information systems/technology offers four main contributions to corporate performance. *First* (beginning in the 1970s with mainframe computers), it is used to automate existing back-office processes, such as payroll, human resource records, and accounts payable and receivable, and to establish huge databases. *Second* (beginning in the 1980s), it is used to automate individual tasks, such as keeping track of clients and expenses, through the use of PCs with word processing and spreadsheet software. Corporate databases are accessed to provide sufficient data to analyze the data and create what-if scenarios. These first two contributions tend to focus on reducing costs. *Third* (beginning in the 1990s), it is used to enhance key business functions, such as marketing and operations. This third contribution focuses on productivity improvements. The system provides customer support and help in distribution and logistics. For example, FedEx found that by allowing customers to directly access its package-tracking database via its Internet web site instead of their having to talk to a human operator, the company saved up to $2 million annually.[64] Business processes are analyzed to increase efficiency and productivity via reengineering. Enterprise resource planning (ERP) application software, such as SAP, PeopleSoft, Oracle, Baan, and J.D. Edwards, are used to integrate worldwide business activities so that employees need to enter information only once, and then that information is available to all corporate systems (including accounting) around the world. *Fourth* (beginning in 2000), it is used to develop competitive advantage. For example, American Hospital Supply (AHS), a leading manufacturer and distributor of a broad line of products for doctors, laboratories, and hospitals, developed an order-entry distribution system that directly linked the majority of its customers to AHS computers. The system was successful because it simplified ordering processes for customers, reduced costs for both AHS and customers, and allowed AHS to provide pricing incentives to the customer. As a result, customer loyalty was high, and AHS' share of the market became large.

A current trend in corporate information systems is the increasing use of the Internet for marketing, intranets for internal communication, and extranets for logistics and distribution. An **intranet** is an information network within an organization that also has access to the external worldwide Internet. An intranet typically begins as a way to provide employees with company information such as lists of product prices, employee benefits, and company policies. It is likely to be converted into an extranet for supply-chain management. An **extranet** is an information network within an organization that is available to key suppliers and customers. The key issue in building an extranet is the creation of fire walls to block extranet users from accessing the firm's or other users' confidential data. Once this is accomplished, the company can allow employees, customers, and suppliers to access information and conduct business on the Internet in a completely automated manner. By connecting these groups, a company hopes to obtain a competitive advantage by reducing the time needed to design and bring new products to market, slashing inventories, customizing manufacturing, and entering new markets.[65]

Supply-Chain Management

The expansion of the marketing-oriented Internet into intranets and extranets is making significant contributions to organizational performance through supply chain management. **Supply-chain management** is the forming of networks for sourcing raw materials, manufacturing products or creating services, storing and distributing goods, and delivering goods to customers and consumers.[66] In a 2003 survey, more than 85% of senior executives stated that improving their firm's supply-chain performance was a top priority. Companies, such as Wal-Mart, Dell, and Toyota, that are known to be exemplars in supply-chain management spend only 4% of their revenues on supply-chain costs compared to 10% by the average firm.[67]

Industry leaders are integrating modern information systems into their corporate value chains to harmonize companywide efforts and to achieve competitive advantage. For example, Heineken distributors input actual depletion figures and replenishment orders to the Netherlands brewer through their linked web pages. This interactive planning system generates time-phased orders based on actual usage rather than on projected demand. Distributors are then able to modify plans based on local conditions or changes in marketing. Heineken uses these modifications to adjust brewing and supply schedules. As a result of this system, lead times have been reduced from the traditional 10–12 weeks to 4–6 weeks. This time savings is especially useful in an industry competing on product freshness. In another example, P&G participates in an information network to move the company's line of consumer products through Wal-Mart's many stores. As part of the network with Wal-Mart, P&G knows by cash register and by store what products have passed through the system every hour of each day. The network is linked by satellite communications on a real-time basis. With actual point-of-sale information, products are replenished to meet current demand and minimize stockouts while maintaining exceptionally low inventories.[68]

5.5 The Strategic Audit: A Checklist for Organizational Analysis

One way of conducting an organizational analysis to ascertain a company's strengths and weaknesses is by using a Strategic Audit, as shown in **Appendix 1.A** at the end of **Chapter 1**. The audit provides a checklist of questions, by area of concern. For example, Part IV of the audit examines corporate structure, culture, and resources. It looks at organizational resources and capabilities in terms of the functional areas of marketing, finance, R&D, operations, human resources, and information systems, among others.

5.6 Synthesis of Internal Factors

After strategists have scanned the internal organizational environment and identified factors for their particular corporation, they may want to summarize their analysis of these factors by using a form such as that given in **Table 5–2**. This **IFAS (Internal Factor Analysis Summary) Table** is one way to organize the internal factors into the generally accepted categories of strengths and weaknesses as well as to analyze how well a particular company's management is responding to these specific factors in light of the perceived importance of these factors to the company. Strategists can use the VRIO framework (Value, Rareness, Imitability, & Organization) to assess the importance of each of the factors that might be considered strengths. Except for its internal orientation, an IFAS Table is built the same way as the EFAS Table described in **Chapter 4** (in **Table 4–5**). To use an IFAS Table, complete the following steps:

1. In **Column 1 (*Internal Factors*)**, list the 8 to 10 most important strengths and weaknesses facing the company.

TABLE 5–2 INTERNAL FACTOR ANALYSIS SUMMARY (IFAS TABLE): MAYTAG AS EXAMPLE

Internal Factors	Weight	Rating	Weighted Score	Comments
1	2	3	4	5
Strengths				
• Quality Maytag culture	.15	5.0	.75	Quality key to success
• Experienced top management	.05	4.2	.21	Know appliances
• Vertical integration	.10	3.9	.39	Dedicated factories
• Employer relations	.05	3.0	.15	Good, but deteriorating
• Hoover's international orientation	.15	2.8	.42	Hoover name in cleaners
Weaknesses				
• Process-oriented R&D	.05	2.2	.11	Slow on new products
• Distribution channels	.05	2.0	.10	Superstores replacing small dealers
• Financial position	.15	2.0	.30	High debt load
• Global positioning	.20	2.1	.42	Hoover weak outside the United Kingdom and Australia
• Manufacturing facilities	.05	4.0	.20	Investing now
Total Scores	1.00		3.05	

Notes:
1. List strengths and weaknesses (8–10) in Column 1.
2. Weight each factor from **1.0** (Most Important) to **0.0** (Not Important) in Column 2 based on that factor's probable impact on the company's strategic position. **The total weights must sum to 1.00.**
3. Rate each factor from **5.0** (Outstanding) to **1.0** (Poor) in Column 3 based on the company's response to that factor.
4. Multiply each factor's weight times its rating to obtain each factor's weighted score in Column 4.
5. Use Column 5 (comments) for rationale used for each factor.
6. Add the individual weighted scores to obtain the total weighted score for the company in Column 4. This tells how well the company is responding to the factors in its internal environment.

Source: T. L. Wheelen and J. D. Hunger, "Internal Factor Analysis Summary (IFAS)." Copyright © 1987, 1988, 1989, 1990, and 2005 by T. L. Wheelen. Copyright © 1991, 2003, and 2005 by Wheelen and Hunger Associates. Reprinted by permission.

2. In **Column 2 (*Weight*)**, assign a weight to each factor, from 1.0 (Most Important) to 0.0 (Not Important), based on that factor's probable impact on the particular company's current strategic position. The higher the weight, the more important this factor is to the current and future success of the company. **(All weights must sum to 1.0, regardless of the number of factors.)**
3. In **Column 3 (*Rating*)**, assign a rating to each factor from 5.0 (Outstanding) to 1.0 (Poor), based on management's specific response to that particular factor. Each rating is a judgment regarding how well the company's management is currently dealing with each specific internal factor.
4. In **Column 4 (*Weighted Score*)**, multiply the weight in **Column 2** for each factor by its rating in **Column 3** to obtain that factor's weighted score. This results in a weighted score for each factor ranging from **5.0** (Outstanding) to **1.0** (Poor), with 3.0 as Average.

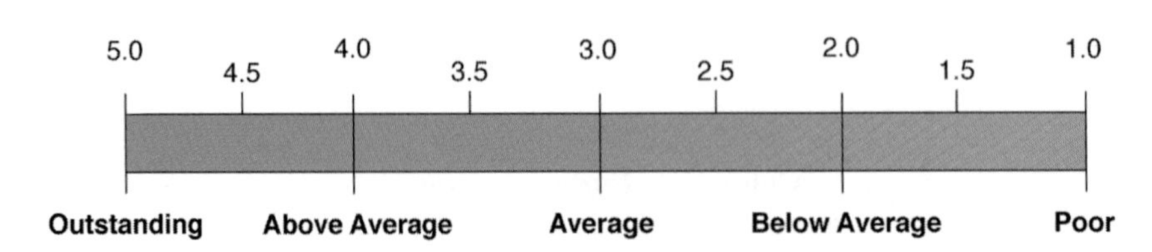

5. In **Column 5** (***Comments***), note why a particular factor was selected and how its weight and rating were estimated.
6. Finally, add the weighted scores for all the internal factors in **Column 4** to determine the total weighted score for that particular company. The **total weighted score** indicates how well a particular company is responding to current and expected factors in its internal environment. The score can be used to compare that firm to other firms in its industry. Check to ensure that the total weighted score truly reflects the company's current performance in terms of profitability and market share. **The total weighted score for an average firm in an industry is always 3.0.**

As an example of this procedure, **Table 5–2** includes a number of internal factors for Maytag Corporation in 1995 (before Maytag sold its European and Australian operations), with corresponding weights, ratings, and weighted scores provided. Note that Maytag's total weighted score is 3.05, meaning that the corporation is about average compared to the strengths and weaknesses of others in the major home appliance industry.

5.7 Conclusion

In 1991, Kentucky Fried Chicken changed its name to KFC in an attempt to broaden its image away from fried chicken. KFC management had noted the societal trend toward healthier eating and was worried that its signature item was in decline. The company responded to this trend by introducing "Colonel's Rotisserie Gold" chicken but was forced to drop it after the roasters kept breaking down. Not wanting to give up, management later introduced an "Oven-Roasted" line of chicken. After promoting the product for only three months, CEO David Novak admitted that the roasted line was a disappointment. "We don't think we came out of the box in the roasted category with the best effort that we could have," explained Novak. Deciding to refocus on its signature fried chicken items, management aired a new pool of television commercials extolling the health benefits of its fried chicken—only to be charged by the Federal Trade Commission of making false claims. Nevertheless, the company continued its preparations for a new line of salads being introduced later in 2004.[69]

Monitoring the external environment is only one part of environmental scanning. Strategists also need to scan a corporation's internal environment to identify its resources, capabilities, and competencies. What are its strengths and weaknesses? At KFC, management clearly noted that the environment was changing in a way that made its primary product less desirable. In attempting to offer a product that was more in line with the changing market, it failed to effectively deal with its weaknesses in new product development and marketing. Its two attempts to introduce roasted chicken were failures. Management's next mistake was using advertising to try to convince the public that its fried chicken was a health food. This is a classic example of a "reactor" company attempting to stay in business by jumping from one ill-advised strategy to another, without realizing that it didn't have the capabilities in key functional areas to support a new strategy.

Strategy Bits

- Countries with the highest percentages of their populations in the workforce are China (56.5%), Switzerland (56.1%), Thailand (54.4%), Iceland (54.2%), and Denmark (53.8%). Canada ranks 8th, at 52.4%, and the United States ranks 25th, at 49.0%.
- Countries with the highest percentages of women in the workforce are Belarus (52.9%), Cambodia (51.6%), Malawi (50.2%), Moldova (50.1%), and The Bahamas (49.4%). The United States ranks 19th, at 46.6%, and Canada ranks 23rd, at 46.0%.[70]

Discussion Questions

1. What is the relevance of the resource-based view of a firm to strategic management in a global environment?
2. How can value-chain analysis help identify a company's strengths and weaknesses?
3. In what ways can a corporation's structure and culture be internal strengths or weaknesses?
4. What are the pros and cons of management's using the experience curve to determine strategy?
5. How might a firm's management decide whether it should continue to invest in current known technology or in new, but untested, technology? What factors might encourage or discourage such a shift?

Strategic Practice Exercises

1. Based on the information presented in the Conclusion to this chapter, what would you recommend to the management of KFC? Should it continue to experiment with healthier menu items, or should it just "stick to its knitting" by staying with fried food? What resources and competencies are needed to adopt a health food strategy?
2. Can you analyze a corporation by using the Internet? Try the following exercise:
   a. Form into teams of around three to five people. Select a well-known publicly owned company to research. Inform the instructor of your choice.
   b. Assign each person a separate task. One might be to find the latest financial statements. Another would be to learn as much as possible about the company's top management and board of directors. Another might be to identify its business model. Another might be to identify its key competitors.
   c. Conduct research on the company by *using the Internet only*.
   d. Meet with your team members to discuss what you have found. What are the company's opportunities, threats, strengths, and weaknesses? Go back to the Internet for more information, if needed.
   e. Prepare a three- to five-page typed report of the company. The report should include information that answers the following questions:
      i. Does the firm have any core competencies? Are any of these distinctive (better than the competition) competencies? Does the firm have any competitive advantage? Provide a SWOT analysis, using EFAS and IFAS Tables.
      ii. What is the likely future of this firm if it continues on its current path?
      iii. Would you buy stock in this company? Assume that your team has $25,000 to invest. Allocate the money among the four to five primary competitors in this industry. List the companies, the number of shares you would purchase of each, the cost of each share as of a given date, and the total cost for each purchase, assuming a typical commission used by an Internet broker, such as E-Trade.

Key Terms

autonomous (self-managing) work team (p. 125)
basic R&D (p. 121)
brand (p. 118)
business model (p. 110)
capability (p. 106)
capital budgeting (p. 120)
center of gravity (p. 112)
cluster (p. 107)
competency (p. 106)
concurrent engineering (p. 125)
conglomerate structure (p. 115)
continuous system (p. 124)
continuum of sustainability (p. 109)
core competency (p. 106)
corporate brand (p. 119)
corporate culture (p. 116)
corporate reputation (p. 119)
cross-functional work team (p. 125)
cultural integration (p. 116)
cultural intensity (p. 116)
distinctive competency (p. 106)
divisional structure (p. 115)
durability (p. 108)
economy of scale (p. 125)
economy of scope (p. 125)
engineering (or process) R&D (p. 121)
experience curve (p. 124)
explicit knowledge (p. 109)
extranet (p. 128)
financial leverage (p. 120)
flexible manufacturing (p. 125)
functional structure (p. 114)
human diversity (p. 127)
IFAS Table (p. 129)
imitability (p. 108)
intermittent system (p. 123)
internal strategic factor (p. 106)
intranet (p. 128)
linkage (p. 113)
market position (p. 118)
market segmentation (p. 118)
marketing mix (p. 118)
mass customization (p. 125)

operating leverage (p. 124)
organizational analysis (p. 106)
organizational structure (p. 114)
primary activity (p. 113)
product life cycle (p. 118)
product R&D (p. 121)
quality of work life (p. 127)
R&D intensity (p. 120)
R&D mix (p. 121)
replicability (p. 108)
resource (p. 106)
reverse engineering (p. 108)
simple structure (p. 114)
strategic business unit (SBU) (p. 115)
support activity (p. 113)
supply-chain management (p. 128)
tacit knowledge (p. 109)
technological competence (p. 121)
technological discontinuity (p. 122)
technology transfer (p. 121)
transferability (p. 108)
transparency (p. 108)
value chain (p. 111)
VRIO framework (p. 106)
virtual team (p. 126)

PART ENDING VIDEO CASE PART TWO

Newbury Comics, Inc.

ENVIRONMENTAL SCANNING AND ORGANIZATIONAL ANALYSIS

Newbury Comics Cofounders, Mike Dreese and John Brusger, parlayed $2,000 and a comic book collection into a thriving chain of 22 stores spanning the New England region. Known to be *the* place to shop for everything from the best of the underground/independent music scene to major label superstars, the chain also stocks a wide variety of non-music related items such as T-shirts, Dr. (doc) Martens shoes, posters, jewelry, cosmetics, books, magazines, and other trendy items.

In Part Two, **"Scanning the Environment**," the video case addresses the identification of external environmental variables, industry analysis, and organizational analysis. Newbury Comics, Inc., Cofounders Mike and John, and Jan Johannet, Manager for one of the New Hampshire stores, reveal more about the development of the company. They discuss factors contributing to the successful growth of Newbury Comics. They describe how their diverse customers plus the emergence of bootlegging (selling illegal copies) and burning discs (copying 1 CD onto another CD) led the company to begin offering used CDs in its stores.

Used CDs have become a very important business for Newbury Comics. Mike Dreese reports that used CDs account for $6 to 7 million in annual sales and $4 million in annual gross profits for the company. This fact is remarkable given that the firm's overall annual sales and pre-tax profits are $75 million and $8 million, respectively. According to John Brusger and Jan Johannet, the new CD market turned "soft" when mass merchandisers like Target and Best Buy began selling CDs and Internet companies, such as Napster, offered the downloading of music. John and Mike wanted another product to supplement their sales of new CDs. They scanned their environment to learn if it made sense to enter this business.

They asked the owners of local specialty music stores for information. These "mom and pop" retailers had been buying and selling used CDs for years and were very familiar with this product. Mike refers to the local mom and pop retailers as his "strategic alliance of information sources." According to John, surveys of current customers revealed that a large number of Newbury Comics customers wanted the company to be in the used CD business. Management analyzed the competition for used CDs in Newbury Comics' market area. Used CDs appeared to have high sales potential. The immediate competition was composed of mom and pop specialty music retailers; no chain stores offered used CDs at that time. According to Mike Dreese, the local stores weren't doing a good job of marketing used CDs.

According to Mike and Jan, Newbury Comics has several internal strengths, which uniquely fit the used CD market. The stores have a wide variety of customers and a staff with "knowledge of the street." The employees live the lifestyle of Newbury Comics' discriminating customers and are thus able to identify trends before the public at large learns of them. Consequently, the stores are able to purchase an excellent selection of underground music in addition to the usual top 50 and older CDs. Mike Dreese states that new entrant specialist shops into the used CD business are "not a threat to us." He is concerned that established chains such as Tower Records, Best Buy, and Music Land might someday enter the used CD business.

Concepts Illustrated in the Video

- Environmental Scanning
- Industry Analysis
- Organizational Analysis
- Identifying Societal Trends
- Rivalry Among Existing Firms
- Threat of New Entrants/Entry Barriers
- Threat of Substitute Products
- Industry Evolution
- Core and Distinctive Competencies
- Corporate Culture

Study Questions

1. How does Newbury Comics conduct environmental scanning? How well is it doing it?
2. Describe the competitors in Newbury Comics' market area. Do they form strategic groups? How do the actions of competitors affect Newbury Comics (and vice versa)?
3. What are the substitutes for CDs? Are they a threat or an opportunity for Newbury Comics?
4. What external factors played a role in the decision to enter the used CD business? What other businesses should the company consider entering?
5. What are the core competencies of Newbury Comics? Are they distinctive? Why?

CHAPTER 6

Strategy Formulation: Situation Analysis and Business Strategy

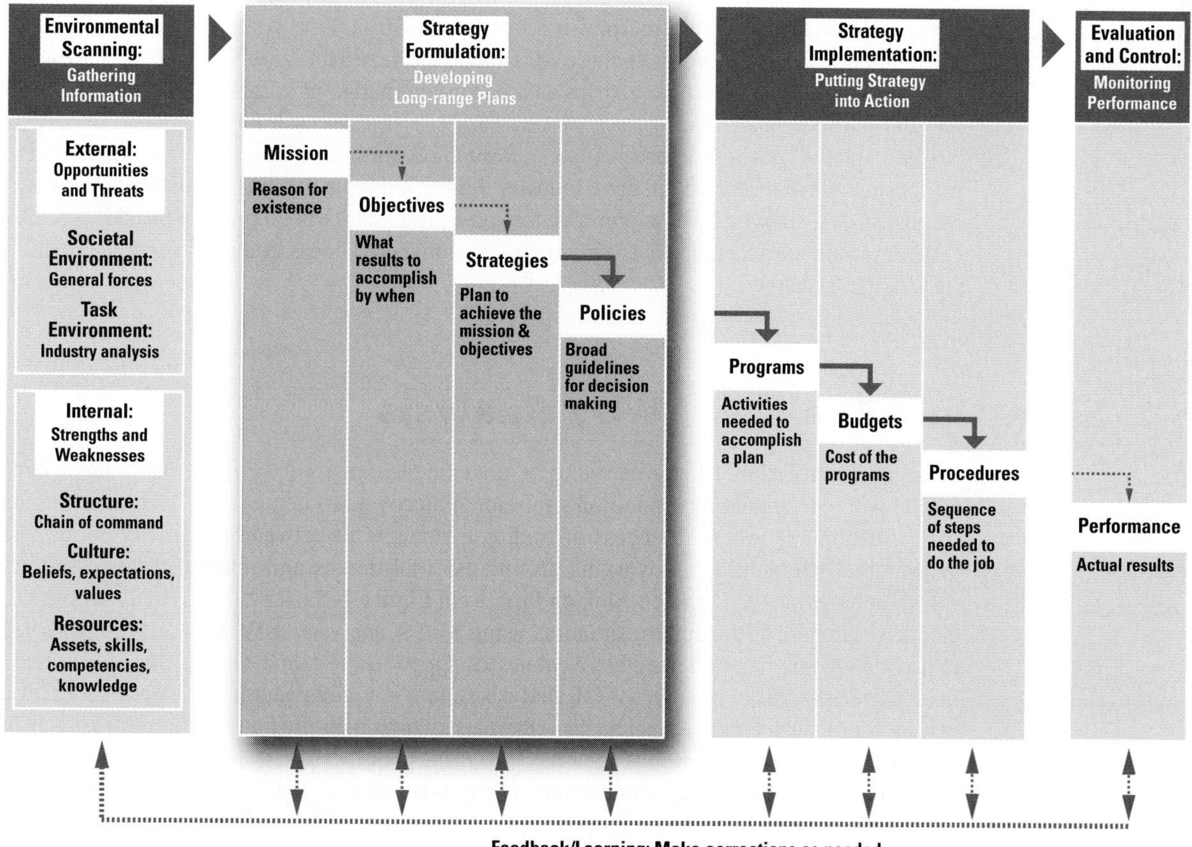

Learning Objectives

After reading this chapter, you should be able to:

- Organize environmental and organizational information by using SWOT analysis and an SFAS Matrix
- Generate strategic options by using the TOWS matrix
- Understand the competitive and cooperative strategies available to corporations
- List the competitive tactics that would accompany competitive strategies
- Identify the basic types of strategic alliances

MIDAMAR CORPORATION IS A FAMILY-OWNED COMPANY IN CEDAR RAPIDS, IOWA, THAT has carved out a growing niche for itself in the world food industry: supplying food prepared according to strict religious standards. The company specializes in halal foods, which are produced and processed according to Islamic law for sale to Muslims. Why did it focus on this one type of food? According to owner-founder Bill Aossey, "It's a big world, and you can only specialize in so many places." Although halal foods are not as widely known as kosher foods (processed according to Judaic law), their market is growing along with Islam, the world's fastest-growing religion. Midamar purchases halal-certified meat from Midwestern companies certified to conduct halal processing. Certification requires practicing Muslims schooled in halal processing to slaughter the livestock and to oversee meat and poultry processing.

Aossey is a practicing Muslim who did not imagine such a vast market when he founded his business in 1974. "People thought it would be a passing fad," remarked Aossey. The company has grown to the point where it now exports halal-certified beef, lamb, and poultry to hotels, restaurants, and distributors in 30 countries throughout Asia, Africa, Europe, and North America. Its customers include McDonald's, Pizza Hut, and KFC. McDonald's, for example, uses Midamar's turkey strips as a bacon-alternative in a breakfast product recently introduced in Singapore.[1]

Midamar is successful because its chief executive formulated a strategy designed to give it an advantage in a very competitive industry. It is an example of a differentiation focus competitive strategy in which a company focuses on a particular target market to provide a differentiated product or service. This strategy is one of the business competitive strategies discussed in this chapter.

6.1 Situational Analysis: SWOT Analysis

Strategy formulation, often referred to as strategic planning or long-range planning, is concerned with developing a corporation's mission, objectives, strategies, and policies. It begins with situation analysis: the process of finding a strategic fit between external opportunities and internal strengths while working around external threats and internal weaknesses. As shown in the Strategic Decision-Making Process in **Figure 1–5**, step 5(a) is "analyzing strategic factors in light of the current situation, using SWOT analysis." **SWOT** is an acronym used to describe the particular Strengths, Weaknesses, Opportunities, and Threats that are strategic factors for a specific company. SWOT analysis should not only result in the identification of a corporation's distinctive competencies—the particular capabilities and resources that a firm possesses and the superior way in which they are used—but also in the identification of opportunities that the firm is not currently able to take advantage of due to a lack of appropriate resources. Over the years, SWOT analysis has proven to be the most enduring analytical technique using in strategic management. For example, a survey of 113 manufacturing and service companies in the United Kingdom reported the five most-used tools and techniques in strategic analysis to be (1) spreadsheet what-if analysis, (2) analysis of key or critical success factors, (3) financial analysis of competitors, (4) SWOT analysis, and (5) core capabilities analysis.[2] It is very likely that these have a similar rate of usage in the rest of the world.

It can be said that the essence of strategy is opportunity divided by capacity.[3] An opportunity by itself has no real value unless a company has the capacity (i.e., resources) to take advantage of that opportunity. This approach, however, considers only opportunities and strengths when considering alternative strategies. By itself, a distinctive competency in a key resource or capability is no guarantee of competitive advantage. Weaknesses in other resource areas can prevent a strategy from being successful. SWOT can thus be used to take a broader view of strategy through the formula SA = O/(S–W) that is, (Strategic Alternative equals Opportunity divided by Strengths minus Weaknesses). This reflects an important issue strategic managers face: Should we invest more in our strengths to make them even stronger (a distinctive competence) or should we invest in our weaknesses to at least make them competitive?

SWOT analysis, by itself, is not a panacea. Some of the primary criticisms of SWOT analysis are:

- It generates lengthy lists.
- It uses no weights to reflect priorities.
- It uses ambiguous words and phrases.
- The same factor can be placed in two categories (e.g., a strength may also be a weakness).
- There is no obligation to verify opinions with data or analysis.
- It requires only a single level of analysis.
- There is no logical link to strategy implementation.[4]

Generating a Strategic Factors Analysis Summary (SFAS) Matrix

The EFAS and IFAS Tables plus the SFAS Matrix have been developed to deal with the criticisms of SWOT analysis. When used together, they are a powerful analytical set of tools for strategic analysis. The **SFAS (Strategic Factors Analysis Summary) Matrix** summarizes an organization's strategic factors by combining the external factors from the EFAS Table with the internal factors from the IFAS Table. The EFAS and IFAS examples given of Maytag Corporation (as it was in 1995) in **Tables 4–5** and **5–2** list a total of 20 internal and external factors. These are too many factors for most people to use in strategy formulation. The SFAS Matrix requires a strategic decision maker to condense these strengths, weaknesses, opportunities, and threats into fewer than 10 strategic factors. This is done by reviewing and revising the weight given each factor. The revised weights reflect the priority of each factor as a determinant of the company's future success. The highest-weighted EFAS and IFAS factors should appear in the SFAS Matrix.

As shown in **Figure 6–1**, you can create an SFAS Matrix by following these steps:

1. In **Column 1** (***Strategic Factors***), list the most important EFAS and IFAS items. After each factor, indicate whether it is a Strength **(S)**, a Weakness **(W)**, an Opportunity **(O)**, or a Threat **(T)**.
2. In **Column 2** (***Weight***), assign weights for all the internal and external strategic factors. As with the EFAS and IFAS Tables presented earlier, **the weight column must total 1.00**. This means that the weights calculated earlier for EFAS and IFAS will probably have to be adjusted.
3. In **Column 3** (***Rating***) assign a rating of how the company's management is responding to each of the strategic factors. These ratings will probably (but not always) be the same as those listed in the EFAS and IFAS Tables.

TABLE 5–2 INTERNAL FACTOR ANALYSIS SUMMARY (IFAS): MAYTAG AS EXAMPLE (SELECTION OF STRATEGIC FACTORS)*

Internal Strategic Factors	Weight	Rating	Weighted Score	Comments
1	2	3	4	5
Strengths				
S1 Quality Maytag culture	.15	5.0	.75	Quality key to success
S2 Experienced top management	.05	4.2	.21	Know appliances
S3 Vertical integration	.10	3.9	.39	Dedicated factories
S4 Employee relations	.05	3.0	.15	Good, but deteriorating
S5 Hoover's international orientation	.15	2.8	.42	Hoover name in cleaners
Weaknesses				
W1 Process-oriented R&D	.05	2.2	.11	Slow on new products
W2 Distribution channels	.05	2.0	.10	Superstores replacing small dealers
W3 Financial position	.15	2.0	.30	High debt load
W4 Global positioning	.20	2.1	.42	Hoover weak outside the United Kingdom and Australia
W5 Manufacturing facilities	.05	4.0	.20	Investing now
Total Scores	1.00		3.05	

TABLE 4–5 EXTERNAL FACTOR ANALYSIS SUMMARY (EFAS): MAYTAG AS EXAMPLE (SELECTION OF STRATEGIC FACTORS)*

External Strategic Factors	Weight	Rating	Weighted Score	Comments
1	2	3	4	5
Opportunities				
O1 Economic integration of European Community	.20	4.1	.82	Acquisition of Hoover
O2 Demographics favor quality appliances	.10	5.0	.50	Maytag quality
O3 Economic development of Asia	.05	1.0	.05	Low Maytag presence
O4 Opening of Eastern Europe	.05	2.0	.10	Will take time
O5 Trend to "Super Stores"	.10	1.8	.18	Maytag weak in this channel
Threats				
T1 Increasing government regulations	.10	4.3	.43	Well positioned
T2 Strong U.S. competition	.10	4.0	.40	Well positioned
T3 Whirlpool and Electrolux strong globally	.15	3.0	.45	Hoover weak globally
T4 New product advances	.05	1.2	.06	Questionable
T5 Japanese appliance companies	.10	1.6	.16	Only Asian presence is Australia
Total Scores	1.00		3.15	

*The most important external and internal factors are identified in the EFAS and IFAS tables as shown here by shading these factors.

Figure 6–1 Strategic Factor Analysis Summary (SFAS) Matrix

1	2	3	4	Duration 5			6
Strategic Factors (Select the most important opportunities/threats from EFAS, Table 4–5 and the most important strengths and weaknesses from IFAS, Table 5–2)	**Weight**	**Rating**	**Weighted Score**	**SHORT**	**INTERMEDIATE**	**LONG**	**Comments**
S1 Quality Maytag culture (S)	.10	5.0	.50			X	Quality key to success
S5 Hoover's international orientation (S)	.10	2.8	.28	X	X		Name recognition
W3 Financial position (W)	.10	2.0	.20	X	X		High debt
W4 Global positioning (W)	.15	2.2	.33		X	X	Only in N.A., U.K., and Australia
O1 Economic integration of European Community (O)	.10	4.1	.41			X	Acquisition of Hoover
O2 Demographics favor quality (O)	.10	5.0	.50		X		Maytag quality
O5 Trend to super stores (O + T)	.10	1.8	.18	X			Weak in this channel
T3 Whirlpool and Electrolux (T)	.15	3.0	.45	X			Dominate industry
T5 Japanese appliance companies (T)	.10	1.6	.16			X	Asian presence
Total Scores	1.00		3.01				

Notes:

1. List each of the most important factors developed in your IFAS and EFAS Tables in Column 1.
2. Weight each factor from 1.0 (Most Important) to 0.0 (Not Important) in Column 2 based on that factor's probable impact on the company's strategic position. **The total weights must sum to 1.00.**
3. Rate each factor from 5.0 (Outstanding) to 1.0 (Poor) in Column 3 based on the company's response to that factor.
4. Multiply each factor's weight times its rating to obtain each factor's weighted score in Column 4.
5. For duration in Column 5, check appropriate column (short term—less than 1 year; intermediate—1 to 3 years; long term—over 3 years).
6. Use Column 6 (comments) for rationale used for each factor.

Source: T. L. Wheelen and J. D. Hunger, "Strategic Factors Analysis Summary (SFAS)." Copyright © 1987, 1988, 1989, 1990, 1991, 1992, 1993, 1994, 1995, 1996 and 2005 by T. L. Wheelen. Copyright © 1997 and 2005 by Wheelen and Hunger Associates. Reprinted by permission.

4. In **Column 4 (*Weighted Score*)** multiply the weight in **Column 2** for each factor by its rating in **Column 3** to obtain the factor's rated score. This results in a weighted score for each factor ranging from **5.0** (outstanding) to **1.0** (Poor), with **3.0** as average.
5. In **Column 5 (*Duration*)**, depicted in **Figure 6–1**, indicate **short-term** (less than one year), **intermediate-term** (one to three years), or **long-term** (three years and beyond).
6. In **Column 6 (*Comments*)**, repeat or revise your comments for each strategic factor from the previous EFAS and IFAS Tables. **The total weighted score for the average firm in an industry is always 3.0**

The resulting SFAS Matrix is a listing of the firm's external and internal strategic factors in one table. The example given in **Figure 6–1** is for Maytag Corporation in 1995, before the firm sold its European and Australian operations. The SFAS Matrix includes only the most important factors gathered from environmental scanning and thus provides information that is essential for strategy formulation. The use of EFAS and IFAS Tables together with the SFAS Matrix deals with some of the criticisms of SWOT analysis. For example, the use of the SFAS Matrix reduces the list of factors to a manageable number, puts weights on each factor, and allows one factor to be listed as both a strength and a weakness (or as an opportunity and a threat).

Finding a Propitious Niche

One desired outcome of analyzing strategic factors is identifying a niche where an organization can use its core competencies to take advantage of a particular market opportunity. A niche is a need in the marketplace that is currently unsatisfied. The goal is to find a **propitious niche**—an extremely favorable niche that is so well suited to the firm's internal and external environment that other corporations are not likely to challenge or dislodge it.[5] A niche is propitious to the extent that it currently is just large enough for one firm to satisfy its demand. After a firm has found and filled that niche, it is not worth a potential competitor's time or money to also go after the same niche.

Finding such a niche is not always easy. A firm's management must be always looking for a **strategic window**—that is, a unique market opportunity that is available only for a particular time. The first firm through a strategic window can occupy a propitious niche and discourage competition (if the firm has the required internal strengths). One company that has successfully found a propitious niche is Frank J. Zamboni & Company, the manufacturer of the machines that smooth the ice at ice skating rinks. Frank Zamboni invented the unique tractor-like machine in 1949, and no one has found a substitute for what it does. Before the machine was invented, people had to clean and scrape the ice by hand to prepare the surface for skating. Now hockey fans look forward to intermissions just to watch "the Zamboni" slowly drive up and down the ice rink, turning rough, scraped ice into a smooth mirror surface—almost like magic. So long as Zamboni's company is able to produce the machines in the quantity and quality desired, at a reasonable price, it's not worth another company's while to go after Frank Zamboni & Company's propitious niche.

As a niche grows, so can a company within that niche—by increasing its operations' capacity or through alliances with larger firms. The key is to identify a market opportunity in which the first firm to reach that market segment can obtain and keep dominant market share. For example, Church & Dwight was the first company in the United States to successfully market sodium bicarbonate for use in cooking. Its Arm & Hammer brand baking soda is still found in 95% of all U.S. households. The propitious niche concept is crucial to the software industry. Small initial demand in emerging markets allows new entrepreneurial ventures to go after niches too small to be noticed by established companies. When Microsoft developed its first disk operating system (DOS) in 1980 for IBM's personal computers, for example, the demand for such open systems software was very small—a small niche for a then very small Microsoft. The company was able to fill that niche and to successfully grow with it.

Niches can also change—sometimes faster than a firm can adapt to that change. A company's management may discover in their situation analysis that they need to invest heavily in the firm's capabilities to keep them competitively strong in a changing niche. South African Breweries (SAB), for example, took this approach when management realized that the only way to keep competitors out of its market was to continuously invest in increased productivity and infrastructure in order to keep its prices very low. See the GLOBAL ISSUE feature to see how SAB was able to successfully defend its market niche during significant changes in its environment.

GLOBAL ISSUE

SAB Defends Its Propitious Niche

Out of 50 beers drunk by South Africans, 49 are brewed by South African Breweries (SAB). Founded more than a century ago, SAB controlled most of the local beer market by 1950 with brands such as Castle and Lion. When the government repealed the ban on the sale of alcohol to blacks in the 1960s, SAB and other brewers competed for the rapidly growing market. SAB fought successfully to retain its dominance of the market. With the end of apartheid, foreign brewers have been tempted to break SAB's near-monopoly but have been deterred by the entry barriers SAB has erected:

Entry Barrier #1: Every year for the past two decades SAB has reduced its prices. The "real" (adjusted for inflation) price of its beer is now half what it was during the 1970s. SAB has been able to achieve this through a continuous emphasis on productivity improvements—boosting production while cutting the workforce almost in half. Keeping prices low has been key to SAB's avoiding charges of abusing its monopoly.

Entry Barrier #2: In South Africa's poor and rural areas, roads are rough, and electricity is undependable. SAB has long experience in transporting crates to remote villages along bad roads and making sure that distributors have refrigerators (and electricity generators if needed). Many of its distributors are former employees who have been helped by the company to start their own trucking businesses.

Entry Barrier #3: Most of the beer sold in South Africa is sold through unlicensed pubs called *shebeens*—most of which date back to apartheid, when blacks were not allowed licenses. Although the current government of South Africa would be pleased to grant pub licenses to blacks, the shebeen owners don't want them. They enjoy not paying any taxes. SAB cannot sell directly to the shebeens, but it does so indirectly through wholesalers. The government, in turn, ignores the situation, preferring that people drink SAB beer than potentially deadly moonshine.

To break into South Africa, a new entrant would have to build large breweries and a substantial distribution network. SAB would, in turn, probably reduce its prices still further to defend its market. The difficulties of operating in South Africa are too great, the market is growing too slowly, and (given SAB's low cost position) the likely profit margin is too low to justify entering the market. Some foreign brewers, such as Heineken, would rather use SAB to distribute their products throughout South Africa. With its home market secure, SAB purchased Miller Brewing to secure a strong presence in North America.

Source: Summarized from "Big Lion, Small Cage," *The Economist* (August 12, 2000), p. 56, and other sources.

6.2 Review of Mission and Objectives

A reexamination of an organization's current mission and objectives must be made before alternative strategies can be generated and evaluated. Even when formulating strategy, decision makers tend to concentrate on the alternatives—the action possibilities—rather than on a mission to be fulfilled and objectives to be achieved. This tendency is so attractive because it is much easier to deal with alternative courses of action that exist right here and now than to really think about what you want to accomplish in the future. The end result is that we often choose strategies that set our objectives for us rather than having our choices incorporate clear objectives and a mission statement.

Problems in performance can derive from an inappropriate statement of mission, which may be too narrow or too broad. If the mission does not provide a *common thread* (a unifying theme) for a corporation's businesses, managers may be unclear about where the company is heading. Objectives and strategies might be in conflict with each other. Divisions might be competing against one another rather than against outside competition—to the detriment of the corporation as a whole.

A company's objectives can also be inappropriately stated. They can either focus too much on short-term operational goals or be so general that they provide little real guidance. There may be a gap between planned and achieved objectives. When such a gap occurs, either the strategies have to be changed to improve performance or the objectives need to be adjusted downward to be more realistic. Consequently, objectives should be constantly reviewed to ensure their usefulness. This is what happened at Coca-Cola Company in 2004, when management failed to note the growing consumer desire for alternatives to soda pop. In a statement to investors, Chairman and CEO Neville Isdell reported that "the emerging consumer trends in health and wellness were missed. . . . We stopped driving carbonated soft drinks, and we're the world leader." Isdell then indicated that weak results should persist into 2005 in the key markets of North America, Germany, and the Philippines. He reported that the company had consequently reduced its sales growth objective for 2005 to 3.5%, down from 5.5%. Operating income growth was also reduced from 10% to 7%. In addition, earnings per share growth was reduced from 12% to less than 10%. Isdell concluded by stating that 2005 "is not going to deliver the kinds of returns that are going to be acceptable to me, as a shareholder."[6]

6.3 Generating Alternative Strategies by Using a TOWS Matrix

Thus far we have discussed how a firm uses SWOT analysis to assess its situation. SWOT can also be used to generate a number of possible alternative strategies. The **TOWS Matrix** (TOWS is just another way of saying SWOT) illustrates how the external opportunities and threats facing a particular corporation can be matched with that company's internal strengths and weaknesses to result in four sets of possible strategic alternatives. (See **Figure 6–2**.) This is a good way to use brainstorming to create alternative strategies that might not otherwise be considered. It forces strategic managers to create various kinds of growth as well as retrenchment strategies. It can be used to generate corporate as well as business strategies.

To generate a TOWS Matrix for Maytag Corporation in 1995, for example, use the External Factor Analysis Summary (EFAS) Table listed in **Table 4–5** from **Chapter 4** and the Internal Factor Analysis Summary (IFAS) Table listed in **Table 5–2** from **Chapter 5**. To build **Figure 6–2**, take the following steps:

Figure 6–2
TOWS Matrix

INTERNAL FACTORS (IFAS) / EXTERNAL FACTORS (EFAS)	**Strengths (S)** List 5 – 10 *internal* strengths here	**Weaknesses (W)** List 5 – 10 *internal* weaknesses here
Opportunities (O) List 5 – 10 *external* opportunities here	**SO Strategies** Generate strategies here that use **strengths** to take **advantage** of **opportunities**	**WO Strategies** Generate strategies here that take **advantage** of **opportunities** by **overcoming weaknesses**
Threats (T) List 5 – 10 *external* threats here	**ST Strategies** Generate strategies here that use **strengths** to **avoid threats**	**WT Strategies** Generate strategies here that **minimize weaknesses** and **avoid threats**

Source: Reprinted from Long-Range Planning, *Vol. 15, No. 2, 1982, Weihrich "The TOWS Matrix—A Tool For Situational Analysis," p. 60. Copyright © 1982 with permission of Elsevier.*

1. In the Opportunities (O) block, list the external opportunities available in the company's or business unit's current and future environment from the EFAS Table (**Table 4–5**).
2. In the Threats (T) block, list the external threats facing the company or unit now and in the future from the EFAS Table (**Table 4–5**).
3. In the Strengths (S) block, list the specific areas of current and future strength for the company or unit from the IFAS Table (**Table 5–2**).
4. In the Weaknesses (W) block, list the specific areas of current and future weakness for the company or unit from the IFAS Table (**Table 5–2**).
5. Generate a series of possible strategies for the company or business unit under consideration based on particular combinations of the four sets of factors:
   - **SO Strategies** are generated by thinking of ways in which a company or business unit could use its strengths to take advantage of opportunities.
   - **ST Strategies** consider a company's or unit's strengths as a way to avoid threats.
   - **WO Strategies** attempt to take advantage of opportunities by overcoming weaknesses.
   - **WT Strategies** are basically defensive and primarily act to minimize weaknesses and avoid threats.

The TOWS Matrix is very useful for generating a series of alternatives that the decision makers of a company or business unit might not otherwise have considered. It can be used for the corporation as a whole (as is done in **Figure 6–3** with Maytag Corporation before it sold Hoover Europe), or it can be used for a specific business unit within a corporation (such as Hoover's floor care products). Nevertheless, using a TOWS Matrix is only one of many ways to generate alternative strategies. Another approach is to evaluate each business unit within a corporation in terms of possible competitive and cooperative strategies.

6.4 Business Strategies

Business strategy focuses on improving the competitive position of a company's or business unit's products or services within the specific industry or market segment that the company or business unit serves. Business strategy can be competitive (battling against all competitors for advantage) and/or cooperative (working with one or more companies to gain advantage against other competitors). Just as corporate strategy asks what industry(ies) the company should be in, business strategy asks how the company or its units should compete or cooperate in each industry.

Porter's Competitive Strategies

Competitive strategy raises the following questions:

- Should we compete on the basis of lower cost (and thus price), or should we differentiate our products or services on some basis other than cost, such as quality or service?
- Should we compete head to head with our major competitors for the biggest but most sought-after share of the market, or should we focus on a niche in which we can satisfy a less sought-after but also profitable segment of the market?

Michael Porter proposes two "generic" competitive strategies for outperforming other corporations in a particular industry: lower cost and differentiation.[7] These strategies are

TABLE 5–2 INTERNAL FACTOR ANALYSIS SUMMARY (IFAS): MAYTAG AS EXAMPLE (SELECTION OF STRATEGIC FACTORS)*

Internal Strategic Factors	Weight	Rating	Weighted Score	Comments
1	2	3	4	5
Strengths				
S1 Quality Maytag culture	.15	5.0	.75	Quality key to success
S2 Experienced top management	.05	4.2	.21	Know appliances
S3 Vertical integration	.10	3.9	.39	Dedicated factories
S4 Employee relations	.05	3.0	.15	Good, but deteriorating
S5 Hoover's international orientation	.15	2.8	.42	Hoover name in cleaners
Weaknesses				
W1 Process-oriented R&D	.05	2.2	.11	Slow on new products
W2 Distribution channels	.05	2.0	.10	Superstores replacing small dealers
W3 Financial position	.15	2.0	.30	High debt load
W4 Global positioning	.20	2.1	.42	Hoover weak outside the United Kingdom and Australia
W5 Manufacturing facilities	.05	4.0	.20	Investing now
Total Scores	1.00		3.05	

TABLE 4–5 EXTERNAL FACTOR ANALYSIS SUMMARY (EFAS): MAYTAG AS EXAMPLE (SELECTION OF STRATEGIC FACTORS)*

External Strategic Factors	Weight	Rating	Weighted Score	Comments
1	2	3	4	5
Opportunities				
O1 Economic integration of European Community	.20	4.1	.82	Acquisition of Hoover
O2 Demographics favor quality appliances	.10	5.0	.50	Maytag quality
O3 Economic development of Asia	.05	1.0	.05	Low Maytag presence
O4 Opening of Eastern Europe	.05	2.0	.10	Will take time
O5 Trend to "Super Stores"	.10	1.8	.18	Maytag weak in this channel
Threats				
T1 Increasing government regulations	.10	4.3	.43	Well positioned
T2 Strong U.S. competition	.10	4.0	.40	Well positioned
T3 Whirlpool and Electrolux strong globally	.15	3.0	.45	Hoover weak globally
T4 New product advances	.05	1.2	.06	Questionable
T5 Japanese appliance companies	.10	1.6	.16	Only Asian presence is Australia
Total Scores	1.00		3.15	

*The most important external and internal factors are identified in the EFAS and IFAS Tables as shown here by shading these factors.

Figure 6–3 Generating TOWS Matrix for Maytag Corporation

Strengths →
Weaknesses →

Internal Factors (IFAS Table 5–2) / **External Factors** (EFAS Table 4–5)	**Strengths (S)**	**Weaknesses (W)**
	S1 Quality Maytag culture S2 Experienced top management S3 Vertical integration S4 Employee relations S5 Hoover's international orientation	W1 Process-oriented R&D W2 Distribution channels W3 Financial position W4 Global positioning W5 Manufacturing facilities
Opportunities (O)	**SO Strategies**	**WO Strategies**
O1 Economic integration of European Community O2 Demographics favor quality O3 Economic development of Asia O4 Opening of Eastern Europe O5 Trend toward super stores	• *Use worldwide Hoover distribution channels to sell both Hoover and Maytag major appliances.* • *Find joint venture partners in Eastern Europe and Asia.*	• *Expand Hoover's presence in continental Europe by improving Hoover quality and reducing manufacturing and distribution costs.* • *Emphasize superstore channel for all non-Maytag brands.*
Threats (T)	**ST Strategies**	**WT Strategies**
T1 Increasing government regulation T2 Strong U.S. competition T3 Whirlpool and Electrolux positioned for global economy T4 New product advances T5 Japanese appliance companies	• *Acquire Raytheon's appliance business to increase U.S. market share.* • *Merge with a Japanese major home appliance company.* • *Sell off all non-Maytag brands and strongly defend Maytag's U.S. niche.*	• *Sell off Dixie-Narco Division to reduce debt.* • *Emphasize cost reduction to reduce break-even point.* • *Sell out to Raytheon or a Japanese firm.*

Opportunities →
Threats →

called generic because they can be pursued by any type or size of business firm, even by not-for-profit organizations:

- **Lower cost strategy** is the ability of a company or a business unit to design, produce, and market a comparable product more efficiently than its competitors.
- **Differentiation strategy** is the ability of a company to provide unique and superior value to the buyer in terms of product quality, special features, or after-sale service.

Porter further proposes that a firm's competitive advantage in an industry is determined by its **competitive scope**—that is, the breadth of the company's or business unit's target market. Before using one of the two generic competitive strategies (lower cost or differentiation), the firm or unit must choose the range of product varieties it will produce, the distribution channels it will employ, the types of buyers it will serve, the geographic areas in which it will sell, and the array of related industries in which it will also compete. This should reflect an understanding of the firm's unique resources. Simply put, a company or business unit can choose a broad target (that is, aim at the middle of the mass market) or a narrow target (that is, aim at a market niche). Combining these two types of target markets with the two competitive strategies results in the four variations of generic strategies depicted in **Figure 6–4**. When the lower-cost and differentiation strategies have a broad mass-market target, they are simply called *cost leadership* and *differentiation*. When they are focused on a market niche (narrow

Figure 6–4 Porter's Generic Competitive Strategies

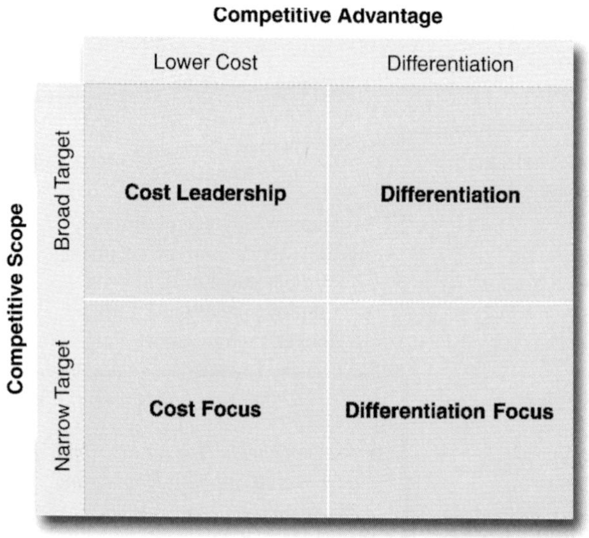

Competitive Advantage

Competitive Scope	Lower Cost	Differentiation
Broad Target	**Cost Leadership**	**Differentiation**
Narrow Target	**Cost Focus**	**Differentiation Focus**

Source: Reprinted with permission of The Free Press, A Division of Simon & Schuster Adult Publishing Group, from THE COMPETITIVE ADVANTAGE OF NATIONS *by Michael E. Porter. Copyright © 1990, 1998 by Michael E. Porter. All rights reserved.*

target), however, they are called *cost focus* and *differentiation focus*. Although research indicates that established firms pursuing broad-scope strategies outperform firms following narrow-scope strategies in terms of ROA (Return on Assets), new entrepreneurial firms have a better chance of surviving if they follow a narrow-scope rather than a broad-scope strategy.[8]

Cost leadership is a lower-cost competitive strategy that aims at the broad mass market and requires "aggressive construction of efficient-scale facilities, vigorous pursuit of cost reductions from experience, tight cost and overhead control, avoidance of marginal customer accounts, and cost minimization in areas like R&D, service, sales force, advertising, and so on."[9] Because of its lower costs, the cost leader is able to charge a lower price for its products than its competitors and still make a satisfactory profit. Although it may not necessarily have the lowest costs in the industry, it has lower costs than its competitors. Some companies successfully following this strategy are Wal-Mart, Dell (computers), Alamo (rental cars), Aldi (grocery stores), Southwest Airlines, and Timex (watches). Having a lower-cost position also gives a company or business unit a defense against rivals. Its lower costs allow it to continue to earn profits during times of heavy competition. Its high market share means that it will have high bargaining power relative to its suppliers (because it buys in large quantities). Its low price will also serve as a barrier to entry because few new entrants will be able to match the leader's cost advantage. As a result, cost leaders are likely to earn above-average returns on investment.

Differentiation is aimed at the broad mass market and involves the creation of a product or service that is perceived throughout its industry as unique. The company or business unit may then charge a premium for its product. This specialty can be associated with design or brand image, technology, features, a dealer network, or customer service. Differentiation is a viable strategy for earning above-average returns in a specific business because the resulting brand loyalty lowers customers' sensitivity to price. Increased costs can usually be passed on to the buyers. Buyer loyalty also serves as an entry barrier; new firms must develop their own distinctive competence to differentiate their products in some way in order to compete successfully. Examples of companies that successfully use a differentiation strategy are Walt Disney Productions, Maytag, Nike, Apple Computer, and Mercedes-Benz. Research suggests that a differentiation strategy is more likely to generate higher profits than is a low-cost strategy because differentiation creates a better entry barrier. A low-cost strategy is more likely, however, to generate increases in market share.[10]

Cost focus is a low-cost competitive strategy that focuses on a particular buyer group or geographic market and attempts to serve only that niche, to the exclusion of others. In using cost focus, a company or business unit seeks a cost advantage in its target segment. A good example of this strategy is Potlach Corporation, a manufacturer of toilet tissue. Rather than compete directly against Procter & Gamble's Charmin, Potlach makes the house brands for Albertson's, Safeway, Jewel, and many other grocery store chains. It matches the quality of the well-known brands but keeps costs low by eliminating advertising and promotion expenses. As a result, Spokane-based Potlach makes 92% of the private-label bathroom tissue and one-third of all bathroom tissue sold in Western U.S. grocery stores.[11]

Differentiation focus, like cost focus, concentrates on a particular buyer group, product line segment, or geographic market. This is the strategy successfully followed by Midamar Corporation, Morgan Motor Car Company (a manufacturer of classic British sports cars), Nickelodeon (a cable channel for children), and local ethnic grocery stores. In using differentiation focus, a company or business unit seeks differentiation in a targeted market segment. This strategy is valued by those who believe that a company or a unit that focuses its efforts is better able to serve the special needs of a narrow strategic target more effectively than can its competition. As explained in **STRATEGY HIGHLIGHT 6.1**, this strategy is followed by Poison, Incorporated, in the marketing of its Grim Reaper cigarettes to a very small segment of the tobacco market: serious risk takers!

Risks in Competitive Strategies

No one competitive strategy is guaranteed to achieve success, and some companies that have successfully implemented one of Porter's competitive strategies have found that they could not sustain the strategy. As shown in **Table 6–1**, each of the generic strategies has risks. For example, a company following a differentiation strategy must ensure that the higher price it charges for its higher quality is not too far above the price of the competition; otherwise, customers will not see the extra quality as worth the extra cost. This is what is meant in **Table 6–1** by the term **cost proximity**. P&G's use of R&D and advertising to differentiate its products had been very successful for many years, until customers in the value-conscious 1990s turned to cheaper private brands. As a result, P&G was forced to reduce costs until it could get prices back in line with customer expectations.

STRATEGY HIGHLIGHT 6.1

Grim Reaper Uses Focused Differentiation Strategy

Cigarettes are bad for your health. The U.S. Surgeon General, many research studies, and practically all health agencies agree that smoking is a primary cause of cancer. So, why would anyone buy a new brand of cigarettes called *Grim Reaper*, with a black-hooded death's head on its package?

After running a construction business for many years in Castle Hayne, North Carolina, Dan Norris founded Poison, Incorporated, to sell cigarettes to risk takers. He came up with this radical idea when he read a news report about a multi-billion-dollar judgment against Philip Morris by a man who claimed that he had no idea cigarettes were hazardous. Poison sold 12,000 cartons in 2003. Norris explains: *My product is just telling you the truth. . . . Our target market is a person who understands the dangers of smoking cigarettes, but is willing to take the chance for the experience of smoking. . . . The smokers of our cigarettes are the ones who climb Mount Everest, scuba through the canyons of Abez, hang glide off the cliffs of Montejerno, and know they have lived their lives to the fullest when they take the final ride with the Reaper.*

Source: Summarized from A. G. Breed, "Little Tobacco," *The (Ames, IA) Tribune* (January 17, 2004), p. C7.

TABLE 6–1 RISKS OF GENERIC COMPETITIVE STRATEGIES

Risks of Cost Leadership	Risks of Differentiation	Risks of Focus
Cost leadership is not sustained: • Competitors imitate. • Technology changes. • Other bases for cost leadership erode.	Differentiation is not sustained: • Competitors imitate. • Bases for differentiation become less important to buyers.	The focus strategy is imitated. The target segment becomes structurally unattractive: • Structure erodes. • Demand disappears.
Proximity in differentiation is lost.	Cost proximity is lost.	Broadly targeted competitors overwhelm the segment: • The segment's differences from other segments narrow. • The advantages of a broad line increase.
Cost focusers achieve even lower cost in segments.	Differentiation focusers achieve even greater differentiation in segments.	New focusers subsegment the industry.

Source: Adapted with the permission of The Free Press, A Division of Simon & Schuster Adult Publishing Group, from *COMPETITIVE ADVANTAGE: Creating and Sustaining Superior Performance* by Michael Porter.

Issues in Competitive Strategies

Porter argues that to be successful, a company or business unit must achieve one of the previously mentioned generic competitive strategies. It is especially difficult to move between a narrow-target strategy and a broad-target strategy. Otherwise, the company or business unit is **stuck in the middle** of the competitive marketplace, with no competitive advantage, and is doomed to below-average performance. An example of a company that is stuck in the middle is Hewlett-Packard (HP). After its acquisition of Compaq in 2002, HP lost its direction and was squeezed between Dell and IBM. Dell stood for low priced simple PCs in an industry where PCs were becoming a commodity. IBM stood for weaving together multiple subsystems in a complex industry to provide integrative customer solutions. HP could neither match Dell's low cost nor IBM's differentiation on the basis of quality service. In referring to CEO Carly Fiorina's attempt to offer "the best customer experience," one analyst stated: "Her problem, in a nutshell, is that HP is trying to be all things to all kinds of customers, and is leaving them more and more plain confused."[12]

Although it may be difficult to move from a narrow- to a broad-target scope strategy (and vice versa) successfully, research does not support the argument that a firm or unit must chose between differentiation and lower cost in order to be successful.[13] What of companies that attempt to achieve *both* a low-cost and a high-differentiation position? The Toyota and Honda auto companies are often presented as examples of successful firms able to achieve both of these generic strategies. Thanks to advances in technology, a company may be able to design quality into a product or service in such a way that it can achieve both high quality and high market share—thus lowering costs.[14] Although Porter agrees that it is possible for a company or a business unit to achieve low cost and differentiation simultaneously, he continues to argue that this state is often temporary.[15] Porter does admit, however, that many different kinds of potentially profitable competitive strategies exist. Although there is generally room for only one company to successfully pursue the mass-market cost leadership strategy (because it is so dependent on achieving dominant market share), there is room for an almost unlimited number of differentiation and focus strategies (depending on the range of possible desirable features and the number of identifiable market niches). Quality, alone, has eight different dimen-

TABLE 6–2 THE EIGHT DIMENSIONS OF QUALITY

1. Performance	Primary operating characteristics, such as a washing machine's cleaning ability.
2. Features	"Bells and whistles," such as cruise control in a car, that supplement the basic functions.
3. Reliability	Probability that the product will continue functioning without any significant maintenance.
4. Conformance	Degree to which a product meets standards. When a customer buys a product out of the warehouse, it should perform identically to that viewed on the showroom floor.
5. Durability	Number of years of service a consumer can expect from a product before it significantly deteriorates. Differs from reliability in that a product can be durable but still need a lot of maintenance.
6. Serviceability	Product's ease of repair.
7. Aesthetics	How a product looks, feels, sounds, tastes, or smells.
8. Perceived Quality	Product's overall reputation. Especially important if there are no objective, easily used measures of quality.

Source: Adapted with the permission of The Free Press, A Division of Simon & Schuster Adult Publishing Group, from *MANAGING QUALITY: The Strategic and Competitive Edge* by David A. Garvin. Copyright © 1988 by David A. Garvin. All rights reserved.

sions—each with the potential of providing a product with a competitive advantage (see **Table 6–2**).

Most entrepreneurial ventures follow focus strategies. The successful ones differentiate their product from those of other competitors in the areas of quality and service, and they focus the product on customer needs in a segment of the market, thereby achieving a dominant share of that part of the market. Adopting guerrilla warfare tactics, these companies go after opportunities in market niches too small to justify retaliation from the market leaders. Veteran entrepreneur Norm Brodsky argues that it's often much easier for a small company to compete against a big company than against a well-run small company. "We beat the giants on service. We beat them on flexibility. We beat them on location and price."[16]

Industry Structure and Competitive Strategy

Although each of Porter's generic competitive strategies may be used in any industry, certain strategies are more likely to succeed than others in some instances. In a **fragmented industry**, for example, where many small- and medium-sized local companies compete for relatively small shares of the total market, focus strategies will likely predominate. Fragmented industries are typical for products in the early stages of their life cycles. If few economies are to be gained through size, no large firms will emerge, and entry barriers will be low—allowing a stream of new entrants into the industry. Chinese restaurants, veterinary care, used-car sales, ethnic grocery stores, and funeral homes are examples. Even though P.F. Chang's (97 outlets) and the Panda Restaurant Group (600 outlets) have firmly established themselves as chains in the United States, local, family-owned restaurants still comprise 87% of Asian casual dining restaurants.[17]

If a company is able to overcome the limitations of a fragmented market, however, it can reap the benefits of a broadly targeted cost leadership or differentiation strategy. Until Pizza Hut was able to use advertising to differentiate itself from local competitors, the pizza fast-food business was a fragmented industry composed primarily of locally owned pizza parlors, each with its own distinctive product and service offering. Subsequently, Domino's used the cost leader strategy to achieve U.S. national market share.

As an industry matures, fragmentation is overcome, and the industry tends to become a **consolidated industry** dominated by a few large companies. Although many industries start out being fragmented, battles for market share and creative attempts to overcome local or niche market boundaries often increase the market share of a few companies. After product standards become established for minimum quality and features, competition shifts to a greater emphasis on cost and service. Slower growth, overcapacity, and knowledgeable buyers combine to put a premium on a firm's ability to achieve cost leadership or differentiation along the dimensions most desired by the market. R&D shifts from product to process improvements. Overall product quality improves, and costs are reduced significantly.

The **strategic rollup** was developed in the mid-1990s as an efficient way to quickly consolidate a fragmented industry. With the aid of money from venture capitalists, an entrepreneur acquires hundreds of owner-operated small businesses. The resulting large firm creates economies of scale by building regional or national brands, applies best practices across all aspects of marketing and operations, and hires more sophisticated managers than the small businesses could previously afford. Rollups differ from conventional mergers and acquisitions in three ways: (1) they involve large numbers of firms, (2) the acquired firms are typically owner operated, and (3) the objective is not to gain incremental advantage but to reinvent an entire industry.[18] Rollups are currently under way in the funeral industry, led by Service Corporation International, Stewart Enterprises, and the Loewen Group; and in the veterinary care industries, by Veterinary Centers of America. Of the 16,000 pet hospitals in the United States, Veterinary Centers of American had acquired 317 by June 2004 and was in the process of buying at least 25 more each year for the foreseeable future.[19]

Once consolidated, an industry has become one in which cost leadership and differentiation tend to be combined to various degrees. A firm can no longer gain high market share simply through low price. The buyers are more sophisticated and demand a certain minimum level of quality for price paid. The same is true for firms emphasizing high quality. Either the quality must be high enough and valued by the customer enough to justify the higher price or the price must be dropped (through lowering costs) to compete effectively with the lower-priced products. This consolidation is taking place worldwide in the automobile, airline, and home appliance industries.

Hypercompetition and Competitive Strategy

In his book *Hypercompetition*, D'Aveni proposes that it is becoming increasingly difficult to sustain a competitive advantage for very long. "Market stability is threatened by short product life cycles, short product design cycles, new technologies, frequent entry by unexpected outsiders, repositioning by incumbents, and tactical redefinitions of market boundaries as diverse industries merge."[20] Consequently, a company or business unit must constantly work to improve its competitive advantage. It is not enough to be just the lowest-cost competitor. Through continuous improvement programs, competitors are usually working to lower their costs as well. Firms must find new ways not only to reduce costs further but also to add value to the product or service being provided.

The same is true of a firm or unit that is following a differentiation strategy. Maytag Corporation, for example, was successful for many years by offering the most reliable brand in major home appliances. It was able to charge the highest prices for Maytag brand washing machines. When other competitors improved the quality of their products, however, it became increasingly difficult for customers to justify Maytag's significantly higher price. Consequently, Maytag Corporation was forced not only to add new features to its products but also to reduce costs through improved manufacturing processes so that its prices were no longer out of line with those of the competition.

D'Aveni contends that when industries become hypercompetitive, they tend to go through escalating stages of competition. Firms initially compete on cost and quality, until an abundance of high-quality, low-priced goods result. This occurred in the U.S. major home appliance industry by 1980. In a second stage of competition, the competitors move into untapped markets. Others usually imitate these moves until the moves become too risky or expensive. This epitomized the major home appliance industry during the 1980s and 1990s, as firms moved first to Europe and then into Asia and South America.

According to D'Aveni, firms then raise entry barriers to limit competitors. Economies of scale, distribution agreements, and strategic alliances made it all but impossible for a new firm to enter the major home appliance industry by the end of the 20th century. After the established players have entered and consolidated all new markets, the next stage is for the remaining firms to attack and destroy the strongholds of other firms. Maytag's 1995 decision to divest its European division and acquire Amana was a prelude to building a North American stronghold, while Whirlpool, GE, and Electrolux were distracted by European and worldwide investments. Eventually, according to D'Aveni, the remaining large global competitors work their way to a situation of perfect competition in which no one has any advantage and profits are minimal.

Before hypercompetition, strategic initiatives provided competitive advantage for many years, perhaps for decades. This is no longer the case. According to D'Aveni, as industries become hypercompetitive, there is no such thing as a sustainable competitive advantage. Successful strategic initiatives in this type of industry typically last only months to a few years. According to D'Aveni, the only way a firm in this kind of dynamic industry can sustain any competitive advantage is through a continuous series of multiple short-term initiatives aimed at replacing a firm's current successful products with the next generation of products before the competitors can do so. Intel and Microsoft are taking this approach in the hypercompetitive computer industry.

Hypercompetition views competition, in effect, as a distinct series of ocean waves on what used to be a fairly calm stretch of water. As industry competition becomes more intense, the waves grow higher and require more dexterity to handle. Although a strategy is still needed to sail from point A to point B, more turbulent water means that a craft must continually adjust course to suit each new large wave. One danger of D'Aveni's concept of hypercompetition, however, is that it may lead to an overemphasis on short-term tactics (discussed in the next section) over long-term strategy. Too much of an orientation on the individual waves of hypercompetition could cause a company to focus too much on short-term temporary advantage and not enough on achieving its long-term objectives through building sustainable competitive advantage.

Which Competitive Strategy Is Best?

Before selecting one of Porter's generic competitive strategies for a company or business unit, management should assess its feasibility in terms of company or business unit resources and capabilities. Porter lists some of the commonly required skills and resources, as well as organizational requirements, in **Table 6–3**.

Competitive Tactics

Studies of decision making report that half the decisions made in organizations fail because of poor tactics.[21] A **tactic** is a specific operating plan that details how a strategy is to be implemented in terms of when and where it is to be put into action. By their nature, tactics are narrower in scope and shorter in time horizon than are strategies. Tactics, therefore, may be viewed (like policies) as a link between the formulation and implementation of strategy. Some of the tactics available to implement competitive strategies are timing tactics and market location tactics.

TABLE 6–3 REQUIREMENTS FOR GENERIC COMPETITIVE STRATEGIES

Generic Strategy	Commonly Required Skills and Resources	Common Organizational Requirements
Overall Cost Leadership	• Sustained capital investment and access to capital • Process engineering skills • Intense supervision of labor • Products designed for ease of manufacture • Low-cost distribution system	• Tight cost control • Frequent, detailed control reports • Structured organization and responsibilities • Incentives based on meeting strict quantitative targets
Differentiation	• Strong marketing abilities • Product engineering • Creative flair • Strong capability in basic research • Corporate reputation for quality or technological leadership • Long tradition in the industry or unique combination of skills drawn from other businesses • Strong cooperation from channels	• Strong coordination among functions in R&D, product development, and marketing • Subjective measurement and incentives instead of quantitative measures • Amenities to attract highly skilled labor, scientists, or creative people
Focus	• Combination of the above policies directed at the particular strategic target	• Combination of the above policies directed at the particular strategic target

Source: Adapted with the permission of The Free Press, A Division of Simon & Schuster Adult Publishing Group, from *COMPETITIVE STRATEGY: Techniques for Analyzing Industries and Competitors* by Michael Porter.

Timing Tactics: When to Compete

A **timing tactic** deals with *when* a company implements a strategy. The first company to manufacture and sell a new product or service is called the **first mover** (or pioneer). Some of the advantages of being a first mover are that the company is able to establish a reputation as an industry leader, move down the learning curve to assume the cost leader position, and earn temporarily high profits from buyers who value the product or service very highly. A successful first mover can also set the standard for all subsequent products in the industry. A company that sets the standard "locks in" customers and is then able to offer further products based on that standard.[22] Microsoft was able to do this in software with its Windows operating system, and Netscape garnered over an 80% share of the Internet browser market by being first to commercialize the product successfully. Research indicates that moving first or second into a new industry or foreign country results in greater market share and shareholder wealth than does moving later.[23] Being first provides a company profit advantages for about 10 years in consumer goods and about 12 years in industrial goods.[24] This is only true, however, if the first mover has sufficient resources to both exploit the new market and defend its position against later arrivals with greater resources.[25] Gillette, for example, has been able to keep its leadership of the razor category (70% market share) by continuously introducing new products.[26]

Being a first mover does, however, have disadvantages. These disadvantages can be, conversely, advantages enjoyed by late-mover firms. **Late movers** may be able to imitate the technological advances of others (and thus keep R&D costs low), keep risks down by waiting until a new market is established, and take advantage of the first mover's natural inclination to ignore market segments.[27] Research indicates that successful late movers tend to be large firms with considerable resources and related experience.[28] Microsoft is one example. Once Netscape had established itself as the standard for Internet browsers in the 1990s, Microsoft used its huge resources to directly attack Netscape's position with its Internet Explorer. It did not want Netscape to also set the standard in the developing and highly lucrative intranet market inside corporations. By 2004, Microsoft's Internet Explorer dominated web browsers, and Netscape was only a minor presence. Nevertheless, research suggests that the advantages and disadvantages of first and late movers may not always generalize across industries because of differences in entry barriers and the resources of the specific competitors.[29]

Market Location Tactics: Where to Compete

A **market location tactic** deals with *where* a company implements a strategy. A company or business unit can implement a competitive strategy either offensively or defensively. An **offensive tactic** usually takes place in an established competitor's market location. A **defensive tactic** usually takes place in the firm's own current market position as a defense against possible attack by a rival.[30]

Offensive Tactics. Some of the methods used to attack a competitor's position are:

- **Frontal Assault:** The attacking firm goes head to head with its competitor. It matches the competitor in every category, from price to promotion to distribution channel. To be successful, the attacker must have not only superior resources but also the willingness to persevere. This is generally a very expensive tactic and may serve to awaken a sleeping giant, depressing profits for the whole industry. This is what Kimberly-Clark did when it introduced Huggies disposable diapers against P&G's market-leading Pampers. The resulting competitive battle between the two firms depressed Kimberly-Clark's profits.[31]
- **Flanking Maneuver:** Rather than going straight for a competitor's position of strength with a frontal assault, a firm may attack a part of the market where the competitor is weak. AMD followed this tactic with its entry into the microprocessor market—a market then almost totally dominated by Intel. Rather than going directly after Intel's microprocessor business, AMD developed low-priced chips to go after the customers Intel didn't mind losing. To be successful, the flanker must be patient and willing to carefully expand out of the relatively undefended market niche or else face retaliation by an established competitor.
- **Bypass Attack:** Rather than directly attacking the established competitor frontally or on its flanks, a company or business unit may choose to change the rules of the game. This tactic attempts to cut the market out from under the established defender by offering a new type of product that makes the competitor's product unnecessary. For example, instead of competing directly against Microsoft's Pocket PC and Palm Pilot for the handheld computer market, Apple introduced the iPod as a personal digital music player. It was the most radical change to the way people listen to music since the Sony Walkman. By redefining the market, Apple successfully sidestepped both Intel and Microsoft, leaving them to play catch-up.[32]
- **Encirclement:** Usually evolving out of a frontal assault or flanking maneuver, encirclement occurs as an attacking company or unit encircles the competitor's position in terms of products or markets or both. The encircler has greater product variety (e.g., a complete product line, ranging from low to high price) and/or serves more markets (e.g., dominates every secondary market). For example, Steinway was a major manufacturer of pianos in the United States until Yamaha entered the market with a broader range of pianos, keyboards, and other musical instruments. Although Steinway still dominates concert halls, it has only a 2% share of the U.S. market.[33]
- **Guerrilla Warfare:** Instead of a continual and extensive resource-expensive attack on a competitor, a firm or business unit may choose to "hit and run." Guerrilla warfare is characterized by the use of small, intermittent assaults on different market segments held by the competitor. In this way, a new entrant or small firm can make some gains without seriously

threatening a large, established competitor and evoking some form of retaliation. To be successful, the firm or unit conducting guerrilla warfare must be patient enough to accept small gains and to avoid pushing the established competitor to the point that it must respond or else lose face. Microbreweries, which make beer for sale to local customers, use this tactic against national brewers such as Anheuser-Busch.

Defensive Tactics. According to Porter, defensive tactics aim to lower the probability of attack, divert attacks to less threatening avenues, or lessen the intensity of an attack. Instead of increasing competitive advantage per se, they make a company's or business unit's competitive advantage more sustainable by causing a challenger to conclude that an attack is unattractive. These tactics deliberately reduce short-term profitability to ensure long-term profitability[34]:

- **Raise Structural Barriers:** Entry barriers act to block a challenger's logical avenues of attack. Some of the most important, according to Porter, are to:
  1. Offer a full line of products in every profitable market segment to close off any entry points (for example, Coca Cola offers unprofitable noncarbonated beverages to keep competitors off store shelves);
  2. Block channel access by signing exclusive agreements with distributors;
  3. Raise buyer switching costs by offering low-cost training to users;
  4. Raise the cost of gaining trial users by keeping prices low on items new users are most likely to purchase;
  5. Increase scale economies to reduce unit costs;
  6. Foreclose alternative technologies through patenting or licensing;
  7. Limit outside access to facilities and personnel;
  8. Tie up suppliers by obtaining exclusive contracts or purchasing key locations;
  9. Avoid suppliers that also serve competitors; and
  10. Encourage the government to raise barriers, such as safety and pollution standards or favorable trade policies.
- **Increase Expected Retaliation:** This tactic is any action that increases the perceived threat of retaliation for an attack. For example, management may strongly defend any erosion of market share by drastically cutting prices or matching a challenger's promotion through a policy of accepting any price-reduction coupons for a competitor's product. This counterattack is especially important in markets that are very important to the defending company or business unit. For example, when Clorox Company challenged P&G in the detergent market with Clorox Super Detergent, P&G retaliated by test marketing its liquid bleach, Lemon Fresh Comet, in an attempt to scare Clorox into retreating from the detergent market. Research suggests that retaliating quickly is not as successful in slowing market share loss as a slower but more concentrated and aggressive response.[35]
- **Lower the Inducement for Attack:** A third type of defensive tactic is to reduce a challenger's expectations of future profits in the industry. Like Southwest Airlines, a company can deliberately keep prices low and constantly invest in cost-reducing measures. With prices kept very low, there is little profit incentive for a new entrant.

Cooperative Strategies

A company uses competitive strategies and tactics to gain competitive advantage within an industry by battling against other firms. These are not, however, the only business strategy options available to a company or business unit for competing successfully within an industry.

A company can also use **cooperative strategies** to gain competitive advantage within an industry by working with other firms. The two general types of cooperative strategies are collusion and strategic alliances.

Collusion

Collusion is the active cooperation of firms within an industry to reduce output and raise prices in order to get around the normal economic law of supply and demand. Collusion may be explicit, in which case firms cooperate through direct communication and negotiation, or tacit, in which case firms cooperate indirectly through an informal system of signals. Explicit collusion is illegal in most countries and in a number of regional trade associations, such as the European Union. For example, Archer Daniels Midland (ADM), the large U.S. agricultural products firm, conspired with its competitors to limit the sales volume and raise the price of the food additive lysine. Executives from three Japanese and South Korean lysine manufacturers admitted meeting in hotels in major cities throughout the world to form a "lysine trade association." The three companies were fined more than $20 million by the U.S. federal government.[36] In another example, Denver-based Qwest signed agreements favoring competitors that agreed not to oppose Qwest's merger with U.S. West or its entry into the long-distance business in its 14-state region. In one agreement, Qwest agreed to pay McLeodUSA almost $30 million to settle a billing dispute in return for McLeod's withdrawing its objections to Qwest's purchase of U.S. West.[37]

Collusion can also be tacit, in which case there is no direct communication among competing firms. According to Barney, tacit collusion in an industry is most likely to be successful if (1) there are a small number of identifiable competitors, (2) costs are similar among firms, (3) one firm tends to act as the price leader, (4) there is a common industry culture that accepts cooperation, (5) sales are characterized by a high frequency of small orders, (6) large inventories and order backlogs are normal ways of dealing with fluctuations in demand, and (7) there are high entry barriers to keep out new competitors.[38]

Even tacit collusion can, however, be illegal. For example, when General Electric wanted to ease price competition in the steam turbine industry, it widely advertised its prices and publicly committed not to sell below those prices. Customers were even told that if GE reduced turbine prices in the future, it would give customers a refund equal to the price reduction. GE's message was not lost on Westinghouse, the major competitor in steam turbines. Both prices and profit margins remained stable for the next 10 years in this industry. The U.S. Department of Justice then sued both firms for engaging in "conscious parallelism" (following each other's lead to reduce the level of competition) in order to reduce competition.

Strategic Alliances

A **strategic alliance** is a partnership of two or more corporations or business units to achieve strategically significant objectives that are mutually beneficial.[39] Alliances between companies or business units have become a fact of life in modern business. The number of strategic alliances grew to more than 10,200 in 2000 alone. Each of the top 500 global business firms now average 60 major alliances.[40] Fully two-thirds of companies surveyed in 2003 expected their dependence on alliances of some sort to increase over the next three years.[41] Some alliances are very short term, only lasting long enough for one partner to establish a beachhead in a new market. Over time, conflicts over objectives and control often develop among the partners. For these and other reasons, around half of all alliances (including international alliances) perform unsatisfactorily.[42] Others are more long lasting and may even be preludes to full mergers between companies.

Many alliances increase profitability of the members and have a positive effect on firm value.[43] A study by Cooper and Lybrand found that firms involved in strategic alliances had

11% higher revenue and 20% higher growth rate than did companies not involved in alliances.[44] It is likely that forming and managing strategic alliances is a capability that is learned over time. Research reveals that the more experience a firm has with strategic alliances, the more likely its alliances will be successful.[45]

Companies or business units may form a strategic alliance for a number of reasons, including:

1. **To obtain technology and/or manufacturing capabilities:** For example, Intel formed a partnership with HP to use HP's capabilities in RISC technology in order to develop the successor to Intel's Pentium microprocessor. A study found that firms with strategic alliances had more modern manufacturing technologies than did firms without alliances.[46]
2. **To obtain access to specific markets:** Rather than buy a foreign company or build breweries of its own in other countries, Anheuser-Busch chose to license the right to brew and market Budweiser to other brewers, such as Labatt in Canada, Modelo in Mexico, and Kirin in Japan. In a survey by the *Economist Intelligence Unit*, 59% of executives stated that their primary reason for engaging in alliances was the need for fast and low-cost expansion into new markets.[47]
3. **To reduce financial risk:** For example, because the costs of developing new large jet airplanes were becoming too high for any one manufacturer, Aerospatiale of France, British Aerospace, Construcciones Aeronáuticas of Spain, and Daimler-Benz Aerospace of Germany formed a joint consortium called Airbus Industrie to design and build such planes. Using alliances with suppliers is a popular means of outsourcing an expensive activity.
4. **To reduce political risk:** Forming alliances with local partners is a good way to overcome deficiencies in resources and capabilities when expanding into international markets.[48] To gain access to China while ensuring a positive relationship with the often-restrictive Chinese government, Maytag Corporation formed a joint venture with the Chinese appliance maker RSD.
5. **To learn new capabilities:** For example, Pittsburgh Brewing Company, maker of Iron City Beer, partnered with Alcoa to produce aluminum bottles that keep beer colder for 50 minutes longer than conventional bottles.[49]

Cooperative arrangements between companies and business units fall along a continuum from weak and distant to strong and close. (See **Figure 6–5**.) The types of alliances range from mutual service consortia to joint ventures and licensing arrangements to value-chain partnerships.[50]

Mutual Service Consortia. A **mutual service consortium** is a partnership of similar companies in similar industries that pool their resources to gain a benefit that is too expensive to develop alone, such as access to advanced technology. For example, IBM of the United States,

Figure 6–5
Continuum of Strategic Alliances

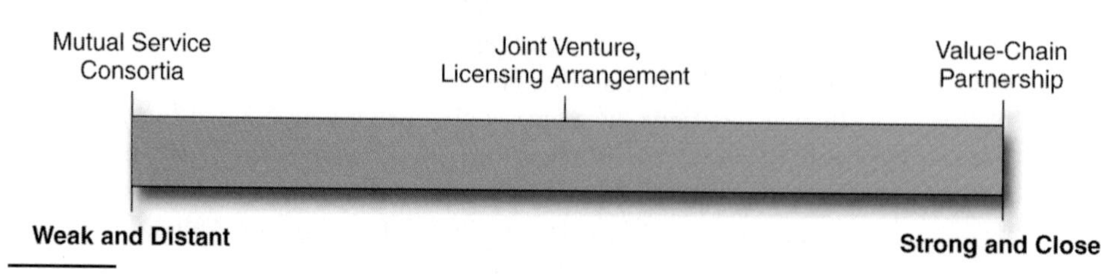

Source: Reprinted by permission of the Harvard Business Review. From "Collaborative Advantage: The Art of Alliances," by R.M. Kanter, July–August 1994. Copyright © 1994 by the Harvard Business School Publishing Corporation; all rights reserved.

Toshiba of Japan, and Siemens of Germany formed a consortium to develop new generations of computer chips. As part of this alliance, IBM offered Toshiba its expertise in chemical mechanical polishing to help develop a new manufacturing process using ultraviolet lithography to etch tiny circuits in silicon chips. IBM then transferred the new technology to a facility in the United States.[51] The mutual service consortia is a fairly weak and distant alliance—appropriate for partners that wish to work together but not share their core competencies. There is very little interaction or communication among the partners.

Joint Ventures. A **joint venture** is a "cooperative business activity, formed by two or more separate organizations for strategic purposes, that creates an independent business entity and allocates ownership, operational responsibilities, and financial risks and rewards to each member, while preserving their separate identity/autonomy."[52] Along with licensing arrangements, joint ventures lay at the midpoint of the continuum and are formed to pursue an opportunity that needs a capability from two companies or business units, such as the technology of one and the distribution channels of another.

Joint ventures are the most popular form of strategic alliance. They often occur because the companies involved do not want to or cannot legally merge permanently. Joint ventures provide a way to temporarily combine the different strengths of partners to achieve an outcome of value to both. For example, Toys 'Я' Us and Amazon.com formed a joint venture called Toysrus.com to act as an online toy store. Amazon agreed to include the joint venture on its web site, ship the products, and handle customer service. In turn, Toys 'R' Us agreed to choose and buy the toys, using its parents' purchasing power to get the most desired toys at the best price.[53]

Extremely popular in international undertakings because of financial and political–legal constraints, forming joint ventures is a convenient way for corporations to work together without losing their independence. Disadvantages of joint ventures include loss of control, lower profits, probability of conflicts with partners, and the likely transfer of technological advantage to the partner. Joint ventures are often meant to be temporary, especially by some companies that may view them as a way to rectify a competitive weakness until they can achieve long-term dominance in the partnership. Partially for this reason, joint ventures have a high failure rate. Research indicates, however, that joint ventures tend to be more successful when both partners have equal ownership in the venture and are mutually dependent on each other for results.[54]

Licensing Arrangements. A **licensing arrangement** is an agreement in which the licensing firm grants rights to another firm in another country or market to produce and/or sell a product. The licensee pays compensation to the licensing firm in return for technical expertise. Licensing is an especially useful strategy if the trademark or brand name is well known but the MNC does not have sufficient funds to finance its entering the country directly. Anheuser-Busch uses this strategy to produce and market Budweiser beer in the United Kingdom, Japan, Israel, Australia, Korea, and the Philippines. This strategy also becomes important if the country makes entry via investment either difficult or impossible. The danger always exists, however, that the licensee might develop its competence to the point that it becomes a competitor to the licensing firm. Therefore, a company should never license its distinctive competence, even for some short-run advantage.

Value-Chain Partnerships. A **value-chain partnership** is a strong and close alliance in which one company or unit forms a long-term arrangement with a key supplier or distributor for mutual advantage. For example, P&G, the maker of Folgers and Millstone coffee, worked with coffee appliance makers Mr. Coffee, Krups, and Hamilton Beach to use technology licensed from Black & Decker to market a pressurized, single-serve coffee-making system called Home Cafe. This was an attempt to reverse declining at-home coffee consumption at a time when coffeehouse sales were rising.[55]

To improve the quality of parts it purchases, companies in the U.S. auto industry, for example, have decided to work more closely with fewer suppliers and to involve them more in product design decisions. Activities that had previously been done internally by an auto maker are now being outsourced to suppliers specializing in those activities. The benefits of such relationships do not just accrue to the purchasing firm. Research suggests that suppliers that engage in long-term relationships are more profitable than suppliers with multiple short-term contracts.[56]

All forms of strategic alliances involve uncertainty. Many issues need to be dealt with when an alliance is initially formed, and others emerge later. Many problems revolve around the fact that a firm's alliance partners may also be its competitors, either immediately or in the future. According to Peter Lorange, an authority in strategy, one thorny issue in any strategic alliance is how to cooperate without giving away the company or business unit's core competence: "Particularly when advanced technology is involved, it can be difficult for partners in an alliance to cooperate and openly share strategic know-how, but it is mandatory if the joint venture is to succeed."[57] It is therefore important that a company or business unit that is interested in joining or forming a strategic alliance consider the strategic alliance success factors listed in **Table 6–4**.

TABLE 6–4
STRATEGIC ALLIANCE SUCCESS FACTORS

- Have a clear strategic purpose. Integrate the alliance with each partner's strategy. Ensure that mutual value is created for all partners.
- Find a fitting partner with compatible goals and complementary capabilities.
- Identify likely partnering risks and deal with them when the alliance is formed.
- Allocate tasks and responsibilities so that each partner can specialize in what it does best.
- Create incentives for cooperation to minimize differences in corporate culture or organization fit.
- Minimize conflicts among the partners by clarifying objectives and avoiding direct competition in the marketplace.
- In an international alliance, ensure that those managing it have comprehensive cross-cultural knowledge.
- Exchange human resources to maintain communication and trust. Don't allow individual egos to dominate.
- Operate with long-term time horizons. The expectation of future gains can minimize short-term conflicts.
- Develop multiple joint projects so that any failures are counterbalanced by successes.
- Agree on a monitoring process. Share information to build trust and keep projects on target. Monitor customer responses and service complaints.
- Be flexible in terms of willingness to renegotiate the relationship in terms of environmental changes and new opportunities.
- Agree on an exit strategy for when the partners' objectives are achieved or the alliance is judged a failure.

Source: Compiled from B. Gomes-Casseres, "Do You Really Have an Alliance Strategy?" *Strategy & Leadership* (September/October 1998), pp. 6–11; L. Segil, "Strategic Alliances for the 21st Century," *Strategy & Leadership* (September/October 1998), pp. 12–16; and A. C. Inkpen and K-Q Li, "Joint Venture Formation: Planning and Knowledge Gathering for Success," *Organizational Dynamics* (Spring 1999), pp. 33–47. Inkpen and Li provide a checklist of 17 questions on p. 46.

6.5 Conclusion

Once environmental scanning is completed, situational analysis calls for the integration of this information. SWOT analysis is the most popular method for examining external and internal information. We recommend using the SFAS Matrix as one way to identify a corporation's strategic factors. Using the TOWS matrix to identify a propitious niche is one way to develop a sustainable competitive advantage by using those strategic factors.

Business strategy is composed of both competitive and cooperative strategy. As the external environment becomes more uncertain, an increasing number of corporations are choosing to simultaneously compete *and* cooperate with their competitors. These firms may cooperate to obtain efficiency in some areas, while each firm simultaneously tries to differentiate itself for competitive purposes. Raymond Noorda, Novell's founder and former CEO, coined the term **co-opetition** to describe such simultaneous competition and cooperation among firms.[58] A careful balancing act, co-opetition involves the careful management of alliance partners so that each partner obtains sufficient benefits to keep the alliance together. A long-term view is crucial. An unintended transfer of knowledge could be enough to provide one partner a significant competitive advantage over the others.[59] Unless that company forebears from using that knowledge against its partners, the alliance will be doomed.

Strategy Bits

- Countries with the highest levels of global competitiveness are Finland, the United States, Sweden, Taiwan, Denmark, Norway, and Singapore, in that order.[60]
- Countries with the highest percentages of pirated software are Vietnam (94%), China (92%), Indonesia (88%), Russia and Ukraine (87%), and Pakistan (83%).[61]

Discussion Questions

1. What industry forces might cause a propitious niche to disappear?
2. Is it possible for a company or business unit to follow a cost leadership strategy and a differentiation strategy simultaneously? Why or why not?
3. Is it possible for a company to have a sustainable competitive advantage when its industry becomes hypercompetitive?
4. What are the advantages and disadvantages of being a first mover in an industry? Give some examples of first-mover and late-mover firms. Were they successful?
5. Why are many strategic alliances temporary?

Strategic Practice Exercise

THE PROBLEM

On January 22, 2002, Kmart Corporation became the largest retailer in U.S. history to seek bankruptcy protection. In Kmart's petition for reorganization under Chapter 11 of the U.S. Bankruptcy Code, Kmart management announced that they would outline a plan for repaying Kmart's creditors, reducing Kmart's size, and restructuring its business so that it could leave court protection as a viable competitor in discount mass-market retailing. Emerging from bankruptcy in May 2003, Kmart still lacked a business strategy to succeed in an extremely competitive marketplace.

By 2004, the discount department store industry had reached maturity, and Kmart no longer possessed a clearly defined position within that industry. Its primary competitors were Wal-Mart, Sears, Target, Kohl's, and JCPenney, with secondary competitors in certain categories. Wal-Mart, an extremely efficient retailer, was known for consistently having the lowest costs (reflected in low prices) and the highest sales in the industry. Having started in rural

America, Wal-Mart was now actively growing internationally. Sears, with the second-highest annual sales, had a strong position in hard goods, such as home appliances and tools. Around 40% of all major home appliance sales continued to be controlled by Sears. Nevertheless, Sears was struggling with slumping sales as customers turned from Sears' mall stores to stand-alone, big-box retailers, such as Lowe's and Home Depot, to buy their hard goods. Target, third in sales but second in profits, behind Wal-Mart, had distinguished itself as a merchandiser of stylish upscale products. Along with Wal-Mart, Target had flourished to such an extent that Dayton-Hudson, its parent company, had changed its corporate name to Target. Kohl's, a relatively new entrant to the industry, operated 420 family-oriented stores in 32 states. JCPenney operated more than 1,000 stores in all 50 states. Both Kohl's and JCPenney emphasized soft goods, such as clothing and related items.

Kmart was also challenged by "category killers" that competed in only one or a few industry categories but in greater depth within any category than could any department store. Some of these were Toys 'Я' Us, Home Depot, Lowe's, and drug stores such as Rite Aid, CVS, Eckerd, and Walgreens.

Kmart had been established in 1962 by its parent company S.S. Kresge as a discount department store offering the most variety of goods at the lowest prices. Unlike Sears, the company chose not to locate in shopping centers but to establish its discount stores in highly visible corner locations. During the 1960s, '70s, and '80s, Kmart prospered. By 1990, however, when Wal-Mart first surpassed Kmart in annual sales, Kmart's stores had become dated and lost their appeal. Other well-known discount stores, such as Korvette's, Grant's, Woolco, Ames, Bradlees, and Montgomery Ward, had gone out of business as the industry had consolidated and reached maturity. Attempting to avoid this fate, Kmart management updated and enlarged the stores, added name brands, and hired Martha Stewart as its lifestyle consultant. None of these changes improved Kmart's financial situation. By the time it declared bankruptcy, it had lost money in 5 of the past 10 years.

Out of bankruptcy, Kmart became profitable—primarily by closing or selling (to Sears and Home Depot) around 600 of its retail stores. Management had been unable to invigorate sales in its stores. Declared guilty of insider trading, Martha Stewart went to prison just before the 2004 Christmas season. In a surprise move, Edward Lampert, Kmart's Chairman of the Board and a major shareholder of Sears, initiated the acquisition of Sears by Kmart for $11 billion in November 2004. The new company was to be called Sears Holdings Corporation. Even though management predicted that the combined company's costs could be reduced by $500 million annually within three years through supplier and administrative economies, analysts wondered how these two struggling firms could ever be successful.[62]

THE ASSIGNMENT

What business competitive strategies were used by each of Kmart's competitors? What business strategy(ies) do you recommend for the new company? Should Kmart and Sears keep their own identities and have unique competitive strategies, or should they be combined in some manner with a new competitive strategy? Defend your answer.

Key Terms

business strategy (p. 145)
collusion (p. 157)
competitive scope (p. 147)
competitive strategy (p. 145)
consolidated industry (p. 152)
cooperative strategy (p. 157)
co-opetition (p. 161)
cost focus (p. 149)
cost leadership (p. 148)
cost proximity (p. 149)
defensive tactic (p. 155)
differentiation (p. 148)
differentiation focus (p. 149)
differentiation strategy (p. 147)
first mover (p. 154)
fragmented industry (p. 151)
joint venture (p. 159)
late mover (p. 154)
licensing arrangement (p. 159)
lower cost strategy (p. 147)
market location tactic (p. 155)
mutual service consortium (p. 158)
offensive tactic (p. 155)
propitious niche (p. 142)
SFAS (Strategic Factors Analysis Summary) Matrix (p. 139)
SO, ST, WO, WT Strategies (p. 145)
strategic alliance (p. 157)
strategic rollup (p. 152)
strategic window (p. 142)
strategy formulation (p. 138)
stuck in the middle (p. 150)
SWOT (p. 138)
tactic (p. 153)
timing tactics (p. 154)
TOWS Matrix (p. 144)
value-chain partnership (p. 159)

CHAPTER 7
Strategy Formulation: Corporate Strategy

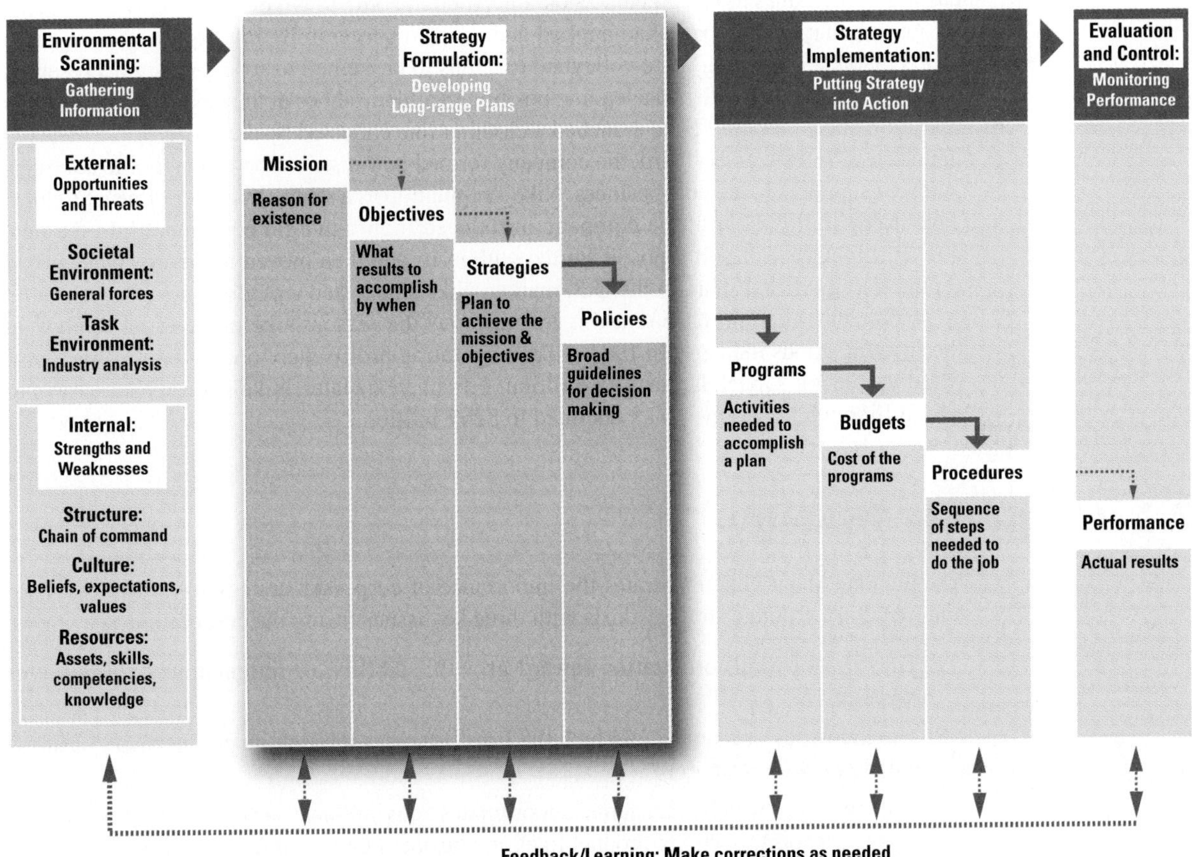

Learning Objectives

After reading this chapter, you should be able to:

- Understand the three aspects of corporate strategy.
- Apply the directional strategies of growth, stability, and retrenchment
- Understand the differences between vertical and horizontal growth as well as concentric and conglomerate diversification
- Identify strategic options to enter a foreign country
- Apply portfolio analysis to guide decisions in companies with multiple products and businesses
- Develop a parenting strategy for a multiple-business corporation

WHAT IS THE BEST WAY FOR A COMPANY TO GROW IF ITS PRIMARY BUSINESS IS MATURING? A study of 1,850 companies by Zook and Allen revealed two conclusions: First, the most sustained profitable growth occurs when a corporation pushes out of the boundary around its core business into adjacent businesses. Second, those corporations that consistently outgrow their rivals do so by developing a formula for expanding those boundaries in a predicable, repeatable manner.[1]

Nike is a classic example of this process. Despite its success in athletic shoes, no one expected Nike to be successful when it diversified in 1995 from shoes into golf apparel, balls, and equipment. Only a few years later, it was acknowledged to be a major player in the new business. According to researchers Zook and Allen, the key to Nike's success was a formula for growth that the company had applied and adapted successfully in a series of entries into sports markets, from jogging to volleyball to tennis to basketball to soccer and, most recently, to golf. First, Nike established a leading position in athletic shoes in the target market—in this case, golf shoes. Second, Nike launched a clothing line endorsed by the sports' top athletes—in this case, Tiger Woods. Third, the company formed new distribution channels and contracts with key suppliers in the new business. Nike's reputation as a strong marketer of new products gave it credibility. Fourth, the company introduced higher-margin equipment into the new market. In the case of golf clubs, it started with irons and then moved to drivers. Once it had captured a significant share in the U.S. market, Nike's next step was global distribution.

Zook and Allen propose that this formula was the reason Nike moved past Reebok in the sporting goods industry. In 1987, Nike's operating profits were only $164 million, compared to Reebok's much larger $309 million. Fifteen years later, Nike's profits had grown to $1.1 billion while Reebok's had declined to $247 million.[2]

7.1 Corporate Strategy

The vignette about Nike illustrates the importance of corporate strategy to a firm's survival and success. Corporate strategy deals with three key issues facing the corporation as a whole:

1. The firm's overall orientation toward growth, stability, or retrenchment (***directional strategy***).
2. The industries or markets in which the firm competes through its products and business units (***portfolio strategy***).
3. The manner in which management coordinates activities and transfers resources and cultivates capabilities among product lines and business units (***parenting strategy***).

Corporate strategy is primarily about the choice of direction for a firm as a whole and the management of its business or product portfolio.[3] This is true whether the firm is a small company or a large multinational corporation (MNC). In a large multiple-business company, in particular, corporate strategy is concerned with managing various product lines and business units for maximum value. In this instance, corporate headquarters must play the role of the organizational "parent," in that it must deal with various product and business unit "children." Even though each product line or business unit has its own competitive or cooperative strategy that it uses to obtain its own competitive advantage in the marketplace, the corporation must coordinate these different business strategies so that the corporation as a whole succeeds as a "family."[4]

Corporate strategy, therefore, includes decisions regarding the flow of financial and other resources to and from a company's product lines and business units. Through a series of coordinating devices, a company transfers skills and capabilities developed in one unit to other units that need such resources. In this way, it attempts to obtain synergy among numerous product lines and business units so that the corporate whole is greater than the sum of its individual business unit parts.[5] All corporations, from the smallest company offering one product in only one industry to the largest conglomerate operating in many industries with many products, must at one time or another consider one or more of these issues.

To deal with each of the key issues, this chapter is organized into three parts that examine corporate strategy in terms of *directional strategy* (orientation toward growth), *portfolio analysis* (coordination of cash flow among units), and *corporate parenting* (the building of corporate synergies through resource sharing and development).[6]

7.2 Directional Strategy

Just as every product or business unit must follow a business strategy to improve its competitive position, every corporation must decide its orientation toward growth by asking the following three questions:

1. Should we expand, cut back, or continue our operations unchanged?
2. Should we concentrate our activities within our current industry, or should we diversify into other industries?
3. If we want to grow and expand nationally and/or globally, should we do so through internal development or through external acquisitions, mergers, or strategic alliances?

A corporation's **directional strategy** is composed of three general orientations (sometimes called *grand strategies*):

- **Growth strategies** expand the company's activities.
- **Stability strategies** make no change to the company's current activities.
- **Retrenchment strategies** reduce the company's level of activities.

Having chosen the general orientation (such as growth), a company's managers can select from several more specific corporate strategies, such as concentration within one product line/industry or diversification into other products/industries. (See **Figure 7–1**.) These strategies are useful both to corporations operating in only one industry with one product line and to those operating in many industries with many product lines.

Growth Strategies

By far the most widely pursued corporate directional strategies are those designed to achieve growth in sales, assets, profits, or some combination. Companies that do business in expanding industries must grow to survive. Continuing growth involves increasing sales and a chance

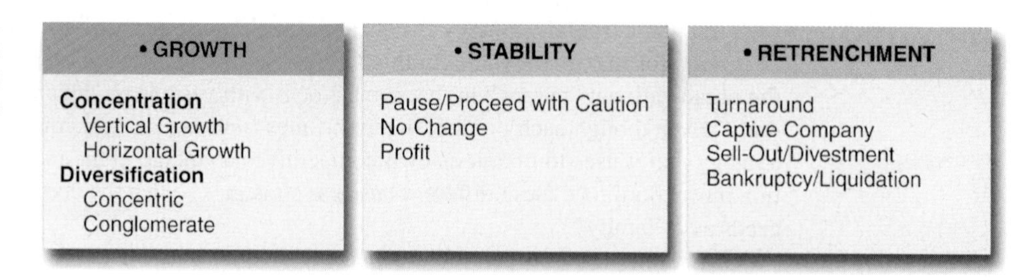

Figure 7–1 **Corporate Directional Strategies**

to take advantage of the experience curve to reduce the per-unit cost of products sold, thereby increasing profits. This cost reduction becomes extremely important if a corporation's industry is growing quickly or consolidating and if competitors are engaging in price wars in attempts to increase their shares of the market. Firms that have not reached "critical mass" (that is, gained the necessary economy of large-scale production) face large losses unless they can find and fill a small, but profitable, niche where higher prices can be offset by special product or service features. That is why Oracle wanted to acquire PeopleSoft, a rival software firm, in 2004. Although still growing, the software industry was maturing around a handful of large firms. According to CEO Larry Ellison, Oracle needed to double or even triple in size by buying smaller and weaker rivals if it was to compete with SAP and Microsoft.[7]

A corporation can grow internally by expanding its operations both globally and domestically, or it can grow externally through mergers, acquisitions, and strategic alliances. A **merger** is a transaction involving two or more corporations in which stock is exchanged but in which only one corporation survives. Mergers usually occur between firms of somewhat similar size and are usually "friendly." The resulting firm is likely to have a name derived from its composite firms. One example is the merging of Allied Corporation and Signal Companies to form Allied Signal. An **acquisition** is the purchase of a company that is completely absorbed as an operating subsidiary or division of the acquiring corporation. Examples are Procter & Gamble's (P&G's) acquisition of Richardson-Vicks, known for its Oil of Olay and Vidal Sassoon brands, and Noxell Corporation, known for Noxzema and Cover Girl.

Acquisitions usually occur between firms of different sizes and can be either friendly or hostile. Hostile acquisitions are often called *takeovers*. A strategic alliance is a partnership between two or more corporations or business units to achieve strategically significant objectives that are mutually beneficial. See **Chapter 6** for a detailed discussion of strategic alliances.

Growth is a very attractive strategy for two key reasons:

- Growth based on increasing market demand may mask flaws in a company—flaws that would be immediately evident in a stable or declining market. A growing flow of revenue into a highly leveraged corporation can create a large amount of **organization slack** (unused resources) that can be used to quickly resolve problems and conflicts between departments and divisions. Growth also provides a big cushion for turnaround in case a strategic error is made. Larger firms also have more bargaining power than do small firms and are more likely to obtain support from key stakeholders in case of difficulty.
- A growing firm offers more opportunities for advancement, promotion, and interesting jobs. Growth itself is exciting and ego-enhancing for CEOs. The marketplace and potential investors tend to view a growing corporation as a "winner" or "on the move." Executive compensation tends to get bigger as an organization increases in size. Large firms are also more difficult to acquire than are smaller ones; thus an executive's job in a large firm is more secure.

The two basic growth strategies are **concentration** on the current product line(s) in one industry and **diversification** into other product lines in other industries.

Concentration

If a company's current product lines have real growth potential, concentration of resources on those product lines makes sense as a strategy for growth. The two basic concentration strategies are vertical growth and horizontal growth. Growing firms in a growing industry tend to choose these strategies before they try diversification.

Vertical Growth. **Vertical growth** can be achieved by taking over a function previously provided by a supplier or by a distributor. The company, in effect, grows by making its own supplies and/or by distributing its own products. This may be done in order to reduce costs, gain control over a scarce resource, guarantee quality of a key input, or obtain access to potential customers. This growth can be achieved either internally by expanding current operations or externally through acquisitions. Henry Ford, for example, used internal company resources to build his River Rouge plant outside Detroit. The manufacturing process was integrated to the point that iron ore entered one end of the long plant, and finished automobiles rolled out the other end, into a huge parking lot. In contrast, Cisco Systems, a maker of Internet hardware, chose the external route to vertical growth by purchasing Radiata, Inc., a maker of chip sets for wireless networks. This acquisition gave Cisco access to technology permitting wireless communications at speeds previously possible only with wired connections.[8]

Vertical growth results in **vertical integration**—the degree to which a firm operates vertically in multiple locations on an industry's value chain, from extracting raw materials to manufacturing to retailing. More specifically, assuming a function previously provided by a supplier is called **backward integration** (going backward on an industry's value chain). The purchase of Carroll's Foods for its hog-growing facilities by Smithfield Foods, the world's largest pork processor, is an example of backward integration.[9] Assuming a function previously provided by a distributor is labeled **forward integration** (going forward on an industry's value chain). FedEx, for example, used forward integration when it purchased Kinko's in order to provide store-front package drop-off and delivery services for the small-business market.[10]

Vertical growth is a logical strategy for a corporation or business unit with a strong competitive position in a highly attractive industry—especially when technology is predictable and markets are growing.[11] To keep and even improve its competitive position, a company may use backward integration to minimize resource acquisition costs and inefficient operations as well as forward integration to gain more control over product distribution. The firm, in effect, builds on its distinctive competence by expanding along the industry's value chain to gain greater competitive advantage.

Although backward integration is often more profitable than forward integration (because of typical low margins in retailing), it can reduce a corporation's strategic flexibility. The resulting encumbrance of expensive assets that might be hard to sell could create an exit barrier, preventing the corporation from leaving that particular industry. Examples of single-use assets are blast furnaces and breweries. When demand drops in either of these industries (steel or beer), these assets have no alternative use but continue to cost money in terms of debt payments, property taxes, and security expenses.

Transaction cost economics proposes that vertical integration is more efficient than contracting for goods and services in the marketplace when the transaction costs of buying goods on the open market become too great. When highly vertically integrated firms become excessively large and bureaucratic, however, the costs of managing the internal transactions may become greater than simply purchasing the needed goods externally—thus justifying outsourcing over vertical integration. This is why vertical integration and outsourcing are situation specific. Neither approach is best for all companies in all situations.[12] STRATEGY HIGHLIGHT **7.1** shows how transaction cost economics helps explain why firms vertically integrate or outsource important activities.

STRATEGY HIGHLIGHT 7.1

Transaction Cost Economics Analyzes Vertical Growth Strategy

Why do corporations use vertical growth to permanently own suppliers or distributors when they could simply purchase individual items when needed on the open market? Transaction cost economics is a branch of institutional economics that attempts to answer this question. Transaction cost economics proposes that owning resources through vertical growth is more efficient than contracting for goods and services in the marketplace when the transaction costs of buying goods on the open market become too great. Transaction costs include the basic costs of drafting, negotiating, and safeguarding a market agreement (a contract) as well as the later managerial costs when the agreement is creating problems (e.g., goods aren't being delivered on time or quality is lower than needed), renegotiation costs (e.g., costs of meetings and phone calls), and the costs of settling disputes (e.g., lawyers' fees and court costs).

According to Williamson, three conditions must be met before a corporation will prefer internalizing a vertical transaction through ownership over contracting for the transaction in the marketplace: (1) A high level of uncertainty must surround the transaction, (2) assets involved in the transaction must be highly specialized to the transaction, and (3) the transaction must occur frequently. If there is a high level of uncertainty, it will be impossible to write a contract covering all contingencies, and it is likely that the contractor will act opportunistically to exploit any gaps in the written agreement—thus creating problems and increasing costs. If the assets being contracted for are highly specialized (e.g., goods or services with few alternate uses), there are likely to be few alternative suppliers—thus allowing the contractor to take advantage of the situation and increase costs. The more frequent the transactions, the more opportunity for the contractor to demand special treatment and thus increase costs further.

Vertical integration is not always more efficient than the marketplace, however. When highly vertically integrated firms become excessively large and bureaucratic, the costs of managing the internal transactions may become greater than simply purchasing the needed goods externally—thus justifying outsourcing over ownership. The usually hidden management costs (e.g., excessive layers of management, endless committee meetings needed for interdepartmental coordination, and delayed decision making due to excessively detailed rules and policies) add to the internal transaction costs—thus reducing the effectiveness and efficiency of vertical integration. The decision to own or to outsource is, therefore, based on the particular situation surrounding the transaction and the ability of the corporation to manage the transaction internally both effectively and efficiently.

Sources: O. E. Williamson and S. G. Winter, eds., *The Nature of the Firm: Origins, Evolution, and Development* (New York: Oxford University Press, 1991); E. Mosakowski, "Organizational Boundaries and Economic Performance: An Empirical Study of Entrepreneurial Computer Firms," *Strategic Management Journal* (February 1991), pp. 115–133; P. S. Ring and A. H. Van de Ven, "Structuring Cooperative Relationships Between Organizations," *Strategic Management Journal* (October 1992), pp. 483–498.

Harrigan proposes that a company's degree of vertical integration can range from total ownership of the value chain needed to make and sell a product to no ownership at all.[13] (See **Figure 7–2**.) Under **full integration**, a firm internally makes 100% of its key supplies and completely controls its distributors. Large oil companies, such as BP Amoco and Royal Dutch Shell, are fully integrated. They own the oil rigs that pump the oil out of the ground, the ships and pipelines that transport the oil, the refineries that convert the oil to gasoline, and the trucks that deliver the gasoline to company-owned and franchised gas stations. If a corporation does not want the disadvantages of full vertical integration, it may choose either taper or quasi-integration strategies.

With **taper integration**, a firm internally produces less than half of its own requirements and buys the rest from outside suppliers (backward taper integration). In the case of Smithfield

Figure 7–2
Vertical Integration Continuum

Full Integration	Taper Integration	Quasi-Integration	Long-Term Contract

Source: Suggested by K.R. Harrigan, Strategies for Vertical Integration *(Lexington, MA: Lexington Books, D.C. Heath, 1983), pp. 16–21. Reprinted by permission of Rowman & Littlefield Publishing Group.*

Foods, its purchase of Carroll's allows it to produce 27% of the hogs it needs to process into pork. In terms of forward taper integration, a firm may sell part of its goods through company-owned stores and the rest through general wholesalers. Although Apple Computer opened 25 company-owned stores in 2001, most of the company's sales continued to be through national chains such as CompUSA and Circuit City and through independent local and regional dealers specializing in Macs.[14]

With **quasi-integration**, a company does not make any of its key supplies but purchases most of its requirements from outside suppliers that are under its partial control (backward quasi-integration). For example, by purchasing 20% of the common stock of a key supplier, In Focus Systems, Motorola guaranteed its access to In Focus' technology, which enabled Motorola to establish a joint venture with In Focus to manufacture flat-panel video displays.[15] An example of forward quasi-integration would be a large pharmaceutical firm acquiring part interest in a drugstore chain in order to guarantee that its drugs have access to the distribution channel. Purchasing part interest in a key supplier or distributor usually provides a company with a seat on the other firm's board of directors, thus guaranteeing the acquiring firm both information and control. A company may not want to invest in suppliers or distributors, but it still wants to guarantee access to needed supplies or distribution channels. In this case, it may use contractual agreements.

Long-term contracts are agreements between two firms to provide agreed-upon goods and services to each other for a specified period of time. This cannot really be considered to be vertical integration unless it is an *exclusive* contract that specifies that the supplier or distributor cannot have a similar relationship with a competitive firm. In that case, the supplier or distributor is really a *captive company* that, although officially independent, does most of its business with the contracted firm and is formally tied to the other company through a long-term contract.

Recently there has been a movement away from vertical growth strategies (and thus vertical integration) toward cooperative contractual relationships with suppliers and even with competitors. These relationships range from **outsourcing**, in which resources are purchased from outsiders through long-term contracts instead of being made in-house (for example, Hewlett-Packard buys its laser engines from Canon for HP's laser jet printers), to strategic alliances, in which partnerships, technology licensing agreements, and joint ventures supplement a firm's capabilities (for example, Toshiba has used strategic alliances with GE, Siemens, Motorola, and Ericsson to become one of the world's leading electronic companies).[16]

Horizontal Growth. A firm can achieve **horizontal growth** by expanding its products into other geographic locations and/or by increasing the range of products and services it offers to current markets. In the latter case, the company expands sideways at the same location on the industry's value chain. One example is Blockbuster's 2004 bid for its rival in movie rentals, Hollywood Entertainment. In another example, General Motors followed a horizontal growth strategy when it extended its operations to China. After it launched Buick in China in 1999, it invested more than $2 billion into an expanded lineup of 14 cars, ranging from the Chevrolet Spark mini car to luxurious Cadillacs. Along with its Chinese partners, GM is investing an additional $3 billion to raise production, develop new engines, and expand R&D in Shanghai.[17] A company can grow horizontally through internal development or externally through acquisitions or strategic alliances with other firms in the same industry.

Horizontal growth results in **horizontal integration**—the degree to which a firm operates in multiple geographic locations at the same point on an industry's value chain. Horizontal integration for a firm may range from full to partial ownership to long-term contracts. For example, KLM, the Dutch airline, purchased a controlling stake (partial ownership) in Northwest Airlines to obtain access to American and Asian markets. KLM was unable to acquire all of Northwest's stock because of U.S. government regulations forbidding foreign ownership of a domestic airline (for defense reasons). Many small commuter airlines engage in long-term contracts with major airlines in order to offer a complete arrangement for travelers. For example, Mesa Airlines arranged a five-year agreement with United Airlines to be listed on United's computer reservations as United Express through the Denver airport.

Diversification Strategies

When an industry consolidates and becomes mature, most of the surviving firms have reached the limits of growth using vertical and horizontal growth strategies. Unless the competitors are able to expand internationally into less mature markets, they may have no choice but to diversify into different industries if they want to continue growing. The two basic diversification strategies are concentric and conglomerate.

Concentric (Related) Diversification. Growth through **concentric diversification** into a related industry may be a very appropriate corporate strategy when a firm has a strong competitive position but industry attractiveness is low. Research indicates that the probability of succeeding by moving into a related business is a function of a company's position in its core business. For companies in leadership positions, the chances for success are nearly three times higher than those for followers.[18] By focusing on the characteristics that have given the company its distinctive competence, the company uses those very strengths as its means of diversification. The firm attempts to secure strategic fit in a new industry where the firm's product knowledge, its manufacturing capabilities, and the marketing skills it used so effectively in the original industry can be put to good use.[19] The corporation's products or processes are related in some way: They possess some common thread.

The search is for **synergy**, the concept that two businesses will generate more profits together than they could separately. The point of commonality may be similar technology, customer usage, distribution, managerial skills, or product similarity. This is the rationale taken by Quebec-based Bombardier, the world's third-largest aircraft manufacturer. In the 1980s, the company expanded beyond snowmobiles into making light rail equipment. Defining itself as a transportation company, it entered the aircraft business in 1986, with its purchase of Canadair, then best known for its fire-fighting airplanes. It later bought Learjet, a well-known maker of business jets. Over a 14-year period, Bombardier launched 14 new aircraft. By 2004, the company was planning to build slightly larger versions of its successful 100-seat commuter jets to directly compete with Airbus and Boeing.[20]

A firm may choose to diversify concentrically through either internal or external means. Bombardier, for example, diversified externally through acquisitions. Toro, in contrast, grew internally in North America by using its current manufacturing processes and distributors to make and market snow blowers in addition to lawn mowers. For some criteria to use when considering concentric diversification alternatives, see **STRATEGY HIGHLIGHT 7.2**.

Conglomerate (Unrelated) Diversification. When management realizes that the current industry is unattractive and that the firm lacks outstanding abilities or skills that it could easily transfer to related products or services in other industries, the most likely strategy is **conglomerate diversification**—diversifying into an industry unrelated to its current one. Rather than maintaining a common thread throughout their organization, strategic managers who adopt this strategy are primarily concerned with financial considerations of cash flow or risk reduction. This is also a good strategy for a firm that is able to transfer its own excellent management system into less well-managed acquired firms. General Electric and Berkshire Hathaway are examples of companies that have used conglomerate diversification to grow successfully. Managed by Warren Buffet, Berkshire Hathaway has interests in furniture retailing, razor blades, airlines, paper, broadcasting, soft drinks, and publishing.[21]

STRATEGY HIGHLIGHT 7.2

Screening Criteria for Concentric Diversification

Market Attractiveness

1. Is the market large enough to be attractive?
2. Is the market growing faster than the economy?
3. Does it offer the potential to increase revenue from current customers?
4. Does it provide the ability to sell existing services to new customers?
5. Does it create a recurring revenue stream?
6. Are average earnings in the industry/market higher than in current businesses?
7. Is the market already taken by strong competitors?
8. Does it strengthen relationships with existing value-chain players?

Market Feasibility

1. Can the company enter the market within a year?
2. Are there any synergies in the geographic region where the market is located?
3. Can existing capabilities be leveraged for market entry?
4. Can existing assets be leveraged for market entry?
5. Can existing employees be used to support this opportunity?
6. Will current and future laws and regulations affect entry?
7. Is there a need for a strong brand in the new market?
8. If there is a need for partners, can the company secure and manage partner relationships?

Source: Summarized from N. J. Kaplan, "Surviving and Thriving When Your Customers Contract," *Journal of Business Strategy* (January/February 2003), p. 20. Republished with permission, Emerald Group Publishing Limited.

The emphasis in conglomerate diversification is on sound investment and value-oriented management rather than on the product–market synergy common to concentric diversification. A cash-rich company with few opportunities for growth in its industry might, for example, move into another industry where opportunities are great but cash is hard to find. Another instance of conglomerate diversification might be when a company with a seasonal and, therefore, uneven cash flow purchases a firm in an unrelated industry with complementing seasonal sales that will level out the cash flow. CSX management considered the purchase of a natural gas transmission business (Texas Gas Resources) by CSX Corporation (a railroad-dominated transportation company) to be a good fit because most of the gas transmission revenue was realized in the winter months—the lean period in the railroad business.

International Entry Options

In today's world, growth usually has international implications. Research indicates that going international is positively associated with firm profitability.[22] A corporation can select from several strategic options the most appropriate method to use in entering a foreign market or establishing manufacturing facilities in another country. The options vary from simple exporting to acquisitions to management contracts. As in the case of KLM's purchase of stock in Northwest Airlines, this can be a part of the corporate strategies previously discussed. See the GLOBAL ISSUE feature to see how Wal-Mart is using international entry options in a horizontal growth strategy to expand throughout the world. Some of the most popular options for international entry are as follows:

- **Exporting:** A good way to minimize risk and experiment with a specific product is **exporting**, shipping goods produced in the company's home country to other countries for marketing. The company could choose to handle all critical functions itself, or it could contract these functions to an export management company. Exporting is becoming

GLOBAL ISSUE

Wal-Mart Looks to International Markets for Growth

How can Wal-Mart continue to grow? From its humble beginnings in Bentonville, Arkansas, the company has successfully grown such that its discount stores can now be found in most every corner of the nation. Wal-Mart long ago surpassed Sears as the largest retailer in the United States. Eight out of ten U.S. households shop at Wal-Mart at least once a year. With $256 billion in annual sales, it is the world's biggest company. Its core domestic discount store business made up 65% of the firm's sales and 85% of its profits in 2004.

According to A. T. Kearney, Wal-Mart's three biggest sources of cost advantage were low corporate overhead, supply-chain efficiencies, and low labor costs. Increasing attempts to unionize Wal-Mart's workers, 8,000 employee lawsuits, and the need to reduce its employee turnover are likely to erode its labor cost advantage. (The company has to hire 600,000 employees every year just to stay at its current size.) The company's expanding human resources, public relations, and legal departments were adding to the firm's overhead costs and eroding its entrepreneurial culture. In addition, Wal-Mart had fewer locations left in the United States on which to build stores. These factors suggested that the company's domestic growth could not be sustained past 2007. Then what?

Wal-Mart's management realized that an increasing percentage of Wal-Mart's growth must come from international markets. Unfortunately, the company's first attempts to expand outside the country in the early 1990s flopped miserably. Wal-Mart offered the wrong products, such as tennis balls that wouldn't bounce in high-altitude Mexico City and 110-volt appliances in Argentina, where 220 volts is the norm. Learning from those early attempts, Wal-Mart opened stores in Canada, Mexico, China, Brazil, Japan, Germany, and Britain.

After closing a losing operation in Indonesia, management altered its strategy to focus on becoming a major retailer in Europe. In December 1997, Wal-Mart purchased the 21-store German Tertkauf chain. A year later, it strengthened its hold in Germany by acquiring 74 Interspar stores. It took months of remodeling the stores with wider aisles, better lighting, and more check-out counters before the stores were re-christened Wal-Mart. Unfortunately, Wal-Mart was unable to make these stores profitable; even by 2004. German price controls, rigid labor laws, and restrictive zoning regulations made it very difficult for Wal-Mart to compete with well-established rivals such as Metro and Aldi. Wal-Mart's expatriate managers suffered from culture-clash, which was not helped by their refusal to learn German. Hiring employees was difficult due to relatively low pay and a frugal policy on managers' business expenses.

Interestingly, Wal-Mart did better in the United Kingdom than in Germany. In 1999, it bought Britain's 229-store Asda Group, the country's third-largest grocery chain. Already a strong retailer, Wal-Mart's Asda soon overtook struggling J. Sainsbury to become the second-largest supermarket chain after Tesco in the UK.

Worldwide, more than 100 million customers visit Wal-Mart stores every week. Of its 4,906 total stores, in 2004, 1,375 (28%) were located outside the United States in nine countries (including 623 in Mexico and 34 in China). In 2004, Wal-Mart's management planned to open 50 new discount stores and more than 220 new supercenters in North America, plus around 140 stores overseas.

Sources: "How Big Can It Grow?" *Economist* (April 17, 2004), pp. 67–69; L. Kim, "Crossing the Rhine," *U.S. News & World Report* (August 14, 2000), p. 39; "Wal-Mart to Buy British Food Chain," *Des Moines Register* (June 15, 1999), p. 9S; P. Geitner, "Wal-Mart Rises in Germany," *Des Moines Register* (December 11, 1999), p. 12S; *Money* (December 1999), p. 162.

increasingly popular for small businesses because of the Internet, fax machines, toll-free numbers, and overnight express services, which reduce the once-formidable costs of going international.

- **Licensing:** Under a **licensing** agreement, the licensing firm grants rights to another firm in the host country to produce and/or sell a product. The licensee pays compensation to the licensing firm in return for technical expertise. This is an especially useful strategy if the trademark or brand name is well known but the company does not have sufficient funds to finance its entering the country directly. Anheuser-Busch uses this strategy to produce and market Budweiser beer in the United Kingdom, Japan, Israel, Australia, Korea, and the Philippines. This strategy is also important if the country makes entry via investment either difficult or impossible.

- **Franchising:** Under a **franchising** agreement, the franchiser grants rights to another company to open a retail store using the franchiser's name and operating system. In exchange, the franchisee pays the franchiser a percentage of its sales as a royalty. Franchising provides an opportunity for a firm to establish a presence in countries where the population or per capita spending is not sufficient for a major expansion effort.[23] Franchising accounts for 40% of total U.S. retail sales. Close to half of U.S. franchisers, such as Toys 'Я' Us, franchise internationally.[24]
- **Joint Ventures:** Forming a joint venture between a foreign corporation and a domestic company is the most popular strategy used to enter a new country.[25] Companies often form joint ventures to combine the resources and expertise needed to develop new products or technologies. A joint venture may also enable a firm to enter a country that restricts foreign ownership. The corporation can enter another country with fewer assets at stake and thus lower risk. For example, when Mexico privatized its railroads in 1996 (two years after the North American Free Trade Agreement was ratified), the Kansas City Southern (KCS) saw an opportunity to form one complete railroad from Mexico's industrialized northeast to Canada. KCS jointly bid with the Mexican shipping line Transportacion Maritima Mexicana (with which it would jointly operate the Mexican rail system) to purchase 80% of Grupo Transportacion Ferroviaria Mexicana (TFM). KCS then formed an alliance with Canadian National Railway to complete the route.[26] A joint venture may be an association between a company and a firm in the host country or a government agency in that country. A quick method of obtaining local management, it also reduces the risks of expropriation and harassment by host country officials.
- **Acquisitions:** A relatively quick way to move into an international area is through acquisitions—purchasing another company already operating in that area. Synergistic benefits can result if the company acquires a firm with strong complementary product lines and a good distribution network. For example, South Africa Breweries (SAB) paid $5.6 billion to purchase Miller Brewing from Philip Morris in 2002. With this acquisition, SAB became SABMiller and obtained a strong position in North America without having to build breweries and a distribution network. It also moved ahead of Anheuser-Busch as the world's second-largest brewer, after Belgium's Interbrew. SABMiller's next international strategic move was to bid for China's Harbin Brewery Group in 2004.[27] Research suggests that wholly owned subsidiaries are more successful in international undertakings than are strategic alliances, such as joint ventures.[28] This is one reason firms more experienced in international markets take a higher ownership position when making a foreign investment.[29] Cross-border acquisitions now account for 19% of all acquisitions in the United States—up from only 6% in 1985.[30] In some countries, however, acquisitions can be difficult to arrange because of a lack of available information about potential candidates. Government restrictions on ownership, such as the U.S. requirement that limits foreign ownership of U.S. airlines to 49% of nonvoting and 25% of voting stock, can also discourage acquisitions.
- **Green-Field Development:** If a company doesn't want to purchase another company's problems along with its assets, it may choose **green-field development**—building its own manufacturing plant and distribution system. Research indicates that firms possessing high levels of technology, multinational experience, and diverse product lines prefer greenfield development to acquisitions.[31] This is usually a far more complicated and expensive operation than acquisition, but it allows a company more freedom in designing the plant, choosing suppliers, and hiring a workforce. For example, Nissan, Honda, and Toyota built auto factories in rural areas of Great Britain and then hired a young workforce with no experience in the industry.

- **Production Sharing:** Coined by Peter Drucker, the term **production sharing** means the process of combining the higher labor skills and technology available in developed countries with the lower-cost labor available in developing countries. It is often called *outsourcing*. One example is Maytag's moving some of its refrigeration production to a new plant in Reynosa, Mexico, in order to reduce labor costs. A current trend is to move data processing and programming activities "offshore" to places such as Ireland, India, Barbados, Jamaica, the Philippines, and Singapore, where wages are lower, English is spoken, and telecommunications are in place.
- **Turnkey Operations: Turnkey operations** are typically contracts for the construction of operating facilities in exchange for a fee. The facilities are transferred to the host country or firm when they are complete. The customer is usually a government agency of, for example, a Middle Eastern country that has decreed that a particular product must be produced locally and under its control. For example, Fiat built an auto plant in Russia to produce an older model of Fiat under a Russian brand name. MNCs that perform turnkey operations are frequently industrial equipment manufacturers that supply some of their own equipment for the project and that commonly sell replacement parts and maintenance services to the host country. They thereby create customers as well as future competitors.
- **BOT Concept:** The **BOT (Build, Operate, Transfer) concept** is a variation of the turnkey operation. Instead of turning the facility (usually a power plant or toll road) over to the host country when completed, the company operates the facility for a fixed period of time, during which it earns back its investment plus a profit. It then turns the facility over to the government at little or no cost to the host country.[32]
- **Management Contracts:** A large corporation operating throughout the world is likely to have a large amount of management talent at its disposal. **Management contracts** offer a means through which a corporation can use some of its personnel to assist a firm in a host country for a specified fee and period of time. Management contracts are common when a host government expropriates part or all of a foreign-owned company's holdings in its country. The contracts allow the firm to continue to earn some income from its investment and keep the operations going until local management is trained.

Controversies in Directional Growth Strategies

Is vertical growth better than horizontal growth? Is concentric diversification better than conglomerate diversification? Although the research is not in complete agreement, growth into areas related to a company's current product lines is generally more successful than is growth into completely unrelated areas.[33] For example, one study of various growth projects examined how many were considered successful—that is, still in existence after 22 years. The results were vertical growth, 80%; horizontal growth, 50%; concentric diversification, 35%; and conglomerate diversification, 28%.[34]

In terms of diversification strategies, research suggests that the relationship between relatedness and performance is curvilinear, in the shape of an inverted U-shaped curve. If a new business is very similar to that of the acquiring firm, it adds little new to the corporation and only marginally improves performance. If the new business is completely different from the acquiring company's businesses, there may be very little potential for any synergy. If, however, the new business provides new resources and capabilities in a different, but similar, business, the likelihood of a significant performance improvement is high.[35]

Is internal growth better than external growth? Corporations can follow the growth strategies of either concentration or diversification through the internal development of new products and services, or through external acquisitions, mergers, and strategic alliances. The value of global acquisitions and mergers has steadily increased from less than $1 trillion in 1990 to

$3.5 trillion in 2000.[36] Research generally concludes, however, that firms growing through acquisitions do not perform financially as well as firms that grow through internal means.[37] For example, on September 3, 2001, the day *before* HP announced that it was purchasing Compaq, HP's stock was selling at $23.11. After the announcement, the stock price fell to $18.87. Three years later, on September 21, 2004, the shares sold at $18.70, down 19% from the first of the year.[38] One reason for this poor performance may be that acquiring firms tend to spend less on R&D than do other firms.[39] Another reason may be the typically high price of the acquisition itself. Studies reveal that over one-half to two-thirds of acquisitions are failures primarily because the premiums paid were too high for them to earn their cost of capital.[40] Another reason for the poor stock performance is that 50% of the customers of a merged firm are less satisfied with the combined company's service two years after the merger.[41] Other research indicates, however, that acquisitions have a higher survival rate than do new internally generated business ventures.[42] It is likely that neither strategy is best by itself and that some combination of internal and external growth strategies is better than using one or the other.[43]

What can improve acquisition performance? A study by Bain & Company of more than 11,000 acquisitions by companies throughout the world concluded that successful acquirers make small, low-risk acquisitions before moving on to larger ones.[44] Research by Porrini reveals that previous experience between an acquirer and a target firm in terms of R&D, manufacturing, or marketing alliances improves the likelihood of a successful acquisition.[45] Realizing that an acquired company must be carefully assimilated into the acquiring firm's operations, Cisco uses three criteria to judge whether a company is a suitable candidate for takeover:

- It must be relatively small.
- It must be comparable in organizational culture.
- It must be physically close to one of the existing affiliates.[46]

Stability Strategies

A corporation may choose stability over growth by continuing its current activities without any significant change in direction. Although sometimes viewed as a lack of strategy, the stability family of corporate strategies can be appropriate for a successful corporation operating in a reasonably predictable environment.[47] They are very popular with small business owners who have found a niche and are happy with their success and the manageable size of their firms. Stability strategies can be very useful in the short run, but they can be dangerous if followed for too long (as many small-town businesses discovered when Wal-Mart came to town). Some of the more popular of these strategies are the pause/proceed-with-caution, no-change, and profit strategies.

Pause/Proceed-with-Caution Strategy

A **pause/proceed-with-caution strategy** is, in effect, a timeout—an opportunity to rest before continuing a growth or retrenchment strategy. It is a very deliberate attempt to make only incremental improvements until a particular environmental situation changes. It is typically conceived as a temporary strategy to be used until the environment becomes more hospitable or to enable a company to consolidate its resources after prolonged rapid growth. This was the strategy Dell followed after its growth strategy had resulted in more growth than it could handle. Explained CEO Michael Dell, "We grew 285% in two years, and we're having some growing pains." Selling personal computers by mail enabled Dell to underprice Compaq and IBM, but it could not keep up with the needs of a $2 billion, 5,600-employee company selling PCs in 95 countries. Dell did not give up on its growth strategy; it merely put it temporarily in limbo until the company was able to hire new managers, improve the structure, and build new facilities.[48]

No-Change Strategy

A **no-change strategy** is a decision to do nothing new—a choice to continue current operations and policies for the foreseeable future. Rarely articulated as a definite strategy, a no-change strategy's success depends on a lack of significant change in a corporation's situation. The relative stability created by the firm's modest competitive position in an industry facing little or no growth encourages the company to continue on its current course, making only small adjustments for inflation in its sales and profit objectives. There are no obvious opportunities or threats, nor is there much in the way of significant strengths or weaknesses. Few aggressive new competitors are likely to enter such an industry. The corporation has probably found a reasonably profitable and stable niche for its products. Unless the industry is undergoing consolidation, the relative comfort a company in this situation experiences is likely to encourage the company to follow a no-change strategy in which the future is expected to continue as an extension of the present. Most small-town businesses probably follow this strategy before Wal-Mart moves into their areas.

Profit Strategy

A **profit strategy** is a decision to do nothing new in a worsening situation but instead to act as though the company's problems are only temporary. The profit strategy is an attempt to artificially support profits when a company's sales are declining by reducing investment and short-term discretionary expenditures. Rather than announce the company's poor position to shareholders and the investment community at large, top management may be tempted to follow this very seductive strategy. Blaming the company's problems on a hostile environment (such as anti-business government policies, unethical competitors, finicky customers, and/or greedy lenders), management defers investments and/or cuts expenses (such as R&D, maintenance, and advertising) to stabilize profits during this period. It may even sell one of its product lines for the cash-flow benefits. For example, Kmart sold some of its retail stores to Home Depot and Sears at a time when its store sales were declining. Obviously, the profit strategy is useful only to help a company get through a temporary difficulty. It may also be a way to boost the value of a company in preparation for going public via an initial public offering (IPO). Unfortunately, the strategy is seductive, and if continued long enough, it will lead to a serious deterioration in a corporation's competitive position. The profit strategy thus tends to be top management's passive, short-term, and often self-serving response to a difficult situation.

Retrenchment Strategies

A company may pursue retrenchment strategies when it has a weak competitive position in some or all of its product lines, resulting in poor performance—sales are down and profits are becoming losses. These strategies impose a great deal of pressure to improve performance. In an attempt to eliminate the weaknesses that are dragging the company down, management may follow one of several retrenchment strategies, ranging from turnaround or becoming a captive company to selling out, bankruptcy, or liquidation.

Turnaround Strategy

Turnaround strategy emphasizes the improvement of operational efficiency and is probably most appropriate when a corporation's problems are pervasive but not yet critical. Research shows that poorly performing firms in mature industries have been able to improve their performance by cutting costs and expenses and by selling assets.[49] Analogous to a weight-reduction diet, the two basic phases of a turnaround strategy are contraction and consolidation.[50]

Contraction is the initial effort to quickly "stop the bleeding" with a general, across-the-board cutback in size and costs. The second phase, **consolidation**, implements a program to stabilize the now-leaner corporation. To streamline the company, plans are developed to reduce unnecessary overhead and to make functional activities cost-justified. This is a crucial time for the organization. If the consolidation phase is not conducted in a positive manner, many of the best people leave the organization. An overemphasis on downsizing and cutting costs coupled with a heavy hand by top management is usually counterproductive and can actually hurt performance.[51] If, however, all employees are encouraged to get involved in productivity improvements, the firm is likely to emerge from this retrenchment period a much stronger and better-organized company. It has improved its competitive position and is able once again to expand the business.[52] See **Strategy Highlight 7.3** for a description of IBM's effective use of the turnaround strategy.

Captive Company Strategy

A **captive company strategy** involves giving up independence in exchange for security. A company with a weak competitive position may not be able to engage in a full-blown turnaround strategy. The industry may not be sufficiently attractive to justify such an effort from either the current management or investors. Nevertheless, a company in this situation faces poor sales and increasing losses unless it takes some action. Management desperately searches for an "angel" by offering to be a captive company to one of its larger customers in

STRATEGY HIGHLIGHT 7.3

Turnaround Strategy at IBM

During the 1970s and 1980s, IBM dominated the computer industry worldwide. It was the market leader in both large mainframe and small personal computers (PCs). Along with Apple Computer, IBM set the standard for all PCs. Even until recently—when IBM no longer dominates the field—PCs are still identified as being either Apple or IBM-style PCs.

IBM's problems came to a head in the early 1990s. The company's computer sales were falling. More companies were choosing to replace their large, expensive mainframe computers with PCs, but they weren't buying the PCs from IBM. An increasing number of firms, such as HP, Dell, Gateway, and Compaq, had entered the industry. They offered IBM-style PC "clones" that were considerably cheaper and often more advanced than IBM's PCs. IBM's falling revenues meant corporate losses—$15 billion in cumulative losses from 1991 through 1993. Industry experts perceived the company as a bureaucratic dinosaur that could no longer adapt to changing conditions. Its stock price fell to $40, with no end in sight.

IBM's board of directors in 1993 hired a new CEO, Louis Gerstner, to lead a corporate turnaround strategy at "Big Blue" (the nickname IBM had earned because of its rigid dress code policies). To stop the flow of red ink, the company violated its long-held "no layoffs" policy by reducing its workforce by 40%. Under Gerstner, IBM reorganized its sales force around specific industries, such as retailing and banking. Decision making was made easier. Previously, according to Joseph Formichelli, a top executive with the PC division, he had "had to go through seven layers to get things done." Firing incompetent employees could take a year, "so you pawned them off on another group." Strategy presentations were hashed over so many times, "they got watered down to nothing." Under Gerstner, however, formal presentations were no longer desired. The emphasis switched to quicker decision making and a stronger customer orientation.

From 1994 to 2000, the company transformed itself from being a besieged computer maker to a dominant service provider. Its Global Services unit grew from almost nothing to a $30 billion business with more than 135,000 employees. In 2004, it divested its PC business.

Source: G. Hamel, "Waking Up IBM," *Harvard Business Review* (July–August 2000), pp. 137–146; I. Sager, "Inside IBM: Internet Business Machines," *Business Week E.Biz* (December 13, 1999), pp. EB20–EB40; B. Ziegler, "Gerstner's IBM Revival: Impressive, Incomplete," *Wall Street Journal* (March 25, 1997), pp. B1, B4.

order to guarantee the company's continued existence with a long-term contract. In this way, the corporation may be able to reduce the scope of some of its functional activities, such as marketing, thus significantly reducing costs. The weaker company gains certainty of sales and production in return for becoming heavily dependent on another firm for at least 75% of its sales. For example, to become the sole supplier of an auto part to General Motors, Simpson Industries of Birmingham, Michigan, agreed to let a special team from GM inspect its engine parts facilities and books and interview its employees. In return, nearly 80% of the company's production was sold to GM through long-term contracts.[53]

Sell-Out/Divestment Strategy

If a corporation with a weak competitive position in an industry is unable either to pull itself up by its bootstraps or to find a customer to which it can become a captive company, it may have no choice but to sell out. The **sell-out strategy** makes sense if management can still obtain a good price for its shareholders and the employees can keep their jobs by selling the entire company to another firm. The hope is that another company will have the necessary resources and determination to return the company to profitability.

If the corporation has multiple business lines and it chooses to sell off a division with low growth potential, this is called **divestment**. This was the strategy Quaker Oats used when it sold its struggling Snapple beverage unit for $300 million—$1.4 billion less than it had paid for the business. When Quaker's management had purchased Snapple, they believed that they could use Quaker's resources to continue Snapple's phenomenal growth. They had hoped to transform the stately old oatmeal company into a soft-drink power. Unfortunately for Quaker, the soft drink market was changing rapidly. New entrants, such as Arizona Iced Tea, Mystic, and Nantucket Nectars, imitated Snapple, while Coke and Pepsi formed alliances with Nestea and Lipton to enter the market.[54]

Bankruptcy/Liquidation Strategy

When a company finds itself in the worst possible situation, with a poor competitive position in an industry with few prospects, management has only a few alternatives—all of them distasteful. Because no one is interested in buying a weak company in an unattractive industry, the firm must pursue a bankruptcy or liquidation strategy. **Bankruptcy** involves giving up management of the firm to the courts in return for some settlement of the corporation's obligations. Top management hopes that once the court decides the claims on the company, the company will be stronger and better able to compete in a more attractive industry. Faced with high debt and declining sales of its Wonder Bread, Twinkies, and Hostess Cup Cakes, Interstate Bakeries declared Chapter 11 bankruptcy in 2004. Because the company had been unable to reduce its high overhead costs, its products were no longer cost-competitive. A new CEO was appointed to do what Interstate's management had been unable to do: slash labor and manufacturing costs while boosting distribution to Wal-Mart and other discount retailers.[55]

In contrast to bankruptcy, which seeks to perpetuate a corporation, **liquidation** is the termination of a firm. When the industry is unattractive and the company is too weak to be sold as a going concern, management may choose to convert as many saleable assets as possible to cash, which is then distributed to the shareholders after all obligations are paid. Liquidation is a prudent strategy for distressed firms with a small number of choices, all of which are problematic.[56] The benefit of liquidation over bankruptcy is that the board of directors, as representatives of the shareholders, together with top management make the decisions instead of turning them over to the bankruptcy court, which may choose to ignore shareholders completely.

At times, top management must be willing to select one of these less desirable retrenchment strategies. Unfortunately, many top managers are unwilling to admit that their company has serious weaknesses for fear that they may be personally blamed. Even worse, top management may not even perceive that crises are developing. When these top managers eventually notice trouble, they are prone to attribute the problems to temporary environmental disturbances and tend to follow profit strategies. Even when things are going terribly wrong, top management is greatly tempted to avoid liquidation in the hope of a miracle. Top management enters a *cycle of decline*, in which it goes through a process of secrecy and denial, followed by blame and scorn, avoidance and turf protection, ending with passivity and helplessness.[57] Thus, a corporation needs a strong board of directors who, to safeguard shareholders' interests, can tell top management when to quit.

7.3 Portfolio Analysis

Chapter 6 deals with how individual product lines and business units can gain competitive advantage in the marketplace by using competitive and cooperative strategies. Companies with multiple product lines or business units must also ask themselves how these various products and business units should be managed to boost overall corporate performance:

- How much of our time and money should we spend on our best products and business units to ensure that they continue to be successful?
- How much of our time and money should we spend developing new costly products, most of which will never be successful?

One of the most popular aids to developing corporate strategy in a multiple-business corporation is portfolio analysis. Although its popularity has dropped since the 1970s and 1980s, when more than half of the largest business corporations used portfolio analysis, it is still used by around 27% of Fortune 500 firms in corporate strategy formulation.[58] Portfolio analysis puts the corporate headquarters into the role of an internal banker. In **portfolio analysis**, top management views its product lines and business units as a series of investments from which it expects a profitable return. The product lines/business units form a portfolio of investments that top management must constantly juggle to ensure the best return on the corporation's invested money. A McKinsey & Company study of the performance of the 200 largest U.S. corporations found that companies that actively managed their business portfolios through acquisitions and divestitures created substantially more shareholder value than companies that passively held their businesses.[59]

Two of the most popular portfolio approaches are the BCG Growth-Share Matrix and GE Business Screen.

BCG Growth-Share Matrix

Using the **BCG (Boston Consulting Group) Growth-Share Matrix**, depicted in **Figure 7–3**, is the simplest way to portray a corporation's portfolio of investments. Each of a corporation's product lines or business units is plotted on a matrix according to both the growth rate of the industry in which it competes and its relative market share. A unit's relative competitive position is defined as its market share in the industry divided by that of the largest other competitor. By this calculation, a relative market share above 1.0 belongs to the market leader. The business growth rate is the percentage of market growth—that is, the percentage by which sales of a particular business unit classification of products have increased. The matrix assumes that, other things being equal, a growing market is attractive.

The line separating areas of high and low relative competitive position is set at 1.5 times. A product line or business unit must have relative strengths of this magnitude to ensure that it

Figure 7–3
BCG Growth-Share Matrix

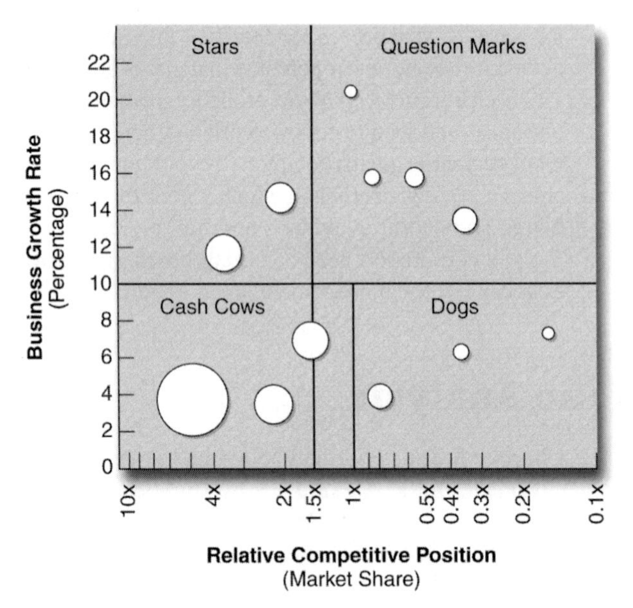

Source: Reprinted from Long Range Planning, *Vol. 10, No. 2, 1977, Hedley, "Strategy and the Business Portfolio," p. 12. Copyright © 1977 with permission from Elsevier.*

will have the dominant position needed to be a "star" or "cash cow." On the other hand, a product line or unit having a relative competitive position less than 1.0 has "dog" status.[60] Each product or unit is represented in **Figure 7–3** by a circle. The area of the circle represents the relative significance of each business unit or product line to the corporation in terms of assets used or sales generated.

The BCG Growth-Share Matrix has a lot in common with the product life cycle. As a product moves through its life cycle, it is categorized into one of four types for the purpose of funding decisions:

- **Question marks** (sometimes called "problem children" or "wildcats") are new products with the potential for success, but they need a lot of cash for development. If such a product is to gain enough market share to become a market leader and thus a star, money must be taken from more mature products and spent on the question mark.
- **Stars** are market leaders that are typically at the peak of their product life cycle and are usually able to generate enough cash to maintain their high share of the market. When their market growth rate slows, stars become cash cows. HP's printer business has been called HP's "crown jewel" by CEO Carleton Fiorina because in 2002 it provided 105% of HP's profits (other units lost money) while accounting for only 28% of HP's sales.[61]
- **Cash cows** typically bring in far more money than is needed to maintain their market share. In this declining stage of their life cycle, these products are "milked" for cash that will be invested in new question marks. Question marks unable to obtain dominant market share (and thus become stars) by the time the industry growth rate inevitably slows become dogs.
- **Dogs** have low market share and do not have the potential (because they are in an unattractive industry) to bring in much cash. According to the BCG Growth-Share Matrix, dogs should be either sold off or managed carefully for the small amount of cash they can generate. For example, DuPont, the inventor of nylon, sold its textiles unit in 2003 because the company wanted to eliminate its low-margin products and focus more on its growing biotech business.[62]

Underlying the BCG Growth-Share Matrix is the concept of the experience curve (discussed in **Chapter 5**). The key to success is assumed to be market share. Firms with the highest market share tend to have a cost leadership position based on economies of scale, among other things. If a company is able to use the experience curve to its advantage, it should be able to manufacture and sell new products at a price low enough to garner early market share leadership (assuming no successful imitation by competitors). Once the product becomes a star, it is destined to be very profitable, considering its inevitable future as a cash cow.

Having plotted the current positions of its product lines or business units on a matrix, a company can project its future positions, assuming no change in strategy. Present and projected matrixes can thus be used to help identify major strategic issues facing the organization. The goal of any company is to maintain a balanced portfolio so it can be self-sufficient in cash and always working to harvest mature products in declining industries to support new ones in growing industries.

The BCG Growth-Share Matrix is a very well-known portfolio concept with some clear advantages. It is quantifiable and easy to use. *Cash cow*, *dog*, and *star* are easy-to-remember terms for referring to a corporation's business units or products. Unfortunately, the BCG Growth-Share Matrix also has some serious limitations:

- The use of highs and lows to form four categories is too simplistic.
- The link between market share and profitability is questionable.[63] Low-share businesses can also be profitable.[64] For example, Olivetti is still profitably selling manual typewriters through mail-order catalogs.
- Growth rate is only one aspect of industry attractiveness.
- Product lines or business units are considered only in relation to one competitor: the market leader. Small competitors with fast-growing market shares are ignored.
- Market share is only one aspect of overall competitive position.

GE Business Screen

General Electric, with the assistance of the McKinsey & Company consulting firm, developed a more complicated matrix. As depicted in **Figure 7–4**, the **GE Business Screen** includes nine cells based on long-term industry attractiveness and business strength/competitive position. The GE Business Screen, in contrast to the BCG Growth-Share Matrix, includes much more data in its two key factors than just business growth rate and comparable market share. For example, at GE, industry attractiveness includes market growth rate, industry profitability, size, and pricing practices, among other possible opportunities and threats. Business strength or competitive position includes market share as well as technological position, profitability, and size, among other possible strengths and weaknesses.[65]

The individual product lines or business units are identified by a letter and plotted as circles on the GE Business Screen. The area of each circle is in proportion to the size of the industry in terms of sales. The pie slices within the circles depict the market shares of the product lines or business units.

To plot product lines or business units on the GE Business Screen, follow these four steps:

1. Select criteria to rate the industry for each product line or business unit. Assess overall industry attractiveness for each product line or business unit on a scale from 1 (very unattractive) to 5 (very attractive).
2. Select the key factors needed for success in each product line or business unit. Assess business strength/competitive position for each product line or business unit on a scale of 1 (very weak) to 5 (very strong).

Figure 7–4
General Electric's Business Screen

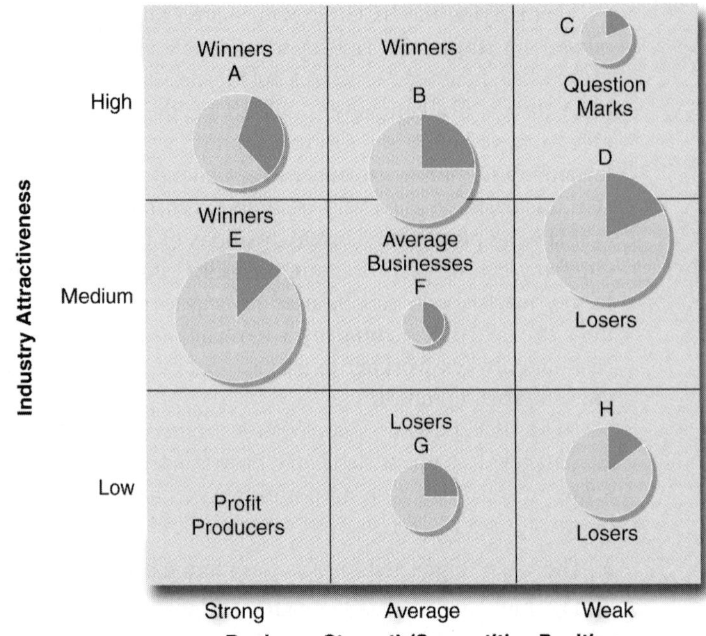

Source: Adapted from Strategic Management in GE, *Corporate Planning and Development, General Electric Corporation. Reprinted by permission of General Electric Company.*

3. Plot each product line's or business unit's current position on a matrix like that depicted in **Figure 7–4**.
4. Plot the firm's future portfolio, assuming that present corporate and business strategies remain unchanged. Is there a performance gap between projected and desired portfolios? If so, this gap should serve as a stimulus to seriously review the corporation's current mission, objectives, strategies, and policies.

Overall the nine-cell GE Business Screen is an improvement over the BCG Growth-Share Matrix. The GE Business Screen considers many more variables and does not lead to such simplistic conclusions. It recognizes, for example, that the attractiveness of an industry can be assessed in many different ways (other than simply using growth rate), and it thus allows users to select whatever criteria they feel are most appropriate to their situation. This portfolio matrix, however, does have some shortcomings:

- It can get quite complicated and cumbersome.
- The numerical estimates of industry attractiveness and business strength/competitive position give the appearance of objectivity, but they are in reality subjective judgments that may vary from one person to another.
- It cannot effectively depict the positions of new products or business units in developing industries.

Advantages and Limitations of Portfolio Analysis

Portfolio analysis is commonly used in strategy formulation because it offers certain *advantages*:

- It encourages top management to evaluate each of the corporation's businesses individually and to set objectives and allocate resources for each.
- It stimulates the use of externally oriented data to supplement management's judgment.

- It raises the issue of cash-flow availability for use in expansion and growth.
- Its graphic depiction facilitates communication.

Portfolio analysis does, however, have some very real *limitations* that have caused some companies to reduce their use of this approach:

- Defining product/market segments is difficult.
- It suggests the use of standard strategies that can miss opportunities or be impractical.
- It provides an illusion of scientific rigor when in reality positions are based on subjective judgments.
- Its value-laden terms, such as cash cow and dog, can lead to self-fulfilling prophecies.
- It is not always clear what makes an industry attractive or where a product is in its life cycle.
- Naively following the prescriptions of a portfolio model may actually reduce corporate profits if they are used inappropriately. For example, General Mills' Chief Executive H. Brewster Atwater cited his company's Bisquick brand baking mix as a product that would have been written off years ago based on portfolio analysis. "This product is 57 years old. By all rights it should have been overtaken by newer products. But with the proper research to improve the product and promotion to keep customers excited, it's doing very well."[66]

7.4 Corporate Parenting

Campbell, Goold, and Alexander, authors of *Corporate-Level Strategy: Creating Value in the Multibusiness Company*, contend that corporate strategists must address two crucial questions:

- What businesses should this company own and why?
- What organizational structure, management processes, and philosophy will foster superior performance from the company's business units?[67]

Portfolio analysis attempts to answer these questions by examining the attractiveness of various industries and by managing business units for cash flow—that is, by using cash generated from mature units to build new product lines. Unfortunately, portfolio analysis fails to deal with the question of what industries a corporation should enter or with how a corporation can attain synergy among its product lines and business units. As suggested by its name, portfolio analysis tends to primarily view matters financially, regarding business units and product lines as separate and independent investments.

Corporate parenting, in contrast, views a corporation in terms of resources and capabilities that can be used to build business unit value as well as generate synergies across business units. According to Campbell, Goold, and Alexander:

> *Multibusiness companies create value by influencing—or parenting—the businesses they own. The best parent companies create more value than any of their rivals would if they owned the same businesses. Those companies have what we call parenting advantage.*[68]

Corporate parenting generates corporate strategy by focusing on the core competencies of the parent corporation and on the value created from the relationship between the parent and its businesses. In the form of corporate headquarters, the parent has a great deal of power in this relationship. According to Campbell, Goold, and Alexander, if there is a good fit between the parent's skills and resources and the needs and opportunities of the business units, the corporation is likely to create value. If, however, there is not a good fit, the corporation is likely to destroy value.[69] Research indicates that companies that have a good fit between their strategy and their parenting roles are better performers than companies that do not have a good fit.[70] This approach to corporate strategy is useful not only in deciding what new businesses to acquire but also in choosing how each existing business unit should be best managed. This appears to be the secret to the success of General Electric under CEO Jack Welch. According to one analyst, "He and his managers really add value by imposing tough standards of profitability and by disseminating knowledge and best practice quickly around the GE empire. If some manufacturing trick cuts costs in GE's aero-engine repair shops in Wales, he insists it be applied across the group."[71]

The primary job of corporate headquarters is, therefore, to obtain synergy among the business units by providing needed resources to units, transferring skills and capabilities among the units, and coordinating the activities of shared unit functions to attain economies of scope (as in centralized purchasing).[72] This is in agreement with the concept of the learning organization discussed in **Chapter 1** in which the role of a large firm is to facilitate and transfer the knowledge assets and services throughout the corporation.[73] This is especially important given that 75% or more of a modern company's market value stems from its intangible assets—the organization's knowledge and capabilities.[74]

Developing a Corporate Parenting Strategy

Campbell, Goold, and Alexander recommend that the search for appropriate corporate strategy involves three analytical steps:

1. **Examine each business unit (or target firm, in the case of acquisition) in terms of its strategic factors:** People in the business units probably identified strategic factors when they were generating business strategies for their units. One popular approach is to establish centers of excellence throughout a corporation. According to Frost, Birkinshaw, and Ensign, a **center of excellence** is "an organizational unit that embodies a set of capabilities that has been explicitly recognized by the firm as an important source of value creation, with the intention that these capabilities be leveraged by and/or disseminated to other parts of the firm."[75]
2. **Examine each business unit (or target firm) in terms of areas in which performance can be improved:** These are considered to be parenting opportunities. For example, two business units might be able to gain economies of scope by combining their sales forces. In another instance, a unit may have good, but not great, manufacturing and logistics skills. A parent company having world-class expertise in these areas could improve that unit's performance. The corporate parent could also transfer some people from one business unit who have the desired skills to another unit that is in need of those skills. People at corporate headquarters may, because of their experience in many industries, spot areas where improvements are possible that even people in the business unit may not have noticed. Unless specific areas are significantly weaker than the competition, people in the business units may not even be aware that these areas could be improved, especially if each business unit monitors only its own particular industry.
3. **Analyze how well the parent corporation fits with the business unit (or target firm):** Corporate headquarters must be aware of its own strengths and weaknesses in terms of resources, skills, and capabilities. To do this, the corporate parent must ask whether it has the characteristics that fit the parenting opportunities in each business unit. It must also ask whether there is a misfit between the parent's characteristics and the strategic factors of each business unit.

Horizontal Strategy and Multipoint Competition

A **horizontal strategy** is a corporate strategy that cuts across business unit boundaries to build synergy across business units and to improve the competitive position of one or more business units.[76] When used to build synergy, it acts like a parenting strategy. When used to improve the competitive position of one or more business units, it can be thought of as a corporate competitive strategy. In **multipoint competition**, large multi-business corporations compete against other large multi-business firms in a number of markets. These multipoint competitors are firms that compete with each other not only in one business unit but in a number of business units. At one time or another, a cash-rich competitor may choose to build its own market share in a particular market, to the disadvantage of another corporation's business unit. Although each business unit has primary responsibility for its own business strategy, it may sometimes need some help from its corporate parent, especially if the competitor business unit is getting heavy financial support from its corporate parent. In such an instance, corporate headquarters develops a horizontal strategy to coordinate the various goals and strategies of related business units.

For example, P&G, Kimberly-Clark, Scott Paper, and Johnson & Johnson (J&J) compete with one another in varying combinations of consumer paper products, from disposable diapers to facial tissue. If (purely hypothetically) J&J just developed a toilet tissue with which it chose to challenge P&G's high-share Charmin brand in a particular district, it might charge a low price for its new brand to build sales quickly. P&G might not choose to respond to this attack on its share by cutting prices on Charmin. Because of Charmin's high market share, P&G would lose significantly more sales dollars in a price war than J&J would with its initially low-share brand. To retaliate, P&G might thus challenge J&J's high-share baby shampoo with P&G's own low-share brand of baby shampoo in a different district. Once J&J had perceived P&G's response, it might choose to stop challenging Charmin so that P&G would stop challenging J&J's baby shampoo.

Multipoint competition and the resulting use of horizontal strategy may actually slow the development of hypercompetition in an industry. The realization that an attack on a market leader's position could result in a response in another market leads to mutual forbearance in which managers behave more conservatively toward multimarket rivals and competitive rivalry is reduced.[77] In one industry, for example, multipoint competition resulted in firms being less likely to exit a market. "Live and let live" replaced strong competitive rivalry.[78] Multipoint competition is likely to become even more prevalent in the future, as corporations become global competitors and expand into more markets through strategic alliances.[79]

7.5 Conclusion

Corporate strategy is primarily about the choice of direction for the firm as a whole. It deals with three key issues that a corporation faces: (1) the firm's overall orientation toward growth, stability, or retrenchment; (2) the industries or markets in which the firm competes through its products and business units; and (3) the manner in which management coordinates activities and transfers resources and cultivates capabilities among product lines and business units. These issues are dealt with through directional strategy, portfolio analysis, and corporate parenting.

One impact of the growth of computers and the Internet is that corporations are rethinking what industries they should be in. For example, Emerson Electric, the 110-year-old St. Louis manufacturer of electric motors, refrigeration components, and industrial tools, recently positioned itself in power backup systems for computers. Realizing that the growth potential of its traditional product lines was limited, Emerson's management decided to move into a more attractive industry. With the power grid reaching its capacity, electrical outages are expected to become more commonplace in the United States as the economy expands. First, the company purchased Jordan Industries Inc.'s telecommunications-products business. Emerson then bought the power supply division of Swedish phone maker Ericsson.

Emerson's acquisitions meant that the company could provide reliable power backup capability for its customers. When the power goes out, Emerson's components act to switch the power from one source to another and regulate the voltage. Emerson provides the generators and fuel cells to generate the temporary electricity. These products have become crucial for any company that relies on the Internet for conducting business. Intira Corp., a St. Louis web-hosting company, suffered a seven-hour outage due to a malfunctioning transformer, but it was able to stay online thanks to Emerson equipment. According to John Steensen, Intira's chief technology officer, "All of our affected customers would have gotten a month of free service if we had gone down, costing us hundreds of thousands of dollars." The acquisitions significantly increased Emerson's sales and made the power unit the largest and fastest-growing of Emerson's five SBUs. Cisco Systems, MCI, and Intel are Emerson customers. Emerson's management is estimating that its high-tech power-systems business will grow at 15% to 20% annually for the foreseeable future.[80]

Strategy Bits

- The least corrupt countries in the world are Finland, New Zealand, Denmark, Iceland, Singapore, and Sweden.[81]
- The most corrupt countries in the world are Angola, Democratic Republic of Congo, Ivory Coast, Georgia, Indonesia, and Tajikistan.[82]

Discussion Questions

1. How does horizontal growth differ from vertical growth as a corporate strategy? from concentric diversification?
2. What are the tradeoffs between an internal and an external growth strategy? Which approach is best as an international entry strategy?
3. Is stability really a strategy or just a term for no strategy?
4. Compare and contrast SWOT analysis with portfolio analysis.
5. How is corporate parenting different from portfolio analysis? How is it alike? Is it a useful concept in a global industry?

Strategic Practice Exercise

On March 14, 2000, Stephen King, the horror writer, published his new book, *Riding the Bullet*, on the Internet before it appeared in print. Within 24 hours, around 400,000 people had downloaded the book—even though most of them needed to download software in order to read the book. The unexpected demand crashed servers. According to Jack Romanos, president of Simon & Schuster, "I don't think anybody could have anticipated how many people were out there who are willing to accept the written word in a paperless format." To many, this announced the coming of the electronic novel. Environmentalists applauded that e-books would soon replace paper books and newspapers, thus reducing pollution coming from paper mills and landfills. The King book was easy to download, and the download took less time than a trip to the bookstore. Critics argued that the King book used the Internet because at 66 pages, it was too short to be a standard printed novel. It was also free, so there was nothing to discourage natural curiosity. Some people in the industry estimated that 75% of those who downloaded the book did not read it.[83]

1. Form into small groups in the class to discuss the future of Internet publishing.
2. Consider the following questions as discussion guides:
   - What are the pros and cons of electronic publishing?
   - Should newspaper and book publishers convert to electronic publishing over paper? (The *Wall Street Journal* and others publish in both paper and electronic formats. Is this a success?)
   - Would you prefer this textbook and others in an electronic format?
   - What business model should publishers use to make money publishing on the Internet?
3. Present your group's conclusions to the class.

Key Terms

acquisition (p. 166)
backward integration (p. 167)
bankruptcy (p. 178)
BCG (Boston Consulting Group) Growth-Share Matrix (p. 179)
BOT (Build, Operate, Transfer) concept (p. 174)
captive company strategy (p. 177)
cash cow (p. 180)
center of excellence (p. 184)
concentration (p. 166)
concentric diversification (p. 170)
conglomerate diversification (p. 170)
consolidation (p. 177)
contraction (p. 177)
corporate parenting (p. 183)
corporate strategy (p. 164)
directional strategy (p. 165)
diversification (p. 166)
divestment (p. 178)
dog (p. 180)
exporting (p. 171)
forward integration (p. 167)
franchising (p. 173)
full integration (p. 168)
GE business screen (p. 181)
green-field development (p. 173)
growth strategy (p. 165)
horizontal growth (p. 169)
horizontal integration (p. 169)
horizontal strategy (p. 185)
licensing (p. 172)
liquidation (p. 178)
long-term contract (p. 169)
management contract (p. 174)
merger (p. 166)
multipoint competition (p. 185)
no-change strategy (p. 176)
organization slack (p. 166)
outsourcing (p. 169)
pause/proceed-with-caution strategy (p. 175)
portfolio analysis (p. 179)
production sharing (p. 174)
profit strategy (p. 176)
quasi-integration (p. 169)
question mark (p. 180)
retrenchment strategy (p. 165)
sell-out strategy (p. 178)
stability strategy (p. 165)
star (p. 180)
synergy (p. 170)
taper integration (p. 168)
transaction cost economics (p. 167)
turnaround strategy (p. 176)
turnkey operation (p. 174)
vertical growth (p. 167)
vertical integration (p. 167)

CHAPTER 8 Strategy Formulation: Functional Strategy and Strategic Choice

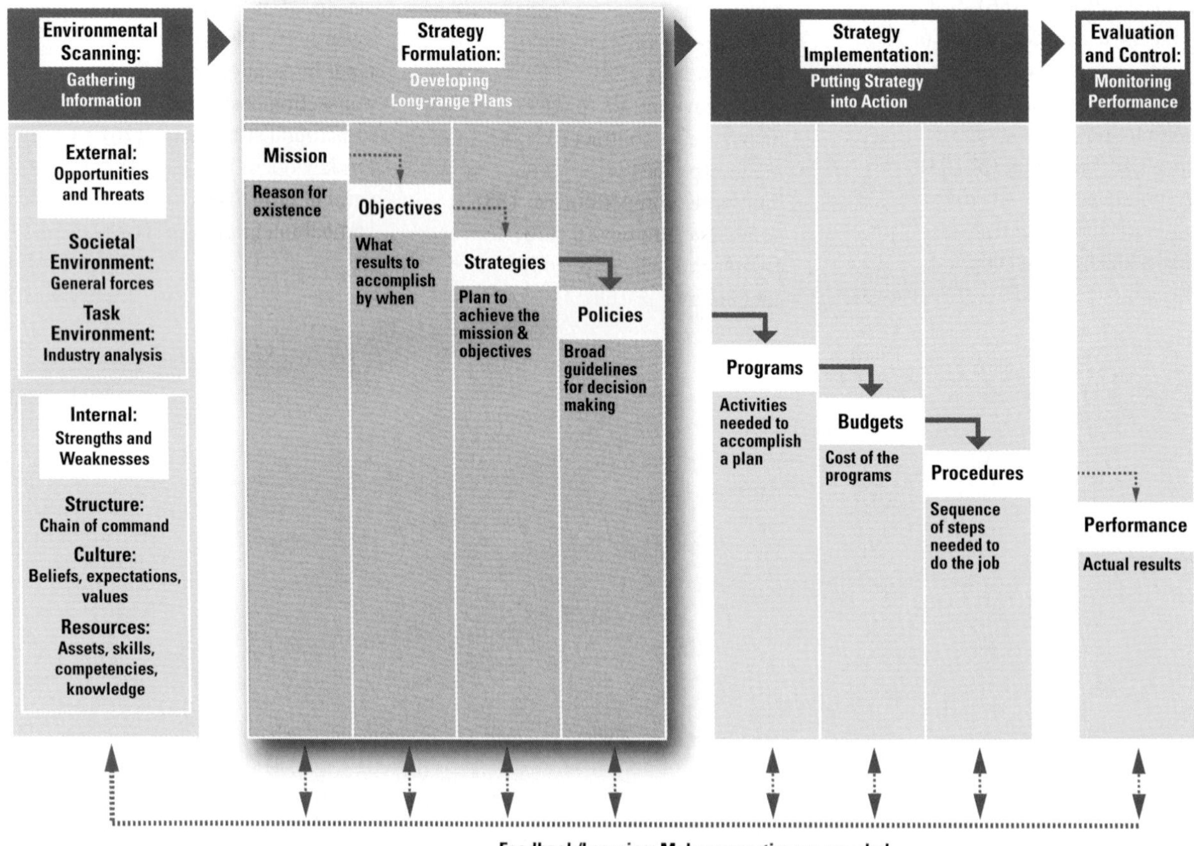

Learning Objectives

After reading this chapter, you should be able to:

- Identify a variety of functional strategies that can be used to achieve organizational goals and objectives
- Understand what activities and functions are appropriate to outsource in order to gain or strengthen competitive advantage
- Recognize strategies to avoid and understand why they are dangerous
- Construct corporate scenarios to evaluate strategic options
- Use a stakeholder priority matrix to aid in strategic decision making
- Develop policies to implement corporate, business, and functional strategies

For almost 150 years, the Church & Dwight Company has been building market share on a brand name whose products are in 95% of all U.S. households. Yet if you asked the average person what products this company makes, few would know. Although Church & Dwight may not be a household name, the company's ubiquitous orange box of Arm & Hammer[1] brand baking soda is common throughout North America. Church & Dwight provides a classic example of a marketing functional strategy called *product development*. Shortly after its introduction in 1878, Arm & Hammer Baking Soda became a fundamental item on the pantry shelf as people found many uses for sodium bicarbonate other than baking, such as cleaning, deodorizing, and tooth brushing. Hearing of the many uses people were finding for its product, the company advertised that its baking soda was good not only for baking but also for deodorizing refrigerators—simply by leaving an open box in the refrigerator. In a brilliant marketing move, the firm then suggested that consumers buy the product and throw it away—deodorize a kitchen sink by dumping Arm & Hammer baking soda down the drain!

The company did not stop there. It looked for other uses of its sodium bicarbonate in new products. Church & Dwight has achieved consistent growth in sales and earnings through the use of *line extensions*, putting the Arm & Hammer brand first on baking soda and then on laundry detergents, toothpaste, and deodorants. By the beginning of the 21st century, Church & Dwight had become a significant competitor in markets previously dominated only by giants such as Procter & Gamble, Unilever, and Colgate-Palmolive—using only one brand name. Was there a limit to this growth? Was there a point at which these continuous line extensions would begin to eat away at the integrity of the Arm & Hammer name?

8.1 Functional Strategy

Functional strategy is the approach a functional area takes to achieve corporate and business unit objectives and strategies by maximizing resource productivity. It is concerned with developing and nurturing a functional capability to provide a company or business unit with a competitive advantage. Just as a multidivisional corporation has several business units, each with its own business strategy, each business unit has its own set of departments, each with its own functional strategy.

The orientation of a functional strategy is dictated by its parent business unit's strategy.[2] For example, a business unit following a competitive strategy of differentiation through high quality needs a manufacturing functional strategy that emphasizes expensive quality assurance processes over cheaper, high-volume production; a human resource functional strategy that emphasizes the hiring and training of a highly skilled, but costly, workforce; and a marketing functional strategy that emphasizes distribution channel "pull," using advertising to increase consumer demand, over "push," using promotional allowances to retailers. If a business unit were to follow a low-cost competitive strategy, however, a different set of functional strategies would be needed to support the business strategy.

Just as competitive strategies may need to vary from one region of the world to another, functional strategies may need to vary from region to region. When Mr. Donut expanded into Japan, for example, it had to market donuts not as breakfast but as snack food. Because the Japanese had no breakfast coffee and donut custom, they preferred to eat the donuts in the afternoon or evening. Mr. Donut restaurants were thus located near railroad stations and supermarkets. All signs were in English, to appeal to the Western interests of the Japanese.

Marketing Strategy

Marketing strategy deals with pricing, selling, and distributing a product. Using a **market development** strategy, a company or business unit can (1) capture a larger share of an existing market for current products through market saturation and market penetration or (2) develop new markets for current products. Consumer product giants such as P&G, Colgate-Palmolive, and Unilever are experts at using advertising and promotion to implement a market saturation/penetration strategy to gain the dominant market share in a product category. As seeming masters of the product life cycle, these companies are able to extend product life almost indefinitely through "new and improved" variations of product and packaging that appeal to most market niches. These companies also follow the second market development strategy by taking a successful product they market in one part of the world and marketing it elsewhere. Noting the success of their presoak detergents in Europe, for example, both P&G and Colgate successfully introduced this type of laundry product to North America under the trade names of Biz and Axion.

Using the **product development** strategy, a company or unit can (1) develop new products for *existing markets* or (2) develop new products for *new markets*. Church & Dwight has had great success by following the first product development strategy, developing new products to sell to its current customers in its existing markets. Acknowledging the widespread appeal of its Arm & Hammer brand baking soda, the company has generated new uses for its sodium bicarbonate by reformulating it as toothpaste, deodorant, and detergent. Using a successful brand name to market other products is called **line extension**, and it is a good way to appeal to a company's current customers. Sara Lee Corporation (famous for its frozen cheesecake) has taken the same approach by putting the Sara Lee name on various food products, such as premium meats and fresh baked goods. Arm & Hammer has successfully followed the second product development strategy by developing new pollution-reduction products (using sodium bicarbonate compounds) for sale to coal-fired electric utility plants—a very different market from grocery stores.

There are numerous other marketing strategies. For advertising and promotion, for example, a company or business unit can choose between "push" and "pull" marketing strategies. Many large food and consumer products companies in the United States and Canada have followed a **push strategy** by spending a large amount of money on trade promotion in order to gain or hold shelf space in retail outlets. Trade promotion includes discounts, in-store special offers, and advertising allowances designed to "push" products through the distribution system. The Kellogg Company decided a few years ago to change its emphasis from a push to a **pull strategy**, in which advertising "pulls" the products through the distribution channels. The company now spends more money on consumer advertising designed to build brand awareness so that shoppers will ask for the products. Research has indicated that a high level of advertising (a key part of a pull strategy) is beneficial to leading brands in a market.[3]

Other marketing strategies deal with distribution and pricing. Should a company use distributors and dealers to sell its products, or should it sell directly to mass merchandisers or even straight to the consumers via the Internet? Using multiple channels simultaneously can lead to problems. In order to increase the sales of its lawn tractors and mowers, for example, John Deere decided to sell the products not only through its current dealer network but also through mass merchandisers such as Home Depot. Deere's dealers were furious. They considered Home Depot to be a key competitor. The dealers were concerned that Home Depot's ability to underprice them would eventually lead to their becoming little more than repair facilities for their competition and left with insufficient sales to stay in business.[4]

When pricing a new product, a company or business unit can follow one of two strategies. For new-product pioneers, **skim pricing** offers the opportunity to "skim the cream" from the top of the demand curve with a high price while the product is novel and competitors are few. **Penetration pricing**, in contrast, attempts to hasten market development and offers the pioneer the opportunity to use the experience curve to gain market share with a low price and then dominate the industry. Depending on corporate and business unit objectives and strategies, either of these choices may be desirable to a particular company or unit. Penetration pricing is, however, more likely than skim pricing to raise a unit's operating profit in the long term.[5] The use of the Internet to market goods directly to consumers allows a company to use **dynamic pricing**, a practice in which prices vary frequently based upon demand, market segment, and product availability.[6]

Financial Strategy

Financial strategy examines the financial implications of corporate and business-level strategic options and identifies the best financial course of action. It can also provide competitive advantage through a lower cost of funds and a flexible ability to raise capital to support a business strategy. Financial strategy usually attempts to maximize the financial value of a firm.

The trade-off between achieving the desired debt-to-equity ratio and relying on internal long-term financing via cash flow is a key issue in financial strategy. Many small- and medium-sized family-owned companies such as Urschel Laboratories try to avoid all external sources of funds in order to avoid outside entanglements and to keep control of the company within the family. Many financial analysts believe, however, that only by financing through long-term debt can a corporation use financial leverage to boost earnings per share—thus raising stock price and the overall value of the company. Research indicates that higher debt levels not only deter takeover by other firms (by making the company less attractive) but also lead to improved productivity and improved cash flows by forcing management to focus on core businesses.[7]

Research reveals that a firm's financial strategy is influenced by its corporate diversification strategy. Equity financing, for example, is preferred for related diversification, whereas debt financing is preferred for unrelated diversification.[8] The recent trend away from unrelated to related acquisitions explains why the number of acquisitions being paid for entirely with stock increased from only 2% in 1988 to 50% in 1998.[9]

A very popular financial strategy is the leveraged buyout (LBO). In a **leveraged buyout**, a company is acquired in a transaction financed largely by debt, usually obtained from a third party, such as an insurance company or an investment banker. Ultimately the debt is paid with money generated from the acquired company's operations or by sales of its assets. The acquired company, in effect, pays for its own acquisition. Management of the LBO is then under tremendous pressure to keep the highly leveraged company profitable. Unfortunately, the huge amount of debt on the acquired company's books may actually cause its eventual decline by focusing management's attention on short-term matters. One study of LBOs (also called MBOs [Management Buy Outs]) revealed that the financial performance of the typical LBO usually falls below the industry average in the fourth year after the buyout. The firm declines because of inflated expectations, utilization of all slack, management burnout, and a lack of strategic management.[10] Often the only solution is to go public once again by selling stock to finance growth.[11]

The management of dividends and stock price is an important part of a corporation's financial strategy. Corporations in fast-growing industries such as computers and computer software often do not declare dividends. They use the money they might have spent on dividends to finance rapid growth. If the company is successful, its growth in sales and profits is reflected in a higher stock price, eventually resulting in a hefty capital gain when shareholders sell their common stock. Other corporations, such as Maytag Corporation, that do not face rapid growth must support the value of their stock by offering consistent dividends. Like Maytag, they may even go into debt to finance these dividends.

A number of firms are supporting the price of their stock by using **reverse stock splits**. Contrasted with a typical forward 2-for-1 stock split in which an investor receives an additional share for every share owned (with each share being worth only half as much), in a reverse 1-for-2 stock split, an investor's shares are split in half for the same total amount of money (with each share now being worth twice as much). Thus, 100 shares of stock worth $10 each are exchanged for 50 shares worth $20 each. A reverse stock split may successfully raise a company's stock price, but does not solve underlying problems. A study by Credit Suisse First Boston revealed that almost all 800 companies that had reverse stock splits in a five-year period underperformed their peers over the long term.[12]

A recent financial strategy being used by large established corporations to highlight a high-growth business unit in a popular sector of the stock market is to establish a tracking stock. A **tracking stock** is a type of common stock tied to one portion of a corporation's business. This strategy allows established companies to highlight a high-growth business unit without selling the business. By keeping the unit as a subsidiary with its common stock separately identified, the corporation is able to keep control of the subsidiary and yet allow the subsidiary the ability to fund its own growth with outside money. It goes public as an IPO and pays dividends based on the unit's performance. Because the tracking stock is actually an equity interest in the parent company (not the subsidiary), another company cannot acquire the subsidiary by buying its shares. Examples of corporations that use tracking stocks as part of their financial strategy are AT&T (AT&T Wireless), Sprint (Sprint PCS), JCPenney (CVS Drugs), and Staples (Staples.com).[13]

Research and Development (R&D) Strategy

R&D strategy deals with product and process innovation and improvement. It also deals with the appropriate mix of different types of R&D (basic, product, or process) and with the question of how new technology should be accessed—through internal development, external acquisition, or strategic alliances.

One of the R&D choices is to be either a **technological leader**, pioneering an innovation, or a **technological follower**, imitating the products of competitors. Porter suggests that deciding to become a technological leader or follower can be a way of achieving either overall low cost or differentiation. (See **Table 8–1**.)

One example of an effective use of the *leader* R&D functional strategy to achieve a differentiation competitive advantage is Nike, Inc. Nike spends more than most in the industry on R&D to differentiate the performance of its athletic shoes from that of its competitors. As a result, its products have become the favorite of serious athletes. An example of the use of the *follower* R&D functional strategy to achieve a low-cost competitive advantage is Dean Foods Company. "We're able to have the customer come to us and say, 'If you can produce X, Y, and Z product for the same quality and service, but at a lower price and without that expensive label on it, you can have the business,'" says Howard Dean, president of the company.[14]

TABLE 8–1 RESEARCH AND DEVELOPMENT STRATEGY AND COMPETITIVE ADVANTAGE

	Technological Leadership	Technological Followership
Cost Advantage	Pioneer the lowest-cost production design. Be the first down the learning curve. Create low-cost ways of performing value activities.	Lower the cost of the product or value activities by learning from the leader's experience. Avoid R&D costs through imitation.
Differentiation	Pioneer a unique product that increases buyer value. Innovate in other activities to increase buyer value.	Adapt the product or delivery system more closely to buyer needs by learning from the leader's experience.

Source: Adapted with the permission of The Free Press, A Division of Simon & Schuster Adult Publishing Group, from *COMPETITIVE ADVANTAGE: Creating and Sustaining Superior Performance* by Michael Porter.

An increasing number of companies are working with their suppliers to help them keep up with changing technology. They are beginning to realize that a firm cannot be competitive technologically only through internal development. For example, Chrysler Corporation's skillful use of parts suppliers to design everything from car seats to drive shafts has enabled it to spend consistently less money than its competitors to develop new car models. Using strategic technology alliances is one way to combine the R&D capabilities of two companies. Maytag Company worked with one of its suppliers to apply fuzzy logic technology to its IntelliSense™ dishwasher. The partnership enabled Maytag to complete the project in a shorter amount of time than if it had tried to do it alone.[15]

A new approach to R&D is **open innovation**, in which a firm uses alliances and connections with corporate, government, and academic labs to learn about new developments. For example, Intel opened four small-scale research facilities adjacent to universities to promote the cross-pollination of ideas. Mattel, Wal-Mart, and other toy manufacturers and retailers use idea brokers such as Big Idea Group to scout for new toy ideas. Big Idea Group invites inventors to submit ideas to its web site (www.bigideagroup.net). It then refines and promotes to its clients the most promising ideas.[16] To open its own labs to ideas being generated elsewhere, P&G's CEO Art Lafley decreed that half of the company's ideas must come from outside, up from 10% in 2000. P&G instituted the use of *technology scouts* to search beyond the company for promising innovations.[17] A slightly different approach is for a large firm such as IBM or Microsoft to purchase minority stakes in relatively new high-tech entrepreneurial ventures that need capital to continue operation. Investing corporate venture capital is one way to gain access to promising innovations at a lower cost than by developing them internally.[18]

Operations Strategy

Operations strategy determines how and where a product or service is to be manufactured, the level of vertical integration in the production process, the deployment of physical resources, and relationships with suppliers. It should also deal with the optimum level of technology the firm should use in its operations processes. See the GLOBAL ISSUE feature to see how differences in national conditions can lead to differences in product design and manufacturing facilities from one country to another.

Advanced Manufacturing Technology (AMT) is revolutionizing operations worldwide and should continue to have a major impact as corporations strive to integrate diverse business

GLOBAL ISSUE

International Differences Alter Whirlpool's Operations Strategy

To better penetrate the growing markets in developing nations, Whirlpool decided to build a "world washer." This new type of washing machine was to be produced in Brazil, Mexico, and India. Lightweight, with substantially fewer parts than its U.S. counterpart, its performance was to be equal to or better than anything on the world market while being competitive in price with the most popular models in these markets. The goal was to develop a complete product, process, and facility design package that could be used in different countries with low initial investment. Originally the plan had been to make the same low-cost washer in identical plants in each of the three countries.

Significant differences in each of the three countries forced Whirlpool to change its product design to adapt to each nation's situation. According to Lawrence Kremer, Senior Vice President of Global Technology and Operations, "Our Mexican affiliate, Vitromatic, has porcelain and glass-making capabilities. Porcelain baskets made sense for them. Stainless steel became the preferred material for the others." Costs also affected decisions. "In India, for example, material costs may run as much as 200% to 800% higher than elsewhere, while labor and overhead costs are comparatively minimal," added Kremer. Another consideration were the garments to be washed in each country. For example, saris—the 18-foot lengths of cotton or silk with which Indian women drape themselves—needed special treatment in an Indian washing machine, forcing additional modifications.

Manufacturing facilities also varied from country to country. Brastemp, Whirlpool's Brazilian partner, built its plant of precast concrete to address the problems of high humidity. In India, however, the construction crew cast the concrete, allowed it to cure, and then, using chain, block, and tackle, five or six men raised each three-ton slab into place. Instead of using one building, Mexican operations used two—one housing the flexible assembly lines and stamping operations, and an adjacent facility housing the injection molding and extrusion processes.

Source: WHEELEN, TOM; HUNGER, J. DAVID, *STRATEGIC MANAGEMENT AND BUSINESS POLICY*, 9th Edition, © 2004, p. 172. Reprinted by permission of Pearson Education, Inc., Upper Saddle River, NJ.

activities by using computer-assisted design and manufacturing (CAD/CAM) principles. The use of CAD/CAM, flexible manufacturing systems, computer numerically controlled systems, automatically guided vehicles, robotics, manufacturing resource planning (MRP II), optimized production technology, and just-in-time techniques contribute to increased flexibility, quick response time, and higher productivity. Such investments also act to increase the company's fixed costs and could cause significant problems if the company is unable to achieve economies of scale or scope. Baldor Electric Company, the largest maker of industrial electric motors in the United States, built a new factory by using new technology to eliminate undesirable jobs with high employee turnover. With one-tenth the employees of its foreign plants, the plant was cost-competitive with plants producing motors in Mexico and China.[19]

A firm's manufacturing strategy is often affected by a product's life cycle. As the sales of a product increase, there will be an increase in production volume ranging from lot sizes as low as one in a **job shop** (one-of-a-kind production using skilled labor) through **connected line batch flow** (components are standardized; each machine functions like a job shop but is positioned in the same order as the parts are processed) to lot sizes as high as 100,000 or more per year for **flexible manufacturing systems** (parts are grouped into manufacturing families to produce a wide variety of mass-produced items) and **dedicated transfer lines** (highly automated assembly lines that make one mass-produced product using little human labor). According to this concept, the product becomes standardized into a commodity over time in conjunction with increasing demand. Flexibility thus gives way to efficiency.[20]

Increasing competitive intensity in many industries has forced companies to switch from traditional mass production using dedicated transfer lines to a continuous improvement production strategy. A **mass-production** system was an excellent method to produce a large number of low-cost, standard goods and services. Employees worked on narrowly defined, repetitious tasks under close supervision in a bureaucratic and hierarchical structure. Quality, however, often tended to be fairly low. Learning how to do something better was the prerogative of management; workers were expected only to learn what was assigned to them. This system tended to dominate manufacturing until the 1970s. Under the **continuous improvement** system developed by Japanese firms, empowered cross-functional teams strive constantly to improve production processes. Managers are more like coaches than like bosses. The result is a large quantity of low-cost, standard goods and services, but with high quality. The key to continuous improvement is the acknowledgment that workers' experience and knowledge can help managers solve production problems and contribute to tightening variances and reducing errors. Because continuous improvement enables firms to use the same low-cost competitive strategy as do mass-production firms but at a significantly higher level of quality, it is rapidly replacing mass production as an operations strategy.

The automobile industry is currently experimenting with the strategy of **modular manufacturing** in which pre-assembled sub-assemblies are delivered as they are needed (i.e., Just-In-Time) to a company's assembly-line workers, who quickly piece the modules together into a finished product. For example, General Motors built a new automotive complex in Brazil to make its new subcompact, the Celta. Sixteen of the 17 buildings were occupied by suppliers, including Delphi, Lear, and Goodyear. These suppliers delivered pre-assembled modules (which comprised 85% of the final value of each car) to GM's building for assembly. In a process new to the industry, the suppliers acted as a team to build a single module comprising the motor, transmission, fuel lines, rear axle, brake-fluid lines, and exhaust system, which was then installed as one piece. GM hoped that this manufacturing strategy would enable it to produce 100 vehicles annually per worker compared to the standard rate of 30 to 50 autos per worker.[21] Ford and Chrysler have opened similar modular facilities in Brazil.

The concept of a product's life cycle eventually leading to one-size-fits-all mass production is being increasingly challenged by the new concept of mass customization. Appropriate for an ever-changing environment, mass customization requires that people, processes, units, and technology reconfigure themselves to give customers exactly what they want, when they want it. In the case of Dell Computer, customers use the Internet to design their own computers. In contrast to continuous improvement, mass customization requires flexibility and quick responsiveness. Managers coordinate independent, capable individuals. An efficient linkage system is crucial. The result is low-cost, high-quality, customized goods and services.

Purchasing Strategy

Purchasing strategy deals with obtaining the raw materials, parts, and supplies needed to perform the operations function. Purchasing strategy is important because materials and components purchased from suppliers comprise 50% of total manufacturing costs of manufacturing companies in the United Kingdom, United States, Australia, Belgium, and Finland.[22] The basic purchasing choices are multiple, sole, and parallel sourcing. Under **multiple sourcing**, the purchasing company orders a particular part from several vendors. Multiple sourcing has traditionally been considered superior to other purchasing approaches because (1) it forces suppliers to compete for the business of an important buyer, thus reducing purchasing costs, and (2) if one supplier cannot deliver, another usually can, thus guaranteeing that parts and supplies are always on hand when needed. Multiple sourcing has been one way for a purchasing firm to control the relationship with its suppliers. So long as suppliers can provide evidence that they can meet the product specifications, they are kept on the purchaser's list of acceptable vendors for specific parts and supplies. Unfortunately, the common practice of accepting the lowest bid often compromises quality.

W. Edwards Deming, a well-known management consultant, strongly recommended **sole sourcing** as the only manageable way to obtain high supplier quality. Sole sourcing relies on only one supplier for a particular part. Given his concern with designing quality into a product in its early stages of development, Deming argued that the buyer should work closely with the supplier at all stages. This reduces both cost and time spent on product design, and it also improves quality. It can also simplify the purchasing company's production process by using the **Just-In-Time (JIT)** concept of having the purchased parts arrive at the plant just when they are needed rather than keeping inventories. The concept of sole sourcing is taken one step further in JIT II, in which vendor sales representatives actually have desks next to the purchasing company's factory floor, attend production status meetings, visit the R&D lab, and analyze the purchasing company's sales forecasts. These in-house suppliers then write sales orders for which the purchasing company is billed. Developed by Lance Dixon at Bose Corporation, JIT II is also being used at IBM, Honeywell, and Ingersoll-Rand. Karen Dale, purchasing manager for Honeywell's office supplies, said she was very concerned about confidentiality when JIT II was first suggested to her. Now she has 5 suppliers working with her 20 buyers and reports few problems.[23]

Sole sourcing reduces transaction costs and builds quality by having the purchaser and supplier work together as partners rather than as adversaries. With sole sourcing, more companies will have longer relationships with fewer suppliers. Sole sourcing does, however, have limitations. If a supplier is unable to deliver a part, the purchaser has no alternative but to delay production. Multiple suppliers can provide the purchaser with better information about new technology and performance capabilities. The limitations of sole sourcing have led to the development of parallel sourcing. In **parallel sourcing**, two suppliers are the sole suppliers of two different parts, but they are also backup suppliers for each other's parts. If one vendor cannot supply all of its parts on time, the other vendor is asked to make up the difference.[24]

The Internet is being increasingly used both to find new sources of supply and to keep inventories replenished. For example, Hewlett-Packard introduced a Web-based procurement system to enable its 84,000 employees to buy office supplies from a standard set of suppliers. The new system enabled the company to save \$60 to \$100 million annually in purchasing costs.[25] See **STRATEGY HIGHLIGHT 8.1** to learn how David Crosier, Vice President for Supply-chain Management at Staples, used the Internet to keep the retailer in Post-It Notes and Scotch tape from 3M.

Logistics Strategy

Logistics strategy deals with the flow of products into and out of the manufacturing process. Three trends related to this strategy are evident: centralization, outsourcing, and the use of the Internet. To gain logistical synergies across business units, corporations began centralizing logistics in the headquarters group. This centralized logistics group usually contains specialists with expertise in different transportation modes, such as rail or trucking. They work to aggregate shipping volumes across the entire corporation to gain better contracts with shippers. Companies such as Georgia-Pacific, Marriott, and Union Carbide view the logistics function as an important way to differentiate themselves from the competition, to add value, and to reduce costs.

Many companies have found that outsourcing logistics reduces costs and improves delivery time. For example, HP contracted with Roadway Logistics to manage its in-bound raw materials warehousing in Vancouver, Canada. Nearly 140 Roadway employees replaced 250 HP workers, who were transferred to other HP activities.[26]

Many companies are using the Internet to simplify their logistical system. For example, Ace Hardware created an online system for its retailers and suppliers. An individual hardware store can now see on the web site that ordering 210 cases of wrenches is cheaper than ordering 200 cases. Because a full pallet is composed of 210 cases of wrenches, an order for a full pallet means that the supplier doesn't have to pull 10 cases off a pallet and repackage them

STRATEGY HIGHLIGHT 8.1

Staples Uses Internet to Replenish Inventory from 3M

David Crosier was mad. As the Vice President for Supply-chain Management for Staples, the office supplies retailer, Crosier couldn't even find a Post-It Note to write down the complaint that his stores were consistently low on 3M products. Crosier would send an order to the Minnesota Mining & Manufacturing Company (3M) for 10,000 rolls of Scotch tape and receive only 8,000. Even worse, the supplies from 3M often arrived late, causing "stock outs" of popular products. Crosier then discovered 3M's new online ordering system for office supplies. The web site enabled 3M to reduce customer frustration caused by paper forms and last-minute phone calls by eliminating error-prone steps in purchasing. Since using 3M's web site, Staples' Crosier reports that 3M's fill rate has improved by 20% and that its on-time performance has almost doubled. "The technology takes a lot of inefficiencies out of the supply-chain process."

This improvement at 3M was initiated by Allen Messerli, information manager at 3M, over a five-year period. Since 1997, 3M has invested $30 million in the project. Ongoing maintenance costs of keeping the system current are $2.6 million. Before implementing this online system, 3M had serious problems with its finished goods inventory, distribution, and customer service. For example, nearly 40% of its customer records (in the U.S. alone) had invalid addresses. Bloated finished goods inventory in 1998 caused a 45% drop in earnings. With more than 70,000 employees around the world, 3M had difficulty linking employees, managers, and customers because of incompatible networks. With its new Global Enterprise Data Warehouse, 3M is now delivering customer, product, sales, inventory, and financial data directly to its employees and partners, who can access the information via the Internet (at www.3m.com). The company reports saving $10 million annually in maintenance and customer-service costs. More accurate and current sales reporting is saving an additional $2.5 million per year. The new technology has improved productivity, boosting global sales. Supply-chain managers such as David Crosier at Staples are pleased with making the Internet an important part of their purchasing strategy.

Source: D. Little, "3M: Glued to the Web" *Business Week E.Biz* (November 2000), pp. EB65–EB70.

for storage. There is less chance that loose cases will be lost in delivery, and the paperwork doesn't have to be redone. As a result, Ace's transportation costs are down 18%, and warehouse costs have been cut 28%.[27] As shown in **STRATEGY HIGHLIGHT 8.1**, 3M's new system enabled it to save $10 million annually in maintenance and customer-service costs.

Human Resource Management (HRM) Strategy

HRM strategy, among other things, addresses the issue of whether a company or business unit should hire a large number of low-skilled employees who receive low pay, perform repetitive jobs, and most likely quit after a short time (the McDonald's restaurant strategy) or hire skilled employees who receive relatively high pay and are cross-trained to participate in *self-managing work teams*. As work increases in complexity, the more suited it is for teams, especially in the case of innovative product development efforts. Multinational corporations are increasingly using self-managing work teams in their foreign affiliates as well as in home country operations.[28] Research indicates that the use of work teams leads to increased quality and productivity as well as to higher employee satisfaction and commitment.[29]

Companies following a competitive strategy of differentiation through high quality use input from subordinates and peers in performance appraisals to a greater extent than do firms following other business strategies.[30] A complete **360-degree appraisal**, in which input is gathered from multiple sources, is now being used by more than 10% of U.S. corporations, and has become one of the most popular tools in developing new managers.[31]

Companies are finding that having a *diverse workforce* can be a competitive advantage. Research reveals that firms with a high degree of racial diversity following a growth strategy have higher productivity than do firms with less racial diversity.[32] Avon Company, for example, was able to turn around its unprofitable inner-city markets by putting African-American and Hispanic managers in charge of marketing to these markets.[33] Diversity in terms of age and national origin also offers benefits. DuPont's use of multinational teams has helped the company develop and market products internationally. McDonald's has discovered that older workers perform as well as if not better than younger employees. According to Edward Rensi, CEO of McDonald's USA, "We find these people to be particularly well motivated, with a sort of discipline and work habits hard to find in younger employees."[34]

Information Technology Strategy

Corporations are increasingly using **information technology strategy** to provide business units with competitive advantage. When FedEx first provided its customers with PowerShip computer software to store addresses, print shipping labels, and track package location, its sales jumped significantly. UPS soon followed with its own MaxiShips software. Viewing its information system as a distinctive competency, FedEx continued to push for further advantage over UPS by using its web site to enable customers to track their packages. FedEx uses this competency in its advertisements by showing how customers can track the progress of their shipments. (Soon thereafter, UPS provided the same service.) Although it can be argued that information technology has now become so pervasive that it no longer offers companies a competitive advantage, corporations worldwide continue to spend over $2 trillion annually on information technology.[35]

Multinational corporations are finding that having a sophisticated intranet allows employees to practice *follow-the-sun management*, in which project team members living in one country can pass their work to team members in another country in which the work day is just beginning. Thus, night shifts are no longer needed.[36] The development of instant translation software is also enabling workers to have online communication with co-workers in other countries who use a different language.[37] For example, Mattel has cut the time it takes to develop new products by 10% by enabling designers and licensees in other countries to collaborate on toy design. IBM uses its intranet to allow its employees to collaborate and improve their skills, thus reducing its training and travel expenses.[38]

Many companies, such as Lockheed Martin and Whirlpool, use information technology to form closer relationships with both their customers and suppliers through sophisticated extranets. For example, General Electric's Trading Process Network allows suppliers to electronically download GE's requests for proposals, view diagrams of parts specifications, and communicate with GE purchasing managers. According to Robert Livingston, GE's head of worldwide sourcing for the Lighting Division, going on the web reduces processing time by one-third.[39]

8.2 The Sourcing Decision: Location of Functions

For a functional strategy to have the best chance of success, it should be built on a capability residing within that functional area. If a corporation does not have a strong capability in a particular functional area, that functional area could be a candidate for outsourcing.

Outsourcing is purchasing from someone else a product or service that had been previously provided internally. Outsourcing is becoming an increasingly important part of strategic decision making and an important way to increase efficiency and often quality. Firms competing in global industries must in particular search worldwide for the most appropriate suppliers. In a study of 30 firms, outsourcing resulted on average in a 9% reduction in costs and a 15% increase in capacity and quality.[40] For example, Boeing is using outsourcing as a way to reduce the cost of designing and manufacturing its new 787 Dreamliner. Up to 70% of the plane is being outsourced. In a break from past practice, suppliers make large parts of the fuselage, including plumbing, electrical, and computer systems, and ship them to Seattle for assembly by Boeing. Outsourcing enables Boeing to build a 787 in 4 months instead of the usual 12.[41]

According to an American Management Association survey of member companies, 94% of the responding firms outsource at least one activity. The outsourced activities are general and administrative (78%), human resources (77%), transportation and distribution (66%), information systems (63%), manufacturing (56%), marketing (51%), and finance and accounting (18%). The survey also reveals that 25% of the respondents have been disappointed in their outsourcing results. Fifty-one percent of the firms reported bringing an outsourced activity back in-house. Nevertheless, authorities not only expect the number of companies engaging in outsourcing to increase, they also expect companies to outsource an increasing number of functions, especially those in customer service, bookkeeping, financial/clerical, sales/telemarketing, and the mailroom.[42] Software programming and customer service, in particular, are being outsourced to India. For example, General Electric's back-office services unit, GE Capital International Services, is one of the oldest and biggest of India's outsourcing companies. From only $26 million in 1999, its annual revenues grew to over $420 million in 2004.[43] As part of this trend, in 2004 IBM acquired Daksh eServices Ltd., one of India's biggest suppliers of remote business services.[44]

Outsourcing does have disadvantages. For example, mounting complaints forced Dell Computer to stop routing corporate customers to a technical support call center in Bangalore, India.[45] GE's introduction of a new washing machine was delayed three weeks because of production problems at a supplier's company to which it had contracted out key work. Some companies have found themselves locked into long-term contracts with outside suppliers that were no longer competitive.[46] Some authorities propose that the cumulative effects of continued outsourcing steadily reduce a firm's ability to learn new skills and to develop new core competencies.[47] A survey of 129 outsourcing firms revealed that half the outsourcing projects undertaken in 2003 failed to deliver anticipated savings. Another survey of software projects, by MIT, found that the median Indian project had 10% more software bugs than did comparable U.S. projects.[48] A study of 91 outsourcing efforts conducted by European and North American firms found seven major outsourcing errors that should be avoided[49]:

1. **Outsourcing activities that should not be outsourced:** Companies failed to keep core activities in-house.
2. **Selecting the wrong vender:** Vendors were not trustworthy or lacked state-of-the-art processes.
3. **Writing a poor contract:** Companies failed to establish a balance of power in the relationship.
4. **Overlooking personnel issues:** Employees lost commitment to the firm.
5. **Losing control over the outsourced activity:** Qualified managers failed to manage the outsourced activity.[50]
6. **Overlooking the hidden costs of outsourcing:** Transaction costs overwhelmed other savings.
7. **Failing to plan an exit strategy:** Companies failed to build reversibility clauses into their contracts.

Sophisticated strategists, according to Quinn, are no longer thinking just of market share or vertical integration as the keys to strategic planning:

Instead they concentrate on identifying those few core service activities where the company has or can develop: (1) a continuing strategic edge and (2) long-term streams of new products to satisfy future customer demands. They develop these competencies in greater depth than anyone else in the world. Then they seek to eliminate, minimize, or outsource activities where the company cannot be preeminent, unless those activities are essential to support or protect the chosen areas of strategic focus.[51]

The key to outsourcing is to purchase from outside only those activities that are not key to the company's distinctive competencies. Otherwise, the company may give up the very capabilities that made it successful in the first place, thus putting itself on the road to eventual decline. This is supported by research reporting that companies that have more experience with a particular manufacturing technology tend to keep manufacturing in-house.[52] J. P. Morgan Chase & Company terminated a seven-year technology outsourcing agreement with IBM because the bank's management realized that information technology (IT) was too important strategically to be outsourced.[53] Therefore, in determining functional strategy, the strategist must:

- Identify the company's or business unit's core competencies
- Ensure that the competencies are continually being strengthened
- Manage the competencies in a way that best preserves the competitive advantage they create

An outsourcing decision depends on the fraction of total value added that the activity under consideration represents and on the amount of potential competitive advantage in that activity for the company or business unit. See the proposed outsourcing matrix in **Figure 8–1**. A firm should consider outsourcing any activity or function that has low potential for competitive advantage. If that activity constitutes only a small part of the total value of the firm's products or services, it should be purchased on the open market (assuming that quality providers of the activity are plentiful). If, however, the activity contributes highly to the company's products or services, the firm should purchase it through long-term contracts with trusted suppliers or distributors. A firm should always produce at least some of the activity or function (i.e., taper vertical integration) if that activity has the potential for providing the company some competitive advantage. However, full vertical integration should be considered

Figure 8–1 Proposed Outsourcing Matrix

Activity's Total Value-Added to Firm's Products and Services

Activity's Potential for Competitive Advantage	Low	High
High	**Taper Vertical Integration:** Produce Some Internally	**Full Vertical Integration:** Produce All Internally
Low	**Outsource Completely:** Buy on Open Market	**Outsource Completely:** Purchase with Long-Term Contracts

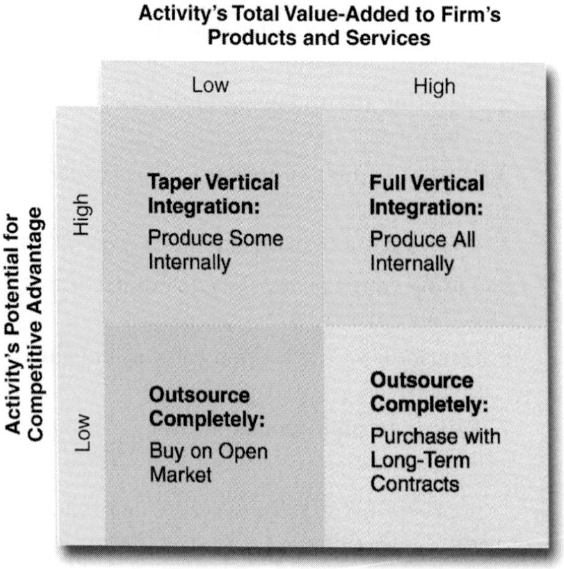

Source: J. D. Hunger and T. L. Wheelen, "Proposed Outsourcing Matrix." Copyright © 1996 and 2005 by Wheelen and Hunger Associates. Reprinted by permission.

only when that activity or function adds significant value to the company's products or services in addition to providing competitive advantage.

8.3 Strategies to Avoid

Several strategies that could be considered corporate, business, or functional are very dangerous. Managers who have made poor analyses or lack creativity may be trapped into considering some of the following **strategies to avoid:**

- **Follow the Leader:** Imitating a leading competitor's strategy might seem to be a good idea, but it ignores a firm's particular strengths and weaknesses and the possibility that the leader may be wrong. Fujitsu Ltd., the world's second-largest computer maker, had been driven since the 1960s by the sole ambition of catching up to IBM. Like IBM, Fujitsu competed primarily as a mainframe computer maker. So devoted was it to catching IBM, however, that it failed to notice that the mainframe business had reached maturity by 1990 and was no longer growing.
- **Hit Another Home Run:** If a company is successful because it pioneered an extremely successful product, it tends to search for another super product that will ensure growth and prosperity. As in betting on long shots in horse races, the probability of finding a second winner is slight. Polaroid spent a lot of money developing an "instant" movie camera, but the public ignored it in favor of the camcorder.
- **Arms Race:** Entering into a spirited battle with another firm for increased market share might increase sales revenue, but that increase will probably be more than offset by increases in advertising, promotion, R&D, and manufacturing costs. Since the deregulation of airlines, price wars and rate specials have contributed to the low profit margins and bankruptcies of many major airlines, such as Eastern, Pan American, TWA, and United.
- **Do Everything:** When faced with several interesting opportunities, management might tend to leap at all of them. At first, a corporation might have enough resources to develop each idea into a project, but money, time, and energy are soon exhausted as the many projects demand large infusions of resources. The Walt Disney Company's expertise in the entertainment industry led it to acquire the ABC network. As the company churned out new motion pictures and television programs such as *Who Wants to Be a Millionaire*, it spent $750 million to build new theme parks and buy a cruise line and a hockey team. By 2000, even though corporate sales had continued to increase, net income was falling.[54]
- **Losing Hand:** A corporation might have invested so much in a particular strategy that top management is unwilling to accept its failure. Believing that it has too much invested to quit, management may continue to throw "good money after bad." Pan American Airlines, for example, chose to sell its Pan Am Building and Intercontinental Hotels, the most profitable parts of the corporation, to keep its money-losing airline flying. Continuing to suffer losses, the company followed this profit strategy of shedding assets for cash until it had sold off everything and went bankrupt.

8.4 Strategic Choice: Selecting the Best Strategy

After the pros and cons of the potential strategic alternatives have been identified and evaluated, one must be selected for implementation. By now, it is likely that many feasible alternatives will have emerged. How is the best strategy determined?

Perhaps the most important criterion is the capability of the proposed strategy to deal with the specific strategic factors developed earlier, in the SWOT analysis. If the alternative doesn't take advantage of environmental opportunities and corporate strengths/competencies, and lead away from environmental threats and corporate weaknesses, it will probably fail.

Another important consideration in the selection of a strategy is the ability of each alternative to satisfy agreed-on objectives with the least resources and the fewest negative side effects. It is, therefore, important to develop a tentative implementation plan in order to address the difficulties that management is likely to face. This should be done in light of societal trends, the industry, and the company's situation, based on the construction of scenarios.

Constructing Corporate Scenarios

Corporate scenarios are *pro forma* (estimated) balance sheets and income statements that forecast the effect each alternative strategy and its various programs will likely have on division and corporate return on investment. (Pro forma financial statements are discussed in **Chapter 15**.) In a survey of *Fortune 500* firms, 84% reported using computer simulation models in strategic planning. Most of these were simply spreadsheet-based simulation models dealing with what-if questions.[55]

The recommended scenarios are simply extensions of the industry scenarios discussed in **Chapter 4**. If, for example, industry scenarios suggest the probable emergence of a strong market demand in a specific country for certain products, a series of alternative strategy scenarios can be developed. The alternative of acquiring another firm having these products in that country can be compared with the alternative of a green-field development (e.g., building new operations in that country). By using three sets of estimated sales figures (Optimistic, Pessimistic, and Most Likely) for the new products over the next five years, the two alternatives can be evaluated in terms of their effect on future company performance as reflected in the company's probable future financial statements. Pro forma balance sheets and income statements can be generated with spreadsheet software, such as Excel, on a personal computer.

To construct a corporate scenario, follow these steps:

1. Use industry scenarios (as discussed in **Chapter 4**) to develop a set of assumptions about the task environment (in the specific country under consideration). For example, 3M requires the general manager of each business unit to describe annually what his or her industry will look like in 15 years. List *optimistic*, *pessimistic*, and *most likely* assumptions for key economic factors such as the GDP (Gross Domestic Product), CPI (Consumer Price Index), and prime interest rate and for other key external strategic factors such as governmental regulation and industry trends. This should be done for every country/region in which the corporation has significant operations that will be affected by each strategic alternative. These same underlying assumptions should be listed for each of the alternative scenarios to be developed.
2. Develop common-size financial statements (as discussed in **Chapter 15**) for the company's or business unit's previous years, to serve as the basis for the trend analysis projections of pro forma financial statements. Use the *Scenario Box* form shown in **Table 8–2**:

   a. Use the historical common-size percentages to estimate the level of revenues, expenses, and other categories in estimated pro forma statements for future years.

   b. Develop for each strategic alternative a set of *optimistic*, *pessimistic*, and *most likely* assumptions about the impact of key variables on the company's future financial statements.

   c. Forecast three sets of sales and cost of goods sold figures for at least five years into the future.

TABLE 8–2 SCENARIO BOX FOR USE IN GENERATING FINANCIAL PRO FORMA STATEMENTS

Factor	Last Year	Historical Average	Trend Analysis	Projections[1]									Comments
				200–			200–			200–			
				O	P	ML	O	P	ML	O	P	ML	
GDP													
CPI													
Other													
Sales units													
Dollars													
COGS													
Advertising and marketing													
Interest expense													
Plant expansion													
Dividends													
Net profits													
EPS													
ROI													
ROE													
Other													

Note:
1. **O** = Optimistic; **P** = Pessimistic; **ML** = Most Likely.

Source: T. L. Wheelen and J. D. Hunger. Copyright © 1987, 1988, 1989, 1990, 1992, and 2005 by T. L Wheelen. Copyright © 1993 and 2005 by Wheelen and Hunger Associates. Reprinted with permission.

d. Analyze historical data and make adjustments based on the environmental assumptions listed earlier. Do the same for other figures that can vary significantly.

e. Assume for other figures that they will continue in their historical relationship to sales or some other key determining factor. Plug in expected inventory levels, accounts receivable, accounts payable, R&D expenses, advertising and promotion expenses, capital expenditures, and debt payments (assuming that debt is used to finance the strategy), among others.

f. Consider not only historical trends but also programs that might be needed to implement each alternative strategy (such as building a new manufacturing facility or expanding the sales force).

3. Construct detailed pro forma financial statements for each strategic alternative:

a. List the actual figures from this year's financial statements in the left column of the spreadsheet.

b. List to the right of this column the optimistic figures for years 1 through 5.

c. Go through this same process with the same strategic alternative, but now list the pessimistic figures for the next five years.

d. Do the same with the most likely figures.

e. Develop a similar set of *optimistic* (O), *pessimistic* (P), and *most likely* (ML) pro forma statements for the second strategic alternative. This process generates six different pro forma scenarios reflecting three different situations (O, P, and ML) for two strategic alternatives.

f. Calculate financial ratios and common-size income statements, and create balance sheets to accompany the pro forma statements.

g. Compare the assumptions underlying the scenarios with the financial statements and ratios to determine the feasibility of the scenarios. For example, if cost of goods sold drops from 70% to 50% of total sales revenue in the pro forma income statements, this drop should result from a change in the production process or a shift to cheaper raw materials or labor costs rather than from a failure to keep the cost of goods sold in its usual percentage relationship to sales revenue when the predicted statement was developed.

The result of this detailed scenario construction should be anticipated net profits, cash flow, and net working capital for each of three versions of the two alternatives for five years into the future. A strategist might want to go further into the future if the strategy is expected to have a major impact on the company's financial statements beyond five years. The result of this work should provide sufficient information on which forecasts of the likely feasibility and probable profitability of each of the strategic alternatives could be based.

Obviously, these scenarios can quickly become very complicated, especially if three sets of acquisition prices and development costs are calculated. Nevertheless, this sort of detailed what if analysis is needed to realistically compare the projected outcome of each reasonable alternative strategy and its attendant programs, budgets, and procedures. Regardless of the quantifiable pros and cons of each alternative, the actual decision will probably be influenced by several subjective factors such as those described in the following sections.

Management's Attitude Toward Risk

The attractiveness of a particular strategic alternative is partially a function of the amount of risk it entails. **Risk** is composed not only of the *probability* that the strategy will be effective but also of the *amount of assets* the corporation must allocate to that strategy and the *length of time* the assets will be unavailable for other uses. Because of variation among countries in terms of customs, regulations, and resources, companies operating in global industries must deal with a greater amount of risk than firms operating only in one country.[56] The greater the assets involved and the longer they are committed, the more likely top management is to demand a high probability of success. Managers with no ownership position in a company are unlikely to have much interest in putting their jobs in danger with risky decisions. Research indicates that managers who own a significant amount of stock in their firms are more likely to engage in risk-taking actions than are managers with no stock.[57]

A high level of risk was why Intel's board of directors found it difficult to vote for a proposal in the early 1990s to commit $5 billion to making the Pentium microprocessor chip—five times the amount of money needed for its previous chip. In looking back on that board meeting, then-CEO Andy Grove remarked, "I remember people's eyes looking at that chart and getting big. I wasn't even sure I believed those numbers at the time." The proposal committed the company to building new factories—something Intel had been reluctant to do. A wrong decision would mean that the company would end up with a killing amount of overcapacity. Based on Grove's presentation, the board decided to take the gamble. Intel's resulting manufacturing expansion eventually cost $10 billion but resulted in Intel's obtaining 75% of the microprocessor business and huge cash profits.[58]

Risk might be one reason that significant innovations occur more often in small firms than in large, established corporations. A small firm managed by an entrepreneur is often willing to accept greater risk than is a large firm of diversified ownership run by professional managers.[59] It is one thing to take a chance if you are the primary shareholder and are not concerned with periodic changes in the value of the company's common stock. It is something else if the corporation's stock is widely held and acquisition-hungry competitors or takeover artists surround the company like sharks every time the company's stock price falls below some external assessment of the firm's value.

A new approach to evaluating alternatives under conditions of high environmental uncertainty is to use real-options theory. According to the **real-options approach**, when the future is highly uncertain, it pays to have a broad range of options open. This is in contrast to using **net present value (NPV)** to calculate the value of a project by predicting its payouts, adjusting them for risk, and subtracting the amount invested. By boiling everything down to one scenario, NPV doesn't provide any flexibility in case circumstances change. NPV is also difficult to apply to projects in which the potential payoffs are currently unknown. The real-options approach, however, deals with these issues by breaking an investment into stages. Management allocates a small amount of funding to initiate multiple projects, monitors their development, and then cancels the projects that aren't successful and funds those that are doing well. This approach is very similar to the way venture capitalists fund an entrepreneurial venture in stages of funding based on the venture's performance.

A survey of 4,000 CFOs found that 27% of them always or almost always used some sort of options approach to evaluating and deciding on growth opportunities.[60] Research indicates that the use of the real-options approach does improve organizational performance.[61] Some of the corporations using the real-options approach are Chevron for bidding on petroleum reserves, Airbus for calculating the costs of airlines changing their orders at the last minute, and the Tennessee Valley Authority for outsourcing electricity generation instead of building its own plant. Because of its complexity, the real-options approach is not worthwhile for minor decisions or for projects requiring a full commitment at the beginning.[62]

Pressures from Stakeholders

The attractiveness of a strategic alternative is affected by its perceived compatibility with the key stakeholders in a corporation's task environment. Creditors want to be paid on time. Unions exert pressure for comparable wage and employment security. Governments and interest groups demand social responsibility. Shareholders want dividends. All these pressures must be given some consideration in the selection of the best alternative.

Stakeholders can be categorized in terms of their (1) interest in a corporation's activities and (2) relative power to influence the corporation's activities.[63] With the **Stakeholder Priority Matrix** depicted in **Figure 8–2**, each stakeholder group can be placed in one of the nine cells.

Strategic managers should ask four questions to assess the importance of stakeholder concerns in a particular decision:

1. How will this decision affect each stakeholder, especially those given high and medium priority?
2. How much of what each stakeholder wants is he or she likely to get under this alternative?
3. What are the stakeholders likely to do if they don't get what they want?
4. What is the probability that they will do it?

Strategy makers should choose strategic alternatives that minimize external pressures and maximize the probability of gaining stakeholder support. In addition, top management can propose a political strategy to influence its key stakeholders. A **political strategy** is a plan to bring stakeholders into agreement with a corporation's actions. Some of the most commonly

Figure 8–2
Stakeholder Priority Matrix

	Low Power	Medium Power	High Power
High Interest	Medium Priority	High Priority	High Priority
Medium Interest	Low Priority	Medium Priority	High Priority
Low Interest	Low Priority	Low Priority	Medium Priority

Source: ACADEMY OF MANAGEMENT EXECUTIVE: THE THINKING MANAGER'S SOURCE by C. ANDERSON. Copyright 1997 by ACAD OF MGMT. Reproduced with permission of ACAD OF MGMT in the format Textbook via Copyright Clearance Center.

used political strategies are constituency building, political action committee contributions, advocacy advertising, lobbying, and coalition building.

Pressures from the Corporate Culture

If a strategy is incompatible with a company's corporate culture, the likelihood of its success is very low. Foot-dragging and even sabotage will result as employees fight to resist a radical change in corporate philosophy. Precedents from the past tend to restrict the kinds of objectives and strategies that can be seriously considered.[64] The "aura" of the founders of a corporation can linger long past their lifetimes because their values are imprinted on a corporation's members.

In evaluating a strategic alternative, strategy makers must consider corporate culture pressures and assess a strategy's compatibility with the corporate culture. If there is little fit, management must decide if it should:

- Take a chance on ignoring the culture
- Manage around the culture and change the implementation plan
- Try to change the culture to fit the strategy
- Change the strategy to fit the culture

Further, a decision to proceed with a particular strategy without a commitment to change the culture or manage around the culture (both very tricky and time-consuming) is dangerous. Nevertheless, restricting a corporation to only those strategies that are completely compatible with its culture might eliminate from consideration the most profitable alternatives. (See **Chapter 10** for more information on managing corporate culture.)

Needs and Desires of Key Managers

Even the most attractive alternative might not be selected if it is contrary to the needs and desires of important top managers. Personal characteristics and experience affect a person's assessment of an alternative's attractiveness.[65] A person's ego may be tied to a particular proposal to the extent that all other alternatives are strongly lobbied against. As a result, the person may have unfavorable forecasts altered so that they are more in agreement with the desired alternative.[66] A key executive might influence other people in top management to favor a particular alternative so that objections to it are overruled. For example, one CEO was able to locate the corporation's 500-person national headquarters in Washington, DC, so that it would be close to his own home.

Industry and cultural backgrounds affect strategic choice. For example, executives with strong ties within an industry tend to choose strategies commonly used in that industry. Other executives who have come to the firm from another industry and have strong ties outside the industry tend to choose different strategies from what is being currently used in their industry.[67] County of origin often affects preferences. For example, Japanese managers prefer a cost-leadership strategy more than do U.S. managers.[68] Research reveals that executives from Korea, the United States, Japan, and Germany tend to make different strategic choices in similar situations because they use different decision criteria and weights. For example, Korean executives emphasize industry attractiveness, sales, and market share in their decisions, whereas U.S. executives emphasize projected demand, discounted cash flow, and ROI.[69]

There is a tendency to maintain the status quo, which means that decision makers continue with existing goals and plans beyond the point when an objective observer would recommend a change in course. Some executives show a self-serving tendency to attribute the firm's problems not to their own poor decisions but to environmental events out of their control, such as government policies or a poor economic climate.[70] Negative information about a particular course of action to which a person is committed may be ignored because of a desire to appear competent or because of strongly held values regarding consistency. It may take a crisis or an unlikely event to cause strategic decision makers to seriously consider an alternative they had previously ignored or discounted.[71] For example, it wasn't until the CEO of ConAgra, a multinational food products company, had a heart attack that ConAgra started producing the Healthy Choice line of low-fat, low-cholesterol, low-sodium frozen-food entrees.

Process of Strategic Choice

There is an old story told at General Motors:

> *At a meeting with his key executives, CEO Alfred Sloan proposed a controversial strategic decision. When asked for comments, each executive responded with supportive comments and praise. After announcing that they were all in apparent agreement, Sloan stated that they were not going to proceed with the decision. Either his executives didn't know enough to point out potential downsides of the decision, or they were agreeing to avoid upsetting the boss and disrupting the cohesion of the group. The decision was delayed until a debate could occur over the pros and cons.*[72]

Strategic choice is the evaluation of alternative strategies and selection of the best alternative. There is mounting evidence that when an organization is facing a dynamic environment, the best strategic decisions are not arrived at through **consensus** when everyone agrees on one alternative. They actually involve a certain amount of heated disagreements—and even conflict.[73] This is certainly the case for firms operating in global industries. Because unmanaged conflict often carries a high emotional cost, authorities in decision making propose that strategic managers use "programmed conflict" to raise different opinions, regardless of the personal feelings of the people involved.[74] Two techniques help strategic managers avoid the consensus trap that Alfred Sloan found:

1. **Devil's Advocate:** The idea of the **devil's advocate** originated in the medieval Roman Catholic Church as a way of ensuring that impostors were not canonized as saints. One trusted person was selected to find and present all the reasons a person should *not* be

canonized. When this process is applied to strategic decision making, a devil's advocate (who may be an individual or a group) is assigned to identify potential pitfalls and problems with a proposed alternative strategy in a formal presentation.

2. **Dialectical Inquiry:** The dialectical philosophy, which can be traced back to Plato and Aristotle and more recently to Hegel, involves combining two conflicting views—the thesis and the antithesis—into a synthesis. When applied to strategic decision making, **dialectical inquiry** requires that two proposals using different assumptions be generated for each alternative strategy under consideration. After advocates of each position present and debate the merits of their arguments before key decision makers, either one of the alternatives or a new compromise alternative is selected as the strategy to be implemented.

Research generally supports the conclusion that the devil's advocate and dialectical inquiry methods are equally superior to consensus in decision making, especially when the firm's environment is dynamic. The debate itself, rather than its particular format, appears to improve the quality of decisions by formalizing and legitimizing constructive conflict and by encouraging critical evaluation. Both lead to better assumptions and recommendations and to a higher level of critical thinking among the people involved.[75]

Regardless of the process used to generate strategic alternatives, each resulting alternative must be rigorously evaluated in terms of its ability to meet four criteria:

1. **Mutual exclusivity:** Doing any one alternative would preclude doing any other.
2. **Success:** It must be doable and have a good probability of success.
3. **Completeness:** It must take into account all the key strategic issues.
4. **Internal consistency:** It must make sense on its own as a strategic decision for the entire firm and not contradict key goals, policies, and strategies currently being pursued by the firm or its units.[76]

8.5 Developing Policies

The selection of the best strategic alternative is not the end of strategy formulation. The organization must then engage in developing policies. Policies define the broad guidelines for implementation. Flowing from the selected strategy, policies provide guidance for decision making and actions throughout the organization. They are the principles under which the corporation operates on a day-to-day basis. At General Electric, for example, Chairman Jack Welch initiated the policy that any GE business unit be Number One or Number Two in whatever market it competes. This policy gives clear guidance to managers throughout the organization. Another example of such a policy is Casey's General Stores' policy that a new service or product line may be added to its stores only when the product or service can be justified in terms of increasing store traffic.

When crafted correctly, an effective policy accomplishes three things:

- It forces trade-offs between competing resource demands.
- It tests the strategic soundness of a particular action.
- It sets clear boundaries within which employees must operate while granting them freedom to experiment within those constraints.[77]

Policies tend to be rather long lived and can even outlast the particular strategy that created them. These general policies—such as "The customer is always right" (Nordstrom) or "Low prices, every day" (Wal-Mart)—can become, in time, part of a corporation's culture.

Such policies can make the implementation of specific strategies easier. They can also restrict top management's strategic options in the future. Thus a change in strategy should be followed quickly by a change in policies. Managing policy is one way to manage the corporate culture.

8.5 Conclusion

This chapter completes the part of this book on strategy formulation and sets the stage for strategy implementation. Functional strategies must be formulated to support business and corporate strategies; otherwise, the company will move in multiple directions and eventually pull itself apart. For a functional strategy to have the best chance of success, it should be built on a capability residing within that functional area. If a corporation does not have a strong capability in a particular functional area, that functional area could be a candidate for outsourcing.

When evaluating a strategic alternative, the most important criterion is the ability of the proposed strategy to deal with the specific strategic factors developed earlier, in the SWOT analysis. If the alternative doesn't take advantage of environmental opportunities and corporate strengths/competencies and lead away from environmental threats and corporate weaknesses, it will probably fail. Developing corporate scenarios and pro forma projections for each alternative are rational aids for strategic decision making. This logical approach fits Mintzberg's planning mode of strategic decision making, as discussed in Chapter 1. Nevertheless, some strategic decisions are inherently risky and may be resolved on the basis of one person's "gut feel." This is an aspect of the entrepreneurial mode and may be used in large, established corporations as well as in new venture startups. Various management studies have found that executives routinely rely on their intuition to solve complex problems. According to Ralph Larsen, Chairman and CEO of Johnson & Johnson, "Often there is absolutely no way that you could have the time to thoroughly analyze every one of the options or alternatives available to you. So you have to rely on your business judgment."[78]

For example, when Bob Lutz, President of Chrysler Corporation, was enjoying a fast drive in his Cobra roadster one weekend in 1988, he wondered why Chrysler's cars were so dull. "I felt guilty: there I was, the president of Chrysler, driving this great car that had such a strong Ford association," said Lutz, referring to the original Cobra's Ford V-8 engine. That Monday, Lutz enlisted allies at Chrysler to develop a muscular, outrageous sports car that would turn heads and stop traffic. Others in management argued that the $80 million investment would be better spent elsewhere. The sales force warned that no U.S. auto maker had ever succeeded in selling a $50,000 car. With only his gut instincts to support him, he pushed the project forward with unwavering commitment. The result was the Dodge Viper—a car that single-handedly changed the public's perception of Chrysler. Years later, Lutz had trouble describing exactly how he had made this critical decision. "It was this subconscious, visceral feeling. And it just felt right," explained Lutz.[79]

Strategy Bits

- Forrester Research projects that 3.3 million U.S. jobs will be outsourced offshore by 2015.[80]
- Deloitte Research projects more than 800,000 financial services jobs and high-tech jobs will migrate from Western Europe to cheaper labor markets in India, Eastern Europe, China, Africa, and Latin America.[81]

Discussion Questions

1. Are functional strategies interdependent, or can they be formulated independently of other functions?
2. Why is penetration pricing more likely than skim pricing to raise a company's or a business unit's operating profit in the long run?
3. How does mass customization support a business unit's competitive strategy?
4. When should a corporation or business unit outsource a function or an activity?
5. What is the relationship of policies to strategies?

Strategic Practice Exercise

Levi Strauss & Company, the California gold rush outfitter whose trademark blue jeans have been an American clothing staple for generations, had fallen on hard times by 2004 and needed a change in strategic direction. At the end of 2003, the company had undergone seven straight years of declining sales after its sales peaked in 1996 at $7.1 billion. Although the company earned $311 million in operating profits in 2003 on $4 billion in revenues, it posted a record $349 million in net losses, largely due to non-cash charges for accounting purposes. The firm's global workforce had shrunk from more than 37,000 in 1996 to around 12,000. According to Walter Loeb, a retail analyst, "There was a time when Levi's was the fashion garment of the day. The exclusivity of the Levi's brand is no longer as important to customers."

Management responded to the decline by moving its manufacturing plants offshore and by introducing a new line of discount jeans. In the early 1980s, the company had 63 manufacturing plants in the United States. Beset by strong competition in the 1990s, the company had hoped to cut costs and invigorate sales by steadily shifting production to overseas contractors. On January 8, 2004, the company closed its San Antonio, Texas, plant, its last U.S. plant. Levi's continued to base its headquarters staff, designers, and sales employees in the United States. According to company spokesperson Jeff Beckman, the company's identity would also stay in the United States. "We're still an American brand, but we're also a brand and a company whose products have been adopted by consumers around the world. We have to operate as a global company," said Beckman.

In July 2003, the company introduced its new line of Signature jeans at Wal-Mart, priced at $21 to $23 a pair. The company had traditionally sold its products in department stores, where prices ranged from $35 for the 501 jeans to $44 for 599 Giant Fit baggy jeans. In 2004, management was considering selling its $1 billion Dockers casual-pants unit in order to reduce its $2.2 billion debt and to refocus on the jeans business.[82]

1. What is Levi's problem?
2. What do you think of its actions to completely outsource its manufacturing overseas and to introduce a new low-priced line of jeans in discount stores?
3. Should it sell its Dockers unit?
4. What would you recommend to Levi's top management to boost company sales and profits?

Key Terms

360-degree appraisal (p. 197)
connected line batch flow (p. 194)
consensus (p. 207)
continuous improvement (p. 195)
corporate scenario (p. 202)
dedicated transfer line (p. 194)
devil's advocate (p. 207)
dialectical inquiry (p. 208)
dynamic pricing (p. 191)
financial strategy (p. 191)
flexible manufacturing system (p. 194)
functional strategy (p. 189)
HRM strategy (p. 197)
information technology strategy (p. 198)
job shop (p. 194)
Just-In-Time (JIT) (p. 196)
leveraged buyout (LBO) (p. 191)
line extension (p. 190)
logistics strategy (p. 196)
market development (p. 190)
marketing strategy (p. 190)
mass production (p. 194)
modular manufacturing (p. 195)
multiple sourcing (p. 195)
net present value (NPV) (p. 205)
open innovation (p. 193)
operations strategy (p. 193)
outsourcing (p. 198)

parallel sourcing (p. 196)
penetration pricing (p. 191)
political strategy (p. 205)
product development (p. 190)
pull strategy (p. 190)
purchasing strategy (p. 195)
push strategy (p. 190)
R&D strategy (p. 192)
real-options approach (p. 205)
reverse stock split (p. 192)
risk (p. 204)
skim pricing (p. 191)
sole sourcing (p. 195)
Stakeholder priority matrix (p. 205)
strategic choice (p. 207)
strategies to avoid (p. 201)
technological follower (p. 192)
technological leader (p. 192)
tracking stock (p. 192)

PART ENDING VIDEO CASE PART THREE

Newbury Comics, Inc.

STRATEGY FORMULATION

Newbury Comics Cofounders Mike Dreese and John Brusger parlayed $2,000 and a comic book collection into a thriving chain of 22 stores spanning the New England region, known to be *the* place to shop for everything from the best of the underground/independent music scene to major label superstars. The chain also stocks a wide variety of non-music related items such as T-shirts, Dr. (doc) Martens shoes, posters, jewelry, cosmetics, books, magazines, and other trendy items.

In Part Three, **"Strategy Formulation,"** the video addresses strategy formulation in terms of situation analysis, business, corporate, and functional strategy. Mike, John, and Jan conduct a SWOT analysis of Newbury Comics in terms of Strengths, Weaknesses, Opportunities, and Threats and how strategy is formulated. They are very much aware of how the company's core competencies provide competitive advantage. Mike explains that he dislikes setting three-year revenue targets (objectives), but prefers to formulate strategy on an experimental basis. Note that even when discussing strategy formulation, Mike talks about implementation. He tells how he assigned the development of the used CD implementation plan to Duncan Brown, Senior Vice President. Brown was to look for long-run roadblocks in case the strategy was successful in the short run. Newbury Comics is a good example of the value of SWOT analysis when formulating strategy. Most of the information, such as the employees' knowledge and competition, was presented in the earlier video dealing with environmental scanning. Some of the threats, however, are mentioned for the first time. Mike notes that the vendor community (suppliers of new CDs) may decide to make it difficult for any retailer to buy new CDs if that retailer sells used ones. He also notes that in four to five years, Napster-type operators who deal in digit-to-digit downloads instead of CDs may dominate the business of music distribution.

The management of Newbury Comics definitely believes that the company has a competitive advantage (edge) in its market. Jan states that the company's prices are cheaper than the mall music stores plus it offers used CDs. Even when competitors like Best Buy have similar prices, Newbury Comics has a better selection plus used CDs. Mike again points out that the company's corporate culture attracts employees with a "knowledge of the street." One-third of the employees play in bands. John adds that Newbury Comics offers hard-to-find material that is sold in "onesies" and "twosies" to the discriminating buyer.

Concepts Illustrated in the Video

- Strategy Formulation
- SWOT Analysis
- Propitious Niche
- Competitive Strategy
- Competitive Tactics (timing)
- Corporate Growth Strategy
- Marketing Strategy
- Human Resource Management Strategy
- Information Systems Strategy
- Management's Attitude Toward Risk

Study Questions

1. Has Newbury Comics found a "propitious niche"?
2. Conduct a SWOT analysis of Newbury Comics. Did you list anything that management failed to list?
3. The video casually mentions mission and objectives for the company. Formulate a mission statement for Newbury Comics.
4. What competitive strategy is being followed by Newbury Comics?
5. What corporate strategy is being followed by Newbury Comics?

PART FOUR

Strategy Implementation and Control

CHAPTER 9 Strategy Implementation: Organizing for Action

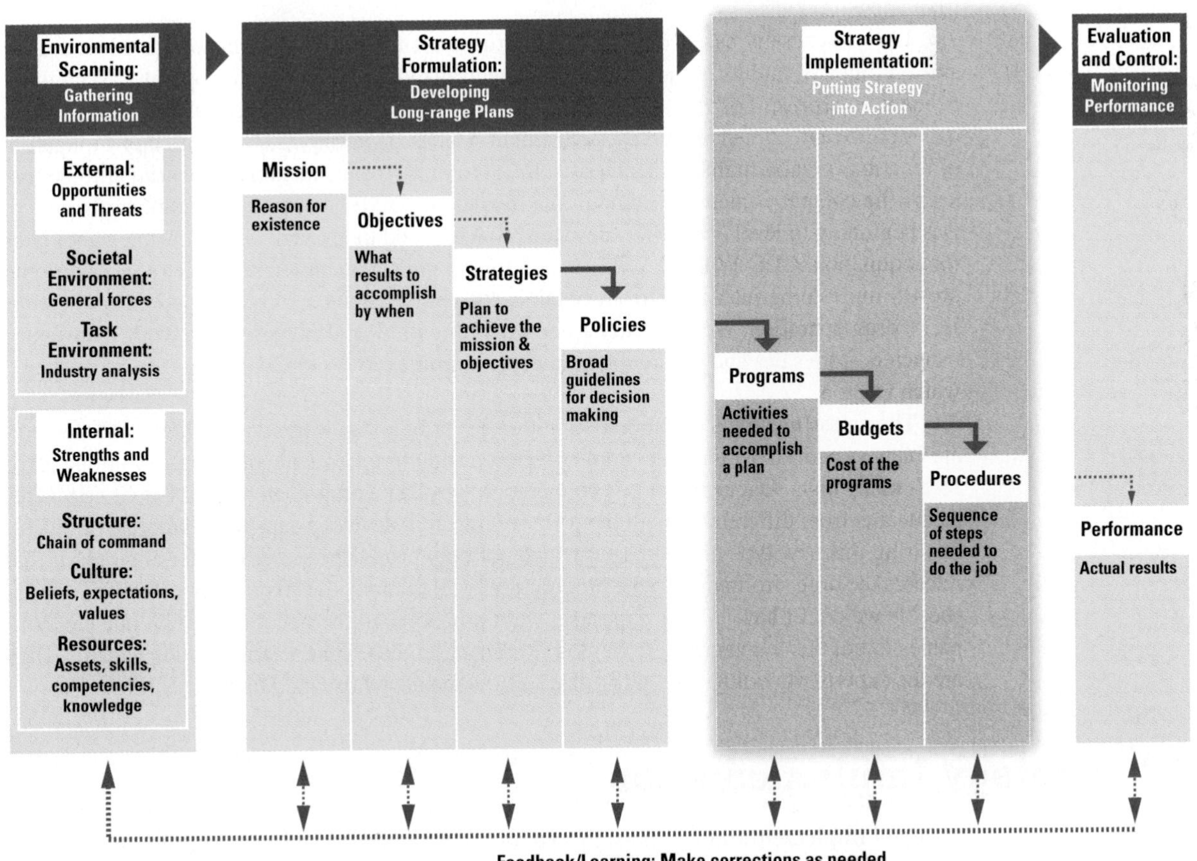

Learning Objectives

After reading this chapter, you should be able to:

- Develop programs, budgets, and procedures to implement strategic change
- Understand the importance of achieving synergy during strategy implementation
- List the stages of corporate development and the structure that characterizes each stage
- Identify the blocks to changing from one stage to another
- Construct matrix and network structures to support flexible and nimble organizational strategies
- Decide when and if programs such as reengineering, Six Sigma, and job redesign are appropriate methods of strategy implementation
- Understand the centralization versus decentralization issue in multinational corporations

JOHNSON & JOHNSON (J&J) IS ONE OF THE MOST SUCCESSFUL HEALTH-CARE COMPANIES IN the world. Founded in 1886, it is composed of 204 different business units, organized into 3 groups: pharmaceutical drugs, medical devices and diagnostics, and consumer products. Although most people know J&J for its Band-Aids and baby powder, its competitors know the company as a fierce rival that combines scientific expertise with intelligent marketing. It regularly develops or acquires innovative products and then sells them more aggressively than most companies. Even though hospitals might prefer to purchase surgical tools from one company and sutures from another, it will likely buy them both from J&J because J&J offers favorable prices to hospitals that buy the whole package. Johnson & Johnson's reputation as an ethical company makes it easy for the company to persuade physicians and consumers to try its new products.

J&J's success is based on its unique structure and culture. J&J is structured as a divisional company, and its authority is very decentralized. Each of its units operates as an independent enterprise. For example, each unit establishes its own business strategy and has its own finance and human resource management (HRM) departments. Although this duplication of functions creates high overhead costs, the autonomy fosters an entrepreneurial attitude that keeps the company intensely competitive overall. By 2003, however, the company's growth was beginning to level off. Drug sales were slowing, and there were fewer feasible candidates for acquisition. CEO William Weldon and his top management team decided that additional growth must come internally, from obtaining synergy among J&J's many units. As head of J&J's drug operation, Weldon had earlier worked to get R&D executives to work with senior managers from sales and marketing on a new committee to decide which projects to push and which to drop.

The cross-functional collaboration within the drug group worked so well that Weldon created new systems to foster better communication and more frequent collaboration among all of J&J's many units. One result of this cooperation was J&J's drug-coated stent, Cypher. J&J created teams from different units in the drug and medical device groups to collaborate on manufacturing this new type of stent. The device not only props open arteries after angioplasty but releases the drug sirolimus into the blood vessel wall to block the creation of excessive scar tissue. "If we didn't have all this expertise, we'd probably still be negotiating with outside companies to put this together," said Weldon. Referring to the Cypher team, Weldon stated: "They are the experts who know the marketplace, know the hospitals, and know the cardiologists."[1]

9.1 Strategy Implementation

Strategy implementation is the sum total of the activities and choices required for the execution of a strategic plan. It is the process by which objectives, strategies, and policies are put into action through the development of programs, budgets, and procedures. Although implementation is usually considered after strategy has been formulated, implementation is a key part of strategic management. Strategy formulation and strategy implementation should thus be considered as two sides of the same coin.

Poor implementation has been blamed for a number of strategic failures. For example, studies show that half of all acquisitions fail to achieve what was expected of them, and one out of four international ventures does not succeed.[2] The most-mentioned problems reported in postmerger integration were poor communication, unrealistic synergy expectations, structural problems, missing master plan, lost momentum, lack of top management commitment, and unclear strategic fit. A study by A. T. Kearney found that a company has just two years in which to make an acquisition perform. After the second year, the window of opportunity for forging synergies has mostly closed. Kearney's study was supported by further independent research by Bert, MacDonald, and Herd. Among the most successful acquirers studied, 70% to 85% of all merger synergies were realized within the first 12 months, with the remainder being realized in year 2.[3]

To begin the implementation process, strategy makers must consider these questions:

- *Who* are the people who will carry out the strategic plan?
- *What* must be done to align the company's operations in the new intended direction?
- *How* is everyone going to work together to do what is needed?

These questions and similar ones should have been addressed initially when the pros and cons of strategic alternatives were analyzed. They must also be addressed again before appropriate implementation plans can be made. Unless top management can answer these basic questions satisfactorily, even the best-planned strategy is unlikely to provide the desired outcome.

A survey of 93 *Fortune 500* firms revealed that more than half of the corporations experienced the following 10 problems when they attempted to implement a strategic change. These problems are listed in order of frequency:

1. Implementation took more time than originally planned.
2. Unanticipated major problems arose.
3. Activities were ineffectively coordinated.
4. Competing activities and crises took attention away from implementation.
5. The involved employees had insufficient capabilities to perform their jobs.
6. Lower-level employees were inadequately trained.
7. Uncontrollable external environmental factors created problems.
8. Departmental managers provided inadequate leadership and direction.
9. Key implementation tasks and activities were poorly defined.
10. The information system inadequately monitored activities.[4]

9.2 Who Implements Strategy?

Depending on how a corporation is organized, those who implement strategy will probably be a much more diverse set of people than those who formulate it. In most large, multi-industry corporations, the implementers are everyone in the organization. Vice presidents of functional areas and directors of divisions or strategic business units (SBUs) work with their subordinates to put together large-scale implementation plans. Plant managers, project managers, and unit heads put together plans for their specific plants, departments, and units. Therefore, every operational manager down to the first-line supervisor and every employee is involved in some way in the implementation of corporate, business, and functional strategies.

Many of the people in the organization who are crucial to successful strategy implementation probably have little to do with the development of the corporate and even business strategy. Therefore, they might be entirely ignorant of the vast amount of data and work that went into the formulation process. Unless changes in mission, objectives, strategies, and policies and their importance to the company are communicated clearly to all operational managers, there can be a lot of resistance and foot-dragging. Managers might hope to influence top management into abandoning its new plans and returning to its old ways. This is one reason why involving people from all organizational levels in the formulation and implementation of strategy tends to result in better organizational performance.

9.3 What Must Be Done?

The managers of divisions and functional areas work with their fellow managers to develop programs, budgets, and procedures for the implementation of strategy. They also work to achieve synergy among the divisions and functional areas in order to establish and maintain a company's distinctive competence.

Developing Programs, Budgets, and Procedures

Strategy implementation involves establishing programs to create a series of new organizational activities, budgets to allocate funds to the new activities, and procedures to handle the day-to-day details.

Programs

The purpose of a **program** is to make a strategy action oriented. For example, when Xerox Corporation undertook a turnaround strategy, it needed to significantly reduce its costs and expenses. In 2002 management introduced a program called *Lean Six Sigma*. This program was developed to identify and improve a poorly performing process. Xerox first trained its top executives in the program and then launched around 250 individual Six Sigma projects throughout the corporation. The result was $6 million in saving in 2003, with even more expected in 2004.[5] (Six Sigma is explained later in this chapter.)

One way to examine the likely impact new programs will have on an existing organization is to compare proposed programs and activities with current programs and activities. Brynjolfsson, Renshaw, and Van Alstyne proposed a **matrix of change** to help managers decide how quickly change should proceed, in what order changes should take place, whether to start at a new site, and whether the proposed systems are stable and coherent. As shown in **Figure 9–1**, target practices (new programs) for a manufacturing plant are drawn on the vertical axis, and existing practices (current activities) are drawn on the horizontal axis. As shown, any new strategy will likely involve a sequence of new programs and activities. Any one of these may conflict with existing practices/activities—and that creates implementation problems. Use the following steps to create the matrix:

1. Compare the new programs/target practices with each other to see if they are complementary (+), interfering (–), or have no effect on each other (leave blank).
2. Examine existing practices/activities for their interactions with each other, using the same symbols as in step 1.
3. Compare each new program/target practice with each existing practice/activity for any interaction effects. Place the appropriate symbols in the cells in the lower-right part of the matrix.

Figure 9–1
The Matrix of Change

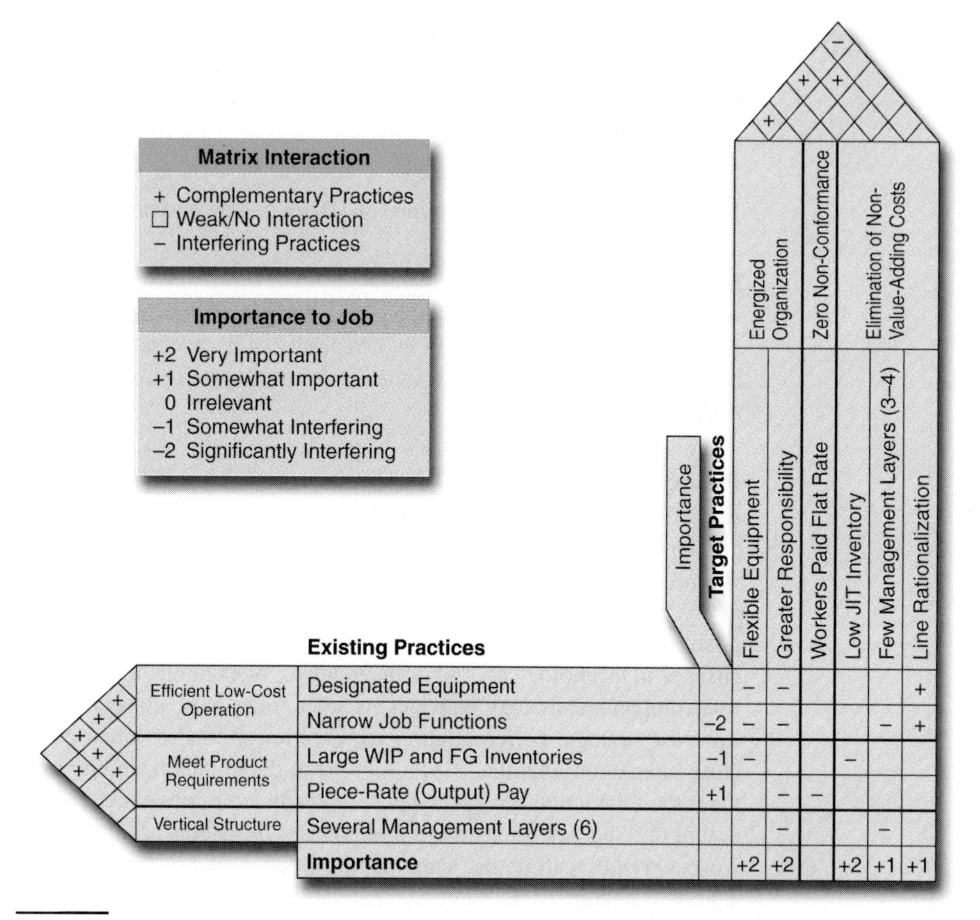

Source: Reprinted from "The Matrix of Change," by E. Brynjolfsson, A. A. Renshaw, and M. Van Alstyne, MIT Sloan Management Review *(Winter 1997), p. 43, by permission of publisher. Copyright © 1997 by Massachusetts Institute of Technology. All rights reserved.*

4. Evaluate each program/activity in terms of its relative importance to achieving the strategy or getting the job accomplished.
5. Examine the overall matrix to identify problem areas where proposed programs are likely to interfere with each other or with existing practices/activities. Note in **Figure 9–1** that the proposed program of installing flexible equipment interferes with the proposed program of assembly-line rationalization. The two new programs need to be changed so that they no longer conflict with each other. Note also that the amount of change necessary to carry out the proposed implementation programs (target practices) is a function of the number of times each program interferes with existing practices/activities. That is, the more minus signs and the fewer plus signs in the matrix, the more implementation problems can be expected.

The matrix of change can be used to address the following types of questions:

- **Feasibility:** Do the proposed programs and activities constitute a coherent, stable system? Are the current activities coherent and stable? Is the transition likely to be difficult?
- **Sequence of Execution:** Where should the change begin? How does the sequence affect success? Are there reasonable stopping points?
- **Location:** Are we better off instituting the new programs at a new site, or can we reorganize the existing facilities at a reasonable cost?

- **Pace and Nature of Change:** Should the change be slow or fast, incremental or radical? Which blocks of current activities must be changed at the same time?
- **Stakeholder Evaluations:** Have we overlooked any important activities or interactions? Should we get further input from interested stakeholders? Which new programs and current activities offer the greatest sources of value?

The matrix offers useful guidelines on where, when, and how fast to implement change.[6]

Budgets

After programs have been developed, the **budget** process begins. Planning a budget is the last real check a corporation has on the feasibility of its selected strategy. An ideal strategy might be found to be completely impractical only after specific implementation programs are costed in detail.

Procedures

After the program, divisional, and corporate budgets are approved, **procedures** must be developed. Often called **Standard Operating Procedures (SOPs)**, they typically detail the various activities that must be carried out to complete a corporation's programs. Also known as *organizational routines*, procedures are the primary means by which organizations accomplish much of what they do.[7] Once in place, procedures must be updated to reflect any changes in technology as well as in strategy. For example, a company following a differentiation competitive strategy manages its sales force more closely than does a firm following a low-cost strategy. Differentiation requires long-term customer relationships created out of close interaction with the sales force. An in-depth understanding of the customer needs provides the foundation for product development and improvement.[8] In a retail store, procedures ensure that the day-to-day store operations will be consistent over time (that is, next week's work activities will be the same as this week's) and consistent among stores (that is, each store will operate in the same manner as the others). For example, to ensure that its policies are carried out to the letter in every one of its fast-food retail outlets, McDonald's has done an excellent job of developing very detailed procedures (and policing them!).

Before a new strategy can be successfully implemented, current procedures may need to be changed. For example, in order to implement Home Depot's strategic move into services, such as kitchen and bathroom installation, the company had to first improve its productivity. Store managers were drowning in paperwork designed for a smaller and simpler company. "We'd get a fax, an e-mail, a call, and a memo, all on the same project," reported store manager Michael Jones. One executive used just three weeks of memos to wallpaper an entire conference room, floor to ceiling—windows included. CEO Robert Nardelli told his top managers to eliminate duplicate communications and streamline work projects. Directives not related to work orders had to be sent separately and only once a month. The company also spent $2 million on workload-management software.[9]

Achieving Synergy

One of the goals to be achieved in strategy implementation is synergy between and among functions and business units. This is the reason corporations commonly reorganize after an acquisition. **Synergy** is said to exist for a divisional corporation if the return on investment (ROI) of each division is greater than what the return would be if each division were an independent business. According to Goold and Campbell, synergy can take place in one of six forms:

- **Shared Know-How:** Combined units often benefit from sharing knowledge or skills. This is a leveraging of core competencies.

- **Coordinated Strategies:** Aligning the business strategies of two or more business units may provide a corporation significant advantage by reducing inter-unit competition and developing a coordinated response to common competitors (horizontal strategy).
- **Shared Tangible Resources:** Combined units can sometimes save money by sharing resources, such as a common manufacturing facility or R&D lab.
- **Economies of Scale or Scope:** Coordinating the flow of products or services of one unit with that of another unit can reduce inventory, increase capacity utilization, and improve market access.
- **Pooled Negotiating Power:** Combined units can combine their purchasing to gain bargaining power over common suppliers to reduce costs and improve quality. The same can be done with common distributors.
- **New Business Creation:** Exchanging knowledge and skills can facilitate new products or services by extracting discrete activities from various units and combining them in a new unit or by establishing joint ventures among internal business units.[10]

Johnson & Johnson's program to improve collaboration among its 204 business units is one example of how J&J hoped to obtain all six forms of synergy, but especially the last one, new business creation.

9.4 How Is Strategy to Be Implemented? Organizing for Action

Before plans can lead to actual performance, a corporation should be appropriately organized, programs should be adequately staffed, and activities should be directed toward achieving desired objectives. (Organizing activities are reviewed briefly in this chapter; staffing, directing, and control activities are discussed in **Chapters 10** and **11**.)

Any change in corporate strategy is very likely to require some sort of change in the way an organization is structured and in the kind of skills needed in particular positions. Managers must, therefore, closely examine the way their company is structured in order to decide what, if any, changes should be made in the way work is accomplished. Should activities be grouped differently? Should the authority to make key decisions be centralized at headquarters or decentralized to managers in distant locations? Should the company be managed like a "tight ship" with many rules and controls, or "loosely" with few rules and controls? Should the corporation be organized into a "tall" structure with many layers of managers, each having a narrow span of control (that is, few employees per supervisor) to better control his or her subordinates; or should it be organized into a "flat" structure with fewer layers of managers, each having a wide span of control (that is, more employees per supervisor) to give more freedom to his or her subordinates?

Structure Follows Strategy

In a classic study of large U.S. corporations such as DuPont, General Motors, Sears, and Standard Oil, Alfred Chandler concluded that **structure follows strategy**—that is, changes in corporate strategy lead to changes in organizational structure.[11] He also concluded that organizations follow a pattern of development from one kind of structural arrangement to another as they expand. According to Chandler, these structural changes occur because the old structure, having been pushed too far, has caused inefficiencies that have become too obviously detrimental to bear. Chandler, therefore, proposed the following as the sequence of what occurs:

1. New strategy is created.
2. New administrative problems emerge.
3. Economic performance declines.
4. New appropriate structure is invented.
5. Profit returns to its previous level.

Chandler found that in their early years, corporations such as DuPont tend to have a centralized functional organizational structure that is well suited to producing and selling a limited range of products. As they add new product lines, purchase their own sources of supply, and create their own distribution networks, they become too complex for highly centralized structures. To remain successful, this type of organization needs to shift to a decentralized structure with several semiautonomous divisions (referred to in **Chapter 5** as *divisional structure*).

Alfred P. Sloan, past CEO of General Motors, detailed how GM conducted such structural changes in the 1920s.[12] He saw decentralization of structure as "centralized policy determination coupled with decentralized operating management." After top management had developed a strategy for the total corporation, the individual divisions (Chevrolet, Buick, and so on) were free to choose how to implement that strategy. Patterned after DuPont, GM found the decentralized multidivisional structure to be extremely effective in allowing the maximum amount of freedom for product development. Return on investment (ROI) was used as a financial control. (ROI is discussed in more detail in **Chapter 11**.)

Research generally supports Chandler's proposition that structure follows strategy (as well as the reverse proposition that structure influences strategy).[13] As mentioned earlier, changes in the environment tend to be reflected in changes in a corporation's strategy, thus leading to changes in a corporation's structure. Strategy, structure, and the environment need to be closely aligned; otherwise, organizational performance will likely suffer.[14] For example, a business unit following a differentiation strategy needs more freedom from headquarters to be successful than does another unit following a low-cost strategy.[15]

Although it is agreed that organizational structure must vary with different environmental conditions, which, in turn, affect an organization's strategy, there is no agreement about an optimal organizational design. What was appropriate for DuPont and General Motors in the 1920s might not be appropriate today. Firms in the same industry do, however, tend to organize themselves similarly to one another. For example, automobile manufacturers tend to emulate General Motors' divisional concept, whereas consumer-goods producers tend to emulate the brand-management concept (a type of matrix structure) pioneered by Procter & Gamble Company. The general conclusion seems to be that firms following similar strategies in similar industries tend to adopt similar structures.

Stages of Corporate Development

Successful corporations tend to follow a pattern of structural development as they grow and expand. Beginning with the simple structure of the entrepreneurial firm (in which everybody does everything), successful corporations usually get larger and organize along functional lines, with marketing, production, and finance departments. With continuing success, the company adds new product lines in different industries and organizes itself into interconnected divisions. The differences among these three structural **stages of corporate development** in terms of typical problems, objectives, strategies, reward systems, and other characteristics are specified in detail in **Table 9–1.**

TABLE 9–1 FACTORS DIFFERENTIATING STAGE I, II, AND III COMPANIES

Function	Stage I	Stage II	Stage III
1. Sizing up: Major problems	Survival and growth dealing with short-term operating problems.	Growth, rationalization, and expansion of resources, providing for adequate attention to product problems.	Trusteeship in management and investment and control of large, increasing, and diversified resources. Also, important to diagnose and take action on problems at division level.
2. Objectives	Personal and subjective.	Profits and meeting functionally oriented budgets and performance targets.	ROI, profits, earnings per share.
3. Strategy	Implicit and personal; exploitation of immediate opportunities seen by owner-manager.	Functionally oriented moves restricted to "one product" scope; exploitation of one basic product or service field.	Growth and product diversification; exploitation of general business opportunities.
4. Organization: Major characteristic of structure	One unit, "one-man show."	One unit, functionally specialized group.	Multiunit general staff office and decentralized operating divisions.
5. (a) Measurement and control	Personal, subjective control based on simple accounting system and daily communication and observation.	Control grows beyond one person; assessment of functional operations necessary; structured control systems evolve.	Complex formal system geared to comparative assessment of performance measures, indicating problems and opportunities and assessing management ability of division managers.
5. (b) Key performance indicators	Personal criteria, relationships with owner, operating efficiency, ability to solve operating problems.	Functional and internal criteria such as sales, performance compared to budget, size of empire, status in group, personal, relationships, etc.	More impersonal application of comparisons such as profits, ROI, P/E ratio, sales, market share, productivity, product leadership, personnel development, employee attitudes, public responsibility.
6. Reward-punishment system	Informal, personal, subjective; used to maintain control and divide small pool of resources for key performers to provide personal incentives	More structured; usually based to a greater extent on agreed policies as opposed to personal opinion and relationships.	Allotment by "due process" of a wide variety of different rewards and punishments on a formal and systematic basis. Companywide policies usually apply to many different classes of managers and workers with few major exceptions for individual cases.

Source: Donald H. Thain, "Stages of Corporate Development," *Ivey Business Journal* (formerly *Ivey Business Quarterly*), Winter 1969, p. 37.

Stage I: Simple Structure

Stage I is typified by the entrepreneur, who founds a company to promote an idea (a product or a service). The entrepreneur tends to make all the important decisions personally and is involved in every detail and phase of the organization. The Stage I company has little formal structure, which allows the entrepreneur to directly supervise the activities of every employee (see **Figure 5–4** for an illustration of the simple, functional, and divisional structures). Planning is usually short range or reactive. The typical managerial functions of planning, organizing, directing, staffing, and controlling are usually performed to a very limited degree, if at all. The greatest strengths of a Stage I corporation are its flexibility and dynamism. The drive of the entrepreneur energizes the organization in its struggle for growth. Its greatest weakness is its extreme reliance on the entrepreneur to decide general strategies as well as detailed procedures. If the entrepreneur falters, the company usually flounders. This is labeled by Greiner as a **crisis of leadership**.[16]

Stage I describes Oracle Corporation, the computer software firm, under the management of its co-founder and CEO Lawrence Ellison. The company adopted a pioneering approach to retrieving data, called Structured Query Language (SQL). When IBM made SQL its standard, Oracle's success was assured. Unfortunately, Ellison's technical wizardry was not sufficient to manage the company. Often working at home, he lost sight of details outside his technical interests. Although the company's sales were rapidly increasing, its financial controls were so weak that management had to restate an entire year's results to rectify irregularities. After the company recorded its first loss, Ellison hired a set of functional managers to run the company while he retreated to focus on new product development.

Stage II: Functional Structure

Stage II is the point when the entrepreneur is replaced by a team of managers who have functional specializations. The transition to this stage requires a substantial managerial style change for the chief officer of the company, especially if he or she was the Stage I entrepreneur. He or she must learn to delegate; otherwise, having additional staff members yields no benefits to the organization. The previous example of Ellison's retreat from top management at Oracle Corporation to new product development manager is one way that technically brilliant founders are able to get out of the way of the newly empowered functional managers. In Stage II, the corporate strategy favors protectionism through dominance of the industry, often through vertical and horizontal growth. The great strength of a Stage II corporation lies in its concentration and specialization in one industry. Its great weakness is that all its eggs are in one basket.

By concentrating on one industry while that industry remains attractive, a Stage II company, such as Oracle Corporation in computer software, can be very successful. Once a functionally structured firm diversifies into other products in different industries, however, the advantages of the functional structure break down. A **crisis of autonomy** can now develop, in which people managing diversified product lines need more decision-making freedom than top management is willing to delegate to them. The company needs to move to a different structure.

Stage III: Divisional Structure

Stage III is typified by the corporation's managing diverse product lines in numerous industries; it decentralizes the decision-making authority. Stage III organizations grow by diversifying their product lines and expanding to cover wider geographical areas. They move to a divisional structure with a central headquarters and decentralized operating divisions—with each division or business unit a functionally organized Stage II company. They may also use a conglomerate structure if top management chooses to keep its collection of Stage II subsidiaries operating autonomously. A **crisis of control** can now develop, in which the various units act to optimize their own sales and profits without regard to the overall corporation, whose headquarters seems far away and almost irrelevant.

Recently, divisions have been evolving into SBUs to better reflect product-market considerations. Headquarters attempts to coordinate the activities of its operating divisions or SBUs through performance- and results-oriented control and reporting systems and by stressing corporate planning techniques. The units are not tightly controlled but are held responsible for their own performance results. Therefore, to be effective, the company has to have a decentralized decision process. The greatest strength of a Stage III corporation is its almost unlimited resources. Its most significant weakness is that it is usually so large and complex that it tends to become relatively inflexible. General Electric, DuPont, and General Motors are examples of Stage III corporations.

Stage IV: Beyond SBUs

Even with its evolution into SBUs during the 1970s and 1980s, the divisional structure is not the last word in organization structure. The use of SBUs may result in a **red tape crisis** in which the corporation has grown too large and complex to be managed through formal programs and rigid systems, and procedures take precedence over problem solving. Under conditions of (1) increasing environmental uncertainty, (2) greater use of sophisticated technological production methods and information systems, (3) the increasing size and scope of worldwide business corporations, (4) a greater emphasis on multi-industry competitive strategy, and (5) a more educated cadre of managers and employees, new advanced forms of organizational structure are emerging. These structures emphasize collaboration over competition in the managing of an organization's multiple overlapping projects and developing businesses.

The matrix and the network are two possible candidates for a fourth stage in corporate development—a stage that not only emphasizes horizontal over vertical connections between people and groups but also organizes work around temporary projects in which sophisticated information systems support collaborative activities. According to Greiner, it is likely that this stage of development will have its own crisis as well—a sort of **pressure-cooker crisis**. He predicts that employees in these collaborative organizations will eventually grow emotionally and physically exhausted from the intensity of teamwork and the heavy pressure for innovative solutions.[17]

Blocks to Changing Stages

Corporations often find themselves in difficulty because they are blocked from moving into the next logical stage of development. Blocks to development may be internal (such as lack of resources, lack of ability, or refusal of top management to delegate decision making to others) or external (such as economic conditions, labor shortages, and lack of market growth). For example, Chandler noted in his study that the successful founder/CEO in one stage was rarely the person who created the new structure to fit the new strategy, and as a result, the transition from one stage to another was often painful. This was true of General Motors Corporation under the management of William Durant, Ford Motor Company under Henry Ford I, Polaroid Corporation under Edwin Land, Apple Computer under Steven Jobs, and Hayes Microcomputer Products under Dennis Hayes. (See **STRATEGY HIGHLIGHT 9.1** for what happened to the company founded by the inventor of the modem.)

Entrepreneurs who start businesses generally have four tendencies that work very well for small new ventures but become Achilles' heels for these same individuals when they try to manage a larger firm with diverse needs, departments, priorities, and constituencies:

- **Loyalty to comrades:** This is good at the beginning but soon becomes a liability as "favoritism."
- **Task oriented:** Focusing on the job is critical at first but then becomes excessive attention to detail.
- **Single-mindedness:** A grand vision is needed to introduce a new product but can become tunnel vision as the company grows into more markets and products.
- **Working in isolation:** This is good for a brilliant scientist but disastrous for a CEO with multiple constituencies.[18]

STRATEGY HIGHLIGHT 9.1

The Founder of the Modem Blocks Transition to Stage II

Would there be an Internet without the modem? Although most large organizations now rent digital T1 lines for fast Internet access, many individuals and small business owners still access the World Wide Web through the same type of modem and command set invented by Dennis Hayes.

Dennis Hayes is legendary not only for inventing the personal computer modem but also for driving his company into bankruptcy—not once but twice. Hayes and retired partner Dale Heatherington founded Hayes Microcomputer Products 20 years ago, when they invented a device called the Hayes Smartmodem that allowed personal computers to communicate with each other through telephone lines via the Hayes Standard AT Command Set. The modem was needed to convert voice analog data into the digital data needed by computers. Modem sales boomed from $4.8 million in 1981 to $150 million in 1985. When competitors developed low-cost modems, Hayes delayed until the early 1990s to respond with its own low-priced version. Sales and profits plummeted. Hayes lost its dominant position to U.S. Robotics. Management problems mounted. Creditors and potential investors looking into the company's books and operations found them a shambles. According to one investment banker, "The factory was in complete disarray." The company reported its first loss in 1994, by which time the company had nearly $70 million in debt. In November 1994, Hayes applied for protection from creditors under Chapter 11 of the U.S. Bankruptcy Code.

Still under the leadership of its founder, the company underwent a turnaround during 1995. Still in second place with a 9.3% market share of modem sales in North America, Dennis Hayes put his company up for sale. He turned down a bid of $140 million from rival Diamond Multimedia Systems and instead accepted only $30 million for 49% of the company from Asian investors. Although the offer required Mr. Hayes to relinquish the title of CEO, Hayes would still be Chairman of the Board. He explained his decision as deriving from his unwillingness to completely let go of his baby. "I'll be able to have input, through the board and as chairman, that will best use my abilities. What I was concerned about was that someone would come in and . . . slash a part of the company without understanding how it fit in."

The company, renamed Hayes Corporation, continued to suffer losses. On October 9, 1998, the company declared **Chapter 11** bankruptcy for the last time. Unable to find further financing to turn things around, the company was forced to sell its brands, manufacturing facilities, and distribution offices to the Canadian firm Zoom Technologies (www.zoom.com), for $5.3 million. It sold its web site domain name, Hayes.com, its service center, and its spare parts inventories to Modem Express (www.modemexpress.com), a seller of refurbished "orphan" products. The company founded by Dennis Hayes now exists only as a division of another company.

Source: D. McDermott, "Asians Rejuvenate Hayes Microcomputer," *Wall Street Journal* (May 6, 1996), p. A10, plus information gathered from company web sites and Hayes Company documents within the SEC's Edgar database.

This difficulty in moving to a new stage is compounded by the founder's tendency to maneuver around the need to delegate by carefully hiring, training, and grooming his or her own team of managers. The team tends to maintain the founder's influence throughout the organization long after the founder is gone. This is what happened at Walt Disney Productions when the family continued to emphasize Walt's policies and plans long after he was dead. Although this may often be an organization's strength, it may also be a weakness—to the extent that the culture supports the status quo and blocks needed change.

Organizational Life Cycle

Instead of considering stages of development in terms of structure, the organizational life cycle approach places the primary emphasis on the dominant issue facing the corporation. Organizational structure is only a secondary concern. The **organizational life cycle** describes how organizations grow, develop, and eventually decline. It is the organizational equivalent of the product life cycle in marketing. These stages are Birth (Stage I), Growth (Stage II), Maturity (Stage III), Decline (Stage IV), and Death (Stage V). The impact of these stages on

TABLE 9–2 ORGANIZATIONAL LIFE CYCLE

	Stage I	Stage II	Stage III*	Stage IV	Stage V
Dominant Issue	Birth	Growth	Maturity	Decline	Death
Popular Strategies	Concentration in a niche	Horizontal and vertical growth	Concentric and conglomerate diversification	Profit strategy followed by retrenchment	Liquidation or bankruptcy
Likely Structure	Entrepreneur dominated	Functional management emphasized	Decentralization into profit or investment centers.	Structural surgery	Dismemberment of structure

Note: *An organization may enter a Revival phase either during the Maturity or Decline stages and thus extend the organization's life.

corporate strategy and structure is summarized in **Table 9–2**. Note that the first three stages of the organizational life cycle are similar to the three commonly accepted stages of corporate development mentioned previously. The only significant difference is the addition of the Decline and Death stages to complete the cycle. Even though a company's strategy may still be sound, its aging structure, culture, and processes may be such that they prevent the strategy from being executed properly. Its core competencies become *core ridgities* that are no longer able to adapt to changing conditions—thus the company moves into Decline.[19]

Movement from Growth to Maturity to Decline and finally to Death is not, however, inevitable. A Revival phase may occur sometime during the Maturity or Decline stages. The corporation's life cycle can be extended by managerial and product innovations.[20] This often occurs during the implementation of a turnaround strategy. This is what happened at Lionel, the maker of toy electric trains. Founded by Joshua Lionel Cowen in 1900 to make electrical devices, Lionel came to define the toy electric train. In 1953, Lionel sold three million engines and freight cars, making it the biggest toy manufacturer in the world. By the mid-1960s, the company was in decline. Electric trains were becoming a historical curiosity. Slot cars and space toys were in demand. Train hobbyists preferred the smaller HO gauge electric train over Lionel's larger train because HO gauge trains were more realistic and used less space. The company barely managed to remain in business over the next three decades. In 1999, Lionel's new owners hired Richard Maddox, a lifelong train enthusiast and an executive close to retirement at toy company Bachmann Industries. Maddox and his executive team worked to update Lionel's trains with new models and the latest technology. He improved the catalog and established dozens of licensing agreements. "We're trying to excel in things whimsical, clever," says Maddox. The unofficial Lionel historian, Todd Wagner, discovered long-forgotten blueprints of trains from the 1920s and 1930s that were gathering dust in old Lionel storerooms. The company decided to use those plans to build more authentic historical models. The reinvigorated company soon saw increased sales and profits.[21]

Unless a company is able to resolve the critical issues facing it in the Decline stage, it is likely to move into Stage V, Death—also known as bankruptcy. This is what happened to Montgomery Ward, Pan American Airlines, Macy's Department Stores, Baldwin-United, Eastern Airlines, Colt's Manufacturing, Orion Pictures, and Wheeling-Pittsburgh Steel, as well as many other firms. So many Internet ventures went bankrupt during 2000 that *Fortune* magazine listed 135 Internet companies on its "Dot-Com Deathwatch."[22] As in the cases of Johns-Manville, International Harvester, Macy's, and Kmart—all of which went bankrupt—a corporation can rise like a phoenix from its own ashes and live again under the same or a different name. The company may be reorganized or liquidated, depending on individual circumstances. For example, Kmart emerged from Chapter 11 bankruptcy in 2003 with a new

CEO and a plan to sell a number of its stores to Home Depot and Sears. These sales earned the company close to $1 billion. Although store sales continued to erode, Kmart had sufficient cash reserves to continue with its turnaround.[23] It used that money to acquire Sears in 2005. Unfortunately, however, fewer than 20% of firms entering Chapter 11 bankruptcy in the United States emerge as going concerns; the rest are forced into liquidation.[24]

Few corporations move through these five stages in order. Some corporations, for example, might never move past Stage II. Others, like General Motors, might go directly from Stage I to Stage III. A large number of entrepreneurial ventures jump from Stage I or II directly into Stage IV or V. Hayes Microcomputer Products, for example, went from the Growth (Stage II) to Decline stage (Stage IV) under its founder Dennis Hayes. The key is to be able to identify indications that a firm is in the process of changing stages and to make the appropriate strategic and structural adjustments to ensure that corporate performance is maintained or even improved. This is what the successful Internet auction firm eBay did when it hired Meg Whitman from Hasbro as CEO to professionalize its management and to improve its marketing.

Advanced Types of Organizational Structures

The basic structures (simple, functional, divisional, and conglomerate) are discussed in **Chapter 5** and summarized under the first three stages of corporate development in this chapter. A new strategy may require more flexible characteristics than the traditional functional or divisional structure can offer. Today's business organizations are becoming less centralized, with a greater use of cross-functional work teams. **Table 9–3** depicts some of the changing structural characteristics of modern corporations. Although many variations and hybrid structures contain these characteristics, two forms stand out: the matrix structure and the network structure.

Matrix Structure

Most organizations find that organizing around either functions (in the functional structure) or products and geography (in the divisional structure) provides an appropriate organizational structure. The matrix structure, in contrast, may be very appropriate when organizations conclude that neither functional nor divisional forms, even when combined with horizontal linking mechanisms such as SBUs, are right for their situations. In **matrix structures,**

TABLE 9–3 CHANGING STRUCTURAL CHARACTERISTICS OF MODERN CORPORATIONS

Old Organization Design	New Organization Design
One large corporation	Minibusiness units and cooperative relationships
Vertical communication	Horizontal communication
Centralized, top-down decision making	Decentralized participative decision making
Vertical integration	Outsourcing and virtual organizations
Work/quality teams	Autonomous work teams
Functional work teams	Cross-functional work teams
Minimal training	Extensive training
Specialized job design focused on individuals	Value-chain team-focused job design

Source: Reprinted from *RESEARCH IN ORGANIZATIONAL CHANGE AND DEVELOPMENT*, Vol. 7, No. 1, 1993, Macy and Izumi, "Organizational Change, Design, and Work Innovation: A Meta-Analysis of 131 North American Field Studies—1961–1991," p. 298. Copyright © 1993 with permission from Elsevier.

Figure 9–2
Matrix and Network Structures

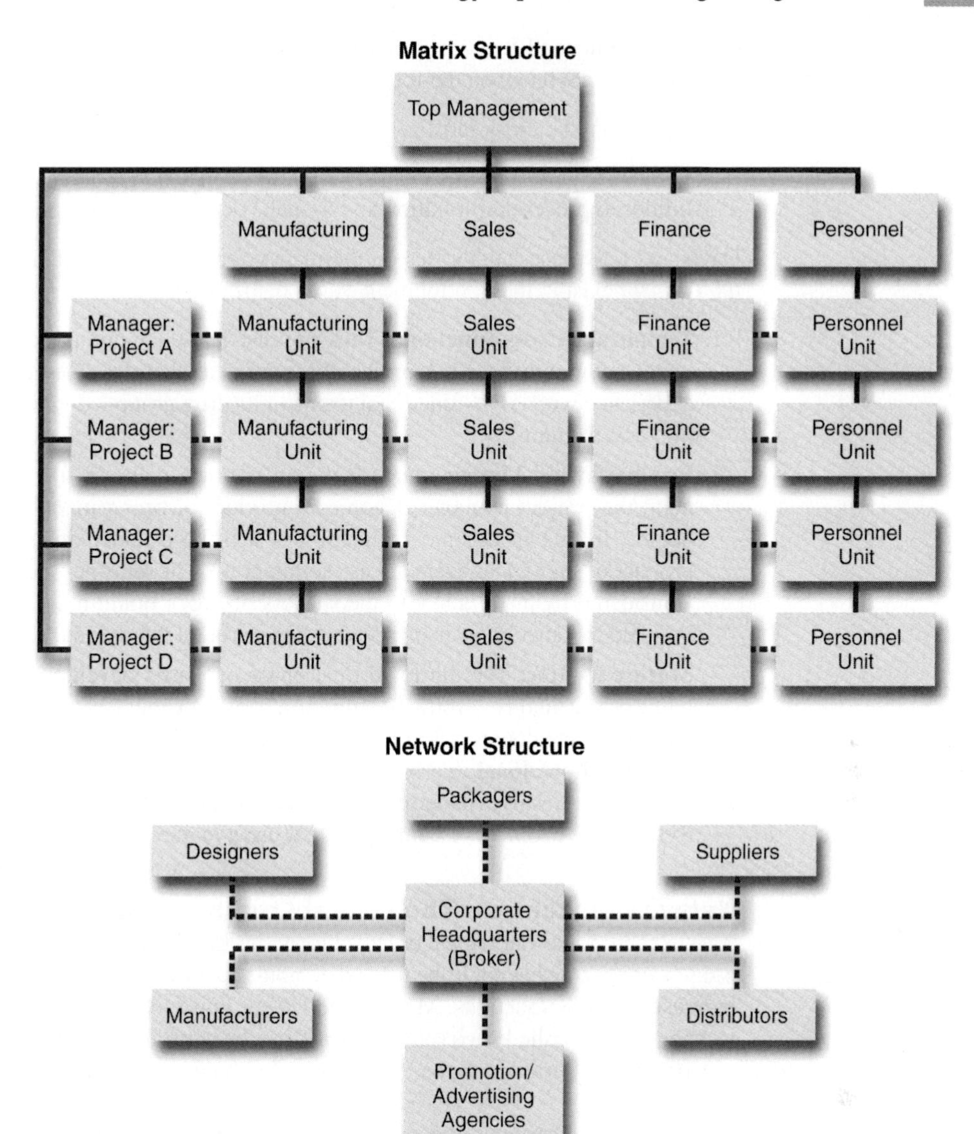

functional and product forms are combined simultaneously at the same level of the organization. (See **Figure 9–2.**) Employees have two superiors, a product or project manager, and a functional manager. The "home" department—that is, engineering, manufacturing, or sales—is usually functional and is reasonably permanent. People from these functional units are often assigned temporarily to one or more product units or projects. The product units or projects are usually temporary and act like divisions in that they are differentiated on a product-market basis.

Pioneered in the aerospace industry, the matrix structure was developed to combine the stability of the functional structure with the flexibility of the product form. The matrix structure is very useful when the external environment (especially its technological and market aspects) is very complex and changeable. It does, however, produce conflicts revolving around duties, authority, and resource allocation. To the extent that the goals to be achieved are vague and the technology used is poorly understood, a continuous battle for power between product and functional managers is likely. The matrix structure is often found in an organization or SBU when the following three conditions exist:

- Ideas need to be cross-fertilized across projects or products.
- Resources are scarce.
- Abilities to process information and to make decisions need to be improved.[25]

Davis and Lawrence, authorities on the matrix form of organization, propose that *three distinct phases* exist in the development of the matrix structure[26]:

1. **Temporary Cross-functional Task Forces:** These are initially used when a new product line is being introduced. A project manager is in charge as the key horizontal link. J&J's experience with cross-functional teams in its drug group led it to emphasize teams crossing multiple units.
2. **Product/brand Management:** If the cross-functional task forces become more permanent, the project manager becomes a product or brand manager, and a second phase begins. In this arrangement, function is still the primary organizational structure, but product or brand managers act as the integrators of semi-permanent products or brands. Considered by many a key to the success of P&G, brand management has been widely imitated by other consumer products firms around the world.
3. **Mature Matrix:** The third and final phase of matrix development involves a true dual-authority structure. Both the functional and product structures are permanent. All employees are connected to both a vertical functional superior and a horizontal product manager. Functional and product managers have equal authority and must work well together to resolve disagreements over resources and priorities. Boeing and TRW Systems are example of companies that use a mature matrix.

Network Structure—The Virtual Organization

A newer and somewhat radical organizational design, the **network structure** (see **Figure 9–2**) is an example of what could be termed a "non-structure" because of its virtual elimination of in-house business functions. Many activities are outsourced. A corporation organized in this manner is often called a **virtual organization** because it is composed of a series of project groups or collaborations linked by constantly changing nonhierarchical, cobweb-like electronic networks.[27]

The network structure becomes most useful when the environment of a firm is unstable and is expected to remain so.[28] Under such conditions, there is usually a strong need for innovation and quick response. Instead of having salaried employees, the company may contract with people for a specific project or length of time. Long-term contracts with suppliers and distributors replace services that the company could provide for itself through vertical integration. Electronic markets and sophisticated information systems reduce the transaction costs of the marketplace, thus justifying a "buy" over a "make" decision. Rather than being located in a single building or area, the organization's business functions are scattered worldwide. The organization is, in effect, only a shell, with a small headquarters acting as a "broker," electronically connected to some completely owned divisions, partially owned subsidiaries, and other independent companies. In its ultimate form, a network organization is a series of independent firms or business units linked together by computers in an information system that designs, produces, and markets a product or service.[29]

An example of a complete network organization is Just Toys. This New York City company licenses characters such as Disney's Little Mermaid, Hanna-Barbera's Flintstones, and Marvel Entertainment's Spiderman to make bendable polyvinyl chloride figures called Bend-Ems. The manufacturing and administrative work for Bend-Ems is contracted out. The company has only 30 employees. If a toy isn't selling well, production can be reduced and shipments stopped almost immediately. It would take Mattel and Hasbro months to react in a similar situation.

Other companies, such as Nike, Reebok, and Benetton, use the network structure in their operations function by subcontracting (outsourcing) manufacturing to other companies in low-cost locations around the world. For control purposes, the Italian-based Benetton maintains what it calls an "umbilical cord" by assuring production planning for all its subcontractors, planning materials requirements for them, and providing them with bills of labor and standard prices and costs, as well as technical assistance to make sure their quality is up to Benetton's standards.

The network organizational structure provides an organization with increased flexibility and adaptability to cope with rapid technological change and shifting patterns of international trade and competition. It allows a company to concentrate on its distinctive competencies while gathering efficiencies from other firms that are concentrating their efforts in their areas of expertise. The network does, however, have disadvantages. Some believe that the network is really only a transitional structure because it is inherently unstable and subject to tensions.[30] The availability of numerous potential partners can be a source of trouble. Contracting out individual activities to separate suppliers or distributors may keep the firm from discovering internal synergies by combining these activities. If a particular firm overspecializes on only a few functions, it runs the risk of choosing the wrong functions and thus becoming noncompetitive.

Cellular Organization: A New Type of Structure?

Miles and Snow et al. propose that the evolution of organizational forms is leading from the matrix and the network to the cellular organizational form. According to them, "a **cellular organization** is composed of cells (self-managing teams, autonomous business units, etc.) which can operate alone but which can interact with other cells to produce a more potent and competent business mechanism." This combination of independence and interdependence allows the cellular organizational form to generate and share the knowledge and expertise needed to produce continuous innovation. The cellular form includes the dispersed entrepreneurship of the divisional structure, customer responsiveness of the matrix, and self-organizing knowledge and asset sharing of the network.[31] As proposed, the cellular structure is similar to a current trend in industry of using internal joint ventures to temporarily combine specialized expertise and skills within a corporation to accomplish a task that individual units alone could not accomplish.[32]

According to Miles and Snow et al., the impetus for such a new structure is the pressure for a continuous process of innovation in all industries. Each cell has an entrepreneurial responsibility to the larger organization. Beyond knowledge creation and sharing, the cellular form adds value by keeping the firm's total knowledge assets more fully in use than any other type of structure. It is beginning to appear in firms that are focused on rapid product and service innovation—providing unique or state-of-the-art offerings.

Reengineering and Strategy Implementation

Reengineering is the radical redesign of business processes to achieve major gains in cost, service, or time. It is not in itself a type of structure, but it is an effective way to implement a turnaround strategy.

Business process reengineering strives to break away from the old rules and procedures that develop and become ingrained in every organization over the years. These may be a combination of policies, rules, and procedures that have never been seriously questioned because they were established years earlier. They may range from "Credit decisions are made by the credit department" to "Local inventory is needed for good customer service." These rules of organization and work design may have been based on assumptions about technology, people, and organizational goals that may no longer be relevant. Rather than attempting to fix existing problems through minor adjustments and fine-tuning of existing processes, the key to reengineering is asking, "If this were a new company, how would we run this place?"

Michael Hammer, who popularized the concept of reengineering, suggests the following principles for reengineering:

- **Organize around outcomes, not tasks:** Design a person's or a department's job around an objective or outcome instead of a single task or series of tasks.
- **Have those who use the output of the process perform the process:** With computer-based information systems, processes can now be reengineered so that the people who need the result of the process can do it themselves.
- **Subsume information-processing work into the real work that produces the information:** People or departments that produce information can also process it for use instead of just sending raw data to others in the organization to interpret.
- **Treat geographically dispersed resources as though they were centralized:** With modern information systems, companies can provide flexible service locally while keeping the actual resources in a centralized location for coordination purposes.
- **Link parallel activities instead of integrating their results:** Instead of having separate units perform different activities that must eventually come together, have them communicate while they work so that they can do the integrating.
- **Put the decision point where the work is performed and build control into the process:** The people who do the work should make the decisions and be self-controlling.
- **Capture information once and at the source:** Instead of having each unit develop its own database and information processing activities, the information can be put on a network so that all can access it.[33]

Studies of the performance of reengineering programs show mixed results. Several companies have had success with business process reengineering. For example, the Mossville Engine Center, a business unit of Caterpillar, Inc., used reengineering to decrease process cycle times by 50%, reduce the number of process steps by 45%, reduce human effort by 8%, and improve cross-divisional interactions and overall employee decision making.[34]

One study of North American financial firms found that "the average reengineering project took 15 months, consumed 66 person-months of effort, and delivered cost savings of 24%."[35] In a survey of 782 corporations using reengineering, 75% of the executives said their companies had succeeded in reducing operating expenses and increasing productivity. Although only 47% stated that their companies had succeeded in generating revenue growth and 37% at raising market share, 70% of the respondents stated that their companies planned to use reengineering in the future.[36] A study of 134 large and small Canadian companies found that reengineering programs resulted in (1) an increase in productivity and product quality, (2) cost reductions, and (3) an increase in overall organization quality, for both large and small firms.[37] Other studies report, however, that anywhere from 50% to 70% of reengineering programs fail to achieve their objectives.[38]

Six Sigma

Originally conceived by Motorola as a quality improvement program in the mid-1980s, Six Sigma has become a cost-saving program for all types of manufacturers. Briefly, **Six Sigma** is an analytical method for achieving near-perfect results on a production line. Although the emphasis is on reducing product variance in order to boost quality and efficiency, it is increasingly being applied to accounts receivable, sales, and R&D. In statistics, the Greek letter *sigma* denotes variation in the standard bell-shaped curve. One sigma equals 690,000 defects per 1 million. Most companies are only able to achieve three sigma, or 66,000 errors per million. Six Sigma reduces the defects to only 3.4 per million—thus saving money by preventing waste. The process of Six Sigma encompasses five steps:

1. *Define* a process where results are poorer than average.
2. *Measure* the process to determine exact current performance.
3. *Analyze* the information to pinpoint where things are going wrong.
4. *Improve* the process and eliminate the error.
5. *Establish* controls to prevent future defects from occurring.[39]

At Dow Chemical, each Six Sigma project has resulted in cost savings of $500,000 in the first year. Six Sigma experts at 3M have been able to speed up R&D and analyze why its top sales people sold more than others. A disadvantage of the program is that training costs in the beginning may outweigh any savings. The expense of compiling and analyzing data, especially in areas where a process cannot be easily standardized, may exceed what is saved.[40]

A new program called **Lean Six Sigma** is becoming increasingly popular in companies. This program incorporates the statistical approach of Six Sigma with the lean manufacturing program originally developed by Toyota. Like reengineering, it includes the removal of unnecessary steps in any process and fixing those that remain. This is the "lean" addition to Six Sigma. Xerox used Lean Six Sigma to resolve a problem with a $500,000 printing press it had just introduced. Teams from supply, manufacturing, and R&D development used Lean Six Sigma to find the cause of the problem and to resolve it by working with a supplier to change the chemistry of the oil on a roller.[41]

Designing Jobs to Implement Strategy

Organizing a company's activities and people to implement strategy involves more than simply redesigning a corporation's overall structure; it also involves redesigning the way jobs are done. With the increasing emphasis on reengineering, many companies are beginning to rethink their work processes, with an eye toward phasing unnecessary people and activities out of the process. Process steps that have traditionally been performed sequentially can be improved by performing them concurrently using cross-functional work teams. Harley-Davidson, for example, has managed to reduce total plant employment by 25% while reducing by 50% the time needed to build a motorcycle. Restructuring through needing fewer people requires broadening the scope of jobs and encouraging teamwork. The design of jobs and subsequent job performance are, therefore, increasingly being considered as sources of competitive advantage.

Job design refers to the study of individual tasks in an attempt to make them more relevant to the company and to the employee(s). To minimize some of the adverse consequences of task specialization, corporations have turned to new job design techniques: **job enlargement** (combining tasks to give a worker more of the same type of duties to perform), **job rotation** (moving workers through several jobs to increase variety), and **job enrichment** (altering the jobs by giving the worker more autonomy and control over activities). The **job characteristics model** is a good example of job enrichment. (See STRATEGY HIGHLIGHT 9.2.) Although each of these methods has its adherents, no one method seems to work in all situations.

A good example of modern job design is the introduction of team-based production by the glass manufacturer Corning, Inc., in its Blacksburg, Virginia, plant. With union approval, Corning reduced job classifications from 47 to 4 to enable production workers to rotate jobs

STRATEGY HIGHLIGHT 9.2

Designing Jobs with the Job Characteristics Model

The job characteristics model is an advanced approach to job design based on the belief that tasks can be described in terms of certain objective characteristics and that these characteristics affect employee motivation. In order for a job to be motivating, (1) the worker needs to feel a sense of responsibility, feel the task to be meaningful, and receive useful feedback on his or her performance, and (2) the job has to satisfy needs that are important to the worker. The model proposes that managers follow five principles for redesigning work:

1. Combine tasks to increase task variety and to enable workers to identify with what they are doing.
2. Form natural work units to make a worker more responsible and accountable for the performance of the job.
3. Establish client relationships so the worker will know what performance is required and why.
4. Vertically load the job by giving workers increased authority and responsibility over their activities.
5. Open feedback channels by providing workers with information on how they are performing.

Research supports the job characteristics model as a way to improve job performance through job enrichment. Although there are several other approaches to job design, practicing managers seem increasingly to follow the prescriptions of this model as a way of improving productivity and product quality.

Source: J. R. Hackman and G. R. Oldham, *Work Redesign* (Reading, MA: Addison-Wesley, 1980), pp. 135–141; G. Johns, J. L. Xie, and Y. Fang, "Mediating and Moderating Effects in Job Design," *Journal of Management* (December 1992), pp. 657–676; R. W. Griffin, "Effects of Work Redesign on Employee Perceptions, Attitudes, and Behaviors: A Long-Term Investigation," *Academy of Management Journal* (June 1991), pp. 425–435.

after learning new skills. The workers were divided into 14-member teams that, in effect, managed themselves. The plant had only two levels of management: Plant Manager Robert Hoover and two line leaders who only advised the teams. Employees worked demanding 12½-hour shifts, alternating three-day and four-day weeks. The teams made managerial decisions, imposed discipline on fellow workers, and were required to learn three "skill modules" within two years or else lose their jobs. As a result of this new job design, a Blacksburg team, made up of workers with interchangeable skills, can retool a line to produce a different type of filter in only 10 minutes—six times faster than workers in a traditionally designed filter plant. The Blacksburg plant earned a $2 million profit in its first eight months of production instead of losing the $2.3 million projected for the startup period. The plant performed so well that Corning's top management acted to convert the company's 27 other factories to team-based production.[42]

9.5 International Issues in Strategy Implementation

An international company is one that engages in any combination of activities, from exporting/importing to full-scale manufacturing, in foreign countries. A **multinational corporation (MNC)**, in contrast, is a highly developed international company with a deep involvement throughout the world, plus a worldwide perspective in its management and decision making. For an MNC to be considered global, it must manage its worldwide operations as if they were totally interconnected. This approach works best when the industry has moved from being *multidomestic* (each country's industry is essentially separate from the same industry in other countries; an example is retailing) to *global* (each country is a part of one worldwide industry; an example is consumer electronics).

The design of an organization's structure is strongly affected by the company's stage of development in international activities and the types of industries in which the company is involved. Strategic alliances may complement or even substitute for an internal functional activity. The issue of centralization versus decentralization becomes especially important for an MNC operating in both multidomestic and global industries.

International Strategic Alliances

Strategic alliances, such as joint ventures and licensing agreements, between an MNC and a local partner in a host country are becoming increasingly popular as a means by which a corporation can gain entry into other countries, especially less developed countries. The key to the successful implementation of these strategies is the selection of the local partner. Each party needs to assess not only the strategic fit of each company's project strategy but also the fit of each company's respective resources. A successful joint venture may require as much as two years of prior contacts between the parties. Research reveals that firms favor past partners when forming new alliances.[43] Key drivers for strategic fit between alliance partners are the following:

- Partners must agree on fundamental values and have a shared vision about the potential for joint value creation.
- Alliance strategy must be derived from business, corporate, and functional strategy.
- The alliance must be important to both partners, especially to top management.
- Partners must be mutually dependent for achieving clear and realistic objectives.
- Joint activities must have added value for customers and the partners.
- The alliance must be accepted by key stakeholders.
- Partners contribute key strengths but protect core competencies.[44]

Stages of International Development

Corporations operating internationally tend to evolve through five common stages, both in their relationships with widely dispersed geographic markets and in the manner in which they structure their operations and programs. These **stages of international development** are:

- **Stage 1 (Domestic Company):** The primarily domestic company exports some of its products through local dealers and distributors in the foreign countries. The impact on the organization's structure is minimal because an export department at corporate headquarters handles everything.
- **Stage 2 (Domestic Company with Export Division):** Success in Stage 1 leads the company to establish its own sales company with offices in other countries to eliminate the middlemen and to better control marketing. Because exports have now become more important, the company establishes an export division to oversee foreign sales offices.
- **Stage 3 (Primarily Domestic Company with International Division):** Success in earlier stages leads the company to establish manufacturing facilities in addition to sales and service offices in key countries. The company now adds an international division with responsibilities for most of the business functions conducted in other countries.
- **Stage 4 (Multinational Corporation with Multidomestic Emphasis):** Now a full-fledged MNC, the company increases its investments in other countries. The company establishes a local operating division or company in the host country, such as Ford of Britain, to better serve the market. The product line is expanded, and local manufacturing capacity is established. Managerial functions (product development, finance, marketing, and so on) are organized locally. Over time, the parent company acquires other related businesses, broadening the base of the local operating division. As the subsidiary in the

host country successfully develops a strong regional presence, it achieves greater autonomy and self-sufficiency. The operations in each country are, nevertheless, managed separately as if each were a domestic company.

- **Stage 5 (Multinational Corporation with Global Emphasis):** The most successful MNCs move into a fifth stage in which they have worldwide personnel, R&D, and financing strategies. Typically operating in a global industry, the MNC denationalizes its operations and plans product design, manufacturing, and marketing around worldwide considerations. Global considerations now dominate organizational design. The global MNC structures itself in a matrix form around some combination of geographic areas, product lines, and functions. All managers are responsible for dealing with international as well as domestic issues.

Research provides some support for the concept of the stages of international development, but it does not necessarily support the preceding sequence of stages. For example, a company may initiate production and sales in multiple countries without having gone through the steps of exporting or having local sales subsidiaries. In addition, any one corporation can be at different stages simultaneously, with different products in different markets at different levels. Firms may also leapfrog across stages to a global emphasis. Developments in information technology are changing the way business is being done internationally. See the GLOBAL ISSUE feature for a possible sixth stage of international development, in which an MNC locates its headquarters and key functions at multiple locations around the world. Nevertheless, the stages concept provides a useful way to illustrate some of the structural changes corporations undergo when they increase their involvement in international activities.

Centralization Versus Decentralization

A basic dilemma an MNC faces is how to organize authority centrally so that it operates as a vast interlocking system that achieves synergy and at the same time decentralize authority so that local managers can make the decisions necessary to meet the demands of the local mar-

GLOBAL ISSUE

Multiple Headquarters: A Sixth Stage of International Development?

In what could be a sixth stage of international development, an increasing number of MNCs are relocating their headquarters and headquarters functions at multiple locations around the world. Of the 800 corporate headquarters established in 2002, 200 of them were in developing nations. The antivirus software company Trend Micro, for example, spreads its top executives, engineers, and support staff throughout the world to improve its ability to respond to new virus threats. "With the Internet, viruses became global. To fight them, we had to become a global company," explained Chairman Steve Chang. Trend Micro's financial headquarters is in Tokyo, where it went public. Its product development is in Taiwan, and its sales headquarters is in America's Silicon Valley.

C. K. Prahalad, strategy professor at the University of Michigan, proposes that this is a new stage of international development. "There is a fundamental rethinking about what is a multinational company. Does it have a home country? What does headquarters mean? Can you fragment your corporate functions globally?" Corporate headquarters are now becoming virtual, with executives and core corporate functions dispersed throughout various world regions. These primarily technology companies are using geography to obtain competitive advantage through the availability of talent or capital, low costs, or proximity to most important customers. Logitech, for example, has its manufacturing headquarters in Taiwan to capitalize on low-cost Asian manufacturing; its business-development headquarters in Switzerland, where it has a series of strategic technology partnerships; and a third headquarters in Fremont, California.

Sources: S. Hamm, "Borders Are So 20th Century," *Business Week* (January 22, 2003), pp. 68–70; "Globalization from the Top Down," *Futurist* (November–December 2003), p. 13.

ket or host government.[45] To deal with this problem, MNCs tend to structure themselves either along product groups or geographic areas. They may even combine both in a matrix structure—the design chosen by 3M Corporation and Asea Brown Boveri (ABB), among others.[46] One side of 3M's matrix represents the company's product divisions; the other side includes the company's international country and regional subsidiaries.

Two examples of the usual international structure are Nestlé and American Cyanamid. Nestlé's structure is one in which significant power and authority have been decentralized to geographic entities. This structure is similar to that depicted in **Figure 9–3**, in which each geographic set of operating companies has a different group of products. In contrast, American Cyanamid has a series of centralized product groups with worldwide responsibilities. To depict Cyanamid's structure, the geographical entities in **Figure 9–3** would have to be replaced by product groups or SBUs.

The **product-group structure** of American Cyanamid enables the company to introduce and manage a similar line of products around the world. This enables the corporation to centralize decision making along product lines and to reduce costs. The **geographic-area structure** of Nestlé, in contrast, allows the company to tailor products to regional differences and to achieve regional coordination. For instance, Nestlé markets 200 different varieties of its instant coffee, Nescafé. The geographic-area structure decentralizes decision making to the local subsidiaries.

As industries move from being multidomestic to more globally integrated, MNCs are increasingly switching from the geographic-area to the product-group structure. Nestlé, for example, found that its decentralized structure had become increasingly inefficient. As a result, operating margins at Nestlé trailed those at rivals Unilever, Group Danone, and Kraft Foods by as much as 50%. CEO Peter Brabeck-Letmathe acted to eliminate country-by-country responsibilities for many functions. In one instance, he established five centers worldwide to handle most coffee and cocoa purchasing. Nevertheless, Nestlé is still using three different versions of accounting, planning, and inventory software for each of its main regions—Europe, the Americas, and Asia, Oceania, and Africa.[47]

Figure 9–3
Geographic Area Structure for an MNC

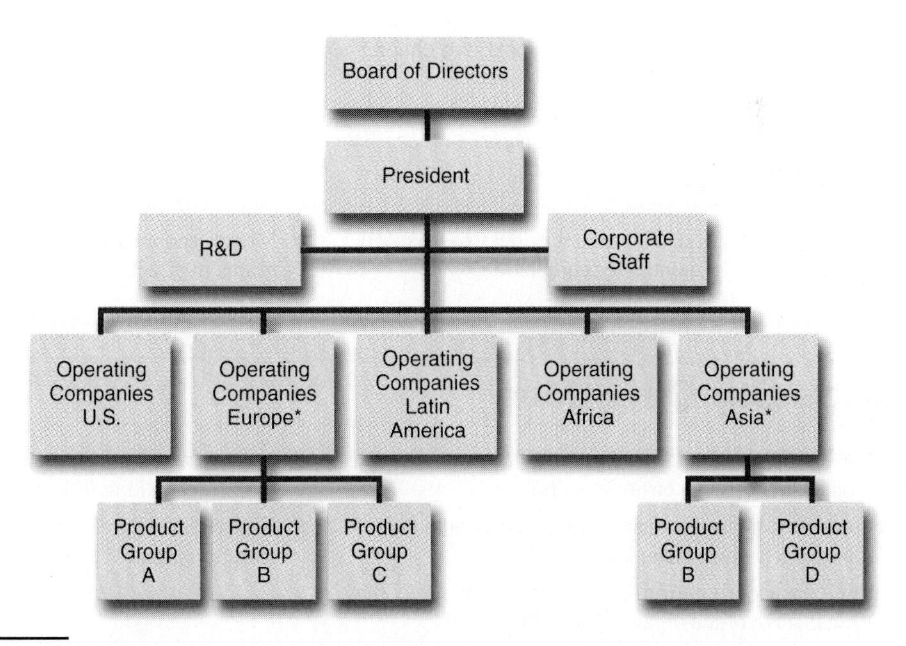

**Note: Because of space limitations, product groups for only Europe and Asia are shown here.*

Simultaneous pressures for decentralization to be locally responsive and centralization to be maximally efficient are causing interesting structural adjustments in most large corporations. This is what is meant by the phrase "think globally, act locally." Companies are attempting to decentralize those operations that are culturally oriented and closest to the customers—manufacturing, marketing, and human resources. At the same time, the companies are consolidating less visible internal functions, such as research and development, finance, and information systems, where there can be significant economies of scale.

9.6 Conclusion

Strategy implementation is where "the rubber hits the road." Environmental scanning and strategy formulation are crucial to strategic management but by themselves are only the beginning of the process. The failure to carry a strategic plan into the day-to-day operations of the workplace is a major reason why strategic planning often fails to achieve its objectives. It is discouraging to note that in one study nearly 70% of the strategic plans were never successfully implemented.[48]

For a strategy to be successfully implemented, it must be made action oriented. This is done through a series of programs that are funded through specific budgets and contain new detailed procedures. This chapter explains how jobs and organizational units can be designed to support a change in strategy. This is what Edward Zander did when he took over as CEO of Motorola in 2003. He knew that in order to turn around Motorola's recent poor performance, he had to dismantle Motorola's bureaucracy and its culture of interdepartmental rivalry. The units were referred to as *smokestacks* or *warring tribes*, with very little inter-unit cooperation but a lot of conflict. Zander's plan was to replace Motorola's product-based divisions with customer-based divisions. He hoped that this structural change would promote a more cooperative atmosphere so that the company could implement its new concept of "seamless mobility," in which people could transfer home phone calls, digital music, or television programs to a mobile phone as they leave the house. Zander followed through by making cooperation a key factor in raises and bonuses.[49] Like Zander, we will continue with issues in strategy implementation in the next two chapters.

Strategy Bits

- The implementation of a strategic decision usually takes from 2 to 16 months for completion.[50]
- Most corporate headquarters have around 10 to 30 programs in effect at any one time.[51]

Discussion Questions

1. How should a corporation attempt to achieve synergy among functions and business units?
2. How should an owner–manager prepare a company for its movement from Stage I to Stage II?
3. How can a corporation keep from sliding into the Decline stage of the organizational life cycle?
4. Is reengineering just another management fad, or does it offer something of lasting value?
5. How is the cellular organization different from the network structure?

Strategic Practice Exercise

The Synergy Game

Yolanda Sarason and Catherine Banbury

SETUP

Put three to five chairs on either side of a room, facing each other, in the front of the class. Put a table in the middle, with a bell in the middle of the table.

PROCEDURE

The instructor/moderator divides the class into teams of three to five people. Each team selects a name for itself. The instructor/moderator lists the team names on the board. The first two teams come to the front and sit in the chairs facing each other. The instructor/moderator reads a list of products or services being provided by an actual company. The winning team must identify (1) possible sources of synergy and (2) the actual company being described. For example, if the products/services listed are family restaurants, airline catering, hotels, and retirement centers, the synergy is ***standardized food service and hospitality settings*** and the company is **The Marriott Corporation**. The first team to successfully name the company *and* the synergy wins the round.

After one practice session, the game begins. Each of the teams is free to discuss the question with other team members. When one of the two teams thinks that it has the answer to both parts of the question, it must be the first to ring the bell in order to announce its answer. If it gives the correct answer, it is deemed the winner of round one. Both parts of the answer must be given for a team to have the correct answer. If a team correctly provides only one part, that answer is still wrong—no partial credit. The instructor/moderator does not say which part of the answer, if either, was correct. The second team then has the opportunity to state the answer. If the second team is wrong, both teams may try once more. If neither chooses to try again, the instructor/moderator may (1) declare no round winner and both teams sit down, (2) allow the next two teams to provide the answer to round one, or (3) go on to the next round with the same two teams. Two new teams then come to the front for the next round. Once all groups have played once, the winning teams play each other. Rounds continue until there is a grand champion. The instructor should provide a suitable prize, such as candy bars, for the winning team.

Source: This exercise was developed by Professors Yolanda Sarason of Colorado State University and Catherine Banbury of St. Mary's College and Purdue University and presented at the Organizational Behavior Teaching Conference, June 1999. Copyright © 1999 by Yolanda Sarason and Catherine Banbury. Adapted with permission.

Note from Wheelen and Hunger

The *Instructors' Manual* for this book contains a list of products and services with their synergy and the name of the company. In case your instructor does not use this exercise, try the following examples:

Example 1: Motorcycles, autos, lawn mowers, generators

Example 2: Athletic footwear, Rockport shoes, Greg Norman clothing, sportswear

For each example, did you guess the company providing these products/services and the synergy obtained? The answers are printed here, upside down:

Example 1: Engine technology by Honda

Example 2: Marketing and distribution for the athletically oriented by Reebok

Key Terms

budget (p. 218)
cellular organization (p. 229)
crisis of autonomy (p. 222)
crisis of control (p. 222)
crisis of leadership (p. 222)
geographic-area structure (p. 235)
job characteristics model (p. 231)
job design (p. 231)
job enlargement (p. 231)
job enrichment (p. 231)
job rotation (p. 231)
Lean Six Sigma (p. 231)
matrix of change (p. 216)
matrix structure (p. 226)
multinational corporation (MNC) (p. 232)
network structure (p. 228)
organizational life cycle (p. 224)
pressure-cooker crisis (p. 223)
procedure (p. 218)
product-group structure (p. 235)
program (p. 216)
red tape crisis (p. 223)
reengineering (p. 229)
Six Sigma (p. 230)
stage of corporate development (p. 220)
stage of international development (p. 233)
standard operating procedures (SOPs) (p. 218)
strategy implementation (p. 214)
structure follows strategy (p. 219)
synergy (p. 218)
virtual organization (p. 228)

CHAPTER 10
Strategy Implementation: Staffing and Directing

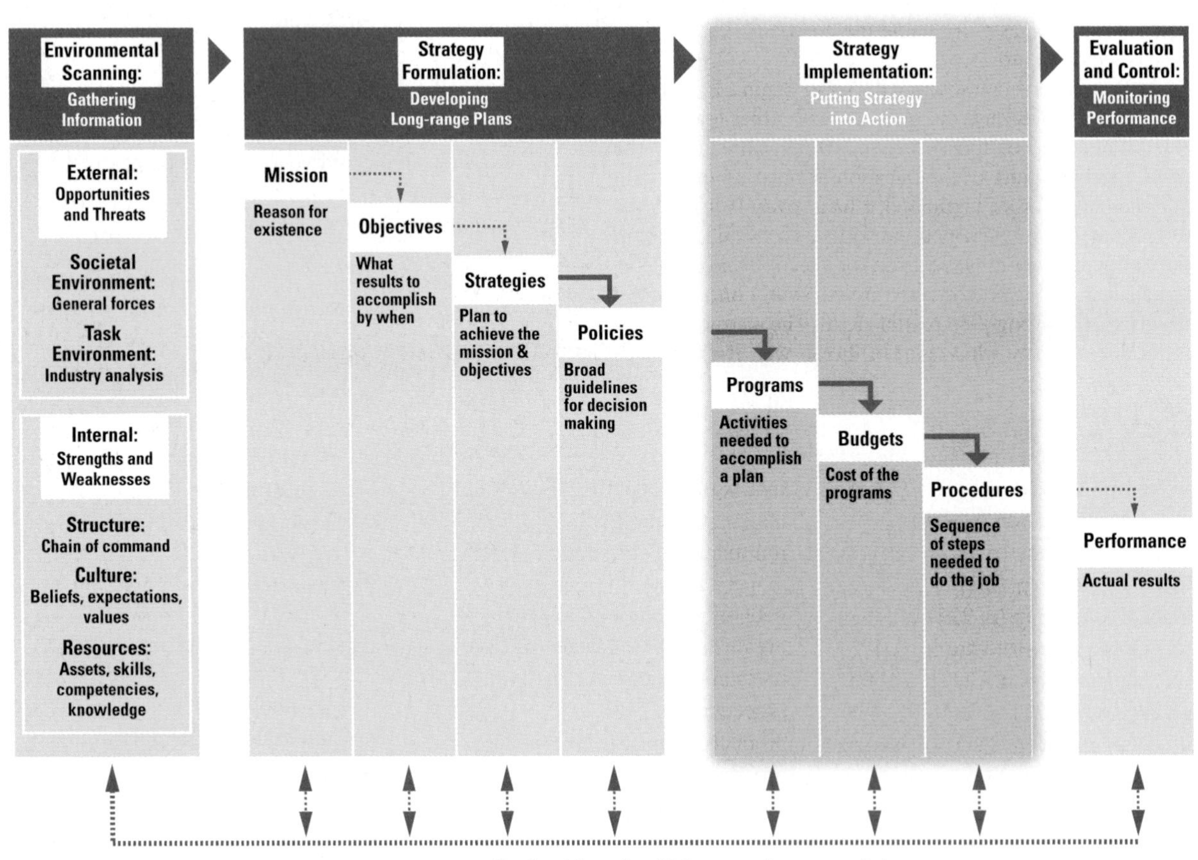

Learning Objectives

After reading this chapter, you should be able to:

- Understand the link between strategy and staffing decisions
- Match the appropriate manager to the strategy
- Understand how to implement an effective downsizing program
- Discuss important issues in effectively staffing and directing international expansion
- Assess and manage the corporate culture's fit with a new strategy
- Decide when and if programs such as MBO and TQM are appropriate methods of strategy implementation
- Formulate action plans

HAVE YOU HEARD OF ENTERPRISE RENT-A-CAR? YOU WON'T FIND IT AT THE AIRPORT WITH Hertz, Avis, or National Car Rental operations. Yet Enterprise owns more cars and operates in more locations than Hertz or Avis. It is the largest rental car company in North America. In ignoring the highly competitive airport market, Enterprise has chosen a differentiation competitive strategy by marketing to people in need of a spare car. Instead of locating many cars at a few high-priced locations at airports, Enterprise sets up inexpensive offices throughout metropolitan areas. As a result, cars are rented for 30% less than they cost at airports. As soon as one branch office grows to about 150 cars, the company opens another rental office a few miles away. People are increasingly renting from Enterprise even when their current car works fine. According to CEO Andy Taylor, "We call it a 'virtual car.' Small-business people who have to pick up clients call us when they want something better than their own car." Why is Enterprise able to follow this competitive strategy so successfully without attracting Hertz and Avis into its market?

The secret to Enterprise's success is its well-executed strategy implementation. Clearly laid-out programs, budgets, and procedures support the company's competitive strategy by making Enterprise stand out in the mind of the consumer. When a new rental office opens, employees spend time developing relationships with the service managers of every auto dealership and body shop in the area. Enterprise employees bring pizza and doughnuts to workers at auto garages across the country. Enterprise forms agreements with dealers to provide replacements for cars brought in for service. At major accounts, the company actually staffs an office at the dealership and has cars parked outside so customers don't have to go to an Enterprise office to complete paperwork.

One key to implementation at Enterprise is *staffing*—hiring and promoting a certain kind of person. Virtually every Enterprise employee is a college graduate, usually from the bottom half of the class. According to COO Donald Ross, "We hire from the half of the college class that makes the upper half possible. We want athletes, fraternity types—especially fraternity presidents and social directors. People people." These new employees begin as management trainees. Instead of regular raises, their pay is tied to branch office profits.

Another key to implementation at Enterprise is *leading*—specifying clear performance objectives and promoting a team-oriented corporate culture. The company stresses promotion from within and advancement based on performance. Every Enterprise employee, including top executives, starts at the bottom. As a result, a bond of shared experience connects all employees and managers. To reinforce a cohesive culture of camaraderie, senior executives routinely do "grunt work" at branch offices. Even Andy Taylor, the CEO, joins the work. "We were visiting an office in Berkeley and it was mobbed, so I started cleaning cars," says Taylor. "As it was happening, I wondered if it was a good use of my time, but the effect on morale was tremendous." Because the financial results of every branch office and every region are available to all, the collegial culture stimulates good-natured competition. "We're this close to beating out Middlesex," grins Woody Erhardt, an area manager in New Jersey. "I want to pound them into the ground. If they lose, they have to throw a party for us, and we get to decide what they wear."[1]

This example from Enterprise Rent-A-Car illustrates how a strategy must be implemented with carefully considered programs in order to succeed. This chapter discusses strategy implementation in terms of staffing and leading. **Staffing** focuses on the selection and use of employees. **Leading** emphasizes the use of programs to better align employee interests and attitudes with a strategy.

10.1 Staffing

The implementation of new strategies and policies often calls for new human resource management priorities and a different use of personnel. Such staffing issues can involve hiring new people with new skills, firing people with inappropriate or substandard skills, and/or training existing employees to learn new skills.

If growth strategies are to be implemented, new people may need to be hired and trained. Experienced people with the necessary skills need to be found for promotion to newly created managerial positions. When a corporation follows a growth through acquisition strategy, it may find that it needs to replace several managers in the acquired company. The percentage of an acquired company's top management team that either quit or was asked to leave is around 25% after the first year, 35% after the second year, 48% after the third year, 55% after the fourth year, and 61% after five years.[2] In addition, executives who join an acquired company after the acquisition quit at significantly higher-than-normal rates beginning in their second year. Executives continue to depart at higher-than-normal rates for nine years after the acquisition.[3] Turnover rates of executives in firms acquired by foreign firms are significantly higher than for firms acquired by domestic firms, primarily in the fourth and fifth years after the acquisition.[4]

It is one thing to lose excess employees after a merger, but it is something else to lose highly skilled people who are difficult to replace. To deal with problems such as this, some companies are appointing special integration managers to shepherd companies through the implementation process. The job of the integrator is to prepare a competitive profile of the combined company in terms of its strengths and weaknesses, draft an ideal profile of what the combined company should look like, develop action plans to close the gap between the actuality and the ideal, and establish training programs to unite the combined company and to make it more competitive.[5] To be a successful **integration manager**, a person should have (1) a deep knowledge of the acquiring company, (2) a flexible management style, (3) an ability to work in cross-functional project teams, (4) a willingness to work independently, and (5) sufficient emotional and cultural intelligence to work well with people from all backgrounds.[6]

If a corporation adopts a retrenchment strategy, however, a large number of people may need to be laid off or fired (in many instances, being laid off is the same as being fired); and top management, as well as the divisional managers, needs to specify the criteria to be used in making these personnel decisions. Should employees be fired on the basis of low seniority or on the basis of poor performance? Sometimes corporations find it easier to close or sell off an entire division than to choose which individuals to fire.

Staffing Follows Strategy

As in the case of structure, staffing requirements are likely to follow a change in strategy. For example, promotions should be based not only on current job performance but also on whether a person has the skills and abilities to do what is needed to implement the new strategy.

Changing Hiring and Training Requirements

Having formulated a new strategy, a corporation may find that it needs to either hire different people or retrain current employees to implement the new strategy. Consider the introduction of team-based production at Corning's filter plant mentioned in **Chapter 9**.

Employee selection and training were crucial to the success of the new manufacturing strategy. Plant Manager Robert Hoover sorted through 8,000 job applications before hiring 150 people with the best problem-solving ability and a willingness to work in a team setting. Those selected received extensive training in technical and interpersonal skills. During the first year of production, 25% of all hours worked were devoted to training, at a cost of $750,000.[7]

One way to implement a company's business strategy, such as overall low cost, is through training and development. A study of 51 corporations in the UK found that 71% of "leading" companies rated staff learning and training as important or very important compared to 62% of the other companies.[8] Another study of 155 U. S. manufacturing firms revealed that those with training programs had 19% higher productivity than did those without such programs. Another study found that a doubling of formal training per employee resulted in a 7% reduction in scrap.[9] Training is especially important for a differentiation strategy emphasizing quality or customer service. For example, Motorola, with annual sales of $17 billion, spends 4% of its payroll on training by providing at least 40 hours of training a year to each employee. There is a very strong connection between strategy and training at Motorola. For example, after setting a goal to reduce product development cycle time, Motorola created a two-week course to teach its employees how to accomplish that goal. It brought together marketing, product development, and manufacturing managers to create an action learning format in which the managers worked together instead of separately. The company is especially concerned with attaining the highest quality possible in all its operations. Realizing that it couldn't hit quality targets with poor parts, Motorola developed a class for its suppliers on statistical process control. The company estimates that every $1 it spends on training delivers $30 in productivity gains within three years.[10]

Training is also important when implementing a retrenchment strategy. As suggested earlier, successful downsizing means that a company has to invest in its remaining employees. General Electric's Aircraft Engine Group used training to maintain its share of the market even though it had cut its workforce from 42,000 to 33,000 in the 1990s.[11]

Matching the Manager to the Strategy

It is possible that a current CEO may not be appropriate to implement a new strategy. Research indicates that there may be a career life cycle for top executives. During the early years of executives' tenure, for example, they tend to experiment intensively with product lines to learn about their business. This is their *learning stage*. Later, their accumulated knowledge allows them to reduce experimentation and increase performance. This is their *harvest stage*. They enter a *decline stage* in their later years, when they reduce experimentation still further, and performance declines. Thus, there is an inverted U-shaped relationship between top executive tenure and the firm's financial performance. Some executives retire before any decline occurs. Others stave off decline longer than their counterparts. Because the length of time spent in each stage varies among CEOs, it is up to the board to decide when a top executive should be replaced.[12]

The most appropriate type of general manager needed to effectively implement a new corporate or business strategy depends on the desired strategic direction of that firm or business unit. Executives with a particular mix of skills and experiences may be classified as an **executive type** and paired with a specific corporate strategy. For example, a corporation following a concentration strategy emphasizing vertical or horizontal growth would probably want an aggressive new chief executive with a great deal of experience in that particular industry—a **dynamic industry expert**. A diversification strategy, in contrast, might call for someone with an analytical mind who is highly knowledgeable in other industries and can manage diverse product lines—an **analytical portfolio manager**. A corporation choosing to follow a stability strategy would probably want as its CEO a **cautious profit planner**, a person with a conservative style, a production or engineering background, and experience with controlling budgets, capital expenditures, inventories, and standardization procedures.

Weak companies in a relatively attractive industry tend to turn to a type of challenge-oriented executive known as a **turnaround specialist** to save the company. For example, Burger King's new CEO, Gregory Brenneman, was hired in 2004 to fix the ailing company because he had built a reputation as a turnaround wizard. After helping Continental Airlines return to profitability in the 1990s, he engineered the sale of PricewaterhouseCoopers to IBM in 2002. Burger King's hamburger market share had fallen from 18.5% in 2001 to 15.6% in 2003—and had taken profits with it. In his first 90 days at Burger King, Brenneman developed a turnaround plan that he hoped to complete with a public offering of Burger King shares in 2006. His plan included improving food offerings and buying back some stores from franchisees to give the company greater control over menus and store design.[13]

If a company cannot be saved, a **professional liquidator** might be called on by a bankruptcy court to close the firm and liquidate its assets. This is what happened to Montgomery Ward, Inc., the nation's first catalog retailer, which closed its stores for good in 2001, after declaring bankruptcy for the second time. Research tends to support the conclusion that as a firm's environment changes, it tends to change the type of top executive to implement a new strategy.[14] For example, during the 1990s, when the emphasis was on growth in a company's core products/services, the most desired background for a U.S. CEO was either in marketing or international experience, contrasted with finance during the 1980s, when conglomerate diversification was popular.[15]

This approach is in agreement with Chandler, who proposes (see **Chapter 9**) that the most appropriate CEO of a company changes as a firm moves from one stage of development to another. Because priorities certainly change over an organization's life, successful corporations need to select managers who have skills and characteristics appropriate to the organization's particular stage of development and position in its life cycle. For example, founders of firms tend to have functional backgrounds in technological specialties, whereas successors tend to have backgrounds in marketing and administration.[16] A change in the environment leading to a change in a company's strategy also leads to a change in the top management team. For example, a change in the U.S. utility industry's environment in 1992, supporting internally focused, efficiency-oriented strategies, led to top management teams being dominated by older managers with longer company and industry tenure, with efficiency-oriented backgrounds in operations, engineering, and accounting.[17] Research reveals that executives having a specific personality characteristic (external locus of control) are more effective in regulated industries than are executives with a different characteristic (internal locus of control).[18]

Other studies have found a link between the type of CEO and a firm's overall strategic type. (Strategic types are presented in **Chapter 4**). For example, successful prospector firms tended to be headed by CEOs from research/engineering and general management backgrounds. High-performance defenders tended to have CEOs with accounting/finance, manufacturing/production, and general management experience. Analyzers tended to have CEOs with a marketing/sales background.[19]

A study of 173 firms over a 25-year period revealed that CEOs in these companies tended to have the same functional specialization as the former CEO, especially when the past CEO's strategy continued to be successful. This may be a pattern for successful corporations.[20] In particular, it explains why so many prosperous companies tend to recruit their top executives from one particular area. At Procter & Gamble (P&G)—a good example of an analyzer firm—for example, the route to the CEO's position has traditionally been through brand management, with a strong emphasis on marketing—and more recently international experience. In other firms, the route may be through manufacturing, marketing, accounting, or finance—depending on what the corporation has always considered its core capability (and its overall strategic orientation).

Selection and Management Development

Selection and development are important not only to ensure that people with the right mix of skills and experiences are initially hired but also to help them grow on the job so that they might be prepared for future promotions.

Executive Succession: Insiders Versus Outsiders

Executive succession is the process of replacing a key top manager. The average tenure of a chief executive of a large U.S. company declined from nearly nine years in 1980 to just over seven years in 2001.[21] Given that two-thirds of all major corporations worldwide replace their CEO at least once in a five-year period, it is important that the firm plan for this eventuality.[22] It is especially important for a company that usually promotes from within to prepare its current managers for promotion. For example, companies using relay executive succession, in which a candidate is groomed to take over the CEO position, have significantly higher performance than those that hire someone from the outside or hold a competition between internal candidates.[23] These "heirs apparent" are provided special assignments, including membership on other firms' boards of directors.[24]

Companies known for being excellent training grounds for executive talent are AlliedSignal, Bain & Company, Bankers Trust, Bristol Myers Squibb, Citicorp, General Electric, Hewlett-Packard, McDonald's, McKinsey & Company, Microsoft, Nike, PepsiCo, Pfizer, and P&G. For example, one study showed that hiring 19 GE executives into CEO positions added $24.5 billion to the share prices of the companies that hired them. One year after people from GE started their new jobs, 11 of the 19 companies they joined were outperforming their competitors and the overall market.[25]

Some of the best practices for top management succession are encouraging boards to help the CEO create a succession plan, identifying succession candidates below the top layer, measuring internal candidates against outside candidates to ensure the development of a comprehensive set of skills, and providing appropriate financial incentives.[26] A survey of U.S. boards by Korn/Ferry International found that 77% had some sort of succession-planning process in place in 2003, compared to only 33% two years earlier.[27] Succession planning has become the most important topic discussed by boards of directors.[28] See **STRATEGY HIGHLIGHT 10.1** to see how Hewlett-Packard identifies those with potential for executive leadership positions.

Prosperous firms tend to look outside for CEO candidates only if they have no obvious internal candidates. For example, only 10% of *Fortune* 100 companies have CEOs appointed from the outside.[29] Hiring an outsider to be a CEO is a risky gamble. CEOs from the outside tend to introduce significant change and high turnover among the current top management.[30] A study of 392 large U.S. firms revealed that only 16.6% of them had hired outsiders to be their CEOs. The outsiders tended to perform slightly worse than insiders but had a very high variance in performance. Compared to that of insiders, the performance of outsiders tended to be either very good or very poor. Although outsiders performed much better (in terms of shareholder returns) than insiders in the first half of their tenures, they did much worse in their second half. As a result, the average tenure of an outsider was 6.6 years compared to 10.9 years for insiders.[31]

Firms in trouble, however, overwhelmingly choose outsiders to lead them.[32] For example, one study of 22 firms undertaking turnaround strategies over a 13-year period found that the CEO was replaced in all but 2 companies. Of 27 changes of CEO (several firms had more than 1 CEO during this period), only 7 were insiders—20 were outsiders.[33] The probability of an outsider being chosen to lead a firm in difficulty increases if there is no internal heir apparent, if the last CEO was fired, and if the board of directors is composed of a large percentage of outsiders.[34] Boards realize that the best way to force a change in strategy is to hire a new CEO

STRATEGY HIGHLIGHT 10.1

How Hewlett-Packard Identifies Potential Executives

Hewlett-Packard identifies those with high potential for executive leadership by looking for six broad competencies that the company believes are necessary:

1. *Practice the HP Way* by building trust and respect, focusing on achievement, demonstrating integrity, being innovative with customers, contributing to the community, and developing organizational decision making.
2. *Lead change and learning* by recognizing and acting on signals for change, leading organizational change, learning from organizational experience, removing barriers to change, developing self, and challenging and developing others.
3. *Know the internal and external environments* by anticipating global trends, acting on trends, and learning from others.
4. *Lead strategy setting* by inspiring breakthrough business strategy, leading the strategy-making process, committing to business vision, creating long-range strategies, building financial strategies, and defining a business-planning system.
5. *Align the organization* by working across boundaries, implementing competitive cost structures, developing alliances and partnerships, planning and managing core business, and designing the organization.
6. *Achieve results* by building a track record, establishing accountability, supporting calculated risks, making tough individual decisions, and resolving performance problems.

Source: Summarized from R. M. Fulmer, P. A. Gibbs, and M. Goldsmith, "The New HP Way: Leveraging Strategy with Diversity, Leadership Development and Decentralization," *Strategy & Leadership* (October/November/December, 1999), pp. 21–29.

who has no connections to the current strategy.[35] For example, outsiders have been found to be very effective in leading strategic change for firms in Chapter 11 bankruptcy.[36]

Identifying Abilities and Potential

A company can identify and prepare its people for important positions in several ways. One approach is to establish a sound **performance appraisal system** to identify good performers with promotion potential. A survey of 34 corporate planners and human resource executives from 24 large U.S. corporations revealed that approximately 80% made some attempt to identify managers' talents and behavioral tendencies so that they could place a manager with a likely fit to a given competitive strategy.[37] Companies select those people with promotion potential to be in their executive development training program. Approximately 10,000 of GE's 276,000 employees take at least one class at the company's famous Leadership Development Center in Crotonville, New York.[38] Doug Pelino, chief talent officer at Xerox, keeps a list of about 100 managers in middle management and at the vice presidential levels who have been selected to receive special training, leadership experience, and mentorship to become the next generation of top management.[39]

A company should examine its human resource system to ensure not only that people are being hired without regard to their racial, ethnic, or religious background but also that they are being identified for training and promotion in the same manner. Management diversity could be a competitive advantage in a multiethnic world. With more women in the workplace, an increasing number are moving into top management. Recent studies are suggesting that female executives score higher than men on motivating others, fostering communication, producing high-quality work, and listening to others, while there is no difference between male and female executives in strategic planning or analyzing issues.[40]

Many large organizations are using **assessment centers** to evaluate a person's suitability for an advanced position. Corporations such as AT&T, Standard Oil, IBM, Sears, and GE have successfully used assessment centers. Because each is specifically tailored to its corporation, these assessment centers are unique. They use special interviews, management games, in-basket exercises, leaderless group discussions, case analyses, decision-making exercises, and oral presentations to assess the potential of employees for specific positions. Promotions into these positions are based on performance levels in the assessment center. Assessment centers have generally been able to accurately predict subsequent job performance and career success.[41]

Job rotation—moving people from one job to another—is also used in many large corporations to ensure that employees are gaining the appropriate mix of experiences to prepare them for future responsibilities. Rotating people among divisions is one way that a corporation can improve the level of organizational learning. General Electric, for example, routinely rotates its executives from one sector to a completely different one to learn the skills of managing in different industries. Jeffrey Immelt, who took over as CEO from Jack Welch, had managed businesses in plastics, appliances, and medical systems.[42] Companies that pursue related diversification strategies through internal development make greater use of interdivisional transfers of people than do companies that grow through unrelated acquisitions. Apparently, the companies that grow internally attempt to transfer important knowledge and skills throughout the corporation in order to achieve some sort of synergy.[43]

Problems in Retrenchment

Downsizing (sometimes called "rightsizing") refers to the planned elimination of positions or jobs. This program is often used to implement retrenchment strategies. Because the financial community is likely to react favorably to announcements of downsizing from a company in difficulty, such a program may provide some short-term benefits, such as raising the company's stock price. If not done properly, however, downsizing may result in less, rather than more, productivity. One study found that a 10% reduction in people resulted in only a 1.5% reduction in costs, profits increased in only half the firms downsizing, and the stock prices of downsized firms increased over three years, but not as much as did those of firms that did not downsize.[44] Why were the results so marginal?

A study of downsizing at automobile-related U.S. industrial companies revealed that at 20 out of 30 companies, either the wrong jobs were eliminated or blanket offers of early retirement prompted managers, even those considered invaluable, to leave. After the layoffs, the remaining employees had to do not only their work but also the work of the people who had gone. Because the survivors often didn't know how to do the departeds' work, morale and productivity plummeted.[45] Downsizing can seriously damage the learning capacity of organizations.[46] Creativity drops significantly (affecting new product development), and it becomes very difficult to keep high performers from leaving the company.[47] In addition, cost-conscious executives tend to defer maintenance, skimp on training, delay new product introductions, and avoid risky new businesses—all of which leads to lower sales and eventually to lower profits.

A good retrenchment strategy can thus be implemented well in terms of organizing but poorly in terms of staffing. A situation can develop in which retrenchment feeds on itself and acts to further weaken instead of strengthen the company. Research indicates that companies undertaking cost-cutting programs are four times more likely than others to cut costs again, typically by reducing staff.[48] This happened at Eastman Kodak and Xerox during the 1990s, but 10 years later the companies were still working to regain their profitable past performance. In contrast, successful downsizing firms undertake a strategic reorientation, not just a bloodletting of employees. Research shows that when companies use downsizing as part of a larger restructuring program to narrow company focus, they enjoy better performance.[49]

Consider the following guidelines that have been proposed for successful downsizing:

- **Eliminate unnecessary work instead of making across-the-board cuts:** Spend the time to research where money is going and eliminate the task, not the workers, if it doesn't add value to what the firm is producing. Reduce the number of administrative levels rather than the number of individual positions. Look for interdependent relationships before eliminating activities. Identify and protect core competencies.
- **Contract out work that others can do cheaper:** For example, Bankers Trust of New York has contracted out its mailroom and printing services and some of its payroll and accounts payable activities to a division of Xerox. Outsourcing may be cheaper than vertical integration.
- **Plan for long-run efficiencies:** Don't simply eliminate all postponable expenses, such as maintenance, R&D, and advertising, in the unjustifiable hope that the environment will become more supportive. Continue to hire, grow, and develop—particularly in critical areas.
- **Communicate the reasons for actions:** Tell employees not only why the company is downsizing but also what the company is trying to achieve. Promote educational programs.
- **Invest in the remaining employees:** Because most "survivors" in a corporate downsizing will probably be doing different tasks from what they were doing before the change, firms need to draft new job specifications, performance standards, appraisal techniques, and compensation packages. Additional training is needed to ensure that everyone has the proper skills to deal with expanded jobs and responsibilities. Empower key individuals/groups and emphasize team building. Identify, protect, and mentor people who have leadership talent.
- **Develop value-added jobs to balance out job elimination:** When no other jobs are currently available within the organization to transfer employees to, management must consider other staffing alternatives. For example, Harley-Davidson worked with the company's unions to find other work for surplus employees by moving into Harley plants work that had previously been done by suppliers.[50]

International Issues in Staffing

Implementing a strategy of international expansion takes a lot of planning and can be very expensive. Nearly 80% of midsize and larger companies send their employees abroad, and 45% plan to increase the number they have on foreign assignment. A complete package for one executive working in another country costs from $300,000 to $1 million annually. Nevertheless, between 10% and 20% of all U.S. managers sent abroad returned early because of job dissatisfaction or difficulties in adjusting to a foreign country. Of those who stayed for the duration of their assignment, nearly one-third did not perform as well as expected. One-fourth of those completing an assignment left their company within one year of returning home—often leaving to join a competitor.[51] One common mistake is failing to educate the person about the customs and values in other countries.

Because of cultural differences, managerial style and human resource practices must be tailored to fit the particular situations in other countries. Because only 11% of human resource managers have ever worked abroad, most have little understanding of a global assignment's unique personal and professional challenges and thus fail to develop the training necessary for such an assignment.[52] Ninety percent of companies select employees for an international assignment based on their technical expertise while ignoring other areas.[53] A lack of knowledge of national and ethnic differences can make managing an international operation extremely difficult. For example, the three ethnic groups living in Malaysia (Malay, Chinese, and Indian) share different religions, attend different schools, and do not like to work in the same factories with each other. Because of the importance of cultural distinctions such as these, multinational corporations (MNCs) are now putting more emphasis on intercultural training for managers being sent on an assignment to a foreign country. This type of training is one of the commonly cited reasons for the lower expatriate failure rates—6% or less—for European and Japanese MNCs, which have emphasized cross-cultural experiences, compared with a 35% failure rate for U.S.-based MNCs.[54]

To improve organizational learning, many MNCs are providing their managers with international assignments lasting as long as five years. Upon their return to headquarters, these expatriates have an in-depth understanding of the company's operations in another part of the world. This has value to the extent that these employees communicate this understanding to others in decision-making positions. Research indicates that an MNC performs at a higher level when its CEO has international experience.[55] Unfortunately, not all corporations appropriately manage international assignments. While out of the country, a person may be overlooked for an important promotion (out of sight, out of mind). Upon his or her return to the home country, co-workers may deprecate the out-of-country experience as a waste of time. The perceived lack of organizational support for international assignments increases the likelihood that an expatriate will return home early.[56]

Out of their study of 750 U.S., Japanese, and European companies, Black and Gregersen found that the companies that do a good job of managing foreign assignments follow three general practices:

- When making international assignments, they focus on transferring knowledge and developing global leadership.
- They make foreign assignments to people whose technical skills are matched or exceeded by their cross-cultural abilities.
- They end foreign assignments with a deliberate repatriation process, with career guidance and jobs where the employees can apply what they learned in their assignments.[57]

Once a corporation has established itself in another country, it hires and promotes people from the host country into higher-level positions. For example, most large MNCs attempt to fill managerial positions in their subsidiaries with well-qualified citizens of the host countries. Unilever and IBM take this approach to international staffing. This policy serves to placate nationalistic governments and to better attune management practices to the host country's culture. The danger in using primarily foreign nationals to staff managerial positions in subsidiaries is the increased likelihood of suboptimization (the local subsidiary ignores the needs of the larger parent corporation). This makes it difficult for an MNC to meet its long-term, worldwide objectives. To a local national in an MNC subsidiary, the corporation as a whole is an abstraction. Communication and coordination across subsidiaries become more difficult. As it becomes harder to coordinate the activities of several international subsidiaries, an MNC will have serious problems operating in a global industry.

Another approach to staffing the managerial positions of MNCs is to use people with an "international" orientation, regardless of their country of origin or host country assignment. This is a widespread practice among European firms. For example, Electrolux, a Swedish firm, had a French director in its Singapore factory. Using third-country "nationals" can allow for more opportunities for promotion than does Unilever's policy of hiring local people, but it can also result in more misunderstandings and conflicts with the local employees and with the host country's government.

Some U.S. corporations take advantage of immigrants and their children to staff key positions when negotiating entry into another country and when selecting an executive to manage the company's new foreign operations. For example, when General Motors wanted to learn more about business opportunities in China, it turned to Shirley Young, a Vice President of Marketing at GM. Born in Shanghai and fluent in Chinese language and customs, Young was instrumental in helping GM negotiate a $1 billion joint venture with Shanghai Automotive to build a Buick plant in China. With other Chinese-Americans, Young formed a committee to advise GM on relations with China. Although just a part of a larger team of GM employees working on the joint venture, Young coached GM employees on Chinese customs and traditions.[58]

MNCs with a high level of international interdependence among activities need to provide their managers with significant international assignments and experiences as part of their training and development. Such assignments provide future corporate leaders with a series of valuable international contacts in addition to a better personal understanding of international issues and global linkages among corporate activities.[59] Research reveals that corporations using cross-national teams, whose members have international experience and communicate frequently with overseas managers, have greater product development capabilities than others.[60] Executive recruiters report that more major corporations are now requiring candidates to have international experience.[61]

10.2 Leading

Implementation also involves leading through coaching people to use their abilities and skills most effectively and efficiently to achieve organizational objectives. Without direction, people tend to do their work according to their personal view of what tasks should be done, how, and in what order. They may approach their work as they have in the past or emphasize those tasks that they most enjoy—regardless of the corporation's priorities. This can create real problems, particularly if the company is operating internationally and must adjust to customs and traditions in other countries. This direction may take the form of management leadership, communicated norms of behavior from the corporate culture, or agreements among workers in autonomous work groups. It may also be accomplished more formally through action planning or through programs such as Management By Objectives (MBO), and Total Quality Management (TQM).

Managing Corporate Culture

Because an organization's culture can exert a powerful influence on the behavior of all employees, it can strongly affect a company's ability to shift its strategic direction. A problem for a strong culture is that a change in mission, objectives, strategies, or policies is not likely to be successful if it is in opposition to the accepted culture of the company. Corporate culture has a strong tendency to resist change because its very reason for existence often rests on preserving stable relationships and patterns of behavior. For example, the male-dominated, Japanese-centered corporate culture of the giant Mitsubishi Corporation created problems for the company when it implemented its growth strategy in North America. The alleged sexual harassment of its female employees by male supervisors resulted in a lawsuit by the U.S. Equal Employment Opportunity Commission and a boycott of the company's automobiles by the National Organization for Women.[62]

There is no one best corporate culture. An optimal culture is one that best supports the mission and strategy of the company of which it is a part. This means that, like structure and staffing, corporate culture should support the strategy. Unless strategy is in complete agreement with the culture, any significant change in strategy should be followed by a modification of the organization's culture. Although corporate culture can be changed, it may often take a

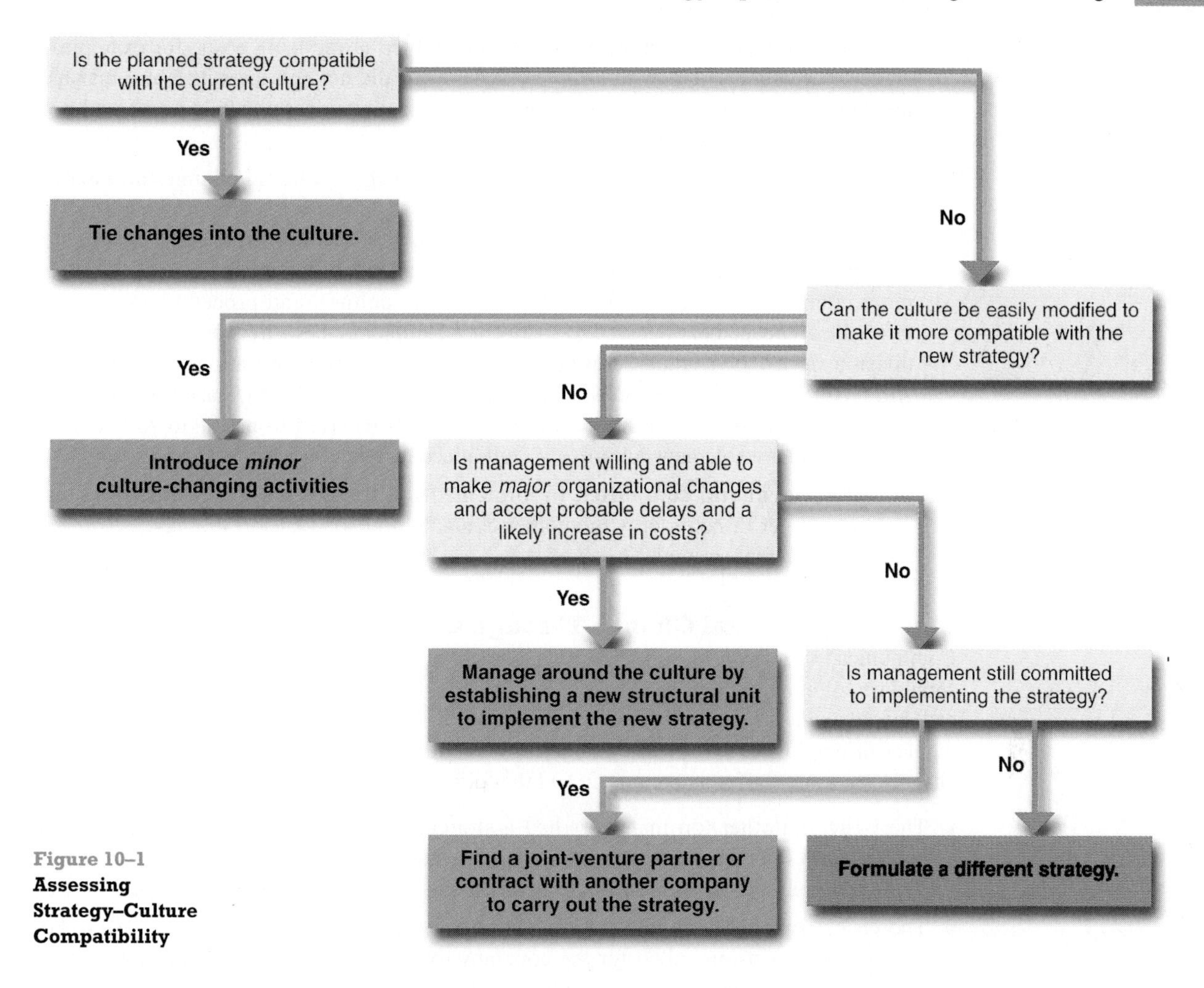

Figure 10–1
Assessing Strategy–Culture Compatibility

long time, and it requires much effort. A key job of management involves managing corporate culture. In doing so, management must evaluate what a particular change in strategy means to the corporate culture, assess whether a change in culture is needed, and decide whether an attempt to change the culture is worth the likely costs.

Assessing Strategy–Culture Compatibility

When implementing a new strategy, a company should take the time to assess **strategy–culture compatibility**. (See **Figure 10–1**.) Consider the following questions regarding a corporation's culture:

1. **Is the planned strategy compatible with the company's current culture?** *If yes*, full steam ahead. Tie organizational changes into the company's culture by identifying how the new strategy will achieve the mission better than the current strategy does. *If not . . .*
2. **Can the culture be easily modified to make it more compatible with the new strategy?** *If yes*, move forward carefully by introducing a set of culture-changing activities such as minor structural modifications, training and development activities, and/or hiring new managers who are more compatible with the new strategy. When P&G's top

management decided to implement a strategy aimed at reducing costs, for example, it made some changes in how things were done, but it did not eliminate its brand-management system. The culture adapted to these modifications over a couple years, and productivity increased. *If not . . .*

3. **Is management willing and able to make major organizational changes and accept probable delays and a likely increase in costs?** *If yes*, manage around the culture by establishing a new structural unit to implement the new strategy. At General Motors, for example, top management realized the company had to make some radical changes to be more competitive. Because the current structure, culture, and procedures were very inflexible, management decided to establish a completely new division (GM's first new division since 1918) called Saturn to build its new auto. In cooperation with the United Auto Workers, an entirely new labor agreement was developed, based on decisions reached by consensus. Carefully selected employees received from 100 to 750 hours of training, and a whole new culture was built, piece by piece. *If not . . .*
4. **Is management still committed to implementing the strategy?** *If yes*, find a joint-venture partner or contract with another company to carry out the strategy. *If not*, formulate a different strategy.

Managing Cultural Change Through Communication

Communication is key to the effective management of change. Rationale for strategic changes should be communicated to workers not only in newsletters and speeches but also in training and development programs. This is especially important in decentralized firms where a large number of employees work in far-flung business units.[63] Companies in which major cultural changes have successfully taken place had the following characteristics in common:

- The CEO and other top managers had a strategic vision of what the company could become and communicated that vision to employees at all levels. The current performance of the company was compared to that of its competition and constantly updated.
- The vision was translated into the key elements necessary to accomplish that vision. For example, if the vision called for the company to become a leader in quality or service, aspects of quality and service were pinpointed for improvement, and appropriate measurement systems were developed to monitor them. These measures were communicated widely through contests, formal and informal recognition, and monetary rewards, among other devices.[64]

For example, when Pizza Hut, Taco Bell, and KFC were purchased by Tricon Global Restaurants (now Yum! Brands) from PepsiCo, the new management knew that it had to create a radically different culture than the one at PepsiCo if the company was to succeed. To begin, management formulated a statement of shared values—"How We Work Together" principles. They declared their differences with the "mother country" (PepsiCo) and wrote a "Declaration of Independence" stating what the new company would stand for. Restaurant managers participated in team-building activities at the corporate headquarters and finished by signing the company's "Declaration of Independence" as "founders" of the company. Since then, "Founder's Day" has become an annual event celebrating the culture of the company. Headquarters was renamed the "Restaurant Support Center," signifying the cultural value that the restaurants were the central focus of the company. People measures were added to financial measures and customer measures, reinforcing the "putting people first" value. In an unprecedented move in the industry, restaurant managers were given stock options and added to the list of performance incentives. The company created values-focused 360-degree performance reviews, which were eventually pushed to the restaurant manager level.[65]

Managing Diverse Cultures Following an Acquisition

When merging with or acquiring another company, top management must give some consideration to a potential clash of corporate cultures. According to a Hewitt Associates survey of 218 major U.S. corporations, integrating culture was a top challenge for 69% of the reporting companies.[66] Cultural differences are even more problematic when a company acquires a firm in another country. DaimlerChrysler's purchase of a controlling interest in Mitsubishi Motors in 2001 was insufficient to overcome Mitsubishi's resistance to change. After investing $2 billion to cut Mitsubishi's costs and improve its product development, DaimlerChrysler gave up. According to one executive, "It's an absolute disaster. We can't sell it. It's worth nothing."[67] It's dangerous to assume that the firms can simply be integrated into the same reporting structure. The greater the gap between the cultures of the acquired firm and the acquiring firm, the faster executives in the acquired firm quit their jobs and valuable talent is lost. Conversely, when corporate cultures are similar, performance problems are minimized.[68]

There are four general methods of managing two different cultures. (See **Figure 10–2.**) The choice of which method to use should be based on (1) how much members of the acquired firm value preserving their own culture and (2) how attractive they perceive the culture of the acquirer to be[69]:

1. **Integration** involves a relatively balanced give-and-take of cultural and managerial practices between the merger partners—and no strong imposition of cultural change on either company. It merges the two cultures in such a way that the separate cultures of both firms are preserved in the resulting culture. This is what occurred when France's Renault purchased a controlling interest in Japan's Nissan Motor Company and installed Carlos Ghosn as Nissan's new CEO to turn around the company. Ghosn was very sensitive to Nissan's culture and allowed the company room to develop a new corporate culture based on the best elements of Japan's national culture. His goal was to form one successful auto group from two very distinct companies.[70]

Figure 10–2
Methods of Managing the Culture of an Acquired Firm

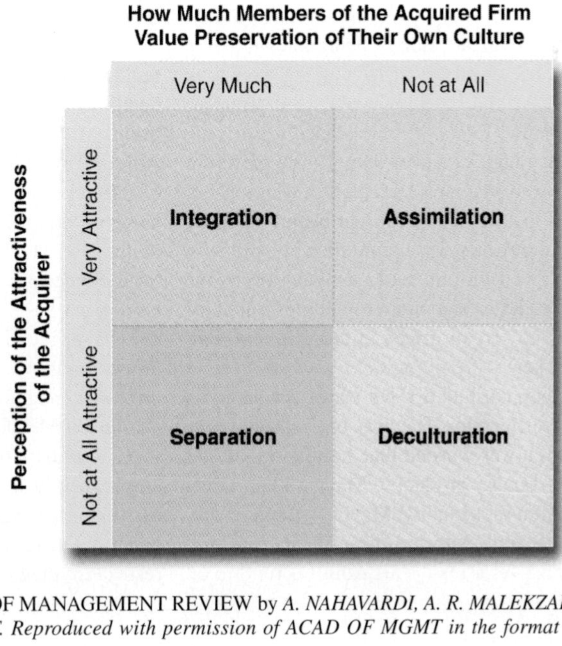

Perception of the Attractiveness of the Acquirer	How Much Members of the Acquired Firm Value Preservation of Their Own Culture: Very Much	Not at All
Very Attractive	**Integration**	**Assimilation**
Not at All Attractive	**Separation**	**Deculturation**

Source: ACADEMY OF MANAGEMENT REVIEW by *A. NAHAVARDI, A. R. MALEKZADEH. Copyright 1988 by the ACAD OF MGMT. Reproduced with permission of ACAD OF MGMT in the format Textbook via Copyright Clearance Center.*

2. **Assimilation** involves the domination of one organization over the other. The domination is not forced, but it is welcomed by members of the acquired firm, who may feel for many reasons that their culture and managerial practices have not produced success. The acquired firm surrenders its culture and adopts the culture of the acquiring company. See **STRATEGY HIGHLIGHT 10.2** describes this method of acculturation when Admiral was acquired by Maytag Corporation.
3. **Separation** is characterized by a separation of the two companies' cultures. They are structurally separated, without cultural exchange. In the Shearson–American Express merger, both parties agreed to keep the fast-paced Shearson completely separate from the planning-oriented American Express. This approach allowed American Express to easily divest Shearson once it discovered that the merger was not working.
4. **Deculturation** involves the disintegration of one company's culture, resulting from unwanted and extreme pressure from the other to impose its culture and practices. This is the most common and most destructive method of dealing with two different cultures. It is often accompanied by much confusion, conflict, resentment, and stress. This is a primary reason so many executives tend to leave after their firm is acquired.[71] Such a merger typically results in poor performance by the acquired company and its eventual divestment. This is what happened when AT&T acquired NCR Corporation in 1990 for its computer business. It replaced NCR managers with an AT&T management team, reorganized sales, forced employees to adhere to the AT&T code of values (called the "Common Bond"), and even dropped the proud NCR name (successor to National Cash Register) in favor of a sterile GIS (Global Information Solutions) nonidentity. By 1995, AT&T was forced to take a $1.2 billion loss and lay off 10,000 people.[72] The NCR unit was sold in 1996.

STRATEGY HIGHLIGHT 10.2

Admiral Assimilates Maytag's Culture

Maytag's corporate culture had been dominated almost from the birth of the company by the concept of quality. Maytag employees took great pride in being known as the "dependability people." Over the years, Maytag Company consistently advertised that its repairmen were "lonely" because Maytag products rarely, if ever, needed repair.

Admiral's history had, however, been quite different from Maytag's. Prior to Maytag's purchase of Magic Chef (and thus Admiral) in 1986, Admiral had been owned by three different corporations. Its manufacturing plant in Galesburg, Illinois, had deteriorated to a dismal level by the time Maytag acquired it. Refrigerators sometimes rolled off the assembly line with screws driven in crooked and temperature balances askew.

Maytag's management had always wanted to have its own Maytag brand refrigerator. That was one reason it purchased Admiral. But it was worried that Admiral might not be able to produce a quality product to Maytag's specifications. To improve Admiral's quality, Maytag's top management decided to integrate Admiral directly into Maytag Company operations. As a result, all Admiral functional departments except marketing reported directly to the Maytag Company president.

Under the direction of Leonard Hadley, while he was serving as Maytag President, a project was initiated to design and manufacture a refrigerator for the Maytag brand at the Admiral plant. When Hadley first visited Admiral's facilities to discuss the design of a Maytag line of refrigerators, Admiral personnel asked Hadley when the name on their plant's water tower would be changed from Admiral to Maytag. Hadley, acknowledging Maytag's cultural concerns regarding quality, responded: "When you earn it."

The refrigerator resulting from the Maytag–Admiral collaboration was a huge success. The project crystallized corporate management's philosophy for forging synergies among the Maytag units, while simultaneously allowing the individual expertise of those units to flourish. Admiral's employees were willing to accept the dominance of Maytag's strong quality-oriented culture because they respected it. In turn, they expected to be treated with some respect for their tradition of skill in refrigeration technology.

Action Planning

Activities can be directed toward accomplishing strategic goals through action planning. At a minimum, an **action plan** states what actions are going to be taken, by whom, during what time frame, and with what expected results. After a program has been selected to implement a particular strategy, an action plan should be developed to put the program in place. **Table 10–1** shows an example of an action plan for a new advertising and promotion program. Take the example of a company choosing forward vertical integration through the acquisition of a retailing chain as its growth strategy. Once it owns its own retail outlets, it must integrate the stores into the company. One of the many programs it would have to develop is a new advertising

TABLE 10–1 EXAMPLE OF AN ACTION PLAN

Action Plan for Jan Lewis, Advertising Manager, and Rick Carter, Advertising Assistant, Ajax Continental

Program Objective: To Run a New Advertising and Promotion Campaign for the Combined Jones Surplus/Ajax Continental Retail Stores for the Coming Christmas Season Within a Budget of $XX.

Program Activities:
1. Identify Three Best Ad Agencies for New Campaign.
2. Ask Three Ad Agencies to Submit a Proposal for a New Advertising and Promotion Campaign for Combined Stores.
3. Agencies Present Proposals to Marketing Manager.
4. Select Best Proposal and Inform Agencies of Decision.
5. Agency Presents Winning Proposal to Top Management.
6. Ads Air on TV and Promotions Appear in Stores.
7. Measure Results of Campaign in Terms of Viewer Recall and Increase in Store Sales.

Action Steps	Responsibility	Start–End
1. A. Review previous programs	Lewis & Carter	1/1–2/1
B. Discuss with boss	Lewis & Smith	2/1–2/3
C. Decide on three agencies	Lewis	2/4
2. A. Write specifications for ad	Lewis	1/15–1/20
B. Assistant writes ad request	Carter	1/20–1/30
C. Contact ad agencies	Lewis	2/5–2/8
D. Send request to three agencies	Carter	2/10
E. Meet with agency acct. execs	Lewis & Carter	2/16–2/20
3. A. Agencies work on proposals	Acct. Execs	2/23–5/1
B. Agencies present proposals	Carter	5/1–5/15
4. A. Select best proposal	Lewis	5/15–5/20
B. Meet with winning agency	Lewis	5/22–5/30
C. Inform losers	Carter	6/1
5. A. Fine-tune proposal	Acct. Exec	6/1–7/1
B. Presentation to management	Lewis	7/1–7/3
6. A. Ads air on TV	Lewis	9/1–12/24
B. Floor displays in stores	Carter	8/20–8/30
7. A. Gather recall measures of ads	Carter	9/1–12/24
B. Evaluate sales data	Carter	1/1–1/10
C. Prepare analysis of campaign	Carter	1/10–2/15

program for the stores. The resulting action plan to develop a new advertising program should include much of the following information:

1. **Specific actions to be taken to make the program operational:** One action might be to contact three reputable advertising agencies and ask them to prepare a proposal for a new radio and newspaper ad campaign based on the theme "Jones Surplus is now a part of Ajax Continental. Prices are lower. Selection is better."
2. **Dates to begin and end each action:** Time would have to be allotted not only to select and contact three agencies but to allow them sufficient time to prepare a detailed proposal. For example, allow one week to select and contact the agencies plus three months for them to prepare detailed proposals to present to the company's marketing director. Also allow some time to decide which proposal to accept.
3. **Person (identified by name and title) responsible for carrying out each action:** List someone—such as Jan Lewis, advertising manager—who can be put in charge of the program.
4. **Person responsible for monitoring the timeliness and effectiveness of each action:** Indicate that Jan Lewis is responsible for ensuring that the proposals are of good quality and are priced within the planned program budget. She will be the primary company contact for the ad agencies and will report on the progress of the program once a week to the company's marketing director.
5. **Expected financial and physical consequences of each action:** Estimate when a completed ad campaign will be ready to show top management and how long it will take after approval to begin to air the ads. Estimate also the expected increase in store sales over the six-month period after the ads are first aired. Indicate whether "recall" measures will be used to help assess the ad campaign's effectiveness plus how, when, and by whom the recall data will be collected and analyzed.
6. **Contingency plans:** Indicate how long it will take to get an acceptable ad campaign to show top management if none of the initial proposals is acceptable.

Action plans are important for several reasons. First, action plans serve as a link between strategy formulation and evaluation and control. Second, an action plan specifies what needs to be done differently from the way operations are currently carried out. Third, during the evaluation and control process that comes later, an action plan helps in both the appraisal of performance and the identification of any remedial actions, as needed. In addition, the explicit assignment of responsibilities for implementing and monitoring the programs may contribute to better motivation.

Management By Objectives

Management By Objectives (MBO) is a technique that encourages participative decision making through shared goal setting at all organizational levels and performance assessment based on the achievement of stated objectives.[73] MBO links organizational objectives and the behavior of individuals. Because it is a system that links plans with performance, it is a powerful implementation technique.

The MBO process involves:

1. Establishing and communicating organizational objectives.
2. Setting individual objectives (through superior–subordinate interaction) that help implement organizational ones.

3. Developing an action plan of activities needed to achieve the objectives.
4. Periodically (at least quarterly) reviewing performance as it relates to the objectives and including the results in the annual performance appraisal.[74]

MBO provides an opportunity for the corporation to connect the objectives of people at each level to those at the next higher level. MBO, therefore, acts to tie together corporate, business, and functional objectives, as well as the strategies developed to achieve them. Although MBO originated the 1950s, 90% of surveyed practicing managers feel that MBO is applicable today.[75] The principles of MBO are a part of self-managing work teams and quality circles.[76]

One of the real benefits of MBO is that it can reduce the amount of internal politics operating within a large corporation. Political actions within a firm can cause conflict and create divisions between the very people and groups who should be working together to implement strategy. People are less likely to jockey for position if the company's mission and objectives are clear and they know that the reward system is based not on game playing but on achieving clearly communicated, measurable objectives.

Total Quality Management

Total Quality Management (TQM) is an operational philosophy committed to *customer satisfaction* and *continuous improvement*. TQM is committed to quality/excellence and to being the best in all functions. Because TQM aims to reduce costs and improve quality, it can be used as a program to implement an overall low-cost or a differentiation business strategy. About 92% of manufacturing companies and 69% of service firms have implemented some form of quality management practices.[77] Not all have been successes. McKinsey & Company reported that two-thirds of the TQM programs it examined had failed to produce expected improvements. In contrast, a recent study of TQM in 193 hospitals found a positive relationship between the degree of TQM implementation and organizational performance.[78] An analysis of the successes and failures of TQM concluded that the key is top management. Successful TQM programs occur in companies in which "top managers move beyond defensive and tactical orientations to embrace a developmental orientation."[79]

TQM has four objectives:

1. Better, less variable quality of the product and service
2. Quicker, less variable response in processes to customer needs
3. Greater flexibility in adjusting to customers' shifting requirements
4. Lower cost through quality improvement and elimination of non–value-adding work[80]

According to TQM, faulty processes, not poorly motivated employees, are the cause of defects in quality. The program involves a significant change in corporate culture, requiring strong leadership from top management, employee training, empowerment of lower-level employees (giving people more control over their work), and teamwork in order to succeed in a company. TQM emphasizes prevention, not correction. Inspection for quality still takes place, but the emphasis is on improving the process to prevent errors and deficiencies. Thus quality circles or quality improvement teams are formed to identify problems and to suggest how to improve the processes that may be causing the problems.

TQM's essential ingredients are:

- **An intense focus on customer satisfaction:** Everyone (not just people in the sales and marketing departments) understands that their jobs exist only because of customer needs. Thus all jobs must be approached in terms of how they will affect customer satisfaction.

- **Internal as well as external customers:** An employee in the shipping department may be the internal customer of another employee who completes the assembly of a product, just as a person who buys the product is a customer of the entire company. An employee must be just as concerned with pleasing the internal customer as in satisfying the external customer.
- **Accurate measurement of every critical variable in a company's operations:** This means that employees have to be trained in what to measure, how to measure, and how to interpret the data. A rule of TQM is that *you only improve what you measure.*
- **Continuous improvement of products and services:** Everyone realizes that operations need to be continuously monitored to find ways to improve products and services.
- **New work relationships based on trust and teamwork:** Important is the idea of empowerment—giving employees wide latitude in how they go about achieving the company's goals. Research indicates that the keys to TQM success lie in executive commitment, an open organizational culture, and employee empowerment.[81]

International Considerations in Leading

In a study of 53 different national cultures, Hofstede found that each nation's unique culture could be identified using five dimensions. He found that national culture is so influential that it tends to overwhelm even a strong corporate culture. (See the numerous sociocultural societal variables that compose another country's culture that are listed in **Chapter 4's Table 4–3**.) In measuring the differences among these **dimensions of national culture** from country to country, Hofstede was able to explain why a certain management practice might be successful in one nation but fail in another[82]:

1. **Power distance (PD)** is the extent to which a society accepts an unequal distribution of power in organizations. Malaysia and Mexico scored highest, whereas Germany and Austria scored lowest. People in countries scoring high on this dimension tend to prefer autocratic to more participative managers.
2. **Uncertainty avoidance (UA)** is the extent to which a society feels threatened by uncertain and ambiguous situations. Greece and Japan scored highest on disliking ambiguity, whereas the United States and Singapore scored lowest. People in nations scoring high on this dimension tend to want career stability, formal rules, and clear-cut measures of performance.
3. **Individualism-collectivism (I-C)** is the extent to which a society values individual freedom and independence of action compared with a tight social framework and loyalty to the group. The United States and Canada scored highest on individualism, whereas Mexico and Guatemala scored lowest. People in nations scoring high on individualism tend to value individual success through competition, whereas people scoring low on individualism (thus high on collectivism) tend to value group success through collective cooperation.
4. **Masculinity-femininity (M-F)** is the extent to which society is oriented toward money and things (which Hofstede labels masculine) or toward people (which Hofstede labels feminine). Japan and Mexico scored highest on masculinity, whereas France and Sweden scored lowest (thus highest on femininity). People in nations scoring high on masculinity tend to value clearly defined sex roles where men dominate and to emphasize performance and independence, whereas people scoring low on masculinity (and thus high on femininity) tend to value equality of the sexes where power is shared and to emphasize the quality of life and interdependence.

5. **Long-term orientation (LT)** is the extent to which society is oriented toward the long versus the short term. Hong Kong and Japan scored highest on long-term orientation, whereas Pakistan scored the lowest. A long-term time orientation emphasizes the importance of hard work, education, and persistence as well as the importance of thrift. Nations with a long-term time orientation tend to value strategic planning and other management techniques with a long-term payback.

Hofstede's work is being extended by Project GLOBE, a team of 150 researchers who are collecting data on cultural values and practices and leadership attributes from 18,000 managers in 62 countries. The project is studying the nine cultural dimensions of assertiveness, future orientation, gender differentiation, uncertainty avoidance, power distance, institutional emphasis on collectivism versus individualism, in-group collectivism, performance orientation, and humane orientation.[83]

The dimensions of national culture help explain why some management practices work well in some countries but not in others. For example, MBO, which originated in the United States, has succeeded in Germany, according to Hofstede, because the idea of replacing the arbitrary authority of the boss with the impersonal authority of mutually agreed-upon objectives fits the low power distance that is a dimension of the German culture. It has failed in France, however, because the French are used to high power distances; they are used to accepting orders from a highly personalized authority. In countries with high levels of uncertainty avoidance, such as Switzerland and Austria, communication should be clear and explicit, based on facts. Meetings should be planned in advance and have clear agendas. In contrast, in low-uncertainty-avoidance countries, such as Greece or Russia, people are not used to structured communication and prefer more open-ended meetings. Because Thailand has a high level of power distance, Thai managers feel that communication should go from the top to the bottom of a corporation. As a result, 360-degree performance appraisals are seen as dysfunctional.[84] Some of the difficulties experienced by U.S. companies in using Japanese-style quality circles in TQM may stem from the extremely high value U.S. culture places on individualism. The differences between the United States and Mexico in terms of the power distance (Mexico 104 vs. U.S. 46) and individualism–collectivism (U.S. 91 vs. Mexico 30) dimensions may help explain why some companies operating in both countries have difficulty adapting to the differences in customs.[85] In addition, research has found that technology alliance formation is strongest in countries that value cooperation and avoid uncertainty.[86]

When one successful company in one country merges with another successful company in another country, the clash of corporate cultures is compounded by the clash of national cultures. For example, when two companies, one from a high-uncertainty-avoidance society and one from a low-uncertainty-avoidance country, are considering a merger, they should investigate each other's management practices to determine potential areas of conflict. With the value of cross-border mergers and acquisitions totaling $720 billion annually, the management of cultures is becoming a key issue in strategy implementation.[87] See the GLOBAL ISSUE feature to learn how differences in national and corporate cultures created conflict when Upjohn Company of the United States and Pharmacia AB of Sweden merged.

MNCs must pay attention to the many differences in cultural dimensions around the world and adjust their management practices accordingly. Cultural differences can easily go unrecognized by a headquarters staff that may interpret these differences as personality defects, whether the people in the subsidiaries are locals or expatriates. When conducting strategic planning in an MNC, top management must be aware that the process will vary based on the culture of the nation where a subsidiary is located. For example, in one MNC, the French expect concepts and key questions and answers. North American managers provide heavy financial analysis. Germans give precise dates and financial analysis. Information is usually late from Spanish and Moroccan operations, and quotas are typically inflated. It is up to management to adapt to the

GLOBAL ISSUE

Cultural Differences Create Implementation Problems in Merger

When Upjohn Pharmaceuticals of Kalamazoo, Michigan, and Pharmacia AB of Stockholm, Sweden, merged in 1995, employees of both sides were optimistic for the newly formed Pharmacia & Upjohn, Inc. Both companies were second-tier competitors fighting for survival in a global industry. Together, the firms would create a global company that could compete scientifically with its bigger rivals.

Because Pharmacia had acquired an Italian firm in 1993, it also had a large operation in Milan. U.S. executives scheduled meetings throughout the summer of 1996—only to cancel them when their European counterparts could not attend. Although it was common knowledge in Europe that most Swedes take the entire month of July for vacation and that Italians take off all of August, this was not common knowledge in Michigan. Differences in management styles became a special irritant. Swedes were used to an open system, with autonomous work teams. Executives sought the whole group's approval before making an important decision. Upjohn executives followed the more traditional American top-down approach. Upon taking command of the newly merged firm, Dr. Zabriskie (who had been Upjohn's CEO), divided the company into departments reporting to the new London headquarters. He required frequent reports, budgets, and staffing updates. The Swedes reacted negatively to this top-down management hierarchical style. "It was degrading," said Stener Kvinnsland, head of Pharmacia's cancer research in Italy before he quit the new company.

The Italian operations baffled the Americans, even though the Italians felt comfortable with a hierarchical management style. Italy's laws and unions made layoffs difficult. Italian data and accounting were often inaccurate. Because the Americans didn't trust the data, they were constantly asking for verification. In turn, the Italians were concerned that the Americans were trying to take over Italian operations. At Upjohn, all workers were subject to testing for drug and alcohol abuse. Upjohn also banned smoking. At Pharmacia's Italian business center, however, waiters poured wine freely every afternoon in the company dining room. Pharmacia's boardrooms were stocked with humidors for executives who smoked cigars during long meetings. After a brief attempt to enforce Upjohn's policies, the company dropped both the no-drinking and no-smoking policies for European workers.

Although the combined company had cut annual costs by $200 million, overall costs of the merger reached $800 million, some $200 million more than projected. Nevertheless, Jan Eckberg, CEO of Pharmacia before the merger, remained confident of the new company's ability to succeed. He admitted, however, that "we have to make some smaller changes to release the full power of the two companies."

Source: Summarized from R. Frank and T. M. Burton, "Cross-Border Merger Results in Headaches for a Drug Company," *Wall Street Journal* (February 4, 1997), pp. A1, A12.

differences.[88] The values embedded in his or her national culture have a profound and enduring effect on an executive's orientation, regardless of the impact of industry experience or corporate culture.[89] Hofstede and Bond conclude: "Whether they like it or not, the headquarters of multinationals are in the business of multicultural management."[90]

10.3 Conclusion

Strategy is implemented through structural change (organizing), selecting the appropriate people to carry out the strategy (staffing), and clear communication regarding how the strategy can be put into action (leading). A number of programs, such as organizational and job design, reengineering, Six Sigma, MBO, TQM, and action planning, can be used to implement a new strategy. Executives must manage the corporate culture and find the right mix of qualified people to put a strategy in place.

Research on executive succession reveals that it is very risky to hire new top managers from outside the corporation. Although this is often done when a company is in trouble, it can be dangerous for a successful firm. This is also true when hiring people for non-executive positions. An in-depth study of 1,052 star stock analysts at 78 investment banks revealed that hiring a star (an outstanding performer) from another company did not improve the hiring company's performance. When a company hires a star, the star's performance plunges, there is a sharp decline in the functioning of the team the person works with, and the company's market value declines. Their performance dropped about 20% and did not return to the level before the job change—even after 5 years. Interestingly, around 36% of the stars left the investment banks that hired them within 36 months. Another 29% quit in the next 24 months.

This phenomenon occurs not because a star doesn't suddenly become less intelligent when switching firms, but because the star cannot take to the new firm the firm-specific resources that contributed to her or his achievements at the previous company. As a result, the star is unable to repeat the high performance in another company until he or she learns the new system. This may take years, but only if the new company has a good support system in place. Otherwise, the performance may never improve. For these reasons, companies cannot obtain competitive advantage by hiring stars from the outside. Instead, they should emphasize growing their own talent and developing the infrastructure necessary for high performance.[91]

It is important not to ignore the 75% of the workforce who, while not being stars, are the solid performers that keep a company going over the years. An undue emphasis on attracting stars wastes money and destroys morale. The CEO of McKesson, a pharmaceutical wholesaler, calls these B players "performers in place. . . . They are happy living in Dubuque. I have more time and admiration for them than the A player who is at my desk every six months asking for the next promotion." Coaches who try to forge a sports team composed of stars court disaster. According to Karen Freeman, former head coach of women's basketball at Wake Forest University, "During my coaching days, the most dysfunctional teams were the ones who had no respect for the B players." In basketball or business, when the team goes into a slump, the stars are the first to whine, Freeman reports.[92]

Strategy Bits

- The number of students leaving their home countries for higher education will triple from 2 million to nearly 6 million per year by 2020.
- The countries attracting the largest number of international students are the United States followed by the United Kingdom.[93]

Discussion Questions

1. What skills should a person have for managing a business unit following a differentiation strategy? Why? What should a company do if no one is available internally and the company has a policy of promotion from within?
2. When should someone from outside a company be hired to manage the company or one of its business units?
3. What are some ways to implement a retrenchment strategy without creating a lot of resentment and conflict with labor unions?
4. How can corporate culture be changed?
5. Why is an understanding of national cultures important in strategic management?

Strategic Practice Exercise

Staffing involves finding the person with the right blend of characteristics, such as personality, training, and experience, to implement a particular strategy. The Keirsey Temperament Sorter is designed to identify different kinds of personality temperament. It is similar to other instruments derived from Carl Jung's theory of psychological types, such as the Myers-Briggs, the Singer-Loomis, and the Grey-Wheelright. The questionnaire identifies four temperament types: **Guardian (SJ)**, **Artisan (SP)**, **Idealist (NF)**, and **Rational (NT)**. ***Guardians*** have natural talent in managing goods and services. They are dependable and trustworthy. ***Artisans*** have keen senses and are at home with tools, instruments, and vehicles. They are risk-takers and like action. ***Idealists*** are concerned with growth and development and like to work with people. They prefer friendly cooperation over confrontation and conflict.

Rationalists are problem solvers who like to know how things work. They work tirelessly to accomplish their goals. Each of these four types has four variants.[94]

Keirsey challenges the assumption that people are basically the same in the ways that they think, feel, and approach problems. Keirsey argues that it is far less desirable to attempt to change others (because it has little likelihood of success) than to attempt to understand, work with, and take advantage of normal differences. Companies can use this type of questionnaire to help team members understand how each person can contribute to team performance. For example, Lucent Technology used the Myers-Briggs Type Indicator to help build trust and understanding among 500 engineers in 13 time zones and 3 continents in a distributed development project.

1. Access the Keirsey Temperament Sorter using your Internet browser. Type in the following URL: *www.advisorteam.com*
2. Complete and score the questionnaire. Print the description of your personality type.
3. Read the information on the web site about each personality type. Become familiar with each.
4. Bring to class a sheet of paper containing your name and your personality type: Guardian, Artisan, Idealist, or Rational. Your instructor will either put you into a group containing people with the same predominant style or into a group with representatives from each type. He or she may then give each group a number. The instructor will then give the teams a project to accomplish. Each group will have approximately 30 minutes to do the project. It may be to solve a problem, analyze a short case, or propose a new entrepreneurial venture. The instructor will provide you with very little guidance other than to form and number the groups, give them the project, and keep track of time. He or she may move from group to group to sit in on each team's progress. When the time is up, the instructor will ask a spokesperson from each group to (1) describe the process the group went through and (2) present orally each group's ideas. After each group makes its presentation, the instructor may choose one or more of the following:

- On a sheet of paper, each person in the class should identify his or her personality type and vote which team did the best on the project.
- The class as a whole should try to identify each group's dominant decision-making style in terms of how it did its assignment. See how many people vote for one of the four types for each team.
- Each member of a group should guess whether he or she was put into a team composed of the same personality types or in one composed of all four personality types.

Key Terms

action plan (p. 253)
analytical portfolio manager (p. 241)
assessment center (p. 244)
assimilation (p. 252)
cautious profit planner (p. 241)
deculturation (p. 252)
dimensions of national culture (p. 256)
downsizing (p. 245)
dynamic industry expert (p. 241)
executive succession (p. 243)
executive type (p. 241)
individualism–collectivism (p. 256)
integration (p. 251)
integration manager (p. 240)
job rotation (p. 245)
leading (p. 240)
long-term orientation (p. 257)
Management By Objectives (p. 254)
masculinity–femininity (p. 256)
performance appraisal system (p. 244)
power distance (p. 256)
professional liquidator (p. 242)
separation (p. 252)
staffing (p. 240)
strategy–culture compatibility (p. 249)
Total Quality Management (p. 255)
turnaround specialist (p. 242)
uncertainty avoidance (p. 256)

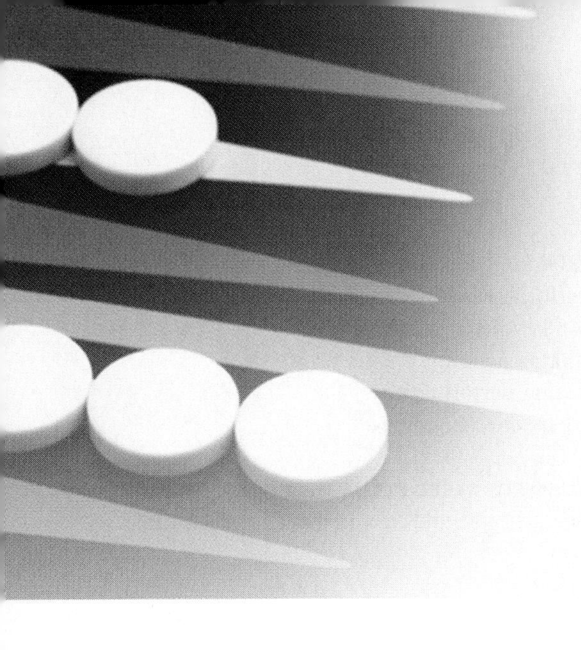

CHAPTER 11 Evaluation and Control

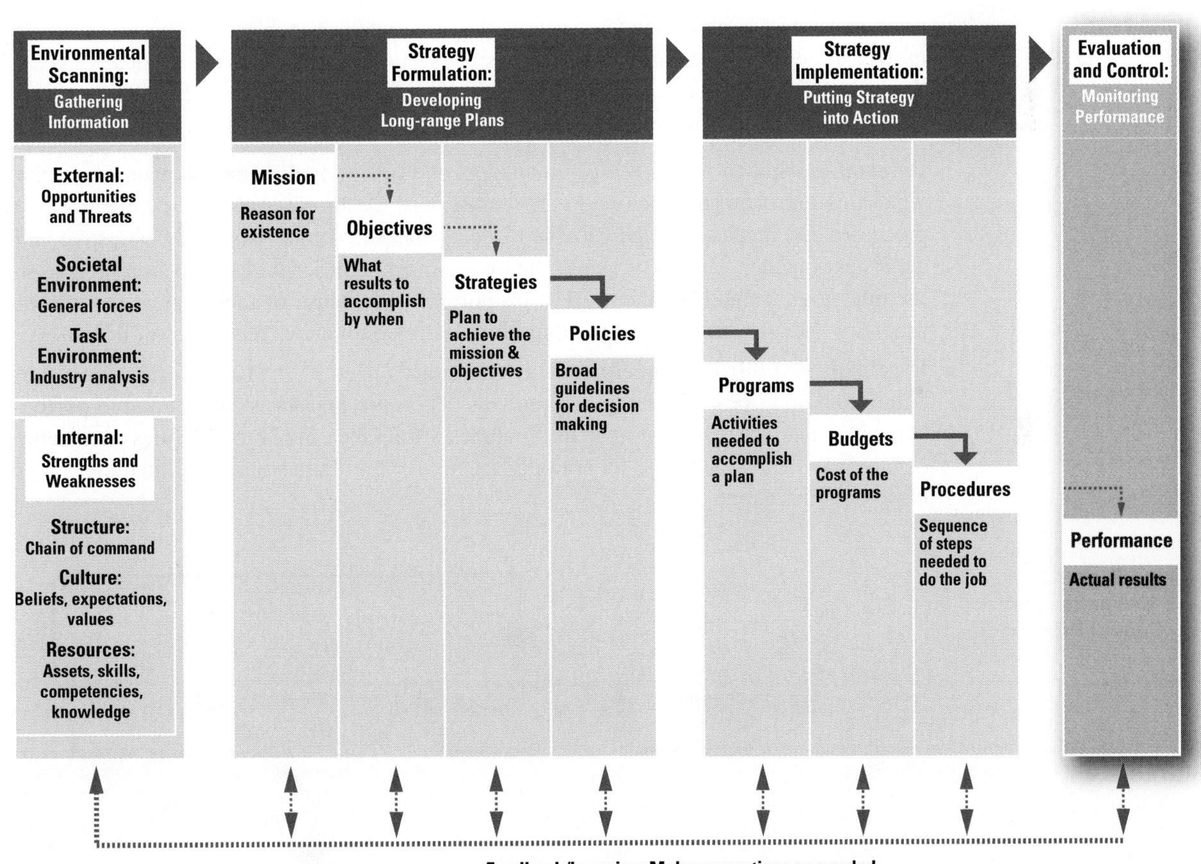

Learning Objectives

After reading this chapter, you should be able to:

- Understand the basic control process
- Choose among traditional measures, such as ROI, and shareholder value measures, such as economic value added, to properly assess performance
- Use the balanced scorecard approach to develop key performance measures
- Apply the benchmarking process to a function or an activity
- Understand the impact of problems with measuring performance
- Develop appropriate control systems to support specific strategies

NUCOR CORPORATION, ONE OF THE MOST SUCCESSFUL STEEL FIRMS OPERATING IN THE United States, keeps its evaluation and control process simple and easy to manage. According to Kenneth Iverson, Chairman of the Board:

> *We try to keep our focus on what really matters—bottom-line performance and long-term survival. That's what we want our people to be thinking about. Management takes care not to distract the company with a lot of talk about other issues. We don't clutter the picture with lofty vision statements or ask employees to pursue vague, intermediate objectives like "excellence" or burden them with complex business strategies. Our competitive strategy is to build manufacturing facilities economically and to operate them efficiently. Period. Basically, we ask our employees to produce more product for less money. Then we reward them for doing that well.*[1]

The **evaluation and control process** ensures that a company is achieving what it set out to accomplish. It compares performance with desired results and provides the feedback necessary for management to evaluate results and take corrective action, as needed. This process can be viewed as a five-step feedback model, as depicted in **Figure 11–1**:

1. **Determine what to measure:** Top managers and operational managers need to specify what implementation processes and results will be monitored and evaluated. The processes and results must be capable of being measured in a reasonably objective and consistent manner. The focus should be on the most significant elements in a process—the ones that account for the highest proportion of expense or the greatest number of problems. Measurements must be found for all important areas, regardless of difficulty.
2. **Establish standards of performance:** Standards used to measure performance are detailed expressions of strategic objectives. They are measures of acceptable performance results. Each standard usually includes a tolerance range that defines acceptable deviations. Standards can be set not only for final output but also for intermediate stages of production output.

Figure 11–1
Evaluation and Control Process

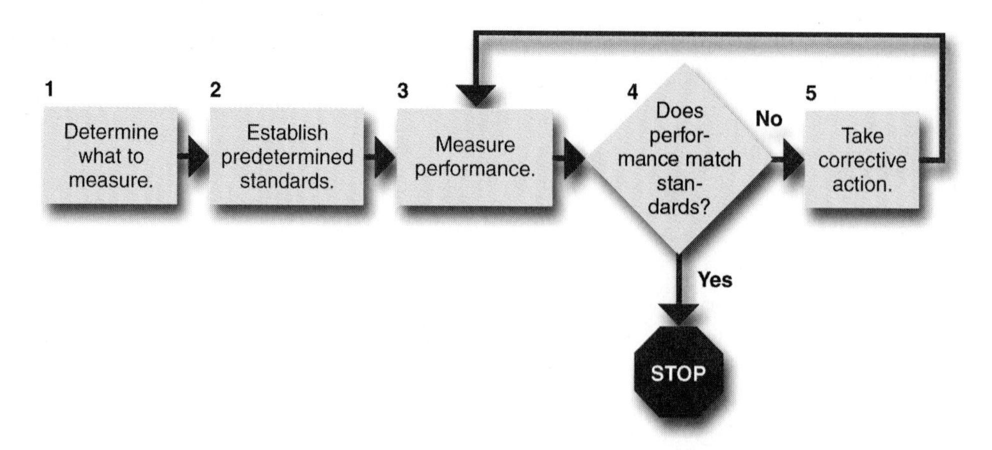

3. **Measure actual performance:** Measurements must be made at predetermined times.
4. **Compare actual performance with the standard:** If actual performance results are within the desired tolerance range, the measurement process stops here.
5. **Take corrective action:** If actual results fall outside the desired tolerance range, action must be taken to correct the deviation. The following questions must be answered:
   a. Is the deviation only a chance fluctuation?
   b. Are the processes being carried out incorrectly?
   c. Are the processes appropriate to the achievement of the desired standard? Action must be taken that will not only correct the deviation but also prevent its happening again.
   d. Who is the best person to take corrective action?

Top management is often better at the first two steps of the control model than it is at the last two follow-through steps. It tends to establish a control system and then delegate the implementation to others. This can have unfortunate results. Nucor is unusual in its ability to deal with the entire evaluation and control process.

11.1 Evaluation and Control in Strategic Management

Evaluation and control information consists of performance data and activity reports (gathered in Step 3 in **Figure 11–1**). If undesired performance results because the strategic management processes were inappropriately used, operational managers must know about it so that they can correct the employee activity. Top management need not be involved. If, however, undesired performance results from the processes themselves, top managers, as well as operational managers, must know about it so that they can develop new implementation programs or procedures. Evaluation and control information must be relevant to what is being monitored. One of the obstacles to effective control is the difficulty in developing appropriate measures of important activities and outputs.

An application of the control process to strategic management is depicted in **Figure 11–2**. It provides strategic managers with a series of questions to use in evaluating an implemented strategy. Such a strategy review is usually initiated when a gap appears between a company's financial objectives and the expected results of current activities. After answering the proposed set of questions, a manager should have a good idea of where the problem originated and what must be done to correct the situation.

11.2 Measuring Performance

Performance is the end result of activity. Which measures to select to assess performance depends on the organizational unit to be appraised and the objectives to be achieved. The objectives that were established earlier in the strategy formulation part of the strategic management process (dealing with profitability, market share, and cost reduction, among others) should certainly be used to measure corporate performance once the strategies have been implemented.

Appropriate Measures

Some measures, such as return on investment (ROI), are appropriate for evaluating a corporation's or division's ability to achieve a profitability objective. This type of measure, however, is inadequate for evaluating additional corporate objectives such as social responsibility or

Figure 11–2
Evaluating an Implemented Strategy

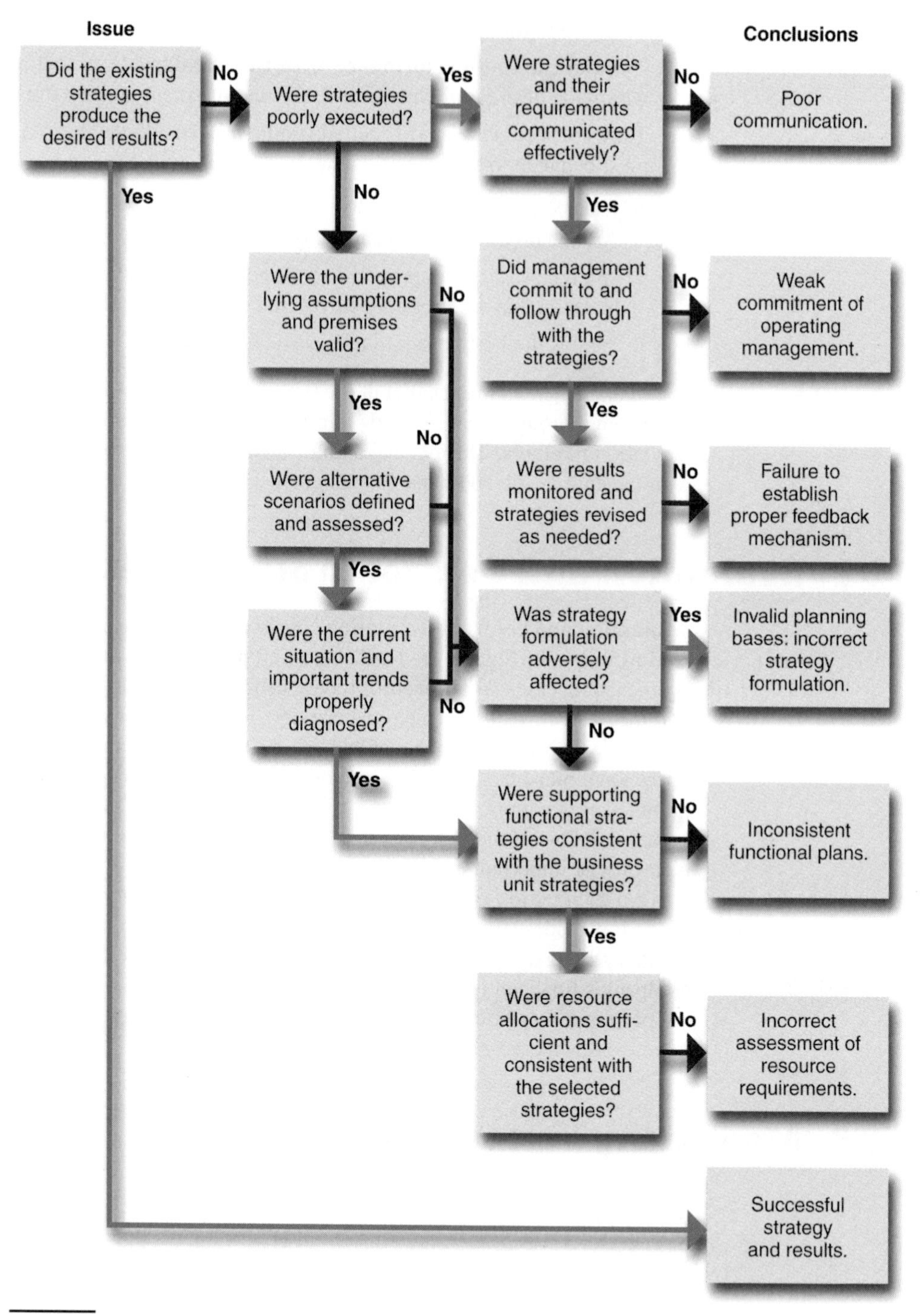

Source: From "The Strategic Review," Planning Review, *Jeffrey A. Schmidt, 1998 © MCB University Press Limited. Republished with permission of Emerald Group Publishing Ltd.*

employee development. Even though profitability is a corporation's major objective, ROI can be computed only after profits are totaled for a period. It tells what happened after the fact—not what is happening or what will happen. A firm, therefore, needs to develop measures that predict likely profitability. These are referred to as **steering controls** because they measure variables that influence future profitability.

One example of a steering control used by retail stores is the *inventory turnover ratio*, in which a retailer's cost of goods sold is divided by the average value of its inventories. This measure shows how hard an investment in inventory is working; the higher the ratio, the better. Not only does quicker-moving inventory tie up less cash in inventories, it also reduces the risk that the goods will grow obsolete before they're sold—a crucial measure for computers and other technology items. For example, Office Depot increased its inventory turnover ratio from 6.9 in 2003 to 7.5 in 2004, leading to increased profits for the year.[2]

Types of Controls

Controls can be established to focus on actual performance results (output), on the activities that generate the performance (behavior), or on resources that are used in performance (input). **Behavior controls** specify how something is to be done through policies, rules, standard operating procedures, and orders from a superior. **Output controls** specify what is to be accomplished by focusing on the end result of the behaviors through the use of objectives and performance targets or milestones. **Input controls** focus on resources, such as knowledge, skills, abilities, values, and motives of employees.[3]

Behavior, output, and input controls are not interchangeable. Behavior controls (such as following company procedures, making sales calls to potential customers, and getting to work on time) are most appropriate when performance results are hard to measure but the cause–effect connection between activities and results is clear. Output controls (such as sales quotas, specific cost-reduction or profit objectives, and surveys of customer satisfaction) are most appropriate when specific output measures have been agreed on but the cause–effect connection between activities and results is not clear. Input controls (such as number of years of education and experience) are most appropriate when output is difficult to measure and there is no clear cause–effect relationship between behavior and performance (such as in college teaching). Corporations following the strategy of conglomerate diversification tend to emphasize output controls with their divisions and subsidiaries (presumably because they are managed independently of each other), whereas corporations following concentric diversification use all three types of controls (presumably because synergy is desired).[4] Even if all three types of controls are used, one or two of them may be emphasized more than another, depending on the circumstances. For example, Muralidharan and Hamilton propose that as a multinational corporation (MNC) moves through its stages of development, its emphasis on control should shift from being primarily output at first, to behavioral, and finally to input control.[5]

Examples of increasingly popular behavior controls are the ISO 9000 and 14000 Standards Series on quality and environmental assurance developed by the International Standards Association of Geneva, Switzerland. Using the **ISO 9000 Standards Series** (composed of five sections, from 9000 to 9004) is a way of objectively documenting a company's high level of quality operations. Using the **ISO 14000 Standards Series** is a way to document the company's impact on the environment. A company wanting ISO 9000 certification would document its process for product introductions, among other things. ISO 9001 would require this firm to separately document design input, design process, design output, and design verification—a large amount of work. ISO 14001 would specify how companies should establish, maintain, and continually improve an environmental management system. Although the average total cost for a company to be ISO 9000 certified is close to $250,000, the annual savings are around $175,000 per company.[6] Overall, ISO 14001–related savings are about equal to the costs, reports Tim Delawder, Vice President of SWD, Inc., a metal finishing company in Addison, Illinois.[7]

Many corporations view ISO 9000 certification as assurance that a supplier sells quality products. Firms such as DuPont, Hewlett-Packard, and 3M have facilities registered to ISO standards. Companies in more than 60 countries, including Canada, Mexico, Japan, the United States (including the entire U.S. auto industry), and the European Union, require ISO 9000 certification of their suppliers.[8] The same is happening for ISO 14000. Both Ford and General Motors require their suppliers to follow ISO 14001. In a survey of manufacturing executives, 51% of the executives found that ISO 9000 certification increased their international competitiveness. Other executives noted that it signaled their commitment to quality and gave them a strategic advantage over noncertified competitors.[9] Since its ISO 14000 certification, SWD, Inc., has become a showplace for environmental awareness. According to SWD's Delawder, ISO 14000 certification improves environmental awareness among employees, reduces risks of violating regulations, and improves the firm's image among customers and the local community.[10]

Another example of a behavior control is a company's monitoring of employee phone calls and PCs to ensure that employees are behaving according to company guidelines. In a study by the American Management Association, nearly 75% of U.S. companies actively monitored their workers' communications and on-the-job activities. Around 54% tracked individual employees' Internet connections, and 38% admitted storing and reviewing their employees' e-mail. About 45% of the companies surveyed had disciplined workers (16% had fired them). For example, Xerox fired 40 employees for visiting pornographic web sites.[11]

Activity-Based Costing

Activity-based costing (ABC) is a recently developed accounting method for allocating indirect and fixed costs to individual products or product lines based on the value-added activities going into that product.[12] This accounting method is thus very useful in doing a value-chain analysis of a firm's activities for making outsourcing decisions. Traditional cost accounting, in contrast, focuses on valuing a company's inventory for financial reporting purposes. To obtain a unit's cost, cost accountants typically add direct labor to the cost of materials. Then they compute overhead from rent to R&D expenses, based on the number of direct labor hours it takes to make a product. To obtain unit cost, they divide the total by the number of items made during the period under consideration.

Traditional cost accounting is useful when direct labor accounts for most of total costs and a company produces just a few products requiring the same processes. This may have been true of companies during the early part of the twentieth century, but it is no longer relevant today, when overhead may account for as much as 70% of manufacturing costs. According to Bob Van Der Linde, CEO of a contract manufacturing services firm in San Diego, California: "Overhead is 80% to 90% in our industry, so allocation errors lead to pricing errors, which could easily bankrupt the company."[13] The appropriate allocation of indirect costs and overhead has thus become crucial for decision making. The traditional volume-based cost-driven system systematically understates the cost per unit of products with low sales volumes and products with a high degree of complexity. Similarly, it overstates the cost per unit of products with high sales volumes and a low degree of complexity.[14] When Chrysler used ABC, it discovered that the true cost of some of the parts used in making cars was 30 times what the company had previously estimated.[15]

ABC accounting allows accountants to charge costs more accurately than the traditional method because it allocates overhead far more precisely. For example, imagine a production line in a pen factory where black pens are made in high volume and blue pens in low volume. Assume that it takes eight hours to retool (reprogram the machinery) to shift production from one kind of pen to the other. The total costs include supplies (the same for both pens), the direct labor of the line workers, and factory overhead. In this instance, a very significant part of the overhead cost is the cost of reprogramming the machinery to switch from one pen to another. If the company produces 10 times as many black pens as blue pens, 10 times the cost of the reprogramming expenses will be allocated to the black pens as to the blue pens under traditional cost accounting methods. This approach underestimates, however, the true cost of making the blue pens.

ABC accounting, in contrast, first breaks down pen manufacturing into its activities. It is then very easy to see that it is the activity of changing pens that triggers the cost of retooling. The ABC accountant calculates an average cost of setting up the machinery and charges it against each batch of pens that requires retooling, regardless of the size of the run. Thus a product carries only those costs for the overhead it actually consumes. Management is now able to discover that its blue pens cost almost twice as much as do the black pens. Unless the company is able to charge a higher price for its blue pens, it cannot make a profit on these pens. Unless there is a strategic reason why it must offer blue pens (such as a key customer who must have a small number of blue pens with every large order of black pens or a marketing trend away from black to blue pens), the company will earn significantly greater profits if it completely stops making blue pens.[16]

Enterprise Risk Management

Enterprise Risk Management (ERM) is a corporatewide, integrated process for managing the uncertainties that could negatively or positively influence the achievement of a corporation's objectives. In the past, managing risk was done in a fragmented manner within functions or business units. Individuals would manage process risk, safety risk, and insurance, financial, and other assorted risks. As a result of this fragmented approach, companies would take huge risks in some areas of the business while overmanaging substantially smaller risks in other areas. ERM is being adopted because of the increasing amount of environmental uncertainty that can affect an entire corporation. As a result, the position Chief Risk Officer is one of the fastest-growing executive positions in U.S. corporations.[17] Microsoft uses scenario analysis to identify key business risks. According to Microsoft's treasurer, Brent Callinicos, "The scenarios are really what we're trying to protect against."[18] The scenarios were the possibility of an earthquake in the Seattle region and a major downturn in the stock market.

The process of rating risks involves three steps:

1. Identify the risks, using scenario analysis or brainstorming or by performing risk self-assessments.
2. Rank the risks, using some scale of impact and likelihood.
3. Measure the risks, using some agreed-upon standard.

Some companies are using value at risk, or VAR (effect of unlikely events in normal markets), and stress testing (effect of plausible events in abnormal markets) methodologies to measure the potential impact of the financial risks they face. DuPont uses earnings at risk (EAR) measuring tools to measure the effect of risk on reported earnings. It can then manage risk to a specified earnings level, based on the company's "risk appetite." With this integrated view, DuPont can view how risks affect the likelihood of achieving certain earnings targets.[19]

Primary Measures of Corporate Performance

The days when simple financial measures such as ROI or EPS were used alone to assess overall corporate performance are coming to an end. Analysts now recommend a broad range of methods to evaluate the success or failure of a strategy. Some of these methods are stakeholder measures, shareholder value, and the balanced scorecard approach. Even though each of these methods has supporters as well as detractors, the current trend is clearly toward more complicated financial measures and an increasing use of non-financial measures of corporate performance. For example, research indicates that companies pursuing strategies founded on innovation and new product development now tend to favor non-financial over financial measures.[20]

Traditional Financial Measures

The most commonly used measure of corporate performance (in terms of profits) is **return on investment (ROI)**. It is simply the result of dividing net income before taxes by the total amount invested in the company (typically measured by total assets). Although using ROI has several advantages, it also has several distinct limitations. (See **Table 11–1**.) Although ROI gives the impression of objectivity and precision, it can be easily manipulated.

Earnings per share (EPS), which involves dividing net earnings by the amount of common stock, also has several deficiencies as an evaluation of past and future performance. First, because alternative accounting principles are available, EPS can have several different but equally acceptable values, depending on the principle selected for its computation. Second, because EPS is based on accrual income, the conversion of income to cash can be near term or delayed. Therefore, EPS does not consider the time value of money. **Return on equity (ROE)**, which involves dividing net income by total equity, also has limitations because it is also derived from accounting-based data. In addition, EPS and ROE are often unrelated to a company's stock price.

Operating cash flow, which involves the amount of money generated by a company before the cost of financing and taxes, is a broad measure of a company's funds. This is the

TABLE 11–1 ADVANTAGES AND LIMITATIONS OF USING ROI AS A MEASURE OF CORPORATE PERFORMANCE

Before using Return on Investment (ROI) as a measure of corporate performance, consider its advantages and limitations.

Advantages

- ROI is a single, comprehensive number that includes all revenues, costs, and expenses.
- It can be used to evaluate the performance of a general manager of a division or SBU.
- It can be compared across companies to see which firms are performing better.
- It provides an incentive to use current assets efficiently and to acquire new assets only when they would increase profits significantly.

Limitations

- ROI is very sensitive to depreciation policy. ROI can be increased by writing down the value of assets through accelerated depreciation.
- It can discourage investment in new facilities or the upgrading of old ones. Older plants with depreciated assets have an advantage over newer plants in earning a higher ROI.
- It provides an incentive for division managers to set transfer prices for goods sold to other divisions as high as possible and to lobby for corporate policy favoring in-house transfers over purchases from other firms.
- Managers tend to focus more on ROI in the short-run over its use in the long-run. This provides an incentive for goal displacement and other dysfunctional consequences.
- ROI is not comparable across industries which operate under different conditions of favorability.
- It is influenced by the overall economy and will tend to be higher in prosperity and lower in a recession.
- It is affected by inventory practices (LIFO or FIFO) and inflation.

company's net income plus depreciation plus depletion, amortization, interest expense, and income tax expense.[21] Some takeover specialists look at a much narrower **free cash flow**: the amount of money a new owner can take out of the firm without harming the business. This is net income plus depreciation, depletion, and amortization less capital expenditures and dividends. The free cash flow ratio is very useful in evaluating the stability of an entrepreneurial venture.[22] Although cash flow may be harder to manipulate than earnings, the number can be increased by selling accounts receivable, classifying outstanding checks as accounts payable, trading securities, and capitalizing certain expenses, such as direct-response advertising.[23]

Because of these and other limitations, ROI, EPS, ROE, and operating cash flow are not by themselves adequate measures of corporate performance. At the same time, these traditional financial measures are very appropriate when used with complementary financial and non-financial measures. (See **Strategy Highlight 11.1** for an example of weird performance measures that have been used instead of the traditional financial measures.)

Stakeholder Measures

Each stakeholder has its own set of criteria to determine how well the corporation is performing. These criteria typically deal with the direct and indirect impacts of corporate activities on stakeholder interests. Top management should establish one or more simple **stakeholder measures** for each stakeholder category so that it can keep track of stakeholder concerns. (See **Table 11–2**.)

Shareholder Value

Because of the belief that accounting-based numbers such as ROI, ROE, and EPS are not reliable indicators of a corporation's economic value, many corporations are using shareholder value as a better measure of corporate performance and strategic management effectiveness. **Shareholder value** can be defined as the present value of the anticipated future stream of cash flows from the business plus the value of the company if liquidated. Arguing that the purpose

STRATEGY HIGHLIGHT 11.1

Eyeballs and MUUs: Questionable Performance Measures

When Amazon.com's investor-relations team went to Denver in September 2000 to seek funding from Marsico Capital Management, a mutual fund company, it presented its usual performance story. Even though the company had never shown a profit, the team told how Amazon.com had a "first to market" advantage and that its web site received an extremely high number of "monthly unique visitors" and "eyeballs." Although such presentations had in the past raised millions of dollars for the company in stock purchases, this one failed. Marsico was more concerned with when the company would become profitable. The Amazon.com team left empty-handed.

Until 2000, investors had been so enamored with new Internet firms that they had made decisions based on novel measures of performance and firm valuation. They looked at measures such as *stickiness* (length of web site visit), *eyeballs* (number of people who visit a web site), and *mindshare* (brand awareness). Mergers and acquisitions were priced on multiples of *MUUs* (monthly unique users) or even on registered users. Since practically all the dot.com (Internet) firms failed to earn a profit, investors and analysts used these measures to estimate what the firms might be worth sometime in the future. Once analysts realized that these valuations were worthless, stock prices dropped to almost nothing, and by 2001 most of the dot.com firms were out of business.

Sources: E. Schonfeld, "How Much Are Your Eyeballs Worth?" *Fortune* (February 21, 2000), pp. 197–204; N. Byrnes, "Eyeballs, Bah! Figuring Dot-Coms' Real Worth," *Business Week* (October 30, 2000), p. 62; R. Barker, "Amazon: Cheaper—But Cheap Enough?" *Business Week* (December 4, 2000), p. 172.

TABLE 11–2 A SAMPLE SCORECARD FOR "KEEPING SCORE" WITH STAKEHOLDERS

Stakeholder Category	Possible Near-Term Measures	Possible Long-Term Measures
Customers	Sales ($ and volume) New customers Number of new customer needs met ("tries")	Growth in sales Turnover of customer base Ability to control price
Suppliers	Cost of raw material Delivery time Inventory Availability of raw material	Growth rates of: Raw material costs Delivery time Inventory New ideas from suppliers
Financial community	EPS Stock price Number of "buy" lists ROE	Ability to convince Wall Street of strategy Growth in ROE
Employees	Number of suggestions Productivity Number of grievances	Number of internal promotions Turnover
Congress	Number of new pieces of legislation that affect the firm Access to key members and staff	Number of new regulations that affect industry Ratio of "cooperative" vs. "competitive" encounters
Consumer advocate (CA)	Number of meetings Number of "hostile" encounters Number of times coalitions formed Number of legal actions	Number of changes in policy due to CA Number of CA-initiated "calls for help"
Environmentalists	Number of meetings Number of hostile encounters Number of times coalitions formed Number of EPA complaints Number of legal actions	Number of changes in policy due to environmentalists Number of environmentalist "calls for help"

Source: R. E. Freeman, *Strategic Management: A Stakeholder Approach* (Boston: Ballinger Publishing Company, 1984), p. 179. Copyright © 1984 by R. E. Freeman. Reprinted by permission of R. Edward Freeman.

of a company is to increase shareholder wealth, shareholder value analysis concentrates on cash flow as the key measure of performance. The value of a corporation is thus the value of its cash flows discounted back to their present value, using the business's cost of capital as the discount rate. As long as the returns from a business exceed its cost of capital, the business will create value and be worth more than the capital invested in it.

The New York consulting firm Stern Stewart & Company devised and popularized two shareholder value measures: economic value added (EVA) and market value added (MVA). A basic tenet of EVA and MVA is that businesses should not invest in projects unless they can generate a profit above the cost of capital. Stern Stewart argues that a deficiency of traditional accounting-based measures is that they assume the cost of capital to be zero.[24] Well-known companies, such as Coca-Cola, General Electric, AT&T, Whirlpool, Quaker Oats, Eli Lilly, Georgia-Pacific, Polaroid, Sprint, Teledyne, and Tenneco have adopted MVA and/or EVA as the best yardstick for corporate performance. According to Sprint's CFO, Art Krause, "Unlike EPS, which measures accounting results, MVA gauges true economic performance."[25]

Economic value added (EVA) has become an extremely popular shareholder value method of measuring corporate and divisional performance and may be on its way to replacing ROI as the standard performance measure. EVA measures the difference between the prestrategy and poststrategy values for the business. Simply put, EVA is after-tax operating income minus the total annual cost of capital. The formula to measure EVA is:

EVA = after-tax operating income – (investment in assets
× weighted average cost of capital)[26]

The cost of capital combines the cost of debt and equity. The annual cost of borrowed capital is the interest charged by the firm's banks and bondholders. To calculate the cost of equity, assume that shareholders generally earn about 6% more on stocks than on government bonds. If long-term treasury bills are selling at 7.5%, the firm's cost of equity should be 13.5%—more if the firm is in a risky industry. A corporation's overall cost of capital is the weighted-average cost of the firm's debt and equity capital. The investment in assets is the total amount of capital invested in the business, including buildings, machines, computers, and investments in R&D and training (allocating costs annually over their useful life). Because the typical balance sheet understates the investment made in a company, Stern Stewart has identified 150 possible adjustments, before EVA is calculated.[27] Multiply the firm's total investment in assets by the weighted-average cost of capital. Subtract that figure from after tax operating income. If the difference is positive, the strategy (and the management employing it) is generating value for the shareholders. If it is negative, the strategy is destroying shareholder value.[28]

Roberto Goizueta, past-CEO of Coca-Cola, explained, "We raise capital to make concentrate, and sell it at an operating profit. Then we pay the cost of that capital. Shareholders pocket the difference."[29] Managers can improve their company's or business unit's EVA by (1) earning more profit without using more capital, (2) using less capital, and (3) investing capital in high-return projects. Studies have found that companies using EVA outperform their median competitor by an average of 8.43% of total return annually.[30] EVA does, however, have some limitations. For one thing, it does not control for size differences across plants or divisions. As with ROI, managers can manipulate the numbers. As with ROI, EVA is an after-the-fact measure and cannot be used as a steering control.[31] Although proponents of EVA argue that EVA (unlike Return on Investment, Equity, or Sales) has a strong relationship to stock price, other studies do not support this contention.[32]

Market value added (MVA) is the difference between the market value of a corporation and the capital contributed by shareholders and lenders. Like net present value, it measures the stock market's estimate of the net present value of a firm's past and expected capital investment projects. As such, MVA is the present value of future EVA.[33] To calculate MVA,

1. Add all the capital that has been put into a company—from shareholders, bondholders, and retained earnings.
2. Reclassify certain accounting expenses, such as R&D, to reflect that they are actually investments in future earnings. This provides the firm's total capital. So far, this is the same approach taken in calculating EVA.
3. Using the current stock price, total the value of all outstanding stock, adding it to the company's debt. This is the company's market value. If the company's market value is greater than all the capital invested in it, the firm has a positive MVA—meaning that management (and the strategy it is following) has created wealth. In some cases, however, the market value of the company is actually less than the capital put into it, which means shareholder wealth is being destroyed.

Microsoft, General Electric, Intel, and Coca-Cola tend to have high MVAs in the United States, whereas General Motors and RJR Nabisco have low ones.[34] Studies have shown that EVA is a predictor of MVA. Consecutive years of positive EVA generally lead to a soaring

MVA.[35] Research also reveals that CEO turnover is significantly correlated with MVA and EVA, whereas ROA and ROE are not. This suggests that EVA and MVA may be more appropriate measures of the market's evaluation of a firm's strategy and its management than are the traditional measures of corporate performance.[36] Nevertheless, these measures consider only the financial interests of the shareholder and ignore other stakeholders, such as environmentalists and employees.

Balanced Scorecard Approach: Using Key Performance Measures

Rather than evaluate a corporation using a few financial measures, Kaplan and Norton argue for a "balanced scorecard" that includes non-financial as well as financial measures.[37] This approach is especially useful given that research indicates that non-financial assets explain 50% to 80% of a firm's value.[38] The **balanced scorecard** combines financial measures that tell the results of actions already taken with operational measures on customer satisfaction, internal processes, and the corporation's innovation and improvement activities—the drivers of future financial performance. Management should develop goals or objectives in each of four areas:

1. **Financial:** How do we appear to shareholders?
2. **Customer:** How do customers view us?
3. **Internal Business Perspective:** What must we excel at?
4. **Innovation and Learning:** Can we continue to improve and create value?

Each goal in each area (for example, avoiding bankruptcy in the financial area) is then assigned one or more measures, as well as a target and an initiative. These measures can be thought of as **key performance measures**—measures that are essential for achieving a desired strategic option.[39] For example, a company could include cash flow, quarterly sales growth, and ROE as measures for success in the financial area. It could include market share (competitive position goal) and percentage of new sales coming from new products (customer acceptance goal) as measures under the customer perspective. It could include cycle time and unit cost (manufacturing excellence goal) as measures under the internal business perspective. It could include time to develop next-generation products (technology leadership objective) under the innovation and learning perspective.

A survey by Bain & Company reported that 50% of *Fortune 1000* companies in North America and about 40% in Europe use a version of the balanced scorecard.[40] Another survey reported that the balanced scorecard is used by over half of *Fortune's Global 1000* companies.[41] A study of the *Fortune 500* firms in the United States and the *Post 300* firms in Canada revealed the most popular non-financial measures to be customer satisfaction, customer service, product quality, market share, productivity, service quality, and core competencies. New product development, corporate culture, and market growth were not far behind.[42] CIGNA, for example, uses the balanced scorecard to determine employee bonuses.[43] Corporate experience with the balanced scorecard reveals that a firm should tailor the system to suit its situation, not just adopt it as a cookbook approach. When the balanced scorecard complements corporate strategy, it improves performance. Using the method in a mechanistic fashion without any link to strategy hinders performance and may even decrease it.[44]

Evaluating Top Management and the Board of Directors

Through its strategy, audit, and compensation committees, a board of directors closely evaluates the job performance of the CEO and the top management team. Of course, it is concerned primarily with overall corporate profitability as measured quantitatively by ROI, ROE, EPS, and shareholder value. The absence of short-run profitability certainly contributes to the firing of any CEO. The board, however, is also concerned with other factors.

Members of the compensation committees of today's boards of directors generally agree that a CEO's ability to establish strategic direction, build a management team, and provide leadership are more critical in the long run than are a few quantitative measures. The board should evaluate top management not only on the typical output-oriented quantitative measures but also on behavioral measures—factors relating to its strategic management practices. The specific items that a board uses to evaluate its top management should be derived from the objectives that both the board and top management agreed on earlier. If better relations with the local community and improved safety practices in work areas were selected as objectives for the year (or for five years), these items should be included in the evaluation. In addition, other factors that tend to lead to profitability might be included, such as market share, product quality, or investment intensity. Although the number of boards conducting systematic evaluations of their CEO is increasing, it is estimated that no more than half of the boards do so.

Only 40% of large corporations conduct formal performance evaluations of their boards of directors. Individual director evaluations are even less common. Corporations that have successfully used board performance appraisal systems are Target, Bell South, Raytheon, and Gillette.[45] *Business Week* annually publishes a list of the best and worst boards of directors in the United States.

Chairman–CEO Feedback Instrument. An increasing number of companies are evaluating their CEO by using a 17-item questionnaire developed by Ram Charan, an authority on corporate governance. The questionnaire focuses on four key areas: (1) company performance, (2) leadership of the organization, (3) team building and management succession, and (4) leadership of external constituencies.[46] After taking an hour to complete the questionnaire, the board of KeraVision, Inc., used it as a basis for a lengthy discussion with the CEO, Thomas Loarie. The board criticized Loarie for "not tempering enthusiasm with reality" and urged Loarie to develop a clear management succession plan. The evaluation caused Loarie to more closely involve the board in setting the company's primary objectives and discussing "where we are, where we want to go, and the operating environment."[47]

Management Audit. Management audits are very useful to boards of directors in evaluating management's handling of various corporate activities. Management audits have been developed to evaluate activities such as corporate social responsibility, functional areas such as the marketing department, and divisions such as the international division. These can be helpful if the board has selected particular functional areas or activities for improvement.

Strategic Audit. The strategic audit presented in the Chapter 1 **Appendix 1.A** is a type of management audit. A strategic audit provides a checklist of questions, by area or issue, that enables a systematic analysis of various corporate functions and activities to be made. It is a type of management audit and is extremely useful as a diagnostic tool to pinpoint corporatewide problem areas and to highlight organizational strengths and weaknesses and environmental opportunities and threats (SWOT).[48] A strategic audit can help determine why a certain area is creating problems for a corporation and help generate solutions to the problem. As such, it can be very useful in evaluating the performance of top management.

Primary Measures of Divisional and Functional Performance

Companies use a variety of techniques to evaluate and control performance in divisions, strategic business units (SBUs), and functional areas. If a corporation is composed of SBUs or divisions, it will use many of the same performance measures (ROI or EVA, for instance) that it uses to assess overall corporate performance. To the extent that it can isolate specific functional units such as R&D, the corporation may develop responsibility centers. It will also use typical functional measures such as market share and sales per employee (marketing), unit costs and percentage of defects (operations), percentage of sales from new products and number of patents (R&D), and turnover and job satisfaction (HRM). For example, FedEx uses Enhanced Tracker software with its COSMOS database to track the progress of its 2.5 to 3.5 million shipments daily. As a courier is completing her or his day's activities, the Enhanced Tracker asks whether the person's package count equals the Enhanced Tracker's count. If the count is off, the software helps reconcile the differences.[49]

During strategy formulation and implementation, top management approves a series of programs and supporting **operating budgets** from its business units. During evaluation and control, actual expenses are contrasted with planned expenditures, and the degree of variance is assessed. This is typically done on a monthly basis. In addition, top management will probably require **periodic statistical reports** summarizing data on such key factors as the number of new customer contracts, the volume of received orders, and productivity figures.

Responsibility Centers

Control systems can be established to monitor specific functions, projects, or divisions. Budgets are one type of control system that is typically used to control the financial indicators of performance. **Responsibility centers** are used to isolate a unit so that it can be evaluated separately from the rest of the corporation. Each responsibility center, therefore, has its own budget and is evaluated on its use of budgeted resources. It is headed by the manager responsible for the center's performance. The center uses resources (measured in terms of costs or expenses) to produce a service or a product (measured in terms of volume or revenues). There are five major types of responsibility centers. The type is determined by the way the corporation's control system measures these resources and services or products:

1. **Standard cost centers: Standard cost centers** are primarily used in manufacturing facilities. Standard (or expected) costs are computed for each operation on the basis of historical data. In evaluating the center's performance, its total standard costs are multiplied by the units produced. The result is the expected cost of production, which is then compared to the actual cost of production.
2. **Revenue centers:** With **revenue centers**, production, usually in terms of unit or dollar sales, is measured without consideration of resource costs (for example, salaries). The center is thus judged in terms of effectiveness rather than efficiency. The effectiveness of a sales region, for example, is determined by comparing its actual sales to its projected or previous year's sales. Profits are not considered because sales departments have very limited influence over the cost of the products they sell.
3. **Expense centers:** Resources are measured in dollars, without consideration for service or product costs. Thus budgets will have been prepared for engineered expenses (costs that can be calculated) and for discretionary expenses (costs that can be only estimated). Typical **expense centers** are administrative, service, and research departments. They cost a company money, but they only indirectly contribute to revenues.
4. **Profit centers:** Performance is measured in terms of the difference between revenues (which measure production) and expenditures (which measure resources). A **profit center** is typically established whenever an organizational unit has control over both its resources and its products or services. By having such centers, a company can be organized into divisions of separate product lines. The manager of each division is given autonomy to the extent that he or she is able to keep profits at a satisfactory (or better) level.

   Some organizational units that are not usually considered potentially autonomous can, for the purpose of profit center evaluations, be made so. A manufacturing department, for example, can be converted from a standard cost center (or expense center) into a profit center; it is allowed to charge a transfer price for each product it "sells" to the sales department. The difference between the manufacturing cost per unit and the agreed-upon transfer price is the unit's "profit."

Transfer pricing is commonly used in vertically integrated corporations and can work well when a price can be easily determined for a designated amount of product. Even though most experts agree that market-based transfer prices are the best choice, only 30%–40% of companies use market price to set the transfer price. (Of the rest, 50% use cost; 10%–20% use negotiation.)[50] When a price cannot be set easily, however, the relative bargaining power of the centers, rather than strategic considerations, tends to influence the agreed-upon price. Top management has an obligation to make sure that these political considerations do not overwhelm the strategic ones. Otherwise, profit figures for each center will be biased and provide poor information for strategic decisions at both the corporate and divisional levels.

5. **Investment centers:** Because many divisions in large manufacturing corporations use significant assets to make their products, their asset base should be factored into their performance evaluation. Thus it is insufficient to focus only on profits, as in the case of profit centers. An **investment center's** performance is measured in terms of the difference between its resources and its services or products. For example, two divisions in a corporation made identical profits, but one division owns a $3 million plant, whereas the other owns a $1 million plant. Both make the same profits, but one is obviously more efficient; the smaller plant provides the shareholders with a better return on their investment. The most widely used measure of investment center performance is ROI.

Most single-business corporations, such as Apple Computer, tend to use a combination of cost, expense, and revenue centers. In these corporations, most managers are functional specialists and manage against a budget. Total profitability is integrated at the corporate level. Multidivisional corporations with one dominating product line (such as Anheuser-Busch) that have diversified into a few businesses but that still depend on a single product line (such as beer) for most of their revenue and income generally use a combination of cost, expense, revenue, and profit centers. Multidivisional corporations, such as General Electric, tend to emphasize investment centers—although in various units throughout the corporation other types of responsibility centers are also used. One problem with using responsibility centers, however, is that the separation needed to measure and evaluate a division's performance can diminish the level of cooperation among divisions that is needed to attain synergy for the corporation as a whole. (This problem is discussed later in this chapter, under "Suboptimization.")

Using Benchmarking to Evaluate Performance

According to Xerox Corporation, the company that pioneered this concept in the United States, **benchmarking** is "the continual process of measuring products, services, and practices against the toughest competitors or those companies recognized as industry leaders."[51] Benchmarking, an increasingly popular program, is based on the concept that it makes no sense to reinvent something that someone else is already using. It involves openly learning how others do something better than one's own company so that the company not only can imitate but perhaps even improve on its current techniques. The benchmarking process usually involves the following steps:

1. Identify the area or process to be examined. It should be an activity that has the potential to determine a business unit's competitive advantage.
2. Find behavioral and output measures of the area or process and obtain measurements.
3. Select an accessible set of competitors and best-in-class companies against which to benchmark. These may very often be companies that are in completely different industries

but perform similar activities. For example, when Xerox wanted to improve its order fulfillment, it went to L.L.Bean, the successful mail-order firm, to learn how it achieved excellence in this area.

4. Calculate the differences among the company's performance measurements and those of the best-in-class companies and determine why the differences exist.
5. Develop tactical programs for closing performance gaps.
6. Implement the programs and then compare the resulting new measurements with those of the best-in-class companies.

Benchmarking has been found to produce best results in companies that are already well managed. Apparently, poorer-performing firms tend to be overwhelmed by the discrepancy between their performance and the benchmark—and tend to view the benchmark as too difficult to reach.[52] Nevertheless, a survey by Bain & Company of 460 companies of various sizes across all U.S. industries indicated that more than 70% were using benchmarking in either a major or limited manner.[53] Cost reductions range from 15% to 45%.[54] Benchmarking can also increase sales, improve goal setting, and boost employee motivation.[55] The average cost of a benchmarking study is around $100,000 and involves 30 weeks of effort.[56] Manco, Inc., a small Cleveland-area producer of duct tape, regularly benchmarks itself against Wal-Mart, Rubbermaid, and PepsiCo to enable it to better compete with giant 3M. The American Productivity & Quality Center, a Houston research group, established the Open Standards Benchmarking Collaborative database, composed of more than 1,200 commonly used measures and individual benchmarks, to track the performance of core operational functions. Firms can submit their performance data to this online database to learn how they compare to top performers and industry peers (see *www.apqc.org*).

International Measurement Issues

The three most widely used techniques for international performance evaluation are ROI, budget analysis, and historical comparisons. In one study, 95% of the corporate officers interviewed stated that they use the same evaluation techniques for foreign and domestic operations. Rate of return was mentioned as the single most important measure.[57] However, ROI can cause problems when it is applied to international operations: Because of foreign currencies, different rates of inflation, different tax laws, and the use of transfer pricing, both the net income figure and the investment base may be seriously distorted.[58]

A study of 79 MNCs revealed that **international transfer pricing** from one country unit to another is primarily used not to evaluate performance but to minimize taxes.[59] Taxes are an important issue for MNCs, given that corporate tax rates vary from over 40% in Canada, Japan, Italy, and the United States to 25% in Bolivia, 15% in Chile, and 10%–15% in Zambia.[60] For example, the U.S. Internal Revenue Service contends that many Japanese firms doing business in the United States have artificially inflated the value of U.S. deliveries in order to reduce the profits and thus the taxes of their American subsidiaries.[61] Parts made in a subsidiary of a Japanese MNC in a low-tax country such as Singapore can be shipped to its subsidiary in a high-tax country such as the United States at such a high price that the U.S. subsidiary reports very little profit (and thus pays few taxes), while the Singapore subsidiary reports a very high profit (but also pays few taxes because of the lower tax rate). A Japanese MNC can, therefore, earn more profit worldwide by reporting less profit in high-tax countries and more profit in low-tax countries. Transfer pricing is an important factor, given that 56% of all trade in the Triad and one-third of all international trade is composed of intercompany transactions.[62] Transfer pricing can thus be one way the parent company can reduce taxes and "capture profits" from a subsidiary. Other common ways of transferring profits to the parent company (often referred to as the **repatriation of profits**) are through dividends, royalties, and management fees.[63]

Among the most important barriers to international trade are the different standards for products and services. There are at least three categories of standards: safety/environmental, energy efficiency, and testing procedures. Existing standards have been drafted by such bodies as the British Standards Institute (BSI-UK) in the United Kingdom, Japanese Industrial Standards Committee (JISC), AFNOR in France, DIN in Germany, CSA in Canada, and American Standards Institute in the United States. These standards traditionally created entry barriers that served to fragment various industries, such as major home appliances, by country. The International Electrotechnical Commission (IEC) standards were created to harmonize standards in the European Union and eventually to serve as worldwide standards, with some national deviations to satisfy specific needs. Because the European Union (EU) was the first to harmonize the many different standards of its member countries, the EU is shaping standards for the rest of the world. In addition, the International Organization for Standardization (ISO) is preparing and publishing international standards. These standards provide a foundation for regional associations to build upon. CANENA, the Council for Harmonization of Electrotechnical Standards of the Nations of the Americas, was created in 1992 to further coordinate the harmonization of standards in North and South America. Efforts are also under way in Asia to harmonize standards.[64]

An important issue in international trade is **piracy**. Firms in developing nations around the world make money by making counterfeit copies of well-known name brand products and selling them globally. See the GLOBAL ISSUE feature to learn how this is being done.

GLOBAL ISSUE

Piracy: 15%–20% of China's Goods Are Counterfeit

"There's more counterfeiting going on in China now than we've ever seen anywhere," states Dan Chow, a law professor at Ohio State University. "We know that 15 to 20 percent of all goods in China are counterfeit." This includes products from Tide detergent and Budweiser beer to Marlboro cigarettes. Yamaha estimates that five out of every six bikes bearing its brand name are fake. Procter & Gamble estimates that 15% of the soaps and detergents under its Head & Shoulders, Vidal Sassoon, Safeguard, and Tide brands in China are counterfeit, costing the company $150 million in lost sales. In Yiwu, a few hours from Shanghai, one person admitted to a *60 Minutes* reporter that she could make 1,000 pairs of counterfeit Nike shoes in 10 days for $4.00 a pair. According to Joseph M. Johnson, president of the China division of Bestfoods Asia Ltd, "We are spending millions of dollars to combat counterfeiting."

Tens of thousands of counterfeiters are currently active in China. They range from factories mixing shampoo and soap in back rooms to large state-owned enterprises making copies of soft drinks and beer. Other factories make everything from car batteries to automobiles. Mobile CD factories with optical disc-mastering machines counterfeit music and software. *60 Minutes* found a small factory in Donguan making fake Callaway golf clubs and bags at a rate of 500 bags per week. Factories in southern Guangdong or Fujian provinces truck their products to a central distribution center, such as the one in Yiwu. They may also be shipped across the border into Russia, Pakistan, Vietnam, or Burma. Chinese counterfeiters have developed a global reach through their connections with organized crime.

According to the market research firm Automotive Resources, the profit margins on counterfeit shock absorbers can reach 80% versus only 15% for the real ones. Counterfeiters charge up to 80% less for an oil filter for a Mercedes than the $24 for an authentic filter.

Counterfeit products can be found around the world—not just in China. The worldwide cost of software piracy is around $12 million annually. For example, 27% of the software sold in the United States is pirated. That figure increases to around 50% in Brazil, Singapore, and Poland, and to over 80% in Vietnam (94%), China (92%), Indonesia (88%), Russia (87%), Ukraine (87%), and Pakistan (83%).

Sources: "The World's Greatest Fakes," *60 Minutes*, CBS News (August 8, 2004); "Business Software Piracy," *Pocket World in Figures 2004* (London: Economist & Profile Book, 2003), p. 60; D. Roberts, F. Balfour, P. Magnusson, P. Engardio, and J. Lee, "China's Piracy Plague," *Business Week* (June 5, 2000), pp. 44–48; "Emerging Market Indicators: Software Piracy," *The Economist* (June 27, 1998), p. 108; "Piracy's Big-Business Victims," *Futurist Update* (December 2000).

Authorities in international business recommend that the control and reward systems used by a global MNC be different from those used by a multidomestic MNC.[65] A *multidomestic MNC* should use loose controls on its foreign units. The management of each geographic unit should be given considerable operational latitude, but it should be expected to meet some performance targets. Because profit and ROI measures are often unreliable in international operations, it is recommended that the MNC's top management, in this instance, emphasize budgets and non-financial measures of performance such as market share, productivity, public image, employee morale, and relations with the host country government.[66] Multiple measures should be used to differentiate between the worth of the subsidiary and the performance of its management.

A *global MNC*, however, needs tight controls over its many units. To reduce costs and gain competitive advantage, it is trying to spread the manufacturing and marketing operations of a few fairly uniform products around the world. Therefore, its key operational decisions must be centralized. Its environmental scanning must include research not only into each of the national markets in which the MNC competes but also into the "global arena" of the interaction between markets. Foreign units are thus evaluated more as cost centers, revenue centers, or expense centers than as investment or profit centers because MNCs operating in a global industry do not often make the entire product in the country in which it is sold.

11.3 Strategic Information Systems

Before performance measures can have any impact on strategic management, they must first be communicated to the people responsible for formulating and implementing strategic plans. Strategic information systems can perform this function. They can be computer based or manual, formal or informal. One of the key reasons given for the bankruptcy of International Harvester was the inability of the corporation's top management to precisely determine its income by major class of similar products. Because of this inability, management kept trying to fix ailing businesses and was unable to respond flexibly to major changes and unexpected events. In contrast, one of the key reasons for the success of Wal-Mart has been management's use of the company's sophisticated information system to control purchasing decisions. Cash registers in Wal-Mart retail stores transmit information hourly to computers at company headquarters. Consequently, managers know every morning exactly how many of each item were sold the day before, how many have been sold so far in the year, and how this year's sales compare to last year's. The information system allows all reordering to be done automatically by computers, without any managerial input. It also allows the company to experiment with new toys without committing to big orders in advance. In effect, the system allows the customers to decide through their purchases what gets reordered.

Enterprise Resource Planning (ERP)

Many corporations around the world have adopted **enterprise resource planning (ERP)** software. ERP unites all of a company's major business activities, from order processing to production, within a single family of software modules. The system provides instant access to critical information to everyone in the organization, from the CEO to the factory floor worker. Because of the ability of ERP software to use a common information system throughout a company's many operations around the world, it is becoming the business information systems' global standard. The major providers of this software are SAP AG, Oracle, J. D. Edwards, Peoplesoft, Baan, and SSA.

The German company SAP AG originated the concept with its R/3 software system. Microsoft, for example, used R/3 to replace a tangle of 33 financial tracking systems in 26 subsidiaries. Even though it cost the company $25 million and took 10 months to install, R/3 annually saves Microsoft $18 million. Coca-Cola uses the R/3 system to enable a manager in Atlanta to use her personal computer to check the latest sales of 20-ounce bottles of Coke Classic in India. Owens-Corning envisions that its R/3 system will allow salespeople to learn what is available at any plant or warehouse and to quickly assemble orders for customers.

ERP is, nevertheless, not for every company. The system is extremely complicated and demands a high level of standardization throughout a corporation. Its demanding nature often forces companies to change the way they do business. There are three reasons ERP could fail: (1) insufficient tailoring of the software to fit the company, (2) inadequate training, and (3) insufficient implementation support.[67] Over the two-year period of installing R/3, Owens-Corning had to completely overhaul its operations. Because R/3 was incompatible with Apple Computer's very organic corporate culture, the company was only able to apply it to its order management and financial operations, but not to manufacturing. Other companies that had difficulty installing and using ERP are Whirlpool, Hershey Foods, and Stanley Works. At Whirlpool, SAP's software led to missed and delayed shipments, causing Home Depot to cancel its agreement for selling Whirlpool products.[68]

Divisional and Functional IS Support

At the divisional or SBU level of a corporation, the information system should be used to support, reinforce, or enlarge its business-level strategy through its decision support system. An SBU pursuing a strategy of overall cost leadership could use its information system to reduce costs either by improving labor productivity or improving the use of other resources such as inventory or machinery. Merrill Lynch took this approach when it developed PRISM software to provide its 500 U.S. retail offices with quick access to financial information in order to boost brokers' efficiency. Another SBU, in contrast, might want to pursue a differentiation strategy. It could use its information system to add uniqueness to the product or service and contribute to quality, service, or image through the functional areas. FedEx wanted to use superior service to gain a competitive advantage. It invested significantly in several types of information systems to measure and track the performance of its delivery service. Together, these information systems gave FedEx the fastest error-response time in the overnight delivery business.

11.4 Problems in Measuring Performance

The measurement of performance is a crucial part of evaluation and control. The lack of quantifiable objectives or performance standards and the inability of the information system to provide timely and valid information are two obvious control problems. According to Meg Whitman, CEO of eBay, "If you can't measure it, you can't control it." That's why eBay has a multitude of measures, from total revenues and profits to *take rate*, the ratio of revenues to the value of goods traded on the site.[69] Without objective and timely measurements, it would be extremely difficult to make operational, let alone strategic, decisions. Nevertheless, the use of timely, quantifiable standards does not guarantee good performance. The very act of monitoring and measuring performance can cause side effects that interfere with overall corporate performance. Among the most frequent negative side effects are a short-term orientation and goal displacement.

Short-Term Orientation

Top executives report that in many situations, they analyze neither the long-term implications of present operations on the strategy they have adopted nor the operational impact of a strategy on the corporate mission. Long-run evaluations are often not conducted because executives (1) don't realize their importance, (2) believe that short-run considerations are more important than long-run considerations, (3) aren't personally evaluated on a long-term basis, or (4) don't have the time to make a long-run analysis.[70] There is no real justification for the first and last reasons. If executives realize the importance of long-run evaluations, they make the time needed to conduct them. Even though many chief executives point to immediate pressures from the investment community and to short-term incentive and promotion plans to support the second and third reasons, evidence does not always support their claims.[71]

At one international heavy-equipment manufacturer, managers were so strongly motivated to achieve their quarterly revenue target that they shipped unfinished products from their plant in England to a warehouse in the Netherlands for final assembly. By shipping the incomplete products, they were able to realize the sales before the end of the quarter—thus fulfilling their budgeted objective and making their bonuses. Unfortunately, the high cost of assembling the goods at a distant location (requiring not only renting the warehouse but also paying additional labor) ended up reducing the company's overall profit.[72]

Many accounting-based measures encourage a **short-term orientation** in which managers consider only current tactical or operational issues and ignore long-term strategic ones. **Table 11–1** indicates that one of the limitations of ROI as a performance measure is its short-term nature. In theory, ROI is not limited to the short run, but in practice it is often difficult to use this measure to realize long-term benefits for a company. Because managers can often manipulate both the numerator (earnings) and the denominator (investment), the resulting ROI figure can be meaningless. Advertising, maintenance, and research efforts can be reduced. Estimates of pension-fund profits, unpaid receivables, and old inventory are easy to adjust. Optimistic estimates of returned products, bad debts, and obsolete inventory inflate the present year's sales and earnings.[73] Expensive retooling and plant modernization can be delayed as long as a manager can manipulate figures on production defects and absenteeism.

Mergers can be undertaken that will do more for the present year's earnings (and the next year's paycheck) than for the division's or corporation's future profits. For example, research on 55 firms that engaged in major acquisitions revealed that even though the firms performed poorly after the acquisition, the acquiring firms' top management still received significant increases in compensation.[74] Determining CEO compensation on the basis of firm size rather than performance is typical and is particularly likely for firms that are not monitored closely by independent analysts.[75]

Research supports the conclusion that many CEOs and their friends on the board of directors' compensation committee manipulate information to provide themselves a pay raise. For example, CEOs tend to announce bad news—thus reducing the company's stock price—just before the issuance of stock options. Once the options are issued, the CEOs tend to announce good news—thus raising the stock price and making their options more valuable.[76] Board compensation committees tend to expand the peer group comparison outside their industry to include lower-performing firms to justify a high raise to the CEO. They tend to do this when the company performs poorly, the industry performs well, the CEO is already highly paid, and shareholders are powerful and active.[77]

Goal Displacement

If not carefully done, monitoring and measuring of performance can actually result in a decline in overall corporate performance. **Goal displacement** is the confusion of means with ends and occurs when activities originally intended to help managers attain corporate objectives become ends in themselves—or are adapted to meet ends other than those for which they were intended. Two types of goal displacement are behavior substitution and suboptimization.

Behavior Substitution

Behavior substitution refers to a phenomenon when people substitute activities that do not lead to goal accomplishment for activities that do lead to goal accomplishment because the wrong activities are being rewarded. Managers, like most other people, tend to focus more of their attention on behaviors that are clearly measurable than on those that are not. Employees often receive little or no reward for engaging in hard-to-measure activities such as cooperation and initiative. However, easy-to-measure activities might have little or no relationship to the desired good performance. Rational people, nevertheless, tend to work for the rewards that the system has to offer. Therefore, people tend to substitute behaviors that are recognized and rewarded for behaviors that are ignored, without regard to their contribution to goal accomplishment. A research study of 157 corporations revealed that most of the companies made little attempt to identify areas of non-financial performance that might advance their chosen strategy. Only 23% consistently built and verified cause-and-effect relationships between intermediate controls (such as number of patents filed or product flaws) and company performance.[78]

A U.S. Navy quip sums up this situation: "What you inspect (or reward) is what you get." If the reward system emphasizes quantity while merely asking for quality and cooperation, the system is likely to produce a large number of low-quality products and unsatisfied customers.[79] A proposed law governing the effect of measurement on behavior is that quantifiable measures drive out non-quantifiable measures.

A classic example of behavior substitution happened a few years ago at Sears. Sears' management thought that it could improve employee productivity by tying performance to rewards. It, therefore, paid commissions to its auto shop employees as a percentage of each repair bill. Behavior substitution resulted as employees altered their behavior to fit the reward system. The results were over-billed customers, charges for work never done, and a scandal that tarnished Sears' reputation for many years.[80]

Suboptimization

Suboptimization refers to the phenomenon of a unit optimizing its goal accomplishment to the detriment of the organization as a whole. The emphasis in large corporations on developing separate responsibility centers can create some problems for the corporation as a whole. To the extent that a division or functional unit views itself as a separate entity, it might refuse to cooperate with other units or divisions in the same corporation if cooperation could in some way negatively affect its performance evaluation. The competition between divisions to achieve a high ROI can result in one division's refusal to share its new technology or work process improvements. One division's attempt to optimize the accomplishment of its goals can cause other divisions to fall behind and thus negatively affect overall corporate performance. One common example of suboptimization occurs when a marketing department approves an early shipment date to a customer as a means of getting an order and forces the manufacturing department into overtime production for that one order. Production costs are raised, which reduces the manufacturing department's overall efficiency. The end result might be that, although marketing achieves its sales goal, the corporation as a whole fails to achieve its expected profitability.

11.5 Guidelines for Proper Control

In designing a control system, top management should remember that controls should follow strategy. Unless controls ensure the use of the proper strategy to achieve objectives, there is a strong likelihood that dysfunctional side effects will completely undermine the implementation of the objectives. The following guidelines are recommended:

1. **Control should involve only the minimum amount of information needed to give a reliable picture of events:** Too many controls create confusion. Focus on the strategic factors by following the **80/20 rule**: Monitor those 20% of the factors that determine 80% of the results. See **STRATEGY HIGHLIGHT 11.2** for some additional rules of thumb used by strategists.
2. **Controls should monitor only meaningful activities and results, regardless of measurement difficulty:** If cooperation between divisions is important to corporate performance, some form of qualitative or quantitative measure should be established to monitor cooperation.
3. **Controls should be timely so that corrective action can be taken before it is too late:** Steering controls, controls that monitor or measure the factors influencing performance, should be stressed so that advance notice of problems is given.
4. **Long-term *and* short-term controls should be used:** If only short-term measures are emphasized, a short-term managerial orientation is likely.
5. **Controls should aim at pinpointing exceptions:** Only activities or results that fall outside a predetermined tolerance range should call for action.
6. **Emphasize the reward of meeting or exceeding standards rather than punishment for failing to meet standards:** Heavy punishment of failure typically results in goal displacement. Managers will "fudge" reports and lobby for lower standards.

STRATEGY HIGHLIGHT 11.2

Some Rules of Thumb in Strategy

Managers use many rules of thumb, such as the 80/20 rule, in making strategic decisions. These "rules" are primarily approximations based on years of practical experience by many managers. Although most of these rules have no objective data to support them, they are often accepted by practicing managers as a way of estimating the cost or time necessary to conduct certain activities. They may be useful because they can help narrow the number of alternatives into a shorter list for more detailed analysis. Some of the rules of thumb used by experienced strategists are described here.

Indirect Costs of Strategic Initiatives

- The R&D Rule of Sevens is that for every $1 spent in developing a new prototype, $7 will be needed to get a product ready for market, and $7 additional will be required to get to the first sale. These estimates don't cover working capital requirements for stocking distributor inventories.
- First-year costs for promoting a new consumer goods product are 33% of anticipated first-year sales. Second-year costs should be 20%, and third year costs 15%.
- A reasonably successful patent-based innovation will require $2 million in legal defense costs.

Safety Margins for New Business Initiatives

- A new manufacturing business should have sufficient startup capital to cover one year of costs.
- A new consumer goods business should have sufficient capital to cover two years of business.
- A new professional services business should have sufficient capital to cover three years of costs.

Source: R. West and F. Wolek, "Rules of Thumb in Strategic Thinking," *Strategy & Leadership* (March/April 1999), p. 34.

If the culture complements and reinforces the strategic orientation of a firm, there is less need for an extensive formal control system. In their book *In Search of Excellence*, Peters and Waterman state that "the stronger the culture and the more it was directed toward the marketplace, the less need was there for policy manuals, organization charts, or detailed procedures and rules. In these companies, people way down the line know what they are supposed to do in most situations because the handful of guiding values is crystal clear."[81] For example, at Eaton Corporation, the employees are expected to enforce the rules themselves. If someone misses too much work or picks fights with co-workers, other members of the production team point out the problem. According to Randy Savage, a long-time Eaton employee, "They say there are no bosses here, but if you screw up, you find one pretty fast."[82]

11.6 Strategic Incentive Management

To ensure congruence between the needs of a corporation as a whole and the needs of the employees as individuals, management and the board of directors should develop an incentive program that rewards desired performance. This reduces the likelihood of the agency problems (when employees act to feather their own nests instead of building shareholder value) mentioned in **Chapter 2**. Incentive plans should be linked in some way to corporate and divisional strategy. Research reveals that firm performance is affected by its compensation policies.[83] Companies using different business strategies tend to adopt different pay policies. For example, a survey of 600 business units indicates that the pay mix associated with a growth strategy emphasizes bonuses and other incentives over salary and benefits, whereas the pay mix associated with a stability strategy has the reverse emphasis.[84] Research indicates that SBU managers having long-term performance elements in their compensation program favor a long-term perspective and thus greater investments in R&D, capital equipment, and employee training.[85] The typical CEO pay package is composed of 21% salary, 27% short-term annual incentives, 16% long-term incentives, and 36% stock options.[86]

The following three approaches are tailored to help match measurements and rewards with explicit strategic objectives and time frames[87]:

1. **Weighted-factor method:** The **weighted-factor method** is particularly appropriate for measuring and rewarding the performance of top SBU managers and group-level executives when performance factors and their importance vary from one SBU to another. One corporation's measurements might contain the following variations: the performance of high-growth SBUs is measured in terms of market share, sales growth, designated future payoff, and progress on several future-oriented strategic projects; the performance of low-growth SBUs, in contrast, is measured in terms of ROI and cash generation; and the performance of medium-growth SBUs is measured for a combination of these factors. (See **Table 11–3**.)
2. **Long-term evaluation method:** The **long-term evaluation method** compensates managers for achieving objectives set over a multiyear period. An executive is promised some company stock or "performance units" (convertible into money or stock) in amounts to be based on long-term performance. A board of directors, for example, might set a particular objective in terms of growth in earnings per share during a five-year period. The giving of awards would be contingent on the corporation's meeting that objective within the designated time. Any executive who leaves the corporation before the objective is met receives nothing. The typical emphasis on stock price makes this approach more applicable to top management than to business unit managers. Because rising stock markets tend to raise the stock prices of mediocre companies, there is a developing trend to index stock

TABLE 11–3 WEIGHTED-FACTOR APPROACH TO STRATEGIC INCENTIVE MANAGEMENT

Strategic Business Unit Category	Factor	Weight
High Growth	Return on assets	10%
	Cash flow	0%
	Strategic-funds programs (developmental expenses)	45%
	Market-share increase	45%
	Total	**100%**
Medium Growth	Return on assets	25%
	Cash flow	25%
	Strategic-funds programs (developmental expenses)	25%
	Market-share increase	25%
	Total	**100%**
Low Growth	Return on assets	50%
	Cash flow	50%
	Strategic-funds programs (developmental expenses)	0%
	Market-share increase	0%
	Total	**100%**

Source: Reprinted from *ORGANIZATIONAL DYNAMICS,* Vol. 13, No. 4, 1984, Paul J. Stonich, "The Performance Measurement and Reward System: Critical to Strategic Management," p. 51. Copyright © 1984 with permission of Elsevier.

options to competitors or to the Standard & Poor's 500.[88] General Electric, for example, offered its CEO 250,000 performance share units (PSUs) tied to performance targets achieved over five years. Half of the PSUs convert into GE stock only if GE achieves 10% average annual growth in operations. The other half converts to stock only if total shareholder return meets or beats the S&P 500.[89]

3. **Strategic-funds method:** The **strategic-funds method** encourages executives to look at developmental expenses as being different from expenses required for current operations. The accounting statement for a corporate unit enters strategic funds as a separate entry below the current ROI. It is, therefore, possible to distinguish between expense dollars consumed in the generation of current revenues and those invested in the future of a business. Therefore, a manager can be evaluated on both a short- and a long-term basis and has an incentive to invest strategic funds in the future. (See **Table 11–4**.)

TABLE 11–4 STRATEGIC-FUNDS APPROACH TO AN SBU'S PROFIT-AND-LOSS STATEMENT

Sales	$12,300,000
Cost of sales	–6,900,000
Gross margin	$ 5,400,000
General and administrative expenses	–3,700,000
Operating profit (return on sales)	$ 1,700,000
Strategic funds (development expenses)	–1,000,000
Pretax profit	$ 700,000

Source: Reprinted from *ORGANIZATIONAL DYNAMICS,* Vol. 13, No. 4, 1984, Paul J. Stonich, "The Performance Measurement and Reward System: Critical to Strategic Management," p. 52. Copyright © 1984 with permission of Elsevier.

An effective way to achieve the desired strategic results through a reward system is to combine the three approaches:

1. Segregate strategic funds from short-term funds, as is done in the strategic-funds method.
2. Develop a weighted-factor chart for each SBU.
3. Measure performance on three bases: The pretax profit indicated by the strategic-funds approach, the weighted factors, and the long-term evaluation of the SBUs' and the corporation's performance.

Genentech, General Electric, Adobe, IBM, and Textron are some firms in which top management compensation is contingent upon the company's achieving strategic objectives.[90]

11.7 Conclusion

Having strategic management without evaluation and control is like playing football without any goalposts. Unless strategic management improves performance, it is only an exercise. In business, the bottom-line measure of performance is making a profit. If people aren't willing to pay more than what it costs to make a product or provide a service, that business will not continue to exist. **Chapter 1** explains that organizations engaging in strategic management outperform those that do not. The sticky issue is: How should we measure performance? Is measuring profits sufficient? Does an income statement tell us what we need to know? The accrual method of accounting enables us to count a sale even when the cash has not yet been received. Therefore, a firm might be profitable but still go bankrupt because it can't pay its bills. Is profits the amount of cash on hand at the end of the year after paying costs and expenses? But what if you made a big sale in December and must wait until January to get paid? Like retail stores, perhaps we need to use a fiscal year ending January 31 (to include returned Christmas items that were bought in December) instead of a calendar year ending December 31. Should two managers receive the same bonus when their divisions earn the same profit, even though one division is much smaller than the other? What of the manager who is managing a new product introduction that won't make a profit for another two years?

Evaluation and control is one of the most difficult parts of strategic management. No one measure can tell us what we need to know. That's why we need to use not only the traditional measures of financial performance, such as net earnings, ROI, and EPS, but we need to consider using EVA or MVA and a balanced scorecard, among other possibilities. On top of that, science informs us that just attempting to measure something changes what is being measured. The measurement of performance can and does result in short-term–oriented actions and goal displacement. That's why experts suggest that we use multiple measures of only those things that provide a meaningful and reliable picture of events: Measure those 20% of the factors that determine 80% of the results. Once the appropriate performance measurements are taken, it is possible to learn whether the strategy was successful. As shown in the model of strategic management depicted at the beginning of this chapter, the measured results of corporate performance allow us to decide whether we need to reformulate the strategy, improve its implementation, or gather more information about our competition.

Strategy Bits

- The five busiest airports in the world are Atlanta Hartsfield, Chicago O'Hare, London Heathrow, Tokyo Haneda, and Los Angeles International, in that order.[91]
- The countries with the most crowded road networks (number of vehicles per kilometer of road) are Hong Kong (286.7), United Arab Emirates (231.6), Germany (194.5), Lebanon (190.6), and Singapore (168.9). The United States ranks 42nd, at only 34.1 vehicles per kilometer (1 kilometer = 0.62 mile).[92]

Discussion Questions

1. Is **Figure 11–1** a realistic model of the evaluation and control process?
2. What are some examples of behavior controls? Output controls? Input controls?
3. Is EVA an improvement over ROI, ROE, or EPS?
4. How much faith can a manager place in a transfer price as a substitute for a market price in measuring a profit center's performance?
5. Is the evaluation and control process appropriate for a corporation that emphasizes creativity? Are control and creativity compatible?

Strategic Practice Exercise

Each year, *Fortune* magazine publishes an article titled, "America's Most Admired Companies." It lists the 10 most admired companies in the United States. Another article lists the top 10 in the world. *Fortune*'s rankings are based on scoring publicly held companies on what it calls "eight key attributes of reputation": innovativeness, quality of management, employee talent, quality of products/services, long-term investment value, financial soundness, social responsibility, and use of corporate assets. *Fortune* asks Clark, Martire & Bartolomeo to survey more than 10,000 executives, directors, and securities analysts. Respondents are asked to choose the companies they admire most, regardless of industry. *Fortune* has been publishing this list since 1982. The *2004 Fortune* list of the top 10 most admired were (starting with number 1) Wal-Mart, Berkshire Hathaway, Southwest Airlines, General Electric, Dell Computer, Microsoft, Johnson & Johnson, Starbucks, FedEx, and IBM. The top 10 outside the United States were Toyota Motor, BMW, Sony, Nokia, Nestlé, Honda Motor, British Petroleum, Singapore Airlines, Cannon, and L'Oreal.[93]

Try one of these exercises:

1. Go to the library and find a "Most Admired Companies" *Fortune* article from the 1980s or early 1990s and compare that list to the latest one. (See *www.fortune.com* for the latest list.) Which companies have fallen out of the top 10? Pick one of the companies and investigate why it is no longer on the list.
2. How much of the evaluation is dominated by the profitability of the company? See how many of the top 10 are very profitable. How many of these companies also appear in *Fortune*'s "The 100 Best Companies to Work For"?
3. Why was Wal-Mart the most admired company in the United States in both 2003 and 2004 (up from 6th place in 1999)? Wal-Mart was sued more than 6,000 times in 2002. It is said to squeeze its suppliers to death and destroy its competitors (often small, local mom-and-pop stores) through brute force. It imports many of its goods from China, thus contributing to the outsourcing of jobs.[94] Shouldn't the most admired company also score highly in "The 100 Best Companies to Work For"?
4. Compare *Fortune*'s list to other lists of corporate reputations. Other lists are compiled by the Reputation Institute (*www.reputationinstitute.com*) and by PricewaterhouseCoopers and Financial Times (available through the web site of the Reputation Institute). Note that the Reputation Institute lists J&J as number 1, whereas PricewaterhouseCoopers/FT lists GE as its most respected company. Why is there a difference among the three ratings?

Key Terms

80/20 rule (p. 282)
activity-based costing (p. 266)
balanced scorecard (p. 272)
behavior control (p. 265)
behavior substitution (p. 281)
benchmarking (p. 275)
earnings per share (p. 268)
economic value added (p. 271)
enterprise resource planning (p. 278)
enterprise risk management (p. 267)
evaluation and control information (p. 263)
evaluation and control process (p. 262)
expense center (p. 274)
free cash flow (p. 269)
goal displacement (p. 280)
input control (p. 265)
international transfer pricing (p. 276)
investment center (p. 275)
ISO 9000 Standards Series (p. 265)
ISO 14000 Standards Series (p. 265)
key performance measure (p. 272)
long-term evaluation method (p. 283)
management audit (p. 273)
market value added (p. 271)
operating budget (p. 274)
operating cash flow (p. 269)
output control (p. 265)

performance (p. 263)
periodic statistical report (p. 274)
piracy (p. 277)
profit center (p. 274)
repatriation of profit (p. 277)
responsibility center (p. 274)
return on equity (p. 268)
return on investment (p. 268)
revenue center (p. 274)
shareholder value (p. 269)
short-term orientation (p. 280)
stakeholder measure (p. 269)
standard cost center (p. 274)
steering control (p. 264)
strategic-funds method (p. 283)
suboptimization (p. 280)
transfer pricing (p. 275)
weighted-factor method (p. 283)

PART ENDING VIDEO CASE PART FOUR

Newbury Comics, Inc

IMPLEMENTATION AND CONTROL

Newbury Comics cofounders Mike Dreese and John Brusger parlayed $2,000 and a comic book collection into a thriving chain of 22 stores spanning the New England region, known to be *the* place to shop for everything from the best of the underground/independent music scene to major label superstars. The chain also stocks a wide variety of non-music related items such as T-shirts, Dr. (doc) Martens shoes, posters, jewelry, cosmetics, books, magazines, and other trendy items.

In Part Four, **"Strategy Implementation and Control,"** the video focuses on Newbury Comics' used CD business. Mike, John, and Jan discuss the development of procedures and control processes for introducing the used CD program. Budgeting is indirectly mentioned in terms of huge expenditures made at the six-month point to greatly expand the program. The video also highlights the importance of having the right staff to implement a strategy.

As pointed out in Part 3 of the Video Case, the project of developing an implementation plan was assigned to Duncan Brown, Senior Vice President. Part of this plan was to begin the used CD program in a few stores and then evaluate how well the program was working. This was a very ad hoc approach to implementation, but it fit the very loose entrepreneurial approach Newbury Comics takes toward strategy formulation. Mike tells us that he is more interested in "continuous improvement" than in setting specific sales or profit objectives. He admits that one reason he wanted to enter the used CD business was because he likes being a "pioneer" (i.e., first mover). But being a pioneer has its problems.

Jan points out that when the used CD program was started, a store would just put up signs saying that it now bought and sold used CDs. It was then up to the manager to set both the buying and selling price for each CD (with no help from any computer). The main office would then print tags for that store. As a result, stores (even the same store) would offer the same CD for a different price. Following Mike's belief in encouraging creativity and individual initiative, there were no attempts to place blame during this implementation period.

Mike points out that the used CD business is much more complicated than dealing with new CDs. Although management saw it as a risky business, they also believed that its potential for the company outweighed the risk. Because of the many complications of the used CD business, it resulted in a series of new activities in implementation, evaluation, and control, such as choosing what CDs to buy at what price, cleaning, and packaging them. These new activities resulted in adding new job duties at the store level, warehouse, and main office—thus changing the structure of the organization from one of being fairly decentralized at the store level to one with much more centralization of decision making at headquarters. The main office took control of pricing. The IBM AS-400 computer was part of the information system developed for the used CD bar code program to integrate information from all the stores. Duties were expanded and positions were added at the headquarters office and warehouse to deal with finding sources of bulk shipments, setting prices, and sorting, cleaning, and packaging used CDs. Special relationships were developed with some bulk suppliers of used CDs to make sure that Newbury Comics would get the first look at a new batch in return for paying more than other purchasers. A system of procedures was developed to sell non-selling used CDs to other retailers.

Concepts Illustrated in the Video

- Strategy Implementation: Programs, Budgets, and Procedures
- Achieving Synergy
- Job Design
- Staffing Follows Strategy
- Evaluation and Control: Measuring Performance
- Strategic Information Systems

Study Questions

1. Why was the used CD program at Newbury Comics a success?
2. What programs and procedures did management use to implement the growth strategy?
3. How important is staffing to this company's success?
4. How does the structure of Newbury Comics help or hinder the company's growth?
5. How is synergy achieved throughout the company?

CHAPTER 12
Strategic Issues in Managing Technology and Innovation

Learning Objectives

After reading this chapter, you should be able to:

- List the differences between successful and unsuccessful innovations
- Understand the importance of lead users and market research as sources of new ideas
- Assess the importance of product and process R&D for success within an industry
- Decide when to innovate internally and when to use alliances
- Propose an appropriate structure and culture to support innovative ideas and products
- Apply appropriate techniques and measures to manage new product development

MOST PEOPLE HAVE TASTED PEPSI COLA, LAY'S POTATO CHIPS, AND FRITO'S CORN CHIPS, but have they tried Quaker Soy Crisps or Gatorade Xtremo Thirst Quencher? These are just 2 of the more than 200 new product variations that PepsiCo annually adds to its already large global portfolio of products. Why does PepsiCo introduce so many new products when its current products are still in demand? According to PepsiCo's Chairman and CEO, Steven Reinemund, "Innovation is what consumers are looking for, particularly in the small, routine things of their life." This emphasis on product development seems to be paying off. PepsiCo's double-digit earnings have been consistent over the years and show no sign of slowing. (Its earnings increased 19% from 2002 to 2003 on a 7% increase in sales.) In 2004, PepsiCo was included in *Business Week*'s list of the 50 best-performing public companies.

PepsiCo constantly monitors its environment for changing tastes and fashions. It then tailors its products to suit those changes. When the public became concerned with obesity, its Frito-Lay division developed several low-fat chips and led its competitors by removing all trans fats from its Lay's, Ruffles, and Doritos brands. In June 2004, it introduced "low-carb" Doritos, Cheetos, and Tostitos. The company looks for new products both internally and externally. To capitalize on the growing market for New Age herbal-enhanced beverages, it acquired SoBe Beverages in 2001. Since then, PepsiCo has used brand extension to offer the energy drink SoBe No Fear to the school-aged market and SoBe Fuerte to the Hispanic market. Noting that the foreign-born segment of the 46 million U.S. Hispanic market didn't like PepsiCo's Latin-flavored versions of Lay's and Doritos chips, the company looked to its Mexican subsidiary, Sabritas. Not wanting to cannibalize Frito-Lay's core U.S. brands, the company limited the distribution of products such as Sabritones chile and lime puffed wheat snacks to smaller retail stores in Mexican-dominated areas. Despite no advertising and minimal distribution, U.S. sales of Sabritas brands doubled from $50 million in 2002 to $100 million in 2004. Distribution increased from 10% to one-third of the U.S. population. Because they were marketed as an ethnic specialty rather than as a Frito-Lay line extension, the Sabritas brands were able to win extra shelf space in grocery stores. Analysts agree that PepsiCo has developed a strong capability in product development. According to Robert van Brugge of Sanford C. Bernstein & Company, "They have been early to see trends and aggressive in targeting them."[1]

PepsiCo is a good example of a company successfully using its resources to create new products for new and existing markets. Properly managing technology and innovation is crucial in a fast-moving global environment. In the high-pressure toys and games industry, for example, about 40% of all products on the market are less than one year old.[2] Over the past 15 years, the top 20% of firms in an annual innovation poll conducted by *Fortune* magazine achieved double the shareholder returns of their peers.[3] Nevertheless, many large firms find it difficult to be continually innovative. A recent survey of business executives reveals that a significant majority are concerned that their companies are losing growth opportunities because they are not able to properly manage new technology (see **Table 12–1**).[4] A survey of 700 companies by Arthur D. Little found that 85% of the executives were "dissatisfied with their ability to manage innovation."[5] Even innovative established companies, such as 3M, Procter & Gamble (P&G), and Rubbermaid, have experienced a slowing in their rate of successful new product introductions.[6]

TABLE 12–1
EXECUTIVES FEAR THEIR COMPANIES ARE BECOMING LESS INNOVATIVE

A survey of business executives conducted by *Fortune* with the consulting firm Integral, Inc., revealed the percentages of those responding either **agree** or **strongly agree** to the following five statements:

Statement	%
Your company has recently lost relatively low-value customers in small market niches or low-end market segments.	55%
Your organization passes up growth opportunities it would have pursued when the company was smaller because the opportunities are now "too small to be interesting."	60%
There is a disconnect between the kind of innovations your frontline troops suggest and the types of innovations upper management invests in.	64%
When your organization sees a potentially disruptive technology, it defines it as a technical problem ("Will our customers accept the product?") instead of a market problem.	58%
New entrants have exploited opportunities where uncertainty over market size and customer needs resulted in inaction by your company.	68%

Source: "Don't Leave Us Behind," *Fortune* (April 3, 2000), p. 250.

In this chapter, we examine strategic issues in technology and innovation as they affect environmental scanning, strategy formulation, strategy implementation, and evaluation and control.

12.1 The Role of Management

Due to increased competition and accelerated product development cycles, innovation and the management of technology are becoming crucial to corporate success. Research conducted by Forbes, Ernst & Young, and the Wharton School of Business found the most important driver of corporate value for both durable and non-durable companies to be innovation.[7] New product development is positively associated with corporate performance.[8] Approximately half the profits of all U.S. companies come from products launched in the previous 10 years.[9] What is less obvious is how a company can generate a significant return from investment in R&D as well as an overall sense of enthusiasm for innovative behavior and risk-taking. One way is to include innovation in the corporation's mission statement. See **STRATEGY HIGHLIGHT 12.1** for mission statements from well-known companies. Another way is by establishing policies that support the innovative process. For example, 3M has a policy of generating at least 25% of its revenue from products introduced in the preceding three years. To support this policy, this $13 billion corporation annually spends nearly $1 billion.[10]

The importance of technology and innovation must be emphasized by people at the very top and reinforced by people throughout a corporation. If top management and the board are not interested in these topics, managers below them tend to echo their lack of interest. When growth in sales and profits stalled at P&G several years ago, the new CEO, Art Lafley, realized that product development was no longer a core competency of the company. In 2002, just 12 of the firm's 250-some brands generated half of P&G's sales and an even larger percentage of its profits.[11] Lafley urged product groups to "connect and develop" by pulling in experts from unrelated brands to help with new product creation. One example of the impact of Lafley's directive was the decision to enter the home car-care business. Instead of a project team trying to develop a new product on its own, P&G looked for and found expertise in different parts of the company. The company's PuR unit's water filter experts knew how to

STRATEGY HIGHLIGHT 12.1

Examples of Innovation Emphasis in Mission Statements

To emphasize the importance of technology, creativity, and innovation to overall future corporate success, some well-known firms have added sections to this effect in their published mission statements. Some of these are listed here:

Proctor & Gamble: "Our success is based on a deep understanding of consumers, their habits, and product needs; our ability to attract and support the best innovations in the world; out ability to acquire, develop, and apply technology across P & G's broad array of product categories; and our capability to collaborate with external innovation partners."

IBM: "We strive to lead in the creation, development, and manufacture of the industry's most advanced information technologies, including computer systems, software, networking systems, storage devices and microelectronics."

Intel: "Delight our customers, employees, and shareholders by relentlessly delivering the platform and technology advancements that become essential to the way we work and live."

Hewlett-Packard: "We want to create the best technology on the planet — and be the best at selling, servicing, and supporting that technology."

Merck & Co: "The mission of Merck is to provide society with superior products and services by developing innovations and solutions that improve the quality of life and satisfy customer needs, and to provide employees with meaningful work and advancement opportunities, and investors with a superior return."

deionize water to get rid of minerals. Its Cascade brand unit already had a compound in its dishwasher detergent that reduced water spots. The project team combined both technologies to make the Mr. Clean AutoDry handheld sprayer, a device that sprays soap on cars and then rinses them without spotting. The result was a doubling of Mr. Clean brand sales in a year.[12]

Management has an obligation to not only encourage new product development but also develop a system to ensure that technology is being used most effectively, with the consumer in mind. Between 33% and 60% of all new products that reach the market fail to make a profit.[13] A study by Chicago consultants Kuczmarski & Associates of 11,000 new products marketed by 77 manufacturing, service, and consumer-product firms revealed that only 56% of all newly introduced products were still being sold five years later. Only 1 in 13 new product ideas ever made it into test markets. Although some authorities argue that this percentage of successful new products needs to be improved, others contend that too high a percentage means that a company isn't taking the risks necessary to develop a really new product.[14]

A study of 111 successful and 86 unsuccessful product innovations found that the *successful innovations* had some or all of the following features:

- They were moderately new to the market.
- They were based on tried-and-tested technology.
- They saved money, met customers' needs, and supported existing practices.

In contrast, the *unsuccessful innovations* had a different set of characteristics:

- They were based on cutting-edge or untested technology.
- They followed a "me-too" approach.
- They were created with no clearly defined solution in mind.[15]

The importance of top management's providing appropriate direction is exemplified by Steve Jobs' management of Apple Computer. Ever since he co-founded the company, Jobs has pushed Apple to provide not just a product but a complete system. For example, Apple decided in 2001 to make a digital music player, the iPod, that would be as easy to use for digital media as the Sony Walkman was for cassette tapes. Jobs realized, however, that the company could not succeed by just making and selling hardware. The digital player would be worthless without an online download store. By painstakingly negotiating digital-rights issues with reluctant record companies, he achieved something never before accomplished: providing easy, legal access to over 1 million songs. By 2004, Apple sold 3.7 million iPods valued at $1 billion in sales. Commenting on the iPod's success, Jobs explained, "We can invent a complete solution that works."[16]

12.2 Environmental Scanning

Issues in innovation and technology influence both external and internal environmental scanning.

External Scanning

Corporations need to continually scan their external societal and task environments for new developments in technology that may have some application to their current or potential products. Research reveals that firms that scan their external environment are more innovative than those that focus inward on their core competencies as a way to generate new products or processes.[17] Stakeholders, especially customers, can be important participants in the new product development process.

Technological Developments

Motorola, a company well known for its ability to invest in profitable new technologies and manufacturing improvements, has a sophisticated scanning system. Its intelligence department monitors the latest technological developments introduced at scientific conferences, in journals, and in trade gossip. This information helps it build "technology roadmaps" that assess where breakthroughs are likely to occur, when they can be incorporated into new products, how much money their development will cost, and which of the developments is being worked on by the competition.[18]

A company's focusing its scanning efforts too closely on its current product line is dangerous. Most new developments that threaten existing business practices and technologies do not come from existing competitors or even from within traditional industries. A new technology that can substitute for an existing technology at a lower cost and provide higher quality can change the very basis for competition in an industry. Managers therefore need to actively scan the periphery for new product ideas because this is where breakthrough innovations will be found.[19] Consider, for example, the impact of Internet technology on the personal computer software industry. Microsoft Corporation had ignored the developing Internet technology during the 1980s and early 1990s while battling successfully with IBM, Lotus, and WordPerfect to dominate operating system software via Windows 95 as well as word processing and spreadsheet programs via Microsoft Office. Ironically, just as Microsoft introduced its new Windows 95 operating system, newcomer Netscape used Java applets in its user-friendly, graphically oriented browser program with the potential to make operating systems unnecessary. By the time Microsoft realized the significance of this threat, Netscape had already established itself as the industry standard for browsers. Microsoft was forced to spend huge amounts of time and resources trying to catch up to Netscape's dominant market share with its own Internet Explorer browser.

One way to learn about new technological developments in an industry is to locate part of a company's R&D or manufacturing in those locations making a strong impact on product development. Large multinational corporations (MNCs) undertake between 5% and 25% of their R&D outside their home country.[20] For example, automobile companies like to have design centers in southern California and in Italy, key areas for automotive styling. Software companies throughout the world know that they must have a programming presence in California's Silicon Valley if they are to compete on the leading edge of technology. The same is true of the semiconductor industry in terms of manufacturing.[21]

Impact of Stakeholders on Innovation

A company should look to its stakeholders, especially its customers, suppliers, and distributors, for sources of product and service improvements. These groups of people have the most to gain from innovative new products or services. Under certain circumstances, they may propose new directions for product development. Some of the methods of gathering information from key stakeholders are using lead users, market research, and new product experimentation.

Lead Users. Research by Von Hippel indicates that customers are a key source of innovation in many industries. For example, 77% of the innovations developed in the scientific instruments industry came from the users of the products. Suppliers are often important sources as well. Suppliers accounted for 36% of innovations in the thermoplastics industry, according to Von Hippel.[22] One way to commercialize a new technology is through early and in-depth involvement with a firm's customers in a process called co-development.[23] This type of customer is called a "lead user."

Von Hipple proposes that companies should look to lead users for help in product development, especially in high-technology industries where things move so quickly that a product is becoming obsolete by the time it arrives on the market. These **lead users** are "companies, organizations, or individuals that are well ahead of market trends and have needs that go far beyond those of the average user."[24] They are the first to adopt a product because they benefit significantly from its use—even if it is not fully developed. At Dow Chemical, for example, scientists solicit feedback from customers before developing a new product in the lab. Once the product is ready for commercialization, Dow gives its lead users the first opportunity to use the product and suggest further development.[25]

At 3M, a product development team in 3M's Medical Surgical Markets Division was charged with creating a breakthrough in the area of surgical drapes—the material that prevents infections from spreading during surgery. At the time, 3M dominated the market but had not developed a new product improvement in almost a decade. After spending six weeks learning about the cause and prevention of infections, the project team spent six more weeks investigating trends in infection control. The team then worked to identify lead users—doctors in developing nations and veterinarians who couldn't afford the current expensive drapes. The team invited several lead users to a 2½-day workshop focused on "Can we find a revolutionary, low-cost approach to infection control?" The workshop generated concepts for six new product lines and a radical new approach to infection control. The team chose the three strongest concepts for presentation to senior management. 3M has successfully applied the lead user method in 8 of its 55 divisions.

Lead user teams are typically composed of four to six people from marketing and technical departments, with one person serving as project leader. Team members usually spend 12 to 15 hours per week on the project for its duration. For planning purposes, a team should allow four to six weeks for each phase and four to six months for the entire project. The four phases of the lead user process are:

1. **Lay the Foundation:** Identify target markets and the type and level of innovations desired.
2. **Determine the Trends:** Research the field and talk with experts who have a broad view of emerging technologies and leading-edge applications.

3. **Identify Lead Users:** Talk with users at the leading edge of the target and related markets to understand their needs.
4. **Develop the Breakthrough:** Host a two- to three-day workshop with several lead users and a half-dozen marketing and technical people. Participants first work in small groups and then as a whole to design the final concepts that fit the company's and the users' needs.[26]

Market Research. A more traditional method of obtaining new product ideas is to use **market research** to survey current users regarding what they would like in a new product. This method has been successfully used by companies, such as P&G, to identify consumer preferences. It is especially useful in directing incremental improvements to existing products. For example, the auto maker BMW solicits suggestions from BMW owners to improve its current offerings and to obtain ideas for new products.

Market research may not, however, necessarily provide the information needed for truly innovative products or services (radical innovation). According to Sony executive Kozo Ohsone, "When you introduce products that have never been invented before, what good is market research?" For example, Hal Sperlich took the concept of the minivan from Ford to Chrysler when Ford refused to develop the concept. According to Sperlich,

> *[Ford] lacked confidence that a market existed because the product didn't exist. The auto industry places great value on historical studies of market segments. Well, we couldn't prove there was a market for the minivan because there was no historical segment to cite. In Detroit most product-development dollars are spent on modest improvements to existing products, and most market research money is spent on studying what customers like among available products. In ten years of developing the minivan we never once got a letter from a housewife asking us to invent one. To the skeptics, that proved there wasn't a market out there.*[27]

A heavy emphasis on being customer driven could actually prevent companies from developing innovative new products. A study of the impact of technological discontinuity (explained in **Chapter 5**) in various industries revealed that the leading firms failed to switch to the new technology not because management was ignorant of the new development but because they listened too closely to their current customers. In all of these firms, a key task of management was to decide which of the many product and development programs continually being proposed to them should receive financial resources. The criterion used for the decision was the total return perceived in each project, adjusted by the perceived riskiness of the project. Projects targeted at the known needs of key customers in established markets consistently won the most resources. Sophisticated systems for planning and compensation favored this type of project every time. As a result, the leading companies continued to use the established technology to make the products its current customers demanded, allowing smaller entrepreneurial competitors to develop the new, more risky technology.[28]

Because the market for the innovative products based on the new technology was fairly small at first, new ventures had time to fine-tune product design, build sufficient manufacturing capacity, and establish the product as the industry standard (as Netscape did with its Internet browser). As the marketplace began to embrace the new standard, the customers of the leading companies began to ask for products based on the new technology. Although some established manufacturers were able to defend their market share positions through aggressive product development and marketing activity (as Microsoft did against Netscape), many firms, finding that the new entrants had developed insurmountable advantages in manufacturing cost and design experience, were forced out of the market. Even the established manufacturers that converted to the new technology were unable to win a significant share of the new market.[29]

New Product Experimentation and Acquisition. Instead of using lead users or market research to test the potential of innovative products, some successful companies are using speed and flexibility to gain market information. These companies have developed their products by probing potential markets with early versions of the products, learning from the probes, and probing again.[30] For example, Seiko's only market research is surprisingly simple. The company introduces hundreds of new models of watches into the marketplace. It makes more of the models that sell; it drops those that don't.

The consulting firm Arthur D. Little found that the use of standard market research techniques has resulted in a success rate of only 8% for new cereals—92% of all new cereals fail. As a result, innovative firms, such as Keebler and the leading cereal makers, are reducing their expenditures for market research and working to reduce the cost of launching new products by making their manufacturing processes more flexible.[31]

Microsoft has successfully followed a strategy of monitoring the competition for new developments. It follows an *embrace and extend* strategy of imitating new products developed by pioneers, refining them, and outmarketing the competition. (This approach is nothing new. P&G used Mr. Clean to defeat the newly introduced Lestoil.) Microsoft's distinctive competency is its ability to change directions and adjust priorities when the market changes.[32] Another approach to new product development is to simply acquire new technology from others. Cisco Systems, for example, kept itself on the cutting edge of making and selling Internet routers by buying a number of high-tech startups. In effect, Cisco outsourced its R&D to California's venture capitalists.[33]

Internal Scanning

In addition to scanning the external environment, strategists should also assess their company's ability to innovate effectively by asking the following questions:

1. Has the company developed the resources needed to try new ideas?
2. Do the managers allow experimentation with new products or services?
3. Does the corporation encourage risk-taking and tolerate mistakes?
4. Are people more concerned with new ideas or with defending their turf?
5. Is it easy to form autonomous project teams?[34]

In addition to answering these questions, strategists should assess how well company resources are internally allocated and evaluate the organization's ability to develop and transfer new technology in a timely manner into the generation of innovative products and services. These issues are important, given that it takes on average seven ideas to generate a new commercial product, according to the Product and Development Management Association.[35]

Resource Allocation Issues

A company must make available the resources necessary for effective research and development. Research indicates that a company's **R&D intensity** (its spending on R&D as a percentage of sales revenue) is a principal means of gaining market share in global competition.[36] The amount of money spent on R&D often varies by industry. For example, the computer software and drug industries spend an average of 11% to 13% of their sales revenue for R&D. Others, such as the food and the containers and packaging industries, spend less than 1%. A good rule of thumb for R&D spending is that a corporation should spend at a "normal" rate for that particular industry, unless its competitive strategy dictates otherwise.[37] Research indicates that consistency in R&D strategy and resource allocation across lines of business improves corporate performance by enabling the firm to better develop synergies among product lines and business units.[38]

Simply spending money on R&D or new projects does not, however, guarantee useful results. One study found that although large firms spent almost twice as much per R&D patent than did smaller firms, the smaller firms used more of their patents. The innovation rate of small businesses was 322 innovations per million employees versus 225 per million for large companies.[39] A recent study by the U.S. Small Business Administration reported that patents obtained by small firms were twice as likely to be among the top 1% of the most widely cited patents as patents obtained by large firms.[40] One explanation for this phenomenon is that large (especially older) firms tend to spend development money on extensions of their current products (incremental innovation) or to increase the efficiency of existing performance.[41] In contrast, small firms tend to apply technology to improving effectiveness through developing completely new products (radical innovation).[42] Other studies reveal that the maximum innovator in various industries often was the middle-sized firm. These firms were generally more effective and efficient than others in technology transfer. Very small firms often do not have sufficient resources to exploit new concepts (unless supported by venture capitalists with deep pockets), whereas the bureaucracy present in large firms rewards consistency over creativity.[43] From these studies, Hitt, Hoskisson, and Harrison propose the existence of an inverted U-shaped relationship between size and innovation. According to Hitt et al., "This suggests that organizations are flexible and responsive up to some threshold size but encounter inertia after that point."[44]

In some cases, firms waste their R&D spending. For example, between 1950 and 1979, the U.S. steel industry spent 20% more on plant maintenance and upgrading for each ton of production capacity added or replaced than did the Japanese steel industry. Nevertheless, the top management of U.S. steel firms failed to recognize and adopt two breakthroughs in steelmaking—the basic oxygen furnace and continuous casting. Their hesitancy to adopt new technology caused them to lose the world steel market.[45]

Time-to-Market Issues

In addition to money, another important consideration in the effective management of R&D is **time to market**. During the 1980s, the time from inception to profitability of a specific R&D program was generally accepted to be 7 to 11 years. According to Karlheinz Kaske, CEO of Siemens AG, however, the time available to complete the cycle is getting shorter. Companies no longer can assume that competitors will allow them the number of years needed to recoup their investment. In the past, Kaske says, "ten to fifteen years went by before old products were replaced by new ones . . . now, it takes only four or five years."[46] Time to market is an important issue because 60% of patented innovations are generally imitated within four years at 65% of the cost of innovation.[47] In the 1980s, Japanese auto manufacturers gained incredible competitive advantage over U.S. manufacturers by reducing new products' time to market to only three years. (U.S. auto companies needed five years.)[48]

12.3 Strategy Formulation

R&D strategy deals not only with the decision to be a leader or a follower in terms of technology and market entry (discussed in **Chapter 8**, in the R&D strategy section) but also with the source of the technology. Should a company develop its own technology or purchase it from others? The strategy also takes into account a company's particular mix of basic versus applied and product versus process R&D (discussed in **Chapter 5**). The particular mix should suit the level of industry development and the firm's particular corporate and business strategies.

Product Versus Process R&D

As illustrated in **Figure 12–1**, the proportion of product and process R&D tends to vary as a product moves along its life cycle. In the early stages, **product innovations** are most important because the product's physical attributes and capabilities most affect financial performance. Later, **process innovations** such as improved manufacturing facilities, increasing

Figure 12–1
Product and Process R&D in the Innovation Life Cycle

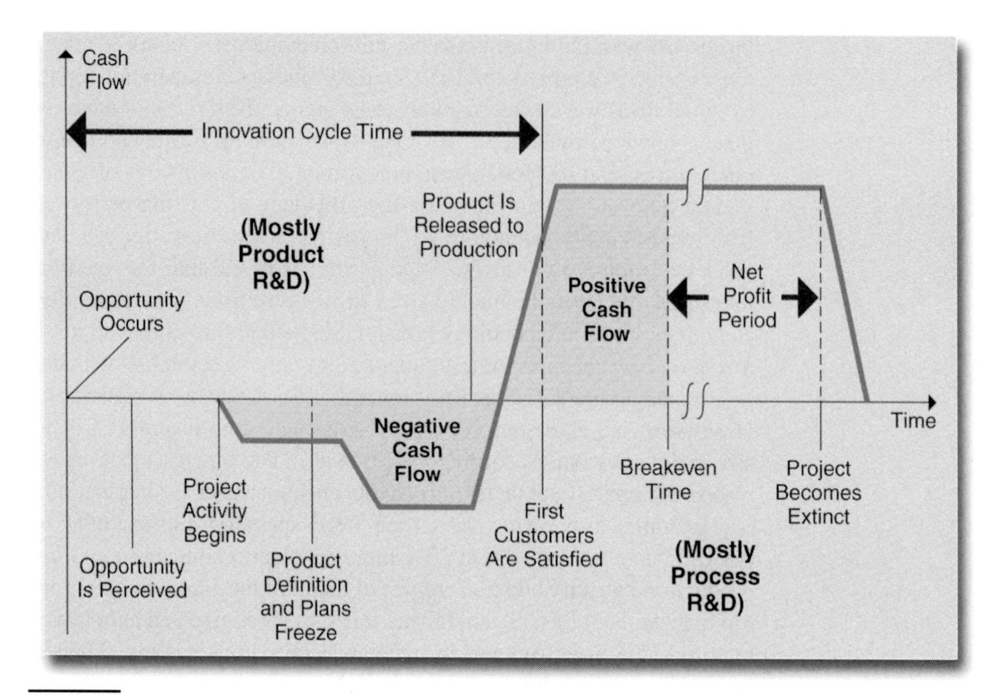

Source: Adapted from M. L. Patterson, "Lessons from the Assembly Line," Journal of Business Strategy *(May/June 1993), p. 43. Republished with permission, Emerald Group Publishing Limited.*

product quality, and faster distribution become important to maintaining the product's economic returns. Generally, product R&D has been key to achieving differentiation strategies, whereas process R&D has been at the core of successful cost-leadership strategies.

Historically, U.S. corporations have not been as skillful at process innovations as have German and Japanese companies. The primary reason has been a function of the amount of money invested in each form of R&D. U.S. firms spend, on the average, 70% of their R&D budgets on product R&D and only 30% on process R&D; German firms, 50% on each form; and Japanese firms, 30% on product and 70% on process R&D.[49] The traditionally heavy emphasis by U.S. major home appliance manufacturers on process R&D is one reason they have such a strong position in the North American market. The emphasis on quality and durability, coupled with a reluctance to make major design changes simply for the sake of change, has resulted in products with an average life expectancy of 20 years for refrigerators and 15 years for washers and dryers. Even though quality has improved significantly over the past 20 years, the average washer, dryer, and refrigerator cost no more than they did 20 years ago and yet last almost twice as long.

To be competitive, companies must find the proper mix of product and process R&D. Research indicates that too much emphasis by a firm on efficiency-oriented process R&D can drive out product R&D.[50] Even though the key to the success of the U.S. major home appliance industry has been its emphasis on process innovation, significant product innovation is more likely to result in a first-mover advantage.[51] For example, Maytag's introduction of the Neptune, a new type of front-loading washing machine, gave it a significant marketing advantage even after Whirlpool and General Electric introduced their versions of the new product.

Technology Sourcing

Technology sourcing, typically a make-or-buy decision, can be important in a firm's R&D strategy. Although in-house R&D has traditionally been an important source of technical knowledge (resulting in valuable patents) for companies, firms can also tap the R&D capabilities of competitors, suppliers, and other organizations through contractual agreements (such as licensing, R&D agreements, and joint ventures) or acquisitions. Each approach has advantages and disadvantages.[52] One example of technology acquisition was Motorola's purchase in 2004 of MeshNetworks, Inc., to obtain a Wi-Fi technology needed in Motorola's government contracting business.[53] When technological cycles were longer, a company was more likely to choose an independent R&D strategy not only because it gave the firm a longer lead time before competitors copied it but also because it was more profitable in the long run. In today's world of shorter innovation life cycles and global competition, a company may no longer have the luxury of waiting to reap a long-term profit.

Firms that are unable to finance alone the huge costs of developing a new technology may coordinate their R&D with other firms through a **strategic R&D alliance**. By the 1990s, more than 150 cooperative alliances involving 1,000 companies were operating in the United States, and many more were operating throughout Europe and Asia.[54] These alliances can be (1) joint programs or contracts to develop a new technology, (2) joint ventures establishing a separate company to take a new product to market, or (3) minority investments in innovative firms wherein the innovator obtains needed capital and the investor obtains access to valuable research. For example, the biotech company Amgen uses strategic alliances as part of its growth strategy. It uses its collegial corporate culture to court entrepreneurial ventures that are normally shy of big companies. "We're trying to have a small company feel," explains Amgen CEO Kevin Sharer. By 2003, Amgen had formed partnerships with 100 companies. It developed its latest drug, Cinacalcet, a treatment for a kidney-related condition called secondary hyperparathyroidism, from a license with one of its partners, NPS Pharmaceuticals.[55]

When should a company buy or license technology from others instead of developing it internally? Following the resource-based view of the firm discussed in **Chapter 5**, a company should buy technologies that are commonly available but make (and protect) those that are rare, valuable, and hard to imitate and that have no close substitutes. In addition, outsourcing technology may be appropriate when:

- The technology is of low significance to competitive advantage.
- The supplier has proprietary technology.
- The supplier's technology is better and/or cheaper and reasonably easy to integrate into the current system.
- The company's strategy is based on system design, marketing, distribution, and service—not on development and manufacturing.
- The technology development process requires special expertise.
- The technology development process requires new people and new resources.[56]

Licensing technology to other companies may be an excellent R&D strategy—especially in a turbulent high-tech environment where being the first firm to establish the standard dominant design may bring competitive advantage.[57] Matsushita successfully used this strategy to overcome the technologically superior Sony beta format with the VHS format for VCRs. When Matsushita freely licensed the VHS format to all other VCR makers, Sony was relegated to a minority position in the market, and Matsushita (through its Panasonic brand) became a dominant VCR manufacturer.[58] Licensing enables a company to enter foreign markets that might not otherwise be possible due to high tariffs, import prohibitions and restrictions, or the high cost and risk of investing in foreign factories. Licensing is an alternative international strategy in situations when exports or local production through a subsidiary or joint venture are impracticable.[59]

A serious issue in the sourcing of new technology is the use of another company's intellectual property without paying for it. **Intellectual property** is special knowledge used in a new product or process developed by a company for its own use and is usually protected by a patent, copyright, trademark, or trade secret. It can be licensed to another firm for a fee. As mentioned earlier, making and selling an imitation of someone else's product (such as Nike shoes) is considered to be piracy. Both the recording industry and the motion picture industry are extremely threatened by the illegal duplication of their products.

The number of patents being issued in the United States is growing at 6% annually and running at nearly twice the level of a decade ago. Similar growth is happening elsewhere in the world. Patents are global. Although a U.S. patent does not function outside the United States, the same idea cannot in theory be patented anywhere else.[60] Countries joining the World Trade Organization (WTO) must agree to Trips (trade-related aspects of intellectual property rights), an international agreement that establishes minimum standards for the legal protection of intellectual property.[61] Because China has recently joined the WTO, a number of companies are attempting to enforce their patents in that country. See the **GLOBAL ISSUE** feature for an example of a Chinese company that was sued by Cisco Systems for intellectual property violations.

Importance of Technological Competence

Firms that emphasize growth through acquisitions over internal development tend to be less innovative than others in the long run.[62] Research suggests that companies must have at least a minimal R&D capability if they are to correctly assess the value of technology developed by others. This is called a company's "absorptive capacity" and is a valuable by-product of rou-

GLOBAL ISSUE

Use of Intellectual Property at Huawei Technologies

Xu Danhua, chief of the pre-research department at Huawei Technologies, works to develop products for digital homes. He is using technologies to link PCs, TVs, stereos, and other devices to the Internet and to each other throughout a building or an apartment. "I like to face the challenges of new technology," says Xu. "Huawei is a company that very quickly takes on the trends of the industry." This is a relatively new direction for a company that until recently was a low-cost manufacturer of equipment developed elsewhere. Huawei intends to sell sophisticated electronic products to international customers. According to the company's head of R&D, "Huawei is a global company with global markets in mind." To take advantage of skilled people in other parts of the world, it is building development centers in Europe, India, and the United States.

Cisco Systems, a maker of networking equipment, launched a lawsuit against Huawei in December 2002, alleging patent and copyright infringement and asking for an injunction to remove certain Huawei products from the market. Cisco had already lined up support from the Chinese government. Having just joined the World Trade Organization (WTO) in 2001, China was eager to shed its image as the world's leading haven for pirated goods. According to an official with China's Ministry of Information Industry, "The government will not give any political help to Huawei."

Huawei protested its innocence but soon announced a global joint venture with Cisco's rival, 3Com Corporation. The venture provides Huawei with 3Com's distribution system, along with a strong base in the United States. When Cisco's Executive Vice President, Charles Giancarlo, was informed of the Huawei–3Com alliance, he said, "I was so mad I couldn't speak for three days." Keeping up the pressure, Cisco filed another suit in east Texas, near Huawei's Dallas office. Huawei typically undersells Western rivals by 30% or more and has a reputation for selling products that look and feel like Cisco's products. It was a major competitor in DSL equipment. "Huawei is a threat to everyone," says Christine Heckart, Vice President for Marketing at Juniper Networks. "They bid on everything that moves."

For Huawei, the lawsuits were part of a painful and risky transition from a position of cheap labor, government support, and lax intellectual property protection in China to the tougher rules of global markets. Eager to shed its "me-too" reputation, Huawei agreed to settle the lawsuit with Cisco Systems in 2004.

Sources: Summarized from P. Burrows and B. Einhorn, "Cisco: In Hot Pursuit of a Chinese Rival," *Business Week* (May 19, 2003), pp. 62–63, and B. Einhorn, M. Kripalani, and J. Ewing, "Huawei: More Than a Local Hero," *Business Week* (October 11, 2004), pp. 180–184.

tine in-house R&D activity.[63] **Absorptive capacity** is a firm's ability to recognize, assimilate, and utilize new external knowledge.[64] Firms that have absorptive capacity are able to use knowledge obtained externally to increase the productivity of their research expenditures.[65] Further, without this capacity, firms could become locked out in their ability to assimilate the technology at a later time. Therefore, a company's absorptive capacity is a dynamic capability that influences the nature and sustainability of that company's competitive advantage.[66]

A corporation that purchases an innovative technology must have the **technological competence** to make good use of it. Some companies that introduce the latest technology into their processes do not adequately assess the competence of their people to handle it. For example, a survey conducted in the United Kingdom in the 1980s found that 44% of all companies that started to use robots met with initial failure, and that 22% of those firms abandoned the use of robots altogether, mainly because of inadequate technological knowledge and skills.[67] One U.S. company built a new plant equipped with computer-integrated manufacturing and statistical process controls, but the employees could not operate the equipment because 25% of them were illiterate.[68]

Categories of Innovation

Innovation can range from incremental to radical. As shown in **Figure 12–2**, a corporation's *capabilities* (existing or new) interact with its *strategic scope* (limited or unlimited) to form four basic categories of innovation. A corporation may emphasize one of these categories or operate in all of them.[69]

Quadrant 1: Improving Core Businesses. This type of innovation focuses on incremental innovations that can be developed rapidly and inexpensively. It includes line extensions and more convenient packaging and is often a part of a horizontal growth strategy. Its potential weakness is market myopia—its emphasis on current products and customers. As illustrated earlier in this chapter, PepsiCo is the master of this type of innovation.

Quadrant 2: Exploiting Strategic Advantages. This type of innovation focuses on taking existing brands and product lines to new customers and markets without requiring major change in current capabilities. It means moving beyond the company's current strategic scope

Figure 12–2
Categories of Innovation

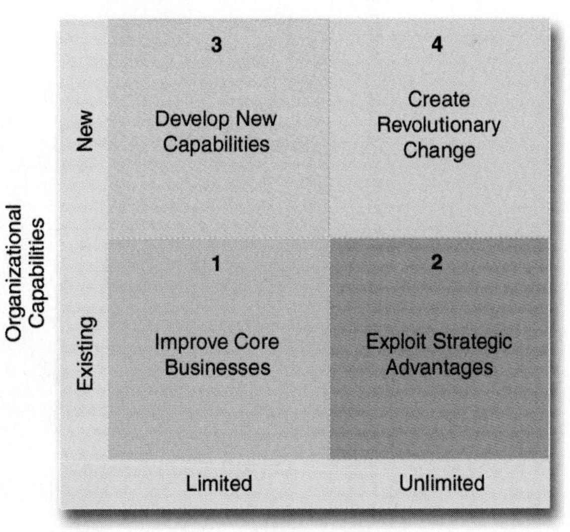

Source: Adapted from C. Hickman and C. Raia, "Incubating Innovation," Journal of Business Strategy *(May/June 2002), p. 15. Reprinted with permission, Emerald Group Publishing Limited.*

by leveraging capabilities by spreading them across a broader range of markets and customers via concentric diversification. Its potential weakness is the relative ease with which competitors with similar capabilities can imitate the innovation. Coleman and Toro are examples of companies that have leveraged their capabilities in camping (Coleman) and lawn (Toro) equipment to move into new products and new markets, such as Coleman gas grills and Toro snow blowers.

Quadrant 3: Developing New Capabilities. This type of innovation focuses on deepening customer satisfaction and loyalty to the brand or product line by adding new organizational capabilities without introducing major changes in strategic scope. The company may develop or purchase new technologies, talents, or businesses to better serve the firm's current scope of customers and markets. It may involve a vertical growth strategy. Its potential weakness is the investment cost and implementation time. Microsoft follows an embrace-and-extend policy to either acquire or imitate a new product in order to offer it to its current customers in the next version of Windows or Office software.

Quadrant 4: Creating Revolutionary Change. This type of innovation focuses on radical innovations that transcend current product lines or brands to make fundamental changes in both its strategic scope and its capabilities. This can mean a new business model and a revolutionary new future for the company. Its potential weakness is a high risk of failure. Sony

Figure 12–3 Product/Market Evolution Portfolio Matrix

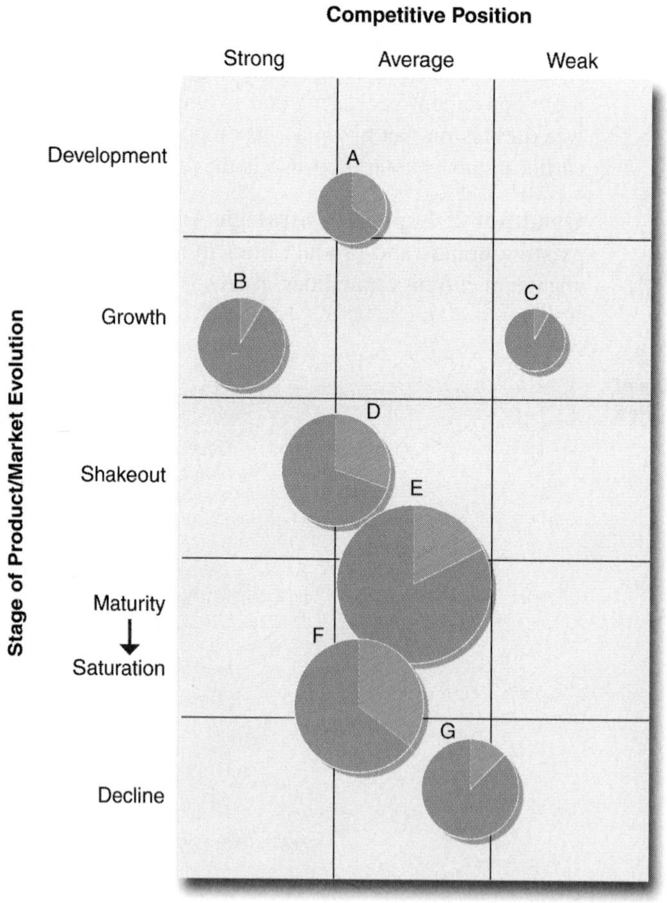

Source: C. W. Hofer and D. Schendel, Strategy Formulation: Analytical Concepts *(St. Paul, MN: West Publishing Co., 1978), p. 34. From C. W. Hofer, "Conceptual Constructs for Formulating Corporate and Business Strategies" (Dover, MA: Case Publishing), no. BP-0041, p. 3. Copyright © 1977 by Charles W. Hofer. Reprinted by permission.*

Corporation is the master of radical innovation. Its pioneering products, such as the Walkman, the Airboard, and the robo-pet Aibo, introduce whole new product categories.

Product Portfolio

Developed by Hofer and based on the product life cycle, the 15-cell **product/market evolution matrix** (shown in **Figure 12–3**) depicts the types of developing products that cannot be easily shown on other portfolio matrixes. Products are plotted in terms of their competitive positions and their stages of product/market evolution. As on the GE Business Screen, the circles represent the sizes of the industries involved, and the pie wedges represent the market shares of the firm's business product lines. Present and future matrixes can be developed to identify strategic issues. In response to **Figure 12–3**, for example, we could ask why Product B does not have a greater share of the market, given its strong competitive position. We could also ask why the company has only one product in the developmental stage. A limitation of this matrix is that the product life cycle does not always hold for every product. Many products, for example, do not inevitably fall into decline but (like Tide detergent and Colgate toothpaste) are revitalized and put back on a growth track.

12.4 Strategy Implementation

If a corporation decides to develop innovations internally, it must make sure that its structure and culture are suitable for such a strategy. It must make sufficient resources available for new products, provide collaborative structures and processes, and incorporate innovation into its overall corporate strategy.[70] It must ensure that its R&D operations are managed appropriately. It must establish procedures to support all six **stages of new product development**. (See **Table 12–2**.) If, like most large corporations, the culture is too bureaucratic and rigid to support entrepreneurial projects, top management must reorganize so that innovative projects can be free to develop.

Developing an Innovative Entrepreneurial Culture

To create a more innovative corporation, top management must develop an entrepreneurial culture—one that is open to the transfer of new technology into company activities and products and services. The company must be flexible and accepting of change. It should include a willingness to withstand a certain percentage of product failures on the way to success. It should be able to manage small, incremental innovations in existing products as well

TABLE 12–2 SIX STAGES OF NEW PRODUCT DEVELOPMENT

1. **Idea Generation.** New product concepts are identified and refined.
2. **Concept Evaluation.** Screening techniques are used to determine the concept's validity and market opportunity. Preliminary market research is conducted, and a strategy is developed. A business plan is developed to present to management.
3. **Preliminary Design.** A new venture team is formed to prepare desired product specifications.
4. **Prototype Build and Test.** A functioning model of the product is built and subjected to numerous tests.
5. **Final Design and Pilot Production.** Final product and process designs are developed to produce small numbers of the product for use in test marketing. Suggestions from the users are fed back to the design team for possible inclusion in the final product.
6. **New Business Development.** The entire company is energized to launch the product.

Source: Managing Corporate Culture, Innovation, and Intrapreneurship, Howard W. Oden. Copyright © 1997 by Quorum Books. Reproduced with permission of Greenwood Publishing, Inc., Westport, CT.

as radical advances that may alter the basis for competition in an industry.[71] Largeness is not a disadvantage. In his classic book *Diffusion of Innovations*, Rogers reveals that innovative organizations tend to have the following characteristics:

- Positive attitude toward change
- Decentralized decision making
- Complexity
- Informal structure
- Interconnectedness
- Organizational slack (unused resources)
- Large size
- System openness[72]

Such a culture has been noted in 3M Corporation and Texas Instruments, among others. R&D in these companies is managed quite differently from traditional methods. First, employees are dedicated to a particular project outcome rather than to innovation in general. Second, employees are often responsible for all functional activities and for all phases of the innovation process. Time is allowed to be sacrificed from regular duties to spend on innovative ideas. If the ideas are feasible, employees are temporarily reassigned to help develop them. These people may become project champions who fight for resources to make the project a success. Third, these internal ventures are often separated from the rest of the company to provide them with greater independence, freedom for short-term pressures, different rewards, improved visibility, and access to key decision makers.[73]

The innovative process often involves individuals at different organizational levels who fulfill three different types of entrepreneurial roles: product champion, sponsor, and orchestrator. A **product champion** is a person who generates a new idea and supports it through many organizational obstacles. A **sponsor** is usually a department manager who recognizes the value of the idea, helps obtain funding to develop the innovation, and facilitates its implementation. An **orchestrator** is someone in top management who articulates the need for innovation, provides funding for innovating activities, creates incentives for middle managers to sponsor new ideas, and protects idea/product champions from suspicious or jealous executives. Unless all these roles are present in a company, major innovations are unlikely to occur.[74]

Companies are finding that one way to overcome the barriers to successful product innovation is by using multifunctional teams with significant autonomy dedicated to a project. In a survey of 701 companies from Europe, the United States, and Japan, 85% of the respondents have used this approach, with 62% rating it as successful.[75] Research reveals that cross-functional teams are best for designing and developing innovative new products, whereas the more traditional bureaucratic structures seem to be best for developing modifications to existing products, line extensions, and me-too products.[76] Chrysler Corporation was able to reduce the development time for new vehicles by 40% by using cross-functional teams and by developing a partnership approach to new projects.[77] International Specialty Products, a maker of polymers, used "product express" teams composed of chemists and representatives from manufacturing and engineering to cut development time in half. "Instead of passing a baton, we bring everyone into the commercialization process at the same time," explained John Tancredi, vice president for R&D. "We are moving laterally, like rugby players, instead of like runners in a relay race."[78]

Organizing for Innovation: Corporate Entrepreneurship

Corporate entrepreneurship (also called intrapreneurship) is defined by Guth and Ginsberg as "the birth of new businesses within existing organizations, that is, internal innovation or venturing; and the transformation of organizations through renewal of the key ideas on which they are

Figure 12–4
Organizational Designs for Corporate Entrepreneurship

Operational Relatedness \ Strategic Importance	Very Important	Uncertain	Not Important
Unrelated	3 Special Business Units	6 Independent Business Units	9 Complete Spin-off
Partly Related	2 New Product Business Department	5 New Venture Division	8 Contracting
Strongly Related	1 Direct Integration	4 Micro New Ventures Department	7 Nurturing and Contracting

Source: Reprinted from R. A. Burgelman, "Designs for Corporate Entrepreneurship in Established Firms." Copyright © 1984, by the Regents of the University of California. Reprinted from the California Management Review, *Vol. 26, No. 3. By permission of The Regents. All rights reserved.*

built, that is, strategic renewal."[79] A large corporation that wants to encourage innovation and creativity within its firm must choose a structure that will give the new business unit an appropriate amount of freedom while maintaining some degree of control at headquarters. Research reveals that corporate entrepreneurship has a positive impact on a company's financial performance.[80]

Burgelman proposes (see **Figure 12–4**) that the use of a particular organizational design should be determined by (1) the strategic importance of the new business to the corporation and (2) the relatedness of the unit's operations to those of the corporation.[81] The combination of these two factors results in nine organizational designs for corporate entrepreneurship:

1. **Direct Integration:** A new business with a great deal of strategic importance and operational relatedness must be a part of the corporation's mainstream. Product champions—people who are respected by others in the corporation and who know how to work the system—are needed to manage these projects. Janiece Webb championed the incorporation of Internet web browsers in Motorola's mobile phones and is now in charge of Motorola's Personal Networks Group. Because Webb's unit only makes software, she works with other divisions to shape their "product maps," which show what they hope to bring to market and when.[82]
2. **New Product Business Department:** A new business with a great deal of strategic importance and partial operational relatedness should be a separate department, organized around an entrepreneurial project in the division where skills and capabilities can be shared. Maytag Corporation did this when it built a new plant near its current Newton, Iowa, washer plant to manufacture the wholly new Neptune line of energy- and water-efficient front-loading washing machines.
3. **Special Business Units:** A new business with a great deal of strategic importance and low operational relatedness should be a special new business unit with specific objectives and time horizons. Teradyne tried this with a new product called Integra. The new product was based on a new, low-cost technology—something that might be good enough in a few years to replace Teradyne's current technology. Because the technology wasn't good enough for Teradyne's high-end applications, Teradyne's management treated

Integra like an entrepreneurial venture. Integra's general manager, Marc Levine, reported to a board of directors composed of Teradyne's top executives. Instead of a budget, Levine had a business plan and venture capital (from Teradyne). This governance structure allowed Integra to operate autonomously by recruiting and purchasing from outside the company. According to Levine, "The idea was to think of this as a business from the start, not an R&D project. The board setup allows more of a coaching attitude." Says Teradyne's Vice President, Edward Rogas, "A division is always pressed to do the next logical thing—and make it compatible with the existing line. We told Marc: Be aggressive on the technology; do something no one else has done."[83]

4. **Micro New Ventures Department:** A new business with uncertain strategic importance and high operational relatedness should be a peripheral project that is likely to emerge in the operating divisions on a continuous basis. Each division thus has its own new ventures department. Xerox Corporation, for example, uses its SBUs to generate and nurture new ideas. Small product-synthesis teams within each SBU test the feasibility of new ideas. Those concepts receiving a "go" are managed by an SBU product-delivery team, headed by a chief engineer, that takes the prototype from development through manufacturing.
5. **New Venture Division:** A new business with uncertain strategic importance that is only partly related to present corporate operations belongs in a new venture division. It brings together projects that either exist in various parts of the corporation or can be acquired externally; sizable new businesses are built. Lucent established an internal venture capital operation to fund the ideas of researchers from its Bell Labs R&D unit that didn't fit into existing business units. One new venture, Visual Insights, sells software that can detect billing fraud by analyzing patterns in large amounts of data. Another, Veridicom, does fingerprint authentication.[84]
6. **Independent Business Units:** Uncertain strategic importance coupled with no relationship to present corporate activities can make external arrangements attractive. Hewlett-Packard established printers as an independent business unit in Boise, Idaho (far from its Palo Alto, California, headquarters), because management was unsure of the desktop printer's future. According to Richard Belluzzo, head of HP's printer business, "We had the resources of a big company, but we were off on our own. There wasn't central planning . . . , so we could make decisions really fast."[85]
7. **Nurturing and Contracting:** When an entrepreneurial proposal might not be important strategically to the corporation but is strongly related to present operations, top management might help the entrepreneurial unit to spin off from the corporation. This allows a friendly competitor, instead of one of the corporation's major rivals, to capture a small niche. Techtronix has extensively used this approach. Because of research revealing that related spin-offs tend to be poorer performers than nonrelated spin-offs (presumably owing to the loss of benefits enjoyed with a larger company), it is especially important that the parent company continue to support the development of the spun-off unit in this cell.[86]
8. **Contracting:** As the required capabilities and skills of the new business are less related to those of the corporation, the parent corporation may spin off the strategically unimportant unit yet keep some relationship through a contractual arrangement with the new firm. The connection is useful in case the new firm eventually develops something of value to the corporation. For example, B.F. Goodrich offered manufacturing rights plus a long-term purchasing agreement to a couple of its managers for a specific raw material Goodrich still used (in declining quantities) in its production process but no longer wanted to manufacture internally.
9. **Complete Spin-off:** If both the strategic importance and the operational relatedness of the new business are negligible, the corporation is likely to completely sell off the business to

STRATEGY HIGHLIGHT 12.2

How *Not* to Develop an Innovative Organization

In their book *Corporate Venturing*, researchers Block and MacMillan state that fostering an organizationwide commitment to new business development means more than paying lip service to innovation. They argue that a superficial commitment is almost worse than no commitment at all. They noted that unsuccessful companies tend to follow the following "rules of the road to certain failure":

1. Announce to the company that from now on, it is going to "become entrepreneurial."
2. Create a separate venture department charged with the job of developing new businesses. Hold no one else responsible.
3. Bring in a horde of consultants and self-professed experts to harangue management and employees at all levels to aggressively seek new business ideas.
4. Hold several one-day senior management retreats to discuss the need to become more entrepreneurial.
5. Make no further changes in management practices or the behavior of senior managers.

Source: Reprinted by permission of the Harvard Business School Press. From "Corporate Venturing: Creating New Business Within the Firm," by Z. Block and I. C. MacMillan, Boston MA, 1993, p. 36.

another firm or to the present employees in some form of Employee Stock Ownership Plan (ESOP). The corporation could also sell off the unit through a leveraged buyout (executives of the unit buy the unit from the parent company with money from a third source, to be repaid out of the unit's anticipated earnings). Because 3M wanted to focus its development money on areas with more profit potential, it decided to spin off its money-losing data storage and medical imaging divisions as a new company called Imation.

Organizing for innovation has become especially important for corporations that want to become more innovative but whose age and size have made them highly bureaucratic, with a culture that discourages creative thinking. These new structural designs for corporate entrepreneurship cannot work by themselves, however. The entrepreneurial units must also have the support of management and sufficient resources. They must also have employees who are risk-takers, willing to purchase an ownership interest in the new venture, and a corporate culture that supports new ventures. This is in contrast to corporations in which top management makes only a superficial commitment to innovation by demanding new ideas without providing the culture necessary to support their development. See **STRATEGY HIGHLIGHT 12.2** for how *not* to develop an innovative organization.

12.5 Evaluation and Control

For innovations to succeed, appropriate evaluation and control techniques must be used to ensure that the end product is what was originally planned. Some of these techniques are the stage-gate process and the house of quality. Appropriate measures are also needed to evaluate the effectiveness of the R&D process. Today's global information technology enables executives to continually assess performance as a product moves from the idea to the finished product stage.

Evaluation and Control Techniques

The **stage-gate process** is a method of managing new product development to increase the likelihood of launching new products quickly and successfully. The process is a series of steps to move products through the six stages of new product development listed in **Table 12–2**. A new concept cannot move beyond any stage until it has been evaluated thoroughly. The stage-gate process is used by companies such as IBM, 3M, General Motors, Corning, and P&G. Corning's managers believe that the process enables them to better estimate the potential payback of any project under consideration. They report that the stage-gate process reduces development time, allows identification of questionable projects, and increases the ratio of internally generated products that result in commercially successful products. It is especially useful for a major platform project (such as a line of new cars) that could be used to create multiple derivative products.[87]

The **house of quality** is another method of managing new product development.[88] Originally developed at Mitsubishi's Kobe shipyards, it is a tool to help project teams make important design decisions by getting them to think about what users want and how to get it to them most effectively.[89] It enhances communication and coordination among engineering, marketing, and manufacturing and ensures better product/customer fit. As shown in **Figure 12–5**, the house of quality is a matrix that maps customer requirements against product attributes. The first step is to identify product requirements and to weight their relative importance from the customer's perspective. For example, market research identified five attributes that customers want from a car door. Each of these are listed in the left column of **Figure 12–5**. The second step is to identify the engineering attributes in measurable terms. As shown in **Figure 12–5**, engineering lists four attributes of the door. In the third step, the team fills in the body of the central matrix (the body of the house). Each cell in the matrix indicates both the direction and the strength of a relationship between an engineering attribute and a customer requirement. **Figure 12–5** shows two negative signs between "easy to open" and "weight of the door," indicating that heavy doors are generally harder to open. The fourth step is to fill in the roof of the house by showing the interaction between design parameters. Thus, the negative sign between door weight and hinge stiffness indicates that a heavy door reduces the stiffness of the hinge. The final bit of information is depicted on the far right side of the house of quality and is a summary of the company's existing product compared with that of its competitors.

Figure 12–5 House of Quality

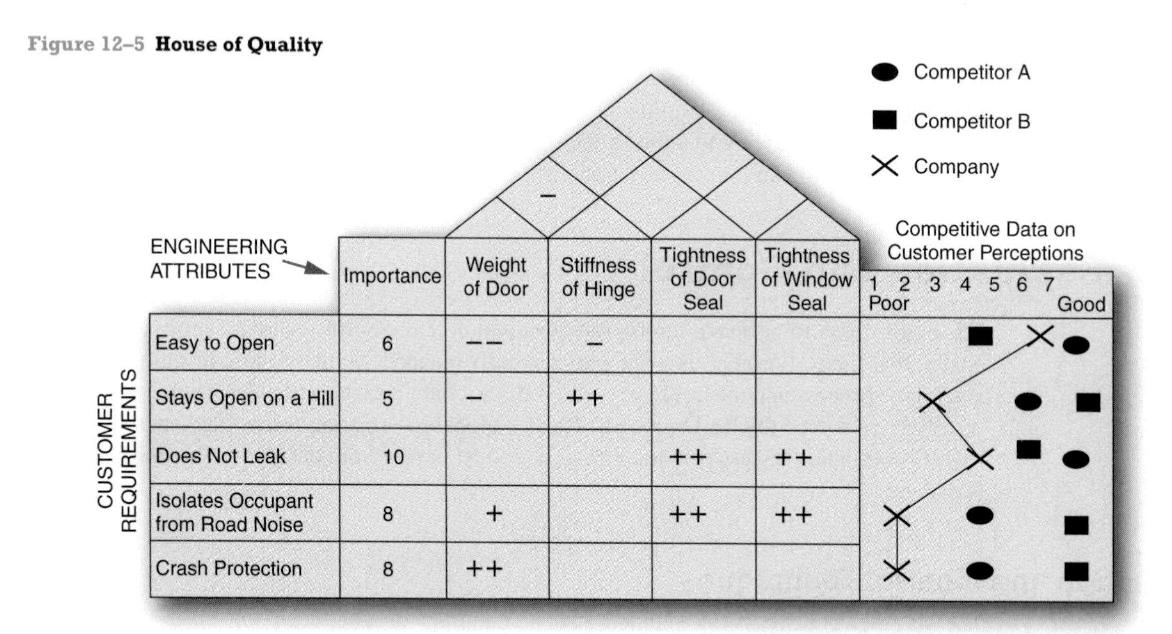

Source: ACADEMY OF MANAGEMENT JOURNAL *by M. A. SCHILLING, C. W. L. HILL. Copyright 1998 by ACAD OF MGMT. Reproduced with permission of ACAD OF MGMT in the format Textbook via Copyright Clearance Center.*

The house of quality provides a common framework within which the project team can interact. It makes the relationship between customer requirements and product attributes clear, emphasizes design trade-offs, highlights the competitive shortcomings of current products, and helps identify what steps should be taken to improve the design. It is very useful for cross-functional project teams and a good technique to ensure that both the customer's desires and production feasibility are included in the end result.[90]

Evaluation and Control Measures

Companies want to gain more productivity at a faster pace from their R&D activities. But how do we measure the effectiveness or efficiency of a company's R&D? This is a problem, given that a company shouldn't expect more than one in seven product ideas from basic research to make it to the marketplace. Some companies measure the proportion of their sales attributable to new products. For example, Hewlett-Packard measures how much of its revenues come from products introduced in the past three years.[91] At BellCore, the effectiveness of basic research is measured by how often the lab's research is cited in other scientists' work. This measure is compiled and published by the Institute for Scientific Information. Other companies judge the quality of research by counting how many patents they file annually.

Pittiglio Rabin Todd & McGrath (PRTM), a high-tech consulting firm, proposes an **index of R&D effectiveness**. The index is calculated by dividing the percentage of total revenue spent on R&D into new product profitability, which is expressed as a percentage. When this measure was applied to 45 large electronics manufacturers, only 9 companies scored 1.0 or higher, indicating that only 20% received a positive payback from their R&D spending. The top companies kept spending on marginal products to a minimum by running frequent checks on product versus market opportunities and canceling questionable products quickly. They

Table 12–3
Thirteen "Best Practices" for Improving R&D

1. Corporate and business unit strategies are well defined and clearly communicated.
2. Core technologies are defined and communicated to R&D.
3. Investments are made in developing multinational R&D capabilities to tap ideas throughout the world.
4. Funding for basic research comes from corporate sources to ensure a long-term focus; funding for development comes from business units to ensure accountability.
5. Basic and applied research are performed either at a central facility or at a small number of labs, each focused on a particular discipline of science or technology. Development work is usually performed at business unit sites.
6. Formal, cross-functional teams are created for basic, applied, and developmental projects.
7. Formal mechanisms exist for regular interaction among scientists, and between R&D and other functions.
8. Analytical tools are used for selecting projects as well as for ongoing project evaluation.
9. The transfer of technology to business units is the most important measure of R&D performance.
10. Effective measures of career development are in place at all levels of R&D.
11. Recruiting of new people is from diverse universities and from other companies when specific experience or skills are required that would take a long time to develop internally.
12. Some basic research is performed internally, but there are also many university and third-party relationships.
13. Formal mechanisms are used for monitoring external technological developments.

Source: From "Benchmarking R&D Productivity," I. Krause and J. Liu, 1993 © MCB University Press Limited. Republished with permission of Emerald Group Publishing Ltd.

also moved new products to market in half the time of the others. As a result, revenue growth among the top 20% of the companies was double the average of all 45 companies.[92]

A study of 15 multinational companies with successful R&D operations focused on three measures of R&D success: (1) improving technology transfer from R&D to business units, (2) accelerating time to market for new products and processes, and (3) institutionalizing cross-functional participation in R&D. The companies participated in basic, applied, and developmental research activities. The study revealed 13 **best practices** that all the companies followed.[93] Listed in **Table 12–3**, they provide a benchmark for a company's R&D activities.

12.6 Conclusion

The management of technology and innovation is crucial in today's fast-moving global environment. In every industry, the leading competitors are the innovators. The list of today's innovators, well-known companies such as Dell, Southwest Airlines, and Starbucks, lead their industry now but will eventually cede this advantage to other companies with even better ideas. The real challenge for strategic management is *sustained innovation*.[94]

Royal Dutch/Shell had traditionally been better at investing in large, low-risk projects yielding a modest return than in small, high-risk projects with the potential to transform the entire industry. In an effort to emphasize radical innovation, the company introduced a new approach called *GameChanger*.[95] Six teams of six people each meet every week at the Exploration and Production Divisions in Houston, Texas, and in Rijswijk, the Netherlands, to consider ideas that have been sent to them by e-mail. Out of these GameChanger teams have come four business initiatives for the corporation. One of them is Shell's new "Light Touch" oil-discovery method—a way of using lasers to sense hydrocarbon emissions released naturally in the air from underground reserves.

Increasing numbers of companies are using the Internet to stimulate and manage innovation. The concept is for small entrepreneurial teams to drive innovation at a rate never before experienced in large corporations. According to Christensen, author of *The Innovator's Dilemma*, "The trend now is to decentralize operations, to build idea factories, or idea markets. This is a way to bring the startup mentality inside."[96]

Companies such as Nortel Networks and P&G are adopting this "knowledge market" approach to innovation. Nortel allocates *phantom stock* to those who volunteer for special high-risk innovative projects. Nortel buys the stock as if the project were an IPO. Employees are paid in chits redeemable for cash once when the project is finished and again after it has been on the market about a year. P&G has created a Corporate New Ventures (CNV) unit as an autonomous idea lab with a mission of encouraging new ideas for products and putting them into speedy production. Ideas bubbling up from P&G's worldwide workforce of 110,000 people are routed to the CNV innovation panel via *My Idea*, a corporate collaboration network. Employees submitting winning ideas are rewarded with stock options. CNV teams then analyze the ideas by using the Internet to analyze markets, demographics, and cost information to learn whether the idea is a feasible opportunity. Once the team agrees on an idea, a project is launched within days. The CNV has the authority to tap any resources in the company to bring a product to market. So far, CNV has generated 58 products into the market. One of these, a cleaning product called Swiffer, was commercialized in just 10 months, less than half the usual time. Swiffer is a disposable cloth that generates static electricity to attract dust and dirt. The idea for it was generated by P&G's paper and cleaning-agent experts during a discussion on the Internet. According to Craig Wynett, CNV President, "It was an exercise in speed, in breaking down the company's traditional division-by-division territories to come up with new ideas."[97]

Strategy Bits

- Japan is the world's robotics leader, with 350,000 industrial robots in 2003. Germany is second, with 105,000, and the United States is third, with 104,000 robots.[98]
- In 2004, 607,000 household robots were in use. Most of these were vacuum cleaner and lawn mower robots. The UN Commission for Europe and the International Federation of Robotics predict that 4.1 million domestic robots will be in use by the end of 2007.[99]
- In 2004, 692,000 companion or entertainment robots, such as Sony's dog-like Aibo, were in use throughout the world.[100]

Discussion Questions

1. How should a corporation scan the external environment for new technological developments? Who should be responsible?

2. What is technology research and how does it differ from market research?

3. What is the importance of product and process R&D to competitive strategy?

4. What factors help determine whether a company should outsource a technology?

5. How can a company develop an entrepreneurial culture?

Strategic Practice Exercise

How Creative Is Your Organization?

One of the keys to managing technology and innovation is to have a creative organization in which people are free to propose and try new ideas. The following questionnaire is taken from "Building a Creative Hothouse" by Barton Kunstler in the January–February 2001 issue of *The Futurist*. It is a simplified version of the Hothouse Assessment Instrument presented in greater detail in the Spring 2000 issue of *Futures Research Quarterly*. This version describes many of the elements of a highly creative organization.

If you work or have worked full time in an organization, answer this questionnaire in light of your experience with that organization. If you have not worked full time anywhere, find someone who is working full time and ask that person to complete this questionnaire. Then discuss the person's answers with him or her.

To assess the level of creativity in your organization's culture, score your level of agreement or disagreement with the statements below as follows: **Strongly Agree** (5 points), **Mildly Agree** (4 points), **Neutral** (3 points), **Mildly Disagree** (2 points), **Strongly Disagree** (1 point).

(1) VALUES

1.___ We believe that our work can change the world.

2.___ The organization actively promotes a positive quality of life in our surrounding communities.

3.___ People here really believe our products and services are vital to others' well-being.

4.___ Virtually all who work here continually study and question the basic nature of their job and the technologies—human, organizational, technical—they work with.

5.___ Working here fills me with a sense of personal well-being and commitment to my higher values.

(2) MISSION AND VISION

6.___ Principles of justice and compassion directly and significantly influence strategy, design, and development.

7.___ We explore the fundamental practices and principles of our industry and its disciplines as a source of creativity, values, and purpose.

8.___ We can fail without fear for our jobs.

9.___ My organization takes the long view.

10.___ Employees are free to develop their own vision of what their jobs entail.

(3) IDEAS

11.___ This organization cultivates the growth of knowledge into wisdom and views wisdom as a guide to action.

12.___ Organizational structure is shaped by innovative, idea-driven approaches to our challenges and tasks.

13.___ Organizational responses to crises are thoughtful and imaginative, not reactive and typical.

14.___ The organization respects thinkers.

15.___ I am respected for all my talents, whether or not they contribute to the bottom line.

(4) EXCHANGE

16.___ My organization rewards those who display mastery at their jobs and seeks their advice, whatever their title or position.

17.___ Institutionalized procedures enable anyone to make suggestions or raise objections.

18.___ Intellectually exciting and stimulating conversation directly influences product development and delivery.

19.___ "Idea people" share their vision with other employees and invite feedback.

20.___ The group uses conflict as an opportunity for personal and organizational growth.

(5) PERCEPTION

21.___ How we perceive our tasks, our expertise, and the group itself is a legitimate object of inquiry.

22.___ Whole-minded thinking, including activities based on movement and heightening awareness of the five senses, is encouraged.

23.___ Employees are taught and encouraged to think creatively.

24.___ We continually re-vision our group's place within its industry and society as a whole.

25.___ Clear problem-solving algorithms are taught, practiced, developed, and applied wherever a need is perceived, without regard to concerns of status, tradition, or company politics.

(6) LEARNING

26.___ To be viewed as a "continuous learner" at work benefits one's career.

27.___ We regularly challenge group norms, and anyone can initiate this process.

28.___ My organization is constantly engaged in learning about itself and the environments in which it operates.

29.___ The organization allocates resources toward employee involvement in cultural events as attendees, participants, or learners.

30.___ Projects are undertaken by integrated teams whose members bring multiple disciplines and diverse perspectives to the task.

(7) SOCIAL

31.___ Our relationships at work are relaxed, irreverent, warm, and crackling with ideas.

32.___ People from different departments and organizational levels socialize together, either during or after work.

33.___ Committee meetings are reasonably productive and amicable.

34.___ When we form teams to work on special projects, the work is integrated into our day-to-day schedules.

35.___ We always produce effective leadership when and where we need it.

(8) FESTIVA

36.___ Social occasions are planned and designed in highly creative ways.

37.___ The line between work and play is virtually nonexistent.

38.___ Developments in art, politics, science, and other fields not directly related to our work are discussed in relation to their impact upon our organization and industry.

39.___ We have a strong group vocabulary of terms and symbols that promotes communication, community, and creativity.

40.___ We are encouraged to play whimsically with ideas, materials, and objects as well as with new ways of doing things.

______ **TOTAL POINTS**

Scoring Your Organization's Creativity

If You Scored:	Organization Is in the Creative . . .
40–79	***Dead Zone***—a place where it is virtually impossible for creativity to flourish
80–159	***I-Zone***—where management thinks in terms of the next quarter and creativity is seldom transmitted from one person or department to another* OR . . . ***O-Zone***—where creativity is valued but not consistently incorporated into the organization's strategy*
160–200	***Hot Zone***—where creativity is intense and productive

**Note:* I-Zone organizations score higher on Values, Ideas, Perception, and Social questions. O-Zone organizations score higher on Mission and Vision, Learning, Exchange, and Festiva questions.

Source: B. Kunstler, "Building a Creative Hothouse," *The Futurist* (January–February 2001), pp. 22–29. Reprinted by permission of the World Future Society.

Key Terms

absorptive capacity (p. 303)
best practice (p. 312)
corporate entrepreneurship (p. 306)
house of quality (p. 310)
index of R&D effectiveness (p. 311)
intellectual property (p. 301)
lead user (p. 296)
market research (p. 297)
orchestrator (p. 306)
process innovation (p. 299)
product champion (p. 306)
product innovation (p. 299)
product/market evolution matrix (p. 305)
R&D intensity (p. 298)
sponsor (p. 306)
stage-gate process (p. 309)
stage of new product development (p. 305)
strategic R&D alliance (p. 301)
technological competence (p. 303)
technology sourcing (p. 300)
time to market (p. 299)

CHAPTER 13

Strategic Issues in Entrepreneurial Ventures and Small Businesses

Learning Objectives

After reading this chapter, you should be able to:

- Differentiate between an entrepreneurial venture and a small business
- Use the strategic decision-making process to form a new venture
- Differentiate between an idea and an opportunity
- Identify sources of innovative concepts
- List the characteristics of the typical entrepreneur
- Understand the importance of moving through the substages of small-business development
- Avoid pitfalls in assessing the financial statements of a small, privately owned company

ONE NIGHT WHILE ATTENDING A PROFESSIONAL BASKETBALL GAME, VINCENT NORMENT noticed a problem on the court. As the game progressed, sweat-soaked headbands kept creeping down into the players' eyes. The athletes seemed to be constantly adjusting their headbands and were distracted from playing their best. Norment concluded that all that was needed to solve the problem was to put a thick strap across the top of the headband. The strap could be made of the same super-absorbent material as the rest of the headband. With this strap, a headband would not only absorb more of the athlete's sweat but also stay in place. With a background in sports-related products, Norment suggested his idea to headband manufacturers. "They looked at the product and said it wouldn't work," reported Norment.

When a patent search found nothing similar on the market, Norment patented his idea for DBands and planned to sell them through his own company, DApparel, Inc. Knowing that the key to success was getting the product used by athletes, Norment promoted DBands at the three-point shooting contest of the 2003 March Madness collegiate basketball playoffs. He asked players for their opinions and persuaded one player to wear the headband on ESPN. Thanks to the exposure, Norment got endorsements from Ron Artest of the Indiana Pacers and Brad Miller of the Sacramento Kings, among others. Now that DBands was starting to get the attention of the market, the next step was securing distribution.

DBands arrived in sporting goods stores such as The Athlete's Foot and Foot Locker in spring 2005, priced between $9.99 and $14.99. Norment expected to sell 50,000 to 100,000 DBands by December 2005. His goal was to make the DApparel brand a household name, one head at the time.[1]

13.1 Importance of Small Business and Entrepreneurial Ventures

Strategic management as a field of study typically deals with large, established business corporations. However, small business cannot be ignored. There are approximately 23 million small businesses—over 99% of all businesses—in the United States. They generate 60% to 80% of net new jobs annually and produce almost 30% of known export value. Studies by the Global Entrepreneurship Monitor have found a strong correlation between national economic growth and the level of entrepreneurial activity in prior years.[2] Research reveals that not only do small firms spend almost twice as much of their R&D budget on fundamental research as do large firms, but also, small companies are roughly 13 times more innovative per employee than large firms.[3] The National Science Foundation estimates that 98% of "radical" product developments result from the research done in the labs of small companies.[4] Nevertheless, not every country is as supportive of new ventures as is the United States. See the GLOBAL ISSUE feature to learn how different countries support entrepreneurship.

Despite the overall success of small businesses, however, every year tens of thousands of small companies fail. Figures from the U.S. Small Business Administration indicate that 50%

GLOBAL ISSUE

Entrepreneurship: Some Countries Are More Supportive Than Others

Entrepreneurship is becoming increasingly important throughout the world. True to economist Joseph Schumpeter's view of entrepreneurship as "creative destruction," much of the world from Eastern Europe to South America to Asia envisions entrepreneurial ventures as the means to build successful free market economies. New entrepreneurial ventures are emerging daily in these countries. Unfortunately, not every country makes it easy to start a new business.

According to the World Bank, countries range from easy to difficult in terms of starting an entrepreneurial venture. The amount of difficulty is usually a function of government requirements and paperwork and can be measured in the number of days it takes to start a new venture. The *quickest* in days are Australia (2), Canada (3), New Zealand (3), Denmark (4), the United States (4), Puerto Rico (6), Singapore (8), Hong Kong (11), Latvia (11), and the Netherlands (11). The *slowest* in days are Zaire (215), Haiti (203), Laos (198), Indonesia (168), Mozambique (153), Brazil (152), Angola (146), Burkina Faso (136), Zimbabwe (122), and Venezuela (119). Not surprisingly, the World Bank analysis of 130 countries concludes that onerous regulation retards economic growth.

Even though entrepreneurship is more difficult in many other parts of the world than in the United States, the situation is changing. For example, investors are flocking to young, fast-growing companies in Europe. Politicians are beginning to see entrepreneurs as part of a solution to unemployment rather than as grasping exploiters. Venture capital is becoming more available. The EASDAQ, founded in 1996, is Europe's version of the NASDAQ. Companies can be listed on the EASDAQ regardless of size or history, so long as they agree to international accounting standards and U.S.-style financial reporting.

There is still an ingrained cultural aversion to the risk-taking so necessary to entrepreneurship. The contradiction between the Marxist ideology and private ownership in China means that business entrepreneurs are not perceived as legitimate. The social stigma attached to business failure is deeply entrenched in many countries. According to Christophe Sapet, the French founder of a computer game company called Infogrames, "When you earn money, (French) people are jealous. They think you have done something wrong."

Sources: "Down to Business," *The Economist* (October 11, 2003), p. 9; J. Kahn, "Suddenly, Startups Are Chic," *Fortune* (February 15, 1999), p. 110; "Financial Indicators," *The Economist* (October 16, 1999), p. 109; "Emerging-Market Indicators," *The Economist* (September 23, 2000), p. 128; E. W. K. Tsang, "In Search of Legitimacy: The Private Entrepreneur in China," *Entrepreneurship Theory and Practice* (Fall 1996), pp. 21–30.

of businesses founded in any one year are not in business four years later.[5] Similar rates occur in the United Kingdom, the Netherlands, Japan, Taiwan, and Hong Kong.[6] Although an increasing number of studies are more positive regarding the survival rate of new entrepreneurial ventures, new businesses are definitely considered risky.[7] The causes of small-business failure (depending on the study cited) range from inadequate accounting systems to inability to cope with growth. The underlying problem appears to be an overall lack of strategic management—beginning with an inability to plan a strategy to reach the customer and ending with a failure to develop a system of controls to keep track of performance.[8]

Definition of Small-Business Firms and Entrepreneurial Ventures

The most commonly accepted definition of a small-business firm in the United States is one that employs fewer than 500 people and that generates sales of less than $20 million annually.

Although the meanings of the terms *small business* and *entrepreneurship* overlap considerably, the concepts are different. A **small-business firm** is independently owned and operated, is not dominant in its field, and does not engage in innovative practices. An **entrepreneurial venture**, in contrast, is any business whose primary goals are profitability and growth and that can be characterized by innovative strategic practices.[9] The basic difference between a small-business firm and an entrepreneurial venture, therefore, lies not in the type of goods or services provided, but in their fundamental views on growth and innovation. According to Donald Sexton, an authority on entrepreneurship, this explains why strategic planning is more likely to be present in an entrepreneurial venture than in a typical small-business firm:

> *Most firms start with just a single product. Those oriented toward growth immediately start looking for another one. It's that planning approach that separates the entrepreneur from the small-business owner.*[10]

The Entrepreneur as Strategist

Often defined as a person who organizes and manages a business undertaking and who assumes risk for the sake of a profit, an **entrepreneur** is the ultimate strategist. He or she makes all the strategic as well as operational decisions. All three levels of strategy—corporate, business, and functional—are the concerns of this founder and owner–manager of a company. This is typical of a new venture, which is usually a Stage I company (discussed in **Chapter 9**, in the stages of corporate development section). As one entrepreneur puts it: "Entrepreneurs are strategic planners without realizing it."

The development of DBands described earlier captures the key elements of an entrepreneurial venture: a basic business idea that has not yet been successfully tried and a gutsy entrepreneur who, while working on borrowed capital and a shoestring budget, creates a new business through a lot of trial and error and persistent hard work. Similar stories can be told of other people, such as Debbie Fields, who created Mrs. Fields Cookies, and Will Parish, who founded National Energy Associates. Both were ridiculed at one time or another for their desire to start businesses. Friends and family members told Fields that starting a business to sell chocolate chip cookies "was a stupid idea." Will Parish, who built a power plant in California's Imperial Valley that burns "pasture patties," was called an "entre-manure." Every day the plant burned 900 tons of manure collected from nearby feedlots to generate 15 megawatts of electricity—enough to light 20,000 homes. The power was sold to Southern California Edison. Parish got the idea from a trip to India, where the fuel used to heat a meal was cow dung. Once the plant was earning a profit, Parish planned to build a larger plant nearby that would burn wheat straw and other crop wastes. The plants provide an environmentally sound as well as profitable way to dispose of waste. Very interested in conservation, Parish says, "I wanted to combine doing well with doing good."[11]

13.2 Use of Strategic Planning and Strategic Management

Research shows that strategic planning is strongly related to small-business financial performance.[12] A survey of the high-growth *Inc. 500* firms revealed that 86% performed strategic planning. Of those performing strategic planning, 94% reported improved profits.[13] Nevertheless, many small companies still do not use the process.[14] A study of 131 firms filing for bankruptcy revealed that 72% lacked mission statements and objectives for their businesses.[15] Around 40% of existing small family-owned businesses do not have written strategic plans.[16] The reasons often cited for the apparent lack of strategic planning practices in many small-business firms are fourfold:

- **Not enough time:** Day-to-day operating problems take up the time necessary for long-term planning. It's relatively easy to justify avoiding strategic planning on the basis of day-to-day crisis management. Some will ask: "How can I be expected to do strategic planning when I don't know if I'm going to be in business next week?"
- **Unfamiliar with strategic planning:** A small-business CEO may be unaware of strategic planning or may view it as irrelevant to the small-business situation. Planning may be viewed as a straitjacket that limits flexibility.

- **Lack of skills:** Small-business managers often lack the skills necessary to begin strategic planning and do not have or want to spend the money necessary to import trained consultants. Future uncertainty may be used to justify a lack of planning. One entrepreneur admits, "Deep down, I know I should plan. But I don't know what to do. I'm the leader, but I don't know how to lead the planning process."
- **Lack of trust and openness:** Many small-business owner–managers are very sensitive regarding key information about the business and are thus unwilling to share strategic planning with employees or outsiders. For this reason, boards of directors are often composed only of close friends and relatives of the owner–manager—people unlikely to provide an objective viewpoint or professional advice.

Degree of Formality

Research generally concludes that the strategic planning process can be far more informal in small companies than it is in large corporations.[17] Some studies have even found that too much formalization of the strategic planning process may actually result in reduced performance.[18] Strategic planning is often forced on an entrepreneur by banks and venture capitalists when the entrepreneur is searching for capital to launch or expand the new venture. It is possible that a heavy emphasis on structured, written plans can be dysfunctional to the small entrepreneurial firm because it detracts from the very flexibility that is a benefit of small size. The process of strategic planning, not the plan itself, is probably the key to improving business performance. Research does show, however, that as an entrepreneurial firm matures, its strategic planning process tends to become more formal.[19]

These observations suggest that new entrepreneurial ventures begin life in Mintzberg's *entrepreneurial mode* of strategic planning (explained in **Chapter 1**) and move toward the *planning mode* as the company becomes established and wants to continue its strong growth. If, after becoming successfully established, the entrepreneur instead chooses stability over growth, the venture moves more toward the *adaptive mode* so common to many small businesses.

Usefulness of the Strategic Management Model

The model of strategic management (presented in **Figure 1–2** in **Chapter 1**) is also relevant to entrepreneurial ventures and small businesses. This basic model holds for both an established small company and a new entrepreneurial venture. As the research mentioned earlier concluded, small and developing companies increase their chances of success if they make a serious attempt to work through the strategic issues embedded in the strategic management model. The key is to focus on what's important—the set of managerial decisions and actions that determines the long-run performance of the company. The list of informal questions presented in **Table 13–1** may be more useful to a small entrepreneurial company than their more formal counterparts used by large, established corporations.

Usefulness of the Strategic Decision-Making Process

As mentioned in **Chapter 1**, one way in which the strategic management model can be made action oriented is to follow the strategic decision-making model presented in **Figure 1–5**. The eight steps presented in that model are just as appropriate for small companies as they are for large corporations. Unfortunately, the process does not fit new entrepreneurial

TABLE 13–1 INFORMAL QUESTIONS TO BEGIN THE STRATEGIC MANAGEMENT PROCESS IN A SMALL COMPANY OR ENTREPRENEURIAL VENTURE

Formal	Informal
Define mission	What do we stand for?
Set objectives	What are we trying to achieve?
Formulate strategy	How are we going to get there? How can we beat the competition?
Determine policies	What sort of ground rules should we all be following to get the job done right?
Establish programs	How should we organize this operation to get what we want done as cheaply as possible with the highest quality possible?
Prepare pro forma budgets	How much is it going to cost us and where can we get the cash?
Specify procedures	In how much detail do we have to lay things out, so that everybody knows what to do?
Determine performance measures	What are those few key things that will determine whether we can make it? How can we keep track of them?

ventures. Such a company must develop a new mission and new objectives, strategies, and policies out of a comparison of its external opportunities and threats to its potential strengths and weaknesses. Consequently, we propose in **Figure 13–1** a modified version of the strategic decision-making process; this version more closely suits a new entrepreneurial venture.

The proposed **strategic decision-making process for entrepreneurial ventures** is composed of the following eight interrelated steps:

1. **Develop the basic business idea—a product and/or service that has target customers and/or markets:** An **idea** is a concept for a product or service that currently doesn't exist or is not currently available in a market niche. It may be a brand-new concept (radical innovation) or an improvement to a current product or service (incremental innovation). The idea can be developed from a person's experience or generated in a moment of creative insight. For example, Vincent Norment conceived of a headband with a stay-on strap while attending a basketball game.
2. **Scan and assess the external environment to locate factors in the societal and task environments that pose opportunities and threats:** The scanning should focus particularly on market potential and resource accessibility.
3. **Scan and assess the internal factors relevant to the new business:** The entrepreneur should objectively consider personal assets, areas of expertise, abilities, and experience, all in terms of the organizational needs of the new venture.
4. **Analyze the strategic factors in light of the current situation, using SWOT:** The venture's potential strengths and weaknesses must be evaluated in light of opportunities and threats. This analysis can be done with a SFAS Matrix (see **Figure 6–1**) of the strategic factors.
5. **Decide go or no go:** If the basic business idea appears to be a feasible business opportunity, the process should be continued. An **opportunity** is an idea for a new product or service with a market that is willing to pay for that product or service so that it can form the basis of a profitable business. Otherwise, further development of the idea should be canceled unless the strategic factors change.

Figure 13–1
Strategic Decision-Making Process for New Ventures

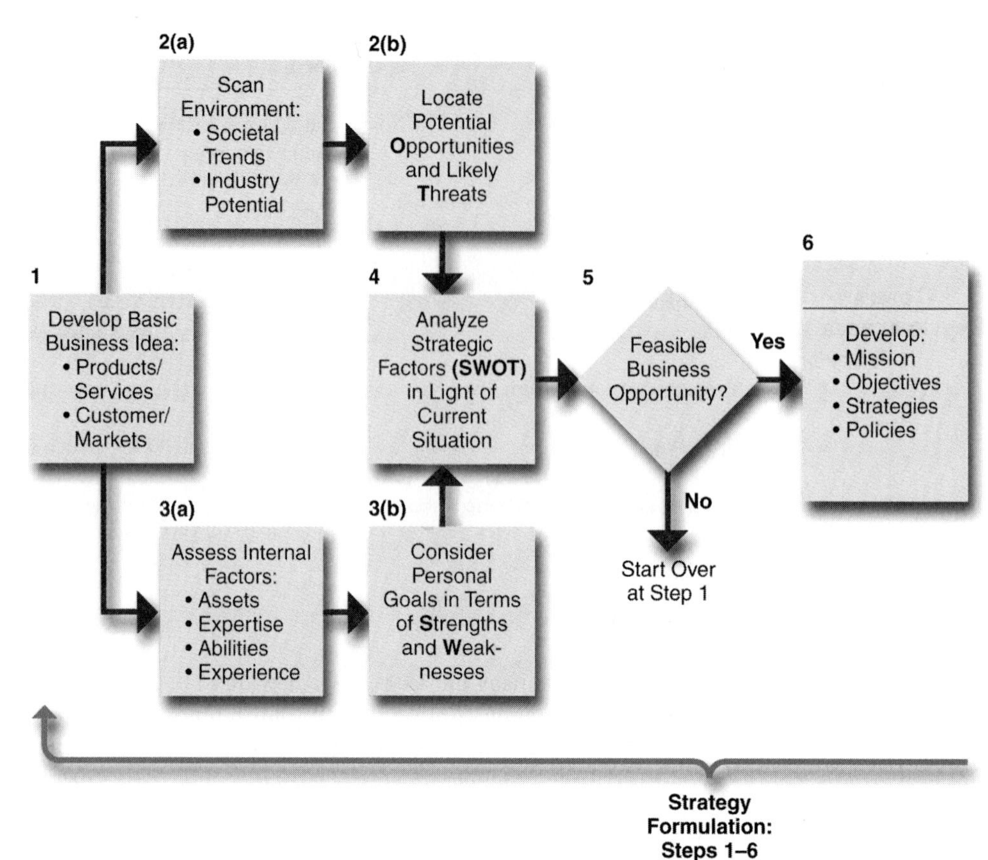

6. **Generate a business plan that specifies how the opportunity will be transformed into reality:** See **Table 13–2** for the suggested contents of a strategic **business plan**. The proposed venture's mission, objectives, strategies, and policies, as well as its likely board of directors (if a corporation) and key managers should be developed. Key internal factors should be specified and performance projections generated. The business plan serves as a vehicle through which financial support is obtained from potential investors and creditors. It increases a new venture's probability of survival and facilitates new product develop-

TABLE 13–2
CONTENTS OF A STRATEGIC BUSINESS PLAN FOR AN ENTREPRENEURIAL VENTURE

I. Table of Contents	X. Human Resources Plan
II. Executive Summary	XI. Ownership
III. Nature of the Business	XII. Risk Analysis
IV. Strategy Formulation	XIII. Timetables and Milestones
V. Market Analysis	XIV. Strategy Implementation—Action Plans
VI. Marketing Plan	XV. Evaluation and Control
VII. Operational Plans—Service/Product	XVI. Summary
VIII. Financial Plans	XVII. Appendixes
IX. Organization and Management	

Note: The Strategic Audit in Appendix 1.A can be used to develop a business plan. It provides detailed questions to serve as a checklist.

Source: Thomas L. Wheelen, "Contents of a Strategic Business Plan for an Entrepreneurial Venture." Copyright © 1988 and 2005 by Thomas L. Wheelen. Reprinted by permission.

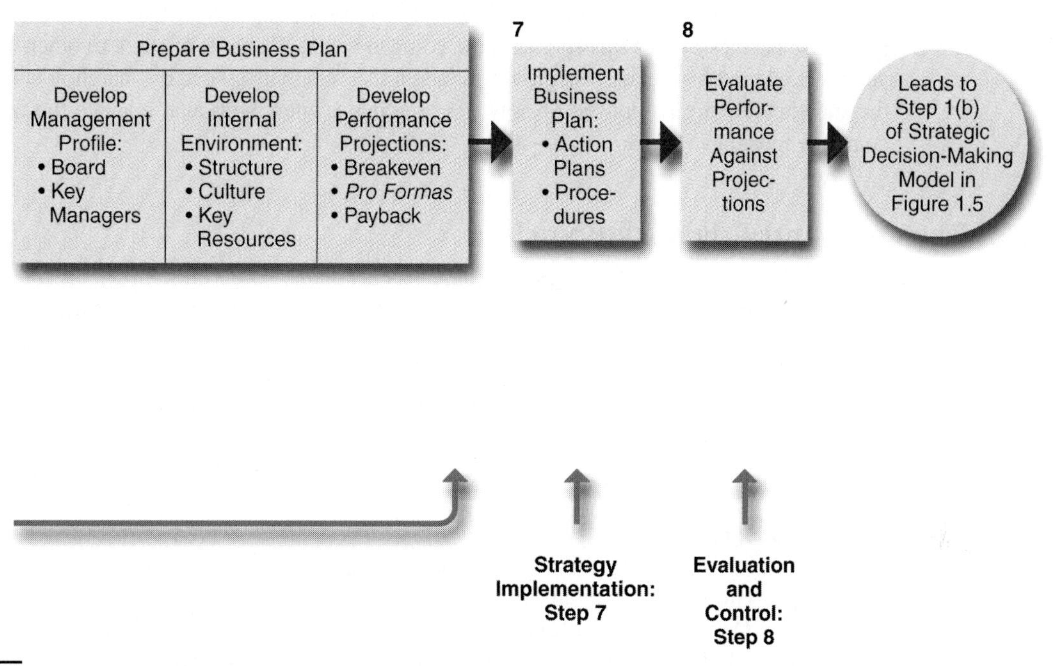

Source: T. L. Wheelen and C. E. Michaels, Jr., "Model for Strategic Decision-Making Process for New Ventures." Copyright © 1987 and 2005 by T. L. Wheelen. Reprinted by permission.

ment.[20] Firms using business plans tend to have higher revenue and sales growth than do those without them.[21] Starting a business without a business plan is the quickest way to kill a new venture.[22] For example, one study of 270 clothing retailers found that 80% of the successful stores had written business plans, whereas 65% of the failed businesses had not.[23]

A strategic audit (see **Appendix 1.A** at the end of **Chapter 1**) can be used to develop a formal business plan. The audit's sections and subsections, along with the questions within them, can be re-aligned to fit the model depicted in **Figure 13–1**. Instead of analyzing the historical events of an existing company, one can use the questions to project the proposed company's future. The questions can be reoriented to follow the outline in **Appendix 1.A**. A crucial building block of a sound business plan is the construction of realistic scenarios for the pro forma financials. The pro formas must reflect the impact of seasonality on the cash flows of the proposed new venture.

7. **Implement the business plan:** Do this through the use of action plans and procedures.
8. **Evaluate the implemented business plan through comparison of actual performance against projected performance results:** This step leads to step 1(b) of the strategic decision-making process shown in **Figure 1–5**. To the extent that actual results are less than or much greater than the anticipated results, the entrepreneur needs to reconsider the company's current mission, objectives, strategies, policies, and programs, and possibly make changes to the original business plan.

13.3 Issues in Corporate Governance

Corporate governance is much simpler in small entrepreneurial ventures than in large, established corporations. For one thing, the owners and the managers are usually the same people—the company founders (or their close relatives). If a venture is not incorporated, there is no need for a board of directors. It may be a sole proprietorship or a simple partnership. Those entrepreneurial ventures wishing to grow quickly or to limit the liability of the owners often incorporate the business. Once incorporated, the company can sell shares of stock to others (such as venture capitalists) to finance its growth. When the company is owned by shareholders (even if the shareholders are composed of only the founding owners who also manage the firm), the company must have a board of directors.

Boards of Directors and Advisory Boards

The boards of directors of entrepreneurial firms are likely to be either very passive or very active. Passive boards exist when the stock is closely held by the founding owners (and their immediate families) who manage the company on a day-to-day basis. As the only stockholders, they elect themselves to board offices and call meetings only when the law requires it—usually as a social occasion. There is no need for an active board since there are no other stockholders and thus no agency problems. The board typically has few or no external directors.[24] In most instances, the primary role of the board is simply to be a figurehead to satisfy the law. This places it on the far left end of the board of directors' continuum shown in Chapter 2's **Figure 2–1**.

Entrepreneurial ventures financed by venture capitalists typically have very active boards of directors. The venture capitalists expect to obtain seats on the board in exchange for their investment.[25] Once on the board, venture capitalists tend to be very powerful members of the board and are highly involved in strategic management.[26] The boards of directors of fast-growth entrepreneurial firms have around five directors, of whom about three are external. Almost 80% of them have written strategic plans with a time horizon of 12 to 24 months.[27] Venture capitalists usually require three years or more of pro forma financial statements broken out on a monthly cash flow basis for the first two years and on a quarterly basis thereafter.

Since closely held entrepreneurial ventures and small businesses tend to have relatively passive boards composed primarily of insiders, this type of business should use an advisory board to provide advice to the owner–managers. An **advisory board** is a group of external business people who voluntarily meet periodically with the owner–managers of the firm to discuss strategic and other issues. The members are usually invited to join the board by the president of the company. The advisory board has no official capacity but is expected to provide management with useful suggestions and act as a sounding board. Since the members typically receive no compensation for serving, quarterly business meetings are often followed by cocktails and dinner at a nearby country club, hotel, or prestigious restaurant. It is important to staff the advisory board with knowledgeable people who have significant business experience or skills who can complement the background and skills of the company's owner–managers. Using an advisory board is an easy way to obtain free professional consulting advice. Research indicates that advisory boards improve the performance of small businesses.[28]

Impact of the Sarbanes-Oxley Act

Complying with the Sarbanes-Oxley Act is becoming a cost burden for small publicly held U.S. companies. Companies face higher audit and legal fees, new internal control systems, and higher directors' and officers' liability insurance premiums, among other expenses.

Compliance costs are estimated at $500,000 for a small firm and in the millions for a large one.[29] As a result, 198 firms "went dark" in 2003 by delisting their stock from stock exchanges. By only trading via "pink sheets" in over-the-counter stocks, these firms do not have to comply with the act's minimum requirements, and they do not have to file with the Securities and Exchange Commission (SEC). Under SEC rules, a company may choose to terminate its registration if the corporation's securities have fewer than 300 holders of record or if there are fewer than 500 holders of record and the company's total assets don't exceed $10 million. A research study of firms going dark indicated that the firms delist their stock not only to avoid compliance costs but also to evade the outside monitoring and additional scrutiny required by Sarbanes-Oxley. According to Christian Leuz, co-author of the study: "We basically find that going dark can serve as a way to conserve cash, but it may also be exploited by insiders trying to avoid the scrutiny of the market. Whether insiders succeed, and whether the decision to go dark is a good or bad one therefore depends on the governance in place."[30]

13.4 Issues in Environmental Scanning and Strategy Formulation

Environmental scanning in small businesses is much less sophisticated than it is in large corporations. The business is usually too small to justify hiring someone to do only environmental scanning or strategic planning. Top managers, especially if they are the founders, tend to believe that they know the business and can follow it better than anyone else. A study of 220 small rapid-growth companies revealed that the majority of CEOs were actively and personally involved in all phases of the planning process, especially in the setting of objectives. Only 15% of the companies used a planning officer or formed a planning group to assist in the planning process. In the rest of the firms, operating managers who participated in strategic planning provided input only to the CEO, who then formulated the plan.[31] Unfortunately, the literature suggests that most small business owner–managers rely more on internal as opposed to external sources of information.[32] Conducting a periodic industry analysis using Porter's forces is just as important for a small business as for a large one. Nevertheless, few small businesses do much competitor analysis. If they do analyze competition, typical small business owners often only look locally, without considering competitors across town or in a nearby city.

A fundamental reason for differences in strategy formulation between large and small entrepreneurial companies lies in the relationship between owners and managers. The CEO of a large corporation has to consider and balance the varied needs of the corporation's many stakeholders. The CEO of a small business, however, is very likely also to be the owner—the company's primary stakeholder. Personal and family needs can thus strongly affect a small business's mission and objectives and can overrule other considerations.[33]

Size can affect the selection of an appropriate corporate strategy. Large corporations often choose growth strategies for their many side benefits for management as well as for shareholders. A small company may, however, choose a stability strategy because the entrepreneur is interested mostly in (1) generating employment for family members, (2) providing the family a "decent living," and (3) being the "boss" of a firm small enough that he or she can manage it comfortably. Some business owners don't pursue a growth strategy because they do not want the loss of control that results from bank debt or the sale of stock to outsiders. Some may even fear that growth will attract attention from larger competitors that might want to take over the company or drive it out of business.[34] Thus the goals of a small business are likely to be the same as the goals of the owner–manager.

Basic SWOT analysis is just as relevant to new entrepreneurial businesses as it is to established large ones. Both the greatest strength and the greatest weakness of a small firm, at least in the beginning, rest with the entrepreneur—the owner–manager of the business. The entrepreneur is the manager, the source of product/market strategy, and the dynamo who energizes the company. That is why the internal assessment of a new venture's strengths and weaknesses focuses in **Figure 13–1** on the founder's personal characteristics—his or her assets, expertise, abilities, and experience. Research reveals that founder competencies, motivations, and connections plus the firm's competitive strategies are direct predictors of new venture growth and success.[35] Intangible assets, such as leadership, strategy, and human and intellectual capital, were found to be more important than traditional financial measures for a venture's success in going public through an IPO.[36]

Just as an entrepreneur's strengths can be the key to company success, personal weaknesses can be a primary cause of failure. For example, the study of clothing retailers mentioned earlier showed that the owner–managers of 85% of the failed stores had no prior retailing experience.

Sources of Innovation

Peter Drucker, in his book *Innovation and Entrepreneurship*, proposes seven sources for innovative opportunity that should be monitored by those interested in starting an entrepreneurial venture, either within an established company or as an independent small business.[37] The first four **sources of innovation** lie within the industry itself; the last three arise in the societal environment. These seven sources are:

1. **The Unexpected:** An unexpected success, an unexpected failure, or an unexpected outside event can be a symptom of a unique opportunity. When Don Cullen of Transmet Corporation spilled a box of very fine aluminum flakes onto his company's parking lot, he discovered that their presence in the asphalt prevented it from turning sticky in high temperatures. His company now produces aluminum chips for use in roofing. Sales have doubled every year since the product's introduction, and Cullen's company will soon dominate the business.
2. **The Incongruity:** A discrepancy between reality and what everyone assumes it to be, or between what is and what ought to be, can create an opportunity for innovation. For example, a side effect of retailing via the Internet is the increasing number of packages being delivered to homes. Since neither FedEx nor UPS can leave a package unless someone is home to sign for it, many deliveries are delayed. Tony Paikeday founded zBox Company to make and sell a hard plastic container that would receive deliveries from any delivery service and would be accessible only by the owner and the delivery services. "We're amazed that it doesn't exist yet," says Paikeday.[38]
3. **Innovation Based on Process Need:** When a weak link is evident in a particular process but people work around it instead of doing something about it, an opportunity is present for the person or company willing to forge a stronger one. Tired of having to strain to use a too-small keyboard on his personal computer, David Levy invented a keyboard with 64 normal-sized keys cleverly put into an area the size of a credit card.[39]
4. **Changes in Industry or Market Structure:** A business is ready for an innovative product, service, or approach to the business when the underlying foundation of the industry or market shifts. Black Entertainment Television, Inc. (BET), was born when Robert Johnson noticed that no television programmer was targeting the increasing number of black viewers. The BET brand has expanded into magazines and is now known by more than 90% of African-Americans.[40]
5. **Demographics:** Changes in the population's size, age structure, composition, employment, level of education, and income can create opportunities for innovation. For exam-

ple, Pam Henderson started a company called Kids Kab to shuttle children and teenagers to private schools, doctor and dentist appointments, lessons, and extracurricular activities. With the trend to dual careers, parents were no longer always available to provide personal transportation for their own children and needed such a service.

6. **Changes in Perception, Mood, and Meaning:** Opportunities for innovation can develop when a society's general assumptions, attitudes, and beliefs change. For example, the increasing dominance of a few national brewers have caused beer drinkers to look for alternatives to the same old national brands. By positioning Yuengling, a local Pennsylvania beer, as a full-flavored beer and providing it with an artsy, nostalgic-looking label, the small company was able to catch the fancy of young, trendy consumers who viewed it as Pennsylvania's version of Anchor Steam, the successful San Francisco beer.
7. **New Knowledge:** Advances in scientific and nonscientific knowledge can create new products and new markets. Advances in two different areas can sometimes be integrated to form the basis of a new product. For example, Medical Foods was formed to make foods that act like medicine to treat conditions from diabetes to arthritis. Its first product, NiteBite, is a chocolate-flavored snack bar designed to help diabetics manage nocturnal hypoglycemia, caused by low blood sugar. NiteBite gradually releases glucose into the bloodstream, where it lasts for six hours or more.[41]

Factors Affecting a New Venture's Success

According to Hofer and Sandberg, three factors have a substantial impact on a new venture's performance. In order of importance, these **factors affecting new venture success** are (1) the structure of the industry entered, (2) the new venture's business strategy, and (3) behavioral characteristics of the entrepreneur.[42]

Industry Structure

Research shows that the chances for success are greater for entrepreneurial ventures that enter rapidly changing industries than for those that enter stable industries. In addition, prospects are better in industries that are in the early, high-growth stages of development.[43] Competition is often less intense. Fast market growth also allows new ventures to make some mistakes without serious penalty. New ventures also increase their chances of success when they enter markets in which they can erect entry barriers to keep out competitors.

Contrary to popular wisdom, however, patents may not always provide competitive advantage, especially for new ventures in a high-tech or hypercompetitive industry. A well-financed competitor could examine a newly filed application for a patent, work around the patent, and beat the pioneering firm to market with a similar product. In addition, the time and cost of filing and defending a patent may not be worth the effort. According to Connie Bagley, author of *The Entrepreneur's Guide to Business Law*:

> *It might take 18 months to get a patent on a product that has a 12-month life cycle. By the time you finally get the damn thing litigated, it's meaningless. So people are focusing less on proprietary assurance and more on first-mover advantage. . . . The law is just too slow for this high-speed economy.*[44]

Most new ventures enter industries that have a low degree of industry concentration (that is, no dominant competitors).[45] Industry concentration is not necessarily bad. It may create market niches being ignored by large firms.[46] Hofer and Sandberg found that a new venture is more likely to be successful entering an industry in which one dominant competitor has a 50% or more market share than entering an industry in which the largest competitor has less than a 25% market share. To explain this phenomenon, Hofer and Sandberg point out that when an industry has one dominant firm, the remaining competitors are relatively weak and are easy prey for an aggressive entrepreneur. To avoid direct competition with a major rival, the new venture can focus on a market segment that is being ignored.

Industry product characteristics also have a significant impact on a new venture's success. First, a new venture is more likely to be successful when it enters an industry with heterogeneous (different) products than when it enters one with homogeneous (similar) products. In a heterogeneous industry, a new venture can differentiate itself from competitors with a unique product; or, by focusing on the unique needs of a market segment, it can find a market niche. Second, a new venture is, according to research data, more likely to be successful if the product is relatively unimportant to the customer's total purchasing needs than if it is important. Customers are more likely to experiment with a new product if its cost is low and product failure will not create a problem.

Business Strategy

According to Hofer and Sandberg, the keys to success for most new ventures are (1) to differentiate the product from those of other competitors in the areas of quality and service and (2) to focus the product on customer needs in a segment of the market in order to achieve a dominant share of that part of the market. Adopting guerrilla-warfare tactics, these companies go after opportunities in market niches too small or too localized to justify retaliation from the market leaders.[47] It is crucial, however, that a new venture analyze its competitors to assess their likely response to the company's entry into the market.

To continue its growth once it has found a niche, an entrepreneurial firm can emphasize continued innovation and pursue natural growth in its current markets. The firm can also expand into related markets in which the company's core skills, resources, and facilities offer the keys to further success. It can leverage its resources by engaging in strategic alliances with other firms. Sixty-three percent of U.S. small business owners report that they are involved in strategic alliances, especially in marketing and distribution. Of those using strategic alliances, half maintain three or more.[48]

Some studies do indicate, however, that new ventures can also be successful following strategies other than going after an undefended niche with a focus strategy. A narrow-market approach may leave the new firm vulnerable and preordained to only limited sales. One possible approach would be to offer products that are substitutable to, but differentiated from, those offered by bigger firms.[49] For some practical suggestions for locating an opportunity and formulating a business strategy, see **STRATEGY HIGHLIGHT 13.1**.

Entrepreneurial Characteristics

Four **entrepreneurial characteristics** are key to a new venture's success. Successful entrepreneurs have:

1. **The ability to identify potential venture opportunities better than most people:** Entrepreneurs focus on opportunities—not on problems—and try to learn from failure. Entrepreneurs are goal oriented and have a strong impact on the emerging culture of an organization. They are able to envision where the company is going and are thus able to provide a strong overall sense of strategic direction. As a result, their firms have a strong entrepreneurial orientation (EO)—that is, are innovative, proactive, and willing to take risks.[50]
2. **A sense of urgency that makes them action oriented:** They have a high need for achievement, which motivates them to put their ideas into action. They tend to have an internal locus of control that leads them to believe that they can determine their own fate through their own behavior. They also have a significantly greater capacity to tolerate

STRATEGY HIGHLIGHT 13.1

Suggestions for Locating an Opportunity and Formulating a Business Strategy

Given that differentiation and focus are the most popular and effective competitive strategies for a new venture, what are some of the ways to identify a new opportunity in which these strategies can be used? *Entrepreneur* magazine provides four interesting approaches:

1. **Tap the countertrend:** For every trend, there is likely to be a potentially lucrative countertrend waiting to be discovered. When a trend is hot, look for its opposite in a small but potentially growing market niche. Note how Hardee's successfully responded to the trend to low-fat and low-carb diets with it own monster-size bacon cheeseburger with more calories, carbs, and fat than its competitors. Because the idea was so outrageous, the Hardee's product received free coverage in newspapers and on television.
2. **Eat off the established company's plate:** Trendwatching.com coined the term "feeder business" for companies that feed off giants such as Amazon or eBay. When Eric Cohen and Joyce Shulman noticed that the typical blank pizza box was 16 inches of available advertising space, they decided to partner with the box makers to print paid advertisements on them for pizzerias. They then branched out into coffee cups and ice bags.
3. **Switch the niche:** A company may be able to identify a successful product or service that caters to a particular market and tailor it to fit a different market niche. For example, when Una Cassidy encountered numerous women looking for beauty products for use during pregnancy, she founded Selph. Cassidy removed all the usual ingredients found in beauty products that would be harmful to a fetus during pregnancy and replaced them with superior products that were gentle on the skin.
4. **Borrow a business model:** Netflix developed a novel business model (discussed in **Chapter 1**) in which members are charged a set monthly fee to borrow an unlimited number of DVDs by mail. This model was picked up quickly by other entrepreneurs such as GameFly, which rents video games by mail, Booksfree.com, which rents paperbacks by mail, and Bag Borrow Or Steal, which rents designer purses by mail.

Sources: K. Axelton, "Fever Pitch," *Entrepreneur* (December 2004), p. 74; N. L. Torres, "Think Outside the Box," *Entrepreneur* (February 2004), pp. 108–111; A. Pennington, "Una Cassidy," *Entrepreneur* (November 2003), p. 24.

ambiguity and stress than do many in established organizations.[51] They also have a strong need for control and may even be viewed as "misfits who need to create their own environment." They tend to distrust others and often have a need "to show others that they amount to something, that they cannot be ignored."[52]

3. **A detailed knowledge of the keys to success in the industry and the physical stamina to make their work their lives:** Successful entrepreneurs have better-than-average education and significant work experience in the industry in which they start their businesses. They often work with partners to form a new venture. (Seventy percent of new high-tech ventures are started by more than one founder.[53]) More than half of all entrepreneurs work at least 60 hours per week in the startup year, according to a National Federation of Independent Business study.[54]
4. **Access to outside help to supplement their skills, knowledge, and abilities:** Over time, entrepreneurs develop a network of people who have key skills and knowledge, whom the entrepreneurs can call on for support. Through their enthusiasm, these entrepreneurs are able to attract key investors, partners, creditors, and employees. For example, the founders of eBay did not hesitate to bring in Meg Whitman as CEO because Whitman had the managerial skills that eBay needed to expand.

In summarizing their conclusions regarding factors affecting the success of entrepreneurial ventures, Hofer and Sandberg propose the guidelines presented in **Table 13–3**.

TABLE 13–3 SOME GUIDELINES FOR NEW VENTURE SUCCESS

- Focus on industries facing substantial technological or regulatory changes, especially those with recent exits by established competitors.
- Seek industries whose smaller firms have relatively weak competitive positions.
- Seek industries that are in early, high-growth stages of evolution.
- Seek industries in which it is possible to create high barriers to subsequent entry.
- Seek industries with heterogeneous products that are relatively unimportant to the customer's overall success.
- Seek to differentiate your products from those of your competitors in ways that are meaningful to your customers.
- Focus such differentiation efforts on product quality, marketing approaches, and customer service—and charge enough to cover the costs of doing so.
- Seek to dominate the market segments in which you compete. If necessary, either segment the market differently or change the nature and focus of your differentiation efforts to increase your domination of the segments you serve.
- Stress innovation, especially new product innovation, that is built on existing organizational capabilities.
- Seek natural, organic growth through flexibility and opportunism that builds on existing organizational strengths.

Source: C. W. Hofer and W. R. Sandberg, "Improving New Venture Performance: Some Guidelines for Success," *American Journal of Small Business* (Summer 1987), pp. 17, 19.

13.5 Issues in Strategy Implementation

Two key implementation issues in a small company are organizing and staffing the growing company and transferring ownership of the company to the next generation.

Substages of Small Business Development

The implementation problems of a small business change as the company grows and develops over time. Just as the decision-making process for entrepreneurial ventures is different from that of established businesses, the managerial systems in small companies often vary from those of large corporations. Those variations are based on their stage of development. The stages of corporate growth and development discussed in **Chapter 9** suggest that all small businesses are either in Stage I or trying to move into Stage II. These models imply that all successful new ventures eventually become Stage II, functionally organized, companies. This is not always true, however. In attempting to show clearly how small businesses develop, Churchill and Lewis propose five **substages of small business development**: (a) existence, (b) survival, (c) success, (d) take-off, and (e) resource maturity.[55] A review of these small-business substages shows in more detail how a company can move through the entrepreneurial Stage I into a functionally oriented, professionally managed Stage II.

Stage A: Existence

At this point, an entrepreneurial venture faces the problems of obtaining customers and delivering the promised product or service. The organizational structure is simple. The entrepreneur does everything and directly supervises subordinates. Systems are minimal. The owner is the business.

Stage B: Survival

Those ventures able to satisfy a sufficient number of customers enter this stage; the rest close when their owners run out of startup capital. Those reaching the survival stage are concerned about generating the cash flow needed to repair and replace capital assets as they wear out and to finance the growth to continue satisfying the market segment they have found.

At this stage, the organizational structure is still simple, but it probably has a sales manager or general supervisor to carry out the owner's well-defined orders. A major problem of many small businesses at this stage is finding a person who is qualified to supervise the business when the owner can't be present but who is still willing to work for a very modest salary. An entrepreneur usually tries to use a family member rather than hire an outsider who lacks the entrepreneur's dedication to the business and (in the words of one owner–manager) "steals them blind." A company that remains in this stage for a long time is often called a "mom and pop" firm. It earns marginal returns on invested time and capital (with lots of psychic income!) and eventually goes out of business when "mom and pop" give up or retire. This type of small business is viewed more as a **lifestyle company** in which the firm is purely an extension of the owner's lifestyle. More than 94% of small private companies are in this category.[56]

Stage C: Success

By this point, the company's sales have reached a level where the firm is not only profitable but has sufficient cash flow to reinvest in itself. The key issue at this stage is whether the company should be used as a platform for growth or as a means of support for the owners as they completely or partially disengage from the company. The company is transforming into a functionally structured organization, but it still relies on the entrepreneur for all key decisions. The two options are disengagement and growth.

Stage C(1): Disengagement. The company can now successfully follow a stability strategy and remain at this stage almost indefinitely—provided that environmental change does not destroy its niche or poor management reduce its competitive abilities. By now functional managers have taken over some of the entrepreneur's duties. The company at this stage may be incorporated, but it is still primarily owned by the founder or the founder's family. Consequently, the board of directors is either a rubber stamp for the entrepreneur or a forum for family squabbles. Growth strategies are not pursued because either the market niche will not allow growth or the owner is content with the company at a size he or she can still manage comfortably. Strategic decisions make limited use of objective information and tend to be intuitive—based on personal desires and the founder's background.[57]

Stage C(2): Growth. The entrepreneur risks all available cash and the established borrowing power of the company in financing further growth. Strategic and operational planning are extensive and deeply involve the owner. Managers with an eye to the company's future rather than for its current situation are hired. This is an entrepreneurial high-growth firm aiming to be included in the *Inc. 500*. The emphasis now is on teamwork rather than on the entrepreneur's personal actions and energy. The personal values and philosophy of the founder are slowly transferred into a developing corporate culture.

Stage D: Take-Off

The key problems in this stage are how to grow rapidly and how to finance that growth. By now the firm is incorporated and has sold or is planning to sell stock in its company via an initial public offering (IPO) or via a direct public offering (DPO).[58] The entrepreneur must learn to delegate to specialized professional managers or to a team of managers who now form the top management of the company.[59] Delegation is a key issue for a company at this stage of development. A functional structure of the organization should now be solidly in place. Operational and strategic planning greatly involve the hired managers, but the company is still dominated by the entrepreneur's presence and stock control. Vertical and horizontal growth strategies are being seriously considered as the firm's management debates when and how to grow. The company is now included in the *Inc. 500* select group of firms.

At this point, the entrepreneur either is able to manage the transition from a small to a large company or recognizes personal limitations, sells his or her stock for a profit, and leaves the firm. The composition of the board of directors changes from dominance by friends and relatives of the owner to a large percentage of outsiders with managerial experience who can help the owner during the transition to a professionally managed company. The biggest danger facing the firm in this stage is the owner's desire to remain in total control (not willing to delegate) as if it were still a small entrepreneurial venture, even though he or she lacks the managerial skills necessary to run an established corporation. One study of small businesses found that fewer than one-third had written succession plans to replace the current owners.[60]

Stage E: Resource Maturity

It is at this point that the small company has adopted most of the characteristics of an established, large company. It may still be a small- or medium-sized company, but it is recognized as an important force in the industry and a possible candidate for the *Fortune 500* someday. The greatest concerns of a company at this stage are controlling the financial gains brought on by rapid growth and retaining its flexibility and entrepreneurial spirit. In terms of the stages of organizational growth and development discussed in **Chapter 9**, the company has become a full-fledged Stage II functional corporation.

Transfer of Power and Wealth in Family Businesses

Small businesses are often **family businesses**. Within the United States, family businesses account for approximately 80% of the total 15 million businesses.[61] It is estimated that over one-third of the U.S. *Fortune 500* companies are either family owned or dominated. Of the world's largest firms, the proportion is over one-half.[62] Some of the world's largest family-owned or controlled firms are Wal-Mart, Ford Motor, Samsung, LG Group, Carrefour Group, Fiat Group, IFI, PSA Peugeot Citroen, Cargill, and BMW.[63] Interestingly, the 177 family companies in the 2003 *S&P 500* financially outperformed non-family companies over the previous 10 year period.[64]

Even though the founders of the companies are the primary forces in starting the entrepreneurial ventures, their needs for business support and financial assistance cause them to turn to family members, who can be trusted, over unknown outsiders of questionable integrity who may demand more salary than the enterprise can afford. Sooner or later, the founder's spouse and children are drafted into business operations either because the family standard of living is directly tied to the business or the entrepreneur desperately needs help just to staff the operation. The children are guaranteed summer jobs, and the business changes from dad's or mom's company to "our" company. The family members are extremely valuable assets to the entrepreneur because they are often also willing to put in long hours at low pay to help the business succeed. Even though the spouse and children might have no official stock in the company, they know that they will somehow share in its future and perhaps even inherit the business. The problem is that only 30% of family firms survive to the second generation, and just 15% survive to the third generation.[65] A common saying among European family businesses is: "The first generation creates, the second inherits, and the third destroys."[66] This saying is supported by research indicating that firm performance declines when descendents take over management of a firm.[67]

TABLE 13–4
TRANSFER OF POWER IN A FAMILY BUSINESS

Phase 1	**Owner-Managed Business:** Phase 1 begins at startup and continues until the entrance of another family member into the business on a full-time basis. Family considerations influence but are not yet a directing part of the firm. At this point, the founder (entrepreneur) and the business are one.
Phase 2	**Training and Development of New Generation:** The children begin to learn the business at the dining room table during early childhood and then through part-time and vacation employment. The family and the business become one. Just as the entrepreneur identified with the business earlier, the family now begins to identify itself with the business.
Phase 3	**Partnership Between Generations:** At this point, a son or daughter of the founder has acquired sufficient business and managerial competence so that he or she can be involved in key decisions for at least a part of the company. The entrepreneur's offspring, however, has to first gain respect from the firm's employees and other managers and show that he or she can do the job right. Another issue is the lack of willingness of the founder to share authority with the son or daughter. Consequently, a common tactic taken by sons and daughters in family businesses is to take a job in a large, established corporation where they can gain valuable experience and respect for their skills.
Phase 4	**Transfer of Power:** Instead of being forced to sell the company when he or she can no longer manage the business, the founder has the option in a family business of turning it over to the next generation as part of their inheritance. Often the founder moves to the position of Chairman of the Board and promotes one of the children to the position of CEO. Unfortunately, some founders cannot resist meddling in operating affairs and unintentionally undermine the leadership position of the son or daughter. To avoid this problem, the founder should sell his or her stock (probably through a leveraged buyout to the children) and physically leave the company and allow the next generation the freedom it needs to adapt to changing conditions.

Source: N. C. Churchill and K. J. Hatten, "Non-Market-Based Transfer of Wealth and Power: A Research Framework for Family Businesses," *American Journal of Small Business* (Winter 1987), pp. 51–64. Reprinted from *Entrepreneurship Theory & Practice* by permission of Baylor University.

Churchill and Hatten propose that family businesses go through four sequential phases from the time in which the venture is strictly managed by the founder to the time in which the next generation takes charge.[68] These phases are detailed in **Table 13–4**. Each of these phases must be well managed if the company is to survive past the third generation. Some of the reasons family businesses may fail to successfully transfer ownership to the next generation are (1) inherited wealth destroys entrepreneurial drive, (2) the entrepreneur doesn't allow for a changing firm, (3) emphasis on business means the family is neglected, (4) the business' financial growth can't keep up with rising family lifestyles, (5) family members are not prepared to run a business, and (6) the business becomes an arena for family conflicts.[69] In addition, succession planning may be ignored because of the founder's or family's refusal to think about the founder's death, the founder's unwillingness to let go of the firm, the fear of sibling rivalry, or intergenerational envy.

According to Joe Astachan of the Cox Family Enterprise Center at Kennesaw State University, families whose businesses survive over time tend to operate on a set of agreed principles that pass from one generation to another. These include the creation of an active board of directors, a process of strategic planning that allows everyone to debate and agree upon the company's direction, and two to four family meetings a year. The surviving businesses tend to have strong boards that usually include a significant proportion of outsiders.[70]

13.6 Issues in Evaluation and Control

As a means by which a corporation's implementation of strategy can be evaluated, the control systems of large corporations have evolved over a long period of time in response to pressures from the environment (particularly the government). Conversely, an entrepreneur creates what is needed as the business grows. Because of his or her personal involvement in decision making, the entrepreneur managing a small business has little need for a formal, detailed reporting system. Thus a founder who has little understanding of accounting and a shortage of cash might employ a bookkeeper instead of an accountant. A formal personnel function might never appear because the entrepreneur lumps it in with simple bookkeeping and uses a secretary to handle personnel files. As an entrepreneurial venture becomes more established, it develops more complex evaluation and control systems, but they are often not the kind used in large corporations and are probably used for different purposes.

Financial statements, in particular, tell only half the story in small, privately owned companies. The formality of the financial reporting system in such a company is usually a result of pressures from government tax agencies, not from management's desire for an objective evaluation and control system. For example, the absence of taxes in Bermuda has been given as the reason why business owners keep little documentation—thus finding it nearly impossible to keep track of inventory, monitor sales, or calculate how much they are owed.[71]

Because balance sheets and income statements do not always give an accurate picture, standard ratios such as return on assets and debt–equity are unreliable. Research reveals systematic differences among liquidity and solvency measures for small compared to large companies. The mean averages of both the current ratio and the debt ratio are systematically larger for the small companies.[72] Cash flow is widely regarded as more important for an entrepreneurial business than is the traditional balance sheet or income statement. Even though a small business may be profitable in the accounting sense, a negative cash flow could bankrupt the company. Levin and Travis provide five reasons why owners, operators, and outside observers should be wary of using standard financial methods to indicate the health of a small, privately owned company[73]:

- **The line between debt and equity is blurred:** In some instances, what appears as a loan is really an easy-to-retrieve equity investment. The entrepreneur in this instance doesn't want to lose his or her investment if the company fails. Another condition is that retained earnings seldom reflect the amount of internal financing needed for the company's growth. This account may merely be a place in which cash is left so that the owner can avoid double taxation. To avoid other taxes, owner–managers may own fixed assets that they lease to the corporation. The equity that was used to buy those assets is really the company's equity, but it doesn't appear on the books.
- **Lifestyle is a part of financial statements:** The lifestyle of the owner and the owner's family is often reflected in the balance sheet. The assets of some firms include beach cottages, mountain chalets, and automobiles. In others, plants and warehouses that are used for company operations are not shown because they are held separately by the family. Income statements may not reflect how well the company is operating. Profitability is not as important in decision making in small, private companies as it is in large, publicly held corporations. For example, spending for recreation or transportation and paying rents or salaries above market rates to relatives put artificially high costs on the books of small firms. The business might appear to be poorly managed to an outsider, but the owner is acting rationally. The owner–manager wants dependable income or its equivalent with the least painful tax consequences. Because the standard profitability measures such as ROI are not useful in the evaluation of such a firm, Levin and Travis recommend return on current assets as a better measure of corporate productivity.

- **Standard financial formulas don't always apply:** Following practices that are in contrast to standard financial recommendations, small companies often use short-term debt to finance fixed assets. The absence of well-organized capital markets for small businesses, along with the typical banker's resistance to making loans without personal guarantees, leaves the private owner little choice. Although a large amount of long-term debt is considered to be a good use of financial leverage by a large publicly held firm, it can drive a smaller firm into bankruptcy by raising its break-even point.
- **Personal preference determines financial policies:** Because the owner is often the manager of the small firm, dividend policy is largely irrelevant. Dividend decisions are based not on stock price (which is usually unknown because the stock is not traded) but on the owner's lifestyle and the tradeoff between taking wealth from the corporation and double taxation.
- **Banks combine personal and business wealth:** Because of the large percentage of small businesses that go bankrupt every year, bank loan officers are reluctant to lend money to a small business unless the owner also provides some personal guarantees for the loan. In some instances, part of the loan may be composed of a second mortgage on the owner's house. If the owner does not want to succumb to this pressure by lenders to include the owner's personal assets as part of the collateral, the owner–manager must be willing to pay high interest rates for a loan that does not put the family's assets at risk.

13.7 Conclusion

Why is it that some entrepreneurial ventures are successful almost immediately and others fail to even reach breakeven? For some, it may be just "dumb luck" or serendipity. For others, it may be a matter of thinking through the idea before taking action. The underlying reason for new venture failure appears to be an overall lack of strategic management—beginning with an inability to plan a strategy to reach the customer and ending with a failure to develop a system of controls to keep track of performance. Many people new to entrepreneurship naively think that all that is needed to start a business is a good idea. Wrong!

An idea is *not* the same as an opportunity. An idea is a concept for a product or service that doesn't exist or is not currently available in a market niche. It may be a brand-new concept or an improvement of a current product or service. The idea can be developed from a person's experience or generated in a moment of creative insight. In contrast, an opportunity is an idea for a new product or service with a market that is willing to pay for that product or service so that it can form the basis of a profitable business.

Research indicates that writing a business plan (an entrepreneur's version of a strategic plan) improves the chances for success. A business plan is the test to see whether an idea is really an opportunity. Research also suggests that differentiation and focus are the competitive strategies that are most likely to lead to success, at least in the startup stage of development. Beyond these suggestions, it is up to the entrepreneur to find the right opportunity that fits the environment and his or her strengths and weaknesses.

One reason a new venture may not get immediate results with a new product or service is because not enough people are willing to try a new product until a sufficient number of others do so. They may be waiting for the tipping point. In epidemiology, the tipping point in an epidemic is the point at which there are enough carriers of a disease to allow an explosion that will infect a large number of people. Malcolm Gladwell proposes that a **tipping point** is also the point in which a situation that may have seemed stable or only very slowly changing suddenly goes through a massive, rapid shift. "It's the boiling point. It's the moment when the line starts to shoot straight upwards," explains Gladwell.[74] Until a product reaches the tipping point, sales may be very slow to develop and usually only to the few people who like to experiment with innovative products or services. The key is to be patient and to cultivate those customers who may influence the larger market that prefers to wait until a new product is perfected or accepted as the standard.[75] This is what happened to the company Research In Motion when it introduced its wireless e-mail gadget, called Blackberry, in 1999. The company hired "evangelists" to lend the devices to executives on Wall Street. Four years later, Blackberry arrived on Oprah Winfrey's "favorite things of 2003" and became an industry wireless standard.[76]

Strategy Bits

- Nations scoring highest on an innovation index measuring human resource skills, market incentive structures, and interaction between business and scientific sectors are the United States, Taiwan, Finland, Sweden, Japan, Israel, Switzerland, Canada, Australia, and Germany.[77]
- Regions in the United States scoring highest on a creativity index measuring technology, talent, and tolerance are Austin (TX), San Francisco (CA), Seattle (WA), Burlington (VT), Boston (MA), Raleigh-Durham-Chapel Hill (NC), Portland (OR), Madison (WI), Boise (ID), and Minneapolis (MN).[78]

Discussion Questions

1. In terms of strategic management, how does a new venture's situation differ from that of an ongoing small company?
2. How should a small entrepreneurial company engage in environmental scanning? To what aspects of the environment should management pay most attention?
3. What are the characteristics of an attractive industry from an entrepreneur's point of view? What role does innovation play?
4. What considerations should small-business entrepreneurs keep in mind when they are deciding whether a company should follow a growth or a stability strategy?
5. How does being family owned (as compared to being publicly owned) affect a firm's strategic management?

Strategic Practice Exercise

Read STRATEGY HIGHLIGHT 13.1, "Suggestions for Locating an Opportunity and Formulating a Business Strategy." Your strategy instructor may form multiple groups of five people each in your strategy class. Each group may be assigned one of the four approaches to identifying some ideas that could be opportunities for an entrepreneurial venture:

1. Tap the countertrend.
2. Eat off the established company's plate.
3. Switch the niche.
4. Borrow a business model.

When your group meets, discuss your assigned approach and identify one or more ideas that could be opportunities. Remember that an idea is a concept for a product or service that doesn't exist or is not currently available in a market niche. An opportunity is an idea for a new product or service with a market that is willing to pay for that product or service so that it can form the basis of a profitable business. This means that the idea has to have the potential to be profitable. Bring your ideas to class and see what your instructor and others in the class think of your ideas. Once all the ideas have been presented, take a vote on which of the ideas have the most likelihood of being opportunities.

(If this concept is not used as a class exercise, you may choose to meet informally with several members of your class over coffee. See if you can come up with an idea for each of the four approaches. Are any of them opportunities?)

Key Terms

advisory board (p. 324)
business plan (p. 322)
entrepreneur (p. 319)
entrepreneurial characteristic (p. 328)
entrepreneurial venture (p. 318)
factor affecting new venture success (p. 327)
family business (p. 332)
idea (p. 321)
lifestyle company (p. 331)
opportunity (p. 321)
small-business firm (p. 318)
source of innovation (p. 326)
strategic decision-making process for entrepreneurial venture (p. 321)
substage of small business development (p. 330)
tipping point (p. 335)

CHAPTER 14
Strategic Issues in Not-for-Profit Organizations

Learning Objectives

After reading this chapter, you should be able to:

- Identify the types of not-for-profit organizations
- Explain how sources of revenue influence not-for-profit strategic decision making
- Compare and contrast the strategic management of profit-making with not-for-profit organizations
- Discuss popular strategies being used by not-for-profit organizations

EIGHT TIMES A DAY, THE REVEREND BERNARD MCCOY SOLEMNLY CHANTS PRAYER IN Latin in the monastery chapel. He then goes back to his computer and telephone to manage LaserMonks. McCoy and four other monks at The Cistercian Abbey of Our Lady of Spring Bank in Sparta, Wisconsin, sell refilled inkjet and laser printer cartridges from their Internet site and telephone mail order center. LaserMonks offers the refills at prices 30% to 90% lower than offered at retail stores. Says McCoy, "You get quality products at great savings. We do good work with the extra income. Plus, the monks pray for you. I don't think Staples ever offered to do that."

Sales increased from $2,000 during their first year of business in 2002 to $500,000 in 2003, with a profit of $30,000. After expenses are paid for the business and the monastery, the money pays for everything from a defibrillator for the local fire department to providing free computer training for orphans in Vietnam. Worried about the monastery's not-for-profit status, LaserMonks was established as a profit-making corporation owned by the abbey. According to McCoy, "through charitable, legal means, we channel money to the abbey, which is how we don't jeopardize our tax-exempt status. . . . We pay business taxes like everybody else." Responding to the concern that a monastery should not be involved in business activities, McCoy states, "We're not selling God; we're selling black dust and ink so we can give our profits away to good causes. But you do have to walk a fine line in your marketing and not be offensive to God, yourself, or any other groups that have various relations to divine things."[1]

LaserMonks is an example of *strategic piggybacking*, a not-for-profit strategy that is as old as Girl Scout cookies and museum gift shops. Today's not-for-profits are using profit-making ventures as a way to diversify their revenue streams in tight financial times.[2] Piggybacking is a way for not-for-profits to earn money in a secondary business activity to support their primary mission, which may be raising orphans or providing a free educational experience.

By the mid-1990s, most not-for-profit organizations were turning to strategic management and other concepts from business to ensure their survival. According to Cynthia Massarsky, Deputy Director of the Yale School of Management—The Goldman Sachs Foundation Partnership on Nonprofit Ventures, "Nonprofits are looking to be more efficient in the way they do things. By taking a few lessons from the business world, perhaps they've learned how to operate a little more efficiently."[3] This is a significant change from past attitudes because most not-for-profit managers have traditionally felt that business concepts were not relevant to their situation. According to Peter Drucker:

> *Twenty years ago, management was a dirty word for those involved in nonprofit organizations. It meant business, and nonprofits prided themselves on being free of the taint of commercialism and above such sordid considerations as the bottom line. Now most of them have learned that nonprofits need management even more than business does, precisely because they lack the discipline of the bottom line.*[4]

A knowledge of not-for-profit organizations is important if only because they account for an average of 1 in every 20 jobs in nations throughout the world. A study by the Johns Hopkins University Institute for Policy Studies found that in nine countries between 1990 and 1995, nonprofit jobs grew by 23% compared to 6.2% for the whole economy.[5] Not-for-profits employ over 25% of the U.S. workforce and own approximately 15% of the nation's private wealth.[6] In the United States alone, in addition to various federal, state, and local government agencies, there are about 10,000 not-for-profit hospitals and nursing homes (84% of all hospitals), 4,600 colleges and universities, more than 100,000 private and public elementary and secondary schools, and almost 350,000 churches and synagogues, plus many thousands of charities and service organizations.[7]

Typically, **not-for-profit organizations (NFP)** include **private nonprofit corporations** (such as hospitals, institutes, private colleges, and organized charities) as well as **public governmental units or agencies** (such as welfare departments, prisons, and state universities). Traditionally, studies in strategic management have dealt with profit-making firms to the exclusion of nonprofit or governmental organizations. This, however, is changing. Increasing numbers of not-for-profit organizations are adopting strategic management.

Scholars and practitioners are concluding that many strategic management concepts and techniques can be successfully adapted for not-for-profit organizations.[8] Although the evidence is not yet conclusive, there appears to be an association between strategic planning efforts and performance measures such as growth.[9] The purpose of this chapter is, therefore, to highlight briefly the major differences between profit-making and not-for-profit organizations, so that the effects of their differences on the strategic management process can be understood.

14.1 Why Not-for-Profit?

The not-for-profit sector of an economy is important for several reasons. First, society desires certain goods and services that profit-making firms cannot or will not provide. These are referred to as **public or collective goods** because people who might not have paid for the goods receive benefits from them. Paved roads, police protection, museums, and schools are examples of public goods. A person cannot use a private good unless he or she pays for it. Generally, once a public good is provided, however, anyone can use or enjoy it.

Certain aspects of life do not appear to be served appropriately by profit-making business firms yet are often crucial to the well-being of society. These aspects include areas in which society as a whole benefits from a particular service but in which a particular individual benefits only indirectly. It is in these areas that not-for-profit organizations have traditionally been most effective. Libraries and museums are examples. Although most people do not visit libraries or museums very often, they are usually willing to pay taxes and/or donate funds to support their existence. They do so because they believe that these organizations act to uplift the culture and quality of life of the region. To fulfill their mission, entrance fees (if any) must be set low enough to allow everyone admission. These fees, however, are not profitable—they rarely even cover the costs of the service. The same is true of animal shelters managed by the Humane Society. Although few people want abandoned pets running wild through city streets, fees charged for the adoption of these animals cannot alone pay the costs of finding and caring for them. Additional revenue is needed—in the form of either donations or public taxation. Such public or collective services cannot generate a profit, yet they are necessary for any successful civilization. Which aspects of society are most suited to being served by not-for-profit organizations rather than by profit-making business organizations? This is an issue that governments face when they privatize what has previously been provided by the state. See the GLOBAL ISSUE feature to learn more about this development.

A second reason why the not-for-profit sector is important is that a private nonprofit organization tends to receive benefits from society that a private profit-making firm cannot obtain. Preferred tax status to nonstock corporations is given in section 501(c)(3) of the U.S. Internal Revenue Service code in the form of exemptions from corporate income taxes. Private non-

GLOBAL ISSUE

Which Is Best for Society: Business or Not-For-Profit?

Many nations throughout the world are attempting to privatize state-owned enterprises to balance their budgets. **Privatization** is (1) the selling of state-owned enterprises to private individuals or corporations or (2) the hiring of a private business to provide services previously offered by a state agency. The British government, for example, sold British Airways, its state-owned airline, to private investors. In the United States, many city governments now allow private companies to collect and dispose of trash—something that had previously been done by the city.

Problems can result, however, if privatization goes too far. For example, in converting from a communist-oriented, centrally managed economy to a more democratic, free-market economy, Eastern European countries are finding that profit-making business firms are unable to satisfy all of society's needs. What used to be provided by the state free of charge (but tax-supported) in Russia and other countries may now be provided only for the rich or not at all. The same problem is evident in the United States in the controversies over the provision of health care, retirement benefits, and private versus public education.

Some of the aspects of life that cannot easily be privatized and are often better managed by not-for-profit organizations are as follows:

- Religion
- Education
- Charities
- Clubs, interest groups, and unions
- Health care
- Government

The privatization of state-owned business enterprises is likely to continue globally because most of these enterprises must expand internationally in order to survive in the increasingly global environment. They cannot compete successfully if they are forced to follow inefficient, socially oriented policies and regulations (emphasizing employment over efficiency) rather than economically oriented, international practices (emphasizing efficiency over employment). The global trend toward privatization will probably continue until each country reaches the point where the efficiency of business is counterbalanced by the effectiveness of the not-for-profit sector of the economy. As political motives overcome economic ones, government will likely intervene in that decision.

profit firms also enjoy exemptions from various other state, local, and federal taxes. Under certain conditions, these firms also benefit from the tax deductibility of donors' contributions and membership dues. In addition, they qualify for special reduced-cost mailing privileges.[10] These benefits are allowed because private nonprofit organizations are typically service organizations, which are expected to use any excess of revenue over costs and expenses (a surplus rather than a profit) either to improve service or to reduce the price of their service. This service orientation is reflected in the fact that not-for-profit organizations do not use the term *customer* to refer to the recipient of the service. The recipient is typically referred to as a *patient, student, client, case*, or simply *the public*.

14.2 Importance of Revenue Source

The feature that best differentiates not-for-profit organizations from each other as well as from profit-making corporations is their source of revenue.[11] A **profit-making firm** depends on revenues obtained from the sale of its goods and services to customers, who typically pay for the costs and expenses of providing the product or service plus a profit. A not-for-profit organization, in contrast, depends heavily on dues, assessments, or donations from its membership, or on funding from a sponsoring agency, such as the United Way or the federal government, to pay for much of its costs and expenses.

Sources of Not-for-Profit Revenue

Revenue is generated from a variety of sources—not just from clients receiving the product or service from the not-for-profit. It can come from people who do not even receive the services they are subsidizing. One study of Minnesota nonprofits found that donations accounted for almost 40%, government grants for around 25%, and program service fees for about 35% of total revenues.[12] In other types of not-for-profit organizations—such as unions and voluntary medical plans—revenue comes mostly from the members, the people who receive the service. Nevertheless, the members typically pay dues in advance and must accept later whatever service is provided, whether they choose it or not and whether it is what they expected or not. The service is often received long after the dues are paid.

In profit-making corporations, there is typically a simple and direct connection between the customer or client and the organization. The organization tends to be totally dependent on sales of its products or services to the customer for revenue and is therefore extremely interested in pleasing the customer. As shown in **Figure 14–1**, a profit-making organization (organization A) tries to influence the customer (through advertising and promotion) to continue to buy and use its services. Either by buying or not buying the item offered, the customer, in turn, directly influences the organization's decision-making process. The business is thus market-oriented.

In the case of a typical not-for-profit organization, however, there is likely to be a very different sort of relationship between the organization providing and the person receiving the

Figure 14–1
The Effects of Sources of Revenue on Patterns of Client–Organization Influence

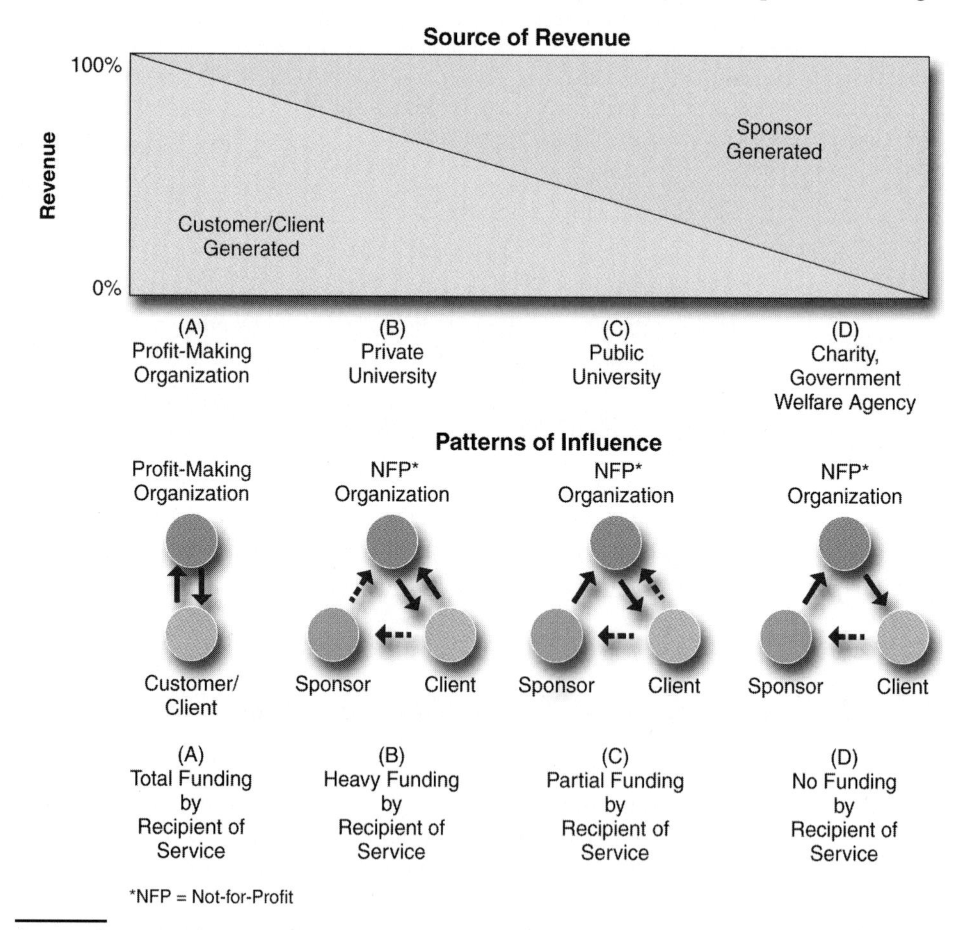

Source: Thomas L. Wheelen and J. David Hunger, "The Effect of Revenue Upon Patterns of Client–Organization Influence." Copyright © 1982 by Wheelen and Hunger Associates. Revised 1991. Reprinted by permission.

service. Because the recipient of the service typically does not pay the entire cost of the service, outside sponsors are required. In most instances, the sponsors receive none of the service but provide partial to total funding for the needed revenues. As indicated earlier, these sponsors can be the government (using taxpayers' money) or charitable organizations, such as the United Way (using voluntary donations). As shown in **Figure 14–1**, a not-for-profit organization can be partially dependent on sponsors for funding (*organizations B and C*) or totally dependent on the sponsors (*organization D*). The less money it receives from clients receiving the service or product, the less market-oriented is a not-for-profit organization.

Patterns of Influence on Strategic Decision Making

The **pattern of influence** on an organization's strategic decision making derives from its sources of revenue.[13] As shown in **Figure 14–1**, a private university (organization B) is heavily dependent on student tuition and other client-generated funds for about 70% of its revenue. Therefore, the students' desires are likely to have a stronger influence (as shown by an unbroken line) on the university's decision making than are the desires of the various sponsors such as alumni and private foundations. The sponsors' relatively marginal influence on the organization is reflected by a broken line. In contrast, a public university (organization C) is more heavily dependent on outside sponsors such as a state legislature for revenue funding. Student tuition and other client-generated funds form a small percentage (often less than 40%) of total revenue. Therefore, the university's decision making is heavily influenced by the sponsors (unbroken line) and only marginally influenced directly by the students (broken line).

In the case of organization D, however, the client has no direct influence on the organization because the client pays nothing for the services received. In this situation, the organization tends to measure its effectiveness in terms of sponsor satisfaction. It has no real measure of its efficiency other than its ability to carry out its mission and achieve its objectives within the dollar contributions it has received from its sponsors. In contrast to other organizations in which the client contributes a significant proportion of the needed revenue, organization D actually might be able to increase its revenue by heavily lobbying its sponsors while reducing the level of its service to its clients!

Regardless of the percentage of total funding that a client generates, the client may attempt to indirectly influence a not-for-profit organization through the sponsors. This is depicted by the broken lines connecting the client and the sponsor in organizations B, C, and D in **Figure 14–1**. Welfare clients or prison inmates, for example, may be able to indirectly improve the services they receive if they pressure government officials by writing to legislators or even by rioting. Students at public universities can lobby state officials for student representation on governing boards.

The key to understanding the management of a not-for-profit organization is thus learning who pays for the delivered services. If the recipients of the service pay only a small proportion of the total cost of the service, strategic managers are likely to be more concerned with satisfying the needs and desires of the funding sponsors or agency than those of the people receiving the service. The acquisition of resources can become an end in itself.

Usefulness of Strategic Management Concepts and Techniques

Some strategic management concepts can be equally applied to business and not-for-profit organizations, whereas others cannot. The marketplace orientation underlying portfolio analysis, for example, does not translate into situations in which client satisfaction and revenue are only indirectly linked. Industry analysis and competitive strategy are primarily relevant to not-for-profits that obtain most of their revenue from user fees rather than from donors or taxpayers. For example, as hospitals find themselves relying increasingly on patient fees for their revenue, they use competitive strategy to gain advantage versus other hospitals. Smaller not-for-profit hospitals stress the "high touch" of their staff over the "high tech" of competitors that have better diagnostic machinery. The concept of competitive advantage is less useful to a typical not-for-profit than the related concept of institutional advantage, which sets aside the profit-making objective of competitive advantage. A not-for-profit can be said to have **institutional advantage** when it performs its tasks more effectively than other comparable organizations.[14]

SWOT analysis, mission statements, stakeholder analysis, and corporate governance are, however, just as relevant to a not-for-profit as they are to a profit-making organization.[15] Portfolio analysis can be very helpful but is used very differently in not-for-profits than in business firms. (See the section on strategic piggybacking later in the chapter.) As with any corporation, nonprofits usually have boards of directors whose job is to ensure that the paid executive director and staff work to fulfill the organization's mission and objectives. Unlike the boards of most business firms, nonprofit boards are often required, however, to take primary responsibility for strategic planning and fund-raising. Many nonprofits find that a well-crafted mission statement not only helps in finding donors but also in attracting volunteers. Take the example of the mission statement of a local animal shelter:

> *To shelter and care for stray, lost, or abandoned animals and to responsibly place animals in new homes and enforce animal laws. We are also here to better educate people in ways to be solutions to animal problems, not causes.*[16]

Strategic management is difficult to apply when an organization's output is difficult to measure objectively, as is the case with most not-for-profit organizations. Thus it is very likely that many not-for-profit organizations have not used strategic management because its concepts, techniques, and prescriptions do not lend themselves to situations where sponsors, rather than the marketplace, determine revenue. The situation, however, is changing. The trend toward privatizing public organizations, such as converting subsidized community hospitals to independent (nonsubsidized) status, usually means that the clients/patients pay a larger percentage of the costs. As these not-for-profits become more market oriented (and thus client oriented), strategic management becomes more applicable and more increasingly used.[17] Nevertheless, various constraints on not-for-profits mean that strategic management concepts and techniques must be modified to be effective.

14.3 Impact of Constraints on Strategic Management

Several characteristics peculiar to a not-for-profit organization constrain its behavior and affect its strategic management. Newman and Wallender list the following five **constraints on strategic management**:

1. **Service is often intangible and hard to measure.** This difficulty is typically compounded by the existence of multiple service objectives developed to satisfy multiple sponsors.
2. **Client influence may be weak.** Often the organization has a local monopoly, and clients' payments may be a very small source of funds.
3. **Strong employee commitments to professions or to a cause may undermine allegiance** to the organization employing them.
4. **Resource contributors may intrude on the organization's internal management.** Such contributors include fund contributors and government.
5. **Restraints on the use of rewards and punishments** may result from constraints 1, 3, and 4.[18]

It is true that several of these characteristics can be found in profit-making as well as in not-for-profit organizations. Nevertheless, as Newman and Wallender state, the "frequency of strong impact is much higher in not-for-profit enterprises."[19]

Impact on Strategy Formulation

The long-range planning and decision making affected by the listed constraints serve to add at least four **complications to strategy formulation**:

1. **Goal conflicts interfere with rational planning:** Because a not-for-profit organization typically lacks a single clear-cut performance criterion (such as profits), divergent goals and objectives are likely, especially with multiple sponsors. Differences in the concerns of various important sponsors can prevent management from stating the organization's mission in anything but very broad terms, if they fear that a sponsor who disagrees with a particular, narrow definition of mission might cancel its funding. For example, a study of 227 public Canadian hospitals found that more than half had very general, ambiguous, and unquantified objectives.[20] According to Heffron, an authority in public administration, "The greater openness within which they are compelled to operate—the fishbowl atmosphere—impedes thorough discussion of issues and discourages long-range plans that might alienate stakeholders."[21] In such organizations, it is the reduced influence of the clients that permits this diversity of values and goals to occur without a clear market check. For example, when a city council considers changing zoning to implement a strategic plan for the city, all sorts of people (including the press) will demand to be heard. A decision might be made based on pressure from a few stakeholders (who make significant contributions or who threaten to stir up trouble) to the detriment of the community as a whole.
2. **An integrated planning focus tends to shift from results to resources:** Because not-for-profit organizations tend to provide services that are hard to measure, they rarely have a net bottom line.[22] Planning, therefore, becomes more concerned with resource inputs, which can easily be measured, than with service, which cannot. Goal displacement (explained in **Chapter 11**) becomes even more likely than it is in business organizations.[23]
3. **Ambiguous operating objectives create opportunities for internal politics and goal displacement:** The combination of vague objectives and a heavy concern with resources allows managers considerable leeway in their activities. Such leeway makes possible political maneuvering for personal ends. In addition, because the effectiveness of a not-for-profit organization hinges on the satisfaction of the sponsoring group, management tends to ignore the needs of the client while focusing on the desires of a powerful sponsor. University administrators commonly say that people will donate money for a new building (which will carry the donor's name) but not for other more pressing needs, such as the maintenance of existing buildings. In this situation, powerful department heads might wine and dine the donor, hoping to get the money for their pet projects. This problem is compounded by the common practice of selecting people to boards of trustees/directors not on the basis of their managerial experience but on the basis of their ability to contribute money, raise funds, and work with politicians. (A major role of a not-for-profit board is to ensure adequate resources—usually translated to mean fund-raising.[24]) Directors usually receive no compensation for serving on the board. Their lack of interest in overseeing management is reflected in an overall not-for-profit board-meeting attendance rate of only 50%, compared with 90% for boards of directors of business corporations. This is one reason why boards of not-for-profits tend to be larger than are boards of business corporations. Eckerd College, for example, has a 52-member, extremely passive board of directors.[25] Board members of not-for-profit organizations tend to ignore the task of determining strategies and policies—often leaving that to the paid (or sometimes unpaid)

executive director. The larger the board, the less likely it is to exercise control over top management.[26]

4. **Professionalization simplifies detailed planning but adds rigidity:** In not-for-profit organizations in which professionals play important roles (as in hospitals or colleges), professional values and traditions can prevent the organization from changing its conventional behavior patterns to fit new service missions tuned to changing social needs. This rigidity, of course, can occur in any organization that hires professionals. The strong service orientation of most not-for-profit organizations, however, tends to encourage the development of static professional norms and attitudes. As not-for-profits attempt to become more business-like, this may be changing. One study of Minnesota nonprofits revealed that 29% of the program directors and 15% of the staff had degrees or experience in business administration.[27]

Impact on Strategy Implementation

The five constraining characteristics also affect how a not-for-profit organization is organized in both its structure and job design. Three **complications to strategy implementation** in particular can be highlighted:

1. **Decentralization is complicated:** The difficulty of setting objectives for an intangible, hard-to-measure service mission complicates the delegation of decision-making authority. Because of the heavy dependence on sponsors for revenue support, the top management of a not-for-profit organization must be always alert to the sponsors' view of an organizational activity. This necessary caution leads to **defensive centralization**, in which top management retains all decision-making authority so that low-level managers cannot take any actions to which the sponsors may object.
2. **Linking pins for external–internal integration become important:** Because of the heavy dependence on outside sponsors, a special need arises for people in buffer roles to relate to both inside and outside groups. This role is especially necessary when the sponsors are diverse (revenue comes from donations, membership fees, and federal funds) and the service is intangible (for instance, a "good" education) with a broad mission and multiple shifting objectives. The job of a *Dean for External Affairs*, for example, consists primarily of working with the school's alumnae and raising funds.
3. **Job enlargement and executive development can be restrained by professionalism:** In organizations that employ a large number of professionals, managers must design jobs that appeal to prevailing professional norms. Professionals have rather clear ideas about which activities are, and which are not, within their province. Enriching a nurse's job by expanding his or her decision-making authority for drug dosage, for example, can cause conflict with medical doctors who believe that such authority is theirs alone. Because a professional often views managerial jobs as nonprofessional and merely supportive, promotion into a management position is not always viewed positively.

Impact on Evaluation and Control

Special **complications to evaluation and control** arising from the constraining characteristics also affect how behavior is motivated and performance is controlled. Two problems, in particular, are often noticed:

1. **Rewards and penalties have little or no relationship to performance:** When desired results are vague and the judgment of success is subjective, predictable and impersonal feedback cannot be established. Performance is judged either intuitively ("You don't

seem to be taking your job seriously") or on the basis of whatever small aspects of a job can be measured ("You were late to work twice last month").

2. **Inputs rather than outputs are heavily controlled:** Because its inputs can be measured much more easily than outputs, a not-for-profit organization tends to focus more on the resources going into performance than on the performance itself.[28] The emphasis is thus on setting maximum limits for costs and expenses. Because there is little to no reward for staying under these limits, people usually respond negatively to such controls.

Because of these and other complications, not-for-profits can waste money in many ways, especially on administrative costs and expenses. Because of this, it is becoming increasingly common to calculate ratios comparing total support and revenue with the amounts spent on specific service activities. For example, analysts become concerned when the total spent on the mission of the organization (e.g., community service) is less than 50% of total income received from sponsors and activities. Other rules of thumb are that a not-for-profit should not spend more than 35% on administrative expenses and that the costs of fund-raising should not account for more than 15% of total income.[29]

14.4 Not-for-Profit Strategies

One of the issues in the strategic management of not-for-profit organizations is the tendency of nonprofits to make program decisions based on a mission rather than on a strategy. Kasturi Rangan points out that many nonprofits don't have a strategy at all; instead, they rally under a particular cause, such as "Fight homelessness" or "Save the children."[30] Because that cause is so worthwhile, nonprofits tend to support any program that's even slightly related to the mission, so long as there is money available (at least in the beginning) to support the new program. Without a clear long-term strategy, this will eventually stretch the not-for-profit's core capabilities into unintended directions and create a budget with more expenses than revenues. The need to attract additional donors forces not-for-profits to go after grants or donations that fit within their broadly defined mission but only slightly fit their existing capabilities. The problem is that such a grant usually contains restrictions that the funding be spent on a particular program or initiative. Starved for money, not-for-profits accept these restrictions in order to obtain the funding. Because the funds barely cover the direct costs of the additional activity, unanticipated indirect costs force the not-for-profit to look for more funding, each time as a larger, less focused, and more cash-starved organization. The result is an organization with large bureaucratic overhead but not enough professionals to carry out all its programs effectively. This leads to increasing pressure to reduce costs and to use more volunteers—both of which may reduce the quality of service to clients. Professional employees become demoralized because of increasing service demands, less support, and marginal pay raises.

The organization's executive director is usually too busy administering a convoluted bureaucracy, dealing with bickering professional employees, and fund-raising to do any serious strategic planning. It is therefore usually left to the board of directors to call a stop to this *activity trap*. The board must define achievable objectives and propose a strategy to make them happen. It must decide not only what the organization will do but also what it will not do. Given that the primary mission is sacrosanct, the board should develop a narrow operational mission with measurable objectives and a strategy to go with them.[31] Once this is done, the organization is free to decide which programs to support and which to curtail.

If a not-for-profit organization has established an operational mission and measurable service objectives, it can consider various ways to support its priority programs without having to accept mission-extending donor requirements. Increasingly, not-for-profits are choosing the strategies of strategic piggybacking, mergers, and strategic alliances.

Strategic Piggybacking

Coined by Nielsen, the term **strategic piggybacking** refers to the development of a new activity for a not-for-profit organization that would generate the funds needed to make up the difference between revenues and expenses.[32] The new activity is typically related in some manner to the not-for-profit's mission, but its purpose is to help subsidize the primary service programs. It appears to be a form of concentric diversification, but it is engaged in not as part of the mission but only for its money-generating value. In an inverted use of portfolio analysis, the organization invests in new, safe cash cows to fund its current cash-hungry question marks and dogs. It is a type of **social entrepreneurship**, in which a not-for-profit organization starts a new venture to achieve social goals.

Although strategic piggybacking is not new, it has recently become very popular. As early as 1874, for example, the Metropolitan Museum of Art retained a professional to photograph its collections and to sell copies of the prints. Profits were used to defray the museum's operating costs. More recently, various income-generating ventures have appeared under various auspices, from the Girl Scouts to UNICEF, and in numerous forms, from cookies and small gift shops to vast real estate developments. A study by the U.S. General Accounting Office revealed that the amount of funds resulting from income-producing activities of not-for-profits has significantly increased since the 1970s. Hospitals are offering wellness programs, ranging from meditation classes to aerobics. Some 70% of colleges and universities now offer "auxiliary" services, such as bookstores, conference rooms, and computer centers, as sources of income.[33] The American Cancer Society earns millions annually by allowing its name to appear on products sold by private drug companies, such as GlaxoSmithKline's Nicorette chewing gum. The Metropolitan Museum of Art now has 16 stores outside the main museum and a fast-growing web site—all of which generate money. The Baptist Hospital of Nashville, Tennessee, built and operates a $15 million, 18-acre office and training-field complex, which it rents to Nashville's professional football team.

The U.S. Small Business Administration, however, views this money-making activity as "unfair competition." The U.S. Internal Revenue Service (IRS) advises that a not-for-profit that engages in a business "not substantially related" to the organization's exempt purposes may jeopardize its tax-exempt status, particularly if the income from the business exceeds approximately 20% of total organizational revenues. The IRS requires not-for-profits to pay an unrelated business income tax on commercial activities that don't relate to the organization's central mission. So far, not-for-profits are still considered tax exempt if their businesses are staffed by volunteers or if almost all their merchandise is donated. According to Marcus Owens, Director of Tax-Exempt Organizations for the IRS, "The ultimate question is should these institutions continue as tax-exempt entities. And it's being raised more than ever before."[34] This has caused many not-for-profits such as The Cistercian Abbey mentioned earlier to establish two separate entities. "Doing all the separate bookkeeping, accounting, and cost allocations can be a bit burdensome, time-consuming and distracting," says Jeffrey Tanenbaum, a lawyer specializing in representing nonprofits.[35]

Although strategic piggybacks can help not-for-profit organizations self-subsidize their primary missions and better use their resources, according to Nielsen, there are several potential drawbacks.[36] First, the revenue-generating venture could actually lose money, especially in the short run. Second, the venture could subvert, interfere with, or even take over the primary mission. Third, the public, as well as the sponsors, could reduce their contributions because of negative responses to such "money-grubbing activities" or because of a mistaken belief that the organization is becoming self-supporting. Fourth, the venture could interfere with the internal operations of the not-for-profit organization. To avoid these drawbacks, a not-for-profit should carefully evaluate its resources before choosing this strategy. See **Strategy Highlight 14.1** to see the resources needed for a piggyback.

STRATEGY HIGHLIGHT 14.1

Resources Needed for Successful Strategic Piggybacking

Based on his experience as a consultant to not-for-profit organizations, Edward Skloot suggests that a not-for-profit should have five resources before engaging in strategic piggybacking:

1. **Something to sell:** The organization should assess its resources to see if people might be willing to pay for goods or services closely related to the organization's primary activity. Repackaging the Boston Symphony into the less formal Boston Pops Orchestra created a way to subsidize the deficit-creating symphony and provide year-round work for the musicians.
2. **Critical mass of management talent:** Enough people must be available to nurture and sustain an income venture over the long haul. This can be very difficult, given that the most competent not-for-profit professionals often don't want to be managers.
3. **Trustee support:** If the trustees have strong feelings against earned-income ventures, they could actively or passively resist commercial involvement. When the Children's Television Workshop began licensing its Sesame Street characters to toy companies and theme parks, many people criticized it for joining business in selling more things to children.
4. **Entrepreneurial attitude:** Management must be able to combine an interest in innovative ideas with business-like practicality.
5. **Venture capital:** Because it often takes money to make money, engaging in a joint venture with a business corporation can provide the necessary startup funds as well as the marketing and management support. For example, Massachusetts General Hospital received $50 million from Hoechst, the German chemical company, for biological research in exchange for exclusive licenses to develop commercial products from particular research discoveries.

Source: Reprinted by permission of the *Harvard Business Review.* From "Should Not-for-Profits Go into Business?" by E. Skloot, January–February 1983.

The U.S. National Association of College and University Business Officers predicts that within a few years, more than 90% of colleges and universities in the United States will be using strategic piggybacks.[37] A similar trend is expected for other not-for-profits that heavily rely on donations and taxpayer support for their revenue.

Mergers

Dwindling resources are leading an increasing number of not-for-profits to consider mergers as a way of reducing costs through economies of scope and reducing program duplication and raising prices because of increased market power.[38] For example, the merger of Baptist Health Systems and Research Health Services created Health Midwest in Kansas City. The New York Hospital–Cornell Medical Center and Columbia–Presbyterian Medical Center combined to form the New York and Presbyterian Hospitals Health Care System. Since 1990, more than 45% of U.S. hospitals have been involved in mergers and acquisitions.[39]

Strategic Alliances

Strategic alliances involve developing cooperative ties with other organizations. Not-for-profit organizations often use alliances as a way to enhance their capacity to serve clients or to acquire resources while still enabling them to keep their identities.[40] Services can be purchased and provided more efficiently through cooperation with other organizations than if they were done alone. For example, four Ohio universities agreed to create and jointly operate a new school of international business. Alone, none of the business schools could afford the $30 million to build the school. The Collaborative Ventures Program of the Teagle Foundation has given more than $4 million in grants to help colleges set up money-saving collaborations. While only a handful of consortia existed in 1995, by 1998 there were at least 21, representing 125 colleges and universities.[41]

Strategic alliances and mergers are becoming commonplace among not-for-profit organizations. The next logical step is strategic alliances between business firms and not-for-profits. Already, business corporations are forming alliances with universities to fund university research in exchange for options on the results of that research. Business firms find it cheaper to pay universities to do basic research than to do it themselves. Universities are in need of research funds to attract top professors and to maintain expensive labs. Such alliances of convenience are being criticized, but they are likely to continue.

14.5 Conclusion

Not-for-profit organizations are an important part of society. Understanding their reasons for existence and their differences from profit-making corporations is therefore important. The lack of profit motive often results in vague statements of mission and unmeasurable objectives. Coupled with a concern for maintaining funding from sponsors, these factors can cause a lack of consideration for the very clients the organization was designed to serve. Programs that have little or no connection with the organization's mission may develop. Nevertheless, not-for-profit organizations are usually established to provide goods and services judged valuable by society that profit-making firms cannot or will not provide. Judging their performance simply on the basis of economic considerations is dangerous because they are designed to deal with conditions under which profit-making corporations could not easily survive.

Strategy Bits

- Countries with the highest number of people in prison per 100,000 population are the United States (707), Russia (638), Belarus (554), Kazakhstan (522), Turkmenistan (489), Bermuda (447), Suriname (437), Bahamas (416), Ukraine (416), and South Africa (404).[42]
- Countries with the most hospital beds per 1,000 population are Japan (17.0), Norway (14.0), Russia (13.1), Moldova (12.9), Estonia (12.0), Belarus (11.8), the Netherlands (11.5), Martinique (10.7), Georgia (10.5), and Kirgizstan (10.4).[43]

Discussion Questions

1. Are not-for-profit organizations less efficient than profit-making organizations? Why or why not?
2. How does the lack of a clear-cut performance measure, such as profits, affect the strategic management of a not-for-profit organization?
3. What are the pros and cons of strategic piggybacking? In what way is it "unfair competition" for not-for-profits to engage in revenue generating activity?
4. What are the pros and cons of mergers and strategic alliances? Should not-for-profits engage in alliances with business firms?
5. A number of not-for-profit organizations in the United States have been converting to profit making. Why would a not-for-profit organization want to change its status to profit making? What are the pros and cons of doing so?

Strategic Practice Exercises

1. Read the **Global Issue** feature in this chapter. It lists six aspects of society that it proposes are better managed by not-for-profit organizations than by profit-making organizations. Do you agree with this list? Should some aspects be deleted from the list? Should other aspects be added?
2. Examine a local college or university—perhaps the one you may be currently attending. What strategic issues is it facing? Develop a SFAS Matrix (see **Figure 6–1**) of strategic factors. Is it attempting to use any strategic management concepts? If so, which ones? What sorts of strategies should it consider for contin-

ued survival and future growth? Is it currently using strategic piggybacks to obtain additional funding? What sorts of additional piggybacks should it consider? Are strategic alliances with another college or university or business firm a possibility?

Key Terms

complication to evaluation and control (p. 346)
complication to strategy formulation (p. 345)
complication to strategy implementation (p. 346)
constraint on strategic management (p. 344)
defensive centralization (p. 346)
institutional advantage (p. 344)
not-for-profit organization (p. 340)
pattern of influence (p. 343)
private nonprofit corporation (p. 340)
privatization (p. 341)
profit-making firm (p. 341)
public governmental unit or agency (p. 340)
public or collective good (p. 340)
social entrepreneurship (p. 348)
strategic piggybacking (p. 348)

analyzing strategy cases. This chapter provides various analytical techniques and suggestions for conducting this kind of case analysis.

15.1 The Case Method

The analysis and discussion of case problems has been the most popular method of teaching strategy and policy for many years. The case method provides the opportunity to move from a narrow, specialized view that emphasizes functional techniques to a broader, less precise analysis of the overall corporation. Cases present actual business situations and enable you to examine both successful and unsuccessful corporations. In case analysis, you might be asked to critically analyze a situation in which a manager had to make a decision of long-term corporate importance. This approach gives you a feel for what it is like to face making and implementing strategic decisions.

15.2 Researching the Case Situation

You should not restrict yourself only to the information written in the case unless your instructor states otherwise. You should, if possible, undertake outside research about the environmental setting. Check the decision date of each case (typically the latest date mentioned in the case) to find out when the situation occurred and then screen the business periodicals for that time period. An understanding of the economy during that period will help you avoid making a serious error in your analysis—for example, suggesting a sale of stock when the stock market is at an all-time low or taking on more debt when the prime interest rate is over 15%. Information about the industry will provide insights into its competitive activities. *Important Note: Don't go beyond the decision date of the case in your research unless directed to do so by your instructor.*

Use computerized company and industry information services such as Compustat, Compact Disclosure, and CD/International, available on CD-ROM or online at the library. On the Internet, Hoover's Online Corporate Directory (www.hoovers.com) and the Security and Exchange Commission's Edgar database (www.sec.gov) provide access to corporate annual reports and 10-K forms. This background will give you an appreciation for the situation as it was experienced by the participants in the case. Use a search engine such as Google or Alta Vista to find additional information about the industry and the company.

A company's **annual report** and **SEC 10-K, 10-Q**, and **14-A forms** from the year of the case can be very helpful. According to the Yankelovich Partners survey firm, 8 out of 10 portfolio managers and 75% of security analysts use annual reports when making decisions.[6] They contain not only the usual income statements and balance sheets but also cash flow statements and notes to the financial statements, indicating why certain actions were taken. 10-K forms include detailed information not usually available in an annual report. 10-Q forms include quarterly financial reports. 14-A forms include detailed information on members of a company's board of directors and proxy statements for annual meetings. Some resources available for research into the economy and a corporation's industry are suggested in **Appendix 15.A**.

A caveat: Before obtaining additional information about the company profiled in a particular case, ask your instructor if doing so is appropriate for your class assignment. Your strategy instructor may want you to stay within the confines of the case information such as the decision date, provided in the book. In this case, it is usually acceptable to at least learn more about the societal environment at the time of the case.

15.3 Financial Analysis: A Place to Begin

Once you have read a case, a good place to begin your analysis is with the financial statements. **Ratio analysis** is the calculation of ratios from data in these statements. It is done to identify possible financial strengths or weaknesses. Thus it is a valuable part of SWOT analysis. A review of key financial ratios can help you assess a company's overall situation and pinpoint some problem areas. Ratios are useful, regardless of firm size, and they enable you to compare a company's ratios with industry averages. **Table 15–1** lists some of the most important financial ratios, which are (1) **liquidity ratios**, (2) **profitability ratios**, (3) **activity ratios**, and (4) **leverage ratios**.

Analyzing Financial Statements

In your analysis, do not simply make an exhibit that includes all the ratios (unless your instructor requires you to do so), but select and discuss only those ratios that have an impact on the company's problems. For instance, accounts receivable and inventory may provide a source of funds. If receivables and inventories are double the industry average, reducing them may provide needed cash. In this situation, the case report should include not only sources of funds but also the number of dollars freed for use. Compare these ratios with industry averages to discover whether the company is out of line with others in the industry. Annual and quarterly industry ratios can be found in the library or on the Internet. (See the resources for case research in **Appendix 15.A**.)

A typical financial analysis of a firm would include a study of the operating statements for five or so years, including a trend analysis of sales, profits, earnings per share, debt-to-equity ratio, return on investment, and so on, plus a ratio study comparing the firm under study with industry standards. As a minimum, undertake the following five steps in basic financial analysis.

1. Scrutinize historical income statements and balance sheets. These two basic statements provide most of the data needed for analysis. Statements of cash flow may also be useful.
2. Compare historical statements over time if a series of statements is available.
3. Calculate changes that occur in individual categories from year to year, as well as the cumulative total change.
4. Determine the change as a percentage as well as an absolute amount.
5. Adjust for inflation if that was a significant factor.

Examination of this information may reveal developing trends. Compare trends in one category with trends in related categories. For example, an increase in sales of 15% over three years may appear to be satisfactory until you note an increase of 20% in the cost of goods sold during the same period. The outcome of this comparison might suggest that further investigation into the manufacturing process is necessary. If a company is reporting strong net income growth but negative cash flow, this would suggest that the company is relying on something other than operations for earnings growth. Is it selling off assets or cutting R&D? If accounts receivable are growing faster than are sales revenues, the company is not getting paid for the products or services it is counting as sold. Is the company dumping product on its distributors at the end of the year to boost its reported annual sales? If so, expect the distributors to return the unordered product the next month, thus drastically cutting the next year's reported sales.

Other "tricks of the trade" need to be examined. Until June 2000, firms growing through acquisition were allowed to account for the cost of the purchased company through the pool-

TABLE 15–1 FINANCIAL RATIO ANALYSIS

	Formula	How Expressed	Meaning
1. **Liquidity Ratios**			
Current ratio	$\frac{\text{Current assets}}{\text{Current liabilities}}$	Decimal	A short-term indicator of the company's ability to pay its short-term liabilities from short-term assets; how much of current assets are available to cover each dollar of current liabilities.
Quick (acid test) ratio	$\frac{\text{Current assets} - \text{Inventory}}{\text{Current liabilities}}$	Decimal	Measures the company's ability to pay off its short-term obligations from current assets, excluding inventories.
Inventory to net working capital	$\frac{\text{Inventory}}{\text{Current assets} - \text{Current liabilities}}$	Decimal	A measure of inventory balance; measures the extent to which the cushion of excess current assets over current liabilities may be threatened by unfavorable changes in inventory.
Cash ratio	$\frac{\text{Cash} + \text{Cash equivalents}}{\text{Current liabilities}}$	Decimal	Measures the extent to which the company's capital is in cash or cash equivalents; shows how much of the current obligations can be paid from cash or near-cash assets.
2. **Profitability Ratios**			
Net profit margin	$\frac{\text{Net profit after taxes}}{\text{Net sales}}$	Percentage	Shows how much after-tax profits are generated by each dollar of sales.
Gross profit margin	$\frac{\text{Sales} - \text{Cost of goods sold}}{\text{Net sales}}$	Percentage	Indicates the total margin available to cover other expenses beyond cost of goods sold and still yield a profit.
Return on investment (ROI)	$\frac{\text{Net profit after taxes}}{\text{Total assets}}$	Percentage	Measures the rate of return on the total assets utilized in the company; a measure of management's efficiency, it shows the return on all the assets under its control, regardless of source of financing.
Return on equity (ROE)	$\frac{\text{Net profit after taxes}}{\text{Shareholders' equity}}$	Percentage	Measures the rate of return on the book value of shareholders' total investment in the company.
Earnings per share (EPS)	$\frac{\text{Net profit after taxes} - \text{Preferred stock dividends}}{\text{Average number of common shares}}$	Dollars per share	Shows the after-tax earnings generated for each share of common stock.
3. **Activity Ratios**			
Inventory turnover	$\frac{\text{Net sales}}{\text{Inventory}}$	Decimal	Measures the number of times that average inventory of finished goods was turned over or sold during a period of time, usually a year.
Days of inventory	$\frac{\text{Inventory}}{\text{Cost of goods sold} \div 365}$	Days	Measures the number of one day's worth of inventory that a company has on hand at any given time.
Net working capital turnover	$\frac{\text{Net sales}}{\text{Net working capital}}$	Decimal	Measures how effectively the net working capital is used to generate sales.
Asset turnover	$\frac{\text{Sales}}{\text{Total assets}}$	Decimal	Measures the utilization of all the company's assets; measures how many sales are generated by each dollar of assets.

TABLE 15–1 (CONTINUED)

	Formula	How Expressed	Meaning
Fixed asset turnover	Sales / Fixed assets	Decimal	Measures the utilization of the company's fixed assets (i.e., plant and equipment); measures how many sales are generated by each dollar of fixed assets.
Average collection period	Accounts receivable / Sales for year ÷ 365	Days	Indicates the average length of time in days that a company must wait to collect a sale after making it; may be compared to the credit terms offered by the company to its customers.
Accounts receivable turnover	Annual credit sales / Accounts receivable	Decimal	Indicates the number of times that accounts receivable are cycled during the period (usually a year).
Accounts payable period	Accounts payable / Purchases for year ÷ 365	Days	Indicates the average length of time in days that the company takes to pay its credit purchases.
Days of cash	Cash / Net sales for year ÷ 365	Days	Indicates the number of days of cash on hand, at present sales levels.
4. **Leverage Ratios**			
Debt to asset ratio	Total debt / Total assets	Percentage	Measures the extent to which borrowed funds have been used to finance the company's assets.
Debt to equity ratio	Total debt / Shareholders' equity	Percentage	Measures the funds provided by creditors versus the funds provided by owners.
Long-term debt to capital structure	Long-term debt / Shareholders' equity	Percentage	Measures the long-term component of capital structure.
Times interest earned	Profit before taxes + Interest charges / Interest charges	Decimal	Indicates the ability of the company to meet its annual interest costs.
Coverage of fixed charges	Profit before taxes + Interest charges + Lease charges / Interest charges + Lease obligations	Decimal	A measure of the company's ability to meet all of its fixed-charge obligations.
Current liabilities to equity	Current liabilities / Shareholders' equity	Percentage	Measures the short-term financing portion versus that provided by owners.
5. **Other Ratios**			
Price/earnings ratio	Market price per share / Earnings per share	Decimal	Shows the current market's evaluation of a stock, based on its earnings; shows how much the investor is willing to pay for each dollar of earnings.
Divided payout ratio	Annual dividends per share / Annual earnings per share	Percentage	Indicates the percentage of profit that is paid out as dividends.
Dividend yield on common stock	Annual dividends per share / Current market price per share	Percentage	Indicates the dividend rate of return to common shareholders at the current market price.

Note: In using ratios for analysis, calculate ratios for the corporation and compare them to the average and quartile ratios for the particular industry. Refer to Standard & Poor's and Robert Morris Associates for average industry data. Special thanks to Dr. Moustafa H. Abdelsamad, Dean, Business School, Texas A&M University–Corpus Christi, Corpus Christi, Texas, for his definitions of these ratios.

GLOBAL ISSUE

Financial Statements of Multinational Corporations: Not Always What They Seem

A multinational corporation follows the accounting rules for its home country. As a result, its financial statements may be somewhat difficult to understand or to use for comparisons with competitors from other countries. For example, British firms such as British Petroleum and The Body Shop use the term *turnover* rather than *sales revenue*. In the case of AB Electrolux of Sweden, a footnote to an annual report indicates that the consolidated accounts have been prepared in accordance with Swedish accounting standards, which differ in certain significant respects from U.S. generally accepted accounting principles (U.S. GAAP). For one year, net income of 4,830m SEK (Swedish kronor) approximated 5,655m SEK according to U.S. GAAP. Total assets for the same period were 84,183m SEK according to Swedish principles, but 86,658m SEK according to U.S. GAAP.

ing of both companies' stock. This approach was used in 40% of the value of mergers between 1997 and 1999. The pooling method enabled the acquiring company to disregard the premium it paid for the other firm (the amount above the fair market value of the purchased company, often called "goodwill"). Thus, when PepsiCo agreed to purchase Quaker Oats for $13.4 billion in PepsiCo stock, the $13.4 billion was not found on PepsiCo's balance sheet. As of June 2000, merging firms must use the "purchase" accounting rules, in which the true purchase price is reflected in the financial statements.[7]

The analysis of a multinational corporation's financial statements can get very complicated, especially if its headquarters is in another country that uses different accounting standards. See the GLOBAL ISSUE for why financial analysis can get tricky at times.

Common-Size Statements

Common-size statements are income statements and balance sheets in which the dollar figures have been converted into percentages. These statements are used to identify trends in each of the categories, such as cost of goods sold as a percentage of sales (sales is the denominator). For the income statement, net sales represent 100%: You calculate the percentage for each category so that the categories sum to the net sales percentage (100%). For the balance sheet, you give the total assets a value of 100% and calculate other asset and liability categories as percentages of the total assets with total assets as the denominator. (Individual asset and liability items, such as accounts receivable and accounts payable, can also be calculated as a percentage of net sales.)

When you convert statements to this form, it is relatively easy to note the percentage that each category represents of the total. Look for trends in specific items, such as cost of goods sold, when compared to the company's historical figures. To get a proper picture, however, you need to make comparisons with industry data, if available, to see whether fluctuations are merely reflecting industrywide trends. If a firm's trends are generally in line with those of the rest of the industry, problems are less likely than if the firm's trends are worse than industry averages. If ratios are not available for the industry, calculate the ratios for the industry's best and worst firms and compare them to the firm you are analyzing. Common-size statements are especially helpful in developing scenarios and pro forma statements because they provide a series of historical relationships (for example, cost of goods sold to sales, interest to sales, and inventories as a percentage of assets) from which you can estimate the future with your scenario assumptions for each year.

Z-Value, Index of Sustainable Growth, and Free Cash Flow

If a corporation being studied appears to be in poor financial condition, use **Altman's Bankruptcy Formula** to calculate its **Z-value**. The Z-value formula combines five ratios by weighting them according to their importance to a corporation's financial strength. The formula is:

$$Z = 1.2x_1 + 1.4x_2 + 3.3x_3 + 0.6x_4 + 1.0x_5$$

where:

x_1 = Working capital/Total assets (%)
x_2 = Retained earnings/Total assets (%)
x_3 = Earnings before interest and taxes/Total assets (%)
x_4 = Market value of equity/Total liabilities (%)
x_5 = Sales/Total assets (number of times)

A score below 1.81 indicates significant credit problems, whereas a score above 3.0 indicates a healthy firm. Scores between 1.81 and 3.0 indicate question marks.[8]

The **index of sustainable growth** is useful to learn whether a company embarking on a growth strategy will need to take on debt to fund this growth. The index indicates how much of the growth rate of sales can be sustained by internally generated funds. The formula is:

$$g^* = \frac{[P(1 - D)(1 + L)]}{[T - P(1 - D)(1 + L)]}$$

where:

P = (Net profit before tax/Net sales) × 100
D = Target dividends/Profit after tax
L = Total liabilities/Net worth
T = (Total assets/Net sales) × 100

If the planned growth rate calls for a growth rate higher than its g*, external capital will be needed to fund the growth unless management is able to find efficiencies, decrease dividends, increase the debt–equity ratio, or reduce assets through renting or leasing arrangements.[9]

Useful Economic Measures

If you are analyzing a company over many years, you may want to adjust sales and net income for inflation to arrive at "true" financial performance in constant dollars. **Constant dollars** are dollars adjusted for inflation to make them comparable over various years. One way to adjust for inflation in the United States is to use the Consumer Price Index (CPI), as given in **Table 15–2**. Dividing sales and net income by the CPI factor for that year will change the figures to 1982–1984 constant dollars (when the CPI was 1.0).

Another helpful analytical aid provided in **Table 15–2** is the **prime interest rate**, the rate of interest banks charge on their lowest-risk loans. For better assessments of strategic decisions, it can be useful to note the level of the prime interest rate at the time of the case. A decision to borrow money to build a new plant would have been a good one in 2003 at 4.12% but less practical in 2000, when the average rate reached 9.23%.

In preparing a scenario for your pro forma financial statements, you may want to use the **gross domestic product (GDP)** from **Table 15–2**. GDP is used worldwide and measures the total output of goods and services within a country's borders. The amount of change from one year to the next indicates how much that country's economy is growing. Remember that scenarios have to be adjusted for a country's specific conditions. For other economic information, see the resources for case research in **Appendix 15.A**.

TABLE 15–2
U.S. ECONOMIC INDICATORS*

Year	GDP (in $ billions) Gross Domestic Product	CPI (for all items) Consumer Price Index	PIR (in %) Prime Interest Rate
1985	4,180.7	1.076	9.93
1986	4,422.2	1.096	8.33
1987	4,693.3	1.136	8.21
1988	5,049.6	1.183	9.32
1989	5,483.7	1.240	10.87
1990	5,743.8	1.307	10.01
1991	5,916.7	1.362	8.46
1992	6,244.4	1.403	6.25
1993	6,553.0	1.445	6.00
1994	6,935.7	1.482	7.15
1995	7,253.8	1.524	8.83
1996	7,661.6	1.569	8.27
1997	8,318.4	1.605	8.44
1998	8,790.2	1.630	8.35
1999	9,268.4	1.666	7.99
2000	9,817.0	1.722	9.23
2001	10,128.8	1.771	6.92
2002	10,487.0	1.799	4.68
2003	11,004.0	1.840	4.12
2004	11,733.5	1.889	4.27

*Note: Gross Domestic Product (GDP) in billions of dollars; Consumer Price Index (CPI) for all items (1982–1984 = 1.0); Prime Interest Rate (PIR) in percentages.

Sources:

1. Gross Domestic Product (GDP) from *Survey of Current Business* (October 2004), Vol. 84, No. 10, Table 1.1.5, p. D-3, and (March 2005), Vol. 85, No. 3, Table 1.1.5, p. D-3.

2. Consumer Price Index (CPI) from U.S. Bureau of Labor Statistics, *Monthly Labor Review*, Vol. 128, No. 2 (February 2005), Table 37, p. 127.

3. Prime Interest Rate (PIR) from *Survey of Current Business*, Vol. 85, No. 1 (January 2005), Table D.1 (Domestic Perspectives), p. D-52.

15.4 Format for Case Analysis: The Strategic Audit

There is no one best way to analyze or present a case report. Each instructor has personal preferences for format and approach. Nevertheless, in **Appendix 15.B** we suggest an approach for both written and oral reports that provides a systematic method for successfully attacking a case. This approach is based on the strategic audit, which is presented at the end of **Chapter 1** in **Appendix 1.A**. We find that this approach provides structure and is very

Figure 15–1
Strategic Audit Worksheet

Strategic Audit Heading	Analysis		Comments
	(+) Factors	(–) Factors	
I. Current Situation			
A. Past Corporate Performance Indexes			
B. Strategic Posture: Current Mission Current Objectives Current Strategies Current Policies			
SWOT Analysis Begins:			
II. Corporate Governance			
A. Board of Directors			
B. Top Management			
III. External Environment (EFAS): Opportunities and Threats (SW<u>OT</u>)			
A. Societal Environment			
B. Task Environment (Industry Analysis)			
IV. Internal Environment (IFAS): Strengths and Weaknesses (<u>SW</u>OT)			
A. Corporate Structure			
B. Corporate Culture			
C. Corporate Resources			
1. Marketing			
2. Finance			
3. Research and Development			
4. Operations and Logistics			
5. Human Resources			
6. Information Systems			
V. Analysis of Strategic Factors (SFAS)			
A. Key Internal and External Strategic Factors (SWOT)			
B. Review of Mission and Objectives			
SWOT Analysis Ends. Recommendation Begins:			
VI. Alternatives and Recommendations			
A. Strategic Alternatives—pros and cons			
B. Recommended Strategy			
VII. Implementation			
VIII. Evaluation and Control			

Note: See the complete Strategic Audit on pages 26–33. It lists the pages in the book that discuss each of the eight headings.

Source: T. L. Wheelen and J. D. Hunger, "Strategic Audit Worksheet." Copyright © 1985, 1986, 1987, 1988, 1989, and 2005 by T. L. Wheelen. Copyright © 1989 and 2005 by Wheelen and Hunger Associates. Revised 1991, 1994, and 1997. Reprined by permission. Additional copies available for classroom use in Part D of *Case Instructors Manual* and on the Prentice Hall Web site (www.prenhall.com/wheelen).

helpful for the typical student who may be a relative novice in case analysis. Regardless of the format chosen, be careful to include a complete analysis of key environmental variables—especially of trends in the industry and of the competition. Look at international developments as well.

If you choose to use the strategic audit as a guide to the analysis of complex strategy cases, you may want to use the **strategic audit worksheet** in **Figure 15–1**. See **Appendix 15.C** for an example of a completed student-written analysis of a 1993 Maytag Corporation case (not the more recent 2002 version) done in an outline form, using the strategic audit format. This is one example of what a case analysis in outline form may look like.

Case discussion focuses on critical analysis and logical development of thought. A solution is satisfactory if it resolves important problems and is likely to be implemented successfully. How the corporation actually dealt with the case problems has no real bearing on the analysis because management might have analyzed its problems incorrectly or implemented a series of flawed solutions.

15.5 Conclusion

Using case analysis is one of the best ways to understand and remember the strategic management process. By applying to cases the concepts and techniques you have learned, you will be able to remember them long past the time when you have forgotten other memorized bits of information. The use of cases to examine actual situations brings alive the field of strategic management and helps build your analytic and decision-making skills. These are just some of the reasons why the use of cases in disciplines from agribusiness to health care is increasing throughout the world.

Strategy Bits

- Zimbabwe had the highest rate of inflation during 2003, with consumer prices rising annually 385%.
- Hong Kong had the least inflation. Its consumer prices declined during 2003 by 2.6%.[10]

Discussion Questions

1. Why should you begin a case analysis with a financial analysis? When are other approaches appropriate?
2. What are common-size financial statements? What is their value to case analysis? How are they calculated?
3. When should you gather information outside a case by going to the library or using the Internet? What should you look for?
4. When is inflation an important issue in conducting case analysis? Why bother?
5. How can you learn what date a case took place?

Strategic Practice Exercise

Convert the following two years of income statements from the Maytag Corporation into common-size statements. The dollar figures are in thousands. What does converting to a common size reveal?

Consolidated Statements of Income: Maytag Corporation

	1992	%	1991	%
Net sales	$3,041,223	100	$2,970,626	100
Cost of sales	2,339,406	___	2,254,221	___
Gross profits	701,817	___	716,405	___
Selling, general, & admin. expenses	528,250	___	524,898	___
Reorganization expenses	95,000	___	0	___
Operating income	78,567	___	191,507	___
Interest expense	(75,004)	___	(75,159)	___
Other—net	3,983	___	7,069	___
Income before taxes and accounting changes	7,546	___	123,417	___
Income taxes	(15,900)	___	(44,400)	___
Income before accounting changes	(8,354)	___	79,017	___
Effects of accounting changes for postretirement benefits	(307,000)	___	0	___
Net income (loss)	$(315,354)	___	$79,017	___

Key Terms

activity ratio (p. 356)
Altman's Bankruptcy Formula (p. 360)
annual report (p. 355)
common-size statement (p. 359)
constant dollars (p. 360)
gross domestic product (p. 360)
index of sustainable growth (p. 360)
leverage ratio (p. 356)
liquidity ratio (p. 356)
prime interest rate (p. 360)
profitability ratio (p. 356)
ratio analysis (p. 356)
red flag (p. 354)
SEC 10-K form (p. 355)
SEC 10-Q form (p. 355)
SEC 14-A form (p. 355)
strategic audit worksheet (p. 363)
Z-value (p. 360)

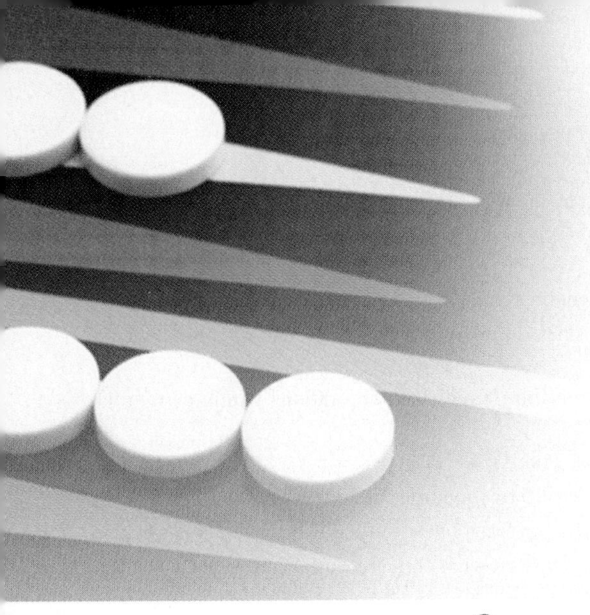

APPENDIX 15.A Resources for Case Research

Company Information

1. Annual reports
2. Moody's *Manuals on Investment* (a listing of companies within certain industries that contains a brief history and a five-year financial statement of each company)
3. Securities and Exchange Commission Report Forms 10-K (annually) and 10-Q (quarterly)
4. Standard & Poor's *Register of Corporations*, Directors, and Executives
5. Value Line's *Investment Survey*
6. Findex's *Directory of Market Research Reports*, Studies and Surveys (a listing by Market Research.com of more than 11,000 studies conducted by leading research firms)
7. Compustat, Compact Disclosure, CD/International, and Hoover's Online Corporate Directory (computerized operating and financial information on thousands of publicly held corporations)
8. Shareholders meeting notices in SEC Form 14-A (proxy notices)

Economic Information

1. Regional statistics and local forecasts from large banks
2. *Business Cycle Development* (Department of Commerce)
3. Chase Econometric Associates' publications
4. U.S. Census Bureau publications on population, transportation, and housing
5. *Current Business Reports* (U.S. Department of Commerce)
6. *Economic Indicators* (U.S. Joint Economic Committee)
7. *Economic Report of the President to Congress*
8. *Long-Term Economic Growth* (U.S. Department of Commerce)
9. *Monthly Labor Review* (U.S. Department of Labor)
10. *Monthly Bulletin of Statistics* (United Nations)
11. *Statistical Abstract of the United States* (U.S. Department of Commerce)
12. *Statistical Yearbook* (United Nations)
13. *Survey of Current Business* (U.S. Department of Commerce)
14. *U.S. Industrial Outlook* (U.S. Department of Defense)

15. *World Trade Annual* (United Nations)
16. *Overseas Business Reports* (by country, published by the U.S. Department of Commerce)

Industry Information

1. Analyses of companies and industries by investment brokerage firms
2. *Business Week* (provides weekly economic and business information, as well as quarterly profit and sales rankings of corporations)
3. *Fortune* (each April publishes listings of financial information on corporations within certain industries)
4. *Industry Survey* (published quarterly by Standard & Poor's)
5. *Industry Week* (late March/early April issue provides information on 14 industry groups)
6. *Forbes* (mid-January issue provides performance data on firms in various industries)
7. *Inc.* (May and December issues give information on fast-growing entrepreneurial companies)

Directory and Index Information on Companies and Industries

1. *Business Periodical Index* (on computers in many libraries)
2. *Directory of National Trade Associations*
3. *Encyclopedia of Associations*
4. Funk and Scott's *Index of Corporations and Industries*
5. Thomas' *Register of American Manufacturers*
6. *Wall Street Journal Index*

Ratio Analysis Information

1. *Almanac of Business and Industrial Financial Ratios* (Prentice Hall)
2. *Annual Statement Studies* (Risk Management Associates; also Robert Morris Associates)
3. *Dun's Review* (Dun & Bradstreet; published annually in September–December issues)
4. *Industry Norms and Key Business Ratios* (Dun & Bradstreet)

Online Information

1. Hoover's Online—financial statements and profiles of public companies (www.hoovers.com)
2. U.S. Securities and Exchange Commission—official filings of public companies in Edgar database (www.sec.gov)
3. Fortune 500—statistics for largest U.S. corporations (www.fortune500.com)
4. Dun & Bradstreet's Online—short reports on 10 million public and private U.S. companies (smallbusiness.dnb.com)
5. Ecola's 24-Hour Newsstand—links to web sites of 2,000 newspapers, journals, and magazines (www.ecola.com)
6. Competitive Intelligence Guide—information on company resources (www.fuld.com)
7. Society of Competitive Intelligence Professionals (www.scip.org)
8. *The Economist*—provides international information and surveys (www.economist.com)
9. Web 100—information on 100 largest U.S. and international companies (www.w100.com).
10. Bloomberg—information on interest rates, stock prices, currency conversion rates, and other general financial information (www.bloomberg.com)
11. Annual Report Gallery (www.reportgallery.com)
12. CEOExpress—links to many valuable sources of business information (www.ceoexpress.com)
13. *Wall Street Journal*—business news (www.wsj.com)
14. CorporateInformation.com—subscription service for company profiles (www.corporate information.com)
15. Kompass International—industry information (www.kompass.com)

16. CorpTech—database of technology companies (www.corptech.com)
17. ZDNet—information technology industry (www.zdnet.com)
18. The Scannery—information on international companies (www.thescannery.com)
19. Guide to Financials—information on how to read a financial statement (www.ibm.com/investor/financialguide)
20. *CIA World Fact Book*—international information by country (www.cia.gov/cia/publications/factbook/index.html)

APPENDIX 15.B
Suggested Case Analysis Methodology Using the Strategic Audit

1. READ CASE

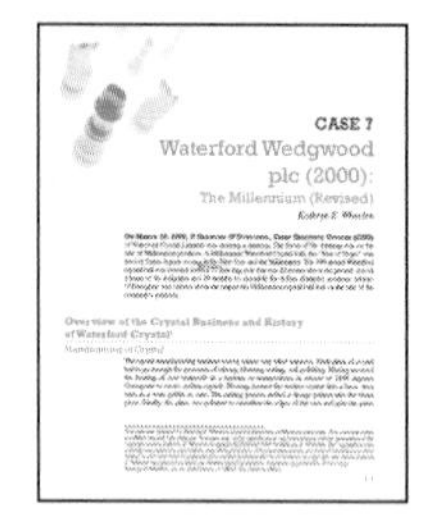
CASE 7
Waterford Wedgwood plc (2000):
The Millennium (Revised)

First Reading of the Case

- Develop a general overview of the company and its external environment.
- Begin a list of the possible strategic factors facing the company at this time.
- List the research information you may need on the economy, industry, and competitors.

2. READ THE CASE WITH THE STRATEGIC AUDIT

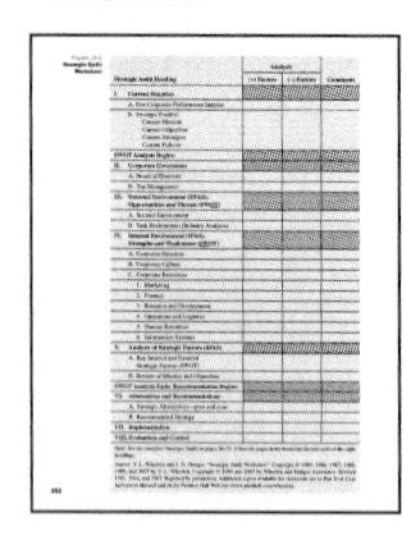

Second Reading of the Case

- Read the case a second time, using the strategic audit as a framework for in-depth analysis. (See **Appendix 1.A** on pages 26–33.) You may want to make a copy of the strategic audit worksheet (**Figure 15–1**) to use to keep track of your comments as you read the case.
- The questions in the strategic audit parallel the strategic decision-making process shown in **Figure 1–5** (pages 22–23).
- The audit provides you with a conceptual framework to examine the company's mission, objectives, strategies, and policies as well as problems, symptoms, facts, opinions, and issues.
- Perform a financial analysis of the company, using ratio analysis (see **Table 15–1**), and do the calculations necessary to convert key parts of the financial statements to a common-size basis.

3. DO OUTSIDE RESEARCH

Library and Online Computer Services

- Each case has a decision date indicating when the case actually took place. Your research should be based on the time period for the case.
- See **Appendix 15.A** for resources for case research. Your research should include information about the environment at the time of the case. Find average industry ratios. You may also want to obtain further information regarding competitors and the company itself (10-K forms and annual reports).

This information should help you conduct an industry analysis. *Check with your instructor to see what kind of outside research is appropriate for your assignment.*

- Don't try to learn what actually happened to the company discussed in the case. What management actually decided may not be the best solution. It will certainly bias your analysis and will probably cause your recommendation to lack proper justification.

4. BEGIN SWOT ANALYSIS

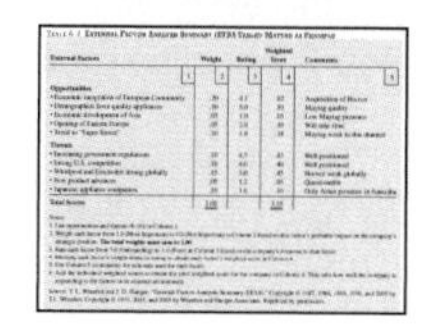

External Environmental Analysis: EFAS

- Analyze the four societal forces to see what trends are likely to affect the industry(s) in which the company is operating.
- Conduct an industry analysis using Porter's competitive forces from **Chapter 4**. Develop an Industry Matrix (**Table 4–3** on page 78).
- Generate 8 to 10 external factors. These should be the *most important* opportunities and threats facing the company at the time of the case.
- Develop an EFAS Table, as shown in **Table 4–5** (page 98), for your list of external strategic factors.
- **Suggestion:** Rank the 8 to 10 factors from most to least important. Start by grouping the 3 top factors and then the 3 bottom factors.

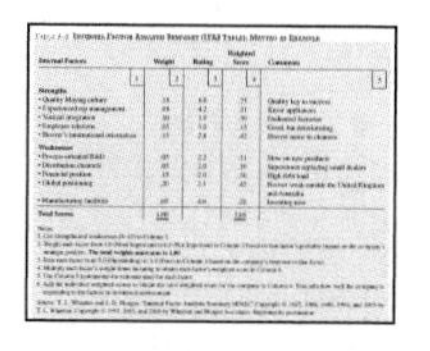

Internal Organizational Analysis: IFAS

- Generate 8 to 10 internal factors. These should be the *most important* strengths and weaknesses of the company at the time of the case.
- Develop an IFAS Table, as shown in **Table 5–2** (page 130), for your list of internal strategic factors.
- **Suggestion:** Rank the 8 to 10 factors from most to least important. Start by grouping the 3 top factors and then the 3 bottom factors.

5. WRITE YOUR STRATEGIC AUDIT: PARTS I TO IV

First Draft of Your Strategic Audit

- Review the student-written audit of an old Maytag case in **Appendix 15.C** for an example.
- Write Parts I to IV of the strategic audit. Remember to include the factors from your EFAS and IFAS Tables in your audit.

6. WRITE YOUR STRATEGIC AUDIT: PART V

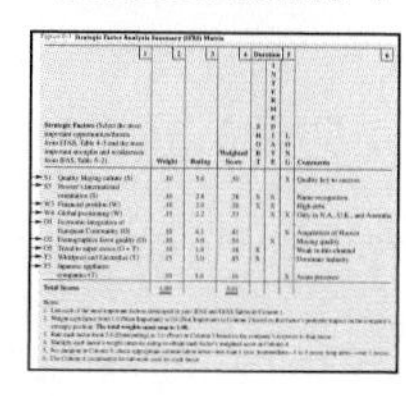

Strategic Factor Analysis Summary: SFAS

- **Condense the list of factors from the 16 to 20 identified in your EFAS and IFAS Tables to only the 8 to 10 most important factors.**
- Select the most important EFAS and IFAS factors. Recalculate the weights of each. The weights still need to add to 1.0.
- Develop a SFAS Matrix, as shown in **Figure 6–1** (page 141), for your final list of strategic factors. Although the weights (indicating the importance of each factor) will probably change from the EFAS and IFAS Tables, the numeric rating (1 to 5) of each factor should remain the same. These ratings are your assessment of management's performance on each factor.
- This is a good time to reexamine what you wrote earlier in Parts I to IV. You may want to add to or delete some of what you wrote. Ensure that each one of the strategic factors you have included in your SFAS Matrix is discussed in the appropriate place in Parts I to IV. Part V of the audit is *not* the place to mention a strategic factor for the first time.
- Write Part V of your strategic audit. This completes your SWOT analysis.
- This is the place to suggest a revised mission statement and a better set of objectives for the company. The SWOT analysis coupled with revised mission and objectives for the company set the stage for the generation of strategic alternatives.

7. WRITE YOUR STRATEGIC AUDIT: PART VI

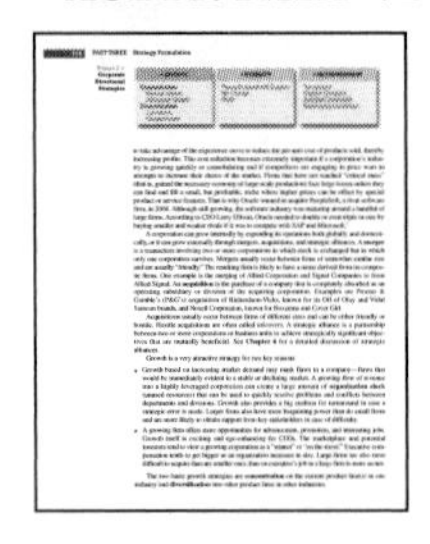

Strategic Alternatives and Recommendation

A. Alternatives

- Develop around three mutually exclusive strategic alternatives. If appropriate to the case you are analyzing, you might propose one alternative for growth, one for stability, and one for retrenchment. Within each corporate strategy, you should probably propose an appropriate business/competitive strategy. You may also want to include some functional strategies where appropriate.
- Construct a corporate scenario for each alternative. Use the data from your outside research to project general societal trends (GDP, inflation, etc.) and industry trends. Use these as the basis of your assumptions to write pro forma financial statements (particularly income statements) for each strategic alternative for the next five years.
- List **pros** and **cons** for each alternative based on your scenarios.

B. Recommendation

- Specify which one of your alternative strategies you recommend. Justify your choice in terms of dealing with the strategic factors you listed in Part V of the strategic audit.
- Develop policies to help implement your strategies.

8. WRITE YOUR STRATEGIC AUDIT: PART VII

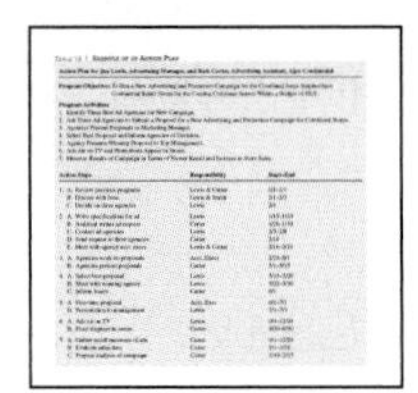

Implementation

- Develop programs to implement your recommended strategy.
- Specify who is to be responsible for implementing each program and how long each program will take to complete.
- Refer to the pro forma financial statements you developed earlier for your recommended strategy. Use common-size historical income statements as the basis for the pro forma statement. Do the numbers still make sense? If not, this may be a good time to rethink the budget numbers to reflect your recommended programs.

9. WRITE YOUR STRATEGIC AUDIT: PART VIII

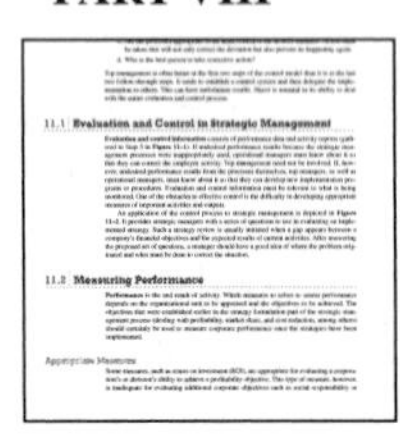

Evaluation and Control

- Specify the type of evaluation and controls that you need to ensure that your recommendation is carried out successfully. Specify who is responsible for monitoring these controls.
- Indicate whether sufficient information is available to monitor how the strategy is being implemented. If not, suggest a change to the information system.

10. PROOF AND FINE-TUNE YOUR AUDIT

Final Draft of Your Strategic Audit

- Check to ensure that your audit is within the page limits of your professor. You may need to cut some parts and expand others.
- Make sure that your recommendation clearly deals with the strategic factors.
- **Attach your EFAS and IFAS Tables, and SFAS Matrix**, plus your ratio analysis and pro forma statements. Label them as numbered exhibits and refer to each of them within the body of the audit.
- Proof your work for errors. If on a computer, use a spell checker.

Special Note: Depending on your assignment, it is relatively easy to use the strategic audit you have just developed to write a written case analysis in essay form or to make an oral presentation. The strategic audit is just a detailed case analysis in an outline form and can be used as the basic framework for any sort of case analysis and presentation.

APPENDIX 15.C
Example of a Student-Written Strategic Audit
(For the 1993 Maytag Corporation Case)

I. CURRENT SITUATION

A. Current Performance

Poor financials, high debt load, first losses since 1920s, price/earnings ratio negative.

- First loss since 1920s.
- Laid off 4,500 employees at Magic Chef.
- Hoover Europe still showing losses.

B. Strategic Posture

1. **Mission**
   - Developed in 1989 for the Maytag Company: "To provide our customers with products of unsurpassed performance that last longer, need fewer repairs, and are produced at the lowest possible cost."
   - Updated in 1991: "Our collective mission is world class quality." Expands Maytag's belief in product quality to all aspects of operations.
2. **Objectives**
   - "To be profitability leader in industry for every product line Maytag manufactures." Selected profitability rather than market share.
   - "To be number one in total customer satisfaction." Doesn't say how to measure satisfaction.
   - "To grow the North American appliance business and become the third largest appliance manufacturer (in unit sales) in North America."
   - To increase profitable market share growth in North American appliance and floor care business, 6.5% return on sales, 10% return on assets, 20% return on equity, beat competition in satisfying customers, dealer, builder and endorser, move into third place in total units shipped per year. Nicely quantified objectives.

3. **Strategies**
   - Global growth through acquisition, and alliance with Bosch-Siemens.
   - Differentiate brand names for competitive advantage.
   - Create synergy between companies, product improvement, investment in plant and equipment.
4. **Policies**
   - Cost reduction is secondary to high quality.
   - Promotion from within.
   - Slow but sure R&D: Maytag slow to respond to changes in market

II. STRATEGIC MANAGERS

A. Board of Directors

1. Fourteen members—eleven are outsiders.
2. Well-respected Americans, most on board since 1986 or earlier.
3. No international or marketing backgrounds.
4. Time for a change?

B. Top Management

1. Top management promoted from within Maytag Company. Too inbred?
2. Very experienced in the industry.
3. Responsible for current situation.
4. May be too parochial for global industry. May need new blood.

III. EXTERNAL ENVIRONMENT (EFAS Table; see Exhibit 1)

A. Societal Environment

1. **Economic**
   a. Unstable economy but recession ending, consumer confidence growing—could increase spending for big-ticket items like houses, cars, and appliances. **(O)**
   b. Individual economies becoming interconnected into a world economy. **(O)**
2. **Technological**
   a. Fuzzy logic technology being applied to sense and measure activities. **(O)**
   b. Computers and information technology increasingly important. **(O)**
3. **Political–Legal**
   a. NAFTA, European Union, other regional trade pacts opening doors to markets in Europe, Asia, and Latin America that offer enormous potential. **(O)**
   b. Breakdown of communism means less chance of world war. **(O)**
   c. Environmentalism being reflected in laws on pollution and energy usage. **(T)**
4. **Sociocultural**
   a. Developing nations desire goods seen on TV. **(O)**
   b. Middle-aged baby boomers want attractive, high-quality products, like BMWs and Maytag. **(O)**
   c. Dual-career couples increases need for labor-saving appliances, second cars, and day care. **(O)**
   d. Divorce and career mobility means need for more houses and goods to fill them. **(O)**

B. Task Environment

1. North American market mature and extremely competitive—vigilant consumers demand high quality with low price in safe, environmentally sound products. **(T)**
2. Industry going global as North American and European firms expand internationally. **(T)**
3. European design popular and consumer desire for technologically advanced appliances. **(O)**
4. **Rivalry Among Existing Firms: High.** Whirlpool, AB Electrolux, GE have enormous resources and developing global presence. **(T)**
5. **Bargaining Power of Buyers: Low.** Technology and materials can be sourced worldwide. **(O)**
6. **Power of Other Stakeholders: Medium.** Quality, safety, environmental regulations increasing. **(T)**
7. **Bargaining Power of Supplying Distributors' Power: High.** Super retailers more important; mom and pop dealers less. **(T)**
8. **Threat of Substitutes: Low. (O)**
9. **Threat of New Entrants: High.** New entrants unlikely except for large international firms. **(T)**

IV. INTERNAL ENVIRONMENT (IFAS Table; see Exhibit 2)

A. Corporate Structure

1. Divisional structure: appliance manufacturing and vending machines. Floor care managed separately. **(S)**
2. Centralized major decisions by Newton corporate staff, with a time line of about three years. **(S)**

B. Corporate Culture

1. Quality key ingredient—commitment to quality shared by executives and workers. **(S)**
2. Much of corporate culture is based on founder F. L. Maytag's personal philosophy, including concern for quality, employees, local community, innovation, and performance. **(S)**
3. Acquired companies, except for European, seem to accept dominance of Maytag culture. **(S)**

C. Corporate Resources

1. **Marketing**
   a. Maytag brand lonely repairman advertising successful but dated. **(W)**
   b. Efforts focus on distribution—combining three sales forces into two, concentrating on major retailers. (Cost $95 million for this reconstructing.) **(S)**
   c. Hoover's well-publicized marketing fiasco involving airline tickets. **(W)**
2. **Finance** (see **Exhibits 3 and 4**)
   a. Revenues are up slightly; operating income is down significantly. **(W)**
   b. Some key ratios are troubling, such as a 57% debt/asset ratio, 132% long-term debt/equity ratio. No room for more debt to grow company. **(W)**
   c. Net income is 400% less than 1988, based on common-size income statements. **(W)**
3. **R&D**
   a. Process-oriented with focus on manufacturing process and durability. **(S)**
   b. Maytag becoming a technology follower, taking too long to get product innovations to market (competitors put out more in last 6 months than prior 2 years combined) lagging in fuzzy logic and other technological areas. **(W)**
4. **Operations**
   a. Maytag's core competence. Continual improvement process kept it dominant in the U.S. market for many years. **(S)**
   b. Plants aging and may be losing competitiveness as rivals upgrade facilities. Quality no longer distinctive competence? **(W)**

5. **Human Resources**
   a. Traditionally very good relations with unions and employees. **(S)**
   b. Labor relations increasingly strained, with two salary raise delays, and layoffs of 4500 employees at Magic Chef. **(W)**
   c. Unions express concern at new, more distant tone from Maytag Corporation. **(W)**
6. **Information Systems**
   a. Not mentioned in case. Hoover fiasco in Europe suggests information systems need significant upgrading. **(W)**
   b. Critical area where Maytag may be unwilling or unable to commit resources needed to stay competitive. **(W)**

V. ANALYSIS OF STRATEGIC FACTORS

A. Situational Analysis (See SFAS Matrix in Exhibit 5)

B. Review of Current Mission and Objectives

1. Current mission appears appropriate.
2. Some of the objectives are really goals and need to be quantified and given time horizons.

VI. STRATEGIC ALTERNATIVES AND RECOMMENDED STRATEGY

A. Strategic Alternatives

1. *Growth Through Concentric Diversification:* Acquire a company in a related industry like commercial appliances.
   a. [***Pros***] Product/market synergy created by acquisition of related company.
   b. [***Cons***] Maytag does not have the financial resources to play this game.
2. *Pause Strategy:* Consolidate various acquisitions to find economies and to encourage innovation among the business units.
   a. [***Pros***] Maytag needs to get its financial house in order and get administrative control over its recent acquisitions.
   b. [***Cons***] Unless it can grow through a stronger alliance with Bosch-Siemens or some other backer, Maytag is a prime candidate for takeover because of its poor financial performance in recent years, and it is suffering from the initial reduction in efficiency inherent in acquisition strategy.
3. *Retrenchment:* Sell Hoover's foreign major home appliance businesses (Australia and UK) to emphasize increasing market share in North America.
   a. [***Pros***] Divesting Hoover improves bottom line and enables Maytag Corp. to focus on North America while Whirlpool, Electrolux, and GE are battling elsewhere.
   b. [***Cons***] Maytag may be giving up its only opportunity to become a player in the coming global appliance industry.

B. Recommended Strategy

1. Recommend pause strategy, at least for a year, so Maytag can get a grip on its European operation and consolidate its companies in a more synergistic way.
2. Maytag quality must be maintained, and continued shortage of operating capital will take its toll, so investment must be made in R&D.

3. Maytag may be able to make the Hoover UK investment work better since the recession is ending and the EU countries are closer to integrating than ever before.
4. Because it is only an average competitor, Maytag needs the Hoover link to Europe to provide a jumping-off place for negotiations with Bosch-Siemens that could strengthen their alliance.

VII. IMPLEMENTATION

A. The only way to increase profitability in North America is to further involve Maytag with the superstore retailers; sure to anger the independent dealers, but necessary for Maytag to compete.

B. Board members with more global business experience should be recruited, with an eye toward the future, especially with expertise in Asia and Latin America.

C. R&D needs to be improved, as does marketing, to get new products online quickly.

VIII. EVALUATION AND CONTROL

A. MIS needs to be developed for speedier evaluation and control. While the question of control vs. autonomy is "under review," another Hoover fiasco may be brewing.

B. The acquired companies do not all share the Midwestern work ethic or the Maytag Corporation culture, and Maytag's managers must inculcate these values into the employees of all acquired companies.

C. Systems should be developed to decide if the size and location of Maytag manufacturing plants is still correct and to plan for the future. Industry analysis indicates that smaller automated plants may be more efficient now than in the past.

Note: The following exhibits were originally attached in their entirety to this strategic audit, but for reasons of space, only their titles are listed here:

Exhibit 1: EFAS Table
Exhibit 2: IFAS Table
Exhibit 3: Ratio Analysis for 5 Years
Exhibit 4: Common-Size Income Statements
Exhibit 5: SFAS Matrix

Notes

Chapter 1

1. S. Holmes and M. Arndt, "A Plane That Could Change the Game," *Business Week* (August 9, 2004), p. 33; D. Carpenter and A. Linn, "Hoping for a Lift," *The (Ames, IA) Tribune* (May 22, 2004), p. C7; S. Holmes, "Will This Idea Really Fly?" *Business Week* (June 23, 2003), pp. 34–35; C. Matlack and S. Holmes, "Mega Plane," *Business Week* (November 10, 2003), pp. 88–92; S. Holmes, "Boeing: What Really Happened," *Business Week* (December 15, 2003), pp. 33–38; H. Jung, "Boeing Must Build 7E7 or Lose Credibility," *Des Moines Register* (December 9, 2003), p. 3D; "Where's Boeing Going?" *Economist* (November 29, 2003), pp. 57–58; B. Acohido, "Boeing Hopes to Reclaim Glory with 7E7," *USA Today* (December 17, 2003), p. 3B; B. Acohido, "Boeing Rips a Page out of Airbus' Book," *USA Today* (October 22, 2003), p. 3B; S. Holmes, "The Battle over a Radical New Plane," *Business Week* (November 25, 2002), pp. 106–108; R. C. Scamehorn, "The Boeing Commercial Airplanes Group: Decision 2001" in T. Wheelen and J. D. Hunger, *Strategic Management and Business Policy*, 9th edition, Upper Saddle River, NJ: Prentice Hall, 2004, pp. 32.1—32.17.
2. F. W. Gluck, S. P. Kaufman, and A. S. Walleck, "The Four Phases of Strategic Management," *Journal of Business Strategy* (Winter 1982), pp. 9–21.
3. M. R. Vaghefi and A. B Huellmantel, "Strategic Leadership at General Electric," *Long Range Planning* (April 1998), pp. 280–294.
4. T. J. Andersen, "Strategic Planning, Autonomous Actions and Corporate Performance," *Long Range Planning* (April 2000), pp. 184–200; C. C. Miller and L. B. Cardinal, "Strategic Planning and Firm Performance: A Synthesis of More Than Two Decades of Research," *Academy of Management Journal* (December 1994), pp. 1649–1665; P. Pekar, Jr., and S. Abraham, "Is Strategic Management Living Up to Its Promise?" *Long Range Planning* (October 1995), pp. 32–44; W. E. Hopkins and S. A. Hopkins, "Strategic Planning—Financial Performance Relationship in Banks: A Causal Examination," *Strategic Management Journal* (September 1997), pp. 635–652; N. O'Regan and A. Ghobadian, "Refocusing Performance: A Strategy-Centered Approach," paper presented to *Academy of Management* (Seattle, WA, 2003).
5. E. J. Zajac, M. S. Kraatz, and R. F. Bresser, "Modeling the Dynamics of Strategic Fit: A Normative Approach to Strategic Change," *Strategic Management Journal* (April 2000), pp. 429–453.
6. K. G. Smith and C. M. Grimm, "Environmental Variation, Strategic Change and Firm Performance: A Study of Railroad Deregulation," *Strategic Management Journal* (July–August 1987), pp. 363–376; J. A. Nickerson and B. S. Silverman, "Why Firms Want to Organize Efficiently and What Keeps Them from Doing So: Inappropriate Governance, Performance, and Adaptation in a Deregulated Industry," *Administrative Science Quarterly* (September 2003), pp. 433–465.
7. I. Wilson, "Strategic Planning Isn't Dead—It Changed," *Long Range Planning* (August 1994), p. 20.
8. D. Rigby, "Management Tools Survey 2003: Usage Up as Companies Strive to Make Headway in Tough Times," *Strategy & Leadership*, Vol. 31, No. 5 (2003), pp. 4–11.
9. R. M. Grant, "Strategic Planning in a Turbulent Environment: Evidence from the Oil Majors," *Strategic Management Journal* (June 2003), pp. 491–517.
10. M. J. Peel and J. Bridge, "How Planning and Capital Budgeting Improve SME Performance," *Long Range Planning* (December 1998), pp. 848–856; L. W. Rue and N. A. Ibrahim, "The Relationship Between Planning Sophistication and Performance in Small Businesses," *Journal of Small Business Management* (October 1998), pp. 24–32; J. C. Carland and J. W. Carland, "A Model of Entrepreneurial Planning and Its Effect on Performance," paper presented to *Association for Small Business and Entrepreneurship* (Houston, TX, 2003).
11. R. M. Grant, "Strategic Planning in a Turbulent Environment: Evidence from the Oil Majors," *Strategic Management Journal* (June 2003), pp. 491–517.
12. Quoted in "Companies that Expand Abroad: 'Knowledge Seekers' vs. Conquerors," *Knowledge@Wharton* (March 24, 2004), p. 1.
13. C. V. Callahan and B. A. Pasternack, "Corporate Strategy in the Digital Age," *Strategy & Business*, Issue 15 (2nd Quarter 1999), p. 3.
14. J. J. Ballow, R. Burgman, and M. J. Molnar, "Managing for Shareholder Value: Intangibles, Future Value and Investment Decisions," *Journal of Business Strategy*, Vol. 25, No. 3 (2004), pp. 26–34.
15. J. A. C. Baum, "Organizational Ecology," in *Handbook of Organization Studies*, edited by S. R. Clegg, C. Handy, and W. Nord (London: Sage, 1996), pp. 77–114.
16. B. M. Staw and L. D. Epstein, "What Bandwagons Bring: Effects of Popular Management Techniques on Corporate Performance, Reputation, and CEO Pay," *Administrative Science Quarterly* (September 2000), pp. 523–556.
17. T. W. Ruefli and R. R. Wiggins, "Industry, Corporate, and Segment Effects and Business Performance: A Non-Parametric Approach," *Strategic Management Journal* (September 2003), pp. 861–879; Y. E. Spanos, G. Zaralis, and S. Lioukas, "Strategy and Industry Effects on Profitability: Evidence from Greece," *Strategic Management Journal* (February 2004), pp. 139–165; E. H. Bowman and C. E. Helfat, "Does Corporate Strategy Matter?" *Strategic Management Journal* (January 2001), pp. 1–23; T. H. Brush, P. Bromiley, and M. Hendrickx, "The Relative Influence of Industry and Corporation on Business Segment Performance: An Alternative Estimate," *Strategic*

Management Journal (June 1999), pp. 519–547; K. M. Gilley, B. A. Walters, and B. J. Olson, "Top Management Team Risk Taking Propensities and Firm Performance: Direct and Moderating Effects," *Journal of Business Strategies* (Fall 2002), pp. 95–114.

18. For more information on these theories, see A. Y. Lewin and H. W. Voloberda, "Prolegomena on Coevolution: A Framework for Research on Strategy and New Organizational Forms," *Organization Science* (October 1999), pp. 519–534, and H. Aldrich, *Organizations Evolving* (London: Sage, 1999), pp. 43–74.

19. C. Gebelein, "Strategic Planning: The Engine of Change," *Planning Review* (September/October 1993), pp. 17–19.

20. R. A. D'Aveni, *Hypercompetition* (New York: The Free Press, 1994). Hypercompetition is discussed in more detail in Chapter 3.

21. R. S. M. Lau, "Strategic Flexibility: A New Reality for World-Class Manufacturing," *SAM Advanced Management Journal* (Spring 1996), pp. 11–15.

22. M. A. Hitt, B. W. Keats, and S. M. DeMarie, "Navigating in the New Competitive Landscape: Building Strategic Flexibility and Competitive Advantage in the 21st Century," *Academy of Management Executive* (November 1998), pp. 22–42.

23. D. Lei, J. W. Slocum, and R. A. Pitts, "Designing Organizations for Competitive Advantage: The Power of Unlearning and Learning," *Organizational Dynamics* (Winter 1999), pp. 24–38.

24. D. A. Garvin, "Building a Learning Organization," *Harvard Business Review* (July/August 1993), p. 80. See also P. M. Senge, *The Fifth Discipline: The Art and Practice of the Learning Organization* (New York: Doubleday, 1990).

25. A. D. Chandler, *Inventing the Electronic Century* (New York: The Free Press, 2001).

26. T. T. Baldwin, C. Danielson, and W. Wiggenhorn, "The Evolution of Learning Strategies in Organizations: From Employee Development to Business Redefinition," *Academy of Management Executive* (November 1997), pp. 47–58.

27. N. Collier, F. Fishwick, and S. W. Floyd, "Managerial Involvement and Perceptions of Strategy Process," *Long Range Planning* (February 2004), pp. 67–83; J. A. Parnell, S. Carraher, and K. Holt, "Participative Management's Influence on Effective Strategic Planning," *Journal of Business Strategies* (Fall 2002), pp. 161–179.

28. E. W. K. Tsang, "Internationalization as a Learning Process: Singapore MNCs in China," *Academy of Management Executive* (February 1999), pp. 91–101; J. M. Shaver, W. Mitchell, and B. Yeung, "The Effect of Own-Firm and Other Firm Experience on Foreign Direct Investment Survival in the U.S., 1987–92," *Strategic Management Journal* (November 1997), pp. 811–824.

29. W. Mitchell, J. M. Shaver, and B. Yeung, "Getting There in a Global Industry: Impacts on Performance of Changing International Presence," *Strategic Management Journal* (September 1992), pp. 419–432.

30. Research supports the use of this model in examining firm strategies. See J. A. Smith, "Strategies for Start-Ups," *Long Range Planning* (December 1998), pp. 857–872.

31. See A. Campbell and S. Yeung, "Brief Case: Mission, Vision, and Strategic Intent," *Long Range Planning* (August 1991), pp. 145–147, and S. Cummings and J. Davies, "Mission, Vision, Fusion," *Long Range Planning* (December 1994), pp. 147–150.

32. J. Cosco, "Down to the Sea in Ships," *Journal of Business Strategy* (November/December 1995), p. 48.

33. J. S. Sidhu, E. J. Nijssen, and H. R. Commandeur, "Business Domain Definition Practice: Does It Affect Organizational Performance?" *Long Range Planning* (June 2000), pp. 376–401.

34. W. C. Symonds, "Thinking Outside the Big Box," *Business Week* (August 4, 2003), pp. 62–63.

35. W. C. Symonds, "Thinking Outside the Big Box," *Business Week* (August 4, 2003), pp. 62–63.

36. K. M. Eisenhardt and D. N. Sull, "Strategy as Simple Rules," *Harvard Business Review* (January 2001), p. 110.

37. N. Nohria, W. Joyce, and B. Roberson, "What Really Works," *Harvard Business Review* (July 2003), p. 46.

38. D. Welch, "Cadillac Hits the Gas," *Business Week* (September 4, 2000), p. 50.

39. S. Holmes, "GE: Little Engines That Could," *Business Week* (January 20, 2003), pp. 62–63.

40. H. A. Simon, *Administrative Behavior*, 2nd edition (New York: The Free Press, 1957), p. 231.

41. M. Useem, "Lenovo Chairman Liu Chuanzhi: 'We Have Decided to Refocus on the PC Business,'" *Knowledge @ Wharton* (25 August–7 September, 2004).

42. H. Mintzberg, "Planning on the Left Side and Managing on the Right," *Harvard Business Review* (July–August 1976), p. 56.

43. See E. Romanelli and M. L. Tushman, "Organizational Transformation as Punctuated Equilibrium: An Empirical Test," *Academy of Management Journal* (October 1994), pp. 1141–1166.

44. S. S. Gordon, W. H. Stewart, Jr., R. Sweo, and W. A. Luker, "Convergence Versus Strategic Reorientation: The Antecedents of Fast-Paced Organizational Change," *Journal of Management*, Vol. 26, No. 5 (2000), pp. 911–945.

45. Speech to the 1998 Academy of Management, reported by S. M. Puffer, "Global Executive: Intel's Andrew Grove on Competitiveness," *Academy of Management Executive* (February 1999), pp. 15–24.

46. D. J. Hickson, R. J. Butler, D. Cray, G. R. Mallory, and D. C. Wilson, *Top Decisions: Strategic Decision-Making in Organizations* (San Francisco: Jossey-Bass, 1986), pp. 26–42.

47. T. A. Fogarty, "Keeping Zippo's Flame Eternal," *USA Today* (June 24, 2003), p. 3B.

48. H. Mintzberg, "Strategy-Making in Three Modes," *California Management Review* (Winter 1973), pp. 44–53.

49. F. Vogelstein, "Mighty Amazon," *Fortune* (May 26, 2003), pp. 60–74.

50. M. Wong, "Once-Prized Encyclopedias Fall into Disuse," *Des Moines Register* (March 9, 2004), p. 3D.

51. L. V. Gerstner, *Who Says Elephants Can't Dance?* (New York: HarperCollins, 2002).

52. J. B. Quinn, *Strategies for Change: Logical Incrementalism* (Homewood, IL: Irwin, 1980), p. 58.

53. R. M. Grant, "Strategic Planning in a Turbulent Environment: Evidence from the Oil Majors," *Strategic Management Journal* (June 2003), pp. 491–517.

54. P. J. Brews and M. R. Hunt, "Learning to Plan and Planning to Learn: Resolving the Planning School/Learning School Debate," *Strategic Management Journal* (October 1999), pp. 889–913; I. Gold and A. M. A. Rasheed, "Rational Decision-Making and Firm Performance: The Moderating Role of the Environment," *Strategic Management Journal* (August 1997), pp. 583–591; R. L. Priem, A. M. A. Rasheed, and A. G. Kotulic, "Rationality in Strategic Decision Processes, Environmental Dynamism and Firm Performance," *Journal of*

Management, Vol. 21, No. 5 (1995), pp. 913–929; J. W. Dean, Jr., and M. P. Sharfman, "Does Decision Process Matter? A Study of Strategic Decision-Making Effectiveness," *Academy of Management Journal* (April 1996), pp. 368–396.

55. T. L. Wheelen and J. D. Hunger, "Using the Strategic Audit," *SAM Advanced Management Journal* (Winter 1987), pp. 4–12; G. Donaldson, "A New Tool for Boards: The Strategic Audit," *Harvard Business Review* (July–August 1995), pp. 99–107.
56. D. C. Hambrick and J. W. Fredrickson, "Are You Sure You Have a Strategy?" *Academy of Management Executive* (November 2001), pp. 48–59.
57. Hambrick and Fredrickson, p. 49.
58. "Free Trade on Trial," *Economist* (January 3, 2004), pp. 13–16; "A Club in Need of a New Vision," *Economist* (May 1, 2004), pp. 25–27; *World in Figures, 2004 Edition*, published by *The Economist* in association with Profile Books (2003), p. 14.
59. P. Jones and L. Kahaner, *Say It & Live It: 50 Corporate Mission Statements That Hit the Mark* (New York: Currency Doubleday, 1995), p. 53.

Chapter 2

1. N. Byrnes and W. C. Symonds, "Is the Avalanche Headed for PriceWaterhouse?" *Business Week* (October 14, 2002), pp. 45–46; W. C. Symonds, "Tyco: How Did They Miss a Scam So Big?" *Business Week* (September 30, 2002), pp. 40–42; H. R. Weber, "Questions Arise about Board Reviewing Tyco's Finances," *The (Ames, IA) Tribune* (July 6, 2002), p. C8; N. Varchaver, "The Big Kozlowski," *Fortune* (November 18, 2002), pp. 123–126; H. R. Weber, "The King Is Gone," *Des Moines Register* (September 18, 2002), p. D1; "Tyco Settles," *Des Moines Register* (October 24, 2002), p. 3D; H. Bray, "Tyco's Walsh Agrees to Pay Back $20 Million," *Des Moines Register* (December 18, 2002), p. 3D; P. N. Levenson, "Tyco's Betrayal of Board Governance," *Directors & Boards* (Summer 2002), pp. 35–38.
2. A. G. Monks and N. Minow, *Corporate Governance* (Cambridge, MA: Blackwell Business, 1995), pp. 8–32.
3. Ibid., p. 1.
4. W. Symonds, "Tyco: The Vise Grows Ever-Tighter," *Business Week* (October 7, 2002), pp. 48–49.
5. A. Demb and F. F. Neubauer, "The Corporate Board: Confronting the Paradoxes," *Long Range Planning* (June 1992), p. 13. These results are supported by a 1995 Korn/Ferry International survey in which chairs and directors agreed that strategy and management succession, in that order, are the most important issues the board expects to face.
6. Reported by E. L. Biggs in "CEO Succession Planning: An Emerging Challenge for Boards of Directors," *Academy of Management Executive* (February 2004), pp. 105–107.
7. A. Borrus, "Less Laissez-Faire in Delaware?" *Business Week* (March 22, 2004), pp. 80–82.
8. L. Light, "Why Outside Directors Have Nightmares," *Business Week* (October 23, 1996), p. 6.
9. "Where's All the Fun Gone?" *Economist* (March 20, 2004), p. 76.
10. *Directors' Compensation and Board Practices in 2003*, Research Report R-1339-03-RR (New York: Conference Board, 2003), p. 35.
11. Nadler proposes a similar five-step continuum for board involvement ranging from the least involved "passive board" to the most involved "operating board," plus a form for measuring board involvement in D. A. Nadler, "Building Better Boards," *Harvard Business Review* (May 2004), pp. 102–111.
12. H. Ashbaugh, D. W. Collins, and R. LaFond, "The Effects of Corporate Governance on Firms' Credit Ratings," unpublished paper (March 2004); W. Q. Judge, Jr., and C. P. Zeithaml, "Institutional and Strategic Choice Perspectives on Board Involvement in the Strategic Choice Process," *Academy of Management Journal* (October 1992), pp. 766–794; J. A. Pearce II and S. A. Zahra, "Effective Power-Sharing Between the Board of Directors and the CEO," *Handbook of Business Strategy*, 1992/93 Yearbook (Boston: Warren, Gorham, and Lamont, 1992), pp. 1.1–1.16.
13. *26th Annual Board of Directors Study* (New York: Korn/Ferry International, 1999), p. 7.
14. The 2003 percentages for Asian Pacific and UK boards are 69% and 84%, respectively. See *30th Annual Board of Directors Study* (New York: Korn/Ferry International, 2003), p. 6.
15. *Current Board Practices,* American Society of Corporate Secretaries, 2002, as reported by B. Atkins in "Directors Don't Deserve Such a Punitive Policy," *Directors & Boards* (Summer 2002), p. 23.
16. D. A. Nadler, "Building Better Boards," *Harvard Business Review* (May 2004), pp. 102–111; L. Lavelle, "The Best and Worst Boards," *Business Week* (October 7, 2002), pp. 104–114.
17. Nadler, p. 109.
18. A. L. Ranft and H. M. O'Neill, "Board Composition and High-Flying Founders: Hints of Trouble to Come?" *Academy of Management Executive* (February 2001), pp. 126–138.
19. D. F. Larcher, S. A. Richardson, and I. Tuna, "Does Corporate Governance Really Matter?" *Knowledge @ Wharton* (September 8–21, 2004); J. Merritt and L. Lavelle, "A Different Kind of Governance Guru," *Business Week* (August 9, 2004), pp. 46–47; A. Dehaene, V. DeVuyst, and H. Ooghe, "Corporate Performance and Board Structure in Belgian Companies," *Long Range Planning* (June 2001), pp. 383–398; M. W. Peng, "Outside Directors and Firm Performance During Institutional Transitions," *Strategic Management Journal* (May 2004), pp. 453–471.
20. *30th Annual Board of Directors Study Supplement: Governance Trends of the Fortune 1000* (New York: Korn/Ferry International, 2004), p. 3.
21. L. L. Carr, "Strategic Determinants of Executive Compensation in Small Publicly Traded Firms," *Journal of Small Business Management* (April 1997), pp. 1–12.
22. *30th Annual Board of Directors Study* (New York: Korn/Ferry International, 2003).
23. W. S. Schulze, M. H. Lubatkin, R. N. Dino, and A. K. Buchholtz, "Agency Relationships in Family Firms: Theory and Evidence," *Organization Science* (March–April 2001), pp. 99–116.
24. J. P. Katz and B. P. Niehoff, "How Owners Influence Strategy—A Comparison of Owner-Controlled and Manager-Controlled Firms," *Long Range Planning* (October 1998), pp. 755–761; M. Kroll, P. Wright, L. Toombs, and H. Leavell, "Form of Control: A Critical Determinant of Acquisition Performance and CEO Rewards," *Strategic Management Journal* (February 1997), pp. 85–96.
25. L. Tihanyi, R. A. Johnson, R. E. Hoskisson, and M. A. Hitt, "Institutional Ownership Differences and International Diversification: The Effects of Boards of Directors and Technological Opportunity," *Academy of Management Journal*

(April 2003), pp. 195–211; A. E. Ellstrand, L. Tihanyi, and J. L. Johnson, "Board Structure and International Political Risk," *Academy of Management Journal* (August 2002), pp. 769–777; S. A. Zahra, D. O. Neubaum, and M. Huse, "Entrepreneurship in Medium-Size Companies: Exploring the Effects of Ownership and Governance Systems," *Journal of Management*, Vol. 26, No. 5 (2000), pp. 947–976.

26. G. Kassinis and N. Vafeas, "Corporate Boards and Outside Stakeholders as Determinants of Environmental Litigation," *Strategic Management Journal* (May 2002), pp. 399–415; P. Dunn, "The Impact of Insider Power on Fraudulent Financial Reporting," *Journal of Management*, Vol. 30, No. 3 (2004), pp. 397–412.

27. W. S. Schulze, M. H. Lubatkin, R. N. Dino, and A. K. Buckholtz, "Agency Relationships in Family Firms: Theory and Evidence," *Organization Science* (March–April 2001), pp. 99–116.

28. M. N. Young, A. K. Bushholtz, and D. Ahlstrom, "How Can Board Members Be Empowered if They Are Spread Too Thin?" *SAM Advanced Management Journal* (Autumn 2003), pp. 4–11.

29. *Directors' Compensation and Board Practices in 2003*, Research Report R-1339-03-RR (New York: Conference Board, 2003), Table 49, p. 38.

30. C. M. Daily and D. R. Dalton, "The Endangered Director," *Journal of Business Strategy*, Vol. 25, No. 3 (2004), pp. 8–9.

31. I. Sager, "The Boardroom: New Rules, New Loopholes," *Business Week* (November 29, 2004), p. 13.

32. *Directors' Compensation and Board Practices in 2003*, Research Report R-1339-03-RR (New York: Conference Board, 2003), Table 49, p. 38.

33. See S. Finkelstein and D. C. Hambrick, *Strategic Leadership: Top Executives and Their Impact on Organizations* (St. Paul, MN: West, 1996), p. 213.

34. R. A. G. Monks, "What Will Be the Impact of Acting Shareholders? A Practical Recipe for Constructive Change," *Long Range Planning* (February 1999), p. 20.

35. "TIAA-CREF's Role in Corporate Governance," *Investment Forum* (June 2003), p. 13.

36. *30th Annual Board of Directors Study Supplement: Governance Trends of the Fortune 1000* (New York: Korn/Ferry International, 2004), pp. 3–4; K. Weisul, "Make Way for the Madame Director," *Business Week* (December 22, 2003), p. 57.

37. J. Daum, "Portrait of Boards on the Cusp of Historic Change," *Directors & Boards* (Winter 2003), p. 56; J. Daum, "SSBI: Audit Committees Are Leading the Change," *Directors & Boards* (Winter 2004), p. 59.

38. *30th Annual Board of Directors Study* (New York: Korn/Ferry International, 2003), p. 38.

39. *Globalizing the Board of Directors: Trends and Strategies* (New York: The Conference Board, 1999).

40. *30th Annual Board of Directors Study Supplement: Governance Trends of the Fortune 1000* (New York: Korn/Ferry International, 2004), pp. 7–11; *Directors' Compensation and Board Practices in 2003*, Research Report R-1339-03-RR (New York: Conference Board, 2003), p. 10.

41. R. W. Pouder and R. S. Cantrell, "Corporate Governance Reform: Influence on Shareholder Wealth," *Journal of Business Strategies* (Spring 1999), pp. 48–66.

42. M. L. Gerlach, "The Japanese Corporate Network: A Blockmodel Analysis," *Administrative Science Quarterly* (March 1992), pp. 105–139.

43. J. D. Westphal, M. L. Seidel, and K. J. Stewart, "Second-Order Imitation: Uncovering Latent Effects of Board Network Ties," *Administrative Science Quarterly* (December 2001), pp. 717–747; M. A. Geletkanycz, B. K. Boyd, and S. Finkelstein, "The Strategic Value of CEO External Directorate Networks: Implications for CEO Compensation," *Strategic Management Journal* (September 2001), pp. 889–898; M.A. Carpenter and J. D. Westphal, "The Strategic Context of External Network Ties: Examining the Impact of Director Appointments on Board Involvement in Strategic Decision Making," *Academy of Management Journal* (August 2001), pp. 639–660.

44. M. Warner, "Inside the Silicon Valley Money Machine," *Fortune* (October 26, 1998), pp. 128–140.

45. D. Jones and B. Hansen, "Chairmen Still Doing Do-Si-Do," *USA Today* (November 5, 2003), p. 3B; J. H. Daum and T. J. Neff, "SSBI: Audit Committees Are Leading the Charge," *Directors & Boards* (Winter 2003), p. 59.

46. J. A. C. Baum and C. Oliver, "Institutional Linkages and Organizational Mortality," *Administrative Science Quarterly* (June 1991), pp. 187–218; J. P. Sheppard, "Strategy and Bankruptcy: An Exploration into Organizational Death," *Journal of Management* (Winter 1994), pp. 795–833.

47. *Directors' Compensation and Board Practices in 2003*, Research Report R-1339-03-RR (New York: Conference Board, 2003), Table 49, p. 38.

48. J. Canavan, B. Jones, and M. J. Potter, "Board Tenure: How Long Is Too Long?" *Boards & Directors* (Winter 2004), pp. 39–42.

49. *30th Annual Board of Directors Study Supplement: Governance Trends of the Fortune 1000* (New York: Korn/Ferry International, 2004), p. 5.

50. D. F. Larcker and S. A. Richardson, "Does Governance Really Matter?" *Knowledge @ Wharton* (September 8–21, 2004).

51. *26th Annual Board of Directors Study* (New York: Korn/Ferry International, 1999), p. 30.

52. *30th Annual Board of Directors Study* (New York: Korn/Ferry International, 2003), pp. 8, 31, 44.

53. *Directors' Compensation and Board Practices in 2003*, Research Report R-1339-03-RR (New York: Conference Board, 2003), p. 37; H. Sherman, Review of "The Recurrent Crisis in Corporate Governance" by MacAvoy and Millstein, *Directors & Boards* (Spring 2004), p. 15.

54. A. Desai, M. Kroll, and P. Wright, "CEO Duality, Board Monitoring, and Acquisition Performance," *Journal of Business Strategies* (Fall 2003), pp. 147–156; D. Harris and C. E. Helfat, "CEO Duality, Succession, Capabilities and Agency Theory: Commentary and Research Agenda," *Strategic Management Journal* (September 1998), pp. 901–904; C. M. Daily and D. R. Dalton, "CEO and Board Chair Roles Held Jointly or Separately: Much Ado About Nothing," *Academy of Management Executive* (August 1997), pp. 11–20; D. L. Worrell, C. Nemec, and W. N. Davidson III, "One Hat Too Many: Key Executive Plurality and Shareholder Wealth," *Strategic Management Journal* (June 1997), pp. 499–507; J. W. Coles and W. S. Hesterly, "Independence of the Chairman and Board Composition: Firm Choices and Shareholder Value," *Journal of Management*, Vol. 26, No. 2 (2000), pp. 195–214; H. Ashbaugh, D. W. Collins, and R. LaFond, "The Effects of Corporate Governance on Firms' Credit Ratings," unpublished paper, March 2004.

55. N. R. Augustine, "How Leading a Role for the Lead Director?" *Directors & Boards* (Winter 2004), pp. 20–23.

56. *30th Annual Board of Directors Study Supplement: Governance Trends of the Fortune 1000* (New York: Korn/Ferry International, 2004), p. 5.
57. *30th Annual Board of Directors Study* (New York: Korn/Ferry International, 2003), p. 5.
58. H. Bray, "Tyco's Walsh Agrees to Pay Back $20 Million," *Des Moines Register* (December 18, 2002), p. 3D.
59. J. D. Westphal, "Board Games: How CEOs Adapt to Increases in Structural Board Independence from Management," *Administrative Science Quarterly* (September 1998), pp. 511–537; J. D. Westphal and P. Khanna, "Keeping Directors in Line: Social Distancing as a Control Mechanism in the Corporate Elite," *Administrative Science Quarterly* (September 2003), pp. 361–398.
60. H. L. Tosi, W. Shen, and R. J. Gentry, "Why Outsiders on Boards Can't Solve the Corporate Governance Problem," *Organizational Dynamics*, Vol. 32, No. 2 (2003), pp. 180–192.
61. *30th Annual Board of Directors Study Supplement: Governance Trends of the Fortune 1000* (New York: Korn/Ferry International, 2004), p. 5. Other committees are succession planning (32%), directors' compensation (31%), finance (30%), corporate responsibility (19%), and investment (16%).
62. Perhaps because of their potential to usurp the power of the board, executive committees are being used less often.
63. "Re-examining the Role of the Chairman of the Board," *Knowledge @ Wharton* (May 20, 2004). Summary of an article originally published December 18, 2002.
64. *30th Annual Board of Directors Study Supplement: Governance Trends of the Fortune 1000* (New York: Korn/Ferry International, 2004), p. 5.
65. "Where's All the Fun Gone?" *Economist* (March 20, 2004), pp. 75–77.
66. J. H. Daum and T. J. Neff, "SSBI: Audit Committees Are Leading the Charge," *Directors & Boards* (Winter 2002), p. 58.
67. *30th Annual Board of Directors Study* (New York: Korn/Ferry International, 2003), p. 25.
68. J. Sonnenfeld, "Good Governance and the Misleading Myths of Bad Metrics" *Academy of Management Executive* (February 2004), pp. 108–113.
69. H. Ashbaugh, D. W. Collins, and R. LaFond, "The Effects of Corporate Governance on Firms' Credit Ratings," unpublished paper (March 2002).
70. *30th Annual Board of Directors Study* (New York: Korn/Ferry International, 2003), pp. 7, 22, 27, 37, 52.
71. I. Sager, "Access Denied: A Private Matter," *Business Week* (January 26, 2004), p. 13; J. Weber, "One Share, Many Votes," *Business Week* (March 29, 2004), pp. 94–95.
72. E. Thorton, "Corporate Control Freaks," *Business Week* (May 31, 2004), p. 86.
73. D. R. Dalton, C. M. Daily, A. E. Ellstrand, and J. L. Johnson, "Meta-Analytic Reviews of Board Composition, Leadership Structure, and Financial Performance," *Strategic Management Journal* (March 1998), pp. 269–290; G. Beaver, "Competitive Advantage and Corporate Governance—Shop Soiled and Needing Attention!" *Strategic Change* (September–October 1999), p. 330.
74. For governance trends in Europe, see A. Cadbury, "What Are the Trends in Corporate Governance? How Will They Impact Your Company?" *Long Range Planning* (February 1999), pp. 12–19.
75. A. Backover, "Sprint to Pay $50M, Alter Board Procedures," *USA Today* (March 20, 2003), p. 5B.
76. A. Borrus and L. Young, "Nothing Like a Little Exposure," *Business Week* (September 13, 2004), p. 92.
77. L. He and M. J. Conyon, "The Role of Compensation Committees in CEO and Committee Compensation Decisions," paper presented to *Academy of Management* (Seattle, WA, 2003).
78. L. Lavelle, "A Fighting Chance for Boardroom Democracy," *Business Week* (June 9, 2003), p. 50; L. Lavelle, "So That's Why Boards Are Waking Up," *Business Week* (January 19, 2004), pp. 72–73.
79. S. Finkelstein and D. C. Hambrick, *Strategic Leadership: Top Executives and Their Impact on Organizations* (St. Louis: West, 1996).
80. D. C. Hambrick, T. S. Cho, and M-J Chen, "The Influence of Top Management Team Heterogeneity on Firms' Competitive Moves," *Administrative Science Quarterly* (December 1996), pp. 659–684.
81. P. Pitcher and A. D. Smith, "Top Management Heterogeneity: Personality, Power, and Proxies," *Organization Science* (January–February 2001), pp. 1–18; M. A. Carpenter and J. W. Fredrickson, "Top Management Teams, Global Strategic Posture, and the Moderating Role of Uncertainty," *Academy of Management Journal* (June 2001), pp. 533–545; M. A. Carpenter, "The Implications of Strategy and Social Context for the Relationship Between Top Management Team Heterogeneity and Firm Performance," *Strategic Management Journal* (March 2002), pp. 275–284; L. Tihanyi, A. E. Ellstrand, C. M. Daily, and D. R. Dalton, "Composition of the Top Management Team and Firm International Expansion," *Journal of Management*, Vol. 26, No. 6 (2000), pp. 1157–1177.
82. "One on One with Steve Reinemund," *Business Week* (December 17, 2001), special advertising insert on leadership by Heidrick & Struggles, executive search firm.
83. D. A. Waldman, G. G. Ramirez, R. J. House, and P. Puranam, "Does Leadership Matter? CEO Leadership Attributes and Profitability Under Conditions of Perceived Environmental Uncertainty," *Academy of Management Journal* (February 2001), pp. 134–143; F. J. Flynn and B. M. Staw, "Lend Me Your Wallets: The Effect of Charismatic Leadership on External Support for an Organization," *Strategic Management Journal* (April 2004), pp. 309–330.
84. J. Burns, *Leadership* (New York: HarperCollins, 1978); B. Bass, "From Transactional to Transformational Leadership: Learning to Share the Vision," *Organizational Dynamics*, Vol. 18 (1990), pp. 19–31; W. Bennis and B. Nanus, *Leaders: Strategies for Taking Charge* (New York: HarperCollins, 1997).
85. L. V. Gerstner, Jr., *Who Says Elephants Can't Dance?* (New York: HarperCollins, 2002), p. 124.
86. M. Lipton, "Demystifying the Development of an Organizational Vision," *Sloan Management Review* (Summer 1996), p. 84.
87. S. Hahn, "Why High Tech Has to Stay Humble," *Business Week* (January 19, 2004), pp. 76–77.
88. J. H. David, F. D. Schoorman, R. Mayer, and H. H. Tan, "The Trusted General Manager and Business Unit Performance: Empirical Evidence of a Competitive Advantage," *Strategic Management Journal* (May 2000), pp. 563–576.
89. D. B. McNatt and T. A. Judge, "Boundary Conditions of the Galatea Effect: A Field Experiment and Constructive Replication," *Academy of Management Journal* (August 2004), pp. 550–565.

90. J. E. Bono and T. A. Judge, "Self-Concordance at Work: Toward Understanding the Motivational Effects of Transformational Leaders," *Academy of Management Journal* (October 2003), pp. 554–571.

91. T. Lowry, R. O. Crockett, and I. M. Kunii, "Verizon's Gutsy Bet," *Business Week* (August 4, 2003), pp. 52–62.

92. G. Tate and U. Malmendier, "Who Makes Acquisitions? CEO Overconfidence and the Market's Reaction," summarized by *Knowledge @ Wharton* (February 25, 2004).

93. M. S. Chae and J. S. Hill, "The Hazards of Strategic Planning for Global Markets," *Long Range Planning* (December 1996), pp. 880–891.

94. T. R. Eisenmann and J. L. Bower, "The Entrepreneurial M-Form: Strategic Integration in Global Media Firms," *Organization Science* (May–June 2000), pp. 348–355.

95. For an in-depth guide to conducting the strategic planning process, see C. D. Fogg, *Team-Based Strategic Planning* (New York: AMACOM, 1994).

96. M. Wiersema, "Holes at the Top: Why CEO Firings Backfire," *Harvard Business Review* (December 2002), pp. 70–77.

97. L. Greiner, T. Cummings, and A. Bhambri, "When New CEOs Succeed and Fail: 4-D Theory of Strategic Transformation," *Organizational Dynamics*, Vol. 32, No. 1 (2003), pp. 1–16.

98. G. Strauss, "Board Pay Gets Fatter as Job Gets Harrier," *USA Today* (March 7, 2005), p. 1B.

Chapter 3

1. M. Conlin, J. Hempel, J. Tanzer, and D. Poole, "The Corporate Donors," *Business Week* (December 1, 2003), pp. 92–96; I. Sager, "The List: Angels in the Boardroom," *Business Week* (July 7, 2003), p. 12.

2. M. Friedman, "The Social Responsibility of Business Is to Increase Its Profits," *New York Times Magazine* (September 13, 1970), pp. 30, 126–127; M. Freidman, *Capitalism and Freedom* (Chicago: University of Chicago Press, 1963), p. 133.

3. W. J. Byron, *Old Ethical Principles for the New Corporate Culture*, presentation to the College of Business, Iowa State University, Ames, Iowa (March 31, 2003).

4. A. B. Carroll, "A Three-Dimensional Conceptual Model of Corporate Performance," *Academy of Management Review* (October 1979), pp. 497–505. This model of business responsibilities was reaffirmed in A. B. Carroll, "Managing Ethically with Global Stakeholders: A Present and Future Challenge," *Academy of Management Executive* (May 2004), pp. 114–120.

5. Carroll refers to discretionary responsibilities as philanthropic responsibilities in A. B. Carroll, "The Pyramid of Corporate Social Responsibility: Toward the Moral Management of Organizational Stakeholders," *Business Horizons* (July–August 1991), pp. 39–48.

6. M. S. Baucus and D. A. Baucus, "Paying the Piper: An Empirical Examination of Longer-Term Financial Consequences of Illegal Corporate Behavior," *Academy of Management Journal* (February 1997), pp. 129–151.

7. J. Oleck, "Pink Slips with a Silver Lining," *Business Week* (June 4, 2001), p. 14.

8. A. McWilliams and D. Siegel, "Corporate Social Responsibility and Financial Performance: Correlation or Misspecification?" *Strategic Management Journal* (May 2000), pp. 603–609; P. Rechner and K. Roth, "Social Responsibility and Financial Performance: A Structural Equation Methodology," *International Journal of Management* (December 1990), pp. 382–391; K. E. Aupperle, A. B. Carroll, and J. D. Hatfield, "An Empirical Examination of the Relationship Between Corporate Social Responsibility and Profitability," *Academy of Management Journal* (June 1985), p. 459.

9. M. M. Arthur, "Share Price Reactions to Work-Family Initiatives: An Institutional Perspective," *Academy of Management Journal* (April 2003), pp. 497–505; S. A. Waddock and S. B. Graves, "The Corporate Social Performance—Financial Performance Link," *Strategic Management Journal* (April 1997), pp. 303–319; M.V. Russo and P. A. Fouts, "Resource-Based Perspective on Corporate Environmental Performance and Profitability," *Academy of Management Journal* (July 1997), pp. 534–559; H. Meyer, "The Greening of Corporate America," *Journal of Business Strategy* (January/February 2000), pp. 38–43.

10. J. D. Margolis and J. P. Walsh, "Misery Loves Companies: Rethinking Social Initiatives by Business," *Administrative Science Quarterly* (June 2003), pp. 268–305.

11. M. F. L. Orlitzky, F. L. Schmidt, and S. L. Rynes, "Corporate Social and Financial Performance: A Meta Analysis," *Organization Studies*, Vol. 24 (2003), pp. 403–441.

12. M. Porter and M. R. Kramer, "The Competitive Advantage of Corporate Philanthropy," *Harvard Business Review* (December 2002), p. 59.

13. P. S. Adler and S. W. Kwon, "Social Capital: Prospects for a New Concept," *Academy of Management Journal* (January 2002), pp. 17–40.

14. L. Gard, "We're Good Guys, Buy from Us," *Business Week* (November 22, 2004), pp. 72–74.

15. S. A. Muirhead, C. J. Bennett, R. E. Berenbeim, A. Kao, and D. J. Vidal, *Corporate Citizenship in the New Century* (New York: The Conference Board, 2002), p. 6.

16. *2002 Sustainability Survey Report*, PricewaterhouseCoopers, reported in "Corporate America's Social Conscience," Special Advertising Section, *Fortune* (May 26, 2003), pp. 149–157.

17. C. L. Harman and E. R. Stafford, "Green Alliances: Building New Business with Environmental Groups," *Long Range Planning* (April 1997), pp. 184–196.

18. D. B. Turner and D. W. Greening, "Corporate Social Performance and Organizational Attractiveness to Prospective Employees," *Academy of Management Journal* (July 1997), pp. 658–672; S. Preece, C. Fleisher, and J. Toccacelli, "Building a Reputation Along the Value Chain at Levi Strauss," *Long Range Planning* (December 1995), pp. 88–98; J. B. Barney and M. H. Hansen, "Trustworthiness as a Source of Competitive Advantage," *Strategic Management Journal* (Special Winter Issue, 1994), pp. 175–190.

19. R. E. Freeman and D. R. Gilbert, *Corporate Strategy and the Search for Ethics* (Upper Saddle River, NJ: Prentice Hall, 1988), p. 6.

20. M. Arndt, W. Zellner, and P. Coy, "Too Much Corporate Power?" *Business Week* (September 11, 2000), pp. 144–158.

21. "Report: CEOs of Companies with Greatest Outsourcing Got Biggest Pay," *Des Moines Register* (August 31, 2004), p. B5.

22. "Andy Grove to Corporate Boards: It's Time to Take Charge," *Knowledge @ Wharton* (September 9—October 5, 2004).

23. "Nearly Half of Workers Take Unethical Actions—Survey," *Des Moines Register* (April 7, 1997), p. 18B.

24. J. Kurlantzick, "Liar, Liar," *Entrepreneur* (October 2003), p. 70.

25. M. Roman, "True Confessions from CFOs," *Business Week* (August 12, 2002), p. 40.

26. J. Kurlantzick, "Liar, Liar," *Entrepreneur* (October 2003), p. 71.
27. J. Hempel and L. Gard, "The Corporate Givers," *Business Week* (November 29, 2004), pp. 100–104.
28. S. Li, S. H. Park, and S. Li, "The Great Leap Forward: The Transition from Relation-Based Governance to Rule-Based Governance," *Organizational Dynamics*, Vol. 33, No. 1 (2004), pp. 63–78; M. Davids, "Global Standards, Local Problems," *Business Strategy* (January/February 1999), pp. 38–43; "The Opacity Index," *Economist* (September 18, 2004), p. 106.
29. K. Kumar, "Ethical Orientation of Future American Executives: What the Value Profiles of Business School Students Portend," *SAM Advanced Management Journal* (Autumn 1995), pp. 32–36, 47; M. Gable and P. Arlow, "A Comparative Examination of the Value Orientations of British and American Executives," *International Journal of Management* (September 1986), pp. 97–106; W. D. Guth and R. Tagiuri, "Personal Values and Corporate Strategy," *Harvard Business Review* (September–October 1965), pp. 126–127; G. W. England, "Managers and Their Value Systems: A Five Country Comparative Study," *Columbia Journal of World Business* (Summer 1978), p. 35.
30. J. F. Veiga, T. D. Golden, and K. Dechant, "Why Managers Bend Company Rules," *Academy of Management Executive* (May 2004), pp. 84–91.
31. H. Collingwood, "The Earnings Game," *Harvard Business Review* (June 2001), pp. 65–74; J. Fox, "Can We Trust Them Now?" *Fortune* (March 3, 2003), pp. 97–99.
32. S. Watkins, "Former Enron Vice President Sherron Watkins on the Enron Collapse," *Academy of Management Executive* (November 2003), p. 122.
33. L. K. Trevino, "Ethical Decision Making in Organizations: A Person–Situation Interactionist Model," *Academy of Management Review* (July 1986), pp. 601–617.
34. L. Kohlberg, "Moral Stage and Moralization: The Cognitive-Development Approach," in *Moral Development and Behavior*, edited by T. Lickona (New York: Holt, Rinehart & Winston, 1976).
35. L. K. Trevino, "Ethical Decision Making in Organizations: A Person–Situation Interactionist Model," *Academy of Management Review* (July 1986), p. 606.
36. J. Keogh, ed., *Corporate Ethics: A Prime Business Asset* (New York: The Business Roundtable, 1988), p. 5.
37. G. F. Kohut and S. E. Corriher, "The Relationship of Age, Gender, Experience and Awareness of Written Ethics Policies to Business Decision Making," *SAM Advanced Management Journal* (Winter 1994), pp. 32–39; J. C. Lere and B. R. Gaumitz, "The Impact of Codes of Ethics on Decision Making: Some Insights from Information Economics," *Journal of Business Ethics*, Vol. 48 (2003), pp. 365–379.
38. *Business Roundtable Institute for Corporate Ethics Announces Key Findings from "Mapping the Terrain" Survey of CEOs*, press release (Charlottesville, VA: Business Roundtable Institute for Corporate Ethics, June 10, 2004).
39. "Reebok Finds Bad Conditions in Two Factories," *Des Moines Register* (October 19, 1999), p. 8S.
40. T. J. Von der Embse and R. A. Wagley, "Managerial Ethics: Hard Decisions on Soft Criteria," *SAM Advanced Management Journal* (Winter 1988), p. 6.
41. G. F. Cavanagh, *American Business Values*, 3rd ed. (Upper Saddle River, NJ: Prentice Hall, 1990), pp. 186–199.
42. B. R. Agle, R. K. Mitchell, and J. A. Sonnenfeld, "Who Matters Most to CEOs? An Investigation of Stakeholder Attributes and Salience, Corporate Performance, and CEO Values," *Academy of Management Journal* (October 1999), pp. 507–525.
43. G. F. Cavanagh, *American Business Values*, 3rd ed. (Upper Saddle River, NJ: Prentice Hall, 1990), pp. 195–196.
44. I. Kant, "The Foundations of the Metaphysic of Morals," in *Ethical Theory: Classical and Contemporary Readings*, 2nd ed., by L. P. Pojman (Belmont, CA: Wadsworth Publishing, 1995), pp. 255–279.
45. J. L. Badaracco, Jr., *Defining Moments* (Boston: Harvard Business School Press, 1997).
46. "Datbit," *Biz Ed* (March/April 2004).

Chapter 4

1. D. Debelak, "All Fired Up," *Entrepreneur* (July 2004), pp. 116–120.
2. J. B. Thomas, S. M. Clark, and D. A. Gioia, "Strategic Sensemaking and Organizational Performance: Linkages Among Scanning, Interpretation, Action, Outcomes," *Academy of Management Journal* (April 1993), pp. 239–270; J. A. Smith, "Strategies for Start-ups," *Long Range Planning* (December 1998), pp. 857–872.
3. V. K. Garg, B. A. Walters, and R. L. Priem, "Chief Executive Scanning Emphases, Environmental Dynamism, and Manufacturing Performance," *Strategic Management Journal* (August 2003), pp. 725–744.
4. P. Lasserre and J. Probert, "Competing on the Pacific Rim: High Risks and High Returns," *Long Range Planning* (April 1994), pp. 12–35.
5. M. J. Cetron, "Economics: Prospects for the 'Dragon' and the 'Tiger,'" *Futurist* (July–August 2004), pp. 10–11.
6. W. E. Halal, "The Top 10 Emerging Technologies," *Special Report* (World Future Society, 2000).
7. F. Dobbin and T. J. Dowd, "How Policy Shapes Competition: Early Railroad Foundings in Massachusetts," *Administrative Science Quarterly* (September 1997), pp. 501–529.
8. A. Shleifer and R. W. Viskny, "Takeovers in the 1960s and the 1980s: Evidence and Implications," in *Fundamental Issues in Strategy: A Research Agenda*, edited by R. P. Rumelt, D. E. Schendel, and D. J. Teece (Boston: Harvard Business School Press, 1994), pp. 403–418.
9. "Europe's Workplace Revolution," *Economist* (July 31, 2004), pp. 51–52.
10. "Old Europe," *Economist* (October 2, 2004), pp. 49–50.
11. "The Incredible Shrinking Country," *Economist* (November 13, 2004), pp. 45–46.
12. J. Wyatt, "Playing the Woofie Card," *Fortune* (February 6, 1995), pp. 130–132.
13. D. Carpenter, "Walgreen Pursues 12,000 Corners of Market," *Des Moines Register* (May 9, 2004), pp. 1D, 5D.
14. D. Pitt, "Winnebago Industries Benefits from Motor Home Boom," *The (Ames, IA) Tribune* (August 30, 2004), p. B5.
15. M. Arndt, "Zimmer: Growing Older Gracefully," *Business Week* (June 9, 2003), pp. 82–84.
16. H. Yen, "Empty Nesters Push Growth of Pet Health Care Businesses," *The (Ames, IA) Tribune* (September 27, 2003), p. C8.
17. A. Bianco, "The Vanishing Mass Market," *Business Week* (July 12, 2004), pp. 61–68.

18. M. Conlin, "UnMarried America," *Business Week* (October 20, 2003), pp. 106–116.
19. N. Irvin II, "The Arrival of the Thrivals," *Futurist* (March–April 2004), pp. 16–23.
20. G. Smith and C. Lindblad, "Mexico: Was NAFTA Worth It?" *Business Week* (December 22, 2003), pp. 66–72.
21. "Multicultural Retailing," *Arizona Republic* (October 10, 2004), p. D4.
22. "Islamic Finance: West Meets East," *Economist* (October 25, 2003), p. 69.
23. J. Naisbitt, *Megatrends Asia* (New York: Simon & Schuster, 1996), p. 79.
24. K. Ohmae, "The Triad World View," *Journal of Business Strategy* (Spring 1987), pp. 8–19.
25. A. Menon and A. Tomkins, "Learning About the Market's Periphery: IBM's WebFountain," *Long Range Planning* (April 2004), pp. 153–162.
26. I. M. Cockburn, R. M. Henderson, and S. Stern, "Untangling the Origins of Competitive Advantage," *Strategic Management Journal* (October–November 2000), Special Issue, pp. 1123–1145.
27. L. Fuld, "Be Prepared," *Harvard Business Review* (November 2003), pp. 20–21.
28. H. Wissema, "Driving Through Red Lights," *Long Range Planning* (October 2002), pp. 521–539; B. K. Boyd and J. Fulk, "Executive Scanning and Perceived Uncertainty: A Multidimensional Model," *Journal of Management*, Vol. 22, No. 1 (1996), pp. 1–21.
29. P. G. Audia, E. A. Locke, and K. G. Smith, "The Paradox of Success: An Archival and a Laboratory Study of Strategic Persistence Following Radical Environmental Change," *Academy of Management Journal* (October 2000), pp. 837–853; M. L. McDonald and J. D. Westphal, "Getting By with the Advice of Their Friends: CEOs Advice Networks and Firms' Strategic Responses to Poor Performance," *Administrative Science Quarterly* (March 2003), pp. 1–32; R. A. Bettis and C. K. Prahalad, "The Dominant Logic: Retrospective and Extension," *Strategic Management Journal* (January 1995), pp. 5–14; J. M. Stofford and C. W. F. Baden-Fuller, "Creating Corporate Entrepreneurship," *Strategic Management Journal* (September 1994), pp. 521–536; J. M. Beyer, P. Chattopadhyay, E. George, W. H. Glick, and D. Pugliese, "The Selective Perception of Managers Revisited," *Academy of Management Journal* (June 1997), pp. 716–737.
30. H. I. Ansoff, "Strategic Management in a Historical Perspective," in *International Review of Strategic Management*, Vol. 2, No. 1 (1991), edited by D. E. Hussey (Chichester, England: Wiley, 1991), p. 61.
31. M. E. Porter, *Competitive Strategy* (New York: The Free Press, 1980), p. 3.
32. This summary of the forces driving competitive strategy is taken from Ibid., pp. 7–29.
33. M. McCarthy, "Rivals Scramble to Topple Nike's Sneaker Supremacy," *USA Today* (April 3, 2003), pp. B1–B2.
34. M. E. Porter, *Competitive Strategy* (New York: The Free Press, 1980), p. 23.
35. A. S. Grove, "Surviving a 10x Force," *Strategy & Leadership* (January/February 1997), pp. 35–37.
36. A fragmented industry is defined as one whose market share for the leading four firms is equal to or less than 40% of total industry sales. See M. J. Dollinger, "The Evolution of Collective Strategies in Fragmented Industries," *Academy of Management Review* (April 1990), pp. 266–285.
37. M. E. Porter, "Changing Patterns of International Competition," *California Management Review* (Winter 1986), pp. 9–40.
38. T. N. Gladwin, "Assessing the Multinational Environment for Corporate Opportunity," in *Handbook of Business Strategy*, edited by W. D. Guth (Boston: Warren, Gorham and Lamont, 1985), pp. 7.28–7.41.
39. K. J. Hatten and M. L. Hatten, "Strategic Groups, Asymmetrical Mobility Barriers, and Contestability," *Strategic Management Journal* (July–August 1987), p. 329.
40. J. D. Osborne, C. I. Stubbart, and A. Ramaprasad, "Strategic Groups and Competitive Enactment: A Study of Dynamic Relationships Between Mental Models and Performance," *Strategic Management Journal* (May 2001), pp. 435–454; A. Fiegenbaum and H. Thomas, "Strategic Groups as Reference Groups: Theory, Modeling and Empirical Examination of Industry and Competitive Strategy," *Strategic Management Journal* (September 1995), pp. 461–476; H. R. Greve, "Managerial Cognition and the Mimities Adoption of Market Positions: What You See Is What You Do," *Strategic Management Journal* (October 1998), pp. 967–988.
41. C. C. Pegels, Y. I. Song, and B. Yang, "Management Heterogeneity, Competitive Interaction Groups, and Firm Performance," *Strategic Management Journal* (September 2000), pp. 911–923.
42. R. E. Miles and C. C. Snow, *Organizational Strategy, Structure, and Process* (New York: McGraw-Hill, 1978). See also D. J. Ketchen, Jr., "An Interview with Raymond E. Miles and Charles C. Snow," *Academy of Management Executive* (November 2003), pp. 97–104.
43. R. A. D'Aveni, *Hypercompetition* (New York: The Free Press, 1994), pp. xiii–xiv.
44. C. W. Hofer and D. Schendel, *Strategy Formulation: Analytical Concepts* (St. Paul: West Publishing Co., 1978), p. 77.
45. "Information Overload," *Journal of Business Strategy* (January–February 1998), p. 4.
46. E. Von Hipple, *Sources of Innovation* (New York: Oxford University Press, 1988), p. 4.
47. "CI of 'Singular Importance,' Says Procter & Gamble's Chairman," *Competitive Intelligence Magazine* (July–September 1999), p. 5.
48. R. G. Vedder, "CEO and CIO Attitudes about Competitive Intelligence," *Competitive Intelligence Magazine* (October–December 1999), pp. 39–41.
49. J. Schlosser, "Looking for Intelligence in Ice Cream," *Fortune* (March 17, 2003), pp. 114–120.
50. S. H. Miller, "Beware Rival's Web Site Subterfuge," *Competitive Intelligence Magazine* (January–March 2000), p. 8.
51. E. Iwata, "More U.S. Trade Secrets Walk Out Door with Foreign Spies," *USA Today* (February 13, 2003), pp. B1, B2.
52. "Twenty-nine Percent Spy on Co-Workers," *USA Today* (August 19, 2003), p. B1.
53. B. Flora, "Ethical Business Intelligence is NOT Mission Impossible," *Strategy & Leadership* (January/February 1998), pp. 40–41.
54. A. L. Penenberg and M. Berry, *Spooked: Espionage in Corporate America* (Cambridge, MA: Perseus Publishing, 2000).
55. T. Kendrick and J. Blackmore, "Ten Things You Really Need to Know About Competitors," *Competitive Intelligence Magazine* (September–October 2001), pp. 12–15.

56. "CI at Avnet: A Bottom-Line Impact," *Competitive Intelligence Magazine* (July–September 2000), p. 5. For further information on competitive intelligence, see C. S. Fleisher and D. L. Blenkhorn, *Controversies in Competitive Intelligence: The Enduring Issues* (Westport, CT: Praeger Publishers, 2003); C. Vibert, *Competitive Intelligence: A Framework for Web-Based Analysis and Decision Making* (Mason, OH: Thomson/Southwestern, 2004); and C. S. Fleisher and B. E. Bensoussan, *Strategic and Competitive Analysis* (Upper Saddle River, NJ: Prentice Hall, 2003).

57. L. M. Grossman, "Families Have Changed But Tupperware Keeps Holding Its Parties," *Wall Street Journal* (July 21, 1992), pp. A1, A13.

58. H. E. Klein and R. E. Linneman, "Environmental Assessment: An International Study of Corporate Practices," *Journal of Business Strategy* (Summer 1984), p. 72.

59. See L. E. Schlange and U. Juttner, "Helping Managers to Identify the Key Strategic Issues," *Long Range Planning* (October 1997), pp. 777–786, for an explanation and application of the cross-impact matrix.

60. This process of scenario development is adapted from M. E. Porter, *Competitive Advantage* (New York: The Free Press, 1985), pp. 448–470.

61. H. C. Sashittal and A. R. Jassawalla, "Learning from Wayne Gretzky," *Organizational Dynamics* (Spring 2002), pp. 341–355.

62. "Fast Food and Strong Currency" *Economist* (June 11, 2005), p. 70.

63. M. E. Porter, *Competitive Strategy: Techniques for Analyzing Industries and Competitors* (New York: The Free Press, 1980), pp. 47–75.

64. M. Treacy and F. Wiersema, *The Discipline of Market Leaders* (Reading, MA: Addison-Wesley, 1995).

65. Presentation by W. A. Rosenkrans, Jr., to the Iowa Chapter of the Society of Competitive Intelligence Professionals, Des Moines, IA (August 5, 2004).

66. B. Gilad, *Early Warning* (New York: AMACOM, 2004), pp. 97–103. Also see C. S. Fleisher and B. E. Bensoussan, *Strategic and Competitive Analysis* (Upper Saddle River, NJ: Prentice Hall, 2003), pp. 122–143.

67. Presentation by W. A. Rosenkrans, Jr., to the Iowa Chapter of the Society of Competitive Intelligence Professionals, Des Moines, IA (August 5, 2004).

68. L. Fahey, "Invented Competitors: A New Competitor Analysis Methodology," *Strategy & Leadership*, Vol. 30, No. 6 (2002), pp. 5–12.

Chapter 5

1. A. Park and L. Young, "Dell Outfoxes Its Rivals," *Business Week* (September 6, 2004), p. 54.

2. A. Serwer, "Dell Does Domination," *Fortune* (January 21, 2002), p. 71.

3. A. Park and P. Burrows, "What You Don't Know About Dell," *Business Week* (November 3, 2003), pp. 77–84.

4. K. Maney, "Dell Business Model Turns to Muscle as Rivals Struggle," *USA Today* (January 20, 2003), pp. 1B–2B.

5. Ibid., p. 2B.

6. M. Javidan, "Core Competence: What Does It Mean in Practice?" *Long Range Planning* (February 1998), pp. 60–71.

7. M. A. Hitt, B. W. Keats, and S. M. DeMarie, "Navigating in the New Competitive Landscape: Building Strategic Flexibility and Competitive Advantage in the 21st Century," *Academy of Management Executive* (November 1998), pp. 22–42; C. E. Helfat and M. A. Peteraf, "The Dynamic Resources-Based View: Capability Life Cycles," *Strategic Management Journal* (October 2003), pp. 997–1010.

8. D. Brady and K. Capell, "GE Breaks the Mold to Spur Innovation," *Business Week* (April 26, 2004), pp. 88–89.

9. J. B. Barney, *Gaining and Sustaining Competitive Advantage*, 2nd edition (Upper Saddle River, NJ: Prentice Hall, 2003), pp. 159–172. Barney's VRIO questions are very similar to those proposed by G. Hamel and S. K. Prahalad in their book *Competing for the Future* (Boston: Harvard Business School Press, 1994) on pages 202–207, in which they state that to be distinctive, a competency must (a) provide customer value, (b) be competitor unique, and (c) be extendable to develop new products and/or markets.

10. Barney, p. 161.

11. R. M. Grant, "The Resource-Based Theory of Competitive Advantage: Implications for Strategy Formulation," *California Management Review* (Spring 1991), pp. 114–135.

12. P. J. Verdin and P. J. Williamson, "Core Competencies, Competitive Advantage and Market Analysis: Forging the Links," in *Competence-Based Competition*, edited by G. Hamel and A. Heene (New York: John Wiley & Sons, 1994), pp. 83–84.

13. M. E. Porter, "Clusters and the New Economics of Competition," *Harvard Business Review* (November–December 1998), pp. 77–90.

14. J. M. Shaver and F. Flyer, "Agglomeration Economies, Firm Heterogeneity, and Foreign Direct Investment in the United States," *Strategic Management Journal* (December 2000), pp. 1175–1193; W. Chung and A. Kalnins, "Agglomeration Effects and Performance: A Test of the Texas Lodging Industry," *Strategic Management Journal* (October 2001), pp. 969–988.

15. J. E. McGee and L. G. Love, "Sources of Competitive Advantage for Small Independent Retailers: Lessons from the Neighborhood Drugstore," *Association for Small Business & Entrepreneurship*, Houston, TX (March 10–13, 1999), p. 2.

16. M. Polanyi, *The Tacit Dimension* (Garden City, NY: Doubleday, 1966).

17. S. K. McEvily and B. Chakravarthy, "The Persistence of Knowledge-Based Advantage: An Empirical Test for Product Performance and Technological Knowledge," *Strategic Management Journal* (April 2002), pp. 285–305.

18. P. E. Bierly III, "Development of a Generic Knowledge Strategy Typology," *Journal of Business Strategies* (Spring 1999), p. 3.

19. S. Abraham, "Experiencing Strategic Conversations about the Central Forces of our Time," *Strategy & Leadership*, Vol. 31, No. 2 (2003), pp. 61–62.

20. C. A. de Kluyver and J. A. Pearce II, *Strategy: A View from the Top* (Upper Saddle River, NJ: Prentice Hall, 2003), pp. 63–66.

21. O. Gadiesh and J. L. Gilbert, "Profit Pools: A Fresh Look at Strategy," *Harvard Business Review* (May–June 1998), pp. 139–147.

22. J. R. Galbraith, "Strategy and Organization Planning," in *The Strategy Process: Concepts, Contexts, and Cases*, 2nd ed., edited by H. Mintzberg and J. B. Quinn (Upper Saddle River, NJ: Prentice Hall, 1991), pp. 315–324.

23. M. Porter, *Competitive Advantage: Creating and Sustaining Superior Performance* (New York: The Free Press, 1985), p. 36.

24. M. Leontiades, "A Diagnostic Framework for Planning," *Strategic Management Journal* (January–March 1983), p. 14.

25. E. H. Schein, *The Corporate Culture Survival Guide* (San Francisco: Jossey-Bass, 1999), p. 12; L. C. Harris and E. Ogbonna, "The Strategic Legacy of Company Founders," *Long Range Planning* (June 1999), pp. 333–343.
26. D. M. Rousseau, "Assessing Organizational Culture: The Case for Multiple Methods," in *Organizational Climate and Culture*, edited by B. Schneider (San Francisco: Jossey-Bass, 1990), pp. 153–192.
27. L. Smircich, "Concepts of Culture and Organizational Analysis," *Administrative Science Quarterly* (September 1983), pp. 345–346.
28. J. B. Sorensen, "The Strength of Corporate Culture and the Reliability of Firm Performance," *Administrative Science Quarterly* (March 2002), pp. 70–91.
29. K. E. Aupperle, "Spontaneous Organizational Reconfiguration: A Historical Example Based on Xenophon's Anabasis," *Organization Science* (July–August 1996), pp. 445–460.
30. J. B. Barney, *Gaining and Sustaining Competitive Advantage* (Reading, MA: Addison-Wesley, 1997), p. 155.
31. D. Brady, R. D. Hof, A. Reinhardt, M. Ihlwan, S. Holmes, and K. Capell, "Cult Brands," *Business Week* (August 2, 2004), pp. 64–69.
32. R. T. Wilcox, "The Hidden Potential of Powerful Brands," *Batten Briefings* (Summer 2003), pp. 1, 4–5.
33. C. Fombrun and C. Van Riel, "The Reputational Landscape," *Corporate Reputation Review*, Vol. 1, Nos. 1 & 2 (1997), pp. 5–13.
34. P. W. Roberts and G. R. Dowling, "Corporate Reputation and Sustained Financial Performance," *Strategic Management Journal* (December 2002), pp. 1077–1093; J. Shamsie, "The Context of Dominance: An Industry-Driven Framework for Exploiting Reputation," *Strategic Management Journal* (March 2003), pp. 199–215; M. D. Michalisin, D. M. Kline, and R. D. Smith, "Intangible Strategic Assets and Firm Performance: A Multi-Industry Study of the Resource-Based View," *Journal of Business Strategies* (Fall 2000), pp. 91–117; S. S. Standifird, "Reputation and E-Commerce: eBay Auctions and the Asymmetrical Impact of Positive and Negative Ratings," *Journal of Management*, Vol. 27, No. 3 (2001), pp. 279–295.
35. R. L. Simerly and M. Li, "Environmental Dynamism, Capital Structure and Performance: A Theoretical Integration and an Empirical Test," *Strategic Management Journal* (January 2000), pp. 31–49.
36. Ibid.; A. Heisz and S. LaRochelle-Cote, "Corporate Financial Leverage in Canadian Manufacturing: Consequences for Employment and Inventories," *Canadian Journal of Administrative Science* (June 2004), pp. 111–128.
37. J. M. Poterba and L. H. Summers, "A CEO Survey of U.S. Companies' Time Horizons and Hurdle Rates," *Sloan Management Review* (Fall 1995), pp. 43–53.
38. "R&D Scoreboard," *Business Week* (June 27, 1994), pp. 81–103.
39. B. O'Reilly, "The Secrets of America's Most Admired Corporations: New Ideas and New Products," *Fortune* (March 3, 1997), p. 62.
40. P. Pascarella, "Are You Investing in the Wrong Technology?" *Industry Week* (July 25, 1983), p. 37.
41. D. J. Yang, "Leaving Moore's Law in the Dust," *U.S. News & World Report* (July 10, 2000), pp. 37–38; R. Fishburne and M. Malone, "Laying Down the Laws: Gordon Moore and Bob Metcalfe in Conversation," *Forbes ASAP* (February 21, 2000), pp. 97–100.
42. P. Pascarella, "Are You Investing in the Wrong Technology?" *Industry Week* (July 25, 1983), p. 38.
43. C. M. Christensen, *The Innovator's Dilemma* (Boston: Harvard Business School Press, 1997).
44. B. J. Pine, *Mass Customization: The New Frontier in Business Competition* (Boston: Harvard Business School Press, 1993).
45. S. L Rynes, K. G. Brown, and A. E. Colbert, "Seven Common Misconceptions About Human Resource Practices: Research Findings Versus Practitioner Belief," *Academy of Management Executives* (August 2002), pp. 92–103.
46. E. E. Lawler, S. A. Mohrman, and G. E. Ledford, Jr., *Creating High Performance Organizations* (San Francisco: Jossey-Bass, 1995), p. 29.
47. A. Versteeg, "Self-Directed Work Teams Yield Long-Term Benefits," *Journal of Business Strategy* (November/December 1990), pp. 9–12.
48. R. Sanchez, "Strategic Flexibility in Product Competition," *Strategic Management Journal* (Summer 1995), p. 147.
49. A. R. Jassawalla and H. C. Sashittal, "Building Collaborative Cross-Functional New Product Teams," *Academy of Management Executives* (August 1999), pp. 50–63.
50. A. M. Townsend, S. M. DeMarie, and A. R. Hendrickson, "Virtual Teams: Technology and the Workplace of the Future," *Academy of Management Executives* (August 1998), pp. 17–29.
51. S. A. Furst, M. Reeves, B. Rosen, and R. S. Blackburn, "Managing the Life Cycle of Virtual Teams," *Academy of Management Executives* (May 2004), pp. 6–20; L. L. Martins, L. L. Gilson, and M. T. Maynard, "Virtual Teams: What Do We Know and Where Do We Go From Here?" *Journal of Management*, Vol. 30, No. 6 (2004), pp. 805–835.
52. A. M. Townsend, S. M. DeMarie, and A. R. Hendrickson, "Virtual Teams: Technology and the Workplace of the Future," *Academy of Management Executives* (August 1998), p. 18.
53. A. Bernstein, "Can This Man Save Labor?" *Business Week* (September 13, 2004), pp. 80–88.
54. D. Welsh, "What Goodyear Got from its Union," *Business Week* (October 20, 2003), pp. 148–149.
55. S. F. Matusik and C. W. L. Hill, "The Utilization of Contingent Work, Knowledge Creation, and Competitive Advantage," *Academy of Management Executives* (October 1998), pp. 680–697.
56. "Part-Time Workers," *Economist* (July 24, 2004), p. 90.
57. A. Bernstein, "At UPS, Part-Time Work Is a Full-Time Issue," *Business Week* (June 16, 1997), pp. 88–90.
58. J. Muller, "A Ford Redesign," *Business Week* (November 13, 2000), Special Report.
59. G. Colvin, "The 50 Best Companies for Asians, Blacks, and Hispanics," *Fortune* (July 19, 1999), pp. 53–58.
60. V. Singh and S. Point, "Strategic Responses by European Companies to the Diversity Challenge: An Online Comparison," *Long Range Planning* (August 2004), pp. 295–318.
61. Ibid., p. 310.
62. J. Bachman, "Coke to Pay $192.5 Million to Settle Lawsuit," *The (Ames, IA) Tribune* (November 20, 2000), p. D4.
63. J. Lee and D. Miller, "People Matter: Commitment to Employees, Strategy, and Performance in Korean Firms," *Strategic Management Journal* (June 1999), pp. 579–593.
64. A. Cortese, "Here Comes the Intranet," *Business Week* (February 26, 1996), p. 76.
65. D. Bartholomew, "Blue-Collar Computing," *InformationWeek* (June 19, 1995), pp. 34–43.

66. C. C. Poirier, *Advanced Supply Chain Management* (San Francisco: Berrett-Koehler Publishers, 1999), p. 2.
67. M. Cook and R. Hagey, "Why Companies Flunk Supply-Chain 101: Only 33 Percent Correctly Measure Supply-Chain Performance; Few Use the Right Incentives," *Journal of Business Strategy*, Vol. 24, No. 4 (2003), pp. 35–42.
68. C. C. Poirier, *Advanced Supply Chain Management* (San Francisco: Berrett-Kohler Publishers, 1999), pp. 3–5.
69. B. Horowitz, "KFC Roast Line Flops After 3 Months," *USA Today* (July 16, 2004), p. 6D.
70. *Economist Pocket World in Figures, 2004 Edition* (London: Profile Books, 2003), p. 54.

Chapter 6

1. A. Fitzgerald, "Cedar Rapids Export Company Serves Muslims Worldwide," *Des Moines Register* (October 26, 2003), pp. 1M–2M.
2. K. W. Glaister and J. R. Falshaw, "Strategic Planning: Still Going Strong?" *Long Range Planning* (February 1999), pp. 107–116.
3. T. Brown, "The Essence of Strategy," *Management Review* (April 1997), pp. 8–13.
4. T. Hill and R. Westbrook, "SWOT Analysis: It's Time for a Product Recall," *Long Range Planning* (February 1997), pp. 46–52.
5. W. H. Newman, "Shaping the Master Strategy of Your Firm," *California Management Review*, Vol. 9, No. 3 (1967), pp. 77–88.
6. "A Teaching Tool Outlining a Special Day with Howard Shultz," Videotaped Interview, Lloyd Greif Center for Entrepreneurial Studies, University of Southern California (2004).
7. M. E. Porter, *Competitive Strategy* (New York: The Free Press, 1980), pp. 34–41, as revised in M. E. Porter, *The Competitive Advantage of Nations* (New York: The Free Press, 1990), pp. 37–40.
8. J. O. DeCastro and J. J. Chrisman,"Narrow-Scope Strategies and Firm Performance: An Empirical Investigation," *Journal of Business Strategies* (Spring 1998), pp. 1–16; T. M. Stearns, N. M. Carter, P. D. Reynolds, and M. L. Williams,"New Firm Survival: Industry, Strategy, and Location," *Journal of Business Venturing* (January 1995), pp. 23–42.
9. M. E. Porter, *Competitive Strategy* (New York: The Free Press, 1980), p. 35.
10. R. E. Caves and P. Ghemawat, "Identifying Mobility Barriers," *Strategic Management Journal* (January 1992), pp. 1–12.
11. N. K. Geranios, "Potlach Aims to Squeeze Toilet Tissue Leaders," *Des Moines Register* (October 22, 2003), p. 3D.
12. "Hewlett-Packard: Losing the HP Way," *Economist* (August 21, 2004), pp. 49–50.
13. C. Campbell-Hunt,"What Have We Learned About Generic Competitive Strategy? A Meta Analysis," *Strategic Management Journal* (February 2000), pp. 127–154.
14. M. Kroll, P. Wright, and R. A. Heiens,"The Contribution of Product Quality to Competitive Advantage: Impacts on Systematic Variance and Unexplained Variance in Returns," *Strategic Management Journal* (April 1999), pp. 375–384.
15. R. M. Hodgetts,"A Conversation with Michael E. Porter: A 'Significant Extension' Toward Operational Improvement and Positioning," *Organizational Dynamics* (Summer 1999), pp. 24–33.
16. N. Brodsky, "Size Matters," *INC.* (September 1998), pp. 31–32.
17. M. Rushlo, "P.F. Chang's Plans Succeed Where Others Have Failed," *Des Moines Register* (May 18, 2004), pp. 1D, 6D.
18. P. F. Kocourek, S. Y. Chung, and M. G. McKenna,"Strategic Rollups: Overhauling the Multi-Merger Machine," *Strategy + Business* (2nd Quarter 2000), pp. 45–53.
19. J. A. Tannenbaum, "Acquisitive Companies Set Out to 'Roll Up' Fragmented Industries," *Wall Street Journal* (March 3, 1997), pp. A1, A6; VCA Antech, Inc., 10Q Statement, June 30, 2004.
20. R. A. D'Aveni, *Hypercompetition* (New York: The Free Press, 1994), pp. xiii–xiv.
21. P. C. Nutt, "Surprising but True: Half the Decisions in Organizations Fail," *Academy of Management Executive* (November 1999), pp. 75–90.
22. Some refer to this as the economic concept of "increasing returns." Instead of the curve leveling off when the company reaches a point of diminishing returns when a product saturates a market, the curve continues to go up as the company takes advantage of setting the standard to spin off new products that use the new standard to achieve higher performance than competitors. See J. Alley, "The Theory That Made Microsoft," *Fortune* (April 29, 1996), pp. 65–66.
23. H. Lee, K. G. Smith, C. M. Grimm, and A. Schomburg,"Timing, Order and Durability of New Product Advantages with Imitation," *Strategic Management Journal* (January 2000), pp. 23–30; Y. Pan and P. C. K. Chi,"Financial Performance and Survival of Multinational Corporations in China," *Strategic Management Journal* (April 1999), pp. 359–374; R. Makadok, "Can First-Mover and Early-Mover Advantages Be Sustained in an Industry with Low Barriers to Entry/Imitation?" *Strategic Management Journal* (July 1998), pp. 683–696; B. Mascarenhas,"The Order and Size of Entry into International Markets," *Journal of Business Venturing* (July 1997), pp. 287–299.
24. At these respective points, cost disadvantages vis-à-vis later entrants fully eroded the earlier returns to first movers. See W. Boulding and M. Christen, "Idea—First Mover Disadvantage," *Harvard Business Review*, Vol. 79, No. 9 (2001), pp. 20–21, as reported by D. J. Ketchen, Jr., C. C. Snow, and V. L. Hoover, "Research on Competitive Dynamics: Recent Accomplishments and Future Challenges," *Journal of Management*, Vol. 30, No. 6 (2004), pp. 779–804.
25. M. B. Lieberman and D. B. Montgomery, "First-Mover (Dis) Advantages: Retrospective and Link with the Resource-Based View," *Strategic Management Journal* (December, 1998), pp. 1111–1125; G. J. Tellis and P. N. Golder, "First to Market, First to Fail? Real Causes of Enduring Market Leadership," *Sloan Management Review* (Winter 1996), pp. 65–75.
26. J. Pope, "Schick Entry May Work Industry into a Lather," *Des Moines Register* (May 15, 2003), p. 6D.
27. For an in-depth discussion of first- and late-mover advantages and disadvantages, see D. S. Cho, D. J. Kim, and D. K. Rhee, "Latecomer Strategies: Evidence from the Semiconductor Industry in Japan and Korea," *Organization Science* (July–August 1998), pp. 489–505.
28. J. Shamsie, C. Phelps, and J. Kuperman, "Better Late Than Never: A Study of Late Entrants in Household Electrical Equipment," *Strategic Management Journal* (January 2004), pp. 69–84.
29. T. S. Schoenecker and A. C. Cooper, "The Role of Firm Resources and Organizational Attributes in Determining Entry

Timing: A Cross-Industry Study," *Strategic Management Journal* (December 1998), pp. 1127–1143.

30. Summarized from various articles by L. Fahey in *The Strategic Management Reader*, edited by L. Fahey (Upper Saddle River, NJ: Prentice Hall, 1989), pp. 178–205.

31. M. Boyle, "Dueling Diapers," *Fortune* (February 17, 2003), pp. 115–116.

32. P. Burrows, "Show Time," *Business Week* (February 2, 2004), pp. 56–64.

33. A. Serwer, "Happy Birthday, Steinway," *Fortune* (March 17, 2003), pp. 94–97.

34. This information on defensive tactics is summarized from M. E. Porter, *Competitive Advantage* (New York: The Free Press, 1985), pp. 482–512.

35. H. D. Hopkins, "The Response Strategies of Dominant U.S. Firms to Japanese Challengers," *Journal of Management*, Vol. 29, No. 1 (2003), pp. 5–25.

36. T. M. Burton, "Archer-Daniels Faces a Potential Blow As Three Firms Admit Price-Fixing Plot," *Wall Street Journal* (August 28, 1996), pp. A3, A6; R. Henkoff, "The ADM Tale Gets Even Stranger," *Fortune* (May 13, 1996), pp. 113–120.

37. B. Gordon, "Qwest Defends Pacts with Competitors," *Des Moines Register* (April 30, 2002), p. 1D.

38. Much of the content on cooperative strategies was summarized from J. B. Barney, *Gaining and Sustaining Competitive Advantage* (Reading, MA: Addison-Wesley, 1997), pp. 255–278.

39. E. A. Murray, Jr., and J. F. Mahon, "Strategic Alliances: Gateway to the New Europe?" *Long Range Planning* (August 1993), p. 103.

40. R. D. Ireland, M. A. Hitt, and D. Vaidyanath, "Alliance Management as a Source of Competitive Advantage," *Journal of Management*, Vol. 28, No. 3 (2002), pp. 413–446.

41. P. Anslinger and J. Jenk, "Creating Successful Alliances," *Journal of Business Strategy*, Vol. 25, No. 2 (2004), pp. 18–22.

42. S. H. Park and G. R. Ungson, "Interfirm Rivalry and Managerial Complexity: A Conceptual Framework of Alliance Failure," *Organization Science* (January–February 2001), pp. 37–53; D. C. Hambrick, J. Li, K. Xin, and A. S. Tsui, "Compositional Gaps and Downward Spirals in International Joint Venture Management Groups," *Strategic Management Journal* (November 2001), pp. 1033–1053; T. K. Das and B. S. Teng, "Instabilities of Strategic Alliances: An Internal Tensions Perspective," *Organization Science* (January–February 2000), pp. 77–101; J. F. Hennart, D. J. Kim, and M. Zeng, "The Impact of Joint Venture Status on the Longevity of Japanese Stakes in U.S. Manufacturing Affiliates," *Organization Science* (May–June 1998), pp. 382–395.

43. N. K. Park, J. M. Mezias, and J. Song, "A Resource-Based View of Strategic Alliances and Firm Value in the Electronic Marketplace," *Journal of Management*, Vol. 30, No. 1 (2004), pp. 7–27; T. Khanna and J. W. Rivkin, "Estimating the Performance Effects of Business Groups in Emerging Markets," *Strategic Management Journal* (January 2001), pp. 45–74; G. Garai, "Leveraging the Rewards of Strategic Alliances," *Journal of Business Strategy* (March–April 1999), pp. 40–43.

44. L. Segil, "Strategic Alliances for the 21st Century," *Strategy & Leadership* (September/October 1998), pp. 12–16.

45. J. Draulans, A. P. deMan, and H. W. Volberda, "Building Alliance Capability: Management Techniques for Superior Alliance Performance," *Long Range Planning* (April 2003), pp. 151–166; P. Kale, J. H. Dyer, and H. Singh, "Alliance Capability, Stock Market Response, and Long-Term Alliance Success: The Role of the Alliance Function," *Strategic Management Journal* (August 2002), pp. 747–767.

46. M. M. Bear, "How Japanese Partners Help U.S. Manufacturers to Raise Productivity," *Long Range Planning* (December 1998), pp. 919–926.

47. P. Anslinger and J. Jenk, "Creating Successful Alliances," *Journal of Business Strategy*, Vol. 25, No. 2 (2004), p. 18.

48. J. W. Lu and P. W. Beamish, "The Internationalization and Performance of SMEs," *Strategic Management Journal* (June–July 2001), pp. 565–586.

49. C. Sheehan, "Brewery Bottles a Cool Idea," *Des Moines Register* (August 26, 2004), p. 6D.

50. R. M. Kanter, "Collaborative Advantage: The Art of Alliances," *Harvard Business Review* (July–August 1994), pp. 96–108.

51. B. Bremner, Z. Schiller, T. Smart, and W. J. Holstein, "Keiretsu Connections," *Business Week* (July 22, 1996), pp. 52–54.

52. R. P. Lynch, *The Practical Guide to Joint Ventures and Corporate Alliances* (New York: John Wiley & Sons, 1989), p. 7.

53. H. Green, "Double Play," *Business Week E-Biz* (October 23, 2000), pp. EB-42–EB-46.

54. L. L. Blodgett, "Factors in the Instability of International Joint Ventures: An Event History Analysis," *Strategic Management Journal* (September 1992), pp. 475–481; J. Bleeke and D. Ernst, "The Way to Win in Cross-Border Alliances," *Harvard Business Review* (November–December 1991), pp. 127–135; J. M. Geringer, "Partner Selection Criteria for Developed Country Joint Ventures," in *International Management Behavior*, 2nd ed., edited by H. W. Lane and J. J. DiStephano (Boston: PWS-Kent, 1992), pp. 206–216.

55. B. Horovitz, "New Coffee Maker May Jolt Industry," *USA Today* (February 18, 2004), pp. 1E–2E.

56. K. Z. Andrews, "Manufacturer/Supplier Relationships: The Supplier Payoff," *Harvard Business Review* (September–October 1995), pp. 14–15.

57. P. Lorange, "Black-Box Protection of Your Core Competencies in Strategic Alliances," in *Cooperative Strategies: European Perspectives*, edited by P. W. Beamish and J. P. Killing (San Francisco: The New Lexington Press, 1997), pp. 59–99.

58. E. P. Gee, "Co-opetition: The New Market Milieu," *Journal of Healthcare Management*, Vol. 45 (2000), pp. 359–363.

59. D. J. Ketchen, Jr., C. C. Snow, and V. L. Hoover, "Research on Competitive Dynamics: Recent Accomplishments and Future Challenges," *Journal of Management*, Vol. 30, No. 6 (2004), pp. 779–804.

60. "Growth Competitiveness," *Economist* (October 16, 2004), p. 98.

61. *Economist Pocket World in Figures, 2004 Edition* (London: Profile Books, 2003) p. 60.

62. R. Beck, "Kmart + Sears = Success?" *The (Ames, IA) Tribune* (November 20, 2004), p. C8.

Chapter 7

1. C. Zook and J. Allen, "Growth Outside the Core," *Harvard Business Review* (December 2003), pp. 66–73.

2. Ibid., p. 67.

3. R. P. Rumelt, D. E. Schendel, and D. J. Teece, "Fundamental Issues in Strategy," in *Fundamental Issues in Strategy: A Research Agenda*, edited by R. P. Rumelt, D. E. Schendel, and D. J. Teece (Boston: HBS Press, 1994), p. 42.

4. This analogy of corporate parent and business unit children was initially proposed by A. Campbell, M. Goold, and M. Alexander. See "Corporate Strategy: The Quest for Parenting Advantage," *Harvard Business Review* (March–April, 1995), pp. 120–132.
5. M. E. Porter, "From Competitive Strategy to Corporate Strategy," *in International Review of Strategic Management*, Vol. 1, edited by D. E. Husey (Chicester, UK: John Wiley & Sons, 1990), p. 29.
6. This is in agreement with Toyohiro Kono, who proposes that corporate headquarters has three main functions: formulate corporate strategy, identify and develop the company's core competencies, and provide central resources. See T. Kono, "A Strong Head Office Makes a Strong Company," *Long Range Planning* (April 1999), pp. 225–236.
7. "Larry Ups the Ante," *Economist* (February 7, 2004), pp. 59–60.
8. "Cisco Buys Wireless Chip-Set Maker," *The (Ames, IA) Tribune* (November 11, 2000), p. B7.
9. J. Perkins, "It's a Hog Predicament," *Des Moines Register* (April 11, 1999), pp. J1–J2.
10. C. Woodyard, "FedEx Ponies Up $2.4B for Kinko's," *USA Today* (December 31, 2003), p. B1.
11. J. W. Slocum, Jr., M. McGill, and D. T. Lei, "The New Learning Strategy: Anytime, Anything, Anywhere," *Organizational Dynamics* (Autumn 1994), p. 36.
12. M. J. Leiblein, J. J. Reuer, and F. Dalsace, "Do Make or Buy Decisions Matter? The Influence of Organizational Governance on Technological Performance," *Strategic Management Journal* (September 2002), pp. 817–833.
13. K. R. Harrigan, *Strategies for Vertical Integration* (Lexington, MA: Lexington Books, 1983), pp. 16–21.
14. H. Norr, "Apple Opening 25 Stores to Showcase Products," *The (Ames, IA) Tribune* (May 4, 2001), p. B7.
15. L. Grant, "Partners in Profit," *U. S. News & World Report* (September 20, 1993), pp. 65–66.
16. For a discussion of the pros and cons of contracting versus vertical integration, see J. T. Mahoney, "The Choice of Organizational Form: Vertical Financial Ownership Versus Other Methods of Vertical Integration," *Strategic Management Journal* (November 1992), pp. 559–584.
17. D. Welch, D. Roberts, and G. Edmondson, "GM: Gunning It in China," *Business Week* (June 21, 2004), pp. 112–115.
18. C. Zook, "Increasing the Odds of Successful Growth: The Critical Prelude to Moving 'Beyond the Core.'" *Strategy & Leadership*, Vol. 32, No. 4 (2004), pp. 17–23.
19. A. Y. Ilinich and C. P. Zeithaml, "Operationalizing and Testing Galbraith's Center of Gravity Theory," *Strategic Management Journal* (June 1995), pp. 401–410.
20. "Flying into Battle," *Economist* (May 8, 2004), p. 60.
21. R. F. Bruner, "Corporation Diversification May Be Okay After All," *Batten Briefings* (Spring 2003), pp. 2–3, 12.
22. A. Delios and P. W. Beamish, "Geographic Scope, Product Diversification, and the Corporate Performance of Japanese Firms," *Strategic Management Journal* (August 1999), pp. 711–727.
23. E. Elango and V. H. Fried, "Franchising Research: A Literature Review and Synthesis," *Journal of Small Business Management* (July 1997), pp. 68–81.
24. T. Thilgen, "Corporate Clout Replaces 'Small Is Beautiful,' " *Wall Street Journal* (March 27, 1997), p. B14.
25. J. E. McCann III, "The Growth of Acquisitions in Services," *Long Range Planning* (December 1996), pp. 835–841.
26. P. Gogoi and G. Smith, "The Way to Run a Railroad," *Business Week* (October 23, 2000), pp. 106–110.
27. J. Ewing and J. Weber, "Brewers: The Beer Wars Come to a Head," *Business Week* (May 24, 2004), p. 68.
28. B. Voss, "Strategic Federations Frequently Falter in Far East," *Journal of Business Strategy* (July/August 1993), p. 6; S. Douma, "Success and Failure in New Ventures," *Long Range Planning* (April 1991), pp. 54–60.
29. A. Delios and P. W. Beamish, "Ownership Strategy of Japanese Firms: Transactional, Institutional, and Experience Approaches," *Strategic Management Journal* (October 1999), pp. 915–933.
30. A. Seth, K. P. Song, and R. R. Pettit, "Value Creation and Destruction in Cross-Border Acquisitions: An Empirical Analysis of Foreign Acquisitions of U.S. Firms," *Strategic Management Journal* (October 2002), pp. 921–940.
31. K. D. Brouthers and L. E. Brouthers, "Acquisition or Greenfield Start-up? Institutional, Cultural, and Transaction Cost Influences," *Strategic Management Journal* (January 2000), pp. 89–97.
32. J. Naisbitt, *Megatrends Asia* (New York: Simon & Schuster, 1996), p. 143.
33. K. Carow, R. Heron, and T. Saxton, "Do Early Birds Get the Returns? An Empirical Investigation of Early-Mover Advantages in Acquisitions," *Strategic Management Journal* (June 2004), pp. 563–585; K. Ramaswamy, "The Performance Impact of Strategic Similarity in Horizontal Mergers: Evidence from the U.S. Banking Industry," *Academy of Management Journal* (July 1997), pp. 697–715; D. J. Flanagan, "Announcements of Purely Related and Purely Unrelated Mergers and Shareholder Returns: Reconciling the Relatedness Paradox," *Journal of Management*, Vol. 22, No. 6 (1996), pp. 823–835; D. D. Bergh, "Predicting Diversification of Unrelated Acquisitions: An Integrated Model of Ex Ante Conditions," *Strategic Management Journal* (October 1997), pp. 715–731.
34. J. M. Pennings, H. Barkema, and S. Douma, "Organizational Learning and Diversification," *Academy of Management Journal* (June 1994), pp. 608–640.
35. L. E. Palich, L. B. Cardinal, and C. C. Miller, "Curvilinearity in the Diversification-Performance Linkage: An Examination of over Three Decades of Research," *Strategic Management Journal* (February 2000), pp. 155–174.
36. "The Great Merger Wave Breaks," *The Economist* (January 27, 2001), pp. 59–60.
37. D. R. King, D. R. Dalton, C. M. Daily, and J. G. Covin, "Meta-Analyses of Post-Acquisition Performance: Indications of Unidentified Moderators," *Strategic Management Journal* (February 2004), pp. 187–200; W. B. Carper, "Corporate Acquisitions and Shareholder Wealth: A Review and Exploratory Analysis" *Journal of Management* (December 1990), pp. 807–823; P. G. Simmonds, "Using Diversification as a Tool for Effective Performance," *Handbook of Business Strategy, 1992/93 Yearbook*, edited by H. E. Glass and M. A. Hovde (Boston: Warren, Gorham & Lamont, 1992), pp. 3.1–3.7; B. T. Lamont and C. A. Anderson, "Mode of Corporate Diversification and Economic Performance," *Academy of Management Journal* (December 1985), pp. 926–936.
38. "The HP–Compaq Merger Two Years Out: Still Waiting for the Upside," *Knowledge@Wharton* (October 6–19, 2004).
39. D. J. Miller, "Firms' Technological Resources and the Performance Effects of Diversification: A Longitudinal Study," *Strategic Management Journal* (November 2004), pp. 1097–1119.

40. R. Langford and C. Brown III, "Making M&A Pay: Lessons from the World's Most Successful Acquirers," *Strategy & Leadership*, Vol. 32, No. 1 (2004), pp. 5–14; J. G. Lynch and B. Lind, "Escaping Merger and Acquisition Madness," *Strategy & Leadership*, Vol. 30, No. 2 (2002), pp. 5–12; M. L. Sirower, *The Synergy Trap* (New York: The Free Press, 1997); B. Jensen, "Make It Simple! How Simplicity Could Become Your Ultimate Strategy," *Strategy & Leadership* (March/April 1997), p. 35.
41. E. Thornton, "Why Consumers Hate Mergers," *Business Week* (December 6, 2004), pp. 58–64.
42. J. M. Pennings, H. Barkema, and S. Douma, "Organizational Learning and Diversification," *Academy of Management Journal* (June 1994), pp. 608–640.
43. L. Selden and G. Colvin, "M&A Needn't Be a Loser's Game," *Harvard Business Review* (June 2003), pp. 70–79; E. C. Busija, H. M. O'Neill, and C. P. Zeithaml, "Diversification Strategy, Entry Mode, and Performance: Evidence of Choice and Constraints," *Strategic Management Journal* (April 1997), pp. 321–327; A. Sharma, "Mode of Entry and Ex-Post Performance," *Strategic Management Journal* (September 1998), pp. 879–900.
44. S. Rovitt, D. Harding, and C. Lemire, "A Simple M&A Model for All Seasons," *Strategy & Leadership*, Vol. 32, No. 5 (2004), pp. 18–24.
45. P. Porrini, "Can a Previous Alliance Between an Acquirer and a Target Affect Acquisition Performance?" *Journal of Management*, Vol. 30, No. 4 (2004), pp. 545–562.
46. F. Vermeulen, "Controlling International Expansion," *Business Strategy Review* (September 2001), pp. 29–36.
47. A. Inkpen and N. Choudhury, "The Seeking of Strategy Where It Is Not: Towards a Theory of Strategy Absence," *Strategic Management Journal* (May 1995), pp. 313–323.
48. P. Burrows and S. Anderson, "Dell Computer Goes into the Shop," *Business Week* (July 12, 1993), pp. 138–140.
49. J. L. Morrow, Jr., R. A. Johnson, and L. W. Busenitz, "The Effects of Cost and Asset Retrenchment on Firm Performance: The Overlooked Role of a Firm's Competitive Environment," *Journal of Management*, Vol. 30, No. 2 (2004), pp. 189–208.
50. J. A. Pearce II and D. K. Robbins, "Retrenchment Remains the Foundation of Business Turnaround," *Strategic Management Journal* (June 1994), pp. 407–417.
51. C. Chadwick, L. W. Hunter, and S. L. Walston, "Effects of Downsizing Practices on the Performance of Hospitals," *Strategic Management Journal* (May 2004), pp. 405–427; J. R. Morris, W. F. Cascio, and C. E. Young, "Downsizing After All These Years," *Organizational Dynamics* (Winter 1999), pp. 78–87; P. H. Mirvis, "Human Resource Management: Leaders, Laggards, and Followers," *Academy of Management Executive* (May 1997), pp. 43–56; J. K. DeDee and D. W. Vorhies, "Retrenchment Activities of Small Firms During Economic Downturn: An Empirical Investigation," *Journal of Small Business Management* (July 1998), pp. 46–61.
52. C. Chadwick, L. W. Hunter, and S. L. Walston, "Effects of Downsizing Practices on the Performance of Hospitals," *Strategic Management Journal* (May 2004), pp. 405–427.
53. J. B. Treece, "U.S. Parts Makers Just Won't Say 'Uncle,' " *Business Week* (August 10, 1987), pp. 76–77.
54. "Quaker Oats Gives Up on Snapple, Sells It at a $1.4 Billion Loss," *Des Moines Register* (March 28, 1997), p. 8S.
55. B. Grow, "Can Wonder Bread Rise Again?" *Business Week* (October 18, 2004), pp. 108–110.
56. D. D. Dawley, J. J. Hoffman, and B. T. Lamont, "Choice Situation, Refocusing, and Post-Bankruptcy Performance," *Journal of Management*, Vol. 28, No. 5 (2002), pp. 695–717.
57. R. M. Kanter, "Leadership and the Psychology of Turnarounds," *Harvard Business Review* (June 2003), pp. 58–67.
58. B. C. Reimann and A. Reichert, "Portfolio Planning Methods for Strategic Capital Allocation: A Survey of Fortune 500 Firms," *International Journal of Management* (March 1996), pp. 84–93; D. K. Sinha, "Strategic Planning in the Fortune 500," *Handbook of Business Strategy, 1991/92 Yearbook*, edited by H. E. Glass and M. A. Hovde (Boston: Warren, Gorham & Lamont, 1991), p. 9.6.
59. L. Dranikoff, T. Koller, and A. Schneider, "Divestiture: Strategy's Missing Link," *Harvard Business Review* (May 2002), pp. 74–83.
60. B. Hedley, "Strategy and the Business Portfolio," *Long Range Planning* (February 1977), p. 9.
61. B. Elgin, "Can HP's Printer Biz Keep Printing Money?" *Business Week* (July 14, 2003), pp. 68–70.
62. A. Fitzgerald, "Going Global," *Des Moines Register* (March 14, 2004), pp. 1M, 3M.
63. C. Anterasian, J. L. Graham, and R. B. Money, "Are U.S. Managers Superstitious About Market Share?" *Sloan Management Review* (Summer 1996), pp. 67–77.
64. D. Rosenblum, D. Tomlinson, and L. Scott, "Bottom-Feeding for Blockbuster Businesses," *Harvard Business Review* (March 2003), pp. 52–59.
65. R. G. Hamermesh, *Making Strategy Work* (New York: John Wiley & Sons, 1986), p. 14.
66. J. J. Curran, "Companies That Rob the Future," *Fortune* (July 4, 1988), p. 84.
67. A. Campbell, M. Goold, and M. Alexander, *Corporate-Level Strategy: Creating Value in the Multibusiness Company* (New York: John Wiley & Sons, 1994). See also M. Goold, A. Campbell, and M. Alexander, "Corporate Strategy and Parenting Theory," *Long Range Planning* (April 1998), pp. 308–318, and M. Goold and A. Campbell, "Parenting in Complex Structures," *Long Range Planning* (June 2002), pp. 219–243.
68. A. Campbell, M. Goold, and M. Alexander, "Corporate Strategy: The Quest for Parenting Advantage," *Harvard Business Review* (March–April 1995), p. 121.
69. Ibid., p. 122.
70. A. van Oijen and S. Douma, "Diversification Strategy and the Roles of the Centre," *Long Range Planning* (August 2000), pp. 560–578.
71. "Jack's Gamble," *The Economist* (October 28, 2000), pp. 13–14.
72. D. J. Collis, "Corporate Strategy in Multibusiness Firms," *Long Range Planning* (June 1996), pp. 416–418; D. Lei, M. A. Hitt, and R. Bettis, "Dynamic Core Competencies Through Meta-Learning and Strategic Context," *Journal of Management*, Vol. 22, No. 4 (1996), pp. 549–569.
73. D. J. Teece, "Strategies for Managing Knowledge Assets: The Role of Firm Structure and Industrial Context," *Long Range Planning* (February 2000), pp. 35–54.
74. R. S. Kaplan and D. P. Norton, "The Strategy Map: Guide to Aligning Intangible Assets," *Strategy & Leadership*, Vol. 32, No. 5 (2004), pp. 10–17; L. Edvinsson, "The New Knowledge Economics," *Business Strategy Review* (September 2002), pp. 72–76; C. Havens and E. Knapp, "Easing into Knowledge Management," *Strategy & Leadership* (March/April 1999), pp. 4–9.

75. T. S. Frost, J. M. Birkinshaw, and P. C. Ensign, "Centers of Excellence in Multinational Corporations," *Strategic Management Journal* (November 2002), pp. 997–1018.
76. M. E. Porter, *Competitive Advantage* (New York: The Free Press, 1985), pp. 317–382.
77. J. Gimeno, "Reciprocal Threats in Multimarket Rivalry: Staking Out 'Spheres of Influence' in the U.S. Airline Industry," *Strategic Management Journal* (February 1999), pp. 101–128; J. Baum and H. J. Korn, "Dynamics of Dyadic Competitive Interaction," *Strategic Management Journal* (March 1999), pp. 251–278; J. Gimeno and C. Y. Woo, "Hypercompetition in a Multimarket Environment: The Role of Strategic Similarity and Multimarket Contact in Competitive De-escalation," *Organization Science* (May/June 1996), pp. 322–341.
78. W. Boeker, J. Goodstein, J. Stephan, and J. P. Murmann, "Competition in a Multimarket Environment: The Case of Market Exit," *Organization Science* (March/April 1997), pp. 126–142.
79. J. Gimeno and C. Y. Woo, "Multimarket Contact, Economies of Scope, and Firm Performance," *Academy of Management Journal* (June 1999), pp. 239–259.
80. D. Little, "Emerson Electric Jump-Starts Itself," *Business Week* (July 24, 2000), pp. 78–80.
81. From *Corruption Perceptions Index 2004*, as reported in "Countries Rated for Corruption," *Des Moines Register* (October 21, 2004), p. 2D.
82. Ibid.
83. "Learning to E-Read," *The Economist Survey E-Entertainment* (October 7, 2000), p. 22.

Chapter 8

1. Arm & Hammer is a registered trademark of Church & Dwight Company, Inc.
2. S. F. Slater and E. M. Olson, "Marketing's Contribution to the Implementation of Business Strategy: An Empirical Analysis," *Strategic Management Journal* (November 2001), pp. 1055–1067; B. C. Skaggs and T. R. Huffman, "A Customer Interaction Approach to Strategy and Production Complexity Alignment in Service Firms," *Academy of Management Journal* (December 2003), pp. 775–786.
3. S. M. Oster, *Modern Competitive Analysis*, 2nd ed. (New York: Oxford University Press, 1994), p. 93.
4. M. Springer, "Plowed Under," *Forbes* (February 21, 2000), p. 56.
5. W. Redmond, "The Strategic Pricing of Innovative Products," *Handbook of Business Strategy, 1992/1993 Yearbook*, edited by H. E. Glass and M. A. Hovde (Boston: Warren, Gorham & Lamont, 1992), pp. 16.1–16.13.
6. A. Kambil, H. J. Wilson III, and V. Agrawal, "Are You Leaving Money on the Table?" *Journal of Business Strategy* (January/February 2002), pp. 40–43.
7. A. Safieddine and S. Titman in April 1999 *Journal of Finance,* as summarized by D. Champion, "The Joy of Leverage," *Harvard Business Review* (July–August 1999), pp. 19–22.
8. R. Kochhar and M. A. Hitt, "Linking Corporate Strategy to Capital Structure: Diversification Strategy, Type and Source of Financing," *Strategic Management Journal* (June 1998), pp. 601–610.
9. A. Rappaport and M. L. Sirower, "Stock or Cash?" *Harvard Business Review* (November–December 1999), pp. 147–158.
10. D. Angwin and I. Contardo, "Unleashing Cerberus: Don't Let Your MBOs Turn on Themselves," *Long Range Planning* (October 1999), pp. 494–504.
11. For information on different types of LBOs, see M. Wright, R. E. Hoskisson, and L. W. Busenitz, "Firm Rebirth: Buyouts as Facilitators of Strategic Growth and Entrepreneurship," *Academy of Management Executive* (February 2001), pp. 111–125.
12. B. Deener, "Back Up and Look at Reasons for Reverse Stock Split," *The (St. Petersburg, FL) Times* (December 29, 2002), p. 3H.
13. S. Scherreik, "Tread Carefully When You Buy Tracking Stocks," *Business Week* (March 6, 2000), pp. 182–184.
14. T. Due, "Dean Foods Thrives on Regional Off-Brand Products," *Wall Street Journal* (September 17, 1987), p. A6.
15. S. Stevens, "Speeding the Signals of Change," *Appliance* (February 1995), p. 7.
16. H. W. Chesbrough, "A Better Way to Innovate," *Harvard Business Review* (July 2003), pp. 12–13.
17. J. Greene, J. Carey, M. Arndt, and O. Port, "Reinventing Corporate R&D," *Business Week* (September 22, 2003), pp. 74–76.
18. G. Dushnitsky and M. J. Lenox, "When Do Firms Undertake R&D by Investing in New Ventures?" Paper presented to annual meeting of the *Academy of Management*, Seattle, WA (August 2003).
19. A. Aston and M. Arndt, "The Flexible Factory," *Business Week* (May 5, 2003), pp. 90–91.
20. J. R. Williams and R. S. Novak, "Aligning CIM Strategies to Different Markets," *Long Range Planning* (February 1990), pp. 126–135.
21. J. Wheatley, "Super Factory—or Super Headache," *Business Week* (July 31, 2000), p. 66.
22. M. Tayles and C. Drury, "Moving from Make/Buy to Strategic Sourcing: The Outsource Decision Process," *Long Range Planning* (October 2001), pp. 605–622.
23. F. R. Bleakley, "Some Companies Let Supplier Work on Site and Even Place Orders," *Wall Street Journal* (January 13, 1995), pp. A1, A6.
24. J. Richardson, "Parallel Sourcing and Supplier Performance in the Japanese Automobile Industry," *Strategic Management Journal* (July 1993), pp. 339–350.
25. S. Roberts-Witt, "Procurement: The HP Way," *PC Magazine* (November 21, 2000), pp. 21–22.
26. J. Bigness, "In Today's Economy, There Is Big Money to Be Made in Logistics," *Wall Street Journal* (September 6, 1995), pp. A1, A9.
27. F. Keenan, "Logistics Gets a Little Respect," *Business Week* (November 20, 2000), pp. 112–116.
28. B. L. Kirkman and Debra L. Shapiro, "The Impact of Cultural Values on Employee Resistance to Teams: Toward a Model of Globalized Self-Managing Work Team Effectiveness," *Academy of Management Review* (July 1997), pp. 730–757.
29. R. D. Banker, J. M. Field, R. G. Schroeder, and K. K. Sinha, "Impact of Work Teams on Manufacturing Performance: A Longitudinal Field Study," *Academy of Management Journal* (August 1996), pp. 867–890; B. L. Kirkman and B. Rosen, "Beyond Self-Management: Antecedents and Consequences of Team Empowerment," *Academy of Management Journal* (February 1999), pp. 58–74.
30. V. Y. Haines III, S. St. Onge, and A. Marcoux, "Performance Management Design and Effectiveness in Quality-Driven Organizations," *Canadian Journal of Administrative Sciences* (June 2004), pp. 146–160.

31. A. S. DeNisi and A. N. Kluger, "Feedback Effectiveness: Can 360-Degree Appraisals Be Improved?" *Academy of Management Executive* (February 2000), pp. 129–139; G. Toegel and J. A. Conger, "360-Degree Assessment: Time for Reinvention," *Academy of Management Learning and Education* (September 2003), pp. 297–311.
32. O. C. Richard, "Racial Diversity, Business Strategy, and Firm Performance: A Resource-Based View," *Academy of Management Journal* (April 2000), pp. 164–177.
33. G. Robinson and K. Dechant, "Building a Business Case for Diversity," *Academy of Management Executive* (August 1997), pp. 21–31.
34. K. Labich, "Making Diversity Pay," *Fortune* (September 9, 1996), pp. 177–180.
35. N. G. Carr, "IT Doesn't Matter," *Harvard Business Review* (May 2003), pp. 41–50.
36. J. Greco, "Good Day Sunshine," *Journal of Business Strategy* (July/August 1998), pp. 4–5.
37. W. Howard, "Translate Now," *PC Magazine* (September 19, 2000), p. 81.
38. H. Green, "The Web Smart 50," *Business Week* (November 24, 2003), p. 84.
39. T. Smart, "Jack Welch's Cyber-Czar," *Business Week* (August 5, 1996), p. 83.
40. B. Kelley, "Outsourcing Marches On," *Journal of Business Strategy* (July/August 1995), p. 40.
41. S. Holmes and M. Arndt, "A Plane That Could Change the Game," *Business Week* (August 9, 2004), p. 33.
42. J. Greco, "Outsourcing: The New Partnership," *Journal of Business Strategy* (July/August 1997), pp. 48–54.
43. "Out of Captivity," *Economist* (November 13, 2004), p. 68.
44. "IBM's Plan to Buy India Firm Points to Demand for Outsourcing," *Des Moines Register* (April 11, 2004), p. 2D.
45. A. Castro, "Complaints Push Dell to Use U.S. Call Centers," *Des Moines Register* (November 25, 2003), p. 1D.
46. J. A. Byrne, "Has Outsourcing Gone Too Far?" *Business Week* (April 1, 1996), pp. 26–28.
47. R. C. Insinga and M. J. Werle, "Linking Outsourcing to Business Strategy," *Academy of Management Executive* (November 2000), pp. 58–70; D. Lei and M. A. Hitt, "Strategic Restructuring and Outsourcing: The Effect of Mergers and Acquisitions and LBOs on Building Firm Skills and Capabilities," *Journal of Management*, Vol. 21, No. 5 (1995), pp. 835–859.
48. S. E. Ante, "Shifting Work Offshore? Outsourcer Beware," *Business Week* (January 12, 2004), pp. 36–37.
49. J. Barthelemy, "The Seven Deadly Sins of Outsourcing," *Academy of Management Executive* (May 2003), pp. 87–98.
50. A. Takeishi, "Bridging Inter- and Intra-Firm Boundaries: Management of Supplier Involvement in Automobile Product Development," *Strategic Management Journal* (May 2001), pp. 403–433.
51. J. B. Quinn, "The Intelligent Enterprise: A New Paradigm," *Academy of Management Executive* (November 1992), pp. 48–63.
52. M. J. Leiblein and D. J. Miller, "An Empirical Examination of Transaction and Firm-Level Influences on the Vertical Boundaries of the Firm," *Strategic Management Journal* (September 2003), pp. 839–859.
53. S. Hamm, "Is Outsourcing on the Outs?" *Business Week* (October 4, 2004), p. 42.
54. R. Grover and D. Polek, "Millionaire Buys Disney Time," *Business Week* (June 26, 2000), pp. 141–144.
55. D. K. Sinha, "Strategic Planning in the Fortune 500," *Handbook of Business Strategy, 1991/1992 Yearbook*, edited by H. E. Glass and M. A. Hovde (Boston: Warren, Gorham and Lamont, 1991), pp. 9.6–9.8.
56. N. Checa, J. Maguire, and J. Berry, "The New World Disorder," *Harvard Business Review* (August 2003), pp. 70–79.
57. T. B. Palmer and R. M. Wiseman, "Decoupling Risk Taking from Income Stream Uncertainty: A Holistic Model of Risk," *Strategic Management Journal* (November 1999), pp. 1037–1062.
58. D. Clark, "All the Chips: A Big Bet Made Intel What It Is Today; Now It Wagers Again," *Wall Street Journal* (June 6, 1995), pp. A1, A5.
59. L. W. Busenitz and J. B. Barney, "Differences Between Entrepreneurs and Managers in Large Organizations: Biases and Heuristics in Strategic Decision-Making," *Journal of Business Venturing* (January 1997), pp. 9–30.
60. T. Copeland and P. Tufano, "A Real-World Way to Manage Real Options," *Harvard Business Review* (March 2004), pp. 90–99.
61. J. Rosenberger and K. Eisenhardt, "What Are Real Options: A Review of Empirical Research," Paper presented to annual meeting of the *Academy of Management*, Seattle, WA (August 2003).
62. P. Coy, "Exploiting Uncertainty," *Business Week* (June 7, 1999), pp. 118–124. For further information on real options, see M. Amram and N. Kulatilaka, *Real Options* (Boston: Harvard University Press, 1999). For a simpler summary, see R. M. Grant, *Contemporary Strategy Analysis*, 5th edition (Malden, MA: Blackwell Publishing, 2005), pp. 48–50.
63. C. Anderson, "Values-Based Management," *Academy of Management Executive* (November 1997), pp. 25–46.
64. H. M. O'Neill, R. W. Pouder, and A. K. Buchholtz, "Patterns in the Diffusion of Strategies Across Organizations: Insights from the Innovation Diffusion Literature," *Academy of Management Executive* (January 1998), pp. 98–114.
65. B. B. Tyler and H. K. Steensma, "Evaluating Technological Collaborative Opportunities: A Cognitive Modeling Perspective," *Strategic Management Journal* (Summer 1995), pp. 43–70; D. Duchan, D. P. Ashman, and M. Nathan, "Mavericks, Visionaries, Protestors, and Sages: Toward a Typology of Cognitive Structures for Decision Making in Organizations," *Journal of Business Strategies* (Fall 1997), pp. 106–125; P. Chattopadhyay, W. H. Glick, C. C. Miller, and G. P. Huber, "Determinants of Executive Beliefs: Comparing Functional Conditioning and Social Influence," *Strategic Management Journal* (August 1999), pp. 763–789; B. Katey and G. G. Meredith, "Relationship Among Owner/Manager Personal Values, Business Strategies, and Enterprise Performance," *Journal of Small Business Management* (April 1997), pp. 37–64.
66. C. S. Galbraith and G. B. Merrill, "The Politics of Forecasting: Managing the Truth," *California Management Review* (Winter 1996), pp. 29–43.
67. M. A. Geletkanycz and D. C. Hambrick, "The External Ties of Top Executives: Implications for Strategic Choice and Performance," *Administrative Science Quarterly* (December 1997), pp. 654–681.

68. M. Song, R. J. Calantone, and C. A. Di Benedetto, "Competitive Forces and Strategic Choice Decisions: An Experimental Investigation in the United States and Japan," *Strategic Management Journal* (October 2002), pp. 969–978.

69. M. A. Hitt, M. T. Dacin, B. B. Tyler, and D. Park, "Understanding the Differences in Korean and U.S. Executives' Strategic Orientation," *Strategic Management Journal* (February 1997), pp. 159–167; L. G. Thomas III and G. Waring, "Competing Capitalisms: Capital Investment in American, German, and Japanese Firms," *Strategic Management Journal* (August 1999), pp. 729–748.

70. J. A. Wagner III and R. Z. Gooding, "Equivocal Information and Attribution: An Investigation of Patterns of Managerial Sensemaking," *Strategic Management Journal* (April 1997), pp. 275–286.

71. J. Ross and B. M. Staw, "Organizational Escalation and Exit: Lessons from the Shoreham Nuclear Power Plant," *Academy of Management Journal* (August 1993), pp. 701–732; P. W. Mulvey, J. F. Veiga, and P. M. Elsass, "When Teammates Raise a White Flag," *Academy of Management Executive* (February 1996), pp. 40–49.

72. R. A. Cosier, and C. R. Schwenk, "Agreement and Thinking Alike: Ingredients for Poor Decisions," *Academy of Management Executive* (February 1990), p. 69.

73. G. P. West III and G. D. Meyer, "To Agree or Not to Agree? Consensus and Performance in New Ventures," *Journal of Business Venturing* (September 1998), pp. 395–422; L. Markoczy, "Consensus Formation During Strategic Change," *Strategic Management Journal* (November 2001), pp. 1013–1031.

74. A. C. Amason, "Distinguishing the Effects of Functional and Dysfunctional Conflict on Strategic Decision Making: Resolving a Paradox for Top Management Teams," *Academy of Management Journal* (February 1996), pp. 123–148; A. C. Amason and H. J. Sapienza, "The Effects of Top Management Team Size and Interaction Norms on Cognitive and Affective Conflict," *Journal of Management*, Vol. 23, No. 4 (1997), pp. 495–516.

75. D. M. Schweiger, W. R. Sandberg, and P. L. Rechner, "Experiential Effects of Dialectical Inquiry, Devil's Advocacy, and Consensus Approaches to Strategic Decision Making," *Academy of Management Journal* (December 1989), pp. 745–772; G. Whyte, "Decision Failures: Why They Occur and How to Prevent Them," *Academy of Management Executive* (August 1991), pp. 23–31; R. L. Priem, D. A. Harrison, and N. K. Muir, "Structured Conflict and Consensus Outcomes in Group Decision Making," *Journal of Management*, Vol. 21, No. 4 (1995), pp. 691–710.

76. S. C. Abraham, "Using Bundles to Find the Best Strategy," *Strategy & Leadership* (July/August/September 1999), pp. 53–55.

77. O. Gadiesh and J. L Gilbert, "Transforming Corner-Office Strategy into Frontline Action," *Harvard Business Review* (May 2001), pp. 73–79.

78. A. M. Hayashi, "When to Trust Your Gut," *Harvard Business Review* (February 2001), pp. 59–65.

79. Ibid., pp. 59–60.

80. D. Kirkpatrick, "The Net Makes It All Easier—Including Exporting U.S. Jobs," *Fortune* (May 26, 2003), p. 146.

81. C. Matlack, M. Kripalani, D. Fairlamb, S. Reed, G. Edmundson, and A. Reinhardt, "Job Exports: Europe's Turn," *Business Week* (April 19, 2004), pp. 50–51.

82. T. A. Badger, "Levi's Factories Fade Away," *Des Moines Register* (January 9, 2004), pp. 1D–2D; L. Lee, "Jean Therapy, $23 a Pop," *Business Week* (June 28, 2004), pp. 91–93.

Chapter 9

1. A. Barrett, "Staying on Top," *Business Week* (May 5, 2003), pp. 60–68.

2. J. W. Gadella, "Avoiding Expensive Mistakes in Capital Investment," *Long Range Planning* (April 1994), pp. 103–110; B. Voss, "World Market Is Not for Everyone," *Journal of Business Strategy* (July/August 1993), p. 4.

3. A. Bert, T. MacDonald, and T. Herd, "Two Merger Integration Imperatives: Urgency and Execution," *Strategy & Leadership*, Vol. 31, No. 3 (2003), pp. 42–49.

4. L. D. Alexander, "Strategy Implementation: Nature of the Problem," *International Review of Strategic Management*, Vol. 2, No. 1, edited by D. E. Hussey (New York: John Wiley & Sons, 1991), pp. 73–113.

5. F. Arner and A. Aston, "How Xerox Got Up to Speed," *Business Week* (May 3, 2004), pp. 103–104.

6. E. Brynjolfsson, A. A. Renshaw, and M. Van Alstyne, "The Matrix of Change," *Sloan Management Review* (Winter 1997), pp. 37–54.

7. M. S. Feldman and B. T. Pentland, "Reconceptualizing Organizational Routines as a Source of Flexibility and Change," *Administrative Science Quarterly* (March 2003), pp. 94–118.

8. S. F. Slater and E. M. Olson, "Strategy Type and Performance: The Influence of Sales Force Management," *Strategic Management Journal* (August 2000), pp. 813–829.

9. B. Grow, "Thinking Outside the Box," *Business Week* (October 25, 2004), pp. 70–72.

10. M. Goold and A. Campbell, "Desperately Seeking Synergy," *Harvard Business Review* (September–October 1998), pp. 131–143.

11. A. D. Chandler, *Strategy and Structure* (Cambridge, MA: MIT Press, 1962).

12. A. P. Sloan, Jr., *My Years with General Motors* (Garden City, NY: Doubleday, 1964).

13. T. L. Amburgey and T. Dacin, "As the Left Foot Follows the Right? The Dynamics of Strategic and Structural Change," *Academy of Management Journal* (December 1994), pp. 1427–1452; M. Ollinger, "The Limits of Growth of the Multidivisional Firm: A Case Study of the U.S. Oil Industry from 1930–90," *Strategic Management Journal* (September 1994), pp. 503–520.

14. D. F. Jennings and S. L. Seaman, "High and Low Levels of Organizational Adaptation: An Empirical Analysis of Strategy, Structure, and Performance," *Strategic Management Journal* (July 1994), pp. 459–475; L. Donaldson, "The Normal Science of Structured Contingency Theory," in *Handbook of Organization Studies*, edited by S. R. Clegg, C. Hardy, and W. R. Nord (London: Sage Publications, 1996), pp. 57–76.

15. A. K. Gupta, "SBU Strategies, Corporate–SBU Relations, and SBU Effectiveness in Strategy Implementation," *Academy of Management Journal* (September 1987), pp. 477–500.

16. L. E. Greiner, "Evolution and Revolution As Organizations Grow," *Harvard Business Review* (May–June 1998), pp. 55–67. This is an updated version of Greiner's classic 1972 article.

17. Ibid., p. 64. Although Greiner simply labeled this as the *"?" crisis*, the term *pressure-cooker* seems apt.

18. J. Hamm, "Why Entrepreneurs Don't Scale," *Harvard Business Review* (December 2002), pp. 110–115.

19. W. P. Barnett, "The Dynamics of Competitive Intensity," *Administrative Science Quarterly* (March 1997), pp. 128–160; D. Miller, *The Icarus Paradox: How Exceptional Companies Bring About Their Own Downfall* (New York: Harper Business, 1990).

20. D. Miller and P. H. Friesen, "A Longitudinal Study of the Corporate Life Cycle," *Management Science* (October 1984), pp. 1161–1183.

21. J. Green, "The Toy-Train Company That Thinks It Can," *Business Week* (December 4, 2000), pp. 64–69.

22. G. David, F. Garcia, and I. Gashurov, "Welcome to the Valley of the Damned.Com," *Fortune* (January 22, 2001), p. 52.

23. R. Berner, "Turning Kmart into a Cash Cow," *Business Week* (July 12, 2004), p. 81.

24. H. Tavakolian, "Bankruptcy: An Emerging Corporate Strategy," *SAM Advanced Management Journal* (Spring 1995), p. 19.

25. L. G. Hrebiniak and W. F. Joyce, *Implementing Strategy* (New York: Macmillan, 1984), pp. 85–86.

26. S. M. Davis and P. R. Lawrence, *Matrix* (Reading, MA: Addison-Wesley, 1977), pp. 11–24.

27. J. G. March, "The Future Disposable Organizations and the Rigidities of Imagination," *Organization* (August/November 1995), p. 434.

28. M. A. Schilling and H. K. Steensma, "The Use of Modular Organizational Forms: An Industry-Level Analysis," *Academy of Management Journal* (December 2001), pp. 1149–1168.

29. M. P. Koza and A. Y. Lewin, "Coevolution of Network Alliances: A Longitudinal Analysis of an International Professional Service Network," *Organization Science* (September/October, 1999), pp. 638–653.

30. For more information on managing a network organization, see G. Lorenzoni and C. Baden-Fuller, "Creating a Strategic Center to Manage a Web of Partners," *California Management Review* (Spring 1995), pp. 146–163.

31. R. E. Miles, C. C. Snow, J. A. Mathews, G. Miles, and H. J. Coleman, Jr., "Organizing in the Knowledge Age: Anticipating the Cellular Form," *Academy of Management Executive* (November 1997), pp. 7–24.

32. J. Naylor and M. Lewis, "Internal Alliances: Using Joint Ventures in a Diversified Company," *Long Range Planning* (October 1997), pp. 678–688.

33. Summarized from M. Hammer, "Reengineering Work: Don't Automate, Obliterate," *Harvard Business Review* (July–August 1990), pp. 104–112.

34. D. Paper, "BPR: Creating the Conditions for Success," *Long Range Planning* (June 1998), pp. 426–435.

35. S. Drew, "BPR in Financial Services: Factors for Success," *Long Range Planning* (October 1994), pp. 25–41.

36. "Do As I Say, Not As I Do," *Journal of Business Strategy* (May/June 1997), pp. 3–4.

37. L. Raymond and S. Rivard, "Determinants of Business Process Reengineering Success in Small and Large Enterprises: An Empirical Study in the Canadian Context," *Journal of Small Business Management* (January 1998), pp. 72–85.

38. K. Grint, "Reengineering History: Social Resonances and Business Process Reengineering," *Organization* (July 1994), pp. 179–201; A. Kleiner, "Revisiting Reengineering," *Strategy + Business* (3rd Quarter 2000), pp. 27–31.

39. M. Arndt, "Quality Isn't Just for Widgets," *Business Week* (July 22, 2002), pp. 72–73.

40. Ibid., p. 73.

41. F. Arner and A. Aston, "How Xerox Got Up to Speed," *Business Week* (May 3, 2004), pp. 103–104.

42. J. Hoerr, "Sharpening Minds for a Competitive Edge," *Business Week* (December 17, 1990), pp. 72–78.

43. S. X. Li and T. J. Rowley, "Inertia and Evaluation Mechanisms in Interorganizational Partner Selection: Syndicate Formation Among U.S. Investment Banks," *Academy of Management Journal* (December 2002), pp. 1104–1119.

44. M. U. Douma, J. Bilderbeek, P. J. Idenburg, and J. K. Loise, "Strategic Alliances: Managing the Dynamics of Fit," *Long Range Planning* (August 2000), pp. 579–598; W. Hoffmann and R. Schlosser, "Success Factors of Strategic Alliances in Small and Medum-Sized Enterprises—An Empirical Survey," *Long Range Planning* (June 2001), pp. 357–381.

45. J. H. Taggart, "Strategy Shifts in MNC Subsidiaries," *Strategic Management Journal* (July 1998), pp. 663–681.

46. C. A. Bartlett and S. Ghoshal, "Beyond the M-Form: Toward a Managerial Theory of the Firm," *Strategic Management Journal* (Winter 1993), pp. 23–46.

47. C. Matlack, "Nestlé Is Starting to Slim Down at Last," *Business Week* (October 27, 2003), pp. 56–57; "Daring, Defying, to Grow," *Economist* (August 7, 2004), pp. 55–58.

48. J. Sterling, "Translating Strategy into Effective Implementation: Dispelling the Myths and Highlighting What Works," *Strategy & Leadership*, Vol. 31, No. 3 (2003), pp. 27–34.

49. R. O. Crockett, "Reinventing Motorola," *Business Week* (August 2, 2004), pp. 82–83.

50. S. Miller, D. Wilson, and D. Hickson, "Beyond Planning: Strategies for Successfully Implementing Strategic Decisions," *Long Range Planning* (June 2004), pp. 201–218.

51. J. Darragh and A. Campbell, "Why Corporate Initiatives Get Stuck?" *Long Range Planning* (February 2001), pp. 33–52.

Chapter 10

1. B. O'Reilly, "The Rent-A-Car Jocks Who Made Enterprise #1," *Fortune* (October 28, 1996), pp. 125–128; J. Schlereth, "Putting People First," an interview with Andrew Taylor, *BizEd* (July/August 2003), pp. 16–20.

2. The numbers are approximate averages from three separate studies of top management turnover after mergers. See M. Lubatkin, D. Schweiger, and Y. Weber, "Top Management Turnover in Related M&Ss: An Additional Test of the Theory of Relative Standing," *Journal of Management*, Vol. 25, No. 1 (1999), pp. 55–73.

3. J. A. Krug, "Executive Turnover in Acquired Firms: A Longitudinal Analysis of Long-Term Interaction Effects," paper presented to annual meeting of *Academy of Management*, Seattle, WA (2003).

4. J. A. Krug and W. H. Hegarty, "Post-Acquisition Turnover Among U.S. Top Management Teams: An Analysis of the Effects of Foreign vs. Domestic Acquisitions of U.S. Targets," *Strategic Management Journal* (September 1997), pp. 667–675; J. A. Krug and W. H. Hegarty, "Predicting Who Stays and Leaves After an Acquisition: A Study of Top Managers in Multinational Firms," *Strategic Management Journal* (February 2001), pp. 185–196.

5. A. Hinterhuber, "Making M&A Work," *Business Strategy Review* (September 2002), pp. 7–9.

6. R. N. Ashkenas and S. C. Francis, "Integration Managers: Special Leaders for Special Times," *Harvard Business Review* (November–December 2000), pp. 108–116.
7. J. Hoerr, "Sharpening Minds for a Competitive Edge," *Business Week* (December 17, 1990), pp. 72–78.
8. "Training and Human Resources," *Business Strategy News Review* (July 2000), p. 6.
9. *High Performance Work Practices and Firm Performance* (Washington, DC: U.S. Department of Labor, Office of the American Workplace, 1993), pp. i, 4.
10. T. T. Baldwin, C. Danielson, and W. Wiggenhorn, "The Evolution of Learning Strategies in Organizations: From Employee Development to Business Redefinition," *Academy of Management Executive* (November 1997), pp. 47–58; K. Kelly, "Motorola: Training for the Millennium," *Business Week* (March 28, 1996), pp. 158–161.
11. R. Henkoff, "Companies That Train Best," *Fortune* (March 22, 1993), pp. 62–75.
12. D. Miller and J. Shamsie, "Learning Across the Life Cycle: Experimentation and Performance Among the Hollywood Studio Heads," *Strategic Management Journal* (August 2001), pp. 725–745.
13. B. Grow, "Fat's in the Fire for This Burger King," *Business Week* (November 8, 2004), pp. 69–70.
14. D. K. Datta and N. Rajagopalan, "Industry Structure and CEO Characteristics: An Empirical Study of Succession Events," *Strategic Management Journal* (September 1998), pp. 833–852; A. S. Thomas and K. Ramaswamy, "Environmental Change and Management Staffing: A Comment," *Journal of Management* (Winter 1993), pp. 877–887; J. P. Guthrie, C. M. Grimm, and K. G. Smith, "Environmental Change and Management Staffing: An Empirical Study," *Journal of Management* (December 1991), pp. 735–748.
15. J. Greco, "The Search Goes On," *Journal of Business Strategy* (September/October 1997), pp. 22–25; W. Ocasio and H. Kim, "The Circulation of Corporate Control: Selection of Functional Backgrounds on New CEOs in Large U.S. Manufacturing Firms, 1981–1992," *Administrative Science Quarterly* (September 1999), pp. 532–562.
16. R. Drazin and R. K. Kazanjian, "Applying the Del Technique to the Analysis of Cross-Classification Data: A Test of CEO Succession and Top Management Team Development," *Academy of Management Journal* (December 1993), pp. 1374–1399; W. E. Rothschild, "A Portfolio of Strategic Leaders," *Planning Review* (January/February 1996), pp. 16–19.
17. R. Subramanian and C. M. Sanchez, "Environmental Change and Management Staffing: An Empirical Examination of the Electric Utilities Industry," *Journal of Business Strategies* (Spring 1998), pp. 17–34.
18. M. A. Carpenter and B. R. Golden, "Perceived Managerial Discretion: A Study of Cause and Effect," *Strategic Management Journal* (March 1997), pp. 187–206.
19. J. A. Parnell, "Functional Background and Business Strategy: The Impact of Executive–Strategy Fit on Performance," *Journal of Business Strategies* (Spring 1994), pp. 49–62.
20. M. Smith and M. C. White, "Strategy, CEO Specialization, and Succession," *Administrative Science Quarterly* (June 1987), pp. 263–280.
21. "Making Companies Work," *Economist* (October 25, 2003), p. 14.
22. A. Bianco, L. Lavelle, J. Merrit, and A. Barrett, "The CEO Trap," *Business Week* (December 11, 2000), pp. 86–92.
23. Y. Zhang and N. Rajagopalan, "When the Known Devil Is Better Than an Unknown God: An Empirical Study of the Antecedents and Consequences of Relay CEO Succession," *Academy of Management Journal* (August 2004), pp. 483–500; W. Shen and A. A. Cannella, Jr., "Will Succession Planning Increase Shareholder Wealth? Evidence from Investor Reactions to Relay CEO Successions," *Strategic Management Journal* (February 2003), pp. 191–198.
24. G. A. Bigley and M. F. Wiersema, "New CEOs and Corporate Strategic Refocusing: How Experience As Heir Apparent Influences the Use of Power," *Administrative Science Quarterly* (December 2002), pp. 707–727.
25. "Coming and Going," Survey of Corporate Leadership, *Economist* (October 25, 2003), pp. 12–14.
26. D. C. Carey and D. Ogden, *CEO Succession: A Window on How Boards Do It Right When Choosing a New Chief Executive* (New York: Oxford University Press, 2000).
27. "Coming and Going," Survey of Corporate Leadership, *Economist* (October 25, 2003), pp. 12–14.
28. "The King Lear Syndrome," *Economist* (December 13, 2003), p. 65.
29. "Coming and Going," Survey of Corporate Leadership, *Economist* (October 25, 2003), pp. 12–14.
30. M. S. Kraatz and J. H. Moore, "Executive Migration and Institutional Change," *Academy of Management Journal* (February 2002), pp. 120–143; Y. Zhang and N. Rajagopalan, "When the Known Devil Is Better Than an Unknown God: An Empirical Study of the Antecedents and Consequences of Relay CEO Succession," *Academy of Management Journal* (August 2004), pp. 483–500; W. Shen and A. A. Cannella, Jr., "Revisiting the Performance Consequences of CEO Succession: The Impacts of Successor Type, Post-Succession Senior Executive Turnover, and Departing CEO Tenure," *Academy of Management Journal* (August 2002), pp. 717–733.
31. C. Lucier and J. Dyer, "Hiring an Outside CEO: A Board's Best Moves," *Directors & Boards* (Winter 2004), pp. 36–38.
32. Q. Yue, "Antecedents of Top Management Successor Origin in China," paper presented to the annual meeting of the *Academy of Management*, Seattle, WA (2003); A. A. Buchko and D. DiVerde, "Antecedents, Moderators, and Consequences of CEO Turnover: A Review and Reconceptualization," paper presented to *Midwest Academy of Management* (Lincoln, NE: 1997), p. 10; W. Ocasio, "Institutionalized Action and Corporate Governance: The Reliance on Rules of CEO Succession," *Administrative Science Quarterly* (June 1999), pp. 384–416.
33. C. Gopinath, "Turnaround: Recognizing Decline and Initiating Intervention," *Long Range Planning* (December 1991), pp. 96–101.
34. K. B. Schwartz and K. Menon, "Executive Succession in Failing Firms," *Academy of Management Journal* (September 1985), pp. 680–686; A. A. Cannella, Jr., and M. Lubatkin, "Succession as a Sociopolitical Process: Internal Impediments to Outsider Selection," *Academy of Management Journal* (August 1993), pp. 763–793; W. Boeker and J. Goodstein, "Performance and Succession Choice: The Moderating Effects of Governance and Ownership," *Academy of Management Journal* (February 1993), pp. 172–186.
35. W. Boeker, "Executive Migration and Strategic Change: The Effect of Top Manager Movement on Product-Market Entry," *Administrative Science Quarterly* (June 1997), pp. 213–236.

36. E. Brockmann, J. J. Hoffman, and D. Dawley, "A Contingency Theory of CEO Successor Choice and Post-Bankruptcy Strategic Change," paper presented to annual meeting of *Academy of Management*, Seattle, WA (2003).
37. P. Lorange and D. Murphy, "Bringing Human Resources into Strategic Planning: System Design Characteristics," in *Strategic Human Resource Management*, edited by C. J. Fombrun, N. M. Tichy, and M. A. Devanna (New York: John Wiley & Sons, 1984), pp. 281–283.
38. M. Leuchter, "Management Farm Teams," *Journal of Business Strategy* (May/June 1998), pp. 29–32.
39. S. Armour, "Playing the Succession Game," *USA Today* (November 24, 2003), p. 3B.
40. R. Sharpe, "As Leaders, Women Rule," *Business Week* (November 20, 2000), pp. 75–84.
41. D. A. Waldman and T. Korbar, "Student Assessment Center Performance in the Prediction of Early Career Success," *Academy of Management Learning and Education* (June 2004), pp. 151–167.
42. "Coming and Going," Survey of Corporate Leadership, *Economist* (October 25, 2003), pp. 12–14.
43. R. A. Pitts, "Strategies and Structures for Diversification," *Academy of Management Journal* (June 1997), pp. 197–208.
44. K. E. Mishra, G. M. Spreitzer, and A. K. Mishra, "Preserving Employee Morale During Downsizing," *Sloan Management Review* (Winter 1998), pp. 83–95.
45. B. O'Reilly, "Is Your Company Asking Too Much?" *Fortune* (March 12, 1990), p. 41. For more information on the emotional reactions of survivors of downsizing, see C. R. Stoner and R. I. Hartman, "Organizational Therapy: Building Survivor Health & Competitiveness," *SAM Advanced Management Journal* (Summer 1997), pp. 15–31, 41.
46. S. R. Fisher and M. A. White, "Downsizing in a Learning Organization: Are There Hidden Costs?" *Academy of Management Review* (January 2000), pp. 244–251.
47. T. M. Amabile and R. Conti, "Changes in the Work Environment for Creativity During Downsizing," *Academy of Management Journal* (December 1999), pp. 630–640; A. G. Bedeian and A. A. Armenakis, "The Cesspool Syndrome: How Dreck Floats to the Top of Declining Organizations," *Academy of Management Executive* (February 1998), pp. 58–67.
48. *Wall Street Journal* (December 22, 1992), p. B1.
49. R. D. Nixon, M. A. Hitt, H. Lee, and E. Jeong, "Market Reactions to Announcements of Corporate Downsizing Actions and Implementation Strategies," *Strategic Management Journal* (November 2004), pp. 1121–1129; G. D. Bruton, J. K. Keels, and C. L. Shook, "Downsizing the Firm: Answering the Strategic Questions," *Academy of Management Executive* (May 1996), pp. 38–45.
50. M. A. Hitt, B. W. Keats, H. F. Harback, and R. D. Nixon, "Rightsizing: Building and Maintaining Strategic Leadership and Long-Term Competitiveness," *Organizational Dynamics* (Autumn 1994), pp. 18–32. For additional suggestions, see W. F. Cascio, "Strategies for Responsible Restructuring," *Academy of Management Executive* (August 2002), pp. 80–91, and T. Mroczkowski and M. Hanaoka, "Effective Rightsizing Strategies in Japan and America: Is There a Convergence of Employment Practices?" *Academy of Management Executive* (May 1997), pp. 57–67.
51. J. S. Black and H. B. Gregersen, "The Right Way to Manage Expats," *Harvard Business Review* (March–April 1999), pp. 52–61.
52. *Ibid.*, p. 54.
53. J. I. Sanchez, P. E. Spector, and C. L. Cooper, "Adapting to a Boundaryless World: A Developmental Expatriate Model," *Academy of Management Executive* (May 2000), pp. 96–106.
54. R. L. Tung, *The New Expatriates* (Cambridge, MA: Ballinger, 1988); J. S. Black, M. Mendenhall, and G. Oddou, "Toward a Comprehensive Model of International Adjustment: An Integration of Multiple Theoretical Perspectives," *Academy of Management Review* (April 1991), pp. 291–317.
55. M. A. Carpenter, W. G. Sanders, and H. B. Gregersen, "Bundling Human Capital with Organizational Context: The Impact of International Assignment Experience on Multinational Firm Performance and CEO Pay," *Academy of Management Journal* (June 2001), pp. 493–511.
56. M. A. Shaffer, D. A. Harrison, K. M. Gilley, and D. M. Luk, "Struggling for Balance Amid Turbulence on International Assignments: Work–Family Conflict, Support, and Commitment," *Journal of Management*, Vol. 27, No. 1 (2001), pp. 99–121.
57. J. S. Black and H. B. Gregersen, "The Right Way to Manage Expats," *Harvard Business Review* (March–April 1999), p. 54.
58. G. Stern, "GM Executive's Ties to Native Country Help Auto Maker Clinch Deal in China," *Wall Street Journal* (November 2, 1995), p. B7.
59. K. Roth, "Managing International Interdependence: CEO Characteristics in a Resource-Based Framework," *Academy of Management Journal* (February 1995), pp. 200–231.
60. M. Subramaniam and N. Venkatraman, "Determinants of Transnational New Product Development Capability: Testing the Influence of Transferring and Deploying Tacit Overseas Knowledge," *Strategic Management Journal* (April 2001), pp. 359–378.
61. J. S. Lublin, "An Overseas Stint Can Be a Ticket to the Top," *Wall Street Journal* (January 29, 1996), pp. B1, B2.
62. P. Elstrom and S. V. Brull, "Mitsubishi's Morass," *Business Week* (June 3, 1996), p. 35.
63. L. G. Love, R. L. Priem, and G. T. Lumpkin, "Explicitly Articulated Strategy and Firm Performance Under Alternative Levels of Centralization," *Journal of Management*, Vol. 28, No. 5 (2002), pp. 611–627.
64. G. G. Gordon, "The Relationship of Corporate Culture to Industry Sector and Corporate Performance," in *Gaining Control of the Corporate Culture,* edited by R. H. Kilmann, M. J. Saxton, R. Serpa, and Associates (San Francisco: Jossey-Bass, 1985), p. 123; T. Kono, "Corporate Culture and Long-Range Planning," *Long Range Planning* (August 1990), pp. 9–19.
65. B. Mike and J. W. Slocum, Jr., "Changing Culture at Pizza Hut and Yum! Brands," *Organizational Dynamics*, Vol. 32, No. 4 (2003), pp. 319–330.
66. T. J. Tetenbaum, "Seven Key Practices That Improve the Chance for Expected Integration and Synergies," *Organizational Dynamics* (Autumn 1999), pp. 22–35.
67. B. Bremner and G. Edmondson, "Japan: A Tale of Two Mergers," *Business Week* (May 10, 2004), p. 42.
68. P. Very, M. Lubatkin, R. Calori, and J. Veiga, "Relative Standing and the Performance of Recently Acquired European Firms," *Strategic Management Journal* (September 1997), pp. 593–614.
69. A. R. Malekzadeh and A. Nahavandi, "Making Mergers Work by Managing Cultures," *Journal of Business Strategy* (May/June 1990), pp. 53–57; A. Nahavandi and A. R. Malekzadeh,

"Acculturation in Mergers and Acquisitions," *Academy of Management Review* (January 1988), pp. 79–90.

70. C. Ghosn, "Saving the Business Without Losing the Company," *Harvard Business Review* (January 2002), pp. 37–45; B. Bremner, G. Edmondson, C. Dawson, D. Welch, and K. Kerwin, "Nissan's Boss," *Business Week* (October 4, 2004), pp. 50–60.

71. M. Lubatkin, D. Schweiger, and Y. Weber, "Top Management Turnover in Related M&Ss: An Additional Test of the Theory of Relative Standing," *Journal of Management*, Vol. 25, No. 1 (1999), pp. 55–73.

72. J. J. Keller, "Why AT&T Takeover of NCR Hasn't Been a Real Bell Ringer," *Wall Street Journal* (September 19, 1995), pp. A1, A5.

73. J. W. Gibson and D. V. Tesone, "Management Fads: Emergence, Evolution, and Implications for Managers," *Academy of Management Executive* (November 2001), pp. 122–133.

74. For additional information, see S. J. Carroll, Jr., and M. L. Tosi, Jr., *Management by Objectives: Applications and Research* (New York: Macmillan, 1973), and A. P. Raia, *Managing by Objectives* (Glenview, IL: Scott, Foresman, and Company, 1974).

75. J. W. Gibson, D. V. Tesone, and C. W. Blackwell, "Management Fads: Here Yesterday, Gone Today?" *SAM Advanced Management Journal* (Autumn 2003), pp. 12–17.

76. J. W. Gibson and D. V. Tesone, "Management Fads: Emergence, Evolution, and Implications for Managers," *Academy of Management Executive* (November 2001), p. 125.

77. S. S. Masterson and M. S. Taylor, "Total Quality Management and Performance Appraisal: An Integrative Perspective," *Journal of Quality Management*, Vol. 1, No. 1 (1996), pp. 67–89.

78. T. J. Douglas and W. Q. Judge, Jr., "Total Quality Management Implementation and Competitive Advantage: The Role of Structural Control and Exploration," *Academy of Management Journal* (February 2001), pp. 158–169.

79. T. Y. Choi and O. C. Behling, "Top Managers and TQM Success: One More Look After All These Years," *Academy of Management Executive* (February 1997), pp. 37–47.

80. R. J. Schonberger, "Total Quality Management Cuts a Broad Swath—Through Manufacturing and Beyond," *Organizational Dynamics* (Spring 1992), pp. 16–28.

81. T. C. Powell, "Total Quality Management as Competitive Advantage: A Review and Empirical Study," *Strategic Management Journal* (January 1995), pp. 15–37.

82. G. Hofstede, "Culture's Recent Consequences: Using Dimensional Scores in Theory and Research," *International Journal of Cross Cultural Management*, Vol. 1, No. 1 (2001), pp. 11–17; G. Hofstede, *Cultures and Organizations: Software of the Mind* (London: McGraw-Hill, 1991); G. Hofstede and M. H. Bond, "The Confucius Connection: From Cultural Roots to Economic Growth," *Organizational Dynamics* (Spring 1988), pp. 5–21; R. Hodgetts, "A Conversation with Geert Hofstede," *Organizational Dynamics* (Spring 1993), pp. 53–61.

83. M. Javidan and R. J. House, "Cultural Acumen for the Global Manager: Lessons from Project GLOBE," *Organizational Dynamics*, Vol. 29, No. 4 (2001), pp. 289–305.

84. Ibid., p. 303.

85. See G. Hofstede and M. H. Bond, "The Confucius Connection: From Cultural Roots to Economic Growth," *Organizational Dynamics* (Spring 1988), pp. 12–13.

86. H. K. Steensma, L. Marino, K. M. Weaver, and P. H. Dickson, "The Influence of National Culture on the Formation of Technology Alliances by Entrepreneurial Firms," *Academy of Management Journal* (October 2000), pp. 951–973.

87. "Emerging-Market Indicators," *The Economist* (October 7, 2000), p. 124.

88. T. T. Herbert, "Multinational Strategic Planning: Matching Central Expectations to Local Realities," *Long Range Planning* (February 1999), pp. 81–87.

89. M. A. Geletkancz, "The Salience of 'Culture's Consequences': The Effects of Cultural Values on Top Executive Commitment to the Status Quo," *Strategic Management Journal* (September 1997), pp. 615–634.

90. G. Hofstede and M. H. Bond, "The Confucius Connection: From Cultural Roots to Economic Growth," *Organizational Dynamics* (Spring 1988), p. 20.

91. B. Groysberg, A. Nanda, and N. Nohria, "The Risky Business of Hiring Stars," *Harvard Business Review* (May 2004), pp. 92–100.

92. D. Jones, "Employers Learning That 'B Players' Hold the Cards," *USA Today* (September 9, 2003), pp. 1B–2B.

93. From a study by the British Council reported in "Studying Abroad," *Futurist* (November–December 2004), p. 2.

94. D. Keirsey, *Please Understand Me II* (Del Mar, CA: Prometheus Nemesis Book Co., 1998).

Chapter 11

1. K. F. Iverson with T. Varian, "Plain Talk," *Inc.* (October 1997), p. 81. Excerpted from Iverson's book, *Plain Talk: Lessons from a Business Maverick* (New York: John Wiley & Sons, 1997).

2. R. Barker, "A Surprise in Office Depot's In-Box," *Business Week* (October 25, 2004), p. 122.

3. R. Muralidharan and R. D. Hamilton III, "Aligning Multinational Control Systems," *Long Range Planning* (June 1999), pp. 352–361. These types are based on W. G. Ouchi, "The Relationship Between Organizational Structure and Organizational Control," *Administrative Science Quarterly*, Vol. 20 (1977), pp. 95–113, and W. G. Ouchi, "A Conceptual Framework for the Design of Organizational Control Mechanisms," *Management Science*, Vol. 25 (1979), pp. 833–848. Muralidhara and Hamilton refer to Ouchi's clan control as input control.

4. W. G. Rowe and P. M. Wright, "Related and Unrelated Diversification and Their Effect on Human Resource Management Controls," *Strategic Management Journal* (April 1997), pp. 329–338.

5. R. Muralidharan and R. D. Hamilton III, "Aligning Multinational Control Systems," *Long Range Planning* (June 1999), pp. 356–359.

6. F. C. Barnes, "ISO 9000 Myth and Reality: A Reasonable Approach to ISO 9000," *SAM Advanced Management Journal* (Spring 1998), pp. 23–30.

7. M. Henricks, "A New Standard," *Entrepreneur* (October 2002), pp. 83–84.

8. M. V. Uzumeri, "ISO 9000 and Other Metastandards: Principles for Management Practice?" *Academy of Management Executive* (February 1997), pp. 21–36.

9. A. M. Hormozi, "Understanding and Implementing ISO 9000: A Manager's Guide," *SAM Advanced Management Journal* (Autumn 1995), pp. 4–11.

10. M. Henricks, "A New Standard," *Entrepreneur* (October 2002), p. 84.

11. L. Armstrong, "Someone to Watch Over You," *Business Week* (July 10, 2000), pp. 189–190.
12. J. K. Shank and V. Govindarajan, *Strategic Cost Management* (New York: The Free Press, 1993).
13. S. S. Rao, "ABCs of Cost Control," *Inc. Technology*, No. 2 (1997), pp. 79–81.
14. R. Gruber, "Why You Should Consider Activity-Based Costing," *Small Business Forum* (Spring 1994), pp. 20–36.
15. "Easier Than ABC," *Economist* (October 25, 2003), p. 56.
16. T. P. Pare, "A New Tool for Managing Costs," *Fortune* (June 14, 1993), pp. 124–129.
17. K. Hopkins, "The Risk Agenda," *Business Week*, Special Advertising Section (November 22, 2004), pp. 166–170.
18. T. L. Barton, W. G. Shenkir, and P. L. Walker, "Managing Risk: An Enterprise-wide Approach," *Financial Executive* (March/April 2001), p. 51.
19. T. L. Barton, W. G. Shenkir, and P. L. Walker, "Managing Risk: An Enterprise-wide Approach," *Financial Executive* (March/April 2001), pp. 48–51; P. L. Walker, W. G. Shenkir, and T. L. Barton, "Enterprise Risk Management: Putting It All Together," *Internal Auditor* (August 2003), pp. 50–55.
20. C. K. Brancato, *New Corporate Performance Measures* (New York: Conference Board, 1995); C. D. Ittner, D. F. Larcker, and M. V. Rajan, "The Choice of Performance Measures in Annual Bonus Contracts," working paper reported by K. Z. Andrews in "Executive Bonuses," *Harvard Business Review* (January–February 1996), pp. 8–9; J. Low and T. Siesfeld, "Measures That Matter: Wall Street Considers Non-Financial Performance More Than You Think," *Strategy & Leadership* (March/April 1998), pp. 24–30.
21. A similar measure, EBITDA (Earnings Before Interest, Taxes, Depreciation, and Amortization), is sometimes used but is *not* determined in accordance with generally accepted accounting principles and is thus subject to varying calculations.
22. J. M. Laderman, "Earnings, Schmernings: Look at the Cash," *Business Week* (July 24, 1989), pp. 56–57.
23. H. Greenberg, "Don't Count on Cash Flow," *Fortune* (May 13, 2002), p. 176; A. Tergesen, "Cash-Flow Hocus-Pocus," *Business Week* (July 15, 2002), pp. 130–132.
24. E. H. Hall, Jr., and J. Lee, "Diversification Strategies: Creating Value or Generating Profits?" paper presented to the annual meeting of the *Decision Sciences Institute*, Orlando, FL (November 18–21, 2000).
25. S. Tully, "America's Best Wealth Creators," *Fortune* (November 28, 1994), p. 143.
26. P. C. Brewer, G. Chandra, and C. A. Hock, "Economic Value Added (EVA): Its Uses and Limitations," *SAM Advanced Management Journal* (Spring 1999), pp. 4–11.
27. D. J. Skyrme and D. M. Amidon, "New Measures of Success," *Journal of Business Strategy* (January/February 1998), p. 23.
28. G. B. Stewart III, "EVA Works—But Not if You Make These Common Mistakes," *Fortune* (May 1, 1995), pp. 117–118.
29. S. Tully, "The Real Key to Creating Wealth," *Fortune* (September 20, 1993), p. 38.
30. A. Ehrbar, "Using EVA to Measure Performance and Assess Strategy," *Strategy & Leadership* (May/June 1999), pp. 20–24.
31. P. C. Brewer, G. Chandra, and C. A. Hock, "Economic Value Added (EVA): Its Uses and Limitations," *Advanced Management Journal* (Spring 1999), pp. 7–9.
32. Pro: K. Lehn and A. K. Makhija, "EVA & MVA As Performance Measures and Signals for Strategic Change," *Strategy & Leadership* (May/June 1996), pp. 34–38. Con: D. I. Goldberg, "Shareholder Value Debunked," *Strategy & Leadership* (January/February 2000), pp. 30–36.
33. A. Ehrbar, "Using EVA to Measure Performance and Assess Strategy," *Strategy & Leadership* (May/June 1999), p. 21.
34. S. Tully, "America's Wealth Creators," *Fortune* (November 22, 1999), pp. 275–284; A. B. Fisher, "Creating Stockholder Wealth: Market Value Added," *Fortune* (December 11, 1995), pp. 105–116.
35. A. B. Fisher, "Creating Stockholder Wealth: Market Value Added," *Fortune* (December 11, 1995), pp. 105–116.
36. K. Lehn and A. K. Makhija, "EVA & MVA As Performance Measures and Signals for Strategic Change," *Strategy & Leadership* (May/June 1996), p. 37.
37. R. S. Kaplan and D. P. Norton, "Using the Balanced Scorecard as a Strategic Management System," *Harvard Business Review* (January–February 1996), pp. 75–85; R. S. Kaplan and D. P. Norton, "The Balanced Scorecard—Measures That Drive Performance," *Harvard Business Review* (January–February, 1992), pp. 71–79.
38. D. I. Goldenberg, "Shareholder Value Debunked," *Strategy & Leadership* (January/February 2000), p. 34.
39. C. K. Brancato, *New Performance Measures* (New York: Conference Board, 1995).
40. A. Gumpus and B. Lyons, "The Balanced Scorecard at Philips Electronics," *Strategic Finance*, Vol. 84 (2002), pp. 92–101.
41. P. D. Heaney, "Can Performance Be Measured?" *Progressive Grocer*, Vol. 82 (2003), pp. 11–13.
42. B. P. Stivers and T. Joyce, "Building a Balanced Performance Management System," *SAM Advanced Management Journal* (Spring 2000), pp. 22–29.
43. D. J. Skyrme and D. M. Amidon, "New Measures of Success," *Journal of Business Strategy* (January/February 1998), p. 22.
44. G. J. M. Braam and E. Nijssen, "Performance Effects of Using the Balanced Scorecard: A Note on the Dutch Experience," *Long Range Planning* (August 2004), pp. 335–349; H. Ahn, "Applying the Balanced Scorecard Concept: An Experience Report," *Long Range Planning* (August 2001), pp. 441–461.
45. J. M. Ivancevich, T. N. Duening, J. A. Gilbert, and R. Konopaske, "Deterring White-Collar Crime," *Academy of Management Executive* (May 2003), pp. 114–127.
46. R. Charan, *Boards at Work* (San Francisco: Jossey-Bass, 1998), pp. 176–177.
47. T. D. Schellhardt, "Directors Get Tough: Inside a CEO Performance Review," *Wall Street Journal Interactive Edition* (April 27, 1998).
48. T. L. Wheelen and J. D. Hunger, "Using the Strategic Audit," *SAM Advanced Management Journal* (Winter 1987), pp. 4–12; G. Donaldson, "A New Tool for Boards: The Strategic Audit," *Harvard Business Review* (July–August 1995), pp. 99–107.
49. H. Threat, "Measurement Is Free," *Strategy & Leadership* (May/June 1999), pp. 16–19.
50. Z. U. Khan, S. K. Chawla, M. F. Smith, and M. F. Sharif, "Transfer Pricing Policy Issues in Europe 1992," *International Journal of Management* (September 1992), pp. 230–241.
51. H. Rothman, "You Need Not Be Big to Benchmark," *Nation's Business* (December 1992), p. 64.
52. C. W. Von Bergen and B. Soper, "A Problem with Benchmarking: Using Shaping as a Solution," *SAM Advanced Management Journal* (Autumn 1995), pp. 16–19.

53. "Tool Usage Rates," *Journal of Business Strategy* (March/April 1995), p. 12.

54. R. J. Kennedy, "Benchmarking and Its Myths," *Competitive Intelligence Magazine* (April–June 2000), pp. 28–33.

55. "Just the Facts: Numbers Runners," *Journal of Business Strategy* (July/August 2002), p. 3; L. Mann, D. Samson, and D. Dow, "A Field Experiment on the Effects of Benchmarking & Goal Setting on Company Sales Performance," *Journal of Management*, Vol. 24, No. 1 (1998), pp. 73–96.

56. S. A. W. Drew, "From Knowledge to Action: The Impact of Benchmarking on Organizational Performance," *Long Range Planning* (June 1997), pp. 427–441.

57. S. M. Robbins and R. B. Stobaugh, "The Bent Measuring Stick for Foreign Subsidiaries," *Harvard Business Review* (September–October 1973), p. 82.

58. J. D. Daniels and L. H. Radebaugh, *International Business*, 5th ed. (Reading, MA: Addison-Wesley, 1989), pp. 673–674.

59. W. A. Johnson and R. J. Kirsch, "International Transfer Pricing and Decision Making in United States Multinationals," *International Journal of Management* (June 1991), pp. 554–561.

60. "Global Economy Makes Taxing Harder," *The Futurist* (March–April 2000), p. 11; "Financial Indicators," *The Economist* (August 26, 2000), p. 89.

61. "Fixing the Bottom Line," *Time* (November 23, 1992), p. 20.

62. T. A. Stewart, "The New Face of American Power," *Fortune* (July 26, 1993), p. 72; G. P. Zachary, "Behind Stocks' Surge Is an Economy in Which Big U.S. Firms Thrive," *Wall Street Journal* (November 22, 1995), pp. A1, A5.

63. J. M. L. Poon, R. Ainuddin, and H. Affrim, "Management Policies and Practices of American, British, European, and Japanese Subsidiaries in Malaysia: A Comparative Study," *International Journal of Management* (December 1990), pp. 467–474.

64. M. Egan, "Setting Standards: Strategic Advantages in International Trade," *Business Strategy Review*, Vol. 13, No. 1 (2002), pp. 51–64; L. Swatkowski, "Building Towards International Standards," *Appliance* (December 1999), p. 30.

65. C. W. L. Hill, P. Hwang, and W. C. Kim, "An Eclectic Theory of the Choice of International Entry Mode," *Strategic Management Journal* (February 1990), pp. 117–128; D. Lei, J. W. Slocum, Jr., and R. W. Slater, "Global Strategy and Reward Systems: The Key Roles of Management Development and Corporate Culture," *Organizational Dynamics* (Autumn 1990), pp. 27–41; W. R. Fannin and A. F. Rodriques, "National or Global?—Control vs. Flexibility," *Long Range Planning* (October 1986), pp. 84–188.

66. A. V. Phatak, *International Dimensions of Management*, 2nd ed. (Boston: Kent, 1989), pp. 155–157.

67. S. McAlary, "Three Pitfalls in ERP Implementation," *Strategy & Leadership* (October/November/December 1999), pp. 49–50.

68. J. B. White, D. Clark, and S. Ascarelli, "This German Software Is Complex, Expensive—And Wildly Popular," *Wall Street Journal* (March 14, 1997), pp. A1, A8; D. Ward, "Whirlpool Takes a Dive with Software Snarl," *Des Moines Register* (April 29, 2000), p. 8D.

69. A. Lashinsky, "Meg and the Machine," *Fortune* (September 1, 2003), pp. 68–78.

70. R. M. Hodgetts and M. S. Wortman, *Administrative Policy*, 2nd ed. (New York: John Wiley & Sons, 1980), p. 128.

71. J. R. Wooldridge and C. C. Snow, "Stock Market Reaction to Strategic Investment Decisions," *Strategic Management Journal* (September 1990), pp. 353–363.

72. M. C. Jensen, "Corporate Budgeting Is Broken—Let's Fix It," *Harvard Business Review* (November 2001), pp. 94–101.

73. D. Henry, "Fuzzy Numbers," *Business Week* (October 4, 2004), pp. 79–88.

74. D. R. Schmidt and K. L. Fowler, "Post-Acquisition Financial Performance and Executive Compensation," *Strategic Management Journal* (November–December 1990), pp. 559–569.

75. H. L. Tosi, S. Werner, J. P. Katz, and L. R. Gomez-Mejia, "How Much Does Performance Matter? A Meta-Analysis of CEO Pay Studies," *Journal of Management*, Vol. 26, No. 2 (2000), pp. 301–339; P. Wright, M. Kroll, and D. Elenkov, "Acquisition Returns, Increase in Firm Size, and Chief Executive Officer Compensation: The Moderating Role of Monitoring," *Academy of Management Journal* (June 2002), pp. 599–608.

76. D. Jones, "Bad News Can Enrich Executives," *Des Moines Register* (November 26, 1999), p. 8S.

77. J. F. Porac, J. B. Wade, and T. G. Pollock, "Industry Categories and the Politics of the Comparable Firm in CEO Compensation," *Administrative Science Quarterly* (March 1999), pp. 112–144.

78. C. D. Ittner and D. F. Larcker, "Coming Up Short," *Harvard Business Review* (November 2003), pp. 88–95.

79. See the classic article by S. Kerr, "On the Folly of Rewarding A, While Hoping for B," *Academy of Management Journal*, Vol. 18 (December 1975), pp. 769–783.

80. W. Zellner, E. Schine, and G. Smith, "Trickle-Down Is Trickling Down at Work," *Business Week* (March 18, 1996), p. 34.

81. T. J. Peters and R. H. Waterman, *In Search of Excellence* (New York: HarperCollins, 1982), pp. 75–76.

82. T. Aeppel, "Not All Workers Find Idea of Empowerment as Neat as It Sounds," *Wall Street Journal* (September 8, 1997), pp. A1, A13.

83. R. S. Allen and M. M. Helms, "Employee Perceptions of the Relationship Between Strategy, Rewards, and Organizational Performance," *Journal of Business Strategies* (Fall 2002), pp. 115–140; M. A. Carpenter, "The Price of Change: The Role of CEO Compensation in Strategic Variation and Deviation from Industry Strategy Norms," *Journal of Management*, Vol. 26, No. 6 (2000), pp. 1179–1198; M. A. Carpenter and W. G. Sanders, "The Effects of Top Management Team Pay and Firm Internationalization on MNC Performance," *Journal of Management*, Vol. 30, No. 4 (2004), pp. 509–528; J. D. Shaw, N. Gupta, and J. E. Delery, "Congruence Between Technology and Compensation Systems: Implications for Strategy Implementation," *Strategic Management Journal* (April 2001), pp. 379–386; E. F. Montemazon, "Congruence Between Pay Policy and Competitive Strategy in High-Performing Organizations," *Journal of Management*, Vol. 22, No. 6 (1996), pp. 889–908.

84. D. B. Balkin and L. R. Gomez-Mejia, "Matching Compensation and Organizational Strategies," *Strategic Management Journal* (February 1990), pp. 153–169.

85. C. S. Galbraith, "The Effect of Compensation Programs and Structure on SBU Competitive Strategy: A Study of Technology-Intensive Firms," *Strategic Management Journal* (July 1991), pp. 353–370.

86. T. A. Stewart, "CEO Pay: Mom Wouldn't Approve," *Fortune* (March 31, 1997), pp. 119–120.

87. P. J. Stonich, "The Performance Measurement and Reward System: Critical to Strategic Management," *Organizational Dynamics* (Winter 1984), pp. 45–57.

88. A. Rappaport, "New Thinking on How to Link Executive Pay with Performance," *Harvard Business Review* (March–April 1999), pp. 91–101.
89. Motley Fool, "Fool's School: Hooray for GE," *The (Ames, IA) Tribune* (October 27, 2003), p. 1D.
90. E. Iwata and B. Hansen, "Pay, Performance Don't Always Add Up," *USA Today* (April 30, 2004), pp. 1B–2B; W. Grossman and R. E. Hoskisson, "CEO Pay at the Crossroads of Wall Street and Main: Toward the Strategic Design of Executive Compensation," *Academy of Management Executive* (February 1998), pp. 43–57.
91. *Pocket World in Figures 2004* (London: The Economist and Profile Books, 2003), p. 70.
92. Ibid., p. 67.
93. A. Harrington, "America's Most Admired Companies," *Fortune* (March 8, 2004), pp. 80–81.
94. J. Useem, "Should We Admire Wal-Mart?" *Fortune* (March 8, 2004), p. 118.

Chapter 12

1. D. Brady, "A Thousand and One Noshes," *Business Week* (June 14, 2004), pp. 54–56.
2. "Don't Laugh at Gilded Butterflies," *Economist* (April 24, 2004), pp. 71–73
3. R. Jonash and T. Sommerlatte, *The Innovation Premium* (Perseus Books, 1999).
4. G. Getz and C. Christensen, "Should You Fear Disruptive Technology?" *Fortune* (April 3, 2000), pp. 249–250.
5. E. Berggen and T. Nacher, "Introducing New Products Can Be Hazardous to Your Company: Use the Right New-Solutions Delivery Tools," *Academy of Management Executive* (August 2001), pp. 92–101.
6. "Fear of the Unknown," *The Economist* (December 4, 1999), pp. 61–62.
7. M. S. Malone, "Which Are the Most Valuable Companies in the New Economy?" *Forbes ASAP* (May 29, 2000), pp. 212–214.
8. F. T. Rothaermel, "Incumbent's Advantage Through Exploiting Complementary Assets via Interfirm Cooperation," *Strategic Management Journal* (June–July 2001), pp. 687–699.
9. S. J. Towner, "Four Ways to Accelerate New Product Development, " *Long Range Planning* (April 1994), p. 57.
10. R. Garud and P. R. Nayyar, "Transformative Capacity: Continual Structuring by Intertemporal Technology Transfer," *Strategic Management Journal* (June 1994), p. 379.
11. J. P. Andrew and H. L. Sirkin, "Innovating for Cash," *Harvard Business Review* (September 2003), pp. 76–83.
12. R. D. Hof, P. Burrows, S. Hamm, D. Brady, and I. Rowley, "Building an Idea Factory," *Business Week* (October 22, 2004), pp. 194–200.
13. M. A. Schilling and C. W. L. Hill, "Managing the New Product Development Process: Strategic Imperatives," *Academy of Management Executive* (August 1998), pp. 67–81.
14. C. Power, K. Kerwin, R. Grover, K. Alexander, and R. D. Hof, "Flops," *Business Week* (August 16, 1993), pp. 76–82.
15. "Expect the Unexpected," *Economist* (September 6, 2003), p. 5. This article summarizes research reported in *Why Innovation Fails* by Carl Franklin (London: Spiro Press, 2003).
16. R. D. Hof, P. Burrows, S. Hamm, D. Brady, and I. Rowley, "Building an Idea Factory," *Business Week* (October 22, 2004), p. 196.
17. L. Rosenkopf and A. Nerkar, "Beyond Local Search: Boundary-Spanning, Exploration, and Impact in the Optical Disk Industry," *Strategic Management Journal* (April 2001), pp. 287–306.
18. G. C. Hill and K. Yamada, "Motorola Illustrates How an Aged Giant Can Remain Vibrant," *Wall Street Journal* (December 9, 1992), pp. A1, A14.
19. L. Huston, "Mining the Periphery for New Products," *Long Range Planning* (April 2004), pp. 191–196; N. Snyder, "Environmental Volatility, Scanning Intensity and Organizational Performance," *Journal of Contemporary Business* (September 1981), p. 16.
20. R. Nobel and J. Birkinshaw, "Innovations in MNCs: Control and Communication Patterns in International R&D Operations," *Strategic Management Journal* (May 1998), pp. 479–496.
21. J. Kerstetter, "An Old Hotbed with New Crops," *Business Week* (October 11, 2004), pp. 164–170; P. Almeida, "Knowledge Sourcing by Foreign Multinationals: Patent Citation Analysis in the U.S. Semiconductor Industry," *Strategic Management Journal* (December 1996), pp. 155–165.
22. E. Von Hippel, *The Sources of Innovation* (Oxford, UK: Oxford University Press, 1988), p. 4. See also S. Thomke and E. Von Hippel, "Customers As Innovators: A New Way to Create Value," *Harvard Business Review* (April 2002), pp. 74–81.
23. M. R. Neale and D. R. Corkindale, "Co-Developing Products: Involving Customer Earlier and More Deeply," *Long Range Planning* (June 1998), pp. 418–425.
24. E. Von Hippel, *The Sources of Innovation* (Oxford, UK: Oxford University Press, 1988), p. 107; E. Von Hippel, S. Thomke, and M. Sonnack, "Creating Breakthroughs at 3M," *Harvard Business Review* (September–October 1999), p. 48.
25. L. Lavelle, "Inventing to Order," *Business Week* (July 5, 2004), pp. 84–85.
26. E. Von Hippel, S. Thomke, and M. Sonnack, "Creating Breakthroughs at 3M," *Harvard Business Review* (September–October 1999), p. 52.
27. G. Hamel and C. K. Prahalad, "Seeing the Future First," *Fortune* (September 5, 1995), p. 70.
28. C. M. Christensen, *The Innovator's Dilemma* (Boston: HBS Press, 1997); J. Wade, "A Community-Level Analysis of Sources and Rates of Technological Variation in the Microprocessor Market," *Academy of Management Journal* (October 1996), pp. 1218–1244.
29. C. M. Christensen and J. L. Bower, "Customer Power, Strategic Investment, and the Failure of Leading Firms," *Strategic Management Journal* (March 1996), pp. 197–218.
30. G. S. Lynn, J. G. Morone, and A. S. Paulson, "Marketing and Discontinuous Innovation: The Probe and Learn Process," *California Management Review* (Spring 1996), pp. 8–37.
31. W. I. Zangwill, "When Customer Research Is a Lousy Idea," *Wall Street Journal* (March 8, 1993), p. A10.
32. S. Baker, "What Every Business Should Learn from Microsoft," *Journal of Business Strategy* (September/October 1998), pp. 36–41.
33. "Don't Laugh at Gilded Butterflies," *Economist* (April 24, 2004), pp. 71–73.
34. D. F. Kuratko, J. S. Hornsby, D. W. Naffziger, and R. V. Montagno, "Implement Entrepreneurial Thinking in Established Organizations," *SAM Advanced Management Journal* (Winter 1993), p. 29.

35. "Business Bulletin," *Wall Street Journal* (May 1, 1997), p. A1. The number improved from 58 ideas in 1967 to 11 in 1990, to 7 in 1995.
36. L. G. Franko, "Global Corporate Competition: Who's Winning, Who's Losing, and the R&D Factor as One Reason Why," *Strategic Management Journal* (September–October 1989), pp. 449–474; See also P. S. Chan, E. J. Flynn, and R. Chinta, "The Strategies of Growing and Turnaround Firms: A Multiple Discriminant Analysis," *International Journal of Management* (September 1991), pp. 669–675.
37. M. J. Chussil, "How Much to Spend on R&D?" *The PIMS-letter of Business Strategy*, No. 13 (Cambridge, MA: The Strategic Planning Institute, 1978), p. 5.
38. J. S. Harrison, E. H. Hall, Jr., and R. Nargundkar, "Resource Allocation as an Outcropping of Strategic Consistency: Performance Implications," *Academy of Management Journal* (October 1993), pp. 1026–1051.
39. S. B. Graves and N. S. Langowitz, "Innovative Productivity and Returns to Scale in the Pharmaceutical Industry," *Strategic Management Journal* (November 1993), pp. 593–605; A. Brady, "Small Is As Small Does," *Journal of Business Strategy* (March/April 1995), pp. 44–52.
40. "Small Firms Make More Than Their Share of Big Inventions," *The Small Business Advocate* (March 2003), pp. 1, 4.
41. J. B. Sorensen and T. E. Stuart, "Aging, Obsolescence, and Organizational Innovation," *Administrative Science Quarterly* (March 2000), pp. 81–112.
42. D. H. Freedman, "Through the Looking Glass," in "The State of Small Business," *Inc.* (May 21, 1996), pp. 48–54.
43. N. Nohria and R. Gulati, "Is Slack Good or Bad for Innovation?" *Academy of Management Journal* (October 1996), pp. 1245–1264.
44. M. A. Hitt, R. E. Hoskisson, and J. S. Harrison, "Strategic Competitiveness in the 1990s: Challenges and Opportunities for U.S. Executives," *Academy of Management Executive* (May 1991), p. 13.
45. T. F. O'Boyle, "Steel's Management Has Itself to Blame," *Wall Street Journal* (May 17, 1983), p. 32.
46. M. Silva and B. Sjogren, *Europe 1992 and the New World Power Game* (New York: John Wiley & Sons, 1990), p. 231.
47. E. Mansfield, M. Schwartz, and S. Wagner, "Imitation Costs and Patents: An Empirical Study," *Economic Journal* (December 1981), pp. 907–918.
48. G. Stalk, Jr., and A. M. Webber, "Japan's Dark Side of Time," *Harvard Business Review* (July–August 1993), p. 99.
49. M. Robert, "Market Fragmentation versus Market Segmentation," *Journal of Business Strategy* (September/October 1992), p. 52.
50. M. J. Benner and M. Tushman, "Process Management and Technological Innovation: A Longitudinal Study of the Photography and Paint Industries," *Administrative Science Quarterly* (December 2002), pp. 676–706.
51. W. T. Robinson and J. Chiang, "Product Development Strategies for Established Market Pioneers, Early Followers, and Late Entrants," *Strategic Management Journal* (September 2002), pp. 855–866.
52. C. L. Nicholls-Nixon and C. Y. Woo, "Technology Sourcing and Output of Established Firms in a Regime of Encompassing Technological Change," *Strategic Management Journal* (July 2003), pp. 651–666.
53. "Business Briefcase," *Des Moines Register* (November 17, 2004), p. 3D.
54. M. Silva and B. Sjogren, *Europe 1992 and the New World Power Game* (New York: John Wiley & Sons), pp. 239–241. See also P. Nueno and J. Oosterveld, "Managing Technology Alliances," *Long Range Planning* (June 1988), pp. 11–17.
55. M. Krantz, "Amgen Thinks Small to Grow," *USA Today* (October 23, 2003), p. 3B.
56. P. R. Nayak, "Should You Outsource Product Development?" *Journal of Business Strategy* (May/June 1993), pp. 44–45.
57. C. W. L. Hill, "Establishing a Standard: Competitive Strategy and Technological Standards in Winner-Take-All Industries," *Academy of Management Executive* (May 1997), pp. 7–25.
58. M. H. Roy and S. S. Dugal, "The Effect of Technological Environment and Competitive Strategy on Licensing Decisions," *American Business Review* (June 1999), pp. 112–118.
59. T. M. Apke, "International Licensing of Technology: Protecting Your Interests," paper presented to the annual meeting of the *Western Decision Sciences Institute* (Honolulu, HI, April 15–19, 2003).
60. "The Cost of Ideas," *Economist* (November 13, 2004), p. 71; "Patent Wars," *Economist* (April 8, 2000), pp. 75–78.
61. "The Right to Good Ideas," *Economist* (June 23, 2001), pp. 21–23.
62. M. A. Hitt, R. E. Hoskisson, R. A. Johnson, and D. D. Moesel, "The Market for Corporate Control and Firm Innovation," *Academy of Management Journal* (October 1996), pp. 1084–1119.
63. W. M. Cohen and D. A. Levinthal, "Absorptive Capacity: A New Perspective on Learning and Innovation," *Administrative Science Quarterly* (March 1990), pp. 128–152.
64. P. J. Lane and M. Lubatkin, "Absorptive Capacity and Interorganizational Learning," *Strategic Management Journal* (May 1998), pp. 461–477.
65. M. B. Heeley, "Appropriating Rents from External Knowledge: The Impact of Absorptive Capacity on Firm Sales Growth and Research Productivity," paper presented to *Babson Entrepreneurship Research Conference* (Wellesley, MA, 1997).
66. S. A. Zahra and G. George, "Absorptive Capacity: A Review, Reconceptualization, and Extension," *Academy of Management Review* (April 2002), pp. 185–203.
67. "The Impact of Industrial Robotics on the World of Work," *International Labour Review*, Vol. 125, No. 1 (1986). Summarized in "The Risks of Robotization," *The Futurist* (May–June 1987), p. 56.
68. M. A. Hitt, R. E. Hoskisson, and J. S. Harrison, "Strategic Competitiveness in the 1990s: Challenges and Opportunities for U.S. Executives,"*Academy of Management Executive* (May 1991), p. 9.
69. C. Hickman and C. Raia, "Incubating Innovation," *Journal of Business Strategy* (May/June 2002), pp. 14–18.
70. D. Dougherty and C. Hardy, "Sustained Product Innovation in Large, Mature Organizations: Overcoming Innovation-to-Organization Problems," *Academy of Management* (October 1996), pp. 1120–1153.
71. C. A. O'Reilly III and M. L. Tushman, "The Ambidextrous Organization," *Harvard Business Review* (April 2004), pp. 74–81.
72. E. M. Rogers, *Diffusion of Innovations*, 4th edition (New York: The Free Press, 1995).
73. C. A. Lengnick-Hall, "Innovation and Competitive Advantage: What We Know and What We Need to Know," *Journal of Management* (June 1992), pp. 399–429.

74. J. R. Galbraith, "Designing the Innovative Organization," *Organizational Dynamics* (Winter 1982), pp. 5–25.

75. P. R. Nayak, "Product Innovation Practices in Europe, Japan, and the U.S.," *Journal of Business Strategy* (May/June 1992), pp. 62–63.

76. E. M. Olson, O. C. Walker, Jr., and R. W. Ruekert, "Organizing for Effective New Product Development: The Moderating Role of Product Innovativeness," *Journal of Marketing* (January 1995), pp. 48–62.

77. D. Rowe, "Up and Running," *Journal of Business Strategy* (May/June 1993), pp. 48–50.

78. N. Freundlich and M. Schroeder, "Getting Everybody Into the Act," *Business Week* (Quality 1991 edition), p. 152.

79. W. D. Guth and A. Ginsberg, "Corporate Entrepreneurship," *Strategic Management Journal* (Summer 1990), p. 5.

80. S. A. Zahra and J. G. Covin, "Contextual Measures on the Corporate Entrepreneurship–Performance Relationship: A Longitudinal Analysis," *Journal of Business Venturing*, Vol. 10 (1995), pp. 43–58.

81. R. A. Burgelman, "Designs for Corporate Entrepreneurship," *California Management Review* (Spring 1984), pp. 154–166; R. A. Burgelman and L. R. Sayles, *Inside Corporate Innovation* (New York: The Free Press, 1986).

82. W. J. Holstein, "Remaking Motorola Isn't Easy," *U.S. News & World Report* (October 23, 2000), p. 52; R. O. Crockett, "A New Company Called Motorola," *Business Week* (April 17, 2000), pp. 86–92.

83. T. A. Stewart, "How Teradyne Solved the Innovator's Dilemma," *Fortune* (June 10, 2000), pp. 188–190.

84. J. Carey, "An Ivory Tower That Spins Pure Gold," *Business Week* (April 19, 1999), pp. 167–170.

85. S. K. Yoder, "How H-P Used Tactics of the Japanese to Beat Them at Their Game," *Wall Street Journal* (September 8, 1994), pp. A1, A6.

86. C. Y. Woo, G. E. Willard, and S. M. Beckstead, "Spin-Offs: What Are the Gains?" *Journal of Business Strategy* (March–April 1989), pp. 29–32.

87. M. A. Schilling and C. W. L. Hill, "Managing the New Product Development Process: Strategic Imperatives," *Academy of Management Executive* (August 1998), pp. 67–81.

88. J. R. Hauser and D. Clausing, "The House of Quality," *Harvard Business Review* (May–June 1988), pp. 63–73.

89. E. H. Kessler, P. E. Bierly III, and S. Gopalakrishnan, "Vasa Syndrome: Insights from a 17th-Century New-Product Disaster," *Academy of Management Executive* (August 2001), pp. 80–91.

90. M. A. Schilling and C. W. L. Hill, "Managing the New Product Development Process: Strategic Imperatives," *Academy of Management Executive* (August 1998), pp. 67–81.

91. J. B. Levin and R. D. Hof, "Has Philips Found Its Wizard?" *Business Week* (September 6, 1993), pp. 82–84.

92. O. Port, "Rating R&D: How Companies Get the Biggest Bang for the Buck," *Business Week* (July 5, 1993), p. 98.

93. I. Krause and J. Liu, "Benchmarking R&D Productivity," *Planning Review* (January/February 1993), pp. 16–21, 52–53.

94. L. Valikangas and P. Merlyn, "How Market-Based Organization Sustains Organic Innovation," *Business Strategy Review* (September 2002), pp. 3–6.

95. *Ibid.*, p. 4.

96. M. Stepanek, "Using the Net for Brainstorming," *Business Week E.Biz* (December 13, 1999), p. EB55. (See note 28 for *The Innovator's Dilemma.*)

97. *Ibid.*, pp. EB55–EB59.

98. "Robots," *Economist* (October 18, 2003), p. 98.

99. J. Fowler, "Vacuums Lead Surge in Household Robots," *Des Moines Register* (October 21, 2004), p. 3D.

100. *Ibid.*, p. 30.

Chapter 13

1. Summarized from N. L. Torres, "No Sweat," *Entrepreneur* (December 2004), p. 126.

2. "Small Business Resources for Faculty, Students, and Researchers: Answers to Frequently Asked Questions," *Small Business Advocate* (May 2004), p. 5.

3. W. J. Baumol, "Entrepreneurial Cultures and Countercultures," *Academy of Management Learning and Education* (September 2004), pp. 316–326; *The State of Small Business: A Report to the President* (Washington, DC: U.S. Government Printing Office, 1987), p. 117.

4. J. Castro, J. McDowell, and W. McWhirter, "Big vs. Small," *Time* (September 5, 1988), p. 49. This is supported by a 2003 study by the U.S. Small Business Administration which found that a small-firm patent is more likely than a large-firm patent to be among the top 1% of most frequently cited patents.

5. B. Headd, "Redefining Business Success: Distinguishing Between Closure and Failure," *Small Business Economics* (August 2003), as reported in "Frequency of Small Business Failure Reassessed by Advocacy Economist," *Small Business Advocate* (October 2003), p. 2.

6. M. J. Foster, "Scenario Planning for Small Businesses," *Long Range Planning* (February 1993), p. 123; M. S. S. El-Namacki, "Small Business—The Myth and the Reality," *Long Range Planning* (August 1990), p. 79.

7. J. Hopkins, "Study: New Company Failure Rate Not So High," *USA Today* (February 18, 2003), p. 1B. This article summarizes Brian Headd's 2003 study for the Small Business Administration. It revealed that after four years, the 50% that had closed included 33% that were considered unsuccessful. The remaining 17% were sold or closed but were considered successful by their founders. According to a study by Dun & Bradstreet of 800,000 small U.S. businesses started in 1985, 70% were still in business in March 1994. Contrary to other studies, this study counted firms as failures only if they owed money at the time of their demise. Also see J. Aley, "Debunking the Failure Fallacy," *Fortune* (September 6, 1993), p. 21.

8. R. N. Lussier, "Startup Business Advice from Business Owners to Would-Be Entrepreneurs," *SAM Advanced Management Journal* (Winter 1995), pp. 10–13.

9. J. W. Carland, F. Hoy, W. R. Boulton, and J. A. C. Carland, "Differentiating Entrepreneurs from Small Business Owners: A Conceptualization," *Academy of Management Review* (April 1984), p. 358; J. W. Carland, J. C. Carland, F. Hoy, and W. R. Boulton, "Distinctions Between Entrepreneurial and Small Business Ventures," *International Journal of Management* (March 1988), pp. 98–103.

10. S. P. Galante, "Counting on a Narrow Market Can Cloud Company's Future," *Wall Street Journal* (January 20, 1986), p. 17. Sexton's statement that entrepreneurial firms engage in more sophisticated strategic planning than do small businesses is supported by C. H. Matthews and S. G. Scott, "Uncertainty and Planning in Small Entrepreneurial Firms: An Empirical Assessment," *Journal of Small Business Management* (October 1995), pp. 34–52. See also W. H. Stewart, Jr., W. E. Watson,

J. C. Carland, and J. W. Carland, "A Proclivity for Entrepreneurship: A Comparison of Entrepreneurs, Small Business Owners, and Corporate Managers," *Journal of Business Venturing* (March 1999), pp. 189–214.

11. D. Fields, "Mrs. Fields' Weekends," *USA Weekend* (February 3–5, 1989), p. 16; M. Alpert, "In the Chips," *Fortune* (July 17, 1989), pp. 115–116.
12. J. S. Bracker, B. W. Keats, and J. N. Pearson, "Planning and Financial Performance Among Small Firms in a Growth Industry," *Strategic Management Journal* (November–December 1988), pp. 591–603; J. Kargar and J. A. Parnell, "Strategic Planning Emphasis and Planning Satisfaction in Small Firms: An Empirical Investigation," *Journal of Business Strategies* (Spring 1996), pp. 1–20; C. R. Schwenk and C. B. Shrader, "Effects of Formal Strategic Planning on Financial Performance in Small Firms: A Meta-Analysis," *Entrepreneurship Theory & Performance* (Spring 1993), pp. 53–64; L. W. Rue and N. A. Ibrahim, "The Relationship Between Planning Sophistication and Performance in Small Businesses," *Journal of Small Business Management* (October 1998), pp. 24–32.
13. W. H. Baker, H. Lon, and B. Davis, "Business Planning in Successful Small Firms," *Long Range Planning* (December 1993), pp. 82–88. Another study of 184 owner–managers of small businesses in the U.S. Midwest found that they were using strategic planning by formally documenting their mission (99%), objectives (95%), and strategies (93%). See D. F. Kuratko, J. C. Goodale, and J. S. Hornsby, "Quality Practices for a Competitive Advantage in Smaller Firms," *Journal of Small Business Management* (October 2001), pp. 293–311.
14. S. C. Perry, "The Relationship Between Written Business Plans and the Failure of Small Businesses in the U.S.," *Journal of Small Business Management* (July 2001), pp. 201–208.
15. D. B. Bradley III, "The Importance of Marketing Planning to Prevent Small Business Failure," paper presented to annual meeting of the Small Business Institute Directors Association (SBIDA) (San Diego, CA, February 7–9, 2002).
16. L. W. Rue and N. A. Ibrahim, "The Status of Planning in Smaller Family-Owned Businesses," *Family Business Review* (Spring 1996), pp. 29–43.
17. A. Thomas, "Less Is More: How Less Formal Planning Can Be Best," in *The Strategic Planning Management Reader*, edited by L. Fahey (Upper Saddle River, NJ: Prentice Hall, 1989), pp. 331–336; C. B. Shrader, C. L. Mulford, and V. L. Blackburn, "Strategic and Operational Planning, Uncertainty, and Performance in Small Firms," *Journal of Small Business Management* (October 1989), pp. 45–60.
18. R. B. Robinson, Jr., and J. A. Pearce II, "The Impact of Formalized Strategic Planning on Financial Performance in Small Organizations," *Strategic Management Journal* (July–September 1983), pp. 197–207; R. Ackelsberg and P. Arlow, "Small Businesses Do Plan and It Pays Off," *Long Range Planning* (October 1985), pp. 61–67.
19. M. Berry, "Strategic Planning in Small High-Tech Companies," *Long Range Planning* (June 1998), pp. 455–466.
20. F. Delmar and S. Shane, "Does Business Planning Facilitate the Development of New Ventures?" *Strategic Management Journal* (December 2003), pp. 1165–1185; S. Shane and F. Delmar, "Planning for the Market: Business Planning Before Marketing and the Continuation of Organizing Efforts," *Journal of Business Venturing* (November 2004), pp. 767–785.
21. T. Mazzarol, "Do Formal Business Plans Really Matter? A Survey of Small Business Owners in Australia," paper presented to the 45th International Conference on Small Business (ICSB) World Conference 2000 (Brisbane, Australia, June 7–10, 2000).
22. S. C. Perry, "The Relationship Between Written Business Plans and the Failure of Small Businesses in the U.S.," *Journal of Small Business Management* (July 2001), pp. 201–208.
23. V. Fowler, "Business Study Focuses on Failures," *Des Moines Register* (August 9, 1992), p. G1. For information on preparing a business plan, see R. Hisrich and M. Peters, *Entrepreneurship*, 6th ed. (New York: Irwin/McGraw-Hill, 2004).
24. M. K. Fiegener, B. M. Brown, D. R. Dreux IV, and W. J. Dennis, Jr., "CEO Stakes and Board Composition in Small Private Firms," *Entrepreneurship Theory & Practice* (Summer 2000), pp. 5–24.
25. L. W. Busenitz, D. D. Moesel, J. O. Fiet, and J. B. Barney, "The Framing of Perceptions of Fairness in the Relationship Between Venture Capitalists and New Venture Teams," *Entrepreneurship Theory & Practice* (Spring 1997), pp. 5–21.
26. V. H. Fried, G. D. Bruton, and R. D. Hisrich, "Strategy and the Board of Directors in Venture Capital–Backed Firms," *Journal of Business Venturing* (November 1999), pp. 493–503.
27. D. L. Sexton and F. I. Steele, *Leading Practices of Fast Growth Entrepreneurs* (Kansas City, MO: National Center for Entrepreneurship Research, 1997).
28. D. J. Garsombke and T. W. Garsombke, "An Empirical Investigation of the Utilization of External and Internal Boards of Directors and Management Advisory Assistance on the Performance of Small Businesses," *Journal of Business Strategies* (Fall 1996), pp. 167–184.
29. "Does Sarbanes-Oxley Hurt Shareholders and Hide Poor Management?" *Knowledge@Wharton* (November 17–30, 2004).
30. *Ibid.*
31. J. C. Shuman and J. A. Seeger, "The Theory and Practice of Strategic Management in Smaller Rapid Growth Firms," *American Journal of Small Business* (Summer 1986), p. 14.
32. R. C. Pineda, L. D. Lerner, M. C. Miller, and S. J. Phillips, "An Investigation of Factors Affecting the Information-Search Activities of Small Business Managers," *Journal of Small Business Management* (January 1998), pp. 60–71.
33. S. Birley and P. Westhead, "Growth and Performance Contrasts Between 'Types' of Small Firms," *Strategic Management Journal* (November–December 1990), pp. 535–557; J. L. Ward and C. E. Aronloff, "How Family Affects Strategy," *Small Business Forum* (Fall 1994), pp. 85–90.
34. P. Westhead, "Company Performance and Objectives Reported by First and Multi-Generation Family Companies: A Research Note," *Journal of Small Business and Enterprise Development*, Vol. 10, No. 1 (2003), pp. 93–105; J. Wiklund, P. Davidsson, and F. Delmar, "What Do They Think and Feel About Growth? An Expectancy-Value Approach to Small Business Managers' Attitudes Toward Growth," *Entrepreneurship Theory & Practice* (Spring 2003), pp. 247–270; A. Morrison, J. Breen, and S. Ali, "Small Business Growth: Intention, Ability, and Opportunity," *Journal of Small Business Management* (October 2003), pp. 417–425.
35. J. R. Baum, E. A. Locke, and K. G. Smith, "A Multidimensional Model of Venture Growth," *Academy of Management Journal* (April 2001), pp. 292–303; J. Florin, M. Lubatkin, and W. Schulze, "A Social Capital Model of High-Growth Ventures," *Academy of Management Journal* (June 2003), pp. 374–384.

36. J. Low and P. C. Kalafut, *Invisible Advantage: How Intangibles Are Driving Business Performance* (New York: Perseus Publishing, 2002), as reported in "Counting Intangible Assets," *Futurist* (September–October 2003), pp. 12–13.
37. P. F. Drucker, *Innovation and Entrepreneurship* (New York: HarperCollins, 1985), pp. 30–129.
38. F. Donnely, "Let zBox Accept Deliveries," *Des Moines Register* (October 31, 2000), p. TW1.
39. D. Stipp, "Inventor on the Verge of a Nervous Breakthrough," *Fortune* (March 29, 1999), pp. 104–117.
40. D. Whitford, "Taking BET Back from the Street," *Fortune* (November 9, 1998), pp. 167–170.
41. A. Bianchi, "Medical-Food Start-up Offers Tasty Treatments," *Inc.* (January 1997), p. 15.
42. C. W. Hofer and W. R. Sandberg, "Improving New Venture Performance: Some Guidelines for Success," *American Journal of Small Business* (Summer 1987), pp. 12–23. See also J. J. Chrisman and A. Bauerschmidt, "New Venture Performance: Some Critical Extensions to the Model," paper presented to the State-of-the-Art Symposium on Entrepreneurship (Ames: Iowa State University, April 12–14, 1992).
43. K. C. Robinson, "An Examination of the Influence of Industry Structure on Eight Alternative Measures of New Venture Performance for High Potential Independent New Ventures," *Journal of Business Venturing* (March 1999), pp. 165–187.
44. Interview with C. Bagley by J. Useem, "Forget Patents, Says Stanford Prof," *Inc.* (October 1996), p. 23.
45. K. C. Robinson, "An Examination of the Influence of Industry Structure on Eight Alternative Measures of New Venture Performance for High Potential Independent New Ventures," *Journal of Business Venturing* (March 1999), pp. 165–187.
46. J. Wade, "A Community-Level Analysis of Sources and Rates of Technological Variation in the Microprocessor Market," *Academy of Management Journal* (October 1996), pp. 1218–1244.
47. Supported by R. C. Shrader and M. Simon, "Corporate Versus Independent New Ventures: Resources, Strategy, and Performance Differences," *Journal of Business Venturing* (January 1997), pp. 47–66; R. Tonge, P. C. Larsen, and M. Ito, "Strategic Leadership in Super-Growth Companies—A Reappraisal," *Long Range Planning* (December 1998), pp. 838–847; G. Qian and L. Li, "Profitability of Small- and Medium-Sized Enterprises in High-Tech Industries: The Case of the Biotechnology Industry," *Strategic Management Journal* (September 2003), pp. 881–887.
48. K. M. Weaver and P. Dickson, "Strategic Alliances," *NFIB National Small Business Poll*, Vol. 4, Issue 4 (2004).
49. J. R. Baum, E. A. Locke, and K. G. Smith, "A Multidimensional Model of Venture Growth," *Academy of Management Journal* (April 2001), pp. 292–303; A. C. Cooper, G. E. Willard, and C. Y. Woo, "A Reexamination of the Niche Concept," in *The Strategy Process: Concepts, Contexts, and Cases*, 2nd ed., edited by H. Mintzberg and J. B. Quinn (Upper Saddle River, NJ: Prentice Hall, 1991), pp. 619–628; P. P. McDougal, J. G. Covin, R. B. Robinson, Jr., and L. Herron, "The Effects of Industry Growth and Strategic Breadth on New Venture Performance and Strategy Content," *Strategic Management Journal* (September 1994), pp. 537–554; C. E. Bamford, T. J. Dean, and P. P. McDougall, "Initial Strategies and New Venture Growth: An Examination of the Effectiveness of Broad vs. Narrow Breadth Strategies," in *Frontiers of Entrepreneurial Research*, edited by P. D. Reynolds, et al. (Babson Park, MA: Babson College, 1997), pp. 375–389; G. H. Lim, K. S. Lee, and S. J. Tan, "SMEs' Market Entry Strategy: Substitution Instead of Niching," paper presented to the International Council for Small Business Conference (Naples, Italy, June 1999).
50. J. Wiklund and D. Shepherd, "Knowledge-Based Resources, Entrepreneurial Orientation, and the Performance of Small and Medium-Sized Businesses," *Strategic Management Journal* (December 2003), pp. 1307–1314; J. Kickul and L. K. Gundry, "Prospecting for Strategic Advantage: The Proactive Entrepreneurial Personality and Small Firm Innovation," *Journal of Small Business Management* (April 2002), pp. 85–97.
51. H. P. Welsch, "Entrepreneurs' Personal Characteristics: Causal Models," paper presented to the State-of-the-Art Symposium on Entrepreneurship (Ames: Iowa State University, April 12–14, 1992); A. Rahim, "Stress, Strain, and Their Moderators: An Empirical Comparison of Entrepreneurs and Managers," *Journal of Small Business Management* (January 1996), pp. 46–58; C. Korunka, H. Frank, M. Lueger, and J. Mugler, "The Entrepreneurial Personality in the Context of Resources, Environment, and the Startup Process—A Configurational Approach," *Entrepreneurship Theory & Practice* (Fall 2003), pp. 23–42.
52. M. Kets de Vries, "The Dark Side of Entrepreneurship," *Harvard Business Review* (November–December 1985), pp. 160–167.
53. A. C. Cooper, F. J. Gimeno-Gascon, and C. Y. Woo, "Initial Human and Financial Capital as Predictors of New Venture Performance," *Journal of Business Venturing* (Volume 9, 1994), pp. 371–395; H. R. Feeser and G. E. Willard, "Founding Strategies and Performance in High-Tech Firms," in *Handbook of Business Strategy, 1991/92 Yearbook*, edited by H. E. Glass and M. A. Hovde (Boston: Warren, Gorham & Lamont, 1991), pp. 2.1–2.18.
54. R. Ricklefs and U. Gupta, "Traumas of a New Entrepreneur," *Wall Street Journal* (May 10, 1989), p. B1.
55. N. C. Churchill and V. L. Lewis, "The Five Stages of Small Business Growth," *Harvard Business Review* (May–June 1983), pp. 30–50. The life cycle concept is supported by research by M. Beverland, "Organizational Life Cycles in Small Enterprises," paper presented to the 45th International Conference on Small Business (ICSB) World Conference (Brisbane, Australia, June 7–10, 2000).
56. J. W. Petty and W. D. Bygrave, "What Does Finance Have to Say to the Entrepreneur?" *Journal of Small Business Finance* (Spring 1993), pp. 125–137.
57. K. D. Brouthers, F. Andriessen, and J. Nicolaes, "Driving Blind: Strategic Decision-Making in Small Companies," *Long Range Planning* (February 1998), pp. 130–138.
58. See C. Farrell, K. Rebello, R. D. Hof, and M. Maremont, "The Boom in IPOs," *Business Week* (December 18, 1995), pp. 64–72, and S. Gruner, "When Mom & Pop Go Public," *Inc.* (December 1996), pp. 66–73.
59. A. Caruana, M. H. Morris, and A. J. Vella, "The Effect of Centralization and Formalization on Entrepreneurship in Export Firms," *Journal of Small Business Management* (January 1998), pp. 16–29.
60. F. David, D. Kelley, and F. David, "Small Business Owner Succession Planning: An Empirical Study," *Management in Practice*, Society for the Advancement of Management, No. 1 (2002), p. 3.

61. M. C. Sonfield, R. N. Lussier, S. Pfeifer, S. Manikutty, L. Maherault, and L. Verdier, "A Cross-National Investigation of First-Generation and Subsequent-Generation Family Members," paper presented to the Small Business Institute Conference (Clearwater, FL, February 12–14, 2004).
62. J. Magretta, "Governing the Family-Owned Enterprise: An Interview with Finland's Krister Ahlstrom," *Harvard Business Review* (January–February 1998), pp. 113–123.
63. "Passing on the Crown," *Economist* (November 6, 2004), pp. 69–71.
64. M. K. Allio, "Family Businesses: Their Virtues, Vices, and Strategic Path," *Strategy & Leadership*, Vol. 32, No. 4 (2004), pp. 24–33; J. Weber, L. Lavelle, T. Lowry, W. Zellner, and A. Barrett, "Family, Inc.," *Business Week* (November 10, 2003), pp. 100–114.
65. S. Birley, D. Ng, and A. Godfrey, "The Family and the Business," *Long Range Planning* (December 1999), pp. 598–608; "Passing on the Crown," *Economist* (November 6, 2004), pp. 69–71.
66. J. Magretta, "Governing the Family-Owned Enterprise: An Interview with Finland's Krister Ahlstrom," *Harvard Business Review* (January–February 1998), p. 119.
67. "Family Business: Why Firms Do Well When Founders Are at the Helm?" *Knowledge @ Wharton* (October 20–November 2, 2004).
68. N. C. Churchill and K. J. Hatten, "Non-Market-Based Transfers of Wealth and Power: A Research Framework for Family Businesses," *American Journal of Small Business* (Winter 1987), pp. 51–64.
69. J. L. Ward and C. E. Aronoff, "Shirt Sleeves to Shirt Sleeves," *Nation's Business* (September 1992), pp. 62–63.
70. "Passing on the Crown," *Economist* (November 6, 2004), pp. 69–71.
71. J. Applegate, "Business People in Bermuda Get Sloppy Without Taxes," *Des Moines Register* (July 6, 1992), p. 8B.
72. P. L. Huff, R. M. Harper, Jr., and A. E. Eikner, "Are There Differences in Liquidity and Solvency Measures Based on Company Size?" *American Business Review* (June 1999), pp. 96–106.
73. R. I. Levin and V. R. Travis, "Small Company Finance: What the Books Don't Say," *Harvard Business Review* (November–December 1987), pp. 30–32.
74. M. Gladwell, *The Tipping Point* (New York: Little, Brown and Co., 2000).
75. M. Henricks, "Big Tippers," *Entrepreneur* (December 2000), pp. 95–96.
76. D. Brady, "The Brains Behind Blackberry," *Business Week* (April 19, 2004), pp. 55–56.
77. *Pocket World in Figures 2004* (London: Economist and Profile Books, 2003), p. 58.
78. R. Florida, "Breakthrough Ideas for 2004: No Monopoly on Creativity," *Harvard Business Review* (February 2004), pp. 14–15.

Chapter 14

1. R. Imrie, "Ink Venture Reaps Profits for High-Tech Monks," *Des Moines Register* (February 27, 2004), p. 3D; G. Williams, "Charity Begins at Work," *Entrepreneur* (December 2005), p. 40.
2. C. Penttila, "Heart of Gold," *Entrepreneur* (September 2004), pp. 19–22.
3. *Ibid.*, p. 22.
4. P. F. Drucker, "What Business Can Learn from Nonprofits," *Harvard Business Review* (July–August 1989), p. 89.
5. "The Non-Profit Sector: Love or Money," *The Economist* (November 14, 1998), pp. 68–73.
6. G. Rudney, "The Scope and Dimensions of Nonprofit Activity," in *The Nonprofit Sector: A Research Handbook*, edited by W. W. Powell (New Haven, CT: Yale University Press, 1987), p. 56; C. P. McLaughlin, *The Management of Nonprofit Organizations* (New York: John Wiley & Sons, 1986), p. 4.
7. M. O'Neill, *The Third America* (San Francisco: Jossey-Bass, 1989).
8. K. Ascher and B. Nare, "Strategic Planning in the Public Sector," *International Review of Strategic Management*, Vol. 1, edited by D. E. Hussey (New York: John Wiley & Sons, 1990), pp. 297–315; I. Unterman and R. H. Davis, *Strategic Management of Not-for-Profit Organizations* (New York: Praeger Press, 1984), p. 2.
9. P. V. Jenster and G. A. Overstreet, "Planning for a Non-Profit Service: A Study of U.S. Credit Unions," *Long Range Planning* (April 1990), pp. 103–111; G. J. Medley, "Strategic Planning for the World Wildlife Fund," *Long Range Planning* (February 1988), pp. 46–54.
10. J. G. Simon, "The Tax Treatment of Nonprofit Organizations: A Review of Federal and State Policies," in *The Nonprofit Sector: A Research Handbook*, edited by W. W. Powell (New Haven, CT: Yale University Press, 1987), pp. 67–98.
11. B. P. Keating and M. O. Keating, *Not-for-Profit* (Glen Ridge, NJ: Thomas Horton & Daughters, 1980), p. 21.
12. K. A. Froelich, "Business Management in Nonprofit Organizations," paper presented to the Midwest Management Society (Chicago, 1995).
13. J. D. Hunger and T. L. Wheelen, "Is Strategic Management Appropriate for Not-for-Profit Organizations?" in *Handbook of Business Strategy, 1989/90 Yearbook*, edited by H. E. Glass (Boston: Warren, Gorham & Lamont, 1989), pp. 3.1–3.8. The contention that the pattern of environmental influence on the organization's strategic decision making derives from the organization's source(s) of income agrees with the authorities in the field. See R. E. Emerson, "Power-Dependence Relations," *American Sociological Review* (February 1962), pp. 31–41; J. D. Thompson, *Organizations in Action* (New York: McGraw-Hill, 1967), pp. 30–31, and J. Pfeffer and G. R. Salancik, *The External Control of Organizations: A Resource Dependence Perspective* (New York: HarperCollins, 1978), p. 44.
14. M. Goold, "Institutional Advantage: A Way into Strategic Management in Not-for-Profit Organizations," *Long Range Planning* (April 1997), pp. 291–293.
15. K. Ascher and B. Nare, "Strategic Planning in the Public Sector," *International Review of Strategic Management*, Vol. 1, edited by D. E. Hussey (New York: John Wiley & Sons, 1990), pp. 297–315; R. McGill, "Planning for Strategic Performance in Local Government," *Long Range Planning* (October 1988), pp. 77–84.
16. Lorna Lavender, Supervisor of Ames (Iowa) Animal Shelter, quoted by K. Petty, "Animal Shelter Cares for Homeless," *ISU Daily* (July 25, 1996), p. 3.
17. E. Ferlie, "The Creation and Evolution of Quasi Markets in the Public Sector: A Problem for Strategic Management," *Strategic Management Journal* (Winter 1992), pp. 79–97. Research has found that profit-making hospitals have more mission statement

components dealing with principal services, target customers, and geographic domain than do not-for-profit hospitals. See R. Subramanian, K. Kumar, and C. C. Yauger, "Mission Statements of Hospitals: An Empirical Analysis of Their Contents and Their Relationship to Organizational Factors," *Journal of Business Strategies* (Spring 1993), pp. 63–78.

18. W. H. Newman and H. W. Wallender III, "Managing Not-for-Profit Enterprises," *Academy of Management Review* (January 1978), p. 26.

19. *Ibid.*, p. 27. The following discussion of the effects of these constraining characteristics is taken from pp. 27–31.

20. J. Denis, A. Langley, and D. Lozeau, "Formal Strategy in Public Hospitals," *Long Range Planning* (February 1991), pp. 71–82.

21. F. Heffron, *Organization Theory and Public Administration* (Upper Saddle River, NJ: Prentice Hall, 1989), p. 132.

22. V. K. Rangan, "Lofty Missions, Down-to-Earth Plans," *Harvard Business Review* (March 2004), pp. 112–119.

23. F. Heffron, *Organization Theory and Public Administration* (Upper Saddle River, NJ: Prentice Hall, 1989), pp. 103–115.

24. R. T. Ingram, *Ten Basic Responsibilities of Nonprofit Boards*, 2nd ed. (Washington, DC: National Center for Nonprofit Boards, 1997), pp. 9–10.

25. A. C. Smith, "Endowment Use Overlooked," *St. Petersburg Times* (June 23, 2000), p. 3B. Eckerd's board was strongly criticized because it had tolerated improper financial practices on the part of the president and had allowed the college's endowment to dissipate.

26. I. Unterman and R. H. Davis, *Strategic Management of Not-for-Profit Organizations* (New York: Praeger Press, 1984), p. 174; J. A. Alexander, M. L. Fennell, and M. T. Halpern, "Leadership Instability in Hospitals: The Influence of Board–CEO Relations and Organizational Growth and Decline," *Administrative Science Quarterly* (March 1993), pp. 74–99.

27. K. A. Froelich, "Business Management in Nonprofit Organizations," paper presented to the Midwest Management Society (Chicago, 1995), p. 9.

28. R. M. Kanter and D. V. Summers, "Doing Well While Doing Good: Dilemmas of Performance Measurement in Nonprofit Organizations and the Need for a Multiple-Constituency Approach," in *The Nonprofit Sector: A Research Handbook*, edited by W. W. Powell (New Haven, CT: Yale University Press, 1987), p. 163.

29. J. P. Dalsimer, *Understanding Nonprofit Financial Statement: A Primer for Board Members*, 2nd ed. (Washington, DC: National Center for Nonprofit Boards, 1997), p. 17.

30. V. K. Rangan, "Loft Missions: Down-to-Earth Plans," *Harvard Business Review* (March 2004), pp. 112–119.

31. *Ibid.*, p. 115.

32. R. P. Nielsen, "SMR Forum: Strategic Piggybacking—A Self-Subsidizing Strategy for Nonprofit Institutions," *Sloan Management Review* (Summer 1982), pp. 65–69; R. P. Nielsen, "Piggybacking for Business and Nonprofits: A Strategy for Hard Times," *Long Range Planning* (April 1984), pp. 96–102.

33. D. C. Bacon, "Nonprofit Groups: An Unfair Edge?" *Nation's Business* (April 1989), pp. 33–34; "Universities Push Auxiliary Services to Generate More Revenue," *Wall Street Journal* (April 27, 1995), p. A1.

34. M. Langley, "Nonprofit Hospitals Sometimes Are That in Little but Name," *Wall Street Journal* (July 14, 1997), p. A1. See also D. Brady, "When Nonprofits Go After Profits," *Business Week* (June 26, 2000), pp. 173–178; E. Skloot, "Should Not-for-Profits Go into Business?" *Harvard Business Review* (January–February 1983), p. 21; E. Felsenthal, "As Nonprofits Add Sidelines, IRS Takes Aim," *Wall Street Journal* (May 3, 1996), p. B1.

35. C. Penttila, "Heart of Gold," *Entrepreneur* (September 2004), p. 22.

36. R. P. Nielsen, "Piggybacking Strategies for Nonprofits: A Shared Costs Approach," *Strategic Management Journal* (May–June 1986), pp. 209–211.

37. "Universities Push Auxiliary Services to Generate More Revenue" (Business Bulletin), *Wall Street Journal* (April 27, 1995), p. A1.

38. R. A. Krishnan, S. Joshi, and H. Krishnan, "The Influence of Mergers on Firms' Product-Mix Strategies," *Strategic Management Journal* (June 2004), pp. 587–611.

39. *Ibid.*

40. K. G. Provan, "Interorganizational Cooperation and Decision Making Autonomy in a Consortium Multihospital System," *Academy of Management Review* (July 1984), pp. 494–504; R. D. Luke, J. W. Begun, and D. D. Pointer, "Quasi-Firms: Strategic Interorganizational Forms in the Health Care Industry," *Academy of Management Review* (January 1989), pp. 9–19.

41. "More Colleges Are Opting for Mergers," *The (Ames, IA) Daily Tribune* (August 12, 1998), p. B3.

42. *Pocket World in Figures 2004* (London: Economist and Profile Books, 2003), p. 95.

43. *Ibid.*, p. 83.

Chapter 15

1. M. Heimer, "Wall Street Sherlock," *Smart Money* (July 2003), pp. 103–107.

2. *Ibid.*, p. 107.

3. *Ibid.*, p. 105.

4. *Ibid.*, p. 105.

5. *Ibid.*, p. 105.

6. M. Vanac, "What's a Novice Investor to Do?" *Des Moines Register* (November 30, 1997), p. 3G.

7. A. R. Sorking, "New Path on Mergers Could Contain Loopholes," *The (Ames, IA) Daily Tribune* (January 9, 2001), p. B7; "Firms Resist Effort to Unveil True Costs of Doing Business," *USA Today* (July 3, 2000), p. 10A.

8. M. S. Fridson, *Financial Statement Analysis* (New York: John Wiley & Sons, 1991), pp. 192–194.

9. D. H. Bangs, *Managing by the Numbers* (Dover, NH: Upstart Publications, 1992), pp. 106–107.

10. "Consumer Prices," *Economist* (May 8, 2004), p. 98.

Cases in Strategic Management

Cases in Strategic Management

CONTENTS

Section A
Corporate Governance, Social Responsibility, and Executive Leadership

Section B
Ethics and Social Responsibility

Section C
International Issues in Strategic Management

Section D
General Issues in Strategic Management

Industry One—Information Technology

Industry Two—Internet Companies

Industry Three—Recreation and Transportation

Industry Four—Mass Merchandising

Industry Five—Specialty Retailers

Industry Six—Entrepreneurial Ventures

Industry Seven—Manufacturing

Industry Eight—Beverage/Food

Section E

Issues in Not-For-Profit Organizations

Section F

Mini-Cases

Alphabetical Listing of Cases

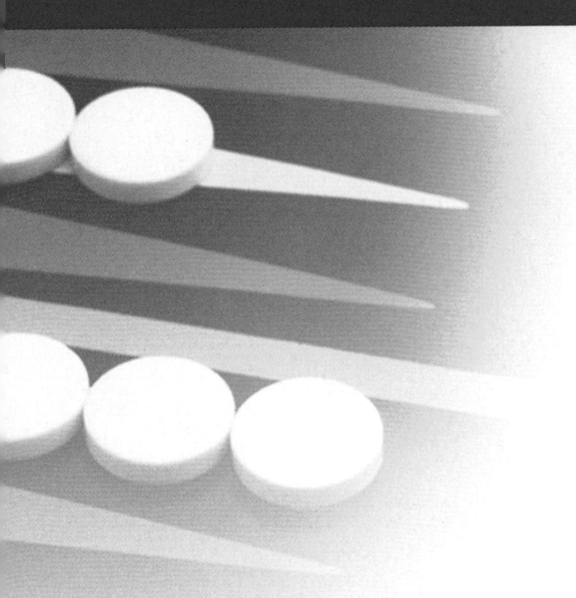

Alphabetical Listing of Cases

Airtran Holdings, Inc., Case 35

Amazon.com, Case 13

AOL Time Warner, Inc., Case 15

Apple Computer and Steve Jobs (2006), Case 10

Audit, Case 4

A.W.A.R.E., Case 33

Boeing Company's Board of Directors Fires the CEO, Case 3

Boise Cascade/Office Max, Case 36

Carey Plant, Case 28

Carnival Corporation & plc (2006), Case 18

Church & Dwight Builds a Corporate Portfolio, Case 32

Dell, Inc., Case 37

eBay, Inc., Case 12

Eli Lilly, Web Case 1

Everyone Does It, Case 5

Gap Inc., Case 21

GlaxoSmithKline's Retaliation Against Cross-Border Sales of Prescription Drugs, Case 6

Google, Case 14

Guajilote Cooperativo Forestal, Honduras Case 9

H. J. Heinz Company, Case 39

Haier Group: U.S. Expansion, Case 26

Harley-Davidson, Inc., 2006, Case 16

Hasbro, Inc., Case 25

Hershey Foods Company, Case 29

Home Depot, Inc. 2006, Case 20

Inner-City Paint Corporation (Revised), Case 24

Invacare Corporation, 2004, Case 27

Intel Corporation, Case 34

JetBlue Airways' Success Story, Case 17

Lowe's Companies, Inc., Case 40

McAfee 2005, Case 11

Movie Gallery, Inc., Case 43

Nike, Inc., Case 41

Oprah Winfrey, Case 23

Outback Steakhouse, Inc., Case 42

Panera Bread Company, Case 30

Pfizer, Inc., Web Case 5

Recalcitrant Director at Byte Products, Inc., Case 1

Six Flags, Inc., Case 38

Southwest Airlines Company, Web Case 8

Starbucks' International Operations, Case 7

Stryker Corporation, Web Case 3

Sykes Enterprises, Web Case 4

Tech Data Corporation, Web Case 2

Tiffany & Co., Case 22

Turkcell, Case 8

Tyson Foods, Inc., Web Case 7

Wallace Group, Case 2

Wal-Mart Stores, Inc., Case 19

Whole Foods Market, Case 31

Williams-Sonoma, Web Case 6

CASE 1

The Recalcitrant Director at Byte Products, Inc.: Corporate Legality Versus Corporate Responsibility

Dan R. Dalton, Richard A. Cosier, and Cathy A. Enz

BYTE PRODUCTS, INC., IS PRIMARILY INVOLVED IN THE PRODUCTION OF ELECTRONIC components that are used in personal computers. Although such components might be found in a few computers in home use, Byte products are found most frequently in computers used for sophisticated business and engineering applications. Annual sales of these products have been steadily increasing over the past several years; Byte Products, Inc., currently has total sales of approximately $265 million.

Over the past six years, increases in yearly revenues have consistently reached 12%. Byte Products, Inc., headquartered in the midwestern United States, is regarded as one of the largest-volume suppliers of specialized components and is easily the industry leader, with some 32% market share. Unfortunately for Byte, many new firms—domestic and foreign—have entered the industry. A dramatic surge in demand, high profitability, and the relative ease of a new firm's entry into the industry explain in part the increased number of competing firms.

Although Byte management—and presumably shareholders as well—is very pleased about the growth of its markets, it faces a major problem: Byte simply cannot meet the demand for these components. The company currently operates three manufacturing facilities in various locations throughout the United States. Each of these plants operates three production shifts (24 hours per day), 7 days a week. This activity constitutes virtually all of the company's production capacity. Without an additional manufacturing plant, Byte simply cannot increase its output of components.

This case was prepared by Professors Dan R. Dalton and Richard A. Cosier of the Graduate School of Business at Indiana University and Professor Cathy A. Enz of Cornell University. The names of the organization, individual, location, and/or financial information have been disguised to preserve the organization's desire for anonymity. This case was edited for SMBP-9th, 10th and 11th Editions. Reprint permission is solely granted to the publisher, Prentice Hall, for the books, Strategic Management and Business Policy—11th Edition and cases in Strategic Management and Business Policy—11th Edition by copyright holders, Dan R. Dalton, Richard A. Cosier and Cathy Enz. Any other publication of this case (translation, any form of electronic or other media), or sold (any form of partnership) to another publisher will be in violation of copyright laws, unless the copyright holders have granted an additional written reprint permission.

James M. Elliott, Chief Executive Officer and Chairman of the Board, recognizes the gravity of the problem. If Byte Products cannot continue to manufacture components in sufficient numbers to meet the demand, buyers will go elsewhere. Worse yet is the possibility that any continued lack of supply will encourage others to enter the market. As a long-term solution to this problem, the Board of Directors unanimously authorized the construction of a new, state-of-the-art manufacturing facility in the southwestern United States. When the planned capacity of this plant is added to that of the three current plants, Byte should be able to meet demand for many years to come. Unfortunately, an estimated three years will be required to complete the plant and bring it online.

Jim Elliott believes very strongly that this three-year period is far too long and has insisted that there also be a shorter-range, stopgap solution while the plant is under construction. The instability of the market and the pressure to maintain leader status are two factors contributing to Elliott's insistence on a more immediate solution. Without such a move, Byte management believes that it will lose market share and, again, attract competitors into the market.

Several Solutions

A number of suggestions for such a temporary measure were offered by various staff specialists but rejected by Elliott. For example, licensing Byte's product and process technology to other manufacturers in the short run to meet immediate demand was possible. This licensing authorization would be short term, or just until the new plant could come online. Top management, as well as the board, was uncomfortable with this solution for several reasons. They thought it unlikely that any manufacturer would shoulder the fixed costs of producing appropriate components for such a short term. Any manufacturer that would do so would charge a premium to recover its costs. This suggestion, obviously, would make Byte's own products available to its customers at an unacceptable price. Nor did passing any price increase to its customers seem sensible, for this too would almost certainly reduce Byte's market share as well as encourage further competition.

Overseas facilities and licensing also were considered but rejected. Before it became a publicly traded company, Byte's founders had decided that its manufacturing facilities would be domestic. Top management strongly felt that this strategy had served Byte well; moreover, Byte's majority stockholders (initial owners of the then privately held Byte) were not likely to endorse such a move. Beyond that, however, top management was reluctant to foreign license—or make available by any means the technologies for others to produce Byte products—as they could not then properly control patents. Top management feared that foreign licensing would essentially give away costly proprietary information regarding the company's highly efficient means of product development. There also was the potential for initial low product quality—whether produced domestically or otherwise—especially for such a short-run operation. Any reduction in quality, however brief, would threaten Byte's share of this sensitive market.

The Solution!

One recommendation that has come to the attention of the Chief Executive Officer could help solve Byte's problem in the short run. Certain members of his staff have notified him that an abandoned plant currently is available in Plainville, a small town in the northeastern United States. Before its closing eight years before, this plant was used primarily for the manufacture of electronic components. As is, it could not possibly be used to produce Byte products, but it could be inexpensively refitted to do so in as few as three months. Moreover, this plant is available at a very attractive price. In fact, discreet inquiries by Elliott's staff indicate that this plant could probably be leased immediately from its present owners because the building has been vacant for some eight years.

All the news about this temporary plant proposal, however, is not nearly so positive. Elliott's staff concedes that this plant will never be efficient and its profitability will be low. In addition, the Plainville location is a poor one in terms of high labor costs (the area is highly unionized), warehousing expenses, and inadequate transportation links to Byte's major markets and suppliers. Plainville is simply not a candidate for a long-term solution. Still, in the short run, a temporary plant could help meet the demand and might forestall additional competition.

The staff is persuasive and notes that this option has several advantages: (1) there is no need for any licensing, foreign or domestic, (2) quality control remains firmly in the company's hands, and (3) an increase in the product price will be unnecessary. The temporary plant, then, would be used for three years or so until the new plant could be built. Then the temporary plant would be immediately closed.

CEO Elliott is convinced.

Taking the Plan to the Board

The quarterly meeting of the Board of Directors is set to commence at 2:00 P.M. Jim Elliott has been reviewing his notes and agenda for the meeting most of the morning. The issue of the temporary plant is clearly the most important agenda item. Reviewing his detailed presentation of this matter, including the associated financial analyses, has occupied much of his time for several days. All the available information underscores his contention that the temporary plant in Plainville is the only responsible solution to the demand problems. No other option offers the same low level of risk and ensures Byte's status as industry leader.

At the meeting, after the board has dispensed with a number of routine matters, Jim Elliott turns his attention to the temporary plant. In short order, he advises the 11-member board (himself, 3 additional inside members, and 7 outside members) of his proposal to obtain and refit the existing plant to ameliorate demand problems in the short run, authorizes the construction of the new plant (the completion of which is estimated to take some three years), and plans to switch capacity from the temporary plant to the new one when it is operational. He also briefly reviews additional details concerning the costs involved, advantages of this proposal versus domestic or foreign licensing, and so on.

All the board members except one are in favor of the proposal. In fact, they are most enthusiastic; the overwhelming majority agree that the temporary plant is an excellent—even inspired—stopgap measure. Ten of the eleven board members seem relieved because the board was most reluctant to endorse any of the other alternatives that had been mentioned.

The single dissenter—T. Kevin Williams, an outside director—is, however, steadfast in his objections. He will not, under any circumstances, endorse the notion of the temporary plant and states rather strongly that "I will not be party to this nonsense, not now, not ever."

T. Kevin Williams, the senior executive of a major nonprofit organization, is normally a reserved and really quite agreeable person. This sudden, uncharacteristic burst of emotion clearly startles the remaining board members into silence. The following excerpt captures the ensuing, essentially one-on-one conversation between Williams and Elliott:

Williams: How many workers do your people estimate will be employed in the temporary plant?

Elliott: Roughly 1,200, possibly a few more.

Williams: I presume it would be fair, then, to say that, including spouses and children, something on the order of 4,000 people will be attracted to the community.

Elliott: I certainly would not be surprised.

Williams: If I understand the situation correctly, this plant closed just over eight years ago, and that closing had a catastrophic effect on Plainville. Isn't it true that a large portion of the community was employed by this plant?

Elliott: Yes, it was far and away the majority employer.

Williams: And most of these people have left the community, presumably to find employment elsewhere.

Elliott: Definitely, there was a drastic decrease in the area's population.

Williams: Are you concerned, then, that our company can attract the 1,200 employees to Plainville from other parts of New England?

Elliott: Not in the least. We are absolutely confident that we will attract 1,200—even more, for that matter virtually any number we need. That, in fact, is one of the chief advantages of this proposal. I would think that the community would be very pleased to have us there.

Williams: On the contrary, I would suspect that the community will rue the day we arrived. Beyond that, though, this plan is totally unworkable if we are candid. On the other hand, if we are less than candid, the proposal will work for us, but only at great cost to Plainville. In fact, quite frankly, the implications are appalling. Once again, I must enter my serious objections.

Elliott: I don't follow you.

Williams: The temporary plant would employ some 1,200 people. Again, this means the infusion of over 4,000 to the community and surrounding areas. Byte Products, however, intends to close this plant in three years or less. If Byte informs the community or the employees that the jobs are temporary, the proposal simply won't work. When the new people arrive in the community, there will be a need for more schools, instructors, utilities, housing, restaurants, and so forth. Obviously, if the banks and local government know that the plant is temporary, no funding will be made available for these projects and certainly no credit for the new employees to buy homes, appliances, automobiles, and so forth.

If, on the other hand, Byte Products does not tell the community of its "temporary" plans, the project can go on. But, in several years when the plant closes (and we here have agreed today that it will close), we will have created a ghost town. The tax base of the community will have been destroyed; property values will decrease precipitously; practically the whole town will be unemployed. This proposal will place Byte Products in an untenable position and in extreme jeopardy.

Elliott: Are you suggesting that this proposal jeopardizes us legally? If so, it should be noted that the legal department has reviewed this proposal in its entirety and has indicated no problem.

Williams: No! I don't think we are dealing with an issue of legality here. In fact, I don't doubt for a minute that this proposal is altogether legal. I do, however, resolutely believe that this proposal constitutes gross irresponsibility.

I think this decision has captured most of my major concerns. These along with a host of collateral problems associated with this project lead me to strongly suggest that you and the balance of the board reconsider and not endorse this proposal. Byte Products must find another way.

The Dilemma

After a short recess, the board meeting reconvened. Presumably because of some discussion during the recess, several other board members indicated that they were no longer inclined to support the proposal. After a short period of rather heated discussion, the following exchange took place:

Elliott: It appears to me that any vote on this matter is likely to be very close. Given the gravity of our demand capacity problem, I must insist that the stockholders' equity be protected. We cannot wait three years; that is clearly out of the question. I still feel that licensing—domestic or foreign—is not in our long-term interests for any number of reasons, some of which have been discussed here. On the other hand, I do not want to take this project forward on the strength of a mixed vote. A vote of 6–5 or 7–4, for example, does not indicate that the board is remotely close to being of one mind. Mr. Williams, is there a compromise to be reached?

Williams: Respectfully, I have to say no. If we tell the truth—namely, the temporary nature of our operations—the proposal is simply not viable. If we are less than candid in this respect, we do grave damage to the community as well as to our image. It seems to me that we can only go one way or the other. I don't see a middle ground.

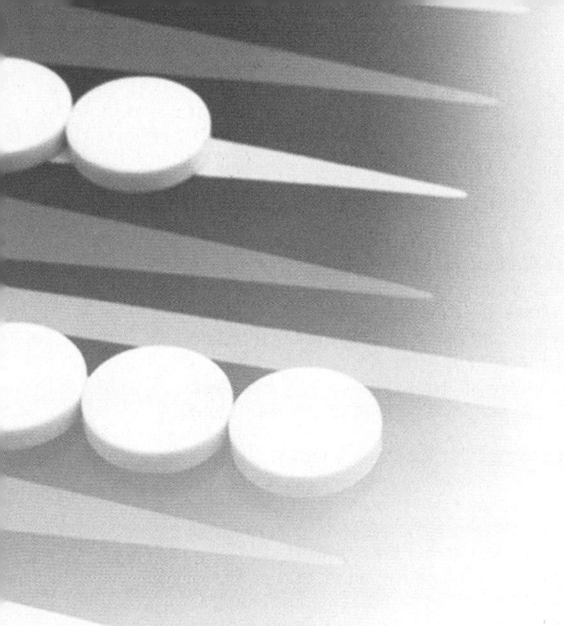

CASE 2
The Wallace Group

Laurence J. Stybel

Frances Rampar, President of Rampar Associates, drummed her fingers on the desk. Scattered before her were her notes. She had to put the pieces together in order to make an effective sales presentation to Harold Wallace.

Hal Wallace was the President of The Wallace Group. He had asked Rampar to conduct a series of interviews with some key Wallace Group employees, in preparation for a possible consulting assignment for Rampar Associates.

During the past three days, Rampar had been talking with some of these key people and had received background material about the company. The problem was not in finding the problem. The problem was that there were too many problems!

Background on The Wallace Group

The Wallace Group, Inc., is a diversified company dealing in the manufacture and development of technical products and systems (see **Exhibit 1**). The company currently consists of three operational groups and a corporate staff. The three groups include Electronics, Plastics, and Chemicals, each operating under the direction of a Group Vice President (see **Exhibits 2, 3,** and **4**). The company generates $70 million in sales as a manufacturer of plastics, chemical products, and electronic components and systems. Principal sales are to large contractors in governmental and automotive markets. With respect to sales volume, Plastics and Chemicals are approximately equal in size, and both of them together equal the size of the Electronics Group.

Electronics offers competence in the areas of microelectronics, electromagnetic sensors, antennas, microwave, and minicomputers. Presently, these skills are devoted primarily to the engineering and manufacture of countermeasure equipment for aircraft. This includes radar detection systems that allow an aircraft crew to know that they are being tracked by radar

Exhibit 1
An Excerpt from the Annual Report

To the Shareholders:

This past year was one of definite accomplishment for The Wallace Group, although with some admitted soft spots. This is a period of consolidation, of strengthening our internal capacity for future growth and development. Presently, we are in the process of creating a strong management team to meet the challenges we will set for the future.

Despite our failure to achieve some objectives, we turned a profit of $3,521,000 before taxes, which was a growth over the previous year's earnings. And we have declared a dividend for the fifth consecutive year, albeit one that is less than the year before. However, the retention of earnings is imperative if we are to lay a firm foundation for future accomplishment.

Currently, The Wallace Group has achieved a level of stability. We have a firm foothold in our current markets, and we could elect to simply enact strong internal controls and maximize our profits. However, this would not be a growth strategy. Instead, we have chosen to adopt a more aggressive posture for the future, to reach out into new markets wherever possible and to institute the controls necessary to move forward in a planned and orderly fashion.

The Electronics Group performed well this past year and is engaged in two major programs under Defense Department contracts. These are developmental programs that provide us with the opportunity for ongoing sales upon testing of the final product. Both involve the creation of tactical display systems for aircraft being built by Lombard Aircraft for the Navy and the Air Force. Future potential sales from these efforts could amount to approximately $56 million over the next five years. Additionally, we are developing technical refinements to older, already installed systems under Army Department contracts.

In the future, we will continue to offer our technological competence in such tactical display systems and anticipate additional breakthroughs and success in meeting the demands of this market. However, we also believe that we have unique contributions to make to other markets, and to that end we are making the investments necessary to expand our opportunities.

Plastics also turned in a solid performance this past year and has continued to be a major supplier to Chrysler, Martin Tool, Foster Electric, and, of course, to our Electronics Group. The market for this group continues to expand, and we believe that additional investments in this group will allow us to seize a larger share of the future.

Chemicals' performance, admittedly, has not been as satisfactory as anticipated during the past year. However, we have been able to realize a small amount of profit from this operation and to halt what was a potentially dangerous decline in profits. We believe that this situation is only temporary and that infusions of capital for developing new technology, plus the streamlining of operations, has stabilized the situation. The next step will be to begin more aggressive marketing to capitalize on the group's basic strengths.

Overall, the outlook seems to be one of modest but profitable growth. The near term will be one of creating the technology and controls necessary for developing our market offerings and growing in a planned and purposeful manner. Our improvement efforts in the various company groups can be expected to take hold over the years with positive effect on results.

We wish to express our appreciation to all those who participated in our efforts this past year.

Harold Wallace
Chairman and President

units on the ground, on ships, or on other aircraft. Further, the company manufactures displays that provide the crew with a visual "fix" on where they are relative to the radar units that are tracking them.

In addition to manufacturing tested and proven systems developed in the past, The Wallace Group is currently involved in two major and two minor programs, all involving display systems. The Navy-A Program calls for the development of a display system for a tactical fighter plane; Air Force-B is another such system for an observation plane. Ongoing production orders are anticipated following flight testing. The other two minor programs, Army-LG and OBT-37, involve the incorporation of new technology into existing aircraft systems.

Exhibit 2 Organizational Chart: The Wallace Group (Electronics)

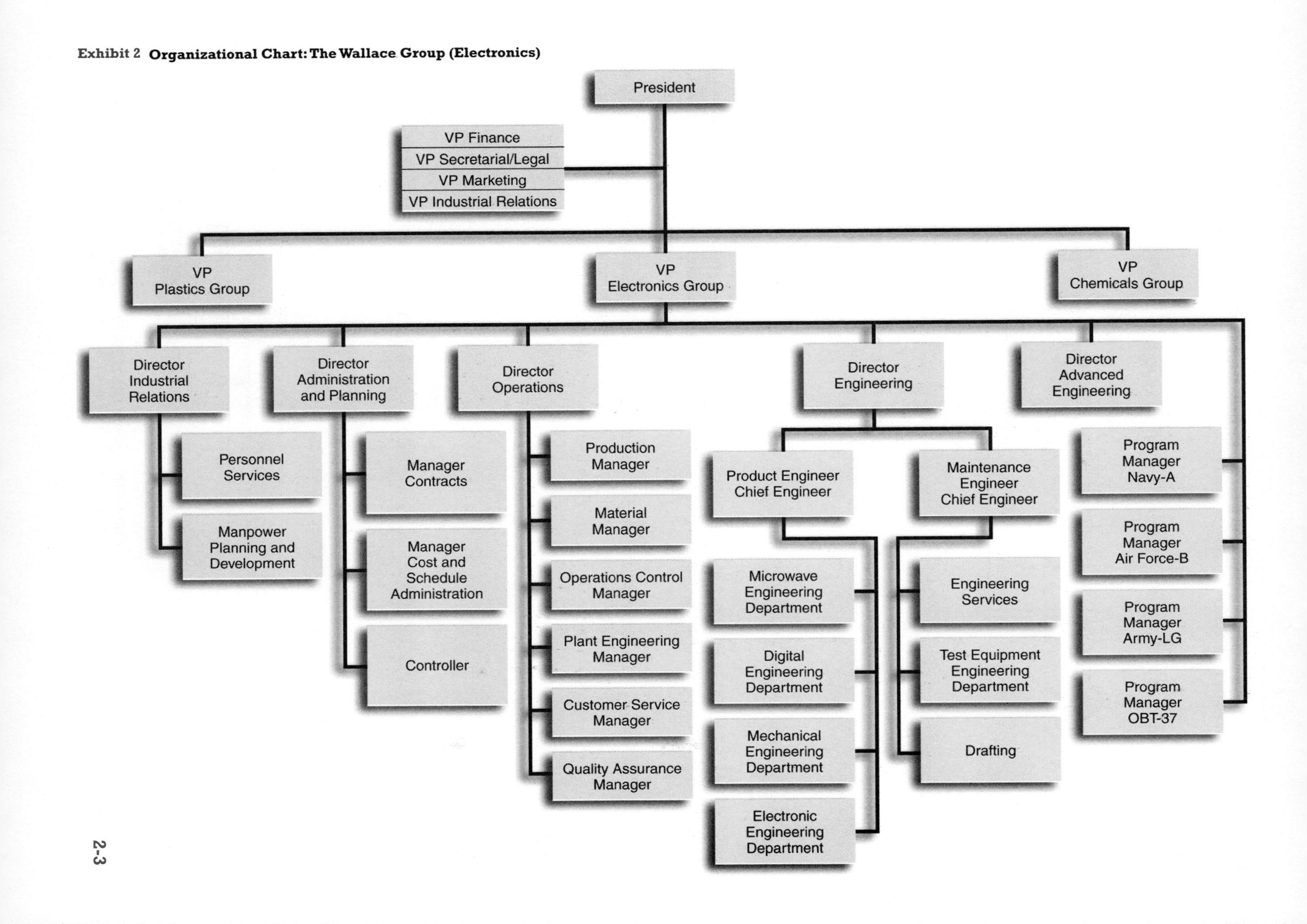

Exhibit 3
The Wallace Group (Chemicals)

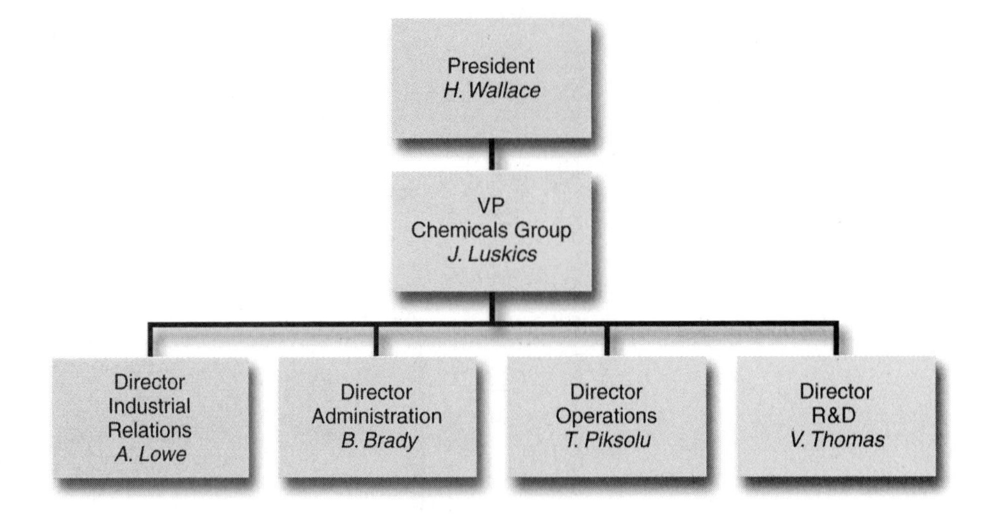

The Plastics Group manufactures plastic components utilized by the electronics, automotive, and other industries requiring plastic products. These include switches, knobs, keys, insulation materials, and so on, used in the manufacture of electronic equipment and other small made-to-order components installed in automobiles, planes, and other products.

The Chemicals Group produces chemicals used in the development of plastics. It supplies bulk chemicals to the Plastics Group and other companies. These chemicals are then injected into molds or extruded to form a variety of finished products.

Exhibit 4
The Wallace Group (Plastics)

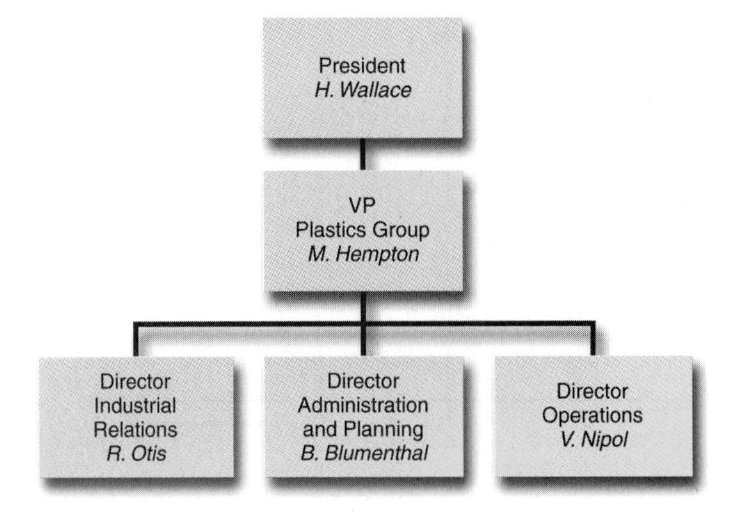

History of The Wallace Group

Each of the three groups began as a sole proprietorship under the direct operating control of an owner/manager. Several years ago, Harold Wallace, owner of the original electronics company, determined to undertake a program of diversification. Initially, he attempted to expand his market through product development and line extensions entirely within the electronics industry. However, because of initial problems, he drew back and sought other opportunities. Wallace's primary concern was his almost total dependence on defense-related contracts. He had felt for some time that he should take some strong action to gain a foothold in the private markets. The first major opportunity that seemed to satisfy his various requirements was the acquisition of a former supplier, a plastics company whose primary market was not defense-related. The company's owner desired to sell his operation and retire. At the time, Wallace's debt structure was such that he could not manage the acquisition and so he had to attract equity capital. He was able to gather a relatively small group of investors and form a closed corporation. The group established a Board of Directors with Wallace as Chairman and President of the new corporate entity.

With respect to operations, little changed. Wallace continued direct operational control over the Electronics Group. As holder of 60% of the stock, he maintained effective control over policy and operations. However, because of his personal interests, the Plastics Group, now under the direction of a newly hired Vice President, Martin Hempton, was left mainly to its own devices except for yearly progress reviews by the President. All Wallace asked at the time was that the Plastics Group continue its profitable operation, which it did.

Several years ago, Wallace and the board decided to diversify further because two-thirds of their business was still defense dependent. They learned that one of the major suppliers of the Plastics Group, a chemical company, was on the verge of bankruptcy. The company's owner, Jerome Luskics, agreed to sell. However, this acquisition required a public stock offering, with most of the funds going to pay off debts incurred by the three groups, especially the Chemicals Group. The net result was that Wallace now holds 45% of The Wallace Group and Jerome Luskics 5%, with the remainder distributed among the public.

Organization and Personnel

Presently, Harold Wallace serves as Chairman and President of The Wallace Group. The Electronics Group had been run by LeRoy Tuscher, who just resigned as Vice President. Hempton continued as Vice President of Plastics, and Luskics served as Vice President of the Chemicals Group.

Reflecting the requirements of a corporate perspective and approach, a corporate staff has grown up, consisting of Vice Presidents for Finance, Secretarial/Legal, Marketing, and Industrial Relations. This staff has assumed many functions formerly associated with the group offices.

Because these positions are recent additions, many of the job accountabilities are still being defined. Problems have arisen over the responsibilities and relationships between corporate and group positions. President Wallace has settled most of the disputes himself because of the inability of the various parties to resolve differences among themselves.

Current Trends

Presently, there is a mood of lethargy and drift within The Wallace Group. Most managers feel that each of the three groups functions as an independent company. And, with respect to group performance, not much change or progress has been made in recent years. Electronics and Plastics are still stable and profitable, but both lack growth in markets and profits. The infusion of capital breathed new life and hope into the Chemicals operation but did not solve most of the old problems and failings that had caused its initial decline. For all these reasons, Wallace decided that strong action was necessary. His greatest disappointment was with the Electronics Group, in which he had placed high hopes for future development. Thus he acted by requesting and getting the Electronics Group Vice President's resignation. Hired from a computer company to replace LeRoy Tuscher, Jason Matthews joined The Wallace Group a week ago.

As of last week, Wallace's annual net sales were $70 million. By group they were:

Electronics	$35,000,000
Plastics	$20,000,000
Chemicals	$15,000,000

Exhibit 5
Selected Portions of a Transcribed Interview with H. Wallace

Rampar: What is your greatest problem right now?

Wallace: That's why I called you in! Engineers are a high-strung, temperamental lot. Always complaining. It's hard to take them seriously.

Last month we had an annual stockholder's meeting. We have an Employee Stock Option Plan, and many of our long-term employees attended the meeting. One of my managers—and I won't mention any names—introduced a resolution calling for the resignation of the President—me!

The vote was defeated. But, of course, I own 45% of the stock!

Now I realize that there could be no serious attempt to get rid of me. Those who voted for the resolution were making a dramatic effort to show me how upset they are with the way things are going.

I could fire those employees who voted against me. I was surprised by how many did. Some of my key people were in that group. Perhaps I ought to stop and listen to what they are saying.

Businesswise, I think we're O.K. Not great, but O.K. Last year we turned in a profit of $3.5 million before taxes, which was a growth over previous years' earnings. We declared a dividend for the fifth consecutive year.

We're currently working on the creation of a tactical display system for aircraft being built by Lombard Aircraft for the Navy and the Air Force. If Lombard gets the contract to produce the prototype, future sales could amount to $56 million over the next five years.

Why are they complaining?

Rampar: You must have thoughts on the matter.

Wallace: I think the issue revolves around how we manage people. It's a personnel problem. You were highly recommended as someone with expertise in high-technology human resource management.

I have some ideas on what is the problem. But I'd like you to do an independent investigation and give me your findings. Give me a plan of action.

Don't give me a laundry list of problems, Fran. Anyone can do that. I want a set of priorities I should focus on during the next year. I want a clear action plan from you. And I want to know how much this plan is going to cost me!

Other than that, I'll leave you alone and let you talk to anyone in the company you want.

Exhibit 6
Selected Portions of a Transcribed Interview with Frank Campbell, Vice President of Industrial Relations

Rampar: What is your greatest problem right now?

Campbell: Trying to contain my enthusiasm over the fact that Wallace brought you in!
Morale is really poor here. Hal runs this place like a one man operation, when it's grown too big for that. It took a palace revolt to finally get him to see the depths of the resentment. Whether he'll do anything about it, that's another matter.

Rampar: What would you like to see changed?

Campbell: Other than a new President?

Rampar: Uh-huh.

Campbell: We badly need a management development program for our group. Because of our growth, we have been forced to promote technical people to management positions who have had no prior managerial experience. Mr. Tuscher agreed on the need for a program, but Hal Wallace vetoed the idea because developing such a program would be too expensive. I think it is too expensive *not* to move ahead on this.

Rampar: Anything else?

Campbell: The IEWU negotiations have been extremely tough this time around, due to excessive demands they have been making. Union pay scales are already pushing up against our foreman salary levels, and foremen are being paid high in their salary ranges. This problem, coupled with union insistence on a no-layoff clause, is causing us fits. How can we keep all our workers when we have production equipment on order that will eliminate 20% of our assembly positions?

Rampar: Wow.

Campbell: We have been sued by a rejected candidate for a position on the basis of discrimination. She claimed our entrance qualifications are excessive because we require shorthand. There is some basis for this statement since most reports are given to secretaries in handwritten form or on audio cassettes. In fact, we have always required it and our executives want their secretaries to have skill in taking dictation. Not only is this case taking time, but I need to reconsider if any of our position entrance requirements, in fact, are excessive. I am sure we do not want another case like this one.

Rampar: That puts The Wallace Group in a vulnerable position, considering the amount of government work you do.

Campbell: We have a tremendous recruiting backlog, especially for engineering positions. Either our pay scales are too low, our job specs are too high, or we are using the wrong recruiting channels. Kane and Smith [Director of Engineering and Director of Advanced Systems] keep rejecting everyone we send down there as being unqualified.

Rampar: Gee.

Campbell: Being head of human resources around here is a tough job. We don't act. We react.

On a consolidated basis, the financial highlights of the past two years are as follows:

	Last Year	Two Years Ago
Net sales	$70,434,000	$69,950,000
Income (pre-tax)	3,521,000	3,497,500
Income (after-tax)	2,760,500	1,748,750
Working capital	16,200,000	16,088,500
Shareholders' equity	39,000,000	38,647,000
Total assets	59,869,000	59,457,000
Long-term debt	4,350,000	3,500,000
Per Share of Common Stock		
Net income	$.37	$.36
Cash dividends paid	.15	.25

Of the net income, approximately 70% came from Electronics, 25% from Plastics, and 5% from Chemicals.

Exhibit 7
Selected Portions of a Transcribed Interview with Matthew Smith, Director of Advanced Systems

Rampar: What is your greatest problem right now?

Smith: Corporate brass keeps making demands on me and others that don't relate to the job we are trying to get done. They say that the information they need is to satisfy corporate planning and operations review requirements, but they don't seem to recognize how much time and effort is required to provide this information. Sometimes it seems like they are generating analyses, reports, and requests for data just to keep themselves busy. Someone should be evaluating how critical these corporate staff activities really are. To me and the Electronics Group, these activities are unnecessary.

An example is the Vice President, Marketing (L. Holt), who keeps asking us for supporting data so he can prepare a corporate marketing strategy. As you know, we prepare our own group marketing strategic plans annually, but using data and formats that are oriented to our needs, rather than Corporate's. This planning activity, which occurs at the same time as Corporate's, coupled with heavy work loads on current projects, makes us appear to Holt as though we are being unresponsive.

Somehow we need to integrate our marketing planning efforts between our group and Corporate. This is especially true if our group is to successfully grow in nondefense-oriented markets and products. We do need corporate help, but not arbitrary demands for information that divert us from putting together effective marketing strategies for our group.

I am getting too old to keep fighting these battles.

Rampar: This is a long-standing problem?

Smith: You bet! Our problems are fairly classic in the high-tech field. I've been at other companies and they're not much better. We spend so much time firefighting, we never really get organized. Everything is done on an ad hoc basis.

I'm still waiting for tomorrow.

Exhibit 8
Selected Portions of a Transcribed Interview with Ralph Kane, Director of Engineering

Rampar: What is your greatest problem right now?

Kane: Knowing you were coming, I wrote them down. They fall into four areas:

1. Our salary schedules are too low to attract good, experienced EEs. We have been told by our Vice President (Frank Campbell) that corporate policy is to hire new people below the salary grade midpoint. All qualified candidates are making more than that now and in some case are making more than our grade maximums. I think our Project Engineer job is rated too low.
2. Chemicals Group asked for and the former Electronics Vice President (Tuscher) agreed to "lend" six of our best EEs to help solve problems it is having developing a new battery. That is great for the Chemicals Group, but meanwhile how do we solve the engineering problems that have cropped up in our Navy-A and OBT-37 programs?
3. As you know, Matt Smith (Director of Advanced Systems) is retiring in six months. I depend heavily on his group for technical expertise, and in some areas he depends heavily on some of my key engineers. I have lost some people to the Chemicals Group, and Matt has been trying to lend me some of his people to fill in. But he and his staff have been heavily involved in marketing planning and trying to identify or recruit a qualified successor long enough before his retirement to be able to train him or her. The result is that his people are up to their eyeballs in doing their own stuff and cannot continue to help me meet my needs.
4. IR has been preoccupied with union negotiations in the plant and has not had time to help me deal with this issue of management planning. Campbell is working on some kind of system that will help deal with this kind of problem and prevent them in the future. That is great, but I need help now—not when his "system" is ready.

Exhibit 9
Selected Portions of a Transcribed Interview with Brad Lowell, Program Manager, Navy-A

Rampar: What is your . . .?

Lowell: . . . great problem? I'll tell you what it is. I still cannot get the support I need from Kane in Engineering. He commits and then doesn't deliver, and it has me quite concerned. The excuse now is that in "his judgment," Sid Wright needs the help for the Air Force program more than I do. Wright's program is one week ahead of schedule, so I disagree with "his judgment." Kane keeps complaining about not having enough people.

Rampar: Why do you think Kane says he doesn't have enough people?

Lowell: Because Hal Wallace is a tight-fisted S.O.B. who won't let us hire the people we need!

Exhibit 10
Selected Portions of a Transcribed Interview with Phil Jones, Director of Administration and Planning

Rampar: What is your greatest problem right now?

Jones: Wheel spinning—that's our problem! We talk about expansion, but we don't do anything about it. Are we serious or not?

For example, a bid request came in from a prime contractor seeking help in developing a countermeasure system for a medium-range aircraft. They needed an immediate response and concept proposal in one week. Tuscher just sat on my urgent memo to him asking for a go/no go decision on bidding. I could not give the contractor an answer (because no decision came from Tuscher), so they gave up on us.

I am frustrated because (1) we lost an opportunity we were "naturals" to win, and (2) my personal reputation was damaged because I was unable to answer the bid request. Okay, Tuscher's gone now, but we need to develop some mechanism so an answer to such a request can be made quickly.

Another thing, our MIS is being developed by the Corporate Finance Group. More wheel spinning! They are telling us what information we need rather than asking us what we want! E. Kay (our Group Controller) is going crazy trying to sort out the input requirements they need for the system and understanding the complicated reports that came out. Maybe this new system is great as a technical achievement, but what good is it to us if we can't use it?

Exhibit 11
Selected Portions of a Transcribed Interview with Burt Williams, Director of Operations

Rampar: What is your biggest problem right now?

Williams: One of the biggest problems we face right now stems from corporate policy regarding transfer pricing. I realize we are "encouraged" to purchase our plastics and chemicals from our sister Wallace groups, but we are also committed to making a profit! Because manufacturing problems in those groups have forced them to raise their prices, should *we* suffer the consequences? We can get some materials cheaper from other suppliers. How can we meet our volume and profit targets when we are saddled with noncompetitive material costs?

Rampar: And if that issue was settled to your satisfaction, then would things be O.K.?

Williams: Although out of my direct function, it occurs to me that we are not planning effectively our efforts to expand into nondefense areas. With minimal alteration to existing production methods, we can develop both end-use products (e.g., small motors, traffic control devices, and microwave transceivers for highway emergency communications) and components (e.g., LED and LCD displays, police radar tracking devices, and word processing system memory and control devices) with large potential markets.

The problems in this regard are:

1. Matt Smith (Director, Advanced Systems) is retiring and has had only defense-related experience. Therefore, he is not leading any product development efforts along these lines.
2. We have no marketing function at the group level to develop a strategy, define markets, and research and develop product opportunities.
3. Even if we had a marketing plan and products for industrial/commercial application, we have no sales force or rep network to sell the stuff.

   Maybe I am way off base, but it seems to me we need a Groups/Marketing/Sales function to lead us in this business expansion effort. It should be headed by an experienced technical marketing manager with a proven track record in developing such products and markets.

Rampar: Have you discussed your concerns with others?

Williams: I have brought these ideas up with Mr. Matthews and others at the Group Management Committee. No one else seems interested in pursuing this concept, but they won't say this outright and don't say why it should not be addressed. I guess that in raising the idea with you I am trying to relieve some of my frustrations.

The Problem Confronting Frances Rampar

As Rampar finished reviewing her notes (see **Exhibits 5–11**), she kept reflecting on what Hal Wallace had told her:

> Don't give me a laundry list of problems, Fran. Anyone can do that. I want a set of priorities I should focus on during the next year. I want a clear action plan from you. And I want to know how much this plan is going to cost me!

Fran Rampar again drummed her fingers on the desk.

CASE 3
The Boeing Company's Board of Directors Fires the CEO

Kathryn E. Wheelen, Richard D. Wheelen,
Thomas L. Wheelen II, and Thomas L. Wheelen

The Announcement

ON MARCH 7, 2005, BOEING ISSUED A SURPRISE NEWS RELEASE STATING THAT BOEING'S Board of Directors, in a special session, had asked for and received the resignation of Harry C. Stonecipher, President, Chief Executive Officer (CEO), and Board member.[1] Stonecipher had joined the board in 1997 and had served as President and CEO for the past 15 months, since the resignation of Phil Conduit.

Background

Conduit had resigned as President and CEO of Boeing on December 1, 2003, because of a major scandal involving the awarding of a $23 billion contract to Boeing for Air Force KC-330 tankers. Conduit was not directly involved in the contract, but it happened during his tenure as CEO.[2] The scandal required the firing of two Boeing executives, who later were sentenced to prison and given fines.[3] Their Department of Defense counterpart was also sentenced to prison.

The Board of Directors then asked Harry Stonecipher to come out of retirement and replace Conduit as President and CEO. Stonecipher had previously served as President and Chief Operating Officer (COO) of McDonnell Douglas Corporation before it had been acquired by Boeing in 1997. He then served as Boeing's President and COO from 1997 until

May 2001 and subsequently as Vice Chairman of the Board from May 2001 until 2002. He retired at age 65, but remained on the board and received pension and benefits of $638,000 in 2003.[4]

During Stonecipher's 15-month tenure as Boeing's CEO, the company's stock price rose 53.4% ($38.00 to $58.30). He resolved a 20-month suspension of Boeing's three business units from bidding on defense contracts. This suspension had been a result of the U.S. Air Force's finding on July 24, 2003, that Boeing had committed "serious and substantial violations of federal law" (regarding the KC-330 tanker contract). Thanks to Stonecipher's efforts, these business units were successfully reinstated with the Air Force on March 4, 2005.[5] Most analysts thought that Stonecipher would retire in May 2006, when he turned 70.

The Incident

On February 25, 2005, Chairman of the Board Lewis Platt learned of a romantic affair between Stonecipher and a female executive. A company employee had notified not only Platt, but also the company's legal and ethics executives. Sources in the company described the employee whistle-blower "as a female, who intercepted 'correspondences' between Stonecipher and a woman executive that were of a romantic nature."[6] The board of directors ordered a comprehensive and immediate investigation of the facts surrounding the relationship, and the claims of the informant.[7]

The subsequent investigation revealed that the relationship between Stonecipher and the woman executive was of a consensual nature and had begun in January 2005.[8] According to Chairman Platt, any allegations that Stonecipher had influenced the women executive's career and salary were untrue.[9] Nevertheless, the board felt that it had to take action. Platt stated: "The Board concluded that the facts reflected poorly on Harry's judgment and would impair his ability to lead the company." Platt further stated in a conference call to reporters and analysts: "It is not the fact he was having an affair—this is not a violation of our *Code of Conduct*." Platt emphasized that the relationship was not the only reason that the board asked for Stonecipher's resignation.[10] (The *Code of Conduct* can be seen on Boeing's web site, *www.Boeing.com*, under the heading *Ethics, General Info & Images*.) Platt stated, "Stonecipher acknowledge the affair."[11] He was asked to resign so his pension and benefits would not be affected. Refusing to go into further details, Platt stated, "We think Harry's entitled to some privacy concerning the details of the relationship."[12]

Fallout

Interestingly, the woman executive, whose name had not been divulged, was neither fired nor asked to resign. On March 8, 2005, after the completion of the investigation and Stonecipher's resignation, four senior Boeing executives named Debra Peabody as the woman who had the affair with Stonecipher. She was a 48-year-old Boeing Vice President for Operations and Commercial Activities in the company's government-relations office in Washington, D.C. She managed office operations for Boeing's chief Washington lobbyist, Vice President Rudy deLeon. Peabody had previously worked in various senior management positions in her 25-year career at Boeing.[13]

Industry experts were split on Stonecipher's forced resignation. One analyst asked, "If the board had true concern for Harry's privacy and his wife, children and grandchildren, then why was the resignation made public through a Boeing press release and Chairman Platt's conference call?" He said, "It could be that the minutes of the board meeting concerning these issues would have become public, if a stockholder requested them or through a lawsuit." The analyst concluded "that it [would] be better if the minutes of the meeting [were] kept private, but the legal issues may have totally controlled Platt's options. Stonecipher's relationship had no direct impact on the company's performance."

The board appointed James Bell (age 56), Chief Financial Officer (CFO), to serve as acting CEO. He would not be a candidate for the job and would continue to oversee the company's financial matters. Bell had been with Boeing for 32 years and had replaced the previous CFO, Michael Sears, who was currently serving prison time for his role in the Air Force tanker scandal.[14]

Stonecipher was paid $1.5 million plus $2.1 million in incentive bonuses in 2004, but had to forfeit his director's option of 3,000 shares. In addition, he did not receive his 2005 incentive award. Harry Stonecipher officially retired from Boeing (for the second time) on April 1, 2005.

On March 11, 2005, Joan Stonecipher filed for divorce from her husband of 50 years. They had celebrated their golden wedding anniversary just a month before. She listed her occupation as a housewife and demanded a "fair and reasonable sum" from her husband. She described her husband as having "substantial income and wealth."[15]

Corporate Governance

Exhibit 1 lists the 11 members of Boeing's Board of Directors in 2005.

Exhibit 1
Board of Directors: Boeing Company

1. John H. Biggs, 67
Former Chairman, President and Chief Executive Officer, Teachers Insurance and Annuity Association—College Retirement Equities Fund

Boeing Board Committees:

Audit and Finance (Chair)

Boeing director since 1997

Boeing director term expires 2007

Director of JP Morgan Chase Co.

Director and former Chairman of the United Way of New York City and the National Bureau of Economic Research

Trustee of Washington University, St. Louis, Missouri

Trustee of the International Accounting Standards Committee

Trustee of the J. Paul Getty Trust

2. John E. Bryson, 60
Chairman of the Board President and Chief Executive Officer, Edison International

Boeing Board Committees:
Compensation (Chair) and Governance, Organization and Nominating

Boeing director since 1995

Boeing director term expires 2007

Director of The Walt Disney Company, Western Asset Fund, Inc., and the W. M Keck Foundation

3. Linda Z. Cook, 45
President and Chief Executive Officer, Shell Canada Limited

Boeing Board Committees:
Audit and Finance

Boeing director since 2003

Boeing director term expires 2007

Former Chief Executive Officer, Shell Gas & Power, Royal Dutch/ Shell Group (London)

Former Director, Strategy & Business Development, Shell Exploration & Production Global Executive Committee (The Hague)

Member of Society of Petroleum Engineers, the Harvard School of

Exhibit 1
(Continued)

Governments Dean's Council, and the Canadian Council of Chief Executives

4. Kenneth M. Duberstein, 59
Chairman and Chief Executive Officer
Duberstein Group

Boeing Board Committees:
Compensation (Chair) and Governance Organization and Nominating

Boeing director since 1997

Boeing director term expires in 2008

Former White House Chief of Staff, 1998–89

Director of ConocoPhillips, Fannie Mae, Fleming Companies, Inc., and St. Paul Companies

Governor of the American Stock Exchange and National Association of Securities Dealers, Inc.

5. Paul E. Gray, 72
President Emeritus and Professor of Electrical Engineering, Massachusetts Institute of Technology (MIT)

Boeing Board Committees
Compensation; Governance, Organization and Nominating; and Special Programs

Boeing director since 1990

Retired at 2005 board meeting

Former Chairman, MIT, 1990–97

Former President, MIT, 1980–90

6. John F. McDonnell, 66
Retired Chairman, McDonnell Douglas Corporation

Boeing Board Committees:
Compensation; Governance, Organization and Nominating

Boeing director since 1997

Boeing director term expires in 2006

Former Chief Executive Officer, McDonnell Douglas Corporation, 1988–94

Chairman of the Board of Trustees of of Washington University, St. Louis, Missouri

Director of Zoltek Companies, Inc.

Director of BJC HealthCare

7. W. James McNerney, Jr., 54
Chairman and Chief Executive Officer, 3M Company

Boeing Board Committees:
Audit and Finance

Boeing director since 2001

Boeing director term expires in 2008

Former President and Chief Executive Officer of GE Aircraft Engines, 1997–2000

Director of The Procter & Gamble Company

8. Lewis E. Platt, 62
Non-Executive Chairman of the Board, The Boeing Company

Boeing Board Committees:
Compensation; and Governance, Organization and Nominating

Boeing director since 1999

Boeing director term expires in 2008

Retired Chairman of the Board, President and Chief Executive Officer, Hewlett-Packard Company

Director of 7-Eleven, Inc.

Serves on the Board of Overseers for the Wharton School of the University of Pennsylvania, Philadelphia, Pennsylvania

Trustee of the David and Lucile Packard Foundation

9. Rozanne L. Ridgway, 68
Former Assistant Secretary of State for Europe and Canada

Boeing Board Committees:
Compensation; and Governance, Organization and Nominating

Boeing director since 1992

Boeing director term expires in 2007

U. S. Foreign Service, 1957–89, including service as Ambassador to German Democratic republic and Finland, Ambassador for Oceans and Fisheries Affairs

Director of Emerson Electric Company, 3M Company, Sara Lee Corporation, Manpower Inc. and the New Perspective Fund

10. John M. Shalikashvilli, 67
Retired Chairman of the Joint Chiefs of Staff, U.S. Department Of Defense

Boeing Board Committees:
Audit (Chair), Finance and Special Program (Chair)

Exhibit 1
(Continued)

Boeing director since 2000

Boeing director term expires in 2006

Formerly Commander-in-Chief of all U.S. Forces in Europe and NATO's 10th Supreme Allied Commander in Europe

Visiting professor at Stanford University's Center for International Security and Cooperation

Director of Frank Russell Trust Company, L-3 Communications Holding, Inc., Plug Power Inc. and United Defense Industries Inc.

11. Harry C. Stonecipher, 67
President and Chief Executive Officer, The Boeing Company

Boeing director since 1997

Boeing director term expires in 2006

Retired Vice Chairman of the Board, The Boeing Company

Former President and Chief Executive Officer of McDonnell Douglas Corporation,1994–97

Former Chairman and Chief Executive Officer of Sundstrand Corporation, 1991–94

Director of PACCAR inc.

The annual fee for a member of the Board of Directors in 2005 was $60,000. In addition, board members were paid $5,000 to chair a committee; $40,000 annual defense stock unit award; and a grant option of 3,000 shares for the member's first annual stock meeting and 2,400 shares for subsequent annual meetings.[16]

John McDonnell owned 11,801,851 shares of Boeing stock (1.40% of total outstanding shares). Harry C. Stonecipher owned 1,755,895 shares. The State Street Bank and Trust Company owned 11.4% of the outstanding stock, and Capital Research and Management owned 5.2%. All directors and officers (26 individuals) owned a total of 1.92% of the outstanding stock.[17]

The company was organized into six principal segments: (1) Commercial Airplanes, (2) Airplanes and Weapon Systems (A&WS), (3) Network Systems, (4) Support Systems, (5) Launch and Orbital Systems (L&OS), *collectively called the Integrated Defense Systems* (IDS), and (6) Boeing Capital Corporation (BCC). These six segments were integrated into the company's three strategic business segments: (1) Boeing Commercial Airplanes, (2) Boeing Integrated Defense, and (3) Boeing Capital Corporation.

Notes

1. "Boeing CEO Harry Stonecipher Resigns; Board Appoints James Bell Interim President and CEO; Lew Platt to Expand Role," Boeing news release (March 7, 2005), p. 1.
2. Abstracted from his profile in 2004. "2004 Annual Meeting and Proxy Statement," *Boeing Company*, p. 5.
3. "Boeing Forces Resignation of CEO." Associated Press (March 7, 2005). *www.msnbc.com*
4. Dave Carpenter, "Boeing Fires CEO for Affair with Exec," Associated Press (web site: *www.news.moneycentral.msn.com*) (March 7, 2005), pp. 1–2.
5. Jim Wolf, "Air Force Ends Boeing Launch Suspension," Reuters (March 4, 2005).
6. Stanley Holmes, "The Affair That Grounded Stonecipher," *BusinessWeek online* (March 8, 2005), p. 1.
7. Carpenter, p. 2.
8. Boeing news release (March 7, 2005), p. 1.
9. Carpenter, p. 2.
10. "Boeing Forces Resignation of CEO," p. 1.
11. Carpenter, p. 2.
12. "Boeing Forces Resignation of CEO," p. 2.
13. Holmes, p. 1.
14. *Ibid.*
15. *Ibid.*
16. "EADS Success Continues in 2004: Ambitious Financial Targets Met for Fifth Consecutive Year," *EADS* (March 9, 2005), pp. 5–8.
17. "Shareholder Structure," *EADS* March 3, 2005); p. 1, and "Board of Directors—Role and Competition," *EADS* (March 7, 2005), p. 1.

CASE 4
The Audit

Gamewell D. Gantt, George A. Johnson and John A. Kilpatrick

Sue was puzzled as to what course of action to take. She had recently started her job with a national CPA firm, and she was already confronted with a problem that could affect her future with the firm. On an audit, she encountered a client who had been treating payments to a large number, but by no means a majority, of its workers as payments to independent contractors. This practice saves the client the payroll taxes that would otherwise be due on the payments if the workers were classified as employees. In Sue's judgment this was improper as well as illegal and should have been noted in the audit. She raised the issue with John, the senior accountant to whom she reported. He thought it was a possible problem but did not seem willing to do anything about it. He encouraged her to talk to the partner in charge if she didn't feel satisfied.

She thought about the problem for a considerable time before approaching the partner in charge. The ongoing professional education classes she had received from her employer emphasized the ethical responsibilities that she had as a CPA and the fact that her firm endorsed adherence to high ethical standards. This finally swayed her to pursue the issue with the partner in charge of the audit. The visit was most unsatisfactory. Paul, the partner, virtually confirmed her initial reaction that the practice was wrong, but he said that many other companies in the industry follow such a practice. He went on to say that if an issue was made of it, Sue would lose the account, and he was not about to take such action. She came away from the meeting with the distinct feeling that had she chosen to pursue the issue, she would have created an enemy.

Sue still felt disturbed and decided to discuss the problem with some of her co-workers. She approached Bill and Mike, both of whom had been working for the firm for a couple of years. They were familiar with the problem because they had encountered the same issue when doing the audit the previous year. They expressed considerable concern that if she went over the head of the partner in charge of the audit, they could be in big trouble since they had failed to question the practice during the previous audit. They said that they realized it was probably wrong, but they went ahead because it had been ignored in previous years, and they knew their supervisor wanted them to ignore it again this year. They didn't want to cause problems. They encouraged Sue to be a "team player" and drop the issue.

This case was prepared by Professors John A. Kilpatrick, Gamewell D. Gantt, and George A. Johnson of the College of Business, Idaho State University. The names of the organization, individual, location, and/or financial information have been disguised to preserve the organization's desire for anonymity. This case was edited for SMBP-9th, 10th and 11th Editions. Presented to and accepted by the refereed Society for Case Research.

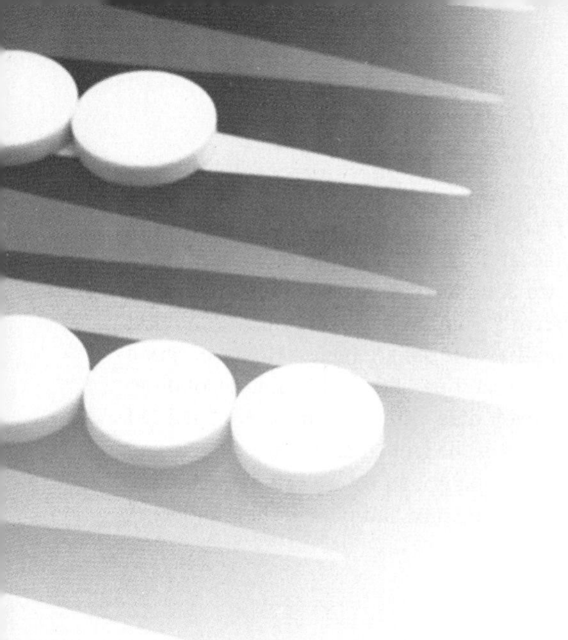

CASE 5
Everyone Does It

Steven M. Cox and Shawana P. Johnson

Jim Willis was the Vice President of Marketing and Sales for International Satellite Images (ISI). ISI had been building a satellite to image the world at a resolution of one meter. At that resolution, a trained photo interpreter could identify virtually any military and civilian vehicle as well as numerous other military and non-military objects. The ISI team had been preparing a proposal for a Japanese government contractor. The contract called for a commitment of a minimum imagery purchase of $10 million per year for five years. In a recent executive staff meeting it became clear that the ISI satellite camera subcontractor was having trouble with the development of a thermal stabilizer for the instrument. It appeared that the development delay would be at least one year and possibly 18 months.

When Jim approached Fred Ballard, the President of ISI, for advice on what launch date to put into the proposal, Fred told Jim to use the published date because that was still the official launch date. When Jim protested that the use of an incorrect date was clearly unethical, Fred said, "Look Jim, no satellite has ever been launched on time. Everyone, including our competitors, publishes very aggressive launch dates. Customers understand the tentative nature of launch schedules. In fact, it is so common that customers factor into their plans the likelihood that spacecraft will not be launched on time. If we provided realistic dates, our launch dates would be so much later than those published by our competitors that we would never be able to sell any advanced contracts. So do not worry about it, just use the published date and we will revise it in a few months." Fred's words were not very comforting to Jim. It was true that satellite launch dates were seldom met, but putting a launch date into a proposal that ISI knew was no longer possible seemed underhanded. He wondered about the ethics of such a practice and the effect on his own reputation.

The Industry

Companies from four nations, the United States, France, Russia, and Israel, controlled the satellite imaging industry. The U.S. companies had a clear advantage in technology and imagery clarity. In the United States, three companies dominated: Lockart, Global Sciences, and ISI. Each of these companies had received a license from the U.S. government to build and launch a satellite able to identify objects as small as one square meter. However, none had yet been able to successfully launch a commercial satellite with such a fine resolution. Currently, all of the companies had announced a launch date within six months of the ISI published launch date. Further, each company had to revise its launch date at least once, and in the case of Global Sciences, twice. Each time a company had revised its launch date, ongoing international contract negotiations with that company had been either stalled or terminated.

Financing a Satellite Program

The construction and ongoing operations of each of the programs was financed by venture capitalists. The venture capitalists relied heavily on advance contract acquisition to ensure the success of their investment. As a result, if any company was unable to acquire sufficient advance contracts, or if one company appeared to be gaining a lead on the others, there was a real possibility that the financiers would pull the plug on the other projects and the losing companies would be forced to stop production and possibly declare bankruptcy. The typical advance contract target was 150% of the cost of building and launching a satellite. Since the cost to build and launch was $200 million, each company was striving to acquire $300 million in advance contracts.

Advance contracts were typically written like franchise licensing agreements. Each franchisee guaranteed to purchase a minimum amount of imagery per year for five years, the engineered life of the satellite. In addition, each franchisee agreed to acquire the capability to receive, process, and archive the images sent to them from the satellite. Typically, the hardware and software cost was between $10 million and $15 million per installation. Because the data from each satellite was different, much of the software could not be used for multiple programs. In exchange, the franchisee was granted an exclusive reception and selling territory. The amount of each contract was dependent on the anticipated size of the market, the number of possible competitors in the market, and the readiness of the local military and civilian agencies to use the imagery. Thus, a contract in Africa would sell for as little as $1 million per year, whereas in several European countries $5–$10 million was not unreasonable. The problem was complicated by the fact that in each market there were usually only one or two companies with the financial strength and market penetration to become a successful franchisee. Therefore, each of the U.S. companies had targeted these companies as their prime prospects.

The Current Problem

Japan was expected to be the third largest market for satellite imagery after the United States and Europe. Imagery sales in Japan were estimated to be from $20 million to $30 million per year. Although the principal user would be the Japanese government, for political reasons the government had made it clear that they would be purchasing data through a local Japanese company. One Japanese company, Higashi Trading Company (HTC), had provided most of the imagery for civilian and military use to the Japanese government.

ISI had been negotiating with HTC for the past six months. It was no secret that HTC had also been meeting with representatives from Lockart and Global Sciences. HTC had sent several engineers to ISI to evaluate the satellite and its construction progress. Jim Willis believed that ISI was currently the front-runner in the quest to sign HTC to a $10 million annual contract. Over five years, that one contract would represent one sixth of the contracts necessary to ensure sufficient venture capital to complete the satellite.

Jim was concerned that if a new launch date was announced, HTC would delay signing a contract. Jim was equally concerned that if HTC learned that Jim and his team knew of the camera design problems and knowingly withheld announcement of a new launch date until after completing negotiations, not only his personal reputation but that of ISI would be damaged. Furthermore, as with any franchise arrangement, mutual trust was critical to the success of each party. Jim was worried that even if only a 12-month delay in launch occurred, trust would be broken between ISI and the Japanese.

Jim's boss, Fred Ballard, had specifically told Jim that launch date information was company proprietary and that Jim was to use the existing published date when talking with clients. Fred feared that if HTC became aware of the delay, they would begin negotiating with one of ISI's competitors, who in Fred's opinion were not likely to meet their launch dates either. This change in negotiation focus by the Japanese would then have ramifications with the venture capitalists whom Fred had assured that a contract with the Japanese would soon be signed.

Jim knew that with the presentation date rapidly approaching, it was time to make a decision.

CASE 6

GlaxoSmithKline's Retaliation Against Cross-Border Sales of Prescription Drugs

Sara Smith Shull and Rebecca J. Morris

War was imminent with Iraq, the relentless bear market was entering its fourth year, personal savings were at an all-time low, and the American consumer was valiantly growing the economy at a meager 1.4% annually. Against this backdrop healthcare costs were spiraling upward year after year. The aging of the largest single population cohort in American history (the Baby Boomers) resulted in greater utilization of healthcare services. Concurrently, the cost of the services themselves (prescription drugs, physician visits, and hospitalizations) was increasing. Cumulatively, these services were responsible for a double-digit increase (10% per capita) in healthcare costs in 2001, the first time in more than a decade that healthcare costs had accelerated so rapidly.[1] Reaching $1.4 trillion, healthcare costs escalated to 14.1% of the gross domestic product (GDP).[2]

GlaxoSmithKline plc (GSK), a prescription drug and personal hygiene consumer products company based in Britain, found itself coping with a new challenge during this period as Americans, especially senior citizens, developed various tactics to deal with the rising drug costs. Discovering that prescription drugs could be acquired from Canadian pharmacies via the Internet at prices substantially lower than those available at pharmacies in the United States, resourceful Americans began to consistently adopt the practice.[3] The flow of drugs from Canadian pharmacies to American consumers captured the attention of GSK and their concern grew as the practice spread. Late in 2002 they attempted to curb the flow of prescription drugs out of Canada into the United States by limiting the drugs shipped to Canadian pharmacies.[4] This challenged pharmacies to provide adequate prescription product for their Canadian customers while shipping product to American customers south of the border. However, GSK discovered Americans, especially seniors, to be loud, persistent, and effective protesters when they threatened to limit drug supplies to Canadian pharmacies. Kate Stahl, the 83-year-old metro president of the Minnesota Senior Federation was defiant: "People in America, including Minnesotans, pay the world's highest prices for drugs. Now, if they (GSK) are going to boycott us, we're going to boycott them."[5] Una Moore echoed support for sanctions against GSK. A retired licensed practical nurse with no pension, she had been compelled to purchase drugs from Canada for years. "I'm terrified that the other companies will follow Glaxo. We have to get together and find a way to beat these guys."[6]

The Basis for GlaxoSmithKline's Decision

The late 1990s and the early years of the 21st century set the stage for GSK's decision. Seeking relief from escalating healthcare costs, many Americans, especially senior citizens, sought alternate channels for acquiring the prescription medicines upon which they increasingly relied. Publicizing the increasing costs and promoting a political agenda, U.S. congressmen from states along the Canadian border began to host bus trips for senior citizens across the border in order to procure prescription drugs at costs as much as 80% lower than those available in the United States. Logistically, relatively small numbers could participate in this practice and make savings on drugs worth the cost of the trip. Americans traveling in Europe, Canada, and Mexico might also acquire small amounts of prescription drugs for personal use at a cost much lower than that available in the United States. However, it was not until the Internet became routinely available in homes, public libraries, and kiosks that prescription drugs from around the world were available at the touch of a button to Americans. In a relatively simple process, seniors and others could take a prescription written by an American physician, send it to a Canadian pharmacy, and within days receive their drugs at home at a substantial discount to what that product cost in the United States.[7] The practice grew rapidly in the early years of the 21st century, as political agendas and budgetary constraints stalled a Medicare prescription drug benefit in the United States. By late 2002, over a million senior citizens indicated that they were seeking prescription drugs over the Internet from an estimated 123 Canadian pharmacies. Precise sales figures attributed to the practice were private record; however, Manitoba pharmacies alone claimed $250 million in sales from approximately 400,000 U.S. customers during 2002.[8] Prices for GSK drugs from a variety of sources are provided in **Exhibit 1**.

GlaxoSmithKline was beginning to feel the economic effects of American consumers acquiring prescription drugs from Canada at lower cost, circumventing the traditional pre-

Exhibit 1 Comparative Patient Drug Costs for GlaxoSmithKline Products (Dollar amounts in U.S. dollars)

Drugs	U.S.A.	Canada (In $US)	Insurance Copay
Advair 50/500mcg diskus	$206.99	$103.18	$30.00–$45.00
Augmentin 875/125mg X28 tabs	66.76	38.72	15.00–25.00
Avandia 8mg X 100 tabs	313.52	219.46	30.00–45.00
Flovent 250mcg inhaler	121.99	63.27	30.00–45.00
Imitrex 50mg X6 injections	117.99	67.84	30.00–45.00
Paxil 30 mg X30 tabs	107.99	47.41	$30.00–$45.00

Note: U.S. prices were taken from a Walgreens Pharmacy in the Minneapolis, Minnesota, area on February 19, 2003. Prices for Augmentin and Avandia were taken from the RailwayRxAssist web site (*www.RailwayRxAssist.com*). Canadian prices do not include shipping. The Canadian exchange rate for U.S. dollars on February 19, 2003, was 0.656938.

scription drug market. Therefore, responding to the growing popularity of cheaper Canadian drugs among American consumers, GSK defended premium pricing in America. "Prescription drugs are generally cheaper in Canada (than the U.S.) primarily because prices are controlled and capped by Canada's Patented Medicines Prices Review Board (through a national health insurance plan)," reiterated the management of GSK on a corporate Website.[9] "But even without price controls, prescription medicines, like most other products, would probably still be cheaper in Canada due to lower wages and buying power there. A Dodge Caravan costs $31,000 in the U.S. but just $21,000 in U.S. dollars in Canada," the site continued. Also, in January 2003 in an action GSK closely compared to that of other consumer good manufacturers, they threatened to stop supplying drug wholesalers and retailers in Canada, unless Canadian pharmacies ceased their cross-border sales. "In response to (U.S.) dealers importing cars from Canada to resell, some U.S. auto-makers threatened to void their warranties or hold back other incentives from the (offending) dealers," declared GSK,[10] ostensibly providing a rationale for their own actions. GSK delayed the deadline once, allowing Canadian pharmacies more time to "self-certify" that they were not exporting drugs to the United States. Then GSK finally cut off the product supply near the end of February 2003. GSK was the only pharmaceutical manufacturer that initiated such action, although all companies selling prescription drugs in America were affected.[11]

The reaction to the GSK decision was immediate and vocal, affecting the public image of the company worldwide. Perceived as mean-spirited, bullying, greedy, and insensitive, GSK faced angry consumers, who for years had tolerated double-digit price increases for their medicines.[12] Detroit resident William Finton, a 65-year-old semi-retired accountant who purchased chronic medications from Canadian pharmacies, remarked, "It really doesn't take a rocket scientist to figure out that they are making excessive profits. Of course they have a lot of expenses in producing these drugs, but once they make the cost back, it really shouldn't be this expensive."[13] "They are beginning to make the tobacco companies look good," quipped Todd Lebor, an equity analyst for Morningstar.[14] Joe Graedon, an author of a syndicated column dedicated to drug issues, wrote of GSK's crackdown to limit Canadian drug supply, "It's like attacking apple pie, Mom, and Chevrolet."[15]

A coalition of ten leading American and Canadian healthcare and business organizations began a national advertising campaign harshly criticizing the drug maker for its ban (Exhibit 2). They maintained that GSK was keeping Americans, especially seniors, from accessing more affordable prescription medications than could be acquired in the United States.[16] Peter Wyckoff, executive director of the Minnesota Senior Federation, a coalition member, declared, "we see this as an issue of unbridled greed, hurting the health and safety of American citizens who have no choice but to look at less costly alternatives (than drugs available in the United States)."[17] The coalition members collectively purchased a full-page ad in the New York Times encouraging healthcare professionals and consumers to pressure GSK to reverse their decision. They insisted that GSK renew delivery of their products to Canadian pharmacies, despite a high likelihood of exportation across the border to the United States. The coalition encouraged readers to contact their legislators and the CEO of GSK, Jean Pierre Garnier, to complain about the ban. They also encouraged senior citizens to consult with their pharmacists and physicians to investigate whether comparable generic agents were available, or whether patients could be switched to drugs manufactured by GSK's competitors and achieve the same therapeutic goal. Consumers were encouraged to sell off GSK stock and boycott over-the-counter or personal hygiene products manufactured by GSK. Jimm Axline, president of the National Association of the Terminally Ill, a nonprofit organization serving families facing terminal illness said,

> With this campaign, we're delivering our message loud and clear to Glaxo, that you cannot steal access to affordable drugs from those who are dying and expect to get away with it. We're urging consumers and healthcare professionals to call their Senators and Congressmen and Glaxo's U.S. CEO, and tell them to give our patients back their affordable drugs.[18]

Exhibit 2
Coalition Ad Critical of Glaxo

Glaxo is taking away your right to affordable prescription drugs!

The world's second largest drug maker, GlaxoSmithKline, has stopped providing its drugs to Canadian pharmacies and wholesalers who supply an estimated one million uninsured and underinsured American seniors with affordable, high quality medications. If Glaxo gets its way, all drugmakers will likely follow its lead and eventually strip seniors of their well-established right to access affordable drugs from alternative sources.

Fight Back to Stop Glaxo Now:

1. Contact the U.S. Congress switchboard in Washington, DC at 1-202-224-3121, ask for the names and phone numbers of your House and Senate members, and call them to share your concerns. Or, visit www.congress.org to learn your legislators' e-mail addresses and send them a note.
2. Call Glaxo's toll-free consumer hotline at 1-888-825-5249, press 3, then press 2, and give your views to the live operator.
3. Write Glaxo's U.S. CEO and tell him to stop the restrictions being placed on Canadian drugs:
   Mr. Jean-Pierre Garnier, CEO, GSK U.S. Pharmaceuticals, Five Moore Drive, P.O. Box 13398, Research Triangle Park, NC. 27709
4. If you have been buying your Glaxo drugs from a Canadian pharmacy and cannot afford the high U.S. pharmacy prices, check with your doctor to see if there is a comparable drug made by another drugmaker that you can switch to.
5. Consider selling any Glaxo stock that you currently hold either directly or through a pension fund. Glaxo stock is listed as "GSK" on the New York Stock Exchange.
6. You may want to consider switching from these Glaxo over-the-counter treatments to those made by other manufacturers. The company's products include the following brands: Beano, Citrucel, Contac, Geritol, Sominex, Sensodyne, Polident, Poligrip, Nytol, Nicoderm, Nicorette, Tegrin, Tums and Vivarin.

This message is brought to you by these American and Canadian organizations who work to keep affordable alternative-sourced drugs available as a safe, reliable and low-cost option for all Americans. The person depicted is a model and the photo is used for illustrative purposes only.

New York State Wide Senior Action Council, Inc.
Albany, New York
www.nysenior.org

Senior Action Network
senior advocacy organization, San Francisco, California
www.senioractionnetwork.org

mail order pharmacy
www.canadameds.com

Action Alliance of Senior Citizens of Greater Philadelphia
senior advocacy group, Philadelphia, Pennsylvania
www.actionseniors.org

AIDS Healthcare Foundation
the nation's largest AIDS organization
Los Angeles, California
www.aidshealth.org

CAARx
Coalition for Access to Affordable Prescription Drugs
Manchester, Vermont
www.caarx.com

crossborderpharmacy.com
mail order pharmacy
www.crossborderpharmacy.com

National Association of the Terminally Ill
nonprofit organization helping families that face terminal illnesses
www.terminallyill.org

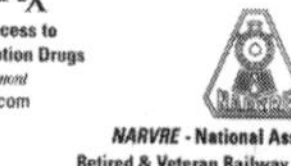

NARVRE - National Association of Retired & Veteran Railway Employees, Inc.
association of American railway workers and retirees nationwide
www.narvre.com

CIPARx
Canadian International Pharmacy Association
national organization of mail order pharmacies serving Canadian and American consumers in need
www.ciparx.com

For more information or if your organization is interested in joining the coalition, call 1-773-769-1616

GSK spokeswoman Nancy Pekarek maintained,

> This is not a financial issue for GlaxoSmithKline. The amount of money we estimate is involved with Internet sales from Canada is less than one percent of our sales in the United States. But, obviously Internet sales are growing, and, as the business increases, so does the potential risk to patients.[19]

Meanwhile, the press and coalition sought to portray GSK as a powerful company more concerned with profits than the health and well-being of American and Canadian consumers. Elizabeth Wennar, MD, spokesperson for the Coalition for Access to Affordable Prescription Drugs, a Vermont-based advocacy group said,

> Strong profit growth is Glaxo's chief concern, not the quality care and the well-being of seniors who cannot pay the exorbitant American prices for their life-saving drugs. If patient care was a genuine worry, Glaxo would have come forward much earlier. They wouldn't have waited nearly three years (during Internet growth) while Canadian pharmacies have grown to serve millions of uninsured and underinsured Americans. Simply put, Glaxo wants a much bigger piece of the sales action.[20]

Glaxo insisted that the decision was simply a tactical maneuver to protect American patients' safety from risks attributed to quality assurance lapses in the reimportation process. However, the Minnesota Senior Federation believed that the drug company was really concerned with the "safety of its sales and profits." Barbara Kaufman, president of the senior group, declared, "The idea that shipping drugs north to Canada . . . and throughout the United States . . . is safe, while shipping drugs south to the U.S. is dangerous is ludicrous."[21] Joe Graedon, in his syndicated column, cast even further doubt on the patient safety rationale for the crackdown, calling it "smoke and mirrors" and emphasizing Canada's own interest in protecting its citizens. "Canadian authorities have rigorous federal supervision of medicines," he said. "You have to assume that if you shop for your Advair at a pharmacy in Toronto, it's going to be just as good as Advair in downtown Durham (North Carolina)."[22] Kris Thorkelson, representing the Manitoba International Pharmacists Association, agreed saying,

> The shipping of drugs across the border and elsewhere has always been and will continue to be safe, ensuring product integrity, and Glaxo's claims about safety are without foundation. Drugs are shipped great distances in similar circumstances every day with no threat to their integrity. The same thing happens in the U.S. and elsewhere, yet the manufacturer is not raising the issue there. Glaxo uses the same shipping techniques to move its products to wholesalers and retailers all over North America.[23]

Industry watchers suggested that the most obvious motivation for the GSK action was the erosion of its American profit picture. A PR newswire out of St. Paul, Minnesota, reinforced this notion by suggesting that Glaxo was attempting to take away the rights of senior citizens under the guise of safety.[24] Formal legal implications were also raised.[25] "What they are doing is restraint of trade,"[26] said Phil Mamber, president of the Massachusetts Senior Action Council.

GlaxoSmithKline, while spending hundreds of millions of dollars annually to advertise its drugs, was losing control over something it couldn't buy: its image. The crackdown on reimportation of Canadian drugs via the Internet had become a lightning rod of controversy, featuring vulnerable, typically elderly patients on one side and a large, multinational, and successful corporation on the other. "(Ironically) GSK is feeding a climate of antipathy toward drug companies that could, in the long term, result in new laws that could have an impact on their sales,"[27] warned Frances Cloud, a pharmaceutical analyst with London's Nomura Securities. Joe Graedon, co-hosting the public radio program, "The People's Pharmacy," agreed,

> (The crack-down) risks alienating a lot of Canadians, and it risks alienating Americans who are fed up with subsidizing the cost of drugs for the rest of the world. The only explanation I can

imagine for why GSK would be willing to risk that is because so many people are now buying their medicines from Canada that GSK is starting to see the effect on the bottom line.[28]

In 2003, the pharmaceutical industry introduced their products into a marketplace decidedly different than other industries. Individuals did not enter the healthcare services marketplace for discretionary purchases. Healthcare services, at one juncture or another, were essential in the lives of most people to maintain optimal health or to treat acute and chronic diseases. However, access to healthcare services and prescription drugs was variable, based on gender, geographic location, socioeconomic factors, and race. Complicating the data interpretation was the weak economy and the prolonged ennui of the American stock markets. While many seniors partook of an active, secure, and stimulating retirement, others, just years short from anticipating a secure retirement, were contemplating remaining at or returning to work, unwillingly, to make ends meet.[29]

GlaxoSmithKline plc

GlaxoSmithKline plc (GSK) was a multinational concern formed from the acquisition of SmithKline Beecham by Glaxo in late 2000. Headquartered in London, England, the company employed more than 100,000 people and distinguished itself as the largest pharmaceutical company in Europe and the second largest pharmaceutical company in the world. Seeing the United States as a key market, GSK struggled to establish itself as the fastest-growing pharmaceutical company there. The 2000 merger resulted in a broad product line that included prescription drugs, vaccines, and consumer health products. Therapeutic targets for GSK products included depression, infectious disease, asthma and chronic obstructive pulmonary disease, migraine headaches, non-insulin dependent diabetes mellitus, chemotherapy-induced nausea and vomiting, and congestive heart failure. Blockbuster products (global sales > £1 billion per annum) included Paxil (depression), Augmentin (Gram positive aerobic bacterial infection), Advair (asthma), Flovent (asthma), Imitrex (migraine headache), and Avandia (non-insulin dependant diabetes mellitus). Consumer health products included Aquafresh toothpaste, Nicorette patches and gum (smoking cessation), and Tums (calcium supplement/ heartburn relief).

GSK was in strong financial condition[30] as shown in **Exhibit 3**. In 2002, they experienced an increase of 7.8% in global sales of pharmaceutical products to nearly $27 billion. U.S. sales of pharmaceutical products increased by 13%. An essential market, the United States represented 54% of all GSK sales. GSK commanded 8.8% of the market share for prescription

Exhibit 3 Profit and Loss Summary: GlaxoSmithKline, plc (Dollar amounts in millions, except per-share data)

Year Ending Dec. 31	2002	2001	Change (%)
Sales			
Pharmaceuticals	$26,993	$24,775	9.0
Consumer health	4,826	4,729	2.1
Total sales	31,819	29,504	7.8
Gross profit	24,906	22,688	9.7
Operating profit	8,327	6,817	22.2
Profit before taxation	8,259	6,504	28.0
Earnings	5,873	4,396	33.5
Earnings per share	$1.99	$1.45	38.0
Shares outstanding	5,912	6,064	(2.5)

Source: GlaxoSmithKline Annual Report, 2002, released February 12, 2003.

Exhibit 4
Global Sales and Growth Rates for Key GlaxoSmithKline Therapeutic Drug Groups and Individual Agents (Dollar amounts in millions)

Therapeutic Class	Global Sales	Global Growth (%)
Central Nervous System	$6.8 billion	17
Paxil	3.1 billion	15 (18% in U.S.)
Respiratory System—Advair	4.4 billion	25
	2.4 billion	96
Anti-infectives—HIV	2.2 billion	13
Metabolic/gastrointestinal—	2.1 billion	1
Avandia	1 billion	19 (15% in U.S.)
Oncology—Zofran	1.1 billion	22 (28% in U.S.)
Cardiovascular—Coreg	459 million	27

drugs in 2001.[31] See GlaxoSmithKline's 2002 Annual Report for complete financial statements at *www.gsk.com.*

Six therapeutic drug groups experienced significant global growth in 2002. Within categories, individual agents also demonstrated significant sales growth. Key figures for these drugs are shown in **Exhibit 4**.

GlaxoSmithKline devoted $4.35 billion to research and development expenditures in 2002, an increase of 14% over 2001. The product "pipeline" included 123 products in clinical development, which consisted of 61 new chemical entities, 23 new vaccines, and 39 line extensions. One agent was in Phase III clinical trials for the prevention of prostate cancer. Five new products were expected to be launched for marketing over the next two years.

In a practice defined as "innovative lifecycle management," GSK's research organization also sought to extend the patent life of established agents by releasing slightly altered forms of already marketed agents. Wellbutrin, an antidepressant, was reformulated as a long-acting, once daily formulation, and was expected to be released in 2003.

Research and development was also committed to extending product lines. Pharmaceutical manufacturers were allowed to resubmit drug applications to the U.S. Food and Drug Administration (FDA) for already marketed agents in order to advertise the drug for expanded uses. GSK expected that new indications approved by the FDA for established agents would contribute to future growth. While physicians often prescribed drugs for "off-label" use, FDA approval legitimized such use and decreased attendant liability. Also, pharmaceutical manufacturers were prohibited by the FDA from encouraging the use of agents for non-approved indications, severely limiting marketing potential. Finally, acquiring new indications for older agents could effectively extend the period of patent protection and discourage generic competition. GSK aggressively sought expanded indications for Paxil, Coreg, Augmentin, and Advair during 2002.[32]

Marketing and general administration costs decreased in 2002 to $12,062 million, a decrease of 0.4%. GSK continued to expand their sales force with a particular focus on new product launches.

Emphasizing an international presence, GSK participated in community service initiatives around the world. Working with the United Nations, the company established fixed, not-for-profit pricing for anti-retroviral (HIV/AIDS) and anti-malarial drugs to public sector customers and nonprofit organizations in the least developed countries and in sub-Saharan Africa. GSK also established preferential pricing to employers that provided HIV/AIDS treatment to their employees in the sub-Sahara. In the United States, GSK initiated the Orange Card program in January 2002, in order to provide medications to the poor that did not have public or private prescription drug coverage. GSK reported worldwide community investment and charitable donations of $104 million in 2001, 2.3% of net income.

The Pharmaceutical Industry

In 2001, prescription drug spending was the fastest growing component of national health expenditures, totaling $141 billion, or 10%, of U.S. national health expenditures.[33] Prescription drug spending had grown 15.7% from the $122 billion spent in 2000. In 2002, drug sales growth slowed but still rose 12%, essentially due to the industry's ability to raise drug prices in the United States by an average of 4%, nearly double the rate of inflation.[34] Two sectors comprised the industry: research-based pharmaceutical companies that developed new branded agents, and generic houses that marketed previously branded drugs that had lost patent protection.

The average revenue growth for the branded pharmaceutical industry slowed from 9.5% in 2001 to 4.5% in 2002.[35] The top ten companies accounted for 60% of all U.S. drug sales. Slowing revenue growth was primarily due to the entry into the market of generic formulations of previous blockbuster products,[36] such as Prilosec (omeprazole) and Prozac (fluoxetine). Concurrent with eroding profits, research and development costs were rising, accelerating to nearly a 17% increase in 2001 up from 8% in 1999. Research and development spending increased 16.6% to $30.3 billion from 2000 to 2001, claiming 13% of revenues. However, the rate at which branded pharmaceutical manufacturers were launching blockbuster products appeared to be slowing.[37] New molecular entities (unique active ingredients at their initial introduction to the pharmaceutical marketplace that had the potential to become blockbuster products) declined to 15 in 2002 compared with the 23 entities brought to market in 1990. Concerns developed that revenue loss to generic formulations was not being offset by the introduction of new agents. Therefore, branded pharmaceutical companies sought strategies to sustain growth that were less research intensive. "Life cycle management" became a strategy to leverage the potential of existing, already marketed agents.[38] This strategy included line extension, the introduction of slightly altered formulations in order to gain patent protection. Aggressive protection of intellectual property through litigation against encroaching generic competitors was another strategy commonly used to manage the life cycle of existing agents.

In 2001, the average branded pharmaceutical company committed 31% of revenues for selling, general, and administrative expenses. Few companies specified the advertising and promotion component of this expense; however, it was estimated to be as high as 12% of revenue in 2001. Marketing spending was divided into direct to consumer advertising (DTC), physician advertising and detailing, and provision of free drug samples as shown in **Exhibit 5**. DTC grew the fastest of the three categories, at a rate of 33% between 1996 and 2000. Marketing dollars were committed to free samples in the hope that patients would not be switched to competing products when a formal prescription was written.

Branded pharmaceutical manufacturers remained highly profitable throughout 2002, with an average 20% profit margin, and were predicted to experience accelerated growth in 2003. Analyst David Reisinger stated, "Despite earnings disappointments, the pharmaceutical

Exhibit 5 Promotional Activity Spending of Pharmaceutical Companies as a Percentage of Total Promotional Spending

Promotional Activity	1996 (%)	2000 (%)
Free samples	53.5%	50.6%
Physician detailing	32.8	30.6
Direct-to-Consumer advertising (DTC)	8.6	15.7
Advertising in professional journals	5.0	3.1
Total promotional spending, in millions	$9,164.3	$15,708.2

Note: As estimated by IMS Health. The 1996 figures add to 99.9%.

industry maintains a very healthy financial position and generates healthy cash flow."[39] Variance in financial performance of individual companies was predicted to continue, however, ultimately separating winners and losers.

The generic drug industry enjoyed explosive growth of 55% in 2001, to nearly $6 billion, and benefited from the patent expirations on several blockbuster branded agents. Although growth slowed in 2002, the fundamentals of the industry remained strong. Cost containment efforts by insurance plans and healthcare systems routinely encouraged the utilization of generic products. In order to encourage use of generic products, such plans offered low out-of-pocket co-payments for these agents, significantly lower than the out-of-pocket cost for comparable, branded agents. However, no generic manufacturer had yet to be included in the top ten U.S. drug companies as of 2001. Indeed, generic drugs accounted for 47% of the dispensed prescriptions in the United States, but only 8% of dollar sales, highlighting the cost differential between generic and branded agents.

Both sectors continued to experience high profits and healthy cash flows. Both outperformed the S&P during the period 1998–2002. While the average stock price to earnings (P/E) multiple for the S&P 500 during that period was 24 times, the average P/E multiple for branded companies was 28 times, while generic manufacturers experienced a stock price that was 29 times earnings.

Health Insurance Coverage in America

The vast majority of Americans in 2003 relied on healthcare insurance benefits to shield them from the major financial impact of illness or accident. In general, Americans that had access to prescription drug coverage during this period did so as part of general healthcare insurance coverage. The Henry Kaiser Family Foundation tracked annual changes in health insurance coverage for all Americans, and in January 2003 released annual statistics for 2001.[40] On average, one in six non-elderly Americans was uninsured during the year. Also, the probability of becoming uninsured varied depending on age, income, work status, race, ethnicity, and other demographic factors. Despite the economic boom of the 1990s, approximately one million adults joined the ranks of the uninsured each year during the decade. The rate slowed perceptibly, even decreased in 1999 and 2000, but began to increase again with the economic downturn in 2001, as the percentage of Americans with employer-sponsored health insurance decreased for the first time since 1993. At the end of 2001, the number of uninsured individuals reached 40.9 million, while the total of uninsured was estimated to be over 43 million in 2003. The 2001 census counted 281.4 million Americans. Hence, 15.3% of Americans were uninsured in 2003. Meanwhile, family incomes for the poor (< 100% of poverty level) and near-poor (between 100%–200% of poverty) shifted downward after 2000.

Non-elderly adults with low incomes were the least likely to have job-based insurance during 2001. Less than half of the persons in low-income families that had two full-time workers had job-based coverage and over 25% were completely uninsured. As a group, only 17% of the poor and 43% of the near poor received a health insurance benefit. Finally, employees in service and labor jobs were far more likely to be uninsured than those with technical, professional, sales, and managerial jobs, even within the same industry and employer.

While Medicaid eligibility requirements for children were more relaxed, adults faced higher hurdles. Therefore, nearly 20% of American adults under the age of 65 were uninsured during 2001, compared to only 12% of children. Racial and ethnic disparities were also detected in patterns of healthcare coverage. Even after adjusting for income differences, minority groups were less likely to have access to health insurance. While minority groups comprised 30% of the non-elderly population in America, they represented nearly 53% of the uninsured.

The Weak Economy Affects Healthcare Benefits

Employers succeeded in modifying insurance benefits during the stagnant economy by transferring greater out-of-pocket costs to employees, or simply declining to contribute to a premium for health insurance at all. More than 43 million Americans were essentially without healthcare insurance. Many of these people were working but unable to afford their contribution to the insurance premium. Caught in a paradox, they had incomes too high to be eligible for public healthcare coverage, such as Medicaid. At the same time, middle class senior citizens that relied on Medicare supplemental insurance benefits as part of a pension package watched as one company after another, old-guard and new, discontinued such coverage. In 1998, 66% of large employers offered retiree health and prescription benefits to retirees. By 2000, less than 40% of such employers did so. Of those that continued to provide health benefits, only 79% offered any type of prescription coverage.[41] By 2003, only 30% of retired seniors carried Medicare supplemental health insurance provided by a former employer.[42] At the same time, 9% of large employers reported in a 2003 survey that they were very likely to eliminate retiree benefits by 2004 for new and current employees that had not yet retired and 6% reported that they would eliminate employee health benefits entirely.[43] A study by the Employee Benefit Research Institute published in 2003 provided some insight into the financial ramifications of being elderly and insured only by Medicare.[44] They estimated that individuals retiring at 65 in 2003 and living until age 85 could expect to pay $100,000 per person out-of-pocket for healthcare over that period. Those that would retire in 2013 (at 65 years and surviving 20 years) could expect to pay at least twice that amount when including Medicare premiums, drugs, and all other out-of-pocket costs.

Prescription Drug Utilization and Spending for Prescription Drugs

Prescription drug use accounted for only 5% of national health expenditures as late as the 1970s. Most insurers did not cover the prescription drug costs. Individuals paid for the relatively few agents that were available out of their own pocket. Perhaps ironically, prescription drug coverage was introduced as a benefit with the advent of managed care in the 1980s. In fact, many beneficiaries of managed care health benefits received pharmaceutical products for no cost. Others paid nominal co-payments of $5–$10 per prescription. Under this system, the out-of-pocket costs contributed by individuals to acquire prescriptions remained low, resulting in burgeoning demand for and utilization of prescription drug products. Private insurance pay-out for prescription drugs was $45 billion in 1991, or 26% of retail drug revenues. By 2001 this figure had ballooned to $141 billion, now 47% of retail drug revenues.[45]

The average individual spent $449 out of his or her own pocket for prescription drugs in 2001, representing 0.9% of personal income. However, the out-of-pocket cost increased significantly with increasing age as portrayed in the **Exhibits 6 and 7**.[46] The American Association for Retired Persons estimated that 80% of Americans 65 years old or older used at least one prescription drug every day. The typical Medicare beneficiary filled a prescription eighteen times per year, a rate of one prescription every twenty days.[47]

A study published by the Department of Health and Human Services in 2001 indicated that customers that paid out-of-pocket paid nearly 15% more for prescription drugs than customers

Exhibit 6
Average Annual Out-of-Pocket Expenditure by Age

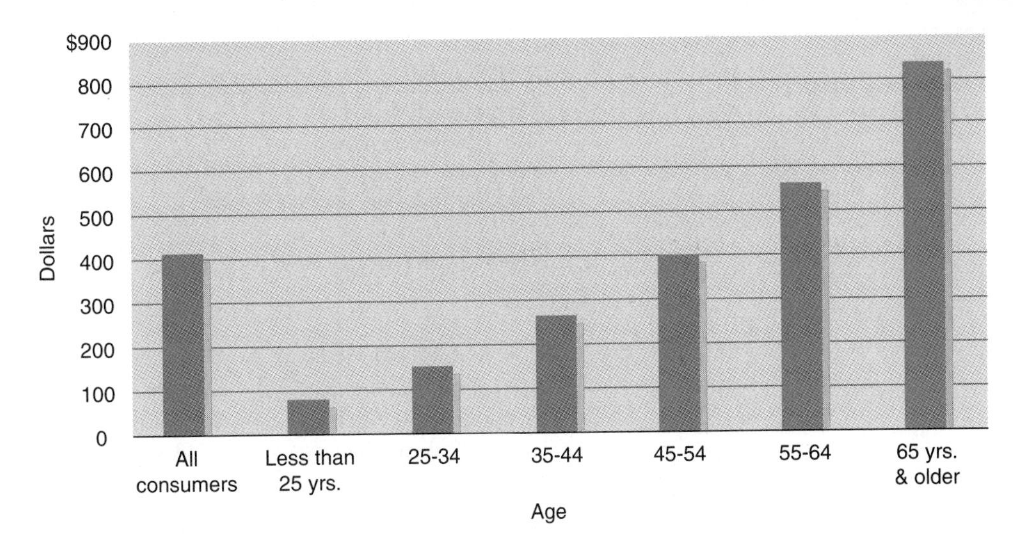

with prescription drug insurance coverage.[48] For the 25% of the most commonly prescribed drugs, this differential was even higher, over 20%. This differential was attributed to the bargaining potential of pharmacy benefit managers (PBMs) that represented prescription drug plans in negotiations with pharmaceutical manufacturers over drug prices. Intense competition between companies to control market share for common therapeutic drug classes resulted in even greater influence of the PBM when negotiating prices for these commonly used agents. The resulting differential outcome strongly reinforced the value of prescription drug insurance coverage.

Medicare was originally created to provide a safety net against rising hospitalization costs for senior citizens. It had never included a benefit for prescription drugs used in the outpatient setting. Few prescription medications were available prior to 1965, the year Medicare was unveiled, and few envisioned the explosion in products resulting from pharmaceutical research. While some Medicare beneficiaries enjoyed prescription drug benefits from other

Exhibit 7
Percentage of Annual Income Spent on Drugs, by Age

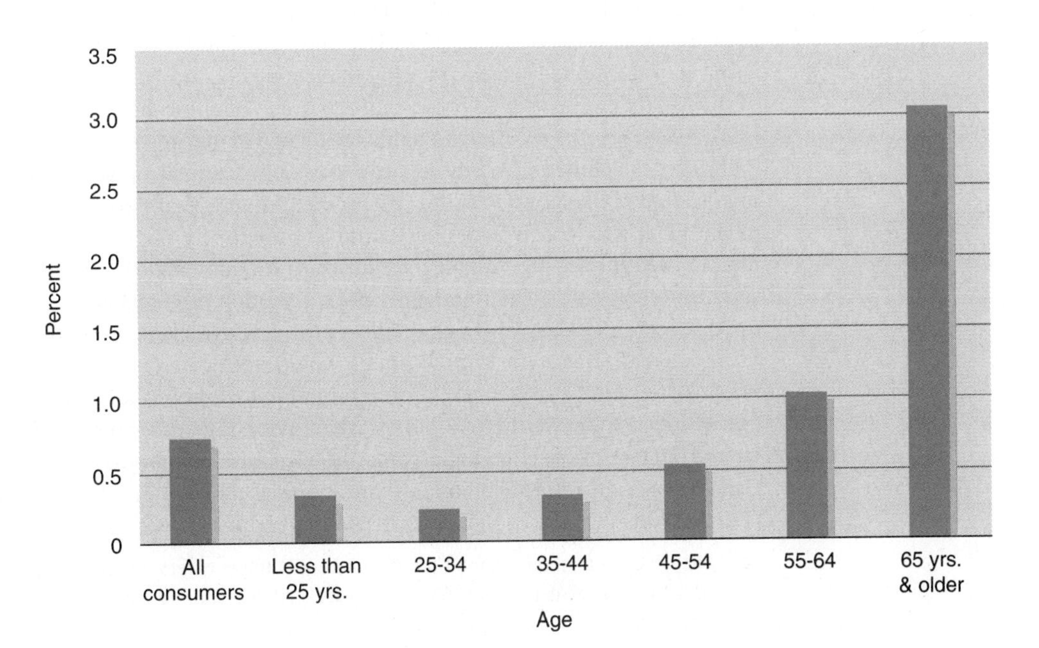

Exhibit 8
Sources of Prescription Drug Coverage for Medicare Beneficiaries

Source of Coverage	1999
Employer sponsored	30.4%
Medicare managed care	15.4%
Medicaid	11.1%
Medigap (privately purchased policies)	11.0%
Other public sources	1.7%
No drug coverage	23.8%

public and private sources, 23.8% of Medicare beneficiaries lacked any type of prescription coverage in 1999. These seniors were more likely to live in rural areas, were 85 years of age or older, and were near poor (income between $10,000–$20,000 per annum). Sources of prescription drug coverage for Medicare beneficiaries in 1999 are summarized in **Exhibit 8**. The beneficiaries with supplementary prescription coverage received an average of $1,131 worth of product, paying 31% or $352 out of their own resources. In contrast, the beneficiary with no supplementary coverage received 45% less, or an average of $617 worth of product, 100% of it covered out of pocket.

In 2002, 13% of Medicare beneficiaries enrolled in managed care programs had no drug coverage, 15% could elect drug coverage for an additional premium, and 72% had limited drug coverage included in the Medicare managed care plan. Almost 1/3 of these plans limited drug choice to generic formulations and enforced relatively low coverage limits, often less than $500.[49]

The Food and Drug Administration's Role

The U.S. Food and Drug Administration (FDA) was responsible for ensuring that drug products made available in the United States were safe and effective. The Division of Import Operations and Policy, a department of the FDA, administered the United States Federal Food, Drug, and Cosmetic Act,[50] which prohibited the interstate shipment (including importation) of unapproved new drugs whether for personal use or otherwise. Unapproved drugs included foreign-made versions of U.S.-approved drugs that had not been manufactured in accordance with and pursuant to FDA approval. Under this act, the FDA could refuse to admit into the United States any drug that "appeared" to be unapproved, placing the burden of proof on the importer to prove that the drug sought to be imported was approved by the FDA. However, the FDA was cognizant of its limited resources in enforcing this act and, therefore, developed a policy regarding its enforcement priorities related to the personal importation of prescription drugs. Under the "Coverage of Personal Importation,"[51] the focus of the FDA was to confiscate only products obviously intended for the commercial resale market (determined by volume), fraudulent products, and those that posed obvious health risks. In other words, small amounts of prescription products (enough for ninety days) destined for personal use and personally carried across the border from outside the United States or mailed into the United States would not normally draw scrutiny as violating the Food, Drug, and Cosmetics Act. In fact, the FDA allowed their own and customs personnel to consider a more permissive policy when assessing such drug products for entry into the United States. In order to understand the impetus for the growth of imported drugs from Canada, one must read the careful wording of the FDA "general guidance" detailed in the "Personal Importation" subchapter of the Regulatory Procedures Manual:

> The statements in this chapter are intended only to provide operating guidance for FDA personnel and are not intended to create or confer any rights, privileges, or benefits on or for any private person.

> FDA personnel may use their discretion to allow entry of shipments of violative FDA regulated products when the quantity and purpose are clearly for personal use, and the product does not present an unreasonable risk to the user. Even though all products that appear to be in violation of statutes administered by the FDA are subject to refusal (for entry), FDA personnel may use their discretion to examine the background, risk, and purpose of the product before making a final decision (to allow entry). Although FDA may use discretion to allow admission of certain violative items, this should not be interpreted as a license to individuals to bring in such shipments.[52]

Under this guidance, the product and its intended use were to be identified, the intended use could not be for the treatment of a serious condition, and the product could not be known to represent a significant health risk.

Alternatively, drugs imported for personal use could be used to treat more serious conditions as long as an effective treatment was not available domestically, there was no known commercialization or promotion of the product to those residing in the United States, the product was not considered to pose an unreasonable risk, the individual importing the drug verified that it was for personal use and included no more than a ninety-day supply, and a U.S. physician was involved in the person's medical care. In such cases, "persons were still breaking the law by acquiring drugs from outside the country, however, the FDA was letting them get away with it," according to an anonymous FDA attorney. Emphasizing that the personal use importation guidance was meant to save FDA resources, and to generally permit medical treatments sought by individuals that were not otherwise available in the United States, the FDA stated that "foreign-made chemical versions of drugs available in the U.S. were not intended to be covered by the personal use policy."[53]

Adopting a relaxed stance under the "personal use guidance," the FDA did little to dissuade the importation of prescription drug products throughout the period from 1995-2003. Despite the growing popularity of Internet pharmacies among Americans, (especially Canadian pharmacies) the FDA did little to inhibit the practice of purchasing foreign drug products online, ostensibly because it did not want to appear unsympathetic to American consumers, especially the elderly.[54] In fact, in the fall of 2002, when American employers and insurers began advocating the use of Canadian pharmacies by covering claims generated there, the FDA associate commissioner for policy and planning, William Hubbard, stated, "If they are not actually importing drugs, I don't know what enforcement role we (FDA) would have."[55] However, the FDA stance appeared to change dramatically in response to GlaxoSmithKline's retaliation to cross-border sales. Quickly, the FDA indicated it would change its regulatory stance and crack down on the importation of drugs, even those clearly destined for personal use.[56] Seeking to distance the agency's harder line from the consumer, Mr. Hubbard implied that insurers that helped Americans import drugs might come under fire. In a February 2003 letter sent to address the questions of an attorney representing health plans, Mr. Hubbard stated,

> Those who aid and abet a criminal violation of the (Food, Drug, and Cosmetic) Act, or conspire to violate the act can also be found criminally liable. Any party participating in an import plan in which a health insurer or claims processor helps arrange a purchase (of drugs) from Canada, does so at its own legal risk.[57]

At the same time, the FDA echoed GSK by citing safety reasons for enforcing the Food, Drug, and Cosmetic Act.[58] Imported drugs might be less likely to be manufactured under exacting specifications and might be mislabeled or otherwise without specific directions for use. The FDA established that this was a public health risk, because Americans had little, if any, recourse if they were exposed to tainted drug product. Sources at the FDA also expressed concern that Canadian pharmacies were diverting drugs from deserving Canadian citizens in order to capture a tidy profit by selling prescription products to Americans. The spread between acquisition cost from pharmaceutical companies and selling price to Americans was enhanced by the attractive exchange rate between American and Canadian dollars at the time. This was true despite the fact that Americans were often purchasing products for as much as 80% less than they would pay for the products in the United States.

European Influence on Pharmaceutical Pricing

The European pricing for prescription drug products influenced pricing of the products in the United States. Due to the administration of national healthcare systems, the European governments set price controls for prescription drug products. In June 2002, the German Health Ministry attempted to cut by 4% the prices it would pay for prescription products to provide public health services.[59] Drug companies balked, as the public health system purchased 80% of all drugs in the country. In a compromise, Chancellor Gerhardt Schroeder agreed to veto the price cut if major drug companies would establish a trust fund designed to finance Germany's soaring healthcare costs. GlaxoSmithKline, along with 37 other multinational pharmaceutical companies, reluctantly agreed to the plan. Worried that other European countries that administer nationalized health systems would follow suit and make the same demands for price cuts, the drug companies had little leverage in Germany and were highly motivated to accept the establishment of the trust fund in lieu of price cuts.

Across the ocean, the outcome of these negotiations directly affected Americans and the prices they paid for prescription drug products. The United States was the only major industrialized country that did not administer some sort of governmental price control for drug products. Pharmaceutical manufacturers openly admitted that as European governments mandated price cuts and eroded the profitability of the European markets, they increased prescription prices in the United States. "Step-by-step, the profitability of European markets is decreasing, and we're depending on the U.S. market more and more," said Jean-Francois Dehecq, chief executive of the French drug maker, Sanofi-Synthelabo.[60] In each of the years prior to 2003, the cost of drugs in the United States had increased by 2%-3% annually, sometimes more, as European governments mandated price cuts in Europe. One company increased prices in the United States by 5.9% annually for three popular medications used to treat heart disease, asthma, and osteoporosis. The result was large differences in the prices that Americans paid for prescriptions versus those paid in other markets. While Europe accounted for the largest single market in the world for prescription drugs, it accounted for just 22% of the dollar sales in the global market. Meanwhile the United States, with fewer people, contributed more than 46% of global dollar sales, and more than 60% of profits.

Donna Shalala, U.S. Secretary of Health and Human Services under President Clinton, commented on the situation. While pointing out that U.S. taxpayers financed much of the basic research that supported the pharmaceutical industry, she remarked, "We have been subsidizing this research and in return we get to pay higher prices (than Europeans)? It's not fair."[61]

Employers and Insurers Join the Debate

Americans were not always acting independently when they acquired necessary prescription medications from Canadian pharmacies via the Internet. Various retirement plans and insurers endorsed the practice to varying degrees. United Health Group, in conjunction with the American Association of Retired Persons (AARP), announced in October 2002 that it was waiving its policy requiring prescriptions eligible for Medicare supplemental insurance coverage to be purchased in the United States or a U.S. territory.[62] Therefore, it would cover the cost of prescription drugs acquired from pharmacies not just in Canada, but also around the world. While not explicitly encouraging the practice of shopping for prescriptions outside the country, the announcement educated more than 400,000 AARP beneficiaries to the possibility.

Meanwhile, some employers and insurers overtly encouraged their retired employees and beneficiaries to purchase prescription drugs from Canadian Internet pharmacies in order to take advantage of cost savings. The National Association of Retired and Veteran Railway Employees Inc.[63] provided a hyperlink to a Canadian Internet pharmacy on its own Web site. The pharmacy site included a catalog of available medications (narcotics were not available) and the cost, in American dollars, of each agent. A selection of "frequently asked questions" instructed users how to use the site and reassured users of the similarity between drug agents available in the United States and Canada. Users were informed that, "prescription drugs coming from Canada are made by the same manufacturers, often at the same plants, as those sold in the U.S." In order to protect Canadian citizens, "Health Canada, the equivalent of the U.S. FDA, provides strict oversight of prescription drugs." The site continued by informing users that a report issued by the Congressional Research Service in Washington DC found that, "pharmaceutical manufacturing practices required by Health Canada and the U.S. FDA are equivalent." The site also informed users of the FDA "general guidance" on personal importation of medication. "While it is technically illegal to purchase medicines from a Canadian pharmacy, the FDA exercises enforcement discretion to allow individuals to import up to a ninety-day supply of prescription drugs for personal use."

Where Elected Officials Stood

Congress had made several attempts to legalize the personal importation of prescription drugs by early 2003, largely due to concern about rapidly rising drug costs for senior citizens.[64] However, the drug industry, applying an aggressive lobbying campaign, had succeeded in preventing the passage of such legislation. During 2002, the Senate voted to allow importation of prescription drugs from Canada, but the proposition never came to a vote in the House of Representatives. A bill legalizing importation from Canadian pharmacies passed both the Senate and the House in 2000. However, the Clinton administration declined to implement the legislation, ostensibly over worries about verifying product safety and little documentation that the practice would actually save money.[65]

Individual elected officials reacted quickly to GSK's policy of limiting drug product to Canadian pharmacies that exported to the United States. Russ Feingold, U.S. Senator from Wisconsin, introduced a bill in Congress to deny tax breaks to pharmaceutical companies that restricted shipment of drugs to Canada.[66] Vermont Representative Bernard Sanders also introduced a bill specifically penalizing GSK for its attempt to cut off U.S. consumer access to Canadian drugs, citing restriction of free trade.[67] Congressman Gil Gutknecht, a Republican from the first district in Minnesota, responded to the shipment restriction,

> Glaxo's brazen attempt to prevent Americans from obtaining lower cost medications from Canada is a textbook example of brazen abuse of monopolistic power. Glaxo is attempting to fix prices. If this isn't a classic example of anti-trust abuse, it should be. It is time for our attorney general to dust off anti-trust laws and enforce them.[68]

By April 2003, legislators were actively accusing the FDA and GlaxoSmithKline of "scaring seniors that are trying to get more affordable medicines."[69] In a raucous hearing, members of the recently formed House Subcommittee on Human Rights and Wellness said the FDA had no evidence of safety problems with drug reimportation and that the agency was shifting its personal importation policy because of drug industry pressure. The committee insisted the FDA should use its efforts to find a way to allow safe importation of drugs from Canada instead. Vermont Representative Sanders criticized the FDA by saying, "You should be putting out pamphlets saying people have been going across the border . . . and there hasn't been one problem."[70]

Meanwhile, busloads of constituents, with their elected officials on-board, continued to make the trip to Canada with the explicit purpose of acquiring prescription drugs at lower cost than was available in the United States. Most prominent, perhaps, was Minnesota Senator Mark Dayton, who donated his annual Senate salary of $145,000 to subsidize monthly trips for senior citizens to purchase drugs in Canada.[71]

GlaxoSmithKline Attempted Discount Card

GSK, in cooperation with other large pharmaceutical manufacturers, began to offer a discount card in 2001 to provide assistance to low-income American families that earned less than $28,000 annually. The card, named Together RX, provided a variable discount for prescription products up to 40% off retail prices. However, in the autumn of 2002, GSK cut the discount, maintaining that the U.S. government would use the low retail prices to demand even lower prices for Medicaid beneficiaries.[72] GSK referred to legislation enacted in 1990 which stipulated that drug manufacturers must treat the Medicaid program as a most-favored customer, meaning that no other buyer could have access to lower prices for prescription product than the Medicaid program. Anxious that the government would accuse GSK of selling prescription drugs to low-income families at a cost lower than that available to Medicaid, they decreased the program discounts to reflect Medicaid pricing. The result was a significant increase in prices for participants in the GSK discount program, while Medicaid beneficiaries continued to pay nominal co-payments to acquire drug products. (Federal and state administrators of the Medicaid program then reimbursed intermediaries for the cost of the prescription at most-favored pricing.) After that time, GSK encouraged concerned Americans to urge Congress to enact a Medicare prescription drug benefit in order to help resolve issues relating to the affordability of medicines.[73]

GSK also provided drugs to qualifying persons through a Patient Assistance Program. In 2002, the program provided free medications valued at $168 million to 400,000 Americans with incomes below $24,000 for a household of two.[74]

Public Perception

The Wall Street Journal conducted a non-scientific, Web-based poll of its readers on March 11, 2003, in order to elicit opinion about Americans that acquired prescription drugs from Internet pharmacies in Canada.[75] The responses to the poll provided some insight into the public image of GSK and other pharmaceutical corporations. The *Journal* received 1,665 answers in response to the question, "Should regulators try to stop Americans from buying prescription drugs from Canada?" Eighty-four percent of respondents said "No," while 16% said "Yes." The poll also provided respondents an opportunity to provide editorial comment on the question. Fifty-two written responses were generated in answer to the preceding question. All but two of the respondents referred negatively to the pharmaceutical industry in their editorial answer. Most respondents complained of "price fixing" by pharmaceutical companies, specifically GSK, in the United States. Others referred to "restraint of free trade," when U.S. citizens were prevented from purchasing prescriptions from Canada. Other editorials suggested that the FDA had altered its stance regarding the personal importation of medications due to political pressure from pharmaceutical companies. Campaign contributions to high-profile officials by pharmaceutical companies were suggested several times as one reason why a price differential for drugs remained between America and the rest of the world. In general, the safety rationale provided by GSK for more stringently regulating imports from Canada was dismissed as rhetorical and not believed to be the authentic reason for GSK's actions.

Two respondents referred to the high cost of pharmaceutical research and Americans' ability to pay higher prices as the primary reason for the cost differential. One respondent worried that the ultimate response by the pharmaceutical industry to the importation issue would be to increase the costs of drugs in Canada, ultimately limiting access for that country as well.

Meanwhile, *The Wall Street Journal* mocked the abrupt crackdown by the FDA with a characterization of the typical "drug trafficker" bringing in medications from abroad.[76] Dubbing elderly Americans as "not your generic smugglers," they described a typical "profile" as "white, elderly, often wearing Bermuda shorts, and American Legion baseball caps." Ostensibly, the detailed "profile" would make it easier for these "traffickers" to be spotted by the FDA. Adopting a serious tone, the author described the motivation of the traffickers. "For many elderly shoppers, cutting the cost of medications is a crucial part of budgeting for retirement." A 76-year-old woman was blunt about her need to leave the country to acquire medicine, "I live on less than $1,200 per month and I saw a $50,000 stock portfolio evaporate since 2000. If I couldn't get cheap meds, I couldn't live."[77]

Americans, especially the elderly, paid the highest prices in the world for prescription drugs.[78] Even though they represented the biggest market for drugs, they had no ability to negotiate prices. Like the 76-year-old woman forced to leave the United States to acquire medicine, a large contingent of the elderly simply could not afford the medications they required to stay alive. But unlike most other developed countries, they received no help from their government to acquire necessary prescriptions.

The Tradeoffs: Health vs. Profits vs. Safety

What was the responsibility of GlaxoSmithKline to see that American patients, especially those with limited means, could have regular access to prescription drug products? Glaxo maintained that patient safety was their primary motivation for the retaliation against cross-border sales from Canada into the United States. Company officials stated, "GSK decided to block the reimportation from Canada out of concern for patient safety. Although consumers may be getting the very same drugs they would buy in the U.S., the drugs may be damaged in transport, mislabeled, or otherwise adulterated."[79]

But was safety the most relevant issue when the product was not a consumer good but rather necessary for health, perhaps even life, but was too expensive for a significant portion of the American population? As University of Minnesota professor Barbara Kaufmann reiterated, "A drug that is not affordable is neither safe nor effective."[80]

What sort of power differential separated GSK from their customers? Did GSK damage their public image through their action? If so, what strategic resources must be committed to repair the resulting damage and restore good public relations to the commerce of GSK?

Notes

1. B. Strunk, P. Ginsburg, and J. Gabel, "Tracking Health Care Costs: Growth Accelerates Again in 2001," *Health Affairs* (September 25, 2002), pp. W299–W310.
2. K. Levit, C. Smith, C. Cowan, et al., "Trends in U.S. Health Care Spending, 2001," *Health Affairs* Vol. 22, No. 1 (2003), pp. 154–164.
3. J. Baglole, "What's New at the Mall of America? Cheaper Drugs from Canada," *The Wall Street Journal* (November 8, 2002).
4. S. Lueck and J. Baglole, "Glaxo Says It Will Retaliate Against Cross-Border Sales," *The Wall Street Journal* (January 13, 2003); J. Baglole, "Glaxo Presses Canadian Firms Not to Resell Its Drugs to U.S.," *The Wall Street Journal* (January 22, 2003); J. Fisher, "GSK Fighting Border Battle," *The News and Observer* (February 13, 2003).
5. W. Wolf, "Seniors Groups Boycott Glaxo over Canada Move," *Star Tribune* (February 23, 2003).

6. A. Dembner, "Rallies Aim to Save Canadian Drug Sales," *The Boston Globe* (February 20, 2003).
7. E. Reguly, "Drugstores That Are Hard to Swallow," *Time Canada* Vol. 16, No. 5 (2003), p. 29.
8. *Ibid.*
9. GlaxoSmithKline, Important Facts Patients Should Know About Cross-Border Internet Sales, *www.gsk.com/media/ca_key.html*.
10. *Ibid.*
11. S. Lueck and J. Baglole, "Glaxo Says It Will Retaliate Against Cross-Border Sales," *The Wall Street Journal* (January 13, 2003); J. Baglole, "Glaxo Presses Canadian Firms Not to Resell Its Drugs to U.S.," *The Wall Street Journal* (January 22, 2003); W. Wolf, "Seniors Groups Boycott Glaxo over Canada Move," *Star Tribune* (February 23, 2003).
12. C. Serres, "Drug Titan Draws Ire," *The News and Observer* (February 14, 2003); A. Krishnan, "GlaxoSmithKline Fights War of Perceptions over Flow of Drugs from Canada," *The (Durham, North Carolina) Herald-Sun* (February 4, 2003).
13. A. Taylor, "Seniors Find Drug Relief in Canada: Congress Will Push Again for Law to Allow Pharmacists to Import Cheaper Medications," *The Detroit News* (August 21, 2001).
14. C. Serres, "Drug Titan Draws Ire," *The News and Observer* (February 14, 2003).
15. A. Krishnan, "GlaxoSmithKline Fights War of Perceptions over Flow of Drugs from Canada," *The (Durham, North Carolina) Herald-Sun* (February 4, 2003).
16. PR Newswire, *Philadelphia Seniors' Organizations Protest Glaxo's Ban on Affordable Drugs* (February 19, 2003), "U.S. & Canadian Organizations Slam Glaxo's Ban Against Affordable Prescription Drugs for American Seniors in Need," *Today's Seniors Network* (February 12, 2003), *http://todayseniornetwork.com/glaxo_ad_campaign.html*; T. Agovino, "Pharmacy Seeks Boycott of Glaxo Products," Associated Press Online (February 4, 2003).
17. A. Dembner, "Rallies Aim to Save Canadian Drug Sales," *The Boston Globe* (February 20, 2003).
18. PR Newswire, *GlaxoSmithKline Actions Threaten Thousands* (February 20, 2003).
19. A. Dembner, "Rallies Aim to Save Canadian Drug Sales," *The Boston Globe* (February 20, 2003).
20. PR Newswire, *GlaxoSmithKline Actions Threaten Thousands* (February 20, 2003).
21. *Ibid.*
22. A. Krishnan, "GlaxoSmithKline Fights War of Perceptions over Flow of Drugs from Canada," *The (Durham, North Carolina) Herald-Sun* (February 4, 2003).
23. Canada NewsWire, *Manitoba On-line Pharmacies Slam Glaxo Drug Ban* (January 12, 2003).
24. PR Newswire, *GlaxoSmithKline Actions Threaten Thousands* (February 20, 2003).
25. T. Cohen, "Wholesaler Cuts GlaxoSmithKline Supplies," Associated Press Online (January 29, 2003).
26. A. Dembner, "Rallies Aim to Save Canadian Drug Sales," *The Boston Globe* (February 20, 2003).
27. C. Serres, "Drug Titan Draws Ire," *The News and Observer* (February 14, 2003).
28. J. Fisher, "GSK Fighting Border Battle," *The News and Observer* (February 13, 2003).
29. K. Green, "Retiree Returns to Early Shift, but This Time at Half Pay," *The Wall Street Journal* (March 5, 2003).
30. GlaxoSmithKline, *Annual Report* (2001); G. Naik and H. Hovey, "Glaxo Profit Rose 28% in 2002: Protest Against Company Urged," *The Wall Street Journal* (February 13, 2003); D. Ranii, "GSK Profit Increases, on This Side of Atlantic," *The News and Observer* (February 13, 2003).
31. T. Scully, L. vander Walde, K. Choi, and J. Higgins, *Health Care Industry Market Update* (Baltimore, MD: Centers for Medicare & Medicaid Services, January 10, 2003), *www.cms.hhs.gov/marketupdate*.
32. GlaxoSmithKline, *Annual Report* (2002).
33. T. Scully, L. vander Walde, K. Choi, and J. Higgins, *Health Care Industry Market Update* (Baltimore, MD: Centers for Medicare & Medicaid Services, January 10, 2003), *www.cms.hhs.gov/marketupdate*.
34. G. Harris, "Drug Sales Growth Slowed, but Still Rose 12% in 2002," *The Wall Street Journal* (February 23, 2003).
35. T. Scully, L. vander Walde, K. Choi, and J. Higgins, *Health Care Industry Market Update* (Baltimore, MD: Centers for Medicare & Medicaid Services, January 10, 2003), *www.cms.hhs.gov/marketupdate*.
36. C. Adams and G. Harris, "Drug Firms Face Growing Pressure over Extensions of Their Patents," *The Wall Street Journal* (March 19, 2002).
37. G. Harris, "Why Drug Makers Are Failing in the Quest for New Blockbusters," *The Wall Street Journal* (April 18, 2002).
38. G. Harris, "Prilosec's Maker Switches Users to Nexium, Thwarting Generics," *The Wall Street Journal* (June 6, 2002).
39. T. Scully, L. vander Walde, K. Choi, and J. Higgins, *Health Care Industry Market Update* (Baltimore, MD: Centers for Medicare & Medicaid Services, January 10, 2003), *www.cms.hhs.gov/marketupdate*.
40. C. Hoffman and M. Wang, *Health Insurance Coverage in America: 2001 Data Update* (The Kaiser Commission on Medicaid and the Uninsured, January 2003), *www.kkf.org*.
41. L. McCormack, J. Gabel, H. Whitmore, et al., "Trends in Retiree Health Benefits: Health Benefits for Retirees Are Eroding Even in the Best of Times," *Health Affairs*, Vol. 21, No. 6 (2003), pp. 169–176.
42. H. Gleckman, "Old, Ill, and Uninsured," *Business Week* (April 7, 2003), pp. 78–79.
43. L. McCormack, J. Gabel, H. Whitmore, et al., "Trends in Retiree Health Benefits: Health Benefits for Retirees Are Eroding Even in the Best of Times," *Health Affairs*, Vol. 21, No. 6 (2003), pp. 169–176.
44. H. Gleckman, "Old, Ill, and Uninsured," *Business Week* (April 7, 2003), pp. 78–79.
45. D. Kreling, D. Mott, J. Wiederholt, et al., *Prescription Drug Trends: A Chartbook Update* (The Kaiser Family Foundation, 2001).
46. T. Scully, L. vander Walde, K. Choi, and J. Higgins, *Health Care Industry Market Update* (Baltimore, MD: Centers for Medicare & Medicaid Services, January 10, 2003), *www.cms.hhs.gov/marketupdate*.
47. Medicare Prescription Drugs: Just the Facts. American Association of Retired Persons. *www.aarp.org/prescriptiondrugs/facts.html*; D. Gross, *Trends in Costs, Coverage, and Use of Prescription Drugs by Medicare Beneficiaries* (AARP, 2001), *http://research.aarp.org/health/dd63_trends.html*.
48. T. Scully, L. vander Walde, K. Choi, and J. Higgins, *Health Care Industry Market Update* (Baltimore, MD: Centers for Medicare & Medicaid Services, January 10, 2003), *www.cms.hhs.gov/marketupdate*.
49. Medicare Prescription Drugs: Just the Facts. American Association of Retired Persons. *www.aarp.org/prescriptiondrugs/facts.html*;

D. Gross, *Trends in Costs, Coverage, and Use of Prescription Drugs by Medicare Beneficiaries* (AARP, 2001), *http://research.aarp.org/health/dd63_trends.html.*

50. M. Blumberg, *Information on Importation of Drugs Prepared by the Division of Import Operations and Policy* (Washington, DC: Office of Regulatory Affairs, U.S. Food and Drug Administration, 1998), *www.fda.gov/ora/import/pipinfo.htm.*
51. "Coverage of Personal Importations," Regulatory Procedures Manual (Washington, DC: Office of Regulatory Affairs, U.S. Food and Drug Administration), *www.fda.gov/ora/compliance_ref/rpm_news2/ch9pers.htm.*
52. *Ibid.*
53. *Ibid.*
54. T. Burton, "FDA Is Cracking Down on Drugs from Canada," *The Wall Street Journal* (March 12, 2003).
55. *Ibid.*
56. J. Baglole, "FDA Effort to Halt Drugs from Canada Stirs Uproar," *The Wall Street Journal* (March 13, 2003).
57. W. Hubbard, *Letter to Robert P. Lombardi Esq. The Kullman Firm, New Orleans La.* (Washington, DC: U.S. Food and Drug Administration, February 12, 2003), *www.fda.gov.*
58. M. Meadows, "Imported Drugs Raise Safety Concerns," *FDA Consumer Magazine* (September/October 2002), *www.fda.gov/fdac/features/2002/502_import.html.*
59. V. Fuhrmans and G. Naik, "In Europe, Drug Makers Fight Against Mandatory Price Cuts," *The Wall Street Journal* (June 7, 2002).
60. *Ibid.*
61. *Ibid.*
62. T. Burton and S. Lueck, "AARP Insurer to Cover Drugs Purchased Outside the U.S.," *The Wall Street Journal* (October 11, 2002).
63. *Low-cost Safe Medicines from Canada: Frequently Asked Questions.* RRxA Railway Rx Assistant, *www.RailwayRxAssist.com/faq.htm.*
64. T. Burton and S. Lueck, "AARP Insurer to Cover Drugs Purchased Outside the U.S.," *The Wall Street Journal* (October 11, 2002).
65. L. McGinley, "Shalala Declines to Implement Law on Importing Prescription Drugs," *The Wall Street Journal* (December 27, 2000).
66. PR Newswire, *GlaxoSmithKline Actions Threaten Thousands* (February 20, 2003).
67. E. Kelly, "Sanders Introduces Prescription Drug Bill," Gannett News Service (February 18, 2003).
68. PR Newswire, *GlaxoSmithKline Actions Threaten Thousands* (February 20, 2003).
69. S. Lueck, "FDA Defends Tougher Stance on Drug Imports," *The Wall Street Journal* (April 4, 2003).
70. *Ibid.*
71. J. Baglole, "What's New at the Mall of America? Cheaper Drugs from Canada," *The Wall Street Journal* (November 8, 2002).
72. J. Graham, "Canada's Mail-Order Drug Houses Plague Glaxo," *The Wall Street Journal* (February 28, 2003).
73. *GlaxoSmithKline Calls for Passage of Medicare Prescription Drug Benefit* (GlaxoSmithKline, February 20, 2003), *www.gsk.com/press2003/press_02202003.htm.*
74. J. Graham, "Canada's Mail-Order Drug Houses Plague Glaxo," *The Wall Street Journal* (February 28, 2003).
75. "Reader Poll: Should Regulators Try to Stop Americans from Buying Prescription Drugs from Canada?" *The Wall Street Journal Online* (March 11, 2003), *www.wsj.com.*
76. J. Millman, "Not Your Generic Smugglers," *The Wall Street Journal* (March 20, 2003).
77. *Ibid.*
78. PR Newswire, *GlaxoSmithKline Actions Threaten Thousands* (February 20, 2003).
79. A. Dembner, "Rallies Aim to Save Canadian Drug Sales," *The Boston Globe* (February 20, 2003).
80. PR Newswire, *GlaxoSmithKline Actions Threaten Thousands* (February 20, 2003).

CASE 7

Starbucks' International Operations

Sanjib Dutta and K. Subhadra

"Internationally, we are in our infancy."
Howard Schultz, Chairman and Chief Global Strategist, Starbucks, March 2003

"The expansion strategy internationally is not bulletproof as it is in the U.S."
Mitchell J. Speiser, Analyst, Lehman Brothers, June 2003

All's Not Well with Starbucks

In March 2003, *Fortune* came out with its annual list of *Fortune 500* companies. For Howard Schultz, Chairman of Starbucks Corp., this list was special as Starbucks featured in the list. It was a dream come true for the Seattle-based entrepreneur.

Though the U.S. economy was reeling under recession and many major retailers were reporting losses and applying for bankruptcy, Starbucks announced a 31% increase in its net earnings and a 23% increase in sales for the first quarter of 2003. Analysts felt that the success of Starbucks showed that a quality product speaks for itself. The fact that Starbucks spent less than 1% of its sales on advertising and marketing strengthened this view. In addition to being a popular brand among customers, Starbucks was also considered the best place to work due to its employee-friendly policies.[1] **Exhibit 1** shows Starbucks' income statement. See Starbucks' 2002 Annual Report, at *http://www.starbucks.com/aboutus/financials.asp*, for complete financial statements.

Exhibit 1 Consolidated Statement of Earnings Starbucks Corporation (Dollar amounts in millions, except per share data)

	Year Ending		
	Sept. 29 2002	Sept. 30 2001	Oct. 1 2000
Net revenues:			
Retail	$2,792,904	$2,229,594	$1,823,607
Specialty	496,004	419,386	354,007
Total net revenues	3,288,908	2,648,980	2,177,614
Cost of sales and related occupancy costs	1,350,011	1,112,785	961,885
Store operating expenses	1,121,108	875,473	704,898
Other operating expenses	127,178	93,326	78,445
Depreciation and amortization expenses	205,557	163,501	130,232
General and administrative expenses	202,161	151,416	110,202
Income from equity investees	35,832	28,615	20,300
Operating income	318,725	281,094	212,252
Interest and other income, net	9,300	10,768	7,110
Internet-related investment losses	–	2,940	58,792
Gain on sale of investment	13,361	–	–
Earnings before income taxes	341,386	288,922	160,570
Income taxes	126,313	107,712	66,006
Net earnings	$ 215,073	$ 181,210	$ 94,564
Net earnings per common share—basic	$ 0.56	$ 0.48	$ 0.25
Net earnings per common share—diluted	$ 0.54	$ 0.46	$ 0.24
Weighted average shares outstanding:			
Basic	385,575	380,566	371,191
Diluted	397,526	394,349	385,999
Ratios (%)			
Cost of sales (%)	41.0	42.0	44.2
Operating income margin (%)	9.7	10.6	9.7
Net profit margin (%)	6.5	6.8	4.3

Source: Starbucks Corporation "2002 Annual Report."

However, analysts felt that the success of Starbucks was due to its profitable domestic operations. It was reported that most of Starbucks' international operations were running into losses. In May 2003, Starbucks' Japanese operations reported a loss of $3.9 million (Japan constituted the largest market for the company outside the United States), and the company also performed badly in Europe and the Middle East. Analysts pointed out that Starbucks' international operations were not as well planned as its U.S. operations. They also observed that the volatile international business environment made it difficult for the company to effectively manage its international operations.

Many analysts felt that it was important for the company to focus on its international operations. With the U.S. market getting saturated, Starbucks would be forced to look outside the United States for revenues and growth.

Background Note

The history of Starbucks dates to 1971, when Jerry Baldwin, Zev Siegl, and Gordon Bowker launched a coffee bean retailing store named Starbucks to sell specialty whole-bean coffee in Seattle. By 1981, the number of Starbucks stores had increased to five, and Starbucks had also established a small roasting facility in Seattle. Around the same time, Schultz, who was working with Hammarplast—a Swedish housewares company that marketed coffee makers—noticed that Starbucks, a small company from Seattle, was ordering more coffee makers than anyone else. In order to find out more about the company, Schultz visited Seattle. Schultz was so impressed by the company and its founders that he offered to work for the company.

In 1982, Schultz joined Starbucks as marketing manager, with an equity stake in the company. During his first year at Starbucks, he studied the various types of coffee and the intricacies of the coffee business. The turning point came in 1983, when Schultz was sent to Milan, Italy, for an international housewares show. There he observed that every street in the city had an espresso coffee bar where people met and spent time. Schultz realized that Starbucks could introduce espresso coffee bars in the United States. He put forward this idea to his partners, but they did not like the idea of selling espresso coffee. However, after a lot of persuasion from Schultz, they agreed to allow him to sell espresso coffee in their retail shop. The business picked up, and by the weekend, they were making more money by selling the beverage than by selling coffee beans. Still, the partners refused to venture into the beverage business, so Schultz decided to quit the company and start out on his own.

In April 1985, Schultz opened a coffee bar called Il Giornale in Seattle, with a seed capital of $150,000 invested by Jerry Baldwin and Gordon Bowker. The rest of the capital was raised through private placement. Soon, the second and third stores were opened in Seattle and Vancouver respectively. During 1987, when Schultz heard that Starbucks' owners were selling off six stores along with a roasting plant and the Starbucks brand name, he raised $3.8 million through private placements and bought Starbucks. Because Starbucks was a more established name, Schultz decided to retain it instead of Il Giornale.

Schultz expanded Starbucks to Chicago, Los Angeles, and other major cities. But with increasing overhead expenses, the company reported a loss of $1.2 million in 1990. However, Schultz was confident of his business plan and continued his expansion spree. He even hired employees from companies such as PepsiCo. By 1991, the number of Starbucks stores had increased to 116, and Starbucks became the first privately owned company to offer employee stock options. In 1992, Starbucks was listed on the New York Stock Exchange at a price of $17 per share.

The strategy Starbucks adopted was to blanket a region with its new stores. By doing so, it could reduce the customers' rush in one store and also increase its revenues through new stores. This helped the company to reduce its distribution costs and the waiting period for customers in its stores, thereby increasing the number of customers. It was reported that on average, a customer visited Starbucks stores 18 times a month, a very high number compared to other American retailers. By 1993 there were around 100 Starbucks stores, which increased to 145 in 1994.

Along with serving coffee, Starbucks also sold merchandise. In 1995, it started selling CDs of its famous in-house music program. It also entered into alliances with various players such as Canadian Airlines, United Air Lines, Starwood Hotels, and Barnes & Noble, Inc., to serve Starbucks coffee.

Analysts attributed the success of Starbucks not only to its aggressive expansion but also to its product innovation. Starbucks came out with new products to attract customers. For instance, in 1995, to cater to the needs of diet-conscious young people, it launched Frappuccino—a low fat creamy iced coffee. In 1996, it launched ice cream and ice cream bars through its subsidiary Starbucks and Dreyer's Grand Ice Cream, Inc. In the same year, it also entered into an agreement with PepsiCo to launch bottled Starbucks Frappuccino. Due to all these initiatives, Starbucks has recorded an average growth of 20% per year since 1991, and its store traffic has increased 6%–8% per year.

However, in the mid 1990s, with the market reaching saturation, Starbucks could no longer depend on the U.S. market for growth. Analysts felt that to maintain its growth rates and to boost revenues, Starbucks should venture abroad. In 1995, Starbucks formed Starbucks

Exhibit 2
Starbucks' International Presence

Country	Type of Entry	Name of Partner	Year
Canada	Wholly owned subsidiary	Starbucks Coffee Canada	1996
Japan	Joint Venture	Sazaby Inc.	1996
Malaysia	Licensee	Berajaya Group bhd	1998
New Zealand	Licensee	Restaurant Brands	1998
Taiwan	Joint Venture	President Coffee Corp.	1998
Kuwait	Licensee	Alshaya	1999
Philippines	Licensee	Rustan's Coffee Corp.	2000
Australia	Joint Venture	Markus Hofer	2000
Israel	Joint Venture	Delek Corporation[2]	2001
Austria	Licensee	Bon Appetit Group[2]	2001
Switzerland	Licensee	Bon Appetit Group[2]	2001
Germany	Joint Venture	Karstadt Qualle AG	2002
Greece	Joint Venture	Marinopoulos Brothers	2002
Mexico	Joint Venture	SC de Mexico	2002
Hawaii	Joint Venture	Café Hawaii Partners	2002
Hong Kong	Joint Venture	Maxim's Caterers Ltd	2000
Indonesia	Joint Venture	PT Mitra A diperkasa	2002
Puerto Rico	Joint Venture	Puerto Rico Coffee Partners LLC	2002
Lebanon	Licensee	Alshaya	N/A
Spain	Joint Venture	Grupo Vips	2002

Notes:
1. This list is not exhaustive.
2. Starbucks closed its operations in Israel and bought out the stakes of its partners in Austria and Switzerland in 2003.

Source: Compiled from various newspaper articles.

Coffee International, a wholly owned subsidiary, to monitor the company's international expansion. In 1996, Starbucks entered Japan through a joint venture with Sazaby Inc. (a leading Japanese teashop and interior-goods retailer), and over the years it expanded into southeast Asia, Europe, and the Middle East. By March 2003, Starbucks had 1,532 stores (23% of its total stores) outside the United States. (See **Exhibit 2** for Starbucks' international presence.)

International Expansion Strategies

Starbucks decided to enter the Asia/Pacific Rim markets first.[2] Growing consumerism in the Asia Pacific countries and eagerness among the younger generation to imitate Western lifestyles made these countries attractive markets for Starbucks.

Starbucks decided to enter international markets by using a three-pronged strategy: joint ventures, licensing, and wholly owned subsidiaries (see **Exhibit 3** for the modes of entry in international markets). Prior to entering a foreign market, Starbucks focused on studying the market conditions for its products in the country. It then decided on the local partner for its business. Initially, Starbucks test-marketed with a few stores that were opened in trendy places, and the company's experienced managers from Seattle handled the operations.

After successful test-marketing, local baristas (brew masters) were given training for 13 weeks in Seattle. Starbucks did not compromise on its basic principles. It ensured similar coffee beverage lineups and *No Smoking* rule in all its stores around the globe.

When Starbucks entered into a joint venture with Sazaby Inc. to open Starbucks stores in Japan, analysts felt that Starbucks was unlikely to succeed. They even advised Starbucks to forego its principles such as its *No Smoking* rule and ensure that the size of the stores would

Exhibit 3
Modes of Entry into International Markets

There are six ways to enter a foreign market: through exporting, turnkey projects, licensing, franchising, joint venture with a host country firm, and setting up a wholly owned subsidiary in the host country. Each mode of entry has advantages and disadvantages. The method a company chooses depends on a variety of factors, including the nature of the particular product or service and the conditions for market penetration in the foreign target market.

Exporting
Most firms begin their global expansion with exports and later switch over to another mode. In the 1990s, the volume of exports in the world economy had increased significantly due to the decline in trade barriers. However, exporting still remains a challenge for smaller firms. Firms planning to export must identify foreign market opportunities, familiarize themselves with the mechanics of exports, and learn to deal with foreign exchange risk.

Turnkey Projects
In a turnkey project, the contractor handles every aspect of the project for a foreign client, including the training of operating personnel. After the completion of the contract, the foreign client is handed the "key" to the plant that is ready for operation. Turnkey projects are common in the chemical, pharmaceutical, and petroleum refining industries.

Licensing
Licensing is an arrangement whereby a company (licenser) grants the rights to intangible property such as patents, inventions, formulas, processes, designs, copyrights, and trademarks to another company (licensee) for a specified period of time. The licenser receives a royalty fee from the licensee. For example, in the early 1960s, Xerox licensed its patented xerographic know-how to Fuji-Xerox. It was initially meant for 10 years, but the license was extended several times. In return, Fuji-Xerox paid Xerox a royalty fee equal to 5% of the net sales revenue that it earned.

Franchising
Franchising is similar to licensing except that it requires long-term commitments. In franchising, the franchiser not only sells intangible property to the franchisee but also insists that the franchisee abide by the rules of the business. In some cases, the franchiser also assists the franchisee in running the business. The franchiser receives a royalty payment that is usually a percentage of the franchisee's revenues. Service companies usually opt for franchising. For example, McDonald's pursues its expansion abroad through franchising. McDonald's sets down strict rules for the franchisees to operate their restaurants. The rules extend to cooking methods, staffing policy, and design and location of the restaurants. McDonald's also organizes the supply chain and provides management training and financial assistance to the franchisees.

Joint Ventures
In contrast to licensing and franchising arrangements, joint ventures allow companies to own a stake and play a role in the management of the foreign operation. Joint ventures require more direct investment and training, management assistance, and technology transfer. Joint ventures can be equity or non-equity partnerships. Equity joint ventures are contractual arrangements with equal partners. Non-equity ventures are ones where the host country partner has a greater stake. In some countries, a joint venture is the only way for a foreign company to set up operations.

Exhibit 3 (continued)

Wholly Owned Subsidiaries

In a wholly owned subsidiary, the firm owns 100% of the stock of the subsidiary. Wholly owned subsidiaries can be established in a foreign country in two ways. A firm can set up new operations in the foreign country or it can acquire a firm and promote its products through that firm. The following are the advantages and disadvantages of various entry modes.

Exporting

Advantage:

Ability to realize location and experience curve economies

Disadvantages:

High Transport Costs
Trade Barriers
Problems with local marketing agents

Turnkey Contracts

Advantages:

Ability to earn returns from process technology skills in countries where FDI is restricted
Creating efficient competitors

Disadvantage:

Lack of long term market presence

Licensing

Advantage:

Low development costs and risks

Disadvantages:

Lack of control over technology
Inability to realize location and experience curve economies
Inability to engage in global strategic coordination

Joint Ventures

Advantages:

Access to local partner's knowledge
Sharing development costs and risks
Politically acceptable

Disadvantages:

Lack of control over technology
Inability to engage in global strategic coordination
Inability to realize location and experience economies

Wholly owned subsidiaries

Advantages:

Protection of technology
Ability to engage in global strategic coordination

Disadvantages:

Ability to realize location and experience economies
High costs and risks

Source: ICFAI Center for Management Research.

not be more than 500 square feet due to the high rents in Japan. However, Starbucks stuck to its *No Smoking* principle, which attracted young Japanese women to the Starbucks stores, and the size of the stores was 1200–1500 square feet—similar to the stores in the United States. Proving analysts wrong, Starbucks became successful and, in the first year, it opened more than 100 stores in Japan.

According to Starbucks sources, listening to its local partner also helped. Starbucks took advantage of its local partner Sazaby's knowledge about Japanese coffee drinking habits and introduced new products such as Green Tea Frappucino, which became popular.

Starbucks was successful in attracting a young crowd in all its Asian markets, as young people in these markets were eager to imitate the American culture. It even adapted itself to the local culture to gain market acceptance. For instance, Starbucks offered curry puffs and meat buns in Asian markets as Asians generally prefer to eat something while having coffee.

Analysts felt that the strong coffee-drinking culture in Europe posed both challenges and opportunities for Starbucks. It would face tough competition from the sidewalk cafes of France, coffeehouses of Vienna, and espresso bars of Italy that had developed a strong coffee-drinking culture across the continent, exposing Europeans to some of the best coffee in the world. However, Starbucks executives commented that Europe used to make great coffees but by the late 1990s, the taste had gone awry. In 1998, Starbucks opened its first store in England, and it soon expanded its presence to Switzerland, Germany, and Greece.

It was generally felt that though old people would stick to the existing coffee houses, the young would be attracted to Starbucks. Said Helmut Spudich, Editor, *Der Standard* (a Vienna-based paper), "The coffeehouses in Vienna are nice, but they are old. Starbucks is considered hip."[3] Another important factor that could lead to the success of Starbucks in Europe was its ambience and *No Smoking* environment, unlike traditional European coffee bars. The self-service mode of operation also attracted the young crowd as it was observed that youngsters did not like to wait for the waiter to come and take orders. According to Starbucks sources, it was successful because it was not selling just coffee but an experience that was unique only to Starbucks stores. Maslen, President of Starbucks International, said, "The coffee is good, but it's just the vehicle. The romance of coffee, the occasion, the community, is what Starbucks is selling."[4] In the Middle East, Starbucks went for licensing (except in Israel, where it had a joint venture). Respecting the culture in the Middle East, Starbucks stores offered segregated sections for women.

In September 2002, Starbucks announced that by 2005 it would increase the number of international stores to 10,000. However, analysts pointed out that it would be difficult for Starbucks to make profits in international markets, and they were soon to be proved right.

Problems in International Markets

From the early 2000s, Starbucks faced many problems in its international operations. (See **Exhibit 4** for the types of risks in international business.) The volatile political environment in the Middle East created serious problems for Starbucks. In July 2002, Arab students called for a boycott of American goods and services, due to the alleged close relationship between the United States and Israel. The boycott targeted U.S. companies including Starbucks, Burger King, Coca-Cola and Estée Lauder. Starbucks topped the list of companies to be boycotted due to Schultz's alleged closeness to the Jewish community.[5]

The problem was aggravated when it was reported that, in one of his lectures to students at the University of Washington, Schultz had said, "One of my missions is to sensitize you; you should not be immune to what is happening in the world. I travel a great deal and one of the things that I see is the rise of anti-Semitism in Europe, especially France and England."[6] His address to Jewish-Americans made matters worse. Schultz said, "What is going on in the Middle East is not an isolated part of the world. The rise of anti-Semitism is at an all time high

Exhibit 4
Types of Risk in International Business

Typically, a firm operating internationally is exposed to different types of risk. These can be listed as environmental, financial, organizational, or strategic risks.

Strategic Risk
MNCs typically face a diverse set of risks, and not all of them can be assessed quantitatively. Michael Porter defines five forces impacting a firm's competitiveness—threat of substitutes, threat of new entrants in the industry, bargaining power of suppliers, bargaining power of customers, and the intensity of competition within the industry. A firm's strategic decisions to respond to these five forces are a source of risk.

Operational Risk
Operational risk arises out of factors internal to the company, such as machinery breakdown, industrial strife, supply and distribution imperfections, excess or shortfall in inventory, etc. It causes downtime in the day-to-day operations of the enterprise. Reducing costs by eliminating waste and reducing variances and lead time by improving processes are important to bring about global efficiency. The greater the number of parts and processes involved in production, the greater the risk of not achieving the desired quality and productivity standards.

Political Risk
Political risk refers to political actions that have a negative impact on the firm's value. The process of establishing a cause-and-effect relationship between political factors and business income is called *political risk analysis*. Political risk is not confined to developing countries. It exists even in highly industrialized economies. While macro-political risks such as war and anti-globalization efforts affect the value of all firms in the country, micro-political risks such as regulation of certain industries adversely affect the value of a firm or firms within that industry.

Country Risk
Country risk is a wider concept that encompasses economic conditions, government policies, political conditions, and security factors. The challenge of country risk analysis is in the aggregation of risk factors.

Technological Risk
Technological risk means the probability of adverse effects on business due to factors such as obsolescence of an existing technology, development costs of new technology, failure of a new technology, and security concerns of electronic transactions.

Environmental Risk
Environmental risk can be of two forms. The company may incur regulators' wrath because it polluted the environment, or there may be a public outcry in the event of environmental damage caused by the company. Environmental risk management might not provide short-term gains like financial risk management does, but in the long run, it can certainly become a source of competitive advantage and also enhance the corporate image.

Source: ICFAI Center for Management Research.

since the 1930s. Palestinians aren't doing their job, they're not stopping terrorism."[7] These comments from Schultz resulted in angry protests from the Arab countries and pro-Palestinian groups across the Middle East and Europe. Analysts felt that Schultz's comments strengthened the feeling that he was acting as an Israeli mouthpiece.

Starbucks distanced itself from Schultz's comments, saying that they represented his personal beliefs and not those of the company. Schultz also denied allegations that he was anti-Palestinian and released a personal statement, saying "My position has always been pro-peace and for the two nations to co-exist peacefully."[8] In addition to these incidents, the U.S. declaration of war on Iraq in early 2003 made matters worse for the company. Due to increasing security threats, Starbucks closed down its six stores in Israel.

Starbucks also faced criticism from Non Governmental Organizations (NGOs) that urged the company to acquire certified coffee beans, ensuring that those coffee beans were grown and marketed under certain economic and social conditions. Furthermore, Starbucks faced problems due to economic recession in countries such as Switzerland, Germany, and Japan in the early 2000s, where it experienced declining sales and revenues.

Starbucks faced stiff competition, high business development costs, and resistance from customers in international markets. Especially in Europe, it was reported that Starbucks faced stiff competition from well-established local players that offered specialty coffee at lower prices than Starbucks. For example, in England, a Starbucks tall latte was sold at $2.93, and a similar drink was available for $2.12 at a local coffee shop.

By the late 1990s, Starbucks noticed that store traffic in Japan, its largest overseas market, had been reducing. It was observed that over a period of time, customers opted for different stores because they did not like the taste of Starbucks coffee. Commented a customer, "I never go to Starbucks if I can help it. The coffee tastes artificial."[9] Starbucks sales in Japan declined by over 17% in 2002. In order to boost its sales, Starbucks introduced food items such as rice and salmon wraps and white peach muffins, yet it failed to gain market acceptance.

Analysts observed that Starbucks was unable to earn enough revenues from its international operations due to its complex joint ventures and licensing agreements. While the company invested huge amounts in imparting training to the employees and promoting its products, it earned only a percentage share in total profits and royalty fees. It was further felt that the company did not have any control over the operational costs.

In addition to its problems in international markets, Starbucks experienced operational problems due to lack of a trained workforce and suitable real estate for its stores. Commenting on the operational hindrances Starbucks faced, Maslen said, "If we could train the people and find the real estate, the expansion could happen tomorrow, almost. There is demand."[10]

Future Prospects

In order to have better control over operational costs, Starbucks decided to go to new suppliers for items such as mugs. It was reported that the company was thinking of sourcing mugs from low-cost Japanese vendors rather than importing them from the United States and that it was planning to source its paper goods (such as plates and cups) from Southeast Asia.

Starbucks also announced that it would slow down its pace of expansion by opening around 80 stores in 2003 (compared to the 115 stores opened in 2002). Company sources also revealed that Starbucks would close down its loss-making stores. However, analysts pointed out that closing the loss-making stores and adopting cost cutting could increase profitability only in the short run and not drive future growth.

Analysts pointed out that Starbucks should rethink its entry strategy in international markets and focus on pricing. They also felt that because the company was relatively debt free and had around $300 million in free cash flows, it should be able to rebuild its foreign operations.

However, they cautioned Starbucks against the external risks resulting from volatile political and business environments around the world. They felt that with increasing tensions between the United States and the rest of the world, the business environment, especially in the Middle East and Southeast Asia, was becoming increasingly volatile. Acknowledging the risks involved in the international markets, Schultz said, "We're not taking our success for granted. We also understand that the burden of proof at times is on us given the fact that a lot is being written and there's more sensitivity than ever before about America and American companies. These are the very early days for the growth and development of the company internationally. Clearly there's a big world out there for Starbucks to expand in."[11]

Only time can tell whether Starbucks will be able to brew its success in the international markets.

Notes

1. Starbucks was the first organization in the United States to offer stock options and health care coverage to part-time employees.
2. Asia/Pacific Rim markets consist of Japan, the Philippines, Indonesia, Thailand, Taiwan, Malaysia, Singapore, China, South Korea, North Korea, New Zealand, Australia, Vietnam, Cambodia, and Papua New Guinea.
3. S. Holmes, D. Bennett, K. Carlisle, and C. Dawson, "Planet Starbucks," *Business Week* (September 9, 2003).
4. "Starbucks Jolts Europe's Coffee Houses," *Seattle Times* (May 19, 2002).
5. In 1998, Schultz was honored with the Israeli 50th Anniversary Tribute Award by the Jerusalem Fund of Aish Ha-Torah (a group supporting Israel).
6. W. McDougall, *Starbucks: The Cup That Cheers*, *www.zmag.org/content/Mideast/99110687698* (July 11, 2002).
7. *Ibid.*
8. *Ibid.*
9. S. Holmes, M. I. Kunii, J. Ewing, and K. Capell, "For Starbucks, There's No Place Like Home," *BusinessWeek* (June 9, 2003).
10. "Starbucks Jolts Europe's Coffee Houses," *Seattle Times* (May 19, 2002).
11. H. Jung, *Starbucks Backlash: The Java Giant's Expansion Brews Dissent Overseas*, *www.globalexchange.org/campaigns/fairtrade/coffee/673.html* (April 16, 2003).

Additional Readings and References

J. Reese, "Starbucks," *Fortune* (December 9, 1996).

L. Ioannau, "King Bean," *Fortune* (May 5, 1998).

"Perky People," *The Economist* (May 28, 1998).

Stone, "Starbucks: The Jolt Is Still There—and Not Just from Java," *BusinessWeek* (April 6, 1999).

N. Schwartz, "Still Perking After All These Years," *Fortune* (May 24, 1999).

M. Gimein, "Behind Starbucks' New Venture: Beans, Beatniks, and Booze," *Fortune* (May 15, 2000).

D. Yang Jones, "An American (Coffee) in Paris—and Rome," *www.ups.edu* (February 19, 2001).

S. Holmes, "Starbucks: Keeping the Brew Hot," *BusinessWeek* (August 6, 2001).

"Coffee with Your Tea?" *The Economist* (October 4, 2001).

S. Erlanger, "Starbucks Proves a Hit in Vienna, Even with Smoking Banned," *www.naplesnews.com* (June 1, 2002).

"Israel to Back out of Starbucks Venture As Arab Boycotts Rage On," *www.inminds.co.uk* (July 11, 2002).

C. Dawson and S. Holmes, "Is Japan Losing Its Taste for Latte Already?" *BusinessWeek* (December 9, 2002).

C. Daniels, "Mr. Coffee," *Fortune* (March 30, 2003).

P. Patsuris, "Can Starbucks Get It Wholesale?" *Forbes* (April 25, 2003).

www.starbucks.com

www.starbucks.co.jp

www.hoovers.com

www.businesswire.com

www.seattletimes.com

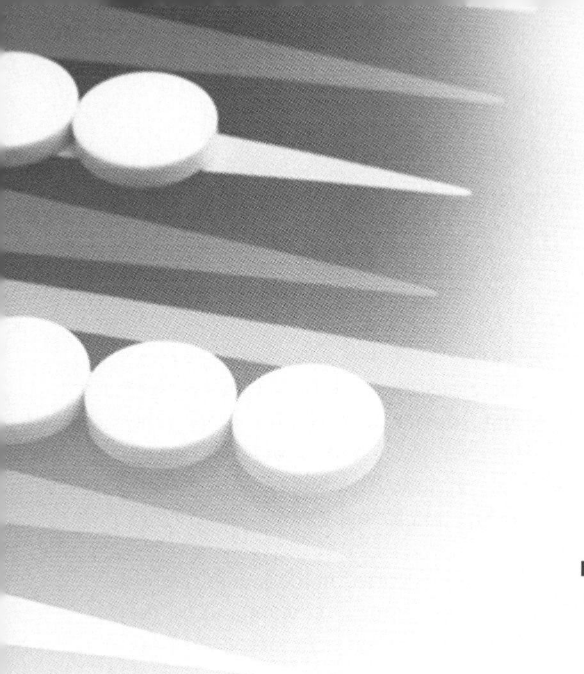

CASE 8

Turkcell:

The Only Turk on Wall Street

Sue Greenfeld

WITH MORE THAN 60% OF THE TURKISH MARKET FOR MOBILE PHONES AND 16.3 MILLION subscribers as of March 31, 2003, Turkcell İletişim Hizmetleri A.Ş., or Turkcell (TKC) for short, is the only Turkish company listed on the New York Stock Exchange. As stated on TKC's web site, "we . . . have developed the premier mobile brand in Turkey by differentiating ourselves from our competition based on quality of service . . . [We] have introduced a wide range of mobile services intended to attract and retain customers with various service needs." Simply put, there is no company in the world like Turkcell. It is a vibrant, full-of-life, and energetic firm that is all over Turkey. This is especially amazing because Turkcell only began operations in 1994.

With more than 100 different consumer services, Turkcell considers itself the leading mobile telecommunications operator in Turkey. Having launched its General Packet Radio Service (GPRS) in 2001 and a Multimedia Messaging Service (MMS) in 2002, Turkcell has believed in remaining at the forefront of technological innovation since its inception. MMS is an application that combines videotext, graphics, and voice into a single message. According to company literature, Turkcell was one of the first mobile operators in Europe to promote MMS technology to its subscribers.

By the end of 2002, Turkcell had total assets of $3.2 billion, revenues of $1.97 billion, net income of $101 million, and more than 2,000 employees. With three additional Turkish market players created since 1994, including Aycell, a state-owned company, and an onerous 66% tax burden, Turkcell wonders what steps it should take to position itself for the twenty-first century. For example, how can it reduce economic risk if the Turkish lira (TRL) takes a nosedive as it did in the year 2000? How can it increase usage per customer aside from increasing its subscriber base? Also, can it afford to take a leadership role in introducing 3G, the third generation of mobile phone systems, into Turkey? Is there anything it can do to influence the Turkish government in order to reduce its 66% tax burden? And with the Turkish government moving toward privatization of numerous industries, why would the government set up a state-owned company in the first place? These are just a few of the questions that the managers of Turkcell are asking as they think about the company and its future.

Country Background

Turkey is a fascinating country with more than 19 civilizations that date back thousands of years. Hittites, Phrygians, Urartians, Lydians, Greeks, and Romans are just a few among the many people who once roamed the rolling landscape. However, the history of modern Turkey begins October 29, 1923, with the revolution and the creation of the Republic of Turkey. This was accomplished through the inspirational leadership of Mustafa Kemal Atatürk, the "Father of the Turks," who transformed and secularized the country.

Turkey is the successor to the great Ottoman Empire, which started in the late thirteenth century but was slowly dismantled throughout the nineteenth century via wars and by the Allied powers during World War I, when the Turks sided with Germany. In fact, one of the worst battles occurred at Gallipoli, when the Australian, British, and New Zealand Armies struggled to destroy the remnants of the Ottoman Empire. More than 100,000 Allied forces and Turks lost their lives at Gallipoli, but the Allied forces were unable to vanquish the Turkish spirit. From this gruesome despair of World War I, Mustafa Kemal Atatürk emerged as a new leader for Turkey, and he quickly realized the need for a new type of government, one more democratic and more secular than had previously existed.

From 1923 to 1929, the Turkish government focused on reducing illiteracy, latinizing the language, nationalizing the economy, and decreasing the 80% dependency on agriculture as a primary source of employment. Some foreign capital was encouraged in the areas of construction and railways. This focus changed during the world depression years of 1929 to 1939, when the emphasis shifted to protectionism, nationalization of foreign firms, and the building up of financial institutions. At that time, the government created its first Five-Year Plan for industrial development, including the establishment of factories for steel, cement, paper, chemicals, sugar, and textiles. The Second Five-Year Plan of 1936 added mines, facilities in natural resources, and other heavier industry, but World War II interrupted this development. During the war years of 1939 to 1945, the government was engaged in a major land reform effort, against the wishes of Turkey's largest landholders.

During World War II, Turkey remained neutral until 1945, when it joined the Allies, and it subsequently became part of the United Nations. It was admitted into the North American Treaty Organization (NATO) in 1952. From 1947 to 1962, Turkey received funds from the Marshall Plan to mechanize agricultural output. Strong encouragement of foreign capital investment began in 1954, while 1963 to 1979 saw rapidly growing international debt. This debt was incurred in part from Turkey's low level of exports in comparison to its high dependence on imported raw material. Since 1986, Turkey has been an associate member of the European Union (EU), and it has since applied for full membership. In December 2002, Turkey received a date from the EU for accession talks to begin in December 2004.

In 2002, Turkey's economy still had a strong 40% agricultural base. Other industries were clothing, textiles, ceramics, food processing, automobiles, mining, steel, petroleum, construction, and glass. About 18.7% of Turkey's exports went to Germany, while 11.4% were directed to the United States. Turkey is highly dependent on oil imports.

Nevertheless, Turkey continues to struggle with an inflation rate that has hovered around 40% for 20 years. **Exhibit 1** indicates the exchange rate of the U.S. dollar for the TRL.

In 2001, there was a major economic crisis when overnight the Turkish lira was drastically devaluated. According to the 2001 Annual Report letter from Chairman Mehmet Emin Karamehmet to Turkcell's shareholders, "the Turkish Lira lost 114% of its value against the U.S. dollar, [Turkish] gross national product decreased by approximately 9.4%, [and] consumer infla-

Exhibit 1
Exchange Rate of the U.S. Dollar for the Turkish Lira

Year	U. S. Dollar ($)	Turkish Lira (TRL)
1996	$1.00	81,405
1997	1.00	151,865
1998	1.00	260,724
1999	1.00	418,783
2000	1.00	677,621
2001	1.00	1,176,560
2002	1.00	1,650,000

Source: www.odci.gov/cia/publications/factbook/geos/tu.html (September 10, 2002).

tion rose by 68% by year end." It was also the first time that Turkcell had posted a net income loss of more than $186 million. Some have blamed the crisis in part on the government printing too much money and having too many state-supported programs, inadequate collection of tax revenues, the severe drop in the Turkish stock market, insufficient privatization of industries, and inadequate reform in the banking area. In 2000, the government took over 22 different Turkish banks that had gone bankrupt and/or were considered corrupt. The International Monetary Fund (IMF) has stepped in more than one time to help assist Turkey. By the end of 2002, Turkey held $16 billion in IMF loans. To make up for lost tax revenues and the underreporting of income, the Turkish government decided to place heavy tax burdens on both the petroleum and mobile communications industries. In the case of petroleum, there is a user tax at the gas pump. In 2002, the equivalent U.S. price for a gallon of gasoline in Turkey was $4.50, and after 1999 the government added a 25% earthquake tax on mobile communications. The 2002 tax rate on Global System for Mobile Communication (GSM) communications operators/subscribers in Turkey, including Turkcell, was approximately 66% of earnings before interest charges.

To enhance foreign investment opportunities in Turkey, a foreign economic relations board (DEIK) was created in 1986. This nonprofit, private organization "attempts to improve the external economic relations with Turkish enterprises and to contribute to the integration of the Turkish economy into the world economy." According to Başak Kızıldemir from DEIK, there are 30 individuals on staff working with business councils in 59 different countries. The Turkish–U.S. Business Council is a part of DEIK. Some member organizations include Microsoft, CNN Türk, Boeing, JPMorgan, and Delta Air Lines, among many others. Literature from the DEIK reminds readers that Turkey is one of the 10 largest emerging economies, has great resiliency, is a long-term trading partner with the United States, and is one of the most trusted allies of the United States. Turkey played a major role in the 1991 Gulf War, helping the United States.

In terms of demographics, Turkey has about 70 million people in a land space approximately the size of Texas (see **Exhibit 2**). Seventy percent of the population is under the age of 35. While the country is secular, without a state-supported religion, 98.8% of Turks identify themselves as Muslim, with less than 1% Jewish or Christian. Turkey has 53 government and 19 private trust-funded universities, and students are admitted through a central placement system. Entry is extremely competitive, and students have to score very well on the multidisciplinary university entrance exam. On the university campus and elsewhere, the Turkish population dresses casually, in Western-style clothing.

History of Telecommunications in Turkey

Like the rest of the world, Turkey has embraced the mobile telephone communication age with a ravenous appetite, and as in many other countries, the postal service and telecommunications in Turkey have been the sole domain of the government. Except for the GSM com-

Exhibit 2
Map of Turkey

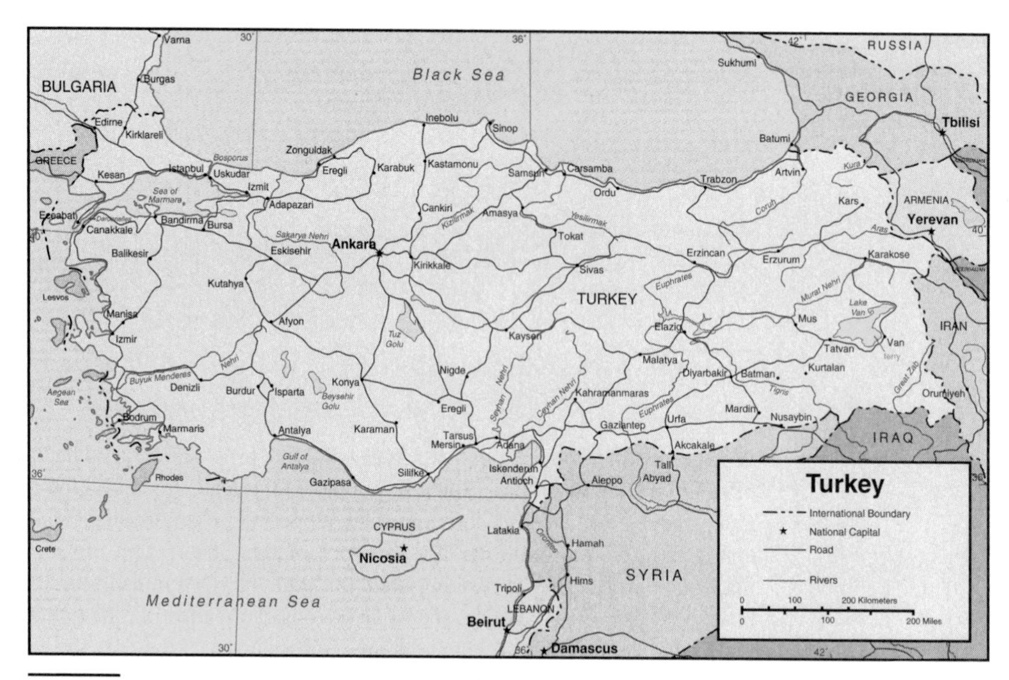

Source: Lonely Planet.

munications, the state-owned Türk Telecom is the only authorized supplier of telecommunications. The Telecommunication Authority regulates all telecommunications activity in Turkey. Telegram and Telephone Law No. 406 was the principal law governing telecommunication, and it gave Türk Telecom complete monopoly power until December 31, 2003. Then the communications world in Turkey became a different ballgame, but the mobile telephone world of GSM had changed 16 years earlier.

In 1987, GSM was created to assist in the unification and integration of mobile communications within the EU, and it is one of four basic digital standards for mobile communications. A key component of GSM is the subscriber's identity, or SIM card. The SIM card allows the user of a handset or mobile phone to be identified. Without a valid SIM card inside, a handset does not function. Under a revenue-sharing agreement with Türk Telecom, Turkcell was formed in 1993 as Turkey's first GSM company. Turkcell started operations the following year, at the same time that a second mobile phone company, TelSim, began. In 1998, upon payment of an up-front license fee of $500 million, Turkcell was a granted a 25-year GSM license to operate in Turkey.

In the mid-1990s, the only services provided were the basic handsets for the sole mobile vocal communication market, but mobile phones in Turkey, as elsewhere, have become personal digital assistants (PDAs), among other features. The infrastructure in Turkey has been constantly updated as new technologies have emerged to provide for better mobile phone services. Turkcell introduced Dual Numbering Service, which enables the creation of two separate numbers on an individual mobile phone. Another technological advance has been the Wireless Application Protocol (WAP), which allows Internet access to anyone with a mobile phone. More specifically, WAP is an application environment and a set of communication protocols for wireless devices, designed to enable manufacturer-, vendor-, and technology-independent access to the Internet and advanced telephony services.

In 2000, the government of Turkey issued two new GSM 1800 licenses. One was to the Iştim consortium, operating under the name Aria. The other new GSM 1800 license was awarded to Türk Telecom, operating under its wholly owned subsidiary Aycell. Aria began offering services on March 21, 2001, and Aycell became operational in December 2001. By the end of 2002, there were four major players in the highly competitive Turkish market: Turkcell, TelSim, Aria, and state-owned Aycell. Each has its own marketing style, and each is working hard to become a household name in Turkey.

While TelSim also started operations in 1994 and held a respectable market share in 2002, it has become embroiled in a long-standing controversy with Motorola, the U.S. communications giant, and Nokia, the Swedish handset vendor. Both Motorola and Nokia have claimed in court papers that TelSim defaulted on $2 billion of vendor financing to help set up TelSim's infrastructure. Motorola wanted the top TelSim CEO to go to jail for up to 24 months for contempt.

Aria is a smaller player and a fast-rising star in Turkey. It is composed of a major consortium of Turkey's largest bank, Işbank, and Telecom Italia. Together, they paid $2.5 billion for the GSM 1800 license, but the real threat to the mobile communications market has been the government's entry, Aycell. Aycell has undercut prices and offers services lower than cost, especially to its own customers calling from an Aycell phone to another Aycell phone, but so far it has gotten away with it. The Turkish government covers any losses of Aycell. Through its lawyers, Turkcell has issued concerns to the regulatory body in Turkey, but wonders whether there is anything else it can do to halt what it thinks is unfair competition.

A new threat from Aycell surfaced in May 2003. The news agency Reuters announced that the Italian telecommunication giant TIM, part of the Telecom Italia group, was merging with Aycell in Turkey. Reuters reported that the two companies "agreed to merge their Turkish wireless operation in a move that would solve TIM's escalating regulatory dispute in the country." The merger of TIM with Aycell would give the Italian company entry into Turkey and would eliminate the need for roaming access to its rivals' networks, which is an important facet of the dispute in Turkey. To combat this challenge, Turkcell realizes that it must be vigilant in case there is an opportunity to merge with or acquire another company itself.

At the end of 2002, it was believed that market penetration of mobile phones ran around 34% in Turkey. This means a lot more growth can be expected if Turkey is to reach the saturation levels of other industrial countries, such as Italy (92%), Finland (82%), Portugal (91%), Spain (81%), the United Kingdom (83%), Greece (83%), Germany (69%), or France (62%). See **Exhibit 3** for mobile phone etiquette.

Exhibit 3
Mobile Phone Etiquette

1. When answering or making a mobile telephone call, it is important to remember a few simple rules. Being polite is the first step.
2. Receiving or making calls should not be disruptive, intrusive, or take priority over face-to-face conversations.
3. Mobile phones should be switched off in meetings, in places of worship, in libraries, and at the cinema, the theater, or a concert.
4. Using a mobile phone should be avoided in elevators, buses, trains, and other small places where the conversation can be overheard.
5. Phones *must* be switched off on airplanes, on sea buses, and in hospitals.
6. Using a mobile phone while driving can be very dangerous. Some U.S. states have made a law against using a phone while driving. Drivers should never endanger themselves or others by using a handheld phone. Only under a dire emergency should a mobile phone be used while driving a car. It is better to pull off to the side of the road to make the call.
7. If calling for business purposes, always call during business hours.

Source: Adapted from S. Delin, "Mobile Manners Maketh Man," Turkcell World: The International Magazine of Turkey's Leading GSM Operator, Issue 2 (Winter 2001).

Company Background

Starting with only 94 employees, Turkcell commenced operations in 1994 under a revenue-sharing agreement with Türk Telecom, the state-owned fixed-line network operator. At that time, there were only 63,500 subscribers in the customer base. This number grew significantly each year to about 2.3 million in 1998, when upon a payment of an up-front license fee of $500 million, Turkcell was granted a 25-year GSM license to operate in Turkey. From 1994 to 1998, Turkcell operated with only TelSim as a primary competitor. Since 1998, the customer base has continued to grow considerably: 5.5 million at the end of 1999, 10.1 million at the end of 2000, 12.2 million at the end of 2001 and 16.3 million by the end of March 2003.

There are two basic types of Turkcell customers: prepaid and postpaid. A prepaid customer purchases a voucher card at a gas station, newsstand, kiosk, retail store, Turkcell's web site, or a bank ATM. He or she scratches the card to reveal the secret 12-digit number. When the customer calls an authorized Turkcell number and provides the 12-digit number, the service is activated or continued for a particular mobile phone. A postpaid customer receives a bill. Both types of customers have risen steadily for Turkcell, to the point where the customer base is two-thirds prepaid and one-third postpaid. By March 21, 2002, there was a nationwide network of more than 520 exclusive handset dealers selling only Turkcell services, and about 13,300 sales points (such as newspaper kiosks) for voucher cards.

In 1999, Turkcell became the first GSM operator in Turkey to be awarded the prestigious ISO 9001. The International Organization for Standardization (ISO) created worldwide guidelines to promote operating efficiency, improve productivity, and reduce costs. The ISO 9000 concept took off in the early 1990s and has helped to define world-class quality systems. There are four levels of ISO 9000: 9001, 9002, 9003, and 9004. The most rigorous of the ISO standards is ISO 9001, which has 20 components. ISO 9001 means the company has certification in design, engineering, and manufacturing.

However, one of Turkcell's most momentous events occurred on July 11, 2000, when the company completed its initial public offering (IPO) of more than 25 billion shares, in the form of ordinary shares on the Istanbul Stock Exchange and American Depository shares on the New York Stock Exchange. There was quite a bit of excitement at Turkcell as numerous company employees were on hand to make the day a big success. Turkcell took over Wall Street with a carnival-like atmosphere. A small Turkish village with street fair tents and kiosks was set up. It featured Turkish food, Turkish coffee and tea, and authentic Turkish crafts. The air had a festive feeling of celebration. There was a man on stilts whose legs were covered with long yellow pants and purple trim saying Turkcell. He wore a matching blue jacket with the Turkcell snabbit logo and a tall hat. It was a sight to behold. And who could forget the blue and white balloons tied together in a gigantic arch overreaching the tents and the wonderful Turkcell banner hanging from the sober columns of the New York Stock Exchange building? None of the Turkcell employees who attended can forget that day. By the end of 2002, they were still talking about the grand Turkcell entrance and quite proud to be the first Turkish company ever listed on the New York Stock Exchange.

In 2001, the company launched one of the world's largest mobile portals, called GPRSLand. GPRS means General Packet Radio Service; it is a data transmission service that provides faster mobile access to the Internet than WAP. GPRS is a standard for wireless communications that runs at speeds up to 115 kilobits per second, compared to GSM's speed of 9.6 kilobits per second. GPRS, which supports a wide range of bandwidths, is an efficient use of limited bandwidth and is particularly suited for sending and receiving small bundles of data, such as in e-mail and web browsing, as well as large volumes of data. GPRS allows Turkcell postpaid customers to have permanent access to their e-mail and the Internet. GPRSLand is a collaborative effort between Turkcell and Ericsson, one of Sweden's largest companies and a supplier of mobile phones. Four software companies have worked to develop the 15 applications included in GPRSLand. GPRSLand is a unique service that has provided Turkcell customers with access to a host of data applications. The applications were segmented into information and entertainment offerings. The launch of GPRSLand was supported by an extensive advertising campaign that made it a well-known service among Turkcell customers. In October 2002, GPRSLand won the "best new service" award at the World Communications Awards in the United Kingdom. "This is how everyone should do it," said the judges of Turkcell's GPRSLand. A panel of judges, including industry leaders, consultants, and representatives from industry groups, also commented, "Turkcell has done a great job putting a package together, not just a network. They've really thought it through and it's great to hear of this kind of sophistication." Currently there are 27 applications on GPRSLand. The business model provides financial incentives for third-party developers as well, encouraging them to create successful applications.

In 2002, Turkcell and Microsoft created another new service, called Office Mobile Service. This service allows subscribers access to Microsoft Outlook and Exchange by using a Microsoft Mobile Information Server (MMIS). Turkcell also provided 100% comprehensive coverage for all cities in Turkey that had populations of 5,000 or more. Turkcell had international roaming agreements with 319 operators in 136 countries as of June 3, 2003. Turkcell started the year 2002 with the appointment of new Chief Executive Officer Muzaffer Akpinar. He became Turkcell's second CEO, following the visionary leadership of CEO Cüneyt Türktan.

The Story of Snabbit

Snabbit is the 1994 creation of Mengül Ertel, a famous Turkish contemporary graphic designer who passed away on March 15, 2000. When Turkcell was about to be launched, the company approached Ertel to design a company logo and emblem that would be very unique and quite memorable. He turned to the animal world and created an animal like no other animal: the snabbit, partly a snail (because of its antennae) and partly a rabbit (because of its speed). According to company literature, the snabbit "reflects the energy, dynamism and total uniqueness that define Turkcell." The snabbit is featured in every Turkcell retail store. It graces numerous promotional items and can be seen at many sporting events. What Ertel produced has become a Turkish icon.

Initially, only one snabbit existed, and he was named Sinyal Bebek. For an important telecommunication fair to be held in September 2001, Sinyal Bebek was renamed Cell-O and given a whole new family. Later, in a *Turkcell World* article, Sevil Delin, a writer and translator, described all the family members. Cell-O is pictured as a technophile and joker, but he is kind-hearted and a visionary. His wife, Celly, is cautious and very economical. She is interested in astrology, and she is a great businesswoman and a great mother. Cellita, the daughter, is environmentally and fashion conscious. She needs her freedom, while Cell, Jr., the son, is an Internet addict, obsessed with soccer, voracious, and enterprising. Finally, the grandfather, Celldede, is just a teenager in his 70s who is an adventurer, a philanderer, and a generous man. By establishing an entire family, Turkcell believed that the Cell family would increase the value of the Turkcell brand and help to ensure brand loyalty to retain subscribers. Each member of the Cell family represents a different segment of Turkcell's customer base. The idea was to target products for those various market segments. Some individuals in Turkey believe the Cell family with its dad, mom, daughter, son and grandfather may have some similarity to the popular show *The Simpsons*, which is shown on TV in English but with Turkish subtitles in Turkey.

Facilities

Turkcell's main headquarters is located at the Turkcell Plaza in Istanbul, Turkey. The highly commercial area is a mixture of upscale retail stores, various types of businesses, mosques, churches, schools, and a tramway. One side of the Turkcell offices faces the famous İstiklal Caddesi (or Independence Street) of Taksim. The headquarters building is nine stories and includes offices, underground parking, a gym, a cafeteria, and a sauna. All lunches are provided by the company through lunch tickets that are given to employees each month. The company pays for parking, and various shops in the nearby area give Turkcell employees special discounts. In the main lobby area is a display case that contains the dozens of awards that Turkcell has received. Among the awards are plaques and certificates from Ericsson, Interpro, and the Lions Club, along with Turkcell's ISO 9001 certification. The building is mostly dedicated to Turkcell's administration, finances, marketing, training, investor relations, and corporate communications.

Maltepe (on the outskirts of Istanbul) is the home of the "brains" of Turkcell—the $10 million Network Control Center, with its state-of-the-art computer technology. It houses 42 technical staff who work in shifts for the 24/7 coverage. Similar to the Houston control center that monitors space shuttle flights, the Turkcell Network Control Center has a series of curved interconnected workstations facing multifaceted sets of maps. When a red light appears, a Turkcell team of technicians is immediately sent to the location to investigate the problem. These 7,500 base stations allow Turkcell to provide 100% mobile communications coverage in Turkey for all cities in Turkey with populations of 5,000 or more. Turkcell also has numerous Turkcell customer care centers throughout Turkey, where subscribers can sign up for various services or resolve their mobile communications or billing issues.

Organizational Philosophy and Social Responsibility

The Turkcell company philosophy has been strongly influenced by the first Turkcell CEO, Cüneyt Türktan, who received bachelor's and master of business administration (MBA) degrees from Bosphorus University in Turkey. In 1980, he joined PriceWaterhouse in New York as an accountant, and then he returned to Turkey in 1985 as an audit supervisor for KPMG, and he worked for Interbank as the Head of Corporate Finance. Then in 1992, he became the Area Finance Director of PepsiCo International, in charge of Turkey and Israel. In 1994, he led the organizational team that created Turkcell.

According to Türktan, writing in a 2002 issue of *Turkcell World*, Turkcell values five structural principles: proactive approach, result orientation, minimum hierarchy, full accountability, and simplicity. The company strongly espouses both creating high employee loyalty and providing extensive employee training. Once a year in Istanbul, the company holds a major Turkcell information day that is designed strictly for the employees, and through its own educational classrooms, Turkcell provides training programs on individual development, functional, conference attending, computer and language training, and organization. The courses are given in English and Russian. Turkcell has more than 2,000 employees, divided into 49% technical, 26% customer care, 16% finance and administration, and 9% marketing. The average age of a Turkcell employee is 28. More than 80% of Turkcell's employees are university educated. Turkcell pays all its employees slightly above industry average.

Carrying on with the organizational philosophy of Turkcell is the second CEO, Muzaffer Akpinar, who was born in 1962 and has worked in the telcom sector since 1993. Akpinar speaks Turkish, French, and English, and he took part in the restructuring of Fintur. He was a founder and managing director of Penta Textile, and he worked as the CEO for KVK Mobil Telfon Hizmetleri, a major importer and distributor of handsets, as well as MV Holding Company. Like the first CEO, Akpinar is a graduate of Bosphorus University in Turkey. He started as the second CEO of Turkcell in January 2002.

Part of Turkcell's philosophy involves good customer relations and social responsibility. This means stressing the importance of customer care and being a good corporate citizen in Turkey. The company wants to increase its customer base and retain its current customers through both marketing and its visibility as a responsible company. For example, in conjunction with the Foundation for Supporting Modern Life, Turkcell has provided 5,000 young girls with scholarships and training in Eastern Turkey. Turkcell targets girls in this program because in rural Turkey, most families prefer to spend their limited funds on their sons. Daughters' educations are generally neglected. For its efforts in this area, Turkcell has received Institute of Public Relations (IPR) excellence awards in the category *Corporate Social Responsibility*. Turkcell also achieved the Cystal Obelisk award for the same project from the Foundation of Women Executives (WEPR) in New York.

As stated by A. Cüneyt Türktan, the former CEO, in an issue of *Turkcell World*, "Turkcell understands and is proud of its role as a corporate citizen and will continue to sponsor important programs." It has also sponsored the restoration of school gyms in Istanbul and the "Sharing Our Toys" campaign for children in rural areas of Turkey, and it helped set up computer laboratories in 53 schools in less developed provinces of Turkey.

Marketing

Turkcell engages in extensive marketing within Turkey. Not only does Turkcell want to increase the number of subscribers, but it wants to increase the call minutes per customer as well. Globally, the year 2001 was a difficult year for mobile telecom operators. These difficulties were compounded in Turkey by economic upheaval that led to a steep depreciation of the currency, lower purchasing power, and a contraction of economic activity. Turkcell had to manage the economic crisis with flexibility and sensitivity by taking decisive measures to control operating and capital expenditures. In order to keep up with the currency's depreciation, Turkcell had to raise the tariffs to subscribers in reasonable increments throughout the year while remaining sensitive to customer expectations and usage patterns.

In addition, Turkey's economic crisis seriously affected the monthly minutes used by subscribers. While subscribers had been using on average more than 100 minutes per month, that number drastically fell to 56.2 minutes monthly as of year end 2003. Ideally, Turkcell would like the monthly minutes per month to match the average of other industrialized or developing countries. The average U.S. subscriber spends more than 430 minutes monthly on a mobile phone, Hong Kong 350, Israel 237, China 199, Egypt 188, Norway 181, Brazil 105, and Greece 105. Turkcell wonders: Are there certain marketing campaigns that might help to achieve an improvement in the average monthly minutes? What type of marketing segmentation should we try? How can Turkish mobile phone users be encouraged to spend more time monthly on a mobile phone? Would educational campaigns be helpful?

For example, some subscribers, especially those in rural areas, appear to be quite resistant to newer technologies such as cell phones and do not know how to best use mobile communication. If an educational campaign were conducted, how much time and effort should Turkcell spend on it? One effort in the year 2000 was quite successful. Should Turkcell do it again? In that year, Turkcell sponsored the "Signal Tour 2000" project, which lasted six months. In this project, a truck was used as a symbol of wireless communication. The truck tour traveled to 82 locations throughout Turkey, met with more than 500,000 people, and covered about 18,000 miles. After the completion of this campaign, Turkcell received the Direct Marketing Association (DMA) International ECHO award, which was presented in Chicago at a gala event in 2001. But such campaigns take time and money. Would sponsorship of other events be more worthwhile? To illustrate, Turkcell also sponsors numerous athletic, cultural, theater, film, and/or music events, including the International Istanbul Jazz Festival and the International Istanbul Film Festival. Which campaigns are best geared at customer retention, getting new subscribers, or getting current consumers to use their mobile phones and services more often?

Financial Issues

The financial structure of Turkcell is highly sophisticated and involves a number of holdings inside and outside Turkey. To illustrate, on August 21, 2002, Turkcell, Sonera, and Cukurova Group, the shareholders of Fintur Holdings B.V., finalized the restructuring of two business divisions of Fintur: the international GSM businesses and the technology businesses. In line with the terms of the transaction, Turkcell bought 16.45% of Fintur International from the Cukurova Group, increasing its stake in Fintur International to 41.45%. At the same time, Sonera bought 23.24% of Fintur International from the Cukurova Group, increasing its holding to 58.8%. As part of this transaction, Turkcell and Sonera sold their entire interest in Fintur Technologies (Internet service providers, digital television, etc.) to the Cukurova Group. But because Cukurova Group is the majority shareholder of Turkcell, it will continue to create group synergies via various projects. Thus Turkcell is one of the major shareholders of Fintur Holdings B.V., which in turn holds a 51.3% interest in Azercell of Azerbaijan, an 83.2% interest in Geocell of Georgia (formerly part of the U.S.S.R.), a 51% interest in K'Cell of Kazakhstan, and a 77% interest in Moldcell of Moldova. Most of these countries have very low penetration of mobile phone usage. For example, only 3% of the Georgian market has mobile phones. Fintur International's GSM business in Azerbaijan, Kazakhstan, Georgia, and Moldova added approximately 500,000 new subscribers and reached a total of approximately 1.6 million subscribers in 2002. The combined revenue of the business was US$240 million in 2002, and the business was EBITDA positive in all countries.

Other holdings of Turkcell outside Turkey include Kuzey Kibris Turkcell (KKTCell) in the Republic of Northern Cyprus. Thus outside Turkey, there is great opportunity for Turkcell to increase its subscriber base, and this explains why Russian is one of the languages included by Turkcell in its training facilities. Should Turkcell expand into other European countries, and, if yes, which ones?

In 2001, Turkcell's loss of more than $186 million was attributed to the severe deflation of the TRL and the subsequent currency translation. Turkcell has to use U.S. funds to repay bank loans, licensing agreements, and purchasing of infrastructure, while revenues from subscribers are received in TRL. Although Turkcell raised its rates to subscribers by 101% in 2001, this was not sufficient to cover the 114% inflation and devaluation of the lira. However, Turkcell announced a $101.8 million net profit as of year end 2002. In 2002, Turkcell made debt repayments of $474.3 million in both principal and interest. At the end of 2002, Turkcell's total outstanding financial debt was reduced to approximately US$1.3 billion at the end of 2002. In addition, during the first quarter of 2003, Turkcell paid a total of $313 million of debt in principal and interest. As of March 31, 2003, Turkcell's total outstanding financial debt was reduced to approximately US$1.0 billion from US$1.3.

Also problematic for Turkcell is the fact that records have to be maintained using two vastly different accounting standards. As a company quoted on the NYSE, Turkcell has to fol-

ings. (Rumors circulated that Suazo was transporting and selling illegally logged mahogany by mixing it with that purchased from Guajilote.)

Munguia: El Caudillo

After renegotiating successfully with the cooperative's distributor, Munguia quickly became the group's caudillo (strong man). The caudillo was a Latin American political and social institution. A caudillo was a (typically male) purveyor of patronage. All decisions went through, and were usually made by, him. A caudillo was often revered, feared, and hated at the same time because of the power he wielded. Munguia was viewed by many in the area as an ascending caudillo because of his leadership of Guajilote.

Guajilote did not operate in a democratic fashion. Munguia made all the decisions—sometimes with input from his second in command and nephew, Miguel Flores Munguia—and handled all of Guajilote's financial matters. Guajilote's members did not seem to have a problem with this management style. The prevailing opinion seemed to be that Guajilote was a lot better off with Munguia running the show by himself than with more involvement by the members. One man put the members' view very succinctly: "Santos, he saved us (from Suazo, from COHDEFOR, from ourselves)."

Guajilote's organizational structure emphasized Munguia's importance. He was alone at the top in his role as decision maker. If, in the future, Munguia became more involved in politics and other ventures that could take him out of Chaparral (possibly for long periods of time), he would very likely be forced to spend less time with Guajilote's operations. Munguia's leadership has been of key importance to Guajilote's maturing as both a work group and as a business. In 1998, there did not seem to be another person in the cooperative that could take Munguia's place.

Guajilote's Members

When founded, the cooperative had been composed of 15 members. Members were initially selected for the cooperative by employees of USAID and COHDEFOR. The number of employees has held steady over time. Since the cooperative's founding, 3 original members have quit; 4 others were allowed to join. Although no specific reasons were given for members leaving, they appeared to be because of personality differences, family problems, or differences of opinion. No money had been paid to them when they left the cooperative. In 1998 there were 16 members in the cooperative.

None of Guajilote's members had any education beyond primary school. Many of the members had no schooling at all and were illiterate. As a whole, the group knew little of markets or business practices.

Guajilote's existence has had an important impact on its members. One member stated that before he had joined Guajilote, he was lucky to have made 2,000 lempiras in a year, whereas he made around 1,000 to 1,500 in one month as a member of the cooperative. He stated that all five of his children were in school, something that he could not have afforded previously. Before joining the cooperative, he had been involved in subsistence farming and other activities that brought in a small amount of money and food. He said that his children had been required previously to work as soon as they were able. As a simple farmer, he often had to leave his family to find work, mostly migrant farm work, to help his family survive. Because of Guajilote, his family now had enough to eat, and he was able to be home with his family.

This was a common story among Guajilote's members. The general improvement in its members' quality of life also appeared to have strengthened the cooperative members' personal bonds with each other.

Financial Situation

No formal public financial records were available. As head of the cooperative, Munguia kept informal records. Guajilote's 1997 revenues were approximately 288,000 lempiras (US$22,153). (Revenues for 1996 were not available.) Guajilote processed around 36,000 feet of wood during 1997. Very little of the money was held back for capital improvement purchases due to the operation's simple material needs. Capital expenditures for 1997 included a mule plus materials needed to maintain Guajilote's large cross-cut saws.

Each of Guajilote's 16 members was paid an average of about 1,500 lempiras (US$113) per month in 1997 and 1,300 lempiras (US$100) per month in 1996. 1998 payments per month had been similar to 1997's payments, according to Guajilote's members. Money was paid to members based on their participation in Guajilote's operations.

There was conjecture, among some workers, that Munguia and his second in charge were paying themselves more than the other members were receiving. When Munguia was asked if he received a higher wage than the others because of his administrative position in the group, he responded that everything was distributed evenly. An employee of COHDEFOR indicated, however, that Munguia had purchased a house in La Union—the largest town in the area. That person conjectured, based on this evidence, that Munguia was likely receiving more from the cooperative than were the other members.

Issues Facing the Cooperative

Guajilote's size and growth potential were limited by the amount of mahogany it could produce in a year. Mahogany was fairly rare in the forest, and Guajilote was legally restricted to downed trees. Moreover, with the difficulties of finding, processing by hand, and then moving the wood out of the forest, Guajilote was further restricted in the quantity of wood it could handle.

Lack of transportation was a major problem for Guajilote. The cooperative had been unable to secure the capital needed to buy its own truck; lending through legitimate sources was very tight in Honduras and enterprises like Guajilote did not typically have access to lines of credit. Although the prices the cooperative was receiving for its wood had improved, the men still thought that the distributor, Juan Suazo, was not paying them what the wood was worth. It was argued that when demand was high for mahogany, the cooperative gave up as much as 10 lempiras per foot in sales to Suazo. Guajilote could conceivably double its revenues if it could somehow haul its wood to Honduras' major market centers and sell it without use of a distributor. The closest market center was Tegucigalpa—three to four hours from Chaparral on dangerous, often rain soaked, mountain roads.

A Possibility

Some of the members of Guajilote wondered if the cooperative could do better financially by skipping the distributor completely. It was possible that some specialty shops (chains and independents) and catalogs throughout the world might be interested in selling high-quality mahogany furniture, i.e., chests or chairs, that were produced in an environmentally friendly manner. Guajilote, unfortunately, had no highly skilled carpenters or furniture makers in its membership. There were, however, a couple towns in Honduras with highly skilled furniture makers who worked on a contract basis.

A U.S. citizen with a furniture export business in Honduras worked with a number of independent furniture makers on contract to make miniature ornamental chairs. This exporter reviewed Guajilote's situation and concluded that the cooperative might be able to make and market furniture very profitably—even if it had to go through an exporter to find suitable markets. Upon studying Guajilote's operations, he estimated that Guajilote might be able to more than treble its revenues. In order to do this, however, the exporter felt that Guajilote would have to overcome problems with transportation and upgrade its administrative competence. Guajilote would need to utilize the talents of its members more if it were to widen its operational scope. It would have to purchase trucks and hire drivers to transport the wood over treacherous mountain roads. The role of administrator would become much more demanding, thus forcing Munguia to delegate some authority to others in the cooperative.

Concerns

In spite of Guajilote's improved outlook, there were many concerns that could affect the cooperative's future. A serious concern was the threat of deforestation through fires, illegal logging (i.e., poaching of mahogany as well as clear cutting), and slash-and-burn agriculture.

Small fires were typically set to prepare soils for planting and to help clear new areas for cultivation. Often these fires were either not well supervised or burned out of the control of the people starting them. Due to the 1998 drought, the number of out-of-control forest fires had been far greater than normal. There seemed to be a consensus among Hondurans that 1998 would be one of the worst years for forest fires. Mahogany and tropical deciduous forests are not fire resistant. Fires not only kill adult and young mahogany trees, but they also destroy their seeds.[3] Mahogany could therefore be quickly eliminated from a site. Each year, Guajilote lost more area from which it could take mahogany.

To make matters worse, many Hondurans considered the area around La Muralla National Park to be a frontier open to settlement by landless campesinos (peasant farmers). In fleeing poverty and desertification, people were migrating to the Olancho province in large numbers.[4] Not only did they clear the forests for cultivation, but they also cut wood for fuel and for use in building their homes. Most of the new settlements were being established in the area's best mahogany growing habitats.

Another concern was that of potential restrictions by CITIES (the international convention on trade in endangered species). Although trade in mahogany was still permitted, it was supposed to be monitored very closely. If the populations of the 12 mahogany species continued to decrease, it was possible that mahogany would be given even greater protection under the CITIES framework. This could include even tighter restrictions on the trade in mahogany or could even result in an outright ban similar to the worldwide ban on ivory trading.

Notes

1. K. Norsworthy, *Inside Honduras* (Albuquerque, NM: Inter-Hemispheric Education Resource, 1993), pp. 133–138.
2. H. Lamprecht, *Silviculture in the Tropics* (Hamburg, Germany: Verlag, 1989), pp. 245–246.
3. *Ibid.*
4. K. Norsworthy, *Inside Honduras* (Albuquerque, NM: Inter-Hemispheric Education Resource, 1993), pp. 133–138.

CASE 10

Apple Computer and Steve P. Jobs (2006): Pixar Animation and Walt Disney Company

Moustafa H. Abdelsamad, Hitesh (John) Adhia, David B. Croll, Alan N. Hoffman, Charles E. Michaels Jr., and Thomas L. Wheelen

Compared to other Fortune 500 companies, Apple Computer has always been an interesting and often exciting firm. It had been the first to make and mass-market a personal computer with its Apple IIc. The company had been the darling of the stock market in the mid-1980s when it cemented its technological advantage through the introduction of its state-of-the-art Macintosh (MAC) personal computer. Nevertheless, the Microsoft Windows operating system and Office software coupled with Intel microprocessors left Apple far behind in PC market share by the mid-1990s. Apple Computer had fallen to being just a niche player in the industry. At that time, it was rumored that the company had little future unless it merged with or sold out to another computer company. With the beginning of the 21st century, Apple's fortunes changed for the better. The introduction of the iPod catapulted Apple back into the spotlight, just at a time when Microsoft and Intel seemed to be losing momentum.

2006 was another exciting year for Apple Computer and for its management and shareholders—full of both good news and bad news.

Good News

On May 23, 2006, Apple and Nike announced a joint-technology running shoe. The new Nike shoe would have a sensor placed in a small pocket of the shoe, and a wireless receiver on the iPod Nano. The two devices were to communicate wirelessly so the runner would be able to track distances covered, calories burned, and time spent exercising. The data was to be accessible in two ways: (1) by clicking on a button and hearing it through headphones, and (2) by looking at a menu on the screen.[1]

On August 2, 2006, Coke and Apple announced that Coke would offer codes for 70 million free iTunes to German and UK Coke customers. Coke was to be allowed to link its web site with Apple's iTunes site.[2]

On August 23, 2006, Apple partnered with General Motors, Ford Motor, and Mazda Motor to make iPods compatible with 2007 model car stereo systems. This would cover about 70% of the cars manufactured by their three companies.[3]

On October 9, 2006, Apple Computer announced that fourth-quarter (ending September 30, 2006) profits rose 27% to $546 million, and revenues rose 32% to $4.84 billion when compared with 2005 results. Mac shipments reached 1.61 million computers, which was the highest sales in the company's history. The sales were driven by the new notebooks with the faster Intel microprocessor. Apple began using the Intel chip in January, and completed the transition in August. Mac sales were up 37% to $2.21 billion. This was the eighth straight quarter that Mac sales were over a million units. Notebooks sales were up 63% and accounted for 61% of computer sales. Notebook sales outpaced the revenues for desktop systems including the Mac. Macs comprised 46% of Apple's revenues, whereas iPods and music sold through iTunes accounted for 42%.[4]

The new iPod nano and the video player with increased storage capacity were released in September 2006. These new products assisted in driving sales up 35.3% to 8.73 million units. Apple had a 75.6% market share of music portable players in the United States, SunDisk had 9.7% and Creative Technology was in third place with 4.3%.[5] Microsoft planned to release its music player for the 2006 Christmas season with a price of $250. During fiscal 2006, Apple Computer sold 41,385,000 iPods, which was more than double the 2005 sales of 20,443,000. The quarterly growth rates from year to year for the iPods ranged from a low of 32% to an extremely high growth rate of 624.2% (see **Exhibit 1**).[6]

Exhibit 1
Quarterly Units Shipped and Percent Change from Year to Year Apple Computer, Inc. (Units in thousands)

Year	Quarter	Macintosh	Year to Year Change (%)	iPod	Year to Year Change (%)
2006	4	1,610	30	8,710	51
	3	1,327	12	8,117	32
	2	1,112	4	8,521	60.1
	1	1,254	20	14,043	207
2005	4	1,236	48	5,751	186.2
	3	1,182	35	6,155	624.2
	2	1,070	43	5,321	559.4
	1	1,046	26	4,580	525
2004	4	836	6	2,010	500
	3	876	14	850	183
	2	748	5	807	909
	1	829	12	733	235

Notes:
The 4th quarter ended on September 30th.
The 3rd quarter ended on June 30th.
The 2nd quarter ended on March 30th.
The 1st quarter ended on December 29th.

Source: Apple Computer, Inc., company quarterly press releases.

On November 8, 2006, Apple's management announced that iTunes Latino would offer Spanish language and bilingual shows in cooperation with NBC Universal's Telemundo. It was also to offer regional Mexican baladas y boleros and pop Latino.[7]

An announcement on November 1, 2006, stated that wireless carrier Cingular was teaming with Napster and Yahoo and did not plan to work with Apple. Napster was to have a $15 monthly fee. Cingular was jointly owned by AT&T and BellSouth. An analyst commented that this strategic alliance was not a major setback for Apple. According to analyst Jonathan Hoopers: "Apple might opt out with its upcoming iPhone to become a 'mobile virtual network operator' which could be a better deal."

On November 12, 2006, Apple announced that it had made an agreement with six airlines, Air France, Continental, Delta, Emirates, KLM and United, to install iPod connections in their in-flight entertainment systems. This was scheduled for mid-2007.[8]

On November 16, 2006, Apple announced that its iPhone, the highly anticipated iPod cell phone, would include a 2.0-megapixel digital camera. An analyst estimated that this phone could add 22% to Apple's earnings in 2007. A Taiwanese source "has confirmed that an Apple iPod iPhone is now in production and that more than 10 million will be available in January, [so] . . . Steve Jobs can formally launch the new [iPhone] at Macworld in January." In addition to the iPhone, an iTV is expected in 2007. An industry analyst predicted "2007 to be one of the most exciting in Apple's history."[9]

Bad News

On August 3, 2006, a French law required Apple Computer to make its iPod player and iTunes online store compatible with rival offerings. This law was initially written to level the playing field to allow smaller rivals to compete with companies such as Sony and Apple. Apple argued that the opening of its formats would encourage software pirates. Other EU countries were looking at similar laws.[10]

On August 24, 2006, Apple management announced the recall of 1.8 million laptop batteries. The batteries were manufactured by Sony. Dell had a similar recall of 4.1 million of these Sony batteries.[11]

On September 1, 2006, the Chinese government told Hongfujin Precision Industry, a supplier of Apple Computer's iPod, to allow more than 200,000 workers to establish a trade union. China did not allow independent labor unions, but the Chinese government had been pressuring foreign-invested companies to allow state-sanctioned labor unions.[12]

On September 5, 2006, SpiralFrog, a new online music service, signed an agreement with EMI Music Publishing to authorize SpiralFrog to use EMI's music catalog for legal downloading in the United States. SpiralFrog had signed a similar deal with Universal Music Group, a unit of Vivendi. Artists covered in these deals included Sting, Nelly Furtado, Jay Z, and Kanye West.[13]

On October 21, 2006, Jon Loch Johansen, age 22, said that he had cracked Apple's iTunes copyright restrictions. The copyright protection stopped iPod users from playing downloaded music from music stores other than iTunes. The copyright protection also stopped music that had been used on an iPod from being played on a competitive music player. Johansen's Norwiegan company, Double Twin Venture, planned to license the code to businesses that could use the code to sell downloadable music for playing on an iPod. Several analysts expected Apple to take legal action against Johansen and his company. In response, Johansen claimed " that he has developed (a legal) way around any restrictions."[14]

When only 15 years of age, Johansen worked with two other European programmers to hack the DVD protection code. The hackers created a free program, DeCSS, which was available on the Internet. DeCSS software allowed the user to unlock a DVD's copy protection.

This allowed users to play and make copies of movies with their computers. Johansen earned the name "DVD Jon" for this hacking effort. There was a series of lawsuits in Norway and the United States.[15]

Real Networks, Inc., the owner of the RealPlayer Music Store, announced on October 21, 2006, that it was introducing a new product, Harmony. Harmony would let customers download music from the RealPlayer online store and allow them to use it on any portable music player. In response, an Apple spokesperson said that the company was looking into Real's actions under various laws, including the Digital Copyright Millennium Act, which prohibited the manufacture, sale, or distribution of code-breaking devices. Real Networks stood firm. A Real Networks executive said, "We remain committed to Harmony and to giving millions of consumers who own portable music devices, including the Apple iPod, choice and compatibility."[16]

Stock Option Investigation

On January 23, 2006, Apple announced "an internal probe uncovered irregularities related to the company's issuance of stock options granted between 1997 and 2001 when its shares fell 3 percent." The board of directors had hired an independent counsel to perform the investigation and to inform the U.S. Securities and Exchange Commission (SEC) of the probe.[17]

The internal probe resulted in examining more than 650,000 e-mails and documents and interviews of more than 40 current and former employees, directors, and advisors. A company representative said that "Jobs knew that some grants had given favorable dates 'in a few instances,' but he did not benefit from them and was not aware of the accounting implications." The investigative report "did not uncover any misconduct by any members of Apple's current management team, but it did raise serious concerns regarding the actions of two former executives." The investigation may have prompted the September 30, 2006, resignation of former Chief Financial Officer (CFO) Fred Anderson from the board.[18]

Steve Jobs stated: "I apologize to Apple's shareholders and employees for these problems, which happened on my watch. They are completely out of character for Apple." He further stated: "We will now work to resolve the remaining issues as quickly as possible and to put the proper remedial measures in place to ensure that this never happens again."[19]

On August 2, 2006, management announced that the company would likely need to restate earnings and delay filing its quarterly SEC report (10-Q) because of additional irregularities the company found in its accounting of stock options. Apple's stock fell 6.6% after this announcement. As of November 12, 2006, the company had not yet filed complete SEC-required financial statements or SEC 10-Q reports for the third and fourth quarters, and its yearly 10-K form.[20]

The problem of backdating stock options in order to maximize executive compensation existed in more than 120 other U.S. companies. Although backdating was not been prohibited under SEC regulations, companies are now required to record non-cash charges for compensation expenses relating to these stock options and to restate past financial statements where this occurred.[21]

On October 10, 2006, McAfee announced that the board had fired President Weiss, and that George Sameriuk, CEO and Chairman, "will retire after stock option investigation into accounting problems that will require financial restatements." The restatements of $100 to $150 million "would cover a 10-year period."[22]

On October 12, 2006, the Minnesota attorney general's office was planning to investigate United Health Group Inc.'s stock options. United Health was already under investigation by federal regulators for "the stock options grant timing for 11 executives of the company."[23]

Apple Threatened with Delisting from the NASDAQ Exchange

In August 2006, Apple and more than a dozen other companies were warned by NASDAQ of their possibly delisting because they were late in filing their quarterly report (third quarter) as these companies worked to untangle their options accounting.[24]

Between 1995 and 2004, more than 7,300 companies were delisted from U.S. stock markets. About half were involuntary delisting. During the period 2000 to 2004, 3,000 companies were delisted from NASDAQ. A Georgetown study by Professor James L. Angel found that "roughly one for every five on the exchange in any given year . . . were delisted."[25]

Apple could have filed a tardy report with the SEC before its requested NASDAQ hearing. The filing was for the third quarter, which ended on July 1, 2005. As of October 10, 2006, the SEC 10-Q had not yet been filed.

History of Apple Computer[26]

The history of Apple Computer can be broken into four separate time periods, each with its own strategic issues and concerns.

1976–1984: The Founders Build a Company

Founded in a California garage on April 1, 1976, Apple created the personal computer revolution with powerful yet easy-to-use machines for the desktop. Steve Jobs sold his Volkswagen bus and Steve Wozniak hocked his HP programmable calculator to raise $1,300 in seed money to start their new company. Not long afterward, a mutual friend helped recruit A.C. "Mike" Markkula to help market the company and give it a million-dollar image. Even though all three founders had left the company's management team during the 1980s, Markkula continued serving on Apple's Board of Directors until August 1997.

The early success of Apple was attributed largely to marketing and technological innovation. In the high-growth industry of personal computers in the early 1980s, Apple grew quickly, staying ahead of competitors by contributing key products that stimulated the development of software for the computer. Landmark programs such as Visicalc (forerunner to Lotus 1-2-3 and other spreadsheet programs) were developed first for the Apple II. Apple also secured early dominance in the education and consumer markets by awarding hundreds of thousands of dollars in grants to schools and individuals for the development of education software.

Even with enormous competition, Apple revenues continued to grow at an unprecedented rate, reaching $583.3 million by fiscal 1982. The introduction of the Macintosh graphical user interface in 1984, which included icons, pull-down menus, and windows, became the catalyst for desktop publishing and instigated the second technological revolution attributable to Apple. Apple kept the architecture of the Macintosh proprietary, that is, it could not be cloned like the "open system" IBM PC. This allowed the company to charge a premium for its distinctive "user-friendly" features.

A shakeout in the personal computer industry began in 1983 when IBM entered the PC market, first affecting companies selling low-priced machines to consumers. Companies that made strategic blunders or that lacked sufficient distribution or brand awareness of their products disappeared.

1985–1997: Professional Managers Fail to Extend the Company

In 1985, amid a slumping market, Apple saw the departure of its founders, Jobs and Wozniak. As Chairman of the Board, Jobs had recruited John Sculley, an experienced executive from PepsiCo, to replace Jobs as Apple's CEO in 1983. Jobs had challenged Sculley when recruiting him by saying, "Do you want to spend the rest of your life selling sugared water, or do you want to change the world?" Jobs willingly gave up his title as CEO so that he could have Sculley as his mentor. In 1985, a power struggle took place between Sculley and Jobs. With his entrepreneurial orientation, Jobs wanted to continue taking the company in risky new directions. Sculley, in contrast, felt that Apple had grown to the point where it needed not only to be more careful in its strategic moves, but also to be better organized and rationally managed. The board of directors supported Sculley's request to strip Jobs of his duties. The board felt that the company needed an experienced executive to lead Apple into its next stage of development.

Jobs then resigned from the company he had founded and sold all but one share of his Apple stock. Under the leadership of John Sculley, CEO and Chairman, the company engineered a remarkable turnaround. He instituted a massive reorganization to streamline operations and expenses. It was during this time that Wozniak left the company. Macintosh sales gained momentum throughout 1986 and 1987. Sales increased 40% from $1.9 billion to $2.7 billion in fiscal 1987, and earnings jumped 41% to $217 million.

In the early 1990s, Apple sold more personal computers than any other computer company. Net sales grew to over $7 billion, net income to over $540 million, and earnings per share to $4.33. The period from 1993 to 1995 was, however, a time of considerable change in the management of Apple. The industry was rapidly changing. Personal computers using Microsoft's Windows operating system and Office software plus Intel microprocessors began to dominate the personal computer market place. (The alliance between Microsoft and Intel was known in the trade as Wintel.) Dell, Hewlett-Packard, Compaq, and Gateway replaced both IBM and Apple as the primary makers of PCs. The new Windows system had successfully imitated the user-friendly "look and feel" of Apple's Macintosh operating system. As a result, Apple lost its competitive edge. In June 1993, Sculley was forced to resign and Michael H. Spindler was appointed CEO of the company. At this time, Apple was receiving a number of offers to acquire the company. Many of the company's executives advocated Apple's merging with another company. When no merger took place, many executives chose to resign.

Unable to reverse the company's falling sales, Spindler was soon forced out and Gilbert Amelio was hired from outside Apple to serve as CEO. Amelio's regime presided over an accelerated loss of market share, deteriorating earnings, and stock that had lost half of its value, Apple's refusal to license the Mac operating system to other manufacturers had given Microsoft the opening it needed to take the market with its Windows operating system. Wintel PCs now dominated the market—pushing Apple into a steadily declining market niche composed primary of artisans and teachers. By 1996, Apple's management seemed be in utter disarray.

Looking for a new product with which Apple could retake the initiative in personal computers, the company bought NeXT for $402 million on December 20, 1996. Steve Jobs had formed the NeXT computer company when he left Apple. Jobs had envisioned his new company as the developer of the "next generation" in personal computers. Part of the purchase agreement was that Jobs would return to Apple as a consultant. In July of 1997, Amelio resigned and was replaced by Steve Jobs as Apple's interim CEO (iCEO). This ended Steve Jobs' 14-year exile from the company that he and Wozniak had founded. In addition to being iCEO of Apple, Jobs also served as CEO of Pixar, a company he had personally purchased from Lucasfilm for $5 million. Receiving only $1.00 a year as CEO of both Pixar and Apple, Jobs held the Guinness World Record as the "Lowest Paid Chief Executive Officer."

1998 to 2001: Jobs Leads Apple "Back to the Future"

Once in position as Apple's CEO, Steve Jobs terminated many of the company's existing projects. Dropped were the iBook and the AirPort products series, which had helped popularize the use of wireless LAN technology to connect a computer to a network.

In May 2001, the company announced the reopening of Apple Retail Stores. Like IBM and Xerox, Apple had opened its own retail stores to market its computers during the 1980s. All such stores had been closed when Wintel-type computers began being sold by mass merchandisers, such as Sears and Circuit City, and through corporate web sites.

The iPod portable digital audio player was introduced, and the company opened its own iTunes music store to provide downloaded music to iPod users. Given the thorny copyright issues inherent in the music business, analysts doubted if the new product would be successful.

2002–2006: A Corporate Renaissance?

In 2002, Apple introduced a redesigned iMac using a 64-bit processor. The iMac had a hemispherical base and a flat-panel all-digital display. Although it received a lot of press, the iMac failed to live up to its sales expectations.

In 2004 and 2005, Apple opened its first retail stores in Europe and Canada. By November 2006, the company had 149 stores in the United States, 4 stores in Canada, 7 stores in the United Kingdom, and 7 stores in Japan.

In 2006, Jobs announced that Apple would sell an Intel-based Macintosh. Previously Microsoft had purchased all of its microprocessors from Motorola. By this time, Microsoft's operating system with Intel microprocessors was running on 97.5% of the personal computers sold, with Apple having only a 2.5% share of the market. The first Intel-based machines, the iMac and MacBook Pro, were introduced.

By this time, Apple's iPod had emerged as the market leader of a completely new industry category, which it had created. In 2006, Apple controlled 75.6% of the market, followed by SunDisk with 9.7%, and Creative Technology in third place with 4.3%. Although one analyst predicted that more than 30 million iPods would be sold in fiscal 2006, Apple actually sold 41,385,000. Taking advantage of its lead in music downloading, the company's next strategic move was to extend its iTunes music stores by offering movies for $9.99 each. An analyst reviewing this strategic move said, "Apple was able to create a $1 billion-a-year market for the legal sale of music. Apple may be able to provide the movie industry with a similar formula."

Steven P. Jobs: Entrepreneur and Corporate Executive[27]

Steve P. Jobs was born on February 24, 1955, in San Francisco and was currently married with three daughters. He was adopted by Paul and Clara Jobs in February 1955. In 1972, Jobs graduated from Homestead High School in Los Altos, California. His high school electronics teacher said, "He was somewhat of loner and always had a different way of looking at things."[28] After graduation, Jobs was hired by Hewlett-Packard as a summer employee. This is where he met Steve Wozniak, a recent dropout from The University of California at Berkeley. Wozniak had a genius IQ and was an engineering whiz with a passion for inventing electronic gadgets. At this time, Wozniak was perfecting his "blue box," an illegal pocket-size telephone attachment that allowed the user to make free long-distance calls. Jobs helped Wozniak sell this device to customers.[29]

In 1972, Jobs enrolled at Reed College in Portland, Oregon, but dropped out after one semester. He remained around Reed for a year and became involved in the counterculture. He enrolled in various classes in philosophy and other topics. In a later speech at Stanford University, Jobs explained, "If I had never dropped in on that single course (calligraphy), that Mac would have never had multiple type faces or proportionally spaced fonts."[30]

In early 1974, Jobs took a job as a video-game designer for Atari, a pioneer in electronic arcade games. After earning enough money, Jobs went to India in search of personal spiritual enlightenment. Later that year, Jobs returned to California and began attending meetings of Steve Wozniak's "Homebrew Computer Club." Wozniak converted his TV monitor into what would become a computer. Wozniak was a very good engineer and extremely interested in creating new electronic devices. Jobs was not interested in developing new devices, but he realized the marketability of Wozniak's converted TV. Together they designed the Apple I computer in Jobs' bedroom and built the first prototype in Jobs' garage. Jobs showed the Apple I to a local electronics retailer, the Byte Shop, and received a $25,000 order for 50 computers. Jobs took this purchase order to Cramer Electronics to order the components needed to assemble the 50 computers.

The local credit manager asked Jobs how he was going to pay for the parts and he replied, "I have this purchase order from the Byte Shop chain of computer stores for 50 of my computers and the payment terms are COD. If you give me the parts on a net 30 day terms, I can build and deliver the computers in that time frame, collect my money from Turrell at the Byte Shop and pay you." With that, the credit manager called Paul Terrell who was attending an IEEE computer conference . . . and verified the validity of the purchase order. Amazed at the tenacity of Jobs, Turrell assured the credit manager if the computers showed up in his stores Jobs would be paid and would have more than enough money to pay for the parts order. The two Steves and their small crew spent day and night building and testing the computers and delivered to Turrell on time to pay his suppliers and have a tidy profit left over for their celebration and next order. Steve Jobs had found a way to finance his soon-to-be multimillion-dollar company without giving away one share of stock or ownership.[31]

Jobs and Wozniak decided to start a computer company to manufacture and sell personal computers. They contributed $1,300 of their own money to start the business. Jobs selected the name Apple for the company based on his memories of a summer job as an orchard worker. On April 1, 1976, Apple Computer Company was formed as a partnership.

During Jobs' early tenure at Apple, he was a persuasive and charismatic evangelist for Apple. Some of his employees have described him at that time as an erratic and tempestuous manager. An analyst said "many persons who look at Jobs' management style forget that he was 30 years old in 1985 and he received his management and leadership education on the job." Jobs guided the company's revenues to $1,515,616,000 and profits of $64,055,000 in 1984. Jobs was cited in several articles as having a demanding and aggressive personality. One analyst said that these two attributes described most of the successful entrepreneurs. Jobs strategically managed the company through a period of new product introduction, rapidly changing technology, and intense competition—a time when many companies have failed.

In 1985, after leaving Apple, Jobs formed a new computer company, NeXT Computer Inc. NeXT was a computer company that built machines with futuristic designs and ran the UNIX-derived NeXT step operating system. It was marketed to academic and scientific organizations. NeXT was not a commercial success, in part because of its high price. Jobs served as Chairman and CEO.[32]

In 1986, Jobs purchased Pixar Animation from Lucasfilm for $5 million. He provided another $5 million in capital, owned 50.6% of the stock, and served as Chairman and CEO. Pixar created three of the six highest domestic grossing (gross revenues) animated films of all time—*Toy Story* (1995), *A Bug's Life* (1998), and *Toy Story II* (1999). These films were released under a partnership with the Walt Disney Company. Each of these films was the highest grossing animated film for the year in which it was released. During this period, Jobs delegated more to his executives. Many analysts felt that the excellent executive staff and animators were prime reasons that Disney management subsequently wanted to acquire Pixar. Jobs served as CEO of NeXT and Pixar from 1985 to 1997. Jobs sold NeXT in 1996 to Apple for $402 million and became iCEO of Apple in July 1997.[33]

At Pixar, Jobs focused on business duties, which was different than his earlier management style at Apple. The creative staff was given a great deal of autonomy. Sources say he spent less than one day a week at the Pixar campus in Emeryville, just across the San Francisco Bay from Apple's headquarters. A Pixar employee said, "Steve did not tell us what to do." He further stated, "Steve's our benevolent benefactor."[34]

Michael D, Eisner, CEO of the Walt Disney Company, did not have a smooth relationship with Jobs during the years of the Pixar/Disney partnership. Critics explained that Eisner was unable to work with Jobs because both men were supremely confident (some said arrogant) that their own judgment was correct—regardless of what others said. In 2005, in response to Eisner's unwillingness to modify Disney's movie distribution agreement with Pixar, Jobs refused to renew the contract. At the time, Disney's own animation unit was faltering and unable to match Pixar's new computer technology and creativity. Concerned with Eisner's leadership style and his inability to support the company's distinctive competence in animation, Roy Disney led a shareholders' revolt. On October 1, 2005, Eisner was replaced by Robert A. Iger as CEO of Disney.[35]

On January 24, 2006, CEO Iger announced that Disney had agreed to pay $7.4 billion in stock to acquire Pixar Animation Studios. Since this deal made Jobs the largest stockholder (6.67%) in Disney, he was appointed to Disney's board of directors.[36]

Edward S. Woodward, Jr., former Chairman of Apple Computer, told Apple's board of directors: "He (Jobs) has a good relationship with you; there is nobody better with you; there is nobody better in the world to work with. Iger made a very wise move, and two years from now everyone will be saying that."[37]

Peter Burrows and Ronald Grover in an article said: "The alliance between Jobs and Disney is full of promise. If he can bring to Disney the same kind of industry-sharing, boundary-busting energy that has lifted Apple and Pixar sky-high, he could help the staid company become the leading laboratory for media convergences. It's not hard to imagine a day when you could fire up your Apple TV and watch net-only spin-offs of popular TV shows from Disney's ABC Inc. (DIS). Or use your Apple iPhone to watch Los Angeles Lakers superstar Kobe Bryant's video biog delivered via Disney's ESPN Inc. 'We've been talking about a lot of things,' said Jobs. 'It's going to be a pretty exciting world looking ahead over the next five years.' "[38]

An expert on Jobs asked, "*So what is Jobs' secret*?" His answer: "There are many, but it starts with focus and a non-religious faith in his strategy." In his return to Apple, he took a proprietary approach as he cut dozen of projects and products. Many on Wall Street were not initially happy with Jobs' new directions for the company, but soon were impressed by the Apple's successful turnaround.[39]

Corporate Governance[40]

Exhibit 2 lists the seven members of the board of directors and the executive officers as of October 8, 2006. Steve Jobs, as CEO, was the only internal board member and the only member who had served on the original board. On September 30, 2006, Fred Anderson, who had joined the board in 2004, resigned from the board over the stock options investigation. On August 28, 2006, Dr. Eric Schmidt, CEO of Google, was appointed to the board. He did not accept the automatic 30,000 stock options available to all new board members. Shaw Nu, analyst, said, "He (Schmidt) gives Jobs and Apple more perspective on dealing with Microsoft. . . . And like Jobs, Schmidt has lost at times against (Microsoft)." As soon as Schmidt's board appointment was announced, speculation began about the potential for future partnerships between Google and Apple.

Exhibit 2
Directors and Executive Officers: Apple Computer Inc.

A. Directors

Name	Position	Age	Since
Fred A. Anderson	Director	61	2004
William V. Campbell	Co-lead Director	65	1997
Millard S. Drexler	Director	61	1999
Albert A. Gore, Jr.	Director	57	2000
Steven P. Jobs	Director and CEO	50	1997
Arthur D. Levinson	Co-lead Director	55	2000
Jerome B. York	Director	67	1997

B. Executives

Steven P. Jobs
CEO, Apple
CEO, Pixar
Director, Apple
Director, Walt Disney

Timothy D. Cook
Chief Operating Officer

Nancy R. Heinen
Senior Vice President
and General Counsel

Ron Johnson
Senior Vice President Retail

Peter Oppenheimer
Senior Vice President
Chief Financial Officer

Dr. Avdias "Avie" Tevanian, Jr.
Chief Software Technology Officer

Jon Rubinstein
Senior Vice President
iPod Divison

Philip W. Schiller
Senior Vice President
Worldwide Product Marketing

Bertrand Seriet
Senior Vice President
Software Engineering

Sina Tamaddon
Senior Vice President, Applications

Source: Apple Computer, Ind., SEC 10-K Report (December 1, 2005), p. 102.

External board members received $50,000 as an annual retainer. In addition, directors were eligible to receive up to two free computer systems, and discounts on the purchase of additional products. On the fourth anniversary of joining the board, each member was entitled to receive an option to acquire 30,000 shares of stock.

Although Steve Jobs' annual salary was only $1.00 as CEO of Apple, the board gave Jobs a bonus of $84 million in 2001, consisting of $43.5 million for a private jet, a Gulfstream V, as well as $40.5 million to pay Jobs' income taxes on this bonus. Jobs owned 10,200,004 (1.25%) of Apple's stock. The closing price on November 21, 2006, was $88.60 per share. Together, the directors and executives owned 16,307,625 (1.94%) shares of stock. Barclay Bank Plc owned 67,094,321 (8.09%) shares and FMR Corporation owned 51,250,663 (6.18%) shares of Apple. These are the two financial institutions with more than 5% ownership.

Management's View of the Company[41]

Apple Computer's 10-K Report for the fiscal year ended September 24, 2005 contained the following analysis of the company by management:

> First, the company designed, manufactured, and marketed personal computers and related software, services, peripherals, and networking solutions. The company also designed, developed, and

marketed a line of portable digital music players along with related accessories and services including the online distribution of third-party music, audio books music videos, short films and television shows. The company's products and services included the Macintosh line of desktop and notebook computers, the iPod digital music player, the Xserve G5 server and the Xserve RAID storage products, a portfolio of consumer and professional software applications, the Mac OS X operating system, the iTunes Music Store, a portfolio of peripherals that support and enhance the Macintosh and iPod product lines, and a variety of other service and support offerings. The company sold its products worldwide through its online stores, its own retail stores, its direct sales force, and third-party wholesalers, resellers, and value added resellers. In addition, the company sold a variety of third-party Macintosh compatible products, including computer printers and printing supplies, storage devices, computer memory, digital camcorders and still cameras, personal digital assistants, and various other computing products and supplies through its online and retail stores. The company sells to *education, consumer, creative, professional, business, and government customers.*

Second, the company's business strategy leveraged its ability, through the design and development of its own operating system, hardware, and many software applications and technologies, to bring to its customers around the world compelling new products and solutions with superior ease-of-use, seamless integration, and innovative industrial design.

Third, the company participated in several highly competitive markets, including *personal computers* with its *Macintosh line* of computers, *consumer electronics* with its *iPod line* of digital music players, and distribution of third-party digital content through its online *iTunes Music Store*. While the company was widely recognized as an innovator in the personal computer and consumer electronic markets as well as a leader in the emerging market for distribution of digital content, these were all highly competitive markets that are subject to aggressive pricing and increased competition. To remain competitive, the company believed that increased investment in research and development (R&D) and marketing and advertising was necessary to maintain and extend its position in the markets where it competes. The company's R&D spending was focused on delivering timely updates and enhancements to its existing line of personal computers displays, operating systems, software applications, and portable music players; developing new digital lifestyle consumer and professional software applications: and investing in new product areas such as rack-mount servers, RAID storage systems, and wireless technologies. The company also believed investment in marketing and advertising programs was critical to increasing product and brand awareness.

Fourth, in June 2005, the company announced its plan to begin using Intel microprocessors in its Macintosh computers. The company planned to begin shipping certain models with Intel microprocessors by June 2006 (which the company did) and to complete the transition of all of its Macintosh computers to Intel microprocessors by the end of calendar year 2007.

Fifth, the company utilized a variety of direct and indirect distribution channels. The company believed that sales of its innovative and differentiated products were enhanced by knowledgeable salespersons who can convey the value of the hardware, software, and peripheral integration, demonstrate the unique digital lifestyle solutions of the Windows platform and networks. The company further believed that providing a high-quality sales and after-sales support experience was critical to attracting and retaining customers. To ensure a high-quality buying experience for its products in which service and education are emphasized, the company had expanded and improved its distribution capabilities by opening its own retail stores in the U.S. and internationally. The company had 124 stores open as of September 24, 2005.

Sixth, the company also staffs selected third-party stores with the company's own employees to improve the buying experience through reseller channels. The company had deployed Apple employees and contractors in reseller locations around the world including the U.S., Europe, Japan, and Australia. The company also sold to customers directly through its online stores around the world.

Seventh, to improve access to the iPod product line, the company had significantly expanded the number of distribution points where iPods are sold. The iPod product line can be purchased in certain department stores, member-only warehouse stores, large retail chains, and specialty retail stores, as well as through the channels listed above.

Business Strategy[42]

The company was committed to bringing the best personal computing and music experience to students, educators, creative professional, businesses, government agencies, and consumers through its innovative hardware, software, peripherals, services, and Internet offerings. The company's business strategy leverages its unique ability through the design and development of its own operating system, hardware, and many software applications and technologies, to bring to its customers new products and solutions with superior ease-of-use, seamless integration, and innovative industrial design. The company believed continual investment in research and development is critical to facilitate innovation of new and improved products and technologies. Besides updates to its existing line of personal computers and related software, services, peripherals, and networking solutions, the company continued to capitalize on the convergence of digital consumer electronics and computers by creating innovations like the iPod and iTunes Music Store. The company's strategy also included expanding its distribution network to effectively reach more of its targeted customers and provide them a high-quality sales and after-sales support experience.

Digital Hub

The company believed personal computing was in an era in which the personal computer functions for both professionals and consumers as the digital hub for advanced new digital devices such as the company's iPod digital music players, personal digital assistants, cellular phone, digital camcorders and still cameras, CD and DVD players, televisions, and other consumer electronic devices. The attributes of the personal computer included a high quality user interface, relatively inexpensive data storage, and the ability to run complex applications and easily connect to the Internet. Apple was the only company in the personal computer industry that controls the design and development of the entire personal computer—from the hardware and operating system to sophisticated application. Additionally, the company's products provided innovative industrial design, intuitive ease-of-use, and built-in networking, graphics and multimedia capabilities. Thus, the company was uniquely positioned to offer integrated digital hub products and solutions.

The company developed products and technologies that adhere to many industry standards in order to provide an optimized user experience through interoperability with peripherals and devices from other companies. The company had played a role in the development, enhancement, promotion, and/or use of numerous of these industry standards.

Expanded Distribution

The company believed that a high quality buying experience with knowledgeable salespersons who can convey the value of the company's products and services was critical to attracting and retaining customers. The company sold many of its products and resold certain third-party products in most of its major markets directly to consumers, education customers, and businesses through its retail and online stores in the U.S. and internationally. The company had also invested in programs to enhance reseller sales, including the Apple Sales Consultant Program, which consisted of the deployment of Apple employees and contractors to selected third-party reseller locations. The company believed providing direct contact with its targeted customers is an efficient way to demonstrate the advantage of its Macintosh computer and other products over those of its competitors. The company had significantly increased the points of distribution for the iPod product family in order to make its products available at locations where its customers shop.

From inception of the retail initiative in 2001 through 2005, the company had opened 116 retail stores in the U.S. and 8 international stores in Canada, Japan, and the U.K. The company opened 2 additional stores in October of 2005. The company had typically located its stores at high traffic locations in quality shopping malls and urban shopping districts.

One of the goals of the retail initiative was to bring new customers to the company and expand its installed base through sales to computer users who currently did not own a

Macintosh computer and first time personal computer buyers. By operating its own stores and building them in desirable high traffic locations, the company was able to better control the customer retail experience and attract new customers. The stores were designed to simplify and enhance the presentation and marketing of personal computing products. To that end, retail stores configurations had evolved into various sizes in order to accommodate market demands. The stores employed experienced and knowledgeable personnel who provided product advice and certain hardware support services. The stores offered a wide selection of third-party hardware, software, and various other computing products and supplies selected to complement the company's own products. Additionally, the stores provided forum in which the company was able to present computing solutions to users in areas such as digital photography, digital video, music, children's software, and home and small business computing.

Education

For more than 25 years, the company had focused on the use of technology in education and had been committed to delivering tools to help educators teach and students learn. The company believed effective integration of technology into classroom instruction can result in higher levels of student achievement, especially when used to support collaboration, information access, and the expression and representation of student thought and ideas. The company created solutions that enable new modes of curriculum delivery, better ways of conducting research, and opportunities for professional development of faculty, students, and staff. The company had designed a range of products and services to help schools maximize their investments in the needs of education customers. These products and services included the eMac™, and the iBook®, video creation and editing solutions, wireless networking, student information systems, high-quality curriculum and professional development solutions, and one-to-one (1:1) learning solutions (primarily in K–12). 1:1 learning solutions typically consisted of iBook portable computers for every student and teacher along with a wireless network connected to a central server.

Creative Professionals

Creative professionals constitutes one of the company's most important markets for both hardware and software products. This market was also important to many third-party developers who provide Macintosh-compatible hardware and software solutions. Creative customers utilized the company's products for a variety of creative activities including digital video and film production and editing; digital video and film special effects, compositing, and titling; digital still photography and workflow management; graphic design, publishing, and print production; music creation and production; audio production and sound design; and web design, development, and administration.

The company designed its high-end hardware solutions, including servers, desktops, and portable Macintosh systems, to incorporate the power, expandability, and features desired by creative professional. The company's operating system, Mac OS X, incorporated powerful graphics and audio technologies and features developer tools to optimize system and application performance when running powerful creative solutions provided by the company or third-party developers. The company also offered various software solutions to meet the needs of its creative customers.

Business Organization[43]

The company managed its business primarily on a geographic basis. The company's reportable operating segments are comprised of the Americas, Europe, Japan, and Retail. The Americas, Japan, and reportable segments did not include activities related to the Retail segments. The Americas segment included both North and South America. The Europe segment included European countries as well as the Middle East and Africa. The Retail segment currently operates Apple-owned retail stores in the U.S., Canada, Japan, and the U.K. Other operating segments included Asia-Pacific, which included Australia and Asia except for Japan, and the company's subsidiary, FileMaker, Inc. Each reportable geographic operating segment provided similar hardware and software products and similar services.

Current Products

Apple Computer designed, manufactured and marketed PCs and related software, services, networking solutions, worldwide and peripherals. The company products and services included the (1) Macintosh line of notebooks and desktop computers (iMac, MacBook, Mac mini, Mac Pro); (2) iPod digital music players (iPod Nano, iPod, iPod Hi-Fi); (3) Mac OS X operating system; (4) Xserve, G5 server, and Xserve RAID storage products; (5) a portfolio of professional and consumer software applications; (6) Mac OS X operating system; (7) iTunes Music Store and (8) a portfolio of peripherals that support and enhance the Macintosh and iPod product lines. The company's pro video peripherals support the Macintosh and iPod product lines. The company offered products and services for the educational industry which included the eMac, iMac, and iBook, creation and editing solutions, wireless networking and student information systems, curriculum and professional development solutions, and one-on-one learning solutions. The company makes announcements on new products and services on a continuous basis

Competition

The company was confronted by aggressive competition in all areas of business. The market for personal computer and related software and peripheral products was highly competitive. This market continued to be characterized by rapid technological advances in both hardware and software that had substantially increased the capabilities and use of personal computers and had resulted in the frequent introduction of new products with competitive price, features, and performance characteristics. Over the past several years, price competition in the personal computer market had been particularly intense. The company's competitors that sold personal computers based on other operating systems had aggressively cut prices and lowered product quality to maintain market share. The company's results of operations and financials can be adversely affected by these and other industry-wide downward pressures on gross margins.

The principal competitive factors in the market for personal computers included price, retail price performance, product qualities and reliability, design innovation, availability of software, product features, marketing and distribution capability, service and support, availability of hardware peripherals, and corporate reputation. Further, as the personal computer industry and its customers placed more reliance on the Internet, an increasing number of Internet devices that are simpler, and less expensive, than traditional personal computers may compete for market share with the company's existing products.

The company was currently taking and will continue to take steps to respond to the competitive pressures being placed on personal computer sales. The company's future operating results and financial condition were substantially dependent on its ability to continue to develop improvements to the Macintosh platform in order to maintain perceived functional and design advantages over competing platforms.

The company's services and products relating to music, and other creative content, had already encouraged significant competition from other companies, many of whom had greater financial, marketing, and manufacturing resources than those of the company. The company faced increasing competition from other companies promoting their own digital and distribution music products services, subscription services, and free peer-to-peer music services. The company anticipated the competition will intensify as hardware, software, and content providers work more collaboratively to offer integrated products competition with the company's offering. However, the company believed it currently maintained a competitive advantage by more effectively integrating an entire solution, including the hardware (iPod), software (iTunes), and distribution of third-party digital content (iTunes Music Store).[44]

including PowerBooks, iBooks, and iPods were performed by third-party vendors in China. Margins on sales of the company's products in foreign countries, and sales of products that included components obtained from foreign suppliers, can be adversely affected by foreign currencies exchange rate fluctuations and international trade regulations, including tariffs and antidumping penalties.

Seasonality[53]

The company had historically experienced increased net sales in the first and fourth quarters compared to other quarters in the fiscal year (ending September 24, 2005) due to seasonal demand related to the holiday season and the beginning of the school year. This historical pattern should not be considered a reliable indicator of the company's future net sales or financial performance.

Raw Materials[54]

Although most components essential to the company's business were generally available from multiple sources, certain key components [including microprocessors and application-specific integrated circuits ("ASIC")] were currently obtained by the company from single or limited sources. Some other key components, while currently available to the company from multiple sources, were at times subject to industry-wide availability constraints and pricing pressures. In addition, the company used some components that were not common to the rest of the personal computers and consumer electronics industries, and new products introduced in the company often initially utilize current components.

Environmental Laws[55]

Compliance with federal, state, local, and foreign laws for the protection of the environment had to date no material effect on the company's capital expenditures, earnings, or competitive position. In the future, these laws could have a material adverse effect on the company.

Production and marketing of products in certain states and countries may subject the company to environmental and other regulations, such as the requirement that the company provide consumers with the ability to return product to the company at the end of its useful life, and place responsibility for environmentally safe disposal or recycling with the company. Such laws and regulations had recently been passed in several jurisdictions in which the company operates, including various European Union member states, Japan, and California. In the future, these laws could have a material adverse effect on the company.

Employees[56]

The company had 14,800 full-time employees and 2,200 temporary employees and contractors.

Legal Proceedings[57]

Apple Computer was subject to certain legal proceedings and claims, which have arisen in the ordinary course of business and had not been fully adjudicated in the opinion of management, the company did not have a potential liability related to any existing legal proceedings and claims that will have a material adverse effect on the financial condition and operating results. In 2005, the company settled several issues and the settlements individually or in the aggregate have a material impact on the company's financial results.

The European Commission had notified the company that it was being investigated relating to the iTune Music Store in the European Union (EU). The case focuses on EU competition law and contended that Apple was charging more for online music in the UK than in Eurozone countries.

An analyst expects legal action against Jon Loch Johansen and RealNetworld, over their breaking of the protection codes on the iPod.

Financial Performance[58]

Management's view of the company's 2005 financial performance (see **Exhibits 3–6**) follows:

> Net sales of iPods rose $3.2 billion during 2005 compared to 2004. Unit sales of iPods totaled 22.5 million in 2005, which represented an increase of 400% from the 4.4 million iPod units sold in 2004. Strong sales of iPods during 2005 continued to be experienced in all the company's operating segments and was driven by a strong demand for the iPod Shuffle introduced in January 2005, the release of an updated version of the iPod Mini in February 2005, the release of the iPod Nano in September 2005, and expansion of the iPod distribution network. Net sales per iPod unit sold decreased 32 percent primarily due to the introduction of the lower priced iPod Shuffle in January 2005, and iPod Mini pricing reductions in February 2005. From the introduction of the iPod in 2002 through 2005, the company sold approximately 28 million iPods.

Other music related products and services consisted of sales associated with the iTune Music Store and iPod services and accessories. Net sales of other music related products and services increased $621 million or 223 percent during 2005 compared to 2004. The company

Exhibit 3
Consolidated Statements of Operations: Apple Computer, Inc. (Dollar amounts in millions, except per share data)

Three fiscal years ending September 24, 2005	2005	2004	2003
Net sales	$ 13,931	8,279	6,207
Cost of sales	9,888	6,020	4,499
Gross margin	4,043	2,259	1,708
Operating expenses:			
Research and development	534	489	471
Selling, general, and administrative	1,859	1,421	1,212
Restructuring costs	—	23	26
Total operating expenses	2,393	1,933	1,709
Operating income (loss)	1,650	326	(1)
Other income and expense:			
Gains on non-current investments, net	—	4	10
Interest and other income, net	165	53	83
Total other income and expense	165	57	93
Income before provision for income taxes	1,815	383	92
Provision for income taxes	480	107	24
Income before accounting changes	1,335	276	68
Cumulative effects of accounting changes, net of income taxes	—	—	1
Net income	$ 1,335	276	69
Earnings per common share before accounting changes:			
Basic	$ 1.65	$ 0.37	$ 0.09
Diluted	$ 1.56	$ 0.36	$ 0.09
Earnings per common share:			
Basic	$ 1.65	$ 0.37	$ 0.10
Diluted	$ 1.56	$ 0.36	$ 0.09
Shares used in computing earnings per share (in thousands):			
Basic	808,439	743,180	721,262
Diluted	856,780	774,622	726,932

Source: Apple Computer, SEC 10-K Report (December 1, 2005), p. 61.

Exhibit 4 Consolidated Balance Sheets: Apple Computer, Inc. (Dollar amounts in millions, except per share data)

Year ending	September 24, 2005	September 25, 2004
ASSETS:		
Current assets:		
Cash and cash equivalents	$ 3,491	$ 2,969
Short-term investments	4,770	2,495
Accounts receivable, less allowances of $46 and $47, respectively	895	774
Inventories	165	101
Deferred tax assets	331	231
Other current assets	648	485
Total current assets	10,300	7,055
Property, plant, and equipment, net	817	707
Goodwill	69	80
Acquired intangible assets, net	27	17
Other assets	338	191
Total assets	$11,551	$ 8,050
LIABILITIES AND SHAREHOLDERS' EQUITY:		
Current liabilities:		
Accounts payable	$ 1,779	$1,451
Accrued expenses	1,705	1,200
Total current liabilities	3,484	2,651
Non-current liabilities	601	323
Total liabilities	4,085	2,974
Commitments and contingencies		
Shareholders' equity:		
Common stock, no par value; 1,800,000,000 shares authorized; 835,019,364 and 782,887,234 shares issued and outstanding, respectively	3,521	2,514
Deferred stock compensation	(60)	(93)
Retained earnings	4,005	2,670
Accumulated other comprehensive income (loss)	—	(15)
Total shareholders' equity	7,466	5,076
Total liabilities and shareholders' equity	$11,551	$8,050

Source: Apple Computer, SEC 10-K Report (December 1, 2005), p. 60.

Exhibit 5 Geographic Data: Apple Computer, Inc. (Dollar amounts in millions)

	2005	2004	2003
Americas:			
Net sales	$6,590	$4,019	$3,181
Operating income	$ 798	$ 465	$ 323
Depreciation, amortization, and accretion	$ 6	$ 6	$ 5
Segment assets (a)	$ 705	$ 563	$ 494
Europe:			
Net sales	$3,073	$1,799	$1,309
Operating income	$ 454	$ 280	$ 130
Depreciation, amortization, and accretion	$ 4	$ 4	$ 4
Segment assets	$ 289	$ 259	$ 252

Exhibit 5
(Continued)

Japan:			
Net sales	$ 920	$ 677	$ 698
Operating income	$ 140	$ 115	$ 121
Depreciation, amortization, and accretion	$ 3	$ 2	$ 3
Segment assets	$ 199	$ 114	$ 130
Retail:			
Net sales	$2,350	$1,185	$ 621
Operating income (loss)	$ 151	$ 39	$ (5)
Depreciation, amortization, and accretion (b)	$ 43	$ 35	$ 25
Segment assets (b)	$ 555	$ 351	$ 243
Other Segments (c):			
Net sales	$ 998	$ 599	$ 398
Operating income	$ 118	$ 90	$ 51
Depreciation, amortization, and accretion	$ 2	$ 2	$ 2
Segment assets	$ 133	$ 124	$ 78

Notes:
(a) The Americas asset figures do not include fixed assets held in the U.S. Such fixed assets are not allocated specifically to the Americas segment and are included in the corporate assets figures below.
(b) Retail segment depreciation and asset figures reflect the cost and related depreciation of its retail stores and related infrastructure. Retail store construction-in-progress, which is not subject to depreciation, is reflected in corporate assets.
(c) Other segments include Asia-Pacific and FileMaker.

Source: Apple Computer, SEC 10-K Report (December 1, 2005), p. 94.

Exhibit 6
Segment Information: Apple Computer, Inc. (Dollar amounts in millions)

Information regarding net sales by product is as follows:

	2005	**2004**	**2003**
Net Sales:			
Desktops (a)	$ 3,436	$2,373	$2,475
Portables (b)	2,839	2,550	2,016
Total Macintosh net sales	6,275	4,923	4,491
iPod	4,540	1,306	345
Other music related products and services (c)	899	278	36
Peripherals and other hardware (d)	1,126	951	691
Software, service, and other net sales (e)	1,091	821	644
Total Net Sales	$13,931	$8,279	$6,207

Notes:
(a) Includes iMac, eMac, Mac mini, Power Mac and Xserve product lines.
(b) Includes iBook and PowerBook product lines.
(c) Consists of iTunes Music Store sales and iPod services, and Apple-branded and third-party iPod accessories.
(d) Includes sales of Apple-branded and third-party displays, wireless connectivity and networking solutions, and other hardware accessories.
(e) Includes sales of Apple-branded operating system, application software, third-party software, AppleCare, and Internet services.

Source: Apple Computer, SEC 10-K Report (December 1, 2005), p. 96.

had experienced strong growth in sales of iPod services and accessories consistent with the increase in overall iPod unit sales for 2005. The increases sales from the iTune Music Store was primarily due to the substantial growth of net sales in the U.S. and expansion in Europe, Canada, and Japan.

Total Macintosh net sales increased $1.4 billion or 27 percent during 2005 compared to 2004. Unit sales of Macintosh systems increased 1.2 million units or 38 percent during 2005 compared to 2004. The increase in Macintosh net sales and unit sales related primarily to strong demand for the company's desktop products, which was experienced in all of the company's operating segments. The company believed that the success of the iPod was having a positive impact on Macintosh net sales by introducing new customers to the company's other products. Desktop demand was stimulated in 2005 due to the new iMac G5 and the introduction of the Mac Mini in January 2005. Net sales and unit sales of desktop products increased 45 percent and 55 percent, respectively, during 2005 compared to 2004. Macintosh net sales and unit sales also included sales of the company's portable products, which increased 11 percent and 21 percent, respectively, compared to 2004.

Future Possibility

On December 11, 2006, a *Fortune* article, "Happiness Is a Warm iPod," discussed the possibility that the Beatles may give Apple Computer's iTunes an exclusive to their recordings. The Beatles had refused for years to allow MP3, Microsoft's MSN, and Rhapsody to use their music.

The Beatles' music was controlled by Apple Corps. Apple Corps had been in and out of courts for more than 20 years over the exclusive use of the name—"Apple." Apple Corps had opposed the use of *Apple* in *Apple* Computer. In May 2006, a London judge ruled in favor of Apple Computer in the use of the word *Apple* in the company's name. This ruling was appealed by the Beatles, and was scheduled to be heard in February 2007. Tim Arango, author of the article, said, "Clearly, if the two Apples wind up in business together, the matter is likely to be dropped."

Britain's EMi Group served as a peacemaker between Steve Jobs and Neil Aspinall, who was the Beatles' road manager and is now serving as the guardian of the Beatles' music as the business manager for Apple Corps.

The Beatles have been very protective of the use of their music. In 1987, Nike used a Beatles song as part of a TV commercial. Nike management believed it had all the legal licenses to use the song, but Nike was sued by the Beatles. Nike got caught in the crossfire between EMi and the Apple Corps. A lawyer said, "The Beatles' position is that they don't sing jingles, or anything else." Jobs would like to be able to link Paul and/or Ringo to the iPod if the deal is finalized. An analyst said that this issue could be a deal breaker. This deal could be worth hundreds of millions of dollars.

Conclusion

Industry analysts were very impressed with Apple Computer's recent history, but were concerned about the company's future. How long would Steve Jobs continue as CEO? Can Apple be successful without Jobs' leadership? Strategically, where should Apple go from here? What does it need to do to keep its competitive advantage in iPods?

Notes

1. Ellen Lee, "Apple, Nike Hocking Runners Up to iPods," *www.SFGate.com,* May 24, 2006.
2. Andrew Ward, "Coke and Apple in iTune Move," *www.FT.com,* August 1, 2006.
3. Mary Wong, "Apple's iPod Sweetens the Ride with Top Automakers," *www.signonsandiego.com,* August 3, 2006.
4. Connie Gugielmo, "Apple Shares Rise on Record Macintosh Shipments, New iPod Sales," *www.Bloomberg.com,* October 19, 2006.
5. Arik Hesseidahl, "Apple's Big Mac," *www.business.com,* October 19, 2006, p. 1.
6. Dan Nystedt, "Apple's New iPods Priced for Profits Not Market Share," *www.playlistmag.com,* September 16, 2006, p. 1.

7. "Apple Launchers iTunes Latino," *www.biz.yahoo.com,* November 1, 2006.
8. Staci D. Kramer, "Six Airlines Integrating iPods into In-Flight Audio, Video Systems," *www.paidcontent.com,* November 14, 2006.
9. Katie Dean, "Apple's iPhone in Tune," *www.thestreet.com,* November, 2006 and "iPhone May Bolster Apple Earnings 22%," *www.macnn.com,* November 25, 2006.
10. Angele Chariton, "French Law on iPod, iTune Takes Effect," *www.biz.yahoo.com,* August 3, 2006.
11. "Apple Get Burned, Toyota Skids," finance.yahoo.com, August 25, 2006 and Philip Goliner, "UPDATE 2-Apple to Recall 1.8 million NoteBook Batteries," *www.yahoo.rueters.com,* August 24, 2006.
12. Elaine Kurtenback, "Report: iPod Supplier Told to Unionize," *www.biz.yahoo.com,* September 1 2006.
13. "Spiral Frog in Deal with EMi Music," *www.biz.yahoo.com,* September 6, 2006.
14. Associated Press, "DVD Jon Says He's Cracked Apples iTunes Copy Restrictions," October 25, 2006, p. 1 of 4.
15. "Net Information About The Jon Johnsen ("DVD JON") Case," *Electronic Fotiport Norge.*
16. "Spiral Frog in Deal with EMi Music,"
17. Duncan Martell, "Apple Probe Found Option Grant 'Irregularities,'" *www.Rueters.com,* June 29, 2006.
18. *Ibid.*
19. Mu Wong, "CEO Apologizes for Apple Stock Practices," *www.yahoo.finance.com.*
20. Arik Heseidahl, "Apple Comes Clean on Options," *www.businessweekonline.com,* October 5, 2006, p. 1.
21. "What Scandal?," *www.Forbes.com,* June 7, 2006, p. 2.
22. "Stock Options Investigation," *www.CBSS.com* (local San Francisco CBS station) October 11, 2006, p. 1.
23. "Minnesota to Expand Investigation of United Health," *www.bizjournals.com,* October 12, 2006, p. 1.
24. *Ibid.*
25. *Ibid.*
26. "This section is a combination of information from previous versions of this book, *Strategic Management and Business Policy* over the past 20 years. Wikipedia, the free encyclopedia, "History of Apple Computer," pp. 1–18.
27. "Steve Jobs," Wikipedia, the free encyclopedia, pp. 1–8.
28. *Ibid,* pp. 1–2.
29. *Ibid,* p. 2.
30. *Ibid.*
31. "History of Apple Computer," pp. 2–3.
32. Previous Apple Computer cases.
33. Pixar, "Corporate Overview," p. 1.
34. "Steve Jobs" Magic Kingdom," *Businessweek online,* p. 3.
35. *Ibid.,* pp. 1-5, and Vandana Sinna, "Disney, Pixar Give Marriage Second Chance," pp. 1–3.
36. "Steve Jobs' Magic Kingdom," p. 1.
37. *Ibid,* p. 2.
38. *Ibid.*
39. *Ibid.*
40. This section was directly quoted from *Apple Computer, Inc.,* "SEC 10-K," September 2, 2005, and (2) "SEC DEF 14A" March 13, 2006.
41. This section was directly quoted from *Apple Computer, Inc.,* "SEC 10-K," September 24, 2005, pp. 27–28.
42. This section was directly quoted from Apple computer, Inc., "SEC 10-K," September 24, 2005, pp. 2–3.
43. *Ibid.,* p. 3.
44. The above 4 paragraphs are directly quoted from "Apple Computer Inc." "SEC 10-K," p. 13.
45. Nick Wingfield and Robert A. Gith, "Microsoft Confirms Plan for Music Video Player," The Wall Street Journal, July 22, 2006, p. A3.
46. Apple Insider, "Apple's Share of U.S. PC Market jumps to 6.1 percent," October 18, 2006, p. 1.
47. The 3 paragraphs directly quoted from *Apple Computer, Inc.,* "SEC 10-K," p. 22.
48. *Ibid.,* p. 5.
49. *Ibid.,* p. 14
50. *Ibid.*
51. *Ibid.,* p. 16
52. *Ibid.,* p. 15
53. *Ibid.*
54. *Ibid.*
55. *Ibid.,* p. 16
56. *Ibid.*
57. *Ibid.*
58. *Ibid.,* p. 32

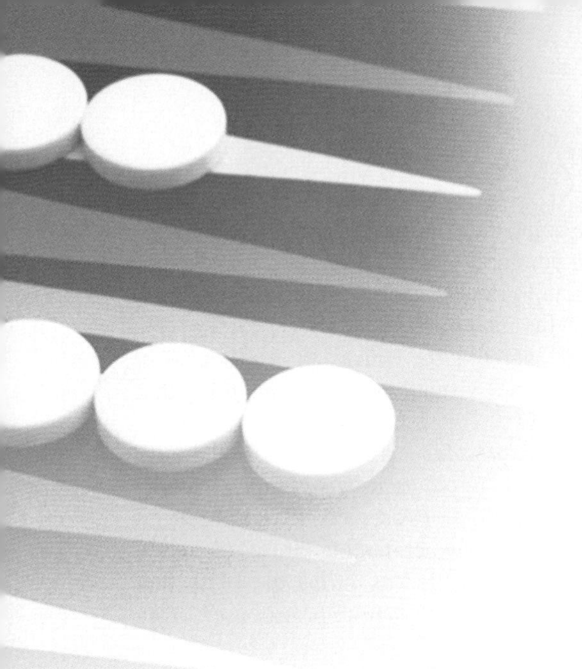

CASE 11

McAfee 2005: Antivirus and Antispyware

Bethany Sweesy and Alan N. Hoffman

McAfee, Inc. proactively secures systems and networks from known and unknown threats, worldwide. Home users, businesses, service providers, the public sector, and our partners all trust McAfee's unmatched security expertise, and have confidence in our comprehensive and proven solutions to block attacks and prevent disruptions.[1]

CEO GEORGE SAMENUK STARED OUT HIS OFFICE WINDOW AND CONSIDERED THE COMPANY'S financial results from 2004. Headquartered in Santa Clara, California, McAfee, as of January 20, 2005, is the "largest dedicated security software company in the industry."[2] In the past year, McAfee had conducted several strategic transactions including the divestiture of two slow-growing product lines and investment in the high-growth security sector, in order to streamline its focus. The strategy appeared to be paying off and McAfee's product portfolio was the strongest ever in the history of the company. Furthermore, having paid down $347 million in debt, McAfee was set to enter 2005 debt-free.

Samenuk knew, however, that in the highly competitive and rapidly changing industry McAfee's success in 2004 would not be sufficient to carry the company through another year. In order to achieve the organization's goal of becoming a "worldwide leader in intrusion prevention and risk management solutions and services,"[3] McAfee must continue to offer customers innovative, quality solutions. With a corporate mission to secure "consumers and businesses from the desktop to the core of the network by delivering best-of-breed products and services that protect . . . global customer's information technology systems and infrastructure"[4] Samenuk knew his work was cut out for him.

 The authors would like to thank Lauren Cotes, David Folding, Mike Howard, Brian Lemberger, Steve Wojtkielo, and Ann Hoffman for their research and contributions to this case.

Industry

The 1960s and 1970s was the era of the mainframe computer. During this period, "rabbits"—programs that cloned themselves—were the most common security threat. Rabbits were a local phenomenon and did not replicate from system to system and were likely to be "mistakes or pranks by system programmers servicing" the mainframes.[5] However, the first epidemic of a computer virus occurred during this time infecting the Univax 1108 system. The virus "merged itself to the end of executable files—[and] virtually did the same thing that modern viruses do."[6]

During the 1980s computers became more and more prevalent, as did viruses. In the early part of the decade, Trojan horses were especially common, as programs were frequently written by private individuals and freely distributed over general access servers. (See **Exhibit 1.**) In the latter half of the decade, several notorious and extremely debilitating viruses including *VirDem*, *Vienna*, and *Jerusalem* affected computers globally.[7] It was during the 1980s that many of the anti-virus software companies began developing software to protect users from the hazards of viruses.

In the 1990s intrusion software became more complex, forcing anti-virus software to follow suit. Additionally, with the approach of 2000 (Y2K), businesses across the globe began dumping enormous amounts of cash in technology. The anti-virus industry felt the effects of this spending and an already competitive industry became even more cutthroat. Companies began underhandedly vying for customers, causing 1997 to be littered with litigation and SEC investigations. McAfee attacked Dr. Solomon for a particular feature in the software; Dr. Solomon counterattacked McAfee for false advertising. Symantec and McAfee also had a bout in court concerning copyright infringement.[8]

Industry shakeout occurred in the early part of the 21st century with the decrease in IT spending and an overall economic slowdown. However, by 2003 conditions had improved and IDC predicted that the security software market would "grow 16.9% annually between 2003 and 2008."[9]

Exhibit 1
Definitions

What is a Virus?
A virus is a manmade program or piece of code that causes an unexpected, usually negative, event. Viruses are often disguised games or images with clever marketing titles such as "Me, nude."

What is a Worm?
Computer Worms are viruses that reside in the active memory of a computer and duplicate themselves. They may send copies of themselves to other computers, such as through email or Internet Relay Chat (IRC).

What is a Trojan Horse?
A Trojan horse program is a malicious program that pretends to be a benign application; a Trojan horse program purposefully does something the user does not expect. Trojans are not viruses since they do not replicate, but Trojan horse programs can be just as destructive. Many people use the term to refer only to non-replicating malicious programs, thus making a distinction between Trojans and viruses.

Source: http://us.mcafee.com/virusInfo/default.asp?cid=10371

History

In 1989, John McAfee formed McAfee Associates to market his anti-virus software. He advertised the company's products on computer bulletin boards, requiring users to pay for the products only if they found them useful. Individuals were so satisfied with the anti-virus software that they recommended it to their companies. Only three years after its humble beginnings, McAfee Associates was so successful that the company decided to go public.[10]

In conjunction with the decision to incorporate, McAfee Associates also "began to diversify and market other types of software compatible with the electronic channel."[11] McAfee Associates expanded product offerings primarily through acquisitions and achieved higher sales through a product bundling strategy. The growth and sales strategies proved profitable and by 1997 annual sales topped $600 million. Also in 1997, McAfee Associates merged with Network General Corporation to form Network Associates. In an effort to achieve the company's vision to become a leading network security and desktop management specialist, Network Associates continued to pursue an acquisition growth strategy acquiring companies such as Trusted Information Systems, Secure Networks, and CyberMedia.

Network Associates' fast track to success came to a sudden halt when in 1999 the company was forced to restate financial results from the previous year. Shareholder lawsuits ensued and the company suffered a loss. The following year several top executives including CEO William Larson resigned after "a surprise earnings warning."[12] This was not the end of the bad news for Network Associates as the company continued to experience repercussions from its aggressive acquisition strategy. In 2003 the company was forced to restate financial results for FYs 1998–2000 after a second SEC investigation revealed improper accounting related to the acquisitions. Despite the setbacks, Network Associates continued to pursue an acquisition growth strategy. This time, however, acquisitions and divestitures streamlined the "business to focus exclusively on security."[13] In late 2004, Network Associates changed its name to McAfee in an effort to reflect the decision to concentrate solely on security products.[14]

Corporate Governance

Exhibit 2A lists the seven members of the board of directors as of January 2005. Only George Samenuk, Chairman and CEO, was an internal member. Board members were elected to staggered three-year terms. The three board committees were audit, compensation, and governance and nominations. All directors except Mr. Semenuk were considered "independent." Mr. Dutkowsky served as lead director. Directors received an annual retainer of $40,000 plus $1,500 for each meeting attended (including committee meetings). The lead director and committee chairs received an additional $10,000 per year.

Exhibit 2B shows the key executives and their salaries. Eric Brown replaced Stephen Richards as Chief Financial Officer in January 2005 when Richards left the company. Raymond Smets, former President of Sniffer Technologies, served as a member of McAfee's top management group from October 2002 when McAfee acquired the company until July 2004 when Sniffer Technology was sold to Network General Division. In addition to salaries and bonuses, the top executives were granted a total of 775,000 shares worth of stock options in 2004.

The executive officers and directors as a group owned 209,847 shares (1.8% of outstanding shares). The financial firms of T. Rowe Price and Lord, Abbett & Company each owned 6% of the outstanding stock.

Exhibit 2
Board of Directors and Key Executives: McAfee, Inc.

A. Board of Directors

George Samenuk, 49
Chief Executive Officer, McAfee, Inc. Chairman of the Board since April, 2001. Previously, he served as President and CEO of TradeOut, Inc., a private online exchange company. He had also served in various senior management positions with IBM. Board member since 2001. Term expires 2006. Owned 175,000 McAfee shares of stock.

Leslie G. Denend, 64
President of McAfee, Inc. 1997–1998. Previously, he served as CEO and President of Network General Corp. prior to its being merged into McAfee, Inc. Board member since 1995. Term expires 2006. Owned 6,297 McAfee shares of stock.

Robert Pangia, 52
General Partner and Managing Member of Ivy Capital Partners. He previously held a number of senior management positions with Paine Webber Inc. Board member since 2001. Term expires 2007. Designated "financial expert" on audit committee. Also member of compensation committee.

Robert B. Bucknam, 54
Sr. Vice President of Cross Match Technologies, Inc., a fingerprint identification provider. He previously served as Chief of Staff, Federal Bureau of Investigation and Deputy Attorney General with the U.S. Dept. of Justice. Board member since 2003. Term expires 2005. Member of governance and nominations committee.

Liane Wilson, 62
Consultant. She previously served as Vice Chairman of Washington Mutual, Inc. Board member since 2002. Term expires 2005. Member of audit and governance and nominations committees.

Robert Dutkowsky, 50
Chairman of the Board, CEO, and President of Engenera, Inc. Previously, he served as President and CEO of J. D. Edwards & Company. He also held executive positions with Teradyne, EMC Corporation, and IBM. Board member since 2001. Term expires 2007. Member of audit and compensations committees. Owned 50 McAfee shares of stock.

Denis J. O'Leary, 48
Private investor. Previously, he was Executive Vice President of J.P. Morgan Chase bank. Board member since 2003. Term expires 2007. Member of compensation and governance and nominations committees.

B. Key Executives

	Salary	Bonus
George Samenuk, 49 Chairman and Chief Executive Officer since January, 2001 when joined firm Previously President & CEO of TradeOut, Inc.	$773,333	$1,075,000
Gene Hodges, 53 President since October, 2001 Held various executive positions since joined firm in 1995	445,833	451,250
Kent H. Roberts, 48 Executive Vice President, Secretary and General Counsel Since January, 2001 Held various legal positions since joined firm in May, 1998	333,333	170,938

Exhibit 2 (*continued*)

Kevin Weiss, 48 Executive Vice President of Worldwide Sales since joined firm in October, 2002 Previously Senior VP of Ariba, Inc.	441,667	463,750
Eric F. Brown, 39 Chief Financial Officer and Executive Vice President since January 2005 when joined firm Previously CFO of MicroStrategy, Inc.	998,000	

Source: 2004 McAfee 10-K Form.

Current Situation

McAfee has unleashed several initiatives to improve financial statement performance. In 2004, the company paid down $347 million in convertible debt and repurchased $220 million in common stock. In addition to altering its capitalization strategy, McAfee also implemented several cost-cutting initiatives. Revenues had declined over the past two years, while net income had increased. (See **Exhibits 3 and 4**.) The initiatives are aimed at achieving a 25% operating margin. Ongoing operations generated over $350 million in cash, ending the fiscal year with nearly $1 billion in cash, cash equivalents, and investments. Deferred revenue for the period increased by $200 million.[15]

McAfee partners with service providers (MSPs, ASPs, Telcos and outsourcing service providers) to sell products.[16] Companies will often opt to outsource the network to a third-party provider for economic reasons. As part of the provider's responsibility it must safeguard the client's network and assets. Rather than develop its own security software, the provider relies on a company such as McAfee to provide the necessary security tools. The partnership enables McAfee to sell multiple products to multiple companies through the convenience of a single provider.

Products

The company provides two categories of products, the McAfee System Protection Solution for desktops and servers and the McAfee Network Protection Solutions for corporate networks. (See **Exhibit 5**.) Customers of both product categories include businesses, governments, and consumers. McAfee distributes products to five main geographic locations including North America, Europe, the Middle East, Africa, Japan, and Latin America.[17]

Desktop and server solutions include anti-virus, anti-hacker and anti-spyware, antispam and anti-abuse, mobile and wireless, and bundled products. Consumers purchase a license for these products and must periodically update the software to keep it current.

- **Anti-Virus**—"McAfee VirusScan detects, blocks, and removes viruses and spyware" that can damage important documents or slow PC processing.[18]
- **Anti-Hacker & Anti-Spyware**—Two products provide hacker and spyware protection. The first is "McAfee Personal Firewall Plus" which "safeguards . . . documents . . . by preventing unwanted Internet connections to or from your PC."[19] "McAfee AntiSpyware detects potentially unwanted programs (PUPs), such as spyware, adware, dialers, tracking cookies, and other unwelcome marketing programs before they compromise . . . information, invade your privacy, or slow the performance of your PC."[20]

Exhibit 3
Income Statement: McAfee, Inc. (Dollar amounts in thousands)

Year ending December 31	2004	2003	2002
Net revenue:			
Product	$ 294,163	$ 513,610	$ 631,550
Services and support	616,379	422,726	411,494
Total net revenue	910,542	936,336	1,043,044
Cost of net revenue:			
Product	73,058	80,895	101,019
Services and support	62,520	57,362	60,539
Amortization of purchased technology	13,331	11,369	3,153
Total cost of net revenue	148,909	149,626	164,711
Operating costs:			
Research and development	172,717	184,606	148,801
Marketing and sales	354,380	363,306	397,747
General and administrative	139,845	129,920	119,393
(Gain) loss on sale of assets and technology	(240,336)	788	(9,301)
Litigation (reimbursement) settlement	(24,991)	—	70,000
Restructuring charges	17,493	22,667	1,116
Amortization of intangibles	14,065	15,637	10,742
Severance/bonus costs related to disposition	10,070	—	—
Reimbursement from transition services agreement	(5,997)	—	—
Provision for (recovery of) doubtful accounts, net	1,716	(1,216)	(219)
Acquisition related costs not subject to capitalization	—	—	16,026
In-process research and development	—	6,600	—
Total operating costs	438,962	722,308	754,305
Income from operations	322,671	64,402	124,028
Interest and other income	15,889	15,917	27,324
Interest and other expenses	(5,315)	(7,543)	(25,085)
(Loss) gain on repurchase of convertible debt	(15,070)	(2,727)	26
(Loss) gain on investments, net	(1,704)	3,076	3,838
Impairment of strategic and other investments	—	—	(198)
Income before provision for (benefit from) income taxes, minority interest and cumulative effect of change in accounting principle	316,471	73,125	129,933
Provision for (benefit from) income taxes	91,406	13,220	(274)
Income before minority interest and cumulative effect of change in accounting principle	225,065	59,905	130,207
Minority interest in income of consolidated subsidiaries	—	—	(1,895)
Income before cumulative effect of change in accounting principle	225,065	59,905	128,312
Cumulative effect of change in accounting principle, net of taxes of $3,590	—	10,337	—
Net income	$ 225,065	$ 70,242	$ 128,312
Other comprehensive income:			
Unrealized losses on marketable securities, net of reclassification adjustment for losses recognized on marketable securities during the period and income tax	$ (2,129)	$ (709)	$ (2,667)
Foreign currency translation (loss) gain	(4,537)	10,578	10,744
Comprehensive income	$ 218,399	$ 80,111	$ 136,389

Note: All notes were deleted

Source: 2004 McAfee 10-K Form, p. 35.

Exhibit 4
Balance Sheet: McAfee, Inc. (Dollar amounts in thousands)

Year ending December 31	2004	2003
ASSETS		
Current assets:		
Cash and cash equivalents	$ 291,155	$ 333,651
Short-term marketable securities	232,929	174,499
Accounts receivable, net of allowance for doubtful accounts of $2,536 and $2,863, respectively	137,520	170,218
Prepaid expenses, income taxes and other current assets	103,687	97,616
Deferred income taxes	200,459	160,550
Assets held for sale	—	24,719
Total current assets	965,750	961,253
Long-term marketable securities	400,597	258,107
Restricted cash	617	20,547
Property and equipment, net	91,715	111,672
Deferred income taxes	220,604	199,196
Intangible assets, net	107,133	105,952
Goodwill	439,180	443,593
Other assets	12,080	20,178
Total assets	$ 2,237,676	$ 2,120,498
LIABILITIES AND STOCKHOLDERS' EQUITY		
Current liabilities:		
Accounts payable	$ 32,891	$ 32,099
Accrued liabilities	197,368	147,281
Deferred revenue	475,621	342,795
Liabilities related to assets held for sale	—	23,310
Total current liabilities	705,880	545,485
Deferred revenue, less current portion	125,752	116,762
Convertible debt	—	347,397
Accrued taxes and other long term liabilities	204,796	222,765
Total liabilities	1,036,428	1,232,409
STOCKHOLDERS' EQUITY		
Preferred stock, $0.01 par value:		
Authorized: 5,000,000 shares; Issued and outstanding: none in 2004 and 2003	—	—
common stock, $0.01 par value: authorized: 300,000,000 shares; Issued:162,266,174 shares and 162,071,798 shares for 2004 and 2003, respectively; outstanding: 162,266,174 shares and 161,721,798 for 2004 and 2003, respectively	1,623	1,621
Treasury stock, at cost: no shares in 2004 and 350,000 shares in 2003	—	(4,707)
Additional paid-in capital	1,178,855	1,087,625
Deferred stock-based compensation	(1,777)	(598)
Accumulated other comprehensive income	27,361	34,027
Accumulated deficit	(4,814)	(229,879)
Total stockholders' equity	1,201,248	888,089
Total liabilities and stockholders' equity	$ 2,237,676	$ 2,120,498

Source: 2004 McAfee 10-K Form, p. 34.

Exhibit 5
McAffee Solution Focus: McAfee, Inc.

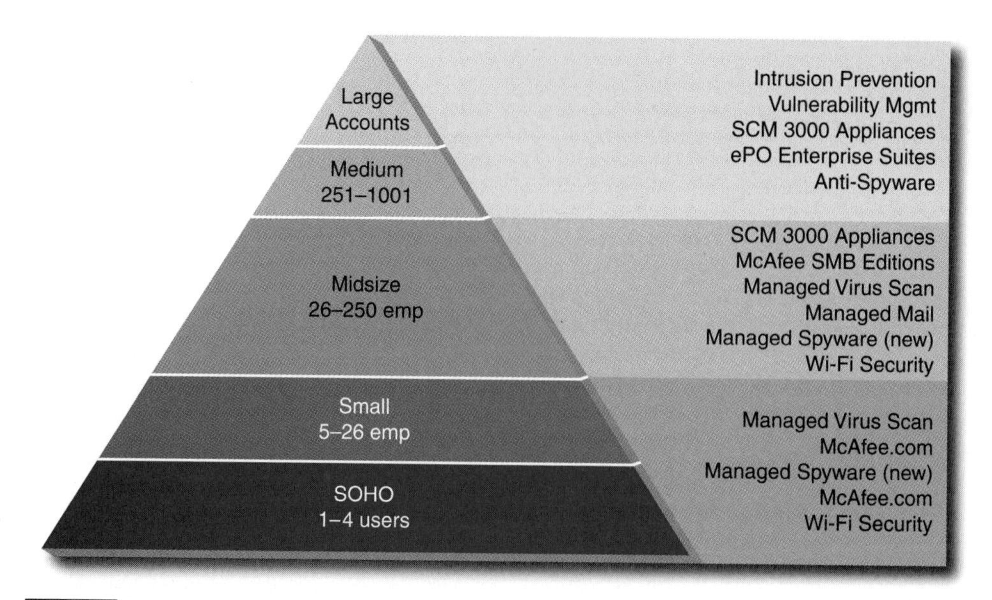

Source: McAfee, Inc.

- **Anti-Spam & Anti-Abuse**—"McAfee SpamKiller" is designed to protect "personal and financial information against known 'phishing' scams by blocking access to known and potentially fraudulent identity theft websites."[21] While "McAfee Privacy Service helps prevent personal information . . . from being transmitted over the Internet." It also allows parents to set controls for the children's Internet activities. "In addition, McAfee Privacy Service helps block online advertisements and filter inappropriate Website, e-mail, and IM content."[22]
- **Wireless & Mobile**—McAfee Virus Scan Mobile protects mobile phones from virus, worms, and Trojan horses that may be transmitted by accessing email, instant messaging or downloads on a wireless phone.[23] The "Wireless Home Network Security encrypts . . . data as it is sent over Wi-Fi and blocks hackers from accessing your wireless network,"[24] protecting personal wireless technologies.

Products are sold on a subscription basis. A single-user, one year license for the home computer Internet security suite is sold for $69.99 before a mail-in rebate of $20. A three-user, one year license is available for $129.99. Products for small businesses are priced depending on the size of the organization and the length of the license.

Network Protection Solutions for corporate networks incorporates two core technologies—IntruShield and Foundstone. McAfee acquired Foundstone Inc. in 2004 and immediately integrated its technology into McAfee's product offerings. Foundstone is a priority-based technology designed to identify the most important assets of the enterprise and assess their vulnerabilities. The system then responds to attacks on the network to remediate the situation. Within the Foundstone technologies, there are five protection solutions:[25]

- **Foundstone Enterprise**—is an "appliance-based solution" that "offers network infrastructure protection to ensure business continuity through asset discovery, inventory, and prioritization; threat intelligence and correlation; and enhanced remediation tracking and reporting."
- **Foundstone FS1000 Appliance**—"is a complete . . . solution that powers Foundstone Enterprise." It "is engineered to manage and mitigate the business risks associated with digital vulnerabilities."

- **Foundstone On-Demand Service**—"performs client vulnerability assessments from the Foundstone Operations Center." It is a "subscription-based, zero deployment solution for effectively assessing vulnerabilities for Internet facing network resources."
- **Foundstone Threat Correction Module**—an add-on module to Foundstone Enterprise that "delivers up-to-the-minute Threat Intelligence Alerts from Foundstone Labs so you can respond immediately to breaking events such as worms and wide-scale attacks."
- **Foundstone Remediation Module**—"is a fully automated and tightly integrated [add-on] module that auto-assigns tickets based on discovered vulnerabilities and auto-closes them once the vulnerabilities have been fixed."

IntruShield is an intrusion prevention system (IPS) combining hardware and software technology that "delivers comprehensive and proactive intrusion prevention to protect business availability and critical network infrastructure by detecting and blocking attacks before they inflict damage."[26] "The . . . architecture integrates patented signature, anomaly, and Denial of Service (DoS) analysis techniques, enabling highly accurate and intelligent attack detection and prevention up to multi-gigabit speeds."

IntruShield has received several awards for technology leadership and was recently recognized as a worldwide market share leader for network based intrusion software by Infonetics Research.[27]

In the future, McAfee hopes to expand its mobile and wireless solutions. McAfee and VeriFone Holdings, Inc., collaborated to be first to market with a virus protection solution for point of sale terminals in the United States. As the trend in merchandising evolves to utilizing Internet Protocol for payment processing, VeriFone and McAfee are seizing the opportunity to provide real-time monitoring and protection for this venue. In the future the companies foresee the virus protection solution being offered on all IP-enabled systems, though for now it is only available on the Omni 3750 Ethernet-enabled payment solution.[28]

Competitors

McAfee competes against companies such as Symantec, Computer Associates, Trend Micro, Sophos, Fescure, Panda and Dr. Ahn's in the security software market (see **Exhibit 6**). The industry is highly competitive, and Symantec is McAfee's most intimidating competitor. **Exhibit 7** shows the rapid growth predicted for security software.

Exhibit 6
McAfee's Competitors

Network Fault Identification and Application Performance Management	Anti-virus Software	Intrusion Detection and Protection Products
Netscout	Symantec	Symantec
WildPackets	Microsoft	Computer Associates
Agilent	Computer Associates	Cisco Systems
Cisco Systems	Trend Micro	Enterasys Security Systems
Compuware Corporation	Sophos	Netscreen
Concord Communications	Fescure	Sourcefire
Finisar	Panda	TippingPont Technologies
Fluke Networks	Dr. Ahn's	
Network Instruments		
Niksun		

Source: McAfee, Inc.

Exhibit 7
Predicted Total Available Market for Security Software

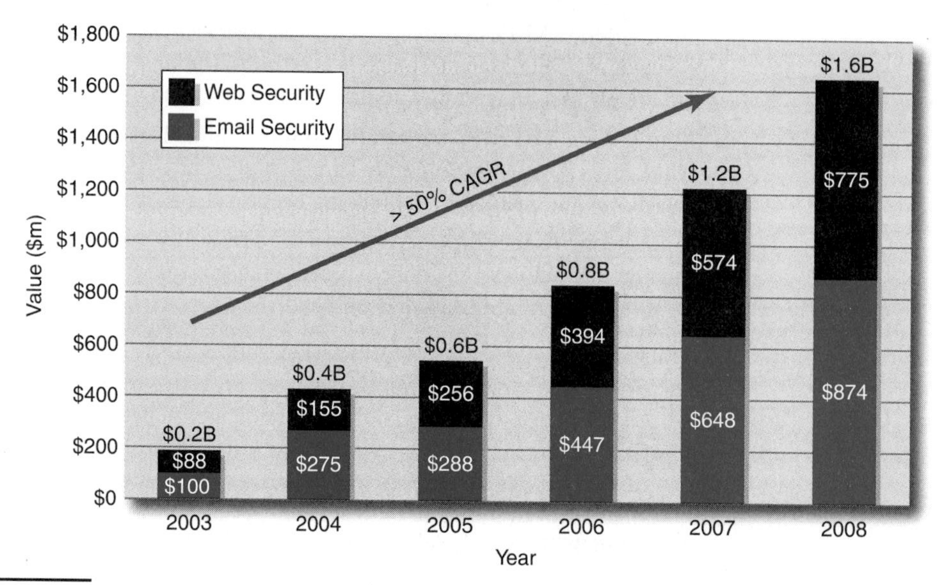

Source: IDC (August 2004). PM and Raymond James Reporting.

Symantec Corporation

Symantec is the industry leader in security solution software and McAfee's strongest competitor. Symantec "provides a variety of content and network security software for both consumers and businesses."[29] The company's product lines include client, gateway, and server security solutions for virus protection; firewalls and VPN networks; vulnerability management; intrusion detection; and security services.

Symantec is most noted for the Norton series of personal computer security solutions. In fact, by capitalizing on the popularity of Norton, Symantec was able to expand into the corporate security market.[30] The company also provides consulting services.

Symantec's premier products include Intruder Alert, NetRecon, Norton AntiVirus, Norton SystemWords, Norton Utilities, pcANYWHERE, Symantec AntiVirus, and Symantec Ghost. These products provide everything from intrusion detection to network vulnerability management, and data transfer from remote PCs to the host. Thus Symantec is able to provide a solution to protect an entire enterprise network from the threat of viruses, worms, and Trojan horses.

Like McAfee, Symantec has also chosen an acquisition growth strategy. The company has a long history of M&A activity, but most notable was the proposed merger with VERITAS. VERITAS was an industry leader in information storage, so a merger with Symantec would enable the corporation to deliver products that incorporated both data storage and protection. Symantec's vision for the future was to enable customers to "bounce back from disruptions" and continue efficient operations.[33]

Symantec has successfully bounced back from its own business disruptions. In 1997, Symantec "filed copyright-infringement charges against Network Associates." The following year anti-virus product users filed a lawsuit against Symantec "alleging that it ignored its warranty by charging to fix a year 2000 software glitch."[34]

Despite the alleged copyright infringement and shareholder lawsuit, Symantec has had strong financial performance. Net profit margin has increased for the past three years; earnings per share has also increased over this time period. Symantec had annual sales of $1.87 billion in FY 2004 and net income of $371 million. The company's stock priced topped out at $48.09 in 2004, $13 per share more than the 2003 high.[36]

Computer Associates

Computer Associates is "one of the world's largest software" providers. Founded in 1976, the company is headquartered in Islandia, NY.[37] CA's product line is extensive and includes solutions for "business intelligence, storage, security, and network management applications."[38] With revenue of $3.5 billion in 2004, the company primarily services *Fortune* 500, Global 1000, and government organizations.[39]

Over the past 10 years the company has made significant investments in systems management and security; currently this segment of the company is greatly expanding.[40] With product offerings that support personal computers, small businesses, and large enterprises and have the ability to be customized by industry, CA delivers security solutions to diverse market segments.[41]

*e*Trust Security Management solution is designed to protect critical information in large enterprises. The software enables the company to enforce privacy policies and comply with regulations while protecting assets from viruses and worms.[42] Similarly, CA offers an *e*Trust product line designed to protect small to medium-sized businesses. Security solutions in the product line include anti-virus, anti-spyware, intrusion detection, content management, and vulnerability management.[43] CA also provides small-business security solutions bundled with their other products. For example, a small business can purchase software that includes security solutions along with backup storage solutions for quick and easy recovery of data.[44] Home and home office security solutions include *e*Trust spyware, virus, and spam protection. A bundled security solution is also available for this market segment.

The company has faced multiple setbacks over the past few years. In 2004, Computer Associates was forced to restate financial results for 2000 and 2001. The investigations began shortly after the dot-com crash in 2001. In 2003 and 2004 several executives were removed from the company. CA signed a Deferred Prosecution Agreement with the Department of Justice in September 2004 accepting full responsibility for previous activities and agreeing to pay restitution to shareholders. However, with a new CEO in place the company was making strides forward.

Panda Software

In 1990, Panda Software was established in Bilbao, Spain. By 1995, Panda had achieved a market leadership position and began international expansion. In 2005, the company employed more than 500 individuals at its headquarters in Spain, and an almost equal number of individuals are employed in subsidiaries and franchises. Products are sold in more than 200 countries around the world. Panda has enjoyed unprecedented growth as a privately owned company, achieving a revenue increase of 55% from 2003 to 2004; this is three times the industry average.[45]

Like the other antivirus vendors, Panda provides solutions for personal computers, small to medium-sized businesses and large enterprises. The company strives to achieve rapid release of updates to customers as well as excellent customer service. One example of the company's focus on customer service is a 24-hour, 7 day a week technical center, available in every country where Panda products are sold.[46]

The software utilizes a signature-based technology to identify known threats and prevent them from damaging assets. "Unlike other companies in the industry, all of Panda Software's products include the same signature-based detection engine, and as a result they all have the same capacity to detect and eliminate threats."[47]

TruPrevent is a patented technology designed to prevent unidentified viruses from infecting the computer or system. Currently, it takes antivirus companies approximately 72 hours to update against a new threat. TruPrevent protects assets during that 72-hour window from discovery of a virus or other intrusion device and the release of an update to uniquely identify and eliminate it.[48]

In addition to its focus on quality products and excellent customer service, the company also implements several socially responsible programs. Specifically, the initiatives focus "on the protection of children, the cooperation in the fight against AIDS and other epidemics, the protection of the environment, etc." Panda also invests in improving local communities in which the company operates.[49]

Trend Micro

Trend Micro Incorporated was founded in 1988 by Steve Chang. The company is headquartered in Tokyo, Japan, and maintains 25 corporate offices throughout the world. Trend Micro has a reputation for innovation with its outbreak solution software. "Trend Micro focuses on . . . providing customers with a comprehensive approach to managing the outbreak lifecycle and the impact of network worms and virus threats to productivity and information."[50]

The company is highly focused and significantly smaller than competitors such as McAfee, Symantec, and Computer Associates. FY 2004 revenues were $587.4 million USD (62.5 billion yen at an exchange rate of JPY105.63/USD). Trend Micro experienced 29% growth in revenue between FY03 and FY04. Earnings during that time period increased by an astounding 71%, causing stockholder equity to increase by 46.5%.[51]

Although Trend Micro does not have the breadth of product offerings of McAfee, Symantec, and Computer Associates, it does have product-line depth. Security solutions include virus protection for enterprises and home users, outbreak life-cycle management, layered network virus protection, email and groupware protection, server gateway and domain protection, file storage and mobile security.[52]

Sophos

Sophos is headquartered in Abingdon, UK, and provides products to more than 150 countries. The company's products are highly scalable and can be used in small businesses, global enterprises, or anything in between. Over the past year and a half, Sophos has focused on consolidating its product portfolio, adding anti-spam and email policy enforcement protection. The company is no longer singularly identified as an anti-virus company but rather as an entire protection solution. Notably, Sophos is recognized for its gateway and endpoint solutions.[53]

Products are designed to protect networks against virus, spam, spyware, and policy abuse. The enterprise solution is a multi-tier, cross-platform application that monitors, updates, and reports threats.[54] Small-business solutions are designed for companies with small IT budgets and less experienced IT professionals. Products are engineered for simplicity and usability. Sophos' Small Business Suite "provides anti-virus and anti-spam protection for desktops, file servers, and email servers" in a single package.[55]

Sophos also provides industry-specific solutions for educational institutions and the government. Security solutions for the education industry are developed to function on multiple platforms while remaining within a specified price point.[56] Government solutions integrate strict security policies and are also designed to function on multi-platforms.[57]

Sophos, a privately held company, has experienced substantial financial success, growing at twice the market rate in FY2004. The British company has plans to increase its workforce by 13% in the coming year to parallel financial growth.

Microsoft: A New Entrant

In an internally generated document in 2004, Microsoft stated that spyware had become a serious problem for PC users and "customers have made it clear that they want Microsoft to deliver effective solutions to protect against the threat."[59] Microsoft developed a twofold plan to assist consumers in the battle against spyware. On December 16, 2004, Microsoft acquired GIANT Company Software, Inc., an anti-spyware leader. Subsequent to the acquisition Microsoft developed a beta version of anti-spyware software that was distributed free to anyone who would like to download the program. Additionally, Microsoft has made Microsoft Windows Malicious Spyware Removal Tool available in monthly updates to assist in ridding PCs of viruses and worms.[60]

Microsoft's entry into the anti-virus, anti-spyware industry poses a serious threat for existing competitors. With nearly $4.9 billion in cash and cash equivalents as of June 30, 2005,[61] the sheer size and purchasing power of Microsoft could potentially eliminate companies such as McAfee.

Looking to the Future

The anti-virus industry is highly competitive with large, all-encompassing solution providers as well as smaller niche players that cater to specific market segments. Overseas competitors also pose a serious threat to McAfee's business. CEO George Samenuk wondered how McAfee could leverage its strengths to compete in the coming months and years. What competitive advantages does McAfee's software have that customers are willing to pay for despite the availability of free anti-spyware software from Microsoft? What strategy should McAfee pursue to remain a market leader in the anti-virus industry? With rapidly changing market conditions and the threat of Microsoft, Samenuk knew the next 12 months would be critical to the survival and success of McAfee.

Notes

1. *http://phx.corporate-ir.net/phoenix.zhtml?c=104920&p=irol-IRHome.* October 26, 2005.
2. Dear shareholders.
3. Dear shareholders.
4. Company's mission statement.
5. *http://www.virus-scan-software.com/virus-scan-help/answers/the-history-of-computer-viruses.shtml.* November 17, 2005.
6. *http://www.virus-scan-software.com/virus-scan-help/answers/the-history-of-computer-viruses.shtml.* November 17, 2005.
7. *http://www.virus-scan-software.com/virus-scan-help/answers/the-history-of-computer-viruses.shtml.* November 17, 2005.
8. *http://www.virus-scan-software.com/virus-scan-help/answers/the-history-of-computer-viruses.shtml.* November 17, 2005.
9. *http://www.sophos.com/pressoffice/news/articles/2005/02/pr_uk_20050207marketgrowth.html.* November 16, 2005.
10. Hoovers Inc., Austin, TX 2005.
11. *http://phx.corporate-ir.net/phoenix.zhtml?c=104920&p=irol-History.*
12. Hoovers Inc., Austin, TX 2005.
13. *http://phx.corporate-ir.net/phoenix.zhtml?c=104920&p=irol-History.*
14. Hoovers Inc., Austin, TX 2005.
15. *http://library.corporate-ir.net/library/10/104/104920/items/155360/AR_042205.pdf.* November 18, 2005. page 2.
16. *http://www.mcafee.com/us/about/partners/msp/default.asp.* November 18, 2005.
17. *http://www.mcafee.com/us/about/home.htm.* October 21, 2005.
18. *http://us.mcafee.com/root/package.asp?pkgid=100&cid=16259.* November 1, 2005.
19. *http://us.mcafee.com/root/package.asp?pkgid=103&cid=16260.* November 1, 2005.
20. *http://us.mcafee.com/root/package.asp?pkgid=206&cid=16261.* November 1, 2005.
21. *http://us.mcafee.com/root/package.asp?pkgid=156.* November 1, 2005.
22. *http://us.mcafee.com/root/package.asp?pkgid=104&cid=16262.* November 1, 2005.
23. *http://us.mcafee.com/root/landingpages/afflandpage.asp?lpname=vs_mobile.* November 1, 2005.
24. *http://us.mcafee.com/root/package.asp?pkgid=250.* November 1, 2005.
25. *http://www.foundstone.com/index.hetm?subnav=products/navigation.htm&subcontent=/products/product overview.htm.*
26. *http://www.mcafee.com/us/local_content/datasheets/ds_instrushieldsecuirtymanagement.pdf*
27. *http://www.monitortoday.com/index.php?page=~~newsitems_9143*
28. *http://global.factiva.com/en/eSrch/ss_hl.asp.* November 1, 2005.
29. Hoover's Inc. Bloomberg, L.P. October 21, 2005.

30. Hoover's Inc. Bloomberg, L.P. October 21, 2005.
31. *http://library.corporate-ir.net/library/89/894/89422/items/163589/Final_Symantec_2005_10Kwrap.pdf.* November 9, 2005.
32. Hoover's Inc. Bloomberg, L.P. October 21, 2005. page 6.
33. *http://library.corporate-ir.net/library/89/894/89422/items/163589/Final_Symantec_2005_10Kwrap.pdf.* November 9, 2005. page 8. Symantec Corp. 2004 Annual Report.
34. Hoover's, Inc. Bloomberg, L.P. October 21, 2005.
35. *http://library.corporate-ir.net/library/89/894/89422/items/163589/Final_Symantec_2005_10Kwrap.pdf.* November 9, 2005. Symantec Corp. 2004 Annual Report.
36. Hoover's Inc. Bloomberg, L.P. October 21, 2005. page 3.
37. *http://www.ca.com/invest/reports/corpprofile/.* November 15, 2005.
38. Hoover's Inc. Bloomberg, L.P. November 10, 2005.
39. *http://investor.ca.com/phoenix.zhtml?c=83100&p=irol-homeprofile.* November 10, 2005.
40. *http://media.corporate-ir.net/media_files/irol/83/83100/reports/2005arpdf.pdf.* November 15, 2005. page 6.
41. *http://www3.ca.com/products/.* November 15, 2005.
42. *http://www3.ca.com/Files/WhitePapers/etrust_security_management_white_paper.pdf.* November 15, 2005. page 2.
43. *http://www3.ca.com/smb/solution.aspx?ID=5276.* November 15, 2005.
44. *http://www3.ca.com/smb/solution.aspx?id=5312&culture=en-us.* November 15, 2005.
45. *http://www.pandasoftware.com/about_panda/about_panda.* December 1, 2005.
46. *http://www.pandasoftware.com/about_panda/press_room/_Best+Performer_BusinesSecure.htm.* December 1, 2005.
47. *http://www.pandasoftware.com/about_panda/technology.* December 1, 2005.
48. *http://www.pandasoftware.com/about_panda/technology.* December 1, 2005.
49. *http://www.pandasoftware.com/about_panda/about_panda.* December 1, 2005.
50. *http://www.trendmicro.com/en/about/investors/company/about/overview.htm.* November 15, 2005.
51. *http://www.trendmicro.com/en/about/investors/accounts/historical/annual.htm.* November 15, 2005.
52. *http://www.trendmicro.com/en/products/global/enterprise.htm.* November 15, 2005.
53. *http://www.sophos.com/pressoffice/news/articles/2005/02/pr_uk_20050207marketgrowth.html.* November 16, 2005.
54. *http://www.sophos.com/products/es/.* November 16, 2005.
55. *http://www.sophos.com/products/sb/sbs/.* November 16, 2005.
56. *http://www.sophos.com/products/education/.* November 16, 2005.
57. *http://www.sophos.com/products/government/.* November 16, 2005.
58. *http://www.sophos.com/pressoffice/news/articles/2005/02/pr_uk_20050207marketgrowth.html.* November 16, 2005.
59. *http://www.microsoft.com/presspass/press/2004/dec04/12-16GIANTPR.mspx.* December 2, 2005.
60. *http://www.microsoft.com/presspass/features/2005/jan05/01-06Spyware.mspx.* December 6, 2005.
61. *http://www.microsoft.com/msft/ar05/flashversion/10k_fr_bal.html.* December 6, 2005.

CASE 12
eBay, Inc.

Darrin Kuykendall, Vineet Walia, and Alan N. Hoffman

"We intend to achieve our mission of becoming the world's most efficient and abundant marketplace by creating marketplace conditions that enable our users' success. By continuing to foster the vibrancy of the world's largest network of buyers and sellers and by making the online trading experience faster, easier and safer, we better enable the success of our user community."

eBay, Annual Report (2002)

ONE OF THE TREMENDOUS ADVANTAGES OF E-COMMERCE IS THAT TRULY ALL OF THE world's shoppers are potential customers for a vendor, no matter their physical location. Not only has eBay handsomely captured a lion's share of the American online auction consumer market, but eBay's offerings also extend to some 18 countries, as well as Latin America.[1] As a result, eBay has emerged as a global organization able to reach a significant customer base. Given its electronic medium, eBay is able to expand its reach much less expensively than a traditional brick-and-mortar business. Philosophically speaking, eBay has created a marketplace where one person's trash is another person's treasure.

In the Beginning: Scarce Resources and Unlimited Wants

Economics is the study of scarce resources and unlimited human wants. Pierre Omidyar, founder of eBay, had a vision of a utopian community founded on the basis of fundamental economics. The vision underlined the concept of having a *self-sustaining platform* that would be able to adapt to user needs without any heavy intervention from a central authority. Omidyar began the business as an online hobby in September 1995, calling it AuctionWeb. The enterprise started out as a sole proprietorship. It was some individual's desired want to own a "broken laser pointer." This *scarce resource* was provided by Omidyar, through his own personal web site auction that he developed. The site was satisfying this individual's want, but Omidyar knew that there was more to his AuctionWeb than met the eye.

AuctionWeb was incorporated in California in May 1996 with partner Jeff Skoll, a Stanford MBA. The company then became known as eBay (for "Electronic Bay"). When Omidyar and Skoll began generating a large amount of traffic and charging customers only $0.25 for listings, their mailboxes were overflowing with checks, and they did not have time to even open the mail. In 1996, eBay then grew to a one-room office, a part-time employee to handle payments, and a salary of $25,000 each for Omidyar and Skoll. eBay, Inc., was reincorporated in Delaware in 1998 and completed its IPO.

As eBay evolved, Omidyar envisioned a world of buyers where scarce resources were reduced. Through an Internet platform and the auction-based business model, this would be very possible. eBay has grown to become a consumer-driven buyer–seller platform. The idea was to develop a community-driven process, where the *community*—an organic, evolving, self-organizing web of individual relationships, formed around shared interests—would handle tasks that other companies handle with customer service operations.

On May 7, 1998, eBay's founder, Omidyar, now former CEO, became Chairman of the Board and brought in a seasoned veteran of consumer marketing, a Harvard Business School MBA, Meg Whitman. Whitman was brought in to direct corporate strategy to continue the accelerated growth rate of eBay. Whitman brought global management and marketing experience through years of service in brand management of Playskool and Mr. Potato Head. Upon Whitman's arrival at eBay, her focus was on expansion and global development: "With more than 10 million auctions completed since eBay's inception, we are changing the face of traditional commerce by giving power to individual consumers, as well as by allowing them to extend their buying and selling reach around the world. I am delighted to be joining eBay,"[2] she said.

Company Background

Whitman followed Omidyar's vision, believing that eBay's success is attributable to the notion that people are inherently good. eBay, Inc., incorporated in May 1996, operates a marketplace in which anyone, anywhere, can buy or sell practically anything. Through eBay's PayPal service, any business or consumer with e-mail and a credit card or bank account can send and receive online payments securely, conveniently, and cost-effectively. Whitman's goal is to create, maintain, and expand the technological functionality, safety, ease of use, and reliability of the trading platform while at the same time supporting the growth and success of its community of users.

Technology is another factor in eBay's success. eBay's trading platform is a fully automated, topically arranged, intuitive, and easy-to-use online service that is available 24 hours a day, 7 days a week (subject to a weekly scheduled two-hour maintenance period). The platform includes software tools and services that are available for free or for a fee and that allow buyers and sellers to more easily trade with one another. Its software tools are designed to make its trading process easy and efficient.

"The depth, breadth and potential of our business gives us great confidence in the future," said Whitman, now President and CEO of eBay. "The eBay marketplace is thriving across geographies, trading categories, pricing formats, listed items, user growth, and the services we offer our community." For Whitman and her executives, this was a major challenge—to uncover eBay's potential.

Corporate Governance

The success of the eBay community and company are fundamentally based on openness, honesty, integrity, and trust. eBay must have a strong board and management team to be effective toward not only stockholders but also stakeholders of the company. eBay's focus is on the effective use of building and strengthening the tools for online relationships. **Exhibit 1** shows biographies of the members of the Board of Directors of eBay, Inc.

Exhibit 1
Board of Directors: eBay, Inc.

Name	Age	Position
Pierre M. Omidyar	35	Founder, Chairman of the Board and Director
Margaret C. Whitman	46	President, Chief Executive Officer and Director
		Senior Vice President and General Manager, Global Online
Matthew J. Bannick	38	Payments
William C. Cobb	46	Senior Vice President and General Manager, eBay International
Rajiv Dutta	41	Senior Vice President and Chief Financial Officer
Michael R. Jacobson	48	Senior Vice President, Legal Affairs, General Counsel and Secretary
Jeffrey D. Jordon	44	Senior Vice President and General Manager, U. S. Business
Maynard G. Webb, Jr.	47	Chief Operating Officer
Philippe Bourguignon	55	Director
Scott D. Cook	50	Director
Robert C. Kagle	47	Director
Dawn G. Lepore	49	Director
Howard D Schultz	49	Director
Thomas J. Tierney	49	Director

Pierre M. Omidyar founded eBay as a sole proprietorship in September 1995. He has been a director and Chairman of the Board since eBay's incorporation in May 1996 and also served as its Chief Executive Officer, Chief Financial Officer, and President from inception to February 1998, November 1997 and August 1996, respectively. Prior to finding eBay, Mr. Omidyar was a developer services engineer at General Magic, a mobile communication platform company from December 1994 to July 1996. Mr. Omidyar co-founded Ink Development Corp. (later renamed eShop) in May 1991 and served as a software engineer there from May 1991 to September 1994. Prior to co-founding Ink, Mr. Omidyar was a developer for Claris, a subsidiary of Apple Computer, and for other Macintosh-oriented software development companies. Mr. Omidyar is currently Chairman and CEO of Omidyar Network. He also serves on Board of Trustees of Tufts University, The Santa Fe Institute, and as a director of several private companies. Mr. Omidyar holds a B.S. degree in Computer Science from Tufts University.

Margaret C. Whitman serves eBay as President and Chief Executive Officer. She has served in that capacity since February 1998 and as a director since March

(continued)

Exhibit 1
(continued)

1998. From January 1997 to February 1998, she was General Manager of the Preschool Division of Hasbro Inc., a toy company. From February 1995 to December 1996, Ms. Whitman was employed by FTD, Inc., a floral products company, most recently as President, Chief Executive Officer and a director. From October 1992 to February 1995, Ms. Whitman was employed by the Stride Rite Corporation, a footwear company, in various capacities, including President, Stride Rite Children's Group and Executive Vice President, Product Development, Marketing & Merchandising, Keds Division. From May 1989 to October 1992, Ms. Whitman was employed by The Walt Disney Company, an entertainment company, most recently as Senior Vice President, Marketing, Disney Consumer Products. Before joining Disney, Ms. Whitman was at Bain & Co., a consulting firm, most recently as a Vice President. Ms. Whitman also serves on the board of directors of The Procter & Gamble Company and Gap Inc. Ms. Whitman holds an A.B. degree in Economics from Princeton University and an M.B.A. degree from the Harvard Business School.

Philippe Bourguignon has served as a director of eBay since December 1999. Mr. Bourguignon has been the Chairman of Aegis Media France, a media communications and market research company since April 2004. From September 2003 to March 2004, Mr. Bourguignon was Co-Chief Executive Officer of The World Economic Forum (The DAVOS Forum). From August 2003 to October 2003, Mr. Bourguignon served as Managing Director of The World Economic Forum. From April 1997 to January 2003, Mr. Bourguignon served as Chairman of the Board of Club Mediterranee S.A., a resort operator. Prior to his appointment at Club Mediterranee S.A., Mr. Bourguignon was Chief Executive Officer of Euro Disney S.A., the parent company of Disneyland Paris, since 1993, and Executive Vice President of The Walt Disney Company (Europe) S.A., since October 1996. Mr. Bourguignon was named President of Euro Disney in 1992, a post he held through April 1993. He joined The Walt Disney Company in 1988 as head of Real Estate development. Mr. Bourguignon holds a Masters Degree in Economics at the University of Aix-en-Provence and holds a post-graduate diploma from the Institut d'Administration des Enterprises (IAE) in Paris.

Scott D. Cook has served as a director of eBay since June 1998. Mr. Cook is the founder of Intuit Inc., a financial software developer. Mr. Cook has been a director of Intuit since March 1984 and is currently Chairman of the Executive Committee of the Board of Intuit. From March 1993 to July 1998, Mr. Cook served as Chairman of the Board of Intuit. From March 1984 to April 1994, Mr. Cook served as President and Chief Executive Officer of Intuit. Mr. Cook also serves on the board of directors of The Procter & Gamble Company. Mr. Cook holds a B.A. degree in Economics and Mathematics from the University of Southern California and an M.B.A. degree from the Harvard Business School.

Robert C. Kagle has served as a director of eBay since June 1997. Mr. Kagle has been a Member of Benchmark Capital, the General Partner of Benchmark Capital Partners, L.P. and Benchmark Founders' Fund, L.P., since its founding in May 1995. Mr. Kagle also has been a General Partner of Technology Venture Investors since January 1984. Mr. Kagle also serves on the board of directors of E-LOAN, Inc. and ZipRealty, Inc. Mr. Kagle holds a B.S. degree in Electrical and Mechanical Engineering from the General Motors Institute (renamed Kettering University in Jaunuary 1998) and an M.B.A. degree from the Stanford Graduate School of Business.

Exhibit 1
(continued)

Dawn G. Lepore has served as a director of eBay since December 1999. Ms. Lepore has served as Chief Executive Officer and Chairman of the Board of drugstore.com, inc., a leading online provider of health, beauty, vision, and pharmacy solutions, since October 2004. From August 2003 to October 2004, Ms. Lepore served as Vice Chairman of Technology, Active Trader, Operations, Business Strategy, and Administration for the Charles Schwab Corporation and Charles Schwab & Co, Inc., a financial holding company. Prior to this appointment, she held various positions with the Charles Schwab Corporation including: Vice Chairman of Technology, Operations, Business Strategy, and Administration from May 2003 to August 2003; Vice Chairman of Technology, Operations, and Administrations from March 2002 to May 2003; Vice Chairman of Technology and Administration from November 2001 to March 2002; and Vice Chairman and Chief Information Officer from July 1999 to November 2001. She also serves on the board of directors of Catalyst, a research and advisory organization working to expand opportunities for women in business, and as a trustee of Smith College. Ms. Lepore holds a B.A. degree from Smith College.

Howard D. Schultz has served as a director of eBay since June 1998. Mr. Schultz is the founder of Starbucks Corporation, a provider of gourmet coffee, and has been its Charirman of the Board and Chief Global Strategist since June 2000. From Starbucks' inception in 1985 to June 2000, he served as its Chariman of the Board and Chief Executive Officer. From 1985 to June 1994, Mr. Schultz also served as President of Starbucks. Mr. Schultz is also one of two founding members of Maveron LLC, a company providing advisory services to consumer-based businesses, and is a member of two LLCs that serve as General Partners of Maveron LLC's affiliated venture capital funds, Maveron Equity Partners LP and Maveron Equity Partners 2000 LP. Mr. Schultz has announced that he will step down from the board when his current term expires at our Annual Meeting in June 2003.

Thomas J. Tierney has served as a director of eBay since March 2003. Mr. Tierney is the founder of The Bridgespan Group, a non-profit consulting firm serving the non-profit sector, and has been its Chairman of the Board since late 1999. Prior to founding Bridgespan, Mr. Tierney served as Chief Executive Officer of Bain & Company, a consulting firm, from June 1992 to January 2000. Mr. Tierney holds a B.A. degree in Economics from the University of California at Davis and an M.B.A. degree with distinction from the Harvard Business School. Mr. Tierney is the co-author of a book about organization and strategy called *Aligning the Stars*.

Executive Officers

Matthew J. Bannick serves eBay as Senior Vice President and General Manager, Global Online Payments and Chief Executive Officer of PayPal. He has served in those capacities since October 2002. From December 2000 to October 2002, Mr. Bannick served as eBay's Senior Vice Persident and General Manager, eBay International. From February 1999 to December 2000, Mr. Bannick served in a variety of other executive positions at eBay. From April 1995 to January 1999, Mr. Bannick was an executive for Navigation Technologies (NavTech), the leading provider of digital map databases for the vehicle navigation and internet mapping industries. Mr. Bannick was President of NavTech North America for three years and also served as

(continued)

Exhibit 1
(continued)

Senior Vice President of Marketing and Vice President of Operations. From June 1992 to August 1992, Mr. Bannick served as a consultant for McKinsey & Company, in Europe and from June 1993 to April 1995 in the U.S. Mr. Bannick also served as a U.S. diplomat in Germany during the period of German unification. Mr. Bannick holds a B.A. in Economics and International Studies from Univeristy of Washington and an M.B.A. degree from the Harvard Business School.

Scott D. Cook has served as a director of eBay since June 1998. Mr. Cook is the founder of Intuit Inc., a financial software developer. Mr. Cook has been a director of Intuit since March 1984 and is currently Chairman of the Executive Committee of the Board of Intuit. From March 1993 to July 1998, Mr. Cook served as Chairman of the Board of Intuit. From March 1984 to April 1994, Mr. Cook served as President and Chief Executive Officer of Intuit. Mr. Cook also serves on the board of directors of The Procter & Gamble Company. Mr. Cook holds a B.A. degree in Economics and Mathematics from the University of Southern California and an M.B.A. degree from the Harvard Business School.

Rajiv Dutta serves eBay as Senior Vice President and Chief Financial Officer. He has served in that capacity since January 2001. From August 1999 to January 2001, Mr. Dutta served as eBay's Vice President of Finance and Investor Relations. From July 1998 to August 1999, Mr. Dutta served as eBay's Finance director. From February 1998 to July 1998, Mr. Dutta served as the World Wide Sales Controller of KLA-Tencor, a manufacturer of semiconductor equipment. Prior to KLA-Tencor, Mr. Dutta spent ten years, from January 1988 to February 1998, at Bio-Rad Laboratories, Inc., a manufacturer and distributor of life science and diagnostic products with operations in over 24 countries. Mr. Dutta held a variety of positions with Bio-Rad, including the group controller of the Life Science Group. Mr. Dutta also serves on the board of directors of Jamadat Mobile Inc., a global publisher of wireless entertainment applications. Mr. Dutta holds a B.A. degree in Economics from St. Stephen's College, Delhi University in India and an M.B.A. degree from Drucker School of Management.

Michael R. Jacobson serves eBay as Senior Vice President, Legal Affairs, General Counsel and Secretary. He has served in that capacity or as Vice President, Legal Affairs, General Counsel, since August 1998. From 1986 to August 1998, Mr. Jacobson was a partner with the law firm of Cooley Godward LLP, specializing in securities law, mergers and acquisitions, and other transactions. Mr. Jacobson holds an A.B. degree in Economics from Harvard College and a J.D. degree from Stanford Law School.

Jeffrey D. Jordan serves eBay as President, PayPal. He has served in that capacity since December 2004. From April 2000 to December 2004, Mr. Jordan served as eBay's Senior Vice President, eBay North America. From September 1999 to April 2000, Mr. Jordan served as eBay's Vice President, Regionals and Services. From September 1998 to September 1999, Mr. Jordan served as Chief Financial Officer for Hollywood Entertainment Corporation, a video rental company, and President of their subsidiary, Reel.com. From September 1990 to September 1998, Mr. Jordan served in various capacities including most recently Senior Vice President and Chief Financial Officer of the Disney Store Worldwide, a subsidiary of the Walt Disney Company. Mr. Jordan holds a B.A. degree in Political Science and Psychology from Amherst College and an M.B.A. degree from the Stanford Graduate School of Business.

Exhibit 1
(continued)

Maynard G. Webb, Jr. serves eBay as Chief Operating Officer. He has served in that capacity since June 2002. From August 1999 to June 2002, Mr. Webb served as President, eBay Technologies. From July 1998 to August 1999, Mr. Webb was Senior Vice President and Chief Information Officer at Gateway, Inc., a computer manufacturer. From February 1995 to July 1998, Mr. Webb was Vice President and Chief Information Officer at Bay Networks, Inc., a manufacturer of computer networking products. From June 1991 to January 1995, Mr. Webb was Director, IT at Quantum Corporation. Mr. Webb also serves on the board of directors of Gartner, Inc., a high technology research and consulting firm and Peribit Networks, a networking company. Mr. Webb holds a B.A.A. degree from Florida Atlantic University.

Source: Adapted from eBay, Inc. (www.ebay.com), SEC 10-K (March 31, 2003), pp. 77–80.

Services

Customer Support

There is intrinsic value in the customer service that eBay provides. eBay does not necessarily provide customer service to buyers and sellers; however, it provides the tools that allow buyers and sellers to easily trade with one another. These software tools are available to buyers and sellers for free or for a fee (see **Exhibit 2**).

eBay prides itself on giving buyers and sellers the opportunity to be able to contact each other through the use of e-mail, text messaging, and phone. eBay enhances the user experience through pretrade and posttrade services. The listing process is simplified through pretrade services including photo hosting, authentication, and seller productivity applications. Posttrade services include insurance, payment processing, vehicle inspections, shipping and postage, and escrow. Services such as these are provided through third-party contracts.

Trust and Safety Programs

The Feedback Forum allows users to provide comments on other eBay users. Feedback is related to specific transactions of trades they personally dealt with. Positive representations are color coded. Users are encouraged to review feedback before making trades with other

Exhibit 2
Software Tools

- eBay Anywhere: Provides wireless connectivity to eBay.
- Seller's Assistant: Allows one to automate e-mail, project management, and list and track listing; provides pictures and HTML and formatting for sellers.
- Turbo Lister: This desktop-based selling tool facilitates creating listings to post on the eBay site. Turbo Lister helps a seller list items on eBay more quickly and easily.
- Selling Manager: Automates the selling process.
- Freight Resource Center: Allows users to calculate shipping costs.
- PayPal: Facilitates online exchange of funds.

Source: Adapted from eBay, Inc. (www.ebay.com), company document.

users. This creates trust within a community of users. The Feedback Forum reduces anonymity and uncertainty of dealing with unknown trading users.

Safeharbor™ Program

This program provides trading guidelines and information regarding disputes and the misuse of the eBay service. In this program, eBay staff are investigators of inappropriate behavior:

> The SafeHarbor™ group is organized into three areas: Investigations, Fraud Prevention and Community Watch. The Investigations team investigates reported trading infractions and misuse of the eBay service. The Fraud Prevention department provides information to assist users with disputes over the quality of the goods sold or potentially fraudulent transactions and, upon receipt of an officially filed, written claim of fraud from a user, will generally suspend the offending user from the eBay service or take other action as appropriate. The Community Watch department investigates the listing of illegal, infringing or inappropriate items on the eBay.com site and our international websites and violations of certain of our policies.[3]

My eBay

This program allows users to receive information about their online eBay activity. This information report includes recent activity, bidding, selling, account balances, favorite categories, and a feedback report. eBay users can also link their personal web pages to the "My eBay" portal. "The About Me home page can include personal information, items listed for sale, eBay feedback ratings, images and links to other favorite sites."[4]

Competitors

"We expect competition to intensify in the future as the barriers to entry into these channels are relatively low, as current offline and new competitors can easily launch online sites at a nominal cost using commercially available software or partnering with any one of a number of successful electronic commerce companies."

eBay, Annual Report (2002)

eBay is in an intensely competitive industry. Profitability can be maintained through preserving and expanding the abundance and diversity of the user community as well as enhancing the user experience. However, Whitman, President and CEO, faces the challenge of high operating expenses, which can lead to declines in net income. The Internet provides new, rapidly evolving and intensely competitive channels for the sale of all types of goods. eBay's broad list of competitors is listed in **Exhibit 3**. In addition, features of eBay's fixed-price business compete with the major Internet portals, such as AOL, MSN, Yahoo!, Amazon.com, and others.

Seasonality is a factor in eBay's globally competitive environment. Users reduce their online activities during holidays such as Thanksgiving and Christmas as well as the change from spring to summer.

Exhibit 3
Competitors by Product Area: eBay, Inc.

Antiques: Bonhams, Christie's, eHammer, Sotheby's, Phillips (LVMH), antique dealers and sellers

Coins & Stamps: Collectors Universe, Heritage, U.S. Mint, Bowers and Merena

Collectibles: Franklin Mint, Go Collect, Collectiblestoday.com, wizardworld.com, Russ Cochran Comic Art Auctions, All Star Auctions

Musical Instruments: Guitar Center, Musician's Friend, Sam Ash, Gbase.com, musical instrument retailers and manufacturers

Sports Memorabilia: Beckett, Collectors Universe, Mastro, Leylands, ThePit.com

Toys, Hobbies, Dolls, Bears: Toys "R" Us, Amazon.com/Toysrus.com, KB Toys/KBToys.com, FAO Inc. (FAO Schwarz, Zany Brainy, the Right Start), Lego, TY Inc.

Premium Collectibles: Bonhams, Christie's, DuPont Registry, Greg Manning Auctions, iCollector, Lycos/Skinner Auctions, Millionaire.com, Phillips (LVMH), Sotheby's, other premium collectibles dealers and sellers

Automotive (used cars and parts): Advance Auto Parts, Autonation.com, AutoTrader.com, Autozone, Barrett-Jackson, California Classics, CarMax, Cars.com, CarsDirect.com, Collectorcartraderonline.com, Dealix, Discount Auto Parts, Dupont Registry, eClassics.com, Edmunds, General Parts (Carquest), Genuine/NAPA, Hemmings, imotors.com, JC Whitney, TraderOnline, Trader Publishing, vehix.com, Wal-Mart, newspaper classifieds, used car dealers, swap meets, car clubs

Books, Movies, Music: Amazon.com, Barnes & Noble/Barnesandnoble.com, Alibris.com, Blockbuster, BMG, Columbia House, Best Buy, CDNow, Express.com, Emusic.com, Tower Records/TowerRecords.com

Clothing and Accessories: Abercrombie.com, AE.com, Amazon.com, Bluefly.com, ColdwaterCreek.com, Delias.com, Dockers.com, Eddie Bauer, The Gap/gap.com, J. Crew/JCrew.com, LandsEnd.com, The Limited, LLBean.com, Macy's, The Men's Wearhouse, Payless.com, Ross, Urbanq.com, VictoriasSecret.com

Computers & Consumer Electronics: Amazon.com, Best Buy, Buy.com, Circuit City, CNET, CompUSA, Dell, Electronics Boutique, Fry's Electronics, Gamestop, Gateway, The Good Guys, MicroWarehouse, PC Connection, Radio Shack, Ritz Camera, Tech Depot, Tiger Direct, Tweeter Home Entertainment, uBid, Computer Discount Warehouse, computer, consumer electronics and photography retailers

Home & Garden: IKEA, Crate & Barrel, Home Depot, Williams-Sonoma Inc. (Pottery Barn, Williams-Sonoma), Bed, Bath & Beyond, Lowes, Linens 'n Things, Pier One, Ethan Allen, Frontgate, Burpee.com

Jewelry: Bluenile.com, Diamond.com, Macy's

Pottery & Glass: Just Glass, Pottery Auction, Pottery Barn, Go Collect, Pier 1 Imports, Restoration Hardware

Sporting Goods/Equipment: Bass Pro Shops, Cabela's, dsports.com, Footlocker, Gear.com, Global Sports, golfclubexchange, MVP.com, Play It Again Sports, REI, Sports Authority, Sportsline.com

Tickets: Ticketmaster, Tickets.com, other ticket brokers

Tool/Equipment/Hardware: Home Depot, HomeBase, Amazon.com, Ace Hardware, OSH

Business-to-Business: Ariba, BidFreight.com, Bid4Assets, BizBuyer.com, Buyer Zone, CloseOutNow.com, Commerce One, Concur Technologies, DoveBid, FreeMarkets, Iron Planet, labx.com, Oracle, Overstock.com, PurchasePro.com, RicardoBiz.com, Sabre, SurplusBin.com, Ventro, Vertical Net

Global Business Strategy

Whitman has seen key opportunities for growth in the United States as well as internationally. Whitman cited international acquisitions, online merchandising, and marketing as levers to achieve the company goals. Overall, eBay receives three major sources of revenue growth: U.S. business, International business, and online payments.

For future expansion, Whitman wants to focus on new user acquisition and marketing. Online auctions, like many online communities, rely on positive relationships among those transacting business. One area of concern for eBay is the threat from fraudulent auctions (e.g., seller has no intention of shipping item), counterfeits, and knockoffs. Each of these areas erodes the trust needed for eBay to flourish. Even though eBay has in place various monitoring measures and de-listing capabilities, unscrupulous individuals or criminals are often one step ahead of eBay and likely will continue to identify means to undermine the trust-based marketplace. As a result, unethical behavior will continue to be a threat to eBay, and its ability to manage such acts, however strong, must be considered a weakness as potential customers may harbor concern about the eBay environment. For example, Jed Conboy, a district attorney in New York, purchased a baseball he believed was signed by Ted Williams for $367 on eBay.[5] The autograph was a fake, and Conboy decided to sue eBay. As in many similar cases, the court ruled in favor of eBay. The primary question is whether eBay is an auction house or a marketplace. If the courts view eBay as a classic auctioneer, the company would have to vouch for the products sold on its site. However, eBay's lawyers have argued successfully that eBay is no more than an independent intermediary that does not take sides in the transaction. Up to this point, the courts have accepted this defense. This legal precedent has allowed eBay to grow and prosper without paying penalties for fraudulent products sold on its site.

Acquisition of PayPal

As a result of the 2001 financial analysts' conference, on October 3, 2002, eBay acquired PayPal, Inc. PayPal enabled any business or consumer with e-mail access and a credit card or bank account in 38 countries to send and receive online payments securely, conveniently, and cost-effectively. Whitman noted, "eBay and PayPal have complementary missions. We both empower people to buy and sell online."[6] eBay's intentions were to accelerate the velocity of trade on eBay by eliminating the various obstacles presented by traditional payment methods. Based on the same financial infrastructure of bank accounts and credit cards, PayPal and eBay created an international payment system. In July 2002, eBay announced plans to acquire PayPal, an online payment company, for $1.5 billion.[7] Although the acquisition provided many opportunities, $7 billion in annual sales on eBay are completed using something other than online payment. And the acquisition of PayPal also came with some legal baggage.

A suit was brought against PayPal by First USA Bank in September 2002 alleging infringement of two patents pertaining to assigning an alias to a credit card. PayPal has a solid defense against this accusation, but even if successful in court, the defense will be costly and divert management's time. A class action suit was also brought against PayPal in February 2002, claiming that the company violated the state's consumer protection laws by restricting customer accounts and failing to promptly unrestrict legitimate accounts. If unsuccessful in its defense, PayPal will have to change its anti-fraud operations in a way that could harm the business in addition to paying significant damages. Even if PayPal is successful in this suit, the trial has damaged the company's reputation and will be costly in terms of legal fees and management's time.

Technology

Much of eBay's success is based on the company's ability to quickly analyze sales trends and capitalize on the movement in specific product categories. In order to compete in this area, eBay requires extensive data mining and data storage software. By taking advantage of the latest product offerings and implementing the software in a coherent architecture, eBay is able to process millions of transactions a day while gathering information on specific segments. It also revamped its application development architecture to support the Java 2, Enterprise Edition, framework. This programming environment adds a new level of flexibility that was not available with the older C++ development tools. Buyers and sellers on eBay make an average of 30 million searches a day.[8] Due to this volume, eBay is constantly trying to improve its search capability. Bidding on items increases dramatically when eBay adds a new search feature; therefore, eBay has constantly invested in improving technology to provide more accurate results as quickly as possible.

Marketing

eBay is recognized as one of the few successful dot-com companies. To realize such achievements, eBay has developed a great number of marketing strengths. Although eBay has advantages as a first mover, to maintain its competitive edge, the company has identified several ways to create and sustain customer relationships. In particular, the company tries to achieve strengths in each of the four P's—price, promotion, product, and place. The fruits of these endeavors is demonstrated by one of the longest "customer hang-times"[9] on the Internet.[10] Furthermore, a strong argument could be made that eBay is synonymous with online auctions and vice versa. eBay's offerings are related to pull rather than push marketing. eBay's product offerings are a result of this user demand. eBay's customers must sell products successfully in order for the digital marketplace to be economically viable; therefore, it is in eBay's best interest to ensure that buyers and sellers alike are satisfied. eBay does not produce the items sold on its site, but it provides the tools and forums that enable the efficient interaction between buyers and sellers. These tools and forums are the keys to eBay's success. For eBay to gain competitive advantage, customers must perceive a value from eBay that exceeds the values of potential rivals or alternatives.

Tremendous brand recognition enables eBay to draw an ever-expanding array of customers. With tens of millions registered users and listings of some 16 million items worldwide, clearly eBay has realized strong product promotion.[11] Surely those wishing to sell or buy items are more inclined to enter a marketplace that has the most significant listing of items. Thus, eBay currently attracts a growing cascade of customers because it appears to be the sensible site for the world of online auctions. Another marketing strength of eBay is its protection of trademarks, copyrights, patents, domain names, trade dress, and trade secrets. eBay employs confidentiality and invention agreements with employees and contractors, as well as nondisclosure agreements with business contacts. Registration and upkeep of these intellectual properties are critical to success.

The value that eBay offers is to make inefficient markets more efficient. Traditional offline marketplaces can be inefficient because:

- They are fragmented and regional in nature, making it difficult and expensive for buyers and sellers to meet, exchange information, and complete transactions
- They offer a limited variety and breadth of goods
- They often have high transaction costs due to intermediaries
- In particular, large markets with broad buyer and seller bases, wide product ranges, and moderate shipping costs have been successful on eBay. Its marketplace is most effective, relative to available alternatives, at addressing markets of new and scarce goods, end-of-life products, and used and vintage items.

eBay has several core competencies that translate into competitive advantages. Competitive advantages are subject to becoming outdated and irrelevant if a company does not work to continuously adapt its strategic outlook. eBay has been able to enable its users to have successful trading experiences through continuous improvements. eBay has also been able to provide exceptional customer service through its Power Seller Program, where people who sell over a certain total dollar value per month receive personal support through an exclusive toll-free phone number.

Financial Performance

eBay's income is mainly generated from transactions fees, third-party advertising, end-to-end services, and offline services in its U.S., International, and Payments segments. eBay's sales have increased every year, from $224.7 million in 1999 to $1,213 million in 2002. This yields a compounded annual growth rate (CAGR) of 75%. Over the same period, net income increased from $9.6 million to $249.9 million. This is a CAGR of 196%. The higher growth rate of net income over sales can probably be attributed to expenses growing at a slower rate than sales.

During the period from 2001 to 2002, eBay's cash holdings have more than doubled from $524 million to $1,109.3 million. This amount of cash is more than enough to cover debt obligations. From 1999 to 2002, long-term debt has decreased from $15 million to $13.8 million, a CAGR of 3%. From 2001 to 2002, long-term debt increased from $12 million to $13.8 million. In eBay's global arena, international sales increased 165% over sales in 2001. International sales make up 26% of total revenues, up from 7% in 2000. **Exhibits 4 and 5** are eBay's income statement and balance sheet, respectively.

The Future

Whitman now faces some critical issues. She notes that eBay's core competencies and competitive advantages are what allow eBay to be successful. Whitman is confident that eBay's business model is sound and the vision of becoming the world's online marketplace is a matter of enhancing the efficient use and effectiveness of eBay's products and services. Whitman faces problems in that eBay needs to be able to develop new services, features,

Exhibit 4 Consolidated Income Statement: eBay, Inc. (Dollar amounts in thousands, except per share amount)

Year Ending December 31	2000	2001	2002
Net revenues	$1,214,100	$748,821	$431,424
Cost of net revenue:	213,876	134,816	95,453
Gross Profit:	1,000,224	614,005	335,971
Operating expenses:			
Sales and marketing	349,650	253,474	166,767
Product development	104,636	75,288	55,863
General and administrative	171,785	105,784	73,027
Payroll taxes on stock option gains	4,015	2,442	2,337
Amortization of intangible assets	15,941	36,591	1,433
Merger related costs	—	—	1,550
Total operating expenses	646,027	473,579	300,977
Income from operations	354,197	140,426	34,994
Interest and other income, net	49,209	41,613	46,337
Interest expenses	(1,492)	(2,851)	(3,374)
Impairment of certain equity investments	(3,781)	(16,245)	—
Income before income taxes and minority interests	398,133	162,943	77,957
Provision for income taxes	(145,946)	(80,009)	(32,725)
Minority interests in consolidated companies	(2,296)	7,514	3,062
Net income	$ 249,891	$ 90,448	$ 48,294
Net income per share:			
Basic	$ 0.87	$ 0.34	$ 0.19
Diluted	$ 0.85	$ 0.32	$ 0.17
Weighted average shares:			
Basic	287,496	268,971	251,776
Diluted	292,820	280,595	280,346

Note: Notes were deleted.

Source: eBay, Inc., SEC Form 10-K (December 2002), p. 95.

and functions in order to stay ahead of its increasing competition. Whitman needs to decide how eBay can exploit its potential and consider the following approaches to ensure future growth of the company:

1. Invest large portions of revenue in research and development in order to develop new service features and functions
2. Make acquisitions and strategic partnerships to increase success in new categories and specialty stores
3. Recruit personnel familiar with certain market segments to allow eBay to develop services better suited to those particular segments
4. Enter the business-to-business auctions market to allow eBay to offer higher-priced items and collect higher commissions
5. Make strategic alliances with shipping companies such as FedEx

In growing, eBay's management will have to take care not to destroy brand value and image as well as remain an auction site, eBay's area of core competence.

Exhibit 5 Consolidated Balance Sheets: eBay, Inc. (Dollar amounts in thousands, except per share amounts)

Year Ending December 31	2002	2001
Assets		
Current assets:		
Cash and cash equivalents	$1,109,313	$ 523,969
Short-term investments	89,690	199,450
Accounts receivable	131,453	101,703
Funds receivable	41,014	—
Other current assets	96,988	58,683
Total current assets	1,468,458	883,805
Long-term investments	470,227	286,998
Restricted cash and investments	134,644	129,614
Property and equipment net	218,028	142,349
Goodwill	1,456,024	187,829
Intangible assets net	279,465	10,810
Deferred tax assets	84,218	21,540
Other assets	13,380	15,584
	$4,124,444	**$1,678,529**
Liabilities and Stockholders' Equity		
Current liabilities		
Accounts payable	$ 47,424	$ 33,235
Funds payable and amounts due to customers	50,396	—
Accrued expenses and other current liabilities	199,323	94,593
Deferred revenue and customer advances	18,846	15,583
Short-term debt	2,970	16,111
Income taxes payable	67,265	20,617
Total current liabilities	386,224	180,139
Long-term debt	12,008	13,798
Deferred tax liabilities	3,629	111,843
Other liabilities	15,864	22,874
Minority interests	37,751	33,232
Total liabilities	249,391	567,971
Commitment		
Stockholders' equity:		
Convertible Preferred Stock, $0.001 par value; 10,000 shares authorized; no shares issued or outstanding	—	—
Common Stock, $0.001 par value; 900,000 shares authorized; 277,259 and 311,277 shares issued and outstanding	311	277
Additional paid-in capital	3,108,443	1,275,240
Unearned stock-based compensation	(5,253)	(2,367)
Retained earnings	414,474	164,633
Accumulated other comprehensive income (loss)	38,498	(8,645)
Total stockholders' equity	3,556,473	1,429,138
Total liabilities and stockholders' equity	$4,124,444	$1,678,529

Note: Notes were deleted.

Source: eBay, Inc., SEC Form 10-K (December 2002), p. 94.

Notes

1. eBay web site, *http://pages.ebay.com/community/aboutebay/overview/index.html* (July 2003).
2. Whitman, 1998.
3. eBay.com, 2003.
4. eBay.com, 2003.
5. M. Mannix, "Sure It's a Great Deal. But Is It Real? Fraud Online Threatens eBay's Money Model," *U.S. News and World Report* (December 11, 2000).
6. Whitman, 2002.
7. M. Richtel, "eBay to Buy PayPal, a Rival in Online Payments," *The New York Times* (July 9, 2002).
8. R. Hof, "Desperately Seeking Search Technology," *BusinessWeek* (September 24, 2001).
9. *Customer hangtime* is an e-commerce term that evaluates the length of time a customer spends on a site at each visit. The greater the length of time per visit, the greater the customer hangtime.
10. eBay web site, *http://pages.ebay.com/community/aboutebay/overview/index.html* (July 2003).
11. *Ibid.*

CASE 13

Amazon.com:

An E-Commerce Retailer

Patrick Collins, Robert J. Mockler, and Marc Gartenfeld

HEADING INTO THE SECOND QUARTER OF 2003, JEFF BEZOS, FOUNDER AND CEO OF Amazon.com, could look back over the last couple sets of quarterly numbers for Amazon.com and be proud. Under pressure from the financial markets to abandon the company's oft-stated goal of sacrificing short-term profits for building long-term growth, market share, and increased shareholder value, Bezos proved that his online retail business model could produce operating profits. Now that Bezos had that issue taken care of, there were a number of new ones that needed to be addressed. Outside the overall economic malaise of the U.S. and world economies, the Internet Tax Moratorium law was up for renewal in November, with no assurance of its being extended, and online stalwarts eBay and Yahoo! were expanding into Amazon.com's markets. Bezos was faced with the task of developing an effective differentiating enterprisewide strategy if Amazon.com was to survive and prosper against aggressive competition over the intermediate and long-term futures.

Amazon.com is considered to be the premier online retailer in the world. Although it originally started out selling only books, it has expanded into numerous other product lines, as shown in **Exhibit 1**. Some of these product lines include CDs, DVDs, and videos. However, in order to offer as large a product line as possible, Amazon.com has entered into contracts with numerous retail partners, such as The Gap and Eddie Bauer, to sell their goods through Amazon.com's web site. Some of these partnership agreements involve Amazon.com running another company's own web site. This type of partnership, known as "powered by Amazon," allows companies to use Amazon.com technology and patented web site capabilities, such as 1-Click Ordering. Two well-known retailers who have participated in this type of arrangement are Target and Toys 'R' Us.

With the number of households having broadband access expected to increase to 29 million by the end of 2003 and the number of Internet users worldwide estimated at 500 million,

---

Exhibit 1
Product Categories: Amazon.com

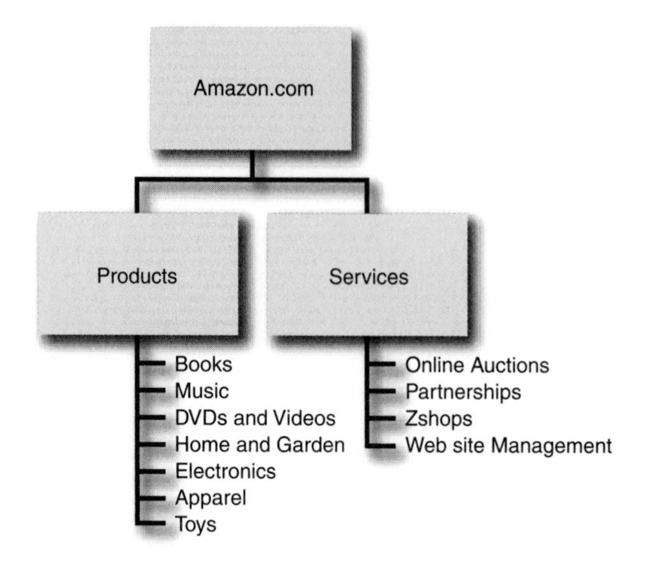

it was becoming easier and easier for a person to shop from the comfort of home.[1] As defined by the Federal Communications Commission (FCC), *broadband* is a new generation of high-speed transmission services that allows users to access the Internet and Internet-related services at significantly higher speeds than by using traditional modems. It has the potential technical capability to meet customers' broad communication, entertainment, information, and commercial needs and desires. And with online retailers commanding a small percentage of retail sales, there is plenty of market to go after.

In an earnings statement announcement released January 23, 2003, Amazon.com showed some outstanding financial numbers. For the fourth quarter, which was the busiest time of year for retailers due to the holiday season, Amazon.com reported record sales of $1.43 billion, an increase of 28% over 2001 fourth quarter sales of $1.12 billion. For the fiscal year ending December 31, 2002, Amazon.com showed an increase of 26% in yearly sales, reporting $3.94 billion in sales for 2002, compared to $3.12 billion for 2001. In addition, for the year ending December 31, 2002, Amazon.com managed its first operating profit of $64.1 million, as compared to a $412.2 million operating loss in 2001. And overall, Amazon.com cut its losses from $567 million to $149 million, an improvement of $418 million.[2] Even though Amazon.com continued to meet its internal goals of focusing on increased market share, expanded product offerings, and overall sales growth, the company was still facing pressure from the stock market to produce consistent operating profits and to prove that its business model worked financially over the long term. This pressure, combined with a decreasing customer confidence level and an increased unemployment rate, had made the retail future look uncertain. The main question for Bezos was how to turn Amazon.com into a consistent moneymaker in the immediate, intermediate, and long-term time frames, while continuing to pursue its corporate objective of expansion at reasonable costs.

History

After graduating from Princeton with a bachelor's degree in electrical engineering and computer science in 1986, Jeff Bezos went to work for a company called Fitel, a startup financial communications firm. From there, Bezos went to Banker's Trust and finally to D. E. Shaw.

While he was in these jobs, Bezos gained invaluable experience in computer programming, finance, and international markets. During his time at D. E. Shaw, Bezos was assigned the job of exploring possible Internet business opportunities. He looked for the best products to sell through the web and put together a list of products that could easily be sold online, including books, computer software, office supplies, apparel, and music.[3] After examining how the retail book business was set up and the fact that there was not a single company that had a stranglehold on the industry, Bezos felt that setting up an online bookstore was the best way to go. He made this recommendation to his company, but his recommendation was rejected. However, the idea of opening an online bookstore became something that Bezos could not let go of, and in 1994 he left D. E. Shaw to chase his dream of commerce on the Internet.

In starting his company, Bezos was faced with a number of questions. Although he had the financial and computer background to run his company, Bezos needed to think about where he was going to establish his company. In doing this analysis, Bezos came up with three criteria for the location of his business. The location had to be an area with people who had the necessary programming talent to develop the software, closeness to a major book wholesaler, and a state with little or no sales tax. After narrowing his options down to four areas that fit his criteria, Bezos decided on Seattle, Washington, as being the best place to start his company.

By the time Bezos got settled in Seattle and went about the process of starting his company, there were a number of online booksellers already in business. Because most people were not familiar with the World Wide Web and were just focusing on using e-mail, their business process model was to take book orders via e-mail, fill them, and ship them—a rather labor-intensive process. To help overcome their first-mover advantage and differentiate his company from the competition, Bezos decided to make his company mission to use the Internet to transform book buying into the fastest, easiest, and most enjoyable shopping experience possible.[4] The competition method was not very cost-effective and was in fact very labor intensive and did not fully maximize the capabilities of the Internet. The second selling method was to develop an online store so that people who had access to the Internet and a web browser, such as Netscape Navigator or Microsoft Explorer, could go and purchase books. To help defray some of the costs for setting up this web store, open-source programming code (which was free) was used.

In 1995, the Internet was becoming easier to use, and Amazon.com's method of sales through its web site started to take off. It was the perfect time to become an online retailer. When Sun Microsystems released Java, a programming language that made it possible to run interactive web pages, web sites became easier for customers to use. This, combined with the increasing number of personal computers, formed a market that was there for the taking. By being one of the first companies to go online and embrace the idea of taking orders through a web site, Amazon.com enjoyed a tremendous first-mover advantage, which it continues to enjoy today. Amazon.com has gone through a number of different changes in its short history, including dividing the company into four different operating segments, as shown in **Exhibit 2**.

Exhibit 2
Operating Segments: Amazon.com

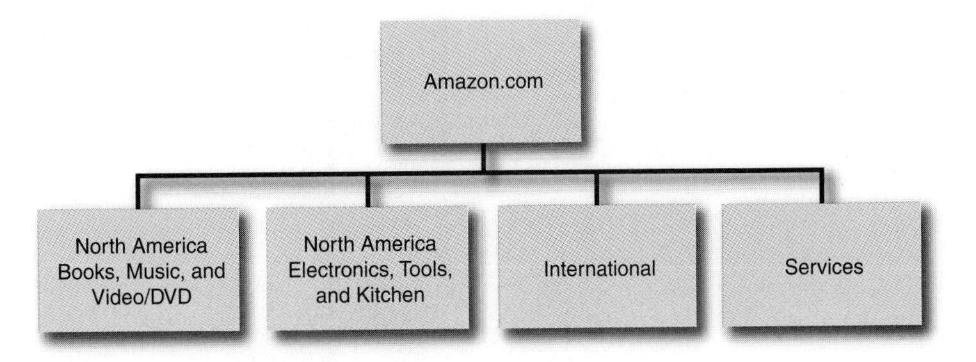

Exhibit 3 **Business Model: Amazon.com**

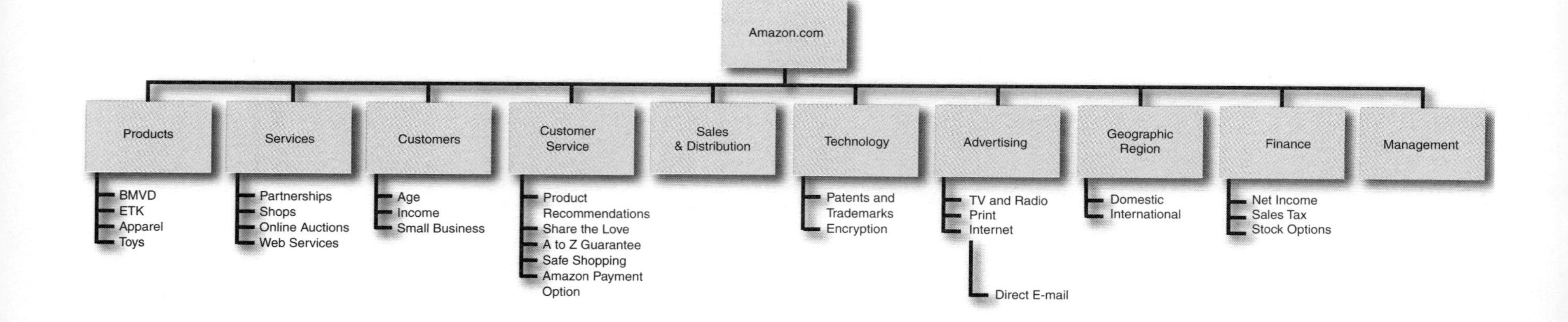

One theme always remained consistent: to get big fast, at all costs. This philosophy, which was stated in Amazon.com's 1997 Letter to Its Shareholders, was developed because it was seen as the best way to spread out costs. Due to its low overhead, the more sales that Amazon.com had, the bigger the increase in profit margin on the items it sold. Amazon.com, like all other retailers, had inventory and administrative costs. But by collecting payments immediately for its sales and floating vendor payments 30 to 40 days, Amazon.com was able to generate a large amount of working capital. Amazon.com also enjoyed an additional competitive advantage over traditional brick-and-mortar retailers in that it did not have to operate physical stores in order to sell its goods and services. Although there were some similarities with brick-and-mortar retailers, there were some unique factors with the online environment, as shown in **Exhibit 3**.

Products

Amazon.com sold a wide variety of products online for both itself and its retail partners. Amazon.com broke down its product line into four areas. The first area was called the Books, Music, and Video/DVD Segment, or BMVD. The second area was called the Electronics, Tools, and Kitchen Segment, or ETK. Apparel and toys made up the remaining two areas.

Books, Music, Video/DVD Segment

The BMVD segment offered books, music, and videos/DVDs for sale. Amazon.com offered these items for sale directly and did not use any of its affiliated partners.

Books

Selling books is what made Amazon.com famous. Amazon.com had more than 5 million titles in stock and available for purchase everyday. Some of the more popular categories included Arts & Photography, Biographies & Memoirs, Business & Investing, Children's Books, Cooking, History, Home & Garden, Horror, Literature & Fiction, Mystery & Thrillers, Nonfiction, Romance, Science Fiction & Fantasy, Sports, and Travel. Books could be purchased in hardcover, paperback, audio, and downloadable formats. Amazon.com offered significant discounts on most categories of books, including those on the *New York Times* bestseller list. To help customers in their selection process, Amazon.com posted book cover art, sample chapters, editorial staff reviews, and professional reviews of the book. In addition to professional reviews, Amazon.com allowed its customers to review books and had them posted online, alongside the professional reviews.

Music

In addition to its wide selection of books, Amazon.com offered a wide selection of music titles. The music could be purchased in a variety of formats, including tapes, compact discs, and downloadable formats, such as MP3s. Some of the more popular categories included Alternative Rock, Blues, Box Sets, Children's Music, Classic Rock, Classical, Country and Western, Hard Rock & Metal, Jazz, Latin, New Age, Opera & Vocal, Pop, Motown, R&B, Rap & Hip-Hop, and Soundtracks. To help customers in their selection process, Amazon.com posted short music clips for customers to listen to. For the more popular music categories, Amazon.com posted its own editorial reviews, as well as customer reviews.

Videos/DVDs

Amazon.com offered a large selection of video and DVD titles for sale. Some of the more popular categories included Action & Adventure, Boxed Sets of Television Series, Classics, Comedy, Cult Movies, Disney Home Video, Documentary, Drama, Horror, Kids & Family,

Musicals, Mystery & Suspense, Science Fiction & Fantasy, Sports, and Westerns. To help customers in their selection process, Amazon.com posted movie summaries as well as movie credits, such as actor and director information. To further help customers, Amazon.com posted its own editorial reviews, as well as customer reviews.

Electronics, Tools, and Kitchen Segment

The ETK segment offered electronic goods, tools, and kitchen supplies. Both Amazon.com and some of its retail partners offered these items for sale.

Electronics

Through its web site, Amazon.com sold a wide variety of electronic goods, including offerings from some of its affiliated partners, such as Target. Some of the categories included Audio & Video Products, Cameras, Camcorders, Cell Phones, Computers, Computer & Video Games, and Software. Amazon.com sold all the major national brands, including Sony, Panasonic, and Canon. Because of the number of accessories needed with some of the electronic goods, such as home theatre systems, Amazon.com posted a list of accessories on the same web page as the main item. To further help customers, Amazon.com made available both professional and staff reviews of products. As it did for books and music, Amazon.com posted product reviews by other customers.

Tools

In order to attract self-proclaimed do-it-yourselfers, Amazon.com offered a wide variety of tools, most of which were carried by its affiliate partners, such as Home Depot. Some of the hardware and tools available for sale included cordless screwdrivers and drills, electric saws and drills, circular saws, and sanders. Some of the brands carried included Black & Decker, Dewalt, and Stanley. Amazon.com posted product information as well as product reviews by its staff and other customers.

Kitchen

To complement its selection of cookbooks, Amazon.com offered a wide selection of kitchen products on its web site, from both itself and its partners, such as Target. Some of the products included small kitchen appliances, cookware, fine china, and flatware. Some of the brands available included Corningware, Calphalon, and Kitchenaid. To help customers make decisions on what products to buy, Amazon.com made available both professional and staff reviews of products. As it did for its other product lines, Amazon.com allowed customers to review and post their reviews online.

Apparel

Because most people were interested in name-brand clothing, Amazon.com did not sell any of its own line of apparel but focused on offering clothing and accessories through its numerous partners. Amazon.com had partnered with some of the country's leading clothing retailers, including The Gap, Target, Eddie Bauer, and Nordstrom.

For women, some of the categories that were available for sale included Lingerie, Sleepwear & Hosiery, Maternity, Outerwear, Pants & Shorts, Shirts & Tops, Skirts & Dresses, Suits & Separates, Sweaters & Sweatshirts, Swim & Athletic Wear, Shoes, and Accessories. All sizes, including petite and plus sizes, were available. Nationally known product lines sold by The Gap, Target, and Mimi Maternity were available, as were the retailers' own private-label brands. For men, some of the categories available for sale included Outerwear, Pants &

Shorts, Shirts, Suits & Sport Coats, Sweaters & Sweatshirts, Swim & Athletic Wear, Underwear, Socks & Sleepwear, Accessories, and Shoes. All sizes, including big and tall, were available. Nationally known product lines sold by companies such as Foot Locker and Eddie Bauer were available, as were the retailers' own private-label brands. For children, a full line of products was made available, the categories including Pants & Shorts, Shirts & Tops, Shoes & Sneakers, Outerwear, Sweaters & Sweatshirts, and Skirts & Dresses. All children's sizes, including infants' and toddlers', were available. Nationally known product lines sold by companies such as OshKosh B'Gosh and Babies 'R' Us, were available, as were the retailers' own private-label brands.

Toys

In order to have as complete a selection of toys as possible, Amazon.com teamed up with the world's biggest toy store, Toys 'R' Us, to offer a wide variety of toys. Some of the categories available included Action Figures, Bikes, Scooters, Dolls, Games, Learning Toys, Preschool Toys, Sports & Outdoor Play, and Video Games. Old favorites such as Lego, Barbie, and G.I. Joe were available, as were more modern games such as Sony PlayStation 2, Nintendo, and Xbox. To help customers in their selection of toys, Amazon.com made available on its web site complete product information and descriptions. In addition, Amazon.com posted both professional and staff reviews of products. As it did for its other product categories, Amazon.com allowed customers to review and post their own product reviews.

Web Operations

Due to its vast selection, Amazon.com was considered to be an online mall. Because of the cost associated with carrying such a large inventory, Amazon.com made use of partnership and affiliation agreements to supplement its own product lines of books, music, videos and DVDs, electronics, tools, and kitchen products. Because it operated online, Amazon.com accepted all major credit cards for payments. Because it did not operate retail stores, Amazon.com had very little overhead and was able to pass these savings along to customers in the form of low prices.

To help customers determine what to buy, Amazon.com posted product reviews from both its staff and outside experts. In addition to these product reviews, Amazon.com allowed its customers to post their own reviews for viewing by other customers. Because all its products were shipped, Amazon.com offered a number of shipping options, including free shipping on many orders over $25. Amazon.com also posted links to shipping companies so its customers could easily track their orders. Product returns needed to be shipped back to Amazon.com by the customer. To help with this, Amazon.com posted shipping instructions and labels on its web site. For those items purchased from its affiliates, in-store product returns were possible.

Services

In order to be the most complete retailer possible, Amazon.com realized that it needed to expand beyond offering its own products for sale. The best way to accomplish this was to use the Amazon.com selling platform as a basis to offer additional goods and services for sale. By turning its focus away from just selling books, music, and movies, some wondered whether Amazon.com would be distracted. However, this was something that the company had always envisioned it would do. In the words of Bezos:

> We want to build a place where people can come to find and discover anything they might want to buy online. You realize very quickly that you can't sell everything people want directly. So instead you need to do that in partnership with thousands and indeed millions of third party sellers in different ways. To try to do that alone, in strictly a traditional retailing model, isn't practical.[5]

Aside from having partnership agreements with other retailers and investing in other online retailers, Amazon.com offered auction services and a store-hosting program for small and medium-sized businesses, called zShops.

Partnerships

In the beginning of 1999, Amazon.com wanted to expand the number of product offerings available on its web site to its customers. Amazon.com decided to go about this in two different ways. The first way was to invest in other online companies that could benefit from the high traffic generated from Amazon.com's web site. To help pay for these investments, Amazon.com used its high stock prices to purchase ownership stakes in other online retailers. Some of the companies that Amazon.com invested in included Pets.com, Homegrocer.com, and Drugstore.com.[6] However, due to the collapse of the stock market, in particular Internet stocks, and years of cumulative losses, most of these companies, in particular Pets.com and Homegrocer.com, ended up going bankrupt and out of business, leading Amazon.com to write off most of these investments, causing a loss of close to $135 million in 2000. In addition to partnering with other online retailers, Amazon.com, due to its patented technology and strategically placed distribution centers, looked at partnering with brick-and-mortar retailers that did not have the e-commerce expertise that Amazon.com had. In 2001, Amazon.com signed deals with brick-and-mortar retailers such as Target, Circuit City, and Borders. These deals called for Amazon.com to run all or part of the other companies' e-commerce operations, selling their products on its own web site.[7]

zShops

Amazon.com got into the store hosting business with its offering called zShops. This was similar to the services offered by Internet portal companies such as Yahoo! and MSN. This service gave small and midsized companies a web site to sell their products. In order to attract people to use this service, Amazon.com offered a guarantee, called A-to-Z Guarantee, which insured the buyer in the event of nondelivery or the supply of a defective product. Both Amazon.com and the merchants benefited from this arrangement. Merchants were given an inexpensive way to sell their products to an already established, loyal customer base. Amazon.com benefited from getting a sales presence in products that it did not carry, which helped to reinforce Amazon.com's motto of offering the earth's largest selection.

Amazon.com made money from sellers in its zShops program in a number of ways. Every seller was required to pay a monthly fee of $39.99 for the right to list as many as 40,000 items. If the number of listed items exceeded 40,000, the seller was charged an additional listing fee of $0.10 per additional item.[8] In addition to the monthly listing fee, if they were willing to pay a merchandising fee, merchants were able to have their listing placed in conjunction with other Amazon.com offerings. Finally, when a sale was completed, a closing fee was charged. It was based on the selling price of the item. If the product sold for between $0.01 and $25.00, Amazon.com collected a 5% closing fee. If the product sold between $25.01 and $1,000.00, Amazon.com collected $1.25 plus a 2.5% commission of any amount above $25. If the product sold for more than $1,000.01, Amazon.com collected $25.63 plus a 1.25% commission on any amount above $1,000. In order to help facilitate the payment for goods purchased in the zShops program (as well as its auction services), Amazon.com set up a program called Amazon Payments, which is explained in the "Customer Service" section of this case study.

Offering this type of service provided many advantages for Amazon.com. It allowed Amazon.com to increase the number of items available on its web site, without the costs of carrying the inventory. By charging monthly management fees and commissions on completed purchases, Amazon.com developed a steady revenue stream without incurring much expense. By offering buyer insurance, Amazon.com was able to protect its loyal customers from fraudulent sellers. Although there were some major advantages of offering this service, there were some potential disadvantages that could materialize in the future. These included the possibility of zShops' merchants offering lower-quality goods, which could dilute Amazon.com's image. It was possible that the zShops could offer goods that competed with the items that Amazon.com sold for itself. There was always the potential of fraudulent sellers. Even though there was buyers' insurance, any fraudulent activity could cause bad public relations for Amazon.com. Finally, there was the possibility that this type of program could distract Amazon.com from its core competencies used in selling its own products.

Online Auctions

In response to the continued profitability and financial success of online auction companies, in particular eBay, Amazon.com announced its own online auction service, Amazon.com Auctions, on March 30, 1999. When online auctions continued to improve in popularity, it seemed to be a natural avenue of expansion for Amazon.com. In order to differentiate itself from established companies and to emphasize that the customer was the important part of retailing, Amazon.com offered a money-back guarantee on goods purchased under $350.

Amazon.com made money from sellers in its online auction program in a number of ways. Every seller was required to pay a listing fee. This fee was $0.10 per listing. Frequent sellers were eligible for the Pro Merchant Subscription monthly fee of $39.99, which gave them the right to list as many as 40,000 items. If the number of listed items exceeded 40,000, the sellers were charged an additional listing fee of $0.10 per additional item.[9] In addition to the listing fee, sellers, if they wanted to draw attention to their listing, were allowed to pay a merchandising fee, which ranged anywhere from $0.05 per item per day to $2.00 per listing. This fee enabled the seller to either promote his or her listing higher in its category or to have it stand out in boldface whenever someone did a search for it. And as in zShops, when a sale was completed, a closing fee was charged, based on the selling price of the item. If the product sold for between $0.01 and $25.00, Amazon.com collected a 5% closing fee. If the product sold between $25.01 and $1,000.00, Amazon.com collected $1.25 plus a 2.5% commission on any amount above $25. If the product sold for $1,000.01 or more, Amazon.com collected $25.63 plus a 1.25% commission on any amount above $1,000.

Amazon Web Services

As a way to help with the interaction with its zShops participants, Amazon.com offered web services, allowing merchants to use some of Amazon.com's patented technology on their own web sites. For bigger merchants, it was a way to help interact with Amazon.com regarding product descriptions and inventory availability.

Amazon.com had developed an online shopping platform that was the envy of the retail world. This platform allowed customers to store billing information and shipping addresses so that each time the customer shopped, it became a one-click process. Amazon.com used this platform to first dominate the online bookselling business and then the online music and movie product industry. When Amazon.com tried to use this platform to sell other goods for itself, such as clothing and toys, it was not as successful. Realizing that trying to sell everything to everyone by using their own fulfillment and shipping centers was a no-win situation, Amazon.com decided to license out its technology to other retailers. Amazon.com wanted to partner with national retailers that had sufficient domestic coverage so as to attain its stated motto of offering the earth's largest selection. Companies such as Target, Toys 'R' Us, Office Depot, and Circuit City decided to partner with Amazon.com. These retailers used Amazon.com's technology on their own web sites as well as offering their wares through Amazon.com's web site. This type of arrangement has worked out for all the parties involved and was something that Amazon.com would continue to do, as evidenced by its announcement of a partnership agreement with the NBA and WNBA.

Customers

Amazon.com catered to people of all ages and descriptions. Amazon.com sold a wide range of products and services that offered something for everyone. Although Amazon.com did not track the demographics of its customers, it had noticed signs that online shopping was starting to become more mainstream. This was evidenced by its best-seller lists reflecting more mainstream tastes, as opposed to its earlier days, when the best-seller titles reflected a more technological focus.[10]

Seniors

Born before or during World War II, seniors accounted for more than 12% of the U.S. population in 2002. By 2015, this age group is expected to comprise nearly 15% of the U.S. population. To entice them to buy, Amazon.com offered low prices and excellent customer service.

Baby Boomers

The baby boom generation, comprising individuals born between 1946 and 1964, constituted some 77 million Americans. In 2002, the baby boomers were in their 40s and 50s. Product lines that appealed to this category included books, home and garden products, kitchenware, and apparel.

Generation X

Generation X comprised approximately 45 million people born between 1965 and 1976. These individuals had reached adulthood in the mid-1980s, and in 2002 were in their 20s and 30s. Product lines that appealed to this category included books, kitchenware, and apparel.

Generation Y

Generation Y included individuals born between 1977 and 1994, representing about 25% of the population in 2002. Product categories that interested this group were apparel, music, books, and toys, in particular electronic games such as Xbox and PlayStation 2 games.

Customer Service

One of the reasons Amazon.com became successful was the tremendous emphasis that the company placed on customer service. From its founding, Amazon.com sought to become the earth's most customer-centric company, where customers could find and discover anything they might have wanted to buy online. Because of the empowerment of the customer, maintaining a high level of customer service was necessary. Being an Internet-only retailer made the job a lot easier. Some of the ways that Amazon.com accomplished great customer service were as follows:

1. It informed the customers, when they purchased, of the predicted and actual shipping times. On larger orders, customers were asked if they would like to wait for the entire order or have it sent piecemeal as the items were ready.
2. It allowed the customers to review products. This helped to build a sense of loyalty among its users.
3. It sent e-mails offering suggestions on other products that they may be interested in purchasing, based on past purchases.
4. By offering numerous ways to search for products (by title, subject, or author), the company made its web site very easy to use.
5. By developing and patenting cutting-edge technology such as its 1-Click Ordering process, the online shopping experience became an easy one.

By having this high level of customer service, combined with an easy-to-use web site, Amazon.com was able to differentiate itself from its competition.

Product Recommendations

As a way to promote sales, while at the same time letting customers know when a certain product was available, Amazon.com sent e-mails out to customers, stating possible recommendations. Amazon.com offered this as a way of making sure that a customer didn't miss the perfect item. Amazon.com determined a customer's interests by examining the items he or she had purchased, items the customer had told Amazom.com he or she owned, and items the customer rated; then it compared the customer's activity on the Amazon.com web site with that of other customers. Using this comparison, Amazon.com was able to recommend other items that may interest the customer. These recommended items would appear in several areas throughout the web site. If the customer needed more information about one area in particular, he or she could click the appropriate link. These recommendations would change when the customer purchased or rated a new item. Changes in the interests of other customers might also affect these recommendations. Because the recommendations would fluctuate, Amazon.com suggested that a customer add items of interest to his or her Wish List or Shopping Cart.

Share the Love

Amazon.com established the Share the Love program to get customers to recommend products to their friends. Each time a customer placed an order for books, music, DVDs, or videos with Amazon.com, the customer was given the opportunity to e-mail friends and give them an additional 10% off the items bought. (The customer selected which items and which friends.) If any of those people purchased one of these items within a week, that customer received a credit to use the next time he or she shopped at Amazon.com. This credit was equal to the dollar amount of the friend's 10% discount. For example, if the customer bought a CD for $15 and decided to Share the Love with a friend on that purchase, that friend would be able to buy the same CD for $13.50. If that friend did purchase the item, the customer would receive a credit for $1.50 (the difference) to use any time in the next 30 days. The customer was eligible to receive one credit per item shared. This was an excellent way for

Amazon.com to build loyalty among its users while offering customers the opportunity to achieve greater discounts.

A-to-Z Guarantee

When a customer bought an item from Amazon Marketplace, Auctions, and zShops sellers, Amazon.com wanted the buyer to feel safe. To address this concern, Amazon.com developed a program called A-to-Z Guarantee. This guarantee concerned the condition of the item purchased and its timely delivery. The buyer was covered as long as he or she provided payment to the seller and either the seller failed to deliver the item or the item was materially different from what was depicted in the seller's description. Buyers who purchased items using Amazon Payments were eligible to receive up to $2,500 of the purchase price, including shipping charges. If the buyer did not pay using Amazon Payments, he or she was eligible to receive up to $250 of the purchase price. Amazon.com provided this coverage at no cost to its buyers, as a demonstration of how committed it was to creating a safe buying experience.

Safe Shopping Guarantee

To address concerns raised about the theft of credit card numbers, Amazon.com started a program called Amazon.com Safe Shopping Guarantee. This guarantee offered protection to the customers while they shopped at Amazon.com so that they never had to worry about credit card safety. In addition to the use of encryption technology called Secure Sockets Layer to process customer transactions, this guarantee covered any liability on unauthorized use of a customer's credit card, up to $50, which was the legal amount a person was liable for under the Fair Credit Billing Act for fraudulent credit card transactions.

Amazon Payment Option

In order to help its loyal customers make payments when they were dealing with a zShops merchant or a seller in the Auctions section, Amazon.com developed a plan called Amazon Payments. Amazon Payments allowed an Amazon.com customer with an account to use the same credit card on file with Amazon.com to pay for other purchases. There were no additional fees involved. And by using this program, the buyer was eligible for both the A-to-z Guarantee and the Safe Shopping Guarantee. All sellers on Auctions or zShops accepted Amazon Payments.

Because it only sold its products online, Amazon.com needed to put its customers at ease when they shopped. Amazon.com had worked to develop numerous programs to accomplish this. Evidence of how successful Amazon.com has been with these customer service initiatives can be seen in the recent score it received from the American Customer Satisfaction Index (ACSI), a customer satisfaction survey. This survey is conducted annually by the National Quality Research Center at the University of Michigan Business School in partnership with the American Society of Quality and the CFI Group, an Ann Arbor, Michigan–based management-consulting group. It measures customer satisfaction when dealing with companies within certain business sectors, such as banking, retail, and e-commerce companies. In the survey conducted for the fourth quarter of 2002, Amazon.com achieved a score of 88, which was the highest ever recorded in the history of the survey.[11] Rather than rest on its laurels, however, Amazon.com was committed to do even better on the next year's survey.

Sales and Distribution

Because selling over the Internet was its only means of contact with customers, Amazon.com needed to ensure that its web site was one that its customers could easily navigate and would feel secure with. In addition to these concerns, Amazon.com had to make sure that the process of ordering an item was not difficult. Part of the way Amazon.com did this was by developing the 1-Click Ordering method, which it patented. The 1-Click Ordering method allowed its customers to store their billing and shipping information on the company's web site. Customers could choose how to pay for their purchases, such as by using credit cards, and choose among multiple shipping addresses, such as home and work. Amazon.com liked customers using this feature because with data mining software, it was able to develop profiles of a customer's buying habits that would help it to develop future product recommendations and marketing programs.

In order to make it as easy as possible for customers, online retailers such as Amazon.com offered a variety of shipping options with the major shipping companies, such as the U.S. Postal Service, UPS, and FedEx. The charges for shipping varied, depending on the level and speed of service chosen. To entice increased order amounts and to address concerns about shipping costs, most online companies, such as Amazon.com and Barnes & Noble.com, offered free shipping when customers ordered over a minimum level and chose normal shipping methods, which could take up to seven days. To help a customer track his or her purchases and determine when an order would be delivered, Amazon.com included on its web site links with their shipping companies, allowing customers to easily monitor the progress of their purchases. To address concerns with product returns, Amazon.com made available on its web site all the necessary shipping information, including mailing labels, for the customer to download and use.

Technology

Because Amazon.com was strictly an online retailer, technology played a significant role in the company's success. Amazon.com implemented numerous web site management, search, customer interaction, recommendation, transaction-processing and fulfillment services, and other systems, using a combination of proprietary technologies and commercially available, licensed technologies. Amazon.com's strategy in 2003 was to focus its development efforts on creating and enhancing the specialized, proprietary software that was unique to its business and to license or acquire commercially developed technology for other applications where available and appropriate. Amazon.com used a set of applications for accepting and validating customer orders, placing and tracking orders with suppliers, managing and assigning inventory to customer orders, and ensuring proper shipment of products to customers. Its transaction-processing systems handled millions of items, a number of different status inquiries, gift-wrapping requests, and multiple shipment methods. These systems allowed the customer to choose whether to receive single or several shipments based on availability and to track the progress of each order. These applications also managed the process of accepting, authorizing, and charging customer credit cards.

Patents and Trademarks

Amazon.com regarded its trademarks, service marks, copyrights, patents, domain names, trade dress, trade secrets, proprietary technologies, and similar intellectual property as critical to its success, and it relied on trademark, copyright, and patent law; trade-secret protection; and confidentiality and/or license agreements with its employees, customers, partners, and others to protect its proprietary rights.[12] Amazon.com had registered a number of domain names and been issued a number of trademarks, service marks, patents, and copyrights by U.S. and foreign governmental authorities. Amazon.com had also applied for the registration of other trademarks, service marks, and domain names and copyrights in the United States and internationally, and it had filed U.S. and international patent applications covering certain parts of its proprietary technology. Amazon.com had licensed in the past, and expected to license in the future, certain aspects of its proprietary rights, such as trademarks, patents, technologies, or copyrighted materials, to third parties. An example of Amazon.com's patented technology that provided a considerable competitive advantage was its 1-Click Ordering method. Amazom.com recognized that one of the biggest drawbacks to online shopping was that the speed of the purchase was slowed if each time a purchase was made, all billing and shipping information had to be entered again. To overcome this, Amazon.com developed a system in which relevant billing and shipping information about the customer was stored for future uses. Amazon.com sued and won a case against Barnes & Noble.com for violating this patent.

Encryption Technology

One of the biggest concerns online shoppers had was that their billing and credit card information were not secure and could be hacked into during the course of a transaction. To help allay this fear, Amazon.com used Secure Sockets Layer (SSL) software, an encryption technology program. This software was the industry standard and considered to be among the best software available at the time for secure online commerce transactions. It encrypted all of a customer's personal information, including credit card number, name, and address, so that it could not be read as it traveled over the Internet.

Wireless Selling Platform

Due to the widespread use of cell phones and PDAs, Amazon.com developed a stripped-down version of its main web site for customers to download and store on their cellular phones and PDAs. With the growing popularity of these devices, Amazone.com needed to address the potential for people to go online through wireless technologies.

Advertising

In order to increase brand recognition, Amazon.com, like most online retailers in 1999 and 2000, spent tremendous amounts of money on advertising. Amazon.com was willing to sacrifice short-term profits for the chance of acquiring greater market share. Because online retailing was a new way of doing business, Amazon.com felt that the best way to differentiate itself from the competition was to spend a tremendous amount of money on advertising its goods and services across all advertising media. However, due to the increasing pressure of producing an operating profit while still offering low prices and free shipping, Amazon was forced to consider cutting operating expenses, in particular advertising. By investing in more online ad activities, such as product recommendations and search engines, Amazon.com had successfully been able to cut back significantly on its marketing budget over the previous two years, as shown in **Exhibit 4**.

Television and Radio

During the 2002 holiday season, Amazon.com spent approximately $5 million on television ads making fun of the hassles of mall shopping. After reevaluating the effectiveness of its ads, Amazon.com decided to suspend all forms of television and radio advertising.

Exhibit 4 Marketing Expenses: Amazon.com (Dollar amounts in thousands)

Marketing Expenses				
2002	2001	2000	1999	1998
$125,383	$138,283	$179,980	$175,838	$67,427

Source: Amazon.com, Form 10-K (2003).

According to Amazon.com's Diego Piacentini, the company realized "that spending money on improving customer experience by dropping prices is definitely more effective than spending the same amount of money to do advertising on TV."[13]

Print

A great cost-effective way to get information out about product offerings is by using circulars, direct mail, and newspaper advertisements, particularly in Sunday newspapers. While it suspended its television advertising campaign, Amazon.com continued to use such inserts to help promote current offerings and coupons touting discounts on future purchases.

Internet

Amazon.com had successfully used the Internet to advertise itself, to both new and old customers. Through the use of data mining software programs and direct e-mail advertisements, Amazon.com was able to notify customers of products that they might be interested in purchasing. The company developed these recommendations based on the customers' prior purchases and comparisons with similar customers with the same purchasing habits. With programs such as Amazon.com Alerts, users could sign up to be notified when the latest releases of authors and artists they were interested in were made available for sale. Through deals with Internet service providers such as AOL and search engine companies such as Google, Amazon.com was able to effectively and directly market its goods and services over the Internet. By signing up more than 900,000 web sites into its Amazon.com Associates program, Amazon.com was able to advertise on a number of individual web sites at a minimal cost.

Because of the cost of running television and radio ad campaigns and concerns over the effectiveness of this type of advertising, Amazon.com focused its attention on advertising through the Internet. Through the use of data mining software programs and prior buying patterns, Amazon.com had developed extensive profiles of its customers. It used the profiles to develop a successful direct e-mail marketing program, alerting customers to items that they might be interested in. In addition, Amazon.com worked with search engine companies such as Google to make sure that its ads were prominently placed on web pages when people got the results of searches. Through its online partners, Amazon.com continually promoted its own web site and products. Because of the low cost of this type of advertising, Amazon.com used money that had previously been spent on ad campaigns to offer free shipping to its customers on many orders of $25 or more. The "buzz" from offering free shipping was better than the "buzz" from any ad campaign.

Geographic Region

Because of its online selling model, Amazon.com was available throughout the entire domestic U.S. market through its web site. Outside the United States, Amazon.com operated web sites in five international markets—Canada, France, Germany, Japan, and the United

Exhibit 5 Geographic Markets: Amazon.com

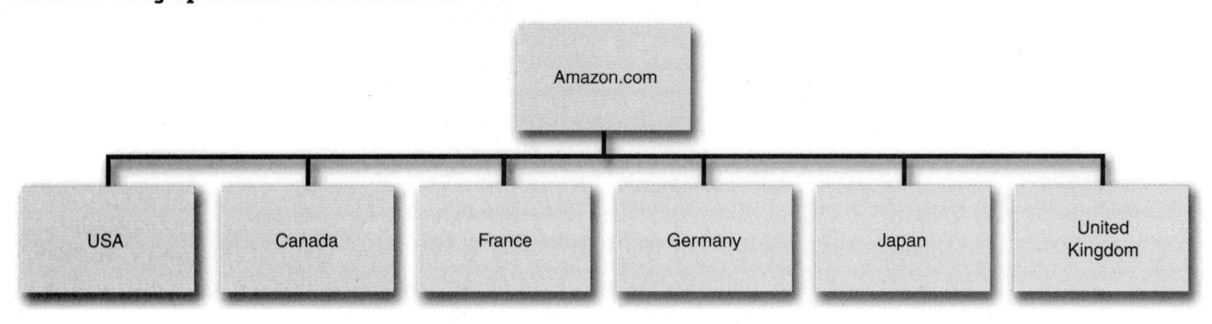

Kingdom, as shown in **Exhibit 5**. In 2002, Amazon.com was not present in any other additional international market.

Domestic

The corporate headquarters for Amazon.com was located in Seattle, Washington. Because Amazon.com conducted all its business over the Internet and did not have the need for any retail outlets, all its orders were processed through fulfillment centers. These fulfillment centers were strategically located throughout the country, to facilitate the delivery of merchandise both to Amazon.com from its distributors and to Amazon.com's customers in a timely fashion. These fulfillment sites were located in states that had low or no sales tax, to limit any potential sales tax expense for Amazon.com's customers. These U.S. centers were located in New Castle, Delaware; Coffeyville, Kansas; and Campbellsville and Lexington, Kentucky. Amazon.com continually evaluated all its real estate holdings to ensure that it had the necessary geographic coverage. In order to provide a high level of customer service, Amazon.com operated four separate customer service centers, located in the following places: Tacoma, Washington; Grand Forks, North Dakota; and Huntington, West Virginia. In addition to these centers, Amazon.com had customer service outsourcing agreements with certain vendors in India, Northern Ireland, and the United States.

International

As shown in **Exhibit 5**, the international markets in which Amazon.com conducted operations included Canada, Japan, France, Germany, and the United Kingdom. Due to the complexities of operating in foreign markets, such as local laws and customs, Amazon.com had set up a separate web site in each country. These international sites shared the common Amazon.com platform but were localized in terms of language, products, customer service, and fulfillment.

Because Amazon.com was an online retailer and did not have the need for any retail outlets, all its orders were taken over the Internet and then processed through fulfillment centers. These fulfillment centers were strategically located throughout its international markets, to facilitate the delivery of merchandise both to Amazon.com from its distributors and to Amazon.com's customers in as timely a fashion as possible. In Japan, Amazon.com outsourced its order fulfillment functions to Nippon Express, and in Canada it outsourced its order fulfillment operations to Assured Logistics. In its other international markets, Amazon.com operated local distribution centers. For these international fulfillment centers, Amazon.com leased and operated the sites in Marston Gate, United Kingdom; Orleans, France; and Bad Hersfeld, Germany.

In order to provide a high level of customer service to its international customers, Amazon.com operated customer service centers in Slough, United Kingdom; Regensburg,

Germany; and Sapporo, Japan. In addition to these centers, Amazon.com had customer service outsourcing agreements with certain vendors in India, Northern Ireland, and the United States.

Financial Position

Amazon.com's first goal was not to produce a profit but to gain market share. Management was willing to sacrifice profits for the potential for growth. As can been seen in its shareholders' deficit on the balance sheet in **Exhibit 6**, Amazon.com did exactly that. It was not until the dot-com bubble burst that Amazon.com began to focus on controlling expenses and producing an operating profit according to generally accepted accounting principles. See Amazon.com's 2002 Annual Report (at *www.amazon.com*) for complete financial statements.

Net Income

Starting in 2001, Amazon.com began to focus on increasing sales and reducing expenses so that it would be able to produce an operating profit. As is shown in **Exhibit 7**, Amazon.com was able to increase its gross profit margin in 2001 and 2002, finally showing an operating profit in 2002. Amazon.com cut advertising expenses tremendously by no longer advertising on television. The costs associated with offering free shipping were evaluated and limited to purchases over $99. However, due to pressure from other online booksellers such as Buy.com offering free shipping, Amazon.com was forced to follow suit and lowered the minimum amount of purchases needed for free shipping to most orders over $25. Despite these pressures, Amazon.com was able to generate sufficient cash to service its debt and capital obligations.

Sales Tax

One of the most important issues facing online retailers in the early 2000s was the issue of sales tax. In early 2003, there was a moratorium on the taxation of e-commerce transactions. But due to the tremendous pressure that state budgets were experiencing at the time, governments were looking for new, recurring revenue streams. The problems with the taxation of

Exhibit 6 Balance Sheet: Amazon.com (Dollar amounts in millions)

Year ending December 31	2002	2001	2000		2002	2001	2000
Cash and Cash equivalents	$ 738	$ 540	$ 822	Accounts payable	$ 618	$ 445	$ 485
Marketable securities	563	456	278	Accrued expenses	315	305	273
Inventories	202	144	175	Unearned revenue	48	88	131
Prepaid exp. + other current assets	113	68	86	Interest payable	72	68	69
Total current assets	1,616	1,208	1,361	Short term debt	13	15	17
Fixed assets, net	239	272	366	Total current liabilities	1,066	921	975
Goodwill, net	71	45	159	Long term debt	2,277	2,156	2,127
Other intangibles, net	3	34	96	Shareholders' deficit	(1,353)	(1,440)	(967)
Other assets	61	78	153	**Total liabilities and stockholders' deficit**	$1,990	$1,637	$2,135
Total Assets	$1,990	$1,637	$2,135				

Sources: Amazon.com, Annual Report (2001); Amazon.com, Form 10-K (2003); and Amazon.com, www.amazon.com (2003).

Exhibit 7
Income Statement: Amazon.com (Dollar amounts in millions)

Year ending December 31,	2002	2001	2000
Sales	$3,932.9	$3,122.4	$2,762.0
Cost of goods sold	2,858.0	2,375.0	2,105.2
Gross profit	1,074.9	747.4	656.8
Gross profit margin (%)	27.3%	23.9%	23.8%
SG&A expense[1]	881.4	848.2	997.6
Depreciation & amortization	87.8	129.9	322.8
Operating income	105.7	(230.7)	(663.6)
Operating margin (%)	2.7%	—	—
Non-operating income	(71.2)	(5.2)	(273.9)
Non-operating expense	142.9	139.2	130.9
Income before taxes	(150)	(556.7)	(1,411.4)
Income taxes	0.0	0.0	0.0
Net loss	(150)	(556.7)	(1,411.4)
Diluted earnings per share	(0.40)	(1.53)	(4.02)

Note:
1. SG&A expenses—Selling, general, and administrative expenses include all salaries, indirect production, marketing, and general corporate expenses.

Source: Hoover's Online, "Company Profiles—Amazon.com," www.hoovers.com.

online transactions had nothing to do with the charging of the tax rates. The issue had to do with how different states categorized products. A recent agreement by 33 states to simplify and help develop a consistent tax platform was pointing in the direction of taxes being levied on these transactions, so a significant competitive advantage was possibly coming to an end. However, the agreement might not succeed if the U.S. Supreme Court issued another ruling forbidding the taxation of interstate commerce by individual states.

Stock Options

As the Financial Accounting Standards Board (FASB) looked at the issue of determining whether to show employee stock options as an expense, companies such as Amazon.com worried. Part of the appeal of working for online companies was the opportunity of striking it rich through stock options. Companies had no problem with issuing the stock options because they were not an expense on the income statement. But with the issue of excessive compensation and financial gimmicks being brought to a head, the FASB was close to issuing a directive on this issue. And with a number of prominent companies such as Citicorp and Coca-Cola already agreeing to show these options as an expense, the stock options situation for Amazon.com needed to be addressed.

Management Strategy

Amazon.com's management has shown a tremendous amount of flexibility in its strategy. In Amazon.com's first years of existence, Bezos had the company solely focused on increasing market share and offering superior customer service. However, once the dot-com bubble burst, along with it Amazon.com's stock price, Bezos had to strike a balance between the company's stated goal of increasing market share and producing a profit.

Although it started out with books and moved into related fields such as movies and music, Amazon.com also wanted to continue to expand the number of products available to its customers. In 1999, by using its high stock price to fund purchases, Amazon.com invested in other online retailers, such as Drugstore.com, Homegrocer.com, and Pets.com. However, none of these formats were ever as successful as Amazon.com, and most were not able to survive the collapse of the dot-com industry in 2000. Doubts were raised in regard to Amazon.com's future survival. So Bezos changed strategies once again.

Bezos focused on proving the viability of his business model. In developing this new strategy, Bezos first had to determine what products to offer for sale and the best way to incorporate them into Amazon.com's sales model. Rather than investing and running web sites in addition to its own, as it had done in the past, Amazon.com decided to form partnerships with other retail companies to cross-sell their products on either Amazon.com's own web sites or on the partners' web sites. Bezos saw this as part of his philosophy to offer everything to everyone. Amazon has been so successful with this strategy that it was running other retailers' web sites in early 2003, earning not only a percentage of sales but also a management fee.

Bezos attempted to produce an operating profit by cutting expenses, in particular advertising expenses. He looked at eliminating the use of expensive television and radio ads and focused on the more inexpensive and personal e-mail ads and reminders. This reduction, along with other cost-saving initiatives, paid off. In the year ending December 31, 2002, Amazon.com produced its first operating profit.

Looking Toward the Future

Although Amazon.com had established itself as one of the premier online retailers in the world, pressure from increased competition, an overall poor economic environment, and the possible repeal of the sales tax exemption afforded e-commerce transactions had put pressure on Amazon.com to evaluate and possibly formulate new strategies in order to remain competitive. CEO Bezos and his management team were faced with two alternatives in order to keep the company ahead of the competition. Both alternatives focused on the services offered by Amazon.com, and both recognized the continued need to expand. However, each one had a different vision to accomplish this.

The **first alternative** was to expand Amazon.com's business in online auctions. Because of the continued need for an intermediary in these types of transactions, Amazon.com would be able to market this additional service to both its current customer base, through the use of personalized e-mails, and to new customers, through a general advertising campaign, including television and print ads.

The benefit of this alternative was that Amazon.com would be expanding on an existing service offering and would not incur any developmental or startup expenses. An additional benefit would be that by aggressively promoting this service, Amazon.com would be able to attract new visitors to its web sites, and these customers might also purchase additional goods and services, such as new books and music that Amazon.com offered.

This alternative was feasible because of the prior experience Amazon.com had developed in expanding and marketing other product lines and services. By learning from past mistakes and successes, Amazon.com would be able to formulate the correct marketing campaign to attract additional traffic to its web sites. The alternative could work because Amazon.com had become one of the premier online brands and had a large enough customer base to compete against eBay and other established online auction services such as Ubid.com and Yahoo! Auctions. In addition to its name recognition, Amazon.com would look to use its large number of customer service programs, such as Amazon Payments and Safe Shopping Guarantee, to address buyer and seller concerns about privacy, fraud, and security while also expanding the number of payment options available to both parties.

The first drawback within this alternative was that Amazon.com would be competing against its own product offerings, as well as those of its retail partners. A second drawback was the fact that it was going head-to-head with one of the few other profitable online companies, eBay. eBay had built a considerably large base of loyal customers who would possibly be reluctant to go to a competitor.

A way around the first drawback was to either set up the auction services in a separate and distinct section on the web site, away from the retail aspect, or set up a new web address for this service line. A way around the second drawback was for Amazon.com to market itself as a less expensive alternative to eBay, setting its pricing structure at a level that was lower than eBay's.

The **second alternative** was to develop and implement a business-to-business (B2B) exchange for suppliers, manufacturers, distributors, and retailers to use. Because the largest percentage of e-commerce sales resulted from transactions conducted on B2B exchanges, this opened up a large potential market for Amazon.com to expand into.

The benefit of this alternative was that Amazon.com could easily market this service to its large number of affiliates and partners that it conducted business with. Having its partners' suppliers and distributors participate in this online exchange would allow their affiliates to achieve greater operational efficiencies in their supply chain. These efficiencies would translate into lower prices for Amazon.com. A second additional benefit for Amazon.com would be the steady cash flow it would receive through the charging of hosting fees and commissions on completed transactions.

This alternative was feasible because Amazon.com would use its past experiences and patented technology to develop a secure, easy-to-use platform that its customers would be comfortable with. It was also feasible because of the large number of midsize to small companies that did not have the necessary capital to develop or run their own exchanges but wished to participate in these auctions in order to increase their own sales and market coverage. This alternative could win against the competition because these additional offerings would be available to all companies—not just companies from one specific industry, which most existing B2B exchanges did (for example, Covisint in the automotive industry). And because Amazon.com would only be acting as an intermediary with these exchanges, costs would be kept to a minimum because Amazon.com would only be the host of the exchange and would not have to hold any inventory.

The drawback to this was that Amazon.com would be entering a business that would require more intense customer service than its other lines of business. This was due to the high dollar amounts of the transactions, as well as the issue of product specifications. An additional drawback would be the issue of payment processing and concerns with the shipping and receiving of goods.

A way around the first drawback was to assign specific customer service personnel to each exchange category. By having an assigned customer service representative handle all aspects of the exchange transaction, Amazon.com's employees would be able to build an excellent relationship with the involved parties, which would help to address any issues that might occur. The way around the second drawback could be broken down into two categories. First, Amazon.com would use its escrow payment service to hold all monies until the goods were received and all parties were satisfied. To help address shipping concerns, Amazon.com, because of its relationship with shipping companies, could negotiate discounted deals with them for their exchange partners to use.

Both alternatives seemed to make sense. They both seemed to have advantages and disadvantages. Both offered ways to increase sales and market share while staying ahead of the competition. Bezos and his management team decided to study both alternatives further, especially within present financial situations, as well as other alternatives in other strategic areas, in order to decide which would be most appropriate.

Notes

1. H. Green, "Retail: The Cart Is Half Full," *BusinessWeek*, No. 3815 (January 13, 2003), pp. 124–125.
2. Hoover's Online, *Company Profiles—Amazon.com*, *www.hoovers.com.* IRS, *www.irs.gov.*
3. R. Spector, *Amazon.com—Get Big Fast* (New York, NY: HarperCollins Publishers, Inc., 2000)
4. Amazon.com, *www.amazon.com.*
5. R. D. Hof, "Q & A: Jeff Bezos: Amazon.com," *BusinessWeek*, No. 3631 (May 31, 1999), p. 137.
6. R. Saunders, *Business the Amazon.com Way* (Milford, CT: Capstone Publishing Limited, 1999).
7. M. Warner, "Can Amazon Be Saved?" *Fortune*, Vol. 144, No. 11 (November 25, 2001), pp. 156–158.
8. Amazon.com, *www.amazon.com.*
9. Ibid.
10. M. Totty, "E-Commerce: Selling Strategies—Demographics: The Masses Have Arrived . . . And E-Commerce Will Never Be the Same," *The Wall Street Journal* (January 27, 2003), p. R8.
11. American Customer Satisfaction Index (ACSI), *www.theacsi.org.*
12. Amazon.com, Form 10-K (2003).
13. N. Wingfield, "eBay Earnings More Than Double—A Surge in Revenue Results from Purchase of PayPal, Big Gains in Core Business," *The Wall Street Journal* (April 23, 2003), p. B7.

References

Amazon.com, Annual Report (2001).

G. Anders and R. Quick, "Amazon.com Files Suit Over Patent on 1-Click Against Barnesandnoble.com," *The Wall Street Journal* (October 25, 1999), p. B18.

Barnes & Noble.com, Form 10-K (2003).

Barnes & Noble.com, *www.barnesandnoble.com.*

C. Bialik, "E-Commerce: B2B—Advertising: Sell First, Advertise Later," *The Wall Street Journal* (October 21, 2002), p. R11.

D. Brady, "How Barnes & Noble Misread the Web," *BusinessWeek*, No. 3667 (February 7, 2000), p. 63.

R. Clarke, "Electronic Data Interchange (EDI): An Introduction," *Business Credit*, Vol. 103, No. 9 (October 2001), pp. 23–25.

J. C. Cooper and K. Madigan, "A Lasting Postwar Surge Will Hinge on the Labor Markets," *BusinessWeek*, No. 3829 (April 21, 2003), pp. 31–32.

E. D. Cordy, "The Legal Regulation of E-Commerce Transactions," *Journal of American Academy of Business*, Vol. 2, No. 2 (March 2003).

J. C. Dooren, "Retail Sales Increase Sharply As Customer Confidence Rises," *The Wall Street Journal* (April 14, 2003), p. A2.

eBay, *www.ebay.com.*

"Amazon Settles Suit Against Online Rival over Buying Shortcut," *The Wall Street Journal* (March 8, 2002), p. B5.

B. Elgin, L. Himelstein, R. Grover, and H. Green, "Inside Yahoo!" *BusinessWeek*, No. 3733 (May 21, 2001), pp. 114–123.

B. Elgin, "Can Yahoo Make 'em Pay? The Net Portal's Turnaround Reaches a Critical Pass," *BusinessWeek*, No. 3798 (September 9, 2002), pp. 92–94.

B. Elgin, "Two Cheers for Yahoo!" *BusinessWeek*, No. 3817 (January 27, 2003) p. 44.

B. Elgin, "Can Yahoo! Make the Bounce Last?" *BusinessWeek*, No. 3820 (February 17, 2003), p. 41.

B. Garrity, "Amazon Now Powering Virgin's Retail Site," *Billboard Magazine,* Vol. 114, No. 27 (July 6, 2002), p. 55.

R. Gavin, "E-Commerce (A Special Report): The Rules—Rules & Regs," *The Wall Street Journal* (January 27, 2003), p. R10.

R. Gold, "E-Commerce: The Rules—Rules & Regs," *The Wall Street Journal* (December 9, 2002), p. R6.

E. Goodridge, "Yahoo's Not Just for Customers Anymore," *InformationWeek,* No. 80 (March 18, 2002), pp.106–108.

R. Greenspan, "Surfing with Seniors and Boomers," *Cyberatlas*, *www. clickz.com/stats/sectors/demographics/article.ph/157-621* (January 23, 2003).

C. Guglielmo, "Don't Write Off Barnes & Noble," *Upside*, Vol. 12, No. 6 (June 2000).

L. Himelstein, "Q&A: Meg Whitman: eBay," *BusinessWeek*, No. 3631 (May 31, 1999), pp. 134–135.

L. Himelstein and G. Khermouch, "Webvan Left the Basics on the Shelf," *BusinessWeek*, No. 3742 (July 23, 2001), p. 43.

R. Hof and M. Roman, "Pets.com: Putting a Sock in It," *BusinessWeek*, No. 3708 (November 20, 2000).

R. D. Hof, "eBay Rules: The Online Marketplace Thrives in Good Times and Bad," *BusinessWeek,* No. 3825A (March 25, 2003), p. 172.

R. D. Hof, "The People's Company," *BusinessWeek,* No. 3760 (December 3, 2001), pp. EB14–EB21.

M. Janofsky, "Deep Cuts Have Not Closed Deficit in Many States, Report Says," *New York Times* (April 26, 2003), p. A20.

F. Keenan, S. Holmes, J. Greene, and R. O. Crockett, "A Mass Market of One," *BusinessWeek,* No. 3810 (December 2, 2002), pp. 68–72.

D. Kirkpatrick, "In the Hands of Geeks, Web Advertising Actually Works," *Fortune*, Vol. 147, No. 7 (April 14, 2003), p. 388.

T. Kontzer, "Amazon's E-Commerce Technology Is on Target," *Information Week*, No. 902 (August 19, 2002), p. 22.

D. J. Lipke, "Mystery Shoppers," *American Demographics*, Vol. 22, No. 12 (December 2000), pp. 41–43.

J. Maness, "Using Pricing Optimization," *Chain Store Age*, Vol. 9, No. 1 (January 2003), p. 109.

T. J. Mullaney, "The Web Is Finally Catching Profits," *BusinessWeek*, No. 3820 (February 17, 2003), p. 68.

S. Patton, "Barnesandnoble.com Settles for Lower Shelf," *CIO*, Vol. 16, No. 4 (November 15, 2002), pp. 64–65.

M. Prior, "eBay Acquires PayPal for $1.5B on Eve of Strong 2Q Report," *DSN Retailing Today*, Vol. 41, No. 14 (July 29, 2002), p. 8.

R. Quick, "Barnes & Noble and Its Online Sibling Enter Alliance Linking Bricks and Clicks," *The Wall Street Journal* (October 27, 2000), p. B10.

S. Reyes, "Tapping Girl Power," *Brandweek*, Vol. 43, No. 16 (April 22, 2002), pp. 26–30.

S. Shepard, "A Talk with Meg Whitman," *BusinessWeek*, No. 3724 (March 19, 2001), pp. 98–99.

J. Soat, "Ah, Spring! Love, Basketball and Taxes," *Information Week*, No. 934 (April 7, 2003), p. 82.

Standard & Poor's, "Retailing: Specialty," *http://netadvantage.standardpoor.com*.

J. Tessler, "E-Commerce: The Basics—Small Investment, Big Results: Entrepreneurs Need Very Little Money—Or Technical Know-how—To Launch a Web Business," *The Wall Street Journal* (November 22, 1999), p. R16.

M. Totty, "E-Commerce: Selling Strategies—So Much Information and So Much Confusion on What It All Means," *The Wall Street Journal* (December 9, 2002), p. R4.

M. Totty, "E-Commerce: The Rules—Regulations: Taming the Frontier—The Internet Was Going to Be a Place Without Rules, Without Borders; A Place Where Anything Goes; Well, Guess What Happened," *The Wall Street Journal* (January 27, 2003), p. R10.

D. Tynan, "The Rebirth of Online Advertising," *Chief Executive*, No. 185 (January/February 2003), pp. 13–14.

UCLA Center for Communication Policy, *Surveying the Digital Future—Year Three*, *www.ccp.ucla.edu/pages/internet-report.asp*.

U.S. Census Bureau, Department of Commerce, *www.census.gov*.

E. White, "Web, Direct Mail Get Larger Share of Marketers' Pie," *The Wall Street Journal* (December 18, 2002), p. B2.

L. Windham and K. Orton, *The Soul of the New Customer* (New York, NY: Allworth Press, 2000).

N. Wingfield, "eBay Conceding Missteps, Will Close Its Site in Japan," *The Wall Street Journal* (February 27, 2002), p. B4.

N. Wingfield, "E-Commerce (A Special Report): Selling Strategies—Delivery—Click and . . . Drive?" *The Wall Street Journal* (July 15, 2002), p. R11.

N. Wingfield, "TV Advertising: Why Web Firms Love It, Hate It," *The Wall Street Journal* (April 24, 2003), p. B1.

Yahoo! Form 10-K (2003).

Yahoo! *www.yahoo.com*.

J. G. S. Yang and W. W. Poon, "Taxable Base of Internet Commerce," *Journal of State Taxation*, Vol. 20, No. 4 (Spring 2002), pp. 70–80.

A. Yegyazarian, "Sales Taxes Hit the Web," *PC World*, Vol. 21, No. 3 (March 2003), p. 34.

CASE 14

Google: An Internet Search Service Company

Joseph Teye-Kofi, Robert J. Mockler, and Marc Gartenfeld

In February of 2005, almost six months after Google's initial public offering (IPO) of stock, CEO Eric Schmidt announced the need to develop an effective company-wide strategy in order to brace for the next level of services and products Google wanted to offer to stay ahead of the competition. In the last quarter of 2004, Google's operating income totaled $321 million, versus $322 million for nine-year-old eBay and $260 million for 10-year-old Yahoo. As an industry market share leader, the overall task at hand was to develop an effective differentiating enterprise-wide strategy especially for the company's Internet search segment, enabling Google to survive and prosper against aggressive competition in the intermediate and long-term future.

The company generated revenue by delivering relevant, cost-effective online advertising. Businesses used the company's AdWords program to promote their products and services with targeted advertising. In addition, the thousands of third-party web sites that made up the Google Network used the Google AdSense program to deliver relevant ads that generated revenue and enhanced the user's experience.

As shown in **Exhibit 1,** Google had many tools and provided many services. Here, common terminologies in Internet search are defined for clarity. A web browser is a program used for displaying and viewing pages on the World Wide Web. A search engine is computer software that compiles lists of documents, most commonly those on the World Wide Web, and the contents of those documents. A blog is an easy-to-use web site, where people can quickly post thoughts and interact with other people, and more. Browser buttons let the user search the Internet simply by highlighting a word (or phrase) on any web page and clicking the Google Search button.

This case was prepared was prepared by Joseph Teye-Kofi, MBA student at St. John's University, under the direction of Dr. Robert J. Mockler and Professor Marc Gartenfeld of St. John's University. Dr. Mockler and Professor Gartenfeld revised and edited this case. This case was reprinted from *Cases in Domestic and Multinational Strategic Management,* Publication (VIII) #44, pp. C5-1 thru C5-21, edited by Robert J. Mockler and Marc Gartenfeld. The copyright holders are solely responsible for the case content. This case was edited for SMBP–11th edition.

Exhibit 1
Google's Tools and Services

Tools	Services
Blogger	Alerts
Browser Buttons	Answers
Desktop Search	Catalogs
Google In Your Language	Images
Picasa Photo Organizer	News Search
Google Tool Bar	Internet search
Translate Tool	Wireless

As for tools, Google's desktop search allowed users to find email, files, web history, and online chat on their computers offline. It allowed users to instantly view web pages, even when not online. Adding Google Browser Buttons to a personal toolbar granted access to Google's search technology, without taking up extra screen space. "Google in Your Language" was a tool that intended to use volunteers to translate all of the world's languages into a database that could be utilized by users of the service. Picasa Photo Organizer was a free software download from Google that helped users instantly find, edit, and share all the pictures on a personal computer.

As for services, Google alerts were email updates of the latest relevant Google results (web, news, etc.) based on users' choice of query or topic. With Google Answers, more than 500 carefully screened analysts in various fields of study were ready to answer questions online for as little as $2.50, usually within 24 hours. Google Catalogs allowed patrons to search and browse mail-order catalogs from various companies online. Google Image Search allowed users to search for images online. Just type in the name of the image and a vast array of specific images were displayed as requested.

Google News allowed users access to more than 4,500 local and international news sources, updated continuously. Google's wireless adaptable search technology could be accessed from any number of devices, such as mobile phones and Palm VII handhelds. Whatever the language or platform, Google let users search the web with ease, speed, and accuracy.

Google's main strength was the fact that it had established itself using superior Internet search technology. It had also made phenomenal strides in the international arena. Moreover, the company's successful IPO gave it the financial leverage needed to expand and easily become a large, independent web portal. A portal or portal site is a computing home site for a web browser. Portals are Internet hubs, more like Grand Central station, that serve as a connection or link to other places that might be of interest to web users. Google's raw materials were the technical proficiency and innovativeness of its employees. The question remained whether or not Google should continue primarily as an Internet search engine or morph into a large web portal.

Google's major weakness was the fact that there were virtually no switching costs in the industry, and Internet search users would try another search engine if they did not find what they were looking for using Google's search technologies. Microsoft's next version of the windows system, code-named "Longhorn" and slated for release in 2006, as "VISTA," presented a potential threat to Google's services. Microsoft's Vice President was quoted as saying, "Google is a very nice system but compared to my vision, it is pathetic."[1] Moreover, Microsoft had all the funding it needed and, if it focused on Internet search technology, was bound to vanquish many big players in the Internet search segment. The main problem to be resolved was how to further differentiate Google's Internet search segment from its competition and to achieve a winning edge over competitors within intensely competitive, rapidly changing immediate, intermediate, and long-term time frames.

Exhibit 2 provides a list of Internet terminology and concepts.

Exhibit 2 A Glossary of Some Relevant Common Internet Technology Concepts/ Terminology

A. General

A **web page** is a location on the World Wide Web: a computer file, encoded in hypertext markup language [HTML] and containing text, graphics files, and sound files, that is accessible through the World Wide Web. Every web page has a unique Uniform Resource Locator URL, or address. For example, when users type `www.stjohns.edu` into an Internet Explorer address bar and press **"enter,"** the page that is displayed would be Saint John's University's web page.

A **toolbar** is a row of icons on a computer screen that are clicked on to perform certain frequently used functions. For example, when I click the printer icon on a computer screen, I convey to the computer my intentions to print that page's contents.

Web hosting is the business of supplying server space for storage of web sites on the Internet, and sometimes the provision of ancillary services such as Web site creation and development. Most portals offer this service. Businesses that intend to grow and market their products and services over the Internet patronize this service, offered mostly by large web portals such as Yahoo and MSN.

After a company is formed, it normally develops a web site under its business name and engages in some form of publicity campaign to attract customers to its web site. It needs space to store the information and communication that ensues from day-to-day transactions on its web site. The more established large portals offer the service of handling a smaller company's storage needs using their servers for a fee.

A **web server** is a computer that stores web documents and makes them available to the rest of the world. A server may be dedicated, meaning its sole purpose is to be a web server, or non-dedicated, meaning it can be used for basic computing in addition to acting as a server.

A **desktop** is a graphical computer representation of an office desk: a visible portion of a software program that forms a background on which icons representing equipment, programs, and files are displayed.

B. Search Services

A **search engine** is a *computer program* that searches for particular keywords and returns a list of documents in which they were found, especially a commercial service that scans documents on the Internet. For example, a web user types "Iraq" in a Google search pane and presses **"enter."** Google's search engine (mathematical algorithms program) scans the entire Internet database for any document containing the word "Iraq" and returns links to these documents in an order based on frequency of the word "Iraq" as it appears in the documents. By definition, therefore, every Internet search company has its own unique search engine (program). The list of responses on a Google "Iraq" search would, therefore, differ from Yahoo search results, which would also differ from AOL search results or Ask Jeeves search results.

A **browser** is computer software that allows an Internet user to search for information on the World Wide Web. It is the vehicle that allows you to travel from one web page to the other just by typing the web address.

A **web browser** is a program used for displaying and viewing pages on the World Wide Web. It is the actual framework that allows all Internet users to see web pages in a particular window.

Spyware is a general term for a program that surreptitiously monitors a user's actions. Although spyware is sometimes sinister, as with a remote control program used by a hacker, software companies have been known to use spyware to gather data about customers. The practice is generally frowned on.

A **pop-up** is an ad that displays in a new browser window. Pop-up windows come in many different shapes and sizes, typically in a scaled-down browser window with only the Close, Minimize, and Maximize commands. Some web surfers strongly resent

Exhibit 2
(Continued)

pop-up ads. Marketers often do not realize the ill-will generated by pop-ups because it is easier to click the "close" button than send an email to complain.

A **portal** or **portal site** is a computing home site for a web browser on the Internet. It is a web site that provides links to information and other web sites. By industry standards, Google is not yet considered a portal. A portal is a much larger and more comprehensive web site because of its extensive links to other equally extensive web pages with different functions. It is the entrance to a maze of related and unrelated web sites. Portals aggregate information from multiple sources into one web-based entry point. Yahoo, MSN, and AOL are considered Internet portals because, aside from the Internet search services they provide, they offer a range of other services not related to search: Web hosting and storage, finance, mail, sports, publishing, personal communications, auto, shopping, and maps and driving directions are but a fraction of the services portals provide.

A **web crawler** is a program used to search through pages on the World Wide Web in order to locate documents containing a particular set of words, a phrase, or a topic. It is tool used by Internet search companies to produce search results.[2]

Source: MSN 2005. "MSN" (online) http://finance.yahoo.com. Accessed March 27, 2005.

Membership Services

The large Internet search companies such as AOL, MSN, and Yahoo were beginning to channel a lot of effort toward maintaining and developing their Internet search capabilities to match Google's current Internet search supremacy. These large companies already had a lot of non–search related member services in place and would enjoy a big advantage if they were able to successfully utilize the information in their large membership database—including email accounts, personals (groups and online dating services), and fantasy sports—to help them advertise to their members based on specific responses to previously asked questions. Google electronically scanned the contents of its Gmail service letters and placed relevant ads based on keywords contained in the letter beside the email once it was opened to be read by a Gmail service member. (Gmail was Google's name for its email service.) The main key to success here remained how to successfully convince members that the confidentiality of their personal information would not be compromised or shared with other marketing entities such as telemarketers.

Competition

The main competitors of Google in Internet search technology were MSN, Yahoo, and AOL. Competition was fierce in this segment for two reasons. First, a great deal of revenue was being generated by the Internet search companies, and the major Internet service providers had been awakened by Google's rise to fame and its ability to generate revenue from ads placed next to its search results. Even though MSN, AOL, and Yahoo offered many other services, they trailed Google in market share and, most importantly, user loyalty, brand identity, and easy name recognition when it came to Internet search. These four big companies all provided search services, but Google was by far the most popular. The other three companies were, however, bigger and offered more variety in non-search Internet services. This was the reason some analysts referred to these relatively bigger companies as Internet portals. The key to the future of Internet search rested with the company that was best able to register its patrons and to successfully utilize that information to advertise even more effectively.

Second, it was difficult to predict the direction in which the Internet search segment was heading with regard to innovation. Every competitor in this segment was trying to be more innovative in search solutions, because quality search results guaranteed customer loyalty and its accompanying advertising dollars.

Yahoo

Yahoo Inc. together with its consolidated subsidiaries was a global Internet brand. The company provided Internet services that were essential and relevant to users and businesses through the provision of online properties to Internet users and a range of tools and marketing solutions for businesses to market to that community of users. The company was focused on extending the marketing platform and access to Internet users beyond the Yahoo Network through the distribution network of third-party entities (affiliates) that had integrated the sponsored search offerings into their web sites. Many of the services offered were free to users. It provided services that allowed businesses to list information on properties on the Yahoo Network. The offerings to users and businesses fell into three categories: Search and Marketplace; Information and Content; and Communications and Consumer Services.

Yahoo placed second to Google in the number of people who utilized search services and was far ahead of the competition when it came to all other Internet services such as email, shopping, online personals, and travel. The opportunity for success was for companies to offer newer and more innovative services in order to build a solid membership base that could be utilized for directory-linked target advertising. Directory-linked target advertising, the future of Internet search's continued revenue generation, first had to overcome its most demanding test of ensuring confidentiality and preventing identity theft. Yahoo had an advantage because it had a huge registered membership already in place owing to the services it offered such as email, auto information, shopping, and driving directions. On the other hand, Yahoo had weaknesses when it came to linking its search engine to an already established information source such as the online *Britannica* encyclopedia, and it also did not have a platform for online auctions.

Yahoo efficiently offered business services such as domain name registration, web site design and development, and web hosting for small and new businesses. This represented a great source of additional revenue. However, Yahoo was relatively weak with regard to assuring registered service members of the confidentiality and security of the personal information they shared with the company. Also, Yahoo was not considered a dominant force in Internet search technology. For the fiscal year ended December 31, 2004, Yahoo's revenues totaled $3.57 billion, up from $1.63 billion. Net income totaled $839.6 million, up from $237.9 million. Results reflected increased marketing services, fees and listings sales results from growth in Yahoo's organic sales and acquisitions and higher investment gains.[3]

AOL

Time Warner Inc. (Time Warner) was a media and entertainment company. It classified its businesses into five fundamental areas: America Online (AOL), consisting principally of interactive services; Cable, consisting principally of interests in cable systems providing video, high-speed data, and digital phone services; Filmed Entertainment, consisting principally of feature film, television, and home video production and distribution; Networks, consisting principally of cable television and broadcast networks; and Publishing, consisting principally of magazine and book publishing. AOL was a subsidiary of Time Warner Inc. It specialized in Internet services provision and more recently began to focus on Internet search services as an additional revenue source. In the Internet search segment, AOL ranked fourth behind Google, Yahoo, and MSN with regard to volume of Internet search patrons.[4]

AOL's strengths were the variety of services it provided. These included online dating services, email services, Internet service provision, news, and sports. The services it provided such as instant messaging allowed it to successfully register all its patrons. This broad membership base could be the needed catalyst for future advertising in the Internet search segment. In addition, AOL had established a very secure web site with virus protection and spam blocking controls for its Internet service subscribers. AOL's international image and popularity remained an Achilles heel. The company, because of its inability to effectively market to non-AOL Internet service subscribers, was not popular outside of the United States and Canada. Moreover, the company's search service was not a dominant one in the Internet search segment when compared to the leading search companies. For the fiscal year ended December 31, 2004, revenues rose 6% to $42.1 billion. Net income from continuing operations and before accounting change rose 2% to $3.21 billion. Results reflected higher worldwide license fees from television series, partially offset by legal reserves expense.[5]

MSN

Microsoft Corporation developed, manufactured, licensed, and supported a wide range of software products for various computing devices. The company's software products included scalable operating systems for servers, personal computers (PCs), and intelligent devices; server applications for client/server environments; information worker productivity applications; business solutions applications; software development tools; and mobile and embedded devices. Microsoft provided consulting services and product support services and trained and certified system integrators and developers. The company sold the Xbox video game console, along with games and peripherals. Its online businesses included the MSN subscription and the MSN network of Internet products and services. The company's seven product segments were Client, Server and Tools, Information Worker, Microsoft Business Solutions, MSN, Mobile and Embedded Devices, and Home and Entertainment.

The MSN network was a subsidiary of Microsoft Corporation and offered Internet services based on membership subscription for emails, online personals, shopping, etc. Recently MSN linked its search engine to its online Encarta encyclopedia software, which was a virtual database of information updated regularly. MSN had the financial backing of Microsoft Corporation and openly expressed its intentions of improving and taking the Internet search business to a new level. MSN also offered business solutions and web page design and development for small new businesses. On the other hand, the company's inability to mount a platform for online auctions and its ineptitude in the sale and distribution of still images and other multimedia products counted as areas that needed improvement. In addition, the company would be able to strongly capture market share only if it was able to bundle very effective search software into Microsoft's Windows computer program without raising any anti-trust concerns.

The company gained prominence when it introduced software that made both business and home computing a breeze for even the most reluctant to embrace computer technology. More recently, it seemed to be losing its technological luster and innovativeness when compared to Google. A key to success would be to successfully recruit technically proficient workers, especially in Internet search technology, and to stop the exodus of its workforce to Google. MSN could also boost its Hotmail email service membership by increasing free storage limits to at least 1 gigabyte, because Yahoo was about to offer 1 gigabyte email storage for its members and Google was already offering 2 gigabytes for its exclusive Gmail service members. For the six months ending December 31, 2004, revenues rose 9% to $20.01 billion. Net income rose 44% to $5.99 billion. Results reflected continued improvements in overall Internet technology spending and lower research and development costs.[6]

The Company

Google was founded in 1998 by Larry Page and Sergey Brin, PhD students at Stanford University who were fed up with the existing Internet search technology companies and their inability to return accurate search results. Google was basically an online company that specialized in developing a reliable Internet search engine. Of all the applications on today's computers, one could argue that the search engine was second in importance only to the web browser (such as Internet Explorer or Mozilla Firefox). This trend reflected the importance of Google as a service provider to the computer services industry.

Google Inc. offered highly targeted advertising solutions, global Internet search solutions through its own destination Internet site, and intranet solutions via an enterprise search appliance. In other words, the company maintained an online index of web sites and other content, which it made available to anyone with an *Internet connection.* Its automated search technology helped people obtain nearly instant access to relevant information from its vast online index. In providing an avenue for search, the company also furnished ads based on keywords in a search inquiry beside the search results.[1]

The company provided an interface for more than 88 languages, and half of Google.com's traffic originated outside the United States. This clearly demonstrated a trend of international popularity and the fact that the company was satisfying an important need in the Internet jungle, where users needed a guide as to where to go looking for specific information, saving time in the process.

Most of Google's revenue came from advertising. This was done through Google AdWords, which was based on an auction system. An advertiser would bid on relevant words, and the placement of the ads was based on the bids. A big benefit for the advertiser was it paid nothing unless a user clicked on its ad. In other words, Google pursued a "performance-oriented" method of advertising. This meant that very little was wasted in terms of advertising dollars spent. Again, the ad system was based on simplicity. There were no flashy ads; instead, the ads were text-based. As a result, an advertiser did not have to spend much time creating an ad campaign. It was also easier for the advertiser to flexibly change ads based on effectiveness. Actually, it took only about 15 minutes to set up an ad campaign at an initial cost of $5.[7] The Google AdWords system had a powerful self-management system. An advertiser could easily adjust a campaign in terms of budgets: They could set a limit on how much they could pay to have their ads posted in a given time frame.

Exhibit 3 shows a detailed description of Google's business model. Each section focuses on strengths and weaknesses in key success areas.

Exhibit 3
Business Model: Google, Inc.

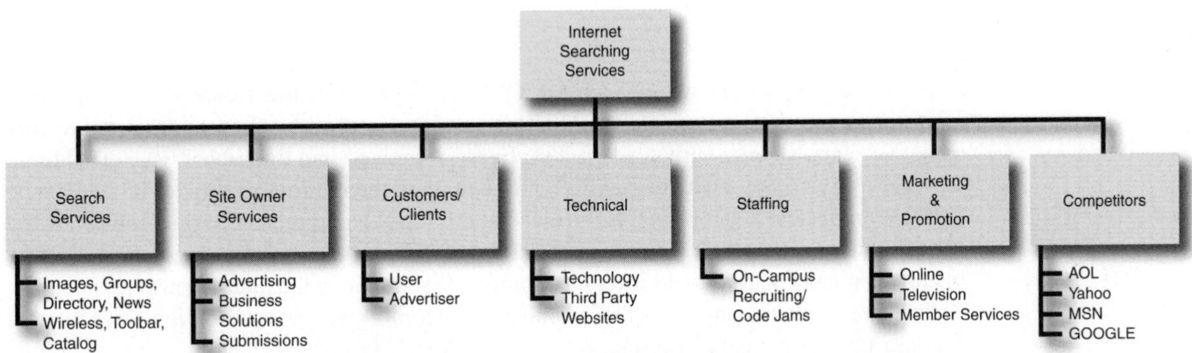

Search Services

Google had developed a broad range of innovative search solutions. Internet search service was the core service from which additional services related to search branched off. Consumers patronized all the additional services even though Google's revenue was solely generated from Internet search services. The company generated all its revenues from selling ads that were placed beside its search results. Google charged its advertisers an undisclosed amount of money any time an ad that was related to a search inquiry was clicked by an Internet search user. The ad clicked did not have to generate a sale for Google to get paid: a phenomenon in Internet search advertising known as "cost per click" pricing. Google had built a financial powerhouse selling ads this way. More recently, the company announced a big change in how it was going to sell ads. Google was going to allow advertisers more control over where their ads appeared online and how the ads were priced. The company would allow advertisers to use flashier animated graphics. The move, which applied to thousands of other web sites (third party) that used Google's search technology, was designed to attract more big-name advertisers and was intended to help Google better tap budgets for advertising of product brands, which represented the bulk of U.S. ad spending.[8]

Images

Google Images contained an index of 425 million still images. With Google Images, for example, a user typed "red sports car" in the Images search pane and pressed "enter." A few seconds later more than a thousand pictures of red sports cars would be made available for the user to choose from. Industry experts predicted a strong demand for multimedia search, given the spread of technology for producing, sharing, and storing digital media files. Images were a strong area for Google because the main competitors had not developed a strong buzz as far as images. With the exception of Yahoo, Google was the automatic choice for images.

Groups

With Google Groups, Google.com users could search for a discussion topic and add postings to a newsgroup. Google acquired the Usenet discussion service from Deja.com, including its archive of more than 500 million postings dating back to 1981. However, Yahoo was more advanced and had many patrons in groups and online personals. Yahoo had several million registered patrons who used its platform for online topic discussions and posting blogs.

Directory

Google used its unique search technology to arrange, by subject category, 1.5 million Uniform Resource Locators (URLs) that had been identified by thousands of volunteers using Netscape's Open Directory project. Every web page had a unique URL, or address. Directory service was a way of classifying or listing all the millions of articles in the Google database into subject categories. AOL, Yahoo, and MSN had directory services. There were not many opportunities for revenue generation with this service on its own; it was just a way of attracting more patrons to discover other profitable services. In the future, however, directory-linked target advertising held the promise of becoming the next direction for effective Internet advertising and marketing.

News

Google News, started in early 2004, was compiled from 4,500 news sources worldwide. Google News employed computer algorithms to identify the most relevant stories within a topic area, then, by story, grouped links to different news sources, allowing users to see how different journalists covered the stories. This service summed up the most-read news articles for busy people who could not sift through volumes of news articles daily. Yahoo's news service could be described as more comprehensive and a leader in this area, which was not a strong service for Google.

Google Wireless

Google's wireless search technology translated web pages into a language understood by handheld devices. Licensees included Sprint PCS, Cingular, Nextel, Bell Mobility (Canada), Yahoo Everywhere, Vizzavi, and Palm. This technology allowed cell-phone and handheld device subscribers to the companies just mentioned the ability to use Google search if they had wireless access to the World Wide Web. The promise of licensing patented technology and intellectual property to other companies needed to be encouraged and developed.

Google Toolbar

Google's downloadable toolbar could be embedded permanently in a user's web browser. In addition to an Internet search box, the Google Toolbar included tools for blocking pop-up ads, automatically filling out web page forms, and creating "blog" postings pointing to a web page (see **Exhibit 4**). Blogs, short for "web logs," were diaries in web page form that presented personal thoughts on almost any topic. In early 2003, Google had acquired Pyra Labs and its web site, Blogger.com, which offered tools for creating web logs. Being able to successfully propagate Google's toolbar on web browsers would be a step in the right direction because Internet search users would not have to go to Google.com to initiate a search query.

Google Catalog

Google's Catalog Search, a beta service started in early 2004, allowed users to search hundreds of print mail-order catalogs not previously available online. The catalogs were scanned, analyzed, and indexed by Google. The company was a pioneer in this area because none of the major competitors—AOL, MSN, and Yahoo—offered this service. This was a very useful service for prospective advertisers, because most patrons of this service had a commercial motivation. A key to success would be to reach an agreement with the companies whose catalogs were indexed to pay a fee to Google any time a sale was finalized through Google catalogs. The online catalog idea was an opportunity to begin collecting

Exhibit 4
Google's Toolbar Embedded in Microsoft's Internet Explorer Web Browser.

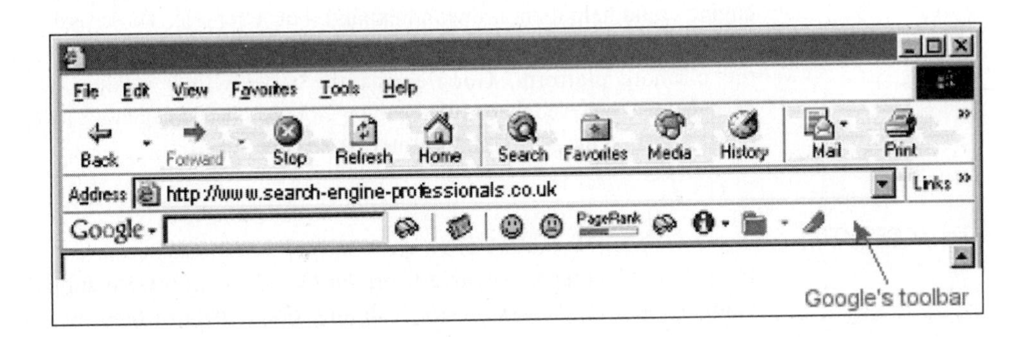

information on products and services that most companies that advertised with Google carried. This information, in the long run, could be used to enhance the quality of directory-linked target ads that were placed next to search results because it would incorporate almost everything in the inventory of advertisers and increase revenues for both Internet search companies and search engines. In addition, the transparency of advertising packages offered and a clear-cut pricing policy were keys to success for Internet search companies.

Site Owner Services

Site owner service referred to a platform that Internet search companies and large Internet services companies used to invite potential advertisers to the variety of advertising packages they offered. It represented a grand standpoint for a web-based company to stake its claim to being in a unique position to help businesses advertise and help them reach a larger audience. This was the link reserved for potential advertisers looking to do business with an Internet search service company such as Google. Google's reluctance to incorporate multimedia banner ads and colorful animated graphics on its home page did not serve as an effective way of letting prospective advertisers get a visual image of Google's advertising packages, because colorful graphics tend to make a better impression.

Advertising

Businesses that intended to advertise beside Google's search results used this link to determine whether Google's offered advertising package was the right choice for their business. A business owner would access this link in order to open a business account as a potential advertiser with Google. Advertising under Site Owner Services was a link reserved only for businesses who intended to do business with Google. For example, Google's AdWords was cost-per-click advertising. Advertisers paid only when users clicked on an ad. It had features that allowed an advertiser to control its costs by setting a budget for what it was willing to spend per day. AdWords-sponsored listings were also shown on Google's partner sites. Yahoo was a segment leader as far as presenting the potential advertiser with the best possible packages and also in terms of the ease with which business was conducted.

Business Solutions

Using this link, businesses were able to assess the various ways Google could help them grow and become more profitable. In other words, with Business Solutions Google marketed the potency of its advertising methods to potential advertisers. Yahoo was the segment leader in this area with MSN and AOL closely in the hunt. All the major players in Internet search were going to great lengths to inform prospective advertisers of the various ways a search engine could help them grow and expand their clientele. The crossing point for Google was the fact that the company refused to advertise on its home page, which was supposed to be the ultimate platform. Google was the most widely visited web site in the world. Management believed that advertising on Google's home page took away from the main reason patrons visited the site—quality Internet search.

Submissions

Case files for prospective advertisers on Google search were submitted through this link. Google had a reputation for not assigning one person or team to a case; rather, they kept switching teams assigned to a particular case. Many prospective advertisers saw Google as filled with arrogant people and found it time-consuming and difficult to do business with the company. Yahoo's effort at making submissions brisk was unmatched in the segment.

Customers and Clients

The Internet searching services' customers and clients consisted primarily of advertisers, Internet search patrons, and large web portals, some of which had their own Internet search services: groups and licensees, among others. Customers and clients were bundled together because of the vague distinction between the two in this segment. Yahoo was a service provider to Google when it displayed Google ads on the Yahoo web site. In this scenario, Google was the customer on Yahoo's web site. On the other hand, if Google displayed a Yahoo service ad beside its search results as a contextual ad, Google became the service provider and Yahoo became a client of Google's search service and its related advertising. Companies in this segment normally provided email services in order to increase the number of people visiting their web sites.

User

Most Internet search users needed guidance in finding information about goods or services in which they were interested, and Internet search engines presented an opportunity to go directly to what users needed without wasting time. Internet search users also ended up buying things or requesting services that they made queries on. This was the lure to advertisers seeking to reach consumers using Internet search companies. Google, since its launch in 1998, had grown explosively to become the most-used web site in the world. Inducted as a verb into the Oxford English dictionary, it was each month used by 165 million people in the United Kingdom and United States alone. In the lives of tens of millions of Internet users, Google was nothing less than the front door to the Internet.[9] Yahoo was closely behind, largely because of its popular free email service, which was patronized worldwide.

Advertiser

Google had numerous loyal web users who used its Internet search services frequently for search solutions on the web. Quality search results made web surfing easier. This loyal pool of patrons presented a great opportunity for advertisers to effectively reach a target audience. As Google continued to develop effective ways of linking search results to specific search-based services, advertisers would keep flocking to Google for ways in which they could help businesses reach a target audience. Contextual ads, which were a Google staple, were Internet search–based ads placed beside search results directing patrons to possible solutions to their internet search query. MSN, Yahoo, and AOL also began to incorporate colorful graphics and multimedia banner ads beside search results. These were more flashy ways of attracting an Internet search user's attention to an ad. Companies in this segment normally provided email services, online shopping, news and sports, online satellite maps, and driving directions services as a way of luring customers to their Internet search services and to also have a registered member base for future directory-linked target advertising. Directory-linked target advertising had not yet been approved because of the privacy and identity theft concerns of Internet service users, especially registered members.

Technical

This section encompasses the technology behind Google's Internet search engines and its policy in relationship to third-party web sites.

Google's Technology

Businesses used the Google's AdWords program to promote their products and services using targeted advertising. In addition, the thousands of third-party web sites that made up the Google network used the Google AdSense program to deliver relevant ads that generated revenue and enhanced the user experience. Google AdWords ads connected businesses with new customers at the very moment when they were looking for a product or service. The Google network reached more than 80% of Internet users. With Google AdWords, prospective advertisers could create their own ads, choose keywords to help Google match their ads to a target audience, and pay only when someone clicked on them.

Google AdSense was a fast and easy way for web site publishers of all sizes to display relevant, unobtrusive Google ads on their web sites' content pages and earn money. Because the ads were related to what users were looking for on a web site, web site publishers could finally both make money and enhance their content pages. It was also a way for web site publishers to provide Google Internet search to their visitors, and earn money by displaying Google ads beside search results.[10] A key to success would be to remain a dominant force in Internet search technology.

Third-Party Web Sites

Google's policy on third-party web sites read: "The sites displayed as search results or linked to by Google services are developed by people over whom Google exercises no control. The search results that appear from Google's indices are indexed by Google's automated machinery and computers, and Google cannot and does not screen the sites before including them in the indices from which such automated search results are gathered. A search using Google services may produce search results and links to sites that some people find objectionable, inappropriate, or offensive. We cannot guarantee that a Google search will not locate unintended or objectionable content and assume no responsibility for the content of any site included in any search results or otherwise linked to by the Google Services."[11] The goal here was to appeal to a large number of third-party web sites in order to reach a larger audience and increase market share in the process.

Staffing

Eric Schmidt, Google's CEO, recently announced the company was having problems recruiting. He claimed the pool of candidates were either not of sufficient quality or not technically proficient enough. The company's headquarters in Mountain View, California, employed a little more than 2,700 people, of whom 900 were techies.

On-Campus Recruiting/Annual Code Jams

The company was notoriously picky when it came to hiring, even though it was hiring about 25 new people a week. A team of 50 recruiters combed through resumes, which had to be submitted online, then dumped them into a program that channels those chosen for an interview to the proper hiring committee and threw the rest in electronic trash. Interviewing for a job at Google could take months in a grueling process that would not guarantee a job. The company also organized annual code jams where programmers from all over the world competed for cash and ultimately a job. The school campus environment at Googleplex—the company's headquarters in Mountain View, California—encouraged employees to stay at work past work hours. There was an around-the-clock free catering service at the cafeteria. Google as well as the main players in the Internet search segment knew the future of the segment depended on the continued development and training of technical staff that came up with more effective ways of enhancing Internet search technology. The key to success, therefore, would be setting up the right administrative mechanisms to effectively handle business operations and to successfully recruit a quality and technically proficient work force while at the same time improving on the competence of existing employees.

Marketing and Promotion

Most of Google's popularity could be attributed to simple word of mouth and quality search results. The company, however, had to shift into a more proactive mode of marketing and promotion on a more serious level. Google needed to communicate to its everyday patrons that it existed, first and foremost, to offer Internet search services but also to get users to accommodate the fact that the company was evolving and was rolling out a bevy of non–search related services.

Online

Companies normally would use their own web sites to promote their services. Google, on the other hand, did not advertise on its home page. This, Google believed, let the user know that the quality of the search result was paramount. Users would be introduced to ads only after typing their inquiries. It must be emphasized that companies encouraged their registered members to customize their web browsers with a preferred company's search pane as the default search engine. Google encouraged its search patrons to download an inbuilt taskbar on their computers for search purposes.

Television

Television ads and radio promotions can be an effective outlet for reaching out to an older, less Internet-savvy audience. Television and radio had not been used traditionally as an outlet for marketing and promotion by Internet search companies, but could be considered as competition between Internet search companies intensified. A need may arise to pursue a marketing strategy that includes television ad campaign.

Member Services

Google needed to expand its membership-grabbing effort by offering new services, such as increasing its 1-gigabyte storage limit for its Gmail users. The company's email services were based on invitation only from an existing Gmail user. How did a person get invited to subscribe to this email service? Few potential users seemed to know. In a nutshell, Google needed to increase its membership service subscription initiatives if it was to compete in the future with companies with a large membership base such as MSN, AOL, and Yahoo.

Competition

Google's main competitors were Yahoo, AOL, and MSN. Google compared favorably with its major competitors in key areas. Google maintained an edge in the U.S. Internet search traffic market share with 31%, while Yahoo and MSN held 26% and 20% shares, respectively.[11] However, Google did not have the size, network, and existing service depth of its competitors.

Google's Internet search engine was by far the most accurate when compared with AOL, MSN, and Yahoo search results. The major concern in this area was the fact that all the major competitors had expressed keen interest in taking over the Internet search segment in a bid to reduce Google's current market share.

The main complaint leveled by Google's clients (prospective advertisers) was the company's inability to assign one team to a project. The company kept changing employees assigned to already established cases and wasted clients' time in the process because they had to start over any time a new team was assigned to an already opened case file.

Finally, Google's main competitors in internet search—Yahoo, MSN, and AOL—were also well-established web portals with a wide range of products and services and millions of registered members. Google was yet to introduce a wide range of services to match its competitors. Google's revenue growth rate of 233.50% (see **Exhibit 5**) surpassed all its competitors across the computer services industry even though the major competitors were by far bigger and more independent web portals. Google's main weakness was the fact that it had to depend on its competitors to propagate its Internet search technology. Others also suggested that Google could do without all the other services and forego the high overhead costs associated with operating a web portal like Yahoo, AOL, and MSN.

Financial Analysis

Google ranked high among the computer services industry's well-run companies. The company's profit margin of 12.52% compared favorably with the industry average. The current management's effectiveness was positively highlighted through its ROA and ROE of 21.05% and 25.97%, respectively.

Google's revenue growth of 117.56% as of December 2004 was phenomenal and further reflected an increase in shareholder value with current revenue per share of $11.692 over the same period. With regard to Internet search technology, Google had the winning search engine. This trend was easily reflected in the company's financial position and by the fact that it was the most visited web site in the world.

Exhibit 5
2004 Direct Competitor Comparison

	Google	MSFT (MSN)	Yahoo	Industry Average
Market Cap ($):	54.05B	279.73B	46.90B	212.81M
Employees:	1,907	57,000	5,500	470
Revenue Growth (%):	117.56%	14.40%	70.50%	10.80%
Revenue ($):	3.19B	38.47B	3.57B	95.93M
Gross Margin (%):	54.29%	83.67%	63.67%	48.74%
EBITDA ($):	788.67M	13.44B	834.28M	6.71M
Operating Margins (%):	20.07%	32.73%	19.26%	8.27%
Net Income ($):	399.12M	10.00B	839.55M	3.13M
EPS ($):	1.442	0.917	0.576	0.13
PE:	137.09	28.04	59.22	27.12
PEG:	1.63	1.73	2.18	1.32
PS:	17.01	7.29	13.24	1.96

Source: http://finance.yahoo.com/q/co?s=GOOG. Accessed February 7, 2005.

Exhibit 6 Consolidated Statements of Income: Google, Inc. (Dollar amounts in thousands, except per share amounts)

	2004	2003	2002
Revenues	$3,189,223	$1,465,934	$439,508
Costs and expenses:			
Cost of revenues	1,457,653	625,854	131,510
Research and development	225,632	91,228	31,748
Sales and marketing	246,300	120,328	43,849
General and administrative	139,700	56,699	24,300
Stock-based compensation	278,746	229,361	21,635
Non-recurring portion of settlement of disputes with Yahoo	201,000	—	—
Total costs and expenses	2,549,031	1,123,470	253,042
Income from operations	640,192	342,464	186,466
Interest income (expense) and other, net	10,042	4,190	(1,551)
Income before income taxes	650,234	346,654	184,915
Provision for income taxes	251,115	241,006	85,259
Net income	$399,119	$105,648	$99,656
Net income per share:			
Basic	2.07	0.77	0.86
Diluted	1.46	0.41	0.45
Number of shares used in per share calculations:			
Basic	193,176	137,697	115,242
Diluted	272,781	256,638	220,633

Source: Google, Inc. 2004 Annual Report, p. 68.

The company made all of its revenues from contextual ads that were placed beside search results. For instance, a business owner arranged with Google to pay for clicks on its ad, to be displayed beside a Google search result any time a particular keyword was searched. A corn distributor might choose "corn" as the keyword that should trigger its ad to be displayed. The business specified the number of clicks it could afford to pay for daily or weekly based on a fee that was agreed on by Google and the advertising company. Businesses were increasingly using this mode of advertising because it yielded better results as far as generating sales: Ads were relevant only to the search inquiry and were more likely to result in a sale.

In a nutshell, Google was one of the fastest growing companies in any industry as reflected in its revenue growth rate. The company's IPO with its Wall Street buzz and the eventual tripling of the company's stock, trading at $180, reflected the confidence that the public had vested in the future direction of the company. Financially, Google was sound. The company's expenses were minimal because it had no inventory. Google's raw materials were the innovativeness of its technical staff. **Exhibits 6 and 7** provide summarized financial information.

Exhibit 7 Consolidated Balance Sheets: Google, Inc. (Dollar amounts in thousands, except par value)

Assets	2004	2003
Current assets:		
Cash and cash equivalents	$426,873	$148,995
Marketable securities	1,705,424	185,723
Accounts receivable, net of allowance of $4,670 and $3,962	311,836	154,690
Income taxes receivable	70,509	—

Exhibit 7
(continued)

	2004	2003
Deferred income taxes, net	19,463	22,105
Prepaid revenue share, expenses and other assets	159,360	48,721
Total current assets	2,693,465	560,234
Property and equipment, net	378,916	188,255
Goodwill	122,818	87,442
Intangible assets, net	71,069	18,114
Deferred income taxes, net, non-current	11,590	—
Prepaid revenue share, expenses and other assets, non-current	35,493	17,413
Total assets	$3,313,351	$871,458
Liabilities, Redeemable Convertible Preferred Stock Warrant and Stockholders' Equity		
Current liabilities:		
Accounts payable	$32,672	$46,175
Accrued compensation and benefits	82,631	33,522
Accrued expenses and other current liabilities	64,111	26,411
Accrued revenue share	122,544	88,672
Deferred revenue	36,508	15,346
Income taxes payable	—	20,705
Current portion of equipment leases	1,902	4,621
Total current liabilities	340,368	235,452
Long-term portion of equipment leases	—	1,988
Deferred revenue, long-term	7,443	5,014
Liability for stock options exercised early, long-term	5,982	6,341
Deferred income taxes, net	—	18,510
Other long-term liabilities	30,502	1,512
Commitments and contingencies		
Redeemable convertible preferred stock warrant	—	13,871
Stockholders' equity:		
Convertible preferred stock, $0.001 par value, issuable in series: 164,782 and 100,000 shares authorized at December 31, 2003 and December 31, 2004, 71,662 and no shares issued and outstanding at December 31, 2003 and December 31, 2004, aggregate liquidation preference of $40,815 and none at December 31, 2003 and December 31, 2004	—	44,346
Class A and Class B common stock, $0.001 par value: 700,000 and 9,000,000 shares authorized at December 31, 2003 and December 31, 2004, 160,866, and 266,917 shares issued and outstanding, excluding 11,987, and 7,605 shares subject to repurchase (see Note 10) at December 31, 2003 and December 31, 2004	267	161
Additional paid-in capital	2,582,352	725,219
Note receivable from officer/stockholder	—	(4,300)
Deferred stock-based compensation	(249,470)	(369,668)
Accumulated other comprehensive income	5,436	1,660
Retained earnings	590,471	191,352
Total stockholders' equity	$2,929,056	$588,770
Total liabilities, redeemable convertible preferred stock warrant and stockholders' equity	3,313,351	871,458

Source: Google, Inc. 2004 Annual Report, p. 67.

Corporate Governance

Exhibit 8 shows Google's Board of Directors and the company's executive management team.

Exhibit 8
Board of Directors and Executive Management Group: Google, Inc.

A. Board of Directors

Dr. Eric Schmidt, Google Inc.
Sergey Brin, Google, Inc.
Larry Page, Google, Inc.
John Doerr, Kleiner Perkins Caufiled & Byers
Michael Mortiz, Sequoia Capital
Ram Sriram, Sherpalo
John Hennessy, Stanford University
Paul Otellini, Intel
Shirley M. Tilghman, Princeton University
Ann Mather

B. Executive Management Group

Dr. Eric Schmidt, Chairman of the Executive Committee and Chief Executive Officer
Larry Page, Co-Founder & President, Products
Sergey Brin, Co-Founder & President, Technology
Shona Brown, Senior Vice President, Business Operations
W. M. Coughran, Jr., Vice President, Engineering
David C. Drummond, Senior Vice President, Corporate Development
Alan Eustace, Senior Vice President, Engineering & Research
Urs Holzle, Senior Vice President, Operations & Google Fellow
Jeff Huber, Vice President, Engineering
Omid Kordestani, Senior Vice President, Global Sales & Business Development
George Reyes, Senior Vice President & Chief Financial Officer
Jonathan Rosenberg, Senior Vice President, Product Management
Elliot Schrage, Vice President, Global Communications & Public Affairs

Source: Google, Inc., "Corporate Information," Google web site.

The Google Culture

Though growing rapidly, Google still maintained a small company feel. At the Googleplex headquarters almost everyone ate in the Google café (known as "Charlie's Place"), sitting at whatever table had an opening and enjoying conversations with Googlers from all different departments. Topics ranged from the trivial to the technical, and whether the discussion was about computer games or encryption or ad serving software, it was not surprising to hear someone say, "That's a product I helped develop before I came to Google."

Google's emphasis on innovation and commitment to cost containment meant each employee was a hands-on contributor. There was little in the way of corporate hierarchy, and everyone wore several hats. The international webmaster who created Google's holiday logos spent a week translating the entire site into Korean. The chief operations engineer was also a licensed neurosurgeon. Because everyone realized they were an equally important part of Google's success, no one hesitated to skate over a corporate officer during a game of roller hockey.

Google's hiring policy was aggressively non-discriminatory and favored ability over experience. The result was a staff that reflected the global audience the search engine served. Google had offices around the globe, and Google engineering centers were recruiting local talent in locations from Zurich to Bangalore. Dozens of languages were spoken by Google staffers, from Turkish to Telugu. When not at work, Googlers pursued interests from cross-country cycling to wine tasting, from flying to Frisbee. As Google expanded its development team, it continued to look for those who shared an obsessive commitment to creating search perfection and having a great time doing it.[12]

Management Strategy

Google's President and CEO, Eric Schmidt, was committed to the continued growth of Google as a premium Internet search company while at the same time striving to further expand beyond just the Internet search–based services the company offered. The company needed to introduce new Internet-related services in order to develop a more enduring company not reliant solely on Internet search technology but diversified enough to remain an enduring entity. The company also had to further develop its international popularity.

In addition, Google needed to improve its general administrative capabilities. The primary complaint leveled by prospective advertisers trying to do business with Google was the fact that its employees were a bunch of brash arrogant people who kept switching teams assigned to cases. This led to unnecessary delays and frustrating experiences when setting up business deals with the company.

Looking to the Future

In 2005, CEO Eric Schmidt and his management team decided that Google needed to effect measures that would allow it to remain competitive as more big players focused on the Internet search segment. Despite the fact that Google was a leader in Internet search technology, the company was introducing a new line of services not related to Internet search. This new situation placed Google in a face-to-face showdown with companies that were previously considered too big to be Google's competitors. These bigger companies, namely MSN (Microsoft), AOL, and Yahoo, were feverishly working to close in on Google's Internet search supremacy and had made public their intentions to participate in the advertising dollars Internet search generates. Google, therefore, needed to differentiate itself from the other competitors in the Internet search services and to remain the household name with the largest market share. It had to achieve this using the immense human, financial, and technological expertise at its disposal.

One alternative proposed by Larry Page, co-founder, suggested the need for Google to keep focusing on doing what it does best—"Internet search solutions." He stressed the need for the company to focus on its distinctive competence by continuing to develop a superior search engine. In essence, Google should remain a company that specialized only in developing the best Internet search engine; and focusing only on Internet search applications and how they could best be utilized to effectively advertise products and services. This would keep Google on top of the pile in the Internet search segment.

The benefit of this alternative was the sustained revenues from advertising that focusing on further developing a proven Internet search engine like Google brings, through online target advertising using contextual ads. This would allow the company to remain focused on developing further what brings the company all of its revenues. It was a winning formula that had been proven because it brought the company sudden fame and fortune.

This alternative was feasible because it focused on further developing Google's main strength—Internet search services. It focused on a path successfully trod by the company—Internet search technology. Google's search engine and its associated contextual ads technology attracted advertisers and had been referred to as the future of advertising.

The alternative could be successful because Google was the segment leader in market share. Despite the hot pursuit by its competitors, Google had established brand name recognition in Internet search technology. Being the Internet search segment leader, Google could further develop its winning search service and focus on capturing market share in the international arena, where Google remained more popular than its competitors. Google could use its brand name recognition in Internet search to generate revenue using its segment-leading contextual ad technology.

The company recently announced that it was going to incorporate colorful and animated multimedia graphics beside its search results. Advertisers were also going to pay for the service whether or not users clicked on an ad. This method of web advertising, known as "cost per impression," was based on the number of people who saw the ads and would be displayed on sites that run Google's search technology. This would allow Google's advertisers to reach more customers while expanding the list of possible advertisers who would want to consider Google as a potential source for advertising, increasing Internet search market share in the process.

A drawback to this alternative was the risk of not having a wide range of services to help absorb the shock of lost revenues in the event Internet search did not live up to its current promise as an effective advertising medium.

Another alternative, being considered by Sergey Brin, co-founder, suggested that in order to differentiate itself from the competition, Google needed to add a broad range of services and communication tools such as instant messaging, travel, news, email, paid jumbo email accounts, web site development and hosting, sports, finance, games, and text messaging to complement its Internet search services. In other words, Google needed to expand as a business if it was to remain competitive in the future.

The benefit of this alternative would be the diverse range of new services offered by Google. It would allow the company to build a solid membership base with the introduction of fantasy sports, instant messaging, travel, and finance and other services in addition to Internet search. This would help build on Google's member services through email services that bring members to Google's web site and also increase the likelihood of generating advertising revenues in the process through increased online activity.

The alternative was feasible, given Google's current profitability and financial flexibility compared to similar companies in the Internet search segment. The company's financial flexibility allowed it to branch off successfully into other areas not related to search. This alternative, therefore, placed Google in a new light as a multi-service provider in this segment. Being the market leader in Internet search technology, Google would be in a great position to introduce new services largely owing to its phenomenal success in Internet search.

The alternative could be successful simply because it made room for Google to survive any future adverse developments in the Internet search segment. By offering a variety of services to complement its Internet search segment, the company would place itself in a position to avoid total collapse should today's revenue-generating Internet search services fail to live up to their future promise. By expanding and offering new services, Google could use its current role as an Internet search powerhouse as a platform to compete and eventually beat already well-established companies such as AOL, MSN, and Yahoo, who offered an array of non–search based Internet services. Non-search Internet services would place Google in a position to have more registered members in their database. This membership database could be an advantage for more effective advertising, especially with directory-linked target advertising, which was yet to be approved but would ultimately allow Internet search companies to use previously collected information on a search user in a member database to help advertise specifically to that particular user.

Furthermore, the future of the industry may depend on directory-linked target advertising: advertising that would incorporate Internet search that analyzed the age, gender, national origin, geographical location, preferences, and previous commercial history of the search inquirer. Even though it was yet to be approved as an advertising medium in Internet search, this was touted as the future of the continued profitability of Internet search, in terms of advertising dollars. Directory-linked target advertising would tend to favor companies that had a database of registered members. This alternative could better prepare Google for competitive advantage in the future should issues of confidentiality and identity theft be tackled effectively by Internet search companies, thus paving the way for directory-linked target advertising. The industry would first have to assure members that the confidentiality of members' personal information would be guaranteed.

A drawback to this alternative was the unforeseen risks associated with rapid expansionary measures, especially in technology-centered companies. In addition, identity theft issues and confidentiality of members' personal information were affecting further development of search-based advertising.

Eric Schmidt, Google's CEO, agreed that these were worthy alternatives. Management needed further deliberation to decide the best course of action that was both efficient and effective for Google to achieve success in Internet search and related services. The best course of action should provide Google a long-term competitive edge.

Notes

1. B. Dudley, "Putting Microsoft Brand on a New Breed: Longhorn," *Seattle Times* (February 28, 2003).
2. *MSN Encarta Encyclopedia Premium, http://encarta.msn.com/dictionary* (March 15, 2005).
3. Dudley (2003).
4. K. Delaney; "In Click Fraud, Web Outfits Have a Costly Problem," *Wall Street Journal* (April 6, 2005).
5. Profile of AOL, *http://finance.yahoo.com/q/pr?s=TWX*, (March 27, 2005).
6. MSN (2005).
7. Eisenmann, T. (2004). "Google, Inc. Case # 9-804-141," p. 4. *http://www.hbs.edu/* (February 8, 2005).
8. Delaney, K., "Google to Target Brands in Revenue Push," *Wall Street Journal* (April 25, 2005).
9. Andrew Murray-Watson. "Gates v. Google: Microsoft Has Declared War on the World's Best Loved Search Engine but It May Find Its Dominance of the Software Industry Works Against It." *http://premium.hoovers.com/subscribe/co/news/list.xhtml?ID=59101&Name=Google&Ticker=GOOG* (February 6, 2005).
10. Google, "Google AdSense," *https://www.google.com/ adsense/?hl=en_US&sourceid=aso&subid=us-et-ads Yahoo.com./finance* (March 18, 2005).
11. Google, "Google AdWords," *https://adwords.google.com/ select/main?cmd=Login&sourceid=AWO&subid=US-ET-ADS&hl=en_US.* (March 18, 2005).
12. Google, "Company Record."

References

"Profile of MSN," *http://finance.yahoo.com/q/pr?s=MSFT* (March 27, 2005).

"Profile of Yahoo," *http://finance.yahoo.com/q/pr?s=YHOO* (March 27, 2005).

T. Taulli *http://www.dealflowmanager.com/documents/ Google%20Research%20Report.doc* (April 26, 2005).

USA Today, *http://asp.usatoday.com/search/search.aspx ?q=where+most+people+click+%22search+engines+with+the+most+visitors%22&spell=1&site=USATODAY_main&client=USATODAY_main&output=xml_no_dtd&num=10&ie=UTF-8&oe=UTF-8&access=p&source=usat* (April 5, 2005).

F. Vogelstein, "Google: Is This Company Worth $165 a Share?" *Fortune* (December 13, 2004).

F. Vogelstein "Search and Destroy," *Fortune* (May 2, 2005).

CASE 15

AOL Time Warner, Inc.: A Bad Idea from the Start?

Vineet Walia, Irene Hagenbuch Sanjana, Stacey Foster, and Alan N. Hoffman

"To become the world's most respected and valued company by connecting, informing and entertaining people everywhere in innovative ways that will enrich their lives."

AOL Time Warner mission statement

Time Warner

The media and entertainment giant Time Warner is the result of a merger of two companies that have grown through mergers and acquisitions. The AOL Time Warner story began in 1918, when Henry Luce and Briton Hadden got the idea for *Time* magazine (incorporated as Time Inc. in 1922) and the Warner brothers opened their first West Coast studio. During the next 50 years, both companies grew to become industry leaders. Time Inc. launched various magazines and acquired a Boston publishing house called Little, Brown and Company. The Warner studio, on the other hand, released the first talking movie in the entertainment industry (Al Jolson's *The Jazz Singer*) and created Warner Bros. Records in 1958. In 1969, the Warner studio (then called Warner-Seven Arts) was acquired by Kinney National Co. and became Warner Communications Inc.

AOL

With the cable industry booming, the computer industry followed suit in 1985, when Steve Case, Jim Kimsey, and Marc Seriff founded Quantum Computer Services to send online information and other services to consumers via PC modems. At that time, the use and knowledge of the possibilities of the World Wide Web did not exist. Over the next four years, Quantum Computer Services was renamed Quantum Online and then America Online. At the same time, Time Inc. acquired Warner Communications Inc., to become Time Warner Inc., the world's largest media and entertainment company.

By the end of the 20th century, AOL reached 27 million members, was an industry leader in its industry, and was continuing its acquisition strategy by purchasing brands such as Netscape, MovieFone, CompuServe, and MapQuest. Time Warner Inc. also further expanded its market potentials in its industry and agreed to its latest and possibly most controversial merger with AOL in January 2001, to become AOL Time Warner.

The Merger That Wasn't

The merger between America Online and Time Warner Inc. was the largest corporate merger in U.S. history. When the merger was made public in January 2001, the transaction was valued at $183 billion. It was the first stock purchase whereby an Internet company—created through the Internet boom—utilized its sky-high stock value to acquire an older, more traditional *Fortune 500* company.

AOL offered $166 billion in stock for Time Warner's real assets and assumed Time Warner's $17 billion debt. This included a 71% premium for former Time Warner stockholders, who received 1.5 shares of AOL Time Warner stock for each Time Warner share they owned at that time. America Online offered a stock value of $110 for each Time Warner share that was selling at $64.75 in the market.[1] AOL shareholders then controlled 55% of the new company's stock, and Time Warner shareholders controlled 45%, which appeared to have left AOL in the driver's seat of the new corporation. While the deal was an amazing offer for Time Warner, analysts in the industry feared that the offer overvalued Time Warner by a tremendous amount. It was felt that this could eventually grow into a costly deal for AOL, particularly because AOL was responsible for paying the corporation's combined debts and meeting overly confident market expectations about future growth.[2]

The merged AOL Time Warner brands included AOL, *Time*, CNN, CompuServe, Warner Bros., Netscape, *Sports Illustrated*, *People*, HBO, ICQ, AOL Instant Messenger, AOL MovieFone, TBS, TNT, Cartoon Network, Digital City, Warner Music Group, Spinner, Winamp, *Fortune*, AOL.com, *Entertainment Weekly*, and Looney Tunes.[3] Before the merger, Time Warner Inc. had been the leading media, entertainment, and news monopoly in the United States. It owned Warner Bros. studio, Warner Music, CNN, HBO, and other cable television networks, and it controlled magazines with a circulation of 130 million. America Online Inc., on the other hand, had grown into the largest dial-up Internet service provider (ISP) and its name had become almost synonymous with the Internet in the public eye. It was the leading e-commerce service, interactive service, Internet technologies, and web brands provider in the world. It held a reputation as the most easy-to-use and convenient interactive service.

America Online and Time Warner believed that their merger was a merger of two synergistic companies. Their marketing concept was to combine new and old media vehicles in order to strengthen overall total position in the market. America Online needed technical capabilities to move into the broadband business. Time Warner, on the other hand, was the second largest cable television operator in the nation. It was a major content provider in the industry that had previously wanted to expand its media empire to become an Internet player. So the merger made perfect theoretical sense to both AOL and Time Warner. In an environment where online services, entertainment, and media meet, the new company's resources would be unparalleled.

The combined company's strategic objectives were:

1. To continue making technology simple for its customers
2. To continue offering simple e-business solutions to the market
3. To accelerate the growth of its cable broadband assets

These objectives were thought to be attainable because of the new combined core competencies, such as Time Warner's cable infrastructure, AOL's ease-of-use trademark, their globally trusted brands, traditional journalistic integrity, and vast Internet expertise.

The Competitive Environment

AOL Time Warner was a distinctive company with multiple business units that spanned many markets. There were numerous national and global competitors in each market, all varying in size and number of years of experience in the marketplace. Most of these competitors were large companies with deep pockets. Similarly to AOL Time Warner, their competitive growth strategy involved mergers and acquisitions of companies with new ideas and promising products or services. The key direct competitors of AOL Time Warner by business line were:

- **Cable Systems:** AT&T Broadband, Cablevision Systems, DIRECTV, Cox Communications, Comcast.
  Barriers to entry—A large up-front investment is required to establish and then maintain the required cable network system. In addition, the large number of already established competitors forces participants to upgrade their equipment and introduce new technology to their product and service lines on a regular basis to stay in the game.
- **Internet:** Earthlink, Prodigy, Terra, Lycos, Yahoo!, Microsoft.
  Barriers to entry—In the Internet arena, a small investment allows any firm to operate its own ISP and to provide e-commerce solutions and online content. Nonetheless, establishing a successful online portal to the world of consumers requires substantial capital to market the new site, maintain and update its content, and ensure efficient operation. Thus, any new entrant to the Internet world needs to weigh the benefits of low entry fees against the need for continuous innovation, maintenance, and updates; operational efficiencies; and strategic positioning of the firm's products and services.
- **Filmed Entertainment:** Vivendi Universal, Viacom, Walt Disney, Sony.
  Barriers to entry—The capital requirements for the film and entertainment industry are very high. While it is not necessary to have high levels of funding for production, this type of business is highly dependent on the talent of the writers, directors, producers, stunt coordinators, actors and actresses, and so forth. In addition, a smaller budget limits promotion capabilities and threatens the success and popularity of any piece produced.
- **Publishing, Music, and Media:** Advance Publications, Bertelsmann, Virgin Group, Sony, News Corp., Primedia, Dow Jones, Tribune, McGraw-Hill, NBC, EMI Group, Pearson, Reed Elsevier Group, Hachette Filipacchi Medias
  Barriers to entry—In the publishing, music, and media industries, the availability of writers, musicians, and ideas for publications is virtually inexhaustible. In all three industries, the already existing players are established in the market and have the necessary capital to find new talent, publish a new book, produce a new record, or print a new publication. In addition, it would be very difficult for a new entrant to gain enough market presence to

sustain the occasional one-off success story over a longer period of time, which thus limits the number of new entrants to this industry segment as well.

Corporate Governance

Richard D. Parsons was Chairman of the Board and Chief Executive Officer of AOL Time Warner Inc., whose businesses included interactive services, cable systems, filmed entertainment, television networks, music, and publishing. He became CEO in May 2002 and Chairman of the Board in May 2003.

Exhibit 1 provides the complete list of the company's Board of Directors.

Ken Novack was Vice Chairman of AOL Time Warner Inc. As a member of the Office of the Chairman, Novack provided strategic counsel and handled special assignments for the Chairman, and he assumed a leading role in major corporate transactions. Formerly the Vice Chairman of America Online and a member of its Board of Directors, he had also served as Vice Chairman of Time Warner, Inc. Novack had played a number of critical roles for the company during the past 11 years. In addition to having broad strategic responsibilities, he oversaw America Online's Legal Department as well as AOL Investments, and he was a key architect of the merger between AOL and Time Warner.

The Marco Environment

One of AOL Time Warner's greatest advantages was that its very brand stood for strong customer service. The company held the unique status of being the only one-stop broadband, Internet, entertainment, media, and communications company in the world.

Exhibit 1
Board of Directors: AOL Time Warner, Inc.

Richard D. Parsons
Chairman of the Board and CEO, Time Warner, Inc.

James L. Barksdale
President and CEO, Barksdale Management Corporation and Co-founder of Netscape

Stephen F. Bollenbach
Co-chairman and CEO, Hilton Hotels Corporation

Stephen M. Case
Co-founder, America Online, Inc.

Frank J. Caufield
Co-founder, Kleiner Perkins Caufield & Byers

R. E. Turner
Founder, Turner Broadcasting System, Inc.

Miles R. Gilburne
Managing Member, ZG Ventures, L.L.C.

Carla A. Hills
Chairman and CEO, Hills & Company, and Former United States Trade Representative

Reuben Mark
Chairman and CEO, Colgate-Palmolive Company

Michael A. Miles
Former Chairman and CEO, Philip Morris Companies Inc.

Kenneth J. Novack
Vice Chairman, Time Warner Inc.

Franklin D. Ranes
Chairman and CEO, Fannie May

Francis T. Vincent, Jr.
Chairman, Vincent Enterprises

Source: AOL Time Warner.

By combining assets and creating new enhanced products and services, the merged corporation was able to increase consumer usage, cross-marketing, and promotion capabilities:

- **eCommerce:** E-commerce and online shopping capabilities can stimulate growth and value for shareholders.
- **Copyright:** Prevailing global copyright advantages let the company produce, distribute, and sell its intellectual property through books, music, movies, entertainment, and broadcasting at a premium price.
- **Connection:** Its established broadband network affords AOL Time Warner the ability to deliver digital content via high-speed Internet access such as cable modems, DSL, satellite, and wireless.

Furthermore, the new AOL Time Warner did not target only a niche market segment or a specific demographic group; instead, it provided products and services to a vast array of consumers. Many of these segments had shifted from being suspicious of technology and e-commerce to being savvy online users.

FCC Changes in Broadband Regulations

Since the late 1990s, analyst and industry experts had predicted that broadband connections would be the future of the Internet and the computing world. It was projected to become the standard connection method for most homes and businesses, delivering new streams of multimedia content,[4] and it could become the most quickly adopted technology in history. Even though the large majority of Internet users in the United States used standard dial-up connections, such projections were worrisome to the more than 6,000 local and national dial-up Internet Service Providers (ISPs). The former America Online was the largest dial-up provider in the country, and numerous other dial-up ISPs felt that the future of their business looked very grim. Those who fell behind in the broadband revolution were at risk of never catching up.[5] The leading player in the broadband market was the cable industry, which in 2002 had a presence in more than two-thirds of all U.S. households and was in the process of upgrading its systems to allow for two-way Internet access.

Lobbying Against Broadband Service Providers

With bleak industry forecasts for dial-up ISPs, major ISPs—including former America Online, one of its most vigorous supporters—were urging the Federal Communications Commission (FCC) to change cable industry regulations. AOL wanted existing cable monopolies, such as AT&T (including its recently acquired TCI and MediaOne), to open their cable networks to unaffiliated ISPs. They demanded that cable industry regulations be adjusted to match the telephone system industry, which until early 2003 was required by law to host the more than 6,000 online access providers on its networks. Cable companies, on the other hand, joined forces in "the battle cry of 'deregulation,'"[6] largely as a means of maintaining business-as-usual in the closed, captive-audience world of cable.

The FCC Ruling

After many months of deliberation and speculation (during which time the former America Online and Time Warner merged), the FCC finally announced its decision on the cable network access issue in February 2002. It ruled that, unlike telephone companies, cable service companies do not have to open and share their networks with other ISPs. It announced the decision "to treat cable-based broadband service as an information service rather than a telecommunications service."[7] This allowed the FCC to work within an industry that had a lower degree of government regulations.

The FCC's second decision came in February 2003. The ruling was in favor of the regional Bell companies, and this resulted in vast changes of the phone and broadband competition rules for the telecommunication services industry. While it did not meet all of the Bell companies' deregulation demands, the FCC declared that the Bells would no longer be required to share their (existing or those planned to be built in the future) high-speed fiber networks with other broadband competitors in residential or business areas. The Bell companies were required to continue leasing a portion (though how much was not specified) of their local copper line networks to independent ISPs at the already existing, deeply discounted price. With such a solution, the FCC believed it was creating a deregulated and competitive broadband industry, which made "it easier for companies to invest in new equipment and deploy the high-speed services that consumers desire."[8]

Financial Performance

In 2002, AOL Time Warner was proud of what it had achieved in its first year of operating as a merged entity. Total revenues rose from $32.2 billion in 2001 to $40.9 billion in 2002 (see **Exhibit 2**). While revenues were on the increase, operating income and net income decreased significantly during this period. In 2002, the net loss was an astounding $98.69 billion in comparison to a loss of $4.93 in 2001 and a profit of $1.12 in 2000 (see **Exhibit 2**). AOL Time Warner attributed the loss in 2002 to a one-time charge due to accounting changes and impairment of goodwill generated at the time of the merger that aggregated to approximately $100 billion. These results illustrated the extremely difficult financial situation that AOL Time Warner was facing. While some difficulties could be attributed to difficult economic and financial times, internal management and cultural turmoil resulting from the merger proved to have more of an effect on the company's performance than originally anticipated. By 2003, the vast potential this firm held through its various publishing, media, entertainment, and Internet businesses was yet to be realized financially. **Exhibit 3** shows the company's consolidated balance sheet.

Leadership Crisis and Management Changes

Many critics argued that AOL should never have acquired Time Warner. Unfortunately, many of them now work for AOL Time Warner. The only reason that AOL was even able to make the acquisition was its inflated stock price during the Internet boom. Today, the "old media" side of the business is keeping the company afloat. This has caused animosity between the AOL and Time Warner units. " 'These companies never should have been merged in the first place,' said veteran media analyst Hal Vogel. 'The Warner side feels cheated and robbed.' "[9]

The main weakness of AOL Time Warner in the human resource area has been its instability in the ranks of upper management, leading to a lack of strategic leadership and infighting among those remaining. Gerald Levin, former Chief Executive at Time Warner, announced his

Exhibit 2 Consolidated Statement of Operations: AOL Time Warner, Inc. (Dollar amounts in millions, except per share data)

Year ending December 31,	2002	2001	2000
Revenues			
Subscriptions	$18,959	$15,657	$4,777
Advertising and commerce	7,680	8,260	2,273
Content and other	14,322	13,249	555
Total revenues[1]	40,961	37,166	7,605
Cost of revenues[1]	(23,315)	(20,533)	(3,866)
Selling, general and administrative[1]	(9,916)	(9,079)	(1,864)
Amortization of goodwill and other intangible assets	(732)	(7,186)	(99)
Impairment of goodwill and other intangible assets	(45,538)	—	—
Merger and restructuring costs	(335)	(250)	(10)
Operating income (loss)	(39,875)	118	1,766
Interest expense, net	(1,783)	(1,353)	275
Other expense, net[1]	(2,498)	(3,567)	(208)
Minority interest income (expense)	(278)	46	—
Income (loss) before income taxes, discontinued operations and cumulative effect of accounting change	(44,434)	(4,756)	1,833
Income tax provision	(140)	(139)	(712)
Income (loss) before discontinued operations and cumulative effect of accounting change	(44,574)	(4,895)	1,121
Discontinued operations, net of tax	113	(39)	—
Income (loss) before cumulative effect of accounting change	(44,461)	(4,934)	1,121
Cumulative effect of accounting	(54,235)	—	—
Net income (loss)	($98,696)	($4,934)	$1,121
Basic income (loss) per common share before discontinued operations and cumulative effect of accounting change	($10.01)	($1.11)	$0.48
Discontinued operations	0.03	—	—
Cumulative effect of accounting change	−12.17	—	—
Basic net income (loss) per common share	($22.15)	($1.11)	$0.48
Average basic common shares	4,545.90	4,429.10	2,323.00
Average diluted common shares	4,521.80	4,584.40	2,595.00

Note:
1. Includes the following income (expenses) resulting from transactions with related companies:

	2002	2001	2000
Revenue	$678	$721	$99
Cost of revenues	(130)	(296)	—
Selling, general and administrative	−83	10	10
Interest income (expense), net	14	30	—
Other income (expense), net	(9)	(19)	—

Source: AOL Time Warner, Inc., "2002 Annual Report," p. 17.

surprise retirement less than a year after the merger. Levin was the driving force behind the decision to sell to AOL, and his departure left few allies of the merger on the Time Warner side. The AOL Time Warner Board ousted Robert Pittman, former Chief Operating Officer, shortly after Levin's exit. Richard Parsons, current CEO of AOL Time Warner restructured the business after Pittman left, splitting the business into two large chunks—the Media & Entertainment Group and the Entertainment & Networks Group. Don Logan and Jeff Bewkes (both from the Time Warner side of the business) took over the management of these two groups. In September 2003, there was a house cleaning in the AOL unit. Jonathan Miller was put in charge

Exhibit 3
Consolidated Balance Sheet: AOL Time Warner, Inc. (Dollar amounts in millions, except per share data.)

Year ending December 31	2002	2001
ASSETS		
Current assets		
Cash and equivalents	$1,730	$719
Receivables, less allowances of $2.379 and $1.889 billion	5,667	6,054
Inventories	1,896	1,791
Prepaid expenses and other current assets	1,862	1,687
Total current assets	11,155	10,251
Noncurrent inventories & film costs	3,351	3,490
Investments, including available-for-sale securities	5,138	6,886
Property, plant & equipment	12,150	12,669
Intangible assets subject to amortization	7,061	7,289
Intangible assets not subject to amortization	37,145	37,708
Goodwill	36,986	127,420
Other assets	2,464	2,791
Total assets	$115,450	$208,504
LIABILITIES AND SHAREHOLDERS' EQUITY		
Current liabilities		
Accounts payable	$2,459	$2,266
Participations payable	1,689	1,253
Royalties and programming costs payable	1,495	1,515
Deferred revenue	1,209	1,451
Debt due within one year	155	48
Other current liabilities	6,388	6,443
Total current liabilities	13,395	12,976
Long-term debt	27,354	22,792
Deferred income taxes	10,823	11,231
Deferred revenue	990	1,048
Other liabilities	5,023	4,839
Minority interests	5,048	3,591
Shareholders' equity		
Series LMCN-V Common Stock, $0.01 par value, 171.2 million shares outstanding in each period	2	2
AOL Time Warner Common Stock, $0.01 par value, 4.305 and 4.258 billion shares outstanding	43	42
Paid-in capital	155,134	155,172
Accumulated other comprehensive income (loss), net	(428)	49
Retained earnings (loss)	(101,934)	(3,238)
Total shareholders' equity	52,817	152,027
Total liabilities and shareholders' equity	$115,450	$208,504

Source: AOL Time Warner, Inc., "2002 Annual Report," p. 16.

of the unit, and several key executives were asked to step down, including Jan Brandt, the architect behind AOL's successful strategy of inundating the nation with free AOL CDs. AOL Time Warner also shut down its controversial Business Affairs office, headed by David Colburn, under suspicion of shady advertising and commerce deals. Many analysts saw these management changes as confirmation that Time Warner management was taking over the company.

Steve Case, the mastermind behind AOL and Time Warner's merger, was blamed for making a bad deal, and several major shareholders wanted him out. John C. Malone, the

Chairman of Liberty Media; Gordon Crawford, a Senior Vice President and Portfolio Manager for the investment firm Capital Research and Management; Fay Vincent, the former Baseball Commissioner; and Stephen F. Bollenbach, the Chief Executive of Hilton Hotels all supported Case's removal. Even Ted Turner, a former supporter of Case, backed his ouster. The 70% decline in AOL Time Warner's stock price had diminished Ted Turner's wealth, which had been over $9 billion at the time of the merger.[10] Case's job became largely advisory; he was removed from the day-to-day operations of the company. Case admitted that there had been a lack of leadership at the AOL unit after the merger, but he continued to believe that his job was safe and that the company was taking steps in the right direction.

What did not appear in the public financial statements was the additional time the newly merged AOL Time Warner began spending on the analysis and integration of the company's differing cultures, employee and management personalities, and operations. All external signs pointed toward a massive AOL Time Warner with combined services and operations that could not be paralleled, but other factors were at play. The combined stock market valuation that was projected, the combined profits and revenues, and the outlined synergies did not happen as expected.

Several factors could be blamed for the worsening AOL Time Warner Internet unit: possible ego and boardroom clashes, the slow-down of the economy, a three-year bear market, the burst of the Internet bubble, the September 11, 2001, terrorist attack, the slow realization of synergy, and the corporation's accounting issues. As one person said, "AOL is a victim of its own success, placing too much faith in the idea that it, like too many others in the dot.com boom, could defy economic gravity."[11] While the unit's poor performance had been linked to vanishing ad revenues, other probable issues included slowing subscriber growth, accounting troubles, investigation by the Department of Justice, impairment of goodwill, and the company's slow move into the broadband business. Furthermore, decreasing value left AOL Time Warner with a tremendous financial loss and high debt levels. This greatly contributed to the internal cultural and managerial tension, and it eventually led to the departures of former AOL Time Warner Chairman of the Board Steve Case and Vice Chairman Ted Turner.

Some analysts argued, "Synergies between traditional media and new media don't exist. Consumers use them for different purposes and to obtain entirely different things."[12] The Internet was used to match one's personal interest with content and to converse with others via specific web sites, chat rooms, or e-mail. Traditional media, on the other hand, were not able to fulfill these requirements. The fundamental limitation of traditional media was the inability to individualize. It was impossible to produce each edition to one user's specific mix of interests. The advantages of traditional media lay in the ability to produce and distribute the same information to everyone, satisfying a generic interest.

Time Warner Drops AOL from Its Name

If and how AOL Time Warner can succeed in the long term is yet to be seen. Until today, the company has held an exceptional position and has always had the potential of turning its business around and becoming very profitable again. The new company must quickly determine how to settle its outstanding battles, including FCC regulations, its approach on traditional versus new distribution and media channels, the Securities and Exchange Commision investigation, the broadband struggle and court case, and anti-trust issues, and it must soothe the bitterness among the company's employees and investors. Potential lenders are not interested in making loans to a company with skyrocketing debt levels, and Wall Street will not see much appeal in floating new stock. Furthermore, AOL Time Warner's new corporate strategy needed to overcome the harsh situation in the financial market, "a lack of qualified buyers [and] a new CEO who insists the merger still will pay off."[13]

On October 16, 2003, AOL Time Warner changed its name to Time Warner Inc., and the earlier Time Warner Inc.'s named was changed to Historic Time Warner Inc. This change confirmed management's belief that the business segments of the merged entity could not be managed under one name and needed their own identities. While its core business was in entertainment, the network, cable, and publishing units continued their steady financial performance. Therefore, the company's brands remained strong, but attention needed to be brought to the Internet division.

There was mixed feedback from the market about the company changing its name from AOL Time Warner to the old Time Warner or Time Warner AOL. Supporters of the change believed that it would encourage investors and employees to concentrate more on the profitable old Time Warner media, publishing, and entertainment properties and less on the downward spiral of the Internet unit. For supporters, employees and investors were the ones the company's name was designed to appeal to. "To them, the AOL ticker symbol is probably synonymous with gut-wrenching stock dives and aggressive accounting practices."[14]

With Case and Turner's departures from the newly renamed Time Warner, the company had various options for the future. The company could choose "a more conservative approach (in other words, the old Time Warner way)"[15] in the future, while its focus was on reducing the debt load and redirecting capital investments. This approach might not be that far-fetched, as more and more former Time Warner senior executives were assuming control over the company. Second, Time Warner could reestablish and redefine guidelines of corporate responsibilities under the current organizational structure. Even with new management's "faith in the recently announced strategy to revamp AOL"[16]—actively growing the number of broadband Internet subscribers, attaining exclusive content deals, and providing premium services—a new corporate concept was required. Despite senior executives' decisions on the firm's future moves, the entire Time Warner corporation will "keep government trust busters busy as they investigate what this new multimedia powerhouse is all about."[17] Time Warner must work to develop and implement the necessary strategies and concepts for a successful future.

In the end, a look at the unaudited 2003 third quarter of Time Warner Inc. indicated that the company was developing a plan—a plan to reduce debt, increase profitability, and raise its stock price. Most importantly, for the nine months ended September 30, 2003, Time Warner Inc. had announced a net profit of $2 billion and positive cash flow from operations.[18] There seemed to be significant reduction in debt. As for the stock price, which at the time hovered around $18, it was better than $9.9, the 52-week low, but it was still not good enough for investors to buy. A lot would depend on the financial results for the fiscal year 2003 yet to be announced by the company.

Notes

1. "AOL Buyout of Time Warner: Merger Frenzy Sweeping Corporate America," *www.wsws.org/articles/2000/jan2000/merg-j14.shtml* (January 14, 2000).
2. *Ibid.*
3. "AOL Time Warner Merger," *www.antiessays.com/show.php?eid=1538.*
4. *www.cme.org/access/broadband/printer.html.*
5. "The Broadband Revolution—Broadband, Networks and Narrow Visions: The Internet at Risk," *www.democraticmedia.org/issues/openaccess/at_risk.html.*
6. *www.cme.org/access/broadband/end_to_end.html.*
7. M. Lewis, "FCC Declines to Hobble Cable Broadband," *www.forbes.com/2002/03/15/0315broadband.html* (March 15, 2002).
8. R. Mark, "FCC Frees Bells of Broadband Restrictions," *http://dc.internet.com/news/article.php/1588441* (February 20, 2003).
9. P. Furman, "AOLTW Feels Pressure to Split into Separate Companies," *Knight Ridder Tribune Business News* (July 16, 2002).
10. D. D. Kirkpatrick, "AOL Chairman's No. 1 Ally Turns into His Biggest Foe," *New York Times* (October 1, 2002).

11. D. Gardner, "Media: Hype Can't Save AOL Time Warner from Scandal," *www.sundayherald.com/26475* (July 28, 2002).
12. V. Crosbie, "AOL Time Warner: It's a New Media, Baby," *http://clickz.com/design/freefee/print.php/1434921* (July 30, 2002).
13. B. Johnson, "Breaking Up AOL Time Warner?" *www.adage.com/news.cms?newsId=35530* (July 23, 2002).
14. J. Glasner, "The Case for AOL Name Change," *www.wired.com/news/business/0,1367,57197,00.html* (January 14, 2003).
15. D. Gardner, "Media: Hype Can't Save AOL Time Warner from Scandal," *www.sundayherald.com/26475* (July 28, 2002).
16. S. Pruitt, "Analysis: AOLTW's Post-merger Depression Lingers On," *www.infoworld.com/article/03/01/30/030130hnaolloss_1.html?business* (January 30, 2003).
17. "AOL Time Warner Merger," *www.antiessays.com/show.php?eid=1538.*
18. *www.timewarner.com/investors/quarterly_earnings/index.adp*

References

"Timeline—Milestones and Key Dates in AOL Time Warner History," *www.aoltimewarner.com/corporate_information/timeline.adp.*

AOL, "Mission and Values," *www.aoltimewarner.com/corporate_information/mission_and_values.adp.*

AOL Time Warner, Annual Report, *www.aoltimewarner.com/investors/annual_reports/pdf/2001ar.pdf* (2001).

S. Lawson, "AOL Raises Red Flags over Three Past Deals," *http://archive.infoworld.com/articles/hn/xml/02/08/14/020814hnaolflag.xml* (August 14, 2002).

D. Gardner, "Media: Hype Can't Save AOL Time Warner from Scandal," *www.sundayherald.com/26475* (July 28, 2002).

"AOL Time Warner Execs Play Down Big Loss," *www.informationweek.com/story/IWK20030129S0009* (January 29, 2003).

AOL, "Board of Directors," *www.aoltimewarner.com/corporate_information/board_of_directors.adp.*

S. Pruitt, "Analysis: AOLTW's Post-merger Depression Lingers On," *www.infoworld.com/article/03/01/30/030130hnaolloss_1.html?business* (January 30, 2003).

"America Online Names AOL Time Warner Insider as New Chief Financial Officer," *www.siliconvalley.com/mld/siliconvalley/business/companies/aol/5286646.htm.*

"AOL Buyout of Time Warner: Merger Frenzy Sweeping Corporate America," *www.wsws.org/articles/2000/jan2000/merg-j14.shtml* (January 14, 2000).

S. Junnarkar and J. Hu, "AOL Buys Time Warner in Historic Merger," *http://news.com.com/2100-1023-235400.html?legacy=cnet* (January 10, 2000).

J. Pelline and M. Yamamoto, "Can New Empire Avoid Titanic Clashes?" *http://news.com.com/2100-1023-235448.html?legacy=cnet* (January 10, 2000).

J. Hu, S. Junnarkar, and B. Lipton Krigel, "How America Online Became a Superpower," *http://news.com.com/2100-1023-235444.html?legacy=cnet* (January 10, 2000).

V. Crosbie, "Viewpoint: AOL Time Warner: It's a New Media, Baby," *www.clickz.com/design/freefee/print.php/1434921* (July 30, 2002).

"AOL Time Warner Merger," *www.antiessays.com/show.php?eid=1538.*

D. Faber, "Clash of Cultures at AOL Time Warner," *http://moneycentral.msn.com/content/CNBCTV/Articles/TVReports/P37848.asp* (January 9, 2003).

S. F. Gale, "Memo to AOL Time Warner: Why Mergers Fail," *www.workforce.com/section/09/feature/23/39/96/* (February 2003).

B. Johnson, "Breaking Up AOL Time Warner?" *www.adage.com/news.cms?newsID=35530* (July 23, 2003).

J. Glasner, "The Case for AOL Name Change," *www.wired.com/news/business/0,1367,57197,00.html* (January 14, 2003).

L. Takeuchi Cullen, "Dialing Up a Departure," *www.time.com/time/archive/preview/from_redirect/0,10987,1101030127-409506,00.html* (January 27, 2003).

www.timewarneraustin.com/company/corporate_information/.

E. Millard, "Time Warner's AOL Problem," *www.newsfactor.com/perl/story/story-start#story-start* (June 4, 2002).

"Dial-Up Vs Broadband," *www.telesolutions.com.au/internet/dialvbroadband.asp.*

"Broadband Vs Dial-Up Internet; What Is DSL?" *http://hankfiles.pcvsconsole.com/answer.php?file=506* (October 21, 2002).

M. Carr, "Dial-up Computer Connections vs. Broadband," *www.gazettearchives.com/cyberspace2001/_disc4/000000cc.htm* (March 19, 2001).

"White Paper: Broadband—Bigger Pipes Mean Better Serving," *Smart Computing*, Vol. 9, No. 6 (June 2001).

K. Schurman, "White Paper: Broadband—Bigger Pipes Mean Better Surfing," *www.smartcomputing.com/editorial/article.asp?article=articles%2Farchive%2Fg0906%2F36g06%2F36g06%2Easp* (June 2001).

L. E. Saris, "White Paper Issues and Statistics on the Subject of Digital Divide," *www.salemcyberspace.org/whitepaper.htm* (July 29, 2002).

M. Cooper, "Consumer Group Kicks Off 'Broadband' Internet Campaign," *www.consumerfed.org/launch1099.htm* (October 7, 1999).

"The Broadband Revolution—What It Is and Why It Matters," *www.cme.org/access/broadband/primer.html.*

"The Broadband Revolution—The End-to-End Internet: No Room for Monopolies," *www.cme.org/access/broadband/end_to_end.html.*

"What the Market Will Bear: Cisco's Vision for Broadband Internet," *www.democraticmedia.org/issues/openaccess/whatthemarketwillbear.html.*

"The Broadband Revolution—Broadband Networks and Narrow Visions: The Internet at Risk," *www.democraticmedia.org/issues/openaccess/at_risk.html.*

G. Larson and J. Chester, "Song of the Open Road: Building a Broadband Network for the 21st Century," *www.democraticmedia.org/resources/articles/openroad4.html* (1999).

"Talking Points on the Broadband Future: Open Access or Closed Networks?" *www.democraticmedia.org/issues/openaccess/AFLTP.html.*

G. O. Larson and J. Chester, "How to Prepare for the Era of the Speedy Internet," *www.democraticmedia.org/resources/articles/prepareforspeedyinternet.html* (2000).

M. Freedman, "Is Broadband All It's Cracked Up to Be?" *http://216.239.37.100/search?q=cache:SvRCk5C0-QMC:www.nop.co.uk/technology/PDF%27s/White%2520Paper%2520-%2520broad-*

band.pdf+broadband%2Binternet%2Bwhite+paper&hl=en&ie=UTF-8 (July 2001).

D. McClure, "The Future of Residential Dial-up Access," *www.internetindustry.com/mag/01_02su/05fut/index.shtml.*

N. Garcia, "How It Works: Dial-Up Networking," *www.pcworld.com/resource/printable/article/0,aid,48467,00.asp* (May 2, 2001).

M. Pastore, "Broadband Technology Boom Predicted," *cyberatlas.internet.com/markets/broadband/article/0,1323,10099_151341,00.html* (January 6, 1999).

"Broadband—High Speed Internet Access," *www.fcc.gov/cgb/broadband.html.*

J. Borland, "Broadband Defectors on the Rise," *http://zdnet.com.com/2100-1106-814343.html* (November 7, 2001).

R. Mark, "FCC Frees Bells of Broadband Restrictions," *http://dc.internet.com/news/article.php/1588441* (February 20, 2003).

M. Lewis, "FCC Declines to Hobble Cable Broadband," *www.forbes.com/2002/03/15/0315broadband.html* (March 15, 2002).

B. Charny, "FCC Loosens Broadband Rules," *http://news.com.com/2100-1033-985313.html* (February 20, 2003).

"New Regulations Could Spur Broadband Investment but Limit Choices," *www.hindustantimes.com/news/181_193657,00030010.htm* (February 22, 2003).

CASE 16

Harley-Davidson, Inc. 2006: The Building of a Second Century

Patricia A. Ryan and Thomas L. Wheelen

We fulfill dreams through the experience of motorcycling by providing to motorcyclists and to the general public an expanding line of motorcycles, branded products and services in selected market segments.[1]

Harley-Davidson Mission Statement

It was a pretty amazing sight: dozens at a time, thousands in a day descending on the Sinclair gas station and Western café in Lusk, Wyoming, on their way to the 2006 Sturgis rally in the blistering heat of early August. Lusk, a town of 1,348 people that lies 147 miles southwest of Sturgis, saw bikers from all walks of life, needing fuel and small supplies, some with tattoos, some with leather to protect themselves from the winds as they cruised at 60 miles per hour along Highway 18 toward Sturgis. Some clearly were businessmen on a weeklong reprieve, others were rougher in appearance. The one thing they all had in common was the love of the ride . . . the ride of the Harley-Davidson motorcycle.

New issues confronted Harley-Davidson in their 104th year of operation—they were facing several potentially costly lawsuits alleging that the company falsely depicted stronger demand than actual in order to charge premium prices for their motorcycles. There were allegations of channel stuffing, a false creation of supply shortage in order to command higher prices: an allegation the company denies. Then there was the customer base: the rockers who grew up in the 1960s and 1970s are graying, and this threatens the growth of Harley-Davidson. As riders approach 60, it is important for Harley-Davidson to recruit new riders from the younger generations. The company's emphasis on recruiting women has been instrumental in recent years. They were faced with an aging Baby Boomer population and needed to focus on growing smaller segments of their business—women bikers and younger bikers, the latter of whom could not traditionally afford a Harley-Davidson motorbike.

Harley-Davidson had enjoyed recent growth, especially in their smaller, more affordable motorbikes, and in August 2006 it was announced that the company was changing their ticker symbol from HDI to HOG. The new ticker symbol was the acronym of the Harley Owners Group, or H.O.G., the lifeblood of the company. Many things were looking good for the 104-year-old motorcycle manufacturer; however, newly installed President and CEO James Ziemer needed to continue the company's strong growth. Harley-Davidson had just opened their first dealership in mainland China, a whole new market for the company. A Harley-Davidson museum was under construction to preserve the history of the company. Ziemer had worked his way up the ranks, staring 36 years earlier as a freight elevator operator and most recently serving a 14-year stint at CFO; but now, in the driver's seat, he faced a different set of responsibilities. As noted by one analyst,

> There are indications that Harley-Davidson is at a turning point. "It's a well managed company with still one of the strongest brand names in consumer products, but I just question whether the company can grow its production 7 to 9 percent in an environment where demand doesn't seem to be growing at that rate"
>
> *Ed Aaron, analyst with BRC Capital Markets*[2]

History[3]

In 1903, William Harley (age 21), a draftsman, and his friend, Arthur R. Davidson, began experimenting with ideas to design and build their own motorcycles. They were joined by Arthur's brothers, William, a machinist, and Walter, a skilled mechanic. The Harley-Davidson Motor Company started in a 10 × 15 foot shed in the Davidson family's backyard in Milwaukee, Wisconsin.

In 1903, three motorcycles were built and sold. The production increased to eight in 1904. The company then moved to Juneau Avenue, which is the site of the company's present offices. In 1907, the company was incorporated.

Ownership by AMF

In 1969, AMF Inc., a leisure and industrial product conglomerate, acquired Harley-Davidson. The management team expanded production from 15,000 in 1969 to 40,000 motorcycles in 1974. AMF favored short-term profits instead of investing in research and development and retooling. During this time, Japanese competitors continued to improve the quality of their motorcycles, while Harley-Davidson began to turn out noisy, oil-leaking, heavily vibrating, poorly finished, and hard-to-handle machines. AMF ignored the Japanese competition. In 1975, Honda Motor Company introduced its "Gold Wing," which became the standard for large touring motorcycles. Harley-Davidson had controlled this segment of the market for years. There was a $2,000 price difference between Harley's top-of-the-line motorcycles and Honda's comparable Gold Wing. This caused American buyers of motorcycles to start switching to Japanese motorcycles. The Japanese companies (Suzuki and Yamaha) continued to enter the heavyweight custom market until the middle 1980s with Harley look-alikes.

During AMF's ownership of the company, sales of motorcycles were strong, but profits were weak. The company had serious problems with poor-quality manufacturing and strong Japanese competition. In 1981, Vaughn Beals, then head of the Harley Division, and 13 other managers conducted a leveraged buyout of the company for $65 million.

Under New Management

New management installed a Materials As Needed (MAN) system to reduce inventories and stabilize the production schedule. Also, this system forced production to work with marketing for more accurate forecasts. This led to precise production schedules for each month, allowing only a 10% variance. The company forced its suppliers to increase their quality in order to reduce customer complaints.

Citicorp, Harley's main lender, refused to lend any more money in 1985. On New Year's Eve, four hours before a midnight that would have meant Harley's demise, the company inked a deal with Heller Financial that kept its doors open. Seven months later, amid a hot market for new stock, Harley-Davidson went public again. Ziemer, the CFO puts it more bluntly: "You throw cash at it, try to grow too fast, you'd destroy this thing."[4]

During the time Harley-Davidson was a privately held firm, management invested in research and development. Management purchased a Computer-Aided Design (CAD) system that allowed the company to make changes in the entire product line and still maintain its traditional styling. These investments by management had a quick payoff in that the break-even point went from 53,000 motorcycles in 1982 to 35,000 in 1986.

In June 1993, more than 100,000 members of the worldwide Harley-Davidson family came home (Milwaukee) to celebrate the company's 90th anniversary. Willie G. Davidson, Vice President–Styling, grandson of the founder, said, "I was overwhelmed with emotion when our parade was rolling into downtown Milwaukee. I looked up to heaven and told the founding fathers, 'Thanks, guys.'"

Acquisitions of Buell and Eaglemark

During 1993, the company acquired a 49% interest in Buell Motorcycle Company, a manufacturer of sport/performance motorcycles. This investment in Buell offered the company the possibility of gradually gaining entry into select niches within the performance motorcycle market. In 1998, Harley-Davidson owned most of the stock in Buell. Buell began distribution of a limited number of Buell motorcycles during 1994 to select Harley-Davidson deals. Buell sales were:[5]

Year	Sales	Units (thousands)
1994	$6 million	576
1995	$14 million	1,407
1996	$23 million	2,762
1997	$40 million	4,415
1998	$53.5 million	6,334
1999	$63.5 million	7,767
2000	$58.1 million	10,189
2001	$61.9 million	9,925
2002	$66.9 million	10,900
2003	$76.1 million	10,000
2004	$79.0 million	9,900
2005	$93.1 million	11,200

Buell's mission "is to develop and employ innovative technology to enhance 'the ride' and give Buell owners a motorcycle experience that no other brand can provide." The European sport/performance market was four times larger than its U.S. counterpart. In 1997, there were 377 Buell dealers worldwide.

On November 14, 1995, the company acquired substantially all of the common stock and common stock equivalents of Eaglemark Financial Services, Inc., a company in which it had held a 49% interest since 1993. Eaglemark provided credit to leisure product manufacturers, their dealers, and customers in the United States and Canada. The transaction was accounted for as a step acquisition under the purchase method. The purchase price for the shares and equivalents was approximately $45 million, which was paid from internally generated funds and short-term borrowings. The excess of the acquisition cost over the fair value of the net assets purchased resulted in approximately $43 million of goodwill, which was amortized on a straight-line basis over 20 years.

Concentration on Motorcycles

On January 22, 1996, the company announced its strategic decision to discontinue the operations of the Transportation Vehicles segment in order to concentrate its financial and human resources on its core motorcycle business. The Transportation Vehicles segment included the Recreation Vehicles division (Holliday Rambler trailers), the Commercial Vehicles division (small delivery vehicles), and B & B Molders, a manufacturer of custom or standard tolling and injection-molded plastic pieces. During 1996, the company completed the sale of the Transportation Vehicles segment for an aggregate sales price of approximately $105 million: approximately $100 million in cash and $5 million in notes and preferred stock.

In the fall of 1997, GT Bicycles manufactured and distributed a 1,000 Harley Limited Edition at a list retail price of $1,700. The pedal-powered bike had a real Harley paint job, signature fenders, a fake gas tank, and chrome of a Harley Softail motorcycle. GT Bicycles manufactured the Velo Glide bikes and was licensed by Harley to produce the limited version. The 4-speed bike weighed 40-plus pounds. Ken Alder, cycle shop owner, said, "It's a big clunker that no one would really want to ride." Nevertheless, the bicycles sold out in less than 4 months to buyers. The resale price for the Limited Edition jumped to $3,500, and one collector advertised his for $5,000. In contrast, a person could purchase an actual Harley XHL 883 Sportster motorcycle for $5,245.

Internal Makeover and New Products

Since 1997, Harley-Davidson has created an internal makeover. The unsung hero of Harley-Davidson's supply-chain makeover was an intense procurement expert named Garry Berryman, 48, vice president of Materials Management/Product Cost. He came to Harley by way of John Deere and Honda Motors. Berryman joined the company in 1995 to find that its supply-chain management has been neglected. There were nine different purchasing departments operating from different plant locations, 14 separate sets of representative terms and conditions, and nearly 4,000 suppliers. Engineers with little or no expertise in supply management were doing the bulk of the buying. To top it off, "the voice of supply management was buried three layers deep in the corporate hierarchy," said Berryman.

While at Honda, Berryman studied Japanese *keiretsu*—huge, vertically integrated companies that foster deep, trusting relationships with suppliers. He wanted to form similar strategic alliances with Harley's top suppliers, bringing them into the design and planning process. Berryman felt that new technology and the web would make it easier than ever to form these bonds and collaborate. He made it clear that relationship and strategy should drive applications, not vice versa. As Dave Cotteleer, the company's manager of planning and control, explained, "We're using technology to cut back on communication times and administrative trivia, like invoice tracking, so we can focus the relationships on more strategic issues. We're not saying, 'Here's a neat piece of technology. Let's jam it into our model.'"[6]

Also, in the 1990s, Harley-Davidson saw the need to build a motorcycle to try to appeal to the younger and international markets who preferred sleeker, faster bikes. Harley-Davidson spent an undisclosed amount of research and development dollars over several years to develop the $17,000 V-Rod motorcycle. The V-Rod, introduced in 2001, had 110 horsepower, nearly double that of the standard Harley bike. The V-Rod was the quickest and fastest production model the company has ever built, capable of reaching 60 miles an hour in 3.5 seconds and 100 mph in a little over 8 seconds. Its top speed was about 140 mph. All in all, the V-Rod was faster and handled better than the traditional bulky Harley bikes.

All other Harley models were powered by 45-degree V-twin air-cooled engines with camshafts in the block; the new V-Rod had a 1,130-cc 60-degree engine with double overhead cams and four valves for each cylinder. The V-Rod had a very long 67.5-inch wheelbase, and it handled better than other Harleys because it was so much lighter. Furthermore, the V-Rod was only 26 inches off the ground, so it would accommodate a wide range of rides.[7] Harley-Davidson hoped to gain some of the younger markets with this new bike.

In 2000, a new Softail model was introduced, and all Softail models were outfitted with the twin Cam 88B engine. Fuel injection was introduced for the Softails in 2001 and in 2000, Buell introduced the Buell Blast with a single cylinder engine. Along with the Buell Blast, Harley-Davidson introduced a new beginner rider's course aimed at the first-time Harley owner and rider. The course was offered in Harley-Davidson and Buell dealerships. The VRSCA V-Rod was introduced in 2002. The V-Rod was the first Harley bike to combine fuel injection, overhead cams, and liquid cooling along with 115 horsepower.

In an attempt to gain further female support, Harley-Davidson announced the introduction of 17-year-old Jennifer Snyder, a champion dirt bike racer, as the newest member of the Harley-Davidson racing team.

In 2003, more than 250,000 Harley owners throughout the world celebrated the 100-year anniversary of Harley-Davidson with a three-week celebration ride, starting in Atlanta, Georgia, and ending in Sturgis, North Dakota.

In 2003, Harley-Davidson introduced the Lightning XBS9. In 2004, the Sporters were refitted with rubber engine mounting, a new frame, and a wider rear tire. The FLHRSI Road King was introduced with low rear suspension and wide handlebars for a beach appearance. In 2005, the XL 883 Sportster 883 Low, featuring a lowered seating position aimed at aging Baby Boomers, was added to the Sportster line. The FLSTNI Softail Deluxe was added to the Softail line with a new sleek appearance reminiscent of the 1939 Harley-Davidson bike. In the same year, the FLSTSC/I Softail Springer Classic revived the late-1940s bike in appearance.

Most recently, in 2006, the Dyna motorcycle line was developed with the first 6-speed transmission. The new FLHX/I Street Glide was introduced as a lower profile touring bike. Most recently, in June 2006, construction commenced on a Harley-Davidson museum to be finished in 2008 in Milwaukee, Wisconsin. In the area of international development, the first dealership was opened in mainland China.

Corporate Governance

Board of Directors

The Board of Directors consisted of 10 members, of which only two were internal members—Jeffrey E. Bluestein, Chairman and James L. Ziemer, President and Chief Executive Officer (CEO). **Exhibit 1** highlights board members at the end of 2005.

The Board of Directors served staggered three-year terms. Since 2003, non-employee directors have not been eligible to receive stock options. The guidelines require that all directors hold 5,000 shares of the common stock and senior executives hold from 5,000 to 30,000 shares of the common stock depending on their level. The directors and senior executives have five years from January 2003 or the date they are elected a director or promoted to a senior executive to accumulate the appropriate number of shares of the Harley-Davidson common stock.

Exhibit 1 Board of Directors: Harley-Davidson, Inc.

Barry K. Allen, *President, Allen Enterprises, LLC*
Barry has been a member of the Board since 1992. His distinguished business career has taken him from the telecommunications industry to leading a medical equipment and systems business and back again. Barry's diverse experience has been particularly valuable to the Board in the areas of marketing and organization transformation.

Richard I. Beattie, *Chairman of the Executive Committee, Simpson Thacher & Bartlett*
Dick has been a valued advisor to Harley-Davidson for nearly 20 years. His contributions evolved and grew with the company over time. In the early 1980s, he provided legal and strategic counsel to the 13 leaders who purchased Harley-Davidson from AMF, taking it back to private ownership. He also advised the team when it was time to take the company public again in 1986. Dick was elected to the Board in 1996.

Jeffrey L. Bluestein, *Chairman of the Board, Harley-Davidson, Inc.*
Jeff began his association with Harley-Davidson in 1975 when he was asked to oversee the engineering group. During his tenure as Vice President–Engineering, Harley-Davidson developed the Evolution engine and established the foundations of our current line of cruiser and touring motorcycles. Jeff has demonstrated creativity and vision across a wide range of senior leadership roles. In 1996, he was elected to the Board, and in June 1997, appointed CEO until his retirement in 2005. He remains on as Chairman of the Board.

George H. Conrades, *Executive Chairman of Akamai Technologies, Inc.*
George has served as a director since 2002 and brings with him extensive experience in e-business. Akamai Technologies is a provider of secure, outsourced e-business infrastructure services and software. He is also a partner with Polaris Venture Partners, an early-stage investment company.

Judson C. Green, *President and CEO, NAVTEQ Corporation*
NAVTEQ is a leading provider of comprehensive digital map information for automotive navigation systems, mobile navigation devices and Internet-based mapping applications. Judson has served as a director since 2004.

Donald A. James, *Vice Chairman and Chief Executive Officer, Fred Deeley Imports, Inc.*
Don's wisdom and knowledge of the motorcycle industry has guided the Board since 1991. As a 31-year veteran of Harley-Davidson's exclusive distributor in Canada, he has a strong sense for our core products. Don has a particularly keen understanding of the retrial issues involved with motorcycles and related products and the competitive advantage inherent in strong, long-lasting dealer relationships.

Sara L. Levinson, *ChairMom and Chief Executive Officer, ClubMom, Inc.*
Sara joined the Board in 1996. She understands the value and power of strong brands, and her current senior leadership role in marketing and licensing, together with her previous experience at MTV, give her solid insights into the entertainment industries and younger customer segments.

George L. Miles, Jr., *President and CEO, WQED Multimedia*
George has been a director since 2002 and currently serves as president and CEO of WQED Multimedia, the public broadcaster for southwestern Pennsylvania.

James A. Norling, *Executive Vice President, Motorola, Inc.; President, Personal Communications Sector, retired*
Jim has been a Board member since 1993. His career with Motorola has included extensive senior leadership assignments in Europe, the Middle East, and Africa, and he has generously shared his international experience and understanding of technological change to benefit Harley-Davidson.

James L. Zeimer, *President and CEO, Harley-Davidson, Inc.*
Jim has been with Harley-Davidson for over 36 years and served as CFO until 2005 when he assumed the role of CEO upon Jeff Bluestein's retirement. He has been a director since 2004.

Source: Harley-Davidson, Inc., 2005 Annual Report, p. 74.

Exhibit 2 Top Management: Harley-Davidson, Inc.

Corporate Officers, Harley-Davidson, Inc.

James L. Ziemer
President and Chief Executive Officer

James M. Brostowitz
Vice President, Treasurer and Acting Chief Financial Officer

Gail A. Lione
Vice President, General Counsel and Secretary

Motor Company Leadership

James L. Ziemer
Chief Executive Officer

Joanne M. Bischmann
Vice President, Marketing

David P. Bozeman
General Manager, Powertrain Operations

James M. Brostowitz
Vice President and Treasurer

Leroy Coleman
Vice President, Advanced Operations

Rodney J. Copes
Vice President and General Manager, Powertrain Operations

Ruth M. Crowley
Vice President, General Merchandise

William B. Dannehl
Vice President, North American Sales and Dealers Services

William G. Davidson
Vice President and Chief Styling Officer

Karl M. Eberle
Vice President and General Manager, Kansas City Operations

Robert S. Farchione
General Manager, Parts and Accessories

Fred C. Gates
General Manager, York Operations

James E. Haney
Vice President and Chief Information Officer

Michael P. Heerhold
General Manager, Tomahawk

John A. Hevey
Vice President, Strategic Planning and New Business Development

Timothy K. Hoelter
Vice President, Government Affairs

Ronald M. Hutchinson
Vice President

Michael D. Keefe
Vice President and Director, Harley Owners Group®

Kathleen A. Lawler
Vice President, Communications

Lara L. Lee
Vice President, Enthusiast Services

Matthew S. Levatich
Vice President, Materials Management

Gail A. Lione
Vice President and General Counsel

James A. McCaslin
President and Chief Operating Officer

Jeffrey A. Merten
Managing Director, Asia Pacific and Latin America

Louis N. Netz
Vice President and Director, Styling

John A. Olin
Vice President, Controller

Steven R. Phillips
Vice President, Quality, Reliability and Technical Services

John K. Russell
Vice President, Managing Director, Europe

Harold A. Scott
Vice President, Human Resources

Kenneth Sutton, Jr.
Vice President, Engineering

Jerry G. Wilke
Vice President, Customer Relationships and Product Planning

Harley-Davidson Financial Services Leadership

Lawrence G. Hund
Vice President, Chief Financial Officer

Kathryn H. Marczak
Vice President, Chief Credit and Administrative Officer

Donna F. Zarcone
President and Chief Operating Officer

Buell Motorcycle Company Leadership

Erik F. Buell
Chairman and Chief Technical Officer

John R. Flickinger
President and Chief Operating Officer

Source: Harley-Davidson, Inc., 2005 Annual Report, p. 76.

Top Management

James C. Ziemer started with Harley-Davidson 36 years ago as a freight elevator operator and served as the CFO from 1991 to 2005. In 2005, on the retirement of Harley veteran Jeffrey Bluestein, Ziemer assumed the top role of President and CEO. He commented, "As we reflect on 2005, Harley-Davidson is strong and well-positioned for the road ahead."[8] Ziemer further commented:

> I believe there are three constants in our success as a company: 1. Our passion for this business, for riding, and for relating to and being one with our customers; 2. Our sense of purpose—in other words, our focus on growing demand by offering great products and unique experiences; and 3. Operational Excellence—which is the continuous, relentless drive to eliminate waste in all aspects of our operations and to run Harley-Davidson better and more efficiently with each passing day. And I believe these three things—being close to our customers, growth and Operational Excellence—hold the keys to the future.[9]

Exhibit 2 shows the corporate officers for Harley-Davidson and its business segments—motor company leadership, Buell leadership, and financial services leadership.

Harley-Davidson continued to receive positive attention from the popular press. In 2006, *Business Week/Interbrand* Annual Rankings Top 100 Global Brands placed Harley-Davidson at number 45, up 1 from 2005. The companies on the list are required to be global in nature with at least 20% of sales outside of their home country.[10] Harley-Davidson had been on this Top 100 list since its inception in 2000. *Fortune* also placed Harley-Davidson in its 2004 list of "Most Admired Companies."[11] Previously, *Forbes* named Harley-Davidson its "Company of the Year" for 2001.

Although retail domestic sales of Harley-Davidson bikes were up 4.2% in 2005 over 2004, not all was rosy for the 104-year-old company. Harley-Davidson, which had fought back from near demise in the 1980s, was to face new rivals in the competitive market, an aging customer base, and a recession. The projected sales figures looked strong through 2006, but what did 2007 hold for Harley-Davidson? These were issues management wrestled with as they planned for the future. One theme was to gain new, younger customers to move Harley-Davidson into its second century.

The Annual Sturgis Rally

Each year, thousands of Harley-Davidson riders from around the country gather in Stugis, South Dakota, the heart of the Black Hills, for the annual Harley-Davidson road rally. The week-long event has an incredible following of bikers from all walks of life who spent several nights in a town transformed for the rally. Each year is a bit different, although much the same. One rider in the 2006 rally commented, "You drive up here thinking you have a nice bike and you find out it is just average, but I always have a great time."[12]

Some ask what burden this places on the small, otherwise quiet town of Sturgis. It is clear the revenue from the rally outweighs any distraction and town residents are happy to give up their quiet secluded life for a few days. In 2006, the Sturgis police department noted:

> In 2005, officers on Rally patrol responded to 1,643 service calls in an eight day period. They make 646 arrests for everything from parking violations and public intoxication to felony drug charges according to Sturgis police Chief Jim Bush. He reported there have been very few accounts of violence though. "There is very little violent crime during recent rallies. I think it is due to the bikers themselves—they want to party, they want to drink, but all in all, they're not really here to harm each other. We don't have a lot of assaults or robberies."[13]

The group can number as high as 250,000, but they are out there to ride and talk with other riders. Few problems arise from the large crowds. Andy Horn, Director of a Harley-Davidson dealership, commented about the riders: "They're doctors, lawyers, policemen, business owners. They're not just the scruffy beer-drinking guys."[14]

Harley Owners Group (H.O.G.)

A special kind of camaraderie marked the Harley Owners Group rallies and other motorcycle events. At events and rallies around the world, members of the H.O.G. came together for fun, adventure, and a love of their machines and the open road. As the largest motorcycle club in the world, H.O.G. offered customers organized opportunities to ride their famed bikes. H.O.G. rallies visibly promoted the Harley-Davidson experience to potential new customers and strengthened the relationships among members, dealers, and Harley-Davidson employees.

According to William G. Davidson, grandson of the co-founder, biker to the core, and known to all as Willie G., "There's a lot of beaners, but they're out on the motorcycles, which is a beautiful thing." He noted that he recently co-led a national rally of Canadian HOG groups with Harley's Chairman Jeff Bleustein.[15]

In 1995, the Buell Riders Adventure Group (BRAG) was created to bring Buell motorcycle enthusiasts together and to share their on-road experiences. In 2005, BRAG held a homecoming event in East Troy, Wisconsin. Harley-Davidson plans to grow both organizations with new members and chapters in the years to come.

Exhibit 3 provides a profile of H.O.G and BRAG clubs. As of 2005, there were about 993,000 H.O.G. members in about 1,200 clubs. The newer BRAG club for Buell riders numbered 110,000 members in more than 55 clubs. Membership in H.O.G was $45 per year or $120 for 3 years.

Exhibit 3 2006 Profile of the H.O.G. and BRAG: Harley-Davidson, Inc.

H.O.G. Sponsored Events: In 2006, H.O.G. continued to sponsor motorcycling events on local, regional, national, and international levels. The 16th annual international H.O.G. Rally drew tens of thousands of members.

H.O.G. Membership: Any owner of a Harley-Davidson motorcycle could become a member of H.O.G. In fact, their first year of membership was included with the purchase of a new Harley-Davidson motorcycle. The number of H.O.G. members had grown rapidly since the motorcycle organization began in 1983 with 33,000 members. There were 993,000 H.O.G. members in 115 countries worldwide. Sponsorship of H.O.G. chapters by Harley-Davidson dealers grew from 49 chapters in 1985 to more than 1,200 chapters in 2005.

A Snapshot of H.O.G.

Created in	1983
Worldwide members	993,000
Worldwide dealer-sponsored chapters	1,200
Countries with members	115

A Snapshot of BRAG (Buell Riders Adventure Group)

Created in	1995
Worldwide members	11,000
Number of clubs	55

Source: Harley-Davidson, Inc. 2005 Annual Report, pp. 28–29, updated from http://www.harley-davidson.com.

The Harley-Davidson Museum

On June 1, 2006, Harley-Davidson launched construction of their museum in Milwaukee, Wisconsin. In true Harley style, the groundbreaking was celebrated, not with a shovel, but rather with a Harley-Davidson XL 883R Sportster motorcycle spinning a burnout and sending dirt flying. The Harley-Davidson Museum was to house a collection of motorcycles and historical mementos from the company's 104-year history. The museum was expected to open in 2008.

Said CEO Ziemer:[6]

> With over one hundred years and millions of motorcycles behind us, Harley-Davidson has a rich history, an exciting present, and a vibrant future. In the years to come, the Harley-Davidson Museum will be a centerpiece of the Harley-Davidson experience. Today's groundbreaking ceremony was a unique way for us to kick off the Museum's construction.

Domestic and Foreign Operations[17]

United States

Domestically, Harley-Davidson sells its motorcycles and related products at wholesale to a network of approximately 667 independently owned full-service Harley-Davidson dealerships. In addition, Harley-Davidson sells at wholesale to the Overseas Military Sales Corporation, an entity that retails the Company's products to members of the U.S. military. The U.S. independent dealer network includes 318 combined Harley-Davidson and Buell dealerships. With respect to sales of new motorcycles, approximately 82% of the U.S. dealerships sell the Harley-Davidson motorcycles exclusively. Independent dealers also sell a smaller portion of parts and accessories, general merchandise, and licensed products through "non-traditional" retail outlets. The "non-traditional" outlets, which are extensions of the main dealership, consist of Secondary Retail Locations (SRLs), Alternate Retail Outlets (AROs), and Seasonal Retail Outlets (SROs). Secondary retail locations are satellites of the main dealership and are developed to meet the service needs of the Company's riding customers. They also provide parties and accessories, general merchandise, and licensed products and are authorized to sell and service new motorcycles. Alternate retail outlets are located primarily in high-traffic locations such as malls, airports, or popular vacation destinations and focus on selling general merchandise and licensed products. Seasonal retail outlets are located in similar high-traffic areas, but operate on a seasonal basis out of temporary locations such as vendor kiosks. There are approximately 90 secondary retail outlets, 65 alternative retail outlets, and 10 seasonal retail outlets in the United States.

Foreign Operations

Total revenue from the sale of motorcycles and related products to independent dealers and distributors located outside of the United States was approximately $1.04 billion, $917 million, and $816 million, or approximately 19%, 18%, and 18% of net revenue of the Motorcycles segment, during 2005, 2004, and 2003, respectively.

Europe/Middle East/Africa

At the end of 2005, there were 359 independent Harley-Davidson dealerships serving 32 European country markets. This includes 292 combined Harley-Davidson and Buell dealerships. Buell is further represented by seven dealerships that do not sell Harley-Davidson motorcycles. They have an established infrastructure in Europe, based out of its headquarters in the United Kingdom, and operate through a network of independent dealers served by eight independent distributors and by five wholly owned sales and marketing subsidiaries in France, Germany, Italy, The Netherlands, and the United Kingdom. The European management team is focused on the expansion and improvement of distributor and dealer relationships through dealer development teams, specialized training programs, retail financing initiatives, ongoing product development, and coordinated Europe-wide and local marketing programs aimed at attracting new customers.

Asia-Pacific

In the Asia/Pacific region, Harley-Davidson sells motorcycles and related products at wholesale to independent dealers and distributors. In Japan, their sales, marketing, and distribution of their products are managed from their subsidiary in Tokyo, which sells motorcycles and related products at wholesale to a network of 118 independent Harley-Davidson dealers. Fifty-one of these 118 dealers sell both Harleys and Buells. There are three dealerships that sell only Buell bikes.

In Australia and New Zealand, the distribution of Harley-Davidson products is managed by independent distributors that purchase products at wholesale directly from the Harley-Davidson U.S. operation. In 2005, the Harley-Davidson subsidiary in Sydney, Australia, began managing the sales, marketing, and distribution of Buell products in this market and is expected to begin managing the distribution of Harley-Davidson products in the later part of 2006. The Australia/New Zealand market is served at retail by a network of 51 independent Harley-Davidson dealerships, including 26 that sell both Harley-Davidson and Buell products.

Latin America

In Latin America, Harley-Davidson sells motorcycles and related products at wholesale to independent dealers. Harley-Davidson supplies all products sold in the Latin-America region directly to independent dealers from its U.S. operations, with the exception of certain motorcycles sold in Brazil, which are assembled and distributed by the Company's subsidiary in Manaus, Brazil.

In Latin America, 12 countries are served by 31 independent dealers. Brazil is the Company's largest market in Latin America and is served by 10 independent dealers. Mexico, the region's second largest market has 11 independent dealers. In the remaining countries in the Latin American region there are 10 independent dealers.

Canada

In Canada the Company sells its motorcycles and related products at wholesale to a single independent distributor, Deeley Harley-Davidson Canada/Fred Deeley Imports Ltd. In Canada, there are approximately 75 independent Harley-Davidson dealerships and three AROs. In Canada, 43 of the 75 dealerships are combined Harley-Davidson and Buell dealerships.

Business Segments

Running a company is like riding a motorcycle. Go too slow, and you tip over. Go too fast, and you crash. At the moment, Harley has a perfect balance.[18]

Harley-Davidson operates in two principal business segments: Motorcycles and Related Products (Motorcycles) and Financial Services. The segments will be discussed in that order. **Exhibit 4** provides financial information on the company's two business segments.

Exhibit 4 Information by Business Segments: Harley-Davidson, Inc.

A. Revenues and Income from Operations
(Dollar amounts in thousands)

Year ending December 31	2005	2004	2003
Net sales and Financial Services income:			
Motorcycles and Related Products net sales	$5,342,214	$5,015,190	$4,624,274
Financial Services income	331,618	305,262	279,459
	$5,673,832	$5,320,452	$4,903,733
Income from operations:			
Motorcycles and Related Products	$1,299,865	$1,189,519	$996,889
Financial Services	191,620	188,600	167,873
General corporate expenses	(21,474)	(16,628)	(15,498)
Operating Income	$1,470,011	$1,361,491	$1,149,264

B. Assets, Depreciation, and Capital Expenditures
(Dollar amounts in millions)

	Motorcycles and Related Products	Financial Services	Corporate	Consolidated
2005				
Identifiable Assets	$1,845,802	$2,363,235	$1,046,172	$5,255,209
Depreciation and Amortization	198,833	6,872	—	205,705
Net Capital Expenditures	188,078	10,311	—	198,389
2004				
Identifiable Assets	$1,646,251	$2,223,796	$1,613,246	$5,483,293
Depreciation and Amortization	206,420	7,536	156	214,112
Net Capital Expenditures	188,122	25,171	257	213,550
2003				
Identifiable Assets	$1,778,566	$1,821,142	$1,323,380	$4,923,088
Depreciation and Amortization	191,118	5,555	245	196,918
Net Capital Expenditures	219,592	7,263	375	227,230

Source: Harley-Davidson, Inc., 2005 Form 10-K, p. 87.

Motorcycles and Related Products Segment

The longer the wait, the more Wall Street loved Harley.[19]

The primary business of the Motorcycles segment is to design, manufacture, and sell premium motorcycles for the heavyweight market. They are best known for their Harley-Davidson motorcycle products, but also offer a line of motorcycles and related products under the Buell brand name. Their worldwide motorcycle sales generated 80.1%, 80.0%, and 80.0%, of the total net sales in the Motorcycles segment during 2005, 2004, and 2003, respectively.

The majority of the Harley-Davidson branded motorcycle products emphasize traditional styling, design simplicity, durability, ease of service, and evolutionary change. Harley's appeal straddles class boundaries, stirring the hearts of grease monkeys and corporate titans

Exhibit 5 Purchaser Demographic Profile: Harley-Davidson, Inc.

	1983	1990	2000	2002	2003	2004	2005
GENDER							
Male	98%	96%	91%	91%	90%	90%	89%
Female	2%	4%	9%	9%	10%	10%	11%
MEDIAN AGE							
Years	34.1	36.7	45.6	46.0	46.7	46.9	46.7
Median Household Income ($000)	$38.3	$47.3	$77.7	$78.6	$80.2	$80.1	$82.5

2005 PURCHASERS

43%	Owned Harley-Davidson motorcycle previously
29%	Coming off of competitive motorcycle
28%	New to motorcycling or haven't owned a motorcycle for at least 5 years

Source: Harley-Davidson Fact Book, http://investor.harley-davidson.com/downloads/factsheet.pdf (August 18, 2006).

alike. Malcolm Forbes, the late owner of *Forbes* magazine, was pivotal in introducing Harleys to the business elite in the early 1980s.[20]

The typical motorcycle rider is a 38-year-old male who is married, has attended college, and earns $44,250 a year. Based on data from the Motorcycle Industry Council owner survey, nearly 1 of every 9 motorcycle owners is female.[21] The average U.S. Harley-Davidson motorcycle purchaser, in contrast, is a married male in his mid-40s, with a household income of approximately $82,500, who purchases a motorcycle for recreational purposes rather than to provide transportation and is an experienced motorcycle rider. Over two-thirds of the firm's U.S. sales of Harley-Davidson motorcycles are to buyers with at least one year of education beyond high school, and 31% of the buyers have college degrees. (See **Exhibit 5.**)

In an effort to grow and recognize the importance of female riders to Harley-Davidson, the company partnered with *Jane* magazine in 2005 in what was called the Spirit of Freedom Contest to recognize women who overcome fears and other obstacles to become Harley riders. The grand prize winner was to receive a new Sportster 883.

"The adrenaline rush of riding a motorcycle out on the open is like no other experience. Through this contest, we are saluting women who embody that spirit of adventure through small gestures, inner strength, and everyday selfless acts" commented Kathleen Lawler, Vice President of Communications, Harley-Davidson.[22]

Buell motorcycle products emphasize innovative design, responsive handling, and overall performance. The Buell motorcycle product line has traditionally consisted of heavyweight performance models, powered by the 1200-cc V-Twin engine. However, in 2000, they introduced the Buell Blast, a new vehicle designed specifically to attract new customers into the sport of motorcycling. This vehicle was considerably smaller, lighter and less expensive than the traditional Buell heavyweight models and is powered by a 492-cc single-cylinder engine. The Buell line has continued to grow since the introduction of the lower priced Buell Blast.

The average U.S. purchaser of the Buell heavyweight motorcycle is a male at the median age of 39 with a median household income of approximately $61,600. Approximately 3% of all Buell heavyweight U.S. retail motorcycle sales are to females. Internal documents indicate that half of Buell Blast purchasers have never owned a motorcycle before, and in excess of 95% of them had never owned a Buell motorcycle before. The median age of Blast purchasers is 38, with over half of them being female.

The motorcycle market comprises four segments: standard, which emphasizes simplicity and cost; performance, which emphasizes handling and acceleration; touring, which emphasizes comfort and amenities for long-distance travel; and custom, which emphasizes styling and individual owner customization.

Harley-Davidson presently manufactures and sells 28 models of Harley-Davidson touring and custom heavyweight motorcycles, with domestic manufacturer's suggested retail prices ranging from approximately $6,595 to $20,195. (See **Exhibit 6.**) The touring segment of the heavyweight market was pioneered by Harley-Davidson and includes motorcycles equipped for long-distance touring with fairings, windshields, saddlebags, and Tour Pak luggage carriers. The custom segment of the market includes motorcycles featuring the distinctive styling associated with classic Harley-Davidson motorcycles. These motorcycles are highly customized through the use of trim and accessories.

Harley-Davidson's traditional heavyweight motorcycles are based on variations of five basic chassis designs and are powered by one of four air-cooled, twin cylinder engines with a 45-degree "V" configuration, which have displacements of 883 cc, 1200 cc, 1450 cc, and 1550 cc. The V-Rod has its own unique chassis design and is equipped with the new Revolution powertrain, a new liquid-cooled, twin-cylinder, 1130-cc engine, with a 60-degree "V" configuration.

Although there are some accessory differences between the top-of-the line touring motorcycles and those of its competitors, suggested retail prices are generally comparable. The prices for the high-end of the Harley-Davidson custom product line range from being competitive to 50% more than its competitors' custom motorcycles. The custom portion of the Harley-Davidson product line represents their highest unit volumes and continues to command a premium price because of the features, styling, and high resale value associated with Harley-Davidson custom products. The smallest displacement custom motorcycle (the 883-cc Sportster) is directly price competitive with comparable motorcycles available in the market. The surveys of retail purchasers indicate that, historically, more than three-quarters of the purchasers of its Sportster model either have previously owned competitive-brand motorcycles or are completely new to the sport of motorcycling or have not participated in the sport for at least five years. Since 1988, research has consistently shown purchasers of Harley-Davidson motorcycles have a repurchase intent in excess of 90%, and management expects to see sales of its 883-cc Sportster model partially translated into sales of its higher-priced products in the normal two- to three-year ownership cycle.

Worldwide Parts and Accessories net sales comprised 15.3%, 15.6%, and 15.4% of net sales in the motorcycles segment in 2005, 2004, and 2003, respectively. Worldwide net sales of general merchandise, which includes MotorClothes apparel and collectibles, comprised 4.6%, 4.5%, and 4.6% of net sales in the Motorcycles segment in 2005, 2004, and 2003, respectively.

Management also provides a variety of services to its dealers and retail customers including service training schools, customized dealer software packages, delivery of its motorcycles, an owners club membership, a motorcycle rental program, and a rider training program that is available in the United States through a limited number of authorized dealers.

President and CEO's Comments[23]

Jim Ziemer was promoted from CFO to CEO in April 2005. Thomas Bergman, 39, was selected to serve as the new Chief Financial Officer. Analysts appear to like Ziemer as the replacement for Jeffrey Bluestein, who continued as Chairman of the Board of Directors. Bluestein had been with Harley-Davidson since 1981, when he was recruited from the faculty ranks at Yale to participate in the management buyout of the company. Ziemer "has the information with where we're going, but he's also rooted in where we've been," commented Kirk Topel, co-owner of Hal's Harley-Davidson dealership in New Berlin, Wisconsin.

Exhibit 6 Price List For 2007 Motorcycles Product Line: Harley-Davidson, Inc.

Motorcycle	MSRP Base Price In Dollars ($)
1. BUELL[1]	
Buell Blast!	4,695
XB12R Buell Firebolt®	10,495
XB9R Buell Firebolt®	8,895
XB12S Buell Lightning®	10,495
XB12Ss Buell Lightning®	10,495
XB9SX Buell Lightning®	8,895
XB12Scg Buell Lightning®	10,495
XB12X Buell Ulysses™	11,495
2. HARLEY DAVIDSON	
SPORTSTER	
XL883 Sportster	6,595
XL883L Sportster 883 Low®	6,995
XL883C or R Sportster Custom	7,795
XL1200C Sportster Custom	9,695
XL1200R Sportster Roadster	8,695
XL 1200L Sportster Low	9,495
XL50 50th Anniversary Sportster	9,795
DYNA	
FXD Dyna™ Glide Super Glider®	12,395
FXDC Dyna™ Super Glide Custom	16,645
FXDB Dyna™ Street Bob™	13,595
FXDL Dyna™ Low Rider	15,795
FXDWG Dyna™ Wide Glider	16,795
SOFTAIL	
FXST Softail® Standard	14,995
FXSTB Softail® Night Train®	15,895
FXSTC Softail® Custom	16,895
FXSTD Softail® Deuce	17,345
FLST Softail® Fat Boy®	17,095
FLSTN Softail® Deluxe	17,345
FLSTSC Softail® Springer Classic	17,545
FLSTC Heritage Softail® Classic	17,820
VRSC (V-Rod)	
VRSCAW V-Rod™	16,495
VRSCD V-Rod™	14,995
VRSCDX Night Rod™ Special	16,495
VRSCX	19,995
VRSCR Street Rod™	15,495
TOURING	
FLHR/FLHRI Road King®	17,345
FLHRCI Road King® Classic	17,695
FLTR/FLTRI Road Glide	17,695
FLHTC/FLHTCI Electra Glide® Standard	16,095
FLHTC/FLHTCI Electra Glide® Classic	18,095
FLHTCU Ultra Classic®	20,195

1. Buell Motorcycle Company partnered with Harley-Davidson in 1993 and was purchased by Harley-Davidson in 1998.

Source: http://www.harley-davidson.com/wcm/Content/Pages/Motorcycles/motorcycles.jsp?locale=en_US

Exhibit 7 Selected United States and World Financial and Sales Information: Harley-Davidson, Inc.

A. Motor Company Revenue, 2005
(Dollar amounts in millions)

Harley-Davidson Motorcycles	$4,183.5
Parts and Accessories	815.7
General Merchandise	247.9
Buell Motorcycles	93.1
Other	2.0
Total	**$5,342.2**

B. Worldwide Motorcycle Shipments
(Units in thousands)

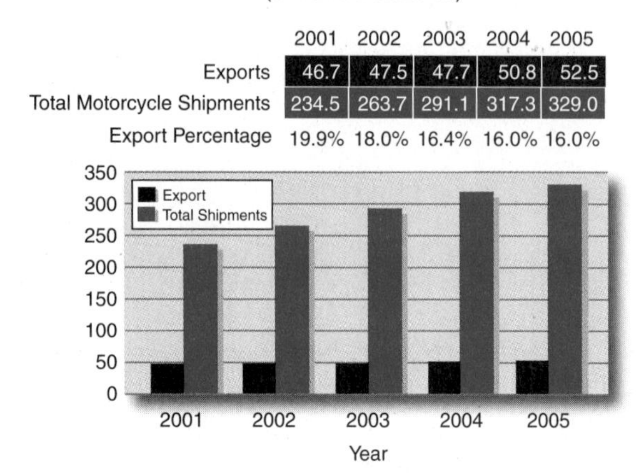

	2001	2002	2003	2004	2005
Exports	46.7	47.5	47.7	50.8	52.5
Total Motorcycle Shipments	234.5	263.7	291.1	317.3	329.0
Export Percentage	19.9%	18.0%	16.4%	16.0%	16.0%

C. Worldwide Parts and Accessories and General Merchandise Revenue
(Dollar amounts in millions)

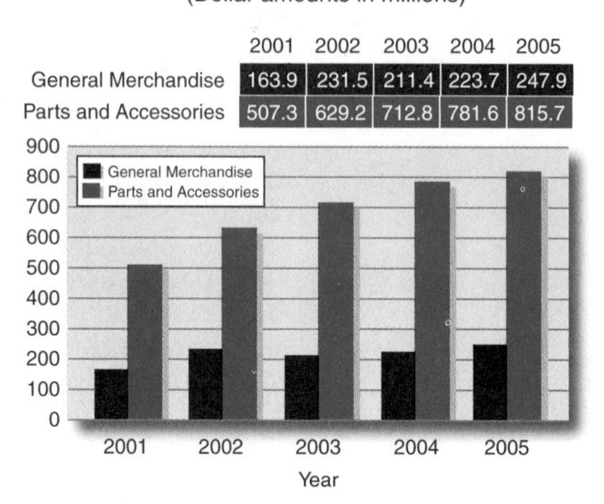

	2001	2002	2003	2004	2005
General Merchandise	163.9	231.5	211.4	223.7	247.9
Parts and Accessories	507.3	629.2	712.8	781.6	815.7

D. Net Income from Continuing Operations
(Dollar amounts in millions)

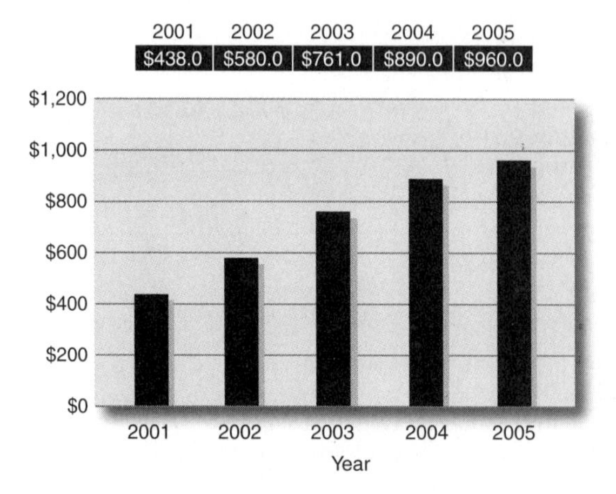

2001	2002	2003	2004	2005
$438.0	$580.0	$761.0	$890.0	$960.0

Source: Harley-Davidson, Inc., 2005 Annual Report and 10-K.

President James C. Ziemer said in his annual letter to the shareholders,

> In 2005, Harley-Davidson consolidated revenue grew to $5.34 billon, a 6.5% increase over 2004, while net income grew 7.8% to 959.6 million. Diluted full-year earnings per share rose 13.7% to $3.41 compared to 2004. We shipped 329,017 new Harley-Davidson motorcycles to dealerships globally. Our dealers again retailed a record number of new Harley-Davidson and Buell motorcycles.

> For the full year, worldwide retail sales of Harley-Davidson motorcycles grew 6.2% to 317,169 units and international retail sales of Harley-Davidson motorcycles climbing 19.9% over the prior year.[24]

Later in the report he discussed Buell sales and sales increases.

> Revenue for Buell motorcycles was $93.1 million in 2005, a 17.8% increase from 2004, on a 13.3% growth in shipments. Buell motorcycles continued to have strong appeal in international markets, which accounted for more than half of the brand's 2005 retail volume. The Buell Ulysses adventure sport bike launched to broad acclaim and sold both in the U.S. and abroad and further established Buell's credentials as a leader in technological innovation.[25]

Exhibits 7 and **8** present data on divisional revenues, worldwide motorcycle shipments, income, and registrations, both worldwide and U.S. and Europe for 2005.

Exhibit 8 World Registrations: Harley-Davidson, Inc.

A. North American 651+cc Motorcycle Registrations
(Units in thousands)

	1996	1997	1998	1999	2000	2001	2002	2003	2004	2005
Total Industry	182.7	206.1	246.2	297.9	365.4	422.8	475.0	495.4	530.8	553.5
Harley-Davidson	86.3	99.3	116.1	142.0	163.1	185.6	220.1	238.2	255.8	264.7
Harley-Davidson Market Share	47.2%	48.2%	47.2%	47.7%	44.6%	43.9%	46.3%	48.1%	48.2%	47.8%

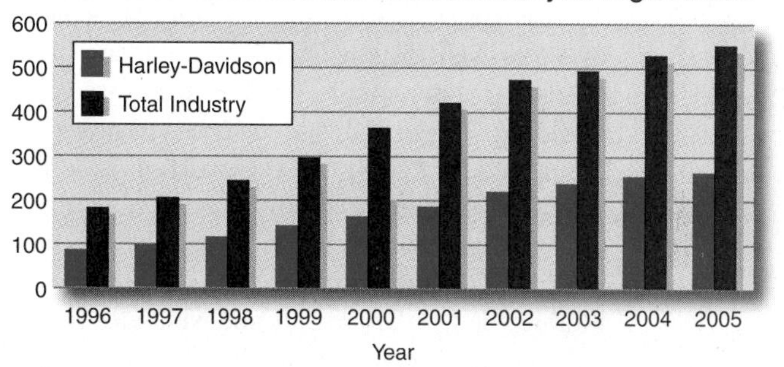

B. European 651+cc Motorcycle Registrations
(Units in thousands)

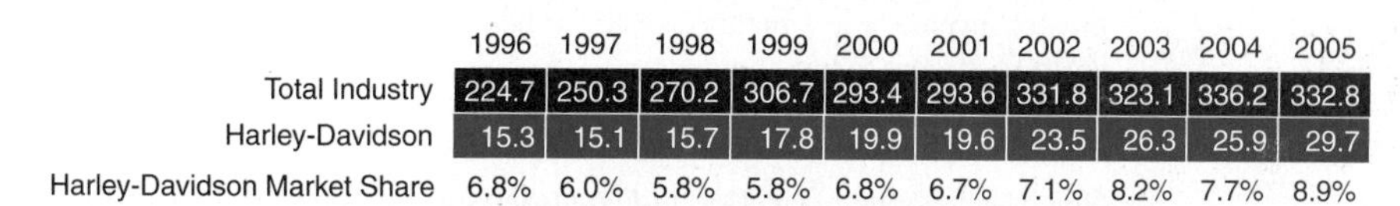

	1996	1997	1998	1999	2000	2001	2002	2003	2004	2005
Total Industry	224.7	250.3	270.2	306.7	293.4	293.6	331.8	323.1	336.2	332.8
Harley-Davidson	15.3	15.1	15.7	17.8	19.9	19.6	23.5	26.3	25.9	29.7
Harley-Davidson Market Share	6.8%	6.0%	5.8%	5.8%	6.8%	6.7%	7.1%	8.2%	7.7%	8.9%

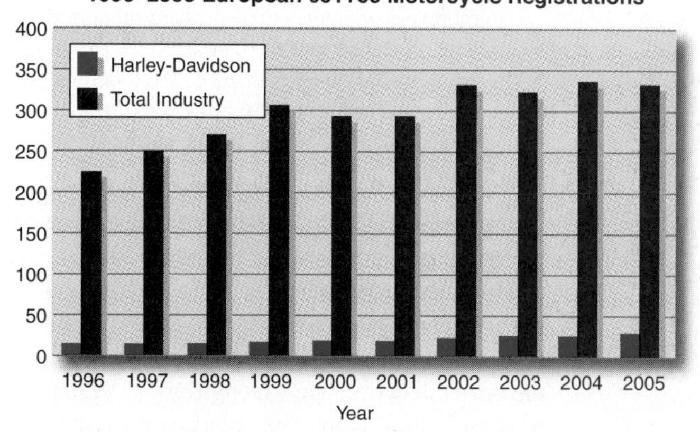

Source: Harley-Davidson, Inc., 2005 Annual Report, p. 40.

Inventory and Legal Issues

The venerable motorcycle company is anything but set in its ways.[26] Consider Harley customer Bob Johnson, 55, vice president of an Orem, Utah, maker of oil-industry tools. Back in 2000, when Johnson bought his Softail Fat Boy, he had to wait five months and pay $1,000 over suggested retail. Even then, he considered himself lucky: In Texas, Harleys were fetching $4,000 to $5,000 over list. But last December, he snared an Electra Glide Classic for $1,200 below retail and rode away on his tricked-out $16,770 touring machine. "They had inventory, and they were actually discounting," he crows.[27]

The customer waiting list for new motorcycles has shrunk from as much as two years to a matter of months. Dealer premiums that used to range between $2,000 and $4,000 have disappeared for most models.

Harley-Davidson faced several lawsuits in 2006, perhaps the most significant of which are the shareholder lawsuits filed in 2005 alleging that senior management violated securities law with regard to information presentation on inventory and sales. The SEC is in the process of investigating the lawsuits and the claims therein. Unspecified damages are sought related to the April 2005 announcement by Harley-Davidson that the company was reducing short-term production growth and planned increases of motorcycle shipments from 317,000 units in 2004 to a new 2005 target of 329,000 units, down 10,000 from the original 2005 target.

The question about the inventory lag is not new to analysts. In the past, there was up to a two-year wait for a new Harley-Davidson bike. Current trends predict the lag will drop to nearly zero, potentially leaving inventory on the dealer's floor, a concept new to Harley-Davidson. "In the end, there's more inventory out there," said Dean Gianoukos, a J. P. Morgan leisure-industry analyst. "The question is, is it because of the economy? Because of people waiting to get the 2003s so they're not buying the 2002 models? Or is it that, if you increase production every year by 15 percent, you're going to eventually hit a wall?" He has a "long-term buy" on the shares, J. P. Morgan's second-highest rating.[28] (See **Exhibit 9** for Motorcycle Unit Shipments and Net Sales for 2004 and 2005.)

In a possible response to the allegations of inventory issues, Ziemer commented as follows:

> Walk into dealer showrooms today and you'll notice something different: they have new motorcycles in stock. It may come as an eye-opener to those who grew used to seeing dealerships largely devoid of new bikes (and who somehow viewed that as the proper order of things), but greater inventory is a planned result to help ensure that our dealers have bikes available when customers want to buy them.[29]

Ziemer continued to say:

> However, let's be clear. Harley-Davidson is a premium product and a premium brand. We're going to continue to run the business to protect the value of the brand by making sure that our motorcycle shipments to dealers are supported by retail growth. That's why we monitor the selling prices of new and used motorcycles so carefully. That's also why we reduced our production growth by 10,000 units in 2005. We took this precautionary step in the second quarter to maintain demand in excess of supply. We know that this action was absolutely the right thing to do to get the 2006 model year off to a great start.[30]

Critics see deeper problems for Harley. They say sales have slowed and that Harley has tried to mask the slowdown by pushing dealers to buy bikes they don't need—known as channel stuffing—and allowing them to borrow to fund the purchases through Harley's financial arm. Dealers may feel the need to take on more inventory because their future allocations of hot models depend on past purchases, bears say. "There's no question there's a lot more inventory on the dealer floor and the parent company has basically shoved merchandise into the dealer network," says Doug Kass of Seabreeze Partners, a hedge fund, who has sold shares of Harley stock short. The company disagrees.[31]

Exhibit 9

A. Motorcycle Unit Shipments and Net Sales: Harley-Davidson, Inc.

	2005	2004	Increase (Decrease)	Percentage Change
Motorcycle Unit Shipments				
Touring motorcycle units	110,193	93,305	16,888	18.1%
Custom motorcycle units	148,609	154,163	(5,554)	(3.6%)
Sportster motorcycle units	70,215	69,821	394	0.5%
Total Harley-Davidson® units	329,017	317,289	11,728	3.7%
Buell® motorcycle units	11,166	9,857	1,309	13.3%
Total motorcycle units	340,183	327,146	13,037	4.0%
Net Sales ($ thousands)				
Harley-Davidson motorcycles	$4,183.5	$3,928.2	255.3	6.5%
Buell motorcycles	93.1	79.0	14.1	17.8%
Total motorcycles	4,276.6	4,007.2	269.4	6.7%
Parts and Accessories	815.7	781.6	34.1	4.4%
General Merchandise	247.9	223.7	24.2	10.8%
Other	2.0	2.7	(0.7)	(25.9)
Total Motorcycles and Related Parts	$5,342.2	$5,015.2	$327.0	6.5%

Source: Harley-Davidson 2005 10-K, p. 31.

B. 2005 Quarterly Motorcycle Shipments: Harley-Davidson, Inc.

	Q1	Q2	Q3	Q4	2005
HARLEY-DAVIDSON					
All 651+cc					
Sportster	17,359	15,238	17,363	20,265	70,225
Custom	34,286	35,371	40,730	38,233	148,620
Touring	25,071	26,519	29,492	29,090	110,172
Total	**76,716**	**77,128**	**87,585**	**87,588**	**329,017**
Domestic	60,878	58,997	72,249	74,383	266,507
International total	15,838	18,131	15,336	13,205	62,510
	76,716	**77,128**	**87,585**	**87,588**	**329,017**
BUELL UNITS					
Buell 651+cc	2,042	2,738	2,616	2,380	9,776
Buell Total	**2,469**	**3,067**	**2,914**	**2,716**	**11,166**

Source: Harley-Davidson Fact Book, http://investor.harley-davidson.com/downloads/factsheet.pdf (August 18, 2006).

New Millennium Bikes: The Buell and the V-Rod

Harley's new V-Rod was introduced in the Los Angeles Convention Center on July 12, 2001. More than 4,000 packed into the center for the company's long-awaited announcement. The cavernous room went black. The engines roared in the darkness. Spotlights clicked on and followed two glinting new hot-rods as they roared onto center stage.[32]

Harley-Davidson deviated from its traditional approach to styling, with the introduction of the V-Rod motorcycle. The new, liquid-cooled V-Rod, inspired by Harley-Davidson's drag racing heritage, combines the characteristics of a performance motorcycle with the styling of a custom.[33] Liquid cooling allows riders to rev a little higher and hotter in each gear, boosting acceleration. It doesn't sound like a big deal, but it was a giant step for a company so stubbornly conservative that it has made only air-cooled engines for 100 years; its designers just couldn't bear the idea of putting a radiator on the front of the bike.[34]

The V-Rod is Milwaukee-based Harley-Davison Inc.'s first truly new motorcycle in more than 50 years. A sleek machine in the making for more than six years, the V-Rod is designed more for speed and handling, unlike the company's immensely popular touring bikes. The V-Rod is one factor behind Harley-Davidson's strong financial performance.

Harley-Davidson's Chief Executive Offer, Jeffrey Bluestein, is well aware of the wait. He's still on a local dealer's list, eagerly awaiting the arrival of the V-Rod he ordered a few months ago.[35]

As it ramped up production, premiums on many models disappeared. Chief Executive Officer James L. Ziemer says Harley wants to "narrow the gap" between supply and demand in order to curb the long-standing—but fast-diminishing—practice of selling bikes at a premium.[36] The new V-Rod's $17,000 price tag failed to win younger buyers.[37] To that end, Harley has poured money into developing new, youth-oriented models. The $17,000 Harley V-Rod—a low-slung, high-powered number known formally as a sport performance vehicle and colloquially as a crotch rocket—is meant for hard-charging youths. Harley has also tried to go young with the Buell Firebolt ($10,000), its answer to Japanese sport bikes, and the Buell Blast ($4,400), a starter motorcycle. But Buell, a subsidiary Harley bought in 1988, has captured just 2% of the sport-bike market, and Harley will make only 10,000 V-Rods in 2005. Bleustein insists that those numbers aren't the point: "These aren't one-shot deals. These are whole new platforms from which many models will proliferate."[38]

At the Detroit Harley-Davidson/Buell dealership in Center Line, owner Jim Loduca commented: "This is the first time in 10 years that I've actually had product on the floor available, but our sales are also up by 14 percent this year. The company has watched this demand curve very carefully. They are simply riding the wave. They know full well that is would be catastrophic to saturate the market." He is also encouraged by Harley's biggest product departure in recent decades—the V-Rod muscle bike.[39]

Clay Wilwert, whose family has owned a dealership in Dubuque since 1959, said, "But guess what, as they rode it, they loved it." They said, "Hey, this is really cool that it doesn't shake my hands asleep."[40]

Some Harley traditionalists say the V-Rod, styled to compete with super-fast European bikes, strays too far from the company's all-American roots, which tend to favor heavier cruising machines. Dealerships sell them for several thousand dollars over the $16,995 list price, and they're the talk of Bike Week.[41]

Licensing[42]

Harley-Davidson endeavored to create an awareness of the "Harley-Davidson" brand among the non-riding public and provides a wide range of product for enthusiasts by licensing the name "Harley-Davidson" and numerous related trademarks. Harley-Davidson had licensed the production and sale of a broad range of consumer items, including tee-shirts, jewelry, small leather goods, toys and numerous other products (Licensed Products). They also license the use of its name in connection with a cafe located in Las Vegas. Although the majority of licensing activity occurs in the United States, Harley-Davidson continues to expand these activities in international markets. Royalty revenues from licensing, included in Motorcycles segment net revenue, were approximately $43 million, $41 million, and $38 million in 2005, 2004, and 2003, respectively.

Marketing and Distribution[43]

Marketing efforts are divided among dealer promotions, customer events, magazine and direct mail advertising, public relations, cooperative programs with Harley-Davidson/Buell dealers, and national television advertising. Harley-Davidson also sponsors racing activities and special promotional events and participates in all major motorcycle consumer shows and rallies.

E-Commerce[44]

Harley-Davidson's e-commerce began in 2001. Their model is unique in the industry in that, although the online catalog is viewed from the Harley-Davidson web site, orders are actually distributed to the participating authorized Harley-Davidson dealer that the customer selects. In turn, those dealers fill the order and handle any after-sale services that the customer may require. In addition to purchasing, customers actively browse the site, create and share product wish lists, and utilize the dealer locator.

International Sales[45]

International sales of motorcycles and related products to independent dealers and distributors outside of the United States was approximately $1.04 billion, $917 million, and $816 million, or approximately 19%, 18%, and 18% of net revenue of the Motorcycles segment, during 2005, 2004, and 2003, respectively.

Distribution[46]

The basic channel of distribution in the United States for its motorcycles and related products consists of approximately 667 independently owned full-service Harley-Davidson dealerships to whom Harley-Davidson sells directly. This includes 318 combined Harley-Davidson and Buell dealerships. With respect to sales of new motorcycles, approximately 82% of the U.S. dealerships sell Harley-Davidson motorcycles exclusively. All dealerships stock and sell genuine replacement parts, accessories, and MotorClothes apparel and collectibles, and perform service for Harley-Davidson's motorcycles.

There are also non-traditional retail outlets for parts, accessories, and general merchandise. There are three types of storefronts: Secondary Retail Locations (SRLs), Alternate Retail Outlets (AROs), and Seasonal Retail Outlets (SROs). SRLs, also known as Harley Shops, are satellites of the main dealership and were developed to meet the service needs of riding customers. Harley Shops also provide replacement parts and accessories and MotorClothes apparel and collectibles and are authorized to sell new motorcycles. AROs are located primarily in high-traffic areas such as malls, airports, or popular vacation destinations and focus on selling the MotorClothes apparel and collectibles and licensed products. SROs are located in similar high-traffic areas, but operate on a seasonal basis out of temporary locations such as vendor kiosks. AROs and SROs are not authorized to sell new motorcycles. In 2005, there were approximately 90 SRLs, 65 AROs, and fewer than 10 SROs in the United States.

Harley-Davidson Customer Base

"Fads don't have 100th birthdays," boasted then-CEO Jeffery Bluestein in 2002.[47]

Harley-Davidson's customers are not what some people might expect. They see the rough-and-tumble riders and do not expect that a good proportion of Harley-Davidson riders are white-collar workers and executives taking the weekend relaxation on their bike. Selected quotes from customers follow:

"It's about an image—freedom of the road, hop on your bike and go, independent living, the loosing of the chains," said Dave Sarnowski, a teacher and Harley rider from La Farge, Wisconsin.[48]

"The Harley people I know go to church, have jobs, shop at the mall, just like everyone else." says Angie Robison, 68, of Daytona Beach, who helps her husband, Joe run a motorcycle repair shop and Harley memorabilia/accessories store. "I can wear my silks over here and my leathers over there, and I'm still the same person."[49]

"I worked at a computer all day for the city, and for me it's pure relaxation. I wear the leathers because they're protective."[50]

"I love the feeling of being out on that bike on the roads—especially in the mountains. You just can't beat it, the feeling you get." Rob Barnett, Harley-Davidson owner.

"In general, the motorcycle industry has increased for 12 years straight, and we're expecting another increase—especially in Harley-Davidson sales—this year." Don Brown, motorcycle analyst with DJB Associates.[51]

"A Harley is a rolling sculpture. A piece of artwork," commented Matt Chase, sales manager of N.F. Sheldon, a Harley store. "You work all week, then on the weekends you put on leathers and everyone's equal . . . all the same, brothers and sisters."[52]

Recession Resistance?

Economics have been hinting about another recession in 2007. How will this affect Harley-Davidson? Harley has seen tremendous sales and stock price growth since 1986. Some analysts now question whether Harley-Davidson will be hurt in a deep recession. For years, Harley-Davidson and the analysts that cover the company have reported that the business is recession-resistant. Given the recent changes in the economic and political landscape, this assertion is being put to the test, and from what we can tell, is ringing true. According to CEO Jim Ziemer, "Motorcycles, the critics say, are easily deferred purchases. We always said we feel we are recession-resistant, not recession-proof."[53]

Competition[54]

The heavyweight (651+cc) motorcycle market is highly competitive. Major competitors are based outside the United States and generally have more financial and marketing resources. They also have larger worldwide sales volumes and are more diversified. In addition to these larger, established competitors, a growing segment of competition has emerged in the United States. The new U.S. competitors generally offer heavyweight motorcycles with traditional styling that compete directly with many of the Harley-Davidson's products. These competitors currently have production and sales volumes that are lower than the Harley-Davidson's and do not hold a significant market share. (See **Exhibits 10, 11,** and **12.**)

Competition in the heavyweight motorcycle market is based on a number of factors, including price, quality, reliability, styling, product features, customer preference, and warranties. Harley-Davidson emphasizes quality, reliability, and styling in its products and offers a one-year warranty for its motorcycles. They support the motorcycling lifestyle in the form of events, rides, rallies, H.O.G. and its financing through HDFS, as a competitive advantage.

Exhibit 10 651+cc Motorcycle Market Regional Comparison by Segment: Harley-Davidson, Inc.

United States	2005	2004	2003	2002	2001
Custom	53.9%	60.4%	61.8%	60.3%	58.9%
Touring	27.2	20.8	20.4	20.2	20.3
Performance	16.0	16.2	15.1	17.3	19.1
Standard	2.9	2.6	2.7	2.2	1.7
Total	100.0%	100.0%	100.0%	100.0%	100.0%
Europe	**2005**	**2004**	**2003**	**2002**	**2001**
Custom	14.3%	13.9%	14.3%	13.8%	15.6%
Touring	6.8	5.8	4.7	4.8	5.2
Performance	57.3	59.7	57.8	61.2	61.6
Standard	21.6	20.6	23.2	20.2	17.6
Total	100.0%	100.0%	100.0%	100.0%	100.0%
Asia/Pacific	**2005**	**2004**	**2003**	**2002**	**2001**
Custom	30.5%	29.9%	32.7%	26.2%	23.8%
Touring	9.0	8.4	9.8	8.2	7.2
Performance	47.6	54.7	53.3	60.0	65.7
Standard	12.9	7.0	4.2	5.6	3.3
Total	100.0%	100.0%	100.0%	100.0%	100.0%

Custom: Characterized by "American Styling." These bikes are often personalized with accessories.

Touring: Designed for long trips with an emphasis on comfort, cargo capacity and reliability. These bikes often have features such as two-way radio for communication with a passenger, stereos, and cruise control.

Performance: Characterized by quick acceleration, top speed, and handling. These bikes are often referred to as sports bikes.

Standard: A basic, no-frills motorcycle with an emphasis on low price. The standard percentage may also include the "adventure touring" niche.

Source: Harley-Davidson Fact Book, http://investor.harley-davidson.com/downloads/factsheet.pdf (August 18, 2006).

In general, resale prices for used Harley-Davidson motorcycles, as a percentage of prices when new, are significantly higher than resale prices for used motorcycles of competitors.

Domestically, Harley-Davidson competes most heavily in the touring and custom segments of the heavyweight motorcycle market, which together accounted for 81%, 81%, and 82% of total heavyweight retail unit sales in the United States during 2005, 2004, and 2003, respectively. The custom and touring motorcycles are generally the most expensive vehicles in the market and the most profitable. During 2005, the heavyweight segment including standard, performance, touring, and custom motorcycles represented approximately 50% of the total U.S. motorcycle market (on- and off-highway motorcycles and scooters) in terms of new units registered.

For the past 18 years, Harley-Davidson has led the industry in domestic (United States) unit sales of heavyweight motorcycles. The market share in the heavyweight market was 48.9% in 2005 compared to 49.5% in 2004. The market share decreased slightly in 2005 as a result of the ongoing capacity constraints; however, this share is still significantly greater than the largest competitor in the domestic market, which ended 2005 with a 16.6% market share.

Exhibit 11 Market Share of U.S. Heavyweight Motorcycles[1] (Engine Displacement of 651+cc)

	2005	2004	2003	2002
New U.S. Registrations (thousands of units):				
Total market new registrations	517.6	494.0	461.2	442.3
Harley-Davidson new registrations	252.9	244.5	228.4	209.3
Buell new registrations	3.6	3.6	3.5	2.9
Total company new registrations	256.5	248.1	231.9	212.2
Percentage (%) Market Share:				
Harley-Davidson motorcycles	48.9%	49.5%	49.5%	47.5%
Buell motorcycles	0.7	0.7	0.8	0.7
Total company	49.6	50.2	50.3	48.2
Honda	16.6	18.7	18.4	19.8
Suzuki	12.4	10.7	9.8	9.6
Yamaha	8.9	8.7	8.5	8.9
Kawasaki	6.5	6.4	6.7	6.9
Other	6.0	5.8	6.3	6.6
Total	100.0%	100.0%	100.0%	100.0%

Note:
1. Motorcycle registration and market share information has been derived from data published by the Motorcycle Industry Council (MIC).

Source: Harley-Davidson, Inc., Form 10-K, 2005, p. 9.

Exhibit 12 Registration Statistics (Units): Harley-Davidson, Inc.[1,2]

	2003	2002	2001	2000	1997	1994	1991
U.S. and Canada							
651+cc volume	495,436	474,955	422,787	366,247	205,407	150,419	100,705
H-D volume	238,243	220,143	185,571	163,984	99,298	69,529	48,260
Buell volume	3,719	3,023	2,695	4,306	1,912	194	n/a
HD total volume	241,962	223,166	188,256	168,290	101,210	69,723	48,260
HOG market share[3]	**48.8%**	**47.0%**	**44.5%**	**45.9%**	**49.3%**	**46.4%**	**47.9%**
Europe							
651+cc volume	323,083	331,790	319,863	338,921	282,378	201,904	194,700
H-D volume	26,299	23,530	22,763	23,230	17,190	14,393	10,996
Buell volume	3,106	1,930	2,312	2,045	785	n/a	n/a
HD total volume	29,405	25,460	25,075	25,275	17,975	14,393	10,996
HOG market share	**9.1%**	**7.7%**	**7.8%**	**7.5%**	**6.4%**	**7.1%**	**5.6%**
Japan and Australia							
651+cc volume	58,941	63,857	62,069	62,667	58,880	39,077	26,995
H-D volume	15,195	13,602	12,662	12,213	9,686	7,588	5,261
Buell volume	989	739	651	658	426	n/a	n/a
HD total volume	16,184	14,341	13,313	12,871	10,112	7,588	5,261
HD market share	**27.5%**	**22.5%**	**21.4%**	**20.5%**	**17.2%**	**19.4%**	**19.5%**

Exhibit 12 *(Continued)*

	2003	2002	2001	2000	1997	1994	1991
Total for Markets Listed							
651+cc volume	877,460	870,602	804,719	767,835	546,665	391,400	322,400
H-D volume	279,737	257,275	220,996	199,427	126,174	91,510	64,517
Buell volume	7,814	5,692	5,658	7,009	3,123	194	n/a
HOG total volume	287,551	262,967	226,654	206,436	129,297	91,704	64,517
HD market share	**32.8%**	**30.2%**	**28.2%**	**26.9%**	**23.7%**	**23.4%**	**20.0%**

Notes:
1. These are actual registrations of motorcycles. The Harley-Davidson, Inc. registrations are typically lower than actual sales due to timing differences.
2. Data provided by R. L. Polk (1994), Giral S. A., Australian Bureau of Statistics, and H-D Japan.
3. HOG represents the new ticker for Harley-Davidson a whole, formerly HDI.

Source: Harley-Davidson Fact Book, http://investor.harley-davidson.com/downloads/factsheet.pdf (August 18, 2006).

Rider Training and Safety

"Increasingly, the motorcycle riders who are getting killed are in their 40s, 50s, and 60s," says Susan Ferguson, vice president for research at the Insurance Institute for Highway Safety, which did the study.[55] Riders over 40 accounted for 40% of all fatalities in 2000, up from 14% in 1990. Part of the reason for the dramatic increase in older bikers' deaths is the growing number of men and women over 40 buying motorcycles, IIHS reports.

In 2000, Harley-Davidson launched an instruction program called Rider's Edge, run through dealers. Rookies pay $225 or so for a 25-hour class. This training program can be credited with bringing in more first-time riders as Harley customers. Forty-five percent are women, 86% buy something, and 25% buy a Harley-Davidson or a Buell within 3 months. "Going into a Harley dealership can be intimidating," says Lara Lee, who runs the program. "We give them a home base and get them riding."[56]

Motorcycle Manufacturing[57]

The ongoing manufacturing strategy is designed to increase capacity, improve product quality, reduce costs, and increase flexibility to respond to changes in the marketplace. Harley-Davidson incorporates manufacturing techniques focused on the continuous improvement of its operations designed to control costs and maintain quality. These techniques, which include employee involvement, just-in-time inventory principles, partnering agreements with the local unions, high-performance work organizations, and statistical process control, are designed to improve product quality, productivity, and asset utilization in the production of Harley-Davidson motorcycles.

The use of just-in-time inventory principles allows it to minimize its inventories of raw materials and work in process, as well as scrap and rework costs. This system also allows quicker reaction to engineering design changes, quality improvements, and market demands. Harley-Davidson has trained the majority of its manufacturing employees in problem solving and statistical methods.

Raw Material and Purchase Components[58]

Harley-Davidson worked hard to establish and/or reinforce long-term, mutually beneficial relationships with its suppliers. Through these collaborative relationships, they have gained access to technical and commercial resources for application directly to product design, development, and commodity price pressures. They anticipate that the focus on collaboration and strong supplier manufacturing initiatives leads to increased commitment from suppliers. This strategy has resulted in improved product quality, technical integrity, application of new features and innovations, reduced lead times for product development, and smoother/faster manufacturing ramp-up of new vehicle introductions. Their initiative to improve supplier productivity and component cost has been instrumental in delivering improvements in cost and in offsetting raw material price increases.

Harley-Davidson continued to work to establish long-term, mutually beneficial relationships with its suppliers. Through these relationships, Harley-Davidson gains access to technical and commercial resources for application directly to product design, development, and manufacturing initiatives. This strategy is resulting in improved product technical integrity, application of new features and innovations, reduced lead times for product development, and smoother/faster manufacturing ramp-up of new vehicle introductions.

Harley-Davidson purchased all of its raw materials, principally steel and aluminum castings, forgings, sheets and bars, and certain motorcycle components, including carburetors, batteries, tires, seats, electrical components, and instruments. Given current economic conditions in certain raw material commodity markets, and pressure on certain suppliers due to difficulties in the automotive industry, Harley-Davidson monitors supply, availability, and pricing for both its suppliers and in-house operations. Harley-Davidson states in their *2005 10-K* that they do not anticipate any significant difficulties in obtaining raw materials or components.

Research and Development[59]

Harley-Davidson views research and development as significant factors in its ability to lead the custom and touring motorcycling market and to develop products for the performance segment. The company's Product Development Center (PDC) brings employees from styling, purchasing, and manufacturing together with regulatory professionals and supplier representatives to create a concurrent product and process development team. The company incurred research and development expenses of $178.5 million, $170.7 million, and $150.3 million during 2005, 2004, and 2003, respectively.

Patents and Trademarks[60]

Harley-Davidson owns patents that relate to its motorcycles and related products and processes for their production. It has increased its efforts to patent its technology and certain motorcycle-related designs and to enforce those patents. Management sees such actions as important as it moves forward with new products, designs, and technologies.

Trademarks are important to the Harley-Davidson's motorcycle business and licensing activities. It has a vigorous global program of trademark registration and enforcement to strengthen the value of the trademarks associated with its products and services, prevent the unauthorized use of those trademarks, and enhance its image and customer goodwill. Management believes the HARLEY-DAVIDSON trademark and the Bar and Shield trademark are each highly recognizable by the public and are very valuable assets. The BUELL trademark is well known in performance motorcycle circles, as is the associated Pegasus logo. They are making efforts to ensure that each of these brands will become better known as the Buell business expands. Additionally, they use numerous other trademarks, trade names, and logos, which are registered both in the United States and abroad. The following are among the trademarks of H-D Michigan, Inc.: Harley-Davidson, H-D, Harley, the Bar & Shield Logo, MotorClothes, the MotorClothes Logo, Rider's Edge, Harley Owners Group, H.O.G., the H.O.G. Logo, Softail, Sportster, and V-Rod. The HARLEY-DAVIDSON trademark has been used since 1903 and the Bar and Shield trademark since 1910. The following are among the trademarks of Buell Motorcycle Company: Buell, the Pegasus Logo, and B.R.A.G. The BUELL trademark has been used since 1984.

Seasonality[61]

In general, Harley-Davidson has not experienced significant seasonal fluctuations in its sales. This has been primarily the result of a strong demand for the Harley-Davidson motorcycles and related products, as well as the availability of floor plan financing arrangements for its North American and European independent dealers. Floor plan financing allows dealers to build their inventory levels in anticipation of the spring and summer selling seasons. Harley-Davidson expressed its belief that efforts to increase the availability of its motorcycles have resulted in an increase in seasonality at its independent dealers. Over the past several years they have been working to increase the availability of Harley-Davidson motorcycles at dealers to improve the customer experience.

Regulations[62]

Federal, state, and local authorities have various environmental control requirements relating to air, water, and noise pollution that affect the business and operations. Harley-Davidson endeavors to ensure that its facilities and products comply with all applicable environmental regulations and standards.

The motorcycles are subject to certification by the U.S. Environmental Protection Agency (EPA) for compliance with applicable emissions and noise standards and by the State of California Air Resources Board (CARB) with respect to CARB's more stringent emissions standards. Motorcycles sold in California are also subject to certain tailpipe and evaporative emissions standards that are unique to California. Their motorcycle products have been certified to comply fully with all such applicable standards. CARB's motorcycle emissions standards will become more stringent in model year 2008. The EPA finalized new tailpipe emission standards for 2006 and 2010, respectively, which are harmonized with the California emissions standards. Additionally, the European Union is considering making its motorcycle emissions standards more stringent and is considering making its motorcycle noise standards more stringent, which already are more stringent than those of the EPA. Similarly, motorcycle noise and emissions levels are becoming more stringent in Japan, as well as in certain emerging markets. Consequently, Harley-Davidson will continue to incur some level of research and development and production costs related to motorcycle emissions and noise for the foreseeable future.

Harley-Davidson, as a manufacturer of motorcycle products, is subject to the National Traffic and Motor Vehicle Safety Act, which is administered by the National Highway Traffic Safety Administration (NHTSA). Harley-Davidson has certified to NHTSA that its motorcycle products comply fully with all applicable federal motor vehicle safety standards and related regulations. Harley-Davidson has, from time to time, initiated certain voluntary recalls. During the past three years, Harley-Davidson initiated 18 voluntary recalls at a total cost of $12.5 million. The Company reserves for all estimated costs associated with recalls in the period that the recalls are announced.

Employees[63]

As of December 31, 2005, the Motorcycles segment had approximately 9,000 employees. Unionized employees at the motorcycle manufacturing and distribution facilities in Wauwatosa, Menomonee Falls, Franklin, and Tomahawk, Wisconsin, and Kansas City,

Missouri, are represented principally by the Paper Allied-Industrial Chemical and Energy Workers International Union (PACE) of the AFL-CIO, as well as the International Association of Machinist and Aerospace Workers (IAM). Production workers at the motorcycle manufacturing facility in York, Pennsylvania, are represented principally by the IAM. The collective bargaining agreement with the Pennsylvania-IAM will expire on February 2, 2007, the collective bargaining agreement with the Kansas City-USW and IAM will expire on August 1, 2007, and the collective bargaining agreement with the Wisconsin-USW and IAM will expire on March 31, 2008.

Approximately 50% of Harley-Davidson's 9,000 employees ride a Harley-Davidson. All employees, including Ziemer and Bluestein, go through a dealer to purchase their bikes. This way, the employees see the customer experience firsthand.

Properties[64]

The following is a summary of the principal operating properties of Harley-Davidson as of December 31, 2005. There are seven facilities that perform manufacturing operations: Wauwatosa and Menomonee Falls, Wisconsin, suburbs of Milwaukee (motorcycle powertrain production); Tomahawk, Wisconsin (fiberglass parts production and painting); York, Pennsylvania (motorcycle parts fabrication, painting and big-twin assembly); Kansas City, Missouri (Sportster assembly); East Troy, Wisconsin (Buell motorcycles assembly); and Manaus, Brazil (assembly of select models for Brazilian market). (See **Exhibit 13.**)

Financial Services Segment[65]

The Financial Services segment has four office facilities: The corporate headquarters are in Chicago, Illinois; retail and insurance operations are in Carson City, Nevada; wholesale, insurance, and retail operations are in Plano, Texas; and European wholesale operations are located in Oxford, England. Ownership and lease structures are outlined in **Exhibit 13.**

Harley-Davidson and Buell[66]

HDFS, operating under the trade name Harley-Davidson Credit, provides wholesale financial services to Harley-Davidson and Buell dealers and retail financing to consumers. HDFS, operating under the trade name Harley-Davidson Insurance, is an agent for the sale of motorcycle insurance policies and also sells extended service warranty agreements, gap contracts, and debt protection products.

Wholesale financial services include floorplan and open account financing of motorcycles and motorcycle parts and accessories, real estate loans, computer loans, and showroom remodeling loans. HDFS offers wholesale financial services to Harley-Davidson dealers in the United States, Canada, and Europe and during 2005; approximately 97% of such dealers utilized those services. Prior to August 2002, HDFS offered wholesale financing to some of the Company's European motorcycle dealers through a joint venture with Transamerica Distribution Finance. In August 2002, HDFS terminated this joint venture relationship and began directly serving the wholesale financing needs of some European dealers. The wholesale finance operations of HDFS are located in Plano, Texas, and Oxford, England.

Retail financial services include installment lending for new and used Harley-Davidson and Buell motorcycles. HDFS' retail financial services are available through most Harley-Davidson and Buell dealers in the United States and Canada. HDFS' retail finance operations are located in Carson City, Nevada, and Plano, Texas.

Exhibit 13 Principal Operating Facilities: Harley-Davidson, Inc.

Type of Facility	Location	Square Feet	Status
Corporate Office	Milwaukee, WI	515,000	Owned
Warehouse	Milwaukee, WI	24,000	Lease expiring 2006
Airplane Hangar	Milwaukee, WI	14,600	Owned
Product Development Center	Wauwatosa, WI	409,000	Owned
Manufacturing	Wauwatosa, WI	422,000	Owned
Manufacturing	Menomonee Falls, WI	479,000	Owned
Manufacturing	Tomahawk, WI	211,000	Owned
Manufacturing	York, PA	1,321,000	Owned
Materials Velocity Center	Manchester, PA	212,000	Owned
Mfg. & Materials Velocity Center	Kansas City, MO	450,000	Owned
Manufacturing	East Troy, WI	40,000	Lease expiring 2008
Product Development & Office	East Troy, WI	54,000	Lease expiring 2008
Distribution Center	Franklin, WI	250,000	Owned
Office	Cleveland, OH	23,000	Lease expiring 2014
Motorcycle Testing	Talladega, AL	24,000	Lease expiring 2010
Motorcycle Testing	Mesa, AZ	29,000	Lease expiring 2014
Motorcycle Testing	Naples, FL	82,000	Owned
Office	Ann Arbor, MI	3,000	Lease expiring 2009
Office	Morfelden-Waldorf, Germany	22,000	Lease expiring 2008
Office and Warehouse	Oxford, England	27,000	Lease expiring 2017
Office	Liederdorp, The Netherlands	9,000	Lease expiring 2010
Office	Paris, France	7,000	Lease expiring 2019
Office and Warehouse	Arese, Italy	17,000	Lease expiring 2009
Office	Zurich, Switzerland	2,000	Lease expiring 2010
Office	Barcelona, Spain	2,000	Lease expiring 2006
Office	Tokyo, Japan	14,000	Lease expiring 2006
Warehouse	Yokohama, Japan	15,000	Lease expiring 2011
Office and Warehouse	Sydney, Australia	2,600	Lease expiring 2006
Office	Shanghai, China	300	Lease expiring 2007
Manufacturing and Office	Manaus, Brazil	35,000	Lease expiring 2006
Office	Chicago, IL	35,000	Lease expiring 2007
Office	Carson City, NV	100,000	Owned
Office	Plano, TX	61,500	Lease expiring 2014
Office	Oxford, England	6,000	Lease Expiring 2017

Source: Harley-Davidson, Inc., 2005 Form 10-K, p. 20.

Motorcycle insurance, extended service contracts, gap coverage, and debt protection products are available through most Harley-Davidson and Buell dealers in the United States and Canada. Motorcycle insurance is also marketed on a direct basis to motorcycle riders. HDFS insurance operations are located in Carson City, Nevada, and Plano, Texas.

Other Manufacturers[67]

Harley-Davidson Financial Services (HDFS) retail aircraft financial service programs are similar to programs for Harley-Davidson and Buell consumers described earlier. HDFS' aircraft business was small portion of its total business and made up less than 4% of total managed loans as of the end of 2005. They face some national competition for wholesale motorcycle finance business. Competitors are primarily regional and local banks and other financial institutions providing wholesale financing to Harley-Davidson and Buell dealers in their local markets.

Funding[68]

HDFS has been financed by operating cash flow, advances, and loans from Harley-Davidson, asset-backed securitizations, commercial paper, revolving credit facilities, senior subordinated debt, and redeemable preferred stock. HDFS also retains an interest in the excess cash flows from the receivable and recognizes income on this retained interest. After the sale HDFS performs billing and portfolio management services for these loans and receives a servicing fee for providing these services.

Competition[69]

The ability to offer a package of wholesale and retail financial services is a significant competitive advantage for HDFS. Competitors compete for business based largely on price and, to a lesser extent, service. HDFS competes based on convenience, service, brand association, strong dealer relations, industry experience, terms, and price.

During 2005, HDFS financed 45% of the new Harley-Davidson motorcycles retailed by independent dealers in the United States, as compared to 40% in 2004. Competitors for retail motorcycle finance business are primarily banks, credit unions, and other financial institutions. In the motorcycle insurance business, competition primarily comes from national insurance companies and from insurance agencies serving local or regional markets. For insurance-related products such as extended service warranty agreements, HDFS faces competition from certain regional and national industry participants.

Seasonality[70]

In the northern United States and Canada, motorcycles are primarily used during warmer months, generally March through August. Accordingly, HDFS experiences significant seasonal variations. Retail customers typically do not buy motorcycles until they can ride them. From mid-March through August, retail financing volume increases and wholesale financing volume decreases as dealers deplete their inventories. From September through mid-March, there is a decrease in retail financing volume while dealer inventories build and turn over more slowly, substantially increasing wholesale financing volume.

Employees

At the end of 2005, the Financial Services segment had approximately 700 employees, none of whom were unionized.

Regulation[71]

The operations of HDFS are subject, in certain instances, to supervision and regulation by state, federal, and various foreign governmental authorities and may be subject to various laws and judicial and administrative decisions imposing various requirements and restrictions, which, among other things, regulate credit-granting activities, including establishing licensing requirements, if any, in applicable jurisdictions; establish maximum interest rates, finance charges, and other charges; regulate customers' insurance coverages; require disclosure to customers; govern secured transactions; set collection, foreclosure, repossession, and claims handling procedures and other trade practices; prohibit discrimination in the extension of credit and administration of loans; and regulate the use and reporting of information related to a borrower's credit experience.

A subsidiary of HDFS, Eaglemark Savings Bank (ESB) is a Nevada state thrift chartered under an Industry Loan Charter. As such, the activities of this subsidiary are governed by federal and State of Nevada banking laws and are subject to examination by federal and state examiners. During 2002, ESB began to originate retail motorcycle and aircraft loans and sell the loans to a non-banking subsidiary of HDFS. This process allows HDFS to offer retail products with common characteristics across the United States and uniformly manage all domestic retail customers.

Corporate Financial and Stock Price Performance

At a time when automakers are cutting their profit margins with zero-percent financing, Harley sells every bike it makes and dealers often charge $2,000 to $4,000 above the sticker price.[72] This was fueled mainly by continued strong demand for most of Harley's bikes, including the Sportster (entry-level motorcycle), Custom (carries the highest margins), Touring (highest selling price, although also the costliest to manufacture), and Buell lines. Further, management's focus on trimming costs, also with increased sales of parts and accessories, resulted in an improved operating margin for the quarter and the full year. The outlook is quite promising for Harley at the moment. (**Exhibits 14** and **15** provide the company's summary of revenue, operating income, and assets, the balance sheet, and the income statement; **Exhibit 16** provides a geographic breakdown of sales.)

Since Harley went public, its shares have risen 18,000%. Harley-Davidson stock has remained strong, even when the general market has weakened. (**Exhibit 17** provides a comparison of Harley-Davidson stock and the Standard and Poor's 500 since the 1986 initial public offering.)

What does the future hold for Harley-Davidson? It really depends how one views the strengths, weaknesses, opportunities, and threats facing the company. Two analysts view the future prospects of Harley-Davidson's stock differently:

"It's an upper-middle-class toy," says Chad Hudson of the Prudent Bear fund, one of a number of prominent short-sellers convinced that Harley will skid. "As people run out of disposable income, that's going to hurt."[73]

Short-sellers—bearish investors who sell borrowed shares, hoping to replace them later with cheaper ones—"are banking on at some point the story cracking," says Chris Cox, a Goldman Sachs analyst who is bullish on Harley shares. "My point is that, if it does, it's not happening any time soon."[74]

Some analysts indicate that one major challenge for Harley-Davidson is to broaden their appeal. "There aren't a lot of the younger generation that can afford to run out and buy a Harley-Davidson," commented Jake Balzer, a senior equity analyst with Guzman and Company.[75]

How does Harley-Davidson move forward and continue to grow at the pace it has seen? Is this a reasonable long-term growth rate? How do they grapple with the aging Baby Boomers, who are generally the individuals who can afford a Harley-Davidson motorcycle? These were but a few of the questions in the minds of senior management as they looked to the future.

Exhibit 14 Harley-Davidson, Inc. Balance Sheet 2001–2005
(Dollar amounts in thousands)

Year ending December 31	2005	2004	2003	2002	2001
Assets					
Current Assets:					
Cash and cash equivalents	$140,975	$275,159	$329,329	$280,928	$439,438
Marketable securities	905,197	1,336,909	993,331	514,800	196,011
Accounts receivable, net	122,087	121,333	112,406	108,694	118,843
Financial receivables held for sale	299,373	456,516	1,001,990	855,771	656,421
Financial receivables held for investment net	1,342,393	1,167,522			
Inventories	221,418	226,893	207,726	218,156	181,115
Deferred Income taxes	61,285	60,517	51,156	41,430	38,993
Prepaid expenses and other current assets	52,509	38,337	33,189	46,807	34,443
Total Current Assets	$3,145,237	$3,683,186	$2,729,127	$2,066,586	$1,665,264
Finance Receivables, net	600,831	488,262	735,859	589,809	379,335
Property, plant and equipment, net	1,011,612	1,024,665	1,046,310	1,032,596	891,820
Prepaid pension costs	368,165	133,322			
Goodwill, net	56,563	59,456	53,678	49,930	49,711
Other Assets	72,801	94,402	358,114	122,296	132,365
Total Assets	$5,255,209	$5,483,293	$4,923,088	$3,861,217	$3,118,495
Liabilities & Shareholder's Equity					
Current Liabilities:					
Accounts Payable	$270,614	$244,202	$223,902	$266,977	$194,683
Accrued expenses and other liabilities	397,525	433,053	407,566	380,496	304,376
Current portion of finance debt	204,973	495,441	324,305	382,579	217,051
Total Current Liabilities	$873,112	$1,172,696	$955,773	$990,052	$716,110
Finance Debt	1,000,000	800,000	670,000	380,000	380,000
Other long-term liabilities	82,281	90,864	86,337	123,353	158,374
Postretirement healthcare benefits	60,975	149,848	127,444	105,419	89,912
Deferred income taxes	155,236	51,432	125,842	29,478	17,816
Total Liabilities	$2,171,604	$2,264,822	$1,965,396	$1,628,302	$1,362,212
Shareholder's Equity:					
Common Stock	$3,310	$3,300	$3,266	$3,254	$3,242
Additional PIC	596,239	533,068	419,455	386,284	359,165
Retained Earnings	4,630,390	3,844,571	3,074,037	2,372,095	1,833,335
Accumulated other comprehensive income	58,653	(12,096)	47,174	(46,266)	(13,728)
Less:					
Treasury Stock	(2,204,987)	(1,150,372)	(586,240)	(482,360)	(425,546)
Unearned Compensation	0	0	0	(92)	(185)
Total Shareholder's Equity	$3,083,605	$3,218,471	$2,957,692	$2,232,915	$1,756,283
Total Liabilities and Shareholder's Equity	$5,255,209	$5,483,293	$4,923,088	$3,861,217	$3,118,495

Source: Harley-Davidson, Inc., 2005 Form 10-K, p. 53.

Exhibit 15 Income Statement 2001–2005: Harley-Davidson, Inc.
(Dollar amounts in thousands)

Year ending December 31	2005	2004	2003	2002	2001
Net Sales	$5,342,214	$5,015,190	$4,624,274	$4,090,970	$3,363,414
COGS	3,301,715	3,115,655	2,958,708	2,673,129	2,183,409
Gross Profit	$2,040,499	$1,899,535	$1,665,566	$1,417,841	$1,180,005
Financial Services Income	331,618	305,262	279,459	211,500	181,545
Financial Services Interest and Operating Expense	139,998	116,662	111,586	107,273	120,272
Operating income from financial services	191,620	188,600	167,873	104,227	61,237
Selling, administrative, and engineering expense	762,108	726,644	684,175	639,366	578,777
Income from operations	$1,470,011	$1,362,491	$1,149,264	$882,702	$662,501
Interest Income, net	22,797	23,101	23,088	16,541	17,478
Other, net	(5,049)	(5,106)	(6,317)	(13,416)	(6,524)
Income before provision for income taxes	$1,487,759	$1,379,486	$1,166,035	$885,827	$673,455
Provision for income taxes	528,155	489,720	405,107	305,610	235,709
Net Income	$959,604	$889,766	$760,928	$580,217	$437,746

Source: Harley-Davidson, Inc., 2005 Form 10-K, p. 52.

Exhibit 16 Geographic Information: Harley-Davidson, Inc.
(Dollar amounts in thousands)

Year ending December 31	2005	2004	2003	2002	2001
Net Revenue[1]:					
United States	$4,304,865	$4,097,882	$3,807,707	$3,416,432	$2,766,391
Europe	530,124	477,962	419,052	337,463	301,729
Japan	192,268	192,720	173,547	143,298	141,181
Canada	143,204	136,721	134,319	121,257	96,928
Other foreign countries	171,753	109,905	89,649	72,520	57,185
Total	$5,342,214	$5,015,190	$4,624,274	$4,090,970	$3,363,414
Financial Services Income[1]					
United States	$308,341	$283,837	$260,551	$199,380	$172,593
Europe	9,135	9,538	8,834	4,524	1,214
Canada	14,142	11,887	10,074	7,596	7,738
Total	$331,618	$305,262	$279,459	$211,500	$181,545
Long-lived assets[2]:					
United States	$1,450,278	$1,246,808	$1,400,772	$1,151,702	$1,021,946
Other foreign countries	38,002	44,300	41,804	36,138	33,234
Total	$1,488,280	$1,291,108	$1,442,576	$1,187,840	$1,055,180

Notes:
1. Net revenue and income is attributed to geographic regions based on location of customer.
2. Long-lived assets include all long-term assets except those specifically excluded under SFAS Number 131, such as deferred income taxes and finance receivables.

Sources: Harley-Davidson 2005 Annual Report, p. 70, and Harley-Davidson 2003 Annual Report, p. 90.

Exhibit 17 Year-End Market Value of $100 Invested on December 31, 1986: Harley-Davidson vs. SP 500

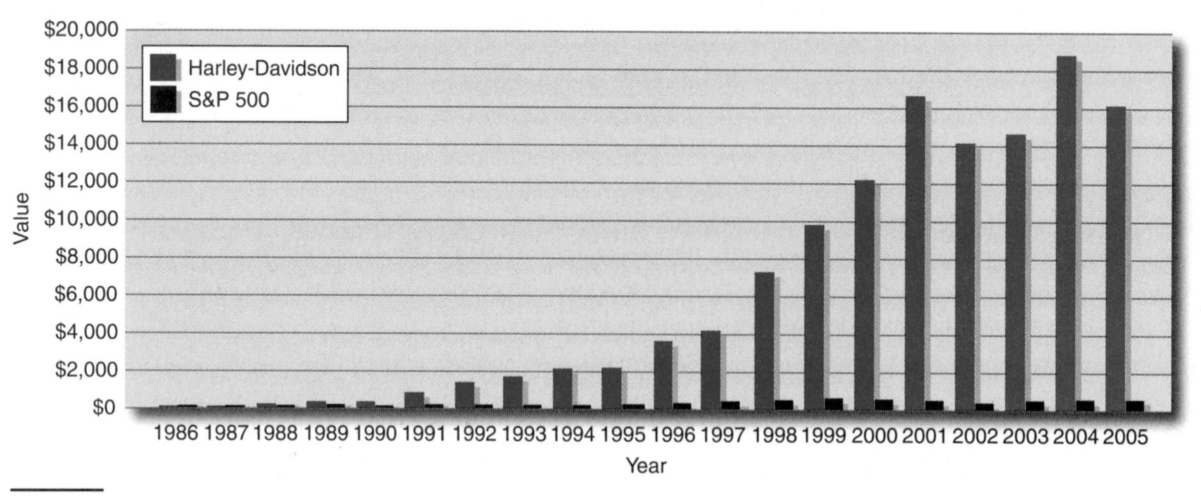

Source: http://investor.harley-davidson.com/HDvsSP500.cfm

Notes

1. *Harley-Davidson Annual Report, 2002,* back cover.
2. Ryan Nakashima, "Potholes Ahead for Harley's New Top Hog," Associated Press Financial Wire (April 13, 2005).
3. Thomas L. Wheelen, Kathryn E. Wheelen, Thomas L. Wheelen II, and Richard D. Wheelen, "Harley-Davidson: The 95th Anniversary," Case 16, *Strategic Management and Business Policy,* 8th edition, Prentice-Hall/Pearson Education, Inc., Upper Saddle River, NJ, 2002.
4. Jonathan Fahey, "Love into Money," *Forbes* (January 7, 2002), pp. 60–65.
5. *Harley-Davidson Annual Reports, 2005, 2003, 2001, 1999, 1997, 1995.*
6. Missy Sullivan, "High-Octane Hog," *Forbes* (September 10, 2002), pp. 8–10. The preceding two paragraphs were directly quoted with minor editing.
7. "A Harley Takes an Engine from Porsche," *The New York Times* (May 26, 2002). Accessed at *http://www.nytimes.com.* The preceding paragraph was directly quoted with minor editing.
8. James C. Ziemer, "Letter to the Shareholders," *Harley-Davidson 2005 Annual Report.*
9. *Ibid.*
10. "The Global Brands Scorecard 2006," *Business Week* (August 7, 2006), cover story.
11. Abrahm Lustgarten, "The List of Industry Champs," *Fortune* (March 7, 2005), http://money.cnn.com/magazines/fortune/fortune_archive/2005/03/07/8253449/index.htm
12. Harley-Davidson rider at 2006 Sturgis rally outside Miner's Restaurant in Keystone, August 18, 2006.
13. "Sturgis Police Department Ramps Up to Keep the Peace During Recent Annual Rally," *Sturgis Motorcycle Rally Magazine* (2006), pp. 28–29.
14. Andy Horn, Director of the Richmond Harley Davidson dealership, *Richmond Times Dispatch.*
15. John Helyar, "Will Harley-Davidson Hit the Wall?" *Fortune* (August 12, 2002), pp. 120–124.
16. Company press release, June 1, 2006, "Harley-Davidson Kicks Off Construction of Its Museum."
17. Harley-Davidson, *2001 10-K.* The following four paragraphs were directly quoted with minor editing.
18. Fahey (2002).
19. Joseph Weber, "Harley Investors May Get a Wobbly Ride," *Business Week* (February 11, 2002), p. 65.
20. Fahey (2002).
21. Discover Today's Motorcycling—Press Release, "Rockefeller Center Motorcycle Show Opens with Today Show Segment and Giant Preview Party" (April 6, 2002).
22. "Harley-Davidson and *Jane* Magazine Roll Out Contest to Honor Women with an Unquenchable Spirit of Freedom," *Market Wire* (June 7, 2005).
23. *Harley-Davidson Annual Report, 2005,* pp. 5–8. Much of this section was directly quoted from President Ziemer's letter to the shareholders with minor editing.
24. *Harley-Davidson Annual Report, 2005,* "Letter to the Shareholders from President and CEO James Ziemer."
25. *Ibid.*
26. M. Schifrin, "100 Year Young," *Forbes* (September 10, 2001), p. 6.
27. Weber, (2002).
28. Ken Brown, "Heard on the Street: Harley-Davidson Growth Engine May Be Stalling," *Wall Street Journal* (February 12, 2002), p. C2.
29. *Harley-Davidson Annual Report, 2005,* "Letter to the Shareholders from President and CEO James Ziemer."
30. *Ibid.*
31. Brown (2002).
32. Sullivan (2002).
33. *Harley-Davidson 10-K,* 2005.
34. Fahey (2002).
35. Rich Rovito, "No Revving Needed for Sales of Harley's V-Rod Motorcycle," *The Business Journal Serving Greater Milwaukee,*

January 14, 2002. Accessed at http://milwaukee.bizjournals.com/milwaukee/stories/2002/01/14/story8.html
36. Weber (2002).
37. "The *Business Week* 50 Ranking," *Business Week* (Spring 2002), p. 54.
38. Helyar (2002).
39. James V. Higgins, "All Hail, Harley-Davidson," *Detroit News* (February 22, 2002). Accessed at http://detnews.com/2002.
40. Fahey (2002).
41. Jerry Shiver, "Richer, Older Harley Riders 'Like Everyone Else,'" *USA Today* (March 8, 2002), pp. 1A–2A.
42. *Harley-Davidson, 2005 10-K.* The following two paragraphs were directly quoted with minor editing.
43. *Ibid.* The second, third, and fourth paragraphs were directly quoted with minor editing.
44. *Ibid.* The paragraph was directly quoted with minor editing.
45. *Ibid.* The paragraph was directly quoted with minor editing.
46. *Ibid.* The following two paragraphs were directly quoted with minor editing.
47. Shiver (2002).
48. "Harley Roars into Its Second Century," *Tribune* (Ames, IA) (July 26, 2002), p. A2.
49. Shiver (2002).
50. *Ibid.*
51. Amanda Ridley, "Spartanburg, S.C., Harley-Davidson Dealer Moving to Expanded Showroom," *Herald-Journal* (July 11, 2004).
52. Tonya M. Pisinski, "Me and My Harley: Hawg Riders Are Downright Passionate about Their Bike Riding and Hitting the Trail," *Worcester Telegram and Gazette* (May 25, 2005).
53. David Wells, "Lehman's Kantor Bets on Harley-Davidson: Call of Day," *Bloomberg* (November 14, 2001).
54. *Harley-Davidson, Form 10-K, 2005.* The following four paragraphs were directly quoted with minor editing.
55. Earle Eldrige, "More Over-40 Motorcyclists Die in Crashes," *USA Today* (January 10, 2002), p. 1B.
56. Fahey (2002).
57. *Harley-Davidson, Form 10-K, 2005.* The following five paragraphs were directly quoted with minor editing.
58. *Ibid.* The first two paragraphs were directly quoted with minor editing.
59. *Ibid.* The following paragraph was directly quoted with minor editing.
60. *Ibid.* The following two paragraphs were directly quoted with minor editing.
61. *Ibid.* The following paragraph was directly quoted with minor editing.
62. *Ibid.* The following three paragraphs were directly quoted with minor editing.
63. *Ibid.* The first paragraph was directly quoted with minor editing.
64. *Ibid.* The following paragraph was directly quoted with minor editing.
65. *Ibid.* The following paragraph was directly quoted with minor editing.
66. *Ibid.* The following two paragraphs were directly quoted with minor editing.
67. *Ibid.* The following paragraph was directly quoted with minor editing.
68. *Ibid.* The following paragraph was directly quoted with minor editing.
69. *Ibid.* The following three paragraphs were directly quoted with minor editing.
70. *Ibid.* The following paragraph was directly quoted with minor editing.
71. *Ibid.* The following two paragraphs were directly quoted with minor editing.
72. Fahey (2002).
73. Helyar (2002).
74. Brown (2002).
75. Nakashima (2005).

CASE 17

JetBlue Airways' Success Story

Sanjib Dutta and Shirisha Regani

"JetBlue has been put together as no other airline has ever been put together before. It has the most capital. It has the best product. So now the question is, can you continue it? And that's what worries me. That's what keeps me up at night. How can we continue what we have started?"

David Neeleman, Founder and CEO of JetBlue

"JetBlue will continue to eat out of the major carriers' rice bowls for quite some time. While they struggle to repair their balance sheets and become more liquid and financially flexible, low-cost airlines like JetBlue will expand into the vacuum the majors have created."

Robert Mann, airline analyst and consultant at R.W. Mann & Co.

JetBlue Beats the Biggies

In early 2003, JetBlue Airways, the three-year-old no-frills U.S. airline, posted a profit of $17.6 million for the first quarter of 2003. In the same period, the U.S. airline industry announced losses of around $2 billion. JetBlue was one of the few bright spots in an industry that had been reeling under the woes of overcapacity and losses for over two years. The company managed to succeed in a period when big names of the U.S. airline industry, like American Airlines, United Air Lines, US Airways, and others, suffered huge losses and were a few steps from bankruptcy.

The U.S. airline industry was in a bad state owing to the effects of terrorism, war, and economic downturn. The major carriers alone were estimated to have an outstanding debt of over $100 billion, as against a combined stock market value of $13 billion in 2002. Passenger traffic was also falling consistently. In early 2003, air traffic was 17% lower than in the same period of 2002 (which was itself 10% lower than the traffic in early 2001).

In this scenario, a number of low-cost airlines began to make their presence felt in the industry. (See **Exhibit 1** for a note on low-cost airlines in the United States.) Southwest

Exhibit 1
A Note on Low-Cost Airlines

No-frills, low-cost carriers seem to be the answer to the problems of the American airline industry. In 2002, when the industry was estimated to have made losses to the tune of $9 billion, Southwest Airlines and JetBlue Airways were the only two major carriers to post profits. Low-cost carriers seemed to be gaining popularity with passengers for short point-to-point trips in the United States. The main features of low-cost carriers are:

- They operate only one kind of aircraft, such as the Boeing 737 or the Airbus 319/320.
- They are one-class carriers that offer standardized treatment to all the passengers.
- They do not offer benefits like lounges, free meals, or drinks.
- Normally there is no seat allocation (JetBlue is an exception).
- Tickets are normally booked over the Internet.

Most low-cost airlines also make efforts to simplify check-in processes by introducing electronic check-ins and simplifying baggage handling.

In 2002 it was estimated that low-cost airlines accounted for 25% of short-haul bookings in the United States.

Some of the prominent low-cost carriers in the United States are:

- Airtran
- American West
- American Trans Air
- Delta Express' Song
- I-Jet
- JetBlue
- Frontier Airlines
- Midwest Express
- Southwest
- Spirit Airlines
- Suncountry
- USA-3000

However, low-frills airlines are not all benefits. Observers say that low-cost carriers charge low fares only when tickets are booked far in advance. Late bookers are penalized with prices equal to or higher than those for premium flights. Analysts also say that the idea that people choose only on the price dimension is wrong. They say that a number of people are willing to pay a premium to be able to fly from good airports and have a comfortable travel experience.

The difference between low-cost and premium airlines, however, is narrowing. The high-cost, full-service airlines are making efforts to control costs, while the low-cost carriers are trying to expand to longer hauls and provide better flight experiences.

Source: Adapted from various newspaper and magazine articles.

Airlines, the highly successful 30-year-old discounter, was the inspiration for most of the low-cost startups. However, not all the startups succeeded. The most important cause for failure was the inability of these low-cost airlines to bring about a balance between cost-cutting and quality of service. The most successful exception to this condition was JetBlue.

JetBlue, which was modeled on Southwest Airlines, managed to succeed in a depressed and highly competitive industry because of its innovative approach to business and its efforts in becoming a cost leader by cutting down on unnecessary frills and wasteful expenses. The airline managed to cut costs without compromising the quality of service. In fact, it provided more amenities than other airlines, including a personal television set for every flyer and comfortable leather seats, creating a feeling of luxury. JetBlue's strategy was to identify and eliminate non-value-adding costs and use the money so saved to provide service of better quality.

Background

JetBlue is the brainchild of David Neeleman, the son of a Mormon missionary, who grew up in Salt Lake City, Utah. Neeleman was a poor student and dropped out of the University of Utah after his freshman year. After dropping out, he spent two years in Brazil as a missionary. Upon returning to the United States, he took up a career in sales, selling condominiums in Hawaii. To boost his business, he started his own travel agency by chartering flights to transport prospective clients to the Hawaiian islands. Neeleman was a hard-seller who even tried to push honeymoon packages onto couples during their weddings.

His reputation as a salesman caught the attention of June Morris, who owned one of Utah's largest travel agencies. Together, they started a Utah-based charter operation in 1984 called Morris Air. Neeleman modeled Morris Air on Southwest Airlines,[1] run by his idol Herb Kelleher. He took ideas from Southwest and tried to improve on them. He adopted a strategy of keeping costs low to increase margins by turning around[2] the planes quickly and having reservationists work from home to save on office rentals. He also developed the industry's first electronic ticketing system, which was easier to operate than manual ones and did not cost much. By 1992, Morris Air had developed into a regular scheduled airline and was poised for an IPO.

Herb Kelleher, impressed with the airline's low-cost, high-revenues strategy, offered to take it over. Southwest bought Morris Air for $129 million. Neeleman gained $22 million from this sale and went to work at Southwest as an Executive Vice President. This arrangement, however, did not work out. Neeleman, accustomed to running his own airline, was unable to adjust to working in a team. Within a year, he parted ways with Southwest. Before he could leave, Kelleher made him sign a non-compete agreement that would be valid for five years.

Neeleman then moved to Canada, where he co-founded a discount airline called West Jet. He also fine-tuned the online reservations system he developed at Morris Air, called it *Open Skies*, and sold it to Hewlett-Packard[3] in 1999, for a reported $22 million.

After his non-compete agreement with Kelleher expired in 1998, Neeleman, along with his lawyer, Tom Kelly, started developing business plans for a new airline that was to be called JetBlue. He raised capital from the same five people who had invested in Morris Air and millionaire investor George Soros. He blew through $30 million before the first plane flew and went back for more capital. But the investors, who were impressed with the success he had made of Morris Air, were ready to lend him more.

Next, he started studying the current scenario in the airline industry to make strategic decisions about his airline. He decided to base his airline in New York's John F. Kennedy International Airport (JFK) rather than the two nearby airports LaGuardia and Newark because he reasoned that, since JFK mostly flew international flights, he would have very little competition from domestic flights at that airport.

He then identified routes that were poorly served by other airlines and decided to concentrate on those. JetBlue would not serve too many routes. Instead, it would concentrate on certain areas, like the West Coast, Northeast, and Florida, flying key routes that were not taken by competitors.

From the beginning, Neeleman was sure that his airline would be a low-cost operator. He studied the price structures of the major airlines over different routes from New York and found that they would not be difficult to undercut, provided that he had the right technology and equipment. To achieve his objective, he used capital equipment that had high initial outlay but was easier on the maintenance side.

He then went after the best people in the industry to work with him for the airline. He roped in Dave Barger, who had led a turnaround at Continental Airlines, to function as

Exhibit 2
Income Statement: JetBlue (Dollar amounts in millions, except per share amounts)

Particulars	December 2002	December 2001	December 2000
Revenue	$635.2	$320.4	$104.6
Cost of Goods sold	212.0	159.4	63.6
Gross Profit	423.2	161.0	41.0
SG&A Expense	291.3	134.3	62.2
Depreciation & Amortization	26.9	—	—
Operating Income/Loss	105.0	26.8	(21.2)
Total Net Income/Loss	$ 54.9	$ 38.5	$(21.3)
Net Profit Margin	8.6%	12.0%	—
Gross Profit Margin	66.6%	50.3%	39.2%
Operating Margin	16.5%	8.4%	—
Diluted EPS	$ 0.84	—	—

Source: www.hoovers.com.

President and COO. He also took two of Southwest's top people to manage finance and human resources at JetBlue.

JetBlue started with initial capital of $160 million. Operations began on February 11, 2000. The inaugural flight was between New York's JFK and Fort Lauderdale, Florida. In early 2002, JetBlue came out with an initial public offer of about 5.5 million shares. The shares, traded on NASDAQ, were offered at a price between $22 and $24 but shot up to around $45 on the first day. The capital raised through the issue was used to buy new planes and to supplement working capital.

In 2002, JetBlue recorded a total net income of $55 million on revenues of $635 million (**see Exhibit 2**). This occurred in a year when the major airlines in the industry were estimated to have lost about $9 billion (**see Exhibit 3**). After posting a 35% increase over the previous year in the first quarter earnings for 2003, the company placed an order for 65 new Airbus A-320 planes, with Airbus Industries, adding to the 41 planes already in the fleet. See the company's *2003 Annual Report* for complete financial statements, at *http://investor.jetblue.com/ireye/ir_site.zhtml?ticker=jblu&script=700.*

Exhibit 3
Loss Position of Airlines in America

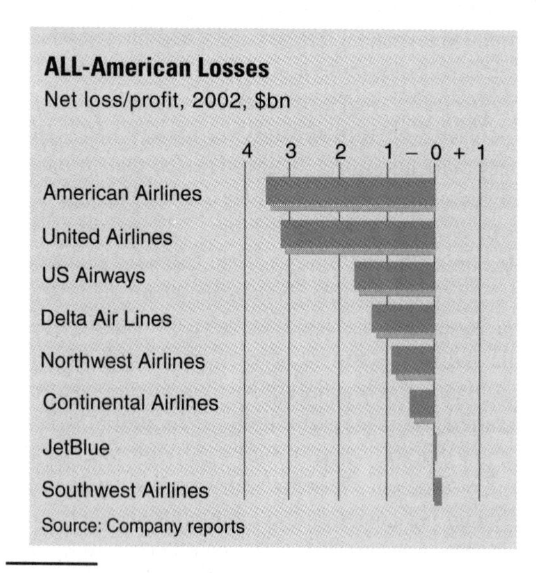

Source: "Flying Dinosaurs," The Economist *(February 6, 2003).*

In its three years of operation, JetBlue flew more than 12 million passengers. The airline received a number of awards for the quality of its service and its success in operations. (**See Exhibit 4** for a list of awards received by JetBlue.)

JetBlue's Success Model

JetBlue succeeded because of its cost advantages and no-nonsense approach to business. The company adopted aggressive cost-cutting measures by doing away with most of the frills other airlines provided that only increased their costs and did not improve customer value, without compromising on quality or comfort. Said Neeleman, "You can be efficient and effective and deliver a great experience at the same time."[4] JetBlue's aim was to create a cost structure that would support low fares without lowering service standards. The fares JetBlue charged for a round trip averaged between $98 to $498, which was more than 50% less than those charged by the majors in the industry. (For instance, a round trip from New York to Florida cost about $500 on the major airlines; JetBlue charged about $140 for the same trip with a seven-day advance purchase.) To support its decision to become a cost leader, JetBlue adopted a number of innovative measures on its flights.

Effective Cost Management

JetBlue decided not to serve meals on its flights, no matter what the distance or duration. Neeleman identified food as an area in which major cost-cutting was possible. He realized that since airline food was notoriously bad, no one was likely to miss it. He, therefore, did away with meals altogether. Instead of meals, JetBlue served light snacks like chips, cookies, and crackers, which cost a fraction of what a regular meal did and also pleased the passengers. All the snacks were piled in a basket, and the customers could help themselves to whatever they wanted. The airline also served coffee and canned drinks, which did not cost much. Neeleman calculated that a normal airline meal cost about $4 per passenger. By choosing to serve snacks that cost 12–14 cents, JetBlue saved a huge amount.

Not serving meals on flights did not affect JetBlue in any way. In fact, analysts felt that JetBlue had identified a very good area for reducing expenses. This innovative approach helped JetBlue save over $3 per passenger, at the same time ensuring that no one went hungry on flights. Passengers also seemed to prefer this kind of snacks to regular, insipid meals, and serving items like chips and animal crackers went well with JetBlue's image as an innovative, fun airline.

The money saved on food was put to better use elsewhere. It was spent mainly on providing personal television sets to all the passengers on the flight. Every passenger was given an individual TV, with a set of headphones. The TV was fixed to the back of the seat in front of each passenger, and passengers could watch 24 channels of satellite television. This idea was a great hit with passengers, who seemed to enjoy the freedom of being able to watch whatever they wanted without having to compromise. (In other airlines, there was normally only one television screen, which all the passengers had to watch together. This left no scope for individual preferences.) There were instances of people choosing JetBlue over other airlines only because of the personal TVs.

Personal TVs provided JetBlue with a good point for differentiation. The company used this feature like a weapon against other domestic airlines, as it was the only one offering personal TVs. The personal TV feature was played up, mentioned in most of the brochures, and it was emphasized in all the advertisements. JetBlue even acquired Live TV, the television

Exhibit 4 Awards Received: JetBlue

Award	Conferred By
1. 2003 Awards	
Top 5 Domestic Airline	Departures, 2003 Readers' Favorite Survey
Best Low Cost Airline	*Entrepreneur* magazine
Best Low Cost Airline	Skytraxx, 2003 Airline of the Year Survey
Airline of the Year	*Airfinance Journal*, 2003 Deal of the Year Awards
North American Corporate Finance Deal of the Year	*Airfinance Journal*, 2003 Deal of the Year Awards
IPO of the Year	*Corporate Finance*
Editors' Choice	Travel-Holiday
Outstanding Inflight Entertainment	*Onboard Services*, 2003 Onboard Services Awards
Outstanding Safety Video	*Onboard Services*, 2003 Onboard Services Awards
2. 2002 Awards	
Best Domestic Airline	*Conde Nast Traveler*, 2002 Readers' Choice Awards
Best Domestic Airline—Coach	*Conde Nast Traveler*, 2002 Business Travel Awards
Best Domestic Airline—Value for Cost	*Conde Nast Traveler*, 2002 Business Travel Awards
Best Domestic Airline	North American Travel Journalists Association, Five-Star Award
#2 Domestic Airline	*Travel and Leisure*, 2002 World's Best Awards
Best Low-Cost Carrier (runner-up)	*Business Traveler*, 2002 Best in Business Travel Awards
"It" Airline	*Entertainment Weekly*, 2002 It List
Editor's Choice	*Worth*
Marketer of the Year	*Advertising Age*
#4 Brand of the Year	*www.brandchannel.com*, 2002 Readers' Choice
Finance Award	*Airline Business*, 2002 Airline Strategy Awards
Market Development Award	*Air Transport World*, 2002 Industry Achievement Awards
Best Overall Airline	*Onboard Services*, 2002 Onboard Service Awards
Best Inflight or Onboard Service	*Onboard Services*, 2002 Onboard Service Awards
Best Onboard Entertainment	*Onboard Services*, 2002 Onboard Service Awards
Best Uniforms (2nd place)	*Onboard Services*, 2002 Onboard Service Awards
3. 2001 Awards	
Best Domestic Airline—Coach	*Conde Nast Traveler*, 2001 Business Travel Awards
#2 Domestic Airline	*Conde Nast Traveler*, 2001 Reader's Choice Awards
#2 Domestic Airline	Zagat, 2001 Airline Survey
Best Domestic Airline	North American Travel Journalists Assn., 2001 Five-Star Award
Best New Airline	*Money*
Favorite U.S. Airline	*Orange County Register*/Knight Ridder
Seal of Approval	*Diversion*
"A" Rating	Planetfeedback, leading online consumer feedback service
#2 Airline	Epinions.com
4. Awards Won by David Neeleman	
Best & Brightest (2003)	*Esquire*
Atlas Award for Guerilla Marketing (2003)	Association of Travel Marketing Executives
Best Visionary (2001)	*Sales & Marketing Management*
Top 20 Most Influential People In Aviation (2001)	*Aviation Daily*
Winners' Circle (2001)	*Travel Agent*
Top Ten Entrepreneurs (2000)	*BusinessWeek*
Travel Industry Innovator (2000)	*Time*
25 Most Influential Executives of 2000	*Business Travel News*
Top 20 Most Influential People in Aviation (2000)	*Aviation Daily*
Winners' Circle (2000)	*Travel Agent*

Source: www.jetblue.com.

station that broadcast the 24 channels onboard, to be able to maintain its advantage over rivals.

The television sets cost about $1 per passenger per flight. That was less than one-third the cost of a meal, so JetBlue did not have to incur any additional expenditure in providing the service. It only diverted resources from an unproductive function to a productive one, which gave the company a competitive advantage over its rivals.

JetBlue did not try to cut costs in all areas. Neeleman realized that cost-cutting must be balanced with good quality for an airline to succeed. Cutting costs in all areas only brought down the quality of service and sometimes turned out to be counterproductive. To avoid this, he sometimes chose items that involved a high initial cost but provided a greater advantage in the long run. For instance, he chose to fit his planes with leather seats instead of cloth ones. Leather furnishings cost twice as much as cloth ones, but they also lasted twice as long. Besides, leather seats were more comfortable for passengers and therefore improved customer value. Passengers really liked the new leather seats, which were also wider and offered more leg room. JetBlue managed to combine luxury with economy. Said Neeleman, "It's different with JetBlue. And people feel different. They don't feel like they are flying on a start-up airline."[5]

Unlike a number of other startup airlines, JetBlue did not use old, cheap planes. By choosing to operate Airbus[6] flights, it dispelled the image of a startup operator functioning on a shoestring budget and created an image of smart efficiency. Neeleman chose the Airbus A-320 over the more popular Boeing 737[7] because he calculated that, although the Airbus cost more initially, it was easier on the maintenance side and was also more fuel-efficient. Fuel-efficiency was an important variable in the decision, in light of rising fuel prices around the world. The planes also came with a five-year warranty, which reduced the maintenance costs drastically and more than made up for the higher initial expenditure.

JetBlue's cost per passenger mile was 6.43 cents, which was only slightly higher than the 6.33 cents of Southwest and much lower than US Airways' 12.45 cents.

Operational Advantage

JetBlue operated only a single fleet of planes, and there was no division into first class, business class, and economy class, unlike with other airline majors. JetBlue figured out that it could save more by offering standard treatment to all passengers and providing good service without distinctions. Flying a single fleet worked to the advantage of the airline as it involved fewer scheduling and maintenance problems. It also helped control costs, as spare parts, furnishings, and crew were interchangeable.

One of the critical factors in the success of JetBlue was that it was able to identify a niche market and cater to it. It did not try to fly too many routes, instead concentrating on New York, Florida, and California. It also flew to secondary airports that did not handle too much air traffic. Neeleman reasoned that he could gain more passengers by flying out of airports his competitors did not use. Secondary airports also offered better business terms than the larger ones, and JetBlue was able to get more terminals and flight slots, enabling it to fly more planes. As a result, JetBlue was able to fly more planes per day than its competitors and, consequently, be more profitable.

Like Southwest, JetBlue also chose point-to-point flights[8] over a hub-and-spoke network.[9] Point-to-point flights were faster and cheaper for the airline as they involved lower travel time and could be accomplished with minimum expenses. (**See Exhibit 5** for JetBlue's route map.)

Another important cost-cutting factor was that JetBlue managed to reduce the turnaround time of flights, which reduced the time spent on the ground. JetBlue flights were ready for their next trip in about 35 minutes, unlike other airlines, whose flights took an hour or more to get ready. This way, JetBlue managed to fly more flights per day than its competitors.

Exhibit 5
Route Map: JetBlue[1]

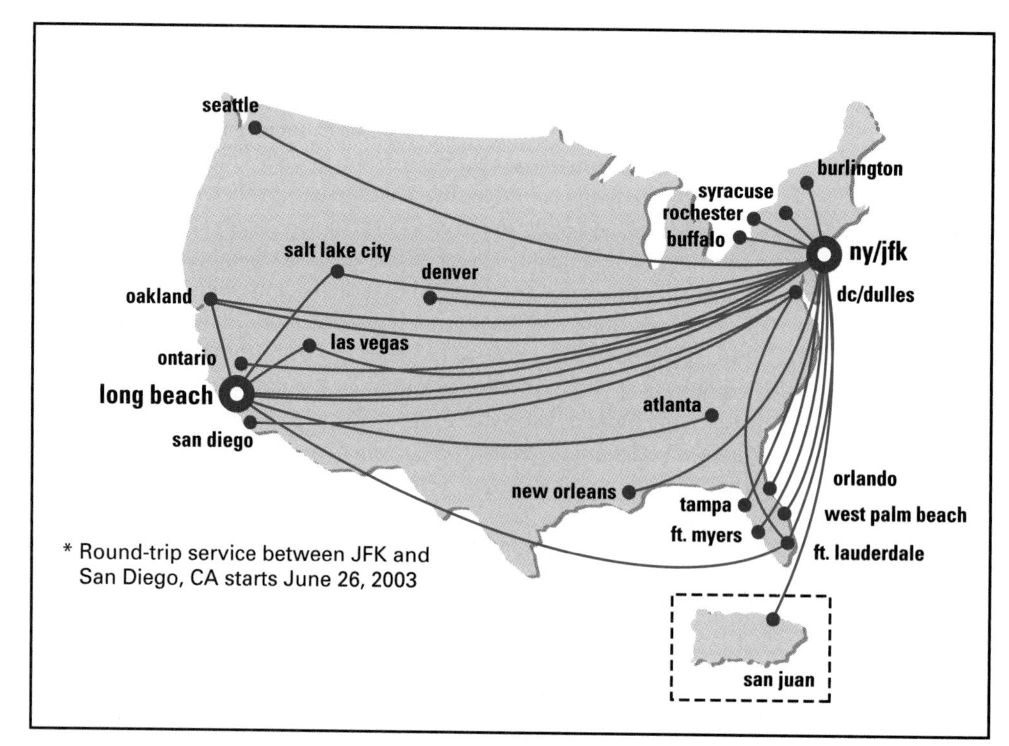

Note:
1. New York and Long Beach are the focus cities.

Source: www.jetblue.com.

Harnessing Technology

To bring about effective cost control and the accomplishment of functions with minimum wastage of time and resources, JetBlue decided to harness the advantages of information systems. Neeleman, who had earlier developed an electronic reservation system, decided to minimize time and costs by allowing the airline's 600-odd reservationists to work from home, using VoIP (Voice over Internet Protocol). Electronic ticketing reduced the hassles of booking tickets and also had the advantage of saving on office rentals. JetBlue also avoided use of travel agents completely by encouraging booking of tickets over the Internet.

JetBlue was also the first airline to introduce the concept of a paperless cockpit by equipping pilots with laptops to access electronic flight manuals and make requisite calculations before take-off. Because of this, they managed to save between 15 and 20 minutes in take-off. First Officer Kevin Carney said, "I used to work for US Airways, and they didn't have anything like this. None of the airlines do."[10]

JetBlue appointed Jeff Cohen as the Chief Information Officer in the first year of business, with a mandate from Neeleman to automate everything. Neeleman wanted a paperless office and highly simplified processes that could be accomplished with minimum manpower. Automation was the key to saving on labor charges and also to completing tasks with a minimum of fuss and delay. Said Cohen, "From the beginning, I've basically had to wake up everyday and figure out how we stay a low-cost airline, without bringing in huge ideas that will cost a huge amount of money and aren't aligned with our business model."[11]

Toward this end, Cohen and his team worked on projects to minimize the CASM (cost per available seat mile, which is the airline industry equivalent of ROI). In 2002, JetBlue's

CASM was 7 cents, which was 25% less than that of other major carriers. Neeleman also tried to avoid outsourcing technologies and programs, preferring instead to develop them in-house. The in-house developers developed a program to track information flight-by-flight and post it on the airline's intranet to keep employees updated about the happenings in the airline. Programs were also developed to enable electronic baggage tagging and automatic check-in, which saved huge amounts of time. Information technology made things easier for customers and also helped JetBlue work with a lean employee force. Having fewer employees allowed the airline to take better care of them and keep them happy.

Customer Focus

JetBlue adopted a proactive, customer-oriented approach to service. Neeleman believed that most airlines did not succeed because they did not give customers their due importance. They looked on them as an annoyance, and subjected them to all kinds of inconveniences and rudeness, without understanding their importance to the business.

JetBlue's philosophy was to keep passengers happy and comfortable. This was reflected in every aspect of the company. Neeleman himself flew in his planes at least once a week and spent time interacting with customers. He also helped the crew serve snacks, handed out baggage, and helped the plane get ready for its next trip. It made customers feel special when the CEO of the airline took the trouble to interact with them and see to their comfort. He also noted customer suggestions and saw that they were attended to as soon as possible.

The airline also made an effort to avoid inconveniencing passengers whenever possible. JetBlue had the best on-time record in the industry, but even when the planes were delayed due to weather or other uncontrollable conditions, the airline ensured that passengers were not put to trouble. There was an instance when Neeleman and his staff called passengers at their homes at 3:00 A.M. to tell them that their 6:00 A.M. flight was delayed so that they did not have to bother coming to the airport early.

Jennifer Klyse, who once flew JetBlue to find out what all the hullabaloo was about, was full of praise for the airline's customer service. She recollected how, when her flight was delayed for two hours in Oakland, the crew apologized to all the passengers at the airport and arranged snacks and drinks. Later, when the plane had to be diverted to San Jose because of weather problems, they gave lunch vouchers to all the passengers. The biggest surprise, however, came when the plane was unable to depart from San Jose because of weather problems. The captain announced that all the passengers would be provided with a free flight segment, which could be redeemed on their next JetBlue flight. All this was done when there was a delay because of the weather, about which there was nothing the airline could have done. This kind of customer orientation won JetBlue a number of loyal customers. The airline estimated that almost 74% of its passengers used this airline for the first time because of good word-of-mouth.

It also helped that JetBlue had an on-time performance record of 80%, as against the 72% for the top 10 airlines in the United States. Luggage-handling errors were also considerably lower, at 2.54 per 1,000 bags handled, compared to the 5.2 of the top 10. On an average, JetBlue received less than 1 complaint for every 100,000 customers flown.

Picking the Right People

To support its customer-centric approach, JetBlue was very careful about the people it employed. Neeleman ensured that the company employed only people who were genuinely service oriented and liked interacting with others. Said Neeleman, "We don't want jaded people working here. If you don't like people, or can't deal with rude customers, you'll be fired."[12] He also ensured that he recruited people who were open-minded and did not hesitate to do things that may not fall into their job descriptions. Only at JetBlue did pilots emerge from the cockpit after every flight to help clean up the plane for the next trip.

Initiative in employees was encouraged and rewarded. Once, when a flight was delayed, the pilot came out from the cockpit and offered his cell phone to customers to use. There were instances when the crew ordered pizza for everyone when a flight was canceled. Employee initiative was recognized. They were usually given free tickets or a vacation to show appreciation.

JetBlue also had a profit-sharing program and attractive bonuses, which motivated employees to contribute their best. New recruits or trainees were also taken care of like regular employees. At other airlines, new recruits were paid a stipend but were asked to look after their own expenses for hotel rooms, food, etc. At JetBlue, those expenses were also taken care of, so new people also came to work grateful and motivated, instead of disgruntled and resentful.

Neeleman motivated his employees by example. Whenever he flew on his flights, he helped clean up the plane and ready it for the next trip. This attitude was adopted by his employees as well. There were no rules at JetBlue except that the customers had to be kept happy at any cost. Every employee knew what was happening in the organization. There was no interdepartmental rivalry, and nobody looked down on any work. Everybody was given equal importance, whether their work was to fly the plane or keep it clean.

Positioning for Fun

JetBlue positioned itself as a fun airline. It used creative advertising to cut through clutter and get its message across effectively. The marketing department at JetBlue, headed by Amy Curtis-McIntyre (who had earlier worked in Virgin Atlantic's marketing department), came up with the hip image JetBlue has. It created advertisements that were "cheap and cheeky" and appealed equally to the affluent and to bargain-seekers. One advertising project included a road show in which cars, painted bright blue, drove through certain identified areas in sets of three, distributing t-shirts and other souvenirs to passers-by to create awareness about JetBlue. Oranges were once distributed in Washington, DC, to promote the airline's flights to Florida. Billboards in New York promised free TVs with every purchase. In Los Angeles, the airline promoted its flights to San Francisco with a "Smog to Fog" punchline. Television spots continued this same theme of fun.

The name JetBlue itself connoted fun and freedom to passengers. It gave an impression of being cool. Naming the airline, however, had not been easy. Neeleman and his team had gone over a number of names, ranging from New Air, to Taxi, to True Blue, before lighting on the name JetBlue. They chose JetBlue because it sounded unique and also conveyed the "young, smart, uncluttered image" the company wanted to maintain. "It works so well for an airline—the blue skies, the wild blue yonder and the idea of openness. Blue creates a happy connotation for the travel experience," said David Polinchock, a branding expert at Location Based Branding in New Jersey.[13] Most of the flight names also have the word *blue* in them, carrying the idea further. The concept was so successful that Virgin Atlantic Airways[14] started an Australian service under the name VirginBlue. Southwest was also planning to paint all its planes blue.

However, JetBlue was not all fun. Customer safety was given utmost importance. After the September 11, 2001, terrorist attacks on America, JetBlue was the first airline to introduce safety measures in planes. It installed monitors in the cockpits so that pilots could see what was happening in the passenger cabins from behind heavy titanium bolted doors.

Looking Ahead

JetBlue succeeded where a number of other airlines had failed. The primary reason for this success was that the airline tried to be different. It built its success on low cost and high standards, which attracted and kept passengers and at the same time helped the airline remain solvent in times when the majors were crumbling to dust.

However, analysts wondered whether this magnitude of success could be sustained for a longer period. JetBlue's cost-leader approach succeeded when the airline was in its growing stage and could yet exercise close control over the business. There were no labor problems because the airline was small enough for all the employees to feel involved and for the management to look after employees well. Things could not be the same forever. With JetBlue growing at a very rapid pace, its real success would be in replicating the same model successfully on a larger scale.

An important factor in JetBlue's success was that it operated in a niche market where it had no competition. It had adopted the Southwest model, but it did not operate in the same markets as Southwest. However, competitors were catching up with JetBlue. Delta Air Lines launched a new discounted fleet called *Song* in April 2003, in direct competition with JetBlue. Song was flying everyday to West Palm Beach from all three airports in New York, which was an advantage over JetBlue (JetBlue still flew only from JFK). Delta was also likely to introduce personal satellite TV, Internet access, and multichannel MP3 audio at a later stage. Virgin Airways was also eyeing the U.S. markets after its success as an inter-city carrier in Europe and Australia. Southwest had better costs than JetBlue and was expected to become JetBlue's biggest competitor, although, in 2003, they were not competing in the same markets.

Another drawback of JetBlue was that it operated only a single fleet of jets. It offered standard treatment to all flyers, without the luxury of first class or business class. It also had more seats than galley space, which made it an essentially short route choice, or the choice of economy class travelers. Business travelers were more likely to prefer airlines that had more space between seats, which was an important factor in comfortable travel. Also, travelers who preferred business class or first class were likely to choose other airlines. The service at JetBlue may have been comparable to first class service, but analysts wondered whether travelers who had the opportunity and means to travel in greater luxury would like traveling with an airline better known for functionality than luxury.

JetBlue's success could well prove to be an example for other airline carriers to emulate. It was one of the very few startups to succeed in the U.S. airline industry from among over 100 that mushroomed after the industry was deregulated in 1978. JetBlue was growing very rapidly. In three years of operations, it had more than 40 planes in its fleet, with more to come. On average, it was adding a plane per month. Its main distinction, however, was that it was one of the few airlines able to remain solvent in difficult times.

Notes

1. Herb Kelleher's Southwest Airways is America's most successful discount airline. The airline has been profitable for a straight 30 years. It is headquartered in Dallas, Texas.
2. Turning aircraft around as fast as possible at the gate is important to minimize the time that aircraft spend on the ground as ground time is non-revenue-producing time for an airline.
3. Hewlett-Packard is a leading provider of IT products, including computing, imaging, and printing. It is headquartered in California.
4. *www.cio.com.*
5. *www.cbsnews.com.*
6. Airbus is a leading manufacturer of aircraft in the world. It was established in 1970 and is headquartered in France.
7. Boeing is a U.S.-based manufacturer of aircraft.
8. In the point-to-point system, the planes have a simple flight route and fly from the origin to the destination.
9. A hub-and-spoke system uses a strategically located airport (the hub) as a passenger exchange point for flights to and from outlying towns and cities (the spokes).
10. *CIO Magazine* (July 1, 2002).
11. *www.cio.com.*
12. *Forbes* (January 31, 2001).
13. *Fortune* (June 19, 2001).
14. Virgin Atlantic Airways is a part of Richard Branson's Virgin group of companies.

Additional Readings and References

"Amazing JetBlue," *Fortune* (April 23, 2003).

M. Arndt and W. Zellner, "American Draws a Bead on JetBlue," *BusinessWeek* (June 24, 2002).

R. Barker, "Is JetBlue Flying Too High?" *BusinessWeek* (April 29, 2002).

J. Boorstin, "Final Boarding Call," *Fortune* (April 29, 2002).

E. Brown, "Neeleman; A Smokeless Herb," *Fortune* (May 22, 2001).

L. DiCarlo, "JetBlue Skies," *Forbes* (January 31, 2001).

S. DiFranco, "Learning from JetBlue," *www.funfactspublishing.com.*

S. Donnelley, "Blue Skies for JetBlue," *Time* (July 10, 2001).

"Flying Dinosaurs," *The Economist* (February 6, 2003).

www.foxnews.com.

www.hoovers.com.

www.jetblue.com.

"JetBlue: Flying Higher?" *www.cbsnews.com*, (October 23, 2002).

"JetBlue Reports More Paying Passengers, Fuller Planes," *South Florida Business Journal* (December 6, 2002).

J. Keeney and D. Neeleman, "JetBlue," *Business 2.0* (March 2001).

J. Keeney, "JetBlue; Cleaning Up," *Fortune* (April 24, 2003).

S. J. Klien, "Naming Your Baby," *Fortune* (June 19, 2001).

http://news.airwise.com.

S. Overby, "JetBlue Skies Ahead," *CIO Magazine* (July 1, 2002).

A. Tsao, "Thinking of Taking Off on JetBlue?" *BusinessWeek* (April 5, 2002).

"A Way Out of the Wilderness," *The Economist* (May 1, 2003).

C. Woodyard, "JetBlue: The Cool Factor," *www.usatoday.com.*

C. Woodyard, "JetBlue Soars on CEO's Creativity," *www.usatoday.com.*

CASE 18

Carnival Corporation & plc (2006): Twelve Distinct Brands Serving Seven Continents

Michael J. Keefe, John K. Ross III, Bill J. Middlebrook, and Thomas. L. Wheelen

MICKEY ARISON, CHAIRMAN AND CEO, NOTED IN HIS 2005 LETTER TO THE STOCKHOLDERS that "Carnival Corporation has become the world's most profitable vacation company, with revenues surpassing $11.6 billion and net income approaching $2.3 billion. Our revenues increased by 14 percent during the past year with 8% driven by the added capacity of new ships and 6 percent from a combination of higher ticket prices, occupancies, and onboard spending." He further stated, "2005 also brought record increases in fuel prices, which cost the company an incremental $0.21 per share and drove the unit costs up 5 percent versus prior years."[1]

Arison explained, "While our targeted brands and strategic growth initiatives remain important ingredients for success, an entrepreneurial spirit is what out company thrives on. . . . Our culture empowers our brand managers to make daily decisions to the best interest of building their respective operating companies. Each brand is accountable for its individual performance."[2]

Overview

In 1972, Ted Arison founded Carnival Cruise Line with one ship, the *Mardi Gras.* Ted Arison's son, Mickey Arison, now serves as Chairman and CEO. In 2006, the company had a portfolio of 12 distinct cruise lines with 79 ships serving 7 continents.

The company's 12 cruise brands were (1) **Carnival Cruise Lines** with 21 ships; (2) **Princess Cruises** with 14 ships; (3) **Holland America Line** with 12 ships; (4) **Costa Cruises** with 10 ships; (5) **P&O Cruises** with 5 ships; (6) **AIDA Cruises** with 4 ships; (7) **Cunard Line** with 2 ocean liners; (8) **P&O Cruises Australia** with 3 ships; (9) **Ocean Village** with 1 ship; (10) **Swan Hellenic** with 1 ship; (11) **Seabourn Cruise Line** with 3 ships; and (12) **Windstar Cruises** with 3 ships. These 79 ships had a capacity of 136,960 passengers. These ships equated to 85% of the company's total assets, and 11% of the operating cost as depreciation.

Carnival also owned a chain of 16 hotels and lodges in Alaska and the Canadian Yukon with 3,000 guest rooms. The company owned 30 domed rail cars, which were run by the Alaska Railroad as sight-seeing trains. Carnival operated two luxury day trips for tours of the glaciers in Alaska and the Yukon River.[3]

The company's occupancy rate for cruises was 105.5%, 104.5%, and 102.6% in 2005, 2004, and 2003, respectively. The company signed agreement with two shipyards to construct 16 additional ships at the cost of $8.1 billion. These 16 ships were scheduled to be delivered between 2006 and September 2009. The company has sold one of these ships. The new ships will increase passenger capacity by 41,816 lower berths or 30.5%. The company stated that it may sell a few older ships and place additional orders for new ships to be delivered in 2008 and 2009.[4]

The global cruise industry carried approximately 14 million passengers in 2005. The U.S. cruise industry grew annually by approximately by 9.1% between 1999 and 2004. In Europe, the compound growth rate was approximately 8.4% for the same time period. In 2005, Carnival had 6,848,386 passengers, which made up 48.9% of the global cruise industry's total number of passengers.

The Evolution of Cruising[5]

With the replacement of ocean liners by aircraft in the 1960s as the primary means of transoceanic travel, the opportunity for developing the modern cruise industry was created. Ships no longer required to ferry passengers from destination to destination became available to investors with visions of a new vacation alternative to complement the increasing affluence of Americans. Cruising, once the purview of the rich and leisure class, was targeted to the middle class, with service and amenities similar to the grand days of first-class ocean travel.

According to Robert Meyers, Editor and Publisher of *Cruise Travel* magazine, the increasing popularity of taking a cruise as a vacation can be traced to two serendipitously timed events. First, television's "Love Boat" series dispelled many myths associated with cruising and depicted people of all ages and backgrounds enjoying the cruise experience. This show was among the top 10 shows on television during the 1970s and provided extensive publicity for cruise operators. Second, the increasing affluence of Americans and the increased participation of women in the workforce gave couples and families more disposable income for discretionary purposes, especially vacations. As the myths were dispelled and disposable income grew, younger couples and families "turned on" to the benefits of cruising as a vacation alternative, creating a large new target market for the cruise product, which accelerated the growth in the number of Americans taking cruises as a vacation.

The Cruise Product[6]

Ted and Mickey Arison envisioned a product in which classical cruise elegance along with modern convenience could be had at a price comparable to land-based vacation packages sold by travel agents. Carnival's all-inclusive package, when compared to packages at resorts or theme parks, such as Walt Disney World, often was priced below these destinations; especially when the array of activities, entertainment, and meals were considered.

A typical vacation on a Carnival cruise ship started when the bags were tagged for the ship at the airport. On arriving at the port of embarkation, passengers were ferried by air-conditioned buses to the ship for boarding. Baggage was taken from the terminal to the cabin of the passenger by cruise/ship staff. Waiters dotted the ship offering tropical drinks to guests while the cruise staff oriented passengers to the various decks, cabins, and public rooms. In a few hours (most ships sailed in the early evening), dinner was served in the main dining rooms, where wine selection rivaled the finest restaurants and the variety of main dishes were designed to suit every palate. Diners could always order double portions if they decide not to save room for the variety of desserts and after-dinner specialties.

After dinner, cruisers could choose from among many forms of entertainment, including live music, dancing, nightclubs, and a selection of movies; or they could sleep through the midnight buffet until breakfast. (Most ships had five or more distinct nightclubs.) During the night, a daily program of activities arrived at the passengers' cabins. The biggest decisions to be made for the duration of the vacation were what to do (or not to do), what to eat and when (usually eight separate serving times, not including the 24-hour room service), and when to sleep. Service in all areas from dining to housekeeping was upscale and immediate. The service was so good that a common shipboard joke said that if you left your bed during the night to visit the head (sea talk for bathroom), your cabin steward would have made the bed and placed chocolates on the pillow by the time you returned to bed.

Carnival History

In 1972 Ted Arison, backed by the (AITS) American Travel Services, Inc., purchased an aging ocean liner from Canadian Pacific Empress Lines for $6.5 million. The new AITS subsidiary, Carnival Cruise Line, refurbished the vessel from bow to stern and renamed it the *Mardi Gras* to capture the party spirit. (Also included in the deal was another ship later renamed the *Carnivale.*) The company's start was not promising, however, as on the first voyage the *Mardi Gras,* with more than 300 invited travel agents aboard, ran aground in Miami Harbor. The ship was slow and guzzled expensive fuel, limiting the number of ports of call and lengthening the minimum stay of passengers on the ship to reach break-even. Arison then bought another older vessel from Union Castle Lines to complement the *Mardi Gras* and the *Carnivale* and named it the *Festivale.* To attract customers, Arison began adding diversions onboard such as planned activities, a casino, nightclubs, discos, and other forms of entertainment designed to enhance the shipboard experience.

Carnival lost money for the next three years, and in late 1974 Ted Arison bought out the Carnival Cruise subsidiary AITS, Inc., for $1 cash and the assumption of $5 million in debt. One month later, the *Mardi Gras* began showing a profit and through the remainder of 1975 operated at more than 100% capacity. (Normal ship capacity was determined by the number of fixed berths [referred to as lower berths] available. Ships, like hotels, could operate beyond this fixed capacity by using rollaway beds, Pullmans, and upper bunks.)

Ted Arison (then Chairman), along with Bob Dickinson (then Vice President of Sales and Marketing) and his son Mickey Arison (then President), began to alter the current approach to cruise vacations. Carnival targeted first-time cruisers and young people with a moderately priced vacation package that included airfare to the port of embarkation and home after the cruise. Per diem rates were very competitive with other vacation packages; Carnival offered passage to multiple exotic Caribbean ports, several meals served daily with premier restaurant service, and all forms of entertainment and activities included in the base fare. The only things not included in the fare were items of a personal nature, liquor purchases, gambling, and tips for the cabin steward, table waiter, and busboy. Carnival continued to add to the shipboard experience with a greater variety of activities, nightclubs, and other forms of entertainment and varied ports of call to increase its attractiveness to potential customers. It was the first modern cruise operator to use multimedia-advertising promotions and established the theme of "Fun Ship" cruises, primarily promoting the ship as the destination and ports of call as secondary. Carnival told the public that it was throwing a shipboard party and everyone was invited. Today, the "Fun Ship" theme still permeates all Carnival Cruise brand ships.

Throughout the 1980s, Carnival was able to maintain a growth rate of approximately 30%—about three times that of the industry as a whole. Between 1982 and 1988, its ships sailed with an average capacity of 104%. Targeting younger, first-time passengers by promoting the ship as a destination proved to be extremely successful. Carnival's customer profile showed that approximately 30% of the passengers at that time were between the ages of 25 and 39, with household incomes of $25,000 to $50,000.

In 1987, Ted Arison sold 20% of his shares in Carnival Cruise Lines and immediately generated over $400 million for further expansion. In 1988, Carnival acquired the Holland America Line, which had four cruise ships with 4,500 berths. Holland America was positioned to appeal to higher-income travelers with cruise prices averaging 25%–35% more than similar Carnival cruises. The deal also included two Holland America subsidiaries, Windstar Sail Cruises and Holland America Westours. This purchase allowed Carnival to begin an aggressive "superliner" building campaign for its core subsidiary. By 1989, the cruise segments of Carnival Corporation carried more than 750,000 passengers in one year, a "first" in the cruise industry.

Ted Arison relinquished the role of Chairman to his son Mickey in 1990, a time when the explosive growth of the industry began to subside. Higher fuel prices and increased airline costs began to affect the industry as a whole. The first Persian Gulf War caused many cruise operators to divert ships from European and Indian ports to the Caribbean area of operations, increasing the number of ships competing directly with Carnival. Carnival's stock price fell from $25 in June of 1990 to $13 later in that year. The company also incurred a $25.5 million loss during fiscal 1990 for the operation of the Crystal Palace Resort and Casino in the Bahamas. In 1991, Carnival reached a settlement with the Bahamian government (effective March 1, 1992) to surrender the 672-room Riviera Towers to the Hotel Corporation of the Bahamas in exchange for the cancellation of some debt incurred in constructing and developing the resort. The corporation took a $135 million write-down on the Crystal Palace for that year.

The early 1990s, even with industry-wide demand slowing, were still a very exciting time. Carnival took delivery of its first two "superliners," the *Fantasy* (1990) and the *Ecstasy* (1991), which were to further penetrate the three- and four-day cruise market and supplement the seven-day market. In early 1991, Carnival took delivery of the third superliner, *Sensation* (inaugural sailing November 1, 1993) and later in the year contracted for the fourth superliner, to be named the *Fascination* (inaugural sailing 1994).

In 1991, Carnival attempted to acquire Premier Cruise Lines, which was then the official cruise line for Walt Disney World in Orlando, Florida, for approximately $372 million. The deal was never consummated because the involved parties could not agree on price. In 1992, Carnival acquired 50% of Seabourn, gaining the cruise operations of K/S Seabourn Cruise Lines, and formed a partnership with Atle Brynestad. Seabourn served the ultra-luxury market with destinations in South America, the Mediterranean, Southeast Asia, and the Baltic.

The 1993 to 1995 period saw the addition of the superliner *Imagination* for Carnival Cruise Lines and the *Ryndam* for Holland America Lines. In 1994, the company discontinued the operations of Fiestamarina Lines, which had attempted to serve Spanish-speaking clientele. Fiestamarina had been beset with marketing and operational problems and had never reached continuous operation. Many industry analysts and observers were surprised at the failure of Carnival to successfully develop this market. In 1995 Carnival sold a 49% interest in the Epirotiki Line, a Greek cruise operation, for $25 million and purchased $101 million (face amount) of senior secured notes of Kloster Cruise Limited, the parent of competitor Norwegian Cruise Lines, for $81 million.

Carnival Corporation continued to expand through internally generated growth by adding new ships. Additionally, Carnival seemed to be willing to continue with its external expansion through acquisitions if the right opportunity arose.

In June 1997, Royal Caribbean made a bid to buy Celebrity Cruise Lines for $500 million and assumption of $800 million in debt. Within a week, Carnival had responded by submitting a counteroffer to Celebrity for $510 million and the assumption of debt. Two days later, Carnival raised the bid to $525 million. Nevertheless, Royal Caribbean announced on June 30, 1997, the final merger arrangements with Celebrity. The resulting company had 17 ships, with more than 30,000 berths.

Not to be thwarted in its expansion, Carnival announced in June 1997 the purchase of Costa, an Italian cruise company and the largest European cruise line, for $141 million. The purchase was finalized in September 2000. External expansion continued when Carnival announced the acquisition of the Cunard Line for $500 million from Kvaerner ASA on May 28, 1998. Cunard was then operationally merged with Seabourn Cruise Line. Carnival owned 100% of the resulting Cunard Line in fiscal 2000. In an attempt at further expansion, Carnival announced on December 2, 1999, a hostile bid for NCL Holding ASA, the parent company of Norwegian Cruise Lines. Carnival was unsuccessful in this acquisition attempt. The terrorist attack on New York's twin towers on 9/11/2001 caused tourists to cancel cruise plans. It caused several companies to go into bankruptcy. Some companies discounted cruise costs. Carnival soon recovered once public fears subsided.[7]

On September 30, 2006, Royal Caribbean announced the acquisition of Pullman, a privately held Spanish cruise and tour operator, for about $551 million. Pulman was the top brand in Spain—Europe's fourth-largest market. The company was very active in South America. The company's five ships ranged in age from 6 to 41 years. Pullman generated two-thirds of its revenue from cruises.[8]

Carnival's Corporate Governance

Board of Directors

Exhibit 1A shows the 14 members of Carnival's Board of Directors, of whom six were internal members. Mickey Arison had beneficial ownership of 188,054,943 shares of stock. He owned 29% of the company's stock. (He also owned the Miami Heat, a basketball team which had won the 2005 NBA Championship.) The Arison family and its trusts controlled 36% of the stock. Mickey's sister, Shari Arison, former Board member, owned 5,103,900 shares. All directors and executive officers as a group owned 190,115,930 shares (29.8% of the total shares).

According to the Board's by-laws, each outside director must own at least 5,000 shares of stock. Each year the external Board members were granted 10,000 stock options. Each director's annual retainer fee was $40,000 for serving on the Board, and extra fees were paid for attending Board and committee meetings.[9]

Exhibit 1B lists Carnival's executive officers. **Exhibit 2** shows compensation for the key executives.

Exhibit 1
Board of Directors and Principal Officers: Carnival Corporation & plc

A. Board of Directors

Mickey Arison
Chairman of the Board and Chief Executive Officer
Carnival Corporation & plc

Robert H. Dickinson
President and Chief Executive Officer
Carnival Cruise Lines

Pier Luigi Foschi
Chairman and Chief Executive Officer
Costa Crociere, S.p.A.

Richard J. Glasier
Former President and Chief Executive Officer
Argosy Gaming Company

A. Kirk Lanterman
Chairman
Holland America Line Inc.

Sir John Parker
Chairman
National Grid plc and The Peninsular and Oriental Steam Navigation Company

Stuart Subotnick
General Partner and Executive Vice President
Metromedia Company

Howard S. Frank
Vice Chairman of the Board and Chief Operating Officer
Carnival Corporation & plc

Baroness Hogg
Chairman
3i Group plc and FrontierEconomicLtd.

Modesto A. Maidique
President
Florida International University

Peter G. Ratcliffe
Chief Executive Officer
P&O Princess Cruises International

Uzi Zucker
Private Investor

B. Directors Emeritus

Ted Arison (1924–1999)
Chairman Emeritus, Carnival Corporation

Meshulam Zonis
Director Emeritus, Carnival Corporation

Mark Birnbach
Director Emeritus, Carnival Corporation

The Lord of Plaistow GCVO, CBE
Life President pf P&O Cruises

Horst Rahe
Life President of AIDA Cruises

Richard G. Capen, Jr.
Former United States Ambassador to Spain
Corporate Director, Author and Business Consultant

Arnold W. Donald
President and Chief Executive Officer
Juvenile Diabetes Research Foundation International

C. Principal Officers

Mickey Arison
Chairman of the Board and Chief Executive Officer

Howard S. Frank
Vice Chairman of the Board and Chief Operating Officer

Gerald R. Cahill
Executive Vice President and Chief Financial and Accounting Officer

Richard D. Ames
Senior Vice President, Management Advisory Services

Pamela C. Conover
Senior Vice President Shared Services

Ian J. Gaunt
Senior Vice President International

Arnaldo Perez
Senior Vice President, General Counsel and Secretary

D. Operations Segments

1. **AIDA CRUISES**
   Michael Thamm
   President
2. **CARNIVAL CRUISE LINES**
   Robert H. Dickinson
   President and Chief Executive Officer
3. **COSTA CROCIERE S.p.A**
   Pier Luigi Foschi
   Chairman of the Board and Chief Executive Officer

4. **CUNARD LINE**
   Carol Marlow
   President and Managing Director
5. **HOLLAND AMERICA LINE**
   Stein Kruse
   President and Chief Executive Officer
6. **PRINCESS CRUISES**
   Alan Buckelew
   President
7. **P&O CRUISES AUSTRALIA**
   Gavin Smith
   Managing Director
8. **P&O CRUISES UK**
   David K. Dingle
9. **P&O PRINCESS CRUISES INTERNATIONAL**
   Peter G. Ratcliffe
   Chief Executive Officer
10. **PRINCESS CRUISES**
    Alan B. Buckelew
    President
11. **SEABURN CRUISE LINE**
    Deborah Natansolm
    President

Source: Carnival Corporation & plc, 2005 Annual Report.

Exhibit 2 Key Executive Compensation: Carnival Corporation & plc

		Annual Compensation			Long-Term Compensation Awards	
Name and Principal Position	**Year**	**Salary ($)**	**Bonus ($)**	**Other Annual Compensation ($)**	**Restricted Stock Awards ($)**	**Number of Securities Underlying Options ($)**
Mickey Arison	2005	800,000	2,900,000	432,600	3,218,400	120,000
Chairman and CEO	2004	700,000	2,400,000	389,000	3,475,200	120,000
	2003	500,000	1,675,000	101,200	2,654,000	120,000
Howard S. Frank	2005	700,000	2,800,000	198,300	2,682,000	100,000
Vice Chairman	2004	600,000	2,300,000	193,400	2,896,00	100,000
and CEO	2003	400,000	1,645,000	198,100	4,913,650	100,000
Robert Dickinson	2005	741,000	1,596,400	160,100	2,070,400	80,000
President and CEO of	2004	400,000	1,393,200	137,600	1,849,200	80,000
Carnival Cruise Lines	2003	400,000	1,256,200	98,900	5,688,400	80,000
Peter G. Ratcliffe	2005	1,100,000	902,000	56,900	1,420,300	50,000
CEO of P&O Princess	2004	1,100,000	814,000	60,500	1,393,200	50,000
Cruises International	2003	966,833	419,800	57,800	864,900	51,188
Pier Luigi Foschi	2005	1,097,000	979,400	237,100	543,600	50,000
Chairman and	2004	981,000	1,033,000	150,000	—	—
CEO of Costa	2003	885,000	490,000	75,000	—	—

Note:
[1] Notes were deleted

Source: Carnival Corporation & plc, SEC- DEF 14A, February 24, 2006, p. 34.

Corporate Organization

Carnival Corporation & plc was a global cruise company and one of the largest vacation companies in the world. Its portfolio of 12 cruise brands (not including Pullman, its most recent purchase) included Carnival Cruise Lines, Princess Cruises, Holland America Line, Windstar Cruises, and Seabourn Cruise Line in North America; P&O Cruises, Cunard Line, Ocean Village and Swan Hellenic in the United Kingdom; AIDA Cruises in Germany; Costa Cruises in Europe; and P&O Cruises in Australia. These brands, which, according to management, comprised the most-recognized cruise brands in North and South America, the United Kingdom, Germany, Southern Europe, and Australia, offered a wide range of holiday and vacation products to a customer base that is broadly varied in terms of cultures, languages, and leisure-time preferences. The corporation also owned two tour companies in Alaska and the Canadian Yukon that complement its cruise operations, Holland America Tours and Princess Tours. Combined, its vacation companies attracted almost 7 million guests annually. Carnival Corporation was incorporated in Panama, and Carnival plc was incorporated in England and Wales.[10]

Mission

According to management, "Our mission is to deliver exceptional vacation experiences through the world's best-known cruise brands that cater to a variety of different lifestyles and budgets, all at an outstanding value unrivaled on land or at sea."[11]

Operating Segments

The principal operating subsidiaries are shown in **Exhibit 3.**

Exhibit 3 Principal Operating Subsidiaries: Carnival Corporation & plc

	Country of Incorporation/ Registration	Percentage of Equity Share Capital Owned at November 30, 2005	Business Description
P&O Princess Cruises International Ltd	England	100%[1]	Shipowner
Alaska Hotel Properties LLC	U.S.A.	100%	Hotel operations
P&O Travel Ltd	England	100%	Travel agent
Royal Hyway Tours Inc.	U.S.A.	100%	Land tours
Tour Alaska LLC	U.S.A.	100%	Rail tours
CC U.S. Ventures, Inc.	U.S.A.	100%	Holding company
Costa Crociere S.p.A.	Italy	99.98%	Passenger cruising
Cozumel Cruise Terminal S.A. de C.V.	Mexico	100%	Port operations
Global Fine Arts, Inc.	U.S.A.	100%	Art sales and picture framing
Holland America Line Inc.	U.S.A.	100%	Hotel operations and land tours and rail tours

Note:
[1] Held directly by the company.

Source: Carnival Corporation & plc, 2005 Annual Report, p. 31.

Corporate Brands[12]

The 12 cruise ship lines competed in all of the three sectors—contemporary, premium and luxury—of the cruise industry.

Carnival Cruise Lines (www.Carnival.com)

Carnival Cruise Lines was the most popular and most profitable cruise line in the world. The leader in the contemporary cruise sector, Carnival operated 21 ships with a total passenger capacity of 47,820. In 2005, it carried a record 3.3 million passengers—the most in the cruise industry. Its newest ship was the *Carnival Miracle.* At that time the line had two new ships, at an estimated cost of $1.0 billion, scheduled for delivery during 2006 and 2007. Carnival ships cruised to destinations in the Bahamas, Canada, the Caribbean, the Mexican Riviera, New England, the Panama Canal, Alaska, and Hawaii, with most cruises ranging from 3 to 7 days.

Princess Cruises (www.princesscruises.com)

Princess Cruises offered a "complete escape" from daily routine. It had 14 ships with a total passenger capacity of 29,152. Princess treated its passengers to world-class cuisine, exceptional service, and a myriad of resort-like amenities onboard, including the Lotus Spa, Movies Under the Stars, lavish casinos, nightclubs, and lounges. Princess was the only cruise line to offer a choice of dining experiences, so guests could dine when and where it was convenient. The Princess Fleet was growing with the addition of the *Crown Princess* in 2006 and the *Emerald Princess* in 2007. The *Crown Princess* carried more than 3,100 passengers and 1,200 crew members. The *Princess* fleet provided more than 90 unique itineraries to more than 270 destinations. Princess was classified in the industry as contemporary premium. The company offered cruises from 7 to 30 days.

Holland America Line (www.hollandamerica.com)

The Holland America Line was a leader in the premium cruise sector. Holland America operated a five-star fleet of 12 ships, with 18,930 passenger capacity. The line had two new ships scheduled for delivery during 2006 and 2007 at an estimated cost of $800 million. Holland America Line visited 280 ports in its primary destinations, which included Alaska, the Caribbean, the Panama Canal, Mexico, South America, Hawaii, Canada, New England, and Europe. The company offered cruises from 2 to 108 days. Its ships sailed to more than 300 ports of call on all seven continents. In 2005, the company had more than 300 cruises.

Seabourn Cruise Line (www.seabourn.com)

Seabourn Cruise Line epitomized luxury cruising aboard each of its three intimate all-suite ships. The Yachts of Seabourn were lavishly appointed with virtually one staff member for every guest, to ensure the highest quality service. The company owned three ships with total capacity of 624 passengers.

Ocean Village (www.oceanvillageholidays.co.uk)

Ocean Village was founded in 2004 in the United Kingdom. Its one ship sailed throughout the Mediterranean and the Caribbean. It was expecting a second ship in November 2007.

P & O Cruises (www.pocruises.com)

P & O Cruises was the largest cruise operator and the best-known contemporary cruise brand in the United Kingdom. The five-ship fleet offered cruises to the Mediterranean, the Baltic, the Norwegian Fjords, the Caribbean, and the Atlantic Islands, as well as around-the-world voyages. The passenger capacity was 8,844 people. Its principal market was the United Kingdom.

Cunard Line (www.cunard.com)

The Cunard Line offered the only regular transatlantic crossing service aboard the world-famous ocean liner *Queen Mary 2.* Her equally famous sister, *Queen Elizabeth 2,* sailed on unique itineraries worldwide serving both U.S. and U.K. guests. The passenger capacity of these two ships was 4,410. The 1,968-passenger *Queen Victoria* joined the fleet in 2005. Cunard's primary market was the United Kingdom and North America. The line proudly carried the legacy of the era of sophisticated floating palaces into the 21st century. These ships were in the luxury sector of the industry.

Swan Hellenic (www.swanhellenic.com)

Swan Hellenic operated a program of discovery cruises, targeted particularly to the United Kingdom. Itineraries included the Mediterranean, North America, South America, the Caribbean, the Indian Ocean, and the Far East.

Costa Cruises (www.costacruises.com)

Costa Cruises was Europe's leading cruise line. Headquartered in Italy, Costa offered guests on its 10 ships a multi-ethnic, multi-cultural, and multi-lingual ambiance. The line had two new ships slated to enter service during 2006 and 2007 at an estimated cost of $1.1 billion. Costa ships, including its newest, the popular *Costa Fortuna,* sailed to destinations in Europe, South America, and the Caribbean.

AIDA (www.aida.com)

AIDA was the best-known cruise brand in the fast growing German cruise industry. With its four club ships, AIDA offered cruises to the Mediterranean, the Baltic, and Norwegian Fjords, Canary Islands, and the Caribbean.

Windstar Cruises (www.windstarcruises.com)

Windstar Cruises offered luxury cruising under sail. The line's three sailing yachts offered its 148 to 308 privileged guests all ocean-view staterooms, five-star service, an eclectic selection of cuisine created by celebrity chef Joachim Splichal, and a water sports program. Windstar Cruises sailed to destinations in Europe, the Caribbean, Central America, and the South Pacific. The passenger capacity was 604. Its target market included people aged 30–50, who liked to explore new places and try new things.

Management's View of the Company[13]

Carnival's management presented its analysis of the company's operations in the 2005 SEC *10-K Report*:

> Worldwide we continue to hear—"Carnival is the wrong end of the market for our client"—which in fact these days could hardly be further from the truth. The "New Carnival," as we have

described the new ship product and delivery, is a world apart from the old Carnival. Carnival Corp. has really lifted the product to a new level where in many ways it completes against Holland America in some areas—even occasionally exceeding them in price points as well. Certainly the older ships are still the product we know from years past—the original "Fun Ships"—but gradually these are being phased out to be replaced by new ships offering every amenity found elsewhere as well as excellent food and service.

As we all know, the European taste is in many ways more subdued than the American. Take a point in question—Costa Cruises—their ships are delightful and tastefully decorated, but done to the European expectation and as such are more "subdued" in their décor. So it should come as no surprise that Carnival has been slow in making ground in the European cruise market. That is until the "NEW Carnival" appeared on the scene.

Carnival's Senior VP Vicki Freed acknowledged that "Carnival could not have had a full season in Europe 10 years ago—not at these price points. We didn't have the quality of the hardware and the quality of the onboard experience that we have now."

Carnival's European ship for the 2005 season was the *Liberty*. It was not only delivered on time, but service was immediately up to the line's standards. Agents who tell clients to be wary of ships less than one year old might want to reassess that message when it comes to Carnival.

Liberty is Carnival's sole new ship this year, but Freed says that's not the only reason it was humming from the get-go. "Remember in 2002 we had three new ships enter service, and they were all totally ready," she says. "We have a very experienced, organized team, and we're willing to spend the money to make sure the targets are made. A lot of the staff on *Liberty* have come from Carnival's *Valor*; they know how to sail on new ships, and that makes a difference."

In a certain sense, the fact that Carnival is succeeding in Europe ties in well with today's Carnival marketing message. "If you look at our price points versus other major contemporary cruise lines, in many cases people are willing to spend a few dollars more for us," says Freed. "We're not the down and dirty pricing leader anymore."

Freed maintains that Carnival's onboard product delivers more than other brands in the contemporary market. "I just cruised on a premium cruise line, and I have to tell you, our food is equal to or better than our sister company," she says. "They won't like me saying that, but definitely our choice, our variety, even our presentation is better. Look at the Versace dishes we're using; look at the flatware, every single dish that comes out of the kitchen is a work of art, even in terms of placement of the vegetables. It's not just about throwing quantity on the plate, it's about putting quality and making it so eye-appealing that people say, 'Wow.' I think that's what today's Carnival is all about, the wow effect."

Freed says the biggest wow factor in terms of the soft goods is the bedding, a feature which has more often been promoted by premium and luxury lines. "People are sick and tired of flowered bed spreads," she notes. "They want the beautiful white clean look. We even have a pillow menu for our suite guests where they can choose from five different types of pillows, whether it's all feathers or synthetic, hard or soft."

Summer in the Tropics (Hurricanes)

Worldwide (Carnival) was fortunately a short-lived victim of hurricane Katrina—our offices lost power late on Thursday evening and happily for us power was restored in the early hours of Monday morning, so in fact we did not lose too many hours. As some of our clients might have noticed, however, more disruptive forces were at work a week or so before when somehow a virus got into our main communications server and caused havoc. After two days of hard work, our technical team was able to rebuild the system, but it was a very different period with a number of programs on the final home run.

Generally speaking, South Florida cruise lines also got fully back to business on Monday after Hurricane Katrina impacted some land-based operations on Friday. Katrina hit Thursday night as a Category 1 hurricane that downed trees and caused flooding and widespread power losses. Many who tried to reach work on Friday encountered dangerous or impassable roadways.

Fort Lauderdale companies were not affected as were those in Miami. Radisson Seven Seas never lost power, so it was business as usual for the staff that could get into the office on Friday. MSC Cruises USA also reopened on Friday, as did Silversea Cruises.

In Miami, Carnival was fully back to business today, as was Norwegian Cruise Line, where everyone was able to get to work. The Royal Caribbean/Celebrity offices reopened after staying closed on Friday. They did suffer some damage—mostly fallen trees and some damage to the roof. Oceania Cruises resumed full operations on Monday afternoon and the reservations department made up for lost time with record call volume.

New Orleans and the Gulf Coast, where Katrina packed a powerful Category 4 punch, has suffered devastating damage, but it could have been even worse as the eye of the storm jogged east at the last moment moving New Orleans out of the worst winds and rain which severe damage and flooding as far over as Mobile and places in western Florida. At this time there is no way of knowing how badly affected the port operations will be and when the cruise lines will be able to return to their New Orleans departures. Worldwide will be monitoring the situation and advising those of our clients with program operating from there as news comes in.

We are devastated to see the news reports coming in from the area and want to take this opportunity—on behalf of all of us and our clients—to send our condolences and best wishes for a speedy resolution to the many problems our friends and their families are having to live through in the effected area. Carnival leased three ships to the government for victims of Katrina.[14]

Advertising

The advertising expenses totaled $455 million, $464 million, and $335 million for 2005, 2004, and 2003, respectively.

Human Resource Management

Shoreside operations had approximately 9,500 full-time and 4,200 part-time/seasonal employees. Carnival also employed approximately 57,500 officers, crew, and staff onboard the 79 ships at any one time. Because of the highly seasonal nature of the Alaskan and Canadian operations, Holland America Tours and Princess Tours increased their workforce during the late spring and summer months in connection with the Alaskan cruise season, employing additional seasonal personnel, which had been included above. Carnival had entered into agreements with unions covering certain employees in the hotel, motor coach, and ship operations. Management considered its employee and union relations to be generally good.

On-board service was labor intensive, employing help from some 51 nations—mostly third-world countries—with reasonable returns to employees. For example, waiters on the *Jubilee* could earn approximately $18,000 to $27,000 per year (base salary and tips), significantly greater than could be earned in their home country for similar employment. Waiters typically worked 10 hours per day with approximately one day off per week for a specified contract period (usually 3 to 9 months). Carnival records showed that employees remained with the company for approximately eight years and that applicants exceeded demand for all cruise positions. Nonetheless, the American Maritime union had cited Carnival (and other cruise operators) several times for exploitation of its crews. The numbers of employees were 71,000, 69,000, 59,000, and 59,000 in 2005, 2004, 2003, and 2002, respectively.[15]

Government Regulations

All of Carnival's ships were registered in a country outside the United States and each ship flew the flag of its country of registration. Carnival's ships were regulated by various international, national, state, and local port authorities' laws, regulations, and treaties in force in the jurisdictions in which the ships operate. In U.S. waters and ports, the ships had to comply with U.S. Coast Guard and U.S. Public Health regulations, the Maritime Transportation Security Act, International Ship and Port Facility Security Code, U.S. Oil Pollution Act of 1990, U.S. Maritime Commission, local port authorities, local and federal law enforcement agencies, and all laws pertaining to the hiring of foreign workers. All cruise ships were inspected for health issues, and received a rating, which was published for potential cruisers to review. Terrorist threats had tightened U.S. security of ports regarding docking facilities, cargo containers and storage areas, and crews.[16]

Environmental Policy

According to Mickey Arison,

> Our corporate culture fosters a deep commitment to preserving the marine environment and in particular the pristine condition of the waters upon which our vessels sail. We are committed to pollution prevention and continuous improvement of our environmental management. We recently announced our goal to become certified in accordance with the international recognized standard ISO 14001, which provides a framework for environmental management and measurement of environmental improvement.[17]

The company had seven stated environmental objectives for 2006. In September 2006, Carnival Corporation & plc earned Environmental Management Certification for meeting the ISO 14001 standards established by the International Organization for Standardization. The certification was granted to Carnival's operating units. The certification was issued by four different recognized maritime regulatory agencies. The agencies were RINA of Italy, who also certified new ships as seaworthy, Germanischer Lloyd of Germany, Lloyd's Register Quality Assurance from North America, and the Maritime and Coastguard Agency of the U.K.

The California Air Resources Board adopted rules to implement legislation that barred cruise ships from burning refuse within three miles of shore. Violations result in a fine of $25,000 per violation. The law was going into effect on January 1, 2007. Similar types of legislation were being proposed for other vessels, such as cargo ships, tankers, and military carriers based in San Diego.

Suppliers

The company's largest purchases were for travel agency services, fuel, advertising, food and beverages, hotel and restaurant supplies and products, airfare, repairs and maintenance and dry-docking, port facility utilization, and communication services, and for the construction of ships. Although Carnival utilized a select number of suppliers for most of its food and beverages and hotel and restaurant supplies and products, most of these items were available from numerous sources at competitive prices. The use of a select number of suppliers enabled management to, among other things, obtain volume discounts. The company purchased fuel and port facility services at some of its ports of call from a limited number of suppliers. In addition, the company performed major dry-dock and ship improvement work at dry-dock facilities in the Bahamas, British Columbia, Canada, the Caribbean, Europe, and the United States. As of January 30, 2006, Carnival had agreements in place for the construction of 16 cruise ships by two shipyards. Management believed there were sufficient dry-dock and shipbuilding facilities to meet the company's anticipated requirements. To better manage price fluctuations, the company hedged the price of fuel oil.

Legal Issues

On July 28, 2006, four law firms filed a lawsuit on behalf of six passengers, who had been injured 10 days earlier on the *Crown Princess* after the ship had suddenly listed (tilted) between 15 and 38 degrees to the right for no apparent reason. The passengers suffered serious physical injuries after being violently thrown against the ship's deck and walls. A total of 12 passengers were seriously injured and about 70 passengers had lesser injuries. Three passengers were hospitalized. One passenger reported, "It felt like (the ship) was going to fall over," and "It was shocking."

Jim Jacobs, co-author of the musical *Grease,* had filed a $100 million class-action lawsuit against 17 cruise lines, many owned by Carnival and Royal Caribbean. Jacobs accused the 17 cruise lines of violating U.S. and international laws and exhorted them to stop producing unlicensed materials written by Jacobs and other writers. According to Jacobs, "They are doing productions not approved by the authors that they would never permit, and then don't pay." Royal Caribbean's Celebrity Cruises had presented 365 performances of *Grease* "without securing the necessary licenses or permissions." *Grease* was reportedly slated to return to Broadway in 2007.

The company was the target of several lawsuits by former employees over overtime pay issues. In addition, Carnival paid $18 million in fines in 2002 for six pollution discharges by its ships. The company pleaded guilty to six felony counts for filing false statements with the U.S. Coast Guard. The company also agreed to cover the company's environmental-safety practices on its ships and Carnival's port facilities around the world. A written statement by the company stated, "Carnival Corp accepts responsibility for the conduct that is the subject of its guilty plea." It also stated, "The company is committed to environmental compliance, and we are adopting a compliance program that will have Carnival the industry leader in sound environmental practices."[18]

The Cruise Industry

International Council of Cruise Lines management described developments in the cruising industry as follows:

> In 2005, the cruise industry experienced a more moderate rate of capacity expansion than in recent years. Four major new cruise ships were launched, but the size of the North American fleet remained unchanged at 192 vessels as an equal number of ships were withdrawn from the market. Due to larger newly-built ships, capacity grew by 2.2 percent for a total combined capacity of 245,755 lower berths. Overall occupancy rose to 106 percent in 2005, due in part, to passenger rescheduling after a number of cruises were cancelled during the hurricane season.
>
> U.S. ports continued to handle 75 percent of all global cruise embarkations in 2005. More than 8.6 million cruise passengers began their cruises from U.S. ports, an increase of 6.3 percent over the previous year. Globally, demand for cruising remained strong in 2005, and the industry increased passenger carryings by 6 percent over 2004 to 11.5 million passengers worldwide. U.S. residents totaled 9.1 million, or 79 percent, of global passengers.
>
> The top 10 cruise embarkation ports—Miami, Port Everglades, Port Canaveral, Los Angeles, Galveston, Tampa, New York, Long Beach, Seattle, and New Orleans—accounted for 84 percent of all U.S. passenger embarkations. Higher 2005 embarkation numbers were posted by Miami (5.3 percent), Los Angeles (30.9 percent), Galveston (22.1 percent), Tampa (6 percent) and Seattle (18.2 percent).[19]

The Top 10 most popular cruise destinations in 2004 were:[20]

Caribbean	45.1%
Europe/Mediterranean	22.4%
Alaska	7.7%
Mexico (West Coast)	6.2%
Panama Canal	3.8%
Hawaii	3.4%
Canada/New England	1.9%
Transatlantic	1.8%
Bermuda	1.7%
South America	1.4%
Others	4.6%

Industry Facts

- Approximately 51 million people (17% of the U.S. population) have cruised at least once. Nearly 2.9 million have taken a cruise in the past three years.
- It was estimated that about 31,028,000 of the U.S. population will take a cruise in the next three years. Non-residents are a substantial number of total passengers.[21]
- Target U.S. market:
  - Total target market—Adults 25+ and household (HH) income
  - Affluent market—Adults 25+ and HH income of $60,000+
  - Very affluent market—Adults 25+ and HH income of $80,000+
  - Ultra affluent—Adults 25+ and HH income of $150,000[22]
- Cost of cruising per person was up $39 in 2005. There were fewer discounts or promotional offers in 2005 (52%) versus 58% in 2004.
- The average airfare was $359.
- In 2005, the cruise industry contributed $32.4 billion to the U.S. economy, a 6% increase over 2004.
- In 2005, passengers and crews were directly responsible for spending $16.2 billion in U.S. goods and services.
- **Exhibit 4** provides additional cruise industry information.
- About 80% of all cruise passengers book some of their travel through a travel agent.

Exhibit 4
The Cruising Industry

A. Cruising Costs[24]

	CRUISERS				
	Cruiser	Destinations	Luxury	Premium	Contemporary
% Receiving discount or promotional offer	52%	40%	49%	59%	54%
Mean cruise + onboard/shore	$1,690	$2,240	$2,580	$2,020	$1,640
Cruise	$1,255	$1,653	$1,948	$1,559	$1,213
Onboard and shore side expenses	$435	$587	$632	$461	$427
% Who flew to cruise	64%	72%	63%	68%	64%
Airfare	$359	$428	$614	$384	$328

Compared to 2004, cruisers report a slightly higher cruise cost per person (up $39), with fewer discounts noted—52% from 58%.

Exhibit 4
(continued)

B. Incidence of Cruising

Approximately 51 million people have cruised at least once; of these, nearly 29 million have cruised in the past three years.

	Ever Cruised	People	Cruised in Past 3 Years	People
Target Market (Age 25+, $40k+)	39%	49,608,000	22%	27,984,000
Total U.S. Population (All ages, all incomes)	17%	51,096,000	10%	28,823,000

C. Cruiser Satisfaction and Perceptions of Travel Agents

- Four out of five cruisers (79%) use travel agents to book at least some of their cruises. (Because of self-reporting, this may be understated due to confusion with 800 numbers and/or agency web sites.)
- Fifty-eight percent (58%) of cruisers and 53% of non-cruisers report high satisfaction levels with their travel agents.
- The majority of cruisers believe that travel agents are:
  - More knowledgeable about travel than they are (55%)
  - Knowledgeable about hotels/resorts and destinations and their unique differences (61%)
  - Remove the hassle from travel planning (51%)
- But cruiser beliefs about travel agents present serious challenges:
  - Get the best deal on vacations—now only 28%
  - Provide good advice (42%)
  - More than half (56%) believe they get better rates when they book on their own.

D. First Cruise

The first cruise for most was in the 1990s or earlier.

Year of First Cruise	Total Cruisers
2002–2005	28%
1999–2001	28%
1990–1998	19%
1980's	13%
1970's	4%
Prior to 1970	6%
TOTAL	**100%**[1]

[1]Actually adds to 98%

E. Summary of Market Projections

- Based on consumer responses, the most likely number of cruisers over the next three years (2006–2003) is 31,028,000.
- These projections understate future cruise passenger volumes.
  - Non-U.S. residents represent a substantial fraction of total passengers but are not in the survey, and . . .
  - Some of our survey respondents will take multiple trips.

Number of U.S. Travelers Likely to Cruise within Next Three Years

	Target Cruise Market[2] $40K + HHI	Affluent Cruise Market $60K + HHI	Very Affluent Cruise Market $80K + HHI	Ultra Affluent Cruise Market $150K + HHI
Best Case	50,396,000	36,766,000	24,552,000	2,254,000
Most Likely	31,028,000	23,028,000	15,444,000	1,453,000

[2]HHI, household income.

F. Criteria for Making Vacation Decisions[25]

	Cruisers	Non-Cruise Vacations
The destination	8.7	8.7
The price	7.3	7.1
Best opportunity to relax and unwind	7.1	7.1
Fit my vacation schedule/days available	6.5	7.0
Offered a unique experience	7.0	6.6
The convenience	6.8	6.6
The particular hotel/resort property or cruise ship	6.5	5.1
Good programs for children and family	3.8	4.4

Note: Data used are based on a 10-point scale where 10 is "most influence" and 1 "did not influence at all."

Source: "TNS," Cruise Industry Report, www.tns-global.com

Competitors

Carnival's primary competitors were Royal Caribbean, Disney, and Norwegian Cruise Line. **Royal Caribbean** operated two brands, Royal Caribbean International and Celebrity Lines. Royal Caribbean operated 20 cruise ships with approximately 45,470 berths. Celebrity cruises operated 16 ships with approximately 16,116 berths. Royal Caribbean was founded in 1968 and based in Miami. The company employed 38,800 employees. In 2005, the company's revenues were $4.90 billion and net income of $663.47 million. The company's gross margin was 63.17% versus Carnival's at 54.25%. In 2005, an unfortunate passenger on his honeymoon aboard a Royal Caribbean ship fell overboard and was never found. Industry-wide, this was the 25th passenger to disappear on a cruise in the past five years.

Celebrity Lines had ordered two new ships, both of which would have 2,850 berths. One ship, the *Solstice,* was to be very large in order to have larger staterooms and more balconies. Condé Nast readers listed *Celebrity* as "The Best Cruise Ship in the World." For 2005, Royal Caribbean placed an order for an energy-efficient ship that would accommodate 5,400 passengers. Royal Caribbean created a new ad campaign, "Create Your Own Adventure," that highlighted vacation experiences told by passengers.[26]

Disney Cruise Line had two cruise ships, each having 877 staterooms (3,508 berths). Disney had its own private island, Castaway Bay. Starting in May 2006, the seven-night itinerary included two stops at the islands. One analyst said, "Carnival should thank Disney for taking children off their ships." Specific areas of the ships were designated for activities preferred by adults, families, teens, and children. People could play together or in separate activities. The following summer, Disney was to have its first Mediterranean cruise.[27]

Norwegian Cruise Line was the industry's fourth largest cruise line. Its new division, "NCL America," provided Hawaii Island hopping, East Coast cruising, and California coastal cruises. No other line covered all of these areas. The ships' atmosphere was "resort casual." The company was Hawaii's cruise leader. Norwegian had two divisions—Norwegian Costal Voyages with 14 ships and 6,092 berths, and Norwegian Cruise Line with 10 ships and 17,890 berths.[28]

Carnival's management briefly described the firm's competition in the following manner:

1. Carnival competed with land-based vacation alternatives throughout the world, including, among others, resorts, hotels, theme parks, and vacation ownership properties located in Las Vegas, Nevada, Orlando, Florida, various parts of the Caribbean, and

Mexico, and Bahamian and Hawaiian Island destination resorts and numerous other vacation destinations throughout Europe and the rest of the world.

2. Carnival's primary cruise competitors in the contemporary and/or premium cruise segments for North American-sourced passengers were Royal Caribbean Cruise Ltd., which owned Royal Caribbean International and Celebrity Cruises Star Cruises, plc, which owned Norwegian Cruise Line and Orient Lines and Disney Cruise Lines.
3. The three primary cruise competitors for European-sourced passengers were My Travel's Sun Cruises, Fred Olsen, Saga and Thomson in the U.K.; Festival Cruises, Hapag-Lloyd, Peter Deilmann, Phoenix Reisen, and Transocean Cruises in Germany; and Mediterranean Shipping Cruises, Louis Cruise Line, Festival Cruises, and Spanish Cruise Line in Southern Europe. We also competed for passengers throughout Europe with Norwegian Cruise Line, Orient Lines, Royal Caribbean International, and Celebrity Cruises.
4. The company's primary competitors in the luxury cruise segment for our Cunard, Seabourn, and Windstar brands included Crystal Cruises, Radisson Seven Seas Cruise Line, and Silversea Cruises.
5. Carnival brands also competed with similar or overlapping product offerings across all of our segments.[29]

Finance

Carnival's management compared the company's 2005 financial results with those of 2004. The following was included in the company's 2005 SEC *10-K Report.*

Revenues

Net cruise revenues increased $1.02 billion, or 13.9% to $8.38 billion in 2005 from $17.36 billion in 2004. (See **Exhibits 5** and **6.**) The 8.5% increase in ALBDs (net revenue yields) between 2004 and 2005 accounted for $638 million of the increase, and the remaining $528 million was from increased net revenue yields, which increased 6.5% in 2005 compared to 2004 (gross revenue yields increased by 4.9%). Net revenue yields increased in 2005 primarily from higher onboard revenues and the weaker U.S. dollar relative to the euro and sterling. Net revenue yields, as measured on a constant dollar basis, increased 6.1% in 2005. Gross cruise revenues increased $1.31 billion, or 13.9%, in 2005 to $10.74 billion from $9.43 billion in 2004 for largely the same reasons as net cruise revenues.

Onboard and other revenues included concession revenues of $2,356 million in 2005 and $2,076 million in 2004. Onboard and other revenues increased in 2005 compared to 2004, primarily because of the 8.5% increase in ALBDs and increased passenger spending on our ships.

Other non-cruise revenues increased $52 million, or 17.3%, to $352 million in 2005 from $300 million in 2004 primarily due to the increase in the number of cruises/tours sold.

Costs and Expenses

Net cruise costs increased $765 million, or 14.0%, to $6.217 million in 2005 from $5.452 billion in 2004. The 8.5% increase in ALBDs between 2004 and 2005 accounted for $387 million of the increase, and the remaining $236 million was from increased net cruise costs per ALBD, which increased 4.8% in 2005 compared to 2004 (gross cruise costs per ALBD increased 3.0%). Net cruise costs per ALBD increased primarily due to a $66 increase in fuel

Exhibit 5
Consolidated Statements of Operations: Carnival Corporation & plc (Dollar amounts in millions, except per share data)

Years ending November 30	2005	2004	2003
Revenues			
Cruise			
Passenger tickets	$ 8,379	$7,357	$5,039
Onboard and other	2,356	2,070	1,420
Other	352	300	259
Total Revenue	$11,807	$9,727	$6,718
Cost and Expenses			
Operating			
Cruise			
Commissions, transportation and other	1,665	1,572	1,021
Onboard and other	408	359	229
Payroll and related	1,145	1,003	744
Food	615	550	393
Fuel	709	493	340
Other ship operating	1,425	1,270	897
Other	250	210	190
Total	$ 6,217	$5,457	$3,814
Selling and administrative	1,329	1,285	936
Depreciation and amortization	902	812	585
	8,448	7,554	5,335
Operating income	2,639	2,173	1,383
Nonoperating (expense) income			
Interest income	28	17	27
Interest expense, net of capitalized interest	(330)	(272)	(195)
Other (expense) income, net	(7)	(5)	8
	(309)	(272)	(160)
Income before income taxes	2,330	1,901	1,223
Income tax expense, net	(73)	(47)	(29)
Net Income	$ 2,257	$1,854	$1,194
Earnings per Share	—	—	—
Basic	$ 2.80	$ 2.31	$ 1.66
Diluted	$ 2.70	$ 2.24	$ 1.63
Dividends per Share	$ 0.80	$0.525	$ 0.44

Source: Carnival Corporation & plc, 2005 Annual Report, p. 5.

cost per metric ton, or 34.0%, to $260 per metric ton in 2005, higher dry-dock amortization expenses, a $23 million MNOPF contribution, and a weaker U.S. dollar relative to the euro and to the pound sterling in 2005. Net cruise costs per ALDB as measured on a constant dollar basis compared to 2004 increased 4.3% in 2005 and were flat excluding fuel costs and the MNOPF contribution, compared to 2004. Gross cruise costs increased $765 million, or 11.8%, in 2004 to $7.24 billion from $6.48 billion in 2004, which was a lower percentage increase than net cruise costs primarily because of the lower proportion of passengers who purchased air transportation from us in 2005.

Other non-cruise operating expenses increased $40 million, or 19.04%, to $250 million in 2005 from $210 million in 2004 primarily due to the increase in the number of cruise/tours sold.

Depreciation and amortization expense increased by $90 million, or 11.1%, to $902 million in 2005 from $812 million in 2004 largely due to the 8.5% increase in ALBDs through the addition of new ships and ship improvement expenditures.

Exhibit 6 Consolidated Balance Sheet: Carnival Corporation & plc (Dollar amounts in millions except per share data)

Years ending November 30	2005	2004
Assets		
Cash and cash equivalents	$ 1,178	$ 643
Short-term investments	9	17
Accounts receivable, net	408	409
Inventories	250	240
Prepaid expenses and other	370	419
Total current assets	2,215	1,728
Property and equipment, net	21,312	20,823
Goodwill	3,206	3,321
Trademarks	1,282	1,306
Other assets	417	458
Total assets	$ 28,432	$ 27,636
Liabilities and Shareholders' Equity		
Current liabilities	—	—
Short-term borrowing	$300	$381
Current portion of long-term debt	1,042	681
Convertible debt subject to current put option	283	600
Accounts payable	690	631
Accrued liabilities and other	832	868
Customer deposits	2,045	1,873
Total current liabilities	5,192	5,034
Long-term debt	5,727	6,291
Other long-term liabilities and deferred income	541	551
Commitments and contingencies (Note 7 and 8)		
Shareholders' equity		
Common stock of Carnival Corporation; $.01 par value; 1,960 shares authorized; 639 shares at 2005 and 634 shares at 2004 issued	6	6
Ordinary shares of Carnival plc; $1.66 par value; 226 shares authorized; 212 shares at 2005 and 2004 issued	353	353
Additional paid-in capital	7,381	7,311
Retained earnings	10,233	8,623
Unearned stock compensation	(13)	(16)
Accumulated other comprehensive income	156	541
Treasury stock; 2 shares of Carnival Corporation at 2005 and 42 shares of Carnival plc at 2005 and 2004, at cost	(1,144)	(1,058)
Total shareholders' equity	16,972	15,760
Total Liabilities and Shareholder's Equity	$ 28,432	$ 27,636

Source: Carnival Corporation & plc, 2005 Annual Report, p. 6.

Other Financial Information

The company's total contracted cash obligations were $1,517,400,000 for the period of 2006 through 2010. Ship future cash costs are forecasted at $7,590,000,000 and $7,052,000,000 for long term debt reduction. The company had repurchased 8.0 million shares for $380 million during the period December 1, 2004 through February 6, 2006. The board had authorized the repurchase of up to $1.0 billion of the common stock.

The company's dividends were 80 cents, 52.5 cents and 41 cents for 2005, 2004 and 2003 respectively. Customers' cruise deposits, which represent unearned revenue, are included in the balance sheet (current liability account) when received and recognized as cruise revenues on completion of the voyage. Customers also were required to pay the full cruise fare (minus deposit) 60 days in advance with the fares being recognized as cruise revenue on completion of the voyage. The customer can make changes aboard ship on his/her credit cards.

In August 2006, the State of Alaska passed a ballot initiative that requires all passengers to pay a $50 head tax. There is also a gaming tax on any gambling that occurs in the state's waters. Carnival management estimated that these two taxes could lower 2007 earnings by about 3 cents per share. Chairman Arison said, "We are disappointed that the Ballot Initiative 2 has passed as we believe this will inhibit the future growth and expansion of Alaska's tourism business." Carnival currently carries about 560,000 passengers a year to Alaska on 16 ships. An analyst wondered when other states and the Caribbean will pass similar legislation.[30]

Exhibit 7 shows revenues by geographical region. The United States generated 58.1%, 59.5%, and 67.1% for 2005, 2004, and 2003, respectively.

Exhibit 7
Revenues by Geographic Regions: Carnival Corporation & plc (Dollar amounts in millions)

Region	2005	2004	2003
U.S.	$6,439	$5,788	$4,513
Continental Europe	1,681	1,549	971
U.K.	1,520	1,341	724
Canada	665	562	231
Australia and New Zealand	311	215	71
Others	471	272	208
Total Revenue	$11,087	$9,727	$6,718

Source: Carnival Corporation & plc, 2005 Annual Report, p. 26.

Notes

1. Carnival Corporation & plc, "2005 Annual Report," p. 2.
2. *Ibid.*
3. *Ibid.*
4. Michael I. Keefe, John K. Ross III, and Bill J. Middlebrook, "Carnival Corporation: Acquiring Princess Cruise Line (2002) in *Strategic Management and Business Policy–10th Edition,* Wheelen and Hunger. This section was directly quoted.
5. *Ibid.*
6. *Ibid.*
7. Carnival Corporation & plc, "Mission," *www.carnivalvcorp.com,* located under Corporate Information–Mission, History.
8. "2005 Annual Report," p. 5.
9. Carnival Corporation & plc, "Mission," *www.carnivalcorp.com,* located under Corporate Information–Mission, History.
10. *Ibid.,* "Carnival Corporate Brands," This section was directly quoted.
11. "The New Carnival," *www.cruiseco.com,* October 2005. This entire section quoted.
12. International Council of Cruise Lines, ICCL— press release. Entire section was directly quoted. *www.icci.org?pressroom/pressrelease.*
13. *Ibid.*
14. *Ibid.,* and Florida–Caribbean Cruise Association, "Cruise Industry Overview–2005."
15. Carnival Corporation & plc, "SEC 10-K," February 9, 2006, p. 19 of 394. Internet version.
16. Royal Caribbean Cruises, Ltd., press release.
17. Royal Caribbean Cruises, Ltd., press release, 1/23/2006.
18. Disney Cruise Lines, press release.
19. Norwegian Cruise Line, company document.
20. "2005 Annual Report," p. 12.
21. *Ibid,* p. 34.
22. *Ibid.*
23. Carnival Cruise Corporation & plc, "Environmental Policy," located at *www.carnivalcorp.com,* Investor Relations–Corporate Responsibility.
24. "Carnival Corp. Earns Environmental Management Information," *www.marinelink.com* 9/12/2006.
25. *Ibid.*
26. "SEC 10-K, p. 36 of 394.
27. *Ibid.*
28. Greg Levine, "Billionaire Arison 'Cruise Line in' Grease Suit," *Forbes.com,* February 13, 2006.
29. "2005 Annual Report," p. 42.
30. Associated Press, "Carnival Disappointed by Alaska Taxes," 8/24/2006.

CASE 19

Wal-Mart Stores, Inc.: Under Attack (2006)

James W. Camerius and J. David Hunger

I am asked often what my father, Sam Walton, who founded Wal-Mart in 1962, would think of our Company today. There is no doubt he'd be proud of our success and the 1.8 million associates who serve our customers every day. He also would be proud that we remain true to the fundamental principles of leadership and business that he was so instrumental in establishing.[1]

Rob Walton
Chairman of the Board
Wal-Mart Stores, Inc.

REFLECTING ON HIS TENURE SINCE 2000 AS CHIEF EXECUTIVE OFFICER, LEE SCOTT, President and CEO of Wal-Mart Stores, Inc., was struck not only by how successful the company had been in terms of growth and financial performance, but also by how much the firm had come under attack for its business practices. On the positive side, the company had received much acclaim for its ability to carry out Sam Walton's vision. Its policy of "everyday low prices" had enabled it to dominate U.S. retailing. In 1999, *Discount Store News* honored Wal-Mart as "Retailer of the Century." In 2000, *Fortune* magazine named it as one of the "100 Best Places to Work." By 2002, Wal-Mart officially became the world's largest company based on its $245 billion in sales—three times the size of France's Carrefour, the second largest retailer in the world. Research revealed that 82% of American households made at least one purchase at Wal-Mart annually. By 2003, not only did it lead the *Fortune* 500, Wal-Mart also sat atop *Fortune*'s list of most admired companies. Economists giddily referred to the "Wal-Mart effect" in which the company's low prices had forced competitors to keep their prices low as well, thus suppressing inflation and increasing U.S. productivity year after year. For example, one study found that a new Wal-Mart store causes competitors' prices to drop 7%–13% for goods such as toothpaste, shampoo, aspirin, and laundry detergent five years after Wal-Mart entered a city. Another study revealed that "big box" retailers, like Wal-Mart, offered households $.25 back for every dollar spent on groceries, or around $450 a year on average.[2]

[1]This case was prepared by Professors J. David Hunger of St. John's University (MN) and Iowa State University and Professor James W. Camerius of Northern Michigan University.

Exhibit 1 Eleven-Year Financial Summary: Wal-Mart Stores, Inc.
(Dollar amounts in millions except per share data)

Fiscal year ending January 31	2006	2005	2004
1. Operating Results			
Net sales	$312,427	$285,222	$256,329
Net sales increase	9.5%	11.3%	11.6%
Comparative store sales increase in the United States(1)	3%	3%	4%
Cost of sales	$240,391	$219,793	$198,747
Operating, selling, general and administrative expenses	56,733	51,248	44,909
Interest expense, net	1,172	986	832
Effective tax rate	33.4%	34.7%	36.1%
Income from continuing operations	11,231	10,267	8,861
Net income	$ 11,231	$ 10,267	$ 9,054
Per share of common stock:			
Income from continuing operations, diluted	$ 2.68	$ 2.41	$ 2.03
Net income, diluted	2.68	2 41	2.07
Dividends	0.60	0.52	0.36
2. Financial Position			
Current assets of continuing operations	$ 43,824	$ 38,854	$ 34,421
Inventories	32,191	29,762	26,612
Property, equipment and capital lease assets, net	79,290	68,118	59,023
Total assets of continuing operations	138,187	120,154	105,405
Current liabilities of continuing operations	48,826	43,182	37,840
Long-term debt	26,429	20,087	17,102
Long-term obligations under capital leases	3,742	3,171	2,997
Shareholders' equity	53,171	49,396	43,623
3. Financial Ratios			
Current ratio	0.9	0.9	0.9
Return on assets(2)	8.91%	9.3%	9.2%
Return on shareholders' equity(3)	22.5%	22.6%	21.3%
4. Other Year-End Data			
Discount stores in the United States	1,209	1,353	1,478
Supercenters in the United States	1,980	1,713	1,471
SAM'S CLUBs in the United States	567	551	538
Neighborhood Markets in the United States	100	85	64
Units outside the United States	2,285	1,587	1,355

(1) Comparative store sales are considered to be sales at stores that were open as of February 2 of the prior fiscal year and have not been expanded or relocated since that date.
(2) Income from continuing operations before minority interest divided by average total assets.
(3) Income from continuing operations before minority interest divided by average shareholders' equity.

Source: Wal-Mart Stores, Inc., 2005 Annual Report, p. 18.

By 2006, Wal-Mart's net sales had increased 9.5% over 2005 to a record $312.4 billion for the fiscal year ending January 31, 2006. At the same time, net income had risen 9.4% to a record $11.2 billion and earnings per share had grown from $2.41 in 2005 to $2.68 in 2006. (See **Exhibits 1–4** for Wal-Mart's financial reports.) Scott was pleased with strong international sales in Argentina, Mexico, and Brazil and with the fact that the company had more than 6,100 stores worldwide. As of January 31, 2006, Wal-Mart was operating 2,285 international stores, buying products from 70 countries, and doing 20% of its business outside the United States. (See **Exhibit 5** for the number of stores by country.)

Exhibit 1 ***(continued)***

2003	2002	2001	2000	1999	1998	1997	1996
$229,616	$204,011	$180,787	$156,249	$130,522	$112,005	$99,627	$89,051
12.6%	12.8%	15.7%	19.7%	16.5%	12.4%	11.9%	13.7%
5%	6%	5%	8%	9%	6%	5%	4%
$178,299	$159,097	$140,720	$121,825	$102,490	$ 88,163	$78,897	$70,485
39,983	35,147	30,822	26,025	21,778	18,831	16,437	14,547
927	1,183	1,196	840	598	716	807	863
35.2%	36.2%	36.5%	36.8%	37.4%	37.0%	36.8%	36.8%
$ 7,818	$ 6,448	$ 6,087	$ 5,394	$ 4,240	$ 3,424	$ 2,978	$ 2,689
7,955	6,592	6,235	5,324	4,397	3,504	3,042	2,737
$ 1.76	$ 1.44	$ 1.36	$ 1.21	$ 0.95	$ 0.76	$ 0.65	$ 0.58
1.79	1.47	1.39	1.19	0.98	0.77	0.66	0.59
0 30	0.28	0.24	0.20	0.16	0.14	0.11	0.10
$ 29,543	$ 26,615	$ 25,344	$ 23,478	$ 20,064	$ 18,589	$17,385	$16,779
24,401	22,053	20,987	19,296	16,361	16,005	15,556	15,667
51,374	45,248	40,461	35,533	25,600	23,237	19,935	18,554
92,900	81,549	76,231	68,983	48,513	44,221	38,571	36,621
32,225	26,795	28,366	25,525	16,155	13,930	10,432	10,944
16,597	15,676	12,489	13,653	6,887	7,169	7,685	8,483
3,000	3,044	3,152	3,000	2,697	2,480	2,304	2,089
39,461	35,192	31,407	25,878	21,141	18,519	17,151	14,757
0.9	1.0	0.9	0.9	1.2	1.3	1.7	1.5
9.2%	8.4%	8.6%	9.8%	9.5%	8.5%	8.0%	7.9%
20.9%	19.4%	21.3%	22.9%	21.4%	19.2%	18.7%	19.6%
1,568	1,647	1,736	1,801	1,869	1,921	1,960	1,995
1,258	1,066	888	721	564	441	344	239
525	500	475	463	451	443	436	433
49	31	19	7	4	—	—	—
1,272	1,154	1,054	991	703	589	314	276

With its purchase of the retail operations of Sonae in Brazil and a majority interest of Seiyu in Japan, Wal-Mart added 537 new international stores and 50,000 new associates (employees). Its recent purchase of a majority interest in CARHCO in Central America added stores in Costa Rica, El Salvador, Guatemala, Honduras, and Nicaragua—thus increasing the number of countries outside the United States in which Wal-Mart operated from 10 to 15. Of the almost 600 stores management planned to open during the 2007 fiscal year (February 1, 2006, to January 31, 2007), more than a third would be outside the United States.[3]

Exhibit 2 Consolidated Statements of Income: Wal-Mart Stores, Inc. (Dollar amounts in millions except per share data)

Fiscal year ending January 31	2006	2005	2004
Revenues:			
Net sales	$312,427	$285,222	$256,329
Other income, net	3,227	2,910	2,352
Total revenue	315,654	288,132	258,681
Costs and expenses:			
Cost of sales	240,391	210,793	198,747
Operating, selling, general and administrative expenses	56,733	51,248	44,909
Operating Income	18,530	17,091	15,025
Interest:			
Debt	1,171	934	729
Capital leases	249	253	267
Interest income	(248)	(201)	(164)
Interest, net	1,172	986	832
Income from continuing operations before income taxes and minority interest	17,358	16,105	14,193
Provision for Income taxes:			
Current	5,932	5,326	4,941
Deferred	(129)	263	177
	5,803	5,589	5,118
Income from continuing operations before minority interest	11,555	10,516	9,075
Minority interest	(324)	(249)	(214)
Income from continuing operations	11,231	10,267	8,861
Income from discontinued operation, net of tax	—	—	193
Net Income	$11,231	$10,267	$9,054
Basic net income per common share:			
Income from continuing operations	$ 2.68	$ 2.41	$ 2.03
Income from discontinued operation	—	—	0.05
Basic net income per common share	$ 2.68	$ 2.41	$ 2.08
Diluted net income per common share:			
Income from continuing operations	$ 2.68	$ 2.41	$ 2.03
Income from discontinued operations	—	—	0.04
Diluted net income per common share	$ 2.68	$ 2.41	$2.07
Weighted-average number of common shares:			
Basic	4,183	4,259	4,363
Diluted	4,188	4,266	4,373
Dividends per common share	$ 0.60	$ 0.52	$ 0.36

Source: Wal-Mart Stores, Inc., 2006 Annual Report, p. 30.

Exhibit 3 Consolidated Balance Sheets: Wal-Mart Stores, Inc.
(Dollar amounts in millions except per share data)

Fiscal year ending January 31	**2006**	**2005**
Assets		
Current assets:		
Cash and cash equivalents	$ 6,414	$ 5.488
Receivables	2,662	1,715
Inventories	32,191	29,762
Prepaid expenses and other	2,557	1,889
Total current assets	43,824	38,854
Property and equipment, at cost:		
Land	16,643	14,472
Buildings and improvements	56,163	46,574
Fixtures and equipment	22,750	21,461
Transportation equipment	1,746	1,530
Property and equipment, at cost	97,302	84,037
Less accumulated depreciation	21,427	18,637
Property and equipment, net	75,875	65,400
Property under capital lease:		
Property under capital lease	5,578	4,556
Less accumulated amortization	2,163	1,838
Property under capital lease, net	3,415	2,718
Goodwill	12,188	10,803
Other assets and deferred charges	2,885	2,379
Total assets	$138,187	$120,154
Liabilities and shareholders' equity		
Current liabilities:		
Commercial paper	$ 3,754	$ 3,812
Accounts payable	25,373	21,987
Accrued liabilities	13,465	12,120
Long-term debt due within one year	1,340	1,281
Obligations under capital leases due within one year	4,595	3,759
Total current liabilities	299	223
	48,826	43,182
Long-term debt	26,429	20,087
Long-term obligations under capital leases	3,742	3,171
Deferred income taxes and other	4,552	2,978
Minority interest	1,467	1,340
Commitments and contingencies		
Shareholders' equity:		
Preferred stock ($0.10 par value: 100 shares authorized, none issued)	—	—
Common stock ($0.10 par value: 11,000 shares authorized, 4,165 and 4,234 issued and outstanding at January 31, 2006 and January 31, 2005, respectively)	417	423
Capital in excess of par value	2,596	2,425
Accumulated other comprehensive income	1,053	2,694
Retained earnings	49,105	43,854
Total shareholders' equity	53,171	49,396
Total liabilities and shareholder's equity	$138,187	$120,154

Source: Wal-Mart Stores, Inc., 2006 Annual Report, p. 31.

Exhibit 4 Consolidated Statements of Cash Flows: Wal-Mart Stores, Inc.
(Dollar amounts in millions except per share data)

Fiscal year ending January 31	2006	2005	2004
Cash flows from operating activities			
Income from continuing operations	$ 11,231	$ 10,267	$ 8,861
Adjustments to reconcile net income to net cash provided by operating activities:			
Depreciation and amortization	4,717	4,264	3,852
Deferred income taxes	(129)	263	177
Other operating activities	620	378	173
Changes in certain assets and liabilities, net of effects of acquisitions:			
Decrease (increase) in accounts receivable	(456)	(304)	373
Increase in inventories	(1,733)	(2,494)	(1,973)
Increase in accounts payable	2,390	1,694	2,587
Increase in accrued liabilities	993	976	1,896
Net cash provided by operating activities of continuing operations	17,633	15,044	15,946
Net cash provided by operating activities of discontinued operation	—	—	50
Net cash provided by operating activities	17,633	15,044	15,996
Cash flows from investing activities			
Payments for property and equipment	(14,563)	(12,893)	(10,308)
Investment in international operations, net of cash acquired	(601)	(315)	(38)
Proceeds from the disposal of fixed assets	1,049	953	481
Proceeds from the sale of McLane	—	—	1,500
Other investing activities	(68)	(96)	78
Net cash used in investing activities of continuing operations	(14,183)	(12,351)	(8,287)
Net cash used in investing activities of discontinued operation	—	—	(25)
Net cash used in investing activities	(14,183)	(12,351)	(8,312)
Cash flows from financing activities			
Increase (decrease) in commercial paper	(704)	544	688
Proceeds from issuance of long-term debt	7,691	5,832	4,099
Purchase of Company stock	(3,580)	(4,549)	(5,046)
Dividends paid	(2,511)	(2,214)	(1,569)
Payment of long-term debt	(2,724)	(2,131)	(3,541)
Payment of capital lease obligations	(245)	(204)	(305)
Other financing activities	(349)	113	111
Net cash used in financing activities	(2,422)	(2,609)	(5,563)
Effect of exchange rate changes on cash	(102)	205	320
Net increase in cash and cash equivalents	926	289	2,441
Cash and cash equivalents at beginning of year	5,488	5,199	2,758
Cash and cash equivalents at end of year	$ 6,414	$ 5,488	$ 5,199
Supplemental disclosure of cash flow information			
Income tax paid	$ 5,962	$ 5,593	$ 4,538
Interest paid	1,390	1,163	1,024
Capital lease obligations incurred	286	377	252

Source: Wal-Mart Stores, Inc., 2006 Annual Report, p. 33.

Exhibit 5
Fiscal 2006 End-of-Year Store Count: Wal-Mart Stores, Inc. January 31, 2006

Country	Discount Stores	Supercenters	SAM's Clubs	Neighborhood Markets
Argentina	0	11	0	0
Brazil	255	23	15	2
Canada	272	0	6	0
China	0	51	3	2
Germany	0	88	0	0
Japan	2	96	0	300
South Korea	0	16	0	0
Mexico	599	105	70	0
Puerto Rico	9	5	9	31
United Kingdom	294	21	0	0
United States	1,209	1,980	567	100
TOTAL	**2,640**	**2,396**	**670**	**435**

Source: Wal-Mart Stores, Inc., 2006 Annual Report, p. 51.

There was a negative side, however, to the Wal-Mart story. The company's stock price had fallen from $56.98 on January 31, 2002 to $46.11 on January 31, 2006. Given the company's continuous growth in sales and earnings, this was a strange development. One analyst commented that an investor who had bought Wal-Mart shares on the first day of trading in 2001 and held them through April 11, 2005, would have seen the investment decline by 9.9%! In contrast, over the same period, Costco Wholesale, Target, and J.C. Penney saw their stock prices climb 12.4%, 49.6%, and 367%, respectively. According to this analyst, the stock's lackluster performance over the previous five years was explained by competition getting tougher and growth prospects getting smaller. Once Wal-Mart had successfully expanded into every small and mid-sized city in the United States where competition was typically weak, further growth required entering large cities and other countries where other discount mass merchandisers, such as Target and Carrefour, were already established. To increase sales, Wal-Mart's management added a series of new retailing concepts. The replacement of traditional discount stores with Wal-Mart Supercenters containing groceries in addition to dry goods led to higher sales, but also to the lower profit margins inherent in the grocery business. Sam's Club's sales growth was good, but far less than that of other Wal-Mart stores. International expansion required acquisition and the conversion of stores to the Wal-Mart system—often expensive, difficult, and time consuming. Investors were not as excited about a business growing at 11% to 13% annually instead of the 20% or more they had come to expect.[4]

The company has been increasingly criticized for the very management practices that had made it so successful. Its low prices, wide selection, and courteous service generated high sales and profits, but its stores tended to drive local "mom and pop" stores out of business, especially in small towns. The United Food and Commercial Workers union contended that the only reason the company could offer such low prices was that Wal-Mart underpaid its workers and offered them substandard benefits. Wal-Mart's almost legendary hard stance with suppliers was being portrayed as an abuse of power. Lawsuits alleging discrimination against women and underage workers operating dangerous machinery, among other examples, added to the firm's public relations problem. It appeared that the company had become a lightning rod for any and all criticism against big business.

Wal-Mart: A Maturing Organization

Genesis of an Idea

Sam Walton started his retail career in 1940 as a management trainee with the J.C. Penney Co. in Des Moines, Iowa. He was impressed with the Penney method of doing business and later modeled the Wal-Mart chain on "The Penney Idea" as reviewed in **Exhibit 6.** The Penney Company found strength in calling employees "associates" rather than clerks. Penney's, founded in Kemerer, Wyoming, in 1902, located stores on the main streets of small towns and cities throughout the United States.

Following service in the U.S. Army during World War II, Sam Walton acquired a Ben Franklin variety store franchise in Newport, Arkansas. He operated this store successfully with his brother, James L. "Bud" Walton (1921–1995), until losing the lease in 1950.

The early retail stores owned by Sam Walton in Newport and Bentonville, Arkansas, and later in other small towns in adjoining southern states, were variety store operations. They were relatively small operations of 6,000 square feet, were located on "main streets," and displayed merchandise on plain wooden tables and counters. Operated under the Ben Franklin name and supplied by Butler Brothers of Chicago and St. Louis, they were characterized by a limited price line, low gross margins, high merchandise turnover, and concentration on return on investment. The firm, operating under the Walton 5 & 10 name with 15 stores, was the largest Ben Franklin franchisee in the country in 1962. The variety stores were phased out by 1976 to allow the company to concentrate on the growth of Wal-Mart discount department stores.

Foundations of Growth

The original Wal-Mart discount concept was not a unique idea. Sam Walton became convinced in the late 1950s that discounting would transform retailing. He traveled extensively in New England, the cradle of "off-pricing." After he had visited just about every discounter in the United States, he tried to interest Butler Brothers executives in the discount store concept. The first Kmart, as a "conveniently located one-stop shopping unit where customers could buy a wide variety of quality merchandise at discount prices," had just opened in Garden City, Michigan. Walton's strategy was to operate a similar discount store in a small community. In that setting, he would offer name-brand merchandise at low prices and would add friendly service. Butler Brothers executives rejected the idea. Undeterred, Walton opened the first "Wal-Mart Discount City" in late 1962 in Rogers, Arkansas.

Exhibit 6 The Penney Idea (1913)

1. To serve the public, as nearly as we can, to its complete satisfaction.
2. To expect for the service we render a fair remuneration and not all the profit the traffic will bear.
3. To do all in our power to pack the customer's dollar full of value, quality, and satisfaction.
4. To continue to train ourselves and our associates so that the service we give will be more and more intelligently performed.
5. To improve constantly the human factor in our business.
6. To reward men and women in our organization through participation in what the business produces.
7. To test our every policy, method, and act in this way: "Does it square with what is right and just?"

Source: V. H. Trimble, Sam Walton: The Inside Story of America's Richest Man (New York: Dutton, 1990).

Wal-Mart stores sold nationally advertised, well-known-brand merchandise at low prices in austere surroundings. As corporate policy, Wal-Mart cheerfully gave refunds, credits, and rain checks. Management conceived the firm as a "discount department store chain offering a wide variety of general merchandise to the customer." Early emphasis was placed on opportunistic purchases of merchandise from whatever sources were available. Health and beauty aids (H&BA) were heavily emphasized in the product line, and "stacking it high" was the manner of merchandise presentation. By the end of 1979, there were 276 Wal-Mart stores located in 11 states.

The firm developed an aggressive expansion strategy. New stores were located primarily in communities of 5,000 to 25,000 in population. The stores' sizes ranged from 30,000 to 60,000 square feet, with 45,000 being the average. The firm also expanded by locating stores in contiguous geographic areas. When its discount operations came to dominate a market area, it moved to an adjoining area. Whereas other retailers built warehouses to serve existing outlets, Wal-Mart built the distribution center first and then spotted stores all around it, pooling advertising and distribution overhead. Most stores were less than a six-hour drive from one of the company's warehouses. The first major distribution center, a 390,000-square-foot facility, opened in Searcy, Arkansas, outside Bentonville in 1978.

Becoming National

At the beginning of 1991, the firm had 1,573 Wal-Mart stores in 35 states, with expansion planned for adjacent states. Wal-Mart had become the largest retailer and the largest discount department store in the United States. By 2006, Wal-Mart had 1,200 discount stores, 1,980 supercenters, 567 Sam's Clubs, and 100 neighborhood markets throughout all 50 states.

As a national discount department store chain, Wal-Mart Stores, Inc., offered a wide variety of general merchandise to the customer. The stores were designed to offer one-stop shopping with 40 departments that included family apparel, health and beauty aids, household needs, electronics, toys, fabric and crafts, automotive supplies, lawn and patio, jewelry, and shoes. A pharmacy, automotive supply and service center, garden center, or snack bar were also operated at certain locations. The firm operated its stores with "everyday low prices" as opposed to putting heavy emphasis on special promotions that called for multiple newspaper advertising circulars. Stores were expected to "provide the customer with a clean, pleasant, and friendly shopping experience."

Although Wal-Mart carried much the same merchandise, offered similar prices, and operated stores that looked much like the competition, there were many differences. In the typical Wal-Mart store, employees wore blue vests to identify themselves, aisles were wide, apparel departments were carpeted in warm colors, store employees followed customers to their cars to pick up their shopping carts, and the customer was welcomed at the door by a "people greeter" who gave directions and struck up conversation. In some cases, merchandise was bagged in brown paper sacks rather than plastic bags because customers seemed to prefer them. The "Wal-Mart" and the slogan "Always Low Prices" on the front of the store served to identify the firm. Yellow smiley faces were used on in-store displays along with the slogan "Watch for Falling Prices." In consumer studies it was determined that the chain was particularly adept at striking the delicate balance needed to convince customers its prices were low without making people feel that its stores were too cheap. In many ways, competitors like Kmart sought to emulate Wal-Mart by introducing people greeters, by upgrading interiors, by developing new logos and signage, and by introducing new inventory response systems.

A "satisfaction guaranteed" refund and exchange policy was introduced to allow customers to be confident of Wal-Mart's merchandise and quality. Technological advancements such as scanner cash registers, handheld computers for the ordering of merchandise, and computer linkages of stores with the general office and distribution centers improved communications and merchandise replenishment. Each store was encouraged to initiate programs that would make it an integral part of the community in which it operated. Associates were encouraged to "maintain the highest standards of honesty, morality, and business ethics" in dealing with the public.

Becoming International

Realizing that there were only so many opportunities for growth within the borders of the United States, Wal-Mart's management embarked on international expansion. It opened its first international store in 1991 when it opened a Sam's Club in Mexico City. Two years later, Wal-Mart International was created to oversee growing global opportunities.

By 2006, Wal-Mart Stores, Inc., of Bentonville, Arkansas, operated mass merchandising retail stores under a variety of names and retail formats, including 2,460 supercenters in the United States, Mexico, Brazil, Germany, the United Kingdom (ASDA), Argentina, South Korea, and Puerto Rico; 1,500 general merchandise stores in the United States, Canada, Puerto Rico, the United Kingdom, and Brazil; 930 food and drug stores in Japan, the United Kingdom, Brazil, the United States, Mexico, Puerto Rico, and China; 189 bodegas in Mexico and Brazil; 670 Sam's Clubs in the United States, Mexico, Brazil, Canada, China, and Puerto Rico; 63 George and Suburbia apparel stores in the United Kingdom and Mexico; 33 soft discount stores in Brazil and Mexico; 10 Maxxi cash and carry stores in Brazil; and 286 Vips restaurants in Mexico. Of these, 2,285 were international stores located outside the United States. Wal-Mart had either total or majority ownership of its international store operations, except for a joint venture in China.

The Sam Walton Spirit

Much of the success of Wal-Mart was attributed to the entrepreneurial spirit of its founder and past Chairman of the Board, Samuel Moore Walton (1918–1992). Many considered him one of the most influential retailers of the century. Sam Walton, or "Mr. Sam," as some referred to him, traced his down-to-earth, old-fashioned, homespun, evangelical ways to growing up in rural Oklahoma, Missouri, and Arkansas. Although he appeared to be remarkably unconcerned about his roots, some suggested that it was his simple belief in hard work and ambition that had "unlocked countless doors and showered upon him, his customers, and his employees . . . the fruits of . . . years of labor in building [this] highly successful company."

"Our goal has always been in our business to be the very best," Sam Walton said in an interview, "and, along with that, we believe that in order to do that, you've got to make a good situation and put the interests of your associates first. If we really do that consistently, they in turn will cause . . . our business to be successful, which is what we've talked about and espoused and practiced." "The reason for our success," he said, "is our people and the way that they're treated and the way they feel about their company." Many have suggested that it was this "people first" philosophy that guided the company through the challenges and setbacks of its early years and allowed it to maintain its consistent record of growth and expansion in later years.

A unique, enthusiastic, and positive individual, Sam Walton was "just your basic homespun billionaire," a columnist once suggested. "Mr. Sam is a life-long small-town resident who didn't change much as he got richer than his neighbors," he noted. Walton had tremendous energy, enjoyed bird hunting with his dogs, and flew a corporate plane. When the company was much smaller, he could boast that he personally visited every Wal-Mart store at least once a year. A store visit usually included Walton leading Wal-Mart cheers that began, "Give me a W, give me an A. . . ." To many employees, he had the air of a fiery Baptist preacher. Paul R. Carter, a Wal-Mart Executive Vice President, was quoted as saying, "Mr. Walton has a calling." He became the richest man in America, and by 1991 had created a personal fortune for his family in excess of $21 billion. Fifteen years later, despite a division of wealth, five family members still controlled around 40% of the Wal-Mart common stock and were ranked among the top ten richest individuals in the United States.[5]

In late 1989 Sam Walton was diagnosed as having multiple myeloma, or cancer of the bone marrow. Nevertheless, he remained active in the firm as Chairman of the Board until his death in 1992.

Corporate Governance

Board of Directors

Exhibit 7 lists the 13 members of Wal-Mart's Board of Directors who were elected at the June 2, 2006, annual shareholders' meeting. Four were affiliated with the company in some manner: (1) S. Robson Walton, Chairman of the Board and son of the founder; (2) David D. Glass, Chairman, Executive Committee and CEO from 1988 to 2000; (3) Jim C. Walton, CEO of Arvest Bank Group and son of the founder; and (4) H. Lee Scott, current President and CEO. Jim Walton had been appointed to the Board September 30, 2005, to replace his older brother, John Walton, who had died in an aircraft accident. The nine other members of the Board were

Exhibit 7 2006 Board of Directors: Wal-Mart Stores, Inc.

Aida M. Alvarez, 56
Former Public Finance VP, First Boston & Bear Stearns
Former member of President Clinton's cabinet
Director since 2006

James W. Breyer, 44
Managing Partner, Accel Partners
Director since 2001

M. Michele Burns, 48
Exec VP & CFO, Marsh & McLennan Consulting Co.
Director since 2003

James J. Cash, Ph.D., 58
Retired Professor, Harvard Business School
Director since 2006

Douglas N. Daft, 63
Retired Chair & CEO, Coca-Cola Co.
Director since 2005

David D. Glass, 70
Past-President & CEO, Wal-Mart
Director since 1977

Roland A. Hernandez, 48
Retired Chair & CEO, Telemundo Group
Director since 1998

H. Lee Scott, 57
President & CEO, Wal-Mart
Director since 1999.

Jack C. Shewmaker, 68
President, J-COM Consulting & Retired Wal-Mart Exec
Director since 1977

Jim C. Walton, 58
Chair & CEO, Arvest Bank Group
Director since September 28, 2005

S. Robson Walton, 61
Chairman, Wal-Mart
Director since 1978

Christopher J. Williams, 48
Chair & CEO, Williams Capital Group Investment Bank
Director since 2004

Linda S.Wolf, 58
Former Chair & CEO, Leo Burnett Worldwide
Director since 2005

Source: Wal-Mart Stores, Inc., Notice of 2006 Annual Shareholders' Meeting, pp. 5–6.

officially considered "independent," as defined by the New York Stock Exchange. In terms of minority membership, the Board was composed of three women, two African Americans, and two Hispanic Americans. The Board was organized into five committees: the Audit Committee; the Compensation, Nominating, and Governance Committee (CNGC); the Executive Committee (EC); the Stock Option Committee (SOC); and the Strategic Planning and Finance Committee (SPFC). The Audit and CNGC committees were composed solely of independent directors, as required by the New York Stock Exchange.

Non-management directors received $60,000 as an annual retainer plus $140,000 worth of Wal-Mart shares on their election to the Board. Those serving as committee chairs additionally received $15,000 to $25,000 for their service. Each non-management director was required by the Board to own within five years from election to the Board an amount of shares equal to five times the annual retainer for the year in which the director was originally elected to the Board. The Board had four regular meetings and three telephone meetings during fiscal 2006. Committee meetings were in addition to the regular Board meetings. Each director attended at least 75% of the Board and committee meetings on which he or she served. The Board typically appointed one of the non-management directors to serve as Presiding Director of any executive sessions of the non-management and independent directors.

Although the officers and directors as a group owned less than 1% of total shares, S. Robson Walton and Jim C. Walton, by virtue of their being two of the five managing members of the family's Walton Enterprises, LLC, represented the Walton family and effectively controlled close to 41% of the shares outstanding.

Top Management and Organization Structure

Exhibit 8 lists the 25 corporate officers. Lee Scott was only the third CEO in the entire history of Wal-Mart when he was elected to the position in January 2000. Its first CEO, Sam Walton, had built the company from the ground up. During the 12 years that David Glass, the previous CEO, held the position, sales grew from $16 billion to $165 billion. Lee Scott had been personally recruited by David Glass 21 years before, from a Springdale, Arkansas, trucking company, to come to Wal-Mart as the manager of the truck fleet. In his years at Wal-Mart, Glass had driven the company to a new level of growth in both domestic and international markets and continued to be active on the firm's board of directors as Chairman of the Executive Committee. Prior to his appointment as President and CEO, Lee Scott had served as Vice Chairman and Chief Operation Officer (COO), Executive Vice-President, and President and CEO of the Wal-Mart Stores unit.

On January 31, 2006, Wal-Mart Stores, Inc., was structured into three business units, Wal-Mart Stores USA, Sam's Club, and Wal-Mart International. The Wal-Mart Stores unit had 3,289 locations and included the company's supercenters, discount stores, and Neighborhood Markets in the United States, as well as walmart.com. The Sam's Club unit had 567 locations and included the warehouse membership clubs in the United States plus samsclub.com. Wal-Mart International had 2,285 locations in 10 countries. The International total was increased though the February 2006 purchase of majority control of CARHCO with 360 locations in five Central American countries. (See **Exhibit 9** for business unit data.)

In September 2005, John Menzer, President and CEO of Wal-Mart International, and Mike Duke, President and CEO of Wal-Mart Stores, USA, were promoted to Vice Chairman positions within the company and effectively traded places. Menzer was given responsibility not only for Wal-Mart Stores USA, but also for the divisions responsible for real estate, logistics, information services, benefits, global procurement, financial services, store planning, and strategic planning. Eduardo Castro-Wright, Executive Vice President and COO of Wal-Mart Stores USA, was promoted to President and CEO of that unit. He was responsible for operations, merchandising, marketing, specialty divisions, and new business development in the

Exhibit 8 2006 Corporate Officers: Wal-Mart Stores, Inc.

Eduardo Castro-Wright
Exec VP, President & CEO
Wal-Mart Stores Division U.S.

M. Susan Chambers
Exec VP
People Division

Patricia A. Curran
Exec VP, Store Operations
Wal-Mart Stores Division U.S.

Douglas J. Degn
Exec VP, Food, Consumables, Hardlines
Wal-Mart Stores Division U.S.

Linda M. Dillman
Exec VP
Risk Mgmt & Benefits Administration

Johnnie Dobbs
Exec V
Logistics & Supply Chain

Michael T. Duke
Vice Chairman
Responsible for Wal-Mart International

Joseph J. Fitzsimmons
Sr VP
Treasurer

John E. Fleming
Exec VP & Chief Marketing Officer
Wal-Mart Stores Division U.S.

Rollin L. Ford
Exec VP & Chief Information Officer

David D. Glass
Chairmand of the Executive Committee
Board of Directors

Mark D. Goodman
Exec VP, Marketing, Membership & E-commerce
SAM'S CLUB

Craig R. Herkert
Exec VP, President & CEO, The Americas
Wal-Mart International

Charles M. Holley, Jr.
Sr VP
Finance

Thomas D. Hyde
Exec VP & Corporate Secretary

Lawrence V. Jackson
Exec VP, President & CEO
Global Procurement

Gregory L. Johnston
Exec VP, Club Operations
Sam's Club

C. Douglas McMillon
Exec VP, President & CEO
Sam's Club

John B. Menzer
Vice Chairman
Responsible for U.S.

Thomas M. Schoewe
Exec VP & Chief Financial Officer

H. Lee Scott
President and Chief Executive Officer

Gregory E. Spragg
Exec VP, Merchandising & Replenishment
Sam's Club

S. Robson Walton
Chairman of the Board

Claire A. Watts
Exec VP, Product Development, Apparel & Home Merchandising, Wal-Mart Stores Division U.S.

Eric S. Zorn
Exec VP
Wal-Mart Realty

Source: Wal-Mart Stores, Inc., 2006 Annual Report, p. 52.

Wal-Mart Stores, Supercenters, and Neighborhood Markets in the United States. Duke took over leadership of Wal-Mart International, the company's fastest-growing unit. According to CEO Lee Scott, Duke's experience heading Wal-Mart's largest operating unit in the United States coupled with his previous experience as head of the company's logistics operations made him uniquely qualified to manage Wal-Mart's International unit. Doug McMillon continued as President and CEO of the Sam's Club business unit.

Exhibit 9 Business Unit Performance: Wal-Mart Stores, Inc.
(Dollar amounts in millions)

	2006		2005		2004	
	Sales	Op. Income	Sales	Op. Income	Sales	Op. Income
Wal-Mart Stores U.S.	$209,910	$15,324	$191,826	$14,163	$174,220	$12,916
Sam's Club	39,798	1,385	37,119	1,280	34,537	1,126
Wal-Mart International	62,719	3,330	56,277	2,988	47,572	2,370
Total	$312,427	$20,039	$285,222	$18,431	$256,329	$16,412

Source: Wal-Mart Stores, Inc., 2006 Annual Report, pp. 22–25.

Competitive Environment

Wal-Mart management was aware that its business operations on a national and international level were subject to a number of factors outside of its control. Any one, or a combination, of these factors could materially affect the financial performance of the firm. These factors included the costs of goods, the cost of electricity and other energy requirements, competitive pressures, inflation, consumer debt levels, interest rate levels, and unemployment levels. They also included currency exchange fluctuations, trade restrictions, changes in tariff and freight rates, and other capital market and economic conditions.

Industry analysts labeled the decades since 1980 as an era of economic uncertainty for retailers. Although the United States had experienced one of the longest periods of economic expansion in its history during this period, increased competitive pressures, sluggish consumer spending, an energy crisis leading to higher fuel prices, lack of worldwide economic growth, and the terrorist events of September 11, 2001, converged to create a very challenging environment for all retailers at the beginning of the 21st century.

Many retail enterprises confronted heavy competitive pressure by restructuring. Sears was one example. Sears, Roebuck and Company, based in Chicago, became a more focused retailer by divesting itself of Allstate Insurance Company and its real estate subsidiaries. In 1993, the company announced it would close 118 unprofitable stores and discontinue the unprofitable Sears general merchandise catalog. It eliminated 50,000 jobs and began a $4 billion, five-year remodeling plan for its remaining multiline department stores. After unsuccessfully experimenting with an "everyday low-price" strategy, management chose to realign its merchandise strategy to meet the needs of middle-market customers, who were primarily women, by focusing on product lines in apparel, home, and automotive. The new focus on apparel was supported with the advertising campaign "The Softer Side of Sears." A later companywide campaign broadened the appeal: "The many sides of Sears fit the many sides of your life." Sears completed its return to its retailing roots by selling off its ownership in Dean Witter Financial Services, Discover Card, Coldwell Banker Real Estate, and Sears mortgage banking operations. In 1999, Sears refocused its marketing strategy with a new program that was designed to communicate a stronger whole-house and event message. A new advertising campaign introduced the slogan "The good life at a great price. Guaranteed." In 2000, a new store format was introduced that concentrated on five focal areas: appliances, home fashions, tools, kids, and electronics. Other departments, including men's and women's apparel, assumed a support role in these stores. In 2001, Sears developed another plan to reposition and restructure its core business: the full-line stores. Alan J. Lacy, Chairman and CEO, announced that this strategy would position Sears in the retail marketplace as "not a department store, not a discount store, but a broad-line retailer with outstanding credit and service capabilities." Sears' sales increased slightly from $39.4 billion in 1999 to $41.1 billion in 2003, but its net income fluctuated from $1.5 billion in 1999 to $735 million in 2001 to $3.4 billion in 2003. The lack of a consistent strategy and marketing image continued until Sears was purchased by Kmart in 2005. It was subsequently merged with Kmart to form a new firm, the Sears Holdings Corporation.

The discount department store industry by 2006 had changed in a number of ways and was thought by many analysts to have reached maturity. Several formerly successful firms such as E. J. Korvette, W. T. Grant, Atlantic Mills, Arlans, Federals, Zayre, Heck's, and Ames had declared bankruptcy and as a result either liquidated or reorganized. Venture announced liquidation in early 1998. Firms such as Target and Shopko began carrying more fashionable merchandise in more attractive facilities and shifted their emphasis to more national markets. Specialty retailers, such as Toys "R" Us, Pier 1 Imports, and Oshman's, had matured and were no longer making big inroads in toys, home furnishings, and sporting goods. The "superstores" of drug and food chains were rapidly discounting increasing amounts of general merchandise. Some firms, such as May Department Stores Company with Caldor and Venture and Woolworth Corporation with Woolco, had withdrawn from the field by either selling their discount divisions or closing them down entirely. Woolworth's remaining 122 Woolco stores in Canada were sold to Wal-Mart in 1994. All remaining Woolworth variety stores in the United States were closed in 1997.

Several new retail formats had emerged in the marketplace to challenge the traditional discount department store format. The superstore, a 100,000 to 300,000-square-foot operation, combined a large supermarket with a discount general-merchandise store. Originally a European retailing concept, these outlets where known as "malls without walls." Kmart's Super Kmart, Target's SuperTarget, and Wal-Mart's Supercenters were examples of this trend toward large operations. Warehouse retailing, which involved some combination of warehouse and showroom facilities, used warehouse principles to reduce operating expenses and thereby offer discount prices as a primary customer appeal. Home Depot combined the traditional hardware store and lumberyard with a self-service home improvement center to become the largest home center operator in the nation.

Some retailers responded to changes in the marketplace by selling goods at price levels 20%–60% below regular retail prices. These off-price operations appeared as two general types: (1) factory outlet stores, such as Burlington Coat Factory Warehouse, Bass Shoes, and Manhattan's Brand Name Fashion Outlet, and (2) independents, such as Loehmann's, T. J. Maxx, Marshall's, and Clothestime, which bought seconds, overages, closeouts, or leftover goods from manufacturers and other retailers. Other retailers chose to dominate a product classification. Some super specialists, such as Sock Appeal, Little Piggie, Ltd., and Sock Market, offered a single narrowly defined classification of merchandise with an extensive assortment of brands, colors, and sizes. Others, as niche specialists, such as Kids Foot Locker and Champs Sports, a division of Foot Locker, Inc. (formerly Woolworth Corporation), targeted an identified market with carefully selected merchandise and appropriately designed stores.

Some retailers, such as Silk Greenhouse (silk plants and flowers), Office Depot (office supplies and equipment), Home Depot (home improvement), and Toys "R" Us (toys), were called "category killers" because they had achieved merchandise dominance in their respective product categories. Stores such as The Limited, Limited Express, Victoria's Secret, and Banana Republic became mini-department specialists by showcasing new lines and accessories alongside traditional merchandise lines. The amount of specialization necessary to be a "category killer" could, however, lead to problems. Toys "R" Us, for example, made most of its sales during the Christmas season and was lucky to make break-even during the rest of the year. Wal-Mart, however, could expand its toy department during the Christmas season and then reduce it in favor of lawn and garden sales during the rest of the year. Once Wal-Mart targeted toys for merchandising emphasis during the Christmas season, Toys "R" Us could not keep up with Wal-Mart's vast selection at lower prices and was forced into bankruptcy in 2005.

Kohl's Corporation, a firm founded in 1962 in Menominee Falls, Wisconsin, operated family-focused, value-oriented department stores in 43 states as of June, 2006. The company's stores averaged 86,500 square feet in size and were typically located near but not within shopping malls. Kohl's offered moderately priced national brand-name apparel, shoes, accessories, and home products targeted to middle-income consumers in suburban areas with convenient parking. During the period 1992 and 2006, the Kohl's operation grew from 76 to 749 stores with its sales increasing from $1.1 billion in 1992 to $13.4 billion in 2006. With a quality image somewhere between J. C. Penney and Target, Kohl's earned $842 million in net income in 2006.

Kmart Corporation, headquartered in Troy, Michigan, celebrated in 1987 the 25th anniversary of its first Kmart store. At that time, it was the world's largest and most successful discount department store chain with sales of $25.6 billion. By 1990, Wal-Mart's sales of $32.6 billion surpassed Kmart's $32.1 billion and Kmart fell to second place in U.S. discount stores. By 2001, Kmart operated 2,114 stores and had sales of $36,151 million but had fallen to third place behind Wal-Mart and Target. In contrast, Wal-Mart's sales had risen to $217,799 million in 2001. Kmart was perceived by many industry analysts and consumers in several independent studies as a laggard. In the same studies, Wal-Mart was perceived as the industry leader, even though, according to the *Wall Street Journal,* "They carry much the same merchandise, offer prices that are pennies apart and operate stores that look almost exactly alike." The newspaper noted, "Even their names are similar." The original Kmart concept of a "conveniently located, one-stop shopping unit where customers could buy a wide variety of quality merchandise at discount prices," had lost its competitive edge in a changing market. As one analyst noted in an industry newsletter: "They had done so well for the past 20 years without paying attention to market changes, now they have to." Kmart changed strategic direction a number of times under different CEOs, but was unable to find a profitable niche in the increasingly competitive discount retailing industry. The firm suffered net losses in 1993, 1995, 1996, 2000, and 2001. Following its extraordinary 2001 loss of $2.4 billion, Kmart filed for bankruptcy under Chapter 11 of the federal bankruptcy laws on January 22, 2002. The firm continued to operate as an ongoing business while reorganizing. Costs were cut and marginal stores were either sold off for cash or closed. In March 2005, key investors in Kmart acquired Sears, Roebuck and Company and merged Kmart and Sears into the Sears Holdings Corporation. The management of Sears Holdings hoped to reduce costs of both Sears and Kmart by finding economies of scale in combining supply chains, IT, finance, legal, and human resources functions. During 2005, management closed 12 more Kmart stores and converted 48 Kmart stores into Sears stores. By 2006, Kmart had 1,479 stores in 49 states, Puerto Rico, and the Virgin Islands. Its stores were organized into Big Kmart stores (84,000–120,000 square feet), Kmart Super Centers (140,000–190,000 square feet), and traditional Kmart stores (80,000–110,000 square feet). For 2005, its first year of operation, Sears Holdings earned $858 million on $55 billion in sales.

Target Corporation was originally a discount unit of Dayton-Hudson, a respected department store chain headquartered in Minneapolis, Minnesota. The success of the Target unit led management to rename the company Target and to sell its department stores in 2004. By June 2006, Target had 1,418 stores in 47 states and 159 SuperTarget Stores in 21 states. Target's management viewed the company as an upscale discounter that provided high-quality, fashionable merchandise at attractive prices in clean, spacious, and guest-friendly stores. In 2003, 2004, and 2005 (years ending end-January of the following year), Target's sales were $42.0 billion, $46.8 billion, and $52.6 billion, respectively. During the same period, net earnings (not counting the sale of its department stores) were $1.6 billion, $1.9 billion, and $2.4 billion, respectively. Target's same-store sales (not including new or acquired stores) increased

5.6% in 2005 (year ending January 28, 2006) from the year earlier. As the nation's second largest retail chain, Target has become the nation's second largest retailer by successfully establishing itself in the upscale discount market niche. About 45% of Target's merchandise consisted of discretionary items, such as furniture, electonics, sporting goods, entertainment, and apparel—areas when trends and fashion were important and margins were wider, compared to only 30% for Wal-Mart, estimated Jeffrey Klinefelter, retail analyst at Piper Jaffray.[6] Wal-Mart was known as the relentless cost-cutter, but Target was the trendier place to shop and save. This upscale image coupled with management's traditional excellence in running quality department stores gave Target a competive advantage when competing against Wal-Mart in urban areas.

Some retailers, such as Kmart, had initially focused on appealing to professional, middle-class consumers who lived in suburban areas and who were likely to be price sensitive. Over time, Kmart attracted more working-class customers. Target went after an upscale consumer. Some firms, such as Fleet Farm and Pamida, served the rural consumer, whereas firms like Value City and Ames Department Stores chose to serve the urban consumer.

In rural communities Wal-Mart's success often came at the expense of established local merchants and units of regional discount store chains. Hardware stores, family department stores, building supply outlets, and stores featuring fabrics, sporting goods, and shoes were among the first to either close or relocate elsewhere. Regional discount retailers in the Sunbelt states, such as Roses, Howard's, T.G.& Y., and Duckwall-ALCO, which had once enjoyed solid sales and earnings, were forced to reposition themselves by renovating stores, opening bigger and more modern units, and re-merchandising. In many cases, stores such as Coast-to-Coast and Ben Franklin closed on a Wal-Mart announcement that it was planning to build in a specific community. "Just the word that Wal-Mart was coming made some stores close up," indicated one local newspaper editor. Ames Department Stores, Inc., which sought bankruptcy protection in 2001, announced in the summer of 2002 that it would close all 237 of its stores and liquidate inventory.

Domestic Strategies and Programs

Domestic strategies and programs at Wal-Mart were based on a set of two priorities that had guided the firm through its growth years. In the first priority, the customer was featured: "Customers would be provided with what they want, when they want it, all at a value." In the second, team spirit was emphasized: "Treating each other as we would hope to be treated, acknowledging our total dependency on our Associate-partners to sustain our success." The growth strategy included aggressive plans for new store openings; expansion to additional states; upgrading, relocating, refurbishing, and remodeling existing stores; and opening new distribution centers. For Wal-Mart management, the 1990s were considered an era in which the firm grew to become a truly nationwide retailer operating in all 50 states.

During the 1980s, Wal-Mart developed a number of new retail formats. The first Sam's Club opened in Oklahoma City, Oklahoma, in 1983. The wholesale club was an idea that had been developed by other firms earlier, but that found its greatest success and growth in acceptability at Wal-Mart. Sam's Clubs featured a vast array of product categories with limited selection of brand and model; cash-and-carry business with limited hours; large (100,000-square-foot), bare-bones facilities; rock-bottom wholesale prices; and minimal promotion. The limited membership plan permitted wholesale members who bought membership and others who usually paid a percentage above the ticket price of the merchandise. A revision in merchandising strategy resulted in fewer items in the inventory mix, with more emphasis on lower prices. A later acquisition of 100 PACE warehouse clubs, which were converted into Sam's Clubs, increased that division's units by more than one-third. A new Sam's Club format was introduced with the opening of a 154,000-square-foot store in 2001 in East Plano, Texas. The store featured an expanded product line with emphasis on fresh food, an open layout, a café, and an Internet kiosk where customers were invited to shop at the www.sams.com Web site. A new Sam's Club slogan, "It's a Big Deal!" referred to the size of the facility and the features of the prototype store.

Wal-Mart Supercenters were large combination stores. They were first opened in 1988 as Hypermarket*USA, a 222,000-square-foot superstore that combined a full general merchandise discount store with a large full-line grocery supermarket, a food court of restaurants, and other service businesses, such as banks or videotape rental stores. A scaled-down version of Hypermarket*USA was called Wal-Mart Supercenter and was similar in merchandise offerings, but with about 180,000 to 200,000 square feet of space. The company proceeded slowly with these plans and later suspended its plans for building any more hypermarkets in favor of the Supercenter concept.

Wal-Mart also tested a new concept called the Neighborhood Market in a number of locations in Arkansas. Identified by the company as "small-marts," these green-and-white stores were stocked with fresh fruits and vegetables, a drive-up pharmacy, a 24-hour photo shop, and a selection of classic Wal-Mart hard goods. Management elected to move slowly on this concept, planning to open no more than 10 a year. The goal was to ring the Superstores with these smaller stores to attract customers who were in hurry and wanted only a few items.

The McLane Company, Inc., a provider of retail and grocery distribution services for retail stores, was acquired by Wal-Mart in 1991. It was never considered a major segment of the total Wal-Mart operation and was divested in 2003.

Several programs were launched in Wal-Mart stores to highlight popular social causes. The "Buy American" program was a Wal-Mart retail program initiated in 1985. The theme was "Bring It Home to the USA," and its purpose was to communicate Wal-Mart's support for American manufacturing. In the program, the firm directed substantial influence to encourage manufacturers to produce goods in the United States rather than import them from other countries. Vendors were attracted into the program by encouraging manufacturers to initiate the process by contacting the company directly with proposals to sell goods that were made in the United States. Buyers also targeted specific import items in their assortments on a state-by-state basis to encourage domestic manufacturing. According to Haim Dabah, president of Gitano Group, Inc., a maker of fashion discount clothing that previously imported 95% of its clothing and now made about 20% of its products in the United States: "Wal-Mart let it be known loud and clear that if you're going to grow with them, you sure better have some products made in the U.S.A." Farris Fashion, Inc. (flannel shirts), Roadmaster Corporation (exercise bicycles), Flanders Industries, Inc. (lawn chairs), and Magic Chef (microwave ovens) were examples of vendors that chose to participate in the program. From the Wal-Mart standpoint, the "Buy American" program centered around value—producing and selling quality merchandise at a competitive price. The promotion included television advertisements featuring factory workers, a soaring American eagle, and the slogan "We buy American whenever we can, so you can too." Prominent in-store signage and store circulars were also included. One store poster read: "Success Stories—These items, formerly imported, are now being purchased by Wal-Mart in the U.S.A."

Wal-Mart was one of the first retailers to embrace the concept of "green" marketing. The program offered shoppers the option of purchasing products that were better for the environment in three respects: manufacturing, use, and disposal. It was introduced through full-page advertisements in the *Wall Street Journal* and *USA Today*. In-store signage identified those products that were environmentally safe. As Wal-Mart executives saw it, "Customers are concerned about the quality of land, air, and water, and would like the opportunity to do something positive." To initiate the program, 7,000 vendors were notified that Wal-Mart had a corporate concern for the environment and asked for their support in a variety of ways. Wal-Mart television advertising showed children on swings, fields of grain blowing in the wind, and roses. Green and white store signs, printed on recycled paper, marked products or packaging that had been developed or redesigned to be more environmentally sound.

The Wal-Mart private brand program began with the "Ol' Roy" brand, the private-label dog food named for Sam Walton's favorite hunting companion. Introduced to Wal-Mart stores in 1982 as a low-price alterative to national brands, Ol' Roy became the biggest seller of all dog-food brands in the United States. "We are a (national) brand-oriented company first," noted Bob Connolly, Executive Vice President of Merchandising of Wal-Mart. "But we also use private label to fill value or pricing voids that, for whatever reason, the brands left behind." Wal-Mart's private-label program included thousands of products that had brand names, such as Sam's Choice, Great Value, Equate, and Spring Valley.

Wal-Mart was the largest clothing seller in the world. Although most of the sales of its clothing business were in basics such as socks, underwear, tee-shirts, and blue jeans, the firm developed a 100-member development team to begin to focus its clothing lines on fashion and style in all sizes. Claire Watts was hired from Limited, Inc., to become the first Director of Product Development. The company also made a significant investment in technology so that all the factors of the development process, from design to production, were coordinated online among Wal-Mart, its suppliers, and factories. Rather than wait for suppliers to bring products to Wal-Mart, merchandise teams traveled to Europe four times a year to visit trendy boutiques and fashion shows and bring back racks of clothes to be evaluated at corporate headquarters on the basis of quality, fashion, and style. In 2002, Wal-Mart introduced a contemporary brand nationwide called George. George, a stylish line of clothing for women and men, had been sold exclusively for 10 years in England's ASDA supermarkets, which Wal-Mart acquired in 1999. Although the George brand was profitable, it was never as successful as management had hoped. In 2005, management put increased emphasis on apparel and music offerings. In an attempt to upgrade its image, the company placed ads featuring women's clothing in *Vogue* magazine.

In 2000, according to DSR Marketing Systems, Wal-Mart became the largest retailer of groceries in the United States, surpassing traditional grocery retailers such as Cincinnati, Ohio–based Kroger, Boise, Idaho–based Albertson's, and Pleasanton, California–based Safeway.

Wal-Mart had become the channel commander in the distribution of many brand-name items. As the nation's largest retailer and in many geographic areas the dominant distributor, it exerted considerable influence in negotiation for the best price, delivery terms, promotion allowances, and continuity of supply. Many of these benefits could be passed on to consumers in the form of quality name-brand items available at lower-than-competitive prices. As a matter of corporate policy, management often insisted on doing business only with producers' top sales executives rather than going through a manufacturer's representative. Wal-Mart had been accused of threatening to buy from other producers if firms refused to sell directly to it. In the ensuing power struggle, Wal-Mart executives refused to talk about the controversial policy or admit that it existed. As a representative of an industry association representing a group of sales agencies representatives suggested, "In the Southwest, Wal-Mart's the only show in town." An industry analyst added, "They're extremely aggressive. Their approach has always been to give the customer the benefit of a corporate saving. That builds up customer loyalty and market share."

Another key factor in the mix was an inventory control system that was recognized as the most sophisticated in retailing. A high-speed computer system linked virtually all the stores to headquarters and the company's distribution centers. It electronically logged every item sold at the checkout counter, automatically kept the warehouses informed of merchandise to be ordered, and directed the flow of goods to the stores and even to the proper shelves. Most importantly for management, it helped detect sales trends quickly and sped up market reaction time substantially. According to Bob Connolly, Executive Vice President of Merchandising, "Wal-Mart has used the data gathered by technology to make more inventory available in the key items that customers want most, while reducing inventories overall." In April 2004, Wal-Mart began a pilot test in 150 stores and Sam's Clubs locations in the Dallas, Texas, area to test the use of radio frequency identification (RFID) to track items through the distribution channel. The new technology resulted in a 16% reduction of out-of-stocks and a threefold increase in replenishing out-of-stock items. RFID was being expanded to nearly 1,000 stores and clubs in 2006 and from 300 suppliers to more than 600 by 2007.

Hired by Wal-Mart in 1978 to help build an information technology system, Randy Mott and colleagues developed a network of computerized distribution centers in the 1980s that made it simple to open and manage new stores efficiently. Promoted to Chief Information Officer in the early 1990s, Mott persuaded managemement to invest in a "data warehouse" that would allow the company to collect and sift customer information to analyze buying trends. The resulting information could indicate which flavor of Pop-Tart sold best at a particular store. Since this concept was new to the industry, it gave the company another significant competitive advantage. From Wal-Mart, Mott moved to Dell and then to Hewlett-Packard to improve their information systems.[7]

At the beginning of 2000, Wal-Mart set up a separate company for its Web site, with plans to go public. Wal-Mart.com, Inc., based in Palo Alto, California, was jointly owned by Wal-Mart and Accel Partners, a Silicon Valley venture-capital firm. The site included a wide range of products and services that ranged from shampoo to clothing to lawn mowers, as well as airline, hotel, and rental car bookings. After launching and then closing a Sam's Club web site, Wal-Mart reopened the site in mid-June 2000, with an emphasis on upscale items such as jewelry, housewares, and electronics and full product lines for small business owners. SamsClub.com was operated by Wal-Mart from the company's Bentonville, Arkansas, headquarters.

International Strategies and Programs

In 1994, Wal-Mart entered the Canadian market with the acquisition of 122 Woolco discount stores from Woolworth Corporation. When acquired, the Woolco stores were losing millions of dollars annually, but operations became profitable within three years. By the end of 2001, the company had 196 Wal-Mart discount stores in Canada. The company's operations in Canada were considered as a model for Wal-Mart's expansion into other international markets. By 2006, the number had grown to 272 discount stores and six Sam's Clubs. With a 35% share of the Canadian discount and department store market, Wal-Mart was the largest retailer in that country.

With a tender offer for shares and mergers of joint ventures in Mexico, the company in 1997 acquired a controlling interest in Cifra, Mexico's largest retailer. Cifra, later identified as Wal-Mart de Mexico, operated stores with a variety of concepts in every region of Mexico, ranging from the nation's largest chain of sit-down restaurants to a softline department store. Retail analysts noted that the initial venture involved many costly mistakes. Time after time it sold the wrong products, including tennis balls that wouldn't bounce in high-altitude Mexico City. Large parking lots at some stores made access difficult as many people arrived by bus. By 2006, Wal-Mart (known as Walmex) operated 599 stores (composed of 187 Bodegas, 16 Mi Bodegas, 1 Mi Bodega Express, 1 Mercamus, 53 Suburbias, 55 Superamas, and 286 Vips stores), 105 Supercenters, and 70 Sam's Clubs in Mexico for a total of 774 outlets, compared to just 551 outlets in 2002. The company had grown to dominate Mexico's retail market with its model of rapid expansion and low prices.

When Wal-Mart entered Argentina in 1995, it also initially faced challenges adapting its U.S.-based retail mix and store layouts to the local culture. Although globalization and U.S.

cultural influences had swept through the country in the early 1990s, the Argentine market did not accept U.S. cuts of meat, bright-colored cosmetics, and jewelry that gave prominent placement to emeralds, sapphires, and diamonds, since most Argentine women preferred wearing gold and silver. The first stores even had hardware departments full of tools wired for 110-volt electric power; the standard throughout Argentina was 220. Compounding the challenges was a store layout that featured narrow aisles; stores appeared crowded and dirty. In 2006, Wal-Mart operated 11 Supercenters in Argentina, the same number as in 2002.

Wal-Mart's management concluded that Brazil offered great opportunities for Wal-Mart because it had the fifth largest population in the world and a population that had a tendency to follow U.S. cultural cues. Although financial data were not broken out on South American operations, retail analysts cited the accounts of Wal-Mart's Brazilian partner, Lojas Americanas SA, to suggest that Wal-Mart lost $100 million in start-up costs for the initial 16 stores. Customer acceptance of Wal-Mart stores was mixed. In Canada and Mexico, many customers had been familiar with the company from cross-border shopping trips. In contrast, many Brazilian customers were not familiar with the Wal-Mart name. In addition, local Brazilian markets were already dominated by savvy local and foreign competitors, such as Grupo Pao de Acucar SA of Brazil and Carrefour SA of France. Wal-Mart's insistence on doing things "the Wal-Mart way" initially alienated many local suppliers and employees. The country's continuing economic problems also presented a challenge. Realizing that it needed to take another approach to growth, management made two acquisitions. The first was Bompreco S. A. Supermercado do Nordeste, a chain of 118 hypermarkets, supermarkets, and mini-markets in Northern Brazil that was purchased in February 2004. The second was Sonae Distribuicao, a retail operation in Southern Brazil consisting of 139 hypermarkets, supermarkets, and warehouse units purchased in December 2005. By 2006, Wal-Mart operated 255 discount stores, 23 Supercenters, 15 Sam's Clubs, and 2 Neighborhood Markets in Brazil for a total of 295 outlets compared to only 12 Supercenters and 8 Sam's Clubs in 2002.

Wal-Mart entered the European market by acquiring three retail chains. Because of complex local regulations, management felt it would be easier for Wal-Mart to buy existing stores in Europe than to build new ones. The response in Europe to Wal-Mart's entry was immediate and dramatic. Competitors scrambled to match Wal-Mart's low prices, long hours, and friendly service. Some firms combined to strengthen their operations. For example, France's Carrefour SA chain of hypermarkets combined forces with competitor Promodes in a $16.5 billion deal. In 2002, Carrefour dominated the European market with three leading formats: hypermarket, supermarket, and hard discount (small food stores with low prices). It was the world's second-largest retailer, with more than 9,200 stores not only in Europe, but in Latin America and Asia as well. In 2005, Carrefour's sales rose 2.5% from the previous year to 74.5 billion euros. Although net income fell 16% to 1.44 billion euros ($1.72 billion) during the same period, the exclusion of one-time charges showed a 1.2% increase in profits to 1.81 euros ($2.15 billion). Carrefour's management planned to invest 10 billion euros ($11.9 billion) to open 100 new hypermarkets in 2006 and a total of 1,000 new stores during 2006–2008. The planned growth in hypermarkets was more than twice the average annual number of openings between 2000 and 2004. Carrefour's management expected that its growth strategy would increase sales by 10% by 2008.[8]

Wal-Mart moved into Germany at the end of 1997 by acquiring 21 stores from hypermarket operator Wertkauf. Also as part of its expansion efforts in Germany, Wal-Mart acquired 74 stores that were a part of the Interspar chain. Soon after the takeover, Wal-Mart quickly filled the top management positions with U.S. expatriates. Within weeks of the purchase, most of the top German managers left the company. Management also discovered that these stores were either cramped, unattractive, or poorly located and needed to be entirely renovated. All of these German stores were identified with the Wal-Mart name and restocked with a new and revamped selection of merchandise. In response to local laws that forced early store closings and forbade Sunday sales, the company simply opened stores earlier, to allow shopping to begin at 7 AM. In January 2000, the company launched its first big "rollback" by cutting prices on several hundred items by up to 23%. Germany was well populated with discounters such as Aldi and Lidl, which ran no-frills, cheap supermarkets. These discounters responded fiercely to price challenge by cutting their prices by up to 25%. As a result, price cuts did not have a dramatic impact on sales. Wal-Mart's store count dropped from 95 Supercenters in 2002 to 88 in 2006, less than 20% of rival Kaufland's stores. Wal-Mart's grocery market share never exceeded 2% of Germany's food sales. In a country where local discounters dominated, the leader was Aldi, which boasted a 19% market share through its 4,000 stores. According to industry analysts, Wal-Mart was in a difficult position because it needed more stores to advertise efficiently and exert purchasing power. Despite Wal-Mart's lackluster performance in Germany, management remained committed to serving this market.[9]

Wal-Mart acquired ASDA, Britain's third largest supermarket group, for $10.8 billion in July 1999. With its own price rollbacks, people greeter, "permanently low prices," and even "smiley" faces, ASDA had emulated Wal-Mart's store culture for many years. Based in Leeds, England, the firm had 232 stores in England, Scotland, and Wales. Although the culture and pricing strategies of the two companies were nearly identical, there were differences, primarily the size and product mix of the stores. The average Wal-Mart Supercenter was 180,000 square feet in size and had about 30% of its sales in groceries. In contrast, the average ASDA store had only 65,000 square feet and did 60% of sales in grocery items. By 2006, Wal-Mart operated 294 discount stores (composed of 236 ASDA stores, 10 George stores, 5 ASDA Living, and 43 ASDA small stores) and 21 Supercenters in the United Kingdom. Although ASDA was still second in the U.K. market with a 16.6% share, its sales were stagnating while its rivals J Sainsbury (16.2% share) and market leader Tesco (30.4% share) were slowly increasing their share of the market. British executives hoped to revitalize the U.K. operations sometime in 2007.[10]

Wal-Mart's initial effort to enter China fell apart in 1996, when Wal-Mart and Thailand's Charoen Pokphand Group terminated an 18-month old joint venture because of management differences. Wal-Mart decided to consolidate its operations with five stores in the Hong Kong border city of Shenzhen, one in Dalian, and another in Kunming. Analysts concluded that the company was taking a low-profile approach because of possible competitive response and government restrictions. Beijing restricted the operations of foreign retailers in China, requiring them, for instance, to have government-backed partners. In Shenzhen, it limited the number of stores Wal-Mart could open. Wal-Mart soon found another joint venture partner and continued its growth. In 2006, Wal-Mart's joint venture operated 51 Supercenters, 3 Sam's Clubs, and 2 Neighborhood Markets. This was a significant increase in China from 2002, when the company operated only 15 Supercenters, three Sam's Clubs, and one Neighborhood Market. Wal-Mart corporate management has targeted China, long a major supplier of its products, as a key market for international store growth. Management planned to open 20 additional stores in China during 2006.[11]

During December 2005, Wal-Mart purchased a majority interest in Seiyu, a retailer in Japan selling apparel, general merchandise, and food in 398 stores. 2005 was the fourth straight year Seiyu operated at a loss. Seiyu, Japan's fourth-largest retailer, had struggled unsuccessfully to adopt Wal-Mart's marketing strategy since 2002 when Wal-Mart acquired a 6% stake. Wal-Mart management was hopeful that its investment would lead to eventual success in an important market. "This market has a lot of promise and because of that we are patiently investing both management as well as capital, and we expect to get a return on that over time," reported Jeff McAllister, COO of Wal-Mart's Japanese operations.[12]

In February 2006, Wal-Mart acquired majority control of the Central American Retail Holding Company, known as CARHCO. With this purchase, Wal-Mart obtained more than 360 supermarkets and other stores in Costa Rica, El Salvador, Guatemala, Honduras, and Nicaragua. CARHCO's 2005 sales were about $2.2 billion.

On May 22, 2006, management announced that Wal-Mart was withdrawing from South Korea by selling all 16 of its outlets to Shinsegae, a local retailer for $882 million. In leaving Korea, Wal-Mart joined Carrefour, Nokia, Nestle, and Google—other firms that had also failed to adjust to South Korean tastes. According to financial analyst Na Hong Seok, "Wal-Mart is a typical example of a global giant who has failed to localize its operations in South Korea. It failed to read what South Korean housewives want when they go shopping." Analysts commented that both Wal-Mart and Carrefour had not opened stores quickly enough to build the sales needed for supply chain economies.

The international expansion accelerated management's plans for the development of Wal-Mart as a global brand along the lines of Coca-Cola, Disney, and McDonald's. "We are a global brand name," said Bobby Martin, an early President of the International Division of Wal-Mart. "To customers everywhere it means low cost, best value, greatest selection of quality merchandise and highest standards of customer service," he noted. Some changes were mandated in Wal-Mart's international operations to meet local tastes and intense competitive conditions. "We're building companies out there," said Martin. "That's like starting Wal-Mart all over again in South America or Indonesia or China." Although stores in different international markets would coordinate purchasing to gain leverage with suppliers, developing new technology and planning overall strategy was being done from Wal-Mart headquarters in Bentonville, Arkansas.

Human Resources and Corporate Culture

One principle that distinguished Wal-Mart was the unusual depth of employee involvement in company affairs. The corporation emphasized human resource management. Employees of Wal-Mart were called "associates," a name borrowed from Sam Walton's early association with the J. C. Penney Co. Input was encouraged at meetings at the store and corporate levels. The firm hired employees locally and provided training programs, and through a "Letter to the President" program, management encouraged employees to ask questions and made words such as "we," "us," and "our" a part of the corporate language. A number of special award programs recognized individual, department, and division achievement. Stock ownership and profit-sharing programs were introduced as part of a "partnership" concept.

The corporate culture was recognized by the editors of the trade publication *Mass Market Retailers,* when it recognized all 275,000 associates collectively as the "Mass Market Retailers of the Year." "The Wal-Mart associate," the editors noted, "has come to symbolize all that is right with the American worker, particularly in the retailing environment and most particularly at Wal-Mart." The "store within a store" concept, as a Wal-Mart corporate policy, trained individuals to be merchants by being responsible for the performance of their own departments as if they were running their own businesses. Seminars and training programs afforded them opportunities to grow within the company. "People development is not just a good 'program' for any growing company but a must to secure our future," was how Suzanne Allford, Vice President of the Wal-Mart People Division, explained the firm's decentralized approach to retail management development.

"The Wal-Mart Way" was a phase used by management to summarize the firm's unconventional approach to business and to the development of its corporate culture. As noted in a report referring to a recent development program: "We stepped outside our retailing world to examine the best managed companies in the United States in an effort to determine the fundamentals of their success and to 'benchmark' our own performances. The name 'Total Quality Management' (TQM) was used to identify this vehicle for proliferating the very best things we do while incorporating the new ideas our people have that will assure our future." In 1999, *Discount Store News* honored Wal-Mart Stores, Inc., as "Retailer of the Century," with a commemorative 200-page issue of the magazine.

In many ways, Wal-Mart's corporate culture was a reflection of the values of its founder, Sam Walton, in its emphasis on everyday low prices, corporate growth, concern for people, and loyalty to the company. According to Chairman David Glass, "Sam has been gone for a number of years now, but he's still alive and well in this company to a great extent. There's not a day that goes by that I don't hear conversations around here about what Sam would do or how he felt about something." An unrelenting focus on cost-cutting led to a continual search to eliminate operating inefficiencies, high pressure on suppliers to reduce costs and provide "just in time" deliveries, and frugal employee benefits. For example, even when CEO Lee Scott and CFO Tom Schoewe went on a business trip they were expected to share hotel rooms. "Sharing rooms is a very symbolic part of what we do," explained Scott.[14]

The company's cultural roots in Bentonville, Arkansas, have been considered by some to be both a key strength and a serious weakness. Management's southern, rural, conservative values provided it a competitive advantage when expanding into small and mid-sized towns throughout America, but created some problems when Wal-Mart expanded into larger cities and other countries. For example, urban shoppers often preferred more fashionable merchandise than what Wal-Mart usually stocked. Brand Keys' 2006 study of top brands revealed that Wal-Mart was behind Target for the second consecutive year. According to Robert Passikoff, President of Brand Keys, "Target means style at accessible pricing. Wal-Mart hasn't reached that point." In addition, Wal-Mart was the last major pharmacy chain to stock the "Plan B" morning-after birth control pill and only did so after it lost a lawsuit brought by three Boston women. Nevertheless, the company continued to keep its "conscientious objector" policy, which allowed employees who didn't feel comfortable dispensing the drugs to refer customers elsewhere. Wal-Mart's non-union stance was acceptable to rural southern communities, but created growing antagonism when the firm added stores in the urban Midwest and northeastern United States and in Canada. A key part of its low-cost competitive strategy, the company's non-union labor costs were 20% less than at unionized supermarkets. Management had also forced suppliers to hide magazine covers the company considered "racy" and refused to stock music or computer games with mature ratings. Nevertheless, most locations offered inexpensive firearms as part of their sporting goods offerings. The strong emphasis on Wal-Mart values offended some employees with different backgrounds. For example, many of the Canadian employees at Wal-Mart's discount store in Jonquiere, Quebec, stood silently through the mandatory Wal-Mart cheer each morning. Employee Sylvie Lavoie explained, "It's not a song. It's a military chant. I found it to be degrading."

Financial Situation

By most financial measures, Wal-Mart was in excellent financial shape and far ahead of its domestic rivals. Its net sales had steadily increased from $89.1 billion in 1996 to $204 billion in 2002 to $312.4 billion in 2006. Net income had followed a similar growth path from $2.7 billion in 1996 to $6.6 billion in 2002 to $11.2 billion in 2006. Wal-Mart's diluted earnings per share increased from $.59 in 1996 to $1.47 in 2002 to $2.68 in 2006. According to CEO Scott, "Comparative store [same store] sales in the U.S. rose a healthy 3.4%" from 2005 to 2006. By comparison, net sales and earnings of Target, its closest rival, were only $52.6 billion and $2.4 billion, respectively, in the 2005 fiscal year ending January 28, 2006. The merger of Sears and Kmart into Sears Holdings Corporation resulted in a $55 billion (in sales) company with a net income of $858 million for the 2005 fiscal year ending January 2006. (See **Exhibits 1, 2, 3,** and **4**).

During 2006, management purchased $3.6 billion of Wal-Mart common stock under a share repurchase program and paid dividends of $2.5 billion. During that year, it also issued $7.7 billion in long-term debt, repaid $2.7 billion of long-term debt, and funded a net decrease in commercial paper of $704 million. Total corporate assets of continuing operations increased from $36,621 million in 1996 to $81,549 million in 2002 to $138,187 million in 2006. Return on assets was 7.9% in 1996, 8.4% in 2002, and 8.9% in 2006. One of management's objectives was to have operating income grow faster than net sales. In fiscal year 2006, however, overall operating income increased by only 8.4% over 2005, compared to a net sales increase of 9.5%. Compared to fiscal 2005, the Wal-Mart Stores USA unit experienced an 8.4% increase in operating income and a 9.4% increase in net sales in fiscal 2006. During the same period, Sam's Club had an 8.2% increase in operating income and a 7.2% increase in net sales. At the same time, the international business unit generated 11.4% increases in both sales and operating income.

Wal-Mart's sales for the first quarter of its 2007 fiscal year ending April 30, 2006, were $79.6 billion, an increase of 12.3% over the same quarter a year earlier. The firm's net income rose to $2.62 billion from $2.46 billion the year before. This 6% increase in profits was better than expected by industry analysts, who also noted Target's 12% first-quarter profit increase.

Of special concern to management was the behavior of the company's stock. Contrary to the upward direction of the firm's sales and profits, the price of Wal-Mart's stock had fallen from $56.98 on January 31, 2002, to $46.11 on January 31, 2006. Even though the board of directors had both repurchased stock and raised dividends per share from $0.52 in 2005 to $0.60 in 2006, the stock failed to respond. When the board further raised dividends to $0.67 per share on March 2, 2006 for the 2007 fiscal year, the stock price fell 11.7% to $45.06 on the New York Stock Exchange.

Challenges to Continued Growth

Wal-Mart's management faced significant challenges in 2006—challenges that could significantly affect the achievement of its growth objectives. The company was being condemned for business practices ranging from low pay and stingy health care benefits to exporting jobs and destroying small businesses. Wal-Mart was also the subject of litigation, including a class action discrimination suit representing 1.6 million current and former female employees who accused the firm of systematic underpayment and lack of promotion. In addition, filmmaker Robert Greenwald premiered a scathing documentary in November 2005 titled *Wal-Mart: The High Cost of Low Prices.* The movie was filled with ex-employees who trashed the company. One activist group, "Wake Up Wal-Mart," which was started in April 2005 by the United Food and Commercial Workers union, gained 115,000 members and aired TV ads to tout the new movie. "Wal-Mart Watch," another activist group, leaked an internal memo to *The New York Times* in October 2005 from Wal-Mart's Executive Vice President for Benefits to Wal-Mart's Board of Directors. The memo stated that 46% of the children of Wal-Mart workers were uninsured or on Medicaid and that Wal-Mart's health plan required such high out-of-pocket payments that the number of employees hit by a very costly illness "almost certainly would end up declaring bankruptcy." The memo proposed that Wal-Mart rewrite job descriptions to involve more physical activity, in part to "dissuade unhealthy people from coming to work at Wal-Mart."[19]

The resulting uproar over Wal-Mart's health benefits led to the Democrat-controlled legislature in Maryland passing a bill on January 12, 2006, requiring any employer with more than 10,000 employees to spend at least 8% of its payroll on health care for its workers. If it spent less, the firm must give the difference to Maryland's Medicaid program. The law was characterized as "the Wal-Mart bill" because Wal-Mart was the only company in Maryland affected. It was noted that as the nation's largest private-sector employer, Wal-Mart provided health insurance to fewer than half of its 1.3 million workers. The new law had been supported by unions who claimed that around 30 states were also considering such legislation. Nevertheless, the bill may be illegal because it could violate the federal Employment

Retirement Income Security Act, which gave Congress the sole authority to regulate employee benefits.[20]

Wal-Mart's reputation took another hit when Wal-Mart's No. 2 executive and Vice Chairman of its Board of Directors, Tom Coughlin, admitted to misappropriating company funds and pleaded guilty to five counts of fraud and one count of tax evasion. Previously, he had served as President and CEO of Wal-Mart Stores and Sam's Club. Coughlin was forced to leave Wal-Mart's board in March 2005. After an internal investigation, two other Wal-Mart employees were fired for financial improprieties.[21]

In 2003, a raid on 60 Wal-Mart stores in 21 states led to the arrests of 245 illegal workers. The company paid $11 million in March 2005 without admitting guilt. In November 2005, federal agents arrested more than 120 workers on immigration violations at the construction site of a Wal-Mart distribution center. Wal-Mart's management argued that those arrested were employees of a subcontractor and that Wal-Mart has contracts with subcontractors requiring them to follow all federal, state, and local laws.[22]

Even though the company required that its suppliers certify that their factories complied with Wal-Mart's workplace standards, Jim Lynn, a Wal-Mart executive, found that these reports were routinely falsified in Honduras. When, as part of his job of checking on suppliers in Central and South America, the executive visited the Glory Garments factory near San Dedro Sula, Honduras, he found a facility "that didn't have potable drinking water, that had no toilet paper in the restrooms, and where the fire exits were padlocked. They did pregnancy testing on the women, and if it came back positive, [the women] were terminated." He also discovered that contrary to Wal-Mart's stated policy, factories received at least three-day advance notification of factory-certification visits—enough time to clean up the facilities. After notifying top management about this situation, Lynn was accused of violating company policies and fired. The case of *James Lynn v. Wal-Mart* was filed in an Arkansas state court in 2005. To its credit, Wal-Mart's management worked to rectify the problems raised by Lynn. Acording to Beth Keck, Wal-Mart's Director of International Affairs, the factories inspected by Lynn were either remedied or terminated as suppliers. Keck acknowledged that outside groups were still not permitted to conduct authorized inspections of their own, though she added that this was a policy that Wal-Mart was working toward.[23] She further reported in a February 13, 2006, news release: "In 2005, Wal-Mart audited on average 35 supplier factories a day or 13,600. We increased the number of unannounced audits to 20 percent."[24]

In general, Wal-Mart's management was not in favor of the unionization of its stores. Keeping labor costs down was key to "everyday low prices." Supermarket rivals paying union wages of $10 an hour and paying most health benefit costs were at a competive disadvantage to Wal-Mart's Supercenters, where employees earned around $8 and hour and paid a higher proportion of their health costs. According to an article appearing in *The Nation,* "During the hiring process, many workers say they have had to sign forms agreeing that they would not support any effort to unionize the store, a clear violation of federal law." Although none of Wal-Mart's U.S. employees were unionized, Wal-Mart had been a defendant in 28 complaints in just one year (2002) brought by the U.S. National Labor Relations Board citing anti-union activities such as threats, interrogations, or disciplining. Critics contended that the company moved quickly to block organizing. For example, when a majority of meat cutters at a store in Jacksonville, Texas, voted to organize, the company closed its butcher departments at Jackson and other stores. When Wal-Mart's store in Jonquiere, Quebec, was certified by the Quebec government as the only unionized Wal-Mart in North America in August 2004, Wal-Mart simply closed the store and left the area. Interestingly, a union certification election two months earlier had been voted down 53% to 47%. After that union defeat, a group of Wal-Mart managers gathered just outside the front door to celebrate for the TV cameras and taunt union supporters as they left the store. Many employees who had voted against the union were so appalled by management's actions that they switched sides. Interestingly, a 2006 study reported by New England Consulting Group found that 60% of union members had visited a Wal-Mart in the past month versus 57% of all shoppers. According to Tom Hayes, a principal in the consulting group, Wal-Mart had more unionized shoppers than any other retailer—double the number for Sears and 40% more than Target. Explained Hays, "The savings are too much to resist."

Even though a recent survey found that only 8% of adults were openly hostile toward Wal-Mart, there was some indication that the company's customers were no longer pleased with the company. Based on interviews conducted in 2003 by Service Industry Research Systems, customer ratings of the staff in terms of courtesy and friendliness dropped more than 20% since 1999. The ratings had fallen to slightly below the industry average, which itself had dropped during the same period.

Opponents of "big box" retail stores were battling Wal-Mart in an increasing number of locations across the country. In 2004, the ethnically mixed Los Angeles suburb of Englewood voted to stop the building of a new Wal-Mart store, partly in the widespread belief that Wal-Mart destroyed local shopkeepers. One person attacked the company as "a modern-day plantation." A major real estate developer dropped plans to include Wal-Mart in a proposed New York City shopping mall in 2005 because of intense opposition from labor unions, neighborhood retailers, and city officials concerned about the effect the store would have on competitors. This would have been Wal-Mart's first New York City location. The company's decision to build a store in Jefferson, Wisconsin, in 2004 created a major battle among its residents. The formation of the Coalition for a Better Jefferson opposing Wal-Mart led to the launch of the pro-Wal-Mart Coalition for the Best Jefferson, headed by 69-year-old Charlotte Goers-Nevin. Goers-Nevin contended: "The number one complaint of the older people is they don't have a place to shop. Wal-Mart was going to be a good tax base for us, and it was going to be nice for the older people." Even though the town's aldermen voted against annexing the land needed for the new store, the controversy divided the city and led to a recall election against the alderman most against Wal-Mart's entry into town.[32]

In their enthusiasm to attack the company, anti-Wal-Mart interest groups sometimes used extreme measures. In December 2005, for example, the union-supported Wake Up Wal-Mart released a TV ad accusing Wal-Mart of violating religious values, supported by a letter from religious leaders attacking the company for paying low wages and offering poor benefits. The letter declared, "Jesus would not embrace Wal-Mart's values of greed and profits at any cost." The campaign was soon jokingly referred to in the media as "Where would Jesus shop?"[33]

By 2006, Wal-Mart's management was beginning to feel as if they were living in a punching bag. It appeared the company was being treated as a scapegoat for any big business wrongdoing and blamed for all of society's ills. It could be argued, for example, that low wages and benefits were typical for the retailing industry as a whole, not just Wal-Mart. Target, Kmart, and other mass merchandisers could be equally criticized for weakening downtowns, extracting public subsidies, and selling clothes made in sweatshops in developing nations. Even though Costco faced a class-action lawsuit alleging systematic discrimination against women, it never received the publicity Wal-Mart lawsuits generated.[34] In an interview with *Business Week,* Scott referred to comments made by a visiting CEO to Wal-Mart executives: "There isn't anything you are faced with, from a class action to the rest of the stuff, that we're not dealing with. The only difference is that yours is played out on the front page of the paper, and you never read about ours."[35] In response to the criticism that Wal-Mart's pay and benefits were too low, CEO Scott countered that people were continuing to apply for Wal-Mart jobs. He stated in Wal-Mart's *2006 Annual Report*: "At a store opening this year just outside Chicago, we received more than 25,000 applications for just 325 jobs."

Corporate Initiatives

To counter social criticism of the company and to regain control of its growth strategy, Wal-Mart management introduced a series of new programs.

Social Initiatives

Throughout its history, Wal-Mart has tried to be a good corporate citizen in those towns where it had facilities. When Hurricane Katrina ravaged America's Gulf Coast, Wal-Mart had its truckers haul $3 million of supplies to the area, arriving in many cases days before the Federal Emergency Management Agency (FEMA). The company also contributed $17 million in cash to relief efforts. Its long-praised efficiency was demonstrated when it reopened all but 13 of its affected stores by September 16, 2005—just three weeks after the storm. By then the company had located 97% of the employees displaced by the storm and offered them jobs at any Wal-Mart operation in the country. Thanks to the ability of Jason Jackson, Wal-Mart's Director of Business Continuity, who was able to plot the likely path of the storm, management was able to get the stores in the zone fully stocked with water, flashlights, batteries, and canned food. The result was a public relations success for the company.[36]

During October 2005, Wal-Mart offered $8.5 million worth of grants from its "Safe Neighborhood Heroes" program to recognize the efforts of hometown fire, police, rescue, and emergency medical service teams with direct financial contributions. "As a community, we must lean on each other to help those we serve," explained Betsy Reithemeyer, head of Wal-Mart & Sam's Club Foundation.[37] In addition, management announced in April 2006 that it planned to build more than 50 stores in struggling urban areas during the next two years. CEO Lee stated that the stores would generate between 15,000 and 25,000 new jobs in neighborhoods with high crime or unemployment rates, on sites that are environmentally contaminated, or in vacant buildings or malls in need of renovation.

Responding to criticism of its health care coverage, Wal-Mart's management introduced a "Value Plan." The new benefits plan offered health coverage to its employees at premiums ranging from $11 to $65 a month. The first three doctors' visits and three prescriptions were mostly paid by the company with only nominal payments needed by the employee. It did, however, contain fairly high deductibles, but the company offered tax-free health savings accounts to help employees pay out-of-pocket expenses up to the deductible amount. Wal-Mart also added health clinics to its stores to provide health care access to its associates and the local community.[38]

To deflect some of the criticism the company had been receiving regarding discrimination against women and minorities, management for the first time made public in April 2006 the data it had been providing the U.S. Equal Opportunity Employment Commission each year. The report stated that 32% of the 1.34 million Wal-Mart U.S. employees were minorities. Minorities were 21% of managers, 20% of professionals, and 33% of sales workers. Women accounted for 60% of the workforce, 39% of managers, and 75% of sales workers.[39]

Wal-Mart management realized that it had to do better in terms of dealing with its many stakeholders. Consequently, in February 2006, it established a new position of Senior Director of Stakeholder Engagement. According to the posted job description, the new position was to report to Wal-Mart's Vice President for Corporate Strategy and "will play a critical role in helping the company . . . create a new model of business engagement that uses market-based changes to create societal value." Explained spokesperson Sarah Clark, "We're trying to centralize our [social responsibility] efforts."[40] In March 2006, management announced that it planned to hire a Director of Global Ethics. The director's job was to manage the company's Global Ethics Office that had been established in 2004 and to ensure that the retailer's code of conduct was being applied across all its operations throughout the world. The person hired would lead the company's global ethics strategy and oversee ethics-related infrastructure, administration, and training.

In its quest for efficiency and low costs, Wal-Mart had inadvertently helped the environment when management decided in the early 1990s that much of the packaging being used by its suppliers was unnecessary. In one example, it told Wal-Mart suppliers to ship deodorants without their paperboard containers. Charles Fishman, in his book *The Wal-Mart Effect,* stated "It's a perfect Wal-Mart moment—the company used its insight and its muscle to help change the world. Millions of trees were not cut down, acres of cardboard were not manufactured only to be discarded, and one billion of deodorant boxes didn't end up in landfills each year. It's all unseen, all unnoticed, and all good."[41] Once they realized that business practice could be aligned with environmental needs, Wal-Mart's management expanded this program to private-label toys and other goods. In an October 24, 2005, presentation by CEO Lee Scott, he presented Wal-Mart's new environmental objectives: (1) to be supplied 100% by renewable energy, (2) to create zero waste, and (3) to sell products that sustain our resources and environment. Wanting to reduce the fuel usage of its trucking fleet, he added: "We will increase our fleet efficiency by 25% over the next three years and double it within ten years." Through improvements in technology, Scott stated that management intended to eliminate 30% of the energy used in Wal-Mart stores. Through a new process called "sandwich balers," at 99 Sam's Clubs and 548 Wal-Mart stores, the company was recycling plastic it used to throw away.

Growth Initiatives

Realizing that Target was its strongest U.S. competitor in discount mass merchandising, Wal-Mart's management felt in 2005 that it needed to overhaul its merchandise mix, stores, and image to go after higher-margin, discretionary sales. Greater emphasis was to be placed on more fashionable merchandise and more attractive advertisements. It wanted to entice its style-conscious customers who went to Wal-Mart to buy food and the basics, but avoided the fashion and home furnishings departments. Management worked to reduce clutter on the Wal-Mart sales floor. Less merchandise was to be stacked at the ends of the aisles. More room was to be allowed between apparel racks. Apparel areas were to receive imitation hardwood floors to suggest more upscale goods. More emphasis was to be placed on the George clothing line originally created in the United Kingdom by the ASDA retail chain. According to CEO Scott, the goal was not to ignore its current customers, but to offer additional goods not currently available to Wal-Mart shoppers. Said Scott: "The first thing you have to do is make sure you have the assortment that is broad enough that includes the customer's tastes and styles. That's where you end up with the new LCD TV, 400-thread-count sheets, and with more fashion."[42] One example of the company's new upscale emphasis was management's decision in April 2006 to double its selection of organic foods in its Supercenters.

In 2003, Wal-Mart broke tradition by opening new stores in a New York City suburban shopping mall and in a Los Angeles mall where a Macy's store had once operated. For the first time, Wal-Mart built its own addition to a regional mall near San Diego. The company was actually being welcomed in cities such as Los Angeles and Portland, Oregon, where its stores' presence helped to revive fading shopping malls that served primarily minority shoppers. Although the shopping mall didn't fit the discounters' traditional model of single-story units surrounded by acres of free parking, it was the only way large retailers could find enough space in urban locations. Target Corporation, in contrast, had been locating its stores in shopping malls for 25 years. A report by Goldman, Sachs & Company estimated that Target's mall stores could grow from 30 in 2003 to 150 by 2012. Real estate analysts calculated that the higher logistical costs of a mall location would be offset by higher store traffic and more sales per square foot.[43]

Wal-Mart's management has long wanted to add financial services to its mix of offerings. Its attempt to purchase an Oklahoma bank in 1999 was thwarted, as was its 2005 attempt to buy a California industrial loan corporation (ILC). Wal-Mart Stores' application to the Federal Deposit Insurance Corporation to charter a bank drew 1,550 mostly negative comments. Most of the negative comments stressed the dangers of an unregulated commercial company owning a federally insured bank. In 2005, Wal-Mart allowed 300 local and community banks to operate branches in more than 1,000 stores on long-term leases. Opponents feared that Wal-Mart might put its own banks in stores and thus devastate community banks. "If they get their hands on an ILC and get into financial trouble, they could swamp the FDIC fund, and we could have a repeat of the savings and loan collapse," stated Camden Fine, CEO of the Independent Community Bankers of America.[44]

Recent Events

During the summer of 2006, Wal-Mart continued to be in the news. Just a few months after announcing that the company was closing its stores in South Korea, management announced that Wal-Mart was also withdrawing from Germany. The sale of its 85 hypermarkets to rival Metro AG resulted in a $863 million pretax loss for the firm. The pullout left the company with only one European operation, ASDA, Britain's second largest supermarket chain.

In a surprise decision, management decided to agree to allow officials from China's state-run union to unionize employees in Wal-Mart's 60 retail stores in China. This amazed most industry analysts because of Wal-Mart's history and because most foreign firms did not have unions in China. According to Jonathan Dong, company spokesman, it was up to the employees at each store to decide if they wished to join the union. As of August 11, 2006, six of the 60 stores had unionized.[45]

On August 8, 2006, Wal-Mart management announced that it was raising starting pay at about a third of its U.S. stores by an average of 6%. It was also introducing wage caps for the first time on each type of job in all stores. This announcement came just two weeks after Chicago's City Council passed an ordinance in July 2006 requiring all retail stores with floor space over 90,000 square feet ("big box" stores) to pay a "living wage" and provide a minimum amount for benefits.[46]

On August 15, 2006 Wal-Mart's management announced that quarterly profits had declined for the first time in 10 years. Higher gasoline prices and the closing of German operations were blamed for a 26% decline in second-quarter profit. Net income fell to $2.1 billion from $2.8 billion a year earlier. With the price of gasoline averaging $2.92 per gallon, up 33% from 2005, Wal-Mart's customers were making fewer trips to the store, but spending more each visit. Net sales for the second quarter of fiscal year 2007 (ending July 31, 2006) were $84.5 billion, an increase of 11.3% over the second quarter of fiscal 2006. Quarterly income from continuing operations was up 4.6% versus a year earlier to nearly $3 billion. The second-quarter profit decline resulted in Wal-Mart's shares falling $.55 to $44.55 at the close of business on August 15, 2006.

What Next?

H. Lee Scott would never forget his first meeting with Sam Walton. "How old are you?" Walton asked the then 30-year-old Scott, who had just taken a job managing Wal-Mart's trucking fleet. "Do you think you can do this job?" asked Walton. When Scott said yes, Walton agreed and said, "I reckon you can." More than 20 years later, as Wal-Mart's CEO, Scott faced his toughest challenge yet: keeping the world's biggest retailer on its phenomenal roll and delivering the huge sales and earnings increases that investors had come to expect from Wal-Mart over the years—all while deflecting increasing criticism of his company's business practices. Analysts had correctly projected that Wal-Mart would surpass General Motors to be ranked number one in revenue on the *Fortune* 500 list in 2000. The combination of growth and acquisition had caused revenue increases every year. Increasing profits followed higher sales. How could this be continued if Wal-Mart's management allowed costs to increase and service to lag?

Wal-Mart Stores, Inc., revolutionized American retailing with its focus on low costs, high customer service, and everyday low pricing to drive sales. Although the company had suffered through some years of lagging performance, it experienced big gains from its move into the grocery business with one-stop Supercenters and into international markets with acquisitions, joint ventures, and new ventures. To keep it all going and growing was a major challenge. As the largest retailer and firm in the world, the company and its leadership were challenged to find new areas to continue to grow sales and profits into the future. Lee Scott knew that an ambitious expansion program was called for to allow the company to meet these objectives, both at home and abroad. The company also needed a strong program to pre-empt its social critics, instead of always being on the defensive. At the same time, Scott realized that Wal-Mart could not allow itself to emphasize social over business objectives.

Notes

1. "Letter to Shareholders," *2006 Annual Report,* Wal-Mart Stores, Inc., p. i.
2. J. Unseem, "One Nation under Wal-Mart," *Fortune* (March 3, 2003), pp. 65–78; A. Bianco and W. Zellner, "Is Wal-Mart Too Powerful?" *Business Week* (October 6, 2003), pp. 100–110; "Opening Up the Big Box," *Economist* (February 25, 2006), p. 80.
3. Letter to Shareholders, *2006 Annual Report,* pp. 12–13.
4. R. Walberg, "Can Wal-Mart's PR Campaign Save Its Stock?" *Street Patrol* (April 14, 2005).
5. "The Top Ten," *Forbes* (October 10, 2005), p. 100 and "Holdings of Major Shareholders," *Notice of 2006 Annual Shareholders' Meeting* (April 14, 2006), p. 26.
6. L. Grant, "Wal-Mart Sets Sights on Target While Keeping Core Customers," *USA Today* (August 5, 2005), pp. 1B and 2B.
7. P. Burrows, "Stopping the Sprawl at HP," *Business Week* (May 29, 2006), pp. 54–56.
8. J. Loades-Carter, "Carrefour to Open 1,000 New Stores as Profits Fall," *Financial Times* (March 9, 2006).
9. J. Ewing, "Wal-Mart: Local Pipsqueak," *Business Week* (April 11, 2005), p. 54.
10. S. Goldstein, "Wal-Mart's U.K. Market Share Eases," *MarketWatch* (March 9, 2006).
11. "Wal-Mart to Hire Up to 150,000 in China," *St. Cloud Times* (March 21, 2006), p. 6A.
12. S. Izumi, "Wal-Mart Sets $1b in Rescue for Seiyu," *Reuters* (November 2, 2005).
13. C. Sang-Hun, "Wal-Mart Selling Stores and Leaving South Korea," *International Herald Tribune* (May 23, 2006).
14. D. Faber, "With a Small-Town Culture, Wal-Mart Dominates," *CNBC* (November 10, 2004).
15. "Wal-Mart Tries to Create Hip Image," *St. Cloud Times* (February 21, 2006), p. 6A.
16. A. Bianco and W. Zellner, "Is Wal-Mart Too Powerful?" *Business Week* (October 6, 2003), pp. 100–110.
17. A. Bianco, "No Union, Please, We're Wal-Mart," *Business Week* (February 13, 2006), p. 80.
18. L. Scott, "To Our Shareholders, Associates, and Customers," *2006 Annual Report,* Wal-Mart Corporation, p. 12.
19. D. McGinn, "Wal-Mart Hits the Wall," *Newsweek* (November 14, 2005), pp. 42–44.
20. "This Year's Political Punch-Bag?" *The Economist* (January 21, 2006), p. 35.
21. C. Rousseau, "Internal Scrutiny Leads to Wal-Mart Request for Director's Resignation," *USA Today* (March 28, 2005), p. 7B.
22. S. Armour and D. Leinwand, "120 Arrested on Immigration Violations at Wal-Mart Site," *USA Today* (November 8, 2005), p. 4B.
23. H. Meyerson, "Former Wal-Mart Executive Jim Bill Lynn Blows Whistle on Factory Inspection Scam," *The American Prospect* (December 2005).
24. B. Keck, "Wal-Mart Files Motion to Dismiss Class Action Lawsuit," *Wal-Mart News Release* (February 13, 2006).
25. L. Grant, "Retail Giant Wal-Mart Faces Challenges on Many Fronts," *USA Today* (November 11, 2003), pp. 1B-2B.
26. L. Featherstone, "Will Labor Take the Wal-Mart Challenge?" *The Nation* (June 28, 2004).
27. A. Bianco (2006), pp. 78–81.
28. J. Hempel, "Labor Loves Wal-Mart's Low Prices," *Business Week* (February 13, 2006), p. 14.
29. D. McGinn (2005), p. 43.
30. "Fewer Smiles in the Aisles," *Business Week* (April 28, 2003), p. 10.
31. "The Behemoth from Bentonville," *The Economist* (February 25, 2006), pp. 85–86.
32. R. Epstein, "Wal-Mart Boosters Try to Oust Jefferson, WI Alderman Who Opposed New Store," *Milwaukee Journal-Sentinel* (July 23, 2005).
33. P. Krugman, "Big Box Balderdash," *The New York Times* (December 12, 2005).

34. J. Milchen, "Is Wal-Mart the Right Target?" *ReclaimDemocracy.org* (November 15, 2005).
35. R. Berner, "Lee Scott on Why Wal-Mart Is Playing Nicer," *Business Week* (October 3, 2005), p. 95.
36. D. Leonard, "The Only Lifeline Was the Wal-Mart," *Fortune* (October 3, 2005), pp. 74–77.
37. Press Release, "Wal-Mart Donates $8.5 Million to Benefit Police, Fire, Rescue and Emergency Medical Teams," *Wal-Mart Company* (October 12, 2005).
38. "Under Fire, a Giant Employer Offers a Useful Health Plan," *USA Today* (November 7, 2005), p. 12A.
39. "Wal-Mart Opens Books on Work Force Diversity," *St. Cloud Times* (April 12, 2006), p. 8A.
40. A. Bernstein, "A Social Strategist for Wal-Mart," *Business Week* (February 6, 2006), p. 11.
41. C. Fishman, *The Wal-Mart Effect,* Penguin Press, as reported by R. Juskalian, "A Fresh Look at Wal-Mart's Power," *USA Today* (January 30, 2006), p. 9B.
42. L. Grant (2005), pp. 1B and 2B.
43. W. Zellner, "Call It Wal-Mart," *Business Week* (July 14, 2003), pp. 40–42.
44. L. Grant, "Wal-Mart Maintains Bank Hopes Despite Greenspan Urging Change in Law," *USA Today* (January 27, 2006), p. 8B.
45. "Wal-Mart to Allow Workers to Join Unions in China," *Reuters* (August 11, 2006).
46. "Wal-Mart Raises Pay, Includes Wage Cap," *St. Cloud (MN) Times* (August 8, 2006), p. 4A.

CASE 20

The Home Depot, Inc. (2006): Executive Leadership

J. David Hunger and Thomas L. Wheelen

Reflecting on the overall performance of Home Depot since he became CEO in December 2000, Bob Nardelli could only be pleased.

> From 2000 to 2005, we opened more than 900 stores, including our 2,000th in December 2005. In 2000, we reported $45.7 billion in annual sales; five years later, our sales nearly doubled, to $81.5 billion. Over the same period, our operating margin grew 230 basis points, from 9.2 percent to 11.5 percent, and our earnings per share more than doubled from $1.10 to $2.72. Since 2000, we returned nearly $13 billion, or approximately 59 percent of our cumulative earnings, to shareholders in the form of dividends and share repurchases. And we achieved EPS growth of at least 20 percent in each of the past four years.
>
> In short, over the past several years, we've been able to deliver sustainable, predictable, and profitable growth, creating a company that has the strongest balance sheet in the industry and tremendous potential for future growth.
>
> Reflecting the hard work and dedication of our 345,000 associates, fiscal year 2005 was another defining year for The Home Depot. We achieved record earnings per share ($2.72, up 20.4 percent), record operating margin (11.5 percent), and record net earnings ($5.8 billion, up 16.7 percent). Our financial success has allowed us to deliver on our commitment to create shareholder value.[1]

Nardelli noted that the average ticket sale per customer had reached an all-time high of $57.98 in 2005, up 5.6% from the previous year. The Home Depot had become an important U.S. retailer of major home appliances. In just a few years, the company had gone from zero to number 3 in the core appliance market share, securing 10% of the U.S. market by the end of 2005. Nardelli had successfully pushed to improve the efficiency of Home Depot's operations though the introduction of self-checkout, Back End Automation and Re-engineering (BEAR), and centralized automated replenishment. The 21.4% growth in services revenue during 2005 was a good indication that the company had successfully extended its business from just selling home improvement products to also installing the products. To better serve the professional contractor market, the company had completed 21 acquisitions. In 2005 alone, Nardelli had announced the purchase of Hughes Supply, the largest acquisition in Home Depot's history. In addition, the company had successfully expanded across the border to become the largest home improvement retailer in both Canada and Mexico. Given this performance, it was easy to understand why Home Depot had been selected by *Fortune* magazine as the "Most Admired Specialty Retailer" for 2005!

With such positive accomplishments, why had Home Depot's common stock fallen 30% since Nardelli had taken charge of the company? The company's own Proxy Statement for the May 25, 2006 shareholders' meeting compared the performance of Home Depot's common stock with that of the S&P 500 Index and the S&P Retail Composite Index. It noted that $100 invested in January 26, 2001, in each would have resulted in $150.09 for the S&P Retail Composite, $102.99 for the S&P 500, but only $92.77 for Home Depot stock!

In addition, Nardelli was increasingly being attacked for having "excessive compensation," given the firm's poor stock performance. One shareholder proposal for the 2006 annual meeting stated the following:

> In each of the last three years, CEO Nardelli has been paid a base salary of more than $1,800,000, well in excess of the IRS cap for deductibility of non-performance-based compensation. His bonus in each of those years has been at least $4,000,000, and he was awarded restricted stock valued at over $8,000,000 in 2002, 2003, and 2004. Mr. Nardelli has also received a disturbingly large amount of compensation in the form of "loan forgiveness" and tax gross-ups related to that forgiveness, which totaled over $3,000,000 in each of the past three years.

In an interview with a *Business Week* reporter in July 2006, Nardelli was asked why he changed the metrics on which he was judged in the middle of the game: "You signed on to the idea that your performance would be gauged relative to stock price. That didn't go well, so you changed it so that your performance is tied with the performance of earnings." He responded that he and the board felt that the leadership team should be measured on things over which the team had direct control, such as earnings per share, instead of stock price compared to the retail index.[2] Even though Nardelli had been able to explain the change in his performance measurement, it didn't help that he was one of the six executives highlighted in a July 24, 2006, *Fortune* article entitled "The Real CEO Pay Problem."[3]

With sales at an all-time high and earnings per share growing 147% in the previous five years, why was the financial community downgrading Home Depot stock and why were the shareholders so upset? Although the stock price had dropped somewhat, cash dividends per share had increased from just $.05 in 1996 to $.16 in 2000 to a high of $.40 in 2005. The company had paid out a total of $857 million in cash dividends to its shareholders in 2005. Isn't Nardelli doing what he is supposed to be doing? What else do they want from a CEO?

The Home Depot, Inc.

Founded in Atlanta, Georgia, in 1978, Home Depot was the world's largest home improvement retailer and the second largest retailer (after Wal-Mart) in the United States based on net sales for the 2005 fiscal year ended January 29, 2006. The Home Depot stores sold a wide assortment of building materials and home-improvement and lawn and garden products, and they provided a number of services such as design and installation. In addition to the Home Depot stores, the company had a store format called EXPO Design Center that sold products and services primarily for home decorating and remodeling projects and two store formats focused on professional customers called Home Depot Supply and Home

Depot Landscaping Supply. As of August 29, 2006, the company operated 1,832 Home Depot stores in all 50 states and the District of Columbia, Puerto Rico, and the Virgin Islands, plus 143 stores in Canada and 57 in Mexico. It also operated 34 EXPO Design Center locations in the United States, 900 Home Depot Supply locations (including 11 Contractor's Warehouse locations) in 44 states and Canada, and 11 Home Depot Landscape Supply stores in the Atlanta and Dallas–Fort Worth areas. The company also had two Home Depot Floor Stores in Texas and Florida that primarily sold flooring products.

The average Home Depot store had approximately 105,000 square feet of indoor selling space and an additional 23,000 square feet of outside garden center, including houseplant enclosures. The stores stocked approximately 35,000–45,000 different kinds of building materials, home improvement products, and lawn and garden supplies. In addition, Home Depot stores offered installation services for many products. Including its recent acquisition of Hughes Supply, the company employed approximately 355,000 associates.

Retail industry analysts had credited Home Depot with being a leading innovator in retailing, by combining the economies of warehouse-format stores with a high level of customer service. Throughout most of its history, the company augmented that concept with a corporate culture that valued decentralized management and decision making, entrepreneurial innovation and risk taking, and high levels of employee commitment and enthusiasm.

One example of the company's operational excellence was its response to Hurricane Katrina in 2005. Home Depot had started mobilizing four days before Katrina hit the U.S. Gulf Coast. Two days before landfall, maintenance teams battened down stores in the hurricane's projected path, while electrical generators and hundreds of extra workers were moved into place. A day after the storm, all but 10 of the company's 33 stores in Katrina's impact zone were open. Within a week, five of its nine New Orleans stores were open.[4]

The stores served the Do-It-Yourself (D-I-Y) person who liked to do his or her own projects and installations, the Do-It-For-Me (D-I-F-M) customer who preferred to pay someone else to do the installations, and Professional Customers, such as home improvement contractors, building maintenance professionals, interior designers, and other professionals. Although the company had been trying to increase its sales to professional customers for a number of years, it had been unable to do so through its retail stores. Home building contractors, for example, did not wish to buy carpet from Home Depot stores because they used outside contractors. The builders wanted a single company to handle both carpet and installation.

In order to better serve the professional customer, Home Depot acquired a number of businesses, such as Apex Supply Company, Contractors' Warehouse, Creative Touch Interiors, National Waterworks, White Cap Construction, Williams Brothers Lumber, and Hughes Supply, to create the Home Depot Supply business unit. Home Depot Supply distributed products and sold installation services primarily to professional business contractors, businesses, and municipalities and operated in three primary areas:

- Maintenance, Repair, and Operations (MRO) supplied maintenance, repair, and operating products primarily to multifamily housing, hospitality, and lodging facilities.
- Builder provided products and arranged installation services for production home builders.
- Professional Supply distributed specialty hardware, tools, and materials to construction contractors.

History

The Home Depot, Inc., was a great success story of three men creating a new business that redefined the industry. By 2000, the company had reached the $40 billion in revenues mark faster than had any retailer in U.S. history. The founders then left the management of the company in the hands of a new management team, who it was hoped would continue the company's success.

Founders Grow an Entrepreneurial Venture: 1978 to 2000[5]

Bernard Marcus began his career in the retail industry in a small pharmacy in Millburn, New Jersey. He later joined the Two Guys Discount Chain to manage its drug and cosmetics departments and eventually became the Vice President of Merchandising and Advertising for the parent company, Vornado, Inc. In 1972 he moved into the Do-It-Yourself home improvement sector as President and Chairman of the Board at Handy Dan/Handy City. The parent company, Daylin, Inc., was chaired by Sanford Sigoloff. He and Marcus had a strong difference of opinion over control, and one Friday at 5:00 PM in 1978, Marcus and two other Handy Dan top executives were discharged.

That weekend, Home Depot was born when the three men—Bernard Marcus, Arthur Blank, and Kenneth G. Langone—laid out plans for the Do-It-Yourself chain. Marcus and Blank were to manage the new venture with Langone providing the seed money to get started. Additional capital was provided by investment firms that included Invemed of New York as well as private investors.

When the first stores opened in Atlanta in 1979, the company leased space in three former Treasury Discount Stores with 60,000 square feet each. All three were suburban locations in the northern half of the city. Industry experts gave Home Depot 10-to-1 odds it would fail. In 1980, a fourth Atlanta stored opened, and the company had annual sales of $22.3 million. The following year, Home Depot ventured beyond Atlanta to open four stores in South Florida and also had its first public offering at $12 a share. By early 1990, its stock had soared by 7,019% and split eight times. In May 1995, an original share was worth $26,300.

The company was voted the "Retailer of the Year" in the home center industry in 1982 and had its first stock splits. By 1983, Marcus was a nationally recognized leader in the Do-It-Yourself industry. Home Depot's strong drawing power became evident as customers passively waited in long checkout lines. In 1984, Home Depot's common stock was listed on the New York Stock Exchange. It was traded under the symbol "HD" and was included in the Standard & Poor's 500 Index.

In 1989 all stores began using Universal Product Code (UPC) scanning systems to speed checkout time. The company's satellite data communications network installation improved management communication and training. On its tenth anniversary, Home Depot opened its 100th store (in Atlanta) and by the year's end had become the nation's largest home center chain.

To handle more volume per store, Home Depot developed and tested in 1990 a new store productivity improvement (SPI) program designed to make more effective use of existing and new store space and to allow for more rapid replenishment of merchandise on the sales floor. The SPI program involved the renovation of portions of certain existing stores and an improved design for new stores with the goal of enhanced customer access, reducing customer shopping time, and streamlining merchandise stocking and delivery. As part of SPI, the company also experimented with modified store layouts, materials handling techniques, and operations.

The company's SPI program proved successful and was implemented in substantially all new stores and in selected existing stores. Home Depot also continued to introduce or refine a number of merchandising programs. Included among such programs were the introduction of full-service, in-store interior decorating centers staffed by designers and an expanded assortment in its lighting department.

In 1991, management created a new division, EXPO Design Centers. EXPO Design Centers appealed to the upscale homeowner through their extensive use of computer-aided design technology by the store's creative coordination. These features were of assistance to customers remodeling their bathrooms and kitchens. From 1991 through 1995, many of the new merchandising techniques developed for the Home Depot EXPO were transferred to the entire chain.

During 1992, the company's "installed sales program," which had been tested in three selected markets in 1990, became available in 122 stores in 10 markets. This program targeted the buy-it-yourself customer, who would purchase an item but did not have either the desire or the ability to install the item.

Home Depot entered the Canadian market in 1994 through its acquisition of Aikenhead's Home Improvement Warehouse. Home Depot's first Mexican store opened in 1998. On a long-term basis, the company anticipated that success in Mexico could lead to more opportunities throughout Central and South America. In 1995, *Fortune* included Home Depot in its list of "America's Most Admired Corporations."

During 1995, the company opened CrossRoads, its first rural chain store, in Quincy, Illinois. A second store was opened in Columbus, Missouri, in 1996. The target market for this chain was farmers and ranchers who shopped in smaller, rural towns across America. At that time, there were about 100 farm and home retailers, with about 850 stores and annual sales of $6 billion. A typical CrossRoads store had 117,000 square feet of inside retail space, plus a 100,000-square-foot lumberyard. In contrast, the average Tractor Supply Company store (a competitor) was about one tenth the size of a CrossRoads store and did not have a lumberyard. In addition to carrying the typical Home Depot products, CrossRoads carried pet supplies, truck and tractor tires and parts, work clothing, farm animal medicines, feed and storage tanks, barbed wire, books (such as *Raising Sheep the Modern Way*), and other items. The company soon terminated this strategy because the stores did not generate sales and profits that Home Depot expected. The existing CrossRoads stores were renamed Home Depot stores.

In 1996, the company acquired Maintenance Warehouse/America Corporation, which was the leading direct mail marketer of maintenance, repair, and operating products to the United States building and facilities in management market. Home Depot's management felt this was "an important step towards strengthening our position with professional business customers."[6] The company's long-term goal was to capture 10% of this market.

During the 1990s, Home Depot built new stores not only within the continental United States, but also in Alaska, Puerto Rico, Canada, and Mexico. This global expansion fit the company's stated vision to be one of the most successful retailers in the next millennium.

During 2000, the company launched its online store, www.homedepot.com. The Home Depot continued to grow internationally by opening its first store in Argentina and establishing the Olympic Job Program in Puerto Rico. The company celebrated the opening of its 1,000th store and its surpassing the one-week $1 billion sales mark for the first time in May. Bernard Marcus and Arthur Blank, the two founders responsible for actively managing the growth of the company, announced that they were retiring from the company and began a search for their replacement.

Expansion Continues in the Nardelli Era: 2001–Present

In December 2000, Arthur Blank retired as President and CEO of Home Depot and joined Bernard Marcus as Co-Chairman of the Board. Blank was replaced by Robert L. Nardelli, who came to the company from a successful career at General Electric. In the last "Founders' Letter" appearing in the *2000 Home Depot Annual Report,* Blank and Marcus gave their blessing to the new management team.

> We're very optimistic. Our optimism is built on our associates' dedication and commitment to our "orange-blooded" entrepreneurial spirit, which embraces change yet retains our core values of excellent customer service, respect for all people and giving back to the community. Our

> optimism is also built on our ability to bring new leadership into the executive ranks—to seek out new talent, experience and vision. That's why we are so excited by Bob Nardelli, one of the country's top business leaders, as President and CEO. His fresh perspective and business insight will take us to the next level. While going outside the businesses in recruiting executive talent is not rare in other industries, it is somewhat rare in retailing. But we're a unique company seeking a unique successor.

Blank left the Board of Directors after the 2001 fiscal year, followed one year later by Marcus—leaving only Kenneth Langone serving on the Board as the last member of the founding team. In addition to serving as President and CEO, Bob Nardelli assumed the position of Chairman of the Board in January 2002.

From 2001 to 2006, Home Depot continued to grow through new store locations, new store formats, and acquisitions. It opened 199 new store locations during 2001, 199 in 2002, 175 in 2003, 183 in 2004, and 152 in 2005, for a total of 908 new Home Depot stores during this period. The 100th Canadian store opened in 2003. In terms of new store formats, the company opened its first Home Depot Landscape Supply store in Atlanta and its first Home Depot Supply store in Dallas during 2002. It also launched the first home improvement online gift registry in 2004. The company spent $14 billion in renovating outdated stores, investing in new technology such as self-checkout lanes and cordless scan guns, and upgrading merchandise. At the end of fiscal 2004, the company entered into an agreement to lease commercial office space in Shanghai to support a future retail initiative in China.

Acquisitions proceeded during this time period at an increasing pace. To expand its position in Mexico, Home Depot acquired Total Home, a Mexican home-improvement chain, in 2001. It then became the market leader in Mexico in 2005 by purchasing Home Mart, the second-largest home improvement retailer in Mexico. To expand its professional service capabilities for housing contractors, the company acquired a number of firms including National Waterworks, Apex Supply Company, Creative Touch Interiors, William Brothers Lumber Company, White Cap Construction, Contractors' Warehouse, and Chem-Dry. The company completed a total of 40 acquisitions from 2001 to 2006 with 21 of these acquisitions being completed in 2005 alone. In 2006, the company acquired Hughes Supply, Inc., a leading distributor of construction and repair products at a cost of $3.5 billion—effectively doubling Home Depot Supply's size and adding $4.0 billion to Home Depot's long-term debt to finance the purchase. With the addition of Hughes Supply, Home Depot became the largest diversified wholesale distributor of construction, repair, and maintenance-related products in the United States. According to *Value Line,* by April 2006, sales at Home Depot Supply accounted for approximately 10 percent of the company's total sales.[7]

Current Strategic Posture

The company adopted a new slogan: "Improve Everything We Touch." This statement was placed on employee wristbands and break-room signs, among other locations. According to CEO Nardelli, the company did a lot of testing to find a slogan that wouldn't be time sensitive. "You can improve everything you touch whether you're a lot attendant, store manager, or chairman of the company."[8]

The company's overall strategy was composed of what Nardelli called the 3Es: *Enhancing the Core, Extending the Business, and Expanding the Market.* Enhancing the Core meant that the Home Depot stores were continually being modernized and their product lines updated to increase sales of current products to current customers. This was measured on the basis of an increasing average ticket paid by store customers and by improving store productivity. Extending the Business meant that the primary retail business of the company was being expanded into multiple channels, such as homedepot.com and catalogs, such as *10 Crescent*

Lane, and by selling new products and services, such as flooring and Chem-Dry carpet-cleaning services. As another example, the company was testing gas stations outside a handful of its U.S. stores. Expanding the Market meant that the corporation was continually expanding into new markets with new products to better serve existing customers and attracts new ones. This was being accomplished by opening Home Depot stores in other countries and by offering new building supply services to professional customers, such as home building contractors. Many of the new products and services, especially those aimed at the professional market, were being obtained through acquisitions of existing companies.

In a January 2006 meeting with the financial community, Home Depot's management announced their plans for the company's growth to 2010. According to CEO Nardelli, "Over the next five years, The Home Depot expects to maintain and grow its leadership position in home improvement retail worldwide. At the same time, we expect to become the nation's largest diversified wholesale distributor, become number one in services and will dramatically increase our direct-to-consumer channels." The company's 2010 targets included:

- Compounded annual sales growth of 9%–12%
- Compounded earnings per share growth of 10%–14%
- 400–500 new store openings—adding 40–55 million new square feet
- Operating margin increases 50–100 basis points
- Cumulative operating cash flow of $50 billion
- Cumulative capital expenditures of $17–20 billion
- Grow Home Depot Supply sales to $23–27 billion

Although the planned number of new Home Depot stores was about half the number opened in the previous five years, CEO Nardelli contended that the slower growth in new retail stores would be made up by the high pace of growth in the retail business overall.[8]

Home Depot's plans for growth hinged on projected market opportunities evolving by 2010:

- $200 billion U.S. do-it-yourself market
- $110 billion services market (representing the labor component)
- More than $250 billion international do-it-yourself market
- More than $410 billion professional market

Carol Liebert, Executive Vice President of Home Depot Stores, announced that the company was leveraging technology to increase efficiency and create a fun, productive shopping environment for customers. New operational initiatives should free associates to spend more time serving customers. By 2010, according to Liebert, the company expected that 70% of operational hours would be dedicated to the selling floor, an industry-leading average. According to Frank Blake, Executive Vice President of Business Development and Corporate Operations, services should continue to grow as a percentage of total revenue. "With more than 11,000 installations per day, The Home Depot is emerging as a major force in the services area, and we expect to continue our double-digit growth through 2010, becoming number one in that market." By 2010, he expected that 5% to 6% of Home Depot sales would come from services. Although the direct-to-consumer division was a small contributor to Home Depot's 2006 revenue, CEO Nardelli felt that this division had the potential to become a billon-dollar business by 2010. He also felt that Home Depot Supply would generate 18% to 19% of overall sales by 2010. By the end of the decade, Nardelli projected that Home Depot Supply would operate more than 1,500 locations in all 50 states. "We are poised for dramatic growth over the next five years across our business," said Nardelli. "Our planned acquisition of Hughes Supply is a great example of how we are rapidly replicating in the professional market the same type of transformation that we brought to the home improvement retail market," he noted.[9]

Management's announcement of Home Depot's new five-year plan received a "lukewarm" response from the financial community. Home Depot's growth in new store openings was clearly slowing as the company reached market saturation. In contrast, rival Lowe's had announced plans to open 150 to 160 new stores in both 2006 and 2007 as it continued its expansion to large U.S. cities. In response to questions, Nardelli stated that the company planned to put fewer stores in direct competition with existing stores. "I don't want to use the word saturation, because that is a sort of self-fulfilling prophecy. . . . The new store growth has been modified to reflect the realities of the market."[10]

Corporate Culture

Entrepreneurial Culture of Founders

The culture at Home Depot had traditionally been characterized by the phrase, "Guess what happened to me at Home Depot?" This phrase showed Home Depot's bond with its customers and the communities in which it had stores and was recognition of superb service. Home Depot called this its "orange-blooded culture."

The orange-blooded culture emphasized individuality, informality, nonconformity, growth, and pride. These traits reflected those of the founders of the company. The culture was "really a reflection of Bernie and me," said Blank. "We're not formal, stuffy folks. We hang pretty loose. We've got a lot of young people. We want them to feel comfortable."[11]

Under the founders, the importance of the individual to the success of the whole venture had been consistently emphasized. Marcus's statements bear this out: "We know that one person can make a difference, and that is what is so unique about The Home Depot. It doesn't matter where our associates work in our company, they can all make a difference."[12] While emphasizing the opportunities for advancement at Home Depot, Marcus decried the kind of "cradle to grave" job that used to be the ideal in America and is the norm in Japan. To him, this was "a kind of serfdom."[13] Home Depot attempted to provide excellent wages and benefits, and superior training and advancement opportunities, while encouraging independent thinking and initiative.

Informality had always been appropriate at Home Depot during the Blank and Marcus years. Spitballs often flew at board meetings and there was always someone around to make sure that ties got properly trimmed. When executives visited stores, they went on their own without an entourage. Most managers had worked the floors and knew the business from the ground up. They were approachable and employees frequently came forward with ideas and suggestions.

Nonconformity had been evident in many different areas of the company—from the initial warehouse concept to the size and variety of merchandise to human resource practices. Both Marcus and Blank had flouted conventional corporate rules that they believed foiled innovation. Training employees at all levels was felt to be one of the most powerful means of transmitting corporate culture, and Home Depot used it extensively. One analyst noted that Home Depot (in a reverse of the "top-to-bottom" training sequence in most organizations) trained the carryout people first: "The logic is that the guy who helps you to your car is the last employee you come in contact with, and they want that contact to be positive."[14]

The Home Depot had been built on a set of values that fostered strong relationships with its key constituencies. The company's management embraced the values of taking care of its people, encouraging an entrepreneurial spirit, treating each other with respect, and being committed to the highest standards. For the customers, management believed that excellent customer service was the key to company success, and that giving back to the communities it served was part of its commitment to the customer. Importantly, management believed that if all employees lived all of these values, they would also create shareholder value.

Blank and Marcus were often asked how the company had managed to grow so fast for as long as it had and still be successful, both financially and with its customers. They responded that aggressive growth required adapting to change, but continued success required holding fast to the culture and values of the company as the company grew.[15]

Culture Change Under New Management

The informal, entrepreneurial culture fostered by the founders, who relied more on instincts than on analytical tools, had successfully built Home Depot. By the end of the 1990s, however, this decentralized culture had, according to analysts, become partially responsible for the firm's stagnation in sales growth. The company "grew so fast the wheels were starting to come off," commented Edward Lawler III, a professor at the University of Southern California.[16]

The job facing Bob Nardelli when he assumed the CEO position in December 2000 was to organize the company and get Home Depot back on the fast track. Five years later, Bob Nardelli was still putting his personal stamp on what had been a decentralized entrepreneurial venture under founders Arthur Blank and Bernie Marcus. The informal (perhaps even chaotic) style of the founders was being replaced by the more military style of Nardelli. Although Nardelli had never actually served in the armed forces, he had always wanted to be in the military. He had been first alternate to the U.S. Military Academy. After graduating from Western Illinois University, his draft number was called, but he did not pass the physical. Nardelli's passion for the military is reflected in his emphasis on military efficiency and in hiring veterans. Of the 1,142 people hired into the store leadership program since it was launched in 2002, 528 of them were junior military officers known as "Bob's Army." By 2006, more than 100 of these ex-officers were managing Home Depot stores. In honor of employees serving in Iraq, Afghanistan, and elsewhere, 1,800 blue star banners hang in the main hallway of corporate headquarters.

Importing ideas, people, and management concepts from the military was one way to reshape an increasingly unwieldy Home Depot into a more centralized and efficient organization. Under Nardelli, the emphasis was on building a disciplined manager corps, one predisposed to following orders, operating in high-pressure environments, and executing with high standards.[17] The constant flow of ideas and suggestions flowing up the organization from Home Depot's many employees was being replaced by major decisions and goals flowing down from top management. According to Joe DeAngelo, Executive Vice President of Home Depot Supply and a previous GE manager, "There's no question; Bob's the general."[18]

The cultural change in Home Depot was making it a very different type of company from Lowe's, a primary competitor. At Lowe's the culture was described as being demanding, but low-profile, collaborative, and collegial.

Interviews by *Business Week* with 11 former Home Depot executives revealed that Nardelli's culture change was facing some stiff resistance. Some described a demoralized staff and reported that a "culture of fear" was causing customer service to decline. Before Nardelli's arrival, most store managers used "tribal knowledge," based on years of experience about what sold and what didn't, to make decisions. Now they nervously clicked through Blackberries at the end of each week, hoping that they "made plan," a combination of sales and profit targets. The once-heavy ranks of full-time store employees had been replaced with part-timers to reduce labor costs. Underperforming managers were routinely asked to leave the company. Since 2001, 98% of Home Depot's 170 top executives had left the company. Fifty-six percent of headquarters personnel were hired from outside the company. Home Depot insiders sometimes referred to the firm as "Home GEpot" because of the increasing number of managers being hired from General Electric. Such poor morale was thought by some to lead to less customer satisfaction.[19]

The University of Michigan's American Customer Satisfaction Index, compiled in 2005, revealed that Home Depot, with a score of 67, had slipped to last place among major U.S. retailers. Home Depot's score had dropped from 73 in 2004 and was 11 points lower than Lowe's and three points lower than Kmart's. A former Home Depot executive stated that Nardelli's effort to measure good customer service, instead of inspiring it, was to blame. "My perception is that the mechanics are there. The soul isn't."[20]

When CEO Nardelli was asked why so many top executives left Home Depot in his first year as CEO, he responded,

> You've got to understand that a lot of these people had made a ton of money. The stock split 12 or 13 times times in the early years and so, financially, they had become independent at an early age. Some said, "Bob I agree we need to transform, but I don't think I want to go through that." There are no hard feelings and I stay in touch.[21]

As of March 8, 2006, every Home Depot employee was expected to keep a copy of a 24-page booklet entitled *How to Be Orange Every Day* in their apron pockets. The booklet contained aphorisms such as "Customers cannot buy what we do not have" and "We create an atmosphere of high-energy fun." This program was introduced by Carl Liebert III, Executive Vice President of Home Depot, in an effort to better align employees with corporate goals and objectives and thus improve customer service. Commented Liebert, "I think about that line from *A Few Good Men* when Jack Nicholson says: 'Are we clear?' and Tom Cruise says: 'Crystal.' I love that." A graduate of the U.S. Naval Academy, Liebert had supervised Six Sigma programs at GE's Consumer Products unit, followed by managing a division at Circuit City. After taking over Home Depot's stores in the United States and Mexico in 2004, Liebert was working to make the company operate with a single mind rather than as a set of independent store operators. "What worked 20 years ago may not work today," explained Liebert. "It's as simple as warfare. We don't fight wars the way we used to."[22] Home Depot executives noted that internal polling showed that customer satisfaction was improving in 2006.

Although the critics of Nardelli's management style admitted to being in awe of his command of minute details, they questioned whether the manufacturing business model that worked well for him at GE—squeezing efficiencies out of the core business while acquiring new businesses—could work in a retail environment where taking care of customers is key. Steve Mahurin, Chief Merchandising Officer at True Value Company and a former Senior Vice President for merchandising at Home Depot, remarked: "Bob has brought a lot of operational efficiencies that Home Depot needed, but he failed to keep the orange-blooded, entrepreneurial spirit alive. Home Depot is now a factory."[23] For his part, Nardelli responded that this was the third time that his business model has been successful and rejected the idea that he has created a culture of fear. "The only reason you should be fearful is if you don't want to make the commitment." He made no apologies for getting rid of underperforming employees and managers in order to achieve financial objectives. "We couldn't have done this by saying, 'Run slower, jump lower, and just kind of get by,'" insists Nardelli. "So I will never apologize for setting the bar high."[24]

Community Involvement and Business Ethics

From its earliest years, Home Depot recognized its role in the community and strove to be known as a good "corporate citizen." In one community, a woman lost her uninsured home and teen-aged son to a fire. Home Depot's management responded, along with other residents, by providing thousands of dollars of free materials and supplies to assist in the rebuilding effort. In another incident, a community organization sponsored a graffiti cleanup, and the Home Depot store in the area donated paint and supplies to assist in the project. These were just a few of the stories that communities told about Home Depot, which had provided over $10 million to help fund many community projects in the United States and Canada. Through its "Team Depot" the company helped build more than 160 homes for Habitat for Humanity and renovated more than 20,000 homes for the elderly and disabled in more than 230 communities as part of Rebuilding Together with Christmas in April.

The Home Depot's traditional concern for its stakeholders continued under the management of Bob Nardelli. As part of its philosophy of doing business, Home Depot indicated that it strove to be the employer, retailer, investment, and neighbor of choice in the home improvement industry. Management stated on the corporate web site that the company had "a daily commitment to living values and principles that recognize our ethical obligations to our shareholders, associates (employees), customers, suppliers, and the communities in which we operate. We understand our responsibility to behave ethically, to understand the impact we have on people and communities and to fairly consider the interests of a broad base of constituencies." Home Depot's *Business Code of Conduct and Ethics* stated:

> Acting with integrity and doing the right thing are the driving forces behind The Home Depot's extraordinary success. From the very beginning, The Home Depot, inclusive of its subsidiaries and affiliates, has been committed to conducting its business in an ethical manner—doing right by our Associates, our customers, our vendors, our suppliers, our communities and our stockholders. . . . All that we do at The Home Depot must be consistent with the values of the Company. We believe in *Doing the Right Thing,* having *Respect for all People,* building *Strong Relationships, Taking Care of Our People, Giving Back,* providing *Excellent Customer Service,* and *Encouraging Entrepreneurial Spirit* and providing strong *Shareholder Returns*.[25]

As part of *Giving Back* to the community, Home Depot made a direct cash donation of $1.5 million in August 2005 to support Hurricane Katrina relief and rebuilding efforts in the U.S. Gulf Coast. In Pass Christian, Mississippi, The Home Depot engaged more than 500 volunteers to build the community's first permanent structure completed after Katrina—a 6,000-square-foot playground, surrounded by dozens of newly planted trees and shrubs, picnic tables, and benches in War Memorial Park. The company also offered 300,000 volunteer hours to communities across North America as part of the Corporate Month of Service in September 2005. Through the Home Depot Foundation, the company supported the building of quality, affordable housing in communities across the country. The company also sponsored a CommUnity Impacts Grant Program that funded nonprofit organizations to construct, maintain, or refurbish play spaces, community gathering spaces, affordable housing, and structures damaged in weather-related disasters. During 2005, Home Depot supported thousands of nonprofit organizations with nearly $40.6 million in material and financial contributions.

The Home Fund was one way the company was implementing *Taking Care of Our People.* The Home Fund was an emergency charitable fund supported by Home Depot associates for fellow associates. During 2005, the fund distributed over $4 million to 4,200 associates in need.

Doing the Right Thing meant that Home Depot showed its concern for the environment by following a set of principles.

- We are committed to improving the environment by selling products that are manufactured, packaged and labeled in a responsible manner, that take the environment into consideration and that provide greater value to our customers.
- We will support efforts to provide accurate, informative product labeling of environmental marketing claims.
- We will strive to eliminate unnecessary packaging.
- We will recycle and encourage the use of materials and products with recycled content.

- We will conserve natural resources by using energy and water wisely and seek further opportunities to improve the resource efficiency of our stores.
- We will comply with environmental laws and will maintain programs and procedures to ensure compliance.
- We are committed to minimizing the environmental health and safety risk for our associates and our customers.
- We will train our employees to enhance understanding of environmental issues and policies and to promote excellence in job performance and all environmental matters.
- We will encourage our customers to become environmentally conscious shoppers.[26]

Corporate Governance

Board of Directors

As of May 25, 2006, the Board of Directors of Home Depot was composed of 11 people, nine of whom were listed as independent according to the standards of the New York Stock Exchange. Robert Nardelli, as CEO of The Home Depot, was an inside director. Milledge Hart was considered a non-independent outside director because of business transactions between a company controlled by Hart and Home Depot. All members of the Nominating and Corporate Governance Committees were considered to be independent. Kenneth Langone served as Lead Director of the board.

Gregory D. Brenneman, *44, had served as director since 2000 and was Chairman and CEO of Burger King Corporation. He had previously served as CEO of Continental Airlines, PWC Consulting, and a private equity firm. He was a member of the the boards of Burger King and Automatic Data Processing. He owned 33,519 shares of Home Depot stock.*

John L. Clendenin, *71, had served as director since 1996 and was retired Chairman and CEO of BellSouth Corporation. He was a member of the boards of four other companies, including Equifax and Kroger Company. He owned 38,832 shares of Home Depot stock and chaired the board's Audit Committee.*

Claudio X. Gonzalez, *71, had served as director since 2001 and was Chairman and CEO of Kimberly-Clark de Mexico. He was a member of the boards of GE, Kellogg Company, Kimberly-Clark, and Investment Company of America. He owned 64,457 shares of Home Depot stock.*

Milledge A. Hart, *III, 72, had served as director since 1978 and was Chairman of DocuCorp International. He was Chairman of two other boards of directors. He owned 3,568,411 shares of Home Depot stock and chaired the board's Information and Technology Advisory Council.*

Bonnie G. Hill, *64, had served as director since 1999 and was President of B. Hill Enterprises, a consulting firm specializing in corporate governance, and Founder and CEO of Icon Blue, Inc., a brand marketing company. She had previously served as CEO of The Times Mirror Foundation and as Vice President of the Times Mirror Company. She was a member of five other boards, including Albertson's, Hershey Foods, and Yum! Brands. She owned 22,370 shares of Home Depot stock and chaired the Leadership Development and Compensation Committee.*

Laban P. Jackson, Jr., *63, had served as director since 2004 and was Chairman of Clear Creek Properties. He was also a member of the boards of J.P. Morgan Chase & Company and IPIX Corporation. He owned 7,400 shares of Home Depot stock.*

Lawrence R. Johnston, *57, had served as director since 2004 and was Chairman and CEO of Albertson's. He had previously been President and CEO of GE Appliances. He owned 5,000 shares of Home Depot stock.*

Kenneth G. Langone, *70, had served as a director since 1978 and was a co-founder of the company. He was Chairman and CEO of Invemed Associates, an investment banking and brokerage firm. He was a member of the boards of ChoicePoint, Yum! Brands, and Unifi, Inc. He owned 16,519,117 shares of Home Depot stock and chaired the board's Nominating and Corporate Governance Committees.*

Angelo R. Mozilo, *67, had served as a director since 2006 and was Chairman and CEO of Countrywide Financial Corporation. He owned 800 shares of Home Depot stock.*

Robert L. Nardelli, *57, had served as a director since 2000 when he was hired as President and CEO of The Home Depot. He previously served as President and CEO of GE Power Systems. He owned 5,332,266 shares of Home Depot stock.*

Thomas J. Ridge, *60, had served as a director since 2005 and was a member of Thomas Ridge, LLC, a lecture and consulting firm. He previously served as Secretary of Homeland Security for the U.S. Federal Government and as Governor of Pennsylvania. He was also a member of the board of Exelon Corporation. He owned no shares of Home Depot stock.*

Each non-management director received an annual retainer of $130,000, paid in the form of $80,000 as deferred shares of stock and $50,000 in the form of cash or stock units. In addition, each non-management director received 9,000 nonqualified stock options plus $2,000 per Board meeting attended (including the annual shareholders' meeting) and $1,500 per committee meeting attended during the year (plus travel and accommodation expenses). Chairs of Board committees were paid an additional amount of $10,000–$15,000.

The Executive Committee included Nardelli (Chair), Clendenin, Hart, and Langone. The Audit Committee included Clendenin (Chair), Brenneman, Gonzalez, Jackson, and Langone. The Nominating and Corporate Governance Committee included Langone (Chair), Brenneman, Jackson, and Ridge. The Leadership Development and Compensation Committee included Hill (Chair), Brown, Clendenin, Gonzalez, and Johnston. The Information Technology Advisory Council included Hart (Chair), Brown, Hill, Johnston, and Ridge.

The 24 directors and officers of the corporation together owned a total of 30,842,591 shares of Home Depot stock, 1.45% of shares outstanding. Stockholders owning more than 5% of the stock were FMR Corporation (5.5%) and Barclays Global Investors (5.3%).

On arriving at the annual shareholders' meeting of Home Depot on May 25, 2006, at the Hotel DuPont in Wilmington, Delaware, shareholders were surprised to note a number of changes from previous annual meetings. For one thing, except for CEO Nardelli, none of the members of the Board of Directors were present. For another, shareholders were allowed to speak about their shareholder proposals, but each had a time limit that was carefully tracked by a giant clock. Nardelli did not present a performance review, refused to acknowledge comments or answer questions, and adjourned the meeting after 30 minutes. "It's very unusual for Home Depot," commented Patrick McGurn, Executive Vice President of Institutional Shareholder Services. "It does beg the question as to whether (Home Depot) was concerned that investors were upset over pay, the performance of the stock or other issues and, as a result, decided to remove the directors from the firing line." According to Richard Metcalf, Corporate Affairs Director for Laborers International Union on North America, "This is one of the worst meetings I've seen in terms of the arrogance coming from the front table."[27]

In addition to the usual election of board members and the appointment of KPMG as the auditing firm, there were eight shareholder proposals being voted on. They dealt with issues ranging from "excessive" senior management compensation, reporting on diversity in management, separating the position of Chairman of the Board from another management position, requiring a majority (instead of plurality) vote for board member elections, shareholder approval for future "extraordinary" retirement benefits for senior executives, reporting on campaign contributions, disclosure of the monetary value of executive benefits, and affirming political non-partisanship of campaign contributions. The votes on these proposals indicated an unusually high level of shareholder dissent, with at least one-third of shareholders voting for every proposal—votes cast before the meeting. The one proposal that was passed asked to change the company's method for electing directors from a plurality to a majority of votes cast. Under the current rules, shareholders could only withhold votes for a director. All director nominees were elected at the 2006 annual meeting even though pension firms and proxy advisors had recommended votes against many Home Depot directors, some of whom had been criticized for a lack of independence. Interestingly, one third of the shareholders withheld votes for CEO Nardelli, even though they knew the vote was meaningless!

In a July 2006 interview with *Business Week*, CEO Nardelli stated that just one week after the 2006 annual meeting he decided to return to the format used at previous shareholder meetings. "I tried a new format; it didn't work. I take full responsibility for it. . . . Directors will be (at the next meeting). . . . We will do a business review."[29] Nardelli was quick to admit that he sometimes made mistakes and that he was willing to reverse himself. For example, when he first arrived at Home Depot as CEO, he made an early decision to improve inventory turnover, which he soon regretted. Said Nardelli, "I didn't understand the complexity. They complied with what I asked, but it hurt sales. We had to step back." In a separate decision, Nardelli changed the staffing mix on the sales floor from 70% full-time to 70% part-time. Unfortunately, this led to a less experienced work force and reduced customer service. Once he realized his mistake, Nardelli returned to the more traditional and heavier staffing with full-time career people.[30] Nardelli did not regret his tendency to push for action—even if it might be the wrong action. "People who do things make mistakes. The biggest mistake is doing nothing."[31]

Top Management

The Home Depot referred to its 13 Executive Officers as its Leadership Team. As of March 29, 2006, the top managers were:

> ***Robert L. Nardelli,** 57, had been President and Chief Executive Officer since 2000 and Chairman since 2002. Previously, he served as President and CEO of GE Power Systems, a division of General Electric.*
>
> ***Francis S. Blake,** 56, had been Executive Vice President of Business Development and Corporate Operations since March 2002. He had previously served as Senior Vice President at General Electric.*
>
> ***Joseph DeAngelo,** 44, had been Executive Vice President of Home Depot Supply since August 2005. He had previously served in other managerial positions at Home Depot and as Executive Vice President of The Stanley Works and as President and CEO of GE TIP/Modular Space, a division of General Electric.*
>
> ***Robert P. DeRodes,** 55, had been Executive Vice President of Information Technology and Chief Information Officer since February 2002. Previously, he had been President and CEO of Delta Technology and Chief Information Officer for Delta Airlines.*
>
> ***Dennis M. Donovan,** 57, had been Executive Vice President of Human Resources since April 2001. Previously, he had been Senior Vice President for Human Resources at Raytheon Company and Vice President of Human Resources at GE Power Systems, a unit of General Electric.*
>
> ***Marvin R. Ellison,** 41, had been Northern Division President since January 2006. He had previously served as Senior Vice President of Logistics and as Vice President of Loss Prevention at The Home Depot since 2002. He had previously been Director of Assets Protection at Target.*
>
> ***Frank L. Fernandez,** 55, had been Executive Vice President–Corporate Secretary and General Counsel since April 2001. Prevously, he had been Managing Partner at a law firm and Assistant Professor at The State University of New York at Albany.*

Carl C. Liebert, III, *40, had been Executive Vice President of The Home Depot Stores since August 2005. He had previously been Senior Vice President of Operations at The Home Depot since August 2003 and a Division President of Circuit City.*

Bruce A. Merino, *52, had been West Coast Division President since May 2000 and President, EXPO Design Center, since October 2005. Previously, he had been Merchandising Vice President at The Home Depot beginning October 1996.*

Julian Paul Raines, *41, had been Southern Division President since February 2005. Previously, he had been a Regional Vice President, VP of Store Operations, and Director of Labor Management beginning in April 2000.*

Thomas V. Taylor, *40, had been Executive Vice President of Merchandising and Marketing since August 2005. He had previously been Executive VP of Home Depot Stores, Eastern Division President, and various other managerial positions at Home Depot beginning in September 1996.*

Carol B. Tome, *49, had been Executive Vice President and Chief Financial Officer since May 2001. Previously, she had been Senior Vice President of Finance and Accounting/Treasurer beginning 1995 and Vice President and Treasurer of Riverwood International Corporation.*

Annette M. Verschuren, *49, had been President of The Home Depot Canada since March 1996. From February 2003 through October 2005, she also was President of EXPO Design Center.*

Thomas Taylor, a 23-year veteran of Home Depot, resigned on July 7, 2006. Industry analysts considered Taylor to be Home Depot's only remaining retail expert and viewed his departure as a serious blow to the company. A report by Credit Suisse First Boston analyst Gary Balter on July 10 questioned if Home Depot had any retail expertise left in the top ranks.[32] This development followed a May 2006 Home Depot announcement that it would no longer report sales at stores open at least a year (same-store sales), an important performance measure in retailing.

Organization Structure

Home Depot, Inc., was legally a set of companies: Home Depot, EXPO Design Center, Home Depot Floor Store, Home Depot Landscape Supply, Home Depot Supply, Home Depot Mexico, and Home Depot Canada. For the purposes of financial reporting, operating decisions, allocation of resources, and performance evaluation, The Home Depot was composed of two business segments, Retail and Supply. The Retail segment was principally engaged in the operation of retail stores located in the United States, Canada, and Mexico. The Supply segment distributed products and sold installation services to business-to-business customers, including home builders, professional contractors, municipalities, and maintenance professionals. The Retail segment included The Home Depot stores, EXPO Design Center stores, The Home Depot Floor Stores, and The Home Depot Landscape Supply. The Retail segment also included the company's retail services business and Home Depot Direct, the company's catalog and online sales business. The Supply segment included water and sewer, industrial fasteners, MRO, professional construction supply, plumbing and HVAC, interiors, lumber, electric utilities, industrial pipes, valves and fittings and electrical products distribution and related services.[33]

The U.S. Home Depot stores were organized and managed by geographic region, such as Southeast, Southwest, West, Northeast, and Midwest. Each geographic division was managed by a president who reported to Carl Liebert, Executive Vice President of Stores. Each store had a Manager, Assistant Managers, and Department Managers. Four to six Assistant Managers usually presided over the store's 10 departments. Each Assistant Manager was responsible for one to three departments. One Assistant Manager was responsible for receiving and the "back end" (stock storage area), in addition to his or her departments. The Assistant Managers were supported by Department Managers who were each responsible for one department. The Department Managers reported directly to the Assistant Managers and had no firing/hiring capabilities. Assistant Managers normally handled ordering, work schedules, and so on. Department Managers handled employees' questions and job assignments.

Marketing

Home Depot's marketing strategy was to offer a broad assortment of high-quality merchandise and services at low prices using knowledgeable, service-oriented personnel and strong advertising and promotion campaigns. The company used major sponsorships, such as NASCAR, the U.S. Olympics team, The Home Depot Center, ESPN College Game Day, and a number of home and garden shows. It also utilized marketing arrangements with television shows of strategic importance, such as *Trading Spaces, While You Were Out,* and *This Old House.* Home Depot's management estimated the company's share of the U.S. home improvement and professional supply market to be approximately 11%.

Advertising and Sponsorships

The company maintained an aggressive campaign, using various media for both price and institutional policy. Print advertising, usually emphasizing price, was prepared by an in-house staff to control context, layout, media placement, and cost. Broadcast media advertisements were generally institutional and promoted the company, its products, and its service, not just its pricing. These advertisements focused on the "You'll feel right at home" and "Everyday Low Pricing" ad slogans, name recognition, and the value of Home Depot's customer service. The 2005 advertising theme was: "You can do it. We can help." Although the company primarily used national advertising, the goal of its advertising was still to project a local flavor. The Western Division maintained its own creative department because of its different time zone and unique product mix. The company attempted to use information for the field in the various markets and put together an effective advertising campaign in English, Spanish, and French-Canadian. The company relied heavily on print media.

Home Depot not only sponsored the 1996 U.S. Summer Olympic Games in Atlanta, but also subsequent winter and summer Olympics, including the 2006 Winter Games in Torino, Italy. The company participated in the Olympic Job Opportunities Program, in which Home Depot provided part-time jobs for hopeful Olympic athletes while they trained for the Olympics. As the leading employer in the U.S. Olympic Committee's Olympic Job Opportunities Program (OJOP), the company had employed more than 500 Olympic and Paralympic athletes since 1992—more than any other company in the world.

Target Markets

According to management, Home Depot stores served three primary customer groups:

- **Do-It-Yourself ("D-I-Y") Customers.** These customers were typically homeowners who purchased products and completed their own projects and installations. To complement the expertise of its associates, The Home Depot stores offered "how-to" clinics taught by associates and merchandise vendors. The typical D-I-Y customer was a married male homeowner, aged 25 to 34, with a high school diploma or some college, and had an annual income of $20,000 to $40,000.
- **Do-It-For-Me ("D-I-F-M") Customers.** These customers were typically homeowners who purchased materials themselves and preferred someone else to complete the project and/or installation. The store arranged for the installation of a variety of The Home Depot

products through qualified independent contractors. The typical D-I-F-M customer was an aging Baby Boomer earning an above-average income.

- **Professional Customers.** These customers were professional remodelers, general contractors, repairpeople, and tradespeople. In many stores, Home Depot offered a variety of programs to these customers, including additional delivery and will-call services, dedicated staff, extensive merchandise selections, and expanded credit programs.

Economic and Seasonal Impacts

With its combination of retail stores and professional supply, the company seemed to be recession-proof. During hard economic times and high interest rates, consumers who could not afford to buy new or bigger homes would maintain or upgrade their existing homes. This would lead to an increase in D-I-Y and D-I-F-M spending. During a period of economic growth and low interest rates, high demand for new or bigger homes would boost sales to professional builders and contractors. Home Depot's business was seasonal with the highest sales volume in the second fiscal quarter (summer) and the lowest volume during the fourth fiscal quarter (winter).

Merchandising Strategy

The merchandising strategy of Home Depot stores followed a three-pronged approach: (1) excellent customer service, (2) everyday low pricing, and (3) wide breadth of products. Merchandising included all activities involved in the buying and selling of goods for a profit. It involved long-range planning to ensure that the right merchandise was available at the right place, at the right time, in the right quantity, and at the right price. Success depended on the firm's ability to act and react with speed, spot changes, and catch trends early.

During 1994, Home Depot refined its merchandising function to be more efficient and responsive to customers. The new structure gave Division Managers responsibility for specific product categories, and specialists in each of these categories made sure the business lines were kept current. There were also field merchants who worked with the stores to ensure proper implementation of new programs as well as the maintenance of any ongoing programs. This approach strengthened product lines, got the right merchandise to the customers, reduced administration costs, and prepared Home Depot to expand into additional product lines. In 1997, Home Depot responded to the demographics of certain markets by expanding its service hours to 24 hours a day in 15 store locations.

EXPO Design Centers were a complete home decorating and remodeling resource for middle- to upper-income D-I-F-M customers. Customers were offered complete project management and installation services in each of the 34 EXPO Design Centers.

Store Location and Direct Marketing

During fiscal 2005, the company opened 140 new Home Depot stores, including four relocations, in the United States. The company also opened 21 new stores in Canada and 10 in Mexico in 2005. Most of the U.S. store openings occurred in existing markets as part of management's clustering strategy. Management intentionally cannibalized sales of existing stores by opening two other stores in a single market area. The short-run effect was to lower same-store sales, but a strategic advantage was created by raising the barrier of entry to competitors. It reduced overcrowding in the existing stores. It also allowed the company to spread its advertising and distribution costs over a larger store base, thereby lowering selling, general, and administrative costs. According to management, approximately 20% of its stores were cannibalized by new stores in 2005.

Home Depot stores were company-owned and managed. The company owned 87% of its buildings in 2005 (up from 74% in 1997 and just 40% in 1989), leasing the remainder. Although management preferred locations surrounded by shopping centers, it was not interested in having a store be attached to a shopping center or mall. Stores were placed in suburban areas populated by members of the Home Depot target market. Ownership provided Home Depot with greater operational control and flexibility, generally lower occupancy loss, and certain other economic advantages. Construction time depended on site conditions, special local requirements, and related factors.

Because of the large number of customers, older stores were being gradually remodeled or replaced with new ones to add room for new merchandise, to increase selling space for what was already there, and sometimes even to add more walking room on the inside—and more parking spaces.

Because merchandising and inventory were centrally organized, product mix varied slightly from store to store. Each, however, sported the Home Depot look: warehouse-style shelves, wide concrete-floored aisles, end displays pushing sale items, and the ever-present orange banners indicating the store's departments. Most stores had banners on each aisle to help customers locate what they were looking for. Regional purchasing departments were used to keep the stores well stocked and were preferred to a single, strong corporate department "since home improvement materials needed in the Southwest would differ somewhat from those needed in the Northeast."

Home Depot Direct offered customers expanded merchandise selection and time convenience through web site and catalog shopping. Through *www.homedepot.com,* Home Depot offered an assortment of more than 30,000 items selected based on their potential for online sales. Home Depot's online sales increased 100% in 2005 from the previous year. Management estimated that its online/catalog sales had the potential to reach $1 billion.[34] In 2005, the company launched *10 Crescent Lane* and *Paces Trading,* catalogs aimed at affluent women, to compete with high-end catalogs from companies such as Williams-Sonoma.

Customer Service

Customer service differentiated Home Depot from its competitors. The availability of sales personnel to attend to customer needs had always been an objective of the Home Depot customer service strategy. The provision of highly qualified and helpful employees, professional clinics, and in-store displays had developed into a customer service approach referred to as "customer cultivation." It gave Do-It-Yourself customers the support and confidence that no home project was beyond their capabilities with Home Depot personnel close at hand. Home Depot employees went beyond simply recommending appropriate products, tools, and materials. Sales personnel cultivated the customer by demonstrating methods and techniques of performing a job safely and efficiently. This unique aspect of the company's service also served as a feedback mechanism—employees helping the next customer learn from the problems and successes of the last one.

For the Do-It-For-Me customer, the Home Depot and EXPO Design Center stores offered a variety of installation services on products such as flooring, carpeting, cabinets, countertops, and water heaters, as well as furnace and central air systems. The company's wholly owned subsidiaries, THD At-Home Services, Inc., and Home Depot Installation Services, Inc., sold and installed roofing, siding, and window programs. With the exception of Home Depot Installation Services, installation services were provided by qualified independent contractors.

All of the retail stores offered hands-on workshops on projects such as kitchen remodeling, basic plumbing, ceramic tile installation, and other activities in which customers in a particular locality had expressed interest. Offered mainly on weekends, the workshops varied in length, depending on complexity. Only the most experienced staff members, many of them former skilled craftsmen, taught at these workshops. Promotion of the workshops was done through direct mail advertising and in-store promotion.

At many Home Depot stores, customers could rent trucks by the hour through Load 'N Go, Home Depot's exclusive truck rental service. The company also expanded a tool rental service to more stores during fiscal 1998.

Home Depot offered credit programs through third-party credit providers to professional, D-I-Y, and D-I-F-M customers. In fiscal 2005, approximately 4 million new Home Depot credit accounts were opened, bringing the total number of Home Depot account holders to about 16 million. Proprietary credit card sales accounted for approximately 26% of store sales in 2005. The company also offered an unsecured Home Improvement Loan program that gave customers the opportunity to finance the purchase of large sales, such as kitchen and bath remodels.

Pricing and Suppliers

Home Depot stressed its commitment to "Everyday Low Pricing." This concept meant across-the-board lower prices and fewer deep-cutting sales. To ensure this, Home Depot employed professional shoppers to check competitors' prices regularly.

One of the major reasons that Home Depot was able to undercut the competition by as much as 25% was a dependable relationship with its suppliers. The company purchased its merchandise from suppliers located throughout the world and was not dependent on any single supplier. Most of the merchandise was purchased directly from manufacturers to eliminate "middleman" costs. The company sourced its products from more than 600 factories in approximately 35 countries. Management believed that competitive sources of supply were readily available for substantially all of the products sold in Home Depot stores.

A survey of manufacturers conducted by Shapiro and Associates found that Home Depot was "far and away the most demanding of customers." Home Depot was most vocal about holding to shipping dates. Manufacturers agreed that increased sales volume had offset concessions made to Home Depot.

Products

A typical Home Depot store stocked approximately 35,000 to 45,000 products, including variations in color and size. The products included different kinds of building materials, home improvement products, and lawn and garden supplies. In addition, Home Depot stores offered installation services for many products. Each store carried a wide selection of quality and nationally advertised brand-name merchandise. The contribution of each product group was as follows.

	Percentage of Sales		
Product Group	**Year Ending 1/29/2006**	**Year Ending 1/30/2005**	**Year Ending 2/1/2004**
Building materials, lumber, and millwork	24.2%	24.4%	23.2%
Plumbing, electrical, and kitchen	29.4	29.0	28.9
Hardware and seasonal	27.1	26.9	27.6
Paint, flooring, and wall covering	19.3	19.7	20.3
Total	100.0%	100.0%	100.0%

Home Depot had formed strategic alliances and exclusive relationships with selected suppliers to market products under a variety of recognized brand names, such as Behr Premium Plus paint, Charmglow gas grills, Hampton Bay lighting, Mills Pride cabinets, Vigoro lawn care products, Husky hand tools, Pegasus faucets, Traffic Master carpets, and Ryobi power tools. Directly working with suppliers enabled the company to improve product features and quality, to import products not currently available to its customers, and to offer products at a lower price than would otherwise be available if the products had been purchased from third-party importers. According to management, this enabled the company to differentiate itself in the marketplace. Through its wholly owned subsidiary, Home TLC, Inc., Home Depot registered a variety of Internet domains, service marks, and trademarks in a number of countries. Some of these were The Home Depot: Home Depot Direct; Hampton Bay fans; Glacier Bay toilets, sinks, and faucets; Workforce tools, tool boxes, and shelving; *www.10CrescentLane.com;* and *www.PacesTrading.com.*

With the acquisition of Hughes Supply, Home Depot Supply in 2006 was composed of 36% infrastructure, 42% construction, 16% maintenance, 4% repair/remodel, and 2% international.[35]

The closest thing to research and development at Home Depot was its 88,000-square-foot Innovation Center, where the company tested everything from riding lawn mowers to displays for patio furniture sets before they arrived at its retail stores. Since it opened as an unidentified building in 2004 somewhere near corporate headquarters in Atlanta, the Center had tested not only new products, but also radically new product categories and store designs. Before the Center was built, executives had no place to test different types of displays lest they tip their hand to spies from competitors, who constantly walked Home Depot stores for new ideas. With the new facility, the company could take an Innovation Center test project to an in-store pilot project in just 30 days.[36]

Logistics

The company had established 16 import distribution centers in the United States and Canada to process its globally sourced merchandise. It also had 30 lumber distribution centers and 10 transit facilities in the United States and Canada. The transit facilities received merchandise from manufacturers and transferred it to trucks for delivery to the stores. By the end of 2005, approximately 40% of the merchandise shipped to Home Depot stores was processed through the company's network of distribution and transit facilities. The remaining merchandise was shipped directly from suppliers to the stores.

Information Systems

Each store was equipped with a computerized point-of-sale system, electronic bar code scanning system, and a UNIX server. Management believed that these systems provided efficient customer checkout, store-based inventory management, rapid order replenishment, labor planning support, and item movement information. To better serve the increasing number of customers applying for credit, the charge card approval process time had been reduced to less than 30 seconds. Store information was communicated to the Store Support Center's computers via a land-based frame relay network. These computers provided corporate, financial, merchandising, and other back-office function support.

The company was continuously assessing and upgrading its information systems to support its growth, reduce and control costs, and enable better decision making. The company opened a second technology center in 2005 in Austin, Texas, to provide redundancy and allow for growth and expansion.

In fiscal 2005, Home Depot completed an installation of back-end scanned receiving to all U.S. and Canadian stores. This system allowed the company to simplify, standardize, and automate how it received its products. By the end of fiscal 2005, self-checkout registers were in 1,272 stores and centralized automatic replenishment was increased to 20% of store sales. A Special Order Services Initiative pilot was implemented in 285 stores. In addition, the company implemented new financial systems for its Mexican retail operations, upgraded call centers, improved its web sites, and launched several new direct-to-consumer brands.

Human Resources

Home Depot had long been noted for its progressive human resources policies, which emphasized the importance of the individual to the success of the company's operations.

Recruitment/Selection

Throughout its entire recruiting process, Home Depot looked for people who shared a commitment to excellence. Also, management recognized that having the right number of people, in the right jobs, at the right time was critical. Employee population varied greatly among stores, depending on store size, sales volume, and the season of the year. In the winter, a store could have had fewer than 75 employees and in the spring would add another 25 to 40 employees. Some of the larger northeastern stores had as many as 280 employees. Full-time employees had filled about 90% of the positions under the founders Blank and Marcus, but in 2005 filled only 68% of the positions.

When a store first opened, it attracted applications through advertisements in local newspapers and trade journals such as *Home Center News.* A new store would usually receive several thousand applications. When seasonal workers and replacements were needed, help-wanted signs were displayed at store entrances. Walk-in candidates were another source, and applications were available at the customer service desk at all times. At the management level, the company preferred to hire people at the Assistant Manager level, requiring them to work their way up to store Manager and beyond. Historically the company often hired outside talent for senior positions. This continued under Bob Nardelli as CEO.

Interviews were scheduled one per day per week; however, if someone with trade experience applied, an on-the-spot interview might be conducted. "Trade" experience included retail, construction, do-it-yourself, or hardware. The company tended to look for older people who brought a high level of knowledge and maturity to the position. In addition to related experience, Home Depot looked for people with a stable work history who had a positive attitude and were excited, outgoing, and hard workers.

The selection process included preemployment tests (honesty, math, and drugs). The stores displayed signs in the windows that said that anyone who used drugs need not apply. Interviews were conducted with three or four people—an initial qualifier, the Administrative Assistant in operations, an Assistant Manager, and the store Manager. Reference checks were completed prior to a job offer. More in-depth background checks (financial, criminal) were conducted on management-level candidates.

To help ensure that Home Depot selected the best qualified people, the company designed a proprietary automated system for identifying the best candidates for store sales associate positions. This system, which had been through extensive validation testing, screened candidates for competencies and characteristics inherent to Home Depot's best sales associates.

Retention

Employee turnover varied from store to store. In the first year of a new store's operations, turnover could run 60% to 70% but would fall below 30% in later years. The company's goal was to reduce turnover to below 20%. The major causes of turnover were students who returned to school, employees who were terminated for poor performance, and tradespeople who considered Home Depot an interim position (often returning to their trade for a position paying as much as $50,000 per year).

Career development was formally addressed during semiannual performance reviews, with goals and development plans mutually set by employees and managers. The company was committed to promotions from within and had a formal job-posting program. Vacancy lists were prepared at the regional level and distributed to the stores. Store managers were promoted from within. Affirmative action plans were used to increase female and minority representation.

Under Nardelli's tenure, people were evaluated on the basis of four performance metrics: financial, operational, customer, and people skills. Dennis Donovan, Home Depot's Executive Vice President for Human Resources (also a GE alumnus), measured the effectiveness of Home Depot workers by using the equation $VA = Q \times A \times E$, where Value Added equals Quality of work multiplied by its Acceptance in the company, times how well the task is Executed.

Compensation

Employee Compensation

Employees were paid a straight salary. Bernard Marcus had said, "The day I'm laid out dead with an apple in my mouth is the day we'll pay commissions. If you pay commissions, you imply that the small customer isn't worth anything." Most management-level employees were eligible for bonuses that were based on such factors as a store's return on assets and sales versus budget. Assistant Managers could receive up to 25% of their base salary in bonuses, and store Managers could earn up to 50% if their stores' performance warranted.

The company maintained two employee stock purchase plans (U.S. and non-U.S. plans). These plans allowed associates to purchase up to 152 million shares of common stock, of which 117 million shares (adjusted for subsequent stock splits) had been purchased from the inception of the plans. Shares could be purchased at 85% of the stock's fair market value. During 2005, 3 million shares were purchased under these plans at an average price of $33.72 a share.

Recognition programs emphasized good customer service, increased sales, safety, cost savings, and length of service. Badges, cash awards, and other prizes were distributed in monthly group meetings.

Executive Compensation

The three components of executive compensation were base salary, annual bonus, and long-term incentives. Base salaries were established by considering total compensation, scope of responsibilities, years of experience, and the competitive marketplace. Merit increases, which occurred in April, were based on an individual's performance over the past year and potential for development. All executive officers participated in the company's Management Incentive Plan (MIP). MIP was a cash-based bonus plan that rewarded executives for the achievement of financial and non-financial objectives that had been established at the beginning of the fiscal year. Long-term incentives were offered in the form of stock options, a performance shares/cash plan, shares of restricted stock, and deferred shares or deferred stock units. These incentives were designed to reward executives for increasing long-term shareholder value and to retain them at the company.

Under the company's Executive Stock Ownership Guidelines, the executive officers were required to hold shares of common stock with a value equal to a specified multiple of base salary. This policy requires executives to hold company stock over the long term to keep their attention on long-term corporate success. The specific multiples were 6 times for CEO, 4 times for Executive Vice Presidents, and 3 times for Division Presidents/Senior Vice Presidents.

CEO Nardelli's salary for fiscal 2005 was $2,225,000. For his performance in fiscal 2005, he was awarded a cash bonus of $7,000,000 and received 380,000 shares of restricted stock, 175,000 of deferred shares, and 90,000 nonqualified stock options. The Leadership Development and Compensation Committee of the corporation's board of directors considered the strong performance of the company during 2005 when it determined compensation for Nardelli. The committee stated that it was especially impressed with the company's achievement of 20.4% growth in diluted earnings per share, net sales growth of 11.5%, comparable store sales growth of 3.8%, and total customer transaction growth of 5.6% in fiscal 2005. In addition, the committee considered progress made over the past year in the development and implementation of programs designed to transform the company to better meet the product and service needs of Home Depot's customers. The committee also used input from two compensation consulting firms to establish appropriate benchmarks for the executive officers.[37]

Training

Home Depot believed that knowledgeable salespeople were one of the keys to the company's success and spent a great deal of time training them to "bleed orange." Training costs to open a new store were about $400,000 to $500,000. Each new employee was required to go through a rigorous week-long orientation, which introduced new hires to Home Depot's culture. Training had been a crucial part of the corporate culture under the founders. When actively involved in the company, Bernard Marcus and Arthur Blank personally conducted many of the management training sessions. At that time, callers to the home office found that corporate executives spent most of their time in the stores training employees. "We teach from the top down, and those who can't teach don't become executives," said one top executive from the Blank/Marcus years. New employees were then paired with experienced associates in the stores to gain first-hand knowledge of customer service and general store operations. They trained an average of four weeks before working on their own. Even then, when there were no other customers in the department, newer employees would watch more experienced employees interact with customers to learn more about products, sales, and customer service. Employees were cross-trained to work in various departments, and even the cashiers learned how to work the sales floor.

Regular employees went through both formal and on-the-job training. Classes were held on product knowledge (giving the employee "total product knowledge . . . including all the skills a trade person might have"); merchandising concepts, and salesmanship (so that they could be sure that a customer had available, and would purchase, everything needed to complete a project); time management; personnel matters; safety and security; and how to interpret the company's various internally generated reports.

The Home Depot Television Network (called HD-TV) allowed the company to disseminate policies and philosophies, product upgrades, and so on. The fact that the programs were broadcast live, with telephone call-ins, enhanced their immediacy and made interaction possible. Every Monday night, for example, Vice Presidents Liebert and Taylor hosted a 25-minute live broadcast called *The Same Page* for senior store staff on the week's most important priorities. In recent years, however, employees had tended to mock HD-TV as "Bobaganda," referring to CEO Nardelli, for its "constant drone" of tips, warnings, and executive messages.[38]

Employees

As of the end of January 2006, the company employed approximately 345,000 people, of whom approximately 26,000 were salaried and the remainder were on an hourly or temporary basis. Approximately 68% of the company's employees were employed on a full-time basis. There were no unions. The company had never suffered a work stoppage. Management felt that its employee relations were very good.

Retail Building and Supply Industry

The retail building supply industry (also known as the home improvement industry) was moving rapidly from one characterized by small, independently run establishments to one dominated by regional and national chains of vast superstores. Home Depot developed the concept of the all-in-one discount warehouse home improvement superstore, designed to be all things to all people. The main rival to Home Depot was Lowe's, which had been expanding throughout the United States and replacing its older, smaller stores with new superstores. Other companies in the industry were facing the challenge by reconfiguring their stores and by targeting niche segments, but some were being forced to sell out to the major competitors or close their stores in the face of increased competition.

In 2006, the U.S. industry continued to be fragmented with estimated sales of approximately $700 billion, comprising of $550 billion of product demand and $150 billion for product installation. This estimate included import and export data and key end-use markets, such as residential repair and remodeling, and nonresidential construction and maintenance. It also included a wide range of product categories, including major appliances and garden supplies.[39] According to *Value Line* in mid-2006, the prospects for the industry remained generally attractive.[40]

The industry was affected by a number of factors in its general (societal) environment. Companies such as Home Depot used econometric models of the economy for planning purposes. These models included a number of variables that had been found to have some effect on home improvement sales. For example, although the U.S. economy was still strong in 2006, rising interest rates were causing a decline in home sales compared to the record-breaking sales of the preceding few years. By July 2006, the Federal Reserve had raised the federal funds rate by 25 basis points to 5.25%. This was the 17th consecutive increase since June 2004 and was in response to strong economic conditions and a low unemployment rate leading to a greater threat of inflation. Analysts were forecasting real disposable income growth of 3.4% in 2006, compared to 1.4% in 2005. Increasing gasoline prices during the spring and summer months affected retail sales as people cut back on discretionary purchases to pay for spiraling travel expenses. According to Bank of America securities analyst David Strasser, "We believe the home improvement sector is facing significant headwinds as housing turnover slows, and interest rates rise." Management at both Home Depot and Lowe's announced that they expected earnings growth for the second half of 2006 to be lower than previously expected. Neverthess, Lowe's CEO Robert Niblock was still optimistic about the long term. He argued that most of his company's products were intended to help with the maintenance and upkeep of older homes. "That's what drives our business," he contended.[41]

A near-record level of U.S. homeownership in 2006 (after a sustained period of low interest rates) provided an established customer base for home maintenance and repair projects. In addition, the large Baby Boom generation was in its 50s—prime income-earning years, when people tended to add to their homes or purchase larger ones. Their declining interest in doing things themselves was leading to growth in the services economy. This was one reason why At-Home Services was one of Home Depot's fastest growing businesses, posting double-digit growth throughout 2005. The millennial generation, the next-largest demographic generation, were in their teens and early 20s and were just beginning to purchase their first homes and fix them up. Hispanic homeownership was growing at three times the national rate. Harvard's

Joint Center for Housing estimated that between 2006 and 2016, immigration would represent at least 40% of household formation.[42]

Developments in information technology were significantly affecting multiple industries. Electronic scanning of merchandise was being used throughout the supply chain. Self-service checkouts and kiosks were being installed in most large retail stores to reduce labor costs and improve inventory procedures. In addition, the Internet was becoming increasingly important as a distribution channel. Internet research firm Nielsen/Net Ratings tracked 92.3 million online purchases in December 2005, up from 61.9 million a year earlier. Online sales by Wal-Mart were already topping $1 billion a year. According to Harvey Seegers, President of Home Depot Direct, 60% of U.S. households in 2006 had broadband Internet capability. "I envision a day when we have complete convergence between cable, satellite, and the Internet," forecasted Seegers.[43]

Home Improvement Competitors

Lowe's

Competition between Home Depot and Lowe's, the two major players in the industry, had intensified recently as Lowe's had been moving into areas previously dominated by Home Depot. As of February 3, 2006, Lowe's operated 1,234 retail stores in 49 states with 140 million square feet of retail selling space and 144,00 full-time and 41,000 part-time non-union employees. Each store averaged 113,000 square feet. Incorporated in North Carolina in 1952, Lowe's was second in market share and working hard to catch up to Home Depot, the industry leader. Lowe's opened 125 stores in 2003, 136 in 2004, and 150 in 2005. Management planned to open 155 stores in 2006—most of them in the Northeastern and Western United States, where the company had few stores. The company also planned to enter Canada with 6 to 10 stores in the Greater Toronto Area in 2007 and grow to 100 stores across Ontario and eventually to other provinces. The percentage of Lowe's stores located in the top 25 and top 100 U.S. markets was increasing (28% and 55%, respectively) at the end of 2005. More than 35% of the 400 approved future locations were in the nation's top 25 markets and more than 65% were in the nation's top 100 markets. Analysts noted that Lowe's was achieving higher increases in sales and profit than its rival Home Depot as it moved into big U.S. markets such as New York.[44]

In terms of financial performance, Lowe's management was proud of the company's growth. Net sales had been steadily rising from $30,838 million in fiscal 2004 (ending January 30, 2004) to $36,464 million in fiscal 2005, to $43,243 in fiscal 2006. During the same three-year period, net earnings increased from $1,844 million in 2004, to $2,176 million in 2005, to $2,771 million in 2006. Its same-store sales increased 6.7% in 2003, 6.6% in 2004, and 6.1% in 2005. The average ticket for comparable stores increased 6.1% in 2005 to $67.67, with comparable-store transactions increasing slightly to 639 million. Diluted earnings per share increased from $2.28 in 2003, to $2.71 in 2004, to $3.46 in 2005. Cash dividends per share had been raised from $.11 in 2003 to $.22 in 2005. Consequently, its stock price had increased from a low of $50.75 and a high of $60.42 in the fourth quarter of 2003 to a low of $59.65 and a high of $69.70 in the fourth quarter of 2005.[45] On June 30, 2006, Lowe's board of directors approved a two-for-one stock split.

Menards

After Home Depot and Lowe's, competitors in the industry were composed of regional and local chains, the most notable being Menards and 84 Lumber. Based on sales, Menards was the third largest home improvement chain in the United States, with estimated annual sales of $5.5 billion and 45,000 employees. Headquartered in Eau Claire, Wisonsin, Menards was a chain of 205 home improvement stores in the 10 Midwestern states of Ohio, Indiana, Illinois, Michigan, Wisconsin, Minnesota, Iowa, Nebraska, and both Dakotas. The privately held company planned to open a store in Saint Joseph, Missouri, in late 2006. Founded in 1962, the company in 2006 was still being operated by the Menard family, led by its founder John Menard, Jr. as CEO and his son, Charlie Menard as COO, and brother Larry Menard as Operations Manager. In 2004, Menard, Inc. ranked 20th on *Forbes*' list of "America's Largest Private Companies." Every Menards store shared a common structure divided by departments: Building Materials, Hardware, Electrical, Millwork, Wall Coverings, Plumbing, Floor Coverings, and Cabinets and Appliances. With distribution centers in Eau Claire, Wisconsin, and Plano, Illinois, the company planned to soon add two additional ones in Shelby, Iowa, and Holiday City, Ohio. In terms of its merchandise mix and its big-box stores, Menards was perceived by customers as being very similar to either Home Depot or Lowe's.

84 Lumber

The 84 Lumber Company was a low-cost (many of its stores had no heat or air conditioning) provider of lumber and building materials that operated in about 35 states—mainly in the East, Southeast, and Midwest parts of the United States. Through more than 450 stores, the company sold building materials, lumber, siding, drywall, windows, and kits to build barns, play sets, decks, and even homes. The CEO as of 2006, Joseph Hardy, Sr. had founded the company in 1956. With estimated sales of $3.5 billion and 8,000 employees, 84 Lumber was a significant regional player in the industry—even though it offered a narrower assortment of merchandise than did the industry leaders. The company's 84 Components subsidiary operated about 20 manufacturing plants that made floor and roof trusses and wall panels.[46]

Other Home Improvement Competitors

A number of other regional home improvement retailers had either gone out of business or sold out to one of the market leaders by 2006. For example, Hechinger was a 64-store chain of home improvement stores founded in 1911 and headquartered in Landover, Maryland, when it was acquired in 1987 by HQ Home Quarters Warehouse. It underwent a massive expansion in the 1990s by opening a series of "big box" stores to better compete with Home Depot and Lowe's. The chain was unable to earn a profit and was sold to private investors in 1997. The new owners merged Hechinger stores with Builders Square, formerly owned by Kmart. After filing for Chapter 11 bankruptcy protection in July 1999, it liquidated its remaining 117 stores that September. In 2004, an online retailer was created to sell to same products as the former Hechinger Company, but it did not operate any retail stores.

Eagle Hardware & Garden of Seattle, Washington, had operated 24 home improvement stores in 1995. Eagle's stores averaged 128,000 square feet, compared to Home Depot's 103,000 square feet. Eagle offered other services, namely, a custom-design section, free chain-cutting station, fences, and an idea center where customers could watch videotapes and live demonstrations of home improvement techniques. In the mid-1990s, Eagle was building the largest stores in the industry in the West Coast and Northwest markets. Eagle Hardware & Garden sold out to Lowe's in 1999 for $1 billion.

Building Supply Competitors

Since both Home Depot and Lowe's sought to expand their business by targeting the professional market, they had been coming into increasing contact with competitors that provided construction services and building products to professional homebuilders and contractors. Some of these were Building Materials Holding Corporation, Lanoga Corporation, and Stock Building Supply.

Building Materials Holding Corporation (BMHC)

Operating through two segments, BMC Construction and BMC West, BMHC was founded in 1987 in San Francisco to provide construction services and building materials to high-volume professional homebuilders and contractors in the western and southern states. BMC Construction (renamed SelectBuild Construction in 2006) provided framing, concrete, plumbing, other construction trades, managing labor, and construction schedules, as well as sourcing materials to production homebuilders. BMC West distributed building products and manufactured building components, such as lumber, millwork, floor and roof trusses, and wall panels. It also provided construction services to professional homebuilders and contractors. In 2005, BMHC had 21,000 employees and earned $137.29 million on sales of $3.44 billion.

Lanoga Corporation

Founded in the mid-1850s, Lanoga was one of the top U.S. retailers of lumber and building materials catering to professional contractors and consumers. Fidelity Capital, through its Pro-Build Holdings, owned Lanoga. Operating more than 320 stores in about 25 states, Lanoga had grown through dozens of small acquisitions. Its seven regional operating divisions included Dixieline in Southern California, Home Lumber Company in Colorado, Lumbermens Building Centers in the Northwest, Arizona, and California, Spenard Builder Supply in Alaska, Parker Lumber in Texas, Wheaton Lumber in Illinois, and United Building Centers in the Midwest and Rocky Mountain states. In February 2006, Lanoga, through its United Building Centers (UBC) subsidiary, purchased Wolohan Lumber, a privately held company in Saginaw, Michigan. UBC operated more than 300 locations with $1.2 billion in sales.

Stock Building Supply

Acquired by the United Kingdom's Wolseley plc in 1986 to be its U.S. division, Stock Building Supply provided a full line of quality building materials and installation services to professional contractors. Rated by industry trade publications as the number one building supply distributor to professional home builders and contractors in the United States, the company had 314 outlets in 33 U.S. states and employed 18,000 workers. It was headquartered in North Carolina and operated a fleet of 4,500 vehicles to move material to hubs, branches, satellites, and customers.[47]

Category Niche Competitors

Given that Home Depot, Lowe's, and Menards stocked hardware and related merchandise, they also competed against national and regional hardware stores, such as True Value Company, Ace Hardware Corporation, and Do It Best. These stores were typically small, locally owned stores with a much narrower and more locally oriented selection of merchandise than the "big box" competitors. With 2005 sales of $3,466 million, Ace Hardware was the leading hardware cooperative in the United States. Ace dealer–owners operated more than 4,600 Ace Hardware Stores, home centers, and lumber and building materials locations in all 50 states and 70 other countries. Like Ace Hardware, True Value (formerly TruServ) competed against the home improvement giants by emphasizing service and a narrower selection of merchandise. With 2005 sales of $2,043 million, the cooperative served 5,800 retail outlets throughout the United States.

As Home Depot, Lowe's, and Menards expanded their merchandise selection to boost sales, they also competed against national, regional, and local stores in individual product categories. Some of these were single category stores, such as the paint retailer Sherwin-Williams, and the flooring retailer CCA Global Partners Company, which competed under the names of Carpet One, Flooring America, Flooring One, ProSource, and International Design Guild. Given the breadth of their offerings, Home Depot, Lowe's, and Menard's also competed in some categories, such as automotive supplies and lighting, with national discounters such as Wal-Mart, Target, and Kmart and with regional discounters such as Mills Fleet Farm and Pamida.

Finance

Fiscal 2005 Performance

Home Depot's net sales for fiscal 2005 increased 11.5% to $81.5 billion from $73.1 billion in fiscal 2004. According to management, this sales growth "was driven by an increase in comparable store sales of 3.8%, sales from new stores opened during fiscal 2005 and fiscal 2004, and sales from our newly acquired businesses." The retail stores contributed 3.0% of same-store sales, with Home Depot Supply contributing the additional 0.8%. The retail store average ticket increased 5.6% to a record $57.98. Services revenue increased to $4.3 billion in fiscal 2005 compared to $3.6 billion in 2004 and $2.8 billion in 2003. Net earnings increased from $5.0 billion in fiscal 2004 to $5.8 billion in fiscal 2005. Diluted earnings per share increased from $2.26 in fiscal 2004 to $2.72 in fiscal 2005. During the four years from 2002 through 2005, the company repurchased approximately 277 million shares of common stock for a total of $9.7 billion. On February 23, 2006, the board authorized an additional $1.0 billion for share repurchases.

The company invested $3.9 billion in capital expenditures during fiscal 2005 for store modernization and technology as well as for 179 new store openings. Five of these stores were relocations of existing stores. The company also closed 22 stores during 2005. The company generated $6.5 billion in cash flow from operations in fiscal 2005. This cash was used to fund $3.9 billion in capital expenditures, $2.5 billion for acquisitions, and $3.9 billion of dividends and share repurchases. At the end of fiscal 2005, the company's return on invested capital (computed on beginning long-term debt and equity for the trailing four quarters) was 22.4% compared to 21.5% for fiscal 2004.

Second Quarter 2006 Results

At the end of the second quarter of the 2006 fiscal year (July 30, 2006), Home Depot reported six-month sales of $47,487 million compared to $41,278 for the same period a year earlier. The retail segment accounted for $41,972 million in sales during 2006 compared to $39,825 million in 2005. The supply segment accounted for $5,624 million in sales during 2006 compared to $1,478 million in 2005. (The figures do not add to total sales because of corporate adjustments.) Net earnings increased during the same period to $3,346 million in 2006 from $3,015 million in 2005. Diluted earnings per share increased to $1.60 compared to $1.40 in 2005. By the end of the second quarter of fiscal 2006, Home Depot's long-term debt to equity ratio was 24.5%, reflecting senior notes issued to purchase Hughes Supply. During the second quarter, the company repurchased 58 million shares for a total of 350 million shares repurchased since 2002—approximately 17% of outstanding shares. Retail sales per square foot were approximately $411 for the second quarter, down 2.3% from the same quarter in 2005.

Concerned about Home Depot's recent drop in customer satisfaction, management added 5.5 million more employee hours to the 2006 Fall/Winter season compared to the same period a year earlier. According to CEO Nardelli, "We are taking this step rather than adjusting payroll down in the second half, as we traditionally do coming off busy spring and summer seasons. Our investment is intended to improve the in-store experience, increase conversion, add customer transactions, and gain share." Meanwhile, Nardelli announced that the company was cutting 300 jobs at its Atlanta headquarters (5.6% of the total staff) as it shifted resources to invest in store improvements. Nardelli also stated: "In the second quarter, we launched a $30 million financial reward program for stores and associates that demonstrate a true passion for serving customers." In addition, the company was completing self-checkout at all stores and revitalizing stores with better lighting and signage. The company also planned to repair and remodel 100 bays in each of its top 500 high-volume stores. Overall, the company was spending $350 million to improve store sales in the second half of the year.[48]

Carol Tome, CFO, reported during the company's Second Quarter 2006 Earnings Conference Call on August 15, 2006, that management was returning to its historical practice of reporting comparable-store sales for the retail segment. CEO Nardelli had previously been heavily criticized for his decision in May 2006 to no longer report same-store sales. According to Tome, "Against a strong retail comp of 3.4 percent in the second quarter of 2005, comp or same store sales were a negative 0.2 percent for the second quarter of 2006. This is slightly down from our first quarter comp, which was a positive 0.2 percent. . . . In the second quarter, we cannibalized about 18 percent of our stores, which had a negative impact on comp sales of approximately 2.1 percent."

Tome also pointed out that Hughes Supply's sales grew 14% from the same quarter in 2005 and that Home Depot's growth rate (not counting acquisitions made since the previous year) was approximately 12%. "This illustrates our success in buying quality companies with strong growth potential," said Tome. She also indicated that in the second quarter Home Depot's consolidated gross margin was 32.2% a decrease of 102 basis points from the same period in 2005. According to Tome,

> Our consolidated gross margin rate reflects our evolving business model. As you know, Supply has a lower gross margin rate than Retail. . . . Supply's gross margin rate was approximately 26.5%. A higher penetration of lower gross margin dollars coupled with a slight decline in the Retail gross margin caused total gross margin compression in the quarter. The retail gross margin rate dropped 26 basis points to 33 percent, reflecting a changing mix of products sold due to growth in appliances. Appliances are now our largest category class.

At the end of the management team's prepared remarks, CEO Nardelli responded to questions regarding the acquisition of Hughes Supply and the strong emphasis being placed by management on new areas for growth.

> We have a balanced approach. We have taken the dividends from 16 cents in FY2000 to 60 cents in FY2005. At the same time, the strategic reinvestment has gone from zero to $12 billion in our Home Depot Supply which certainly broadens our customer base. . . . In 12 months we now have a billion dollar catalog business. In three years we have a billion dollar business in Mexico. . . . We have additional leverage—increasing our long-term debt to equity ratio where last year it was 9 percent. We have a tremendous amount of cash that comes off of our business; our stores are cash cows and we have access to tremendous leverage outside of the business. So we can do whatever we need to do.

Exhibits 1 through 3 provide the company's consolidated statements of earnings, balance sheets, and 10-year selected financial and operating income highlights.

Exhibit 1
Consolidated Statements of Earnings: Home Depot, Inc. and Subsidiaries (Dollar amounts in millions, except per share data)

Fiscal Year Ending[1]	January 29, 2006	January 30, 2005	February 1, 2004
NET SALES	$ 81,511	$ 73,094	$ 64,816
Cost of Sales	54,191	48,664	44,236
GROSS PROFIT	27,320	24,430	20,580
Operating Expenses:			
Selling, General and Administrative	16,485	15,256	12,713
Depreciation and Amortization	1,472	1,248	1,021
Total Operating Expenses	17,957	16,504	13,734
OPERATING INCOME	9,363	7,926	6,846
Interest Income (Expense):			
Interest and Investment Income	62	56	59
Interest Expense	(143)	(70)	(62)
Interest, net	(81)	(14)	(3)
EARNINGS BEFORE PROVISION FOR	9,282	7,912	6,843
INCOME TAXES	9,282	7,912	6,843
Provision for Income Taxes	3,444	2,911	2,539
NET EARNINGS	$ 5,838	$ 5,001	$ 4,304
Weighted Average Common Shares	2,138	2,207	2,283
BASIC EARNINGS PER SHARE	$ 2.73	$ 2.27	$ 1.88
Diluted Weighted Average Common Shares	2,147	2,216	2,289
DILUTED EARNINGS PER SHARE	$ 2.72	$ 2.26	$ 1.88

[1] Fiscal years ended January 29, 2006, January 30, 2005, and February 1, 2004, include 52 weeks.
Source: 2003 Annual Report, The Home Depot p. 36.

Exhibit 2
Consolidated Balanced Sheets: Home Depot, Inc. and Subsidiaries (Dollar amounts in millions, except per share data)

Fiscal Year Ending	January 29, 2006	January 30, 2005
ASSETS		
Current Assets:		
Cash and Cash Equivalents	$ 793	$ 506
Short-Term Investments	14	1,659
Receivables, net	2,396	1,499
Merchandise Inventories	11,401	10,076
Other Current Assets	742	533
Total Current Assets	15,346	14,273
Property and Equipment, at cost:		
Land	7,924	6,932
Buildings	14,056	12,325
Furniture, Fixtures and Equipment	7,073	6,195
Leasehold Improvements	1,207	1,191
Construction in Progress	843	1,404
Capital Leases	427	390
	31,530	28,437
Less Accumulated Depreciation and Amortization	6,629	5,711
Net Property and Equipment	24,901	22,726
Notes Receivable	348	369
Cost in Excess of the Fair Value of Net Assets Acquired	3,286	1,394
Other Assets	601	258
Total Assets	$ 44,482	$ 39,020

Exhibit 2
(continued)

LIABILITIES AND STOCKHOLDERS' EQUITY		
Current Liabilities		
Short-Term Debt	$ 900	$ —
Accounts Payable	6,032	5,766
Accrued Salaries, and Related Expenses	1,176	1,055
Sales Taxes Payable	488	412
Deferred Revenue	1,757	1,546
Income Taxes Payable	388	161
Current Installments of Long-Term Debt	513	11
Other Accrued Expenses	1,647	1,504
Total Current Liabilities	12,901	10,455
Long-Term Debt, excluding current installments	2,672	2,148
Other Long-Term liabilities	977	871
Deferred Income Taxes	1,023	1,388
STOCKHOLDERS' EQUITY		
Common Stock, par value $0.05: authorized: 10,000 shares; issued 2,401 shares at January 29, 2006 and 2,385 shares at January 30, 2005: outstanding 2,124 shares at January 29, 2006 and 2,185 shares at January 30, 2005	120	119
Paid-In Capital	7,287	6,650
Retained Earnings	28,943	23,962
Accumulated Other Comprehensive Income	409	227
Unearned Compensation	(138)	(108)
Treasury Stock, at cost, 277 shares at January 29, 2006 and 200 shares at January 30, 2005	(9,712)	(6,692)
Total Stockholders' Equity	26,909	24,158
Total Liabilities and Stockholders' Equity	$ 44,482	$ 39,020

Source: 2005 Annual Report, The Home Depot, p. 37.

Exhibit 3 10-Year Summary of Financial and Operating Results: Home Depot, Inc. and Subsidiaries
(Dollar amounts in millions, except per share data)

Fiscal Year	10-Year Compound Annual Growth Rate	2005	2004	2003	2002	2001[1]	2000	1999	1998	1997	1996[1]
STATEMENT OF EARNINGS DATA											
Net sales	18.1%	$ 81,511	$ 73,094	$ 64,816	$ 58,247	$ 53,553	$ 45,738	$ 38,434	$ 30,219	$ 24,156	$ 19,535
Net sales increase (%)	—	11.5	12.8	11.3	8.8	17.1	19.0	27.2	25.1	23.7	26.3
Earnings before provision for income taxes	22.8	9,282	7,912	6,843	5,872	4,957	4,217	3,804	2,654	1,898	1,535
Net earnings	23.1	5,838	5,001	4,304	3,664	3,044	2,581	2,320	1,614	1,160	938
Net earnings increase (%)	—	16.7	16.2	17.5	20.4	17.9	11.3	43.7	31.9	23.7	28.2
Diluted earnings per share ($)[2]	23.1	2.72	2.26	1.88	1.56	1.29	1.10	1.00	0.71	0.52	0.43
Diluted earnings per share increase (%)	—	20.4	20.2	20.5	20.9	17.3	10.0	40.8	29.1	20.9	26.5
Diluted weighted average number of common shares	—	2,147	2,216	2,289	2,344	2,353	2,352	2,342	2,320	2,287	2,195
Gross margin—% of sales	—	33.5	33.4	31.8	31.1	30.2	29.9	29.7	28.5	28.1	27.8
Total operating expenses—% of sales	—	22.0	22.6	21.2	21.1	20.9	20.7	19.8	19.7	19.8	20.0
Net interest income (expense)—% of sales	—	—	—	—	0.1	—	—	—	—	—	0.1
Earnings before provision for income taxes—% of sales	—	11.4	10.8	10.6	10.1	9.3	9.2	9.9	8.8	7.9	7.9
Net earnings—% of sales	—	7.2	6.8	6.6	6.3	5.7	5.6	6.0	5.3	4.8	4.8
BALANCE SHEET DATA AND FINANCIAL RATIOS											
Total assets	19.7%	$ 44,482	$ 39,020	$ 34,437	$ 30,011	$ 26,394	$ 21,385	$ 17,081	$ 13,465	$ 11,229	$ 9,342
Working capital	6.9	2,445	3,818	3,774	3,882	3,860	3,392	2,734	2,076	2,004	1,867
Merchandise inventories	18.0	11,401	10,076	9,076	8,338	6,725	6,556	5,489	4,293	3,602	2,708
Net property and equipment	18.8	24,901	22,726	20,063	17,168	15,375	13,068	10,227	8,160	6,509	5,437
Long-term debt	14.0	2,672	2,148	856	1,321	1,250	1,545	750	1,566	1,303	1,247
Stockholders' equity	18.4	26,909	24,158	22,407	19,802	18,082	15,004	12,341	8,740	7,098	5,955
Book value per share ($)	18.5	12.67	11.06	9.93	8.38	7.71	6.46	5.36	3.95	3.23	2.75
Long-term debt-to-equity (%)	—	9.9	8.9	3.8	6.7	6.9	10.3	6.1	17.9	18.4	20.9
Total debt-to-equity (%)	—	15.2	8.9	6.1	6.7	6.9	10.3	6.1	17.9	18.4	20.9
Current ratio	—	1.19:1	1.37:1	1.40:1	1.48:1	1.59:1	1.77:1	1.75:1	1.73:1	1.82:1	2.01:1
Inventory turnover	—	4.8x	4.9x	5.0x	5.3x	5.4x	5.1x	5.4x	5.4x	5.4x	5.6x
Return on invested capital (%)	—	22.4	21.5	20.4	18.8	18.3	19.6	22.5	19.3	16.1	16.3

STATEMENT OF CASH FLOWS DATA											
Depreciation and amortization	24.2%	$ 1,579	$ 1,319	$ 1,076	$ 903	$ 764	$ 601	$ 463	$ 373	$ 283	$ 232
Capital expenditures[3]	11.5	3,881	3,948	3,508	2,749	3,393	3,574	2,618	2,094	1,464	1,248
Cash dividends per share ($)	25.3	0,400	0.325	0.26	0.21	0.17	0.16	0.11	0.08	0.06	0.05
STORE DATA[4]											
Number of stores	17.1%	2,042	1,890	1,707	1,532	1,333	1,134	930	761	624	512
Square footage at fiscal year-end	17.2	215	201	183	166	146	123	100	81	66	54
Increase in square footage (%)	—	7.0	9.8	10.2	14.1	18.5	22.6	23.5	22.8	23.1	21.6
Average square footage per store (in thousands)	—	105	106	107	108	109	108	108	107	106	105
STORE SALES AND OTHER DATA											
Comparable store sales increase (%)[5][6][7]	—	3.8	5.4	3.8	—	—	4	10	7	7	7
Weighted average weekly sales per operating store (in thousands)	(0.3)%	$ 763	$ 766	$ 763	$ 772	$ 812	$ 864	$ 876	$ 844	$ 829	$ 803
Weighted average sales per square foot ($)[4][5]	(0.3)	377	375	371	370	388	415	423	410	406	398
Number of customer transactions[4]	13.6	1,330	1,295	1,246	1,161	1,091	937	797	665	550	464
Average ticket ($)[4]	3.3	57.98	54.89	51.15	49.43	48.64	48.65	47.87	45.05	43.63	42.09
Number of associates at fiscal year-end	15.6	344,810	323,149	298,800	280,900	256,300	227,300	201,400	156,700	124,400	98,100

(1) *Fiscal years 2001 and 1996 include 53 weeks, all other fiscal years reported 52 weeks.*
(2) *Diluted earnings per share for fiscal 1997, excluding a $104 million non-recurring charge, were $0.55.*
(3) *Excludes payments for businesses acquired (net in millions) for fiscal years 2005 ($2,546), 2004 ($727), 2003 ($215), 2002 ($235), 2001 ($190), 2000 ($26), 1999 ($101), 1998 ($6) and 1997 ($61).*
(4) *Excludes all non-store locations since their inclusion may cause distortion of the data presented due to operational differences from our retail stores. The total number of the excluded locations and their total square footage are immaterial to our total number of locations and total square footage.*
(5) *Adjusted to reflect the first 52 weeks of the 53-week fiscal years in 2001 and 1996.*
(6) *Includes Net Sales at locations open greater than 12 months, including relocated and remodeled stores, and Net Sales of all the subsidiaries of The Home Depot, Inc. Stores and subsidiaries became comparable on the Monday following their 365th day of operation and include certain locations acquired in the current year by existing subsidiaries. Comparable store sales is intended only as supplemental information and is not a substitute for Net Earnings presented in accordance with generally accepted accounting principles.*
(7) *Beginning in fiscal 2003, comparable store sales increases were reported to the nearest one-tenth of a percentage. Comparable store sales increases in fiscal years prior to 2003 were not adjusted to reflect this change.*

Source: 2005 Annual Report, The Home Depot pp. F1 and F 2.

Notes

1. B. Nardelli, "Letter to Shareholders," *2005 The Home Depot Annual Report* (March 29, 2006), p. 1.
2. M. Bartiromo, "Bob Nardelli Explains Himself," *Business Week* (July 24, 2006), pp. 98–100.
3. R. Kirkland, "The Real CEO Pay Problem," *Fortune* (July 10, 2006), pp. 78–81.
4. J. Fox, "A Meditation on Risk," *Fortune* (October 3, 2005), pp. 50–80.
5. The company's early history was summarized from Paul M. Swiercz's case "The Home Depot, Inc." in *Cases in Strategic Management,* 4th ed., Thomas L. Wheelen & J. David Hunger (Reading, MA: Addison-Wesley, 1993), pp. 367–397.
6. "Home Depot to Scale Back New-Store Openings," *Reuters* (January 19, 2006).
7. "Home Depot," *Value Line* (July 7, 2006).
8. D. Jones, "Home Depot CEO Aims for Next Level," *USA Today* (July 17, 2006), p. 3B.
9. "The Home Depot Unveils 2010 Growth Targets," *Home Depot News Release* (January 21, 2006).
10. H. R. Weber, "Investors Lukewarm About Home Depot Plan," *Associated Press* (January 19, 2006).
11. *St. Petersburg Times* (December 24, 1990), p. 11.
12. *Business Atlanta* (November 11, 1988).
13. *Ibid.*
14. *Chain Store Executive* (April 1983), p. 9–11.
15. The Home Depot, Inc., *1997 Annual Report,* p. 13. This was directly quoted with minor editing.
16. B. Grow, "Renovating Home Depot," *Business Week* (March 6, 2006), p. 52.
17. *Ibid.,* pp. 50–58.
18. *Ibid.,* p. 52.
19. *Ibid.,* pp. 50–58.
20. *Ibid.,* p. 56.
21. D. Jones, "Home Depot CEO Aims for Next Level," *USA Today* (July 17, 2006), p. 3B.
22. B. Grow (March 6, 2006), p. 55.
23. *Ibid.* pp. 57–58.
24. *Ibid.,* p. 58.
25. "Business Code of Conduct and Ethics," The Home Depot, Inc. (January 26, 2006), *http://ir.homedepot.com/governance/ethics.cfm.*
26. "Environmental Principles," The Home Depot (September 14, 2006), (*www.homedepot.com*) corporate web site.
27. "Lifting the Lid: Home Depot's No-Show Board Raises Ire," *Reuters* (May 26, 2006).
28. "Shareholders Still Fuming After Snub at Home Depot Meeting," *St. Petersburg Times* (June 10, 2006), p. 8D.
29. M. Bartiromo (2006), p. 98.
30. L. Grant, "CEO Bob Nardelli Sees Expansion in Home Depot's Future," *USA Today* (July 28, 2005), p. 3B.
31. D. Jones (2006), p. 3B.
32. M. Bartiromo, (2006), p. 100.
33. The first quarter of 2006 was the first time the company reported two business segments. This was due to the acquisition of Hughes Supply and the subsequent enlargement of Home Depot Supply and related activities. See The Home Depot *Report Form 10-Q* for the second quarter ending July 30, 2006.
34. K. Jacobs, "Home Depot Moves to Expand Online Sales," *Reuters* (February 20, 2006).
35. "Second Quarter 2006 Earnings Conference Call," Home Depot, Inc. (August 15, 2006).
36. B. Grow, "A Lab in a Secure, Undisclosed Spot," *Business Week* (March 6, 2006), p. 58.
37. "Proxy Statement & Notice of 2006 Annual Meeting of Shareholders," *Home Depot* (April 14, 2006), pp. 40–41.
38. B. Grow, (March 6, 2006), p. 56.
39. *Annual Report Form 10-K,* Lowe's Companies, Inc. (2005), p. 4.
40. "Retail Building Supply Industry," *Value Line* (July 7, 2006), p. 876.
41. E. Gartner, "Lowe's Expects Slowdown," *USA Today* (August 22, 2006), p. 4B.
42. *Annual Form 10-K,* Lowe's Companies, Inc. (2006), p. 3.
43. K. Jacobs, "Home Depot Moves to Expand Online Sales," *Reuters* (February 20, 2006).
44. "Lowe's First-Quarter Profit Tops Estimates," *Reuters* (May 22, 2006).
45. *Annual Form 10-K,* Lowe's Companies, Inc. (2005).
46. "84 Lumber Company Company Profile," *Yahoo! Finance* (September 11, 2006).
47. Company-owned web site, *www.wolseley.com* (September 11, 2006).
48. "Quarterly Message from the CEO," Home Depot web site (*www.homedepot.com*) (August 30, 2006).

Jose, California, eight months later, and by the end of 1970, there were six Gap stores. The Gap went public six years later.

In the beginning, the Fishers catered almost exclusively to teenagers, but in the 1970s they expanded into active wear that would appeal to a larger spectrum of customers. Nevertheless, by the early 1980s, The Gap—which had grown to about 500 stores—was still dependent on its large teenage customer base. However, it was less dependent on Levi's (about 35% of sales) due to its growing private labels.

In a 1983 effort to revamp the company's image, Fisher hired Mickey Drexler, a former president of Ann Taylor who had a very successful apparel industry track record, as The Gap's new president. Drexler immediately overhauled the motley clothing lines to concentrate on sturdy, brightly colored cotton clothing. He also consolidated the stores' many private clothing labels into the Gap brand. As a final touch, Drexler replaced circular clothing racks with white shelving so that clothes could be neatly stacked and displayed. Also in 1983, The Gap bought Banana Republic, a unique chain of jungle-themed stores that sold safari clothing. The company expanded the chain, which enjoyed tremendous success in the mid-1980s but slumped after the novelty of the stores wore off late in the decade. In response, Drexler introduced a broader range of clothes (including higher-priced leather items) and dumped the safari lines in 1988. By 1990, Banana Republic was again profitable, and in 1995 it opened its first two stores outside the United States, both in Canada.

The first GapKids store opened in 1985 after Drexler couldn't find clothing that he liked for his son. In 1990, Gap Inc. introduced babyGap in 25 GapKids stores, featuring miniature versions of its GapKids line. The Gap announced in 1991 that it would no longer sell Levi's (which had fallen to less than 2% of total sales) and would sell nothing but private-label items.

In 1994, The Old Navy Clothing Co. was launched, named after a bar Drexler saw in Paris.

Robert Fisher (the founders' son) became the President of the Gap division (including babyGap and GapKids) in 1997 and was charged with reversing the segment's sales decline. The company refocused its Gap chain on basics (jeans, t-shirts, and khakis) and helped boost its performance with a high-profile advertising campaign focusing on those wares. Later in 1997, the Gap opened an online Gap store. In 1998, the retailer opened its first GapBody stores and introduced its only catalog (for Banana Republic). In late 1999, amid sluggish Gap division sales, Fisher resigned, and CEO Drexler took over his duties. Beginning in 2000, Gap Inc. started to report its store count based on the number of concepts for the Gap brand. This meant that any GapAdult, GapKids, babyGap, or GapBody meeting a certain square footage threshold was counted as a separate store, even when residing within a single physical location. GapMaternity was a part of babyGap, but it did not have separate stores. Gap concepts are shown in **Exhibit 3**.

In 2000, Gap misjudged fashion trends, which resulted in disappointing earnings. In May 2002, Drexler announced that he wanted to retire and that he would do so as soon as a replacement was found. On September 26, 2002, Pressler was named President and Chief Executive Officer of Gap Inc. In September 2002, the company reported its 28th straight month of declines in sales at stores open at least one year.

The focus of this case study is on the Gap division of Gap Inc. (see **Exhibit 4**).

Gap Division's Products

The Gap brand name could be divided into five product concepts. Each of them offered different products for different customers.

Overall, Gap had a strong brand name. The division's products were high quality. The fashions and colors appealed to the customers. Products were attractively displayed on white

Exhibit 3
Divisions Gap Inc.

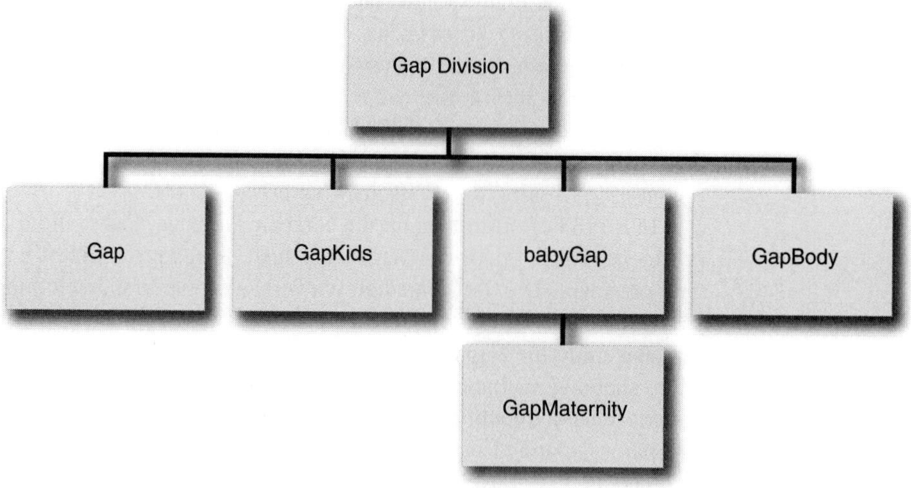

Gap Division

- Gap
- GapKids
- babyGap
  - GapMaternity
- GapBody

Exhibit 4 Structure of Gap Division

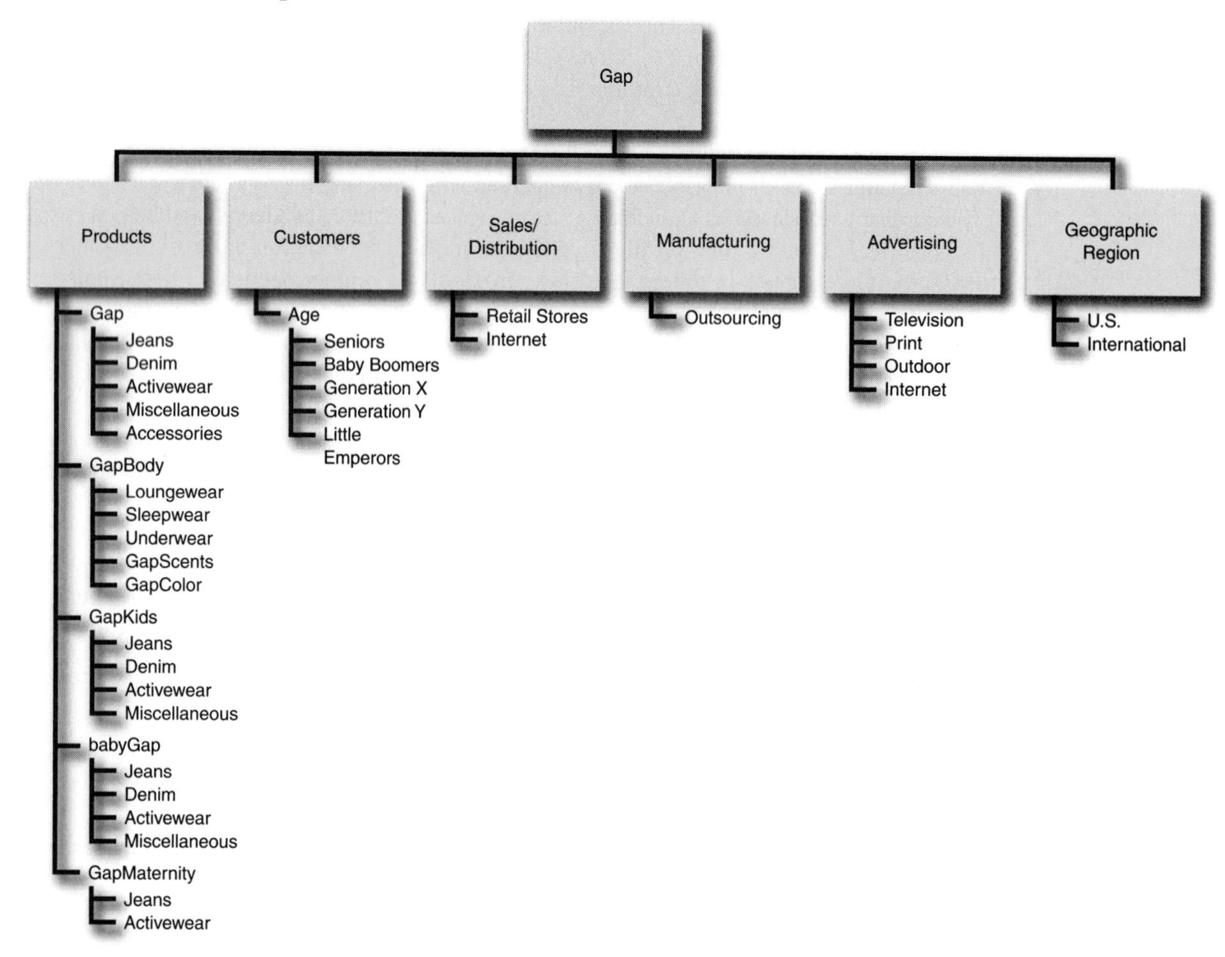

shelving. Products' labels were clear and understandable, and they provided sufficient product information. Gap often marked down the prices of different products. The company had some problems with inventory management, low-turnover products occupied shelf space for too long, and there were cases of inadequate inventory of high-turnover items.

The Gap

Gap, or Gap Adult, as some sources referred to it, offered activewear, denim products, accessories, jeans, and miscellaneous products to both men and women, all of which came in a variety of fits, colors and washes, and fabrics:

- **Jeans and pants:** This is what made Gap famous. Gap offered a variety of jeans and pants. They came in a variety of styles, fabrics, and colors. Women's jeans included boot cut, long and lean, lowrise boot cut, flare, modern boot cut, classic, loose fit, square pocket, utility, sidewinder, carpenter, and patch pocket. They were available in dark faded, light faded, stretch brown tinted, stretch faded, stretch black, stretch rinsed, stretch sandblasted, sandblasted, stonewashed, khaki, dark khaki, dark cement, and black. The men's selection included boot fit, easy fit, standard fit, relaxed fit, loose fit, wide leg, carpenter, worker, and straight fit. They came in vintage, faded, antiqued, brown tinted, rustic, black tinted, stonewashed, rinsed, black, dark blasted, black blasted, dark sandblasted, tinted rinsed, and black.
- **Denim:** Denim products included shirts, blouses, jackets, skirts, dresses, accessories, and shoes.
- **Activewear:** Activewear included sweatshirts, hooded sweatshirts, fleece sweatshirts, sweatpants, t-shirts, and tops.
- **Miscellaneous:** Miscellaneous products included sweaters, turtlenecks, v-necks, blouses, shirts, dresses, jackets, coats, peacoats, trench coats, vests, tops, t-shirts, and polos.
- **Accessories:** Accessories included bags, handbags, backpacks, tote bags, belts, hats, scarves, gloves, mittens, socks, shoes, flip-flops, and slides.

GapBody

With a focus on everyday essentials, GapBody offered loungewear, sleepwear, and underwear; GapScents; and GapColor:

- **Loungewear, Sleepwear, and Underwear:** GapBody offered loungewear, sleepwear, women's bras and panties, and men's underwear. One of the most popular products was the GapBody seamless-style t-shirts, tanks, and camisoles, with no seams or bulky edges. They were created on a cylinder, which made it possible to eliminate side seams.
- **GapScents:** Body lotions, body mists, and eau de toilette were available in "So Pink," "Dream," and "Heaven" fragrances. Gap also introduced "G," a men's fragrance composed of crisp white cotton, juniper, and musk. "G" eau de toilette, aftershave balm, hair and body wash, body lotion, soap on a rope, and gift sets were available. Gap also introduced "Simply White," a new women's fragrance with floral top notes of honeysuckle and jasmine and warm, woodsy bottom notes. Eau de toilette, shower gel, moisturizing soap, body mist, body lotion, intensified fragrance lotion, shimmer lotion, and gift sets were available in this fragrance line.
- **GapColor:** GapBody introduced GapColor, a new line of wearable, high-quality cosmetics. Offered in a range of versatile colors for lips, eyes, face, and nails, some of the products included lip glaze, lip gloss in 10 shades, lip color in 25 shades, lipstick in 10 shades,

lip care in 4 shades, lip liners in 5 shades, nail color in 12 shades, eye color in 20 shades, face powder in 8 shades, and 5 kinds of brushes.

GapKids

GapKids' products included activewear styles, jackets, sweaters, pants, and jeans. As always, the emphasis on quality was shown in the details: from embellished denim for girls and knit tops for boys, to expanded washes in jeans and bright, simple colors across the assortment. Highlights for girls included flare, boot cut, and classic jeans; embellished jeans were also available—glitter flares, glitter patch pockets, charm and heart styles—as were polos, cotton cardigans, yoga pants, zip hoodies, velour and tricot track suits, boots, clogs, and slip-ons. Some highlights for boys included jeans (basic five-pocket jeans, carpenter, and cargo, all in stonewash blast, antique blast, dark sandblast, and whisker antique), basic tops, polos, Oxford shirts, track suits, hooded sweatshirts, sneakers, and slip-ons. GapKids also offered bags, small backpacks for younger kids, premier backpacks for older students, and messenger-style bags.

babyGap

babyGap offered products for little kids, from newborns up to age 5. Products included bodysuits, playwear, overalls, tops, cardigans, sweaters, socks, and shoes, in denim and cozy fabrics.

GapMaternity

GapMaternity did not have its own separate stores. It was a section of babyGap stores and sold online. The products for moms-to-be included jeans and activewear. According to Rachel DiCarlo, vice president of fashion public relations for Gap, "These are the same jeans women wear when they're not pregnant."[3] The favorite items from Gap were translated into maternity wear so women could maintain their sense of style throughout their pregnancy. A wide range of fits and washes were available. Maternity jeans took on a modern look in different styles. Jeans included stretch patch pocket, a worker-inspired jean with front patch pockets, a sandblasted stretch long-and-lean style that fit slim through the leg and had a demi belly panel that sat slightly lower at the waist, and stretch boot cut. The stretch fabric in all the jeans styles improved fit, maximized comfort, and provided ease of movement. GapMaternity also offered activewear, which included stretch hoods, pants, and jackets. Stores carried sizes from XS to XL. Styles were designed for comfort throughout pregnancy, with stretch fabrics and special features such as four comfortable belly panels (the new demi panel, no panel, side panel, and full panel) to ensure that jeans fit perfectly at every stage.

Customers

Gap catered to women and men of almost all ages. Different Gap brands targeted different age groups. Gap paid close attention to the age distribution and priorities of potential customers in its markets. Gap targeted women and men through all its store concepts. Women accounted for 80% of household spending and 83% of all purchases.[4] Most women worked full time, which for apparel retailers such as Gap was good news because it meant not only more income at the disposal of the most important customer but also a need to buy new clothing suitable for their work. Women bought not only clothes for themselves but also for their kids. In addition, they had a great influence on what their husbands were buying. Men were spending a growing percentage of their apparel money on casual wear because of the changes in the dress codes for many white-collar workers. This was a good change for specialty retailers such as Gap that specialized in casual clothing.

Management classified its customers into five generation clusters: seniors, baby boomers, Generation X, Generation Y, and the little emperors.

Seniors

Seniors comprised individuals 65 years and older. They were born before or during World War II and they accounted for more than 12% of the U.S. population in 2002. By 2015, this age group was expected to comprise nearly 15% of the U.S. population. Gap and GapBody targeted seniors.

Baby Boomers

The baby boom generation, comprising individuals born between 1946 and 1964, constituted some 77 million Americans. In 2002, the boomers were in their 40s and 50s. Gap and GapBody targeted these consumers.

Generation X

This group comprised approximately 45 million people born between 1965 and 1976. These individuals had reached adulthood in the mid-1980s and were in their 20s and 30s in 2002. Products from Gap, GapBody, and GapMaternity targeted this group.

Generation Y

This group included individuals born between 1977 and 1994, representing about 25% of the population in 2002. Gap, GapBody, and GapKids targeted this segment.

The Little Emperors

This group included the population of children born after 1994. Gap sold to these markets via its GapKids and babyGap stores.

Gap sold high-quality products at competitive price levels. Consumers were able to shop whenever it was convenient for them, by either going to a physical store or to the Gap web sites. Gap also offered a store credit card for its customers. Gap offered products in sizes 0–14, a limited selection of products in plus-sizes, and no extended plus-sizes. Another important strength of Gap was the customer service the company provided. The division's stores had bright lighting, and products were attractively displayed on shelves. A sufficient number of cash registers provided speedy checkout for customers. Sales associates and other store personnel were trained to answer customers' questions about fabric, fit, and fashion, and to help them select merchandise that would be perfect for them.

Sales and Distribution

The Gap division was headquartered with Gap Inc. in the San Francisco Bay area, Gap Inc.'s product development offices were in New York City, and its distribution operations and offices coordinating sourcing activities were located around the globe. Third-party manufacturers shipped merchandise to distribution centers, which sorted and redistributed it to the stores. Strategically placed throughout the United States, Canada, the United Kingdom, the Netherlands, and Japan, the distribution centers were the backbone of Gap Inc.'s worldwide operations. The company used bar coding and electronic data interchange systems in inventory management. The company operated all its stores, did not franchise or enter into joint ventures, and did not wholesale its products or serve as a supplier to other companies.

Retail Stores

Gap's stores were attractively located. Gap used stand-alone stores and mall locations. Gap leased most of its store premises. Store layout and design was strategic, and products often bought together were placed in close proximity. Products were attractively displayed on white shelving, and mannequins provided ideas and inspiration for customers. Sales associates and other store personnel were trained to answer customers' questions about fabric, fit, and fashion, and to help them select merchandise that would be perfect for them.

Internet

Gap products were available through Gap web sites, including gap.com, gapbody.com, gapkids.com, and babygap.com. Shopping on those web sites was safe, quick, and simple. Customers were able to return products bought online to the company's retail stores. Ordered products were sent to the customer directly from one of the distribution centers. However, customers were not able to pick up their online orders in retail stores.

Manufacturing

Gap Inc.'s goods were produced in approximately 3,600 factories in more than 50 countries. The company did not manufacture any of the goods itself; it neither owned nor operated any garment factories. Instead, it was almost always one of a manufacturer's many customers. Gap Inc. was a designer and marketer.

Gap Inc. developed a set of principles and operating standards for garment manufacturers that reflected its values, beliefs, and business ethics. These standards were set out in its Code of Vendor Conduct, which was first written in the early 1990s and updated in 1996. The Code focused on compliance with local labor laws, working conditions, and the natural environment. It also spelled out to vendors Gap's expectations regarding wages, child labor, health, and safety issues; respecting the right of workers to unionize; and much more. It was written in order to help vendors understand and apply these standards to their day-to-day operations and adopt them as "company policy." Few factories, if any, in the United States or anywhere else were in total compliance all the time.

Gap Inc.'s Global Compliance department comprised more than 90 full-time employees dedicated exclusively to working with potential and current vendors to help them understand and achieve compliance with the Code. Before Gap approved or placed an order with a vendor, the Global Compliance team was involved. First, before any orders were placed, a manufacturer and the factories it intended to use were subjected to a comprehensive approval process to make sure they could operate under the Code of Vendor Conduct. Second, if a garment factory was eventually approved, the Global Compliance team monitored compliance on an ongoing basis. In addition, other Gap employees visited factories—from quality assurance and production experts to employees who determined whether a vendor was capable of producing a specific kind of garment.

Advertising/Promotion

Gap, Inc. advertised its products in a number of ways. Each of the three main brands, including Gap, had its own marketing team headquartered in the San Francisco Bay area. In-house marketing teams created everything from hangtags and in-store posters to billboards and TV commercials. One recent campaign was titled "For Every Generation." This global campaign included television, print, outdoor, and online initiatives.

Television

Gap TV spots were aired in the United States, the United Kingdom, Canada, and Japan. TV spots in the United States were shown during primetime programs, including *Friends, Will & Grace, West Wing, Law & Order, Ed, Scrubs*, and *ER* on NBC; *Alias, The Practice*, and *My Wife & Kids* on ABC; *CSI* and *Survivor* on CBS; and *Malcolm in the Middle* and *Boston Public* on Fox. In those TV spots Gap turned to celebrities such as Lauren Hutton and Bridget Hall to serve as spokespersons.[5]

Print

Print ads appeared in more than 40 international magazines, including *Vogue, Harper's Bazaar, Marie Claire, InStyle, Details, Vanity Fair, W, ESPN, GQ, Spin, Sports Illustrated, Rolling Stone*, and *Interview*. Ads also appeared in major newspapers.

Outdoor

Gap used major-market outdoor billboards, walls, and transit posters in high-visibility markets throughout the United States, Canada, Europe, and Japan.

Internet

Gap pop-up ads and banners appeared on various popular web pages, such as *www.aol.com* and *www.yahoo.com*. Those ads were used not only to promote the Gap brand name but also to announce new product lines and sales. Although Gap took advantage of various channels of promotion, some customers complained that the message of the advertisements was sometimes unclear and confusing. This highlighted another problem in the company: It took a long time for Gap to react to the negative customer feedback and reaction.

Gap worked hard to earn a good reputation and establish a strong brand name. To enhance and exceed the expectations of every customer, Gap store designers were constantly evolving everything that touched the customers—from store signage and merchandise displays to dressing rooms and inventory systems. Their goal was to create a relaxed shopping environment that intensified Gap's bold brand expression and enhanced the sales associates' ability to provide outstanding service. These design changes were designed to help support Gap's growth and future vision and to make the customers' experiences the best of any retailer. Gap wanted its customers to know that when they visited a Gap store, they were not just walking into a store, they were walking into a brand.

High-quality products, good customer service, and a distinct shopping environment ensure a company a good reputation, but these things are often not enough. In 1977, Gap Inc. established a charitable arm, Gap Foundation. In order to make a name for itself, Gap, through the Gap Foundation, engaged in a number of partnerships. It funded two national organizations that shared a commitment to helping underserved youth: Boys & Girls Clubs of America and the Lorraine Monroe Leadership Institute aim to help students develop self-esteem, stay in school, and succeed academically so they can lead more rewarding and fulfilling lives. To help teens make sound educational decisions, explore career opportunities, and prepare for the workforce, Gap funded a career exploration and mentoring program for more than 2,600 Boys & Girls Clubs nationwide. Gap Inc. employees were also in charge of workshops, conducted Career Day sessions at their local Boys & Girls Clubs, and provided job-shadowing opportunities for youth at headquarters and store locations. Dr. Lorraine Monroe acknowledged the challenges of education in underserved urban areas. By embracing these challenges—adding a mix of first-rate teachers, a creative but disciplined environment, and the expectation of perfection—Monroe has helped transform the future of public urban education. This is the premise of the Lorraine Monroe Leadership Institute, which focuses on developing leaders for public schools who are committed to educating underserved youth. Through funding from Gap Foundation, the Institute created Demonstration Schools to train teachers and administrators in Dr. Monroe's extraordinary leadership principles. In addition to the major partnerships with Boys & Girls Clubs of America and the Lorraine Monroe Leadership Institute, Gap Inc. supported nonprofit organizations serving kids in local communities around the world. Although it focused primarily on education and youth development, Gap, Banana Republic, and Old Navy supported many other organizations in areas such as health and human services, civics and arts, and the environment.[6]

Geographic Region

Gap stores were located in five countries outside the United States—the United Kingdom, Canada, France, Japan, and Germany—as shown in **Exhibit 5**. The company had been successful in expanding into international markets. It was not present in any emerging markets, such as Eastern and Central Europe or Asian or South American countries.

Because it was a sole owner of all its subsidiaries, and it operated its stores by itself, Gap was able to avoid any problems associated with loss of control. Because it did not enter into joint ventures or franchises, its expansion was slower than it could have been.

Exhibit 5
Division Stores in Operation as of August 3, 2002: Gap, Inc.[1]

Domestic Stores	
Gap Adult	1,024
GapKids	819
babyGap	193
GapBody	154
Gap Outlet	133
Total Gap Domestic Stores	**2,323**
International Stores	
Canada	192
United Kingdom	235
France	54
Japan	155
Germany	20
Total Gap International Stores	**656**
Total Stores Worldwide	**2,979**

Note:
1. For the past two years, Gap Inc. reported store count based on the number of concepts for Gap brand. This means that any Gap, GapKids, babyGap, or GapBody meeting a certain square footage threshold was counted as a separate store, even when residing within a single physical location.

Source: Gap Inc., company web site www.gapinc.com (2002).

Exhibit 6 Domestic Location by States, as of August 3, 2002: Gap, Inc.

State	Number of Concepts	State	Number of Concepts	State	Number of Concepts
Alaska	29	Louisiana	35	Ohio	89
Arkansas	20	Massachusetts	105	Oklahoma	27
Arizona	35	Maryland	39	Oregon	27
California	235	Maine	12	Pennsylvania	132
Colorado	36	Michigan	51	Puerto Rico	12
Connecticut	50	Minnesota	39	Rhode Island	18
District of Columbia	5	Missouri	37	South Carolina	25
Delaware	8	Mississippi	14	South Dakota	5
Florida	145	Montana	6	Tennessee	38
Georgia	61	North Carolina	51	Texas	179
Hawaii	16	North Dakota	4	Utah	31
Iowa	31	Nebraska	11	Virginia	47
Idaho	8	New Hampshire	17	Vermont	6
Illinois	97	New Jersey	86	Washington	40
Indiana	34	New Mexico	14	Wisconsin	31
Kansas	23	Nevada	19	West Virginia	10
Kentucky	20	New York	212	Wyoming	1
Total stores 2,323					

Source: Gap Inc., company web site, www.gapinc.com (2002).

Gap operated 2,323 store concepts domestically, 235 in the United Kingdom, 192 in Canada, 155 in Japan, 54 in France, and 20 in Germany, as shown in **Exhibit 5**. The actual number of stores was lower because in some instances multiple concepts were located in a single store.

Although Gap was present in all states of the United States, it concentrated mostly on highly populated areas, such as in California, Florida, New York, and Texas, as shown in **Exhibit 6**.

Financial Position

Exhibit 7 shows Gap Inc.'s consolidated statement of operations, and **Exhibit 8** shows Gap Inc.'s consolidated balance sheet. See Gap's 2001 *Annual Report* at *www.gapinc.com*, for complete financial statements.

Due to misjudgment of fashion trends in 2000 and 2001, Gap's revenue grew more slowly than the cost of goods sold, as shown in **Exhibit 7**. Between January 2001 and January 2002, revenues grew less than 2%. At the same time, costs of goods sold grew more than 10%. As a result, gross profit margin fell from more than 41% to 35.8%, as shown in **Exhibit 7**.

Comparable store sales by division for the second quarter of 2002 were as follows: Gap Domestic reported –13% versus –8% in 2001, and Gap International reported –12% versus –6% in 2001.

Total sales by division for the second quarter of 2002 were as follows: Gap Domestic reported $1.1 billion versus $1.2 billion in 2001, and Gap International reported $374 million versus $388 million in 2001.

Comparable store sales by division, year-to-date 2002, were as follows: Gap Domestic reported –17% versus –6% in 2001, and Gap International reported –15% versus –7% in 2001.

Exhibit 7 Consolidated Statement of Operations: Gap, Inc. (Dollar amounts in thousands, except per share data)

Year Ending	February 2 2002	February 3 2001	January 29 2000
Net Sales	$13,847,873	$13,673,460	$11,635,398
Cost and expenses			
Cost of goods sold and occupancy expenses	9,704,389	8,599,442	6,775,262
Operating expenses	3,805,968	3,629,257	3,043,432
Interest expenses	109,190	74,891	44,966
Interest income	(13,315)	(12,015)	(13,211)
Earnings before income taxes	241,641	1,381,885	1,784,949
Income taxes	249,405	504,388	657,884
Net earnings (loss)	($7,764)	877,497	1,127,065
Weighted-average number of shares—basic	860,255,419	879,810,658	853,804,176
Weighted-average number of shares—diluted	860,255,419	879,137,194	895,029,176
Earnings (loss) per share—basic	($0.01)	$1.03	$1.32
Earnings (loss) per share—diluted[1]	($0.01)	1.00	1.26

Note:
1. Diluted losses per share for the 52 weeks ended February 2, 2002, are computed using basic weighted average number of shares outstanding and exclude 13,395,045 dilutive shares as their effects are antidilutive when applied to losses.

Source: Gap Inc., "2001 Annual Report," p. 27.

Total sales by division for year-to-date 2002 were as follows: Gap Domestic reported $2.1 billion versus $2.4 billion in 2001, and Gap International reported $692 million versus $765 million in 2001, as shown in **Exhibit 9**.

Comprehensive earnings included net earnings and other comprehensive earnings (losses). Other comprehensive earnings (losses) included foreign currency translation adjustments and fluctuations in the fair market value of certain derivative financial instruments. **Exhibit 10** presents comprehensive earnings for the 13 and 26 weeks ended August 3, 2002, and August 4, 2001, respectively.

Although Gap, Inc. was still able to raise capital, the worsening situation has made doing so more expensive. On February 14, 2002, Moody's reduced Gap's long- and short-term senior unsecured credit ratings from Baa to Ba and from Prime-3 to Not Prime, respectively, with a negative outlook on long-term ratings. Standard & Poor's reduced the long- and short-term credit ratings from BBB+ to BB+ and from A-2 to B, respectively, with a stable outlook on long-term ratings. On February 27, 2002, Moody's reduced the long-term senior unsecured credit ratings from Ba2 to Ba3 and stated that its outlook on the long-term ratings was stable. On May 9, 2002, and May 24, 2002, the outlook on Gap's credit ratings was changed from stable to negative by Standard & Poor's and Moody's, respectively.

As a result of the downgrades in the long-term credit ratings, effective June 15, 2002, the interest rates payable by Gap, Inc. on $700 million of outstanding notes increased by 175 basis points to 9.90% per annum on $200 million of outstanding notes due in 2005 and to 10.55% per annum on $500 million of outstanding notes due in 2008. The interest rates payable on these notes would be decreased only upon upgrades of long-term credit rating by these rating agencies. Any further downgrades of those ratings by these rating agencies would result in further increases in the interest rates payable on the notes.

Exhibit 8
Consolidated Balance Sheets: Gap, Inc. (Dollar amounts in thousands, except per share data)

Year Ending	Feb. 3, 2002	Feb. 3, 2001
Assets		
Current Assets		
Cash and equivalents	$1,035,749	$ 408,794
Merchandise inventory	1,677,116	1,904,153
Other current assets	331,685	335,103.0
Total current assets	3,044,550	2,648,050
Property and Equipment		
Leasehold improvements	2,127,966	1,899,820
Furniture and equipment	3,327,819	2,826,863
Land and buildings	917,055	558,832
Construction-in-progress	246,691	615,722
	6,619,290	5,901,237
Accumulated depreciation and amortization	(2,458,241)	(1,893,552)
Property and equipment, net	4,161,290	4,007,685
Lease rights and other assets	385,486	357,173
Total assets	$7,591,326	$7,012,908
Liabilities and Shareholder's Equity		
Current Liabilities		
Notes payable	$ 41,889	$ 779,904
Current maturities of long-term debt	—	250,000
Account payable	1,105,117	1,067,207
Accrued expenses and other current liabilities	564,115	505,279
Total current liabilities	2,056,233	2,799,144
Long-Term Liabilities		
Long-term debt	1,961,397	780,246
Deferred lease credits and other liabilities	564,115	505,279
Total long-term liabilities	2,525,512	1,285,525
Total Liabilities	4,581,745	4,084,669
Shareholders' Equity		
Common stock $.05 par value		
Authorized 2,300,000,000 shares: issued 948,597,949 and 939,222,871 shares; outstanding 865,726,890 and 853,996,984 shares	47,430	46,961
Additional paid-in capital	461,408	294,967
Retained earnings	4,890,375	4,974,773
Accumulated other comprehensive losses	(61,824)	(20,173)
Deferred compensation	(7,245)	(12,162)
Treasury stock, at cost	(2,320,563)	(2,356,127)
Total shareholders' equity	3,009,581	2,928,239
Total liabilities and shareholders' equity	$7,591,326	$7,012,908

Source: Gap Inc., "2001 Annual Report," p. 18.

Exhibit 9
Second Quarter Store Sales for Domestic and International Units: Gap, Inc.

	Gap Domestic		Gap International	
	2002	2001	2002	2001
Comparable Store Sales for Second Quarter	(13%)	(8%)	(12%)	(6%)
Total Sales for Second Quarter	$1.1 billion	($1.2 billion)	$347 million	($388 million)
Comparable Store Sales for Year-to-date	(17%)	(6%)	(15%)	(7%)
Total Sales for Year-to-date	$2.1 billion	($2.4 billion)	$692 million	($765 million)

Source: Gap Inc., "2002 Form 10-Q," p. 13.

Exhibit 10 Comprehensive Earnings: Gap, Inc. (Dollar amounts in thousands)

	13 Weeks Ended		26 Weeks Ended	
	August 3, 2002	August 4, 2001	August 3, 2002	August 4, 2001
Net earnings	56,780	89,751	93,458	205,231
Other comprehensive earnings (losses)	18,664	(7,488)	25,433	(19,647)
Comprehensive earnings	75,444	82,263	118,891	185,584

Source: Gap Inc., Form 10-Q *(2002).*

As a result of the downgrades in the short-term credit ratings, Gap Inc. no longer had meaningful access to the commercial paper market. In addition, it was expected that both the recent and any future lowering of the ratings on Gap Inc.'s debt would result in reduced access to the capital markets and higher interest costs on future financing. The increase in interest expense in the second quarter and first half of fiscal 2002 as compared to the same periods in fiscal 2001 was primarily due to an increase in long-term borrowings and higher interest rates on new debt issuance. Long-term debt as of August 3, 2002, was equal to $2,873,132,000, up 46% from $1,961,397,000 on August 4, 2001.[7]

Corporate Management and Strategy

Gap Inc.'s management has demonstrated that it is very proactive, especially when it comes to looking for opportunities for growth. For example, in 1983 the company seemed to have become stagnant, so Drexler was brought in as president. Since then, Gap Inc. has grown tremendously, the store's image has changed, and new store concepts have been started, such as GapKids, babyGap, and Old Navy. The firm has also expanded, with the acquisition of Banana Republic in 1983.

Gap Inc. opened 663 new stores between October 1999 and October 2000 but had slowed new-store openings in 2001 and 2002, as it continued to be plagued by the merchandising, marketing, and logistical problems that had wreaked havoc since spring 2000. Long accustomed to spectacular growth and flashy television advertising, Gap Inc. revamped its strategies in 2001, as competition in the apparel industry continued to increase and the absence of new merchandise offerings and new trends turned up the heat even more.

Gap Inc. pursued a hybrid strategy containing elements of both cost leadership and differentiation, as defined by Michael Porter. It relied on strong brand differentiation and had made considerable investment in brand image as well as customer service. At the same time, the strategy also involved several characteristics affiliated with the cost-leadership approach, including economies of scale and scope, simple product designs, and low-cost distribution. Because of all the problems, which involved mainly the Gap division, changes in management were made. On August 8, 2002, Gap Inc. announced that Gary Muto, President, Banana Republic, had been named President of Gap U.S. On September 26, 2002, it was announced that Paul Pressler had been named President and Chief Executive Officer of Gap Inc., effective immediately.[8]

Looking Toward the Future

Although Gap had strong and well-established brand recognition in the specialty apparel retailers' market, the mistakes that were made within the company, the increasing competition, and changing consumer groups and tastes all put pressure on this division to reevaluate its strategies in order to remain competitive. The new CEO of Gap Inc., Pressler, and the new President of Gap U.S., Muto, were faced with various alternatives in order to put the company ahead of the competition. Both alternatives focused on customers and the mix of products offered to them. Both maintained that changes were needed. Each one, however, had a different view on what exactly needed to be done.

The **first alternative** was to extend the customer base. It proposed that Gap target the plus-sizes (sizes 16–26) and extended plus-sizes (sizes 28–34) markets. In a sense, Gap would offer the same mix of products, such as clothing, accessories, and body care products to an expanded customer base. The benefit of this alternative was that Gap would get into major unsaturated markets with substantial growth opportunities.

The alternative was feasible because of the brand recognition Gap had in the market, which could be extended into new customer groups. It was also feasible because of the widely recognized high quality of Gap products. This alternative could win against competition, because Gap had good relationships with its vendors and would be able to produce the goods in the new sizes, which would not differ from existing ones as far as quality and the fabrics of the products were concerned. Gap monitored its vendors closely and had high standards when choosing new ones. This could also be a winning strategy for Gap because the competition present in that market, including H&M; some discounters, such as Wal-Mart and Target; and department stores, such as Macy's, offered only a limited selection of those products, often of poor quality and style, while Gap was known for classic and comfortable styles and high-quality, durable fabrics. Gap was also better than the competition because among those offering plus-sizes it was the only one with a widely recognized, strong brand name, while others were either just beginning to build a brand name, such as H&M, or did not sell products under private labels, such as department stores or discounters. The drawback of this alternative was that creating clothes in plus-sizes would be difficult. The same trajectory of sizing up could not be continued; it required drawing new patterns because necks, for example, don't get larger above a certain weight, but backs, thighs, and tummies do. A way around this drawback was to utilize the good relationships with vendors and pay extra attention to the new designs by hiring designers with experience in this area. With good designs prepared by Gap employees and close monitoring by the Global Compliance department, the quality could be achieved.

The **second alternative** was to maintain the same customer base but to extend the product line offered. Besides jeans, casual wear, activewear, loungewear, sleepwear, underwear, accessories, and body care products, Gap could also offer various home goods, such as picture frames, throw rugs, pillows, sheets, pillowcases, comforters, and towels. The benefit of this alternative was that Gap would be stretching the brand that was widely known and identified with quality.

This alternative was feasible because Gap could use the experiences of its sister division Banana Republic to better plan and execute this strategy. It was also feasible because through Banana Republic, Gap would also have access to already tested and reliable vendors that were selected using high standards and that were monitored by the Global Compliance department.

Gap would be able to win against the competition because the company would be able to offer a broader range of products than most of its competitors. The only competitors that offered a substantially wider product range were discounters and department stores. The goods offered by discounters, such as Target and Wal-Mart, often lacked the quality that Gap was able to provide. Gap was also better than most department stores, such as JCPenney or Macy's, because through extensive data gathering, it was able to establish a one-to-one relationship with its customers and offer them reliable customer service and product information. Through its efforts at getting to know the customers, Gap was able to develop customer loyalty, which would help persuade customers that the new product lines offered by Gap were as good as the ones they had already gotten used to and trusted. Gap would also be using a recognized brand name and image to market the products, while competitors, such as H&M, were only beginning to build their brand names. The drawback of this alternative was that creating a new product line could stretch the brand too much and diminish the quality brand image that Gap had worked hard to create. It could also use valuable store space currently given to apparel. Or the store size would need to be expanded, which is not always possible. The way around this drawback was to continue using the highest-quality materials and designs, using the same high standards when choosing the vendors as with other Gap products, and then to ensure close monitoring by the Global Compliance department.

Both alternatives seemed to make sense. They both seemed to have advantages and disadvantages. Both presented views about how to achieve the same result of maintaining and increasing the market share and getting ahead of competitors. Muto and Pressler decided to study both alternatives further, especially within present financial situations, as well as other alternatives in other strategic areas, in order to decide which would be most appropriate. The only sure thing at this point in time was that if Gap was to stay competitive, immediate action needed to be taken.

Notes

1. E. Kaiser, "Interview—New Gap CEO Starting at the Bottom," *MarketWatch*, *http://cbs.marketwatch.com* (2002).
2. Standard & Poor's, "Retailing: General," *www.netadvantage.standardpoor.com* (2002).
3. Gap Inc., company web site, *www.gapinc.com* (2002).
4. S. Reyes, "Tapping Girl Power," *Brandweek*, Vol. 43, No. 16 (April 22, 2002), pp. 26–30.
5. S. Brown, "Gap Customers Get Reassurance; Ads Emphasize Store's Classic Style," *Denver Post* (August 22, 2002), p. F1.
6. Gap Inc., company web site, *www.gapinc.com* (2002).
7. Gap Inc., *Form 10-Q* (2002).
8. S. Day, "The Gap Chooses Next Chief," *The New York Times* (September 27, 2002).

References

S. Barta, M. Jason, J. Frye, and M. Woods,"Trends in Retail Trade," Oklahoma State University, *www.agweb.okstate.edu/pearl/agecon/resource/wf-565.pdf* (November 1999).

Board of Governors of the Federal Reserve System, "Monetary Policy Report to the Congress," *www.federalreserve.gov/boarddocs/hh/2002/July/FullReport.pfd* (July 16, 2002).

C. DeNavas-Walt and R. Cleveland, "Money Income in the United States: 2001," *Current Population Reports, U.S. Census Bureau* (September 2002).

L. Downes, "Perpetual Strategy: Building an Information Supply Chain," *Presentation, Foresight on the Future: An Executive Form, New York: Business Objects and IBM DB2* (October 3, 2001).

S. Ellison, "Obese America: Retailer Bets Super-Size Women Will Buy Clothes That Fit—Catherine's Expands Plus Line for Those Who Need A 28 or 34; Studying How Body Gets Larger," *Wall Street Journal* (June 21, 2002), p. B1.

Gap Inc., *Annual Report* (2000).

Gap Inc., *Annual Report* (2001).

S. Hansell, "A Retailing Mix: On Internet, in Paint and in Store," *The New York Times* (December 14, 2002), p. C1.

D. Hazel, "Is Branding Working? Developers Hope the Name Game Will Pay Off," *Shopping Centers Today*, *www.icsc.org/srch/sct/current/sct9909/02.html* (September 1, 1999).

Hoover's Online, "Company Profiles," *www.hoovers.com* (2002).

T. Howard, "Gap Counts on Known, New Stars; Chain Puts Fresh Face on Classic Clothing," *USA Today* (August 8, 2002), p. B2.

T. Howard, "Gap Goes Back to Basics; Turnaround Plan Is About a Lot More Than Fashion," *USA Today* (August 8, 2002), p. B1.

L. Huff, "Apparel Specialty Stores: A Year to Forget," *Chain Store Age*, Vol. 78, No. 8 (August 2002), pp. A14–A15.

S. Konicki, "Sophisticated Supply," *InformationWeek* (December 10, 2001).

L. Lee, "Buried Alive in Khakis," *BusinessWeek*, Vol. 3747, No. 40 (July 9, 2002), p. 40.

D. Lipke, "Mystery Shoppers," *American Demographics* (December 2002), pp. 41–43.

S. Murray, "The Second Coming," *American Demographics* (April 2001), pp. 28–30.

J. Rendon, "The Supply Chain's RFID Gambit," *Mbusiness* (March 2002).

Standard & Poor's, "Retailing: Specialty," *www.netadvantage.standardpoor.com* (2002).

A. Stein, "The Money in the Middle: Step Right Up to the Roaring 2000s," *American Demographics* (April 1, 2000).

J. Strasburg, "Gap Gets Ready to Try On a New Leadership Style," *San Francisco Chronicle* (August 11, 2002), p. G1.

B. Tadeschi, "As Women Start to Use Internet More for Shopping, the Prospects Sharply Improve for On-line Retailers," *The New York Times* (July 12, 1999), p. 4.

V. Valkin, "Gap Taps Ex-Disney Executive As CEO," *Financial Times* (September 26, 2002).

J. Waters, "Gap Finds a New Leader from Disney," *MarketWatch*, *http://cbs.marketwatch.com* (2002).

CASE 22

Tiffany & Co.:
A Specialty Fine Jewelry Retailer

Marcia Chan, Robert J. Mockler, and Marc Gartenfeld

ON JANUARY 31, 2003, TIFFANY & CO. (COMMONLY KNOWN AS TIFFANY) ANNOUNCED that William R. Chaney would retire as Chairman of the Board but would continue to serve on Tiffany's Board of Directors. Michael J. Kowalski would assume the role of Chairman of the Board and continue as Chief Executive Officer (CEO). As Chairman and CEO, Kowalski faced the continuing pressures to implement strategies that would better position Tiffany and continue to create long-term shareholder value in an increasingly competitive environment. In such leadership roles, he faced the pressures of developing an effective differentiating enterprisewide strategy for Tiffany if the company was to survive and prosper against growing global competition over the intermediate and long-term futures as the world's premier luxury brand of fine jewelry.[1]

Fine jewelry was known for its quality, craftsmanship, value, price, and brand. Its quality was nearly perfect, with minimal flaws. The craftsmanship was characterized by excellence because time and patience were required to create each fine jewelry piece. The value was determined by the fine jewelry's quality and craftsmanship. If these criteria were strong and superior, then the value was strong. The prices of fine jewelry were usually high because of its quality, craftsmanship, and value attributes. Fine jewelry brands were well known because they offered the highest standard of these attributes.

Tiffany was a retailer, designer, manufacturer, and distributor of luxury fine jewelry. As of January 31, 2003, Tiffany had 44 company-operated stores in the United States and 82 company-operated international stores. Jewelry represented approximately 79% of its net sales in 2003, followed by 6% for tableware and 4% for timepieces, with all other categories aggregating to 11%. Tiffany's jewelry designs sold under the Tiffany brand, exclusively at company-operated stores, online, and via catalog. In 2003, Tiffany had the following fine jewelry collections: 1837, Atlas, Elsa Peretti, Etoile, Garland, Paloma Picasso, Return to Tiffany, Schlumberger, The Tiffany Mark, Tiffany Biscayne, Tiffany Bubbles, Tiffany Lace, Tiffany Pearls, and Tiffany Roundel.[2] In addition to having stores in the United States, Tiffany had stores in Canada, Mexico, Brazil, England, France, Germany, Italy, Switzerland, Australia, China, Guam, Hong Kong, Japan, Korea, Malaysia, Singapore, and Taiwan. The United States represented approximately 59% of Tiffany's net sales. Tiffany's international presence brought in net sales of 28% from Japan, 6% from other Asia-Pacific countries, 4% from Europe, and the remainder from Canada, Latin America, and the Middle East. However, its international presence produced less than 42% of net sales, even though the number of company-operated stores outside the United States was nearly double the number of U.S stores.[3]

With international stores nearly doubling the number of domestic stores but producing less net sales, Tiffany had to incorporate into its enterprisewide strategy ways to increase its international net sales. One way was to explore developing potential overseas markets. As China became a member of the World Trade Organization (WTO) in 2002, for example, every major organization in the fine jewelry industry positioned itself for the emerging fine jewelry trade in China. China's membership to the WTO had opened an opportunity for the fine jewelers both because of its growing consumer market and because it had low-cost production for custom work and fine craftsmanship.[4] Tiffany tried to capitalize on the market share by establishing one company-operated store, in December 2001, at The Palace Hotel in Beijing, China. It was also to take advantage of the growing trend in high-end luxury brands desired by the Chinese with sales growing during 2000 and 2001. However, Tiffany quickly realized that it took more than just one company-operated store to be successful in the promising fine jewelry market of China, as well as in other potentially strong markets, such as Brazil and Canada.

Besides China, Brazil was also a potential market because the fine jewelry industry was growing there due to lower design and operation costs. This caused fine jewelers to migrate to Brazil and position themselves in the growing market to utilize the low costs. Tiffany opened a company-operated store in San Paolo, Brazil, where it was able to tap the market's potential to help increase net sales. However, similarly to the case in China, Tiffany needed to do more than just open one company-operated store there. Canada was another growing market in the fine jewelry industry because of the growing popularity of diamonds. Most of the thriving diamond industry mines were in this area. Fine jewelers were looking to invest in Canada by investing in Canadian diamond mines. Being a pioneer in the fine jewelry industry by investing in diamond mines was expected to help enhance a specialty fine jeweler's diamond holdings and help streamline its sourcing process. As a result of having larger holdings of diamonds, this generally also meant a larger portion of the market share could be obtained in Canada.[5]

Exhibit 1
Five-Year Stock Price: Tiffany & Co.

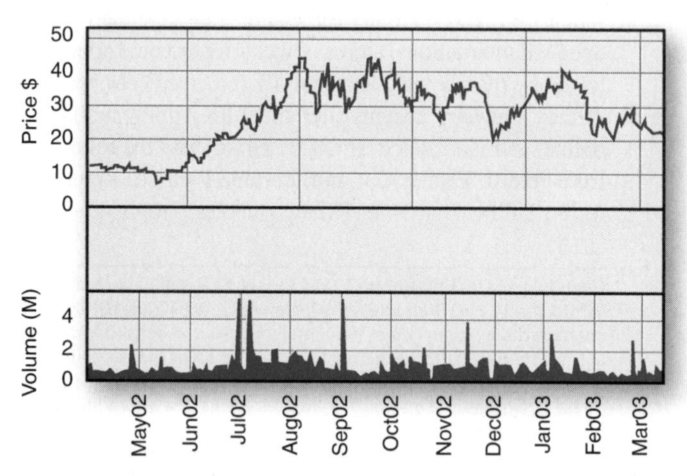

Source: Hoover's Online, "Tiffany & Co. 5 Year Quote," http://quotes.hoovers.com/thomson/chart.html?p=&t=TIF&n=Tiffany+%26+Co.&e=NYSE&c=1481&templ=4&frame=5+Year&index=&ticker=TIF&threed=2&x=5&y=7. Accessed February 25, 2003.

As Tiffany started to make its way into potential overseas markets, its competitors' proactive efforts in expansion and innovation became increasingly aggressive in these potential markets, as well as in the existing markets. Tiffany's competitors' aggressiveness in the industry was taking a toll on Tiffany's stock price. As shown in **Exhibit 1**, Tiffany's stock price had dramatically declined to a price of $23.06 per share as of March 2003, from a high of $41.38 per share in January 2003. This decline was attributed to factors such as increased competition, economic recession post–September 11, and, most recently, severe acute respiratory syndrome (SARS). The SARS epidemic spreading from China in 2003 affected retail sales from tourists because many people were hesitant to travel.

In light of these internal problems and increasing competition, the strategic question that Tiffany needed to resolve was how to expand on its product designs, customer base, manufacturing operations, retail stores, and international presence while enhancing, not hurting, its brand image. In doing this, Tiffany's most important focus of strategic concern was how to differentiate itself from its competitors in the global arena and ultimately achieve a winning edge over its competitors in the immediate, intermediate, and long-term time periods.

History

Tiffany & Co. was a retailer, designer, manufacturer, and distributor of fine jewelry. Its product category had expanded since it originated in 1837 as a stationery store in downtown Manhattan, New York. Established by Charles Lewis Tiffany and his schoolmate John Young, Tiffany's first day of sales in 1837 totaled $4.98. By 2002, fine jewelry made up about 79% of its sales. Other products included timepieces, stationery, chinaware, crystal, sterling silverware, fragrances, and gifts and accessories. It had stores in the United States as well as in international markets around the world. With Charles Tiffany's vision of establishing the grandest preeminent house of design and the world's premier jewelry house, his vision has held true even over a century later.[6] Tiffany had hit the "2001 Top 40 Plus," the National Jeweler's Annual Report that ranks the largest U.S. and Canadian retail jewelry chain sales. With a strong number of retail locations and four new stores in the United States, Tiffany's rank increased five notches, to 17th place.

Exhibit 2 shows Tiffany's organizational chart.

Products

Fine jewelry made up about 79% of Tiffany's sales. Other products included timepieces, stationery, chinaware, crystal, sterling silverware, fragrances, and gifts and accessories.[7] Known for its quality, craftsmanship, and value, Tiffany had established a brand name for itself in the specialty fine jewelry retail sector of luxury goods. Through its strong advertising campaigns, diversified portfolio of products, and license arrangements with third-party designers such as Elsa Peretti and Paloma Picasso, Tiffany was able to produce innovative designs that were signature Tiffany style brands. These signature products contributed to its established brand name and success.

Its quality and durable pieces helped project a positive brand name. However, its small use of celebrity sponsors only modestly supported the Tiffany brand name. With its strong utilization of different metals and stones, and detailed designs and styles with minimal flaws, Tiffany was able to offer quality and durable pieces. Simultaneously, it provided a brand name and long-term value synonymous with the Tiffany name. Its differentiated products through signature products such as the Return to Tiffany collection that were highly trendy and fashionable pieces, offered as everlasting pieces for every occasion to its customers. Tiffany also offered effective competitive pricing at various price ranges to compete in the industry. It offered a sterling silver collection that

Exhibit 2 Organizational Chart: Tiffany & Co.

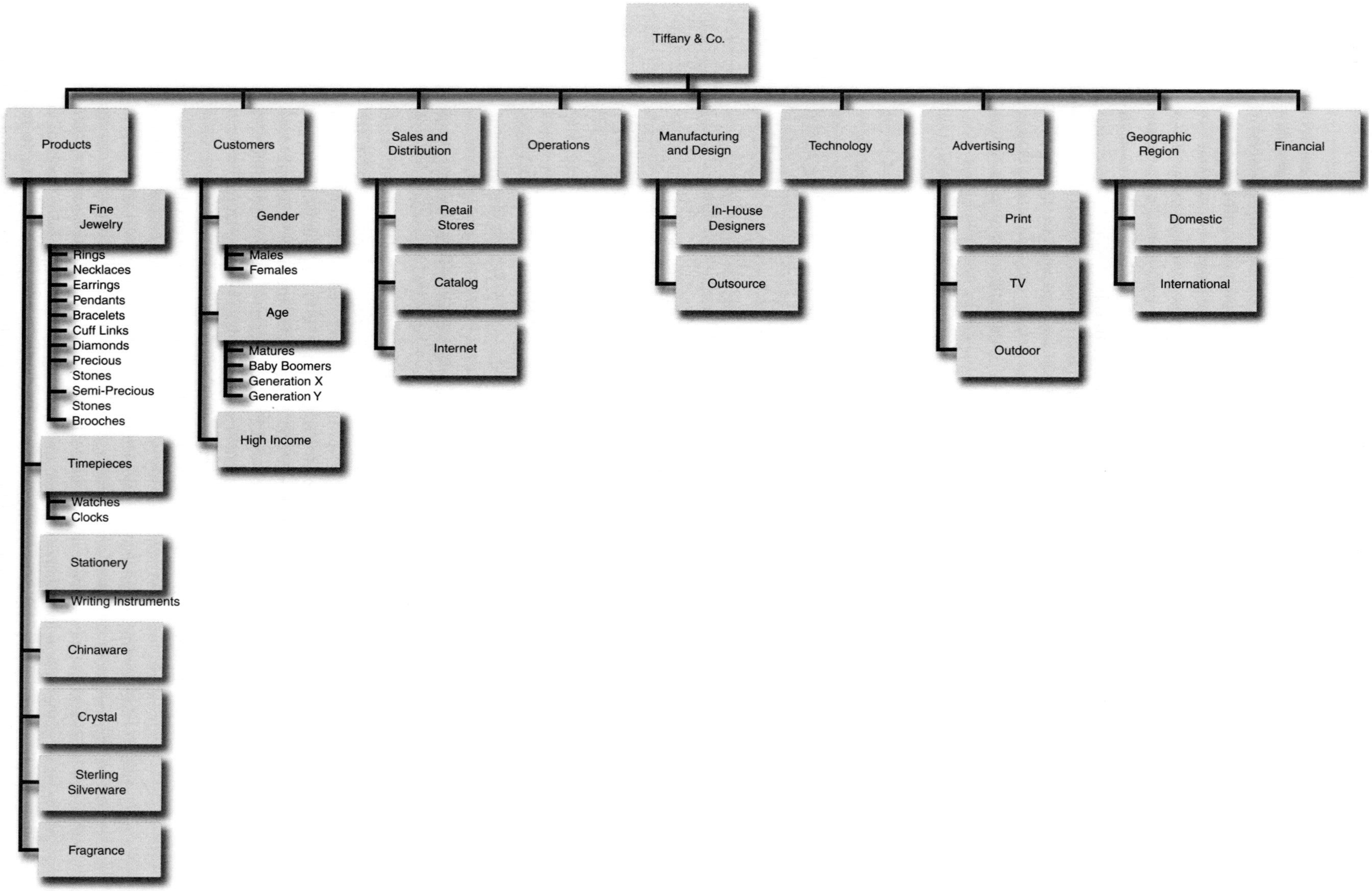

- Tiffany & Co.
  - Products
    - Fine Jewelry
      - Rings
      - Necklaces
      - Earrings
      - Pendants
      - Bracelets
      - Cuff Links
      - Diamonds
      - Precious Stones
      - Semi-Precious Stones
      - Brooches
    - Timepieces
      - Watches
      - Clocks
    - Stationery
      - Writing Instruments
    - Chinaware
    - Crystal
    - Sterling Silverware
    - Fragrance
  - Customers
    - Gender
      - Males
      - Females
    - Age
      - Matures
      - Baby Boomers
      - Generation X
      - Generation Y
    - High Income
  - Sales and Distribution
    - Retail Stores
    - Catalog
    - Internet
  - Operations
  - Manufacturing and Design
    - In-House Designers
    - Outsource
  - Technology
  - Advertising
    - Print
    - TV
    - Outdoor
  - Geographic Region
    - Domestic
    - International
  - Financial

Exhibit 3
Top Purchase Motivators for Luxury Goods

Top Purchase Motivators for LuxuryGoods/Services	Respondents Rating Among Their Top 5
To buy things I know would last	76.65%
For my well-being	61.10%
To enjoy my favorite brands	51.74%
To feel good about myself	50.47%
To indulge myself	49.53%
To express myself	46.37%
To be able to rationalize my purchase	36.28%
To feel successful	30.60%
To be optimistic	29.97%
To be lighthearted	23.34%
To make an impression	17.03%
To be impulsive	12.62%
To be fabulous	7.89%
As a status symbol	6.00%

Source: Advertising Age, www.adage.com/news.cms?newsId=34174 (2002). Accessed February 26, 2003.

was priced less than its other fine jewelry pieces. This attracted a market that made purchase decisions based on price. Tiffany offered different product collections and lines at different prices. However, its very weak attempt to expand the men's product categories was hurting its overall sales and potential revenue. It currently had a limited selection of products for men.

Tiffany's effective inventory management allowed it to deliver its products in a timely manner. A well-stocked inventory on hand was a strength of Tiffany's because this allowed it to cater to customers and deliver the goods its customers desired. When Tiffany's fine jewelry pieces were worn, they maintained their luster through the years and fulfilled the desire for well-being. **Exhibit 3** shows the Top Purchase Motivators for Luxury Goods, as surveyed by *Advertising Age*, and conducted by Ziccardi Partners' Frierson Mee.

Customers

Tiffany catered to the wealthiest segments of all age groups. By capturing those segments, Tiffany could strategically position itself to be a brand representing preeminence for years to come for men, women, and all generations. Tiffany's reacted to new market trends that strategically helped position itself in the market by developing products desired by its target market. Its strong customer relations had helped it succeed with these genders and age groups.

Gender

Tiffany targeted both males and females.

Males

Males purchased jewelry pieces for themselves as well as expensive fine jewelry as gifts for others. Also, men were more involved in shopping because they grew up in households where their mothers were often successful career women. Their mothers would send them to purchase their own clothes, buy groceries for the house, and run errands. Men also became more involved with shopping for apartment furniture and selecting items for the bridal registry. This was an opportunity for Tiffany to cater to this market. Tiffany's weak attempt to expand on men's product categories had reduced the potential revenue to be made. However, even with its limited men's products, its effective use of different metals and stones had helped it maintain partial market share in the men's line.

Females

Females were entering the workforce and relied more on convenience when shopping. They enjoyed purchasing fine jewelry to lavish themselves and decorate to their style. More women were entering the workforce and had little time to shop. This opportunity encouraged Tiffany to use Internet technology to cater to this group with effective shopping convenience efforts. Tiffany was strong in offering various price ranges, the latest trends, beautiful and detailed styles, an easy return and exchange policy, and availability of products at stores, online, and via the catalog to make it easier for working women to shop. However, Tiffany's weak efforts in offering later store hours of operation to accommodate working women drove more women to shop online or via catalog if they could not make it to a retail store in time.

Age

Matures

The age group composed of those 60 years and older was expected to comprise nearly 15% of the U.S. population by 2015. Tiffany was effective in catering to this group with features such as bright lighting, large signs, convenient parking, mass transportation near retail stores, and store layout. Because classic and antique jewelry designs were very popular with this age group, Tiffany offered antique-looking designs such as its Tiffany Bubbles collection

Baby Boomers

This generation, currently in their 40s and 50s, focused on luxury, travel, and leisure. With their kids not living at home, this generation was also known as "empty nesters." They also represented 40 million credit card users, which was about 50% of credit card owners in the United States.[8] Tiffany was strong in catering to their discretionary income and focused on luxury with the different Tiffany collections, diamonds, and gemstones by offering exclusive fine jewelry items and diversified products. Tiffany was also strong in offering store credit cards to reach the baby boomer generation since they preferred to make purchases with credit cards.

Generation X

Generation Xers, currently in their 20s and 30s, were born in the dawning of the Information Age. Specialty retailers gave the Generation Xers experiences that fit their lifestyle and aspirations, and information that kept them informed. Purchases via the Internet were high in this age group. Tiffany was strong in offering sales via the Internet for this age group and others for the convenience and ease of shopping. Its strong security online and in store made it safe and easy for customers to shop with confidence. Also, its sterling silver collections (i.e., Return to Tiffany and Elsa Peretti) were priced accordingly to cater to this age group. This made its collections more price competitive with other specialty fine jewelry retailers in this market.

Generation Y

Generation Y was composed of those primarily in their teens and early 20s. They made their own purchase choices but were influenced by their parents' spending habits. This age segment, which was starting to work, was price conscious and made many purchase decisions based on price. Tiffany targeted this group with its lower-priced collections, such as Return to Tiffany sterling silver jewelry and gifts, while still offering the Tiffany brand that represented quality, craftsmanship, value, and brand in each fine jewelry piece. Tiffany's strength with Generation Y was offering trendy and fashionable pieces, shopping convenience through availability of products online, secure online and store purchases, and strong customer relations.

Income

High-income individuals were affluent and enjoyed luxury items. Because of their taste for luxury, Tiffany offered diamonds, gemstones, and higher-karat metals to these individuals. The Tiffany brand provided status that high-income individuals sought. Also, the pricing of products denoted quality, craftsmanship, and value synonymous to its price range that high-income level individuals looked for in the Tiffany name. In addition, Tiffany's offered this segment convenient shopping through the acceptance of credit cards, easy payment transactions, and great customer service.

Sales and Distribution

Tiffany operated three channels of sales and distribution: (1) U.S. and international retail through company-operated retail stores, (2) Internet sales within the U.S. and wholesale sales to independent retailers and distributors in certain markets, such as in Japan, and (3) direct marketing via catalog sales and Internet sales in the United States.[9] By offering product quality, craftsmanship, value, and innovative designs, as well as expanding its channels of sales and distribution, Tiffany had strategically positioned itself in both the domestic and international markets. However, there was always room for expansion in new sales and distribution channels.

Retail Stores

Tiffany stores were located in prime retail space areas that had high visibility and high traffic. This contributed to the convenience factor for working women and for other target markets. The locations of the stores were in high-end areas to support the high-income individuals targeted. The stores were company operated with knowledgeable sales staffs. With Tiffany's effective decor and layout, excellent lighting, attractive merchandising of "Tiffany Blue" displays, beautiful packaging, excellent inventory on hand, and elegant store atmosphere, customers were attracted to the positive shopping experience Tiffany offered. This meant expanding selections of products, presented in an elegant, warm environment that celebrated the Tiffany name. This experience was offered to increase revenue per square foot of retail selling space and to increase repeat customer purchases.

Besides selling its products in company-operated retail stores, Tiffany also sold to independent retailers and distributors in certain markets, such as in Japan. Some of these independent retailers in Japan and stores such as Macy's and Tourneau carried Tiffany fragrances or timepieces. However, Tiffany's core operations of selling fine jewelry remained in its company-operated retail stores, where its knowledgeable sales staff could respond to all of its clients' questions, needs, and concerns.

Catalogs

Tiffany offered a Tiffany Business catalog, a Tiffany Diamond and the Measure of Brilliance catalog, and a Tiffany Selections catalog. Tiffany's catalogs contained appealing pictures, quality paper stock, and product lines that fell into the category that fit the individual customer or customer's choice of purchase. The Tiffany Business catalog offered business-related products such as writing instruments, business cardholders, and the like. These were gifts designed for clients or for colleagues. The catalogs had limited inventory compared to shopping in the retail store. However, there were items offered in the catalog that were exclusive, giving customers an incentive to shop via the catalogs. Tiffany's strong efforts in the collection of customer data through its customer purchases via the catalogs helped Tiffany understand its customers. If certain customers sought lower-priced items, Tiffany's effective way to reach these customers was to offer various price ranges by sending catalogs with its sterling silver collection, one of its lower-priced collections. The convenient policy of returning catalog purchases at retail stores was a key to its catalogs' success. Customers sought hassle-free returns and exchanges when making purchases, and Tiffany offered this through either returning the item via mail where postage was paid by Tiffany or by bringing the item to a Tiffany retail store.

Internet

Tiffany offered its products via the company web site, *www.tiffany.com*, for shopping convenience. The highly effective security, easy search feature and navigation, and a strong availability of products online offered its customers choice on where to shop and when. The site was divided into collections as well as product categories, so searching for a particular product was made easy. The online shop also provided the VeriSign secure logo, which indicated that shopping on the Tiffany web site was secure. To further ensure secure credit card payments online, Tiffany's encryption codes helped protect identity as well as credit card numbers. After an order was placed online, each fine jewelry piece purchased was individually wrapped and delivered in the famous "Tiffany Blue" packaging. The shopping experience online, from the quality product being purchased down to the last little detail of individually wrapped items in the "Tiffany Blue" box and bag, were things that kept customers satisfied and coming back for repeat purchases.

When a customer visited the Tiffany web site, the technology allowed for effective efforts in an automatic collection of information about the customer. For instance, the web server automatically recognized only the visitor's domain name (not the email address) and recorded the visitor's browser and platform type (such as Netscape browser or Microsoft platform). Cookies were used to record the visitor's session, such as the visitor's shopping selections, when ordering. User-specific information was also recorded, such as the pages the visitor selected for viewing. Also, visitor-keyed information, such as registrations and transaction information, was kept to build its customer database, to later reach the customers through other means such as via catalog, or to send them notifications of promotions. All this data was helpful to Tiffany and was key in helping it improve its Internet web site, promote brand image, promote brand recognition, and understand customer needs.

Tiffany acquired an approximate 5.4% equity interest in *Della.com* Inc. in February 2000. *Della.com* was a provider of online wedding gift registry services. After the acquisition, the company entered into a gift registry service agreement, and the company offered its products through Della's site. Della developed an online wedding gift registry for Tiffany. Later in 2000, *Della.com* merged with the *WeddingChannel.com*. Tiffany saw the growing bridal trend and was proactive in developing a gift registry for this segment. Noticing the growing trend in the bridal market, Tiffany had tried to incorporate products that were relevant to this category. For instance, Tiffany's signature solitaire engagement ring had made the Tiffany brand more popular. The "Tiffany Solitaire" name was a universal name used for a six-prong, solitaire diamond ring setting in the fine jewelry industry. By establishing a popular, signature product, Tiffany was able to help promote its brand image through this product in an industry that equated brand to quality, craftsmanship, and value.

Tiffany's various price ranges offered its customers a selection of different products. Its sterling silver collection was its lower-priced collection, to target the younger age groups in Generations X and Y.

Operations

Tiffany's linked communication between suppliers and personnel had enabled a strong relationship to be built. This helped in its sales operation by replenishing inventory and meeting customer demands through its effective real-time data. The supplier relationship had been built using total quality management, inventory control, and just-in-time operations. Feedback and constant communication helped build the relationship stronger, and, as a result, create quality products effectively and in the most cost-effective manner. Once the products were produced, the timely delivery of the products (just-in-time) was important. Tiffany's inventory management and schedule were timely and effective so that inventory would always be on hand. When products were received by the retail store, the knowledgeable sales force sold the fine jewelry. Besides purchasing a fine jewelry piece, customers received information about what they were purchasing through the trained sales force.

Manufacturing and Designing

Tiffany had manufacturing and design plants domestically and internationally.

In-House Manufacturing and Design

Tiffany recently set up a diamond-cutting factory in the tundra town of Yellowknife, Canada, to cut part of the mine's production, which it sourced through an agreement with junior partner Aber Resources. The $70 million cost of the investment in Aber was a strategic move because Aber held a 40% interest in the Diavik Diamonds Project in Canada's Northwest Territories, an operation developed to mine gem-quality diamonds. In addition, Tiffany had entered into a diamond purchase agreement with Aber. This strong relationship with its vendor helped Tiffany secure a good portion of its future diamond needs.

Outsourcing

Tiffany's strong ability to outsource helped it reduce costs since this process was less costly compared to in-house operations. Tiffany's licensed agreements with designers, such as Elsa Peretti and Paloma Picasso, who specifically designed for Tiffany, had helped it create signature, innovative products synonymous with Tiffany. Their innovative designs, which sold exclusively at Tiffany, provided additional leverage in the competitive environment.

Technology

Tiffany's strength in real-time data capability helped enhance its operations. With real-time data, suppliers and the company could communicate with each other and had up-to-the-minute data regarding production and operations. This information not only would help Tiffany's weak collaboration with its suppliers but also better serve and meet the demands of the customers. In early 2003, Tiffany's software was upgraded, and it was looking to incorporate QAD software into its processes. Its technology, however, had been upgraded to better collect customer data at retail stores and online. Its strong use of the Internet for business and reaching customers had been effective in reaching an audience and delivering a convenience factor.

Advertising

With its marketing and advertising programs that promoted the quality, craftsmanship, value, and design of its products, Tiffany enhanced customer awareness through various forms of advertising media and markets that it served. The shade of blue known as the trademark "Tiffany Blue" symbolized elegance and exclusivity available only at Tiffany stores. This was a key to its success in establishing its brand image and awareness. Tiffany's main advertising media were print, television, and outdoor. These media were used for visibility of brand awareness and helped sustain long-term sales growth.

Print

Tiffany's strength was advertising in high-end, luxury, and fashion magazines with large circulation. Print ads appeared in *InStyle, New Yorker, Cigar Aficionado*, and the like. Print ads included advertising in newspapers. Large and attractive ads were taken out in newspapers for greater visibility, such as a quarter of the page in *The New York Times*. The affluent market, the market that Tiffany catered to, read *The New York Times* and high-end, luxury, and fashion magazines.

Television

Since TV was the largest and usually the most expensive medium, financial resources had to be available for this type of advertising. Tiffany spent about $68.1 million on media (including television), $65.4 million on production, and $57.3 million on catalogs in 2002. Media was the most expensive because it caused the most impact on the target market. Production costs were the costs associated with producing television ads and print advertising, such as drawing the ad, using quality paper stock, and using quality photography. Since costs associated with advertising were high, choosing the right medium that had the largest reach and frequency was important. Research was implemented in choosing the right medium. This was based on the target market's lifestyle and interests. Tiffany's use of Nielsen television ratings data maximized its advertising dollars by researching its target market's television programming choices and networks based on its lifestyle and interests. It offered demographic information for all television shows and network views, indicated the type of shows the targeted demographic watched, indicated what commercials were watched by the specific demographic, and specified the ratings data for that demographic during certain time slots. Tiffany's strength in reaching its market through these high-rated shows and selection of networks had helped it reach its target market as well as making this medium effective for advertising. However, Tiffany's weak use of celebrity sponsors wearing Tiffany jewelry at galas and award shows reduced Tiffany's visibility to the public.

Outdoor

Tiffany advertised on billboards where there was high traffic and strong visibility. Bus depots were another place where Tiffany effectively advertised in the United States, as well as abroad. This helped with promoting the brand image and Tiffany's products by conditioning the consumer's mind with the messages or pictures advertised.

Geographic Region

Tiffany had 44 U.S. company-operated retail stores and 82 international company-operated retail stores. Its U.S. sales were greater, even though the number of international company-operated stores was nearly double. Tiffany's biggest concern was how to increase sales revenue in its international stores.

Domestic

Tiffany's strength was its presence in major U.S. cities, such as New York, San Francisco, and St. Louis. Tiffany's focus on expanding its retail locations both domestically and internationally was a strength in helping it increase its revenue, brand image, and respectable reputation. Its presence in target demographic areas, such as its flagship store on Fifth Avenue in New York, helped reach its clients and catered to their fine jewelry needs. The flagship store was a model store. For example, the flagship store was a lot larger than most of its regular retail stores. The Fifth Avenue flagship store was 124,000 square feet, with 40,000 devoted to retail selling and the remainder to executive and administrative offices, jewelry manufacturing, storage, and product services. Tiffany's U.S. stores totaled approximately 385,000 gross square feet. Individually, other stores were smaller than its flagship store. As a result, these smaller stores were not able to offer as much as the flagship store. For instance, some merchandise might not be displayed, but if asked for, would be brought out from inventory storage. Another strength of Tiffany was its location within major U.S. cities. Its domestic retail stores were located in prime retail space that was accessible by mass transit or driving based on nearby infrastructure. Tiffany's large presence in targeted demographic areas allowed for its target market to easily shop. However, most of the high-income individuals lived in suburbs, but Tiffany had limited presence in these areas. Its stores were mainly located in urban areas, similar to its competitors.

International

Tiffany had 82 company-operated retail stores internationally. Its presence in international markets and in a large number of locations had helped it build brand image as well as generate revenues to help with future expansion. Its largest international market, generating the highest international sales, was Japan. The total approximate gross square feet of its international stores was 224,000 compared to 385,000 square feet per store in the United States. Japan offered a greater shopping experience per square foot of selling space through its product offering, sales staff, store layout and decor, and its "Tiffany Blue" packaging. All these factors contributed to the higher purchase per visit by a customer per square foot of selling space in its Japanese store.

Tiffany opened company-operated stores in markets with strong potential, such as China, Brazil, and Canada. Since China's membership in the WTO in 2001, expansion of free trade had reduced the global cost of production and caused rising global trade. Since rising global trade increased economies of scale, Tiffany looked for low-cost sources of production in China and in Brazil. China was excellent for custom designing and cheap labor, while Brazil was great for its low design and operation costs. This new collaboration with the Brazilians and Chinese helped Tiffany with low-cost sources of production and producing innovative products. Tiffany's strength was not only producing innovative and fashionable pieces to cater to its market but also its streamlined process. With Canada's growing trend in diamonds, Tiffany purchased a diamond mine in Canada to help it gain a hold on the diamonds in the industry and to cater to the growing trend. As new trends developed in the future, Tiffany would explore other potential markets.

Financial Position

Exhibit 4 is Tiffany's financial highlights of 2002 and 2001. Its liquidity needs were expected to remain the same because of its seasonal working capital and capital expenditures, which had increased due to its expansion. Working capital and the corresponding current ratio were $612,978,000 and 2.8:1 at January 31, 2003, compared to $667,647,000 and 3.0:1 on January 31, 2002. See Tiffany's 2002 *Annual Report* for complete financial statements online at *www.tiffany.com*.

Capital expenditures and payment of a capital lease purchase obligation were $210,291,000 in 2002 and $108,382,000 in 2001. A portion of the capital expenditures was related to the renovation and expansion of stores and investment in new systems, office facilities, and internal jewelry manufacturing. Tiffany suffered a loss in 2001 due to economic conditions, especially post–September 11 results. Many retailers suffered due to people being out of jobs and having very little discretionary income, especially for luxury goods. Tiffany's stock price had decreased. However, Kowalski was to improve Tiffany's financial position, increase its stock price, and build brand image. His ongoing strategy was to help Tiffany maintain competitiveness as well as produce greater presence in the fine jewelry retail industry by offering a greater shopping experience per square foot of retail selling space; building brand image through vivid television, print, and outdoor advertising; and offering more products to its customers through detailed, innovative designs. As a specialty

Exhibit 4 Financial Highlights of 2002 and 2001: Tiffany & Co.[1] (Dollar amounts in thousands, except per share data)

Year Ending January 31	2003	2002	Increase (Decrease)
A. Earnings Data			
Net sales	$1,706,602	$1,605,535	6%
Worldwide comparable store Sales (on constant exchange rate basis)	$1,282,808	$1,393,836	(1)%
Gross profit	1,011,448	943,477	7%
Earnings from operations	$319,197	$309,897	3%
Net earnings	$189,894	$173,867	9%
B. Ratio Analysis and Other Data			
Net earnings per diluted share	$1.28	$1.15	11%
Cash dividends per share	$0.1600	$0.1606	
Weighted average number of diluted common shares	146,591	150,517	
Earnings from operations as a percentage of net sales	18.7%	19.3%	
Net earnings as a percentage of net sales	11.1%	10.8%	
Return on average assets	10.7%	10.9%	
Return on average stockholders' equity	16.9%	17.7%	
Net–debt as a percentage of total capital	13.8%	8.6%	

Note:
1. The company's fiscal year ends on January 31 of the following calendar year. All references to years relate to fiscal rather than calendar year.

Source: Tiffany & Co. (2002). Annual Report, p. 20.

fine jewelry retailer, the company's business was seasonal in nature. This meant that typically the fourth quarter represented a greater percentage of annual sales and earnings from operations and cash flow.

Management and Strategy

Tiffany's management strategy had grown and continued to evolve in the luxury goods and specialty fine jewelry retailer sector. With new stores opened in 2002, Tiffany was making a presence domestically as well as abroad. With its recent acquisition of Little Switzerland, Tiffany would have a wholly owned subsidiary. Little Switzerland was headquartered in St. Thomas, U.S. Virgin Islands, and was a specialty retailer of luxury items. It had operating stores in the Caribbean and Alaska, which helped cater to the tourists in those areas.[10] Tiffany had recently renovated its New York flagship store, opened four more company-operated stores, and expanded into potential markets such as Brazil, China, and Canada. Additionally, the investment in Aber Resources would help Tiffany secure a portion of its future diamond needs, giving it control over some of the resources.

When China entered the WTO in 2001, China became the newest potential market for specialty fine jewelry retailers. This market had the greatest potential for expansion as well as the fastest-growing fine jewelry market in Asia due to its low-cost production. Considerations of expanding in potential markets such as China, Brazil, and Canada were part of management's strategy. Expanding on the number of company-operated retail stores in untapped markets and expanding per square foot of retail space in already existing stores were considerations in the growth of Tiffany and its management.

While tapping into potential markets might have been a big step, building brand image and brand recognition were very important when dealing with international markets. International customers needed to be able to recognize the Tiffany name in order to be successful in that market. New products and designs catering to the markets' culture would help the customers realize that Tiffany was sensitive to the markets' culture and its needs.

Looking Toward the Future

Although Tiffany had increased its brand awareness that stood for luxury brand quality, craftsmanship, and value jewelry, it still faced increasing competition and environmental pressures. As Tiffany continued to expand the number of company-operated retail stores in domestic and international markets, it continued to face decisions that needed to be made to improve its strategy in order to remain competitive. Decisions regarding product, customers, sales and distribution, operations, manufacturing and design, technology, advertising, and geographic scope were in the hands of Kowalski. His decisions would determine the fate of Tiffany as a specialty fine jewelry retailer.

The ***first alternative*** considered was to expand the number of stores and square feet of gross international selling space in potential markets like Brazil, Canada, and China.

The benefit of this alternative was that these were growing markets for precious and semiprecious jewelry with innovative designs. Canada had diamond mines that could be beneficial to operations, and China's membership in the WTO made it a potential market for low-cost sourcing. Tiffany also had one company-operated store in each of these potential markets, giving it leverage in obtaining a larger market share since other competitors had not shown much presence in the areas. Also, the benefit of expanding the number of stores and square feet of gross international selling space would help increase its total international sales.

This alternative was feasible because Tiffany had brand recognition in these areas, which was needed to be successful when expanding in potential markets. Tiffany wanted its customers to be proud to wear the fine jewelry purchases branded with the Tiffany name. This not only helped promote brand image and recognition for Tiffany, but it gave the customers a sense of "status" and "well-being" when the fine jewelry piece was worn. The "Tiffany Blue" symbolized exclusive luxury fine jewelry, which was a brand already recognized by all markets, both potential and in which it operated. Because of Brazil and China's low-cost manufacturing and production facilities, Tiffany could use its financial position to help expand its operations and utilize its resources to its advantage. Besides cost-effectiveness in these markets, the fine jewelry trend was vastly growing in these areas as well as Canada. Tiffany had the ability to outsource some of its processes if needed in these areas since it was cost-effective in these areas. So catering to the potential markets was easy because of outsourcers and manufacturing facilities in these areas.

This alternative could win against competition because competitors, like David Yurman, had little international presence. Its major presence was in New York and California. Zales Corporation had a large presence in North America, while Harry Winston had stores in major cities such as New York, Paris, Beverly Hills, Geneva, and Tokyo. Since Tiffany retail stores were company-operated stores, its close relationships with the customers helped management better understand the customers' needs in those markets. Unlike its competition, which sold a larger portion of fine jewelry through major department stores or other independent retailers, Tiffany used company-operated retail stores. Therefore, the high prices that department stores were forcing some of Tiffany's competitors to pay were holding Tiffany's competitors from producing innovative fine jewelry pieces that were important in staying ahead in the industry. Tiffany already had one company-operated store in each of the potential markets of Brazil, Canada, and China. Tiffany's head start in these potential markets gave it a strong leverage to win over the competition. Many of its competitors did not have any presence in these markets or even strong international presence for that matter.

The drawback with this alternative was that Tiffany had to be prepared to face competitive pressures if it decided to expand in the Brazil, Canada, and China markets. Tiffany needed more than one company-operated store in each of these regions. Even though Tiffany was one of the earlier fine jewelers to grab the market share in the potential markets, this would not prevent competitors like Harry Winston and David Yurman from reacting to Tiffany's expansion. In addition, Tiffany would face competition from local competitors in the potential markets. The local competitors had been established for many years, and the residents of those areas recognized the local competitors' brands.

A way around this drawback was to expand per square foot in each of the stores it already had established. With a flagship store already established with the brand name, customers would recognize and feel the experience that Tiffany had to offer. The product lines, customer relations, value, quality, craftsmanship, and experience would be offered to the customers all under one roof. The local competitors would find it hard to compete with Tiffany because of its enormous size and offerings per square foot of selling space.

The ***second alternative*** was to collaborate with international local competitors in existing and potential markets.

The benefit of this alternative was to decrease or eliminate local competitors by working together with them. Tiffany could use these local competitors as independent retailers of Tiffany fine jewelry. Tiffany would utilize the local competitors to its advantage by building a reputation with their loyal customers.

This alternative was feasible because Tiffany would not only increase revenues in international existing markets but also in potential markets. With the help and recognition of the local competition, Tiffany would be able to use the competition's leverage to gain presence and customer loyalty through selling its fine jewelry in local competitors' stores. In addition, local competitors could use the introduction of Tiffany jewelry into their product lines as a way to promote customers to look at their new merchandise. New merchandise usually drew the attention of customers to a retail store.

Tiffany would be able to win against competition because it would be able to offer its merchandise in additional areas and stores in the international and potential markets through its local competitors as independent retailers. With its additional local competitors selling the Tiffany brand products, this would help increase gross international square feet of selling space.

The drawback of this alternative was that it would take huge efforts to come to agreements with local competition to sell Tiffany fine jewelry at their stores. The way around this drawback was for Tiffany to pay a certain percentage of sales to local competitors for each piece of Tiffany jewelry sold at their store. Usually, commission was an incentive to sell a product.

Notes

1. Tiffany & Co., *Annual Report* (2001).
2. Tiffany & Co., *www.tiffany.com.*
3. Tiffany & Co., *www.tiffany.com.*
4. V. Gomelsky, "China: The Once and Future Kingdom," *National Jeweler Online*, *www.nationaljeweler.com.*
5. V. Gomelsky, "China: The Once and Future Kingdom," *National Jeweler Online*, *www.nationaljeweler.com.*
6. Tiffany & Co., *www.tiffany.com.*
7. Tiffany & Co., *Annual Report* (2001).
8. E-Com Profits, "Baby Boomer Facts," *http://e-comprofits.com/babboomfac.html.*
9. Tiffany & Co., *Annual Report* (2001).
10. Tiffany & Co., *www.tiffany.com.*

References

About.com, *http://jewelry.about.com/cs/costumejewelry/index.htm.*

Advertising Age, *www.adage.com/news.cms?newsId=34174* (2002).

The Business Journal, "Holiday Sales Fall Flat for Specialty Stores," *http://tampabay.bizjournals.com/tampabay/stories/2003/01/06/daily7.html* (January 6, 2003).

P. Danziger, "The Tabletop Report, 2002: The Market, the Competitors, the Trends," *http://retailindustry.about.com/library/bl/02q4/bl_um101002.htm* (2002).

P. Danziger, "Today's Jewelry Market," *www.refresher.com/!umi.html* (2002).

Diamonds International, "Couples Confirm 'Love Is in the Air,' " *www.diamondsintl.com/about.cfm?page=press* (2003).

Ernst & Young, "Retail Newsletter," *www.ey.com* (2002).

Federal Trade Commission, *www.ftc.gov.*

B. Green, "Tiffany Granted Preliminary Injunction Against Counterfeit Jewelry Sales," *National Jeweler Online*, *www.nationaljeweler.com/nationaljeweler/search/search_display.jsp?vnu_content_id=1798850.*

J. Harris, "What Is Retailing?" *www.fiu.edu/~retail/whatis.html* (2000).

Harry Winston, *www.harrywinston.com.*

G. E. Hoover, "What Happens After All the Categories Are Killed?" *Arthur Anderson—Retailing Issues Letter.* Vol. 8, No. 4 (1996), pp. 1–4.

Hoover's Online, "Company Capsule," *www.hoovers.com/co/capsule/1/0,2163,11481,00.html.*

Hoover's Online, "Tiffany & Co. 5 Year Quote," *http://quotes.hoovers.com/thomson/chart.html?p=&t=TIF&n=Tiffany+%26+Co.&e=NYSE&c=11481&templ=4&frame=5+Year&index=&ticker=TIF&threed=2&x=5&y=7.*

LVMH, *www.lvmh.com.*

R. Molofsky, "FBI Raids Manhattan for Fake Tiffany Jewels," *www.nationaljeweler.com/nationaljeweler/search/search_display.jsp?vnu_content_id=1871560* (April 23, 2003).

Nielsen Media Research, *www.nielsenmedia.com.*

Professional Jeweler, "Jewelry Store Sales by Products Stats," *www.professionaljeweler.com/archives/features/stats/stats_prod.html*

QAD Inc., "David Yurman Selects QAD to Make Its Worldwide Manufacturing Operations Sparkle," *http://biz.yahoo.com/bw/021202/20232_1.html* (2002).

Retail Industry, "Catalog Sales Growth Continues to Outpace Overall Retail Growth," *http://retailindustry.about.com/library/bl/q2/bl_dma060401a.htm* (June 4, 2001).

Retail Industry, "The Global Luxury Retailing Sector," *http://retailindustry.about.com/library/bl/02q1/bl_ri020602.htm* (2002).

Retail Jewelers Organization, "Buying Fine Jewelry," *www.rjo.polygon.net/docs/buyingfine.html* (2002).

T. Rozhon, "Squeezed, a Jewelry Designer Closes Shop," *The New York Times* *www.nytimes.com/2003/04/04/business/04GEMS.html* (April 4, 2003).

R. S. Russell and B. W. Taylor III, *Operations Management*, 4th edition (New York: Prentice Hall, 2003), pp. 33–53.

Standard & Poor's, "Stocks Remain in the Red," *www.standardandpoors.com.*

Tiffany & Co., *Annual Report* (2002).

Unity Marketing, "Consumers' Appetite for Jewelry Is Vigorous in the First Half of 2002," *www.unitymarketingonline.com/reports/jewelry/pr1.html* (2002).

U.S. Census Bureau, "1992 Census of Retail Trade, Definitions of Industries," *www.census.gov/epcd/www/rc92sics.html* (1992).

M. Vargas, "Jewelry Sales Reach $39.8 Billion," *http://retailindustry.about.com/library/bl/q2/bl_um041701.htm* (April 17, 2001).

WetFeet, "Retail Industry Profile," *www.wetfeet.com/asp/industryprofiles_overview.asp?industrypk=28.*

WSL Strategic Retail, "Convenience Is Key," *http://retailindustry.about.com/library/uc/02/uc_wls1.htm.*

CASE 23

Oprah Winfrey:

The Story of an Entrepreneur

A. Mukund and A. Neela Radhika

"Oprah Winfrey arguably has more influence on the culture than any university president, politician, political or religious leader, except perhaps the pope."

Vanity Fair magazine, in 1994

"[Oprah] may be uncomfortable talking about [money], but when it comes to making it, she sure knows what she's doing."

Fortune magazine, in March 2002

The Mad Cow Controversy: A Talk Show Queen in Trouble

IN MID-1996, OPRAH WINFREY, ONE OF THE WORLD'S MOST WELL-KNOWN MEDIA PERSONalities and the host of *The Oprah Winfrey Show*, was entangled in a major controversy. The controversy arose because of statements made by Oprah and Howard Lyman (Lyman, a founder/member of the Humane Society of the United States) during an episode of *The Oprah Winfrey Show* telecast on April 16, 1996.[1] The show, based on the theme "Dangerous Food," talked about the mad cow disease[2] and the threat it supposedly posed to beef consumers in the United States.

On the show, Lyman blamed the practice of feeding rendered livestock (protein derived from cattle remains) to cattle for outbreak of the disease in Europe, which resulted in the death of more than 1.5 million cattle and 20 people in 1996. Lyman's statements suggested that beef consumers in the United States could also contract the human form of the mad cow disease as a similar practice of feeding livestock was followed in the United States. On the show, Oprah swore that she would never eat a hamburger again in her life.

In May 1996, some cattle producers filed a $10.3 million suit against Oprah and Lyman in the Texas state court, under the Texas False Disparagement of Perishable Food Products Act,[3] claiming business disparagement, negligence, and defamation. They said Oprah created fear regarding the consumption of beef, when she vowed that she would never again eat a burger in her life. David Mullin, an Attorney representing cattle producers, said, "The message of the show was never meant to be where opinions are shared. The show was meant to be scary."

The cattle producers claimed that Oprah knowingly aired false and defamatory comments about the threat of mad cow disease in the United States. The show reportedly had a devastating impact on cattle prices and sales in the United States. Prices fell to a 10-year low within a week of the show, causing losses exceeding $12 million to the cattle producers. However, Chip Babcock, Oprah's Attorney, claimed that the show in question was fair and did not suggest that beef was unsafe. Commenting on the decline in cattle prices following the show, Oprah's attorneys said that the decline in prices was due to factors such as drought and oversupply.

Oprah soon aired a second show on the mad cow disease, with cattle industry representatives on the discussion panel to arrive at a balanced perspective on the issue. Commenting on this, Bill O'Brien, a co-owner of the Texas Beef Group, said, "I do not think it repaired the damage. She did not go on the program and eat a hamburger before the world." In February 2000, a federal court dismissed the suit against Oprah, stating that though Oprah's show melodramatized the issue, it did not give false information to defame cattle producers. The court also acquitted Lyman, stating that his statements, though strongly stated, were based on established facts.

The issue attracted media attention all over the world, highlighting Oprah's immense popularity and influence over her viewers. Oprah, with a business empire worth over $1 billion in 2002, was unarguably the most successful female media personality ever. How this lady overcame her disturbed, troubled childhood and several other problems to become so popular and successful is essentially a story of her entrepreneurial and leadership skills.

Oprah's Rags-to-Riches Journey

The *talk show Queen*, Oprah was born out of wedlock to Vernon Winfrey and Vernita Lee on January 29, 1954, in Kosciusko, Mississippi. Named Orpah Gail Winfrey, she became Oprah after Orpah was misspelled in her school records. Her parents separated when she was very young. Following this, she was sent to live with her grandmother, Hattie Mae Lee, on a small farm. Hattie laid the foundation of Oprah's career when she taught her to read the Bible. At the age of three, Oprah spent hours reading Bible stories to the animals on the farm. Hattie also taught her many lessons about God and faith. These lessons inspired her (at that tender age) to become strong and help people in need. She believed that she had a higher calling and she was sent to "do good" to others.

Public speaking skills were evident in Oprah right from her childhood. In 1957, at less than four years of age, Oprah recited sermons from the Bible at her local church. Oprah loved the attention and applause she received after her recitals. Oprah was an intelligent child who reportedly asked her teachers to advance her to higher grades.

At the age of six, Oprah was sent to live with her father in Nashville, Tennessee. Her father and her stepmother, Zelma, noticed her interest in reading and encouraged her by buying more books. Her voracious reading helped her always stay ahead of her classmates.

Later that year, she was sent to her mother in Milwaukee. Oprah led a few painful years of her childhood at her mother's. She was sexually abused by her male relatives and acquaintances. These experiences had a profound effect on her, and she turned into a promiscuous and problematic teenager. Her mother tried to admit her to a home for troubled teens, but as the home was full, Oprah was sent to live with her father again. The shift to her father's place was a turning point for Oprah. It reportedly put her life back on track. Oprah referred to the reunion with her father as "my saving grace."

Oprah said that her father was a tough taskmaster, insisting on hard work and discipline. This attitude helped her improve herself in all aspects. In Oprah's words, "As strict as he was, he had some concerns about me making the best of my life, and would not accept anything less than what he thought was my best."

Oprah's father encouraged her to participate in various competitions. Participation in such activities helped her develop self-confidence and improved her communication skills. Oprah organized and directed a series of presentations (especially on *God's Trombones*, written by James Weldon Johnson) at various local churches. Oprah used these presentations to raise funds to buy new robes for the youth choir of her church. She actively participated in Sunday church activities and spoke frequently in church. She also worked hard at her studies and, as a result, won a scholarship to attend Tennessee State University, where she specialized in speech communications and performing arts.

In 1971, at the age of 17, Oprah got her first broadcasting job. She worked as a part-time radio announcer for WVOL radio station (targeting mainly African-Americans) in Nashville. In 1972, she won the "Miss Black Tennessee" title. In 1973, after graduating from Tennessee State University, she joined WTVF-TV in Nashville as a reporter. In 1976, she joined WJZ-TV, a major affiliate of ABC[4] in Baltimore, as a news anchor. She worked at WJZ-TV until 1983. During her tenure at WJZ-TV, she got a chance to host a talk show.[5] She was the co-host for *People Are Talking*, a popular talk show in those days.

In 1984, Oprah moved to WLS-TV Chicago (an affiliate of ABC) to host a local TV talk show, *A.M. Chicago*. Oprah deviated from the general talk show format, referred to as "report talk." She introduced a new format, referred to as "rapport talk," that involved back-and-forth conversation between the host and the audience. Oprah's show became an instant hit with women, mostly in the 30–50 age group. According to analysts, Oprah's show was a success because the conversational mode formed the basis of female bonding. Many of the people in her audience felt that Oprah had made the talk show more personal and confessional.

By the end of the year, the talk show became very successful. As a result of the show's success and Oprah's increasing popularity, the show was renamed *The Oprah Winfrey Show*, and its duration was increased from 30 minutes to one hour. In 1986, the show went national and became the country's number one talk show within one year of being nationally syndicated.

During the mid-1980s, Oprah began her acting career with a role in Steven Spielberg's *The Color Purple* (1985). For her performance in the movie, Oprah was nominated for an Oscar and a Golden Globe Award in the category of Best Supporting Actress. Her performance in her second movie, *Native Son* (1986), also won applause from critics.

Oprah's love for acting and her desire to offer quality entertainment led to the establishment of Harpo Productions Inc. (Harpo is Oprah spelled backward). With Harpo, Oprah became the third woman in U.S. history to own a movie production studio (the pioneers were Mary Pickford and Lucille Ball). In October 1988, Harpo Productions acquired the ownership and production rights to *The Oprah Winfrey Show* from ABC. This made Oprah the first woman in the history of TV to own and produce her own talk show.

In 1992, Oprah got engaged to Stedman Graham, a former basketball player and a public relations executive, with whom she had been living since 1986. During the late-1980s and 1990s, Oprah won many awards and garnered recognition for her work in TV and films. In 1994, she was included in the TV Hall of Fame. (Refer to **Exhibit 1** for details of the awards won by Oprah.)

For over a decade, Oprah's talk show, like other talk shows, focused on dysfunctional families and their problems. However, in 1994, Oprah announced a change in her program format. She decided to stop the dysfunctional-group–based shows and began focusing on positive shows that inspired people to rise above their limitations and achieve their dreams. The

Exhibit 1
Awards Won By Oprah

Year	Award
1971	Crowned Miss Fire Prevention, Nashville, TN
1971	Won Miss Black Tennessee pageant
1987	Daytime Emmy (Outstanding Talk/Service Show Host, *The Oprah Winfrey Show*)
1988	International Radio and Television Society, Broadcaster of the Year; youngest recipient
1989	Daytime Emmy (Outstanding Talk/Service Show, *The Oprah Winfrey Show*)
1991	Daytime Emmy (Outstanding Talk/Service Show Host, *The Oprah Winfrey Show*)
1991	Daytime Emmy (Outstanding Talk/Service Show, *The Oprah Winfrey Show*)
1991	NAACP Image (Outstanding News, Talk or Information Series, *The Oprah Winfrey Show*)
1992	Daytime Emmy (Outstanding Talk/Service Show Host, *The Oprah Winfrey Show*)
1992	Daytime Emmy (Outstanding Talk/Service Show, *The Oprah Winfrey Show*)
1993	Daytime Emmy (Outstanding Talk/Service Show Host, *The Oprah Winfrey Show*)
1993	Daytime Emmy (Outstanding Children's Special, *Shades of a Single Protein*, ABC after-school special)
1994	Daytime Emmy (Outstanding Talk/Service Show Host, *The Oprah Winfrey Show*)
1994	Daytime Emmy (Outstanding Talk/Service Show, *The Oprah Winfrey Show*)
1995	Daytime Emmy (Outstanding Talk/Service Show Host, *The Oprah Winfrey Show*)
1995	Daytime Emmy (Outstanding Talk/Service Show, *The Oprah Winfrey Show*)
1996	George Foster Peabody Individual Achievement Award
1996	Daytime Emmy (Outstanding Talk/Service Show, *The Oprah Winfrey Show*)
1997	People's Choice Award, Favorite Female Television Performer
1997	Daytime Emmy (Outstanding Talk Show, *The Oprah Winfrey Show*)
1997	NAACP Image (Outstanding News, Talk or Informational Special, *Dinner with Oprah: A Lifetime Exclusive—Toni Morrison*; shared award)
1997	NAACP Image (Outstanding News, Talk or Informational Series, *The Oprah Winfrey Show: Oprah's Book Club—Dinner with Maya Angelou*; shared award)
1998	People's Choice (Favorite Female Performer in a TV Series, *The Oprah Winfrey Show*)
1998	Daytime Emmy (Lifetime Achievement; presented by the National Academy of Television Arts and Sciences)
1998	Daytime Emmy (Outstanding Talk Show Host, *The Oprah Winfrey Show*; tied with Rosie O'Donnell)
1999	National Book Foundation's 50th Anniversary Gold Medal (for influential contribution to reading and books).
2001	Woman of the Century Award from *Newsweek*
2002	Emmy (Bob Hope Humanitarian Award)

Source: www.eonline.com

aim of this new format was to entertain, enlighten, and empower the millions of viewers who watched the show around the world.

The new format thus offered direction, advice, and help to people through entertainment mixed with therapy. Oprah introduced Dr. Phil McGraw, a renowned psychologist, as a weekly guest on the show, to help guests and the audience gain insights into their problems. Thus, while other talk shows continued to focus on entertainment and shock value, Oprah's shows (and her various ventures) helped change lives for the better.

The Oprah Harpo Empire

During the 1990s, Oprah expanded her business into many areas besides television. She entered various fields, such as publishing, music, film, health and fitness, and education. In 1994, Oprah's initiatives for the protection of children against abuse were rewarded when then U.S. President Bill Clinton signed the "Oprah Bill," a new law designed to protect children against abuse.

In 1996, Oprah headed the list of Forbes' highest-paid entertainers with earnings of $171 million, beating even celebrities such as Steven Spielberg, Michael Jackson, Arnold Schwarzenegger, and Jim Carrey. In September 1996, Oprah launched *Oprah's Book Club* on TV, which was aimed at inculcating and encouraging reading among people. *Oprah's Book Club* was a great success; most of her fans chose to read the books she selected for the Book Club. Reportedly, sales of all the books selected for the club increased substantially (on average by 10 times) and found a place in the bestsellers lists.

Harpo Films Inc., Oprah's film production division, signed a long-term agreement with the ABC television network in the mid-1990s to produce the *Oprah Winfrey Presents* series of telefilms. Some of the major projects under the *Oprah Winfrey Presents* banner were "Amy and Isabelle," "Tuesdays with Morrie," "David and Lisa," "The Wedding," and "Before Women Had Wings." Oprah even acted in some of these telefilms (such as "The Women of Brewster Place," "Before Women Had Wings," and "There Are No Children Here") and received critical acclaim for her performance. The telefilms venture met with reasonable success and generated $4 million in revenues in 2001.

Oprah also signed an exclusive agreement with the Walt Disney Motion Picture Group in the mid-1990s to produce feature films for Disney. The first film produced by the Harpo Group for Disney was Touchstone Pictures' *Beloved*, in which Oprah played the lead role. By the end of the 1990s, Oprah had reportedly become one of the very few people in the world who were recognized immediately by their first name alone. She had become so popular that in 1998, she was voted the second most admired woman in the United States, next only to President Clinton's wife, Hillary Rodham Clinton.

In November 1998, the Harpo Group launched Oxygen Media LLC in partnership with Geraldine Laybourne's GBL LLC, an entertainment company, and Carsey Werner Mandabach (CWM) LLC.[6] Harpo had a 25% stake in Oxygen. Oxygen Media, aimed at women, was an integrated media company that combined the advantages of both cable television and the Internet. Geraldine Laybourne was the chairman and CEO of Oxygen Media. The company's cable network featured a range of programs that included talk shows, music, health, news, comedy, movies, cartoons, and sports. *Oprah Goes Online*, the first program featured on the Oxygen cable network, was a 12-episode course on using the Internet. Oprah also produced and hosted the show *Use Your Life* on Oxygen Media. Oxygen Media's web sites included *Oxygen.com*, *Oprah.com*, and *ThriveOnline.com*. Oprah's web site, *www.oprah.com*, which offered the latest information regarding *The Oprah Winfrey Show* (and later the Angel Network and *O* Magazine), was reportedly viewed over 7 million times every month in 1999 and received more than 2,000 e-mails every day.

Oprah's popularity and ratings had surged ahead of those of other talk show hosts, including veterans such as Phil Donahue (the pioneer of talk shows), Regis Philbin (*Live with Regis*), Kelly Ripa (*Kelly*), Sally Jessy Raphael (*The Sally Jessy Raphael Show*), Jerry Seinfeld, Jerry Springer, and David Letterman. (See **Exhibit 2** for details of popular TV personalities in the United States from 1993 to 2000.) The Harpo empire entered the magazine business in early 2000. By 2002, Oprah headed Harpo Inc., Harpo Productions Inc., Harpo Video Inc., Harpo Films Inc., and Harpo Studios Inc. as the Harpo Group's Chairman.

In April 2000, Harpo Entertainment and Hearst Magazines jointly launched *O, The Oprah Magazine*, in New York City. The magazine was positioned as a personal growth guide for women in the 21st century. *O* addressed various aspects of a woman's life, such as her inner well-being, fashion, health and fitness, relationships, self-discovery, books, home design, and food, among others. The magazine, targeted at women between 25 and 49 years of age, was circulated across the country. Speaking about *O*, Oprah, who was also its editorial director, said, "I believe you are here to become more of yourself, to live your best life. The magazine will present articles and stories of other people to help women look at their lives differently."

Exhibit 2
A. Favorite TV Personalities: Ranks: Harris Poll

	1993	1994	1995	1996	1997	1998	1999	2000	2001
Drew Carey	*	*	*	10	6	8	1	3	1
Regis Philbin	*	*	*	*	*	*	*	2	2
Oprah Winfrey	2	2	3	3	3	1	2	1	3
David Letterman	6	6	4	5	7	*	*	6	4
Ray Romano	*	*	*	*	*	*	*	7	5
Jay Leno	*	8	10	10	8	6	*	7	6
Bill O'Reilly	*	*	*	*	*	*	*	*	7
Kelsey Grammar	*	*	8	8	9	5	5	5	8
Katie Couric	*	*	*	*	*	*	*	*	9
Rosie O'Donnell	*	*	*	8	5	6	8	9	10

Note:
*Not rated in that year.

Source: www.harrisinteractive.com

B. Favorite TV Personalities Among Different Groups: Harris Poll[1]

Gender-Based	
Men	Drew Carey
Women	Oprah Winfrey
Age-Based	
Age 18–24	Drew Carey
Age 25–29	David Letterman
Age 30–39	Drew Carey
Age 40–49	Regis Philbin
Age 50 and over	Regis Philbin
Race-Based	
White	Regis Philbin
African-American	Drew Carey
Hispanic	David Letterman

Note:
1. The Harris Poll was conducted (online) in the United States between December 20, 2001, and January 1, 2002. The sample size of the poll was 2,098 adults from a cross-section of audiences across the country.

Source: www.harrisinteractive.com

Columns in *O* included "Live Your Best Life," "Make Your Dreams Come True" (a step-by-step planning guide), and "Tell it Like It Is" (by Dr. Phil), "Dream Big" (a profile of a person who took steps to live out his or her dream), and "My Journal" (a profile of a celebrity's intimate thoughts).

O was reportedly the most successful startup in the magazine industry. In 2001, its revenues amounted to over $140 million. According to Cathleen Black, President, Hearst Magazines, most successful magazines took nearly five years to become as profitable as *O* did in only two years. Analysts noted that though the market was down and many magazines had posted losses in 2001, *O*'s advertising revenues increased by 43% over its revenues in 2000. *O*'s paid-up circulation amounted to an estimated 2.5 million copies, which was more than those of leading magazines such as *Vogue* and *Martha Stewart Living*. *O* targeted the premium segment, which had an average income of $63,000 and patronized premium brands such as Lexus, Coach, and Donna Karan (which were key advertisers for *O*).

Oprah described *O* as a personal growth manual and took an active part in the content development of the magazine. Analysts remarked that *O* was a reflection of Oprah's personality. The success of *O* was primarily attributed to Oprah's popularity. Commenting on the high revenues earned by the magazine in terms of advertising revenue, Black said, "Advertisers have unanimously responded to the powerful presence of Oprah. The magazine is a new voice for a new time—a lifestyle magazine with heart and soul."

However, Oprah's talk show continued to be her biggest success, generating revenues of over $300 million annually. The show was aired in over 107 countries in the world and was watched by 26 million people in the United States alone. It remained the number one talk show in the daytime slot for 16 years, despite competition from over 50 rivals. According to Bob Iger, President of Walt Disney, the Oprah show contributed significantly to the company's profits (Walt Disney's ABC Network syndicated *The Oprah Winfrey Show* in many major markets). The show appealed primarily to women in the age group 30–50 years. Since most of the audience was from the middle class, the show attracted huge advertising revenues from companies such as Wal-Mart, Procter & Gamble, and Sears.

Oprah, the Entrepreneur

Despite the fact that she was the owner of a huge business empire, Oprah reportedly did not even know how to read a balance sheet and did not follow any corporate models. She had declined offers from many companies such as AT&T, Intel, and Ralph Lauren to be on their boards, stating that "she did not understand what she would do on their boards." Oprah was once reported to have hoarded $50 million in cash, which she called her personal "bag-lady fund," as she was afraid of investing in the stock market, being totally ignorant about it.

Interestingly, she did not like being referred to as a businesswoman. Commenting on her ignorance of doing business the usual way, she said, "If I called a strategic-planning meeting, there would be dead silence, and then people would fall out of their chairs laughing."

According to analysts, Oprah was not in the "business of business"; she was in the "business of soothing souls." The kind of intimacy Oprah enjoyed with her audiences was something that reportedly no other talk show host had ever achieved. Oprah's message, "You are responsible for your own life," acted as her unique selling proposition (USP), just like "convenience" and "everyday low prices" were the USPs of McDonald's and Wal-Mart, respectively.

The Harpo empire, however, did not function purely on Oprah's personal skills. She had put in place a team that dedicatedly worked toward keeping the business running. Dennis Swanson[7] and Jeff Jacobs,[8] President, Harpo Group, contributed greatly to Oprah's success as a talk show host as well as a businesswoman over the years. Explaining Oprah's business, Jacobs said, "We bet on ourselves. We are an intellectual property company, and our partners [ABC, Hearst, Oxygen] are distributors. Core content is developed here and has never left our home base."

Jacobs said that controlling content was a difficult task as Oprah was not only the chief content creator but also the chief content itself. For instance, every issue of *O* sported a bold and winning picture of Oprah on its cover page; in her columns in *O*, she gave details of her personal life, such as her battle against abuse, her triumph over adversity, and her attempts at losing weight. She also discussed her painful experiences as a victim of child abuse and racism. Commenting on the content, Oprah said, "I bring all my stuff with me."

Analysts felt that Oprah's life was central to her brand. They believed that by making herself and her struggle against adversity the central theme of her messages, she successfully touched the American psyche and motivated Americans to become self-reliant. Oprah won the audience's trust by sharing her personal experiences with them on daytime TV to help them deal with their problems and become accountable for their own lives. This strategy reportedly kept Oprah ahead of her competitors.

Analysts believed that Oprah was reluctant to lose control of her brand because she was aware of its power. Oprah consistently refused requests from major companies to use her name on their products, such as perfumes, clothing, books, and food. One of the Oprah's friends remarked that everybody wanted "a part of Oprah's brand," but she was not ready to cede control over it. Analysts said that though some of her competitors (such as Martha Stewart) had lent their names to various products, Oprah firmly refused to do so. Since many of the products marketed by celebrities had failed in the market, analysts felt that Oprah was right in refusing to dilute her brand equity.

Oprah was also against taking the Harpo Group public. She held 90% of the Harpo Group herself. She claimed that by selling her name or a part of her business, she would be selling herself. In Oprah's words, "If I lost control of the business, I would lose myself or at least the ability to be myself. Owning myself is a way to be myself." This clearly indicated how Oprah perceived her businesses and the extent to which her businesses were based on Oprah herself.

Analysts felt that Jacobs' business acumen also contributed greatly to Harpo's success. Oprah and Jacobs were rather an odd pair to be running a business as they had very different management styles. According to analysts, Oprah followed a management-by-instinct technique and took all her decisions on the basis of her gut feelings, while Jacobs believed in careful planning and execution. While Jacobs described Harpo's strategy as multipurposing the content in various media, Oprah explained it as reaching out to a larger audience (through different media) to help people better their lives. However, the success of Harpo Group made it evident that the relationship worked.

According to company sources, Jacobs acted as Oprah's strategic advisor and dealmaker. In Oprah's words, "He is a piranha and that is a good thing for me to have." Remembering his meeting with Jacobs and his commitment towards Oprah, Iger said, "I remember being put off initially, but Jeff Jacobs has one thing in mind: his client. And he serves her very well."

Despite his many contributions to the company, Jacobs preferred to remain in the background and referred to himself as a "behind-the-scenes guy." Besides being the President of Harpo, he also acted as Oprah's personal agent, making her deals and agreements. This arrangement resulted in a saving of over 25% on Oprah's income, which would have gone in payments to agents and managers. Commenting on the financial success of Oprah, Jacobs said, "We understand it is not just how much you make but how much you keep."

Oprah was known for making sudden decisions on the basis of gut feelings. Oprah decided to launch *O*'s first international edition (in early 2002) when watching a documentary on Africa that showed some women in a beauty parlor in Nairobi reading *True Love* and *Hello* magazines. Commenting on this, Oprah said, "I thought, 'African women have no business sitting in a beauty shop reading *Hello!* and *True Love*." Soon after, she launched *O* in Africa!

Interestingly, Oprah's business decisions (based on her gut feelings) were often successful. Her decision to place the table of contents of *O* on page 2 was not common business practice. Most publishers placed it in the middle of the magazine so that readers had to go through a couple of advertisements in search of the table of contents. This practice was aimed at benefiting advertisers, but Oprah, in her own words, wanted to "put the readers first."

The fact that *O* was an instant success proved Oprah's decision right. Commenting on the magazine's success, Oprah said, "I am most proud of the magazine, because I did not know what I was doing." Media reports claimed that *O*, which was mostly developed by Oprah, reflected her ability to balance practicality and preaching. Analysts believed that Oprah knew that such balance would sell—and it did. According to them, this was the same strategy that made her talk show such a success. Oprah maintained a balance between the issues or persons she chose for her show. For example, if one day she discussed the entertainment industry with a celebrity, the very next day she examined a grave issue such as the problems of women in Afghanistan.

Reportedly, Oprah followed the same balanced approach with her finances. Though she did not track her costs closely, she was aware of their magnitude and was sure to draw the strings when necessary. For instance, when Oprah found that the production costs of her show amounted to $50 million annually (which was double the expenditure incurred by other daytime talk shows), she called up Doug Pattison, Harpo's CFO, and said "That is okay, but that is also enough. I think we can keep it at $50 million."

As far as her employees were concerned, Oprah paid them well and expected quality for the money. Reportedly, she did not care about ratings as long as her shows and magazines achieved their objectives. Commenting on this, she said, "Ratings go down when we do an Oprah's Book Club show, but that does not matter. We are getting people to read." Thus, Oprah did not pressure her employees to achieve ratings; instead, she emphasized creativity and quality. According to her employees, Oprah took care that her staff did not measure its success on the basis of media reports. She showered praises on her staff once a project was completed; but when that project was recognized by the world and won ratings or awards, her staff received no special treatment from her. In the words of Kate Forte, President, Harpo Films, "But if it wins big ratings or awards, the boss is mum. It is her reminder that we should not do anything for the external reward."

Though there was great demand for Harpo-produced movies and television films, Oprah did not bend her rules to exploit that demand. According to Iger, though Disney wanted Harpo to produce more films, Oprah's standards and rules limited Harpo's output to one film per year. Commenting on this, Iger said, "Just because there is a buyer does not mean she is a seller."

Oprah's business decisions were based largely on trust (she referred to this as taking leaps of faith). It was reported that she asked only one question before she made a decision: "Can I trust you?" Commenting on this, Nancy Petersman, Executive Vice President, Allen & Co. (an investment banking firm), said "It is all about character with Oprah. We investment bankers do the same sort of thing—try to figure out what people are made of—but with Oprah, it is like someone is looking into your soul."

Trust and control over a project were major factors in Oprah's decision-making process. Hearst succeeded in winning Oprah's assent for *O* despite competition from AOL Time Warner and Conde Nast by winning Oprah's trust. Hearst promised her that the magazine would reflect her values and would work toward translating her message into the written word. To ensure this, Hearst entrusted Oprah with total editorial control of the magazine.

It was the same story with Oprah's investment decisions. Geraldine Laybourne, Co-founder of Oxygen, won Oprah's trust by telling her that she was planning a cable network aimed at providing content and service to women. The idea appealed to Oprah—in fact, she had something similar in her mind—and on an impulse, she invested $20 million in the project and also transferred certain rights to *The Oprah Winfrey Show* library. In return, she received a 25% stake in Oxygen Media.[9]

Oprah, Serving the People

Since Oprah had been a victim of child abuse, she constantly raised the issue in her show and made constant efforts to protect children from such abuse. In 1991, she demanded that the government pass a new law (The National Child Protection Act) against child abuse. Oprah even testified before the Senate Judiciary Committee of the United States to help establish a database of convicted child abusers in the United States. In December 1993, Oprah's efforts were rewarded, when the Oprah Bill (The National Child Protection Act) was made a law.

On principle, Oprah had donated at least 10% of her annual earnings to charity during her adult life. Reportedly, most of these donations were made anonymously. However, in the

1990s, Oprah made such donations openly. She reportedly donated millions of dollars to institutes of higher education (Spelman College, Morehouse College, and Tennessee State University) and established scholarships that helped hundreds of students.

In September 1997, Oprah launched Oprah's Angel Network to encourage people to extend their help to those in need. Oprah asked her audience to help the less fortunate by donating their spare change to the Angel Network. By 2000, Angel Network had received more than $3.5 million in spare change, which was used to give scholarships to poor students and fund Habitat for Humanity homes. In April 2000, Angel Network announced the Use Your Life Award for people who "made others' lives better." The award, which carried a cash prize of $100,000, was given every Monday on *The Oprah Winfrey Show*.

Oprah was chosen to host the interfaith prayer service held at New York City's Yankee Stadium on September 23, 2001, to mourn the victims of the September 11 terrorist attacks on the World Trade Center. Rudy Giuliani, Mayor of New York City, believed that Oprah was the only national personality who had the ability to host such a profoundly religious service that involved people from different faiths. Oprah lived up to his expectations; her service both comforted and inspired mourners.

She said that "loved ones turned to angels after death and are always near to the people's hearts." Oprah reminded the people that hope, prayer, and love never die and asked them to use every moment of their lives to create a deeper meaning to their lives and to find out what really matters. According to an article published in April 2002, Oprah had become an icon of "church-free spirituality" and a spiritual guru to her over 22 million devoted viewers. Her influence was such that the *Wall Street Journal* even credited Oprah with introducing a new technique of interpersonal communication, "Oprahfication" (i.e., "public confession as a form of therapy").[10] This technique became so popular that a magazine even used Oprah as a verb: "I did not want to tell her, but she Oprah'd it out of me." Reportedly, this technique also became popular with politicians, who began holding Oprah-style town meetings to understand their constituents.

The Other Side of Oprah?

Not surprisingly, Oprah had many critics. Over the years, many of her personal as well as business-related policies had been criticized. Though employees at Harpo agreed that the pay and benefits offered by the company were exceptional compared to industry standards, some criticized the strict rules and regulations enforced. They said that Oprah forced her employees to sign a lifelong confidentiality agreement, which bound them from making any revelations about Harpo in their lifetime. In a lawsuit filed by a former employee against the company, Harpo was described as a narcissistic workplace.

Some employees even criticized Oprah for being a tough taskmaster who drove her employees hard to meet her expectations. A former Harpo employee described the environment at Harpo as "an environment of dishonesty and chaos," and said, "everyone undermines everybody else to get more access to Oprah, and I think she encourages it."

Oprah accepted the fact that she gave her employees a tough time. However, regarding the confidentiality agreement, Oprah said, "You would not say it is harsh if you were in the tabloids all the time." Oprah did not respond to other criticism about the work culture at Harpo.

Oprah's decision to invest in Oxygen Media also tarnished her reputation. In 2001, it was reported that the message boards on Oxygen Media offered links to web sites featuring sex themes and kinky-pleasure content (Oprah banned such material on her talk show in the initial years). This was attributed to the alliance between Oxygen Media and ThriveOnline, a women's health site. Though Harpo's spokesperson defended Oprah by saying that Oprah was away on a vacation and was ignorant of these aspects of Oxygen Media, some people suspected Oprah of permitting such material on the web site.

Some sections of Oprah's audiences criticized her spirituality shows, such as *One Way to Live* and *Remembering Your Spirit*. They said that in the early 21st century Oprah had become more of a preacher woman than a confidante and a friend. Some viewers even felt that Oprah was a hypocrite. They said that while she preached about the need to disregard material things and focus on the spiritual aspects of life, *O* featured advertisements of luxury items from companies such as BMW, Louis Vuitton, and Lancome, earning huge revenues for Harpo. They even criticized Oprah for keeping the ticket price for her popular *Live Your Best Life* series of shows as high as $185.

Other controversies, such as the one surrounding the mad cow disease issue, added to Oprah's negative publicity. However, they failed to do any major damage to her popularity. Such was her popularity that even the critics were shocked when in 2001 she announced her decision to quit the show in the near future. Oprah explained, "I am sick of people sitting in chairs stating their problems. Then we roll the videotape, then we have our experts on the topic. I truly do not know what to replace it with. As soon as I do, I am pulling those people from their chairs." She added, "I am in the 'what's next?' phase of my career."

The Show Goes On

Much to the delight of her fans, Oprah changed her mind, and in mid-2002 renewed her contract for the show until 2006. Media reports mentioned that this was typical of Oprah as she generally changed her decisions rather easily. Though Oprah renewed the contract, she said that she was exploring the options she had after exiting the show. However, she was quick to add that she would not leave TV.

Analysts remarked that if Oprah did leave the show in the future, her options were unlimited. A few analysts even said that with the kind of influence and power she had, she could even someday become the President of the United States.

However, Oprah's story was not about power and influence; rather, it was about ability and the determination to leverage entrepreneurial and personal skills to make it big. According to analysts, the most remarkable aspect about Oprah was the way she dealt with the success, wealth, and fame she acquired through the years.

It was reported that with the passage of time, Oprah was evolving, becoming more adaptive, stronger, deeper, and more spiritual. Her admirers believed that Oprah's confidence and belief in herself were growing as well—something that was the key to her success, first as a talk show host, then as a businesswoman, and, perhaps most importantly, as a compassionate human being.

Notes

1. The discussion panel comprised Oprah Winfrey (Host), Howard Lyman (Executive Director, Humane Society, U.S.), Gary Weber (Representative, National Cattlemen's Beef Association) and Dr. Will Hueston (Representative, United States Department of Agriculture).
2. Mad cow disease, scientifically called "Bovine Spongiform Encephalophy" (BSE), is a nervous system disorder. The major symptoms of the disease in cattle are belligerence, poor coordination, confusion and death. According to medical analysts, the disease (in cows) became an epidemic due to the modern farming practices adopted by cattle ranchers, such as feeding cows with rendered livestock. The mad cow disease is linked with a variant of the Creutzfeldt-Jakob disease (CJD), found in beef-consuming human beings. This variant is incurable and fatal. It kills its victims by filling their brain with microscopic spongy holes.
3. Under this Act, people can be held liable if they make false and disparaging statements regarding perishable food products.
4. ABC, a subsidiary of Walt Disney Company, is one of the leading broadcasting companies in the U.S. It broadcasts through a network of more than 230 affiliate stations across the U.S. It also owns over 60 radio stations and 10 TV stations in all the major markets of the country.

5. A talk show is an interactive session between two or more people. Such shows generally involve interaction between a host, guest(s), and the audience.
6. CWM LLC is one of the major independent production studios in America, distributing programming content in over 175 countries.
7. Dennis Swanson was the head of WLS-TV, Chicago. He appointed Oprah as a talk show host and convinced her that she could succeed even though she was overweight and an African American. Such was his belief in Oprah's capability that he ran her show opposite Chicago's number one talk show hosted by Phil Donahue. Within one month, Oprah's show replaced Donahue's in ratings.
8. Jeff was an entertainment lawyer in Chicago. He helped Oprah handle legal formalities regarding her contracts. However, by 1986 he convinced Oprah to establish her own company instead of lending her talent to outsiders. This led to the formation of Harpo Entertainment Inc., in which Jeff was given 5% share. Jeff joined Harpo as President in 1989. In recognition of his contribution to the company, Jeff's stake in the company was increased to 10% later on.
9. In March 2002, it was reported that Oprah regretted her decision to impart certain rights to *The Oprah Winfrey Show* library to Oxygen Media. She felt that by doing so, she had traded her soul. To undo this mistake, Oprah acquired her rights back and in return she agreed to do a special program on Oxygen Media, "Oprah After the Show."
10. *www.christianitytoday.com*, April 1, 2002.

Additional Readings and References

www.achievement.org

www.auditionagency.com

B. Bridget, "Oprah Going, Sally Gone," *www.eonline.com* (March 11, 2002).

B. Byrne, "Oprah Heading to PrimeTime," *www.eonline.com* (June 11, 2002).

"Cattleman: 2nd Oprah Show 'Too Little, Too Late,'" *www.cnn.com* (January 26, 1998).

"Creating *Oprah: The Magazine*," *http://foliomag.com* (September 1, 1999).

"Court Upholds Dismissal of Oprah Lawsuit Without Testing 'Veggie Libel' Law," *www.mediainstitute.org* (February 2000).

"Hearst Magazines Introduces *O*, The Oprah Magazine," *www.broadcast.com* (April 2000).

www.jumptheshark.com

www.leatherquest.com

www.mcspotlight.org

www.oprah.com

"Oprah Accused of Whipping Up Anti-Beef 'Lynch Mob,'" *www.cnn.com* (January 21, 1998).

"Oprah's Angel," *www.etonline.com* (June 18, 2001).

O. Winfrey, *The African American Almanac*, 7th edition (Gale, 1997).

"Oprah Winfrey," *www.businessweek.com* (January 14, 2002).

"Oprah Winfrey," *www.forbes.com* (December 13, 2001).

"Oprah Winfrey: The Well Rounded Interview," *www.well-rounded.com* (July 1998).

"Oprah Wraps Up 'Life,'" *www.etonline.com* (July 2, 2001).

P. Sellers, "The Business of Being Oprah," *Fortune* (March 17, 2002).

"Shut Up and Eat," *www.prwatch.org* (Second Quarter 1997).

H. Taylor, "Oprah Winfrey Recaptures Top Spot As Nation's Most Popular TV Personality," *www.harrisinteractive.com* (December 27, 2000).

CASE 24

Inner-City Paint Corporation (Revised)

Donald F. Kuratko and Norman J. Gierlasinski

History

STANLEY WALSH BEGAN INNER-CITY PAINT CORPORATION IN A RUN-DOWN WAREHOUSE, which he rented, on the fringe of Chicago's "downtown" business area. The company is still located at its original site.

Inner-City is a small company that manufactures wall paint. It does not compete with giants such as Glidden and DuPont. There are small paint manufacturers in Chicago that supply the immediate area. The proliferation of paint manufacturers is due to the fact that the weight of the product (52½ pounds per 5-gallon container) makes the cost of shipping great distances prohibitive. Inner-City's chief product is flat white wall paint sold in 5-gallon plastic cans. It also produces colors on request in 55-gallon containers.

The primary market of Inner-City is the small- to medium-sized decorating company. Pricing must be competitive; until recently, Inner-City had shown steady growth in this market. The slowdown in the housing market combined with a slowdown in the overall economy caused financial difficulty for Inner-City Paint Corporation. Inner-City's reputation had been built on fast service: it frequently supplied paint to contractors within 24 hours. Speedy delivery to customers became difficult when Inner-City was required to pay cash on delivery (C.O.D.) for its raw materials.

Inner-City had been operating without management controls or financial controls. It had grown from a very small two-person company with sales of $60,000 annually five years ago, to sales of $1,800,000 and 38 employees this year. Stanley Walsh realized that tighter controls within his organization would be necessary if the company was to survive.

Equipment

Five mixers are used in the manufacturing process. Three large mixers can produce a maximum of 400 gallons, per batch, per mixer. The two smaller mixers can produce a maximum of 100 gallons, per batch, per mixer.

Two lift trucks are used for moving raw materials. The materials are packed in 100-pound bags. The lift trucks also move finished goods, which are stacked on pallets.

A small testing lab ensures the quality of materials received and the consistent quality of their finished product. The equipment in the lab is sufficient to handle the current volume of product manufactured.

Transportation equipment consists of two 24-foot delivery trucks and two vans. This small fleet is more than sufficient because many customers pick up their orders to save delivery costs.

Facilities

Inner-City performs all operations from one building consisting of 16,400 square feet. The majority of the space is devoted to manufacturing and storage; only 850 square feet is assigned as office space. The building is 45 years old and in disrepair. It is being leased in three-year increments. The current monthly rent on this lease is $2,700. The rent is low in consideration of the poor condition of the building and its undesirable location in a run-down neighborhood (south side of Chicago). These conditions are suitable to Inner-City because of the dusty, dirty nature of the manufacturing process and the small contribution of the rent to overhead costs.

Product

Flat white paint is made with pigment (titanium dioxide and silicates), vehicle (resin), and water. The water makes up 72% of the contents of the product. To produce a color, the necessary pigment is added to the flat white paint. The pigment used to produce the color has been previously tested in the lab to ensure consistent quality of texture. Essentially, the process is the mixing of powders with water, then tapping off of the result into 5- or 55-gallon containers. Color overruns are tapped off into 2-gallon containers.

Inventory records are not kept. The warehouse manager keeps a mental count of what is in stock. He documents (on a lined yellow pad) what has been shipped for the day and to whom. That list is given to the billing clerk at the end of each day.

The cost of the materials to produce flat white paint is $2.40 per gallon. The cost per gallon for colors is approximately 40% to 50% higher. The 5-gallon covered plastic pails cost Inner-City $1.72 each. The 55-gallon drums (with lids) are $8.35 each (see **Exhibit 1**).

Selling price varies with the quantity purchased. To the average customer, flat white sells at $27.45 for 5 gallons and $182.75 for 55 gallons. Colors vary in selling price because of the

Exhibit 1
Paint Cost Sheet: Inner-City Paint Corporation

	5 Gallons	55 Gallons
Sales price	$ 27.45	$ 182.75
Direct material	(12.00)	(132.00)
Pail and lid	(1.72)	(8.35)
Direct labor	(2.50)	(13.75)
Manufacturing overhead ($1/gallon)	(5.00)	(5.00)
Gross margin	$ 6.23	$ 23.65
Gross profit ratio	22.7%	12.9%

variety in pigment cost and quantity ordered. Customers purchase on credit and usually pay their invoices in 30 to 60 days. Inner-City telephones the customer after 60 days of nonpayment and inquires when payment will be made.

Management

The President and majority stockholder is Stanley Walsh. He began his career as a house painter and advanced to become a painter for a large decorating company. Walsh painted mostly walls in large commercial buildings and hospitals. Eventually, he came to believe that he could produce a paint that was less expensive and of higher quality than what was being used. A keen desire to open his own business resulted in the creation of Inner-City Paint Corporation.

Walsh manages the corporation today in much the same way that he did when the business began. He personally must open *all* the mail, approve *all* payments, and inspect *all* customer billings before they are mailed. He has been unable to detach himself from any detail of the operation and cannot properly delegate authority. As the company has grown, the time element alone has aggravated the situation. Frequently, these tasks are performed days after transactions occur and mail is received.

The office is managed by Mary Walsh (Walsh's mother). Two part-time clerks assist her, and all records are processed manually.

The plant is managed by a man in his twenties, whom Walsh hired from one of his customers. Walsh became acquainted with him when the man picked up paint from Inner-City for his previous employer. Prior to the eight months he has been employed by Walsh as Plant Manager, his only other experience has been that of a painter.

Employees

Thirty-five employees (20 workers are part-time) work in various phases of the manufacturing process. The employees are nonunion, and most are unskilled laborers. They take turns making paint and driving the delivery trucks.

Stanley Walsh does all of the sales work and public relations work. He spends approximately one half of every day making sales calls and answering complaints about defective paint. He is the only salesman. Other salesmen had been employed in the past, but Walsh felt that they "could not be trusted."

Customer Perception

Customers view Inner-City as a company that provides fast service and negotiates on price and payment out of desperation. Walsh is seen as a disorganized man who may not be able to keep Inner-City afloat much longer. Paint contractors are reluctant to give Inner-City large orders out of fear that the paint may not be ready on a continuous, reliable basis. Larger orders usually go to larger companies that have demonstrated their reliability and solvency.

Rumors abound that Inner-City is in difficult financial straits, that it is unable to pay suppliers, and that it owes a considerable sum for payment on back taxes. All of the above contribute to the customers' serious lack of confidence in the corporation.

Financial Structure

Exhibits 2 and **3** are the most current financial statements for Inner-City Paint Corporation. They have been prepared by the company's accounting service. No audit has been performed because Walsh did not want to incur the expense it would have required.

Exhibit 2
Balance Sheet for the Current Year Ending June 30: Inner-City Paint Corporation

Current assets		
Cash	$ 1,535	
Accounts receivable (net of allowance for bad debts of $63,400)	242,320	
Inventory	18,660	
Total current assets		$262,515
Machinery and transportation equipment	47,550	
Less accumulated depreciation	15,500	
Net fixed assets		32,050
Total assets		$294,565
Current liabilities		
Accounts payable	$217,820	
Salaries payable	22,480	
Notes payable	6,220	
Taxes payable	38,510	
Total current liabilities		$285,030
Long-term notes payable		15,000
Owners' equity		
Common stock, no par, 1,824 shares outstanding		12,400
Deficit		(17,865)
Total liabilities and owners' equity		$294,565

Future

Stanley Walsh wishes to improve the financial situation and reputation of Inner-City Paint Corporation. He is considering the purchase of a computer to organize the business and reduce needless paperwork. He has read about consultants who are able to quickly spot problems in businesses, but he will not spend more than $300 on such a consultant.

The solution that Walsh favors most is one that requires him to borrow money from the bank, which he will then use to pay his current bills. He feels that as soon as business conditions improve, he will be able to pay back the loans. He believes that the problems Inner-City is experiencing are due to the overall poor economy and are only temporary.

Exhibit 3
Income Statement for the Current Year Ending June 30: Inner-City Paint Corporation

Sales		$1,784,080
Cost of goods sold		1,428,730
Gross margin		$ 355,350
Selling expenses	$ 72,460	
Administrative expenses	67,280	
President's salary	132,000	
Office Manager's salary	66,000	
Total expenses		337,740
Net income		$ 17,610

CASE 25
Hasbro, Inc.

Kristina Fogg, Robert J. Mockler, and Marc Gartenfeld

In February 2005, Hasbro, Inc., a worldwide leader in children's and family leisure time and entertainment products, including the design, manufacture, and marketing of games and toys ranging from traditional to high-tech, announced that its fourth quarter earnings rose 7.2%, after cutting costs to offset a tougher retail environment and declines in its U.S. Toys unit. During this period, in general, revenue in the U.S. Toys segment fell to $263 million from $318.9 million in 2004.[1] Chairman and Chief Executive Officer Alan G. Hassenfeld and President and Chief Operating Officer Alfred J. Verrecchia blamed this decline on the problems and closings of retail outlets such as Toys R' Us and FAO Schwarz. Many companies in the industry were looking at non-traditional outlets and e-commerce as new ways to sell their products. Non-traditional outlets meant avenues that were not widely used to distribute and sell a company's products, such as drug and convenience stores. The task of these two men was to develop an effective differentiating enterprise-wide strategy if Hasbro was to survive and prosper against aggressive competition over the intermediate and long-term future.

In early 2005, Hasbro, located in Pawtucket, Rhode Island, was the second-largest toy maker in the United States after Mattel and had been stimulating the creativity and imagination of children since the early 1920s. Its portfolio of products included such childhood favorites as Monopoly, Scrabble, Candy Land, My Little Pony, G.I. Joe, Transformers, and Mr. Potato Head. After disappointing sales in 2000, Mr. Verrecchia and Mr. Hassenfeld set a new strategic direction for the company that would focus on growing core brands, developing new and innovative products, and decreasing its reliance on licensed products. Through this strategic decision, they were able to bring many of their past products back to life after years in the storage closet.

Despite this success, in 2003 and 2004 the toy industry suffered because of toy store closures, price competition among the various major mass market and toy specialty store retailers, and increased competition from other product categories such as video games and consumer

---

This case was prepared was prepared by Kristina Fogg, MBA student at St. John's University, under the direction of Dr. Robert J. Mockler and Professor Marc Gartenfeld of St. John's University. Dr. Mockler and Professor Gartenfeld revised and edited this case. The copyright holder is solely responsible for the case content. This case was reprinted from *Cases in Domestic and Multinational Strategic Management,* Publication (VIII) #44 , pp. C4-1 through C4-29, edited by Robert J. Mockler and Marc Gartenfeld. This case was edited for SMBP–11th Edition.

Exhibit 1 United States Toys and Games Market Value (Dollar amounts in billions) 1999–2003

A. United States Toys and Games Market Value, 1999–2003

Year	$Billion	% Growth
1999	25.9	
2000	27.4	5.8
2001	29.3	6.9
2002	30.6	4.4
2003	30.2	−1.30

B. United States Toys and Games Market Value Forecast, 2004–2008

Year	$Billion	% Growth
2004	*30.9*	*2.32*
2005	*31.1*	*0.65*
2006	*31.9*	*2.6*
2007	*32.6*	*2.2*
2008	*33.8*	*3.7*

Source: Datamonitor (2003). "Hasbro, Inc.: Company Profile," http://www.datamonitor.com/~d697a180f4254493a6e722feeef50e07~/companies/company/?pid=1B81864B-E7C8-465C-AC5C-3B4FEDFFCB88 (March 23, 2005).

electronics.[2] As seen in **Exhibit 1,** the market value of the Toys & Games market decreased by 1.30% from 2002 to 2003 after steadily increasing from 1999 to 2002.

As a result of these competitive market conditions, Hasbro needed to make several decisions if it wanted to gain market share, increase sales, and win against the competition. Should the company shift its focus away from large retail stores and concentrate on selling to non-traditional outlets? Or should it continue relying on the large toy stores and weather the storm? Also, should they continue focusing on core brands, or reinvest in licensed products? These and other strategic questions needed answering. The main question to be resolved was how to differentiate Hasbro from its competition and so achieve a winning edge over competitors within intensely competitive, rapidly changing immediate, intermediate, and long-term time frames.

The Entertainment Industry

Entertainment is an amusement or distraction that was intended to hold the attention of an audience or an individual. As shown in **Exhibit 2,** key segments in the entertainment industry consisted of motion pictures, television and radio, sports and recreation, music, literature, tourism, and toys and games.

Exhibit 2 The Entertainment Industry

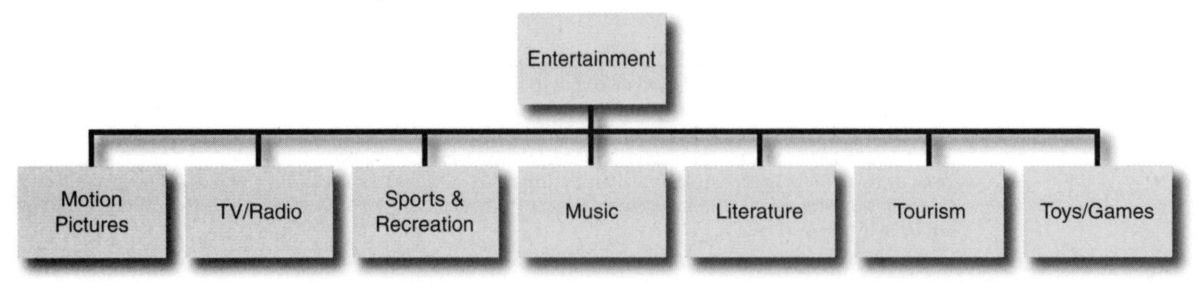

Motion Pictures

During the time period, movies were typically made under a contract between a major distributor, a production company, and a collection of various actors and actresses.

With a major theatrical film, a distributor typically funded a movie from start to finish or provided a portion of the financing in return for fees and a share of the proceeds. In some cases, a producer granted theatrical distribution rights to one party and sold home video rights to another. After arranging to have videos manufactured, the distributor sold them to video retailers. They also distributed them through a revenue-sharing agreement, through which the distributor and retailer shared consumers' rental fees for a video title. Six film distribution companies—Walt Disney, Viacom, Sony, Fox Entertainment Group, Time Warner, and NBC Universal—accounted for approximately 70% of domestic box-office revenues.[3]

For many films at the time, movie theater sales were no longer the primary source of revenues. Profitability of the motion picture often depended heavily on contributions from various home video and television markets. For distributors of filmed entertainment, revenues from selling videos and from licensing films to television outlets in the United States likely exceeded $10 billion in 2003, compared with the approximately $4 billion that they received as their share of movie theater ticket sales.[4]

TV/Radio

The availability of more channels via cable systems and satellite dishes had led to a dramatic shift in the audience market share of "over-the-air" broadcast stations. It was estimated that about 83% of U.S. households received television programming via cable or satellite dish in 2003, compared with about 56% in 1990.[5] During that same period, the prime-time audience share of all broadcast stations fell from about 80% to approximately 55%. As audiences for cable or satellite-based channels grew, advertisers had moved their ad spending in that direction. Since 1990, the share of TV advertising dollars going to channels that depended on cable or satellite dish delivery had increased from 9% to about 28%. Cable- or satellite-based TV networks were expected to continue taking audience and advertiser spending market share from broadcast outlets, which included both networks and individual TV stations.[6]

Sports and Recreation

Included in this segment were companies that owned and operated professional sports teams and organizations; golf courses and golfing centers; motor racetracks; exercise and fitness facilities; dance schools and studios; and other related sports activities.

Music

At the time, the music industry continued to get most of its business from younger consumers. However, its audience demographics had been changing. A survey conducted for the Recording Industry Association of America (RIAA) indicated that consumers aged 10 to 34 years made about 51% of purchases in 2003, down from 70% in 1990. According to the same survey, consumers aged 40 and older accounted for about 37% of music sales in 2003, up significantly from about 19% in 1990. This most likely reflected both the general aging of the population and older consumers' greater ability to afford compact discs.[7]

Literature

Literature included books, magazines, newspapers, and other printed materials. Newspapers and magazines generated income from a mixture of advertising revenue and circulation revenue. Book publishing revenue was derived primarily from sales to readers. Books, magazines, and newspapers competed for readers and buyers based on content, service, and price as perceived by the individual reader. Newspapers also competed for readership with other metropolitan, suburban, and national newspapers.[8] Magazines often competed with other magazines focusing on the same topics. Books competed for readers by subject matter. All three forms of publishing were up against other media for the consumer's time and money.

Tourism

Tourism represented all travel for both learning and recreational purposes. After September 11, 2001, tourism fell rapidly throughout the United States and the rest of the world. However, tourism had been on the rise subsequently. According to TIA's Annual Travel Forecast, overall traveler spending by domestic and international visitors in the U.S. was forecast to increase 6.9% by the end of 2004 to nearly $593 billion, up from $555 billion in 2003. An expected additional 5.3% increase in 2005 would bring expenditures to well beyond the $600 billion mark ($624 billion).[9]

The focus of this case, the toy and games segment of the entertainment industry, is discussed in detail in the following section.

Industry and Competitive Market Segment: Toys and Games

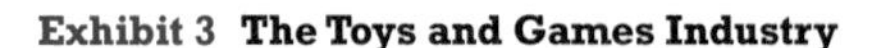

The U.S. toys and games market reached a value of $30.2 billion in the year 2003, having grown with a compound annual growth rate of 4% in the 1999–2003 period.[10] The toy and game segment of the entertainment industry consisted of many different parts, as detailed in **Exhibit 3.**

Exhibit 3 The Toys and Games Industry

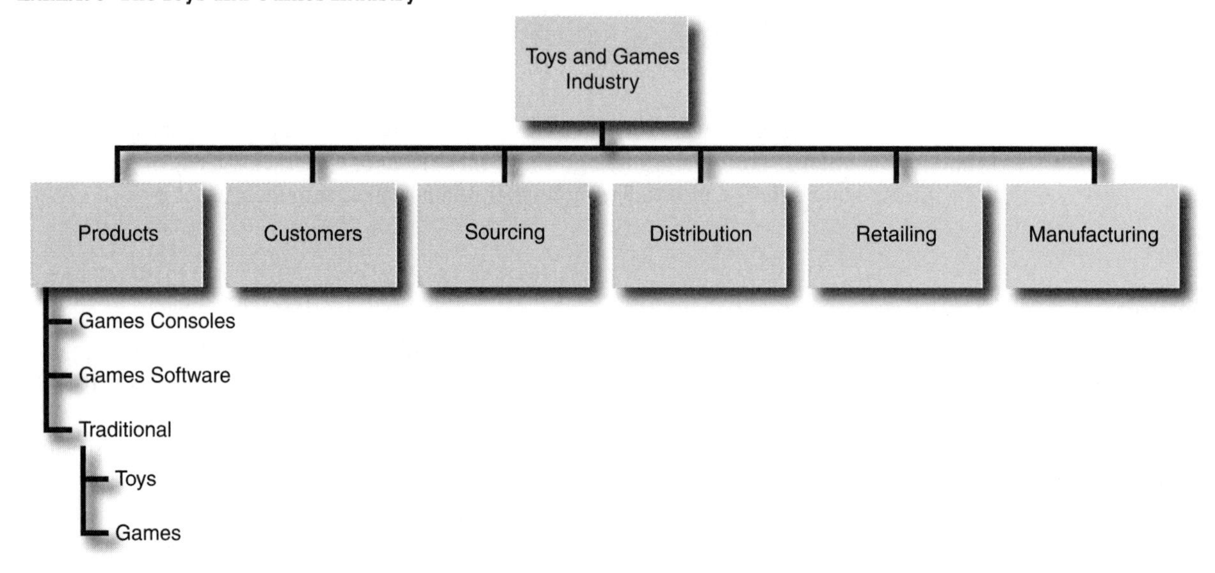

Exhibit 4 2003 vs. 2004 State of the Industry Sales Reflect Total U.S. Industry (Listed alphabetically)

Category	Annual 2003	Annual 2004	% Change
Actions Figures & Accessories	$1.2B	$1.2B	0
Arts & Crafts	$2.4B	$2.5B	−4.0
Building Sets	$629.1M	$621.9M	1.6
Dolls	$2.8B	$2.5B	12
Games/Puzzles	$2.4B	$2.3B	4.3
Infant/Preschool	$2.6B	$2.8B	−7.1
Learning & Exploration	$421.2M	$510.4M	−17.5
Outdoor & Sports Toys	$2.3B	$2.2B	4.5
Plush	$1.4B	$1.2B	16.7
Vehicles	$2.0B	$1.8B	11.1
All Other Toys	$2.5B	$2.5B	0
TOTAL TOY INDUSTRY	**$1069.9B**	**$1151.3B**	**−7.07**

Note: There may be variances due to rounding.

Source: Toy Industry Association (2004). "State of the Industry," http://www.toy-tia.org/Content/NavigationMenu/Press_Room/ Statistics3/State_of_the_Industry/ 2004_vs_2003.htm (February 2, 2005).

The toys and games market of the toy industry was divided into three primary product sectors: games consoles, games software and traditional toys and games. The leading revenue source for this market in 2003 was the traditional toys and games sector, which was worth $20.7 billion. Games software was the second largest sector, which generated $6.9 billion. Games consoles sales were expected to increase dramatically as new consoles were introduced in the future.[11]

Exhibit 4 gives a detailed listing of sales figures by product category for the toy/game industry for the years 2003 and 2004.

Educational aspects of toys were increasingly being emphasized because parents liked to buy toys that were beneficial to their child's development. Parents also believed that the education their child received at school was not sufficient. Because of this, the market for educational toys was expected to rise over the next five years.[12]

There was also a rebirth in the popularity and manufacturing of older style toys because many Generation Xers were becoming parents and purchasing toys for their children that reminded them of the warm memories of their childhood. Hasbro had reintroduced its My Little Pony, GI Joe, and Transformer brands, among many others, to take advantage of this trend. **Exhibit 5** gives the absolute dollar growth of properties from 2002 to 2003.

Competition

Because of the wide variety of products that Hasbro produced, they encountered many different types of competitors. There were both large competitors and smaller, specialty competitors. Although some companies did not manufacture the same types of products as Hasbro, they were still considered competitors because it came down to the choice in the outlet: either the competitor's product, or Hasbro's.

Exhibit 5 Old Becomes New "HIT" Properties

Product Type	Absolute Growth (Dollar Amounts in Millions) Annual 2003 vs. 2002
The Hulk	$156
Care Bears	$136
Disney Princess	$ 81
Strawberry Shortcake	$ 60
Ninja Turtles	$ 58
My Little Pony	$ 56
Polly Pocket	$ 56
Transformers	$ 50
My Scene Barbie	$ 43

Source: Toy Industry Association (2004). "State of the Industry," http://www.toy-tia.org/Content/NavigationMenu/Press_Room/Statistics3/State_of_the_Industry/2004_vs__2003.htm (February 2, 2005).

Larger Competitors

Although there were many toy manufacturing companies competing in the market, three were the most threatening competitors to Hasbro. These companies included Mattel, Lego, and Jakks Pacific. These companies were very different in both the products that they produced and the manner in which they operated.

Mattel

Mattel was the world's number one toy maker at the time. They manufactured products such as Barbie dolls, Fisher-Price toys, Hot Wheels and Matchbox cars, American Girl dolls and books, and various *Sesame Street, Barney,* and other licensed items. Mattel also produced action figures and toys based on Walt Disney movies and the Harry Potter children's books. Some key numbers for the company can be seen in **Exhibit 6**.

Mattel operates under two market segments—Domestic and International. The product lines for both segments are similar, with some products designed for the specific segments. In 2002, their market share in terms of retail dollar sales was 13.8% for infant and preschool, 12% for dolls, 10.8% for arts and crafts, 10.4% for vehicles, and 10.3% in games.[13]

Exhibit 6 Mattel's Key Numbers

Company Type	Public (NYSE: MAT)
2004 Sales (millions)	$5,102.8
1-Year Sales Growth	2.9%
2004 Net Income (millions)	$572.7
1-Year Net Income Growth	6.5%
2004 Employees	25,000
1-Year Employee Growth	0.0%

Source: Hoovers Online (2005). "Mattel, Inc. Factsheet," http://premium.hoovers.com/subscribe/co/factsheet.xhtml?ID=10966 (April 1, 2005).

Like Hasbro, Mattel's strategy in 2004 was to focus on reinventing its core brands. The company was also expanding its interactive learning segment to target the different developmental stages of toddlers and preschoolers. Facing increasing competition in the doll segment, Mattel's strategy was to combine Barbie dolls with storytelling, developing individual storylines for a small line of dolls. Also, Mattel opened American Girl retail stores in New York City and Chicago. Called the American Girl Place, these retail stores offered an imaginative experience for girls where they could have brunch, afternoon tea, or dinner with their dolls. There was also a café and a theatre. These retail stores were attracting little girls from across the United States. Hasbro had been trying to surpass Mattel for years without success. Mattel had managed to sustain their position as the number one toy maker in the United States for years, and they were strong in essentially all key success areas. To begin with, all successful companies must have good leadership, and Mattel's was strong. Mattel was headed by Robert A. Eckert, Chairman of the Board and Chief Executive Officer. In 2002, Eckert had been recognized by *Business Week* as one of the "Top Twenty-Five Managers of the Year." His leadership had helped Mattel maintain their position at the top of the toy manufacturing industry.

Mattel's strengths also included their wide variety of products and their mass-market presence. Their strongest product lines were Barbie, Hot Wheels, Matchbox cars, Tyco R/C vehicles, Fisher-Price, American Girl Dolls, and Harry Potter. All of these brands were number one in their corresponding toy category. One of Mattel's weaknesses was in their game division. For example, UNO games, which consisted of various card games, was lagging in sales.

Barbie dolls, first introduced in 1959, catapulted Mattel to the forefront of the toy industry, where they still remain today. One of Mattel's strongest areas was in creating toys for the girls' market segment. Barbie dolls were continually being reinvented to incorporate the latest fashion trends and technology. All Barbie dolls were sold with accessories and were dressed up in the latest fashion. They also produced dolls whose appearance could be altered by changing their hair color, makeup, or outfit. Their flexible and cost-efficient production lines had allowed them to keep up with the latest trends.

Mattel was also very strong in licensing. Their portfolio of licensing partners included Disney, Sesame Street, Winnie the Pooh, Nickelodeon, Looney Toons, Batman, Mary Kate and Ashley Olson, and Blue's Clues, among many others. Mattel created an online store, where consumers could buy products directly from the web site, which helped the company maintain sales in the tough retail environment. This was the company's major marketing direction at the time. It also points to Mattel's strength in knowing where consumers shop, which is an important aspect of the toy manufacturing industry. Because of the sheer size and bargaining power of the company, it was always able to acquire top-notch designers and inventors, which helped Mattel to keep pushing the edge of innovation.

Mattel's biggest problem at the time, like Hasbro's, was that it relied on larger retailers such as Wal-Mart and Toys "R" Us for a large percentage of their sales. Price cutting by these larger retailers resulted in toy manufacturers taking a hit. Also, retail store sales were declining, causing many stores to close down. Their reliance on these larger retailers in the future could hurt the company.

Lego

Lego, with operations in about 30 countries, manufactured interlocking plastic toys that had become favorites around the world. It also offered Lego kits to build PC-programmable robots, and its Bionicle line featured an evolving story line on the Internet. The company also owned four Lego theme parks in California, Denmark, Germany, and the United Kingdom, as well as Lego retail outlets in the United States and Europe. Lego was a unique

Exhibit 7 Lego's Key Numbers

Company Type	Private
2003 Sales (million)	$1,421.8
1-Year Sales Growth	(11.8)%
2003 Net Income (million)	($180.7)
2003 Employees	8,278
1-Year Employee Growth	(0.2)%

Source: Hoovers Online (2005). "LEGO Fact Sheet," http://premium.hoovers.com/subscribe/co/factsheet.xhtml?ID=42877 (April 1, 2005).

competitor. Although none of the products that they manufactured were in the same product category as those that Hasbro produced, the two companies still competed directly with each other because it came down to one product choice over another. Lego had teamed up with Star Wars to create Lego kits and games that would be on shelves for the release of *Revenge of the Sith,* the last movie in the *Star Wars* saga that began in 1977. Toys "R" Us held a midnight opening to sell the first wave of Star Wars merchandise.

Lego also owned and operated Legoland, theme parks that featured more than 5,000 Lego models, interactive attractions, roller coasters, and other rides. There were four parks in California, Denmark, England, and Germany. In April 2005, the company announced that it would be selling its four theme parks for financial reasons. It also cut hundreds of jobs the previous year while moving more of its production overseas.

Some key numbers for the company can be seen in **Exhibit 7.**

Lego began in 1932 with an original idea to create interlocking blocks that children could use to build imaginative creations. Lego's strengths included its product quality and unique product design, as well as its mass-market presence. (Lego had created a name for itself throughout the years, which had allowed it to acquire top-notch inventors and designers to keep up with the needs of youth, and to allow the company to continually reinvent itself).

Lego's weaknesses included its lack of a wide product line and its inflexible production lines. This was because the basis for the majority of Lego's products was various sizes and shapes of blocks. Also, Lego's products did not emphasize the educational aspect of toys that was increasingly becoming popular. Another weakness of the company, as with many of the larger toy manufacturers, was its reliance on traditional outlets such as Toys "R" Us. This translated into a lack of knowledge of where consumers shop. Lego was also weak in the girls' market segment. Although Lego manufactured products for girls, it did not include many characteristics that today's girls want in a toy. For example, Lego for the most part did not include accessories with products or incorporate the latest fashion trends.

Jakks Pacific

Jakks, one of the top toy companies in the United States, made and sold action figures (including an exclusive license for the Worldwide Wrestling Entertainment figures), activity sets (Flying Colors), die-cast and plastic cars (Road Champs and Remco), preschool toys (Child Guidance), pens and markers (Pentech), and fashion dolls. Other hits included Cabbage Patch Kids and Care Bears, as well as SpongeBob SquarePants. The company also introduced the "TV Games" concept—a battery-operated joystick that plugged into the TV, which allowed users to play classic arcade games of the past such as Pac-Man and Asteroids. The joystick contained up to 13 games and sold for approximately $20. This unique product broke into the game segment because it eliminated the need for expensive game consoles, such as Xbox or Playstation. The low price and retro design allowed the company to sell

Exhibit 8 Jakks Pacific's Key Numbers

Company Type	Public (NASDAQ: JAKK)
2004 Sales (mil.)	$574.3
1-Year Sales Growth	81.9%
2004 Net Income (millions)	$45.9
1-Year Net Income Growth	122.8%
2004 Employees	419
1-Year Employee Growth	32.6%

Source: Hoovers Online (2005). "Jakks Pacific Fact Sheet," http://premium.hoovers.com/subscribe/co/factsheet.xhtml?ID=51594 (April 1, 2005).

their games in nontraditional outlets such as Sakks Fifth Avenue, Bed Bath & Beyond, and Urban Outfitters.

At the time, Jakks Pacific had a pending lawsuit from the WWE alleging that the company engaged in illegal bribes to secure WWE licensing rights. Jakks denied any wrongdoing in the matter. The litigation caused two price drops in the company's stock.[14]

Some key numbers for the company can be seen in **Exhibit 8.**

Jakks Pacific's strengths included its ability to obtain profitable licensing agreements. This is seen through its agreements with WWE and NASCAR, which proved to be very profitable partnerships. However, depending on the outcome of the pending lawsuit, the firm was at risk of losing its licensing agreement with WWE. Another strength of the company was its ability to create unique, entertaining products that appealed to the masses. Its products were very easy to use and were equipped with easily understandable directions. Its "TV Games" joystick generated approximately $66 million per year, or 15% or the company's revenue, and sales of the product had doubled over the past year. Jakks' unique design skills and knowledge of where consumers shop allowed to company to break into non-traditional retail outlets. The company's ability to manufacture the "TV Games" joystick and sell it for only $20 illustrated that Jakks' strengths include securing price competitive resources and maintaining cost-efficient production lines.

In the area of advertising and promotion, Jakks had strong advertising and sales promotions. (Its attractive ad design and ability to keep its target market's interest were strengths in this area as well.)

Although Jakks Pacific had solely secured the WWE as a licensing client, it was unable to strengthen its other core brands. Also, like Lego, Jakks failed to recognize the educational aspect of toys and games that was increasingly being emphasized Another weakness of the company was its inability to manage its licensing deals. As stated previously, the company was at risk of losing WWE—the firm's most profitable licensing partner. Because Jakks was not as large as Hasbro and Mattel, it was weak in the area of acquiring the best inventors and designers.

Specialty Niche Competitors

Hasbro not only competed against the three largest toy manufacturers, it also competed with many smaller, specialty companies.

Dakin

Dakin, previously named Applause, created characters from books, movies, and television. The company designed and marketed its own line of stuffed toys such as Dream Pets and Dakin infant toys and stuffed animals, as well as other licensed characters such as those from *Winnie the Pooh, Bob the Builder, Lord of the Rings,* and *The Simpsons.*

Bandai

Bandai's products included the Tamagotchi virtual pet and its popular Digimon toys. Bandai's toy division also produced toys such as the Mighty Morphin' Power Rangers action figures and Hyper Yo-Yos. It had more than 35 subsidiaries in eight countries, including Sunrise (animated film production), Bandai Networks (content for mobile phones), and Banpresto (amusement machines and software for game consoles).

Electronic Arts

Electronic Arts, EA, was the number one video game publisher in the United States, with more than 100 popular titles such as *NBA Street, Madden NFL 2004, SimCity 4, Need for Speed*, and *Medal of Honor*. It developed games under such brand names as EA Games, EA Sports, and EA Sports Big. It also distributed titles for third-party labels and published games based on *The Lord of the Rings*, Harry Potter, and James Bond.

PlayMobil

PlayMobil, Germany's largest toy maker at the time, made plastic figures with moveable heads, arms, and legs. It also made accessories such as vehicles, animals, dollhouses, and other buildings; licensed its name for products such as books and CD-ROMs; and ran theme parks in France, Germany, Greece, Malta, and the United States.

Marvel Enterprises

Marvel Enterprises was one of the world's leading comic-book publishers and licensed its characters to makers of movies, TV shows, clothing, video games, and other products. Marvel Enterprises' success rested on the strength and marketability of its characters. Toys included action figures and games based on Marvel characters, items with non-Marvel characters (characters from the *Lord of the Rings* movies), and proprietary products.

Ohio Art

The Ohio Art Company manufactured Etch-A-Sketch and other drawing devices, drums for tots, child-sized sports sets, and the Betty Spaghetty family of dolls. Almost half of its sales came from metal lithographed and molded plastic products, including serving trays, film canisters, and auto trim.

Playmates

Playmates made dolls and action figures through licensing agreements with companies such as Disney and Nickelodeon. The company's products included objects from *The Simpsons, Teenage Mutant Ninja Turtles,* Speedeez miniature cars and playsets, and Disney's Little Princess (featuring characters such as Ariel, Cinderella, and Belle from both classic and newer animated films). It also made a line of Hilary Duff fashion dolls.

Poof-Slinky

Founded in the early 1980s, Poof-Slinky, formerly POOF Products, made and sold polyurethane foam toys, including airplanes, rockets, and sporting equipment. The company also manufactured Slinky-brand toys and Slinky Science toys (activity books, science kits, and puzzles).

Radio Flyer

Radio Flyer manufactured the well-known "little red wagon." The #18 Classic Red Wagon had been manufactured for more than 70 years—an American toy industry record, and the reason Radio Flyer owned a majority of the U.S. market. The company also made bicycles and tricycles for children, as well as scooters and pedal-powered cars.

Spin Master

Spin Master created products such as radio-controlled airplanes, dolls, and magically shrinking bits of plastic called Shrinky Dinks. Spin Master's products were sold in major toy and department stores worldwide. Spin Master had a hit with its first toy: Earth Buddy, a novelty product that grew "hair" when it was watered.

Toy Quest

Toy Quest was among the world's largest private makers of electronic games and toys. The company made robotic pets such as Tekno the Robotic Puppy and the interactive doll Cindy Smart, who could speak, as well as "see" shapes, letters, pictures, and objects. Other products included Stretch Screamers, role-play costume sets, MTV-branded electronic music-making devices, and Aqua Blast.

Ty

Ty manufactured the well-known Beanie Babies. Since 1993 Ty had produced more than 365 different Beanie Babies. Other products include Beanie Buddies (bigger versions of traditional Beanies), Ty Classics (stuffed animals), Beanie Boppers (pre-teen dolls), and Punkies (squeezable beanbag pals).

Wham-O

Wham-O created the Wham-O slingshot, the Frisbee, the Hula-Hoop, the Hacky Sack, and Slip'n' Slide. The toy maker also offered other outdoor toys, child Baskin-Robbins ice-cream makers, and surf and snow items under the Malibu, Morey Boogie, and SLEDZ brands. Products were sold in toy and sporting goods stores worldwide. Wham-O was named for the sound made by slingshots hitting their marks. Wham-O was once owned by Mattel, which sold it in 1997 to a group of investors led by Charterhouse Group International.

Zindart

Zindart made die-cast and injection-molded toys and collectibles, as well as paper products such as children's pop-up and novelty books, puzzles, and board games. Zindart made scale models of airplanes, trucks, buses, and cars. These included Corvettes and Mustangs, with up to 200 moveable parts; Mattel's line of replica toy cars; and private-label products such as Texaco trucks. Zindart also produced Hallmark's Keepsake Ornaments line of Christmas collectibles.

These smaller competitors were strong in the sales forces segment, because employees could be more involved with the smaller company. The sales staff, for the most part, were knowledgeable and well-trained. However, it was harder for these companies to maintain relationships with larger store managers because of their smaller sales.

Because they were not as large as the top four competitors, they did not have the bargaining power that the larger companies did. This translated into weaknesses in securing price-competitive resources and in cost-efficient and flexible production lines. Pricing was also a weakness because of their lack of bargaining power for resources. It was also hard for these companies to obtain inventors and designers, because they were in competition with the larger companies. However, the smaller companies were usually strong in employee relations.

The Company

According to Hasbro's Mission Statement, "The heart of Hasbro's business is making great games, toys, lifestyle and entertainment products that are enjoyed by people of all ages worldwide. Hasbro intends to be the number-one company in the toy and game industry; the leading provider of play; and the number-one marketer, pioneer and partner to all channels and all customers." Externally, a major problem facing the company in the near future was the fading Pokemon craze, which had caused losses for Hasbro. In an attempt to overcome these losses, the company was focusing less on licensing and more on other favorites. With the Pokemon fad disappearing, Hasbro had to be sure that its other toys, games, and puzzles could stand up to Mattel's Barbie. This was the same situation with all fad toys. Eventually, the demand would fade and the company had to have something ready to keep profits steady. Another possible problem was the focus away from traditional toys to cyber toys. Although Hasbro had its hands involved in high-tech toys, it had to also keep its older toys alive.

Volatility of consumer preferences and the high level of competition in the family entertainment industry made it difficult to maintain the long-term success of existing product lines and to continually introduce successful new products.[15] Hasbro was an extremely innovative company, but it would have to continue this in the future to be successful. Another threat to top toy companies was the shift in consumer buying patterns. It used to be that toys were sold in toy stores, but time-challenged consumers did not always have time to make the special trip to the toy store. As a result, products had to be available in non-traditional outlets such as clothing stores, drug stores, and music stores. Leading toy retailers Toy "R" Us and KB Toys Inc., were both operating under Chapter 11 bankruptcy protection because of a sharp decline in sales. Because both Hasbro and Mattel relied on Toys "R" Us for approximately 16% of their respective sales, they might have wanted to consider alternative avenues of distribution before it was too late.[16]

Design/Manufacturing

Hasbro manufactured its products in a variety of facilities that were either company owned or outsourced.

Company-Owned Manufacturing Facilities

Hasbro owned three manufacturing facilities located in East Longmeadow, Massachusetts; Waterford, Ireland; and Valencia, Spain. In the fourth quarter of 2003, manufacturing at the Valencia, Spain, facility ceased as a result of changes in the global marketplace. Another incentive for closing the plant was to take advantage of cost efficiencies through sourcing of the products using lower-cost production alternatives.

Strengths in this area included Hasbro's ability to obtain price-competitive resources, because of the large size of the company. Their flexible and cost-efficient production lines were major strengths in this area. Hasbro stressed the importance of good working standards and valued its workers. Another key for success in this area was good employee relations, which led to increased efficiency and output. Because many retailers were ordering products closer to the time of purchase by consumers, Hasbro utilized quick-response inventory management. This pointed to Hasbro's strength in understanding the company's operations, its ability to accurately forecast demand for its products, and its ability to fulfill orders accurately and on time.

Outsourcing

Products not manufactured by Hasbro were manufactured by third-party facilities in the Far East, particularly the People's Republic of China. China constituted the largest manufacturing center of toys in the world. Strengths in this area included Hasbro's constant communication with foreign manufacturers, and its strict control measures on product-specific actions. Also, Hasbro was able to protect its intellectual property while outsourcing, which is a major strength.

Hasbro stressed corporate governance and took precautions when outsourcing. Hasbro was committed to the safety and health of its employees worldwide. This included all employees of vendors making Hasbro products throughout the world. Providing and maintaining a safe work environment and instituting and following work practices to safeguard employees was one of the firm's primary considerations.

Products

Hasbro's wide array of products were categorized as either Toys or Games. In the general product area, Hasbro was strong in its flexible production lines, which enabled them to create a variety of products at a relatively low cost. This allowed the company to pass these cost savings on to the consumer.

Toys

The U.S. Toys segment was responsible for the design, marketing, and selling of boys' action figures, vehicles and playsets, girls' toys, preschool toys and infant products, children's consumer electronics, electronic interactive products, creative play, and toy-related specialty products.

Boys' Toys

Hasbro's boys' toys included a wide range of core properties such as G.I. Joe and Transformers action figures, and the Tonka line of trucks and interactive toys. Other products included licensed products, such as Star Wars and Beyblade. The year 2004 marked the 40th anniversary of the introduction of the G.I. Joe action figure. To commemorate this anniversary, Hasbro reintroduced some of the classic figures with replicas of the original gear and packaging. Strengths in this segment included its unique product design and high product quality. The G.I. Joe action figure had been bringing in revenue for years. The reintroduction of older figures for the product's anniversary was supported with strong sales promotion and advertising, which had continually led to strong sales throughout the years. During this time when the United States was at war, G.I. Joe dolls had increased in popularity. The reintroduction and increased sales promotion for the product pointed to the company's ability to anticipate trends.

In the licensing area, Hasbro had the ability to accurately reproduce licensed characters. However, Hasbro's weakness in this segment stemmed from its struggling licensing program. For example, Hasbro acquired an exclusive contract with Star Wars for the release of the last movie in the trilogy *Star Wars Episode III: Return of the Sith*. This contract gave Hasbro the exclusive right to make and sell Star Wars games until 2018. However, sales in this product category were not as strong as expected, leaving Hasbro's management to contemplate their investment. Also, there were many complaints that Hasbro had manufactured an overabundance of Star Wars and other action figures, but not enough playsets to use with them.

Girls' Toys

Girls' toys included the My Little Pony line, Secret Central, and Raggedy Ann and Andy. My Little Pony was reintroduced in 2003 to support Hasbro's strategy to expand its core brands. In 2004, a new My Little Pony story line was introduced and was supported by a licensing program in publishing, video, and other girl-directed consumables. Strengths in this segment included the company's ability to develop, introduce, and gain consumer acceptance of its products. The reintroduction of the My Little Pony line and the Easy Bake oven were examples of this. Also, the fact that these products had been popular throughout the years indicated a long product life and unique product design, which created a constant cash inflow for the company.

Hasbro's weakness in the girls' toys segment was again its struggling licensing program. Their portfolio of licensed products for girls was small compared to those of their competitors.

Preschool

Preschool products included several brands marketed under the Playskool trademark. Brands in this area include Mr. Potato Head, Sit N' Spin, Gloworm, Busy Ball Popper, Step Start Walk N' Ride, and 2-in-1 Tummy Time Gym. In 2004, the Weebles brand was reintroduced and the Magic Talkin' Kitchen was added to the Cool Crew lineup. Strengths in this segment included a wide product line. Products ranged from plush toys to dolls to learning and exploration, indicating a vast amount of products for consumers to choose from. Reinventing and redesigning many of these classic toys time after time indicated Hasbro's strength in acquiring top-line inventors and designers. Also, many of the products in this segment had been around for generations, which showed strength in protecting intellectual property rights.

Children's Consumer Electronics

Children's Consumer Electronics included Hitclips micro music systems and Kidclips Disney Tunes, which contain Disney tunes on easy-to-use players. Also included in this segment was the Furreal Friends brand, which was a line of electronic toy pets. In 2003, VideoNow was launched, which was a personal video player that featured 3-inch discs that could play up to 30 minutes of uninterrupted content, allowing children to watch their favorite show anytime, anywhere. Strengths in this segment included Hasbro's ability to anticipate trends. The VideoNow product showed Hasbro's knowledge of its target market's increasing desire for high-tech gadgets. It also exemplified the company's ability to continually acquire successful inventors and designers that would consistently produce quality, profit-making products.

Creative Play

Creative Play products included classics such as Play-Doh, Easy-Bake Oven, Lite-Brite, and the Spirograph toys. The Play-Doh line, the company's strongest product line in this segment, was expanded in 2004 with the introduction of Dohville, a town intended to bring fun and classic preschool themes to life. Strengths in this segment included its unique product design. The Easy-Bake Oven, when introduced, was on the Christmas lists of children around the world. Kids were finally able to cook treats such as cookies and brownies without the help of their parents. Also, the Play-Doh line of products, which had been around for years, was continually expanding its already wide product line to meet the ever-changing tastes of children.

Other Products

Other products included the Super Soaker line of water gun products and the Nerf line of soft foam sports action toys. In 2003, the Power Air Surfer Sky Wolf was introduced, which was a remote-controlled airplane that took off straight from the ground.

The creation of a remote-controlled airplane that took off from the ground illustrated Hasbro's continuing ability to acquire creative inventors and designers. Hasbro's weakness in this segment included a recent lack of sales promotion and advertising. Years earlier, Nerf and Super Soaker products had been advertised continually and were desired by children throughout the world. However, lack of advertising for these products has resulted in decreased sales.

Games

The Games segment was responsible for the development, manufacturing, marketing, and selling of traditional board and card games, handheld electronic games, and trading card and role-playing games, as well as learning aids and puzzles.

According to Hasbro's President and COO Alfred Verrecchia, the popularity of board games was an illustration of the social phenomenon that "kids are growing up faster and adults are staying young longer" (Pereira, 2004). Hasbro, in order to take advantage of this trend, promoted its highly successful "family night," where parents and children played games on designated nights. With both Milton Bradley and Parker Brothers, both successful game makers now under the Hasbro umbrella, the company had the opportunity to expand this sector and take advantage of the trend.

Hasbro's Game Division was the company's strongest segment. Hasbro's games were sold through the brand names Milton Bradley and Parker Brothers. The core game items included Monopoly, Battleship, Game of Life, Scrabble, Chutes and Ladders, Candy Land, Trouble, Mousetrap, Operation, Hungry Hungry Hippos, Connect Four, Twister, Yahtzee, Jenga, Clue, Sorry!, Risk, Boggle, Ouija, Diplomacy, Acquire, and Trivial Pursuit. All of these games came with easily understandable directions, which led to a more enjoyable play experience.

In 2002, Trivial Pursuit 20th Anniversary Edition was introduced, which included questions on events, people, and places of the past 20 years. This edition of Trivial Pursuit was the top-selling new game and the top-selling board game overall in 2002. The company continued the success of the Trivial Pursuit brand with the introduction of Trivial Pursuit 1990s Edition in 2004.

In order to combat lagging board game sales, Hasbro expanded several of its well-known brands such as Clue, with new sculpted game pieces that represented each suspect, and Twister, with the introduction of Twister Moves, which combined mat-based play using the classic Twister game and the hip-hop form of dancing. The year 2004 marked the 55th anniversary of the Candy Land game. Hasbro introduced updated and refreshed characters as well as new packaging, board art, and playing pieces. This shows Hasbro's strength in continuous innovation and unique design and concept. It also points to Hasbro's ability to generate an upbeat mood through a fun variety of games. Strengths in this segment also included the remarkable ability to consistently create entertaining, age-appropriate products, as new games were released regularly.

Jigsaw Puzzles

Jigsaw puzzles included a line of puzzles for both children and adults, including the brands Big Ben and Croxley. Strengths in this segment included their ability to create puzzles that would entertain families or individuals for hours, as well as their unique design of puzzles. Hasbro's puzzles were challenging to individuals, which is an important aspect of this segment. Hasbro's weakness in this area was their lack of advertising and promotion. Hasbro's collection of puzzle products was not promoted as heavily as other product areas.

Trading Cards

Trading cards included the Wizards of the Coast trading card and role-playing games, such as Magic: The Gathering and Dungeons and Dragons. Magic: The Gathering had more than 6 million players in more than 75 countries. In 2002, Magic: The Gathering Online was introduced. Here, players could purchase digital cards, trade and play digital cards with other players, build and customize their own decks, and organize their card collections on their PCs. In 2003, there were more than 140,000 registered accounts. Also in 2004, Hasbro introduced Duel Masters—a trading card game that was very popular in Japan. Strengths in this segment included unique abilities in design and concepts, evident in Magic: The Gathering. The company incorporated playing cards with the concept of a game, as well as an online world where players could interact with each other. This also indicated their strength in creating a mass appeal for their products.

Sales

Hasbro used a combination of both an in-house sales force and independent distributors to sell its products throughout the world.

In-House Sales Force

Hasbro's own sales force accounted for the majority of the sales of its products. Hasbro maintained showrooms in New York and several other major cities worldwide. Hasbro's strengths in this area included its knowledgeable and well-trained sales staff. Hasbro's strong reputation allowed it to continually attract successful salespeople (and maintain relationships with outlet managers). Hasbro also used a part-salary, part-commission program for its salespeople, as well as specific sales quotas that were expected to be met. This led to increased sales for the company. The showrooms that Hasbro owned and operated throughout the world allowed buyers to interact with sales staff who were able to answer any questions or concerns about the company's products.

Independent Sales

Sales not accounted for by Hasbro's own sales force were generated by independent distributors who sold Hasbro products mostly in areas of the world where the company did not otherwise maintain a direct presence. Hasbro's strength in this area was Hasbro's choice of distributors with local-area expertise. Independent sales staff also received commission incentives and had to reach certain sales quotas, as Hasbro's own sales staff was required to do. In order to communicate with its independent sales staff, Hasbro created a secure network that allowed these individuals access to Hasbro's wealth of information with the click of a mouse. In this way, Hasbro maintained constant contact with independent distributors.

Outlets

Hasbro sold its products through a variety of outlets, both traditional and non-traditional.

Traditional

Hasbro sold its products through traditional wholesale and retail outlets. Traditional wholesale outlets included catalog stores and mail-order houses. Traditional retail outlets included small independent toy stores, large toy retailers, and general merchandise discount chains. Strengths in this area included Hasbro's ability to accurately forecast demand for products. Hasbro was able to estimate seasonal demands even with their wide variety of products and the great number of outlets to which they delivered products. In addition to this, Hasbro was able to deliver these orders accurately and on time. The wide variety of products was another strength. Because these traditional retailers, especially larger retailers such as Wal-Mart and Target, sold products at such low prices, pricing was a key strategy. Hasbro's strength in this area was its ability to accurately price its products. In order to get products on the shelves at these larger retailers, a company must have a mass-market presence, which was another of Hasbro's strengths.

When dealing with larger retailers, one firm's products competed with many other products on the shelves. Although Hasbro had literally hundreds of products on the shelves at these outlets, its advertising and promotion were weak. In addition, traditional retailers were declining in popularity in the toy industry. Hasbro, in order to move forward in the future, might need to find new places to distribute and sell their products. Previously, Hasbro had owned and operated its own retail stores for Wizards of the Coast trading cards. Although the card game was extremely popular, the retail stores did not fare so well, and were subsequently closed.

Non-traditional

Hasbro also sold its products through a variety of non-traditional outlets, which were the up-and-coming new market for children's toys. Hasbro's strengths in this area included its mass-market presence and its strong relationships with store managers, which were necessary to sell products in non-traditional outlets. Although Hasbro was one of the largest and most profitable toy manufacturers at the time, it was lagging in the area of non-traditional markets. It seemed that management lacked the knowledge of where consumers shopped, which led to the company's heavy reliance on larger retailers.

Customers/Consumers

The ultimate consumers of Hasbro's products included all ages, genders, and income levels, because of the wide variety of products that the company offered.

Age

Products were targeted to different age groups because of the differences in demand, play patterns, and product usage.

Infants/Toddlers

Infants and toddlers ranged from birth to age 3. Products manufactured by Hasbro that were marketed toward this age group included Mr. Potato Head, Sit N' Spin, Gloworm, Busy Ball Popper, Step Start Walk N' Ride, and 2-in-1 Tummy Time Gym. Hasbro's strengths in marketing to this age group included its ability to create products with bright colors, distinctive textures, movement, and sound effects. The 2-in-1 Tummy Time Gym was a toy that allowed babies, while lying on their backs, to play with dangling animals, listen to music, and spin colorful roller balls. Another strength was Hasbro's ability to incorporate the educational element into their products. Hasbro's weakness in this area was its ineffective licensing of products, which had caused sluggish sales within this age group.

Children

Children ranged from age 4 to age 7 and were more influential in purchasing decisions than were infants and toddlers. Because children were also more vocal than infants and toddlers, they were able to express exactly what they wanted and talk their parents into buying it for them. Products manufactured by Hasbro that were marketed toward children included Hit Clips, Furreal Friends, Play-Doh, and the Easy-Bake Oven. Hasbro's strengths in this age group included their manufacturing of products that allowed children to simulate adult tasks. For example, the Easy-Bake Oven allowed children to safely cook on their own without their parents' help. This also illustrated Hasbro's ability to continually create unique products. Hasbro's weakness in this area was its sales promotion and advertising. As stated previously, this was very important in this age group because children were more influential in purchasing decisions. Also, Hasbro was weaker in the area of licensing for this segment.

"Tweens"

A "tween" was an individual between childhood and adolescence, from around age 8 to age 12. Tweens were at the age when they were developing their identities and self-image. Products manufactured by Hasbro that were marketed to this age group included Spirographs, VideoNow, Super Soakers, and Nerf products. Hasbro's strengths in marketing to this age group included its pricing strategy, which allowed the company to manufacture products that these cash-strapped youngsters could afford. Also, Hasbro's ability to continuously innovate, apparent in its technologically advanced VideoNow and ChatNow products, indicated another of the company's strengths. Despite weaknesses in advertising and promoting to other age groups, Hasbro was strong in the tween market. This allowed the company to maintain strong relationships with this age group through branding.

Teenagers

Teenagers ranged from age 13 to age 17 and were making it increasingly hard for toy companies to market to them. Toy companies had been complaining for years that children were growing up faster and abandoning their toys at younger ages. Products manufactured by Hasbro that were targeted toward this age group included the VideoNow and ChatNow products, laser tag products, and the Mission Paintball toy, which allowed users to play paintball through their television sets. Hasbro was in the midst of launching its ChatNow product targeted at this market. The new product allowed kids to call or send text messages to each other using technology similar to a walkie-talkie. Parents were hesitant to buy real mobile phones for children of this age, so Hasbro was attempting to fill this void. Hasbro's strengths in this area included the ability to continuously innovate, the ability to anticipate trends, and the uniqueness of the company's products. Also, because of the strength of Hasbro's brand names, it was able to build strong relationships with teenagers that could last for many years.

Adults

Adults were included in this industry because many toy manufacturers created adult games. Products manufactured by Hasbro that were targeted toward this age group included many of their board games, including Monopoly, Trivial Pursuit, and Clue. Hasbro's strengths in this segment included the ability to create quality, entertaining products. This was evident from the fact that games such as Monopoly and Trivial Pursuit continued to sell year after year.

Also, Hasbro's advertising campaign emphasizing family game nights indicated its strong advertising and sales promotion to this age group.

Gender

Toy consumers were broken down by gender because many manufactured toys were gender specific. With the exception of infant/preschool toys and many games, which were mainly unisex, most other toys were classified as either boys' or girls' products.

Girls

As previously stated, many products manufactured by Hasbro were marketed toward girls, including My Little Pony, Secret Central, and Raggedy Ann and Andy. Hasbro's strengths in this segment included its ability to include accessories with products as well as incorporating the latest fashion trends, creating physically attractive products, and allowing girls to alter the appearance of the dolls. For example, one of the Secret Central dolls came with her own locker, a handwritten note, a yearbook photo sticker sheet, pink shoes, a belt, a zodiac necklace, and a day planner. Also available were snap-ons to accessorize the doll that were sold separately. Hasbro also produced a Bratz Passion for Fashion board game. Including feminine colors and looks into products designed for girls was also one of Hasbro's strengths. The company was also strong in the area of creating toys that emphasize creativity. An example of this was their How to Draw My Little Pony drawing book and kit, which guided girls step by step to recreate their favorite characters.

Boys

As previously stated, products manufactured by Hasbro that were targeted toward boys included G.I. Joe and Transformers action figures, and the Tonka line of trucks and interactive toys. Other products included licensed products, such as Star Wars and Beyblade. Hasbro's strengths in this area included the fact that they manufactured many products in sets that could be collected. An example of this was the G.I. Joe brand, which included numbered dolls, such as Marine Pilot #18. This enticed boys to collect the entire set of dolls. Another of Hasbro's strengths included its attractive product design and its inclusion of a competitive aspect in its products. An example of this is the Lazer Tag line, which allowed children to compete against each other in a fast-paced game of laser tag. Hasbro's weakness in this area was its slim selection of products that allowed children to build things. Hasbro manufactured a Wood Car Model Kit that allowed children to build and paint a fully functioning toy car, but these products were few and far between.

Income

The markets that Hasbro targeted consisted of families with varying incomes. However, most products manufactured by Hasbro were priced at levels affordable to the majority of households. Hasbro's strength in this segment included price-competitive resources and cost efficient production lines, which enabled them to place products on shelves at reasonable prices. Also, Hasbro's strong brand name and quality products were strengths in this segment.

Geographic Markets

Because Hasbro was such a large company, it operated throughout the United States and in more than 25 countries.

Domestic

Hasbro operated in all areas of the United States. Its strengths in this area included its mass-market presence and its pricing strategy. Because they sold products in such a large number of areas, however, it was hard for the company to have in-depth local market knowledge, which translated into a weakness for the company.

International

Hasbro operated in more than 25 countries outside of the United States. The company sold a range of toy and game products marketed in the United States, together with some items sold internationally only. In 2004, the company had approximately 7,500 customers internationally, many of which were individual retail stores. Hasbro's strengths in this area included their cost-efficient distribution and their in-depth understanding of foreign cultures. The company was also strong at accurately pricing its products depending on the country.

Advertising/Promotion

In 2003, Hasbro spent $363,876,000 on advertising, promotion, and marketing programs, compared with $296,549,000 in 2002 and $290,829,000 in 2001. This increased to $387,525,000 in 2004. In general, Hasbro's strengths in this area included a good knowledge of the consumer and adequate financial resources. The timing of promotions and knowledge of local markets was weak, however.

Internet

Hasbro advertised on the Internet mainly through its own home page. Many times, online stores carrying Hasbro's products promoted them for the company. Hasbro's strengths in this area included its ability to create attractive advertisements, as well as its ability to obtain and keep the consumer's interest.

Because of the increase in Internet use by the general population, many companies were considering online advertising. Hasbro was weak, however, in Internet advertising, online sales promotion, and choosing appropriate web sites on which to advertise.

Exhibit 9 shows changes in Internet usage by age group.

Exhibit 9
Percentage of Age Groups as Internet Users

	Internet Users (Percent)	
Age Group	**2001**	**2003**
Age 3–4	17.6	19.9
Age 4–9	41.0	42.0
Age 10–13	66.7	67.3
Age 14–17	76.4	78.8
Age 18–24	66.6	70.6
Age 25–49	65.0	68.0
Age 50+	38.3	44.8

Source: U.S. Department of Commerce, "A Nation Online: Entering the Broadband Age," http://www.ntia.doc.gov/reports/anol/NationOnlineBroadband04.htm (March 20, 2005).

Television

Hasbro advertised the majority of its toy and game products extensively on television. Its advertising highlighted selected items in its various product groups in a manner designed to promote the sale not only of the advertised item, but also of other items offered in the specific product group. Hasbro's strengths in advertising on television included its choice of channels and programs on which to advertise, which stemmed from its in-depth knowledge of its target market. Also, Hasbro continually created age-appropriate advertisements, depending on its target market.

Trade Fairs

Many new products introduced by Hasbro were showcased at the American International Toy Fair in New York City every February. The American International Toy Fair was the largest toy trade show in the Western Hemisphere. More than 1,500 manufacturers, distributors, importers, and sales agents from 30 countries showcased their toy and entertainment products (Toy Industry Association, 2004). Hasbro's strengths in this area included its unique, innovative products, and its knowledgeable, energetic presenters.

Product Previews to Customers

During the course of the year, Hasbro introduced products to major customers that would be available for purchase the following year. This allowed the company to create interest in its products ahead of time and increase sales in the long run. Hasbro's strengths in this area included its good relationships with store managers and its knowledgeable sales staff's ability to make quality, informative presentations.

Print

Occasionally, Hasbro would release print advertisements of some of its brands in various publications, including magazines for mothers-to-be and children. Hasbro's strength in this area included its in-depth knowledge of what publications its target market was reading. This knowledge came from continuous marketing research that enabled the company to gain a better understanding of target markets. Also, Hasbro's ads continually emphasized the educational aspect of its products.

Radio

From time to time, Hasbro would promote some of its products during children's shows on the radio. Hasbro's strengths in this area were its ability to create descriptive ads with catchy phrases in order to gain the target market's attention, as well as choosing appropriate channels on which to advertise. For example, Hasbro's Family Game Night ads described friends getting together for a relaxing night to bond over classic board games.

Sponsorship

At the time, Hasbro did not employ sponsorship as part of its advertising and sales promotion.

Regulatory

Hasbro was regulated by governing bodies both in the United States and in the foreign countries in which they operated.

United States

Consumer Product Safety Act (CPSA)

The Consumer Product Safety Act empowered the Consumer Product Safety Commission to take action against hazards presented by consumer products, including the formulation and implementation of regulations and uniform safety standards. This Commission had the authority to seek to declare a product a banned hazardous substance and to ban it from commerce. The CPSC could also order equitable remedies such as recall, replacement, repair, or refund for the product.

Federal Hazardous Substances Act (FHSA)

The Federal Hazardous Substances Act of 1960 established labeling requirements for consumer products containing hazardous substances. If a product contained a hazardous substance, the front label had to include a warning and a description of the hazard.

Flammable Fabrics Act (FFA)

In 1953, Congress enacted the Flammable Fabrics Act of 1953. As enacted in 1953 and amended in 1954, the FFA prohibited the importation, manufacture for sale, or sale in commerce of any article of wearing apparel that was so highly flammable as to be dangerous when worn by individuals.

Food and Drug Administration (FDA)

The FDA was an agency of the United States Department of Health and Human Services. Part of the Public Health Service, the FDA administered the Federal Food, Drug and Cosmetic Act of 1938 and related laws to ensure that foods were pure and wholesome and produced under sanitary conditions; that drugs and therapeutic devices were safe and effective for their intended uses; that cosmetics were safe and made from appropriate ingredients; and that labels and packaging of products were truthful, informative, and not deceptive. The FDA also enforced the federal Hazardous Substances Act to ensure proper labeling and safety of chemical products, toys, and other articles used in the home.

Children's Television Act of 1990

In 1990, Congress enacted the Children's Television Act (CTA) to increase the amount of educational and informational programming available on television. CTA required each broadcast television station in the United States to serve the educational and informational needs of children through its overall programming, including programming specifically designed to serve these needs ("core programming"). It also limited the amount of time broadcasters could devote to commercial matter during children's programs.

International

Hasbro was also regulated in its international dealings by the specific laws and regulations of the countries in which it operated. There were also generic international standards, governed by the International Organization for Standardization (ISO). The ISO Safety of Toys Part I communicated the safety aspects related to mechanical and physical aspects of products. There were also stipulations about flammability and the migration of certain materials. In the European Union, there were stipulations regarding electronic toys, warning labels on toys, and regulations regarding chemistry sets.

Financials

The year 2004 was a challenging year for Hasbro because of price-cutting by large chain stores, such as Wal-Mart and Target. In 2004 nearly 50% of Hasbro's sales came from its top three customers—Wal-Mart (21%), Toys "R" Us (15%), and Target (10%). The fact that such a large percentage of Hasbro's sales came from these retailers explains the lackluster 2004 sales. Hasbro's 2004 Income Statement and Balance sheet can be seen in **Exhibits 10 and 11.**

Revenue in the company's domestic toy segment slipped to $263.7 million from $318.9 million, because of the slow retail environment. The sluggish retail environment was in a large part due to the financial problems of larger retailers such as FAO Schwarz and Toys "R" Us. **Exhibit 12** details Hasbro's consolidated net revenues by segment from 2000 through 2004.

Exhibit 10
Hasbro, Inc., and Subsidiaries Consolidated Statements of Operations Fiscal Years Ended in December (Dollar amounts in thousands except per share data)

Fiscal Year Ending	December 26 2004	December 27 2003	December 28 2002
Net revenues	$2,997,510	3,138,657	2,816,230
Cost of sales	1,251,657	1,287,962	1,099,162
Gross profit	1,745,853	1,850,695	1,717,068
Expenses			
Amortization	70,562	76,053	94,576
Royalties	223,193	248,423	296,152
Research and product development	157,162	143,183	153,775
Advertising	387,523	363,876	296,549
Selling, distribution and administration	614,401	674,544	656,725
Total expenses	1,452,841	1,506,079	1,497,777
Operating profit	293,012	344,616	219,291
Nonoperating (income) expense			
Interest expense	31,698	52,462	77,499
Other expense, net	1,226	48,090	37,704
Total nonoperating (income) expense	32,924	100,552	115,203
Earnings before income taxes and cumulative effect of accounting change	260,088	244,064	104,088
Income taxes	64,111	69,049	29,030
Net earnings before cumulative effect of accounting change	195,977	175,015	75,058
Cumulative effect of accounting change, net of tax	—	(17,351)	(245,732)
Net earnings (loss)	$ 195,977	157,664	(170,674)
Per common share			
Net earnings before cumulative effect of accounting change			
Basic	$ 1.11	1.01	.43
Diluted	$ .96	.94	.43
Net earnings (loss)			
Basic	$ 1.11	.91	(.99)
Diluted	$ .96	.85	(.90)
Cash dividends declared	$ .24	.12	.12

Source: Hasbro 2004 Annual Report, p. 47.

Exhibit 11
Hasbro, Inc., and Subsidiaries Consolidated Balance Sheets (Dollar amounts in thousands except per share data)

Fiscal Year Ending	December 26 2004	December 28 2003
Assets		
Current assets		
Cash and cash equivalents	$ 725,002	520,747
Accounts receivable, less allowance for doubtful accounts of $37,000 in 2004 and $39,200 in 2003	578,705	607,556
Inventories	194,780	168,979
Prepaid expenses and other current assets	219,735	211,981
Total current assets	1,718,222	1,509,263
Property, plant and equipment, net	206,934	199,854
Other assets		
Goodwill	469,726	463,680
Other intangibles, net	637,929	710,639
Other	207,849	279,940
Total other assets	1,315,504	1,454,259
Total assets	$3,240,660	3,163,376
Liabilities and Shareholders' Equity		
Current liabilities		
Short-term borrowings	$ 17,959	23,354
Current portion of long-term debt	324,124	1,333
Accounts payable	167,585	158,969
Accrued liabilities	638,943	746,399
Total current liabilities	1,148,611	930,055
Long-term debt, excluding current portion	302,698	686,871
Deferred liabilities	149,627	141,210
Total liabilities	1,600,936	1,758,136
Shareholders' equity		
Preference stock of $2.50 par value. Authorized 5,000,000 shares; none issued	—	—
Common stock of $.50 par value. Authorized 600,000,000 shares; issued 209,694,630 shares in 2004 and 2003	104,847	104,847
Additional paid-in capital	380,745	397,878
Deferred compensation	(98)	(679)
Retained earnings	1,721,209	1,567,693
Accumulated other comprehensive earnings	82,388	30,484
Treasury stock, at cost, 32,379,369 shares in 2004 and 34,195,301 shares in 2003	(649,367)	(694,983)
Total shareholders' equity	1,639,724	1,405,240
Total liabilities and shareholders' equity	$3,240,660	3,163,376

Source: Hasbro 2004 Annual Report, p. 47.

Corporate Governance

Exhibit 13.A shows the 13 members of the board of directors, of whom two were internal members. **Exhibit 13.B** shows the 9 members of the management team.

Exhibit 12
Consolidated Net Revenues by Segment (2000–2003): Hasbro,Inc. (Dollar amounts in thousands)

Segment	2004	2003	2002	2001	2000
Boys' toys	$662,500	$962,500	$871,400	$657,300	$865,800
Games and Puzzles	1,276,100	1,207,100	1,121,200	1,259,600	1,653,200
Electronic toys	347,000	266,500	118,000	213,900	179,600
Preschool toys	235,100	215,500	225,400	222,000	240,200
Creative Play	179,700	198,100	195,500	211,600	200,400
Girls' toys	162,800	104,000	122,500	111,900	56,700
Other	134,310	184,957	162,230	180,039	591,315
Net Revenues	**$2,997,510**	**$3,138,657**	**$2,816,230**	**$2,856,339**	**$3,787,215**

Source: Hasbro Annual Reports, 2004, 2003, and 2002.

Exhibit 13 Board of Directors and the Executive Officers: Hasbro, Inc.

A. Board of Directors

Alan G. Hassenfeld
Chairman
Alfred J.Verrecchia
President and Chief Executive Officer
Basil L. Anderson
Vice Chairman
Staples, Inc.
Alan R. Batkin
Vice Chairman
Kissinger Associates, Inc.
Frank J. Biondi, Jr.
Senior Managing Director
Walter View Advisers LLC
Jack M. Connors
Chairman
Hill, Holiday, Connors, Cosmopulos, Inc.
E. Gordon Gee
Chancellor
Vanderbilt University
Jack M. Greenberg
Retired Chairman and Chief Executive Officer
McDonald's Corporation
Claudine B. Malone
President and Chief Executive Officer
Financial and Management Consulting, Inc.
Edward M. Phillip
President and Chief Executive Officer
Decision Matrix Group.Inc.
E. John Rosenwald, Jr.
Vice Chairman
Bear, Sterns & Co. Inc.
Eli J. Segal
Chairman
SchoolSports, Inc.
Paula Stern
Chairwoman
The Stern Group, Inc.

B. Executive Officers

Alan G. Hassenfeld
Chairman
Alfred J. Verrechia
President and Chief Executive Officer
Brian Golder
President, U.S. Toy Segment
David D.F. Hargreaves
Senior Vice President and Chief Financial Officer
Richard B. Holt
Senior Vice President and Chief Audit and Fiscal Compliance Officer
Barry Wagner
Senior Vice President and Controller
Deborah Thomas Slater
Senior Vice President and Treasurer
Martin R. Trueb
Senior Vice President and Treasurer
E. David Wilson
President, Games Segment

Management Strategy

After a disappointing year in 2000, Hasbro's management team sat down to create a new strategy that would better position the company to deliver reliable and sustainable growth. The focus of the company would be on growing its portfolio of core brands, developing new and innovative products, reducing its reliance on licensed products, improving its operating margins, and strengthening its balance sheet.

On May 13, 2003, Alfred J. Verrecchia, who had previously been the company's President and Chief Operating Officer, was promoted to Chief Executive Officer. Verrecchia had been a part of the Hasbro family for many years. He started with the company in 1965 as a junior accountant and had served in a variety of key senior executive positions on his way to the top.

While serving as CEO, Verrecchia's goal was to increase shareholder value despite the challenges of the toy industry. The company focused on ways to grow revenue and manage the company as efficiently as possible. Innovation continued to be the key to future growth. Hasbro's management planned to develop and introduce innovative toys and games that consumers wanted, by anticipating marketplace trends, and to deliver those products wherever consumers were shopping.

Looking to the Future

Chairman and Chief Executive Officer Alan G. Hassenfeld knew that many decisions had to be made regarding the future of his company. He called a conference with some of the brightest minds in his business to debate their opinions on the path that Hasbro should take in the future. One employee suggested that Hasbro focus on manufacturing fad items and securing licensing agreements.

The benefits of this strategic alternative were that it would both immediately increase the company's profits and bring attention to the company. Fad items were the biggest moneymakers for companies and would increase their market share in the short run.

This alternative was feasible because Hasbro was already a leader in securing profitable licensing agreements, as it had with Pokemon. Focusing all of its efforts on this would allow the company to manufacture more successful fad products. At the time, research and development continued in an attempt to find new ways to reinvent Hasbro's core products. Shifting its focus away from core products would free up the research and development money. This money could then be used to seek out and obtain more profitable licensing partners.

This alternative could be successful because Hasbro would gain both profit and market share, and it would strengthen Hasbro's already strong presence in the toy manufacturing industry. Hasbro was strong in all areas of licensing, including obtaining profitable licensing agreements and accurately reproducing licensed characters. Lego, one of Hasbro's main competitors, was weak in this area. Its core business did not focus on licensing opportunities and contracts. Also, Jakks Pacific was involved in a lawsuit regarding their licensing agreement with WWE. Its inability to manage licensing contracts was a weakness that Hasbro could use to its advantage. Mattel, the most threatening competitor, was strong in the licensing area. However, it was currently focused on its core brands. Barbie sales were decreasing and the company was spending more and more time trying to find ways to keep her on the shelves. If Hasbro focused all of their attention on creating the newest, hottest items, Mattel might be left behind and would have to catch up.

A drawback of this alternative was that fad products were often short-lived. Although they made the company a lot of money in a relatively short period of time, they died out quickly, and holding on to product for too long could cause disastrous losses. A way around this drawback was for Hasbro to focus on several fad items at once, and not put all of its money into one product. Management's ability to anticipate trends would allow them to realize what was hot and what was not. This would help the company realize new opportunities and know when to turn its focus away from dying products.

Another employee suggested that, although Hasbro would continue to manufacture fad products, the company should instead focus on reinventing and redesigning its core products.

A benefit of this alternative was that focusing on reinventing and redesigning the company's core products would be a more secure source of revenue for the long run. The core products had made money in the past and should continue to do so in the future. Recreating yesterday's products for today's generation should draw attention to the company. Parents would buy their children toys that they played with when they were growing up. This would in turn increase Hasbro's revenues in the long run.

This alternative was feasible because Hasbro's core products were what the company knew best. It was known for its unique, long-lived products. Redesigning these products for today's generations of children would be relatively easy for Hasbro. Research and development was already underway to find new strategies to make old products attractive to today's youth.

This alternative could be successful because of Hasbro's ability to develop, introduce, and gain consumer acceptance of its products. Although Jakks Pacific and Lego had unique core products, they had never been able to gain the market share that Hasbro was able to achieve. Mattel, the number one toy maker at the time, had strong core products. However, it was experiencing lagging sales of Barbie, which it had relied on for a large percentage of its sales. Hasbro's ability to anticipate trends should allow it to redesign its products to fit the needs of today's children.

A drawback of this alternative was that although focusing on core products was a safer route than focusing on licensing, licensing was the quick moneymaker. A way to get around this drawback would be to incorporate new innovation in old products. Hasbro's ability to obtain top-notch inventors and designers could allow it to combine cutting-edge technology with unique product design.

After listening to both suggestions, Hassenfeld commented that he liked both strategic alternatives and would consider them when defining the future of the company.

References

S. Chartrand, "Inventing Toys from an Adult View," *The New York Times, http://toysngames.com/ir/comments. php?id5P134_0_1_10* (March 23, 2005).

Federal Communications Commission, "Consumer Facts," *http://www.fcc.gov/cgb/consumerfacts/childtv.html* (March 23, 2005).

Filcomedia (2004) "Covert Advertising Techniques," *http://www.adamranson.freeserve.co.uk/covertbrand.htm* (March 6, 2005).

Kenneth L. Fisher, "End Your Gloom," *Forbes http://cpprod.stjohns.edu/cp/tn/fs?tn5wl* (April 15, 2005).

Microsoft Encarta Online Encyclopedia, "Food and Drug Administration," *http://encarta.msn.com* (March 23, 2005).

Wilma Hammet, "Household Hazardous Products," *http://www.healthgoods.com/Education/Healthy_Home_Information/Home_Health_Hazards/household_hazardous_products.htm* (March 23, 2005).

Hasbro Annual Report, 2002.

Hasbro Annual Report, 2003.

Hoovers Online, "Mattel, Inc. Factsheet," *http://premium.hoovers.com/subscribe/co/factsheet.xhtml?ID10966* (April 1, 2005).

Hoovers Online, "LEGO Fact Sheet," *http://premium.hoovers.com/subscribe/co/factsheet.xhtml?ID42877* (April 1, 2005).

Hoovers Online, "JAKKS Pacific Fact Sheet," *http://premium.hoovers.com/subscribe/co/factsheet.xhtml?ID=51594* (April 1, 2005).

Hoovers Online, "Hasbro Inc. Financials: Income Statement," *http://premium.hoovers.com/subscribe/co/fin/annual.xhtml?ID=12007* (April 2, 2005).

Hoovers Online, "Hasbro Inc. Financials: Balance Sheet," *http://premium.hoovers.com/subscribe/co/fin/annual.xhtml?ID=12007* (April 2, 2005).

International Council on Toy Industries, (2001), "Toy Safety Standards Used Around the World," *http://www.toy-icti.org/info/worldsafetystandards.htm* (April 18, 2005).

Geoff Keighley, (2004), "New Life for Old Games," *Business 2.0, http://cpprod.stjohns.edu/cp/tn/fs?tn=wl* (April 15, 2005).

LexisNexis, "Hasbro Profits Up Despite Weak Sales," *http://web.lexis-nexis.com/universe/document?_m=1f606ff320278834b7f2944583d958e2&_docnum=12&wchp=dGLbVzz-zSkVA&_md5=bffd6c8897f01dc8a7b04fdf32ab26c3* (April 4, 2005).

583d958e2&_docnum=12&wchp=dGLbVzz-zSkVA&_md5=bffd6c8897f01dc8a7b04fdf32ab26c3 (April 4, 2005).

Bill McCartney, "Tweens," *http://promisekeepers.ibelieve.com/content.asp?CID=15464* (March 23, 2005).

J. Pereira, "Trends (a Special Report): It's a Whole New Game," *Wall Street Journal,* (November 22, 2004), p. 9.

Ann Pomeroy, "Head of the Class," *HR Magazine; http://www.findarticles.com/p/articles/mi_m3495/is_1_50/ai_ n11841249* (March 23, 2005).

Toy Industry Association, (2004), *"State of the Industry," http://www.toy-tia.org/Content/NavigationMenu/Press_Room/Statistics3/State_of_the_Industry/2004_vs_2003.htm* (February 2, 2005).

Ralph F. Wilson, (2000), "The Eight Essential Types of Internet Promotion," *Web Marketing Today, http://www.wilsonweb.com/wmt5/plan-4promotion.htm* (March 4, 2005).

Notes

1. Reuters, "Cost-cutting Boosts Hasbro's Earnings," *http://www.reuters.com/newsSearchResultsHome.jhtml?query=hasbro&qtype=a* (March 15, 2005).
2. NPD Group, "2004 U.S. Toy Industry Sales Stabilize Thanks in Large Part to Strong December Sales and Increased Sales of Electronic Toys," *http://www.npd.com/dynamic/releases/press_050218.html* (March 12, 2005).
3. Tom Graves, (2004). "Movies & Home Entertainment," *Standard & Poor's, http://jerome.stjohns.edu:151/docs/indsur/pdf/mhe_1199.pdf* (March 15, 2005).
4. *Ibid.*
5. *Ibid.*
6. *Ibid.*
7. *Ibid.*
8. William H. Donald, (2004). "Publishing," *Standard & Poor's, http://jerome.stjohns.edu:151/NASApp/NetAdvantage/showIndustrySurvey.do?code=pb&date=/pub_0904.htm* (March 12, 2005).
9. PR Newswire US (2004). "Travel Industry Optimistic for 2005," *http://sev.prnewswire.com/travel/20041029/DCF06029102004-1.html* (March 4, 2005).
10. Datamonitor (2004). "Toys and Games in the United States: Industry Profile," *http://cpprod.stjohns.edu/cp/tn/fs?tn=wl* (March 19, 2005).
11. *Ibid.*
12. *Ibid.*
13. *Ibid.*
14. Datamonitor (2003)."Hasbro, Inc.: Company Profile." [Online]. *http://www.datamonitor.com/~d697a180f4254493a6e722feeef50e07~/companies/company/?pid=1B81864B-E7C8-465C-AC5C-3B4FEDFFCB88* (March 23, 2005).
15. *Ibid.*
16. *Ibid.*

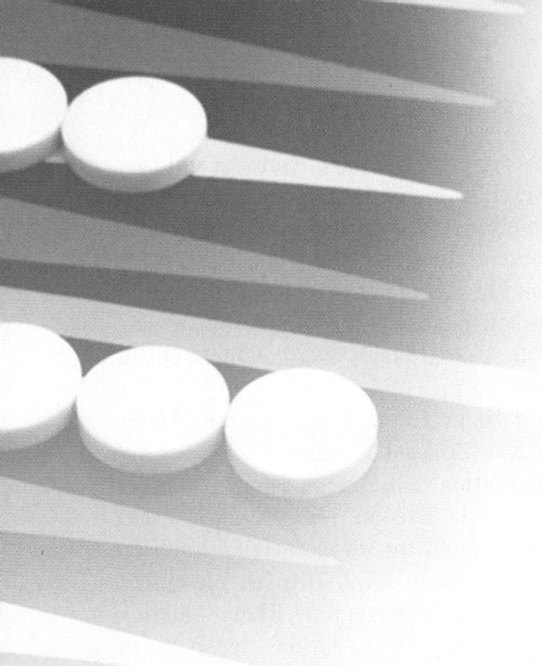

CASE 26

The Haier Group: U.S. Expansion

YongJun Lu, Robert J. Mockler, and Marc Gartenfeld

ON FEBRUARY 23, 2004, THE HAIER GROUP (PRONOUNCED "HIGH-ER"), A MAJOR HOME electrical appliance maker in China, was listed as the only Chinese name brand among the world's 100 most recognizable brands in a global name brand list edited by World Brand Laboratory.[1] The 20-year-old Haier had built a network composed of 18 design centers, 10 industrial parks, 30 overseas factories and manufacturing bases, 58,800 sales offices, and 96 product group categories ranging from refrigerators, washing machines, and air conditioners to cell phones and televisions. As China's domestic markets had mushroomed over the past two decades, Haier had built a reputation at home for quality, innovation, and customer service. It enjoyed leading domestic market share positions in washing machines, refrigerators, vacuum cleaners, and air conditioners.

Encouraged by the Chinese government, Haier strove to become truly international. Haier's executives believed that they could extend the company's strong domestic brand reputation into the West by introducing innovative products for niche consumer markets and then expanding into bigger markets—a strategy that would enable the company to enjoy the higher margins that came with brand sales instead of slugging it out as a low-cost supplier to Western companies.

Haier started out in 1984 as a government-owned enterprise with imported refrigerator production technology from Germany. It subsequently engaged in technical innovation, scientific management, capital operations, mergers and acquisitions, and international expansion. By 2004, it had completed its long march from a small enterprise burdened with a debit of 1.47 million RMB ($177,536) to its current position as the number one domestic electrical appliance producer in China.

Zhang Ruimin, CEO of the Haier Group, announced in November 2004 that the main goal of the company was to continuously increase the volume of products sold in the United

This case was prepared by YongJun Lu under the direction of Dr. Robert J. Mockler and Professor Marc Gartenfeld of St. John's University. Dr. Mockler and Professor Gartenfeld revised and edited this case. The copyright holder is solely responsible for the case content. This case was reprinted from *Cases in Domestic and Multinational Strategic Management*, Publication (VIII) #44 , pp. C7-1 through C7-26, edited by Robert J. Mockler and Marc Gartenfeld. This case was edited for SMBP–11th Edition.

States, and to modify the company's products to meet American demand.[2] Subsequently, on December 22, 2004, Haier selected A&E Factory Service, one of the leading service companies in the United States, to be its primary service provider for repairs on products under warranty and service contracts in the United States and Puerto Rico. This agreement reflected Haier's commitment to the U.S. market and to the aggressive pursuit of quality assurance. The task for Ruimin was to develop an effective strategy for Haier Group to survive and prosper against aggressive competition in the United States over the intermediate and long-term future.

In 2004, the Haier Group was organized into Haier China, Haier Europe, Haier America, Haier Middle East, Haier Spain, and Haier New Zealand divisions. Each company had its own manufacturing base and sales and marketing department. Haier America, founded in 1999, was originally a U.S. sales and marketing division. That year, it invested $40 million to purchase land in Camden, South Carolina, for its new Haier America Industrial Park. It also established a design center in Boston in 1999. Two years later, the Camden plant produced Haier's first products in America—refrigerators. Haier America also spent $15 million in 2002 to purchase the landmark Greenwich Savings Bank in Manhattan, New York City, to serve as its U.S. headquarters. In 2004, the Camden plant mainly produced large (standard-size in the United States) refrigerators to be primarily sold in the U.S. major home appliance market. Most of Haier's other products that were sold in the United States were imported from Haier China or other subsidiaries of the Haier Group that had a production cost advantage.

Although Haier had a good reputation in "white goods" (white goods referred to major home appliances such as refrigerators, washing machines, and stoves, whereas "brown goods" referred to consumer electronics such as radios and televisions), the brand was still relatively new in the United States, and the company faced a number of long-term decisions in order to build an American presence. Some of the decisions included (1) how to integrate itself with the locality and build brand recognition, (2) how to create the products that could meet American needs, (3) how to achieve the cost control needed to maintain its price advantage, and (4) how to continuously improve its services to build the trust of local customers. The main problem to be resolved for Haier was how to differentiate itself from General Electric, Whirlpool, Maytag, and Electrolux in white goods and from Sony, Panasonic, Philips, and LG in brown goods and thus achieve a winning competitive advantage in the U.S. market.

The Home Appliances and Consumer Electronics Segments of the U.S. Durable Goods Industry

Home appliances and consumer electronics were segments of the durable goods industry. Durable goods were manufactured products capable of long use (over three years), such as automobiles, jewelry, furnishings, home appliances, and consumer electronics. The durable goods industry was sensitive to business cycles. The performance of the durable goods industry was tied to the overall economy, especially to interest rates. Purchases of durable goods were typically postponed during poor economic conditions, but increased during good ones. In 2004, total durable goods shipments increased 10.3% over the previous year.[3] Home appliances included both major and small appliances. Major appliances generally included dishwashers, microwaves, washers and dryers, ranges, refrigerators, and air conditioners, whereas small appliances included less costly electric items, such as food mixers, coffee makers, and can openers. Consumer electronics included stereos, televisions, video cameras, and CD and DVD players/recorders.

For the fourth quarter of 2004, U.S. industry demand for major home appliances increased 10.7% from the prior year. For the full year, industry unit shipments grew 8.3%. Economists expected industry shipments in 2005 to increase approximately 2%. Based on sales from manufacturers to dealers, the U.S. market for consumer electronics products was expected to total $125.7 billion in 2005, up 11% from 2004's estimated level, according to projections from the Consumer Electronics Association.[4]

Benefiting from a growing economy, U.S. consumer disposable income increased, and relatively low mortgage rates maintained a fairly high demand for new homes. These positive factors stimulated people's consumption of durable goods including home appliances and consumer electronics. The U.S. economy performed well in 2004, with consumer spending, fiscal stimulus, and low interest rates boosting a 4.1% increase of gross domestic product (GDP), up from a 3.1% increase in 2003. In addition, consumer disposable spending remained strong, ending the year at 6.1%, up from 5.2% in 2003. The number of U.S. jobs increased by 2.2 million in 2004, the best year for job growth since 1999.[5]

U.S. consumer spending on appliances and furniture outpaced overall spending, rising 7.6% for the year, compared to 2.7% for 2003. Consumer confidence was strong, with the Consumer Board's consumer confidence index at 103.4 as of January 2005, the highest level since July 2004. Housing sales were also strong, with sales of new and existing homes in 2004 up 9.4% and 8.9%, respectively, from 2003, according to the National Association of Realtors, a U.S. real estate trade association.[6] Residential housing patterns and increased remodeling activity had contributed to fairly steady growth for major home appliances since 1991. The national median existing-home price in the United States was $171,600 in late 2004, 6.6% higher than a year earlier when the median price was $161,100.[7]

Homes were also getting larger in the United States. Increased total floor space and a greater number of rooms per house translated into more appliance sales. In 2002, new homes averaged 2,320 square feet versus 1,645 square feet in 1975, according to the U.S. Census Bureau. Approximately 36% of all new houses had four or more bedrooms, up from approximately 20% in 1975.

In contrast to home appliances, the demand for consumer electronics was driven by technological innovation—especially in digital technology. The consumer electronics industry had fared better than most other industries in times of flux. Technological advances and ever-changing product lines had helped the industry avoid major saturation problems by making existing products appear outdated. The success of digital products—video players, TVs, phones, and home theater systems—had proven that consumers would often succumb to the urge to own the latest and greatest electronic gadgets, in spite of economic concerns. The consumer electronics industry surged ahead in recent years with all-time records for consumer electronics sales. DVD players, one of the fastest-selling electronics products, led this surge. In 2003, DVD rentals surpassed videocassette rentals for the first time.

As digital technology continued to fuel industry growth, products were getting quicker, smaller (except for TVs), faster, and cheaper. Rapid growth had been seen in home networking, photography, navigation, LCD, plasma, and digital radio. Sensing devices, broadband, and wireless were helping define the industry's future. Driven by demand for digital audio, video, and home information products, U.S. consumer electronics sales soared by 10.7% in 2004 to an all-time record $113.5 billion. Equally strong sales growth was anticipated for 2005, with sales expected to climb to $125.7 billion, according to the Consumer Electronics Administration.[8]

The aging of the Baby Boom generation was expected to escalate spending on appliances and electronics. With most of these people in their prime income-earning years, they were replacing old, inexpensive electronic products with new, higher-quality products and renovating their kitchens with state-of-the-art major home appliances.

Products and Markets

The common element among home appliances and consumer electronics was that they both had useful lives of more than three years. For example, the average useful life of a major home appliance in 2004 was 9 years for dishwashers, 13 years for clothes dryers, 11 years for freezers, 9 years for microwave ovens, 13 years for electric ranges, 15 years for gas ranges, 13 years for large refrigerators, 9 years for compact refrigerators, and 10 years for clothes washers and room air conditioners. In consumer electronics, the average life expectancy of color televisions was 8 years and that of VCRs was 5 years. For small home appliances, the average life expectancy ranged from 7 years for coffee percolators to 4 years for food processors.[9]

Each manufacturer tried to differentiate itself by offering products with unique features or technologically advanced products to attract either general consumers or some specific consumer bases. Further, to gain price advantage, manufacturers put more emphasis on streamlining production and implementing cost control of both production processes and supply chain and distribution management. Because competition was intense within the industry, manufacturers had been trying to gain advantages by launching aggressive mass media advertising campaigns or by doing frequent in-store promotions.

Home Appliances

Manufacturers of major home appliances generally produced washing machines, clothes dryers, dishwashers, ranges, refrigerators, freezers, and microwave ovens, and sometimes air conditioners, vacuum cleaners, and small appliances. Opportunities for home appliances were a low saturation rate (percentage of households with a particular appliance) for a particular product category and an increasing demand for new features on products. The saturation rate of major home appliances in 2004 in the United States was 100% for ranges (gas and electric), 99% for refrigerators, 98% for vacuum cleaners, 96% for microwave ovens, 95% for washing machines, 84% for clothes dryers (gas and electric), 60% for dishwashers, and 17% for compact refrigerators.[10] Some major home appliances, such as full-size refrigerators, clothes washers, and ranges, achieved significant U.S. market saturation rates decades ago. Others, such as microwave ovens, dishwashers, electric dryers, and compact refrigerators, had seen steadily rising saturation rates in recent years. For example, microwave ovens had increased from just 65.9% of U.S. homes in 1987, and compact refrigerators, which were not tracked in 1987, increased from only 7.4% saturation in 1987.[11]

The U.S. home appliance market was mature, but was still the largest market in the world. In 2004, 58,653,000 major home appliance units were sold in the United States plus 5,458,000 more in Canada.[12] Major home appliances already had high saturation levels, and no breakthrough products were looming on the horizon to create a dramatic new demand. Key factors in the appliance area were strong brand recognition, high quality of products and services, capability to provide a wide range of product categories, a strong ability to design new features on existing products, the ability to meet local consumers' needs, and price attractiveness. Brand recognition represented manufacturers' market recognition for providing consistent quality products and consistent maintenance and services in the long term.

In major home appliances, the threat of substitute products came largely from incremental improvements (such as energy-efficient washers and dryers or timed coffee makers) rather than from wholly new products that made previous products obsolete (such as the invention of the electric refrigerator, which replaced the icebox). Thus, to more effectively meet local needs, participants could devote more R&D resources to improving existing products than to developing new product categories. Manufacturers could increase their competitiveness by improving the capability of new feature designs, such as the convertible refrigerator/freezer. To continuously gain price attractiveness in a market of rising material costs in 2004, manufacturers needed to have premium product lines and raise sales in the high-end segment to offset the losses caused by increased costs. To ensure their competitive position, firms invested in technology development leading to new products, such as the robot vacuum cleaner or the home PAD refrigerator (which detected the shelf life of food and automatically displayed a list of items stored in the fridge on the door).

Because of relatively high saturation levels in the United States, the market for major home appliances was driven primarily by the demand for replacing worn-out appliances. Generally speaking, replacements accounted for 75% of sales, new housing for 20%, and new household formation for about 5% of sales of major home appliances. On average, each new home directly or indirectly represented the sales of four or five new appliances, including a refrigerator, a dishwasher, an oven and cook top (or a range), and laundry equipment.

Although housing starts had been at a relatively high level in recent years, specialists predicted that they would fall over the next several years.[13] Major home appliance manufacturers would then need to depend more on replacement demand (including purchases made during remodeling) than on housing starts. In such an environment, companies would need innovative, stylish, and attractively priced products to stimulate sales.

Consumer Electronics

Manufacturers of consumer electronics usually produced stereos, TV, CDs, DVD players/recorders, and video cameras. Opportunities for consumer electronics were the steady growth rate in such product categories as plasma TVs and DVD players/recorders and strong demand for electronic products driven by digital technology and services that offered consumers a convenient, affordable means of accessing information and communicating with other people. Benefiting from a recovering economy in 2003, sales increased 3.5%, almost hitting $100 billion. Digital TV (DTV) continued its ascent as the fastest-growing technology of all time in terms of sales. The Consumer Electronics Association projected that the sales of DTV would reach 6.97 million in 2004, 10.77 million in 2005, 16.77 million in 2006, 23.25 million in 2007, and 27.05 million in 2008.[14] Digital growth was on the rise in nearly every product category across the consumer electronics spectrum, including audio, video, imaging, information technologies, networking, and mobile electronics. The fastest growing products in 2003 as measured by sales were digital cameras, MP3 players, DVD players/recorders, and plasma TVs.

New opportunities were the flat HDTV, large LCD, plasma TV, and new display technologies with paper-thin visual displays. Despite their high prices, plasma TVs became a hot item in 2003. HDTV had become more and more popular as a subscription service in the United States, especially in public outlets such as bars and gyms. Along with the HDTV capability, plasma TVs offered a much crisper and higher-quality video and audio experience. Many specialized retail outlets, such as Best Buy, had reconfigured some of their stores to feature home theater demonstrations with plasma screen TVs. Manufacturers had responded with a continuous stream of new plasma TV products.

Key factors in consumer electronics were brand recognition, high quality of products and services, wide ranges of products, the speed of development of new technologies, and price competitiveness. Manufacturers were able to capture the high-end market by investing in new technology development and quickly translating it to technologically advanced products with unique designs. They also could satisfy some low-end market needs by offering the basic functional products with fewer features and fewer technological advances at relatively lower prices. By offering a wide range of products, manufacturers could satisfy varying needs and provide the convenience of one-stop shopping. In addition, attractive appearance design was very important for manufactures to capture consumer attention.

Manufacturing and R&D

Economic activity in the U.S. manufacturing sector grew in January 2005 for the 20th consecutive month while the overall economy grew for the 39th consecutive month, according to a report from the Institute of Supply Management.[15] The production of home appliances and consumer electronics were capital intensive; there were significant up-front and ongoing costs. Manufacturing facilities were highly mechanized, with assembly lines designed for long production runs. Consequently, the industry's fixed costs were moderately high. However, the business also had a significant variable cost element; it was somewhat sensitive to price changes in raw materials and components.

Research and development (R&D) involved ongoing expenses. New products and features must be continually introduced for a company's goods to remain competitive with otherwise undifferentiated products. In addition, consumer demand forced manufacturers to create innovative features and styles that better suited customer needs. However, in the short run, R&D spending could be reduced when cash needed to be conserved.

Home Appliances

In 2004, while many manufacturers were enjoying strong sales, major home appliance makers were significantly affected by increases in material and logistics costs. Material prices increased at an alarming rate in 2004, causing some financial loss for several companies during the third quarter of 2004. Consequently, Whirlpool, General Electric, and Maytag had passed the 5%–10% increases to their costumers. Whirlpool, an industry leader, estimated that the material cost base would increase an additional 7% to 8% during 2005.[16] Prices of electric appliances in China were in the process of rising at least 5% in 2005. For example, the price of room air conditioners was increasing 5% to 8% because of increases in costs of raw materials, such as plastics (where prices had gone up as much as 30%), steel (up 15%), and copper (up 20%).[17]

The recently volatile economy had forced most manufacturers to explore outsourcing. Many companies saw it as an opportunity to reduce costs, improve flexibility, and streamline production processes. For example, Maytag had been a vertically integrated organization for many years. However, the appliance manufacturer realized that this model was not always efficient. As a result, in 2003 Maytag developed a corporate strategy to look at each business unit and use outsourcing if it was cost effective. The company had entered into an agreement under which Daewoo Electronics of Seoul, South Korea, would manufacture top-freezer refrigerators for Maytag.

Because of the industry's high level of automation, labor was a relatively small percentage of appliance makers' costs. Labor expenses could generally be reduced when product runs were suspended temporarily, but equipment and facilities still needed to be maintained, although at a lower cost than when in full operation. As material costs increased significantly in 2004, companies worked to absorb them. Manufacturers increased productivity, restructured facilities and management, and focused on increasing product innovation. Despite attempts to curb costs, the appliance industry found itself having no choice but to pass a portion of the cost increases to consumers. Appliance manufacturers were hoping to move consumer purchases to higher-end products, where profit margins were better.

Technology was leading to improvements in products. "Smart" computerized appliances were being introduced that were expected to make life easier for users. Examples included Whirlpool's Polara combination oven/refrigerator that automatically started cooking at a programmed time and kept food either hot or cold. In Europe, Electrolux was selling the Trilobite, a robot vacuum cleaner.

The "smart kitchen" concept had captured the attention of both the appliance industry and companies that traditionally specialized in kitchen products. For instance, Samsung had introduced the "Home PAD Refrigerator," which detected the shelf life of food and automatically displayed a list of items stored in the fridge on the door. Via an Internet connection, owners of the Samsung refrigerator could retrieve that information from a remote location. LG Electronics had launched a TV refrigerator, which included a cable-ready, 13.5-inch TV screen, FM radio, two speakers, and a TV tuner.

Some new appliances used a mix of old and new technologies, such as barcode readers to recognize food items in the fridge. The engine of the smart kitchen was a broadband-equipped home network that connected all of the kitchen's products with the family's remote devices, such as a cell phone, a pager, and an office computer or a laptop. The smart kitchen featured such novelties as ovens that could download and execute recipes via the Internet, and ovens that could be temperature-controlled during the day so they could store and eventually cook food via a cell phone request while owners were still at the office.

It was becoming very important for manufacturers to continuously anticipate the trends in such new technologies as "smart appliances" and "smart kitchens" as well as to emphasize product developments and new feature designs. The manufacturer needed to maintain a highly creative and motivated technical team and achieve commitment at the corporate level to provide strong support for such development. Speed to convert innovations into mass production was another important factor that could affect the sales of the new products.

Consumer Electronics

Consumer electronics manufacturers had learned to live in a world where price, brand sensitivity, short windows for product life cycles, and the bargaining power of retailers were the norm, making time to market and time to volume the driving concerns. In order to thrive in an industry punctuated by dramatic swings in demand and short product life cycles, manufacturers had to deliver technical innovations and satisfy customer demands while containing costs. These competitive imperatives had led to the adoption of outsourced manufacturing strategies in order to reduce costs while enhancing operational flexibility.

Manufacturers either used electronics manufacturing service (EMS) providers to handle the entire product design and manufacturing process or outsourced just the manufacturing process. EMS providers offered customers a comprehensive, integrated, lower total cost of ownership approach to product design and manufacturing services. The object was to reduce total manufacturing costs and provide higher manufacturing responsiveness to changes in volume. Either way, tightly managing production and coordinating delivery to multiple distribution points had become key to supply chain profitability in these virtual supply chains.

Opportunities for consumer electronics were being generated by the U.S. transition of television broadcasting from an analog to a digital platform. Profit opportunities abounded from consumers replacing old analog televisions or adding new big-screen sets to their home theater systems. These buyers were opting to purchase displays capable of the better pixel resolution and higher-frequency scan rates of digital television (DTV) signals and took advantage of the improved video fidelity offered by popular DVD players. CEA (Consumer Electronics Administration) forecasted DTV factory revenue to climb 33% to more than $8 billion by the end of 2004, and DTV product sales to climb more than 39% to 5.8 million units. Factory sales of DTV displays exceeded CEA forecasts in 2003, with wholesale volume growing by 41% to nearly $6 billion.[18]

Portable entertainment devices were the current trend in consumer electronics. Advances in technology were changing not only the types of portable entertainment devices consumers used, but also how they were used. The outcome of this digital movement was that consumers could access their content—especially entertainment content—wherever they went. A number of consumer electronic products had emerged to meet rising consumer demand for more cutting-edge on-the-go audio and video applications. Another trend was a personal media player that integrated digital music and video from electronic files. These products allowed consumers to play back digital music much like an MP3 player, but with integrated color screens; they also enabled consumers to view digital photos and play back digitized movies, home videos, and even recorded TV shows.

Technology shifts, shorter product life cycles, and other unanticipated requirements had become part of the industry's new dynamics, but chipmakers and consumer electronics manufacturers were clearly experiencing pressure to produce new and compelling products with new features and better performance at lower production costs. It was important for manufacturers to keep up-to-date in new technologies, such as portable entertainment devices and personal media players, to continuously anticipate the trends in product development, and to improve the appearance of existing products. Time cycles to convert new technology into mass-produced products were becoming much shorter. How well manufacturers would anticipate new trends and how fast they could respond to them in a cost-efficient way were critical to their success.

Industry Supply Chain and Distribution Channels

Manufacturers had some control over retail distribution—through either outlet chain stores or independent stores. Most major manufacturers and retailers had regional distribution facilities located strategically near a cluster of stores. However, because of their high-volume purchases, major retailers such as Sears often received shipments directly from the manufacturing facility to their own warehouses. For example, Samsung put a supply-chain management program in place to reduce the number of logistics steps and deliver directly to customers' warehouses. This prompted manufacturers to provide prompt delivery of items, reduce inventory requirements at individual stores, and undertake more efficient production runs.

Manufacturers were working closely with retailers to increase the efficiency of the supply chain—from source to consumer. Manufacturers and retailers were reducing order cycle time by sharing information through collaborative planning, forecasting, and replenishment (CPFR). CPFR enabled trading partners to gain visibility into each other's demand chain, order forecasts, and promotional plans. For example, Wal-Mart created a partnership with vendors in which both sides shared information to streamline the flow of goods. Vendors tapped into the chain's computers to get a scorecard of performance and manage their own in-store inventory. A 2001 study conducted by Grocery Manufacturers of America (GMA) showed that 57% of companies using CPFR improved trading partner relationships and 38% improved service levels, stock outs, and sales. Intense pricing pressures and the drive to grow share in oversaturated markets were making the efficiency and effectiveness of the supply chain ever more important.

To enhance distribution efficiency, companies often used sophisticated cantilever racking and computer-controlled random-access inventory storage. In addition, many manufacturers employed their own drivers (rather than subcontracting the work), maintained a fleet of trucks and trailers to ensure quality control, and offered customers delivery and setup at no additional cost.

Retail distribution of home appliances and consumer electronics had historically been dominated by department stores, such as Sears Roebuck. Sears was traditionally so strong in major home appliance sales that it alone accounted for nearly two out of every five major home appliances sold in the United States. In addition to selling brand name home appliances, Sears strongly promoted its own line of Kenmore home appliances, for which it contracted with appliance manufacturers such as Whirlpool and Electrolux. These traditional retailers encountered stiff competition from mass merchandise discounters such as Wal-Mart and home improvement retailers such as Home Depot and Lowe's. Sears and other traditional retailers typically sold goods at the manufacturer's suggested retail price (Kenmore products, however, were promoted at lower prices), drawing customers with their well-stocked inventories and knowledgeable salespeople. In contrast, Wal-Mart and Home Depot sold household appliances at a discount below the suggested retail price. Although they kept limited inventory in the store and provided fewer customer services, they provided information kiosks where consumers could browse for more selections.

Sears had responded to increasing competition by lowering prices and increasing advertising, while continuing other promotional efforts such as offering low-cost financing. These recent shifts in retailing had further pressured selling prices. On the manufacturing level, appliance and electronics makers had introduced more value-added products, such as the convertible freezer/refrigerator, to differentiate their offerings and to avoid competing on price alone. Consumer demand for premium appliances and electronics with new features had helped to alleviate the industry's long-running price competition.

Because more than 80% of home appliances and consumer electronics were purchased by consumers from chain store outlets, a manufacturer's relationship with chain stores was the most important factor to affect sales performance. Good relationships translated into more shelf space, better exhibition area, and more aggressive in-store promotion. Furthermore, discount chains store such as Wal-Mart, Target, and Costco usually sold standard products with fewer features at relatively lower prices. More specialized chain stores such as Sears, Circuit City, and Bed Bath & Beyond offered more choices of a wider range of features and better services at reasonable prices.

Most major home appliances were purchased by consumers from retail outlets. The primary reason was that large products such as washers, dryers, and refrigerators usually needed professional installation, which retail outlets were able to provide by keeping trained workers on staff. In addition, consumers typically wished to inspect major appliances in person before purchasing.

Consumer electronics were generally purchased by consumers from electronics stores, such as Best Buy, Circuit City, and Radio Shack. These stores had well-trained employees who had special knowledge of the consumer electronics products and could provide appropriate recommendations to customers according to their specific needs.

Competitors in the U.S. Market

Competition in major home appliances and consumer electronics in the U.S. market came from multinational companies that manufactured both home appliances and consumer electronics as well as some large international and domestic players that focused either on home appliances or on consumer electronics. Some multinational companies, such as Matsushita, LG, and Haier, participated in both product categories. Electrolux, GE, Whirlpool, and Maytag focused mainly on major home appliances. Electrolux and Whirlpool (plus LG and Haier) had a significant presence in air conditioners, but GE and Maytag did not. Although GE had previously divested its small appliance unit to Black & Decker, Whirlpool was still active in small appliances with a 2.9% market share in 2004. Sony, Sanyo, and Philips focused mostly on consumer electronics.

Major Home Appliances

Whirlpool

Whirlpool, a worldwide manufacturer and marketer of major home appliances, was first in U.S. sales with a 33.4% market share in 2004 (see **Exhibit 1**).[19] Whirlpool manufactured in 13 countries under nine brand names and marketed products to distributors and retailers in more than 170 countries. It marketed a line of appliances and related products, primarily for home use. In addition to its presence in major home appliances, Whirlpool had a 7.1% share of the U.S. air conditioning market in 2004.

Exhibit 1 Shares of U.S. and Western European Market in White Goods (Including dishwashers, dryers, ranges, ovens, refrigerators, washers)

UNITED STATES COMBINED MARKET SHARE BY COMPANY

Company	Home Country	2001	2004	Brands
Whirlpool	USA	39.2%	33.4%	Estate, Inglis, KitchenAid, Roper, Whirlpool
GE	USA	23.2%	25.7%	GE, Hotpoint, Monogram, Profile, RCA
Maytag	USA	21.6%	15.1%	Admiral, Amana, Jenn-Air, Magic Chef, Maytag
Electrolux	Sweden	15.0%	19.0%	Frigidaire, Gibson, Kelvinator, Tappan, White-Westinghouse
Others	—	1.0%	6.8%	LG, Haier, Bosch-Siemens, Sub-Zero, Viking, etc.

WESTERN EUROPEAN COMBINED MARKET SHARE BY COMPANY

Company	Home Country	2004
Electrolux	Sweden	16.9%
Bosch-Siemens	Germany	15.1%
Indesit/Merloni	Italy	14.2%
Whirlpool	U.S.	9.4%
Koc Group	Turkey	5.7%
Candy	Italy	3.4%
Others	—	35.3%

Sources: "28th Annual Report of the U.S Appliance Industry," Appliance *(September 2005), Special Insert; "Portrait of the European Appliance Industry,"* Appliance *(November 2005), pp. 71–74.*

With steel, aluminum, oil, and copper costs soaring in 2004, Whirlpool took several actions to curb the rising raw material costs:

- **Product specification.** The company worked to make improvements on and take material content out of products in order to allocate engineering and resources appropriately.
- **Conversion cost consideration.** This was achieved by utilizing six-sigma and lean manufacturing practices.
- **Target setting.** Specific cost reduction targets were set for upcoming quarters.
- **Innovation rate ramp-up.** Whirlpool had introduced 25 new products in the past 3 years and it planned to double that pace in the next 2 years.

Whirlpool's strengths were its dominant U.S. market share and strong U.S. brand recognition. The company owed its leadership position to its 50-plus year relationship with Sears, to which it had been the primary supplier of Kenmore (Sears' own brand label) appliances. Even though Sears began offering appliance brands other than Kenmore in the 1990s, Whirlpool continued to be a key supplier. Whirlpool offered a wide range of product categories, high-quality products with unique designs, and a well-serviced maintenance network. Whirlpool was familiar with its major buyers' needs and responded quickly to shifts in local trends because the company designed and manufactured its major products locally. For example, Whirlpool's large refrigerators with ice-maker, water filter, and water dispenser had become the most popular multi-functional refrigerator in the U.S. market. Whirlpool dominated U.S. sales of dishwashers, washers, and dryers and had a strong international and nationwide supply chain and distribution system. It maintained good relationships with chain stores, individual stores, and Internet sellers. To ensure its dominant position in the U.S. major home appliance market, the company invested heavily in R&D and spent heavily on marketing. It also had some manufacturing plants in Mexico where costs were lower.

Maytag's weaknesses were its high amount of debt and relatively slow responsiveness to market shifts. Although Maytag spent a large amount on new technology development, it had difficulty in developing appropriate products to satisfy new market trends. Compared with the other major appliance manufacturers, Maytag had a relatively weak network with retail chain stores and Internet sellers. The company's products did not appeal to young people because of its conservative designs and relatively higher prices. The company's sales and promotions on the Internet and mass media were also slightly weaker than those of its major competitors, such as Whirlpool. The company's ability to absorb rising material costs was weak given that most of its products were made in the United States. Unlike its competition, Maytag was primarily a domestic company and was just beginning to establish manufacturing facilities in Mexico where costs were lower.

As a result of its acquisitions of Magic Chef, Hoover, and Amana, among others, Maytag had taken on a high amount of debt. Maytag's low profit margins had made it virtually impossible for the company to be as competitive as its peers in negotiating with retailers, leading to a significant loss of valuable store floor space.

Others

Other companies were making and selling a significant amount of major home appliances in the United States. Nevertheless, their total market share was only 6.8% in 2004—still a considerable increase from just 1% in 2001. Bosch-Siemens Hausgerate (BSH), a German joint venture between Robert Bosch and Siemens with the second largest major home appliance sales in Europe (see **Exhibit 1**), had built a dishwasher plant in North Carolina in 1997 and had expanded it in 2002 to produce cooking and laundry appliances. It also had factories in Tennessee and California. BSH made high-quality major home appliances, such as its stainless-steel dishwasher, for sale to affluent U.S. consumers. As the largest market for major home appliances in the world, the United States was considered to be a key part of Bosch-Siemens' future growth. According to CEO Kurt-Ludwig Gutberlet in a 2004 interview, "We will no doubt more than double our business in the U.S. in the next 3 to 4 years."[20]

After importing refrigerators into the U.S. since 1997, Haier built a refrigerator plant in South Carolina. By 2004 Haier's share of the standard-size refrigerator market had risen to 2% for fifth place (behind GE, Electrolux, Whirlpool, and Maytag) and 20% of the compact refrigerator market (ahead of GE's 17%) for first place in this category.

South Korea's LG Electronics (LGE) had also become a serious competitor in U.S. major home appliances. Although LGE's overall share of the U.S. major home appliance market was still low in 2004, it ranked first in U.S. microwave oven sales with a 38% market share, up from only 8% in 1999. LGE was second in the U.S. air conditioner market with a 13.8% market share. LG intended to be a global player in the industry. LGE's management wanted to achieve $14 billion in global sales by 2007, up from $8.5 billion in 2004.[21] Among the large U.S. major home appliance retailers, Best Buy was the first to carry a wide range of LG appliances, followed by Home Depot in January 2005.

In addition to Bosch-Siemens, Haier, and LGE, there were a few smaller niche competitors operating in North America, such as Sub-Zero, Viking Range, W.C. Wood, and Brown Stove Works. Most of them manufactured and sold only one category of appliance, such as specialized ranges or freezers sold at premium prices.

Competitors in Other Major Home Appliance Categories

Air conditioners and floor care appliances were not usually included with U.S. major home appliances when market shares were calculated. For example, room air conditioners were typically listed under "comfort conditioning" along with unitary (central) air conditioners and heat pumps, dehumidifiers, and furnaces. In 2004, the market share leaders in the U.S. room air conditioner market were LG Electronics (29%), Fedders (22%), Electrolux (11%), Whirlpool (11%), Haier (6%), Samsung (6%), Sharp (4%), Matsushita (2%), and Friedrich (2%), with others accounting for the remaining 7%. In the dehumidifier category, Whirlpool (35%) and LG Electronics (30%) dominated the market with the remainder going to Fedders (11%), W. C. Wood (8%), Electrolux (7%), Samsung (3%), Ebco (3%), and others (3%). The leading competitors in floor care appliances in 2004 were Panasonic and Electrolux (Eureka) in canister vacuum cleaners and Electrolux (Eureka) and Maytag (Hoover) in upright vacuum cleaners.[22] Floor care appliances were an extremely competitive category of home electric appliances.

Consumer Electronics

Sony

Sony's PlayStation home video game system was highly profitable and PlayStation 2 dominated the game console market with about 70% of global sales in 2004. Sony, one of the world's top consumer electronics firms, also made a host of other products, including PCs, digital cameras, Walkman stereos, and semiconductors. The company's TVs, stereos, and other consumer electronics accounted for more than 60% of its sales. Sony's entertainment products included recorded music and video, motion pictures, DVDs, and TV programming. In addition, Sony sold mobile phones via Sony Ericsson, its joint venture with Ericsson. Sony also owned an 8% stake in the music club Columbia House.

Internationally, Sony was the overall consumer electronics leader in market share and technology development, through a highly respected brand name, a wider variety of products than most of its competitors, greater market presence through advertising and wholly owned stores, and a higher perceived level of overall quality of its products in most sectors. Sony had a well-earned reputation for producing high-quality electronic products with unique design, attractive appearance, and good warranty service. The company had the capability to use new technology to develop and launch new products in a relatively short time. Consumers could buy Sony products either through its wide Internet networks or from its broad sales and distribution networks almost anywhere in the world. Sony had eight major manufacturing sites in North America and could respond quickly to shifts in local trends. It mainly targeted middle- and upper-income consumers.

Sony paid less attention to developing lower cost products in satisfying the low end of the market. Its weaknesses were its relatively higher prices, its cost control, and fewer in-store promotions.

Matsushita

Matsushita Electric Industrial, one of the world's top consumer electronics makers, might have had an unfamiliar name, but its brands were recognizable: Panasonic, Quasar, Technics, and JVC, to name a few. Its AVC Network sector produced TVs, VCRs, CD and DVD players, PCs, cellular phones, and fax machines. Matsushita also sold components (batteries, electric motors, displays, semiconductors), home appliances (washing machines, vacuum cleaners), and factory automation equipment (industrial robots, welding equipment). The Matsushita group included about 380 consolidated companies around the globe; its products were sold worldwide.

On February 17, 2005, Matsushita Electric Industrial Co., Ltd., at an extraordinary general meeting of shareholders, announced that it was changing the company name to Panasonic Shikoku Electronics Co., Ltd., effective April 1, 2005. The name change was part of the company's strategy to unify global brands under the Panasonic name.

Matsushita's strength was its wide range of product categories including its AVC network, home appliance, industrial equipment, and components and devices. The company offered moderate prices and relatively high-quality products with simplified functions and good warranty services. Its broad global manufacturing and distribution networks provided the company cost control advantages on production and sales. The company also cultivated good relationships with chain stores, individual stores, and Internet sellers. Technological prowess played a significant role for Matsushita to achieve its long-term goal of the ubiquitous networking society and coexistence with a global environment. With its cutting-edge technologies, the company continued to deliver "security and brand loyalty," "ease-of-use and convenience," and "inspiring" products to customers around the globe in a timely manner.

Matsushita's weakness was its diversification strategy. The company's products and brands were so broad that sometimes the company lost concentration on its core products. This was likely to improve with the name change to Panasonic.

Philips

Royal Philips Electronics made consumer electronics, including TVs, VCRs, DVD player/recorders, phones, and fax machines, as well as light bulbs (number one worldwide), electric shavers (number one) and other personal care appliances, picture tubes, semiconductors, and medical systems. Consumer electronics and small appliances accounted for about a third of the company's sales. Philips had sold its major home appliance division to Whirlpool in 1991 and was no longer involved in this industry segment. Philips had been dumping noncore businesses, such as its stake in music giant PolyGram, and acquiring and forming joint ventures in its core sectors (e.g., LG Philips Displays, a CRT display joint venture with LG Electronics).

The United States was a key market for Philips, accounting for one third ($8.9 billion) of the company's worldwide sales in 2003. All five of Philips' product divisions had a presence in the United States. Each operated independently, yet coordinated closely in sharing technologies and in developing products for the consumer and business-to-business marketplaces. Under the leadership of its corporate center in Amsterdam, this collaboration was required to unlock the full potential of the Philips brand.

Philips' strengths were its strong brand recognition, good warranty and services, and intimacy to local markets' needs. The company also implemented heavy advertising and promotion activity and built good relationships with a wide range of chain stores, individual stores, and Internet sellers. Manufacturing locally improved its response rate to the shifts of local consumption trends. Philips' strong brand image made it highly competitive in the broad product categories it provided. Another strength was its advanced technological capability. For example, Philips' high-tech campus in Eindhoven, The Netherlands, was a world-renowned technology center; the campus provided advanced facilities and an optimized working culture for thousands of top-notch engineers. It focused on crucial technological areas such as microsystems, devices, embedded systems, signal processing, and nanotechnology. Like Sony, Philips had the capability to use new technology to develop and offer new products in a relatively short time.

Philips' weaknesses were relatively high production costs and prices. Its styles and features on products that targeted the middle and low end of the market fell slightly behind its major competitors (such as Panasonic and LGE). Philip's products were so diversified that sometimes it lost concentration on its core product development, and its products did not catch much attention from young people because of their relatively high price and complicated functions.

LG Electronics (LGE)

Founded in 1958 as Gold Star, LGE was a member of South Korea's LG Group. The LG Group had 70-plus subsidiaries that designed and manufactured display and media products (TVs, VCRs, plasma display panels), home appliances (refrigerators, microwaves, air conditioners), and telecommunications devices (wireless phones, handsets, switchboards). LGE owned Zenith Electronics and launched a flat-panel display joint venture with Philips Electronics (LG Philips Displays). After Asia, LGE generated most of its sales revenue from North America; the company had established a North American headquarters in 2004. LG Electronics' new vision was to reach the top in quality and quantity by 2005 and become the best global company that had a brand synonymous with customer satisfaction and a workplace that employees were proud to call their own.

LG Electronics was best known as a leading manufacturer of televisions, VCRs, plasma display panels, and telecommunications equipment, but its share of the U.S. home appliance market was growing. Unlike its U.S. competitors, LGE had not implemented price increases to offset rising commodity costs, instead favoring aggressive efforts to increase market share.

LGE's strengths were its broad product categories, quality products with good warranty and services, and highly competitive prices compared with most of its major competitors (such as Sony, Philips, and Panasonic). LGE's products had simplified functions and were very attractive to lower-income young people. The strategic partnerships of LGE with GE, JBL, PBS, and Philips helped it secure world-leading technologies and a base from which to move forward as a leader in the multimedia business. Because LGE had established its manufacturing in Huntsville, Alabama, and Mexico, the company could quickly respond to shifts in the U.S. market. The company also had a strong capability in technology and in launching new products in a relatively short time. Its cost control ability was another one of its strengths. LGE had built good relationships with chain stores, individual stores, and Internet sellers and had implemented aggressive store promotions and mass media advertising. Internet sellers were familiar with its products and were very effective in promoting its products.

LGE's weakness was its relatively weak brand recognition in the high-end U.S. market. Its TV ads were weaker than those of its major competitors (such as Sony and Philips).

The Company

Haier had been founded in China in 1984 to produce mainly household refrigerators. Over the past 20 years, the company had witnessed significant growth and was now a transnational organization widely recognized in the world community. In 2004, Haier's global sales hit RMB100 billion ($12 billion) and the Haier brand was valued at RMB 61.6 billion ($7.4 billion), topping all Chinese trademarks in a nationwide survey. Haier's leadership position in the Chinese home appliance industry had been solidified by obtaining a domestic market share of 21% of overall appliances, far ahead of all its competitors, with 34% of major home appliances and 14% of small electric appliances.

Haier's international promotion framework encompassed global networks for design, procurement, production, distribution, and after-sales services. According to *Euromonitor Statistics* (the world's leading provider of global business intelligence and market analysis), Haier was ranked fourth in global sales revenue of white goods in 2004. According to CEO Zhang Ruimin, Haire was on track to reaching its goal of becoming the third largest appliance maker in the world. Ruimin indicated that reaching that goal meant that the Camden facility would need to be expanded from 400,000 units in 2003 to 500,000 units in order to reach the company's objective of a 10% market share in U.S. refrigerator sales in 2005.[23]

Globally, Haier had gained first place in the United States in sales of compact refrigerators and wine coolers, in Iran for washing machines, and in Cyprus for air conditioners. The company was planning a joint venture with the Taiwan-based Sampo (an appliance manufacturer) to make compressors for air conditioners. The company had joined forces with Fujitsu Hitachi Plasma Display (a joint venture between Fujitsu and Hitachi) to develop and market plasma TVs. It had also announced plans to enter the Japanese market through partnerships with Sanyo Electric and Samsung.

On March 4, 2002, Haier opened its American headquarters in New York City, an indication that Haier had moved into a new phase in the globalization of product design, manufacturing, and sales. Haier had a strong commitment to long-term development in the United States. On August 20, 2003, Haier erected an electric billboard in the shopping district of Ginza, Tokyo, symbolizing Haier's determination to also reach the Japanese marketplace.

Haier's major markets for its consumer electronics were in China and elsewhere in Asia, where the Haier brand had broad consumer acceptance. Haier had a competitive position in the consumer electronics industry in China because of the company's strong brand recognition, rich feature designs, and well-serviced networks.

In 2004, the Haier Group acquired a controlling interest in the mobile phone company Haier-CCT Holdings Ltd., a business in which it already had a stake. Effective January 31, 2005, the name of the subsidiary was changed to Haier Electronics Group Company, Limited. The Haier Group then transferred its top-loading washing machine business to its Haier Electronics subsidiary. Haier Group management planned to eventually transfer other appliances to this unit as part of its plan to become one of the global "top three" in white goods.

In the United States, Electrolux, GE, Whirlpool, and Maytag dominated the major home appliance market with a total share of 93.2% of the major home appliance market in 2004, leaving Haier a small percentage of the total market. According to sales figures, Matsushita, Sony, Philips Electronics, Sanyo, and LG Electronics dominated the consumer electronics market in the United States. Compared with most of these major brands, Haier's consumer electronics products had no competitive advantages either in technology advances or in product quality, except for their relatively lower prices.

Products

Since the company had began exporting to the United States in the early 1990s, Haier had captured 20% of the U.S. market for compact refrigerators, the kind seen in college dorms or hotel rooms. It also pioneered electric wine cellars—inexpensive stand-alone cabinets for wine lovers. Haier started with three refrigerator products in 1998 and had advanced to more than 250 products including both home appliances and consumer electronics by 2004.

Home Appliances

Haier offered a variety of home appliance products, which included, but was not limited to, wine cellars, refrigerators, freezers, air conditioners, dishwashers, laundry products, and small appliances. Haier's core products were its major home appliances, including room air conditioners. Since 2002, Haier had grown in the major home appliance market by offering higher quality and a wider range of appliances with relatively low prices.

Haier America introduced a new line of microwave ovens at the 2005 CES Show, held during January in Las Vegas. The new line offered models ranging from compact to 1.4-cubic-foot convection grills. The units would be available in white, black, and silver colors. The company had made a long-term commitment to this category and was looking for strong and steady growth in it for years to come.

Haier's compact refrigerators were originally developed for the Chinese market, where most people liked small or medium-sized refrigerators that could save room in overcrowded living spaces. Haier applied the same concept to America and captured the niche market in college dorms, small apartments, and hotels. For example, Haier introduced a new compact refrigerator with two wooden flaps on the sides that could be folded out to make a computer table.

College students could put their computer on the refrigerator. The flaps could be folded back down when extra space in the apartment was needed. Haier's new wine cellar had become one of its hottest selling products in the United States.

Other than large refrigerators made at its Camden factory, Haier America imported its products from China or the other subsidiaries of the Haier Group, where labor costs were much lower than in America. This created a price advantage for products sold in America. The company moved the production of its 14-cubic-foot refrigerator back to China in 2003 to make room for its new 21-cubic-foot models at Camden. According to Allan Guberski, VP and General Manager of Haier America Refrigerators, "It's more cost-effective to ship the 14-cubic-foot model because of how many refrigerators you can get in a container as opposed to the 21-cubic-foot."[24] Because of its lower-cost manufacturing facilities in Asia, Haier was better able to absorb rising material costs than were its U.S. competitors.

In order to increase its competitiveness and provide more consumer-friendly services, Haier had contracted with A&E Factory Service to be its primary service provider for repairs of products under the warranty and service contract in the United States and Puerto Rico.

Haier had a capability for advanced feature design on its major appliances. In terms of production, Haier tried to analyze consumer groups and understand their needs thoroughly so as to provide specific products for each distributor or customer group. For example, Haier's wine cooler had a digital thermostat operated by remote control. Its chest freezer had an innovative cooling section in addition to the freezing compartment. Unlike some portable room air conditioner models on the U.S. market, which used a water bucket that had to be emptied, all Haier's portable AC models had an "auto evaporation" function, which allowed continuous operation without water removal.

Haier did, however, have weak brand recognition in the U.S. market. Although Haier had entered the United States in 1998, the company mainly targeted niche markets, such as college dorms, hotel rooms, and the wine cellar market. Haier's aggressive expansion to the major home appliance market had captured some attention from the low end of the market, but such a strategy was not as effective in attracting the middle and high-end market segments. These segments were composed of higher-income young people and baby boomers, which together represented the largest consumer market in the U.S. major home appliance industry. Haier's unique design capability for large refrigerators fell behind its major competitors, such as GE and Whirlpool. Its development of technologically advanced products, such as smart appliances (e.g., the robot vacuum cleaner) fell slightly behind its major competitors.

Consumer Electronics

Haier offered consumer electronic products, which included plasma and flat-screen television sets, VCDs, DVDs, and TV/DVD combos. Consumer electronics was its secondary product line, a diversification designed to leverage the synergy of its existing consumer bases.

Haier's strengths were its relatively low prices and the unique designs and appearance of its electronics products. For example, at the 2005 Consumer Electronics Show in Las Vegas, Haier introduced the Haier P7 cell phone using cutting-edge technology in a unique design. The sleek P7 cell phone could be easily clipped onto a shirt pocket. It was another step forward in the evolution of the cell phone and a benchmark in the development of the Haier brand.

Haier's weaknesses were its weak brand recognition in the U.S. market and limited range of product choices. Its electronic products had no competitive advantages in either quality or warranty and services compared with the other major brands such as Sony and Philips.

Marketing

Home Appliances

For home appliances, the company primarily targeted lower-income young people and college students by offering relatively low prices on its compact appliance products. Haier was working to capture the attention of middle- and higher-income people with its large-capacity refrigerators. Middle-aged and older people preferred well-known brands such as Whirlpool, Maytag, and GE. They cared about the warranty and services of the products, but were somewhat price sensitive. If courted appropriately, they might be willing to try a new brand, especially since brand loyalty in the U.S. major home appliance industry was only 35%.[25]

Haier's primary problem was its low brand awareness in the middle and high-end markets in the United States. The company's large refrigerators, produced mainly for U.S. consumers, had not yet attracted much attention from middle- or higher-income young people, Baby Boomers, and older people. Depending so much on importing its products retarded its responsiveness to shifts in local market needs.

Consumer Electronics

For consumer electronics, Haier mainly targeted lower-income young people and college students. At the time, Haier imported most of its electronics from the Asian and Chinese manufacturing bases, where labor costs were much less than in America. Haier's price advantages on such imported electronics as the TV/DVD combo, LCD, and DVD attracted some attention from the low-end markets. Mid- to high-income and older people preferred major brand products with a reputation for quality, such as Sony and Panasonic. After-sale services were also important to these market segments.

Haier's relatively low prices on such products as the TV/DVD combo and DVD player/recorders made them attractive to younger and lower-income people. The unique designs on some of its high-tech products (e.g., the P7 cell phone) and simplified function designs attracted some attention from these consumer segments.

Haier's problem was its low brand awareness outside of its target market. Its major electronics products had no comparative advantages and had not gained recognition in the middle and high-end markets in the United States. A slow response rate to local market needs was another weakness.

Manufacturing

The Haier Group had 30 factories around the world; the one in South Carolina currently mainly manufactured large-capacity refrigerators for the American market. Although Haier had only one manufacturing base in America, the land available was large enough for continuous expansion.

Haier had a strongly motivated technician team, which was able to increase the company's product competitiveness by applying more features and style designs on its existing products. Haier could make a wide range of products in small production lots because most retailers wanted to offer products with a variety of features. To manage the costs of manufacturing many different product models, Haier designed common basic platforms. Periodically, the company changed the modules of components and subsystems to add some new features to its basic models.

Haier was relatively fast in developing new products. A large international manufacturer might spend 18 months in developing a new wine storage cabinet, but Haier took only 5 months. Because Haier could identify and meet consumer needs quickly, the company had won more than 50% of the total U.S. market share in the wine storage segment; Haier made 55,000 of the 100,000 units sold in 2002.

Haier had no advantage, however, in cost control with its large refrigerator products, making it harder to compete with such well-known brands as Whirlpool, GE, Electrolux (Frigidaire), and Maytag. Furthermore, excessive dependence on imports could cause a low response rate to local trends and relatively low speed of inventory replenishment.

Supply Chain and Distribution

In 2004, most of products that Haier sold in the United States were imported from its Asian and Chinese manufacturing facilities. The supply and distribution functions were extremely important to Haier's business development because they would determine how fast the company could respond to emerging market needs and how well the company could control its logistics costs. On October 25, 2004, COSCO, China's largest oversea shipping company, and Haier reached a strategic cooperation agreement. Under the new agreement, COSCO would provide supply-chain management based on its strong global network resources and help Haier explore business opportunities worldwide. Haier designated COSCO to be one of the leading logistics service providers for Haier's transportation and distribution of home electric appliances and supply of its raw materials and parts.

Haier's product distribution in the United States was nationwide, and its products could be found in most major chain retailers. A brief listing of outlets included Wal-Mart, Lowe's, Best Buy, Home Depot, Office Depot, Target, Sam's Club, Fortunoff, Menards, Bed Bath & Beyond, P.C. Richards, BJ's, Fry's, ABC, and BrandsMart. The list was growing every day. In 800 Wal-Mart stores, Haier had 100% of the room air-conditioner shelf space, 80% of refrigerators, and 100% of one of two SKUs in freezers. In Target stores, Haier had one of two SKUs in refrigerators. Best Buy carried Haier's digital wine cooler and advertised it as an electronic product. It was a strong, high-margin item for Best Buy.

Haier America had a strong distribution network and good relationships with both chain and individual stores. The company's recent collaboration with COSCO could further strengthen its cost savings in transportation and consolidate its price advantage.

Haier America's problems were its lack of American distribution centers and its limited exhibition space of standard appliance products compared with the other major brands such as Whirlpool, GE, Maytag, and Electrolux.

Sales and Promotion

Like most other manufacturers, Haier sold its home appliances and consumer electronics both in stores and through the Internet.

Sales

Store Sales

Since 2001, Haier products had entered the top 10 retail chain stores in the world and major chain stores in China. About 85% of Haier's orders in America and Europe came from the top 10 chain stores in those two areas. Retail sales staffs were familiar with Haier's appliances. Retailers were not as familiar, however, with Haier's electronics products, because most of them had just been introduced into the United States and the stores' shelves were already filled with products of other major brands, such as Sony, Philips, Panasonic, and LG.

Internet Sales

Haier America had broad networks with the major Internet sellers such as eBay, Amazon, and AJMadison. Haier's products could also be found on the web sites of the top chain stores in the United States. Haier America had a broad network and good relationships with Internet sellers. Haier had price advantages over its competitors, which made it possible for Haier to offer better deals to most of the major Internet sellers. Haier did have an outdated web site design, however, putting it behind Whirlpool, GE, Sony, and Panasonic.

Promotion

The Haier Group promoted Haier not as a Chinese or American brand, but as a global brand. The company's slogan was "What the World Comes Home To." To boost its brand image, Haier introduced its Two Brothers logo into the U.S. market.

At first, the company promoted the Haier brand mostly through outdoor advertising, airports and magazines, heavy advertising in trade publications, and on the Internet. Haier infrequently launched in-store promotions on its overstocked and outdated products. In 2004, the company sponsored an Australian basketball team, known as the Melbourne Haier Tigers.

Haier America used aggressive advertising on the Internet. The company had periodically implemented aggressive in-store promotions. Because of its labor cost advantage, Haier was able to discount its older styles or overstocked products. It did little TV advertising. Compared with heavy advertising by GE, Whirlpool, and Sony, Haier's advertising had been limited to airports, buses, billboards, and newspapers. Haier planned to launch more aggressive TV campaigns and provide sponsorships for sports teams to improve its brand recognition.

Technology

Haier had a good feature design capability in its core appliance products. The company needed relatively less time than many of its competitors to launch new products to satisfy different consumer needs. To succeed as a brand in the U.S. market, Haier had been trying to apply different features on each of its products. For example, Haier's convertible freezer/refrigerator provided the option of additional freezer or refrigerator space within one unit. Two separate temperature controls made it possible to create the type of storage needed most.

Nevertheless, Haier fell somewhat behind its major competitors in new appliance technology development. For example, Whirlpool introduced the Polara combination oven/refrigerator that could automatically start cooking at a programmed time and keep food either hot or cold. In Europe, Electrolux was selling the Trilobite, a robot vacuum cleaner. Samsung's "Home PAD Refrigerator" detected the shelf life of food and automatically displayed a list of items stored in the fridge on the door. Compared with other major brand names in consumer electronics, such as Sony, Matsushita, and LG, Haier had no competitive advantage on either product quality or technical advances. Haier's electronic products were therefore not very attractive to potential consumers in comparison with trusted and well-advertised brands such as Philips, Sony, and Panasonic.

Haier's relatively sluggish new technology development could weaken its competitiveness when facing even more serious competition in the future. Haier needed to be more effective in developing new technology for "smart appliances" and addressing more of the "smart kitchen" concept development.

International Expansion

Haier's initial stage of internationalization mainly focused on developing countries (first in Southeast Asia) to build volume and acquire international experience before it moved to the United States. In 1999, Haier established a design center in Boston, a marketing center in New York, and a manufacturing facility in South Carolina. Its strategy of localizing everything from design and manufacturing to sales and distributions indicated that Haier had a strong long-term commitment in the United States.

Haier's successful experience in the United States market supported its subsequent investment and operations in Europe and developing countries. In June 2001, Haier acquired an Italian refrigerator company. This company was to produce Haier refrigerators based on the designs provided by French and Dutch engineers. The products would be sold in the European market. Haier also implemented a strategy to localize designing and manufacturing, as well as sales and distribution. Nevertheless, Haire had no significant market share position in any major home appliance category in any European country in 2004.

In January 2002, the Haier Group signed an inclusive collaboration agreement with Japan's Sanyo Electric Co., which involved a wide-ranging business agreement to market consumer electronics products in both countries. Under the agreement, Sanyo's products would be sold in China through Haier's sales networks under the Sanyo and Haier brand names, while sales of Haier's products in Japan would be promoted by a joint venture, Sanyo-Haier Co. The Sanyo-Haier Co. started operations in April 2002 and initially sold Haier's refrigerators, freezers, and washing machines.

Warranty and Service

Haier America had recently contracted with A&E Factory Service to be its primary service provider for products under its warranty and service contract in the United States and Puerto Rico. Haier was transfering these services to A&E with the target date of February 15, 2005, for full implementation. One of the nation's leading service providers, A&E covered approximately 90% of the United States. It also serviced companies such as Whirlpool, Electrolux, Sears, GE, Fisher & Paykel, and Sharp. The commitment between Haier and A&E would provide customers with professional, courteous service from highly trained technicians and prompt service delivery using cutting-edge dispatch routing software. Only one telephone number would be needed for service inquiries and technician dispatch.

As of 2004, Haier had not yet found appropriate service providers for its consumer electronics products.

Financials

During the 17-year period from 1984 to 2001, the Haier Group had experienced a rapid growth, with an average annual growth rate of 78%, expanding from a small collectively run factory with a debt of $177,000 to the number one Chinese household appliance giant with a global sales of $7.25 billion.

In 2001, Haier group's exports from China totaled $280 million. Haier America's sales revenue at that time was $250 million. In 2002, Haier group's global sales reached $8.66 billion; its exports reached $400 million. In the United States, Haier America's sales increased to $300 million. In 2003, Haier Group's global sales reached $10 billion, its exports from China were $500 million, and it was ranked as the number one domestic electrical appliance producer in China.

In the first half of 2004, the Haier Group exported $530 million worth of products, a rise of 107% year-to-year. The Haier Group posted a 12% rise in fourth-quarter net earnings in 2004, even as fierce competition, soaring raw-materials costs, and a cut in export tax rebates reduced profits. Haier was the first Chinese brand to have more than 100 billion yuan ($12 billion) in assets. The Haier Group reported exports worth more than 1 billion U.S. dollars. Sales in the U.S. market also reached half a billion dollars. By the end of 2004, the Haier Group ranked fourth in major appliance sales worldwide behind Electrolux, Bosch-Siemens, and Whirlpool. In the United States, the company earned a 9% share of the 2,516,000-unit freezer

Exhibit 2
Haier Group Financial Data 2001–2004

Net Sales	2001	2002	2003	2004
Haier Group	$7.25b	$8.60b	$10.00b	$12.00b
Export	$280mil.	$400mil.	$500mil.	$1b
Haier America	$250mil.	$300mil.	$420mil.	$500mil.
Brand Value	$5.26b	$5.90b	$6.40b	$7.44b

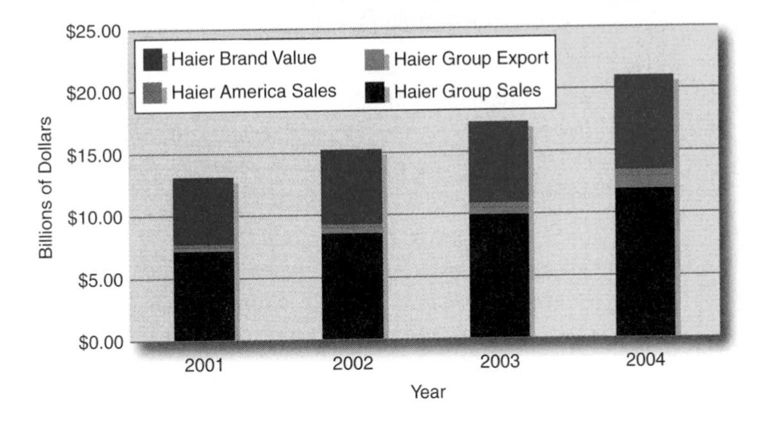

market, a 20% share of the 2,567,000-unit compact refrigerator market, a 6% share of the 8,802,000-unit room air-conditioner market, and a 2% share of the 10,922,000-unit standard-sized refrigerator market. It was also the market share leader in home wine coolers. It had no significant U.S. market share in any other appliance category in 2004.

Exhibit 2 shows Haier's financial data from 2001 to 2004. The Haier Group's annual sales grew 1.7 times during that time, and its sales in the U.S. market doubled over the same period. Haier's total exports more than tripled, reaching $1 billion in 2004. Its brand value increased by 40% and Haier became the most valuable brand in China. Because the Haier Group was owned by the Chinese government, no other financial data were available. Haier Electronics, the Haier Group's publicly held subsidiary, which manufactured and marketed cell phones in 2004, reported sales figures of HK$3,153 million with a loss of HK$42.5 million for that year.

Strategy and Programs

To improve Haier's management efficiency, Zhang Ruimin, the CEO of the Haier Group, combined Chinese traditional culture and Western industrial experience by establishing the OEC (Overall Every Control and Clear) market-chain system. The philosophy of OEC management was to quickly identify problems, search for the causes of these problems, and find solutions one by one. On the basis of the Haier OEC management system, Haier had broken free from traditional management systems by practicing "market chain business flow renovation" and set up an order processing system comprising material, commodity, and capital subsystems, which helped realize a zero-distance contact with customers. Zhang Ruimin's management system had been widely acknowledged as superior by domestic and overseas management professionals.

Facing the challenges brought by e-commerce and China's joining the WTO, Haier began a management-restructuring program in 1998 backed by the efficient Haier market-chain system. During the first 5 years, Haier focused on organizational restructuring and management decentralizing with application of advanced information and network systems in order fulfillment, market-chain performance, logistics, capital operation, after-sales service, product inventory, and operational cost reduction. During the second 5-year period from 2003 to 2008, Haier was implementing a new management program called the "Strategic Business Units" to stimulate employee enthusiasm and to enhance Haier's competitiveness in the global marketplace. Similar to decentralized management, this program encouraged each employee to act as the manager of his or her own business unit, whether it be one job or an entire department.

Haier's growth strategy could be divided into three stages:

The first stage was the Brand Name Strategy (1984–1991). It took Haier seven years to build up a strong brand name in refrigerators through a well-planned TQC (total quality control) system. Haier products became known for quality and innovation. When Zhang Ruimin took in charge of Haier in 1984, his first act was to smash 76 poor-quality refrigerators with a hammer to drive home his intention to improve product quality.

The second stage was the Diversified Development Strategy (1992–1998). Haier spent these six years diversifying a product catalog to avoid having all of the company's eggs in one basket. When it was founded, the company had only one product and a staff of 800. By 2004, more than 30,000 Haier employees were making more than 13,000 products in 86 categories.

The third stage was the Going Multinational Strategy (1998 on). Haier's first overseas manufacturing subsidiaries were set up in developing countries, mainly in Southeast Asia. Then it entered the United States. After its successful experience in the United States, it ventured into Europe in 2001, Japan in 2002, and then into other developing countries. In early 2005, Haier had 62 distributors and more than 30,000 retail outlets around the world. The company's eventual goal was to be listed among the Fortune 500 successful companies.

Looking to the Future

Zhang Ruimin, the Haier Group's CEO, and his colleagues had turned Haier from a collectively run workshop into an international enterprise. From 2001 to 2004, Haier had won access to major U.S. distributors, but its brand still remained unfamiliar to most U.S. consumers. Many analysts were convinced that Haier had put its eggs in too many baskets, and that it ought to be focusing on appliances—its core products, which did not yet have a solid reputation in the U.S. and Europe. Haier needed to build brand recognition and enhance its brand image. There already had been some stumbling blocks, notably in personal computers, which the company exited in 2001 after four unimpressive years. Haier now faced its biggest challenge: expanding its modest U.S. footprint and becoming a genuine global brand.

Haier's management had established a goal of expanding its U.S. market share, but was not yet sure which alternative strategy to follow. Two alternatives appeared to be feasible.

The *first strategic alternative* was for Haier to introduce a wider range of products into the U.S. market. This could be achieved by building distribution centers to more effectively supply chain and individual retailers. Under this alternative, Haier would continue to import most of its products from Haier Group global manufacturing bases. Haier would improve the efficiency of its distribution networks by implementing collaborative planning, forecasting, and replenishment (CPFR).

One benefit of this alternative was that Haier could take advantage of the strength of the Haier Group as a whole and offer more choices in a wide range of product categories that could satisfy different kinds of needs. Haier could thus increase its U.S. market share by providing high-quality products at relatively low prices. This alternative was feasible because Haier America had already established fairly good relationships with most of the large chains and individual retailers and the company had the financial resources needed to build regional distribution centers. Haier products had a significant pricing advantage compared with most of its U.S. competitors because most of Haier's imported products were from its Chinese or

Asian manufacturing facilities, where labor costs were much lower than in the United States. Haier's recent strategic cooperation with COSCO, China's biggest overseas logistics service provider, was expected to allow the company to save more on its supply-chain management and distribution. All of these factors could contribute more to the cost and price advantage of Haier's products and increase its competitiveness against rivals in the U.S. market.

This alternative could succeed against Asian-based multinational firms, such as Matsushita and LG, because Haier would increase its competitiveness in the low-end market segment by improving and streamlining its distribution function to solidify its cost advantage and offer relatively low prices on its newly introduced products. In addition, Haier would probably attract some consumers from the middle market segment because of the firm's ability to absorb rising material costs. It would widen Haier's range of high-quality and simplified function–designed products in both home appliances and consumer electronics. This would be attractive to one-stop shoppers, who want to stick to a quality brand with a good warranty and after-sales service. Haier had already captured 20% of the U.S. market in compact refrigerators and 2% of the U.S. standard refrigerator market, and its wine cellar was the hottest-selling product in its category in the United States. Haier's new introductions should be welcomed by its present consumer base and attract some new consumers in the low end of the U.S. market by continuously offering relatively lower prices on its even broader product categories. Because the new introductions would be produced in Haier's low-cost Chinese and other Asian manufacturing plants, Haier could achieve a price advantage on such products as microwaves and plasma TVs in the U.S. market. This could create another opportunity for Haier to attract some middle market share from its competitors.

A problem with this alternative was Haier's low response rate to shifts in local consumption trends and its relatively long lead times in transportation, which could cause temporary overstocking or a shortage of certain products. Because such a strategy mainly focused on increasing sales by offering relatively low prices of imported products, it could not help Haier build a long-term quality image in the United States. Because most of Haier America's products would continue to be sourced from Asia, import duties would reduce Haier's America's potential profits.

A *second strategic alternative* was for Haier America to develop new features for the consumer electronics and home appliances it currently sold and to expand the South Carolina facility to manufacture other home appliances, such as air conditioners, washers, and dryers. Eventually, Haier America would manufacture all its core products locally. Haier America would improve its existing refrigerator product lines by changing the modules of the components and subsystems to add new versions, such as upright freezers, chest freezers, and refrigerators with freezers on the bottom.

The benefit of this alternative was that it would enable the company to more quickly capture and respond to trends in local markets and to increase the company's competitiveness by providing more appropriate products that could satisfy specific local needs. It was also an effective way for the company to build its brand image by offering both high quality and attractive features on its products, with reasonable prices and effective after-sale services. An increase in local manufacturing would reduce import duties on goods supplied from Asia.

This alternative was feasible because Haier America had already set up a 350,000-square-foot plant on 110 acres in South Carolina, with plenty of room for both improving existing product lines and setting up new product lines. Haier had the necessary financial capability to support such an expansion. Haier also had a strong innovative design team, which could quickly and effectively add new features to its existing products in a very cost-effective way to differentiate its products from other major brands, such as Whirlpool and Maytag, and at the same time meet local market needs.

This alternative could succeed against U.S.-based major home appliance competitors because Haier should be able to implement cost controls on its manufacturing process by implementing its OEC (Overall Every Control and Clear) management to ensure its price advantages in the U.S. market. When Whilpool, GE, and Maytag increased prices in January, 2005, this created an opportunity for Haier to steal some middle market share from its U.S.-based competitors.

Haier would continue to focus on quality control and rich feature design in its core products and launch heavy advertising campaigns. For example, Haier's new compact refrigerator having two wooden flaps on the sides that could be folded out to make a computer table was a strong feature design that satisfied college students' specific needs. Most large manufacturers were not paying attention to such minor details. Haier was able to develop new features for products to satisfy customer needs faster than its competitors. By localizing manufacturing for its core appliance products in the United States and by designing more features into them, Haier could increase its sales and market share in the short run and increase its brand recognition and reputation over the long run.

Drawbacks of this alternative were the required high initial investment in new product lines and advertising, higher local manpower rates, and higher investments in research and development, which could erode the company's profit in the short term. Nevertheless, this alternative lessened the distance between the market and the manufacturing process. Based on consumption trends fed back from the market, a design center in the manufacturing facility could quickly convert this trend information into either new feature designs or new functional products. This could increase the company's competitiveness and benefit its long-term development.

CEO Ruimin needed to decide what strategic direction to take to make Haier a major player in the U.S. market. Was there another alternative that needed to be considered?

Notes

1. Xinhua, "Haier Listed in World's Top 100 Recognizable Brands" (February 3, 2004), *http://www.china.org.cn/english/BAT/86101.htm.*
2. *Business Week* (November 8, 2004), *http://www.businessweek.com/magazine/content/04_45/b3907008.htm.*
3. Washington, "Goods Orders Rise 0.6% in December" (January 27, 2005), *http://www.mabico.com/en/news/20050127/foreign_exchange/article16574/.*
4. Usernomics (January 17, 2005), *http://www.usernomics.com/news/2005/01/1257-bln-of-consumer-electronics-will.html.*
5. R. W. Latella, "National Retail Market Overview"(March, 2005), *http://www.valuation.cushwake.com/Documents/22305.pdf.*
6. A. Glynn, and M. Normand, *Home Furnishings & Appliances Analyst* (March 17, 2005).
7. NAR, "Most Metro Area Home Price Gains Strong but Cooler—NAR" (Feb. 12, 2004), *http://www.realtor.org/publicaffairsweb.nsf/Pages/MetroPrices4thQtr03?OpenDocument.*
8. Twice, "CEA Says '05 Sales Will Grow 10.7%" (January 22, 2005), *http://www.twice.com/article/CA498488.html?verticalid=820&industry−By+The+Numbers&industryid=23106&pubdate=01/24/2005.*
9. "28th Annual Portrait of the U.S. Appliance Industry," *Appliance* (September, 2005), p. P-5.
10. *Ibid.*, pp. P-6 and P-7.
11. A. Tewary, "Home Furnishings & Appliances Analyst" (May 6, 2004), Online.
12. "Portrait of the Canadian Appliance Industry," *Appliance* (August, 2005), pp. 57–61.
13. Russell, J., "53rd Annual Appliance Industry Forecasts—North America" (January 2005), *http//www.appliancemagazine.com/zones/consumer/07_ce/editorial.php?article=699&zone=7&first=1.*
14. CEA, "CEA Announces Another All-Time High for DTV as Cumulative Sales Top 13 Million Units" (November 22, 2004), *http://www.ce.org/press_room/press_release_detail.asp?id=10616.*
15. ISM Report, "January Manufacturing ISM Report on Business" (February 1, 2005), *http://www.ism.ws/ISMReport/ROB022005.cfm.*
16. Whirlpool Reports Record 2004 Sales," *Appliance* (February 3, 2005), *http://www.appliancemagazine.com/news.php?article58084&zone=0&first=101.*
17. China, "China's Electric Appliance Prices Expected to Rise," *Appliance* (February 17, 2005), *http://www.appliancemagazine.com/news.php?article=8145&zone=0&first=51.*
18. CEA, "Video Trends in 2003-2004," *http://www.ce.org/publications/books_references/digital_america/video/default.asp.*
19. "28th Annual Portrait of the U.S. Appliance Industry," *Appliance* (September 2005), p. P-3. All 2004 U.S. market share figures come from this article.
20. L. Bonnema, "Expanding Its Reach," *Appliance* (April 2004), p. B-8.
21. E. Biesen, "Investing in the Future," *Appliance* (September 2005), pp. 53–54.
22. "28th Annual Portrait" (2005), p. P-2.
23. L. Bonnema, "Haier: Working Its Way Up," *Appliance* (October 2003), pp. 32–37.
24. *Ibid.*, p. 33.
25. C. Miller, VP of Marketing, North American Appliance Group, Whirlpool Corporation, quoted by R. J. Babyak and J. Jancsurak in "Product Design & Manufacturing Process for the 21st Century," *Appliance Manufacturer* (November 1994), p. 59.

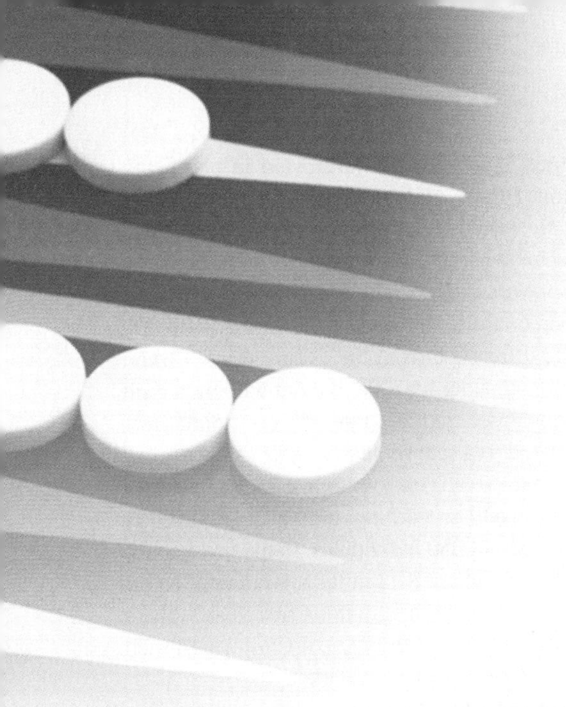

CASE 27
Invacare Corporation, 2004

Walter E. Greene and Jeff Totten

IF YOU HAD ONLY $10,000, WOULD YOU TRY TO RAISE $7.8 MILLION? MALACHI MIXON DID just that to buy Invacare from Johnson & Johnson in 1979. As the new year 2004 dawned, Mixon's concerns centered on how the changing Medicare rules on the eligibility of power wheelchairs for the elderly, intensified advertising by competitors such as The Scooter Store, and the passage of The Medicare Prescription Drug, Improvement, and Modernization Act of 2003 would affect Invacare's aggressive positioning for the near future.

History

Invacare Corporation's roots went back to the year 1885 when the Worthington Company of Elyria, Ohio, began producing "vehicles" designed for the physically handicapped. The Worthington Company merged with a manufacturer of rubber tire wheels and casters in the early 1900s and became the Colson Company. The Colson Company became a major supplier of bicycles and placed little emphasis on the wheelchair product. When the Colson Company moved its headquarters in 1952, three of its employees purchased the wheelchair operations and renamed the company Mobilaid, Inc. By 1960, Mobilaid, Inc., had annual sales of $150,000 and employed 15 individuals. It continued to grow modestly during the 1960s and was acquired in 1970 by Technicare Incorporated (Technicare), which renamed Mobilaid, Inc., as Invacare Corporation (Invacare) in 1971. Invacare focused most of its resources into the medical diagnostic imaging field and indeed became a leading manufacturer of such equipment. Invacare continued to grow at a modest rate, but with little direction and not much in the way of new products. Invacare was acquired by medical giant Johnson & Johnson in 1978.

Mal Mixon, a 39-year-old Technicare manager, became very interested in acquiring Invacare; however, the asking price was $7.8 million. Mixon, though he had only $10,000 to invest, was not dismayed by the large asking price. He believed that there was a strong growth potential for the home health care industry. Mixon was able to get real estate brokers, Cleveland-based investors, and a Chicago bank to put up approximately $7.6 million. Mixon invested his $10,000, borrowed $40,000 from two personal friends, and an additional $100,000 from the company to come up with the approximate difference from the asking price. Mixon accomplished a leveraged buyout that many would not consider feasible, but not without a high cost in debt and equity. For example, the bank loan was secured at a rate of three points over prime, which, at that time in December of 1979, equated to a rate of nearly 20%.

The buyout was structured in such a way that enabled Mixon to retain a 15% interest in Invacare. In 1979, Invacare's sales were about $19 million and net earnings after acquisition costs were approximately $100,000.[1] Invacare employed only about 350 individuals. In the first year of operations under Mixon, the profits of Invacare, which were about $1.4 million, were drained off by the high cost of debt. To further add to the obstacles of the company in its first year(s) were several well-established competitors, primarily E&J (Everest & Jennings), a California-based home health care company, which had more than 80% of the wheelchair market.

Mixon studied Invacare's product lines and eliminated those that were considered obsolete or unprofitable. In January 1981, Invacare entered the home care bed business with the acquisition of a small startup company in Sanford, Florida. Also in 1981, Invacare followed a growth strategy by expanding its product line, entering the respiratory business through the acquisition of Prime Air, Inc., a manufacturer of oxygen concentrators in Hartford, Connecticut. This operation was later moved to the Cleveland area facility in Elyria, Ohio, in 1985. Invacare entered more markets and penetrated current markets more deeply through acquisitions and partnerships throughout the 1980s and 1990s.[2] (See **Exhibit 1** for a partial list of acquisitions.) In January 1988, Invacare began operations of it newly constructed maquiladora plant (a 78,000-square-foot manufacturing facility in Rio Bravo, Mexico, across the border from McAllen, Texas), named Invamex. This manufacturing plant enabled Invacare to manufacture low-cost manual wheelchairs that could compete with those of other foreign competitors from the Far East.

Exhibit 1
Partial List of Invacare's Acquisitions

Date	Firm Acquired	Product
1979	Technicare (Invacare)	Wheelchairs
1981	Home Bed Care	Home beds
1981	Prime Air, Inc.	Oxygen concentrators
1984	Carters, Ltd.	Wheelchairs
1984	Gunter & Meier	Wheelchairs
1988	Invamex	Wheelchairs
1991	Canadian Posture & Seating Centre, Inc.	
1991	Canadian Wheelchair Manufacturing, Ltd.	
1992	Hovis Medical	Home medical equipment
1992	Perry Oxygen Systems	Oxygen systems
1992	Cofipar/Poirier, S.A.	Wheelchairs
1993	Top End	Athletic wheelchairs
1993	Dynamic Control, Ltd.	Wheelchairs
1993	Geomarine Systems, Inc.	Low-air-loss therapy systems
1994	Beram, AB	Wheelchairs
1994	Patient Solutions, Inc.	Ambulatory infusion pumps
1994	Rehadap, S.A.	Wheelchairs
1994	Genus Medical, Inc.	Motorized wheelchairs
1995	Special Health Systems	Wheelchair seating

Exhibit 1
(Continued)

1995	Medical Equipment Repair Service	Aftermarket oxygen parts and repairs
1995	Paratec, AG	Wheelchairs
1995	Group Pharmaceutical, Ltd.	Wheelchair distributor
1995	Thompson Rehab	Wheelchairs
1995	Bencraft Ltd.	Wheelchairs and seating
1995	Patient Solutions	Ambulatory infusion pumps
1995	PinDot Products	Custom seating systems
1996	Fabriorto, Lda.	Wheelchair/walking aids manufacturer
1996	Roller Chair Pty. Ltd.	Power wheelchair manufacturer
1997	Silcraft Corporation	Patient aid manufacturer
1998	Suburban Ostomy Supply Co.*	Medical supplies wholesaler
1999	Adaptive Switch Laboratories	Wheelchair devices manufacturer
1999	Dynamic Systems	Wheelchair devices manufacturer
1999	Scandinavian Mobility Int'l A/S	Bed/mobility aids manufacturer
2003	Pinnacle Medsources Inc.	Home med equipment distributor
2003	Mecc San SrL	Home med equipment manufacturer
2003	Carroll Healthcare, Inc.	Long-term-care furniture manufacturer
2003	Motion Concepts, Inc.	Seating and positioning products

*Renamed Invacare Supply Group in 2000.

Sources: Invacare Reports; Datamonitor (December 8, 2003), p. 6; "Introduction to Invacare: Acquisitions," Investor Relations, www.invacare.com (January 22, 2005).

Invacare Today

The company operated in the home medical equipment (HME) industry segment. "Invacare Corporation is the world's leading manufacturer and distributor of non-acute health care products based upon its distribution channels, the breath of its product line and sales. The company designs, manufactures and distributes an extensive line of health care products for the non-acute care environment, including the home health care, retail and extended care markets."[3]

Invacare continuously revised and expanded its product lines to meet changing market demand and offered more than two dozen product lines. The company's products were sold principally to more than 25,000 home health care and medical equipment provider locations in the United States, Australia, Canada, Europe, and New Zealand, with the remainder of its sales being primarily to government agencies and distributors. Invacare's products were sold through its worldwide distribution network by its sales force, telesales associates, and various organizations of independent manufacturers' representatives and distributors. The company also distributed medical equipment and related supplies manufactured by others.[4]

Trends in the North American Market

The home medical equipment (HME) market included home health care products, physical rehabilitation products, and other non-disposable products used for the recovery and long-term care of patients. The company believed that sales of domestic home medical equipment products would continue to grow during the next decade and beyond as a result of several factors:

- Growth in population over age 65: "The older population in 2030 is projected to be twice as large as their counterparts in 2000, growing from 35 million to 71.5 million and representing nearly 20 percent of the total U.S. population."[5]

- Treatment trends: Medical professionals and patients preferred home health care to institutional care.
- Technological trends: Medical equipment advances made home health care preferred over institutional care.
- Health care cost containment trends: The nation's health care spending was projected to increase to $3.1 trillion, growing at an annual rate of 7.3%.
- Society's mainstreaming of people with disabilities due to the 1991 Americans with Disabilities Act (ADA).
- Distribution channels: Products were now available through retail drug stores; surgical supply houses; rental, hospital, and HMO-based stores; home health agencies; direct sales; etc.

Trends in Foreign Market

The company believed that although many of the market factors influencing demand in the U.S. were also present in Europe and Australasia—aging of the population, technological trends, and society's acceptance of people with disabilities—each of the major national markets within Europe and Australasia had distinctive characteristics. The health care industry was more heavily socialized and, therefore, was more influenced by government regulations and fiscal policies. Variations in product specifications, regulatory approvals, distribution requirements, and reimbursement policies required the company to tailor its approach to each national market. Management believed that as the European markets became more homogeneous and the company continued to refine its distribution channels, the company could more effectively penetrate these markets. Likewise, the company expected to increase its sales in the highly fragmented Australian and New Zealand markets.

The home health care market in Europe was different in several aspects from that in the United States. In most European countries, socialized medicine was the norm. Consequently, governments were the largest single customers of home health care products. The rental market in countries with socialized medicine was virtually nonexistent in a market oriented more toward price than durability. In some European countries, such as Germany, the market was strongly geared toward quality and product features. Several companies, each of which possessed particular strengths in one or more countries, also dominated the European market.

A distribution network that relied on direct government outlets and on some independent medical equipment dealers characterized the European market. As the home health care equipment industry continued to develop, the roles of the medical equipment dealers were expected to strengthen.

Structure

Invacare was a highly centralized firm with headquarters in Elyria, Ohio. Invacare had a unique organizational structure that combined the benefits of both centralized and decentralized operations. During 1995 and 1996, Invacare reorganized domestic operations into a business unit to further decentralize and push decision making down to lower levels, to enable more rapid market response. Invacare realigned its management organization into three operating groups (North American, European, and Invacare Technologies), reporting to its Chief Operating Officer, Gerald Blouch. Each group consisted of several dedicated business units. Externally, Invacare had one "face to the customer" as products were sold through a single domestic sales and service organization with complete account responsibility.

Exhibit 2
Executive Officers: Invacare Corporation

A. Malachi Mixon, III	Chairman of the Board; Chief Executive Officer
Gerald B. Blouch	President; Chief Operating Officer; Director
Joseph B. Richey, II	President—Invacare Technologies; Senior VP—Electronic & Design Engineering; Director
Gregory C. Thompson	Senior VP; Chief Financial Officer
Diane J. Davie	Senior VP—Human Resources
Louis F. J. Slangen	Senior VP—Sales & Marketing
Kenneth A. Sparrow	President—Invacare Europe

Sources: Summary Annual Report 2003; Datamonitor (December 8, 2005), p. 7.

Executive officers are listed in **Exhibit 2.** Mixon, Blouch, and Richey are the three internal members of the 10-member Board of Directors.

Invacare continued acquisitions over the years and in 2003 bought four businesses for cash at a total cost of $70,555,000. The four companies included the assets of Pinnacle Medsources, Inc., a Georgia corporation and distributor of home medical equipment; Mecc San SrL., an Italian corporation and manufacturer of home medical equipment; Carroll Healthcare, Inc. ("Carroll"), a Canadian corporation and a leading manufacturer of beds and furniture for the long-term care industry in North America; and Motion Concepts, Inc. ("Motion"), a Canadian corporation and a leading manufacturer of seating and positioning products in North America.

In 2003, Invacare had 34 plants in North America including four in Canada and the one in Reynosa, Mexico. Their Australasian operations comprised nine facilities, including one in Ohio and two in the United Kingdom. In Europe, Invacare operated from some 26 facilities. In total, Invacare operated more than 60 subsidiaries in approximately two dozen countries. As of December 31, 2003, the company had approximately 5,300 employees. Invacare had managed to work successfully with its employees and had no unions to contend with in the United States. That was not the case in the European market, where the labor forces were well organized up to this time. Invacare had had very little interference from the European organized labor forces, primarily because of the sluggish worldwide economy. Future labor negotiations might be an important measure of how well Invacare would perform in the European market.

Invacare made a commitment in 2004 to build a manufacturing plant in Suzhou Industrial Park in China. This followed up on the opening of an Asian procurement office in Hong Kong in 2000–2001. The company expected to achieve a low-cost delivery position in its basic product lines through overseas sourcing and manufacturing at its China plant. Additional manufacturing capacity at this plant was also planned for, while minimizing the loss of full-time jobs at its Ohio plant.[6]

Financials

Invacare issued annual audited consolidated financial statements in accordance with regulations established by the Securities and Exchange Commission. The consolidated financial statements included the accounts of Invacare Corporation and its subsidiaries. European subsidiaries were consolidated using a November 30 fiscal year-end. All significant company transactions were eliminated. Substantially all of the assets and liabilities of the company's foreign subsidiaries were translated to U.S. dollars at year-end exchange rates.[7]

See **Exhibit 3** for selected financial information over five fiscal years (1999 to 2003) and **Exhibits 4–6** for financial performance over the most recent of those fiscal years.

Exhibit 3 Selected Financial Information: Invacare Corporation (Dollar amounts in thousands, except per share data and ratios)

	2003	2002	2001*	2000	1999†
1. **Earnings**					
Net Sales	$1,247,176	$1,089,161	$1,053,639	$1,013,162	$882,774
Net Earnings‡	71,409	64,770	35,190	59,911	41,494
Net Earnings per Share—Basic	2.31	2.10	1.15	1.99	1.38
Net Earnings per Share—Assuming Dilution	2.25	2.05	1.11	1.95	1.36
Dividends per Common Share	0.05000	0.05000	0.05000	0.05000	0.05000
Dividends per Class B Common Share	0.04545	0.04545	0.04545	0.04545	0.04545
2. **Balance Sheet**					
Current Assets	$474,722	$398,812	$428,401	$432,408	$418,620
Total Assets	1,108,213	906,703	914,537	951,855	955,285
Current Liabilities	228,604	168,226	167,453	197,387	173,119
Working Capital	246,118	230,586	260,948	235,021	245,501
Long-Term Debt	232,038	234,134	342,724	384,316	440,795
Shareholders' Equity	613,188	480,312	381,550	349,773	318,872
3. **Other Data**					
Research and Development Expenditures	$19,130	$17,934	$17,394	$16,231	$15,534
Capital Expenditures, net of Disposals	30,129	19,718	19,486	26,268	32,155
Depreciation and Amortization	27,235	26,638	33,448	31,469	25,978
4. **Key Ratios**					
Return on Sales	5.7%	5.9%	3.3%	5.9%	4.7%
Return on Average Assets	7.1%	7.1%	3.8%	6.3%	4.9%
Return on Beginning Shareholders' Equity	14.9%	17.0%	10.1%	18.8%	14.8%
Current Ratio	2.1:1	2.4:1	2.6:1	2.2:1	2.4:1
Debt-to-Equity Ratio	0.4:1	0.5:1	0.9:1	1.1:1	1.4:1

*Reflects non-recurring and unusual charge of $31,950 ($25,250 after tax of $0.80 per share assuming dilution).
†Reflects non-recurring and unusual charge of $14,800 ($9,028 after tax or $0.29 per share assuming dilution).
‡Amortization of goodwill ceased in 2002, net earnings for prior years includes amortization expense of $8,972 in 2001, $8,899 in 2000 and $7,258 in 1999.

Source: Invacare, 2003 10-K Form.

Exhibit 4 Consolidated Statement of Earnings: Invacare Corporation and Subsidiaries (Dollar amounts in thousands, except per share data)

Years Ending December 31	2003	2002	2001
Net sales	$1,247,176	$1,089,161	$1,053,639
Cost of products sold	872,515	761,763	735,292
Gross Profit	374,661	327,398	318,347
Selling, general & admin. expenses	262,015	220,296	195,574
Amortization of goodwill	—	—	8,972
Non-recurring and unusual items	—	—	31,950
Interest expense	11,710	15,122	22,764
Interest income	(5,473)	(4,550)	(7,303)
Earnings before Income Taxes	106,409	96,530	66,390
Income taxes	35,000	31,760	31,200
Net Earnings	$ 71,409	$ 64,770	$ 35,190

Exhibit 4
(continued)

Net Earnings per Share—Basic	$2.31	$2.10	$1.15
Weighted Average Shares Outstanding	30,862	30,867	30,620
Net Earnings per Share—Diluted	$2.25	$2.05	$1.11
Weighted Average Shares Outstanding—Assuming Dilution	31,729	31,664	31,683

Source: Invacare Corporation, 2003 10-K Form.

Exhibit 5
Balance Sheet: Invacare Corporation and Subsidiaries (Dollar amounts in thousands, except per share data)

Year Ending December 31	2003	2002
Assets		
Current Assets		
Cash and cash equivalents	$16,074	$13,086
Marketable securities	214	1,350
Trade receivables, net	255,534	200,388
Installment receivables, net	7,755	20,953
Inventories, net	130,979	111,382
Deferred income taxes	24,573	26,053
Other current assets	39,593	25,600
Total Current Assets	474,722	398,812
Other Assets	53,263	51,031
Other Intangibles	14,678	4,779
Property and Equipment, net	150,051	130,963
Goodwill	415,499	321,118
Total Assets	$1,108,213	$906,703
Liabilities and Shareholders' Equity		
Current Liabilities		
Accounts payable	$110,178	$80,511
Accrued expenses	97,148	67,187
Accrued income taxes	19,107	16,049
Current maturities of long-term debt	2,171	4,479
Total Current Liabilities	228,604	168,226
Long-Term Debt	232,038	234,134
Other Long-Term Obligations	34,383	24,031
Shareholders' Equity		
Preferred Shares (Authorized 300 shares; none outstanding)	—	—
Common Shares (Authorized 100,000 shares; 30,739 and 30,294 issued in 2003 and 2002)	7,686	7,580
Class B Common Shares (Authorized 12,000 shares; 1,112, issued and outstanding)	278	278
Additional paid-in-capital	109,015	98,995
Retained earnings	477,113	407,235
Accumulated other comprehensive earnings (loss)	45,941	(18,729)
Unearned compensation on stock awards	(1,458)	(1,204)
Treasury shares (770 and 387 shares in 2003 and 2002, respectively)	(25,387)	(13,843)
Total Shareholders' Equity	613,188	480,312
Total Liabilities and Shareholders' Equity	$1,108,213	$906,703

Source: Invacare Corporation, 2003 10-K Form.

Exhibit 6 Performance by Region, 2002 vs. 2003: Invacare Corporation (Dollar amounts in millions)

Region	Net Sales 2003	% Increase over 2002	% Adjusted for Foreign Currency	Net Sales 2002	% Increase over 2001	% Adjusted for Foreign Currency
North American	$897.2	13%	n/a	$793.5	3%	N/A
European	$279.8	11%	−8%	$252.07	7%	2%
Australasia	$77.44	74.8%	27%	$44.3	1%	−8%

Note:
2002 net sales for European region and 2003 net sales for Australasia region were calculated using reported percentage increases and net sales.

Sources: Invacare Corporation Summary Annual Report 2003, *third printed page;* Datamonitor Report *(December 8, 2003), p. 18.*

Products and Promotion

Invacare both manufactured and distributed prescription power and custom manual wheel chairs, standard wheelchairs, respiratory equipment (e.g., liquid oxygen systems), hospital-type beds for the home, motorized scooters, and other patient aids and equipment (e.g., incontinence products, canes, walkers, and shower chairs).[8]

Its products were distributed through a worldwide network of more than 25,000 home health care and medical equipment provider locations in the United States, Australia, Canada, Europe, and New Zealand, with the remainder of its sales being primarily to government agencies and distributors.[9]

The standard wheelchairs were generally purchased by older people and therefore normally reimbursed by Medicare/Medicaid. They were regarded as a commodity item and therefore a price-driven type of sale. The general price range could be from about $350 to $1,000. The power wheelchairs were Invacare's most attractive product line, with prices approaching $5,000 or higher. Power wheelchairs were purchased by people with more severe disabilities than those who purchased manual wheelchairs. Typically, users were quadriplegics who had some motor skills in at least one arm. The power wheelchair was usually controlled by a joystick, which accelerated, turned, and stopped the chair. The user needed enough control in his or her arm to operate the joystick; if not, more sophisticated "sip and puff" controls were used. Invacare was the only manufacturer who designed and manufactured its own controllers (an electronic microprocessor that controls the chair's movements). Invacare began in May of 1991 to manufacture its "Action" line of wheelchairs. These ultralight wheelchairs were the second-fastest growing segment of the market. Younger, active users with permanent disabilities generally purchased ultralight wheelchairs. These chairs allowed people with disabilities to play sports and were used in the 1996, 2000, and 2004 Paralympic games. They were light by any wheelchair standard, generally made of aluminum, and allowed the user greater mobility. However, the latest advancements in materials had enabled the production of carbon composite frames, which was lighter than the then-current frame materials.

New products introduced by the company after 2001 included the Storm Series TDX line of power wheelchairs; unbranded, low-price wheelchairs through its independent subsidiary, Professional Medical Imports; the Zoom HMV scooter; the HomeFill II oxygen system; and, for the European market, the Typhoon line of wheelchairs. Invacare also planned to enter the sleep apnea/therapy market with a new line of sleep therapy aids in 2004.[10]

New products were crucial to Invacare's success:

> Exiting 2003, newly introduced products from the last three home care trade shows accounted for 73% of North American equipment sales in the home care channel. . . . Invacare has additional

> new products for sleep and its other product lines totaling a planned 40 new product introductions for 2004. . . . Invacare Europe has an aggressive product development plan to energize revenue growth . . . [and] Australasia benefited from a new non-healthcare customer that helped drive the top line and keep manufacturing near capacity.[11]

In 2004, through its co-op advertising program, Invacare continued to offer direct-response television commercials designed to generate demand for Invacare power chairs and scooters sold by the HME (Home Medical Equipment) provider. These commercials featured Arnold Palmer, Invacare's worldwide spokesperson. Mr. Palmer had become an integral part of Invacare's "Yes, you can" promotional and marketing efforts, encouraging consumers to achieve personal independence and participate in the activities of life, facilitated by the home health care products that Invacare manufactured, distributed, or marketed throughout the world. "Current advertising specifically highlights the HomeFill II and power mobility products."[12]

Distribution

Early on after the Mixon group acquired Invacare, marketing of its products became a priority. In a very competitive field, Mixon's strategy was to become dealer oriented. That is, in an industry that was influenced not so much by doctors but rather by therapists or dealers, Mixon began a strategy to win over the dealers because they were, for the most part, the representatives of the home health medical equipment market. In the early years, contacts and product orientation were about all they could offer dealers. In 1984 after the successful public stock offering, Invacare implemented an aggressive distribution strategy of offering dealers prepaid freight, 48-hour delivery, cheap financing, money for cooperative advertising, and volume discounts. Dealers became very familiar with Invacare's products because of the more available financing, volume discounts, etc.

During 1995, Invacare entered into retail distribution channels. Invacare kept its Invacare, Action, and PinDot brands exclusively for the HME provider channel. In early 1996, Invacare acquired Frohock-Stewart, Inc., a manufacturer of personal care products. For the first time, that acquisition permitted Invacare to offer a complete range of off-the-shelf home health care products through retail distribution channels that had no association with the company's key brands.

Evolution of the "One Stop Shopping" Proposition

Invacare's basic product strategies were simple: make its products the most attractive products for HME dealers. Invacare was known for its One Stop Shopping marketing strategy. Invacare was the only manufacturer committed to being the one source for the approximately 3,500 home health care and medical equipment dealers in the United States. Invacare distributed approximately 85% of what dealers needed. In 1992, Invacare began its One Stop Shopping Plus, a program that provided discounts to dealers as their percentage of sales exceeded 65% of Invacare products. As dealers stepped up through the percentage break point (65%), the program amounted to an exclusive distribution agreement with Invacare for the dealer in that area. The company had 100 dealers signed up for the program.

The One Stop Shopping concept was extended to Invacare's European Operations during 1995. It has since evolved into today's Total One Stop Shopping proposition, which has been credited for helping the company reach record net sales of $1.09 billion for fiscal year 2002.[13]

Competition

The home health care industry was quickly changing and becoming a global market. Former giant Everest & Jennings International (E&J) struggled and ended up becoming part of Graham-Field Health Products.[14] Other major competitors included The Scooter Store (dealer), Sunrise Medical, Pride Mobility Products, American HomePatient, Medline Industries, Mallinckrodt (Tyco Healthcare), Hillenbrand, Instrumentarium (General Electric), and Respironics. See **Exhibit 7** for a competitor matrix (brands and health care segments).

Government Regulation

The company was directly affected by government regulation and reimbursement policies in virtually every country in which it operated. Government regulations and health care policy differed from country to country and within some countries. Most notably the United States,

Exhibit 7 Major Competitors: Brands and Health Care Industry Segments

Segments Competitors	Wheel chairs	Beds/Medical Rehab Equipment	Surgical Supplies	Sleep Therapy	Respiratory Equipment	Patient Aids
American HomePatient	X	X		X	X	X
Graham-Field	X (E&J, LaBac)	X (Smith & Davis)			X (John Bunn)	X (Lumex)
Hillenbrand Industries		X (Hill-Rom)			X (Vest System)	
Instrument-arium Corp. (GE)		X (Soredex, Ohmeda)			X (System 5, Ultraview)	
Mallinckrodt Inc. (Tyco)				X	X (Puritan Bennett)	
Medline Industries	X	X				
Pride Mobility	X (Jazzy, Pride)	X (Quantum Rehab, Go Chairs/Lifts)				
Respironics				X (REMstar)	X	
Scooter Store	X					
Sunrise Medical	X (Breezy, Quickie, Guardian)	X		X (DeVilbiss)	X (DeVilbiss)	X

Sources: Plunkett's Health Care Industry Almanac 2004, *pp. 210, 389, 410, 450, 577, 612;* Hoover's Online, *www.hoovers.com (January 11 and January 20, 2005; subscription required); www.pridemobility.com (January 18, 2005); www.medline.com (January 20, 2005); & www.grahamfield.com (January 18, 2005).*

Australia, and Canada had policy differences that varied from state to state or province to province. Changes in regulations and health care policy took place frequently and often affected the size, growth potential, and profitability of products sold in each market.

Although there were a number of reimbursement-related issues in most of the countries in which Invacare competed, the issues of primary importance were in the United States. Two critical issues for Invacare were eligibility of power wheelchairs for elderly patients and the provisions of the legislation related to prescription drug coverage under Medicare.

There was a regulatory push by the Centers for Medicare and Medicaid Services (CMS) toward limiting eligibility to patients who cannot take a single step on their own. This limitation would confine many elderly patients, who are now mobile in power wheelchairs, to their beds. The impetus for the eligibility restrictions was extensive fraud that was uncovered after demand for motorized wheelchairs and scooters soared (more than 300% sales growth from 1999 through early 2003).[15] "Claims for power wheelchairs increased from 62,000 in 1999 to 168,000 in 2003. Payments in 1995 came to $22.3 million; in 2003, they rose to $666.5 million. In November 2003, The Associated Press reported the HHS inspector general identified $167 million in fraudulent power wheelchair claims and had 50 active investigations in close to 24 states."[16] CMS' "Operation Wheeler Dealer" began in Harris County, TX, home to 31,000+ power wheelchair payments in 2002 (versus 3,000+ in 2001); as a result, for example, fraudulent claims worth $84 million were found in that county alone, along with a multimillion dollar fraud uncovered in Florida, where a supplier sold $2,000 motorized scooters but billed Medicare for $6,000 power wheelchairs.[17]

In November 2003, Congress passed legislation related to providing prescription drug coverage for the elderly under the Medicare program. As part of funding the costs of this new program, a number of changes to Medicare home care reimbursement rules would take effect over the next few years. First, the home care provider (who was Invacare's customer) would not receive a cost-of-living adjustment for three years, 2004, 2005, and 2006. Also, in 2005 reimbursement for oxygen, along with several types of home care beds, wheelchairs, nebulizers, and supplies, would be lowered to the median reimbursement levels in the Federal Employee Health Benefit Plans. Third, in 2007, Congress authorized competitive bidding in the largest 10 metropolitan regions of the United States for six or fewer items and services, and the program was to be extended to 80 metropolitan regions in 2009.[18] As the law pertained specifically to power wheelchairs, section 302 stated that

> payment may not be made for such covered item unless a physician (as defined in section 1861(r)(1)), a physician assistant, nurse practitioner, or a clinical nurse specialist (as those terms are defined in section 1861(aa)(5)) has conducted a face-to-face examination of the individual and written a prescription for the item.[19]

Invacare's Mixon had this to say about the power wheelchair crackdown: "They've thrown the baby out with the bathwater. They're trying to stop the fraud, but instead, they've decided to kill the program."[20] Andrew Imparato, CEO of the American Association of People with Disabilities, stated, "They are going to force people to impoverish themselves in institutional settings. People who have not committed fraud are penalized, and the punishment doesn't fit the crime."[21]

What Next?

Invacare Corporation had grown from a minor player in the home medical equipment/health care industry to the world's largest manufacturer of home medical equipment/health care products. The company's success had come about because of the strategies it had always followed since 1979: (1) to aggressively introduce new cutting-edge products, (2) to build brand awareness and recognition in partnership with its dealers, and (3) to aggressively pursue key acquisitions that broadened its product offerings.[22] Invacare's goal for 2006 was $2 billion in sales.[23] The challenge for Mixon and his leadership team was to decide what to do about the government regulations, in particular, and the competitive environment, in general, to see that the 2006 goal was not sidetracked.

Notes

1. Invacare Corporation, "Company Profile, History," *Datamonitor* (December 8, 2003), p. 6.
2. "History," *Datamonitor* (December 8, 2003), p. 6.
3. "Business Description," *Datamonitor* (December 8, 2003), p. 5.
4. *Ibid.*
5. *Older Americans 2004: Key Indicators of Well-Being,* "Indicator 1, Number of Older Americans," p. 2.
6. Invacare, *Summary Annual Report 2003*, several printed pages.
7. Invacare, *1991 Annual Report.*
8. "Invacare Corporation, Products/Operations," *Hoovers Online, www.hoovers.com* (January 11, 2005).
9. Jack W. Plunkett, *Plunkett's Health Care Industry Almanac 2004,* p. 418.
10. Invacare, *Summary Annual Report 2003,* several printed pages.
11. *Ibid.,* third printed page.
12. *Ibid.,* fourth printed page.
13. *Datamonitor* (December 8, 2003), p. 17.
14. For more information about Graham-Field, see its web site: *www.grahamfield.com/about.aspx* (January 18, 2005).
15. Markian Hawryluk, "Medicare to Rein In Power Wheelchair Prescriptions, Sales," *American Medical News* (October 6, 2003), p. 9.
16. "Medicare: Power Wheelchair Industry Starts Lobbying," *Medical Devices & Surgical Technology Week* (March 28, 2004), p. 167.
17. Hawryluk (October 6, 2003); Markian Hawryluk, "DME: The Hard Sell," *American Medical News* (September 1, 2003), p. 5+; Michael Janofsky, "Costs and Savings in Medicare Change on Wheelchairs," *The New York Times* (January 30, 2004), *http://www.aapd-dc.org/News/medicare/powerchaircov.html* (January 6, 2005).
18. Invacare, *Summary Annual Report 2003,* fifth printed page.
19. *The Medicare Prescription Drug, Improvement, and Modernization Act of 2003,* section 302(a)(2)(E)(iv), p. H.R. 1–159, *http://frwebgate.access.gpo.gov/cgi-bin/getdoc.cgi?dbname=108_cong_bills&docid=fih1enr.txt.pdf* (January 6, 2005).
20. Janofsky (January 30, 2004).
21. *Ibid.*
22. Invacare, *Summary Annual Report 2003,* fourth printed page.
23. *Ibid.,* fifth printed page.

Bibliography

Brenda Hayslett, telephone interview with Human Resources, Invacare Corporation (April 12, 1993).

Invacare Corporation, *2001 Annual Report,* Elyria, OH.

Invacare Corporation, *2001 Consolidated Financial Statements,* Elyria, OH.

Invacare Corporation, *2002 Consolidated Financial Statements,* Elyria, OH.

Invacare Corporation, *2003 Consolidated Financial Statements,* Elyria, OH.

Javier Ledesma, Personal interview with Controller of Reynosa plant (April 5, 1993).

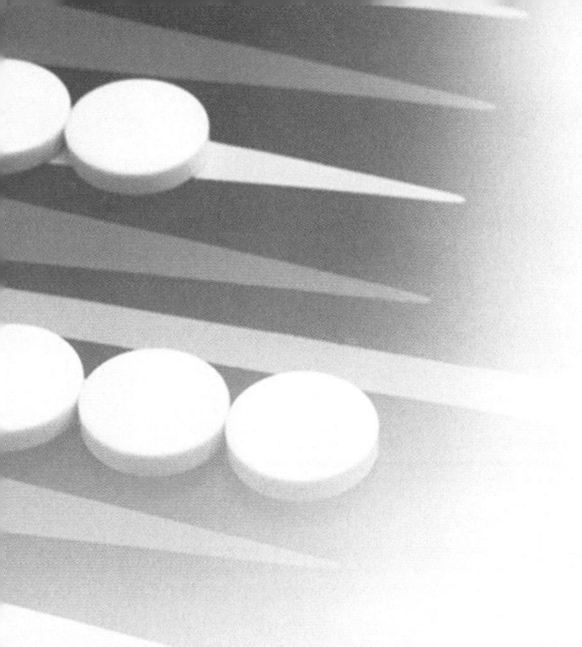

CASE 28
The Carey Plant

Thomas L. Wheelen and J. David Hunger

The Gardner Company was a respected New England manufacturer of machines and machine tools purchased by furniture makers for use in their manufacturing process. As a means of growing the firm, the Gardner Company acquired Carey Manufacturing three years ago from James Carey for $3,500,000. Carey Manufacturing was a high quality maker of specialized machine parts. Ralph Brown, Gardner's Vice President of Finance, had been the driving force behind the acquisition. Except for Andy Doyle and Rod Davis, all of Gardner's Vice Presidents (**Exhibit 1**) had been opposed to expansion through acquisition. They preferred internal growth for Gardner because they felt that the company would be more able to control both the rate and direction of its growth. Nevertheless, since both Peter Finch, President, and R. C. Smith, Executive Vice President, agreed with Brown's strong recommendation, Carey Manufacturing was acquired. Its primary asset was an aging manufacturing plant located 400 miles away from the Gardner Company's current headquarters and manufacturing facility. The Gardner Company was known for its manufacturing competency. Management hoped to add value to its new acquisition by transferring Gardner's manufacturing skills to the Carey Plant through significant process improvements.

James Carey, previous owner of Carey Manufacturing, agreed to continue serving as Plant Manager of what was now called the Carey Plant. He reported directly to the Gardner Company Executive Vice President, R. C. Smith. All functional activities of Carey Manufacturing had remained the same after the acquisition, except for sales activities being moved under Andy Doyle, Gardner's Vice President of Marketing. The five Carey Manufacturing salesmen were retained and allowed to keep their same sales territories. They exclusively sold only products made in the Carey Plant. The other Carey Plant functional departments (Human Resources, Engineering, Finance, Materials, Quality Assurance, and Operations) were supervised by Managers who directly reported to the Carey Plant Manager. The Managers of the Human Resources, Engineering, Materials, and Operations Departments also reported indirectly (shown by dotted lines in **Exhibit 1**) to the Vice Presidents in charge of their respective function at Gardner Company headquarters.

Exhibit 1 Gardner Company Organization Chart

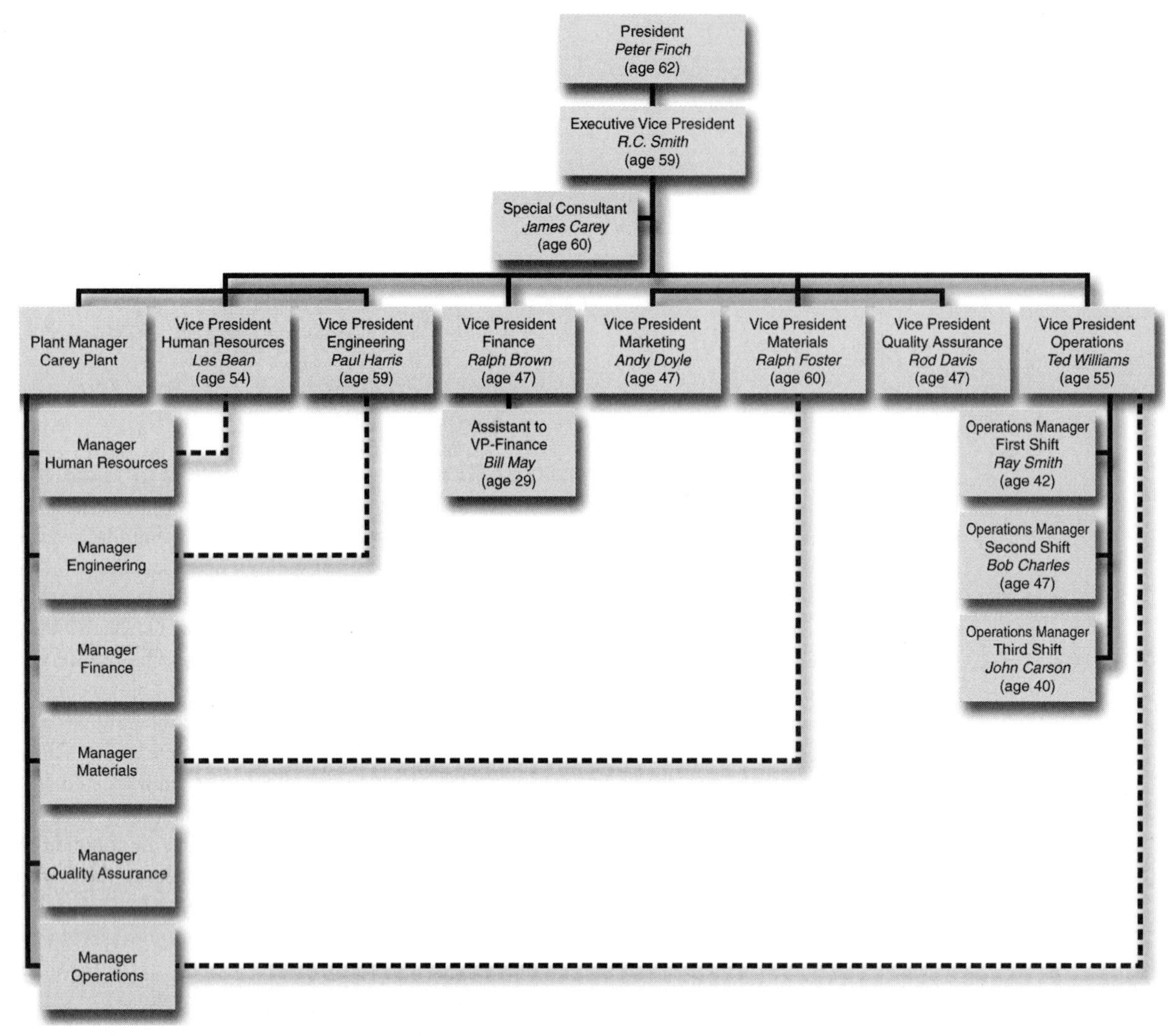

Note: Dotted lines show an indirect reporting relationship.

Until its acquisition, Carey Manufacturing (now the Carey Plant) had been a successful firm with few problems. Following its purchase, however, the plant had been plagued by labor problems, increasing costs, a leveling of sales, and a decline in profits (**Exhibit 2**). Two years ago, the Carey Plant suffered a 10-week strike called by its union in response to demands from the new management (Gardner Company) for increased production without a corresponding increase in pay. (Although Gardner Company was also unionized, its employees were represented by a different union than were the Carey Plant employees.) Concerned by both the strike and the poor performance of the Carey Plant since its purchase two years earlier, Ralph Brown initiated a study last year to identify what was wrong. He discovered that the poor performance of the Carey Plant resulted not only from its outdated and overcrowded manufacturing facility, but also from James Carey's passive role as Plant Manager. Gardner's Executive Committee (composed of the President and eight Vice Presidents) had been aware of the poor condition of the Carey Plant when it had agreed to the acquisition. It had therefore initiated plans to replace the aging plant. A new state-of-the-art manufacturing

Exhibit 2
Carey Plant: Recent Sales and Profit Figures

Year	Sales	Profits
5 Years Ago	$12,430,002	$697,042
4 Years Ago	13,223,804	778,050
3 Years Ago	14,700,178	836,028
2 Years Ago	10,300,000	(220,000)[1]
Last Year	13,950,000	446,812

Note:
1. Ten-week strike during October, November, and December.

facility was being built on available property adjacent to the current plant and should be completed within a few months. The information regarding James Carey was, however, quite surprising to the Committee. Before Gardner's purchase of Carey Manufacturing, James Carey had been actively involved in every phase of his company's operations. Since selling the company, however, Carey had delegated the running of the plant to his staff, the Department Managers. One of his Managers admitted that "He was the driving force of the company, but since he sold out, he has withdrawn completely from the management of the plant."

After hearing Brown's report, the Executive Committee decided that the Carey Plant needed a new Plant Manager. Consequently, James Carey was relieved of his duties as Plant Manager in early January this year and appointed special consultant to the Executive Vice President, R. C. Smith. The current staff of the Carey Plant was asked to continue operating the plant until a new Plant Manager could be named. Vice Presidents Brown and Williams were put in charge of finding a new Manager for the Carey Plant. They recommended several internal candidates to the Executive Vice President, R. C. Smith.

The Offer

On January 31 of this year, Smith offered the Plant Manager position of the Carey Plant to Bill May, current Assistant to Ralph Brown. May had spent six years in various specialist capacities within Gardner's Finance Department after being hired with an MBA. He had been in his current position for the past two years. Brown supported the offer to May with praise for his subordinate. "He has outstanding analytical abilities, drive, general administrative skills and is cost conscious. He is the type of man we need at the Carey Plant." The other executives viewed May not only as the company's efficiency expert, but also as a person who would see any job through to completion. Nevertheless, several of the Vice Presidents expressed opposition to placing a staff person in charge of the new plant. They felt the Plant Manager should have a strong technical background and line management experience. Brown, in contrast, stressed the necessity of a control-conscious person to get the new plant underway. Smith agreed that Gardner needed a person with a strong finance background heading the new plant.

Smith offered May the opportunity to visit the Carey Plant to have a private talk with each of his future staff. Each of the six Department Managers had been with the Carey Plant for a minimum of 18 years. They were frank in their discussions of past problems in the plant and in its future prospects. They generally agreed that the plant's labor problems should decline in the new plant, even though it was going to employ the same 405 employees (half the size of Gardner) with the same union. Four of them were concerned, however, with how they were being supervised. Ever since the acquisition by the Gardner Company, the Managers of the Operations, Materials, Human Resources, and Engineering Departments reported not only to James Carey as Plant Manager, but also to their respective functional Vice Presidents and staff at Gardner headquarters. Suggestions from the various Vice Presidents and staff assistants often conflicted with orders from the Plant Manager. When they confronted James Carey about the situation, he had merely shrugged. Carey told them to expect this sort of thing after an acquisition. "It's important that you get along with your new bosses, since they are the ones who will decide your future in this firm," advised Carey.

Bill May then met in mid-February with Ralph Brown, his current supervisor, to discuss the job offer over morning coffee. Turning to Brown, he said, "I'm worried about this Plant Manager's position. I will be in a whole new environment. I'm a complete stranger to those Department Managers, except for the Finance Manager. I will be the first member of the Gardner Company to be assigned to the Carey Plant. I will be functioning in a line position without any previous experience and no technical background in machine operations. I also honestly feel that several of the Vice Presidents would like to see me fail. I'm not sure if I should accept the job. I have a lot of questions, but I don't know where to get the answers." Looking over his coffee cup as he took a drink, Brown responded, "Bill, this is a great opportunity for you. What's the problem?" Adjusting himself in his chair, May looked directly at his mentor. "The specific details of the offer are very vague in terms of salary, responsibilities, and authority. What is expected of me and when? Do I have to keep the current staff? Do I have to hire future staff members from internal sources or can I go outside the company? Finally, I'm concerned about the lack of an actual job description." Brown was surprised by his protégé's many concerns. "Bill, I'm hoping that all of these questions, except for salary, will soon be answered at a meeting Smith is scheduling for you tomorrow with the Vice Presidents. He wants it to be an open forum."

The Meeting

The next morning, May took the elevator to the third floor. As he walked down the hall to the Gardner Company Executive Committee conference room, he bumped into Ted Williams, Vice President of Manufacturing, who was just coming out of his office. Looking at Bill, Ted offered, "I want to let you know that I'm behind you 100%. I wasn't at first, but I do think you may have what it takes to turn that place around. I don't care what the others think." As the two of them entered the conference room, May looked at the eight Gardner Vice Presidents. Some were sitting at the conference table and working on their laptops while others were getting some coffee from the decanter in the corner. R. C. Smith was already seated at the head of the table. Ralph Brown, sitting on one side of the table, motioned to May to come sit in an empty chair beside him. "Want some coffee?" Brown asked. "Good idea," responded May as he walked over to the decanter. Pouring cream into his coffee, May wondered, "What am I getting myself into?"

CASE 29

Hershey Foods Company: Board of Directors and Stakeholders Conflict over Sale

Cynthia Clark Williams

IN SEPTEMBER 2002, ROBERT C. VOWLER, THE CEO OF THE HERSHEY TRUST COMPANY (HTC) that owned 77% voting control of the Hershey Foods Company, was facing one of the most challenging decisions of his 25-year career as a trust officer: whether or not to recommend to his Board that the American chocolate-making icon be sold. After a summer of community opposition, including a petition to oust the Trust's Board and a lawsuit from the Pennsylvania Attorney General (AG), the HTC Board called a meeting to vote on two offers to buy Hershey Foods Company. On September 14, HTC had received two bids, one from Wm. Wrigley Jr. Co. and one from Nestle SA/Cadbury-Schweppes PLC. Although Wrigley's offer had some attractive features, including the purchase price of $12.5 billion and the promise of expanding local employment and retaining the company name and headquarters, the deal included a 60% stock purchase and 40% in cash. The second offer was a joint bid by Nestle and Cadbury-Schweppes and was an all-cash deal of $11 billion.

The Board meeting was scheduled for September 17, 2002. With the Trust having 77% voting control through its class B shares, the meeting's outcome was, in fact, the final decision regarding the fate of Hershey Foods Company, provided that the U.S. Justice Department's antitrust division approved the deal.[1]

Stepping into the conference room at the Hilton Valley Forge on September 17, Vowler considered how to phrase his recommendation to his fellow Board members seated around the rectangular table.

Events Leading Up to HTC Board Meeting Events

Richard H. Lenny, who had been the CEO of Hershey Foods since March 2001, faced a number of challenges in addition to the potential sale. Competition from Nestle and Mars had increased in recent years, causing profit margins to decline. In an effort to boost margins,

The author prepared this case for the sole purpose of providing material for class discussion. It is not intended to illustrate effective or ineffective handling of a managerial decision or decisions. The author wishes to thank David Wylie, Thomas L. Wheelen, three anonymous reviewers, and the journal editors for their valuable insights and guidance. Reprinted by permission from the *Case Research Journal.* This case was published in *The Case Research Journal*, Volume 26, Issue 1, Winter 2006, pp. 13–28.

Lenny announced a new "value-enhancing" strategy in October 2001.[2] The plan included a $275 million business realignment that called for a voluntary workforce reduction program, the closing of three manufacturing plants and a distribution center, the elimination of non-strategic brands, a realignment of the sales force, and the outsourcing of all cocoa production.[3] However, many community members and employees were growing critical of Lenny's management style and the new strategy.[4] Shareholders, of course, were anxiously awaiting the benefits of the change in strategy. Adding to the CEO's concerns was the recent six-week strike by the local chapter of the Chocolate Worker's Union over health benefits, in the spring of 2002, following Lenny's proposed reductions to employee health coverage. The strike had been the longest in the company's history.[5]

When Lenny learned of HTC's decision to explore a sale, in March 2002, he became determined to seek alternatives. In May 2002 he met with Robert Vowler and proposed a stock buyback of the HTC's shares over a 3- to 5-year period at a 10% premium. But Vowler declined the proposal on behalf of HTC's investment committee. He reiterated that the Trust, its investment banker Morgan Stanley and the AG's office, which had oversight of all charitable trusts, wanted to explore a sale, an idea that had become increasingly popular among HTC Board members in the wake of scandals at Enron and WorldCom. Vowler thought Lenny's buyback offer left the company open to a hostile takeover, as Hershey Foods would have to accumulate debt to finance a buyback.[6] After reportedly being threatened by some of HTC's Board members that he would be fired, Lenny backed off of his buyback proposal and agreed to have his investment banker, Credit Suisse First Boston, solicit bids from potential buyers.[7] A short list was developed that included Coca-Cola, Kraft Foods, Wrigley, and Nestle. Meanwhile, Vowler made his all-cash deal preference clear to the bankers at Morgan Stanley.[8]

Vowler's pressures were also beginning to mount in the months leading up to the September board meeting. He knew after spending a lot of time on the phone with them that some of the HTC's Board members were having second thoughts. He was no doubt aware that the investment bankers and the remaining shareholders might push for the sale because they stood to earn a large sum. The fact that the relationship between the Hershey Foods' board and the HTC board had become more fractious in recent years didn't help matters either (see **Exhibit 1** for chronology). Likewise, the wishes of Pennsylvania's Attorney General (AG) were a concern. The office had just concluded an investigation into alleged mismanagement at the Milton Hershey School, for which the HTC had oversight, calling for it to sell its Hershey Foods' shares in order to diversify

Exhibit 1 Chronology of Key Events

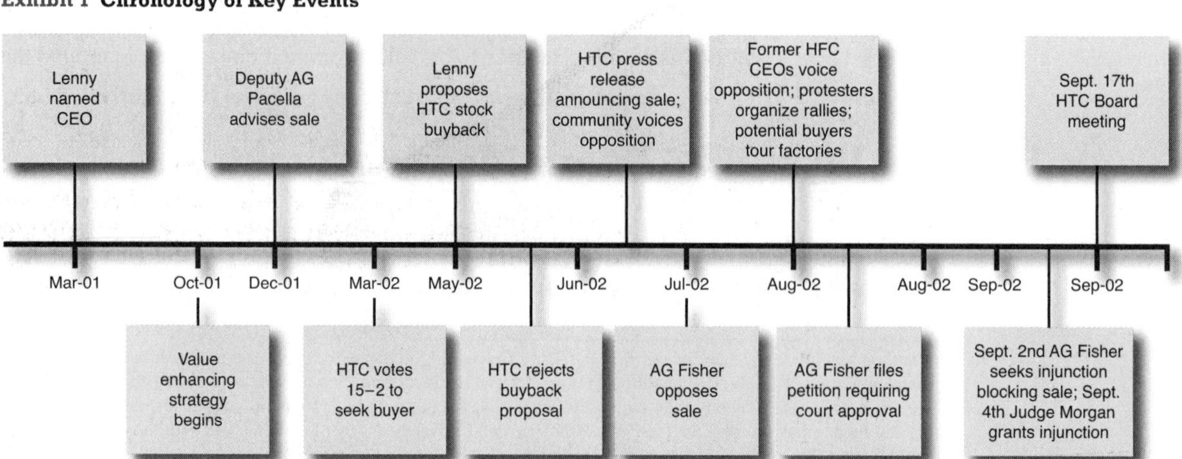

Source: Various articles quoted in case.

and meet its future capital requirements. The local community of Hershey, PA—largely dependent on Hershey Foods for economic stability—was rife with sale rumors that summer.[9]

Hershey Foods Company and the Town of Hershey, PA

The Hershey Foods Company was founded in 1905 by Milton S. Hershey and went public in 1927. In 2001, its sales were $4.6 billion, which represented 43% of the domestic chocolate market. The company was headquartered in Hershey, Pennsylvania, an unincorporated village within the Derry Township, and employed some 6,200 of the township's 21,000 residents.[10]

Hershey Foods was divided into three product groups: the chocolate and confectionery group, restaurant operations, and the food products and services group. The most well-known group was the chocolate and confectionery group; it was responsible for producing such popular brands as Hershey's Kisses, Reese's Peanut Butter Cups, Twizzlers, Mounds, and Kit Kat.[11] Industry experts noted that the chocolate market was not growing. Some saw this as an explanation for the HTC's motivation to sell all of its shares.[12]

Although Hershey Foods controlled a large portion of the chocolate market, in 2002 it had increasing competition from Mars and Nestle and was determined to maintain its market share, having wrestled control from Mars in 1988.[13] Mars, a private company, held approximately 27% of the market, whereas Nestle, a public company, held 12%.[14] The more diversified companies of Mars and Nestle, both of whom sold cat and dog food products among other non-chocolate items, had sales of $64.3 billion and $16.2 billion in 2002, respectively.[15]

Exhibits 2 and 3 are the consolidated income statements and balance sheets of the Hershey Foods Corporation for 1999 through 2001.

Exhibit 2 Consolidated Statements of Income: Hershey Foods Company (Dollar amounts in millions)

Year Ending December 2001	2001	2000	1999
Net Sales	$4,557,241	$4,220,976	$3,970,924
Costs and Expenses:			
Cost of Sales	2,665,566	2,471,151	2,354,724
Selling, marketing and administrative	1,269,964	1,127,175	1,057,840
Business realignment and asset impairments	228,314	—	—
Gain on the sale of business	(19,237)	—	(243,785)
Total costs and expenses	4,144,607	3,598,326	3,168,779
Income Before Interest and Income Taxes	412,634	622,650	802,145
Interest expense, net	69,093	76,011	74,271
Income Before Income Taxes	343,541	546,639	727,874
Provision for income taxes	136,385	212,096	267,564
Net Income	**$207,156**	**$334,543**	**$460,310**
Net Income Per Share—Basic	$1.52	$2.44	$3.29
Net Income Per Share—Diluted	$1.50	$2.42	$3.26
Cash Dividends Paid Per Share (in dollars):			
Common Stock	1.165	1.08	1.00
Class B Common Stock	1.05	0.975	0.905

Note: All notes were deleted.

Source: Hershey Foods Corporation, 2002 Annual Report, p. A-16.

Exhibit 3 Consolidated Balance Sheets Hershey Foods Company (Dollar amounts in thousands)

Year Ending December 31	2001	2000	1999
ASSETS			
Current Assets:			
Cash and cash equivalents	$134,147	$31,969	118,078
Accounts receivable—trade	361,726	379,680	352,750
Inventories	512,134	605,173	602,202
Deferred income taxes	96,939	76,136	80,303
Prepaid expenses and other	62,595	202,390	126,647
Total current assets	1,167,541	1,295,348	1,279,980
Property, Plant and Equipment, Net	1,534,901	1,585,388	1,510,460
Intangibles Resulting from Business Acquisitions, Net	429,128	474,448	450,165
Other Assets	115,860	92,580	106,047
Total Assets	**$3,247,430**	**$3,447,764**	**3,346,652**
LIABILITIES AND STOCKHOLDERS' EQUITY			
Current Liabilities:			
Accounts payable	$133,049	$149,232	136,567
Accrued liabilities	462,901	358,067	292,497
Accrued income taxes	2,568	1,479	72,159
Short-term debt	7,005	257,594	209,166
Current portion of long-term debt	921	529	2,440
Total current liabilities	606,444	766,901	712,829
Long-term Debt	876,972	877,654	878,213
Other Long-term Liabilities	361,041	327,674	330,938
Deferred Income Taxes	255,769	300,499	326,045
Total liabilities	2,100,226	2,272,728	2,248,025
Stockholders' Equity:			
Preferred Stock, shares issued: none in 2001 and 2000	—	—	—
Common Stock, shares issued: 149,517,064 in 2001 and 149,509,014 in 2000	149,516	149,508	149,507
Class B Common Stock, shares issued: 30,433,808 in 2001 and 30,441,858 in 2000	30,434	30,442	30,443
Additional paid-in capital	3,263	13,124	30,079
Unearned ESOP compensation	(15,967)	(19,161)	(22,354)
Retained earnings	2,755,333	2,702,927	2,513,275
Treasury—Common Stock shares, at cost: 44,311,870 in 2001 and 43,669,284 in 2000	(1,689,243)	(1,645,088)	(1,552,708)
Accumulated other comprehensive loss	(86,132)	(56,716)	(49,615)
Total stockholders' equity	1,147,204	1,175,036	1,098,627
Total Liabilities and Stockholders' Equity	**$3,247,430**	**$3,447,764**	**$3,346,652**

Note: All notes were deleted

Source: Hershey Foods Corporation, 2002 Annual Report, p. A-17, 1999 Annual Report, p A-12.

The Sweetest Place on Earth

Milton S. Hershey had two goals when he created the Hershey Foods Company: to be a pioneer in the mass production of chocolate and to create a utopian community. His company not only was a producer of chocolate, but was the builder of houses and public buildings, manager of the town's transportation system and utilities, and creator of the town bank, the Hershey Trust Company. Milton Hershey's goal was to create the "sweetest place on earth," complete with Hershey Kiss–shaped street lights and streets named for cocoa bean producing locales such as Caracas and Java.[16] Hershey Foods is a focal point of the town with an amusement park called Hershey Park, Hotel Hershey, and the Hershey Theater, a 7,000-seat arena.[17] Tourists flocked to the town as did entertainers such as the World Wrestling Federation, Cher, and the Harlem Globetrotters. As one resident and long-time employee put it, "Hershey Foods is the life-blood of this town."[18]

Lenny's New Vision

Although the town of Hershey remained committed to the original Hershey Company's goals, as its new CEO, Lenny's primary focus had been the shareholder. Lenny was a former vice president of Kraft Foods, with oversight of its Nabisco Biscuit unit, and was the first outsider ever to head Hershey Foods. The chocolate maker had seen profits suffer in the past several years, but by 2002, Lenny had increased earnings by 10% in just three months. Part of this success was due to cost cutting from plant closures and cocoa production outsourcing, two main features of the value-enhancing strategy.

Lenny's vision for Hershey Foods Company was clearly different from that of Milton Hershey. The new CEO described his intentions by stating, "I'm here to do what the shareholders want me to do, which is increase shareholder value."[19]

Employees and community members had begun to openly express their concern with Lenny's strategy. According to Art Long, a union member at the Hershey plant for 24 years, "Lenny came here from Nabisco with an ax." Debbie Keyton, a local bar owner whose father worked at the plant, agreed: "People were angry because Hershey wasn't founded on greed."[20]

Hershey Foods' Board of Directors

As with any public company, Hershey Foods had in place a Board of Directors with overall company governance authority. In 2002 the Hershey Foods' Board of Directors consisted of nine members (see **Exhibit 4**). Each director's compensation was $55,000 annually plus $40,000 in restricted stock unit grants each year. On average the Board met six times a year with 97% of its members in attendance.[21]

Hershey Trust Company and the Milton Hershey School

In 2002, the Hershey Trust Company was headed by president and CEO, Robert Vowler, a native of Harrisburg. He and his wife Holly decided to settle there, seeing it as a good place to raise their family.[22] Vowler became an active member in the community by serving on the Harrisburg Regional Chamber of Commerce and the Susquehanna Alliance, an economic development group. He quickly rose through the ranks at various Hershey-related

Exhibit 4 Board of Directors Hershey Foods Company

	Director Since	Audit	Compensation and Executive Organization Committee	Committee on Directors, Corporate Governance	Executive
Jon Boscia	2001	●			
Robert Campbell	1995	●		●	
Gary Coughlan	2001	●			
Bonnie Hill	1993	●	●		
J. Robert Hillier	2001			●	
John C. Jamison	1974	C			●
Richard Lenny	2001			●	C
Mackey McDonald	1996		C		●
John M. Pietruski	1987		●	C	●

Jon A. Boscia, age 49, Chairman and Chief Executive Officer of Lincoln Financial Group in Philadelphia, PA.

Robert H. Campbell, age 64, retired in 2000 as Chairman of the Board and CEO of Sunoco, Inc. in Philadelphia, PA.

Gary P. Coughlan, age 58, retired on March 31, 2002, as the Senior Vice President and CFO of Abbott Laboratories in Abbott Park, IL.

Bonnie G. Hill, age 60, President of B. Hill Enterprises in Los Angeles, CA.

J. Robert Hillier, age 64, Chairman of the Board and founder, The Hillier Group, Princeton, NJ. Served also on Hershey Trust Board.

John C. Jamison, age 67, Chairman of Mallardee Associates, Williamsburg, VA. Chair of Audit Committee.

Richard H. Lenny, age 50, Chairman of the Board, President and CEO of Hershey Foods Corporation, Hershey, PA. Chair of Executive Committee.

Mackey J. McDonald, age 55, Chairman, President and CEO of VF Corporation, Greensborough, NC. Chair of Compensation and Executive Organization Committee.

John M. Pietruski, age 69, Chairman of the Board of Texas Biotechnology Corporation, Houston, TX. Chair of Directors and Corporate Governance Committee.

Source: Hershey Food Corporation, SEC DEF-14A (March 15, 2002), pp. 3–5.

organizations as well. He was president of the Hershey Foundation and a member of its Board of Managers. Prior to being named CEO of the HTC, he had served as the Chief Financial Officer since 1987. From 1980 to 1987 he held several financial management positions with Hershey Entertainment and Resorts, where he remained a member of the Board of Directors.[23]

The HTC not only was the community's first bank, but was trustee for the Milton Hershey School and the Hershey Foundation.[24] The HTC owned approximately 32% of Hershey Foods total equity but its class B shares, each carrying 10 votes, comprised 77% voting control as of December 31, 2002.[25] The HTC was responsible for the M.S. Hershey Foundation, the Milton S. Hershey School, and the Milton Hershey School Trust while also serving its own investment clients. The Hershey Foundation operated the Hershey Museum, Hershey Gardens, Hershey Theatre, and the Hershey Community Archives. See **Exhibit 5** for a description of the organizations owned by HTC.

The Hershey School's original purpose had been to train orphaned boys and had eventually included girls and minorities from underprivileged backgrounds in grades K–12. The school was headed by William L. Lepley, who was a voting member of the HTC and was its highest-paid member.[26]

Student-related costs, including education, food, clothing, health services and housing, were $76.9 million, and in the 2000–2001 school year 1,152 students were enrolled.[27] Over 50% of the HTC's assets were common stock holdings of Hershey Foods, 27% were common

Exhibit 5
Hershey Entities Organizational Chart, Hershey Trust Company

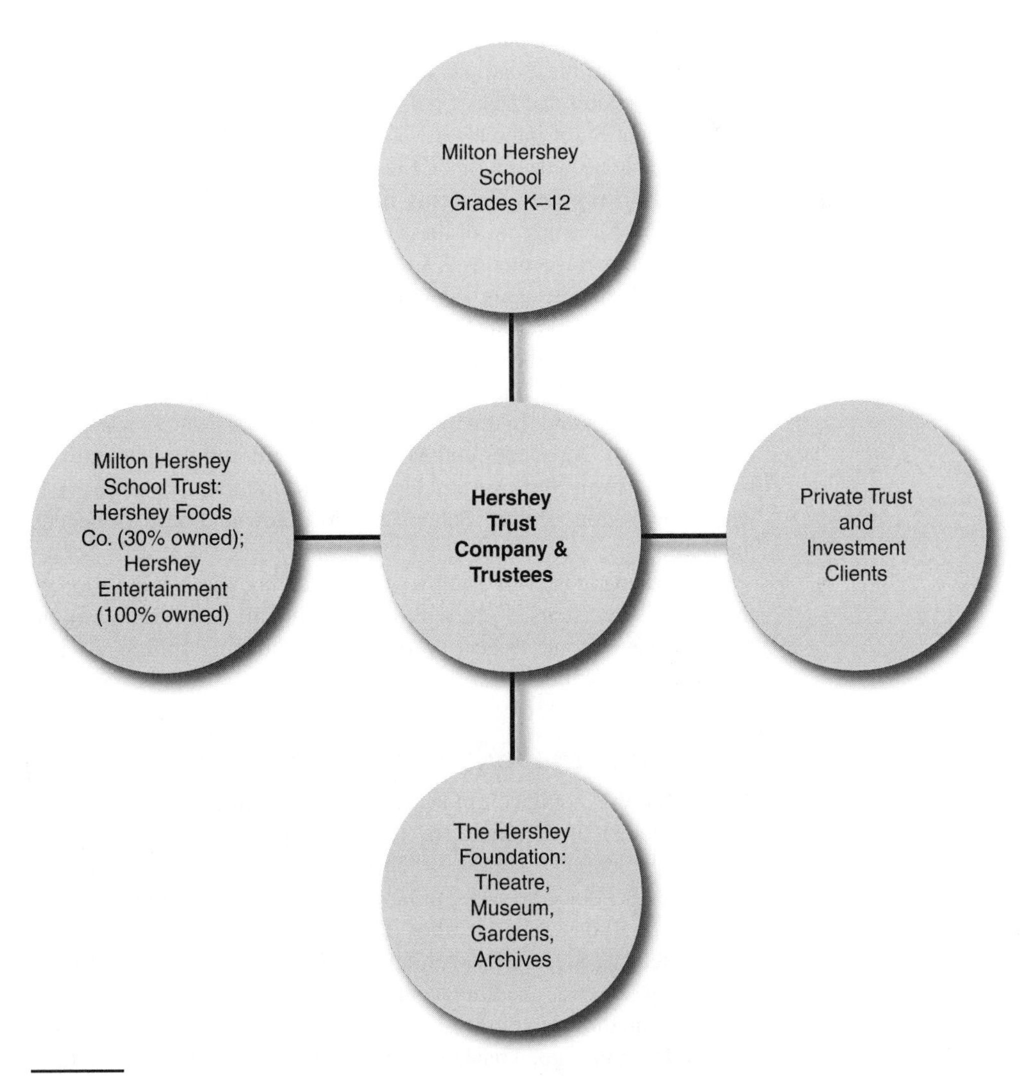

Source: Adapted from HTC organizational chart, http://www.hersheytrust.org.

stock of other companies, 12% were bond holdings, and the remainder was sprinkled among property, equipment, cash, and other investments. Stock in Hershey Foods was valued at $2.5 billion as of July 31, 2001, and unrealized gains were $770 million.[28]

The HTC Board

The Trust Board's relationship with the Hershey Foods Company Board had become more distant following Milton Hershey's death in 1945. Some described it as "frosty" at times.[29] Over the years the shared values of Hershey Trust and Hershey Foods began to appear more like conflicts of interest. Gone were the days when Milton Hershey served as the chairman of both boards. Likewise, the competitive climate began to require a sharper focus on strong numbers for shareholders. During his tenure as Hershey Foods CEO from 1994 to 2001, Ken Wolfe had laid off 400 employees to reduce fixed costs and refused to allow the school to advertise on Hershey candy bars, a long-standing goodwill gesture.

By the mid-1990s the Hershey Foods Board was mostly made up of independent directors. The HTC Board, at the behest of school president Lepley, voted on whether to remove Wolfe and Dick Zimmerman, Hershey Foods CEO from 1984 to 1993. The Trust voted against their removal, but the relationships became more fractured, with each executive stepping down from the Board on leaving his CEO post. Lepley reportedly resented the executives' higher status and lack of willingness to defer to the Trust.[30] In 2001, also to eliminate the apparent conflict of interest between running Hershey Foods and being a controlling shareholder, Lenny became the first CEO not to sit on HTC's Board, according to Vowler.[31]

The Hershey Trust Company had 17 Board members with equal voting rights in 2002 (see **Exhibit 6**).[32] Only six of these members lived in the central Pennsylvania area, and three of these members—Anthony J. Colistra, William H. Alexander, and Robert C. Vowler—were seen as likely to vote against the sale.[33] Average full-time Board member compensation at fiscal year end July 2002 was $152,950.[34]

Bob Hillier was the only Board member at the time to also sit on the board of directors at Hershey Foods (refer back to **Exhibit 4**). Ms. Pennington and Ms. Lipsitz had strong backgrounds in education. Likewise, Mr. Colistra was a former superintendent and an alumnus of the school. Mr. Alexander and Mr. Vowler were both investment professionals, and Vowler had a degree from Northwestern University's Graduate Trust School. Mr. Senser was an alumnus of the Milton Hershey School, and Ms. Rowland brought gender and racial diversity to the Board.

According to Rowland and Vowler, the community's opposition was not a factor in any of the Board's decisions.[35] Yet, with legal, political, and community pressure mounting, such pressure would come to bear on the decision-making abilities of any group facing accountability to external demands.

A Lack of Trust: The Attorney General's Investigation

Although it was not uncommon for public companies to be majority owned by a single large shareholder or to dominate the town's employee base,[36] the HTC's involvement added another challenging element to the situation: it was also a charitable trust for the Milton S. Hershey School. According to James Negley, manager of the Derry Township, "Everything here is incestuous, The Hershey Trust, Hershey Foods, Hershey Entertainment and the Milton Hershey School. Everything goes back to the school."[37] Even though selling all of its controlling shares at one time would fetch the best price and help HTC to diversify, some felt it was yet another sign of the growing separation of HTC and the township of Derry.

"It does make good business sense, but they don't have to cut the heart out of the town to do it. They're out for top dollar, and they're going to do it at the expense of the community,"

Exhibit 6 Hershey Trust Board Members in 2002

Name	Position	Comments
William H. Alexander	Managing Director, Snider Entrepreneurial Center, University of Pennsylvania	HSY (6,091 shares), PA
Robert F. Cavanaugh	Managing Director, DLJ Real Estate Partners, a Credit Suisse Company	Member, Investment Committee
Anthony J. Colistra	Superintendent, Cumberland Valley School District	PA
Don Cornwell	CEO, Granite Broadcasting, New York	Chairman, HTC Investment Committee
John Gabig, Esq.	Retired Partner, Miller & Chevalier	HSY (100 shares), Chairman, HTC Board
Lucy D. Hackney	Former Senior Advisor for Child Care Policy, U.S. General Services Administration	PA
Bob Hillier	CEO, Hillier Group Architects	HSY (1,097 shares) Member, Investment Committee
Dr. William L. Lepley	President of Milton S. Hershey School	HSY (549 shares), PA
Dr. Joan S. Lipsitz	Independent consultant and author of two books on adolescence	
Dr. Michael W. Matier	Director, Institutional Research & Planning, Cornell University	
Rev. John S. McDowell, Jr.	St. James the Less Episcopal Church	HSY (864 shares)
Hilary C. Pennington	Co-President, Jobs for the Future	
Wendy D. Puriefoy	President of Public Education Network	
Juliet C. Rowland	CEO, United Way of Ohio	
Joseph M. Senser	Restaurant owner in Minnesota	
Robert C. Vowler	CEO of HTC	PA, Member, Investment Committee
A. Morris Williams, Jr.	President, Williams & Company	PA

Key: PA, resident of Pennsylvania; HSY, holds stock in Hershey Foods Co.
Notes: McCollister Evarts, MD, of Hershey, PA, and Kenneth Wolfe, former CEO of Hershey Foods and resident of Hershey, PA, were board members until January 2002.

Sources: Hershey School, Trust board members. Harrisburg Patriot (July 26, 2002), p. A15; Hershey School and School Trust IRS form 990; Marcy, B. Cutting the Ties That Bind: without Father, It's No Longer a Close-knit Hershey Family, Sunday Patriot-News Harrisburg (July 28, 2002), p. A1; Marcy, B., Hershey Trust Board Would See Little Profit from Sale, Harrisburg Patriot (August 16, 2002), p. A1.

said Kathleen Lewis, president of the Derry Township Historical Society.[38] Bruce McKinney, a former HTC board director, said of these fissures, "I think the trust in the trust is gone."[39]

The breakdown in the relationship between the HTC and the community had begun in December 2001 with the presentation of the AG's findings. A year earlier, the Pennsylvania AG's office began receiving a number of complaints, mostly from alumni of the school, concerning Lepley, subpar education, and teacher misdeeds. In response, the office stepped in to investigate the allegations. The Public Protection Division of the AG's office oversaw all property in Pennsylvania committed to charitable purposes. The AG's jurisdiction included a mandate to ensure that the assets of the charity, in this case the Milton S. Hershey School, were being properly administered for the benefit of the public.

During the investigation, Deputy Attorney General Mark Pacella began meeting with the HTC. In these meetings he kept repeating that the Trust needed to make some changes.[40] In a meeting on December 4, 2001, he recommended that the trust diversify its holdings so that it might be better equipped to fulfill its financial obligations and manage the school's foundation. In this meeting, Pacella also proposed that the Trust explore the idea of divesting its Hershey Foods shares.[41] According to one report, Pacella implied that the trustees would be breaching their fiduciary responsibility to shareholders by passing up a financial windfall from the sale.[42] Because the HTC had controlling interest through the stock class structure, such a move would effectively force the sale of the company as a whole.

Several months later, at its quarterly meeting in March 2002, the HTC had voted 15–2 to diversify its portfolio by finding a buyer for the Hershey Foods Corporation. Juliet Rowland and Joseph Senser were the only two trustees who voted against exploring a potential sale.[43] In a statement, Mr. Vowler said, "The Trust has been extremely pleased with the Company's management. This is simply a matter of meeting our fiduciary responsibilities to diversify the assets of the Trust."[44]

Very few members of the HTC were willing to speak publicly following the investigation and had apparently made a pact against doing so, including Don Cornwell, the chair of the committee, and Bob Hillier, who also sat on the Hershey Foods Board.[45] Cornwell and Hillier were selected to meet with Richard Lenny and discuss their findings and recommendations. But as pressure on the board began to escalate in late summer, some board members decided to speak out. HTC Board Chairman John Gabig; Anthony Colistra, superintendent of Cumberland Valley School District; and Lucy Hackney, a child care policy advisor, all felt that the sale of Hershey Foods stock was a necessary, albeit painful, step. According to Gabig, "The community, in general, believes that this is their company. Well, it is a public company with shareholders, and everybody knows that a publicly held company has to be responsible to it shareholders."[46]

Public Disclosure: Company and Community Opposition

Because the buyback proposal had been rejected, Lenny preferred that the company remain under trust ownership—even though he stood to gain financially—because he relished the challenge of building the company's brands in partial fulfillment of his value-enhancing strategy.[47] Throughout the early part of the summer, the company and the Trust tried to keep the possible sale quiet as the investment bankers developed their short list.[48]

However, the HTC's intention to explore a sale was leaked to the *Wall Street Journal* on July 25, 2002.[49] Rick Kelly, a public relations specialist who had been hired by Vowler to handle the press, received a call from the newspaper telling him that it planned run the story within hours.[50] Quickly, Kelly organized a news release to be sent from Hershey Foods. In the release issued later that morning, Lenny was quoted as follows:

> Recognizing the School Trust's controlling position and its determination to explore a possible sale, the Hershey Foods Board of Directors has concluded that it is in the best interests of the Company and its stockholders for Hershey Foods and the School Trust to work together in a cooperative manner in this effort.[51]

In a memo to Hershey employees, Lenny expressed his disappointment this way: "I came here to build our brands and build our people, not to manage a potential sale and subsequent integration process. Having been your CEO for only one year, I had hoped to work with you for a long time to come."[52]

The announcement caused Hershey Foods share price to soar to $80 per share—well above its 2002 trading range of $30–$40 (see **Exhibit 7**), but also caused a strong reaction from the community.[53] The week after the announcement, community leaders, school alumni, Hershey employees, and government officials mobilized. The decision to sell was seen as "a

Exhibit 7 Stock Prices on July 25, 2002 and September 17, 2002: Hershey Foods Company

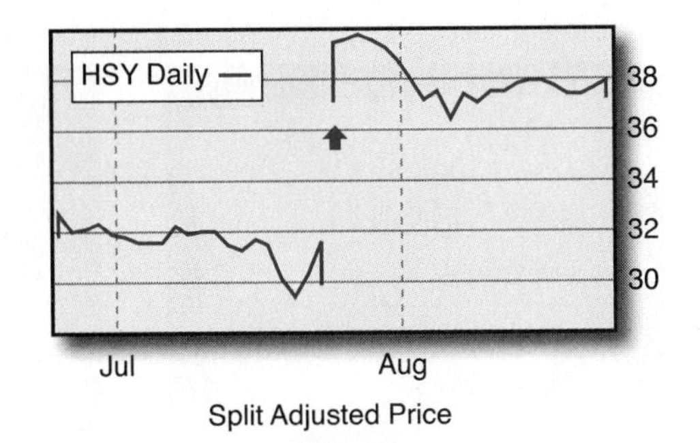

Hershey Foods Corporation

Wednesday, July 24, 2002

Closing Price: **62.50** Open: **60.08** High: **62.95** Low: **59.50** Volume: **965,700**

Thursday, July 25, 2002

Closing Price: **78.30** Open: **75.60** High: **78.80** Low: **74.25** Volume: **9,543,000**

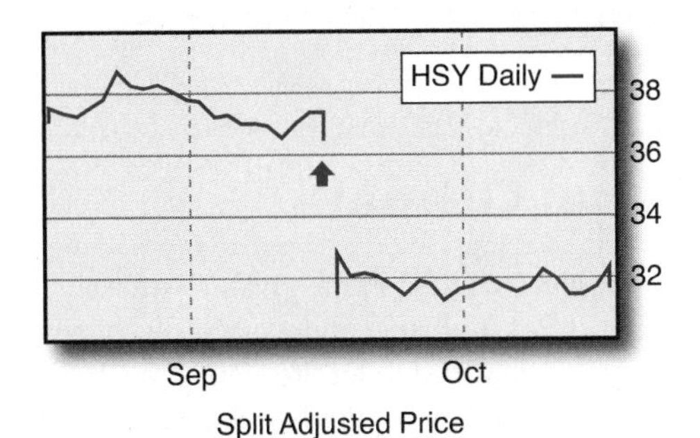

Hershey Foods Corporation

Monday, September 16, 2002

Closing Price: **74.81** Open: **73.67** High: **74.84** Low: **73.52** Volume: **695,600**

Tuesday, September 17, 2002

Closing Price: **73.81** Open: **74.81** High: **74.81** Low: **73.22** Volume: **1,047,600**

Source: http://www.bigcharts.com (October 2, 2005).

threat to an American icon and insult to Milton Hershey," according to the Derry Township paper, *Morning Call.*[54] Former trustee Bruce McKinney positioned himself as a leader in the opposition movement, along with two former Hershey Food's CEOs, Kenneth Wolfe and Richard Zimmerman, who claimed the sale would lead to major layoffs of local workers.[55] McKinney had particularly strong ties to the community and to the company itself. Not only had he been a student at the Milton Hershey School in the 1950s, but he had served as the Board chairman, CEO, and later a trustee of the Hershey Estates (named HERCO in 1976).[56]

On August 2, 2002, McKinney led a crowd of more than 500, including town citizens, alumni, employees and politicians, to Chocolatetown Square in the center of Hershey, PA.[57] An hour-long rally followed the march. The grassroots opposition grew to include an online petition to expel HTC board members, a "derail the sale" yard sign campaign, and union protests in the state capital of Harrisburg, about 20 miles from the town of Hershey[58] (see **Exhibit 8**).

The opposition also had tee-shirts made up with pictures of Milton Hershey and the slogan "Save the Dream" for the protesters to wear during the march. McKinney was quoted as saying, "Fortunately, the community came together in a firestorm of protest. The media across

Exhibit 8 Signs of Opposition

Source: The Friends of Hershey Foods.

Pennsylvania, the country and even most of Western Europe was behind us."[59] A group called Friends of Hershey Foods was organized to oppose the sale and also held rallies at the middle school auditorium.

The Political and Legal Climate

Other voices of dissent included Pennsylvania Attorney General Mike Fisher, who was running for Governor of Pennsylvania and was currently behind in the polls. According to news articles, Fisher could not afford to let the state's most recognizable name be sold and needed mid-state voters from Hershey to win his election.[60] Members of the Trust Board, including Vowler, had previously believed that Fisher would support or ignore the sale.[61]

In reality, his response to the news was quite the contrary. Not only did Pennsylvania government officials move to enact legislation that would require companies to consider the impact the sale would have on the community, but Fisher announced his intent to legally block the company's sale and on August 12 filed a petition with Judge Morgan of the Dauphin County Orphan's Court asking that the sale be subject to its approval because of the court's jurisdiction over the HTC.

On September 3, 2002, the Dauphin County Court heard the attorney general's request for a temporary injunction to prevent the sale of Hershey Foods, which cited the potential and irreparable harm to the local community. Richard Zimmerman testified to try to stop the sale at the injunction hearing.[62] Judge Morgan granted the injunction on September 4 and stated, "The sale appears to be excessive and unnecessary."[63] The Trust then appealed the ruling by stating that the court had no jurisdiction as Hershey was incorporated in the state of Delaware.

The HTC Board Meeting

The HTC Board members met for close to 11 hours on September 17, 2002 (see **Exhibit 6**). The offer from Nestle and Cadbury-Schweppes would result in various Hershey brands being divided between the two companies. Hershey had long-standing licensing agreements with Cadbury, but reportedly shareholders from Nestle believed the $11 billion offer was too high.[64] The Wm. Wrigley Jr. Company offered a combination cash and stock bid of $12.5 billion to form a new company called Wrigley Hershey. After a series of negotiations, a deal was reached with Wrigley whereby it pledged to keep the Hershey factories intact and maintain the local workforce. The Wrigley bid reportedly represented a 42% premium over the pre-auction price of Hershey Foods stock.[65]

During the September 17 meeting, Bill Wrigley, Jr., the CEO of the Wrigley empire, spoke. The meeting began with the investment bankers from both Morgan Stanley and Credit Suisse walking the 17 Board members through each proposal. Nestle representatives were not present, but the appearance by Wrigley did not appear to persuade the HTC members.[66]

During lunch an investment banker from Morgan Stanley whispered to Vowler in the buffet line that the meeting didn't appear to be going well. Vowler mentioned again that he preferred an all-cash deal.

The meeting would last for approximately eight more hours. Sometime before 11 PM, Vowler moved to call for a vote. He began by asking each member to speak for 5 or 10 minutes to express their thoughts about the sale offers.[67] As Vowler listened to the board members' comments, he knew he'd have to address the board and present the final vote on the fate of Hershey Foods Company—his own.

Notes

1. Class B shares typically carry more votes than common shares. In HTC's case, each class B share held 10 votes, whereas common shares held one vote. HTC held 99.6% of class B shares (see Hershey Food Corporation, "SEC DEF-14A," [March 15, 2002], pp. 9–10). Approximately 64% of the largest companies worldwide have controlling shareholders, and 30% of these are family owned (see R. La Porta, F. L. De Silanes, and A. Shleifer (1999). "Corporate Ownership Around the World," *Journal of Finance*, 54:471–517).
2. Company news release, "Hershey Announces Value-Enhancing Strategy," *http://www.hersheyfoods.com/news/release.asp?releaseID=219683* (May 7, 2006).
3. *Ibid.*
4. D. Shope, "Hershey Victory Bittersweet," *The Morning Call* (October 26, 2003), p. D1.
5. Associated Press, "Bitterness Coats Sweet Hershey," *Seattle Times* (May 30, 2002).
6. B. Marcy, "Hershey Trustees Were Blindsided, Besieged," *Knight Ridder Tribune Business News* (September 22, 2001), p. 1.
7. R. Frank and S., Ellison, "Meltdown in Chocolatetown—Controlling Trust at Hershey Bows to Opposition to Sale; Company Faces Future Alone," *Wall Street Journal* (September 19, 2002), p. B1.
8. The case author conducted an hour-long personal interview with Robert Vowler on June 3, 2005, in which he described the events leading up to the sale, the issues surrounding the sale, and the Trust's sale preferences. This interview was used throughout this case to inform or confirm the media accounts. See also D. Ackman, "Hershey Says No, Bankers Cry Foul," *Forbes.com* (September 18, 2002), *http://www.forbes.com*; R. Frank and S. Ellison, "Meltdown in Chocolatetown—Controlling Trust at Hershey" Bows to Opposition to Sale; Company Faces Future Alone, *Wall Street Journal* (September 19, 2002), p. B1.
9. Shope (2003).
10. W. Tanaka, "*Hershey Trust Again Defends Proposed Sale*," *Philadelphia Inquirer* (August 17, 2002); Shope (2003).
11. *http://www.thehersheycompany.com* (May 13, 2005).
12. Tanaka (2002).
13. J. Helyar, "Sweet Surrender," *Fortune* (October 14, 2002), p. 224.
14. Deborah Ball, "Nestle Says a Takeover of Hershey Wouldn't Pass Antitrust Muster," *Wall Street Journal* (August 30, 2002), p. A1.
15. *http://www.hoovers.com* (April 24, 2006).
16. Shope (2003).
17. *http://www.thehersheycompany.com* (May 13, 2005).
18. Shope (2003).
19. Associated Press (2002).
20. Shope (2003).
21. Hershey Food Corporation, *SEC DEF-14A* (March 15, 2002), p. 7.
22. Tanaka (2002).
23. *http://www.hersheytrust.org* (May 26, 2005).
24. All recreation and tourism facilities in Hershey were owned by HERCO (Hershey Entertainment and Resort Company), a separate and distinct corporation wholly owned by the Milton Hershey School Trust. Hershey's Chocolate World, however, was owned by Hershey Foods Corporation. *http://www.hersheyinvestorrelations.com/ireye/ir_site.zhtml?ticker=HSY&script=1801.*
25. HTC held 43,046,247 total shares (common and class B) in Hershey Foods Corporation as of March 1, 2002 (see Hershey Food Corporation, *SEC DEF-14A* [March 15, 2002], p. 10).
26. Helyar (2002).
27. *Milton Hershey School Annual Report, 2000–01.*
28. *Ibid.* and Hershey School and School Trust IRS form 990.
29. *Ibid.*; see also Frank and Ellison (2002).
30. Helyar (2002).
31. Marcy, B. "Cutting the Ties That Bind: Without Father, It's No Longer a Close-knit Hershey Family," *Patriot-News* (July 28, 2002), p. A1.
32. *Ibid.*
33. *Ibid.*
34. Hershey School and School Trust IRS Form 990.
35. *Ibid.*
36. "Passing On the Crown," *The Economist* (November 6, 2004), pp. 69–71.
37. Shope (2003).
38. Marcy (July 28, 2002).
39. B. Marcy, "Hershey Fate Rests with Out-of-Towners," *Patriot News* (September 16, 2002).
40. Frank and Ellison (2002).
41. B. Marcy, "Hershey Trustees Were Blindsided, Besieged," *Knight Ridder Tribune Business News* (September 22, 2002), p. 1.
42. *Ibid.*
43. B. Sulon, Harrisburg, PA—Area Trustees Prove Key in Hershey Decision. Knight Ridder Tribune Business News, (September 23, 2002), p. 1.
44. *http://www.hersheytrust.org* (May 13, 2005).
45. Tanaka (2002).

46. Marcy (September 22, 2002).
47. Sulon, B. "Hershey Foods Chief Spells Out Sale Discussion," *Patriot News* (July 31, 2002). See also B. March, "Hershey Trust Board Would See Little Profit," *Patriot-News* (August 16, 2002), p. A1. Lenny's change-of-control agreement entitled him to three times his $750,000 salary if his employment was terminated because of an ownership change.
48. Marcy (September 22, 2002).
49. *Ibid.*
50. *Ibid.*
51. *www.thehersheycompany.com/news/* (September 20, 2005).
52. Sulon (2002).
53. Historical financial data retrieved April 24, 2006, from *www.hoovers.com*. Authorized common shares as of December 31, 2002, were 450,000,000, authorized class B common shares were 75,000,000, and 132,220,137 were outstanding; see *Hershey Foods 2002 Annual Report*, p. 49.
54. Shope (2003).
55. Marcy (September 22, 2002).
56. Hershey Estates was part of the reorganization led by Milton S. Hershey during the Depression. It was charged with administering all the non-chocolate interests in the town; including the Hershey department store, the nursery and greenhouse, its water, electricity, laundry, hospital, sewer, and transit authorities, the Hershey Park, and all other public buildings. At the time of this reorganization, Hershey Estates and the Hershey Chocolate Company as well as its sugar company were held together by the Hershey Trust Company, which, as trustee for the School, owned and operated all three interests. In 1980, HERCO, Inc., became Hershey Entertainment and Resorts Company to better describe the change in focus over the years.
57. *www.friendsofhershey.org* (October 9, 2003).
58. *Ibid.*
59. Shope (2003).
60. *Ibid.*
61. Marcy (September 22, 2002).
62. Helyar (2002).
63. B. Marcy and P. Decoursey, "Hershey Sale Off," *Patriot-News* (September 18, 2002).
64. D. Ackman, "Hershey Says No; Bankers Cry Foul," *Forbes.com* (September 18, 2002).
65. *Ibid.*
66. Marcy (September 22, 2002).
67. The accounts of the board meeting were based on the June 3, 2005, interview with Robert Vowler. See also B. Marcy, "Hershey Trust's CEO Says Three Criteria, Not Protests, Drove Decision," *Knight Ridder Tribune Business News* (September 19, 2002).

CASE 30

Panera Bread Company: Rising Fortunes?

Ted Repetti and Joyce P. Vincelette

BREAD, ESSENTIAL AND BASIC, BUT NONETHELESS SPECIAL, TRANSCENDS MILLENNIA. A master baker combines simple ingredients to create what has been an integral part of society and culture for over 6,000 years. Sourdough bread, a uniquely American creation, is made from a "culture," or "starter." Sourdough starter contains natural yeasts, flour, and water and is the medium that makes bread rise. In order to survive, a starter must be cultured, fed, and tended to by attentive hands in the right environment. Without proper care and maintenance, the yeast, or the growth factor, would slow down and die. Without a strong starter, bread would no longer rise.

Ronald Shaich, CEO and Chairman of Panera Bread Company, created the company's "starter." Shaich, the master baker, combined the ingredients and cultivated the leavening agent that catalyzed the company's phenomenal growth. Under Shaich's guidance, Panera's total systemwide (both company and franchisee) revenues rose from $350.8 million in 2000 to $977.1 million in 2003. However, new unit expansion fueled this growth. In total, 419 Panera bakery-cafes were opened between 1999 and 2003. New unit growth masked a slowdown in the growth of average annualized unit volumes (AUVs) and year-to-year comparable sales. In 2000, systemwide comparable sales and AUVs increased 9.1% and 12.0%, respectively. Growth of these two key metrics declined in each consecutive year thereafter. In 2003, systemwide comparable sales and AUVs increased only 0.2% and 0.5%. Clearly, growth has slowed. In order to continue to rise, Panera's "starter" needs to be fed and maintained. In addition to new unit growth, new strategies and initiatives must be folded into the mix.

History

Panera Bread Company's roots began with the company that could be considered the grandfather of the fast casual restaurant concept: Au Bon Pain. In 1976, French oven manufacturer Pavailler opened the first Au Bon Pain (a French colloquialism for "where good bread is") in Boston's Faneuil Hall as a demonstration bakery.[1] Struck by its growth potential, Louis Kane, a veteran venture capitalist, purchased the business in 1978.[2] Between 1978 and 1981, Au Bon Pain struggled; it had opened 13 and subsequently closed 10 stores in the Boston area and piled up $3 million in debt.[3] Kane was ready to declare bankruptcy when he gained a new business partner in Ronald Shaich.[4]

A recent Harvard Business graduate, Shaich had opened the Cookie Jar bakery in Cambridge, Massachusetts, in 1980.[5] Shortly after opening the Cookie Jar, Shaich befriended Louis Kane. Shaich was interested in adding bread and croissants to his menu to stimulate his morning sales. Shaich recalled that "50,000 people a day were going past my store, and I had nothing to sell them in the morning."[6] In February 1981, the two merged the Au Bon Pain bakeries and the cookie store to form one business, Au Bon Pain Co., Inc. The two served as Co-CEOs until Kane's retirement in 1994. They had a synergistic relationship that made Au Bon Pain successful: Shaich was the hard-driving, analytical strategist focused on operations, and Kane was the seasoned businessman with a wealth of real estate and finance connections.[7] Between 1981 and 1984, the team expanded the business, worked to decrease the company's debt, and centralized facilities for dough production.[8]

In 1985, the partners added sandwiches to bolster daytime sales, as they noticed a pattern in customer behavior: "We had all of these customers coming and ordering a baguette cut in half. Then they'd take out these lunch bags full of cold cuts and start making sandwiches. We didn't have to be marketing whizzes to know that there was an opportunity there," recalled Shaich.[9] It was a "eureka" moment and the birth of the fast casual restaurant category.[10] According to Shaich, Au Bon Pain was the "first place that gave white collar folks a choice between fast food and fine dining."[11] Au Bon Pain became a lunchtime alternative for urban dwellers who were tired of burgers and fast food. Differentiated from other fast food competitors by its commitment to fresh, quality sandwiches, bread, and coffee, Au Bon Pain attracted customers who were happy to pay more money ($5 per sandwich) than they would have paid for fast food.[12]

In 1991, Kane and Shaich took the company public. By that time, the company had $68 million in sales and was a leader in the quick service bakery segment. By 1994, the company had 200 stores and $183 million in sales, but that growth masked a problem. The company was built on a limited growth concept, what Shaich called, "high density urban feeding."[13] The main customers of the company were office workers in locations like New York, Boston, and Washington, DC. The real estate in such areas was expensive and hard to come by. This strategic factor limited expansion possibilities.[14]

Au Bon Pain acquired the St. Louis Bread Company in 1993 for $24 million.[15] Shaich saw this as the company's "gateway into the suburban marketplace."[16] The acquired company was founded in 1987 by Ken Rosenthal and consisted of a 19-store bakery-cafe chain located in the St. Louis area. The concept of the cafe was based on San Franciscan sourdough bread bakeries.[17] The acquired company would eventually become the platform for what is now Panera.

Au Bon Pain management spent two years studying St. Louis Bread Co., looking for the ideal concept that would unite Au Bon Pain's operational abilities and quality food with the broader suburban growth appeal of St. Louis Bread.[18] Scott Davis, Panera's Chief Concept Officer, recalled the time spent trying to figure out what the new business should look like. "We didn't just look at restaurants and coffee houses," he stated. "We spent a lot of time looking at retailers. That's where our front-of-the-house bakery displays came from. We knew that people buy with their eyes, so we wanted them to walk in and crave baked goods."[19]

The restaging and development of the St. Louis Bread Co. concept was also affected by the management team's understanding of a consumer backlash against the commoditization of food service—a trend that began in the 1950s and spawned a coast-to-coast sameness (e.g., McDonald's).[20] The management team understood that a growing number of consumers wanted a unique expression of tastes and styles. Shaich and his team wrote a manifesto that spelled out what St. Louis Bread would be, from the type of food it would serve to the kind of people behind the counters and the look and feel of the physical space.[21]

Au Bon Pain began pouring capital into the chain when Shaich had another "eureka" moment in 1995. He entered a St. Louis Bread store and noticed a group of business people meeting in a corner. The customers explained that they had no other place to talk.[22] This experience opened Shaich's eyes to the fact that the potential of the neighborhood bakery-cafe concept was greater than that of Au Bon Pain's urban store concept. The bakery-cafe concept capitalized on a confluence of current trends: the welcoming atmosphere of coffee shops, the food of sandwich shops, and the quick service of fast food.[23]

While Au Bon Pain was focusing on making St. Louis Bread a viable national brand, the company's namesake unit was faltering. Rapid expansion of its urban outlets had resulted in operational problems, bad real estate deals,[24] and debt over $65 million.[25] Operating margins were on a steady decline. For example, from 1993 to 1994, margins fell from 11.5% to 8.5%.[26] Margins continued to contract because of higher food costs, stagnant sales, and decreased comparable store sales. Stiff competition from bagel shops and coffee chains such as Starbucks compounded operational difficulties. Another concern was that the fast food ambiance of the stores was not appealing to customers who wanted to sit and enjoy a meal or a cup of coffee.[27] On the other hand, the cafe-style atmosphere of St. Louis Bread, which was known as Panera (Latin for "time for bread") outside the St. Louis area, was proving to be successful. In 1996, comparable sales at Au Bon Pain locations declined 3%, while same-store sales in the Panera unit were up 10%.[28]

Lacking the capital to overhaul the ambiance of the Au Bon Pain segment, the company decided to sell the unit. This left the company the time and resources to strategically focus solely on the more successful Panera chain. Unlike Au Bon Pain, Panera was not confined to a small urban niche and had greater growth potential. Panera's per-store profit of $1.3 million over Au Bon Pain's $1 million (at the time of the sale) also proved more promising. On May 16, 1999, Shaich sold the Au Bon Pain unit to investment firm Bruckman, Sherrill, and Co. for $73 million. At the time of the divestiture, the company changed its corporate name to Panera Bread Company. The sale left Panera Bread Company debt-free, and the cash allowed for the immediate expansion of its bakery-cafe stores.[29]

General Business

From what was once a small chain acquired by Au Bon Pain, Panera Bread Company grew into the leader in the fast casual dining industry. The Panera concept combined and exploited several food service qualities: (1) the casual atmosphere of coffee shops, (2) the quality food of sandwich shops, and (3) the quick service of fast food chains. The company specialized in meeting five consumer-dining needs: breakfast, lunch, daytime "chill-out," lunch in the evening, and take-home bread. Daytime chill-out is the time between breakfast and lunch and between lunch and dinner when customers stop in to take a break from their daily activities. This niche of consumers included seniors, matineegoers, shoppers, business and sales people, and students.[30] Panera provided diners with high-quality foods, including fresh baked goods, made-to-order sandwiches on fresh baked breads, soups, salads, custom roasted coffees, and other cafe beverages. Panera targeted suburban dwellers and workers by offering a premium specialty bakery and cafe experience with a neighborhood emphasis.[31] Panera was the first in the bakery-cafe segment, and its unique concept and operational strengths led it to its leading position in the fast casual dining category.

Panera's concept was designed around meeting the needs and desires of consumers, specifically the need for efficient, time-saving service and the desire for a higher-quality dining experience—something not delivered by traditional fast food chains. The company's goal was to make Panera Bread a nationally dominant brand. Its menu, quality of operations, and design and real estate strategies were vital to the company's success.

Fast Casual

Panera's predecessor Au Bon Pain was a pioneer of the fast casual restaurant category. Fast casual, also known as quick casual, emerged to fill the gap between fast food and full-service restaurants. Technomic Information Services originally coined the term to describe restaurants that offer the speed, efficiency, and inexpensiveness of fast food with the hospitality, quality, and ambiance of a full-service restaurant. Technomic defined a fast casual restaurant by whether it met the following four criteria. *One*, the restaurant had to offer a limited-service or self-service format. *Two*, the average check had to be between $6 and $9, whereas fast food checks averaged less than $5. This pricing scheme placed fast casual between fast food and casual dining. The *third* criterion was that the food had to be made-to-order. Consumers perceived newly prepared, made-to-order foods as fresh. Fast casual menus usually also had more robust and complex flavor profiles than the standard fare at fast food restaurants. The *fourth* criterion required that the decor had to be upscale or highly developed. Decor inspired a more enjoyable experience for the customer as the environment of fast casual restaurants was more akin to that of a neighborhood bistro or casual restaurant. The decor also created a generally higher perception of quality.[32]

The fast casual market had enjoyed double-digit aggregate growth since 1999 and was expected to continue to grow by double digit figures.[33] Fast casual chain sales were expected to reach $50 billion in the next decade.[34] This large growth in fast casual was expected to come at the expense of the fast food industry.

Diverse dining offerings and higher profitability contributed to the industry's growth. Food concepts within the fast casual category ranged from Mexican, to bakeries, to Chinese. Unlike fast food restaurants that construct stand-alone stores, fast casual chains locate in strip malls, on small-town main streets, and in preexisting properties. As a result, the opening costs of a fast casual store are about a third of its average annual sales volume of $1.5 million.[35] The diversity and profitability of fast casual allowed many new players to enter the market offering new concepts and menu items.

The maturation of two large segments of the U.S. population, baby boomers and their children, was largely responsible for the growth in fast casual. Both segments had little time for cooking and grew tired of fast food, and they desired a high-quality, fresher, healthier dining experience, but did not have the time for a full dining experience. Dining trends caused fast casual to emerge as a legitimate trend in the restaurant industry as it bridged the gap between casual dining and the burgers-and-fries fast food industry.

Corporate Governance

Panera's corporate headquarters was located in St. Louis, Missouri.

Board of Directors

Shaich was the only internal board member. The biographical sketches for the board members are shown below[36]:

> ***Ronald M. Shaich*** *(age 50), Director since 1981, Co-Founder, Chairman of the Board since May 1999, Co-Chairman of the Board from January 1988 to May 1999, Chief Executive Officer since May 1994, and Co-Chief Executive Officer from January 1988 to May 1994. Shaich has served as a Director of Lown Cardiovascular Research Foundation.*

Larry J. Franklin *(age 55), Director since June 2001. Franklin has been the President and Chief Executive Officer of Franklin Sports, Inc., a leading branded sporting goods manufacturer and marketer, since 1986. Franklin joined Franklin Sports, Inc., in 1970 and served as its Executive Vice President from 1981 to 1986. Franklin has served on the Board of Directors of Bradford Soap International, Inc., The Sporting Goods Manufacturers Association, The Retail Industry Leadership Association, and The New England Chapter of the Juvenile Diabetes Research Foundation.*

Fred K. Foulkes *(age 62), Director since June 2003. Professor Foulkes has been a Professor of Organizational Behavior and the Director of the Human Resources Policy Institute at Boston University School of Management since 1981 and has taught courses in human resource management and strategic management at Boston University since 1980. From 1968 to 1980, Professor Foulkes was a member of the Harvard Business School faculty. Foulkes has served on the Board of Directors of Bright Horizons Family Solutions and the Society for Human Resource Management Foundation.*

Domenic Colasacco *(age 55), Director since March 2000. Colasacco has been President and Chief Executive Officer of Boston Trust & Investment Management, a trust company formed under Massachusetts state law, since 1992. He joined Boston Trust in 1974, after beginning his career in the research division of Merrill Lynch & Co. in New York City.*

Thomas E. Lynch *(age 44), Director since June 2003. Lynch has been a Senior Managing Director of Mill Road Associates, a financial advisory firm that he founded in 2000. From 1997 through 2000, Lynch was the founder and Managing Director of Lazard Capital Partners, a private equity firm affiliated with the investment bank Lazard. From 1990 to 1997, Lynch was a Managing Director at the Blackstone Group, where he was a senior investment professional for Blackstone Capital Partners. Prior to Blackstone, Lynch was a senior consultant at the Monitor Company. Lynch has served on the Board of the City Center.*

George E. Kane *(age 99), Director since November 1988. Kane was also a company Director from December 1981 to December 1985 and a Director Emeritus from December 1985 to November 1988. Kane retired in 1970 as President of Garden City Trust Company (now University Trust Company) and served as an Honorary Director of University Trust Company from December 1985 to January 2000. Kane became a nonvoting Honorary Director Emeritus after May 2004.*

The Compensation Committee included Franklin, Foulkes, and Colasacco. The Committee on Nominations included Franklin, Lynch, and Kane. The Audit Committee included Foulkes, Colasacco, Lynch, and Kane.

Directors who were not employees received a quarterly fee ranging from $3,000 to $3,500 for serving on the Board, plus reimbursement of out-of-pocket expenses for attendance at each Board or committee meeting. Under the Directors' Plan, each Director who is not an employee or a principal stockholder received a one-time grant of an option to purchase 10,000 shares of Class A Common Stock when he or she was first elected. Each independent Director in office at the end of the fiscal year also received an option to purchase an additional 10,000 shares of Class A Common Stock.

Exhibit 1 shows the common stock ownership in the company. There were two classes of stock: (1) Class A Stock with 28,345,754 shares outstanding and one vote per share, and (2) Class B Common Stock with 1,761,521 shares outstanding and three votes per share.

Top Management

Key Executive Officers of Panera who did not also serve on the Board (as did Shaich) were as follows[37]:

Paul E. Twohig *(age 50), Executive Vice President, Chief Operating Officer since January 2003. From 1993 to 2003, Twohig served as an executive at Starbucks Coffee Company, most recently as*

Exhibit 1 Stock Ownership: Panera Bread Company

Name and, with Respect to Owner of More Than 5%, Address	Class A Common		Class B Common		Combined Voting Percentage
	Number	Percent	Number	Percent	
Ronald M. Shaich c/o Panera Bread Company 6710 Clayton Road Richmond Heights, MO 63117	601,660	2.1%	1,666,381	94.6%	16.5%
Domenic Colasacco	48,862	<1%	—	—	<1%
Larry J. Franklin	40,000	<1%	—	—	<1%
George E. Kane	45,912	<1%	—	—	<1%
Fred K. Foulkes	24,000	<1%	—	—	<1%
Thomas E. Lynch	20,000	<1%	—	—	<1%
Paul E. Twohig	1,000	<1%	—	—	<1%
Mark A. Borland	—	—	—	—	—
Michael E. Hood	—	—	—	—	—
Michael J. Nolan	—	—	—	—	—
All directors, director nominees, and executive officers as a group (14 persons)	818,771	2.8%	1,666,381	94.6%	17.0%
Brown Capital Management, Inc. 1201 N. Calvert Street Baltimore, MD 21202	2,014,695	7.1%	—	—	6.0%
FMR Corp 82 Devonshire Street Boston, MA 02109	4,209,696	17.9%	—	—	12.5%

Source: Panera Bread Company, Inc., 2004 Notice of Annual Meeting of Stockholders, *pp. 16–17.*

Senior Vice President responsible for retail operations development and human resources for more than 1,200 Starbucks stores in 17 states and 5 Canadian provinces. From 1986 to 1991, Twohig was a franchisee and owned and operated four Burger King units in West Palm Beach, Florida. From 1968 to 1986, Twohig was with Burger King Corporation, serving in a variety of roles, including regional manager in New England.

***Neal J. Yanofsky** (age 46), Executive Vice President, Chief Administrative Officer, and Corporate Staff Officer since June 2003. From June 1999 to June 2003, Yanofsky was an independent business consultant with a practice focused on strategy development for high-growth firms, including Panera. From April 1990 to June 1999, Yanofsky was Vice President of Fidelity Ventures, the private equity arm of Fidelity Investments, and served in additional capacities with Fidelity Capital, including Chief Financial Officer at Boston Coach.*

***Mark A. Borland** (age 51), Senior Vice President, Chief Supply Chain Officer since August 2002. Borland joined the company in 1986 and held management positions within Au Bon Pain and Panera Bread divisions until 2000, including Executive Vice President, Vice President of Retail Operations, Chief Operating Officer, and President of Manufacturing Services. From 2000 to 2001, Borland served as Senior Vice President of Operations at RetailDNA and then rejoined Panera as a consultant in the summer of 2001.*

***Scott G. Davis** (age 40), Senior Vice President, Chief Concept Officer since May 1999. Davis joined the company in 1987 and from May 1996 to May 1999 served as Vice President, Customer Experience. From June 1994 to May 1996, Davis served as Director of Concept Services and Customer Experience.*

***Mark E. Hood** (age 51), Senior Vice President, Chief Financial Officer since April 2003. Hood joined the company in August 2002, and from August 2002 to April 2003 served as Senior Vice President, Finance and Administration. From August 2000 to April 2002, Hood served as the*

Chief Financial and Administrative Officer of the U.S. Loyalty Corporation. From June 1995 to September 1999, Hood served as an executive at Saks Fifth Avenue, most recently as Executive Vice President and Chief Financial and Administrative Officer. Prior to joining Saks, Hood held a number of financial positions with the May Department Stores Co. from 1983 to 1995.

***Michael J. Kupstas** (age 46), Senior Vice President, Chief Franchise Officer since September 2001. Kupstas joined the company in 1996. Between August 1999 and September 2001, Kupstas served as Vice President, Franchising and Brand Communication. Between January 1996 and August 1999, Kupstas was Vice President, Company and Franchise Operations. Between April 1991 and January 1996, Kupstas was Senior Vice President/Division Vice President for Long John Silver's, Inc.*

***John M. Maguire** (age 38), Senior Vice President, Chief Company and Joint Venture Operations Officer since August 2001. Maguire joined the company in April 1993. From April 2000 to July 2001, Maguire served as Vice President, Bakery Operations. From November 1998 to March 2000, Maguire served as Vice President, Commissary Operations. From April 1993 to October 1998, Maguire was a Manager and Director of Au Bon Pain/Panera Bread/St. Louis Bread.*

***Michael J. Nolan** (age 44), Senior Vice President, Chief Development Officer since he joined the company in August 2001. From December 1997 to March 2001, Nolan served as Executive Vice President & Director for John Harvard's Brew House, L.L.C., and Senior Vice President, Development, for American Hospitality Concepts, Inc. From March 1996 to December 1997, Nolan was Vice President of Real Estate & Development for Apple South Incorporated, and from July 1989 to March 1996, Nolan was Vice President of Real Estate and Development for Morrison Restaurants Inc. Prior to 1989, Nolan served in various real estate and development capacities for Cardinal Industries, Inc., and Nolan Development and Investment.*

Exhibit 2 shows the executive compensation for the five highest-paid principal executives.

Exhibit 2 Summary Compensation Table for Executives: Panera Bread Company

		Annual Compensation			Long-Term Compensation
Name of Principal Position(s)	**Year**	**Salary ($)**	**Bonus ($)**	**Other Annual Compensation ($)**	**Securities Underlying Options (#)**
Ronald M. Shaich	2003	397,616	—	$49,881[2]	100,000
Chairman and Chief	2002	331,500	—[1]	$144,909[2]	40,000
Executive Officer	2001	338,000	375,000	—	—
Paul E. Twohig	2003	306,250	68,250	—	50,000
Executive Vice President,	2002	—	—	—	130,000
Chief Operating Officer	2001	—	—	—	—
Mark A. Borland	2003	238,462	47,304	—	—
Senior Vice President,	2002	120,536	30,777	—	50,000
Chief Supply Chain Officer	2001	—	—	—	—
Mark E. Hood	2003	243,365	35,551	—	5,000
Senior Vice President,	2002	83,077	18,300	—	80,000
Chief Financial Officer	2001	—	—	—	—
Michael J. Nolan	2003	238,462	51,684	—	5,000
Senior Vice President,	2002	196,153	40,000	—	—
Chief Development Officer	2001	6,539	15,821	—	80,000

Notes:
1. Shaich declined his $375,000 bonus for 2002 earned under the bonus plan approved by the Compensation Committee, in light of the chartered plane benefits he received during 2002.
2. Shaich received $144,909 in personal chartered air travel (based on the aggregate incremental cost of such travel to Panera), $5,500 in matching contributions to the 401(k) plan, and $1,947 in life insurance premiums.

Source: Panera Bread Company, Inc., 2004 Notice of Annual Meeting of Stockholders, *p. 10.*

Concept and Strategy[38]

The company's concept focused on the Specialty Bread/Bakery-Cafe category. Its artisan breads, which were breads made with all-natural ingredients and an artisan's attention to quality and detail, and overall award-winning bakery expertise were at the heart of the concept's menu. The concept was designed to deliver against the key consumer trends, specifically the need for a responsive and more special dining experience than that offered by traditional fast food. The company's goal was to make Panera Bread a nationally dominant brand name. Its menu, prototype, operating systems, design, and real estate strategy allowed it to compete successfully in several sub-businesses: breakfast, lunch, PM chill-out, lunch in the evening, and take-home bread. On a systemwide basis, annualized AUVs increased 0.7%, to $1,852,000, for the 52 weeks ended December 27, 2003, compared to $1,840,000 for the 52 weeks ended December 28, 2002 (see **Exhibit 3**).

Exhibit 3 Selected Financial Information: Panera Bread Company (Dollar amounts in thousands)

A. Systemwide Bakery-Cafe Revenues

	For Fiscal Year Ending			
	December 27, 2003	December 28, 2002	December 29, 2001	December 30, 2000
Systemwide	$977,100	$755,400	$529,400	$350,800

B. Year-to-Year Comparable Sales

	Fifty-Two Weeks Ending				
	December 27, 2003	December 28, 2002	December 29, 2001	December 30, 2000	December 25, 1999
Company-owned	1.7%	4.1%	5.8%	8.1%	3.3%
Franchise-operated	–0.4%	6.1%	5.8%	10.3%	2.0%
Systemwide	0.2%	5.5%	5.8%	9.1%	2.9%

C. Annualized Unit Volume (AUVs)

	For Fiscal Year Ending				
	December 27, 2003	December 28, 2002	December 29, 2001	December 30, 2000	December 25, 1999
Company-owned	$1,831,000	$1,764,000	$1,636,000	$1,471,000	$1,330,000
Franchise-operated	$1,860,000	$1,871,000	$1,800,000	$1,710,000	$1,568,000
Systemwide	$1,850,000	$1,840,000	$1,748,000	$1,617,000	$1,444,000

D. Year Percentage Change in AUVs

	For Fiscal Year Ending			
	December 27, 2003	December 28, 2002	December 29, 2001	December 30, 2000
Company-owned	3.8%	7.8%	11.2%	10.6%
Franchise-operated	–0.6%	3.9%	5.3%	9.1%
Systemwide	0.5%	5.3%	8.1%	12.0%

Sources: Panera Bread Company, Inc., Media Kit *and* 1999 Form 10-K *through* 2003 Form 10-K.

Exhibit 4 Company-Owned and Franchise-Operated Bakery-Cafes: Panera Bread Company

	For Fiscal Year Ending				
	December 27, 2003	December 28, 2002	December 29, 2001	December 30, 2000	December 25, 1999
Number of bakery-cafes:[1]					
Company-owned:					
Beginning of period	132	110	90	81	70
Bakery-cafes opened	29	23	21	11	12
Acquired from franchisee	15	3	—	—	—
Bakery-cafes closed	(3)	(4)	(1)	(2)	(1)
End of period	173	132	110	90	81
Franchise operated:					
Beginning of period	346	259	172	102	47
Bakery-cafes opened	102	92	88	70	56
Sold to company[2]	(15)	(3)	—	—	—
Bakery-cafes closed	(4)	(2)	(1)	—	(1)
End of period	429	346	259	172	102
System-wide:					
Beginning of period	361	252	145	66	—
Bakery-cafes opened	131	115	109	81	68
Bakery-cafes closed	(7)	(6)	(2)	(2)	(2)
End of period	485	361	252	145	66

Notes:
1. Includes majority-owned.
2. In January 2002, the company purchased the area development rights and 3 existing bakery-cafes in the Jacksonville, Florida, market from franchisees. During fiscal 2003, the company acquired 15 operating bakery-cafes' area development rights in the Louisville/Lexington, Kentucky; Dallas, Texas; Toledo, Ohio; and Ann Arbor, Michigan, markets from franchisees.

Sources: Panera Bread Company, Inc., 2003 Form 10-K, *p. 2, and* 2001 Form 10-K, *pp. 2–3.*

The distinctive nature of the company's menu offerings, the quality of its bakery-cafe operations, the company's signature cafe design, and the prime locations of its cafes were integral to the company's success. The company believed its concept had significant growth potential, which it hoped to realize through a combination of company and franchise efforts. Franchising was a key component of the company's success. Utilization of franchise operating partners enabled the company to grow more rapidly because of the added resources and capabilities they provided to implement the concepts and strategy developed by Panera. As of December 27, 2003, there were 429 franchised bakery-cafes operating and signed commitments to open an additional 409 bakery-cafes. In addition, there were 173 wholly or majority-owned company bakery-cafes operating at December 27, 2003. **Exhibit 4** shows the number of bakery-cafes for the last five years.

Competition[39]

The company experienced competition from numerous sources in its trade areas. The company's bakery-cafes competed based on customers' needs for breakfast, lunch, daytime chill-out, lunch in the evening, and take-home bread sales. The competitive factors included location, environment, customer service, price, and quality of products. The company competed for leased space in desirable locations. Certain competitors had capital resources that exceeded those available to the company. Primary competitors included specialty food and casual dining restaurant retailers, including national, regional, and locally owned concepts.

Menu[40]

The menu was designed to provide the company's target customers with products that built on the strength of the company's bakery expertise and met customers' new and ever-changing tastes. The key menu groups were fresh baked goods, made-to-order sandwiches, soups, and cafe beverages. Included within these menu groups were a variety of freshly baked bagels, breads, muffins, scones, rolls, and sweet goods; made-to-order sandwiches; hearty, unique soups; and custom roasted coffees and cafe beverages such as hot or cold espresso and cappuccino drinks. The company's concept emphasized the sophisticated specialty and artisan breads that supported a take-home bread business.

The company regularly reviewed and revised its menu offerings to satisfy changing customer preferences and to maintain customer interest within its target customer groups, the "bread loving trend-setters" and the "bread loving traditionalists." Both of these target customer groups sought a quality experience that reflected their discriminating tastes. The major characteristic that set these two groups apart was the more enthusiastic embrace of new and nutritional menu items by the *trend-setters*. New menu items were developed in test kitchens and then introduced in a limited number of the company's bakery-cafes to determine customer response and verify that preparation and operating procedures maintained product consistency, high quality standards, and profitability. If successful, they were then introduced in the rest of the company's bakery-cafes and franchise bakery-cafes.

Franchises[41]

Panera management believed that its specialty bakery-cafe concept had significant growth potential, which it hoped to realize through a combination of owned, franchised, and joint venture–operated stores. Franchising was a key component of the company's growth strategy. Expansion through franchise partners had enabled the company to grow more rapidly as the franchisees contributed the resources and capabilities necessary to implant the concepts and strategies developed by Panera.

The company began a broad-based franchising program in 1996. The company was actively seeking to extend its franchise relationships beyond its current franchisees and annually filed a Uniform Franchise Offering Circular to facilitate sales of additional franchise development agreements. The company offered two types of franchise opportunities: independent third-party franchisees and Area Development Agreements (ADAs). ADAs transferred all development rights within a specified geographic area to the owner of that contract and required the developer to adhere to a predetermined development time line. Franchisees were required to develop a specified number of bakery-cafes on or before specific dates. If franchisees failed to develop bakery-cafes on schedule, the company had the right to terminate the ADA and to develop company-owned locations or develop locations through new ADA developers in that market.

The franchise agreement typically required the payment of an up-front franchise fee of $35,000 (broken down into $5,000 at the signing of the ADA and $30,000 at or before the bakery-cafe opened) and continuing royalties of 4%–5% on sales from each bakery-cafe.

Franchise-operated bakery-cafes followed the same standards for product quality, menu, site selection, and bakery-cafe construction as did company-owned bakery-cafes. The franchisees were required to purchase all of their dough products from sources approved by the company. The company's fresh dough facility system supplied fresh dough products to most franchise-operated bakery-cafes. The company did not finance franchisee construction or ADA purchases. In addition, the company did not hold an equity interest in any of the franchised bakery-cafes.

The company had entered into franchise ADAs with 32 franchisee groups as of December 27, 2003. Also, as of December 27, 2003, there were 429 franchised bakery-cafes open and commitments to open 409 additional franchised bakery-cafes (see **Exhibit 5**). The company did not have any international franchise development agreements.

The high volume of franchise applicants allowed Panera to be very selective in granting franchises. Panera preferred executives with retail and restaurant franchising experience. The

Exhibit 5
Panera Bread/St. Louis Bread Co. Bakery-Cafes

State	Company Bakery-Cafes	Franchise-Operated Bakery-Cafes	Total Bakery-Cafes
Alabama	4	—	4
Arkansas	—	2	2
California	—	5	5
Colorado	—	14	14
Connecticut	1	4	5
Delaware	—	1	1
Florida	5	43	48
Georgia	8	6	14
Iowa	—	13	13
Illinois	34	32	66
Indiana	3	15	18
Kansas	—	14	14
Kentucky	4	1	5
Massachusetts	2	18	20
Maryland	—	18	18
Maine	—	2	2
Michigan	32	8	40
Minnesota	—	20	20
Missouri	36	16	52
North Carolina	1	17	18
Nebraska	—	7	7
Nevada	—	2	2
New Hampshire	—	7	7
New Jersey	—	25	25
New York	5	3	8
Ohio	6	55	61
Oklahoma	—	15	15
Pennsylvania	7	27	34
Rhode Island	—	3	3
South Carolina	—	2	2
Tennessee	1	9	10
Texas	2	9	11
Virginia	20	1	21
West Virginia	—	2	2
Wisconsin	—	15	15
Totals	173	429	602

Source: Panera Bread Company, Inc., 2003 Form 10-K, *p. 8.*

company chose only very strong and capable franchising partners, many of whom had experience with well-known chains, such as McDonald's and Burger King.[42] Franchisees needed to have access to financing since the company did not finance franchisee construction or ADA purchases.

Panera also saw potential in implementing a joint venture structure as an alternative to company-owned or franchised bakery-cafes to facilitate the development and operation of bakery-cafes. Unlike with franchise agreements, Panera was the major financier (where a specified interest is invested by the joint venture partner) of the bakery-cafes and earned revenues from operations. The joint venture partner managed the bakery-cafes and was entitled to a specified percentage of cash flows. The joint venture agreements forbade the partner from transferring or selling its interest to another party without the consent of Panera. After a specified term, the company had the right to purchase the joint venture partner's interest at a determined value, and the joint venture partner had the right to sell its interest back to the company at a lower value. The company saw the joint venture structure as an opportunity to attract and retain experienced and motivated operators who would want the opportunity to participate in the success of the bakery-cafes.

In 2001, Richard Postle, Panera's former Chief Operating Officer and President, left the company and through an indirect subsidiary entered into a joint venture agreement to develop 50 bakery-cafes in northern Virginia and central Pennsylvania. Under this agreement, there were 27 bakery-cafes operating in these markets at December 27, 2003. After October 2006, the company and the minority-interest owner would each have rights that could, if exercised, permit/require the company to purchase the bakery-cafes at contractually determined values based on multiples of cash flows.

Bakery Supply Chain[43]

According to Ronald Shaich, "Panera has a commitment to doing the best bread in America."[44] Freshly baked bread made with fresh dough was integral to honoring this commitment. Systemwide, bakery-cafes used fresh dough for sourdough and artisan breads and bagels. The company's fresh dough facility system supplied fresh dough to both company-owned and franchise-operated bakery-cafes daily. The company supplied both company-owned and franchise-operated bakery-cafes with fresh dough daily through its commissary system. The company's 16 commissaries (see **Exhibit 6**) prepared fresh, preservative-free dough daily.

The commissaries assured product quality and consistency at both company-owned and franchised bakery-cafes. Panera's master artisan baker, Mile Marino, had been with the company since 1987 and oversaw all baking operations at the fresh dough facilities. A fleet of 98 temperature-controlled trucks leased by Panera and driven by Panera employees distributed the fresh dough to bakery-cafes. The optimal distribution limit was approximately 200 miles. An average distribution route delivered dough to 6 bakery-cafes. The fresh dough was then baked overnight in a $50,000 stone-bottom oven, standard in all bakery-cafes.

The company focused its expansion in areas served by commissaries in order to continue to gain efficiencies through leveraging the fixed cost of its current commissary structure. Panera selectively entered new markets that required the construction of additional facilities until a sufficient number of bakery-cafes could be opened to permit efficient distribution of the fresh dough.

The remaining baked goods that were not prepared with fresh dough (sweet goods) were prepared with frozen dough. In 1996, the company constructed a state-of-the-art frozen dough facility in Mexico, Missouri. In 1998, the company sold the facility and its frozen dough business to Bunge Food Corporation for approximately $13 million in cash. At the time of the

Exhibit 6
Leased Fresh Dough Facilities: Panera Bread Company

Facility	Square Footage
Franklin, MA	40,300
Chicago, IL	30,900
Cincinnati, OH	14,000
Washington, DC (located in Beltsville, MD)	17,900
Warren, OH	16,300
St. Louis, MO	30,000
Orlando, FL	16,500
Atlanta, GA	18,000
Greensboro, NC	9,600
Kansas City, KS	17,000
Detroit, MI	13,500
Dallas, TX	7,800
Minneapolis, MN	8,900
Ontario, CA	13,900
Fairfield, NJ	20,200
Denver, CO	10,000

Source: Panera Bread Company, Inc., 2003 Form 10-K, *p. 8.*

sale, Panera entered into a five-year contract with Bunge for the supply of substantially all of its frozen dough. In November 2002, the company signed an agreement with Dawn Food Products, Inc., to prepare and deliver frozen dough from 2003 through 2007. The agreement was structured as a cost-plus agreement.

All frozen dough and related food materials were distributed to the bakery-cafes through independent distributors. Contract vendors delivered virtually all food products and supplies for retail operations (i.e. paper goods, coffee, smallwares) to the distributors, which then delivered to the individual bakery-cafes. Franchised bakery-cafes operated under individual contracts with either the company's distributor or other regional distributors. As of December 27, 2003, there were three primary distributors serving the Panera Bread system.

Marketing[45]

Panera did not rely heavily on advertising to promote its stores. In 2001, the company spent only $700,000 on media, a low 2.1% ad-to-sales ratio compared to the category average of 4%.[46] The company attempted to increase its per-location sales through menu development, product merchandising, and promotions at everyday prices and by sponsorship of local community charitable events. Advertising was intended to promote the company but not to create an identifiable image that would be synonymous with Panera, such as the McDonald's golden arches.

Franchised bakery-cafes contributed 0.4% of sales to a company-run national advertising fund and 0.4% of sales as a marketing administration fee and were required to spend 2.0% of sales in their local markets on advertising. The company contributed similar amounts from company-owned bakery-cafes toward the national advertising fund and marketing administration fee. The national advertising fund and marketing administration fee contributions received from franchised bakery-cafes were consolidated with company amounts in the company's financial statements. Liabilities for unexpended funds were included in accrued expenses in the consolidated balance sheets. The company's contributions to the national advertising fund and marketing administration fee, as well as its own media costs, were recorded as part of other operating expenses in the consolidated statements of operations. The company utilized external media when deemed appropriate and cost-effective in specific markets.

Most marketing was done through product promotion and word-of-mouth marketing. According to Shaich, "when a new store is opened in an established market, the new store benefits from the buzz and consumer familiarity created by existing locations."[47] This was akin to the "Krispy Kreme Phenomenon," which occurred when consumers greatly anticipated a new store opening in their neighborhood due to word-of-mouth praise for the quality of the food products.

Another way Panera used word-of-mouth marketing was through local charity and community work. Panera strove to add value to its surrounding neighborhoods through its products, service, employment opportunities, and citizenship and believed it had a responsibility to participate and sponsor local events. The company's most well-known program began in 1992. The "Operation Dough-Nation" program ensured that every purchase at Panera would give back in some way to the community. Cash donations could be made inside the store, with the amounts matched with fresh baked bread donated to local food drives. In addition, the company donated all unsold bread to local hunger relief agencies. The company's second community outreach program, "Dough for Funds," gave nonprofit groups a means to raise funds by profiting from the sales of Panera coupons.

The company did not compete on the basis of pricing only; its main selling point was its specialty dining experience. Yet pricing was key to promoting the company's concept. Pricing was structured so customers perceived good value with high-quality food at reasonable prices to encourage frequent visits. The company's average check per transaction at company-owned bakery-cafes for 2003 was $6.61. The average check per transaction varied by the time of day: breakfast, $4.86; lunch, $7.65; PM chill-out, $6.67; and lunch in the evening, $7.42 (see **Exhibit 7**).

The company used its store locations to market its brand image. When choosing a location to open a new store, the company carefully selected the geographic area. Better locations needed less marketing, and the bakery-cafe concept relied on a substantial volume of repeat business. Management used demographic and competitive information to identify areas with the best opportunity for success and that best promoted Panera's neighborhood concept. Location, real estate, and marketing teams worked in conjunction to select ideal locations. In evaluating a potential location, the company studied the surrounding trade area, obtained demographic information within that area, and examined information on breakfast and lunch competitors. Based on analysis of this information, including utilization of predictive modeling using proprietary software, the company determined projected sales and return on investment. The Panera concept had proven successful in a number of different types of real estate (i.e., in-line strip centers, regional malls, and freestanding) in 35 states.

The company also used the actual bakery-cafe as a marketing tool to promote its brand image. The company designed each bakery-cafe to provide a differentiated environment and

Exhibit 7
Average Check per Transaction: Panera Bread Company

	2003	2002	2001	2000	1999
Breakfast	$4.86	$4.49	$4.30	$4.03	$3.76
Lunch	7.65	7.32	7.26	6.89	6.41
PM "Chill Out"	6.67	6.30	5.39	N/A	N/A
Evening lunch	7.42	7.02	N/A	N/A	N/A
Overall	6.61	6.26	6.19	5.80	5.44

Sources: Panera Bread Company, Inc., 1999 Form 10-K *through* 2003 Form 10-K.

Exhibit 8
Average Opening Costs and Square Footage: Panera Bread Company

	2003	2002	2001	2000	1999
Opening Costs	$850,000	$737,000	$760,000	$700,000	$656,000
Square Footage	4,330	4,400	4,250	4,000	3,500

Sources: Panera Bread Company, Inc., 1999 Form 10-K *through* 2003 Form 10-K.

in many cases used fixtures and materials complementary to the neighborhood location of the bakery-cafe. Many locations incorporated the warmth of a fireplace and cozy seating areas and groupings that facilitated utilization as a gathering spot. The design visually reinforced the distinctive difference between the company's bakery-cafes and other bakery-cafes serving breakfast and lunch. Many of the company's cafes also featured outdoor cafe seating.

The average construction, equipment, furniture and fixture, and signage cost for the 29 company-owned bakery-cafes opened in 2003 was $850,000 per bakery-cafe after landlord allowances (see **Exhibit 8**). The average bakery-cafe size was 4,330 square feet (see **Exhibit 8**).

All company-owned bakery-cafes were in leased premises. Lease terms were typically 10 years, with one, two, or three 5-year renewal option periods thereafter. Leases typically had charges for minimum base occupancy, a proportionate share of building and common area operating expenses and real estate taxes, and contingent-percentage rent based on sales above a stipulated sales level.

Management Information Systems[48]

Each company-operated bakery-cafe had computerized cash registers to collect point-of-sale transaction data, which was used to generate pertinent marketing information, including product mix and average check. All product prices were programmed into the system from the company's corporate office. The company allowed franchisees who elected to do so to have access to certain proprietary bakery-cafe systems and systems support.

The company's in-store information system was designed to assist in labor scheduling and food cost management, to provide corporate and retail operations management quick access to retail data, and to reduce managers' administrative time. The system supplied sales, bank deposit, and variance data to the company's accounting department on a daily basis. The company used this data to generate weekly consolidated reports regarding sales and other key elements, as well as detailed profit and loss statements for each company-owned bakery-cafe every four weeks. Additionally, the company monitored the average check, customer count, product mix, and other sales trends. The fresh dough facilities had computerized systems that allowed the fresh dough facilities to accept electronic orders from the bakery-cafes and deliver the ordered product to the bakery-cafes. The company also used network/integration systems, encompassing e-mail and all major financial systems, such as general ledger database systems, and all major operational systems, such as store operating performance database systems.

Human Resources[49]

From the beginning, Panera realized that the quality of its employees was a critical part of a successful product and a unique company. It was the company's belief that the key ingredients in the successful development of Panera ranged from the type of food served to the kind of people behind the counters. Employees included full-time associates in general or administrative positions, commissary operators, bakers, and associates at the bakery-cafes. As of December 27, 2003, the company had 3,924 full-time associates (defined as associates who averaged 25 hours or more per week), of whom 344 were employed in general or administrative functions principally at or from the company's support centers (executive offices); 676 were employed in the company's fresh dough facility operations; and 2,904 were employed in the company's bakery-cafe operations as bakers, managers, and associates. The company also had 4,078 part-time hourly associates at the bakery-cafes. There were no collective bargaining agreements. The company considered its employee relations to be good. The company placed priority on staffing its bakery-cafes, fresh dough facilities, and support center operations with skilled associates and invested in training programs to ensure the quality of its operations. Incentive programs and bonuses were available to salaried employees. Employees also received product discounts and were invited to join employee stock ownership plans. Panera believed that providing bakery-cafe operators the opportunity to participate in the success of the bakery-cafe enabled the company to attract and retain experienced and highly motivated personnel, which resulted in a better customer experience. The company developed a program and began implementation in certain markets in 2003 to allow unit general managers and multi-unit managers to own a minority interest in a bakery-cafe. Prior to full implementation of the program, the company modified the program from an ownership structure to a multi-year bonus structure, which allowed operators to participate in the success of a bakery-cafe. The company expected to continue implementation of this bonus structure where appropriate as an alternative to its traditional company-owned or franchised bakery-cafes to facilitate the development and operation of bakery-cafes.

Finance[50]

Exhibits 9 through **11** show the consolidated statement of operations, common size income statement, and consolidated balance sheets, respectively, for the company for the fiscal years ended 1999 through 2003.

The company's revenues were derived from company-owned bakery-cafe sales, fresh dough sales to franchisees, and franchise royalties and fees. Fresh dough sales to franchisees were the sales of dough products to franchisees. Franchise royalties and fees included royalty income and franchise fees. The cost of food and paper products, labor, occupancy, and other operating expenses related to company-owned bakery-cafe sales. The cost of fresh dough sales related to the sale of fresh dough products and sweet goods to franchisees. General and administrative, depreciation, and pre-opening expenses related to all areas of revenue generation.

Systemwide bakery-cafe sales for the 52 weeks ended December 27, 2003, for the company increased 29.3%, to $977.1 million from $755.4 million, for the 52 weeks ended December 28, 2002. Comparable sales increases and increases in AUVs were lower during the 52 weeks ended December 27, 2003, than during the 52 weeks ended December 28, 2002 (**see Exhibit 3**).

Total company revenues for the 52 weeks ended December 27, 2003, increased 28.1%, to $355.9 million compared to $277.8 million, for the 52 weeks ended December 28, 2002 (**see Exhibit 9**). The growth in total revenues for the 52 weeks ended December 27, 2003, as compared to the prior year, was primarily due to the opening of 131 new bakery-cafes in 2003, as well as the increase in systemwide average weekly sales (excluding closed locations) of 0.7% for the 52 weeks ended December 27, 2003.

Bakery-cafe sales for the 52 weeks ended December 27, 2003, for the company increased 25.1%, to $265.9 million from $212.6 million, for the 52 weeks ended December 28, 2002. Bakery-cafe sales increased primarily due to the impact of a full year's operations of the 23

Exhibit 9 Consolidated Statement of Operations: Panera Bread Company (Dollar amounts in thousands, except per share information)

Year Ending	December 27, 2003	December 28, 2002	December 29, 2001
Revenues:			
Bakery-cafe sales	$265,933	$212,645	$157,684
Franchise royalties and fees	36,245	27,892	19,577
Fresh dough sales to franchisees	53,708	37,215	23,856
Total revenue	355,886	277,752	201,117
Costs and expenses:			
Bakery-cafe expenses:			
Cost of food and paper products	73,727	63,255	48,253
Labor	81,152	63,172	45,768
Occupancy	17,990	14,619	11,345
Other operating expenses	36,804	27,971	20,729
Total bakery-cafe expenses	209,673	169,017	126,095
Fresh dough cost of sales to franchisees	47,151	33,959	21,965
Depreciation and amortization	19,487	13,965	10,839
General and administrative expenses	28,140	24,986	19,589
Pre-opening expenses	1,531	1,051	912
Nonrecurring charge	—	—	—
Total costs and expenses	305,982	242,978	179,400
Operating profit	49,904	34,774	21,717
Interest expense	48	32	72
Other expense (income), net	1,227	287	213
Minority interest	365	180	8
Income before income taxes	48,264	34,275	21,424
Income taxes	17,616	12,510	8,272
Income (loss) before cumulative effect of accounting change and extraordinary items	30,648	21,765	13,152
Cumulative effect of accounting change, net	(239)	—	—
Extraordinary loss from early extinguishments of debt, net	—	—	—
Net Income (loss)	**$ 30,409**	**$ 21,765**	**$ 13,152**
Per share data:			
Basic earnings per common share:			
Before cumulative effect of accounting change	$ 1.03	$ 0.75	$ 0.47
Cumulative effect of accounting change	(0.01)	—	—
Net income (loss)	$ 1.02	$ 0.75	0.47
Diluted earnings per common share:			
Before cumulative effect of accounting change	$ 1.01	$ 0.73	$ 0.46
Cumulative effect of accounting change	(0.01)	—	—
Net income (loss)	$ 1.00	$ 0.73	$ 0.46
Weighted average shares of common and common equivalent shares outstanding:			
Basic	29,733	28,923	27,783
Diluted	30,423	29,891	28,886

Sources: Panera Bread Company, Inc., 2003 Form 10-K, *p. 30, and* 2001 Form 10-K, *p. 28.*

Exhibit 10 Common Size Statement: Panera Bread Company (Dollar amounts in thousands, except per share information)

Year Ending	December 27, 2003	December 28, 2002	December 29, 2001	December 30, 2000	December 25, 1999[1]
Revenues:					
Bakery-cafe sales	74.7%	76.6%	78.4%	82.9%	91.5%
Franchise royalties and fees	10.2%	10.0%	9.7%	8.0%	4.3%
Fresh dough sales to franchisees	15.1%	13.4%	11.9%	9.1%	4.2%
Total revenue	100.0%	100.0%	100.0%	100.0%	100.0%
Costs and expenses:					
Bakery-cafe expenses:[1]					
Cost of food and paper products	27.7%	29.7%	30.6%	32.7%	33.4%
Labor	30.5%	29.7%	29.0%	28.9%	29.0%
Occupancy	6.8%	6.9%	7.2%	7.4%	9.9%
Other operating expenses	13.8%	13.2%	13.1%	12.8%	12.9%
Total bakery-cafe expenses	78.8%	79.5%	80.0%	81.8%	84.3%
Fresh dough cost of sales to franchisees[2]	87.8%	91.3%	92.1%	88.6%	89.7%
Depreciation and amortization	5.5%	5.0%	5.4%	5.6%	3.7%
General and administrative expenses	7.9%	9.0%	9.7%	10.8%	10.0%
Pre-opening expenses	0.4%	0.4%	0.5%	0.3%	0.0%
Non-recuring charge	0.0%	0.0%	0.0%	0.3%	3.2%
Operating profit	14.0%	12.5%	10.8%	7.1%	2.2%
Interest expense	0.0%	0.0%	0.0%	0.1%	1.6%
Other expense (income), net	0.3%	0.1%	0.1%	(0.3%)	0.4%
Minority interest	0.1%	0.1%	0.0%	0.0%	0.0%
Income before income taxes	13.6%	12.3%	10.7%	7.3%	0.2%
Income taxes	4.9%	4.5%	4.1%	2.8%	0.3%
Income (loss) before cumulative effect of accounting change and extraordinary items	8.6%	7.8%	6.5%	4.5%	(0.1%)
Cumulative effect of accounting change, net	(0.1%)	0.0%	0.0%	0.0%	0.0%
Extraordinary loss from early extinguishments of debt, net	0.0%	0.0%	0.0%	0.0%	0.2%
Net Income (loss)	8.5%	7.8%	6.5%	4.5%	(0.4%)

Notes:
1. As a percentage of bakery-cafe sales.
2. As a percentage of fresh dough facility sales to franchisees.

Sources: Panera Bread Company, Inc., 2003 Form 10-K, *p. 14, and* 2001 Form 10-K, *pp. 12–13.*

company-owned bakery-cafes opened in 2002, the opening of 29 company-owned bakery-cafes in 2003, and the 1.7% increase in comparable bakery-cafe sales for the 52 weeks ended December 27, 2003.

Franchise royalties and fees rose 29.7%, to $36.2 million, for the 52 weeks ended December 27, 2003, from $27.9 million for the 52 weeks ended December 28, 2002. The increase in royalty revenue was attributed to the impact of a full year's operations of the 92 franchised bakery-cafes opened in 2002 and the addition of 102 franchised bakery-cafes in 2003.

Fresh dough facility sales to franchisees increased 44.4%, to $53.7 million, for the 52 weeks ended December 27, 2003, from $37.2 million for the 52 weeks ended December 28, 2002. The increase was primarily driven by the increased number of franchise bakery-cafes opened, as well as a shift in certain products being distributed through the fresh dough facility system rather than third parties.

The cost of food and paper products included the costs associated with the fresh dough operations that sell fresh dough products to company-owned bakery-cafes, as well as the cost of food and paper products supplied by third-party vendors and distributors. The costs associated with the fresh dough operations that sell fresh dough products to the franchised bakery-cafes were excluded and are shown separately as fresh dough cost of sales to franchisees in the consolidated statements of operations. The cost of food and paper products decreased to 27.7% of bakery-cafe sales for the 52 weeks ended December 27, 2003, compared to 29.7% of bakery-cafe sales for the 52 weeks ended December 28, 2002. This decrease in the cost of food and paper products as a percentage of bakery-cafe sales was primarily due to the company's improved leveraging of its fresh dough manufacturing and distribution costs as it opened more bakery-cafes in fiscal 2003. For the 52 weeks ended December 27, 2003, there was an average of 32.7 bakery-cafes per fresh dough facility compared to an average of 27.3 for the 52 weeks ended December 28, 2002. Additionally, lower ingredient costs, including the benefits of a new sweet goods contract that commenced during the first quarter of fiscal 2003, further benefited food cost.

Labor expense was $81.2 million, or 30.5% of bakery-cafe sales, for the 52 weeks ended December 27, 2003, compared to $63.2 million, or 29.7% of bakery-cafe sales, for the 52 weeks ended December 28, 2002. The labor expense as a percentage of bakery-cafe sales increased between the 52 weeks ended December 27, 2003, and the 52 weeks ended December 28, 2002, primarily as a result of customer service initiatives in fiscal 2003 related to quality and speed of service as well as table delivery service testing and the continued commitment to training and staffing at bakery-cafes.

Occupancy costs were $18.0 million, or 6.8% of bakery-cafe sales, for the 52 weeks ended December 27, 2003, compared to $14.6 million, or 6.9% of bakery-cafe sales, for the 52 weeks ended December 28, 2002. The occupancy cost as a percentage of bakery-cafe sales declined for the 52 weeks ended December 27, 2003, due to the leveraging of these costs over higher sales volumes.

Other bakery-cafe operating expenses, which included advertising, retail field overhead, utilities, and other cafe expenses, were $36.8 million, or 13.8% of bakery-cafe sales, for the 52 weeks ended December 27, 2003, compared to $28.0 million, or 13.2% of bakery-cafe sales, for the 52 weeks ended December 28, 2002. The increase in other bakery-cafe operating expenses as a percentage of bakery-cafe sales for the 52 weeks ended December 27, 2003, was primarily due to increased organizational costs for field management, costs associated with new markets opened that did not yet have multi-unit leverage, and increased recruiting and training, repair and maintenance, and advertising costs.

For the 52 weeks ended December 27, 2003, fresh dough facility cost of sales to franchisees was $47.2 million, or 87.8% of fresh dough facility sales to franchisees, compared to $34.0 million, or 91.3% of fresh dough facility sales to franchisees, for the 52 weeks ended December 28, 2002. The decrease in the fresh dough cost of sales rate in fiscal 2003 was pri-

Exhibit 11 Consolidated Balance Sheets: Panera Bread Company (Dollar amounts in thousands, except per share information)

Year Ending	December 27, 2003	December 28, 2002	December 29, 2001	December 30, 2000	December 25, 1999
ASSETS					
Current assets:					
Cash and cash equivalents	$ 42,402	$ 29,924	$ 18,052	$ 9,011	$ 1,936
Investments in government securities	5,019	4,102	—	—	—
Trade accounts receivable, net	9,646	7,462	4,559	3,105	2,686
Other accounts receivable	2,748	2,097	597	—	—
Inventories	8,066	5,191	3,459	2,442	1,880
Prepaid expenses	1,294	1,826	1,649	1,027	484
Refundable income taxes	—	—	—	474	98
Deferred income taxes	1,696	8,488	7,289	5,193	5,473
Other	—	172	399	—	—
Total current assets	70,871	59,262	36,004	21,252	12,557
Property and equipment, net	132,651	99,313	79,693	59,857	47,191
Other assets:					
Notes receivable	—	—	—	—	35
Investments in government securities	4,000	5,047	—	—	—
Goodwill	32,743	18,970	17,530	17,790	18,779
Deferred financing costs	—	—	—	24	88
Deposits and other	5,678	5,554	5,020	4,731	3,960
Deferred income taxes	—	294	5,687	8,035	8,419
Total other assets	42,421	29,865	28,237	30,580	31,281
Total assets	**$245,943**	**$188,440**	**$143,934**	**$111,689**	**$91,029**

LIABILITIES AND STOCKHOLDERS' EQUITY					
Current liabilities:					
Accounts payable	$ 8,072	$ 5,987	$ 5,271	$ 5,396	$ 3,535
Accrued expenses	35,552	24,935	16,433	12,086	12,237
Current portion of deferred revenue	1,168	1,403	677	—	—
Current portion of computer equipment financing	—	—	—	374	—
Total current liabilities	44,792	32,325	22,381	17,856	15,772
Deferred income taxes	328	—	—	—	—
Other long-term liabilities	1,115	262	1,125	2,245	2,011
Total liabilities	46,235	32,587	23,506	20,101	17,783
Minority interest	3,771	2,197	556	—	—
Stockholders' equity:					
Common stock, $.0001 par value: Class A, shares authorized 75,000,000; issued 28,296,581 and outstanding 28,187,581 in 2003 and issued 27,446,448 and outstanding 27,337,448 in 2002	3	3	3	1	1
Class B, shares authorized 10,000,000; issued and outstanding 1,847,221 in 2003 and 1,977,363 in 2002	—	—	—	—	—
Treasury stock, carried at cost	(900)	(900)	(900)	(900)	—
Additional paid-in capital	121,992	110,120	98,101	82,971	70,581
Retained earnings	74,842	44,433	22,668	9,516	2,664
Total stockholders' equity	195,937	155,853	120,428	91,588	73,246
Total liabilities and stockholders' equity	**$245,943**	**$188,440**	**$143,934**	**$111,689**	**$91,029**

Sources: Panera Bread Company, Inc., 2003 Form 10-K, *p. 29, and* 2001 Form 10-K, *p. 27.*

marily due to favorable ingredient costs and the impact of the favorable change in the sweet goods supply agreement, which took effect during the first quarter of fiscal 2003.

Depreciation and amortization was $19.5 million, or 5.5% of total revenue, for the 52 weeks ended December 27, 2003, compared to $14.0 million, or 5.0% of total revenue, for the 52 weeks ended December 28, 2002. The increase in depreciation and amortization as a percentage of total revenue for the 52 weeks ended December 27, 2003, compared to the 52 weeks ended December 28, 2002, was primarily due to the impact of a full year's depreciation of the prior year's capital expenditures and increased capital expenditures in the current year.

General and administrative expenses were $28.1 million, or 7.9% of total revenue, and $25.0 million, or 9.0% of total revenue, for the 52 weeks ended December 27, 2003, and December 28, 2002, respectively. The decrease in the general and administrative expense rate between 2003 and 2002 resulted primarily from higher revenues, which helped leverage general and administrative expenses, and from decreased bonus costs.

Pre-opening expenses, which consisted primarily of labor and food costs incurred during in-store training and preparation for opening, exclusive of manager training costs, which were included in other operating expenses, of $1.5 million, or 0.4% of total revenue, for the 52 weeks ended December 27, 2003, were consistent with the $1.1 million, or 0.4% of total revenue, of pre-opening expenses for the 52 weeks ended December 28, 2002.

Profit for the 52 weeks ended December 27, 2003, increased to $49.9 million, or 14.0% of total revenue, from $34.8 million, or 12.5% of total revenue, for the 52 weeks ended December 28, 2002. Operating profit for the 52 weeks ended December 27, 2003, rose as a result of operating leverage that results from opening 29 company bakery-cafes in 2003 as well as the factors described above.

Other expenses for the 52 weeks ended December 27, 2003, increased to $1.2 million, or 0.3% of total revenue, from $0.3 million, or 0.1% of total revenue, for the 52 weeks ended December 28, 2002. The increase in other expense resulted primarily from increased operating fee payments to the minority interest owners. Minority interest represented the portion of the company's operating profit that was attributable to the ownership interest of the minority interest owners. The provision for income taxes increased to $17.6 million for the 52 weeks ended December 27, 2003, compared to $12.5 million for the 52 weeks ended December 28, 2002. The tax provisions for the 52 weeks ended December 27, 2003, and December 28, 2002, reflects a consistent combined federal, state, and local effective tax rate of 36.5%.

Net income for the 52 weeks ended December 27, 2003, increased $8.6 million, or 39.7%, to $30.4 million, or $1.00 per diluted share, compared to net income of $21.8 million, or $0.73 per diluted share, for the 52 weeks ended December 28, 2002. The increase in net income in 2003 is consistent with the factors described above.

Notes

1. Hoover's Inc., "Overview: Panera Bread Company."
2. Hoover's Inc., "Overview: Panera Bread Company."
3. L. Tischler, "Vote of Confidence," *Fast Company*, No. 65 (December 2002), pp. 102–112.
4. P. O. Keegan, "Louis I. Kane & Ronald I. Shaich: Au Bon Pain's Own Dynamic Duo," *Nation's Restaurant News*, Vol. 28, No. 37 (September 19, 1994), p. 172.
5. *Ibid.*
6. Quoted in L. Tischler, "Vote of Confidence," *Fast Company*, No. 65 (December 2002), pp. 102–112.
7. P. O. Keegan, "Louis I. Kane & Ronald I. Shaich: Au Bon Pain's Own Dynamic Duo," *Nation's Restaurant News*, Vol. 28, No. 37 (September 19, 1994), p. 172.
8. R. L. Allen, "Au Bon Pain's Kane Dead at 69; Founded Bakery Chain," *Nation's Restaurant News*, Vol. 34, No. 26 (June 26, 2000), pp. 6–7.
9. Quoted in P. O. Keegan, "Louis I. Kane & Ronald I. Shaich: Au Bon Pain's Own Dynamic Duo," *Nation's Restaurant News*, Vol. 28, No. 37 (September 19, 1994), p. 172.
10. L. Tischler, "Vote of Confidence," *Fast Company*, No. 65 (December 2002), pp. 102–112.
11. Quoted in *Ibid.*
12. P. Kemp, "Second Rising," *Forbes*, Vol. 166, No. 13 (November 13, 2000), p. 290.
13. L. Tischler, "Vote of Confidence," *Fast Company*, No. 65 (December 2002), pp. 102–112.

14. *Ibid.*
15. Hoover's Inc., "Overview: Panera Bread Company."
16. *Ibid.*
17. *Ibid.*
18. L. Tischler, "Vote of Confidence," *Fast Company*, No. 65 (December 2002), pp. 102–112.
19. *Ibid.*
20. *Ibid.*
21. *Ibid.*
22. C. Y. Kwok, "Bakery-Café Idea Smacked of Success from the Very Beginning; Concept Gives Rise to Rapid Growth in Stores, Stock Price," *St. Louis Dispatch* (May 20, 2001), p. E1.
23. *Ibid.*
24. R. L. Allen, "Au Bon Pain Co. Pins Hopes on New President, Image," *Nation's Restaurant News*, Vol. 30, No. 47 (December 2, 1996), pp. 3–4.
25. P. Kemp, "Second Rising," *Forbes*, Vol. 166, No. 13 (November 13, 2000), p. 290.
26. R. L. Papiernik, "Au Bon Pain Mulls Remedies, Pares Back Expansion Plans," *Nation's Restaurant News*, Vol. 29, No. 34 (August 28, 1995), pp. 3–4.
27. "Au Bon Pain Stock Drops 11% on News That Loss Is Expected," *Wall Street Journal* (October 7, 1996), p. B2.
28. *Ibid.*
29. A. Caffrey, "Heard in New England: Au Bon Pain's Plan to Reinvent Itself Sits Well with Many Pros," *Wall Street Journal* (March 10, 1999), p. NE.2.
30. M. Sheridan, "Time Trials," *Restaurants & Institutions*, Vol. 112, No. 12 (May 15, 2002), pp. 93–102.
31. G. LaVecchia, "Fast Casual Enters the Fast Lane," *Restaurant Hospitality*, Vol. 87, No. 2 (February 2003), pp. 43–47.
32. *Ibid.*
33. M. Pethokoukis, "Bye-Bye Burgers," *US News & World Report*, Vol. 133, No. 21 (December 2002), p. 36.
34. *Ibid.*
35. S. Brooks, "Feeling Hot, Hot, Hot," *Restaurant Business*, Vol. 101, No. 15 (September 2002), p. 36.
36. Panera Bread Company, Inc., *2004 Notice of Annual Meeting of Stockholders*, pp. 4–6.
37. *Ibid.*, pp. 7–8.
38. Panera Bread Company, Inc., *2003 Form 10-K*, p. 3. This was directly quoted, with minor editing.
39. *Ibid.*, p. 5.
40. *Ibid.*, p. 4.
41. Panera Bread Company, Inc., *2003 Form 10-K*, pp. 6–7. Some sentences in this section were directly quoted, with minor editing.
42. B. R. Hook and A. Stevenson, "Rising Dough," *Kiplinger's Personal Finance*, Vol. 56, No. 1 (January 2002), p. 71.
43. Panera Bread Company, Inc., *2003 Form 10-K*, pp. 5–6. Some sentences in this section were directly quoted, with minor editing.
44. L. Tischler, "Vote of Confidence," *Fast Company*, No. 65 (December 2002), pp. 102–112.
45. Panera Bread Company, Inc., *2003 Form 10-K*, pp. 4–5. Some paragraphs and sentences in this section were directly quoted, with minor editing.
46. B. Sperber, "Fast Casual Dining Ahead," *Brandweek*, Vol. 43, No. 31 (September 2, 2002), pp. 16–20.
47. J. Peters, "No Loafing Around: Panera Bread Raises Projections for Unit Growth," *Nation's Restaurant News*, Vol. 36, No. 23 (June 10, 2002), p. 12.
48. Panera Bread Company, Inc., *2003 Form 10-K*, p. 6. This section was directly quoted, with minor editing.
49. Panera Bread Company, Inc., *2003 Form 10-K*, pp. 3, 6. Sentences 4 through 8 of the first paragraph and the entire second paragraph were directly quoted, with minor editing.
50. Panera Bread Company, Inc., *2003 Form 10-K*, pp. 13–19. This section was directly quoted, with minor editing.

CASE 31

Whole Foods Market (2005): Will There Be Enough Organic Food to Satisfy a Growing Demand?

Patricia Harasta and Alan N. Hoffman

Reflecting back over his three decades of experience in the grocery business, John Mackey smiled to himself over his previous successes. His entrepreneurial history began with a single store, which he had now grown to the nation's leading natural food chain. Although proud of the past, John had concerns about the future direction of the Whole Foods Market chain. Whole Foods Market was an early entrant into the organic food market and had used their early mover advantage to solidify their position and continue their steady growth.

With the changing economy and a more competitive industry landscape, John Mackey was uncertain about how to meet the company's aggressive growth targets. Whole Foods Market's objective was to reach $10 billion in revenue with 300+ stores by 2010 without sacrificing quality and their current reputation. This would not be an easy task, and John was unsure of the best way to proceed.

Company Background

Whole Foods carried both natural and organic food, offering customers a wide variety of products. "Natural" refers to food that is free of growth hormones or antibiotics; "certificated organic" food conforms to the standards defined by the U.S. Department of Agriculture in October 2002.[1] Whole Foods Market was the world's leading retailer of natural and organic foods, with 172 stores in North America and the United Kingdom. John Mackey, current President and cofounder of Whole Foods, opened the Safer Way natural grocery store in 1978. The store had limited success, as it was a small location allowing only for a limited selection, focusing entirely on vegetarian foods.[2] John joined forces with Craig

 The authors thank Ann Hoffman, Christopher Ferrari, Robert Marshall, Julie Giles, Jennifer Powers, and Gretchen Alper for their research and contributions to this case.

Weller and Mark Skiles, founders of Clarksville Natural Grocery (founded in 1979), to create Whole Foods Market.[3] This joint venture took place in Austin, Texas, in 1980, resulting in a new company, a single natural food market with a staff of 19.

In addition to the supermarkets, Whole Foods owned and operated several subsidiaries. Allegro Coffee Company was formed in 1977 and purchased by Whole Foods Market in 1997; it then acted as their coffee roasting and distribution center. Pigeon Cove was Whole Foods' seafood processing facility, which was founded in 1985 and known as M & S Seafood until 1990. Whole Foods purchased Pigeon Cove located in Gloucester, MA, in 1996. The company is now the only supermarket to own and operate a waterfront seafood facility.[4] The last two subsidiaries are Produce Field Inspection Office and Select Fish, which was Whole Foods' West Coast seafood processing facility, acquired in 2003.[5] In addition to the foregoing, the company had eight distribution centers, seven regional bake houses, and four commissaries.[6]

"Whole Foods Market remains uniquely mission driven: The company is highly selective about what they sell, dedicated to stringent quality standards, and committed to sustainable agriculture. They believe in a virtuous circle entwining the food chain, human beings and Mother Earth: each is reliant upon the others through a beautiful and delicate symbiosis."[7] The message of preservation and sustainability is followed while providing high-quality goods to customers and high profits to investors.

Whole Foods has grown over the years through mergers, acquisitions, and several new store openings.[8] Today, Whole Foods Market is the largest natural food supermarket in the United States.[9] The Company consists of 32,000 employees operating 172 stores in the United States, Canada and United Kingdom with an average store size of 32,000 square feet.[10] While the majority of Whole Foods locations are in the US, the company has made acquisitions expanding its presence in the UK. European expansion provides enormous potential growth due to the large population and it holds "a more sophisticated organic-foods market than US in terms of suppliers and acceptance by the public."[11] Whole Foods targets their locations specifically by an area's demographics. The Company targets locations where 40% or more of the residents have a college degree, as they are more likely to be aware of nutritional issues.[12]

Exhibit 1 lists the company's Board of Directors and key executives. John Mackey, co-founder, CEO, and Chairman of the Board, was the only internal member. A 12-year term limit was imposed on Board members in 2003.

Exhibit 1 Board of Directors and Key Executives: Whole Foods Market

A. Board of Directors

John P. Mackey	Chairman and CEO, Whole Foods Market
David W. Dupree	Managing Director, The Halifax Group
Dr. John B. Elstrott	Professor of Entrepreneurship, Tulane University
Gabrielle E. Greene	Chief Financial Officer, Villanueva Companies
Linda A. Mason	Co-founder & Chair, Bright Horizons Family Solutions
Morris J. Siegel	Managing Partner, Capitol Peaks investment firm
Dr. Ralph Z. Sorenson	Managing Partner, Sorenson Limited Partnership

B. Key Executive Officers

John P. Mackey	Chairman and CEO
Glenda Flanagan	Executive President and Chief Financial Officer
A.C. Galloxs	Co-president and Chief Operating Officer
Walter Robb	Co-president and Chief Operating Officer
James P. Sud	Executive Vice President of Growth and Business Development

Whole Foods Market's Philosophy

The corporate web site defined the company philosophy as follows:

> Whole Foods Market's vision of a sustainable future means our children and grandchildren will be living in a world that values human creativity, diversity, and individual choice. Businesses will harness human and material resources without devaluing the integrity of the individual or the planet's ecosystems. Companies, governments, and institutions will be held accountable for their actions. People will better understand that all actions have repercussions and that planning and foresight coupled with hard work and flexibility can overcome almost any problem encountered. It will be a world that values education and a free exchange of ideas by an informed citizenry; where people are encouraged to discover, nurture, and share their life's passions.[13]

Although Whole Foods recognized that it was only a supermarket, they were working toward fulfilling their vision within the context of their industry. In addition to leading by example, they strove to conduct business in a manner consistent with their mission and vision. By offering minimally processed, high-quality food, engaging in ethical business practices, and providing a motivational, respectful work environment, management believed they were on the path to a sustainable future.[14]

Whole Foods incorporated the best practices of each location back into the chain.[15] This could be seen in the company's store product expansion from dry goods to perishable produce, including meats, fish, and prepared foods. The lessons learned at one location were absorbed by all, enabling the chain to maximize effectiveness and efficiency while offering a product line customers loved. Whole Foods carried only natural and organic products. According to management, the best tasting and most nutritious food available was found in its purest state — unadulterated by artificial additives, sweeteners, colorings, and preservatives.[16]

Whole Foods continually improved customer offerings, catering to its specific locations. Unlike business models for traditional grocery stores, Whole Foods products differed by geographic regions and local farm specialties.

Employee and Customer Relations

Whole Foods encouraged a team-based environment, allowing each store to make independent decisions regarding its operations. Teams consisted of up to 11 employees and a team leader. The team leaders typically headed up one department or another. Each store employed anywhere from 72 to 391 team members.[17] The manager was referred to as the "store team leader." The store team leader was compensated by an Economic Value Added (EVA) bonus and was also eligible to receive stock options.[18]

Whole Foods tried to instill a sense of purpose among its employees and had been named one of the "100 Best Companies to Work for in America" by *Fortune* for the preceding six years. In employee surveys, 90% of its team members stated that they always or frequently enjoyed their jobs.[19]

The company strove to take care of its customers, realizing that they were the "lifeblood of our business," and the two were "interdependent on each other."[20] Whole Foods' primary objective went beyond 100% customer satisfaction, with the goal to "delight" customers in every interaction.

Competitive Environment

American shoppers spent nearly $45.8 billion on natural and organic products in 2004, according to research published in the "*24th Annual Market Overview*" in the June issue of *Natural Foods Merchandiser.* In 2004, natural products sales increased 6.9% across all sales channels, including supermarkets, mass marketers, direct marketers, and the Internet. Sales of organic products rose 14.6% in natural products stores. As interest in low-carb diets waned, sales of organic baked goods rose 35%. Other fast-growing organic categories included meat, poultry, and seafood, up 120%; coffee and cocoa, up 64%; and cookies, up 63%.

At the time of Whole Foods' inception, there was almost no competition, with fewer than six small other natural food characteristics in the United States. Later, the organic foods industry was growing, and Whole Foods found itself competing hard to maintain its elite presence. As the population became increasingly concerned about its eating habits, natural food stores, such as Whole Foods, were flourishing. Other successful natural food grocery chains included Trader Joe's Co. and Wild Oats Market.[21] (See **Exhibit 2.**)

Trader Joe's, originally known as Pronto Markets, had been founded in 1958 in Los Angeles by Joe Coulombe. By expanding its presence and product offerings while maintaining high quality at low prices, the company had found its competitive niche.[22] The company had 215 stores, primarily on the West and East Coasts of the United States. The company "offers upscale grocery fare such as health foods, prepared meals, organic produce and nutritional supplements."[23] A low cost structure allowed Trader Joe's to offer competitive prices while still maintaining its margins. Trader Joe's stores had no service department and averaged just 10,000 square feet in store size. A privately held company, Trader Joe's enjoyed sales of $2.5 million in 2003, a 13.6% increase from 2002.[24]

Wild Oats was founded in 1987, in Boulder, Colorado. Its founders had no experience in the natural foods market, relying heavily on their employees to learn the industry. Acknowledging the increased competition within the industry, Wild Oats was committed to strengthening and streamlining its operations in an effort to continue to build the company.[25] Its product offerings ranged from organic foods to traditional grocery merchandise. Wild Oats, a publicly owned company on NASDAQ, was traded under the ticker symbol of OATS and was "the third largest natural foods supermarket chain in the United States in terms of sales." Although it fell behind Whole Foods and Trader Joe's, the company enjoyed $1,048,164 in sales in 2004, a 7.5% increase over 2003. Wild Oats operated 100 full-service stores in 24 states and Canada.[26]

Additional competition had arisen from grocery stores, such as Stop 'N Shop and Shaw's, which had begun to incorporate natural foods sections in their conventional stores, placing them in direct competition with Whole Foods. Because larger grocery chains had more flexibility in their product offerings, they were more likely to promote products through sales, a strategy Whole Foods rarely practiced.

Exhibit 2 Sales of Competitors in Natural and Organic Foods

Sales (Dollar amounts in Millions)							
Company	2000	2001	% Growth	2002	% Growth	2003	% Growth
Whole Foods Market*	$1,838	$2,272	23.6%	$2,690	18.4%	$3,148	17.0%
Trader Joe's Company†	$1,670	$1,900	13.8%	$2,200	15.8%	$2,500	13.6%
Wild Oats Market‡	$ 838	$ 893	6.6%	$ 919	2.9%	$ 969	5.5%

* *Hoover's Online; http://www.hoovers.com/whole-foods/–ID_10952–/free-co-factsheet.xhtml (December 1, 2004).*
† *Hoover's Online; http://www.hoovers.com/trader-joe's-co/–ID-47619–/free-co-factsheet.xhtm (December 1, 2004).*
‡ *Hoover's Online; http://www.hoovers.com/wild-oats-markets/–ID_41717–/free-co-factsheet.xhtml (December 1, 2004).*

Despite being in a highly competitive industry, Whole Foods maintained its reputation as "the world's #1 natural foods chain."[27] As the demand for natural and organic food continued to grow, pressures on suppliers was rising. Only 3% of U.S. farmland was organic, so there was limited output.[28] The increased demand for these products might further elevate prices or result in goods being out of stock, with possible price wars looming.

The Changing Grocery Industry

Before the emergence of the supermarket, the public was largely dependent on specialty shops or street vendors for dairy products, meats, produce, and other household items. In the 1920s, chain stores began to threaten independent retailers by offering convenience and lower prices through procuring larger quantities of products. The emergence of the supermarkets in the 1930s was a result of three major changes in American society:

1. The shift in population from rural to urban areas
2. An increase in disposable income
3. Increased mobility through ownership of automobiles[29]

Perhaps the earliest example of the supermarket as we know it today was King Kullen, "America's first supermarket," which was founded by Michael Cullen in 1930. "The essential key to his plan was volume, and he attained this through heavy advertising of low prices on nationally advertised merchandise." As the success of Cullen's strategy became evident, others such as Safeway, A&P, and Kroger adopted it as well. By the time the United States entered World War II, 9,000 supermarkets accounted for 25% of industry sales.[30]

Low prices and convenience continued to be the dominant factors driving consumers to supermarkets. The industry was characterized by low margins and continuous downward pressure on prices made evident by coupons, weekly specials, and rewards cards. Over the years firms introduced subtle changes to the business model by providing additional conveniences, such as the inclusion of bakeries, banks, pharmacies, and even coffee houses co-located within the supermarket. Throughout their existence, supermarkets had also tried to cater to the changing tastes and preferences of society such as healthier diets, the Atkins diet, and low-carbohydrate foods. The moderate changes to strategy within supermarkets were imitated by competitors, which were returning the industry to a state of price competition. Supermarkets themselves faced additional competition from wholesalers such as Costco, BJ's, and Sam's Club.

A Different Shopping Experience

The setup of the organic grocery store was a key component in Whole Foods' success. The store's setup and its products were carefully researched to ensure that they were meeting the demands of the local community. Locations were primarily in cities and were chosen for their large space and heavy foot traffic. According to Whole Foods' *10-K Form*, "Approximately 88% of our existing stores are located in the top 50 statistical metropolitan areas."[31] The company used a specific formula to choose their store sites that was based on several metrics, which included but were not limited to income levels, education, and population density.

On entering a Whole Foods supermarket, it became clear that the company attempted to sell the consumer on the entire experience. Team members (employees) were well trained and the stores themselves were immaculate. There were in-store chefs to help with recipes, wine tasting, and food sampling. There were "Take Action food centers"[32] where customers could access information on the issues that affected their food such as legislation and environmental factors. Some stores offered extra services such as home delivery, cooking classes, massages, and valet parking.[33] Whole Foods went out of their way to appeal to the above-average income earner.

Whole Foods used price as a marketing tool in a few select areas, as demonstrated by the 365 Whole Foods brand-name products, priced less than similar organic products that were carried within the store. However, the company did not use price to differentiate itself from competitors.[34] Rather, Whole Foods focused on quality and service as a means of standing out from the competition.

Whole Foods spent only 0.5%[35] of their total sales from the fiscal year 2004 on advertising; they relied on other means to promote their stores. The company relied heavily on word-of-mouth advertising from their customers to help market themselves in the local community. They were also promoted in several health-conscious magazines, and each store budgeted for in-store advertising each fiscal year.

Whole Foods also gained recognition via their charitable contributions and the awareness that they brought to the treatment of animals. The company donated 5% of their after-tax profits to not-for-profit charities.[36] The company was also very active in establishing systems to make sure that the animals used in their products were treated humanely.

Aging Baby Boomers

The aging of the Baby Boomer generation was to expand the senior demographic over the next decade as their children grew up and left the nest. Urban singles were another group that had extra disposable income because of their lack of dependents. These two groups presented a growth opportunity for Whole Foods. Americans spent 7.2% of their total expenditures on food in 2001, making it the seventh highest category on which consumers spent their money.[37] Additionally, U.S. households with income of more than $100,000 per annum represented 22% of aggregate income compared with 18% a decade earlier.[38]

This shift in demographics created an expansion in the luxury store group, while slowing growth in the discount retail market.[39] To that end, there was a gap in supermarket retailing between consumers who could only afford to shop at low-cost providers such as Wal-Mart, and the population of consumers who preferred gourmet food and were willing to pay a premium for perceived higher quality.[40] "'The Baby Boomers are driving demand for organic food in general because they're health-conscious and can afford to pay higher prices,' says Professor Steven G. Sapp, a sociologist at Iowa State University who studies consumer food behavior."[41]

The perception that imported, delicatessen, exotic, and organic foods were of higher quality, therefore commanding higher prices, continued to bode well for Whole Foods Market. As John Mackey explained, "We're changing the [grocery-shopping] experience so that people enjoy it . . . It's a richer, [more fun], more enjoyable experience. People don't shop our stores because we have low prices."[42] The consumer focus on a healthy diet was not limited to food. More new diet plans had emerged in America in the last half of the 20th century than in any other country. This trend had also increased the demand for nutritional supplements and vitamins.[43]

In recent years, consumers had made a gradual move toward the use of fresher, healthier foods in their everyday diets. Consumption of fresh fruits and vegetables and of pasta and other grain-based products had increased.[44] This was evidenced by the aggressive expansion by consumer products companies into healthy food and natural and organic products.[45] "Natural and organic products have crossed the chasm to mainstream America."[46] The growing market could be attributed to the acceptance and widespread expansion of organic product offerings, beyond milk and dairy.[47] Mainstream acceptance of the Whole Foods offering could be attributed to this shift in consumer food preferences as consumers continued to list taste as the number one motivator for purchasing organic foods.[48]

With a growing percentage of women working outside the home, the traditional role of home-cooked meals, prepared from scratch, had waned. As fewer women had the time to devote to cooking, consumers were giving way to the trend of convenience through prepared foods. Sales of ready-to-eat meals had grown significantly. "The result is that grocers are starting to specialize in quasi-restaurant food."[49] Just as women entering the workforce had propelled the sale of prepared foods, it also increased consumer awareness of the need for the one-stop shopping experience. Hypermarkets such as Wal-Mart, which offered non-food items and more mainstream product lines, allowed consumers to conduct more shopping in one place rather than moving from store to store.

The growth in sales of natural foods was expected to continue at the rate of 8–10% annually, according to the National Nutritional Foods Association. The sale of organic food had largely outpaced traditional grocery products because of the consumer perception that organic food was healthier.[50] The purchase of organic food was perceived by 61% of consumers to be beneficial to consumer health, according to a Food Marketing Institute (FMI)/*Prevention* magazine study. Americans believed organic food could help improve fitness and increase longevity.[51] Much of this perception had grown out of fear of the way non-organic foods were treated with pesticides during growth and then preserved for sale. Therefore, an opportunity existed for Whole Foods to contribute to consumer awareness by funding non-profit organizations that focused on educating the public on the benefits of organic lifestyles.

Operations

Whole Foods purchased most of their products from regional and national suppliers. This allowed the company to leverage its size to receive deep discounts and favorable terms with their vendors. The company still permitted stores to purchase from local producers to keep the stores aligned with local food trends and was seen as supporting the community. The company owned two procurement centers and handled the majority of procurement and distribution themselves. Whole Foods also owned several regional bake houses, which distributed products to their stores. The largest independent vendor was United Natural Foods, which accounted for 20% of Whole Foods' total purchases for fiscal year 2004.[52] Product categories at Whole Foods included, but were not limited to:

- Produce
- Seafood
- Grocery
- Meat and poultry
- Bakery
- Prepared foods and catering
- Specialty (beer, wine, and cheese)
- Whole body (nutritional supplements, vitamins, body care, and educational products such as books)
- Floral
- Pet products
- Household products[53]

Although Whole Foods carried all the items that one would expect to find in a grocery store (and plenty that one would not), their "heavy emphasis on perishable foods is designed to appeal to both natural foods and gourmet shoppers."[54] Perishable foods accounted for 67% of their retail sales in 2004 and were the core of Whole Foods' success.[55] This was demonstrated by their own statement, "We believe it is our strength of execution in perishables that has attracted many of our most loyal shoppers."[56]

Whole Foods also provided fully cooked frozen meal options through their private label Whole Kitchen, to satisfy the demands of working families. For example, the Whole Foods Market located in Woodland Hills, CA, redesigned its prepared foods section more than three times[57] in response to a 40% growth in prepared foods sales.[58]

Whole Foods did not put just any product on its shelves. In order to make it into the Whole Foods grocery store, products had to undergo a strict test to determine whether they were "Whole Foods material." The quality standards that all potential Whole Foods products must meet included:

- Food that was free of preservatives and other additives
- Food that was fresh, wholesome, and safe to eat
- Food that was organically grown
- Food and products that promoted a healthy life[59]

Meat and poultry products had to adhere to a higher standard:

- No antibiotics or added growth hormones
- An affidavit from each producer that outlined the whole process of production and how the animals were treated
- An annual inspection of all producers by Whole Foods Market
- Successful completion of a third-party audit to attest to these findings[60]

Also, because of the lack of available nutritional brands with a national identity, Whole Foods decided to enter the private-label product business. They had three private-label product lines, with a fourth program called Authentic Food Artisan, which promoted distinctive products that were certified organic. The three private-label brands were (1) 365 Everyday Value, a well-recognized and trusted brand that met the standards of Whole Foods and was less expensive than the regular product lines; (2) Whole Kids Organic, healthy items that were directed at children; and (3) 365 Organic Everyday Value, all the benefits of organic food at reduced prices.[61]

When opening a new store, Whole Foods stocked it with almost $700,000 worth of initial inventory, which their vendors partially financed.[62] Like most conventional grocery stores, the majority of Whole Foods' inventory was turned over fairly quickly; this was especially true of produce. Fresh organic produce was central to Whole Foods' existence and turned over on a faster basis than other products.

Financial

Whole Foods Market focused on earning a profit while providing job security to its workforce to lay the foundation for future growth. The company was determined not to let profits deter the company from providing excellent service to its customers and a quality work environment for its staff. Their mission statement defined their recipe for financial success.

> Whole Foods, Whole People, Whole Planet—emphasizes that our vision reaches far beyond just being a food retailer. Our success in fulfilling our vision is measured by customer satisfaction,

Exhibit 3 Un-audited Quarterly Statements for the Fiscal Year ending September 26, 2004: Whole Foods Market (Dollar amounts in thousands)

Fiscal Year 2004	First Quarter	Second Quarter	Third Quarter	Fourth Quarter
Sales	**$1,118,148**	**$902,141**	**$917,355**	**$927,306**
Cost of goods sold and occupancy costs	733,721	582,597	600,961	606,537
Gross profit	**384,427**	**319,544**	**316,394**	**320,769**
Direct store expenses	282,596	229,995	232,649	240,800
General and administrative expenses	35,869	28,783	27,551	27,597
Pre-opening and relocation costs	4,073	4,040	4,966	5,569
Operating income	**61,889**	**56,726**	**51,228**	**46,803**
Other income (expense)				
Interest expense	(2,478)	(1,859)	(1,319)	(1,593)
Investment and other income	1,464	1,503	1,782	1,707
Income before income taxes	60,875	56,370	51,691	46,917
Provision for income taxes	24,350	22,548	20,676	18,767
Net income	**$ 36,525**	**$ 33,822**	**$ 31,015**	**$ 28,150**
Basic earnings per share	$ 0.61	$ 0.55	$ 0.50	$ 0.45
Diluted earnings per share	$ 0.57	$ 0.52	$ 0.47	$ 0.43
Dividends per share	$ 0.15	$ 0.15	$ 0.15	$ 0.15

Team Member excellence and happiness, return on capital investment, improvement in the state of the environment, and local and larger community support.[63]

Whole Foods also capped the salary of its executives at no more than 14 times the average annual salary of a Whole Foods worker; this included wages and incentive bonuses as well.[64]

Over a five-year period from 2000 through 2004, the company experienced an 87% growth in sales, with sales reaching $3.86 billion in 2004. Annual sales increases during that period were equally dramatic: 24% in 2001, 18% in 2002, 17% in 2003, and 22% in 2004.[65] This growth was perhaps more impressive, given the relatively negative economic environment and recession in the United States.

Whole Foods' strategy of expansion and acquisition had fueled growth in net income since the company's inception. This was particularly evident when looking at the net income growth in 2002 (24.47%), 2003 (22.72%), and 2004 (27.94%).[66]

The ticker for Whole Foods, Inc. was WFMI. A review of the performance history of Whole Foods stock since its IPO revealed a mostly upward trend. The 10-year price trend showed the company increasing from under $10 per share to a high of over $100 per share, reflecting an increase of over 1,000%.[67] During 2004, the stock was somewhat volatile, but with a mostly upward trend. The August 2005 price of $136 with 65.3 million shares outstanding gave the company a market valuation of $8.8 billion.[68] See **Exhibits 3, 4,** and **5.**

Code of Conduct

From its inception, the company had sought to be different from conventional grocery stores, with a heavy focus on ethics. Besides an emphasis on organic foods, management also established a contract of animal rights, which stated that the company would only do business

Exhibit 4 Balance Sheet: Whole Foods Market (Dollar amounts in thousands)

Year Ending	September 26, 2004	September 28, 2003	September 29, 2002
Assets			
Current Assets			
Cash and cash equivalents	$ 221,537	$ 165,779	$ 12,646
Short-term investments	—	—	—
Net receivables	94,421	61,554	42,356
Inventory	152,912	123,904	108,189
Other current assets	16,702	12,447	8,950
Total Current Assets	**485,572**	**363,684**	**172,141**
Long-Term Investments	—	2,206	4,426
Property Plant and Equipment	904,825	718,240	644,688
Goodwill	112,186	80,548	80,548
Intangible Assets	24,831	26,569	22,889
Accumulated Amortization	—	—	—
Other Assets	20,302	5,573	11,159
Deferred Long-Term Asset Charges	—	—	7,350
Total Assets	**1,547,716**	**1,196,820**	**943,201**
Liabilities			
Current Liabilities			
Accounts payable	328,977	233,778	170,509
Short/current long-term debt	5,973	5,806	5,789
Other current liabilities	—	—	—
Total Current Liabilities	**334,950**	**239,584**	**176,298**
Long-Term Debt	164,770	162,909	161,952
Other Liabilities	1,581	2,301	3,774
Deferred Long-Term Liability Charges	77,760	15,850	12,091
Minority Interest	—	—	—
Negative Goodwill	—	—	—
Total Liabilities	**579,061**	**420,644**	**354,115**
Stockholders' Equity			
Misc. Stocks Options Warrants	—	—	—
Redeemable Preferred Stock	—	—	—
Preferred Stock	—	—	—
Common Stock	535,107	423,297	341,940
Retained Earnings	431,495	351,255	247,568
Treasury Stock	—	—	—
Capital Surplus	—	—	—
Other Stockholders' Equity	2,053	1,624	(422)
Total Stockholders' Equity	968,655	776,176	589,086
Total Liabilities and Stockholders' Equity	**$1,547,716**	**$1,196,820**	**$943,200**

Source: http://finance.yahoo.com/q/bs?s=WFMI&annual (May 26, 2005).

Exhibit 5 Income Statement: Whole Foods Market (Dollar amounts in thousands)

Year Ending	September 26, 2004	September 28, 2003	September 29, 2002
Total Revenue	**$3,864,950**	**$3,148,593**	**$2,690,475**
Cost of Revenue	2,523,816	2,067,939	1,757,213
Gross Profit	**1,341,134**	**1,080,654**	**933,262**
Operating Expenses			
Research & development	—	—	—
Selling general and administrative	1,107,797	893,229	771,631
Non-recurring	11,449	12,091	12,485
Others	—	—	—
Total Operating Expenses	1,119,246	905,320	784,116
Operating Income	**221,888**	**175,334**	**149,146**
Income from Continuing Operations			
Total Other Income/Expenses Net	6,456	5,593	2,056
Earnings Before Interest and Taxes	228,344	180,927	151,202
Interest Expense	7,249	8,114	10,384
Income Before Tax	221,095	172,813	140,818
Income Tax Expense	88,438	69,126	56,327
Minority Interest	—	—	—
Net Income from Continuing Ops	$ 132,657	$ 103,687	$ 84,491
Non-recurring Events			
Discontinued Operations	—	—	—
Extraordinary Items	—	—	—
Effect Of Accounting Changes	—	—	—
Other Items	—	—	—
Net Income	**132,657**	**103,687**	**84,491**

Source: http://finance.yahoo.com/q/is?s=WFMI&annual, (July 27, 2005).

with companies that treated their animals humanely. Although they realize that animal products are vital to their business, they oppose animal cruelty.[69]

The company has a unique 14-page Code of Conduct document that addresses the expected and desired behavior for its employees. The code is broken down into the following four sections:

- Potential conflicts of interest
- Transactions or situations that should never occur
- Situations where a person may need the authorization of the Ethics committee before proceeding
- Times when certain actions must be taken by executives of the company or team leaders of individual stores[70]

This Code of Conduct covered, in detail, the most likely scenarios a manager of a store might encounter. It included several checklists that were to be filled out on a regular, or at least an annual, basis by team leaders and store managers. After completion, the checklists had to be signed and submitted to corporate headquarters and copies retained on file in the store.[71] They ensured that the ethics of Whole Foods were being followed by everyone. The ethical efforts of Whole Foods did not go unrecognized; they were ranked number 70 out of the "100 Best Corporate Citizens."[72]

Scarce Resources

Prime store locations and the supply of organic foods were potential scarce resources and could be problematic for Whole Foods Market in the future.

Whole Foods liked to establish a presence in highly affluent cities, where their target market resided. The majority of Whole Foods customers were well educated, which generally meant high salaries that enabled them to afford the company's higher prices. Whole Foods was particular when deciding on new locations, as location was extremely important for top- and bottom-line growth. However, there were a limited number of communities where 40% of the residents had college degrees.

Organic food was another possible scarce resource. Organic crops yielded a lower quantity of output and were rarer, accounting for only 3% of U.S. farmland usage.[73] Strict government requirements had to satisfied; these were incredibly time consuming, more effort intensive, and more costly to adhere to. With increased demands from mainstream super markets also carrying organics, the demand for such products could outreach the limited supply. The market for organic foods grew from $2.9 billion in 2001 to $5.3 billion in 2004, an 80.5% increase in the three-year period.[74]

Whole Foods recognized that the increasing demand for organic foods might adversely affect their earnings and informed their investors accordingly:

> Changes in the Availability of Quality Natural and Organic Products Could Impact Our Business. There is no assurance that quality natural and organic products will be available to meet our future needs. If conventional supermarkets increase their natural and organic product offerings or if new laws require the reformulation of certain products to meet tougher standards, the supply of these products may be constrained. Any significant disruption in the supply of quality natural and organic products could have a material impact on our overall sales and cost of goods.[75]

Notes

1. *http://www.organicconsumers.org/organic/most 071904.cfm.*
2. Julia Boorstin, *Fortune* (September 15, 2003), p. 127. "No Preservatives, No Unions, Lots of Dough."
3. Whole Foods, *http://www.wholefoods.com/company/timeline.html* (November 4, 2004).
4. Boorstin (2003).
5. Whole Foods, *http://www.wholefoods.com/company/facts.html* (November 5, 2004).
6. Whole Foods, *http://www.wholefoods.com/issues/org_comments-standards0498.html* (November 5, 2004).
7. Whole Foods, *http://www.wholefoods.com/company/index.html* (November 5, 2004).
8. Whole Foods, *http://www.wholefoods.com/company/history.html* (November 5, 2004).
9. "The Natural: Whole Foods Founder John Mackey Builds an Empire on Organic Eating," *Time,* Inc., 2002.
10. Whole Foods, *http://www.wholefoods.com/company/facts.html* (November 11, 2004).
11. "Whole Foods Buying chain of stores based in London: $38 million deal marks U.S. health-Food retailer's initial thrust into overseas market" Robert Elder Jr. (January 17, 2004.)
12. Jeanne Lang Jones, "Whole Foods is bagging locations," *Puget Sound Business Journal: Seattle* (August 13, 2004), p. 1.
13. Whole Foods, *http://www.wholefoodsmarket.com/company/sustainablefuture.html* (November 5, 2004).
14. *Ibid.*
15. Boorstin (2003).
16. *http://www.wholefoodsmarket.com/products/index.html* (July 25, 2005).
17. Whole Foods, *10K-Q 2003 http://www.wholefoodsmarket.com/investor/10K-Q/2003_10K.pdf* (November 11, 2004), p. 7
18. *Ibid.*

19. Whole Foods, *10K-Q 2004 http://www.wholefoodsmarket.com/investor/10K-Q/2004_10KA.pdf (August 15, 2005)*, p. 10.
20. *http://www.wholefoodsmarket.com/company/decla-ration.html* (July 29, 2005).
21. Hoovers Online: *http://www.hoovers.com/whole-foods/–ID10952–/free-co-factsheet.xhtml*: (November 8, 2004).
22. Trader Joe's Company, *www.traderjoes.com* (November 8, 2004).
23. Hoover's Online, *http://www.hoovers.com/trader-joe's-co/–ID-47619–/free-co-factsheet.xhtm* (November 8, 2004).
24. *Ibid.*
25. Wild Oats Market, *www.wildoats.com* (November 8, 2004).
26. Hoover's Online, *http://www.hoovers.com/wild-oats-markets/–ID_41717–/free-co-factsheet.xhtml* (November 8, 2004).
27. Hoover's Online, *http://www.hoovers.com/whole-foods/–ID10952–/free-co-factsheet.xhtml* (November 8, 2004).
28. Paul Grimaldi, "Providence, RI, Grocery Targets New Approach to Pricing,"; *Knight Ridder Tribune Business News* (September 28, 2004), p. 1.
29. David Appel, "The Supermarket: Early Development of an Institutional Innovation," *Journal of Retailing*, Vol. 48, No. 1 (Spring 1972), p. 40.
30. *Ibid.* p. 47.
31. Whole Foods, *10K-Q for 2003*, *http://www.wholefoodsmarket.com/investor/10K-Q/2003_10K.pdf* (November 11, 2004), p. 8.
32. *Ibid.*
33. *Ibid.*
34. *Ibid.*, p. 10.
35. Whole Foods, *10K-Q 2004 http://www.wholefoodsmarket.com/investor/10K-Q/2004_10KA.pdf* (August 15, 2005), p. 10.
36. Whole Foods, *10K-Q 2003*, p. 9.
37. Consumer Lifestyles in the United States (May 2003), 12.2 Expenditure on Food. *Euromonitor*. Solomon Smith Baker Library, Bentley College, Waltham, MA. (November 1, 2004).
38. John. Gapper, "Organic Food Stores Are on a Natural High," *Financial Times* (September 2004).
39. *Ibid.* 2004
40. *Ibid.*
41. Richard Murphy McGill, "Truth or Scare," *American Demographics*, Vol. 26, No. 2, (March 2004) p. 26.
42. Bob Sechler, "Whole Foods Picks Up the Pace of Its Expansion," *Wall Street Journal* (Eastern edition, September 29, 2004), p. 7.
43. Consumer Lifestyles in the United States (May 2003) 12.7 What Americans Eat. *Euromonitor*. Solomon Smith Baker Library, Bentley College, Waltham, MA. (November 1, 2004).
44. Consumer Lifestyles in the United States (May 2003) 12.4 Popular Foods. *Euromonitor*. Solomon Smith Baker Library, Bentley College, Waltham, MA. (November 1, 2004).
45. "Profile in B2B Strategy: Supermarket News Sidles into Natural, Organic Trend with New Quarterly," *Business CustomerWire*, Regional Business News (October 25, 2004).
46. *Ibid.*
47. The World Market for Dairy Products (January 2004). 4.5 Organic Foods. 4.5.1 Global Market Trends in Organic Foods. *Euromonitor*. Solomon Smith Baker Library, Bentley College, Waltham, MA. (November 1, 2004).
48. The World Market for Dairy Products (January 2004). 4.5 Organic Foods. 4.5.1 Global Market Trends in Organic Foods. *Euromonitor*. Solomon Smith Baker Library, Bentley College, Waltham, MA. (November 1, 2004).
49. "Supermarkets' Prepared Meals Save Families Time," *KRTBN Knight-Ridder Tribune Business Daily News* (September 13, 2004).
50. Packaged Food in the United States (January 2004) 3.4 Organic Food. *Euromonitor*. Solomon Smith Baker Library, Bentley College, Waltham, MA. (November 1, 2004).
51. Packaged Food in the United States (January 2004) 3.4 Organic Food. *Euromonitor*. Solomon Smith Baker Library, Bentley College, Waltham, MA. (November 1, 2004).
52. Whole Foods, *10K-Q for 2004*, *http://www.wholefoodsmarket.com/investor/10K-Q/2004_10KA.pdf* (August 15, 2005), p. 10; *http://www.wholefoodsmarket.com/investor/10K-Q/2003_10K.pdf* (November 11, 2004), p. 8.
53. Whole Foods, *10K-Q for 2003*, p. 6.
54. *Ibid.*, p. 5.
55. Whole Foods, *10K Q 2004 http://www.wholefoodsmarket.com/investor/10K-Q/2004_10KA.pdf* (August 15, 2005), p. 14.
56. Whole Foods, *10K-Q 2003*, *http://www.wholefoodsmarket.com/investor/10K-Q/2003_10K.pdf* (November 13, 2004), p. 6.
57. "Supermarkets' Prepared Meals," (2004).
58. *Ibid.*
59. Whole Foods, *10K-Q 2003*, *http://www.wholefoodsmarket.com/investor/10K-Q/2003_10K.pdf* (November 13, 2004), p. 5.
60. *Ibid.*, p. 6.
61. *Ibid.*, p. 7.
62. *Ibid.*, p. 8.
63. Whole Foods, *www.WholeFoodsmarket.com/company/declaration.html* (November 7, 2004).
64. *Ibid.*
65. Whole Foods, *10K-Q for 2003*, *www.WholeFoodsmarket.com/investor/10k-Q/2003_10k.pdf* (November 7, 2004).
66. *Ibid.*
67. Nasdaq.com, "Market Symbol for Whole Foods Is WFMI," *http://quotes.nasdaq.com/quote.dll?page=charting&mode=basics&intraday=off&timeframe=10y&charttype=ohlc&splits=off&earnings=off&movingaverage=None&lowerstudy=volume&comparison=off&index=&drilldown=off&symbol=WFMI&selected=WFM* (November 11, 2004).
68. *Ibid.*
69. Whole Foods, *10K-Q for 2003*, *http://www.wholefoodsmarket.com/investor/10K-Q/2003_10K.pdf* (November 11, 2004), p. 6.
70. Whole Foods Code of Conduct found at company web site, *http://www.wholefoodsmarket.com/investor/codeofconduct.pdf* (November 11, 2004).
71. *Ibid.*, p. 11.
72. Business Ethics, "100 Best Companies to Work For," *http://www.business-ethics.com/100best.htm* (November 12, 2004).
73. Grimaldi (2004).
74. *http://www.preparedfoods.com/PF/FILES/HTML/Mintel_Reports/Mintel_PDF/Summaries/sum-OrganicFoodBeverages-Aug2004.pdf*
75. Whole Foods, *10K for 2004*, *http://www.wholefoodsmarket.com/investor/10K-Q/2004_10KA.pdf*, p. 14.

CASE 32

Church & Dwight Builds a Corporate Portfolio

Roy A. Cook

"**CHURCH & DWIGHT HAS UNDERGONE A SUBSTANTIAL TRANSFORMATION IN THE PAST DECADE** largely as a result of three major acquisitions which doubled the size of the total Company, created a well balanced portfolio of household and personal care businesses, and established a much larger international business."[1] As a new top management team worked to digest and integrate this series of acquisitions while scouting for new acquisition targets in consumer products, it struggled with maintaining market share in its historically core businesses. The top-line numbers looked good, but previously issued commitments to generate annual sales growth from historic core businesses of 15% had been lowered once to the $12\frac{1}{2}\%$ – 15% range and then to the 10% – 12% range. Had the pieces finally been put in place for the company to compete successfully with other well-known giants in the consumer products arena, or would it remain in their shadows?

Background

For more than 160 years, Church & Dwight Co., Inc., had been working to build market share on a brand name that is rarely associated with the company. When consumers are asked, "Are you familiar with Church & Dwight products?" the answer is typically "No." Yet, a variety of Church & Dwight consumer products can be found in 95% of all U.S. households. As the world's largest producer and marketer of sodium bicarbonate–based products, Church & Dwight has achieved fairly consistent growth in both sales and earnings as new and expanded uses were found for its core sodium bicarbonate products. Although Church & Dwight may not be a household name, many of its core products bearing the Arm & Hammer name are easily recognized.

Shortly after its introduction in 1878, Arm & Hammer Baking Soda became a fundamental item on the pantry shelf as homemakers found many uses for it other than baking, such as cleaning and deodorizing. The ingredients that can be found in that ubiquitous yellow box of baking soda in almost every refrigerator can also be used as a dentrifice, a chemical agent to absorb or neutralize odors and acidity, a kidney dialysis element, a blast medium, an environmentally friendly cleaning agent, a swimming pool pH stabilizer, and a pollution control agent.

Finding expanded uses for sodium bicarbonate and achieving orderly growth had been consistent targets for the company. Over the past 30 years, average company sales had increased 10% to 15% annually. Although top-line sales growth had historically been a focal point for the company, a shift may have occurred in management's thinking as more emphasis seemed to be placed on bottom-line profitability growth. President and Chief Executive Officer James R. Craigie may have signaled this change when he stated, "Our long-term objective is to maintain the Company's track record, and continue to achieve sustained earnings growth, which we currently define as 10–12% earning per share growth on an organic basis excluding acquisitions."[2] All of this happened as Church & Dwight appeared to be shifting roles from an acquirer to an operator.

Craigie took over the helm of Church & Dwight from Robert A. Davies III in July 2004. Setting the stage to build on the successful legacy he inherited from his predecessor, Craigie proposed a new strategy of "building a portfolio of strong brands with sustainable competitive advantages."[3] The results of both Davies' and Craigie's efforts to reshape the company through acquisitions and organic growth can be seen in the financial statements shown in **Exhibits 1** and **2.**

Management

The historically slow but steady course Church & Dwight had traveled over the decades reflected stability in the chief executive office and a steady focus on long-term goals. The ability to remain focused might be attributable to the fact that about 25% of the outstanding

Exhibit 1 Consolidated Statements of Income: Church & Dwight Co., Inc. (Dollar amounts in thousands, except per share data)

Year ending December 31	2005	2004	2003
Net Sales	$1,736,506	$1,462,062	$1,056,874
Cost of sales	1,099,506	928,674	738,883
Gross Profit	637,000	533,388	317,991
Marketing expenses	183,422	161,183	88,807
Selling, general and administrative expenses	240,802	200,452	117,333
Income from Operations	212,776	171,753	111,851
Equity in earnings (loss) of affiliates	4,790	15,115	28,632
Investment earnings	3,985	3,225	1,322
Loss on early extinguishment of debt	(1,241)	(22,871)	(4,127)
Other income (expense), net	(1,329)	1,628	(313)
Interest expense	(44,098)	(41,407)	(20,400)
Income before minority interest and taxes	174,883	127,443	116,965
Minority interest	(91)	4	30
Income before taxes	174,974	127,439	116,935
Income taxes	52,068	38,631	35,974
Net Income	$ 122,906	$ 88,808	$ 80,961

Exhibit 2 Consolidated Balance Sheets: Church & Dwight Co., Inc. (Dollar amounts in thousands)

Year ending December 31	2005	2004	2003
Assets			
Current Assets			
Cash and cash equivalents	$ 126,678	$ 145,540	$ 75,634
Accounts receivable	187,863	166,203	107,553
Inventories	156,149	148,898	84,176
Deferred income taxes	11,217	7,600	14,109
Notes receivable—current	1,150	1,015	942
Net assets held for sale	—	13,300	—
Prepaid expenses	11,381	11,240	6,808
Total Current Assets	494,438	493,796	289,222
Property, plant and equipment (net)	326,903	332,204	258,010
Notes receivable	6,134	7,751	8,766
Equity investment in affiliates	10,855	13,255	152,575
Long-term supply contract	4,094	4,881	5,668
Trade names and other intangibles	541,970	474,285	119,374
Goodwill	523,676	511,643	259,444
Other assets	54,047	40,183	26,558
Total Assets	$1,962,117	$1,877,998	$1,119,617
Liabilities and Stockholders' Equity			
Current Liabilities			
Short-term borrowings	$ 105,563	$98,239	$ 62,337
Accounts payable and accrued expenses	255,438	242,024	148,958
Current portion of long-term debt	15,719	5,797	3,560
Income taxes payable	32,990	11,479	17,199
Total Current Liabilities	$ 409,710	$ 357,539	$ 232,054
Long-term debt	635,261	754,706	331,149
Deferred income taxes	124,882	108,216	61,000
Deferred and other long-term liabilities	40,823	39,384	33,164
Pension, postretirement and postemployment benefits	54,305	57,836	23,459
Minority interest	258	287	297
Stockholders' Equity			
Common Stock—$1 par value	69,991	69,991	69,991
Additional paid-in capital	65,110	47,444	27,882
Retained earnings	618,071	510,480	435,588
Accumulated other comprehensive income (loss)	(454)	(3,110)	(13,962)
	752,718	624,805	519,588
Less common stock in treasury, at cost	(55,840)	(64,775)	(81,094)
Stockholders' Equity Total	696,878	560,030	438,494
Total Liabilities and Stockholders' Equity	$1,962,117	$1,877,998	$1,119,617

shares of common stock were owned by descendants of the company's co-founders. Dwight C. Minton, a direct descendant of Austin Church, actively directed the company as CEO from 1969 through 1995 and remained on the Board as Chairman Emeritus. He passed on the duties of CEO to the first non–family member in the company's history, Robert A. Davies III, in 1995. During his almost 10 years of leadership, Davies tripled the size of the company. Next, the future direction of the company was in the hands of James Craigie, who was serving as Chairman. **Exhibit 3** shows the 13 board members, of whom three are internal members.

Exhibit 3 Board of Directors: Church & Dwight Co., Inc.

T. Rosie Albright — Retired President
Carter Products Division
Carter-Wallace, Inc.
Director since 2004
James R. Craigie — President and Chief Executive Officer
Church & Dwight Co., Inc.
Director since 2004
Robert A Davies, III — Chairman
Church & Dwight Co., Inc.
Director since 1985
Rosia B. Dixon, MD — Physician and Consultant
Director since 1979
J. Richard Leaman, Jr. — Retired President and Chief Executive Officer
S. D. Warren Company
Director since 1985
Robert D. LeBlanc — Consultant, retired President and Chief Executive Officer
Handy & Harman
Director since 1998
John D. Leggett, III, PhD — President
Sensor Instruments Co., Inc.
Director since 1979
John F. Maypole — Managing Partner
Peach State Real Estate Holding Co.
Director since 1999
Robert A. McCabe — Chairman
Pilot Capital Corporation
Director since 1987
Dwight C. Minton — Chairman Emeritus
Church & Dwight Co., Inc.
Director since 1965
Lionel L. Nowell, III — Senior Vice President and Treasurer
PepsiCo, Inc.
Director since 2003
Burton B. Staniar — Chairman
Knoll, Inc.
Director since 1999
John O. Whitney — Lead Director
Professor Emeritus of Management
Columbia Business School
Director since 1992

Many companies with strong brand names in the consumer products field have been susceptible to leveraged buyouts and hostile takeovers. However, a series of calculated actions had spared Church & Dwight's board and management from having to make last-minute decisions to ward off unwelcome suitors. Besides maintaining majority control of the outstanding common stock, the Board amended the company's charter, giving current shareholders four votes per share but requiring future shareholders to buy and hold shares for four years before receiving the same privilege. The Board of Directors was also structured into three classes with four directors in each class serving staggered three-year terms. According to Minton, the objective of these moves was to "give the Board control so as to provide the best results for shareholders."[4]

As a further deterrent to would-be suitors or unwelcome advances, the company entered into an employee severance agreement with key officials. This agreement provides severance pay of up to two times (three times for Mr. Craigie) the individual's highest annual salary and bonus plus benefits for two years (three years for Mr. Craigie) if the individual was terminated within one year after a change in control of the company. Change of control was defined as the acquisition by a person or group of 50% or more of company common stock; a change in the majority of the board of directors not approved by the pre-change board of directors; or the approval by the stockholders of the company or a merger, consolidation, liquidation, dissolution, or sale of all the assets of the company.[5]

As Church & Dwight pushed more aggressively into consumer products outside of sodium bicarbonate–related products and into the international arena, numerous changes were made in key personnel and positions, especially in the marketing area. These changes can be seen by reviewing **Exhibits 4 and 5.** Comparing these two exhibits, which present rosters of key officers along with their ages, positions, and original dates of employment for the years 2002 and 2005, shows many changes. Although Davies had retired because of age, Casper, Kornhauser, and Koslow, who had been brought in for their marketing expertise, were no longer with the company. To fill this void, several of the newer additions to a streamlined management team, including Craigie, Fleming, Huns, and Tursi, brought extensive marketing experience to the top management team from organizations such as Spalding Sports Worldwide, Johnson & Johnson, Vlasic Foods, and Carter-Wallace. In addition, Fleming and Huns along with Siracusa brought significant international experience to the team as an increasing emphasis was placed on markets outside the United States.

In addition to the many changes that had taken place in key management positions, changes had also been made in the composition of the Board of Directors. Six of the 10-member Board had served for 10 years or more; three had served for three years or less. Two women served on the board and ages of members ranged from 52 to 78. Although in a less active role as Chairman Emeritus, Dwight Church Minton, who became a board member in 1965, continued to provide leadership and a long legacy of "corporate memory."

Changing Directions

Entering the 21st century, "Management recognized a major challenge to overcome... was the Company's small size compared to its competitors in basic product lines of household and personal care. They also recognized the value of a major asset, the Company's pristine Balance Sheet, and made the decision to grow."[6] According to Craigie, "Church & Dwight has undergone a substantial transformation in the past decade largely as a result of three major acquisitions which doubled the size of the total company, created a well balanced portfolio of household and personal care businesses, and established a much larger international business."[7] The Mentadent, Pepsodent, Aim, and Close-Up brands of toothpaste products were purchased from Unilever in October of 2003; the purchase of the remaining 50% of Armkel, the acquisition vehicle that had been used to purchase Carter-Wallace's consumer brands such as Trojan, was completed in May of 2004; and Spinbrush was purchased from Procter & Gamble in October of 2005. The numbers spoke for themselves, as these acquisitions had pumped up total revenues. In 1995 total company sales were less than $500 million; in 2001, they had jumped to over $1 billion; and in 2005, they reached $1.7 billion.

Exhibit 4 Key Officers, Management Positions, and Tenure with Company — *2002*

Name	Age	Position	Anniversary Date
Robert A. Davies, III	66	President & Chief Executive Officer	1995
Raymond L. Bendure, Ph.D.	58	Vice President Research and Development	1995
Mark A. Bilawsky	54	Vice President, General Counsel and Secretary	1976
Bradley A. Casper	42	Vice President, President, Domestic Personal Care	2002
Mark G. Conish	49	Vice President Operations	1993
Steven P. Cugine	39	Vice President Human Respirces	1999
Zvi Eiref	63	Vice President Finance and Chief Financial Officer	1995
Henry Kornhauser	69	Vice President Creative Services	1997
Dennis M. Moore	51	Vice President Arm & Hammer Division Sales	1980
Joseph A. Sipia, Jr.	53	Vice President, President and Chief Operating Officer/Specialty Products Division	2002
John R. Burke	50	Vice President Financial Analysis and Planning for the Arm & Hammer Division	1985
Robert J. Carroll	43	Vice President MIS	1989
Kenneth S. Colbert	46	Vice President Logistics	1979
Anthony J. Falotico	47	Vice President Research and Development, Household Products	1980
Alfred H. Falter	52	Vice President Procurement	1979
W. Patrick Fiedler	53	Vice President Basic Chemicals, Specialty Products Division	1995
Roger Fingerhut	59	Vice President Manufacturing	2001
Gary P. Halker	51	Vice President, Controller and Chief Information Officer	1977
Jaap Ketting	50	Vice President International Finance, Specialty Products Division	1987
Allison Lukacsko	51	Vice President Research and Development Personal Care	2001
Larry B. Koslow	50	Vice President Marketing, Arm & Hammer Division	1995
Ronald D. Munson	59	Vice President Animal Nutrition, Specialty Products Division	1983

Source: Church & Dwight Co., Inc., *Notice of Annual Meeting of Stockholders and Proxy Statement* (2001), pp. 5–7.

Explosive growth through acquisitions transformed a once-small company focused on a few consumer and specialty products into a much larger competitor, across not only a broader range of products, but also geographic territory. Consumer products now encompassed a broad array of personal care, deodorizing and cleaning, and laundry products, whereas specialty products offerings were expanded to specialty chemicals, animal nutrition, and specialty cleaners. And, international consumer product sales, which had been an insignificant portion of total revenue at the turn of the century, now accounted for 17% of sales. Still, in the face of consumer products behemoths such as Procter & Gamble and Colgate-Palmolive with 2005 sales of $61.7 billion and $11.4 billion, respectively, Church & Dwight was not a major market force and struggled to retain market share.

Exhibit 5 Key Officers, Management Positions, and Tenure with Company — 2005

Name	Age	Position	Anniversary Date
James R. Craigie	52	President & Chief Executive Officer	2004
Mark G. Conish	53	Vice President, Global Operations	1975
Steven P. Cugine	43	Vice President, Global New Products Innovation	1999
Jacquelin J. Brova	52	Vice President, Human Resources	2002
Zvi Eiref	67	Vice President Finance and Chief Financial Officer	1995
Bruce F. Fleming	48	Vice President and Chief Marketing Officer	2006
Susan E. Goldy	52	Vice President, General Counsel and Secretary	2003
Joseph A. Sipia, Jr.	57	Vice President, President, and Chief Operating Officer, Specialty Products Division	2002
Gary P. Halker	55	Vice President, Finance and Treasurer	1977
Adrian J. Huns	58	Vice President, President International Consumer Products	2004
Paul A Siracusa	49	Vice President, Global Research and Development	2005
Louis H. Tursi	45	Vice President, Domestic Consumer Sales	2004

Source: Church & Dwight Co., Inc., *Notice of Annual Meeting of Stockholders & Proxy Statement* (2006), pp. 9–10.

Consumer Products

Prior to its acquisition spree, the company's growth strategy had been based on finding new uses for sodium bicarbonate. Using an overall family branding strategy to penetrate the consumer products market in the United States and Canada, Church & Dwight introduced additional products displaying the Arm & Hammer logo. This logoed footprint remains significant as the Arm & Hammer brand controls a commanding 85% of the baking soda market. By capitalizing on its easily recognizable brand name, logo, and established marketing channels, Church & Dwight moved into such related products as laundry detergent, carpet cleaners and deodorizers, air deodorizers, toothpaste, and deodorant/antiperspirants. This strategy worked well, allowing the company to promote multiple products using only one brand name, but it limited growth opportunities "in highly competitive consumer product markets, in which cost efficiency, new product offering and innovation are critical to success."[8]

From the company's founding until 1970, it produced and sold only two consumer products: Arm & Hammer Baking Soda and a laundry product marketed under the name Super Washing Soda. In 1970 under Minton, Church & Dwight began testing the consumer products market by introducing a phosphate-free, powdered laundry detergent. Several other products, including a liquid laundry detergent, fabric softener sheets, an all-fabric bleach, tooth powder and toothpaste, baking soda chewing gum, deodorant/antiperspirants, deodorizers (carpet, room, and pet), and clumping cat litter, had been added to the expanding list of Arm & Hammer brands. However, simply relying on baking soda extensions and focusing on niche markets to avoid a head-on attack from competitors with more financial resources and marketing clout limited growth opportunities.

Church & Dwight faced the same dilemma as other competitors in a mature domestic market for consumer products. New consumer products had to muscle their way into markets by taking market share from larger competitors' current offerings. With the majority of company sales concentrated in the United States and Canada, where sales are funneled through

Exhibit 6 Selected Consumer Product Categories

United States	Canada	United Kingdom
Laundry Products	Pure Baking Soda	Oral Care
Pure Baking Soda	Antiperspirants	Condoms
Carpet & Room Deodorizer	Oral Care	Antiperspirants
Cleaning Products	Bathroom Cleaners	Depilatories
Cat Litter	Carpet & Room Deodorizers	Pregnancy Kits
Pet Care Products	Condoms	Feminine Hygiene
Bathroom Cleaners	Depilatories	
Toilet Bowl Cleaner	Pregnancy Kits	**Spain**
Antiperspirants	Laundry Products	Depilatories
Oral Care Products		Skin Care
Condoms	**France**	
Depilatories	Skin Care	**Mexico**
Pregnancy Kits	Oral Care	Condoms
Laxatives	Depilatories	Depilatories
	Diagnostics	Oral Care
Australia		Pregnancy Kits
Baby Products	**Brazil**	
Depilatories	Skin Care	
Oral Care	Diagnostics	
Pregnancy Kits		

Source: Church & Dwight Co., Inc., *2005 Annual Report,* pp. 10–11.

mass merchandisers such as Wal-Mart and Walgreens, Church & Dwight was well equipped to gain market share with its low-cost strategy. However, in the international arena, where growth is more product driven and less marketing sensitive, the company was less experienced. To compensate for this weakness, Church & Dwight relied on acquisitions and management changes to improve its international footprint and reach.

So, in the late 1990s, the company departed from its previous strategy of developing new product offerings in-house and bought several established consumer brands such as Brillo, Parsons Ammonia, Cameo Aluminum & Stainless Steel Cleaner, Rain Drops water softener, Sno Bowl toilet bowl cleaner, and Toss 'N Soft dryer sheets from one of its competitors, Dial Corporation. An even broader consumer product assortment including Trojan, Nair, and First Response was added to the company's mix of offering with the acquisition of the consumer products business of Carter-Wallace in partnership with the private equity group Armkel. The breadth of its expanded consumer product offerings and brand names can be seen in **Exhibits 6** and **7.**

According to Minton as the company grew, "We have made every effort to keep costs under control and manage frugally."[9] A good example of this approach to doing business could be seen in the Armkel partnership. "Armkel borrowed money on a non-recourse basis so a failure would have no impact on Church & Dwight, taking any risk away from shareholders."[10] As mentioned previously, the remaining interest in Armkel was purchased in 2005, an

Exhibit 7 Representative Brand Names

Arm & Hammer	Arrid	Nair
Xtra	Aim	Trojan
Brillo	Pepsodent	Natura Lamb
Scrub Free	Spinbrush	First Response

Exhibit 8 U. S. Market Share Position

Product Category	Position
Laundry Detergent	3
Cat Litter	2
Bathroom Cleaner	1
Antiperspirants	5
Condoms	1
Depilatories	2
Home Pregnancy Test Kits	2

important move that cleared the way to increase marketing efforts behind Trojan, a brand that controlled 71% of the market.[11]

With its new stable of products and expanded laundry detergent offerings, Church & Dwight found itself competing head-on with both domestic and international consumer product giants such as Procter & Gamble, Colgate-Palmolive, Clorox, and Unilever. Even though it was smaller in size, Church & Dwight was an aggressive competitor, as its market share positions in key product categories show in **Exhibit 8.**

As more and more products were added to the consumer line-up, Church & Dwight brought many of its marketing tasks in-house as well as stepping out with ground-breaking marketing campaigns. The first major in-house marketing projects were in dental care. Although it entered a crowded field of specialty dental products, Church & Dwight rode the crest of increasing interest by both dentists and hygienists in baking soda for maintaining dental health, enabling it to sneak up on the industry giants. The company moved rapidly from the position of a niche player in the toothpaste market to that of a major competitor.

In a ground-breaking marketing campaign that some consider controversial, the company was to air commercials for condoms on prime-time television. "Church & Dwight executives say their new campaign is designed to shake people up, particularly those who don't think they need to use condoms. Attempts will be made to shock them out of complacency and grab their attention."[12] The company's increasing marketing strength has caught the attention of others as is evidenced by its partnership with Quidel Corporation, a provider of point-of-care diagnostic tests, to meet women's health and wellness needs. "The partnership combines Church & Dwight's strength in the marketing, distribution and sales of consumer products with Quidel's strength in the development and manufacture of rapid diagnostic tests."[13]

For the most part, Church & Dwight's acquired products and entries into the consumer products market had met with success. However, potential marketing problems might be looming on the horizon for its Arm & Hammer line of consumer products. The company could fall into the precarious line-extension snare. Placing a well-known brand name on a wide variety of products could cloud the brand's image, leading to consumer confusion and loss of marketing pull. In addition, competition in the company's core laundry detergent market continued to heat up as the market matured and sales fell, with major retailers such as Wal-Mart and Target wringing price concessions from all producers.[14] Would the addition of such well-known brand names as Xtra, Nair, Trojan, and First Response provide new avenues for consumer products growth?

Specialty Products

In addition to a large and growing stable of consumer products, Church & Dwight also had a very solid core of specialty products. The Specialty Products Division basically consisted of the manufacture and sale of sodium bicarbonate for three distinct market segments: specialty

Exhibit 9 Percent of Net Sales

	2005	2004	2003	2002	2001
Consumer Products	87	86	82	85	82
Specialty Products	13	14	18	15	18

chemicals, animal nutrition products, and specialty cleaners. Manufacturers utilized sodium bicarbonate performance products as a leavening agent for commercial baked goods; an antacid in pharmaceuticals; a chemical in kidney dialysis; a carbon dioxide release agent in fire extinguishers; and an alkaline in swimming pool chemicals, detergents, and various textile and tanning applications. Animal feed producers used sodium bicarbonate nutritional products predominantly as a buffer, or antacid, for dairy cattle feeds and made a nutritional supplement that enhanced milk production of dairy cattle. Sodium bicarbonate had also been used as an additive to poultry feeds to enhance feed efficiency.

"Church & Dwight has long maintained its leadership position in the industry through a strategy of sodium bicarbonate product differentiation, which hinges on the development of special grades for specific end users."[15] Management's apparent increased focus on consumer products had only recently affected the significance of specialty products in the overall corporate mix of revenues, as shown in **Exhibit 9.**

Church & Dwight was in an enviable position to profit from its dominant niche in the sodium bicarbonate products market, because it controlled the primary raw material used in its production. The primary ingredient in sodium bicarbonate was produced from the mineral trona, which was extracted from the company's mines in southwestern Wyoming. The other ingredient, carbon dioxide, was a readily available chemical that could be obtained from a variety of sources. Production of the final product, sodium bicarbonate, for both consumer and specialty products was completed at one of the two company plants located in Green River, Wyoming, and Old Fort, Ohio.

The company maintained a dominant position in the production of the required raw materials for both its consumer and industrial products. It manufactured almost two-thirds of the sodium bicarbonate sold in the United States and, until recently, had been the only U.S. producer of ammonium bicarbonate and potassium carbonate. The company had the largest share (approximately 75%) of the sodium bicarbonate capacity in the United States and was the largest consumer of baking soda as it filled its own needs for company-produced consumer and industrial products.[16]

Just like the Consumer Products Division, the Specialty Products Division focused on developing new uses for the company's core product, sodium bicarbonate. Additional opportunities continued to be explored for Armex Blast Media. This is a sodium bicarbonate-based product used as a paint stripping compound. It gained widespread recognition when it was utilized successfully for the delicate task of stripping the accumulation of years of paint and tar from the interior of the Statue of Liberty without damaging the fragile copper skin. It was being considered for other specialized applications in the transportation and electronics industries and in industrial cleaning because of its apparent environmental safety. Armex also had been introduced into international markets.

Specialty cleaning products were found in blasting (similar to sand blasting applications) as well as many emerging aqueous-based cleaning technologies such as automotive parts cleaning and circuit board cleaning. Safety-Kleen and Church & Dwight teamed up through a 50–50 joint venture, Armakleen, to meet the parts cleaning needs of automotive repair shops. Safety-Kleen's 2,800-strong sales and service team marketed Church & Dwight's aqueous-based cleaners as an environmental friendly alternative to traditional solvent-based cleaners.[17]

The company's Armakleen product was also used for cleaning printed circuit boards. This non-solvent-based product may have an enormous potential market because it may be able to replace chlorofluorocarbon-based cleaning systems. Sodium bicarbonate also had been used to remove lead from drinking water and, when added to water supplies, coated the inside of pipes and prevented lead from leaching into the water. This market could grow in significance with additions to the Clean Water Bill. The search for new uses of sodium bicarbonate from pharmaceutical to environmental protection continued in both the consumer and industrial products divisions.

International Operations

Church & Dwight traditionally enjoyed a great deal of success in North American markets and was attempting to gain footholds in international markets through acquisitions. The company's first major attempt to expand its presence in the international consumer products markets was with the acquisition of DeWitt International Corporation, which manufactured and marketed personal care products including toothpaste. The DeWitt acquisition provided the company not only with increased international exposure but also with much-needed toothpaste production facilities and technology. However, until the 2001 acquisition of the Carter-Wallace line of products, only about 10% of sales were outside the United States. By 2005, international sales of consumer products had grown to 17% of total revenues.

As the company cautiously moved into the international arena of consumer products, it also continued to pursue expansion of its specialty products into international markets. Attempts to enter international markets met with limited success, probably for two reasons: (1) lack of name recognition and (2) transportation costs. Although Arm & Hammer was one of the most recognized brand names in the United States (in the top 10), it did not enjoy the same name recognition elsewhere. In addition, on a historical basis, international transportation costs were at least four times as much as domestic transportation costs. However, export opportunities continued to present themselves as 10% of all U.S. production of sodium bicarbonate was exported. Whereas Church & Dwight dominated the United States sodium bicarbonate market, Solvay Chemicals was the largest producer in Europe and Ashi Glass was the largest producer in Asia. Although demand was particularly strong in Asia, "Little of the chemical produced in North America and Europe is exported to Asia because of prohibitive transportation costs."[18]

Church & Dwight's Future

According to Craigie, developing a strong portfolio of competitive brands required a relentless commitment to the following areas:

- Improving brand positioning to ensure brands stay relevant to consumers
- Accelerating new product development to meet changing consumer needs
- Delivering significant improvement in gross margins through cost improvement programs
- Increasing global leverage through expanding product offerings into current markets and large emerging markets through global marketing campaigns and supply-chain efficiencies
- Continuing to create value through acquisitions
- Securing superior leaders for the company to ensure functional excellence[19]

The core business and foundation on which the company had been built remained the same after more than 160 years. However, as management looked to the future, could they successfully achieve a balancing act based on finding growth through expanded uses of sodium bicarbonate while assimilating a divergent group of consumer products into an expanding international footprint?

Notes

1. Church & Dwight Co, Inc., Annual Report, 2005, p. 3.
2. *Ibid.,* p. 5.
3. *Ibid.,* p. 3.
4. Dwight Church Minton, personal interview (October 2, 2002).
5. *8-K, 2006.*
6. Church & Dwight, Co., Inc., *Annual Meeting, 2001*, p. 1.
7. Church & Dwight Co, Inc. Annual Report, 2006, p. 3.
8. *10K, 2006*, p. 20.
9. Minton (2002).
10. *Ibid.*
11. Jack Neff, "Trojan," *Advertising Age* (November 7, 2005).
12. Mary Ann Liebert, "Condom Maker Wants to Go Prime Time," Drug Development and STD News, *AIDS Patient Care and STDs,* Vol. 19, No. 7 (2005), p. 470.
13. Church & Dwight Co. Press Release, 2006, p. 1.
14. Doris de Guzman, "Household Products Struggle," *Chemical Market Reporter,* Vol. 269, No. 11 (2006).
15. Church & Dwight Co., *Annual Report, 2000*, p. 17.
16. Lisa Jarvis, "Church & Dwight Builds Sales Through Strength in Bicarbonate," *Chemical Market Reporter* (April 10, 2002).
17. Helena Harvilicz, "C&D's Industrial Cleaning Business Continues to Grow," *Chemical Market Reporter*, Vol. 257, No. 20 (May 15, 2000).
18. Gordon Graff, "Sodium Bicarb Supply Strong, Tags Level with Producer Costs," *Purchasing* (April 6, 2006), p. 28C1.
19. Church & Dwight Co, Inc., Annual Report, 2005, pp. 3–4.

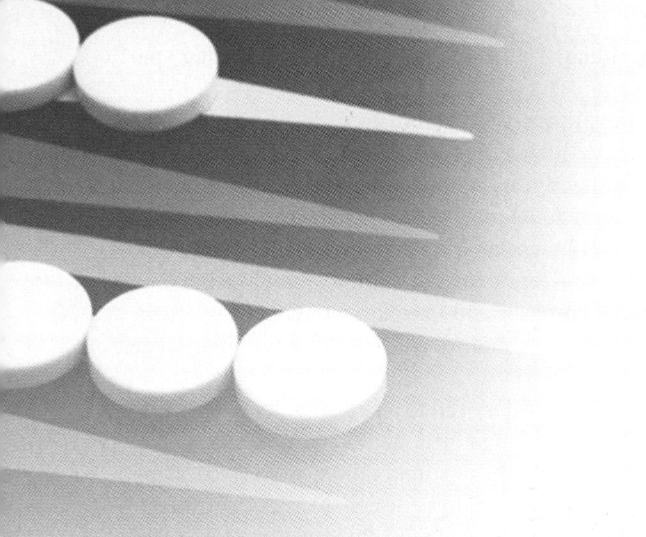

CASE 33

A.W.A.R.E.

John K. Ross III and Eric G. Kirby

IT WAS A TYPICALLY BEAUTIFUL MORNING IN CENTRAL TEXAS AS SHERRY STOOD AT THE office door watching the bustle of activity in the arena. It was just before the first client arrived and Bobby, the Lead Instructor, and several volunteers were getting Duke ready for Cindy. Duke was a 1,000-pound horse that would be led from his stall, groomed, tacked, and then provide Cindy an hour of physical and emotional therapy. Cindy was a beautiful nine-year-old girl with cerebral palsy who used a small walker and leg braces to walk and would, for a short time, allow Duke to be her legs—and her friend.

With a grin and a bang, Cindy opened the screen door to the office and entered as fast as she could. Sherry turned to help her put on her helmet, and within minutes Cindy was being assisted into the arena and onto the mounting blocks, where Bobby and Duke waited. Cindy's smile grew wider as she approached Duke and carefully climbed the mounting blocks. With the help of Bobby and the volunteers, Cindy lifted one leg up and over the saddle, and she was ready to ride. After carefully leaving the mounting blocks Cindy excitedly said "Walk on" and Duke, Cindy, Bobby, and the volunteers began an hour of intense physical therapy, which for Cindy would seem to pass like minutes and would be the highlight of her week.

History

This was A.W.A.R.E. (Always Wanted A Riding Experience). Located in San Marcos, Texas (30 miles south of Austin), A.W.A.R.E. was a not-for-profit therapeutic horseback riding center under the provisions of Section 501(c)3 of the U.S. Internal Revenue Service. Cathy Morgan founded A.W.A.R.E. in October of 1986, using her personal horse, four horses borrowed from friends, and a small arena borrowed from another friend. Cathy was a certified special education teacher and horse-riding expert. For years she had dreamed of combining

The authors wish to thank the fine people at A.W.A.R.E. for their cooperation and assistance. Although A.W.A.R.E. is real, the names used in this case have been changed. This case was prepared by Professors John K. Ross, III and Eric G. Kirby of Southwest Texas State University. This case was edited for SMBP and Cases in SMBP–9th, 10th and 11th Editions.

her love for special children and horseback riding. There was a ready clientele for her specialized type of therapy and growth occurred quickly.

Horseback riding as physical and emotional therapy began in Europe, probably in the 1600s. The modern therapeutic benefits were not realized until Liz Hartel of Denmark won the silver medal for dressage at the 1952 Helsinki Olympic Games—despite having paralysis from polio. Within a short period of time, medical and equine professionals had begun riding centers for rehabilitation purposes in England and then in North America by the 1960s. The first professional organization, North American Riding for the Handicapped Association (NARHA), was formed in 1969 for educational purposes and later to accredit active centers. Today, the number of NARHA-affiliated centers totals more than 550, providing more than 30,000 individuals with riding experiences (*www.narha.org*).

Within two years of founding A.W.A.R.E., Cathy had moved to a larger outdoor arena with nine stalls and lights for night riding. By then she had found three additional riding experts to become instructors and was soon "riding" clients from 9:00 A.M. until 9:00 P.M. She was charging $10 for a one-hour riding lesson and providing scholarships (discounted rates or free-of-charge) for some clients. A small Board of Directors, comprised of Cathy's acquaintances, had been formed and they provided some assistance. For the most part they were not a strong Board, being comprised of well-meaning individuals who were not members of the community's "movers and shakers" and not particularly savvy at running a business. Cathy was able to continue offering the therapeutic riding services, but, as in many small not-for-profits, cash flow was a continual problem. In fact, some weeks her instructors did not get paid until a client paid.

In 1992 Cathy began a letter-writing campaign for donations to help support A.W.A.R.E. with operating expenses, to provide scholarships, and to move to a covered arena. Their facilities were unusable when it rained, at which time the arena turned into a quagmire. Additionally, riders and volunteers were suffering from the heat and sun during the long Texas summers when afternoon temperatures in the 100s were not uncommon. The fund-raising campaign paid off when two locally owned corporations joined together and donated 20 acres with a covered arena, worth about $250,000. For the next year Cathy and a group of volunteers worked to refurbish the land and arena to meet NARHA accreditation standards.

During that same time A.W.A.R.E. put on a successful fundraiser dinner-dance-auction that netted approximately $19,000, and Cathy decided to return to teaching. The Board searched to replace Cathy but was unable to successfully find a long-term Executive Director. After two Executive Directors left within a short time because of the long hours, hard work, and meager salary, one of the volunteers, Sherry Ross (a local CPA who was working as a full-time volunteer), took over the functions of Executive Director and began exercising tight fiscal control of the operation.

Current Situation

A.W.A.R.E. was located on donated property seven miles south of San Marcos, approximately one-quarter mile off an interstate highway and directly behind one of the country's largest outlet malls. Recently the property across the street had begun to be developed into an upscale residential community. A.W.A.R.E. had 13 horses, over 100 clients per session (a 16-week period of time equivalent to a university semester), an unpaid Executive Director, two full-time paid instructors, four part-time paid instructors, and over 200 volunteers per session. A typical day began when Yvonne (who lived in a mobile home on the A.W.A.R.E. property as part of her salary) fed the horses at 7:00 A.M. Classes then began sometime after 8:00 A.M. and continued throughout the day, ending around 9:00 P.M.

For a typical lesson, the instructor began preparations 30 minutes prior to its start by reviewing previous lessons and goals for that client, organized aids (toys for fine motor skills, etc.), then assisted the volunteers as they groomed and tacked the horse. Once the client arrived, they donned a helmet and mounted their horse. During the lesson, one volunteer would be the "horse handler" and also had responsibility for observing and controlling the horse. One or two other volunteers would walk beside the horse as "sidewalkers" (spotters) for safety reasons and to interact with the client. The instructor then guided the class, leading the client through a series of activities designed to focus on verbal, gross or fine motor skills, balance, flexibility, or some other specific goal. Frequently these activities were disguised as games or play and may have included singing, interactions with other riders, and other "fun" activities. All of this was accomplished while the client was sitting, lying, or standing on the horse's back. At the conclusion of the hour lesson, the client was dismounted and returned with the instructor to the office area, returned his or her helmet, and talked briefly with the instructor. The volunteers untacked the horse and returned it to its stall. The instructor would then make notes about the current lesson in the client's file for future reference. Up to six clients may have ridden in a group lesson and been supervised by one instructor.

The Executive Director was also an instructor and, with the help of the Lead Instructor, performed all of the office work necessary to keep A.W.A.R.E. operating. This included preparing financial records, correspondence, payroll, schedule preparation, and the like. To begin a typical semester session, A.W.A.R.E. must contact previous riders to confirm continuing riding, select others who might want to ride from a waiting list, advertise for volunteers and conduct volunteer training, schedule lesson times that match both rider and instructor needs, perform routine maintenance on the facilities, and so forth. The workload was very heavy and the Executive Director generally worked 60 to 70 hours per week. **Exhibit 1** shows the current organizational structure for A.W.A.R.E.

The Lead Instructor typically worked 40 to 50 hours per week, and the one other full-time instructor worked a 40-hour week (both were paid about $10/hour). All other instructors were part time and were paid $8 per hour. Instructors had to be trained in the dual disciplines of horsemanship and physical therapy. A.W.A.R.E. would not ride a client unless a physician had approved horse riding as a beneficial therapy and the instructors had been able to provide not just a pony ride, but a therapeutic riding experience. The instructors continuously supported each other with ideas to improve their lessons and the sharing of knowledge about instructional pedagogy. Additionally, A.W.A.R.E. supported instructors attending specialized conferences on therapeutic horseback riding. However none of the instructors were certified physical therapists.

Exhibit 1 Organizational Structure: A.W.A.R.E.

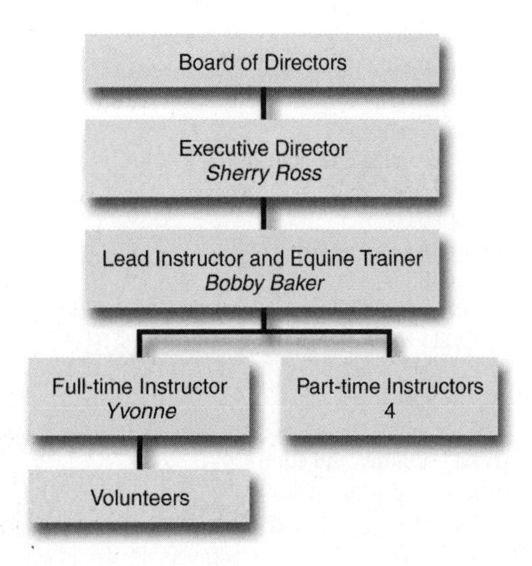

The Board of Directors for A.W.A.R.E was comprised of six volunteers from the local community and included two physicians, a university business professor, the wife of the local newspaper editor, the spouse of a local prominent lawyer, and a local businessperson. Although the Board members were good, well-intentioned individuals, the Board, as a whole, was not strong. They had put on two successful fund-raising events and seemed prepared to attempt another. However, the average tenure of the current Board member was well over five years, which was much too long to remain effective in a not-for-profit such as A.W.A.R.E. With only six members, the work of the Board could be demanding, and burnout could occur.

A.W.A.R.E. had a very good reputation in the local community as a well-run, efficient, and caring organization. The staff and volunteers were active in community affairs, A.W.A.R.E. received funds from the United Way, participated in local and state equestrian Special Olympics (where their riders generally took home most of the gold medals), and cooperated with other not-for-profits in local events. A.W.A.R.E. also had an excellent reputation amongst the equestrian community throughout the state.

Financials

When A.W.A.R.E. was located in a small arena, the majority of the expenses concerned involved payroll and horses. These were still the two largest expense items, however, maintenance and upkeep on the much larger facility had increased expenses dramatically. Additionally, expenses from several other items, like insurance, taxes, and veterinary care, had also increased drastically. Revenues came almost entirely from client fees, supplemented by donations. (See **Exhibits 2** and **3**.)

The contributors of the land placed a stipulation that for the first five years, only therapeutic horseback riding was to be allowed on the property. That time had now expired; however, no other revenue sources had been attempted. Clients were charged $25 for a one-hour

Exhibit 2
Balance Sheet: A.W.A.R.E.

Year Ending December 31	1999	1998	1997	1996	1995
Assets					
Current assets					
Checking and savings	$ 17,336	$ 20,229	$ 20,312	$ 8,608	$ 19,961
Accounts receivable	(864)	(1,189)	(659)	(362)	(187)
Total current assets	16,472	19,040	19,653	8,246	19,774
Fixed assets					
Buildings and land	265,419	265,000	265,000	265,000	265,000
Horses	10,551	10,850	7,550	4,401	4,400
Equipment	32,486	31,485	18,622	27,195	28,073
Accumulated depreciation	(85,195)	(70,622)	(24,087)	(22,034)	(11,329)
Total fixed assets	223,261	236,713	267,085	274,562	286,144
Total Assets	$239,733	$255,753	$286,738	$282,808	$305,918
Liabilities and equity					
Liabilities					
Current liabilities	$ 157	$ 0	$ 0	$ 0	$ 124
Total liabilities	157	0	0	0	124
Equity					
Retained earnings	239,576	255,753	286,738	282,808	305,794
Total equity	239,576	255,753	286,738	282,808	305,794
Total liabilities and equity	$239,733	$255,753	$286,738	$282,808	$305,918

Note: Rounding errors on total.

Exhibit 3
Profit and Loss Statement: A.W.A.R.E.

Year Ending December 31	1999	1998	1997	1996	1995
Ordinary income/expenses					
Income					
Rider fees	$ 50,097	$49,703	$44,894	$ 28,863	$42,184
Donations	10,670	12,716	8,056	4,051	6,579
United Way	7,653	423	5,550	3,982	3,924
Other income	4,095	1,451	3,275	4,367	25,089
Total income	72,515	64,293	61,775	41,263	77,767
Expenses					
Hay and feed	5,097	5,832	6,094	8,866	1,685
Facility maintenance	2,555	2,015	1,229	1,214	1,602
Insurance	3,294	1,875	1,900	1,864	1,265
Payroll	38,381	29,615	22,780	26,194	31,057
Other expenses	37,938	25,034	26,053	17,074	27,156
Total expenses	87,265	64,371	58,056	55,212	62,765
Net ordinary income	(14,750)	(78)	3,719	(13,949)	15,002
Other income/expenses					
In-kind donations	3,960	2,500	7,400	0	350
Net other income	3,960	2,500	7,400	0	350
Net income	$(10,790)	$ 2,422	$11,119	$(13,949)	$15,352

riding session with one of A.W.A.R.E.'s instructors. A modified fee could be charged for group lessons, and some clients were given scholarships. Hippotherapy, horseback riding with a certified physical therapist (PT), billed out as physical therapy and was covered by insurance. Currently, a local physical therapist brought a group of her clients to A.W.A.R.E. once a week. A.W.A.R.E. charged only the regular riding fees, and the PT billed the insurance companies at her regular rates.

Decision Time

Sherry, still standing at the door to the arena, frowned as she began to ponder several recent events that had placed A.W.A.R.E. in a precarious position. She was worried about, and unsure of, both the short-term and long-term viability of the organization. Over the past several years, the summer session had been very profitable for A.W.A.R.E. During the summer, a diagnostic camp for children was run by a national social organization that had brought 12 to 14 riders per day as part of their planned activities. This cash flow paid the summer salaries for the instructors, bought a year's supply of hay for the horses, and allowed A.W.A.R.E. to net around $7,000 for the summer. The camp had informed A.W.A.R.E. only weeks before the summer session was to begin that they were not participating this summer. The loss of cash flow could severely impact both the summer and fall programs. The loss of additional future revenues could force A.W.A.R.E. to scale back operation significantly.

Cash flow would also be impacted when Sherry stepped down as Executive Director. Sherry had been the volunteer Executive Director for over six years, and a medical condition was forcing her to retire. It would be expensive to replace her with a paid Executive Director (a typical salary range might be $36,000 per year) and an additional full-time instructor.

While these problems could be overcome, Sherry was worried about the future. What would A.W.A.R.E. be in 5 to 10 years? Would it even be in existence, operating as it did at present, or would it be something completely different? What would be best for the short- and long-term viability of A.W.A.R.E.? As volunteer Executive Director, Sherry realized there were a number of alternatives, ranging from closing A.W.A.R.E. to creating a nationwide network of similar programs. More realistically, A.W.A.R.E. could offer profit-generating activities such as riding camps for well children or perhaps holding another fund-raiser and hiring a new Executive Director. Other options might include partnering with the local hospital or other not-for-profits in the surrounding area. Sherry realized that due to the success and proximity of the outlet mall, the current property could be sold for about $750,000.

When Cathy Morgan first began A.W.A.R.E., she envisioned the eventual development of an entire therapy complex with staff physicians, live-in clients, and extensive therapy programs. However, Cathy was no longer with the program, and Sherry was unsure what direction A.W.A.R.E. should take and how to get there.

References and Sources for Additional Information

North American Riding for the Handicapped Association, *www.narha.org*.

San Marcos home page, *http://ci.san-marcos.tx.us*.

San Marcos Chamber of Commerce, *www.sanmarcostexas.com*.

CASE 34
Intel Corporation

J. David Hunger

In 1968, Robert N. Noyce, the co-inventor of the integrated circuit, and Gordon E. Moore left Fairchild Semiconductor International to form a new company. They took with them a young chemical engineer, Andrew Grove, and called the new firm Intel, short for integrated electronics. The company successfully made money by manufacturing computer memory modules. The company produced the first microprocessor (also called a "chip") in 1971. A key turning point for the new company was IBM's decision in the early 1980s to select Intel's processors to run IBM's new line of personal computers. Today, more than 80% of the world's PCs run on Intel microprocessors.

One of the company's early innovations was centralizing its manufacturing in giant chip fabrication plants. This allowed Intel to make chips at a lower cost than its competitors who made custom chips in small factories. The founders encouraged a corporate culture of "disagree and commit" in which engineers were encouraged to constantly think of new ways of doing things faster, cheaper, and more reliably.

Massive investment by Japanese competitors in the late 1970s led to falling prices in computer memory modules. Faced with possible bankruptcy, CEO Moore, with Grove as his second in command (Noyce had retired from active management), made the strategic decision in 1985 to abandon the computer memory business to focus on microprocessors. Projected growth in microprocessors was based on Moore's prediction that the number of transistors on a chip would double every 24 months. In what was soon called "Moore's Law," Gordon Moore argued that microprocessor technology would improve exponentially, regardless of the state of the economy, the industry, or any one company. Thus, a company had to be at the cusp of innovation or risk falling behind. According to Moore, "If you lag behind your competition by a generation, you don't just fall behind in chip performance, you get undercut in cost."

To raise money, Intel's management agreed to sell 12% of the company's stock to IBM for $250 million, a stake it later repurchased. Moore's Law soon became part of the corporate culture as a fundamental expectation of all employees. Andy Grove replaced Gordon Moore as Intel's CEO in 1987. Moore continued to serve on Intel's board of directors until 2001. During Grove's tenure as CEO from 1987 to 1998, Intel's stock price rose 31.6% annually and revenues grew from $1.9 billion to $25.1 billion. With 55% of its sales coming from outside the United States, Intel was transformed into a global corporation. The company became central to the growth of personal computers, cell phones, genomic research, and computer-aided design.

Strategic Decisions Lead to Market Dominance

In order to succeed in this high-tech business, management was forced to make a number of risky strategic decisions. For example, Intel's board of directors found it difficult to vote for a proposal in the early 1990s to commit $5 billion to making the Pentium microprocessor chip—five times the amount needed for its previous chip. In looking back on that board meeting, then-CEO Andy Grove remarked, "I remember people's eyes looking at that chart and getting big. I wasn't even sure I believed those numbers at the time." The proposal committed the company to building new factories—something Intel had been reluctant to do. A wrong decision would mean that the company would end up with a killing amount of overcapacity. Based on Grove's presentation, the board decided to take the gamble. Intel's resulting manufacturing expansion eventually cost $10 billion, but resulted in Intel's domination of the microprocessor business and huge cash profits.

In 1994, soon after the introduction of the Pentium microprocessor, users noticed a small defect in the chip and began demanding replacement chips. The company soon fixed the problem and quickly sent their computer-maker customers new Pentium chips to replace the defective ones. Even though Intel had no obligation to deal directly with end users, the people to whom the computer makers sold their PCs, Grove and the board decided to replace all defective Pentium chips wherever they might be. This was an expensive decision, but one for which the firm received high praise throughout the industry.

Realizing that future development of microprocessors would involve RISC technology—a technology Intel did not then have—CEO Grove persuaded Hewlett-Packard's CEO in 1994 to combine HP's work in RISC technology with Intel's ability in product development. This joint venture took on the multibillion-dollar expense of creating 64-bit chip architecture—thought to be crucial to Intel's continued success.

Along with Bill Gates at Microsoft and Steve Jobs at Apple, Andy Grove had become a major figure in the computer industry at the dawn of the 21st century. Although Grove retired as CEO in 1998, he continued to serve until 2005 as Intel's Chairman of the Board. Like Noyce and Moore before him, Grove took on the mantle of corporate guru. His 1996 book, *Only the Paranoid Survive*, in which Grove described how companies should deal with new competitors that emerge suddenly and change the fundamental shape of the industry, was widely read. Even with no official title, Grove continued to serve the company as its "senior adviser."

Intel After Andy Grove: A New Strategic Direction

Craig Barrett replaced Andy Grove as Intel's CEO from 1998 to 2005. He was able to persuade the board in 2002 to invest $28 billion in the latest manufacturing plants and technologies during the longest downturn in the chip industry's history. The board had been worried that new plants could burden the Intel with overcapacity if demand failed to materialize. By 2005, five factories were able to make 2½ times more chips than the older-generation fabrication plants—1.25 million chips daily. Because of the huge cost to build this type of plant, rivals TI, AMD, and IBM each had only one plant of this advanced type in 2006. TI conceded that its capacity to produce the latest-technology chips was limited to only 250,000 per day.

During Barrett's tenure, the company also invested billions of dollars in businesses outside the computer market that largely failed. In 2001, the firm exited from making cameras and other consumer electronics gear after key customers Dell and Hewlett-Packard (HP) complained that Intel was competing against them. In 2002, Intel took a $100 million charge against earnings when it cancelled its entry into Web hosting. In 2004, Intel attempted to go after Texas Instruments with its version of digital signal processors, a key ingredient in cell phones. Unfortunately, cell-phone manufacturers ignored Intel's product in favor of those by TI. Industry analysts concluded that Intel had a steep learning curve outside of personal computers.

Even with this checkered history outside the PC business, in 2004 CEO Barrett launched an ambitious strategic move. Instead of "Intel Inside," the plan was to be "Intel Everywhere." Under the new strategic plan, Intel would offer chips that would be used in all sorts of applications, including PCs, cell phones, flat-panel TVs, portable video players, wireless home networking, and medical diagnostic equipment. The company targeted 10 new product areas for its chips, primarily in the consumer electronics and communications markets. This plan was based on the movement in multiple industries from an analog to a digital format. According to Barrett, "Communication is going digital. Entertainment is going digital. We are able to bring our expertise into different areas where we really had no unique capability before." Supporting this announcement, Intel introduced a chip based on a new technology called WiMax that could be used to deliver high-speed wireless Internet access throughout a small city for about $100,000, one-tenth the cost of fiber-optic lines.

Competition Heats Up

Meanwhile, Intel's PC chip business was running into some difficulty. When, in 2004, Intel and Hewlett-Packard released the Itanium server chip they had jointly developed three years earlier, critics called it "the Itanic." Delivered two years late at a cost of $2 billion, the 64-bit chip performed more slowly than Intel's own 32-bit chip and seemed to have no future. In February 2004, CEO Barrett announced that the company would reconfigure its 32-bit Xeon chip for servers and its Pentium 4 for desktops so that they could handle 64-bit applications. Unfortunately, Advanced Micro Devices (AMD) had already begun selling its Opteron server chip in April 2003. The Opteron had the capability of running both 32-bit and 64-bit applications. Surprisingly, Intel's joint venture partner HP decided to sell servers with AMD's Opteron chip along with Intel's products. By December 2003, AMD had obtained 3.9% of the mainstream server market and was taking aim at the PC market as well.

Since 2003, AMD's chips had been faster, used less power, generated less heat, and cost less than did Intel's. As a result, Intel's share of the market in servers fell from almost 100% in 2001 to less than 85% in 2006. Its market share in laptop PCs declined from 88% in 2001 to 86% in 2006. Its share in desktops also dropped from 80% in 2000 to 74% in 2006. Dell, the biggest PC maker in terms of sales, decided in May 2006 to abandon its policy of only using Intel chips in its PCs by offering AMD chips in its computer servers. This was a serious blow to Intel's continued dominance of the market.

AMD was able to make a significant dent in Intel's market share by focusing its limited resources on microprocessors for PCs and servers and letting others supply the remaining chips. When Intel ran into a parts shortage for its desktop PCs in December 2005, AMD quickly dispatched its sales people to fill the void. AMD-based desktop PCs began to dominate the shelves at Best Buy, Circuit City, and other stores. By mid-2006, AMD held a 26% share of the U.S. server chip market and a 48% share of the multi-core processors, which put at least two chips on a single piece of silicon. As a result, AMD's gross margin of 58.6% exceeded Intel's of 55.1% during the first quarter of 2006.

In response, Intel began offering the first in a family of revamped chips called Core 2. These chips used less energy while offering better performance. Intrigued by AMD's success, industry analysts wondered if AMD would be able to continue offering innovative products without succumbing to the supply problems that had dogged it in the past.

Reinventing the Company

In May 2005, Craig Barrett transferred the CEO position to Paul Otellini and became Chairman of the Board. Past-President of Intel under Barrett, Otellini continued Barrett's strategic decision to push the company into multiple fields with new chip "platforms." PC growth was slowing. Cellular and handheld devices were now competing for the primary spot in people's lives. Otellini agreed that he must reinvent Intel or face a future of eventual decline. The PC business appeared to have reached maturity. Revenue growth had averaged 13% from 2002 to 2005, but analysts were estimating that the company's sales would only grow 7% in 2006 to $42.2 billion. Profits, which had been increasing on average 40% annually from 2002 to 2005, were expected to rise only 5% in 2006 to $9.5 million.

Ortellini proposed that Intel should not just make PC microprocessors, but should also create many types of chips, as well as software, and then combine them into what he called "platforms." Since taking over as CEO, Ortellini had reorganized the company, created business units for each product area, and scattered the processor experts among the units. He added 20,000 people in 2005. (Note: Intel's annual and quarterly reports and SEC filings are available via the company's web site at *www.intel.com*.)

Paul Ortellini was the first non-engineer to serve as Intel's CEO. He put particular emphasis on marketing because he thought that the only way Intel could succeed in new markets was by communicating more clearly what technology could do for customers. This went contrary to the corporate culture in which engineers had been the key players who made ever-faster chips and then let marketers try to sell them. Ortellini created development teams with people having a cross-section of skills. Chip engineers, software developers, marketers, and market specialists now worked together to develop breakthrough innovations. Many engineers were frustrated with the changes and their loss in status. Some of the design specialists who had been working on the Pentium 4 before it was cancelled left Intel for jobs at TI or AMD.

Ortellini's ultimate goal was to provide the manufacturers of everything from laptops and entertainment PCs to cell phones and hospital gear with complete packages of chips and software. The old logo of "Intel Inside" was to disappear, replaced by an updated Intel logo with a swirl to signify movement and a tagline of "Leap Ahead." Meanwhile, the Pentium brand was to be slowly phased out and replaced by Viiv, Centrino, and Core. Intel was on a new path. It was leaving the Grove era behind and moving into uncharted territory. This was not the first time that the company had bet everything on a new strategy. Would Intel succeed with its new strategic direction?

CASE 35

AirTran Holdings, Inc.

Maryanne M. Rouse

AirTran Airways' ability to grow, in what has arguably been the worst environment in years for airlines, adds an unexpected new chapter to one of the most unlikely turnaround stories in the airline industry. In 1996, when the carrier was known as ValuJet, it grounded all flights for three months after the crash of its Flight 592 in the Everglades killed all 110 people on board. Fortunately, the carrier had floated a package of $150 million in junk bonds just prior to the Everglades crash, and these cash resources proved critical as the company addressed safety concerns during the shutdown and the 11 successive loss quarters that followed. In 1997, ValuJet merged with AirTran Airways Corporation to form AirTran Holdings, Inc. (AAI).

At the end of December 2004, AirTran operated 508 daily flights to 48 destinations, primarily in the eastern United States, making it the second-largest "affordable-fare" scheduled airline in the United States in terms of departures (just behind Southwest).

Although the company moved its headquarters from Atlanta to Orlando, Florida, after the 1996 crash, it still flies most of its flights to and from Atlanta, providing both point-to-point and one-stop flights through its Hartsfield hub. AirTran offers a business class any business can afford, all-assigned seating, a generous frequent flier program, and a corporate program dubbed "A2B"; unlike its competitors, the carrier never requires a round-trip purchase or a Saturday night stay.

The company's regional jet operation, AirTran JetConnect, operated by joint-venture partner Air Wisconsin, flies 50-seat Canadair Regional jets in short-haul markets to and from the airline's hub at Hartsfield Atlanta International Airport. AirTran JetConnect serves Greensboro, North Carolina; Pensacola, Florida; and Savannah, Georgia—all of which were previously served by AirTran. The new service will allow the company to redeploy its 717s to increase frequencies in longer-haul, more profitable markets and facilitate growth in larger markets not currently served. In addition, AirTran JetConnect will allow the airline to expand into other short-haul markets as well as increase frequencies in underserved markets.

Marketing and Operations

AirTran's marketing strategy is to develop an innovative brand identity that sets it apart from its low-fare and full-service competitors. The company targets two primary segments: price-sensitive business travelers and leisure travelers, primarily in the eastern United States. To attract business travelers, the carrier launched a business class product that is, in terms of comfort, the equivalent of the first class service offered by its full-service rivals. The business class cabin is configured with 2 × 2-foot oversized seats, providing considerably more leg and seat room than a typical coach cabin. Targeted to the price-sensitive business flier, upgrades to business class from coach are just $25.

AirTran offers a range of fares based on advance purchases of 14 days, 7 days, 3 days, and "walk-up" fares. All fares are one-way, and most are nonrefundable; however, reservations can be changed prior to departure, with a service charge.

The company also offers a popular frequent flier program, A+ Rewards, that allows members to earn free travel more quickly than its competitors and, for twice the number of flight credits, will even buy members a free domestic ticket on any major carrier. The A+ Rewards program offers a number of ways to earn free travel, including the use of the AirTran Visa card, Hertz car rentals, and bonus earnings for Business Class.

In spring 2003, AirTran introduced a new standby program targeted broadly to young travelers (and specifically to college students) between the ages of 18 and 22. Dubbed the X-Fares Standby Program (*www.xfares.com*), this marketing initiative allows those who are eligible to fly standby to almost any AirTran destination for $55 per segment ($75 per "long-haul" segment).

In addition to targeting individual business travelers, AirTran has focused on developing travel partnerships with companies of all sizes, from one- and two-person small businesses to such large corporations as BellSouth, State Farm, and John Deere. Under the terms of its A2B corporate travel program, employees of registered companies get free confirmed upgrades to business class when paying full coach fares, fee waivers for ticket refunds or changes, and advance seat assignment. Unlike rival Southwest, AirTran has established interline ticketing and baggage agreements with Delta, United, US Airways, and American Trans Air and has ticketing arrangements with major online travel services such as Orbitz, Priceline, Expedia, and Travelocity.

AirTran has been aggressive in lining up corporate and community support via public–private partnerships that allow the carrier to shift more of the risk of expansion to communities and businesses expected to benefit from overall lower fares in their markets. The "public" part comprises revenue guarantees by cities, counties, or other municipal entities to protect AirTran against losses during the initial phase of operations; the "private" part builds "travel banks" in which businesses pledge to spend a specified amount on tickets. Both elements help to build a loyal following and serve as a cushion against the early losses of expanding into a new city and the invariable backlash from bigger competitors, which often respond by slashing their own fares and expanding service. Because AirTran's arrival in a market typically drives down fares by as much as 50%, both cities and businesses view the partnership guarantees as money well spent. For example, when AirTran began service to Wichita, Kansas, in May 2002, the average full fare on the Wichita–Washington, DC, flight dropped from $1,667 to $460. Wichita, which was competing with other cities to lure AirTran, estimates that the entry of the low-fare carrier could lead to annual airfare savings of $43 million for business and leisure travelers.

In December 2004, AirTran lost a bidding war to buy leases on 14 gates at Midway Airport in Chicago from ATA Holdings, a company now in bankruptcy. The company, which added seven daily flights from Midway to Florida destinations in January 2004, had planned to create a Midwestern hub and diversify its route system by adding more east–west flights. Despite the disappointing loss of gates to Southwest, AirTran believes it can grow profits by adding new destinations—Sarasota, Indianapolis, and three unnamed cities—and by adding flights to connect cities already in its system.

Named "Best Low-Fare Airline" for 2001 and 2002 by *Entrepreneur* magazine, AirTran's cost structure is among the lowest in the domestic airline industry in terms of cost per Average Seat Miles (ASM). The company's low-cost position is supported by an emphasis on cost controls, lower distribution costs (reservations, ticketing), and high employee productivity. The company's labor costs are equivalent to approximately 25% of revenue—the same percentage as Frontier and JetBlue—below Southwest's 30% and significantly below the full-service carriers' 40+%. An award-winning web site that makes it easy to book flights online has helped AirTran shift 52.5% of its sales to the site—one of the highest percentages in the industry—with an additional 13% of bookings coming from other travel sites. The company estimates its cost per booking online at less than $1—a significant saving over the $8.50 average cost of booking through a travel agent.

In September 1999, the company became the launch customer for the new Boeing 717, an innovative, cost-efficient, and environmentally friendly commercial aircraft that has reduced the higher fuel and maintenance costs associated with the DC-9s with which it had begun operations. (The company's current fleet comprises 77 Boeing 717-200s and 5 Boeing 737-700s.) AirTran has also forged close ties with Boeing and Boeing Capital Corporation, a full-service provider of financial services, including asset-based lending and leasing. Boeing Capital, an indirect wholly owned subsidiary of the Boeing Company, refinanced $201 million of AirTran's junk bonds in 2001 (and also agreed to finance the 20 Boeing 717s to be delivered in 2002, 22 used and 1 new 717 in 2003, and 5 737-700s delivered through June 2004), enabling AirTran to continue its rapid fleet modernization.

Finance

AirTran was one of the few domestic airlines to report profitable operations for the year ended December 31, 2003, recording operating income of $86.3 million and net income of $100.5 million. The company also strengthened its balance sheet by issuing $145.9 million in common stock and $125.0 million of convertible debt at 7% while paying down $76.5 million of long-term debt at 11.27%, paying down $12.7 million of long-term debt at 13%, and converting $5.5 million of 7.75% convertible debt to equity, all of which greatly improved AirTran's debt-to-equity ratio.

Despite a sea of red ink, overcapacity, and threatened bankruptcies in the industry, the company overcame intense fare wars and weak October bookings to eke out a profit of $1.1 million, or 1 cent per share for fourth quarter 2004. Although this was down from $21.7 million or 24 cents a share in fourth quarter 2003, AirTran beat analysts' consensus estimate of a 9 cent loss. Both domestic fare wars and escalating fuel costs hurt the company's profit yield. (The company reported a 70.3% increase in fuel costs.) AirTran's load factor for the period declined 0.5%, to 69.3, compared with fourth quarter 2003; however, revenue passenger miles increased 22.6% as capacity rose 23.4%.

The four hurricanes that struck the state of Florida in 2004 have had and will continue to have a major economic impact on the state in the affected area, which represents about 51% of the airline's normal traffic flows and seriously disrupted flights over the normally busy Labor Day holiday. Both the company's Orlando headquarters and its aircraft hangar in Orlando suffered damage that further hampered operations. The impact of the hurricanes, coupled with a weak revenue environment and record high fuel costs, affected AirTran's financial results for both the third and fourth quarters.

For the full year, AirTran reported a profit of $12.3 million, or 14 cents per share, to become one of only two U.S. airlines (the other was Southwest) to post an overall profit for the year.

Complete annual and quarterly financial information is available from the company's web site (*www.airtran.com*), *The Wall Street Journal* (*www.wsj.com*), and FreeEdgar.

The Industry

On the morning of September 11, 2001, terrorist attacks shut down the U.S. airline industry. The Federal Aviation Administration (FAA) suspended all commercial flights within hours after the attacks on the World Trade Center's Twin Towers and the Pentagon and, although some flights resumed three days later, on September 14, the industry still had not recovered nine months later. Continuing concerns about the safety of flying, a weaker-than-expected economic recovery, and delays resulting both from tighter security and fewer flights led to a passenger traffic year-over-year decline of approximately 12% among the nine major U.S. airlines in the first three quarters of 2002.

Major airlines, many of which deferred or cancelled new aircraft deliveries, pared down flight schedules, and furloughed employees in the wake of 9/11, have been slow to increase capacity to previous levels. Some majors have permanently retired up to 5% of their total capacity, mostly large, older, gas-guzzling planes such as DC-10s and 727s. And, while analysts and airline financial officers agree that retiring inefficient aircraft is a positive step toward profitability in an industry that had suffered from overcapacity, a great deal of that capacity is being replaced by low-fare startups, most of which are still growing, and by small-jet regional carriers. For example, New York–based JetBlue Airways, while still small (500 million revenue passenger miles in April 2002, about 10% of what Continental carried in the same period), has won over a significant number of business travelers on the long-haul routes that have been the province of big, full-service carriers for years. JetBlue is strongly capitalized and well run, and analysts predict that it can grow at an aggressive 25% per year for the next five years by taking market share from the majors. Similarly, both Frontier Airlines and American Trans Air have made traffic gains at the expense of United Airlines in Denver and other western cities.

The airline industry is highly competitive in terms of fares, frequent flier benefits, routes, and service. Profit levels in the industry are highly sensitive to changes in operating and capital costs and the extent to which competitors attempt to match each other's fares and services, as well as to general economic trends. Energy prices continue to be unpredictable: Favorable prices in the first quarter of 2002 were followed by sharp increases in April and May. The airlines have racked up higher costs for the security tax assessed on tickets; for the monthly security fees paid to the Department of Transportation (DOT); for a war-risk insurance premium; for implementing federally mandated directives such as stronger cockpit doors; and for the first class seats dedicated to federal air marshals. Recently testifying before a Congressional committee, airline executives noted that if the United States does strike Iraq, the results will be disastrous for the industry because travel, particularly international travel, will fall off sharply at the same time that oil prices surge.

Of increasing concern to carriers is the number of business travelers who are practicing what one industry analyst calls "Airline Avoidance." Poor service and complex pricing, further exacerbated by arcane rules, regulations, and restrictions on reservation changes, have created an environment in which companies and individuals are purchasing planes, purchasing fractional ownership in planes, or choosing to drive. So many travelers are choosing the latter that Delta Air Lines (DAL) launched a fare sale at the end of March 2002 specifically to provide additional customer incentive to fly rather than drive. The short-haul market is crucial to profitability for full-service carriers because, in general, travelers pay more per mile to fly short trips.

Increasing numbers of travelers are using web sites to book airline tickets, hotel rooms, and car rentals. According to the Internet analysis group Jupiter Media Metrix, consumers were expected to spend about $36.8 billion on travel sites in 2004, up from $24 billion in 2001. Concerned about prices and practices of online travel services, Congress created a nine-member commission to investigate the pricing, practices, and exclusive marketing agreements of various airline and independent sites.

The industry is subject to regulation by a number of federal, state, and local departments and agencies. The DOT has regulatory jurisdiction over passenger airlines, with the FAA regulating aircraft maintenance and operations, including equipment, ground facilities, licensing, and communications. The Aviation and Transportation Security Act of 2001 established a new Transportation Security Administration (within the DOT) with responsibility for aviation security functions including passenger and baggage screening.

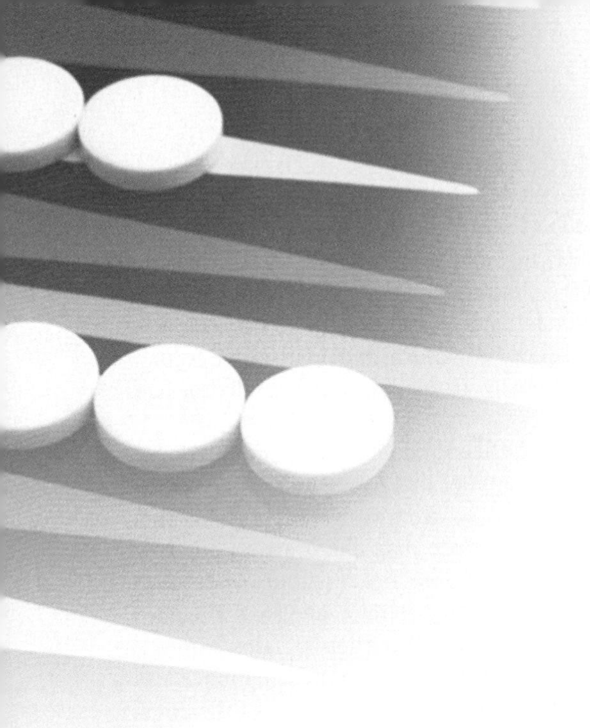

CASE 36

Boise Cascade/ OfficeMax

Maryanne M. Rouse

Boise Cascade Corporation (BCC), long an integrated forest products company, had been attempting for some time to shift its emphasis from manufacturing to distribution. In a move that surprised many who thought Boise would move more gradually, the 91-year-old paper and lumber products company announced in late July 2004 that it would sell its land and plants, its headquarters building in Boise, Idaho, and even its name to Madison Dearborn Partners, a Chicago equity investment firm. When the $3.7 billion deal was completed, probably by mid-November, what was then Boise Cascade would take the name OfficeMax (OMX).

When Boise acquired office supplies catalog/retailer OfficeMax late in 2003, many industry analysts thought the acquisition sent a clear signal that the company might eventually leave the volatile and regulated timber market and key segments of the paper business altogether—but thought it would do so gradually. At the same time that Boise announced the OfficeMax acquisition, the company revealed that it would review alternatives for its non-retail paper and building products businesses, which have combined annual sales exceeding $3.6 billion. Although Boise's best-performing line of business had been its office solutions segment, which alone accounted for $4.022 billion of the company's total sales in 2003, it was thought unlikely that Boise would pursue an immediate sale of its other businesses. Boise had argued for a "mill-to-desktop" model for its paper business, giving the company a good reason not to sell. And, although net income for the paper business had declined substantially over the past few years, it had contributed $1.9 billion to sales and $38.6 million to Boise's bottom line in 2003.

The Company

Boise had been a major distributor of office products and building materials and an integrated manufacturer and distributor of paper, packaging, and wood products. The company currently competed in three segments: Boise Office Solutions, Boise Building Solutions, and Boise Paper Solutions. Although there were significant intersegment transactions, each was managed as a separate business because products, services, markets, and competitive factors differed. Once the acquisition was complete, the company planned to report results for two segments: contract sales and retail sales.

Boise Office Solutions (formerly Boise Cascade Office Products) was a multinational distributor of products for the office, including office supplies and paper, technology products, and office furniture. While office papers were sourced from Boise Paper Solutions, substantially all other products were purchased from outside manufacturers or industry wholesalers. The Office Solutions segment sold directly to large and small businesses and government purchasers in the United States, Canada, Mexico, Australia, and New Zealand. This segment served customers via 63 distribution centers, 2 outbound sales centers, 4 customer service centers, and more than 100 retail stores. This segment included the operating results for OfficeMax. Boise Office Solutions accounted for 48.4% of the company's sales and 58.6% of the company's operating segment profits in 2003, compared to 47.8% of the company's sales and 61% of the profit of the three operating segments in 2002.

Boise Paper Solutions manufactured and sold free-sheet papers, containerboard, corrugated containers, newsprint, and market pulp. This segment operated five pulp and paper mills, two paper converting facilities, six paper distribution facilities, and five corrugated container plants in the United States. Boise Paper Solutions accounted for 34.6% of the company's sales and 48.4% of segment profits in 2003 versus 18.9% of the company's 2002 sales and 19.1% of the profit of the three operating segments. Uncoated free sheet represented 57% of the segments revenue for 2002. Approximately 38% of the segment's free sheet (including 74% of office papers) was sold through Boise Office Solutions; the equivalent of 54% of containerboard was transferred to the company's corrugated container plants. With the exception of newsprint, sales were made by the company's own sales force.

Boise Building Solutions manufactured plywood, oriented strand board (OSB), lumber, laminated veneer lumber (LVL), particleboard, and engineered wood products at 25 manufacturing facilities in the United States, Canada, and Brazil. The segment also operated 28 distribution facilities that provided a broad line of building materials, including wood products manufactured by Boise, to retail lumber dealers, home centers, home improvement "big box" stores, and industrial customers. Boise Building Solutions accounted for 16.45% of Boise's segment sales and a loss of 7% for fiscal 2003, compared to 33% of the company's 2002 sales and 19.7% of the profit of the three operating segments.

Boise owned or controlled approximately 2.4 million acres of timberland in the United States. The timberland was managed as part of the company's Building Solutions and Paper Solutions segments, with the impact on operating results included in those segments. Although Boise's timber resources represented a relatively small part of the company's overall operations, this aspect of the business had been the source of continuing public relations problems for the company. And, while the company's competitors in forest products had also been the target of environmental groups, Boise had been the environmental movement's "poster child" for forest mismanagement and environmental irresponsibility. Because much of the criticism related to the company's logging operations in old-growth forests, Boise's recent announcement that it would no longer engage in this practice was expected to mitigate the negative publicity.

The OfficeMax Acquisition

In December 2003, Boise paid approximately $1.4 billion in cash, stock, transaction costs, and debt assumed for the number-three U.S. office supply chain, OfficeMax. The acquisition created an $8.3 billion company that was expected to be better able to battle rivals Staples and Office Depot. On the plus side, analysts agreed that the combined OfficeMax and Boise Office Solutions would be a much stronger competitor. Although there was some concern that the acquisition, which was financed with a combination of 40% cash and 60% equity, would result in significantly higher debt, an increase in intangible assets and goodwill, much higher lease payments (reflecting OfficeMax's principal mode of financing), and heightened business risk, it was hoped that the recent announcement of the deal with Madison Dearborn Partners would allay many of those concerns.

OfficeMax sold discount-priced office supplies and equipment through nearly 1,000 stores in the United States, the U.S. Virgin Islands, and Puerto Rico, as well as via a majority-owned subsidiary in Mexico. The company also sold more than 40,000 name-brand and private-label office products online and via catalogs. The stores combined office supplies with in-store FurnitureMax (office furniture) and CopyMax (printing services) outlets. Through an alliance with Hewlett-Packard, OfficeMax sold computers and related products in most of its stores. As part of its strategy to focus on meeting the needs of small businesses, OfficeMax offered Internet connection services through EarthLink and shipping services through Airborne. The company's retail operations were supported by 3 PowerMax inventory distribution facilities, 17 delivery centers, and 2 national customer service centers.

The company's financial performance had reflected both a weak economy and strong competitors. OfficeMax reported net income of $76.165 million on sales of $4.775 billion for 2002; however, $57.5 million of earnings resulted from the use of tax loss carryforwards. For Quarter 3 2003, the company reported a loss of $26.7 billion on sales of $1.046 billion. OfficeMax reacted to a string of quarterly losses by developing new store formats to boost sales and reach new markets. OfficeMax PDQ (Pretty Darn Quick) was a smaller-format store that featured CopyMax. OfficeMax's current plans included using its Mexican stores as a platform for expansion into other Spanish-speaking countries.

Financial Position/Performance

Boise's 2003 net income of $17.1 million on total sales of $8.245 billion was an improvement over the company's disappointing $11.34 million in profit on $7.412 billion in sales for 2002. Approximately 90% of the company's sales were in the United States. Analysts believed that Boise's restructuring would leave the company in a stronger financial position, with low debt levels and adequate cash to fund aggressive store and supply-chain improvement as well as growth in its retail and contract segments. However, Boise was seen as lacking the marketing expertise and merchandising strategies of its two larger rivals. Information about Boise's financial position and performance is available in the company's annual reports, quarterly reports, and 10-K forms (*www.officemax.com*).

Key Competitors

International Paper

International Paper (IP) was the world's largest forest products company. It had significant global businesses in paper and paper distribution, packaging, and forest products, including building materials. The company had operations in nearly 40 countries, employed more than

90,000 people, and exported its products to more than 120 nations. Sales of $24.976 billion for 2002 were derived from businesses located primarily in the United States, Europe, Latin America, Asia/Pacific, and Canada; the company reported a net loss of $880 million for 2002. In International Paper's Quarter 3 2003 results, released September 27, the company reported earnings of $122 million on sales of $6.4 billion.

International Paper produced plywood, paper, pulp, and packaging, and it processed chemicals such as crude tall oil and crude sulfate turpentine (byproducts of the paper making process). Arizona Chemical, an International Paper subsidiary, produced resins and inks. International Paper controlled approximately 9 million acres of forest in the United States and 1.5 million in Brazil; it also held interests in forests in New Zealand. The company distributed paper products via its xpedx subsidiary in North America and its subsidiaries Papeteries de France, Scaldia (the Netherlands), and Impap (Poland). About 75% of International Paper's sales were in the United States.

International Paper had pursued an aggressive restructuring strategy, divesting approximately $3 billion of non-core operations from mid-2000 through year-end 2002. The company had also announced that it would sell 1.5 million of the 9 million acres of U.S. timberland it owned in the Southern United States before 2009. (International Paper had planned to sell its Industrial Paper and Arizona Chemical businesses, but it had not received what it considered to be acceptable offers.) International Paper planned to exit the cellulose pulp business and close its mill in Natchez, Mississippi, by the end of 2003. At the same time, International Paper had made a number of acquisitions, including Union Camp, Shorewood Packaging, and Champion International.

Georgia-Pacific

Georgia-Pacific (GP) was the world's second-largest forest products company. Georgia-Pacific operated in two key lines of business: building products (plywood, lumber, OSB, gypsum, wallboard, particleboard, adhesives) and consumer products (Brawny, Coronet, Dixie, Quilted Northern). The company's on-again, off-again portfolio realignment strategies had confused investors and analysts alike.

In a move that would allow the company to develop a sharper focus on its core businesses, Georgia-Pacific announced on September 22, 2003, that it was exploring strategic alternatives for its building products distribution business, including a possible sale. Divesting this segment would allow the company to focus on operating its established building products manufacturing businesses and maintaining its leading supplier role in the wholesale distribution channel. And, although Georgia-Pacific had noted a desire to create shareholder value by sharpening focus on its more stable, consumer-oriented businesses and its goals of reducing debt and strengthening its balance sheet, the company contemplated and then withdrew a planned $1 billion spinoff of its consumer products and packaging businesses, citing poor market conditions.

Georgia-Pacific had reported a loss of approximately $735 million on $23.271 billion in sales for 2002. On October 16, 2003, the company reported quarterly earnings of $1.369 million on $1,369 million in sales (*www.gp.com*).

Weyerhaeuser

One of the largest U.S. forest products companies and North America's largest producer of softwood lumber, Weyerhaeuser (WY) managed 8 million acres of timberland, mainly in the Southern United States and Pacific Northwest. The company also held cutting licenses on about 35 million acres in Canada and had holdings in New Zealand, France, Ireland, and Uruguay. The company had grown both internally and via acquisition. It had bought rival

Willamette Industries for $6.1 billion in early 2002. In addition to timberlands, Weyerhaeuser's operating segments included Wood Products, Containerboard, Packaging and Recycling, Pulp and Paper, and Real Estate.

The wood products segment produced lumber, plywood, OSB, and engineered wood. Weyerhaeuser's real estate operations (home building and master-planned communities) were conducted through its Weyerhaeuser Real Estate Company subsidiary, principally in selected metropolitan areas of southern California, Maryland, Nevada, Texas, Virginia, and Washington.

Weyerhaeuser had reported 2002 net income of $241 million on sales of $18.521 billion. On October 24, 2003, the company reported quarterly earnings of $82 million on revenues of $5.2 billion.

Staples

Staples (SPLS), the largest office supply superstore in the United States and the largest global competitor in this segment, targeted small businesses, home office professionals, and consumers. It sold office products, furniture, computers, and printing and photography services at over 1,500 Staples and Staples Express stores in the United States, Canada, Belgium, France, Germany, Italy, the Netherlands, Portugal, Spain, and the United Kingdom. The company's superstores, which average 20,000 square feet, offer approximately 7,500 SKUs, including computers, other business machines and equipment, office furniture, and office supplies, as well as complementary services, including printing, binding, and copying.

Although Staples superstores generated most of the company's revenues and profits, Staples also operated Staples Business Delivery (a combination of its Staples Direct small business catalog and staples.com), Quill Corporation (catalogs and related web sites), and Staples Contract (contract office supplies). The company's market penetration strategy had focused on opening superstores in city suburbs and smaller Staples Express stores in urban areas. The company had also pursued growth via acquisition in its European operations.

Staples reported earnings of $446.10 million on $11.596 billion in sales for the fiscal year ended February 1, 2003. On August 17, 2003, the company reported Quarter 2 earnings of $139.353 million on quarterly sales of $2.878 billion.

Office Depot

Office Depot (ODP) was the second-largest global chain of office supply stores. In addition to office supplies, Office Depot's 1,000+ company-owned and licensed stores offered computer hardware and software, furniture, and art and engineering supplies, as well as printing and copying services. Most of the warehouse-type stores' sales were to small firms, home offices, and individual customers. Ink Depot, a "corralled" shop dedicated to ink, toner, and fax supplies, currently operated at over 500 Office Depot superstores and would soon be added to all Office Depot locations. In 2002, OPD formed a two-year alliance with the U.S. Chamber of Commerce that would provide members a 5% discount on most office supplies.

Office Depot had closed its concept chains, including Furniture at Work, to focus on aggressively growing its retail stores in North America. Although Office Depot planned to add some stores in Europe and Asia, the company was concentrating on Internet and catalog sales to serve those markets because the operational costs of doing so were significantly lower. In response to a growing concern about ecological issues, Office Depot had entered into an alliance with the environmental consulting firm Green Order to help customers comply with environmental standards in their procurement practices.

Retail sales accounted for just under 60%, with more than 40% of Office Depot's sales generated by its business services group via delivery and contract services to medium and large companies. The company also sold through its Office Depot and Viking Office Products catalogs. (Viking sold office products worldwide.) Office Depot had reported net income of $310.7 on overall sales of $11.357 billion for 2002; 3rd quarter earnings of 2003 were $91.666 million on sales of $3.2 billion.

Industry Environment

Growing and harvesting timber were subject to numerous federal and state government laws and policies to protect the environment, water resources, and wildlife. Most competitors operated under the Sustainable Forestry Initiative (SFI), a certification standard designed to supplement government regulatory programs with voluntary landowner initiatives to further protect public resources. SFI certification was also a key element in repairing the poor social responsibility ratings timber and logging operations had earned for their lack of environmental concern. SFI was an independent standard overseen by a governing board comprising conservation organizations, academia, the forest products industry, and large and small forest landowners. Regulatory and nonregulatory initiatives had increased operating costs, resulted in changes in the valuation of timber, and had made it more difficult to respond to rapid changes in markets, extreme weather, or other unexpected circumstances. The industry faced a protracted squeeze on profits as global competitors flooded the market with lumber and other commodity wood products. Cyclical factors such as the current global recession and the relative strength of the U.S. dollar had negatively affected sales and profits, while other factors, including the increased demand for lumber, plywood, and OSB as a result of the expansion of home building and the increase in repair/remodeling activity in the United States, had had positive effects on demand.

The slowing global economy had resulted in a decreasing demand for pulp and uncoated free sheet, while the strength of the U.S. dollar had made pulp products less competitive overseas, especially in Europe. The demand for paper was expected to lag behind historical rates as a result of electronic substitution in some paper applications. In the containerboard segment, the global recession had reduced manufacturers' demand for corrugated containers, particularly in the United States. In addition, costs for old corrugated containers, a primary raw material for containerboard production, had increased during 2002 and 2003 as a result of increased demand as Asian competitors increased containerboard capacity.

Weak prices, high energy costs, and increased cheap paper imports from Europe had negatively affected the paper sector. For the balance of 2003 and 2004, demand and prices were expected to be flat because competitors may not be able to sustain previously announced price increases. As business levels and employment increase, the demand for certain grades, including uncoated free sheet, were expected to improve.

The business-to-business and business-to-consumer office products markets were highly competitive. Competition was based principally on price and service. Although business demand was strongly influenced by economic conditions and employment levels, consumer demand was considerably less volatile. If market research by Office Depot was any indication, all three companies had ground to make up in brand building/differentiation. Office Depot had found that about half of customers who bought office supplies were uncertain afterward which of the three chains' stores they had shopped in.

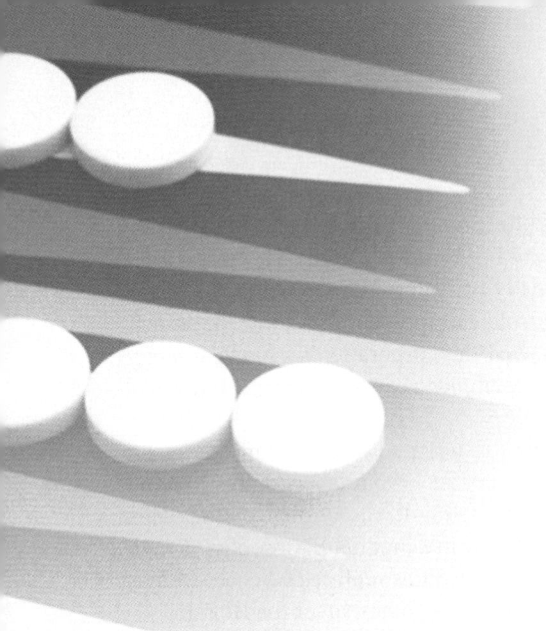

CASE 37
Dell, Inc.

J. David Hunger

Dell, Inc., was founded in 1984 by Michael Dell at age 19 while he was a student living in a dormitory at the University of Texas. As a college freshman, he bought personal computers (PCs) from the excess inventory of local retailers, added features such as more memory and disk drives, and sold them out of the trunk of his car. He withdrew $1,000 in personal savings, used his car as collateral for a bank loan, hired a few friends, and placed ads in the local newspaper offering computers at 10%–15% below retail price. Soon he was selling $50,000 worth of PCs a month to local businesses. Sales during the first year reached $600,000 and doubled almost every year thereafter. After his freshman year, Dell left school to run the business full time.

Michael Dell began manufacturing his own computers in 1985 and marketed them through ads in computer trade publications. Two years later, his company witnessed tremendous change: it launched its first catalog, initiated a field sales force to reach large corporate accounts, went public, changed its name from PCs Limited to Dell Computer Corporation, and established its first international subsidiary in Britain. Michael Dell was selected "Entrepreneur of the Year" by *Inc.* in 1989, "Man of the Year" by *PC Magazine* in 1992, and "CEO of the Year" by *Financial World* in 1993. In 1992, the company was included for the first time among the *Fortune* 500 roster of the world's largest companies.

By 1995, with sales of nearly $3.5 billion, the company was the world's leading direct marketer of personal computers and one of the top five PC vendors in the world. In 1996, Dell supplemented its direct mail and telephone sales by offering its PCs via the Internet at *dell.com*. By 2001, Dell ranked first in global market share and number one in the United States for shipments of standard Intel-architecture servers. The company changed its name to Dell, Inc., in 2003 as a way of reflecting the evolution of the company into a diverse supplier of technology products and services. In 2005, Dell topped *Fortune's* list of "Most Admired Companies." In fiscal year 2006, the company earned $3,572 million in net income on $55,908 million in net revenue. Dell shipped more than 10 million systems during the fourth quarter of 2006—making it the best sales quarter in Dell's history. (Note: Dell's annual and quarterly reports and SEC filings are available via the company's web site at *www.dell.com*.)

Problems of Early Growth

The company's early rapid growth resulted in disorganization. Sales jumped from $546 million in fiscal 1991 to $3.4 billion in 1995. Growth had been pursued to the exclusion of all else, but no one seemed to know how the numbers really added up. When Michael Dell saw that the wheels were beginning to fly off his nine-year-old entrepreneurial venture, he sought older, outside management help. He temporarily slowed the corporation's growth strategy while he worked to assemble and integrate a team of experienced executives from companies such as Motorola, Hewlett-Packard, and Apple.

The new executive team worked to get Dell's house in order so that the company could continue its phenomenal sales growth. Management decided in 1995 to abandon distribution of Dell's products through U.S. retail stores and return solely to direct distribution. This enabled the company to refocus Dell's efforts in areas that matched its philosophy of high emphasis on customer support and service. By 2004, Kevin Rollins replaced Michael Dell as Chief Executive Officer, allowing the founder to focus on being Chairman of the Board.

Business Model

Dell's business model was simple: Dell machines were made to order and delivered directly to the customer. Dell had no distributors or retail stores. Dell PCs had consistently been listed among the best PCs on the market by *PC World* and *PC Magazine*. Cash flow was never a problem because Dell was paid by customers long before Dell paid its suppliers. The company held virtually no parts inventory. As a result, Dell made computers more quickly and cheaply than any other company.

Dell Computer became the master of process engineering and supply-chain management. It spent only $463 million annually on R&D, contrasted to $534 million by Apple Computer and $4 billion by HP, but it focused all of its spending on improving its manufacturing process. Instead of spending its money on new computer technology, Dell waited until a new technology became a standard. Michael Dell explained that soon after a technology product arrived on the market, it was a high-priced, high-margin item made differently by each company. Over time, the technology standardized—the way PCs standardized around Intel microprocessors and Microsoft operating systems. At a certain point between the development of the standard and its becoming a commodity, that technology became ripe for Dell. When the leaders were earning 40% or 50% profit margins, they were vulnerable to Dell making a profit on far smaller margins. Dell drove down costs further by perfecting its manufacturing processes and using its buying power to obtain cheaper parts. Its reduction of overhead expenses to only 9.6% of revenue meant that Dell earned nearly $1 million in revenue per employee—three times the revenue per employee at IBM and almost twice HP's rate.

Although the company outsourced some operations, such as component production and express shipping, it had its own assembly lines throughout the world. The Winston-Salem, North Carolina, plant was opened in 2005 as Dell's third American plant. It was able to manufacture a complete desktop computer every five seconds.

Product Line and Structure

Over the years, Dell, Inc., broadened its product line to include not only desktop and laptop computers, but also servers, storage systems, printers, software, peripherals, and enhanced services, such as infrastructure services. By 2006, net revenue by product line was composed of desktop PCs (38%), mobility (25%), software and peripherals (15%), servers and networking (10%), enhanced services (9%), and storage (3%).

Dell's corporate headquarters was located in Round Rock, Texas, near Austin. The company was structured into three geographic business units: Dell Americas (North and South America), located in Round Rock, Texas; Dell Asia Pacific (Pacific Rim and Australia), located in Singapore; and Dell Europe, Middle East, and Africa, located in Bracknell, England. The company manufactured computer systems in seven plants in Austin, Texas; Nashville, Tennessee; Winston-Salem, North Carolina; Eldorado do Sul, Brazil; Limerick, Ireland; Penang, Malaysia; and Xiamen, China. Its 2006 revenue by region was 65% from the Americas, 23% from Europe, and 12% from the Asia-Pacific unit.

Environmental Change

By 2006, the once-torrid growth in PC sales had slowed to about 5% a year. The percentage of 2005 PC sales via the phone and Internet fell in the United States as the sales through U.S. retail stores rose. Consumers seemed to be more interested in new high-featured digital products, such as Apple's iPod, than in commodity products such as plain beige PCs. Meanwhile, Dell's rivals were becoming more competitive. Gateway, for example, had found ways to reduce its costs and had fought its way back to profitability. The same was true for Hewlett-Packard (HP) once it had digested its acquisition of Compaq. HP's market share increased from 13.8% to 14.9% in 2005, while Dell's shrank slightly. Competitors were pricing their products more aggressively and taking advantage of being in thousands of retail stores. Lenovo (previously Legend), with $13 billion in sales and 8% of the worldwide PC market, was reentering the retail notebook market with the ThinkPad it had acquired from IBM. Based in China, Lenovo specialized in consumer PCs and low-cost manufacturing. It already dominated the PC market in China with 26% market share. Contrasted with Dell, Lenovo sold its products through retailers, corporate resellers, and the IBM sales force, in addition to direct marketing.

Dell, in early 2006, was the largest PC vendor in the world, commanding 20% of the global market, 32% of the American market, and 13% of the European market. Nevertheless, the company's chief advantages—direct marketing and power over suppliers—were losing their punch. Even though the company slashed prices in 2005, it failed to gain market share. Ironically, by driving down supplier costs, Dell had also reduced its rivals' costs. In addition, the sales growth in the computer industry was in the consumer market and in emerging countries rather than in the corporate market in which Dell sold about 85% of its products. The consumer market was expected to grow 10% in 2007 versus only 7.8% for the corporate market. Consumers' desire to see and touch multiple products before a purchase made Dell's direct marketing channel less attractive to them. Sales in countries outside the United States and Canada were often based on the advice of sales staff, putting Dell's "direct only" business model at a disadvantage.

Dell's absence in retail stores had hurt the company's attempts to expand beyond PCs into consumer electronics, such as televisions. As corporate buyers increasingly purchased their computer equipment as part of a package of services to address specific problems, service-oriented rivals such as IBM and HP had an advantage over Dell. Dell's close relation with Intel had been a significant advantage in past years, but this single-source agreement had created a problem recently when Intel's rival AMD offered cheaper and, in some cases, better-performing microprocessors. Taken together, these facts made it clear that the environment no longer favored Dell's business model.

Internal Issues

Dell had grown in size to the point that its usual double-digit sales increases were proving to be unsustainable. Its sales growth dropped from 18.7% in fiscal year 2005 to 13.6% in 2006. Meanwhile, Dell's customer service had fallen to a new low. In 2005, Dell's customer service rating fell 6.3% to a score of 74 (average for the industry) in a survey by the University of Michigan. More than 45% of calls to Dell required at least one transfer. The Better Business Bureau reported that complaints about Dell more than doubled in 2005 to 1,533. It was not surprising to analysts when Dell's U.S. market share fell to 28% during the first quarter of 2006. Consequently, Dell's stock dropped from $40 a share in August 2005 to $25 in June 2006.

Although the company was working to improve customer satisfaction by adding more service people, more people meant increased costs. Even though more sales growth was expected in the consumer than in the corporate market, the consumer market had its disadvantages. For one thing, sales to U.S. consumers carried margins of only 6% compared with 11% for corporate buyers. Second, products had to be physically present in retail stores to compete with Gateway, HP, and Lenovo, among others.

Dell's management was working hard to regain sales growth and cut costs. It was spending more than $100 million in 2006, far more than it had spent in 2005 when its expenses were 9% of sales, compared to 13% for Apple and HP. To boost its customer service, it was expanding call centers to house 1,000 to 3,000 representatives. It was hoped that this would increase the chance that any caller's problem could be solved by someone within the building. Dell was also installing large monitors to let workers see the number of callers on hold. By early 2006, hold times had already been cut in half from those in 2005 and internal surveys of 5,000 customers revealed a 35% increase in customer satisfaction from a year earlier. To cut costs, Dell was redefining what it meant by "free shipping" for its low-end PCs. Instead of delivering them to the customer's home, Dell was planning to mail them to the nearest post office for pickup. Home delivery was an extra charge, but standard with more expensive models.

With rivals such as HP matching or undercutting its PC prices, Dell's management decided to go on the offensive. In June 2006, Dell announced a new policy of accepting old PCs, printers, and other products made by Dell for free recycling throughout the world. Management also decided to no longer single-source its purchases of microprocessor chips from Intel, but to also buy them from AMD for use in a new line of servers and desktop PCs.

In a surprise move, the company introduced its new XPS M2010, a cross between a desktop and a laptop targeted to the entertainment enthusiast. The $3,500 PC featured a detachable wireless keyboard and a monitor with adjustable height. Its black, leather-like exterior, when closed, resembled a luxury briefcase. Meanwhile, Dell's new $1,990 XPS 700 desktop was aimed at video "gamers"—a market segment that had ignored Dell's conservative offerings in the past. The company also acquired Alienware Corporation, whose sleek PCs were modeled after the beast from the movie *Alien,* to appeal to hard-core game players. Management hoped that its "gamer" PCs would generate positive responses that would spill over to Dell's other lines.

On August 17, 2006, Dell's management announced that the company's second-quarter profit fell 36% to $605 million, far short of expectations. It also admitted that the company was cooperating with an informal investigation by the Securities and Exchange Commission. This announcement came just days after Dell voluntarily recalled 4.1 million potentially flammable batteries supplied by Sony Corporation.

Future Prospects

Michael Dell refused to become negative about the future of his company. Back in the 1990s, he recalled, critics had claimed that there were limits to the firm's direct-sales model, and even suggested that Dell would never be able to make laptops or servers. Said Dell, "People say the sky has fallen, that it's the beginning of the end. I don't agree. There are lots of markets with room to grow." Management hoped to double or even triple its market share in Europe. Sales in The Netherlands, for example, were growing by 40% a year. In June 2006, Michael Dell purchased 2.9 million shares of Dell common stock for an average price of $23.99 each, his first purchase of common stock since 2001.

Analysts, nevertheless, continued to be ambivalent about the firm's prospects in a changing industry. Should the company follow the consumer market down in price and adjusts its costs accordingly, or should it focus on business products—sacrificing market share and sales growth for profits?

CASE 38

Six Flags, Inc.: The 2006 Business Turnaround

Patricia A. Ryan

"The business was broken," commented Daniel Snyder in June 2006, the new Chairman of the Board of Six Flags.[1] Fixing the business would not occur overnight for Snyder, who owned the Washington Redskins, but clearly he thought it would be doable and profitable, as was the proxy fight to run the theme park company in late 2005. According to Mark Shapiro, CEO of Six Flags:

> We're investing more in our operations because the health of the business depends on bringing back families. Our first priority is to fix the operation and that is not going to happen overnight. We see this as a long-term investment.[2]

Over the past five years, Six Flags stock had underperformed relative to Cedar Fair, its closest competitor, as well as compared to market indices. In May 2001, Six Flags stock traded at $23.25, and it sank nearly 80% in value to the $5 range in 2005. In 2004, Snyder's company, RedZone, increased its ownership in Six Flags, as did Bill Gates' investment vehicle, Cascade Investments. Together, the two parties owned over 20% of the stock, and they demanded changes to improve financial and operating performance. Snyder and Gates used their ownership to try to influence the Board to make some drastic changes, but the parties were at odds as how to improve the performance of the company. Snyder then made a successful move to remove the old Board of Directors and senior management, replacing them with his own hand-picked executives and board members. The fight for the company was over. In 2006, Snyder had Six Flags in his hands—it was now time to implement the changes he saw necessary to increase the value of his investment.

"The company was so ground down; it won't reverse in a year or two," commented Dennis L. Speigel, President of Consultancy International Theme Park Services.[3] Clearly, it would take skill and time to turn this company around.

The Business

Six Flags operated the largest regional theme park company in the world with a sole focus on theme and water parks. Six Flags operated 29 theme parks as listed in **Exhibit 1.** Regional theme park companies such as Six Flags located parks within a day's drive for visitors and worked to place its parks near large population bases within 50 and 100 miles for a one- or two-day mini-vacation. Unlike national entertainment parks such as Disneyworld and Universal Studios, they were more likely to attract visitors for a day or two as opposed to being a vacation destination. Six Flags' management estimated that their parks were within 150 miles of two thirds of the U.S. population. Specific population bases for each park are given in **Exhibit 1.**

Six Flags was founded in 1961 by Angus G. Wynne with the opening of Six Flags over Texas, a pirate-themed adventure theme park. Over the next 45 years, the company grew into

Exhibit 1 Theme Parks by Focus, Location, Population, and Size: Six Flags, Inc.

Theme Park	Type of Park	Location	Population Within 50 and 100 Miles, Respectively (in millions)	Size (acres)
Six Flags America	Theme and water	Largo, Maryland	7.4 , 12.4	523
Six Flags Darien Lake and Camping Resort	Theme and water	Darien Center, New York	2.1, 3.1	978
Six Flags Elitch Gardens	Theme and water	Denver, Colorado	2.9, 3.9	67
Six Flags Fiesta Texas	Theme and water	San Antonio, Texas	2.0, 3.6	216
Six Flags Great Adventure, Six Flags Hurricane Harbor, Six Flags Water Safari	Theme, water, safari (three separate parks)	Jackson, New Jersey	14.3, 28.1	2279
Six Flags Great America	Theme and water	Gurnee, Illinois	8.8, 13.5	324
Six Flags Kentucky Kingdom	Theme and water	Louisville, Kentucky	1.5, 4.8	59
Six Flags Magic Mountain and Six Flags Hurricane Harbor	Theme and water (two separate parks)	Valencia, California	10.6, 17.7	262
Six Flags Marine World	Theme and mammals	Vallejo, California	5.7, 10.7	135
Six Flags Mexico	Theme	Mexico City, Mexico	NA, 30	107
Six Flags New England	Theme and water	Springfield, Massachusetts	3.2, 15.8	263
Six Flags New Orleans*	Theme	New Orleans, Louisiana	NA	140
Six Flags over Georgia and Six Flags White Water Atlanta	Theme and water (two separate parks)	Atlanta, Georgia	4.8, 7.7	290
Six Flags over Texas, Six Flags Hurricane Harbor	Theme and water	Arlington, Texas	5.7, 6.8	285
Six Flags Splashdown	Water	Houston, Texas	5.1, 6.3	60
Six Flags St. Louis	Theme and water	Eureka, Missouri	2.7, 3.9	503
Six Flags Waterworld Parks	Water (two parks)	Concord and Sacramento, California	7.6, 11.3	NA
Enchanted Village and Wild Waves	Water and rides	Seattle, Washington	3.5, 4.6	66
Frontier City†	Western theme	Oklahoma City, Oklahoma	1.3, 2.6	113
La Ronde	Theme	Montreal, Canada	4.3, 5.8	146
The Great Escape and Six Flags Great Escape Lodge and Indoor Waterpark	Theme and water (two parks)	Lake George, New York	1.1, 3.2	351
White Water Bay†	Tropical theme	Oklahoma City, Oklahoma	1.3, 2.6	21
Wyandot Lake	Water and rides	Columbus, Ohio	2.2, 6.8	18

* Closed for 2006 season because of hurricane damage from Hurricane Katrina.

† Scheduled to close at the end of the 2006 season.

a chain of theme parks with such parks as Six Flags over Georgia, and Great America in Gurnee, Illinois. Known for their fast roller coasters and adventure rides, the company successfully built a group of theme and water parks under the Six Flags name.

The theme parks changed hands several times over the 45 year history and in 1991 were sold to Time Warner. In 1998, Time Warner sold the theme parks to Premier Parks. Premier Parks continued the rapid expansion of Six Flags, using the Six Flags name for several smaller theme parks that Premier had developed including Darien Lake, Elitch Gardens, and Adventure World (CITIES). The Six Flags name was adopted for the entire firm in 2000 and by the end of 2005, the company was the largest amusement operator in the United States.

Six Flags held licenses for multiple Warner Brothers and DC Comics characters including Bugs Bunny, Tweety Bird, Daffy Duck, Yosemite Sam, Batman, and Superman. This meant they could market these characters through merchandise sold in the parks, as well as use the characters to enhance the park experience and for advertising the parks.

Multiple factors affected the business success of Six Flags. The theme parks were seasonal, with 85% of theme park attendance in the second and third quarters of the calendar year.[4] Given the outdoor nature of the theme parks, adverse weather conditions affected attendance and thus revenue. There were multiple competitors for family entertainment dollars; competition came both from direct competitors, such as Cedar Fair and Busch Entertainment, and other competitors, such as Walt Disney World, Disneyland, Sea World, and family fun centers. Cedar Fair owned 12 amusement parks and five outdoor parks including Knott's Berry Farm in California and Cedar Point in Ohio. Busch Entertainment, a subsidiary of Anheuser-Busch, owned nine theme parks in five states. It included Sea World parks in California, Florida, and Texas and two Busch Gardens parks.

The Financial Picture

Six Flags had not turned a profit since 1998. In the last six years, its net losses had been $51,959,000 in 2000, $58,102,000 in 2001, $105,698,000 in 2002, $61,713,000 in 2003, $464,809,000 in 2004, and $110,938,000 in 2005. During that time, its revenues totaled $1,041,197,000 in 2000, $1,075,989,000 in 2001, $1,059,095,000 in 2002, $1,048,643,000 in 2003, $1,037,692,000 in 2004, and $1,089,682,000 in 2005. It had been the huge loss of $5.23 per share in 2004 that had forced a management change at the company. Furthermore, long-term debt had been continually increasing during the past six years. This left Six Flags burdened with excessive debt payments. In 2000, long-term debt accounted for 52.34% of total assets, whereas at the end of 2005, long term debt had increased to 60.94% of total assets. Six Flags was burdened with about $2,242.4 million in total indebtedness at the end of 2005. On August 2, 2006, Moody's downgraded Six Flags' $2.4 million in debt from B2 to B3. It further lowered Six Flags' senior unsecured debt to lower junk level at Caa2 from Caa3. The ratings agency expressed concern about potential higher future expense associated with management's changes on the currently weak financial position.[5] On the day the debt was downgraded, the stock price fell 22.7% to $5.76. Clearly, the stock market interpreted this as a negative signal, and one that was a surprise to the market. The annual maturities of long-term debt subsequent to December 31, 2005 were as follows:[6]

2006	$113,601,000
2007	7,148,000
2008	317,675,000
2009	314,400,000
2010	299,754,000
Thereafter	1,189,779,000
Total	$2,242,357,000

After 2000, the company had lost money each year, with losses skyrocketing in 2004 to 17.08% of sales. Total operating costs were over 80% of revenue in all but one year, with interest payments on debt swallowing the rest of the revenue. Nevertheless, the company's operating income (before debt payments and park closing costs) had been consistently positive at $195,686,000 in 2000, $205,454,000 in 2001, $230,389,000 in 2002, $188,723,000 in 2003, $149,573,000 in 2004, and $183,347,000 in 2005. The company's overall poor performance was reflected in its falling stock price. Although the stock showed strong gains during the exuberant market of the late 1990s, since the market decline in 2000 Six Flags had struggled to maintain its value in the stock market. (For financial statements, see *www.sixflags.com*.)

In October 2005, Six Flags AstroWorld in Houston was closed. The 104-acre site was placed on the market and Six Flags planned to use the proceeds to retire some of its debt. Six Flags New Orleans sustained extensive damage from Hurricane Katrina in August 2005 and did not open for the 2006 season. The company was in negotiation with its insurance carrier for insurance claims and planned to rebuild the park.

In January 2006, Six Flags announced it intended to sell its Oklahoma City theme and water parks after the 2006 season. The proceeds were to be used to repay some of the debt. Six Flags, according to industry analysts, had considerable potential in the theme park industry, but Snyder had his work cut out for him. Would he succeed?

Enter Bill Gates

Bill Gates, founder of Microsoft, one of the world's wealthiest men and a major shareholder of Six Flags, was not pleased with the company's recent performance. His ownership was under the name of his Canadian investment company, Cascade Investments. Gates began buying Six Flags stock in 1999 and accumulated 10,810,120 shares, which accounted for 11.5% of the firm's stock in 2004, at a market value of $54 million. It was stated in SEC filings that Gates had become increasingly dissatisfied with the financial performance of Six Flags over the past five years.[7] He expressed intent to discuss with Six Flag's board the company's strategic decision making and recent financial and operating performance.

When Gates began investing in Six Flags, the stock price had fallen about 80%.[8] Rather than recovering over time, the stock fell further. Gates and Snyder combined owned over 20% of the company's stock, and the pressure to remove old management was great.

Enter Daniel Snyder and Mark Shapiro

In 2005, there was a full management and board turnover. Unsatisfied with how things were being run, Daniel M. Snyder, owner of the Washington Redskins and Red Zone LLC, entered a proxy fight to gain control of Six Flags. Successful in his bid, he became Chairman of the Board in late 2005. Additionally, two of his designates joined the board. This included Mark Shapiro, the new President and CEO. Shortly after this change, there were six new directors placed on the Board and five resignations, two of which were new directors.

Mark Shapiro became CEO of Six Flags on December 14, 2005. For the previous year, Shapiro had served as CEO of RedZone LLC, a private investment firm founded by Daniel Snyder. Snyder held an 11.5% interest in Six Flags.

Although the management turnaround may have been exactly what Six Flags needed, the new management team and directors did not have a proven success record with Six Flags. The management was young in age and in tenure with Six Flags. Only four members had been associated with Six Flags prior to 2005. The rest of the management team and board were new to the company in 2005 or 2006. Given the change in management and the new operational plan to turn around Six Flags, the risks of failure must be assessed.

Turnaround

At the end of 2005, Six Flags employed about 2,500 full-time employees with an additional 31,500 seasonal employees. Many of the seasonal employees were college students. According to CEO Shapiro,

> While we see 2006 as a transitional year, by reaffirming previous management's guidance we are underscoring confidence that our redefined strategy, coupled with celebration of our 45th anniversary, will broaden our customer base by attracting families as well as teenagers, boosting our per capita revenue.[9]

In June 2006, Six Flags announced that it was considering the closure of six more of its 30 theme parks. These were Six Flags Darien Lake near Buffalo, New York; Six Flags Waterworld in Concord, California; Six Flags Elitch Gardens in Denver, Colorado; Six Flags Spashtown in Houston, Texas; Wild Waves and Enchanted Village near Seattle; and Hurricane Harbor outside Los Angeles, California.[10]

Six Flags Darien Lake, one of the six parks facing closure, announced that it would close four weeks early for the 2006 season, closing October 1 rather than November 1. The situation was becoming dire for the company. According to Robert Niles, founder of *themeparkinsider.com,* "In many respects, they've slid to a point where they resemble a souped-up county fair more than world-class theme parks."[11]

The Future

Six Flags changed its ticker symbol from PSK to SIX on June 5, 2006. On August 17, 2006, Shapiro rang the closing bell on the NYSE to celebrate the new ticker symbol. He commented:

> The 2006 season is winding down, and we've witnessed families returning to our parks, spending more, and driving our guest approval ratings to a five-year high. We're proud of what our employees have accomplished in this transitional year, and we're looking ahead to new horizons in 2007.[12]

There were many challenges facing Six Flags. Shapiro felt that the company's new strategy of closing the less productive theme parks and working to increase spending from guests who were in the parks was working. Management eliminated the deep discounts to maintain sales and instead focused on stronger sales techniques. Shapiro felt that the new strategy was working.

> Increased guest spending is continuing at a strong pace—a clear indication that our strategy is working. The drop-off in attendance was driven primarily by an anticipated decline in our season pass sales, which we are no longer deeply discounting in an effort to restore price brand integrity, and to wean ourselves from those teens who don't spend money in the park.[13]

Looking to the future, Shapiro felt that management had clarified the company's mission. They were repositioning Six Flags as a set of themed parks, rather than as a collection of individual amusement parks. They were increasing the bang for the buck for visitors hoping they would stay longer, spend more, and return faster. The emphasis on customer satisfaction was stronger—as indicated by Shapiro's comments:

> This means Six Flags will get back to being genuine theme parks—not merely amusement parks. It means we will restore diversified entertainment offerings such as the Chinese acrobats. It means reinvigorating the parks with "streetmosphere"—a process of enhancing the spaces between the rides with a variety of entertainment offerings. It means that daily parades, in-park celebrations, acrobatic and juggling acts will dazzle our guests. It means the casts of our Looney Tunes characters and Justice League superheroes will expand dramatically from one or two per park in 2005 to at least 30 in every Six Flags branded park, every hour of every operating day, mingling with the crowds, greeting our customers, posing with them for photographs, even riding the rides. By offering a true character program, we will have created new revenue streams that are sorely needed.[14]

Six Flags faced a number of challenges as it ended the 2006 season. Management was in the middle of implementing a new operational plan and there was uncertainly about its success. Management was young and energetic, but fairly new to the company. Given that 85% of park attendance occurred in the second and third quarters of the calendar year, Six Flags faced the challenges of managing a seasonal business.[15] This was a problem for Six Flags given that a number of its parks were in northern locations. As more recreation facilities competed for the consumer's recreation dollar, pressures would surely intensify. Finally, there was the huge mound of debt from which Six Flags needed to unbury itself. There was a risk that the company would not be able to meet its debt obligations. This would affect management's ability to obtain future funding as well as possibly force the company into bankruptcy.

What lay ahead for Six Flags? Would management's turnaround strategy save the firm, or would the heavy debt burden eventually sink the company?

Endnotes

1. "The Batman and Robin of Six Flags," *Business Week* (May 8, 2006).
2. "6 Flags Mulling Future of 6 Parks," Associated Press (June 22, 2006).
3. "Batman and Robin" (2006).
4. Six Flags, *2005 Annual Report,* 20.
5. "Moody's Downgrades Six Flags Debt," Associated Press (August 2, 2006).
6. *Six Flags 2005 10-K,* F-25.
7. *Six Flags 13-D* (August 27, 2004).
8. Matt Krantz, "Add Bill Gates to List of Unhappy Six Flags Investors," *USA Today* (September 1, 2004).
9. Six Flags Company Press Release (March 8, 2006).
10. Associated Press (June 22, 2006).
11. "Batman and Robin" (2006).
12. "Six Flags President and CEO Mark Shapiro Rings NYSE Closing Bell to Celebrate Company's New Stock Ticker Symbol, SIX," Six Flags Press Release (August 17, 2006).
13. Associated Press (June 22, 2006).
14. "Annual Letter to the Shareholders," *Six Flags 2005 Annual Report.*
15. *Six Flags 2005 10-K,* 22.

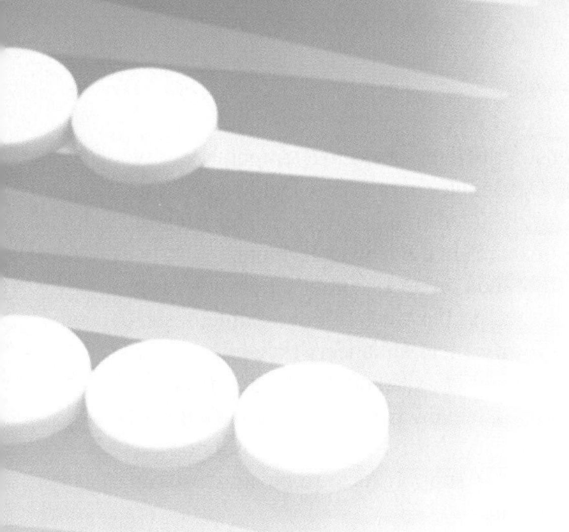

CASE 39

H.J. Heinz Company

Maryanne M. Rouse

H.J. HEINZ COMPANY (HNZ) AND ITS SUBSIDIARIES MANUFACTURED AND MARKETED AN extensive line of processed and minimally processed food and related products throughout the world. The company's products were organized into two core businesses: meal enhancers and meals and snacks. Heinz distributed its products via its own sales force, independent brokers, agents, and distributors to chain, wholesale, cooperative, and independent grocery accounts; mass merchants and superstores; pharmacies; club stores; food service distributors; and institutions, including schools and government agencies.

The Del Monte Merger

In June 2002, Heinz announced that it would spin off and then merge its slower-selling products with Del Monte Foods, Inc., in an effort to simplify its business. After positive votes by both Heinz and Del Monte shareholders and approval by the IRS, the transaction, completed on December 21, 2002, gave Heinz shareholders approximately 75% of the new, much larger Del Monte. The product lines/segments shifted to Del Monte included Heinz's U.S. and Canadian pet food and pet snacks businesses; U.S. tuna; U.S. private-label soups and gravies, as well as College Inn soups; and U.S. infant feeding. The affected brands included StarKist, 9 Lives, Kibbles 'n Bits, Nature's Goodness baby food, and College Inn soups. The merger was expected to reduce Heinz's annual revenue by approximately 20%, or $1.8 billion, while doubling Del Monte's size.

Under the terms of the merger, Heinz shareholders received 0.45 share of stock in the new Del Monte for every share of Heinz stock owned, while Del Monte assumed approximately $1.1 billion of Heinz's debt (about 21% of Heinz's total debt). Heinz also announced that it would reduce its dividend by 33%. (The dividend reduction was expected to free up substantial cash flow, which Heinz planned to use to pay down debt and underwrite additional marketing.) The merger was effected in several steps, including the transfer of Heinz assets to a temporary entity, SKF, which was then merged, along with the existing Del Monte, into a "new Del Monte." The complicated deal, referred to as a *reverse Morris Trust*, resulted in a tax-free transfer because Heinz shareholders would ultimately own a majority of shares in the new Del Monte.

In addition to allowing Heinz to sell its sluggish brands on an essentially tax-free basis, the company noted that the smaller, less-diverse Heinz would become a more flexible, faster-growing company focused on two strategic food platforms: meal enhancers (ketchup, condiments, sauces) and meals and snacks (frozen and shelf-stable meals and snacks, food service frozen products, and infant feeding in non-U.S. markets). The new Heinz would have a global structure, which the company believed would enhance its ability to compete outside the United States. Reducing debt would enable Heinz to better support its core businesses with added investments in product development and advertising.

Investors reacted coolly to the merger announcement, sending Heinz shares down and resulting in only modest gains for Del Monte. By year-end 2002, both companies' stock prices had posted further declines, reflecting weakness in the broader market. (Some industry observers believed the merger could be win–win for Heinz shareholders *only* if there was an end game that involved selling the slimmer and more attractive Heinz.) By mid-January 2005, however, Heinz's stock price had recovered to just under $38, $3 below its 52-week high of $40.67, and Del Monte had managed to regain some strength, closing at $11.17 on January 13, 2005.

The New Growth Strategy

Shortly after the completion of the Del Monte merger, Heinz announced an aggressive growth strategy based on four key initiatives:

- Drive profitable growth through superior products and packaging, everyday price/value, accelerated innovation, and creative marketing
- Remove the "clutter" both by focusing on core businesses and products and by creating a simplified business structure
- Reduce costs (especially fixed costs) by creating a more efficient supply chain, improving cash and working capital management, and making focused capital expenditures
- Measure and recognize performance through a "balanced scorecard" that tied management compensation to key financial and non-financial performance measures and drivers

As part of the company's emphasis on core products, Heinz realigned its SBUs into two core businesses:

- **Meal enhancers:** This segment comprised key brands from the former Ketchup and Condiments unit. Although sales in this segment had been driven by ketchup, which had always been the company's flagship brand, acquisitions and new product development (Jack Daniel's grilling sauces and Mr. Yoshida's marinades, Classico pasta sauces) had given Heinz a growing presence both on the grill and in the kitchen. With global ketchup sales in excess of $1 billion, Heinz had over 50% of the domestic ketchup market and approximately 34% of the global market. Packaging innovations such as the E-Z Squirt bottle had helped drive Heinz's global market share in ketchup up 15%, to 60%. (Heinz had a 75% share in the United Kingdom; the company claimed that 5 points were directly related to the new bottle.) As U.S. fast food chains increased in global popularity, Heinz expected strong growth in both single-serving packet and bulk ketchup and condiment (barbecue sauce, soy sauce, steak sauce, etc.) sales. However, Heinz ketchup faced challenges from other brand-name ketchups, private-label ketchups, and salsa. The increased popularity of salsa and other ethnic condiments, as well as the lower cost structures for private-label brands, were expected to threaten Heinz's market share.

- **Meals and snacks:** This segment brought together branded shelf-stable and frozen meals and snacks from the previous Soup, Beans, and Pasta Meals and Frozen Foods units as well as non-U.S. infant feeding and frozen or shelf-stable products for the institutional market.

  The company's growing frozen meal/snack product line included such best-selling U.S. brands as Ore-Ida potatoes, Boston Market HomeStyle Meals, and Weight Watchers and Smart Ones entrees and desserts. (Heinz, which had acquired Weight Watchers in 1978, sold the international weight control segment of that business in 1999 as part of an initiative to focus on core businesses; however, the company retained the processed food segment.) Popular U.S. snack brands, including Bagel Bites, T.G.I. Friday's, Delimex, and Poppers, were being managed as part of this segment.

  Heinz expected its UK and other non-U.S. brands in this category, such as Weight Watchers from Heinz and Main Street Bistro entrees and Linda McCartney meat-free meals, to drive growth outside the United States. For example, Wattie's was among the most powerful brands in New Zealand, offering a wide range of meal solutions; and the Honig and HAK brands provided Dutch consumers a wide variety of dried soups, meals, and vegetables. And, while Heinz included its U.S. tuna business in the spin-off, it retained such European brands as John West and Petit Navire and the Australian Greenseas tuna brand.

  The company was developing a strong presence in food service frozen products, with varieties such as Chef Francisco and Quality Chef soups and Alden Merrill frozen desserts. Although Heinz's retail private-label soups and gravies and College Inn broths were spun off to Del Monte, the company hoped to grow market share in both U.S. and global markets via such innovations as microwaveable Soup Cups—a convenience concept imported from Australia.

  Also included in this segment was infant feeding. Although Heinz included its U.S. infant feeding business in the spin-off to Del Monte, the company retained both its Heinz branded baby foods, which held top positions in the United Kingdom, Canada, Venezuela, Australia, and China, and Plasmon, its Italian infant feeding business.

A New Organizational Structure

In the first quarter of fiscal 2004, Heinz changed its segment reporting to reflect changes in organizational structure and management:

- **North American Consumer Products:** This segment manufactured, marketed, and sold ketchup, condiments, sauces, pasta meals, frozen potatoes, entrees, snacks, and appetizers to grocery channels in the United States and Canada. North American Consumer Products accounted for approximately 24.5% of sales and 31.6% of profits in fiscal 2004.
- **U.S. Foodservice:** This segment manufactured, marketed, and sold branded and private-label products (including ketchup, condiments, sauces, frozen soups, and desserts) to commercial and non-commercial food outlets and distributors. U.S. Foodservice accounted for approximately 17% of sales and 14.1% of profits in fiscal 2004.
- **Europe:** This segment sold products across categories and channels in Europe; it accounted for approximately 39% of sales and 42.6% of profits in fiscal 2004.
- **Asia/Pacific:** This segment included operations across product categories and channels in New Zealand, Australia, Japan, China, South Korea, Indonesia, Singapore, and Thailand; it contributed approximately 15% of sales and 9.7% of profits in fiscal 2004.
- **Other Operating Entities:** This segment sold products across categories and channels in Africa, India, Latin America, the Middle East, and other geographic areas. This segment accounted for approximately 4.5% of sales and 2% of profits in fiscal 2004.

Financial Position/Performance

In accordance with generally accepted accounting principles, Heinz's financial statements for prior years had been restated to reflect the merger (show revenues, expenses, assets, and liabilities, excluding the entities that were later spun off to Del Monte) and the new segment reporting structure. On that basis, revenues for fiscal 2004 (fiscal year ended April 28, 2004) of $8.41 billion showed an increase of just under 2.2% over the prior year compared to an 8.2% revenue increase from 2002 to 2003. However, gross profit performance improved to 36.7% of sales in 2004 compared to 35.4% of sales in 2003. (Despite cost-cutting initiatives, Heinz's gross profit as a percentage of sales had decreased from 36.93% in 2001 to 35.4% in 2003.)

Net income for fiscal 2004 reflected discontinued operations of the company's Northern Europe bakery business as well as write-downs and reorganization costs; net income for fiscal 2003 reflected both income from discontinued operations ($88.74 million) and the cumulative effect of a change in accounting principles related to goodwill (–$77,812), and it represented a 6.88% return on sales, significantly below 2002's 10.95% but slightly ahead of 2001's 6.84%. In a less positive development, S&P downgraded the company's long- and short-term debt ratings to reflect Heinz's increased financial leverage.

Sales for the six months ended October 27, 2004, increased $216.6 million, or 5.4%, to $4.20 billion. Sales volume increased 1.2% over the same period in the previous fiscal year, while exchange translations added 4.2% to sales. Acquisitions, net of divestitures, increased sales by 0.5%, while lower pricing decreased sales by 0.5%. Despite cost-cutting initiatives, gross profit as a percentage of sales decreased to 36.6% from 37.3%, mainly due to lower pricing and increased product costs in Europe and Latin America. SG&A increased $65.5 million, or 8.3%, to $855.7 million, and increased as a percentage of sales to 20.4% from 19.8% for the six-month period. Operating income decreased $15.0 million, or 2.1%, to $683.1 million, and decreased as a percentage of sales to 16.3% from 17.5%. Income from continuing operations for the first six months of fiscal 2005 (ended on October 27, 2004) was $392.1 million compared to $378.3 million in the same period a year earlier, an increase of 3.6%. On a segment basis, North American Consumer Products accounted for 25% of sales and 34.5% of operating income; U.S. Foodservice contributed 17% of sales and 15.7% of operating income; Europe contributed 38% of sales and 39.2% of operating income; Asia/Pacific contributed 14% of sales and 10.5% of operating income. (Complete SEC filings are available via a link from the company's web site *www.heinz.com* or *www.wsj.com.*)

Acquisition Strategies

Heinz had pursued global growth via market penetration and product/market development achieved principally via acquisition. In September 1999, Heinz acquired a 19.5% interest in The Hain Food Group, Inc., for nearly $100 million, forming a strategic alliance for global production of natural and organic foods and soy-based beverages. Hain was the leading U.S. natural and organic foods company, with more than 3,500 products sold under such brands as Health Valley cereals, bakery products, and soups; Terra Chips snacks; and Westsoy, the largest soy beverage marketer. As part of the alliance, Heinz was to provide procurement, manufacturing, and logistics expertise, with Hain providing marketing, sales, and distribution services.

Other recent acquisitions included the Borden Food Corporation's pasta sauce, dry bouillon, and soup business; the Linda McCartney and Ethnic Gourmet brands; and Anchor Food Products' branded retail business, which included the licensing rights to the T.G.I. Friday's brand of frozen snacks and the Poppers brand of appetizers. The company also completed its acquisitions of Delimex, a leading maker of frozen Mexican food products. Heinz had financed its acquisition strategy principally via debt (in 2004, approximately $5.6 billion), resulting in a total debt to equity ratio of 3.63, twice the industry average.

In fiscal 1999, the company began a growth and restructuring initiative named "Operation Excel." This multiyear program established manufacturing centers of excellence, focused on the product portfolio, realigned the company's management teams, and invested in growth initiatives. The total cost of Operation Excel was estimated at $1.2 billion; pretax savings generated from the program were estimated to be $70 million in fiscal 2000 and $135 million in fiscal 2001. Cost savings were projected to grow to approximately $185 million in 2002 and $200 million in fiscal 2003 and thereafter. In the fourth quarter of fiscal 2001, the company announced a restructuring initiative, named "Streamline," designed to decrease overhead and other operating costs via such steps as closure of the company's tuna operations in Puerto Rico, consolidation of the company's North American pet food production, and the divestiture of the company's U.S. fleet of fishing boats.

The Food Service Market

Heinz was the largest prepared food supplier (ketchup and condiments, salad dressings, frozen foods, soup concentrate, etc.) to the U.S. food service market, which comprised restaurants and other away-from-home eating places. The food service industry, which had seen flat growth as the U.S. economy stalled in recession, was expected to improve as U.S. economic growth strengthened and U.S. families increased the proportion of food dollars spent away from home (slightly over 50% in 2003, up from about 33% in the 1970s). Industry analysts expected strong growth in global food service demand (especially in Europe and Asia) over the next five years. Key competitors included Kraft, Unilever, Sara Lee, Campbell Soup Company, and Dole Food Company, Inc. Because Heinz drew approximately 17% of its revenues from food service operations (restaurants, stadiums, airports, etc.), the company had suffered more than most processed food firms from the after-effects of September 11.

Processed Food Industry

As a whole, the packaged food industry outperformed the S&P 500 for the first seven months of 2004, posting a 5.7% versus a 2.1% decline for the broader index. Cost pressures were a key concern for the industry, primarily from increased commodity, pension, and fuel costs. While many commodities were below recent highs, they remained above 2003 levels. An additional concern was the vulnerability of input prices to weather and export demand. However, industry profit margins were expected to benefit from cost reductions resulting from mergers and acquisitions and the aggressive restructurings undertaken by most major companies in the previous several years.

Sales of frozen and prepared foods in the United States had grown significantly over the previous three years, driven by quality improvements and convenient packaging, factors that promised to make those products still more attractive in the future. Retailers' adjustments virtually guaranteed this: In the previous three years, Wal-Mart and Albertsons had increased their frozen food departments by 25%–40% throughout their chains.

Key competitors in this industry segment included Kraft, Kellogg Company, ConAgra, General Mills, Unilever, Dole, and Sara Lee. Eighty percent of total food, drug, and mass merchandiser sales in the United States went to national brands and, according to one recent study, 46% of Americans were "national brand loyalists" who gravitated strongly to national brands. However, brand loyalty was eroding in all age groups. The benchmark annual index from Interbrand, a brand consultancy, showed 41 of the top brands a year earlier declining in value in 2004.

The industry had experienced aggressive consolidation (13 mergers among publicly traded packaged food companies since the beginning of 2000), which had eliminated all the obvious takeover targets. Industry consolidation plus the maturity of the U.S. market for processed foods (1% growth, low inflation, increasing popularity of generics) made competition for market share intense and left little latitude for price increases. Continued consolidation in the grocery industry via the acquisition of niche players and the emergence of superstores and wholesale clubs would also exert downward pressure on prices.

The Westernization of eating habits, together with rising incomes in developing countries and the appeal of American brand names abroad, was expected to contribute to increased growth among U.S. processed food companies; however, new dietary guidelines from the U.S. Department of Agriculture, which cautioned consumers about the consumption of trans fats, could negatively impact sales of some shelf-stable products.

Heinz has created a special link for students: *www.heinz.com/jsp/students.jsp*.

CASE 40

Lowe's Companies, Inc.

Maryanne M. Rouse

LOWE'S COMPANIES (LOW), THE SECOND LARGEST U.S. HOME IMPROVEMENT RETAILER, competed in the highly fragmented $400+ billion home improvement industry. Capitalizing on historically high rates of home ownership, the company had grown from 15 stores selling commodity-type products to new home builders in 1962 to a chain of almost 1,000 stores in 45 states with over 99.5 million square feet of selling space in 2004. (The total includes 46 stores opened between January 31, 2003, and August 1, 2004, the end of the second quarter of Lowe's fiscal year.) In 1989, the company redefined its business and positioned itself as a "big-box" home-improvement retailer, selling a wide array of higher-margin merchandise. Lowe's opened its first 100,000+ square-foot big-box store in 1992. Between 2003 and 2004, the company developed two prototype stores: the larger had 116,000 square feet of selling space plus an additional 31,000 square feet dedicated to lawn and garden products, while the store developed for smaller markets provided 94,000 square feet of selling space plus an additional 26,000 feet devoted to lawn and garden product lines. A typical store stocked more than 40,000 SKUs, with hundreds more available through the company's special order system. Product lines included plumbing and electrical products, tools, building materials, hardware, outdoor hardlines, appliances, lumber, mill work, paint and decorative products, cabinets, furniture, and nursery and gardening products.

Lowe's served both retail and commercial business customers. Retail customers were primarily do-it-yourself homeowners and others buying for personal and family use. Commercial business customers included repair and remodeling contractors, electricians, landscapers, painters, plumbers, and commercial and residential building maintenance professionals. Approximately 73% of the company's sales were to retail customers, with the balance to commercial customers.

Growth Strategies

With no plans for international expansion in 2004, Lowe's planned to grow domestic square footage at an annual rate of 16%–17% over the next two to three years, with 150 store openings planned for 2005 and another 150–160 store openings for 2006. The company was aggressively targeting metropolitan markets with populations of 500,000 or more, noting that currently the company's highest-volume stores were in metropolitan markets. Stores in these larger markets accounted for approximately 65% of the company's new store openings in 2003 and 2004. In line with this strategy, Lowe's announced plans to add more than 40 stores in the New York/New Jersey metro market as well as in Chicago by year-end 2005. Through September 30, 2004, Lowe's opened over 48 new stores, bringing the company's total above 1,000:

	2003	2002	2001	2000	1999
Number of stores, beginning of year	854	744	650	576	520
New stores opened	125	112	101	80	60
Relocated stores opened	5	11	14	20	31
Stores closed (including relocated stores)	(6)	(13)	(21)	(26)	(35)
Contractor yards sold	(26)	—	—	—	—
Total number of stores, end of year	952	854	744	650	576

The company believed there were significant product/market growth opportunities in three key areas: installed sales, special order sales, and commercial business customers. Additional growth strategies included increasing sales per square foot and adding high-quality product lines.

In 1998, Lowe's began a major expansion into the Western United States, with plans to build 100+ new stores in three to four years. In early 1999, the company acquired Eagle Hardware and Garden, a 41-store chain of home improvement and garden centers, accelerating Lowe's West Coast expansion and providing a stepping-stone to 10 new Western states, including a number of key metropolitan markets.

Finance

Net earnings for 2003 increased 27%, to $1.9 billion, or 6.1% of sales, compared to $1.5 billion, or 5.6% of sales, for 2002. Return on beginning assets, defined as net earnings divided by beginning total assets, was 11.7% for 2003, compared to 10.7% for 2002 and 9.0% for 2001. Return on beginning shareholders' equity, defined as net earnings divided by beginning shareholders' equity, was 22.6% for 2003, compared to 22.0% for 2002 and 18.6% for 2001. The company recorded sales of $30.8 billion in 2003, an 17% increase over 2002 sales of $26.1 billion. Sales for 2002 were 20% higher than 2001 levels. Average ticket amounts increased 4.2%, from $56.80 in 2002 to $59.21 in 2003, due in part to the success of the up-the-continuum initiative as well as the Lowe's credit programs. Comparable-store sales in 2003 increased by 6.7%, with the strongest sales increases in lumber, building materials, outdoor power equipment, paint, flooring, and home organization.

The company reported consistent sales gains across all categories, from appliances to outdoor plants. Percentage contributions to sales by product line are summarized below (dollar amounts in millions):

Category	2003	2002
Appliances	11%	11%
Lumber/Plywood	9	9
Outdoor Fashion	7	7
Millwork	7	7
Nursery	6	6
Flooring	6	6
Fashion Electrical	6	6
Fashion Plumbing	6	6
Paint	7	7
Tools	5	5
Hardware	6	6
Building Materials	5	5
Cabinets/Furniture/Shelving	4	4
Outdoor Power Equipment	3	4
Rough Plumbing	3	3
Walls/Windows	3	3
Rough Electrical	3	2
Home Organization	2	2
Other	1	1
Total sales (millions)	$30,838	$26,112

Sales in the second quarter of fiscal 2004 exceeded $10 billion for the first time in the company's history, increasing 17.3% over sales in the second quarter of fiscal 2003. For the six months ended July 30, 2004, sales increased 19.4%, and comparable-store sales increased 7.2%. Net earnings increased 17.9%, to $704 million, compared to the previous year's second quarter results. The gross margin was 33.3% of sales for the quarter ended July 30, 2004, compared to 30.3% for the previous year's comparable quarter. The gross margin for the six months ended July 30, 2004, was 33.2% versus 30.7% for the first six months of 2003. The company's aggressive new store growth gave Lowe's additional leverage with vendors, which, together with improved inventory management, resulted in a decline in cost of goods sold as a percentage of sales for fiscal 2003 and the first two quarters of 2004. (Lowe's annual and quarterly reports and SEC filings are available via the company's web site *www.lowes.com* or *www.wsj.com*.)

Logistics

To help maintain appropriate inventory levels in stores and to improve distribution efficiency, Lowe's operated 10 highly automated regional distribution centers (RDCs). In 2004, the RDCs were strategically located in North Carolina, Georgia, Indiana, Pennsylvania, Texas, California, Ohio, Wyoming, and Florida. Each Lowe's store was served by one of these RDCs. The company also operated nine smaller support facilities to distribute merchandise that required special handling due to size or type of packaging, such as lumber, various imports, and building materials. Approximately 50% of the merchandise purchased by the company was shipped through its distribution facilities, while the remaining portion was shipped directly to stores from vendors.

Promotion

Lowe's reached target customers through a promotional mix that included television, radio, direct mail, newspaper, event sponsorships, and in-store programs. The company had developed a strategic alliance with the HGTV network, one of a half-dozen media partnerships created to build the image and equity of the Lowe's brand while complementing core media and marketing programs. Lowe's also hosted customer hospitality events through its Team 48 NASCAR sponsorship, supported the wide-ranging activities of Lowe's Home Safety Council, and used its proprietary credit programs to drive customer traffic and purchases. The easy-to-navigate Lowe's web site was a key element in its promotional strategy. The site allowed customers to search the company's inventory on a store-by-store basis, compare products and prices, and order online or for store pickup.

Other Marketing Initiatives

In response to significant growth in the "buy-it-yourself" (BIY, or "do-it-for-me") market, Lowe's developed an installed sales program that allowed customers to arrange for installation of products in over 30 categories. A BIY customer chose and purchased the product but relied on professionals to handle installation. Lowe's had added kiosks in departments such as appliances, home decor/flooring, electrical, lighting, millwork, hardware, seasonal, plumbing, and tools to facilitate special orders. Some of these kiosks were technology based and some were literature based, but all facilitated the ability of the customer to special order to fit their home improvement needs. Special order sales allowed Lowe's to offer a variety of unique items without the investment in inventory.

The design of Lowe's stores had attracted customers, particularly women, who disliked the warehouse shopping layout of rival Home Depot. Lowe's featured wider aisles, brighter lighting, and more signs, and it stocked a larger selection of products for home decorating, including lamps, window treatments, and designer towels, than is found in a typical Home Depot.

In both 2003 and 2004, Lowe's developed a series of initiatives to better serve commercial business customers, including enhanced ordering and credit programs, increased delivery options, an increase in professional-preferred brands, and a policy of increasing in-stock quantities for bigger jobs in an effort to win the loyalty of commercial customers. Analysts estimated potential sales to this segment of the market at almost three times sales to the traditional DIY market.

Suppliers

Excluding special order vendors, Lowe's sourced its products from approximately 7,000 merchandise vendors worldwide, with no single vendor accounting for more than 4% of total purchases; however, the company had begun to develop vendor alliances with key partners under a vendor certification program. Lowe's used its Global Sourcing Division to purchase directly from foreign manufacturers and avoid higher-cost third-party importers. Growing demand for steel, plywood, and other building products, especially from China and other developing economies, had placed pressure on both suppliers and prices.

The Industry

According to the Home Improvement Research Institute (HIRI), the total retail home improvement market in the United States reached $187.6 billion in 2001 and was expected to climb to $236.7 billion in 2006. Industry sales were sensitive to a number of factors, including interest rates, housing turnover, consumer debt levels, and concern about job security. Although new housing starts were important, the sales opportunity from housing turnover was three times larger than from the sales of new homes. Even when a weakening economy forced some homeowners to delay the purchase of new homes, industry research showed that they were likely to continue to invest in improving their existing homes. Aggressive interest rate cuts during 2001, 2002, and 2003 and continued low fixed and variable first and second mortgage rates had allowed consumers to borrow more to fund home improvement projects.

Homeowners spent more to maintain and improve their living spaces than did renters. The U.S. Census Bureau estimated that home ownership increased to 69.2% in third quarter 2004, up from 65% in 1995. In addition, as baby boomers spent more time at home with their families, they were likely to spend a larger portion of disposable income on their homes than in prior years. With the bulk of the U.S. population entering the post-40 age group, demand for household products and remodeling/renovation were likely to experience strong growth.

Competition

The home improvement industry was highly fragmented, with the two largest players, Home Depot and Lowe's, controlling approximately 32% of the $192 billion do-it-yourself market and less than 5% of the $245 billion professional/commercial market. Key competitive factors in the home improvement retailing business were price, location, customer service, product and brand selection, and name recognition. As Lowe's and Home Deport pursued aggressive growth strategies, industry analysts expected consolidation, with less competitive players closing, being acquired, or merging with other retailers.

The industry leader was Home Depot, with 1,788 stores in 50 states, the District of Columbia, 5 Canadian provinces, Puerto Rico, and Mexico and an overall market share estimated at 18%, compared to 9% for Lowe's. The company's stores marketed a wide range of building materials, home improvement supplies, and lawn and garden products; EXPO Design Center stores offered interior design products and installation services.

Home Depot targeted the same three customer groups as Lowe's and, although Home Depot and Lowe's pursued many of the same competitive strategies, Home Depot's size provided the company with significant economies of scale and cost advantages. In September 2004, Home Depot opened a 105,000-square-foot superstore just off Broadway on West 23rd street, replete with such big-city touches as doormen and home delivery. After two lackluster years, Home Depot's stock had rebounded, nearly doubling to around $40 from January 2003 to mid-October 2004. Although profits at Lowe's were rising faster, Home Depot's shares were cheaper.

Other direct competitors included Building Materials Holdings, House 2 Home, Inc., Wolohan Lumber Company, Wickes, Inc., and Payless Cashways. Lowe's also competed with traditional hardware, plumbing, electrical, appliance, and home supply retailers, and with lumber yards in most of its market areas. In addition, Lowe's competed in some product categories with discount stores and membership warehouse clubs.

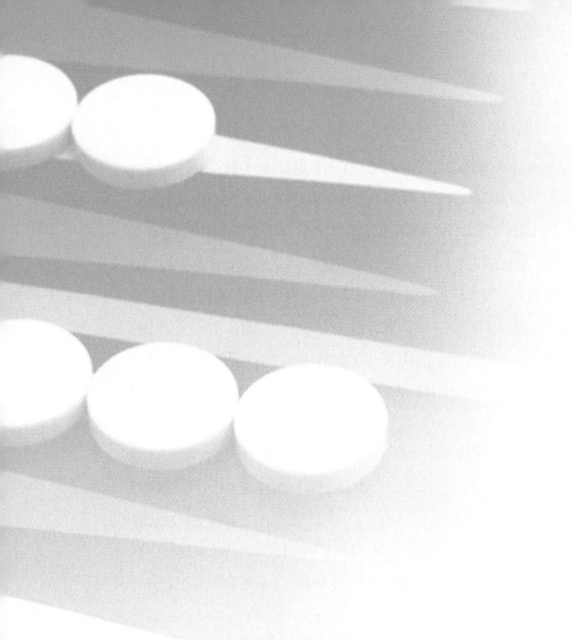

CASE 41
Nike, Inc.

Maryanne M. Rouse

CAN NIKE (NKE) FIND ENOUGH SHELF SPACE TO MAKE UP FOR LOWER SALES TO ITS TOP customer? In February 2002, Foot Locker told Nike that it wanted to reduce the number of Nike's marquee shoes—the Air Jordans, Shox, and others that sell for well over $100—because the retailer believed that consumers were turning more to midpriced shoes. Because Nike refused to change its product mix to support Foot Locker's product line reshuffling, Foot Locker, the dominant global footwear retailer, with over 3,600 stores, cancelled approximately $150 million in Nike orders. (Nike's premium segment accounts for approximately 15%–20% of total global revenues and although neither company discloses details of total orders, Nike noted in its 2002 10-K form that sales to Foot Locker represented approximately $1 billion of Nike's $9.9 billion worldwide sales.)

According to Foot Locker, Nike retaliated by cutting the retailer's allotment of key products, including the highly popular Air Force One. The feud escalated in December, when Nike announced that Foot Locker would no longer be its launch customer for marquee products and, in fact, gave rival FootAction access to high-end basketball shoes that had been exclusive to Foot Locker. In mid-February 2003, Nike's "Hall of Hoops" displays in Foot Locker stores came down and were replaced by Reebok's "Above the Rim" campaign. In 2004, Nike was aggressively lining up new outlets, while Foot Locker faced a significant challenge in maintaining a broad, attractive, and profitable product line (for 2002, Nike comprised 47% of Foot Locker's sales).

The Company

Nike designed, developed, and marketed athletic and casual footwear, active sports and leisure apparel, sports equipment, and accessories under the Nike, Bauer, Cole-Haan, and Hurley brands. Nike was the largest seller of athletic footwear and apparel in the world, with a U.S. market share exceeding 40%. The company's products were sold through approximately 18,000 retail accounts in the United States, including footwear stores, department stores, and sporting goods stores. Nike, with the broadest product line of all competitors, also distributed to specialty, skate, tennis, and golf shops. The company operated several retail formats in the United States: 78 Nike Factory Stores (primarily close-out merchandise), 4 Nike stores, 13 Niketown "showcase" stores, 4 employee-only stores, and 61 Cole-Haan stores. Sales in the United States accounted for 53% of total revenues in 2002. Nike sold its products outside the United States through independent distributors, licensees, and subsidiaries in 140 countries.

In addition to performance equipment (sports balls, timepieces, eyewear, skates, and other equipment designed for sports activities), Nike sold hockey equipment and related accessories under the Bauer and Nike brand names. In April 2002, Nike acquired Hurley International LLC, a California-based designer and distributor of sports apparel for surfing, skateboarding, and snowboarding as well as youth lifestyle apparel. Footwear accounted for 58% of fiscal 2002 revenues; apparel, 29%; equipment, 8%; and other, 5%.

Almost all Nike brand apparel was manufactured by approximately 700 independent contractors, 99% of which were located in Southeast Asia. The reasons for locating shoe production in Southeast Asia were many, but the most important was the cost of labor. In addition to having lower labor costs, Asia provided access to the raw material suppliers and satellite industries (tanneries, textiles, plastics) necessary in athletic shoe manufacturing. A third important factor driving the location of athletic shoe production was the current complex system of differential tariffs.

Working conditions and wages, as well as allegations of harassment and abuse, had been a source of heated debate between Nike and a broad array of special interest groups and journalists for a decade. Critics accused Nike of abandoning countries as they developed better pay and employment rights in favor of countries such as China with lower wages and little regulation of employment practices. In several cases relating to physical or verbal abuse and child labor, Nike agreed that employment practices were problematic, and the company responded with what the Global Alliance agreed were serious and reasonable remediation plans. The company's argument that many of the charges were based on old and/or inaccurate information and did not reflect current operations had done little to satisfy activists. Although Nike had implemented a series of social and environmental initiatives and Nike's largest competitors had pursued almost identical manufacturing strategies, Nike continued to be the focus of activists opposing manufacturing practices in developing countries.

Because Nike didn't actually produce shoes, the company's focus was on R&D and marketing. Nike considered its product design and ability to quickly take advantage of technological advances key sources of competitive advantage. Celebrity spokespersons (Michael Jordan, Tiger Woods, Lance Armstrong, Mia Hamm, etc.) and team endorsements (such as the long-term agreement with Manchester United) were important elements of what had been a very successful promotional strategy. According to the company's annual report, Nike's spending for "demand creation" was $1,027.9 million for 2002—10.4% of revenue. R&D costs, estimated at close to $1 billion, were not separately disclosed.

While Nike was fairly well diversified across price points, the company's marquee shoes, which accounted for 15%–20% of global revenue, had been a strong contributor to profits and had created the "buzz" to move lower-priced models. Declining demand for these premium sneakers was exacerbated by growing unemployment rates, a worsening economy, uncertain geopolitical events, falling consumer confidence, and competition from other teen and young adult "must haves," such as cell phones, PDAs, and other new gizmos; fickle consumer tastes and preferences and the spat with Foot Locker were factors as well.

Although Nike's fiscal 2002 revenue of $9,893 million was the highest in company history, top-line growth was slower (4.3%) than in the previous year (5.5%). Slower sales of athletic shoes in the U.S. region were balanced by increases in footwear sales in other regions and increases in apparel and equipment sales in all regions. Despite downward pressure on prices and markdowns, the company was able to increase gross margin as a percentage of sales to 39.3% for the year. Selling and administrative expenses increased from 28.3% of sales in 2001 to 28.5% in 2002, reflecting both lower sales and increased marketing costs. Operating profit showed definite improvement in 2002, at 10.2% of sales, versus 9.3% in the prior year. Complete financial information is available in Nike's 10-K form for 2002 (*www.nike.com*).

The Industry

In 2003, growth in sales of athletic footwear in the United States could best be described as sluggish. The one bright spot in an otherwise dismal year was the women's segment. In 2003, women's casual tennis footwear was the hottest category, driven by both the retro fashion trend and growth in the casual lifestyle segment. As footwear providers focused on international demand to grow revenue, it was hoped that a continued weak U.S. dollar would prop up global sales.

The non-athletic shoe segment had experienced a major shift away from dress to casual shoes, reflecting the more casual dress environment of the workplace. Lower-priced competition in this segment would make overseas sourcing, effective marketing, and operating efficiencies keys to profits in the near term. According to SportscanINFO, the following trends were expected to continue to influence global sales growth in both shoe segments in 2003:

- Continued growth in the casual, non-performance athletic footwear segment
- A decline in the demand for premium-priced performance athletic shoes
- Price deflation as the middle-range price points continued to shift down and casual styles increased in importance
- Decent but not spectacular growth in basketball shoes (the huge increases predicted for 2002 never did materialize), coupled with better-than-expected growth in running shoes
- The implosion of White/White Retro shoes, which had been aggressively overpromoted, especially by mall retailers

Analysts expected weak growth in equipment, with potentially strong growth in casual apparel.

Competition

The athletic footwear, apparel, and equipment segments were intensely competitive both in the United States and globally. Key competitors included Reebok, New Balance, and Adidas in athletic footwear and sports apparel.

New Balance

Privately held New Balance Athletic Shoe, Inc., headquartered in Boston, Massachusetts, was a leading manufacturer of technically innovative, width-sized footwear and athletic apparel for women, men, and children. The range of product categories included running, walking, cross-training, basketball, tennis, adventure sports, and kids. In 1998, New Balance acquired Dunham Bootmakers to expand into work and hiking boots, sandals, boat shoes, and rugged casuals without diluting the New Balance brand. In 2001, the company acquired PF Flyers to pursue the comfort/casual market.

The company, which has remained committed to a domestic manufacturing strategy, employed more than 2,400 people around the globe. New Balance, long a staple in such outlets as Sports Authority, Foot Locker, and Champs, expanded its distribution channels in 2000 to include independently owned retail stores that would provide the opportunity to showcase the full brand and were to carry New Balance apparel, accessories, and the Dunham line of casual shoes. At the end of 2001, 55 of these independently owned stores, which generated about $46.4 million in sales—4% of New Balance's $1.16 billion in revenue—had opened. By the end of 2002, the company was distributing to over 90 independent retailers. New Balance surprised analysts and industry watchers alike with its vault to the number three spot both worldwide and in the United States, with a 25% year-over-year sales increase from 2001 to 2002, estimated athletic shoe market share of more than 11%, and full line sporting goods market share of 19%.

Adidas

German-based Adidas-Salomon AG held the number four spot in the United States in 2002, with an estimated 11% market share. With global sales of almost $7 billion, a 7.7% increase from 2001 and a record for the company, Adidas was the number two footwear and apparel company worldwide, behind Nike. Industry analysts noted that double-digit sales increases in both North American and Asian markets helped fuel the company's growth. Although analysts expected a sales boost in Asia (the World Soccer Cup matches were played in Japan and South Korea), the company's gains in the North American market were interpreted as a strong indicator of Adidas' success.

Adidas suffered a setback in 2002, when its most important endorser, Kobe Bryant of the L.A. Lakers, bought out his contract (he was expected to sign with either Nike or Reebok). Although the company's new "marquee endorser," Tracy McGrady, was a popular NBA player, he played for the Orlando Magic, a losing team in what was considered a small market. The Adidas group comprised three distinct divisions: Adidas Sports Performance, Adidas Sports Heritage, and Adidas Sports Style. The Sports Performance group housed the current footwear and apparel lines and accounted for 80% of the business; Sports Heritage was the retro division that put out the classic, old-style sneakers targeted to the urban audience; Sports Style, introduced in February 2003, was an upscale sportswear collection to be sold in 150 retailers, including Barney's New York, where the launch was held. Although it accounted for just 20% of the company's revenue, Adidas Sports Style was expected to make significant contributions to both the top and bottom lines.

Reebok

Reebok International, with a 12.2% market share, was the number two U.S. maker of athletic shoes, behind Nike, and ranked fourth globally. In addition to athletic shoes, sportswear, and accessories, Reebok's product lines included the Greg Norman line of men's casual wear, Rockport walking and casual shoes, and Ralph Lauren and Polo dress and athletic shoes. An athletic shoe powerhouse in the mid-1980s and early 1990s, Reebok couldn't compete with Nike when the emphasis shifted from fitness to team sports.

Reebok reached its low point in 1999, when its share price fell to about $7; however, industry observers believed that, with the return of Paul Fireman, the company was once again on the move and appeared to be gaining market share on several fronts. In December 2000, Reebok signed a 10-year licensing contract with the NFL that gave the company the exclusive right to sell "authentic, on-field stuff." Reebok's marketing budget for 2003 was reported to be

$40 million, a 38% increase from the previous year. That increase was expected to help cover the cost of endorsement deals with a roster of younger basketball stars, such as Steve Francis of the Houston Rockets. In 2003, Reebok had deals with 17 of the 26 NBA teams and, by November 2004, was expected to have signed all 26.

The Challenge

Although Nike's 2002 acquisition of Hurley had further diversified its product line, it was essentially still an athletic shoe company. Aggressive competition from Reebok, New Balance, and Adidas; the Foot Locker fiasco; Michael Jordan's retirement—which was expected to seriously impact the company's $350 million Jordan business; increasingly fickle consumers; and a worsening economy all posed significant threats to the growth of Nike's top and bottom lines. What is the company's next strategic move? Can Nike continue to "Just do it"?

CASE 42

Outback Steakhouse, Inc.

Maryanne M. Rouse

WITH 1,185 RESTAURANTS IN 50 STATES AND 21 FOREIGN COUNTRIES IN 2004, OUTBACK Steakhouse, Inc. (OSI), was one of the largest casual dining restaurant companies in the world. Founded in 1988 with a single restaurant in Tampa, Florida, OSI now comprised eight unique themed concepts: Outback Steakhouse (884 company-owned, franchised, and development joint venture units), Carrabba's Italian Grill (171), Bonefish Grill (66), Fleming's Prime Steakhouse and Wine Bar (31), Roy's (18), Lee Roy Selmon's (2), Cheeseburger in Paradise (11), and Paul Lee's Chinese Kitchen (2).

At the end of January 2005, 1,120 of the existing restaurants were company owned. The balance were more joint ventures—the preferred route to entering new markets—than franchises. Because OSI continued to buy back franchises, only three geographic franchises remained.

In August 2004, OSI acquired designation rights for the 76-unit Chi-Chi's restaurant chain from the then-defunct Prandium for $42.5 million. The properties included 23 locations with owned land and buildings, 15 sale-leaseback properties with reversion rights and purchase options, 23 ground leases, and 15 leases. Included in the price were real property, furniture, fixtures, equipment, and liquor licenses. OSI had not disclosed final disposition, but the company had noted that it might convert the sites to one of its existing concepts under its current expansion plans.

Not all of OSI's concepts had been successful. The company shut down its two-location southern Louisiana-themed Zazarac concept because it appeared to lack broad appeal. The per person tab at Zazarac had grown to more than $46, an average higher ticket than OSI had planned for but which was required to make the concept reasonably profitable.

Outback Steakhouse

The atmosphere at an Outback Steakhouse, OSI's Australian-themed flagship brand, was casual and fun, with generous portions, moderate prices (average check per person of $17.50–$20.00), and great service. In addition to its popular beef menu items, Outback offered a continually evolving menu of chicken, fish, seafood, and salad choices, as well as such signature appetizers as "Shrimp on the Barbie" and the "Bloomin' Onion." Alcohol accounted for approximately 13% of Outback Steakhouse revenues.

Two recent initiatives, Call-Ahead Seating and Curbside Take-Away, were designed to enhance the customer experience while increasing same-store sales. Although Outback did not use a conventional reservation system, Call-Ahead Seating had shortened wait times that could exceed an hour on busy weekend nights. Curbside Take-Away rooms plus convenient designated parking places for take-out customers were introduced to capitalize on a growing meal replacement trend across all demographics.

The Outback Steakhouse concept was the company's revenue driver. For the nine months ended September 30, 2004, the Outback Steakhouse segment contributed just over 75% of OSI's company-owned restaurant sales. In 2004, 723 of the 884 Outback locations were company owned. International operations, principally in Asia, comprised a growing percentage of the concept's overall revenue.

Carrabba's Italian Grill

Once considered ethnic, flavorful Italian cooking had become firmly a part of the mainstream of American dining, both at and away from home. OSI's popular Carrabba's Italian Grill concept, designed around an open kitchen, offered a wide range of Italian classics, including pasta, chicken, seafood, and wood-fired pizza, complemented by a versatile wine list. The average per person check at a Carrabba's was $18–$20; alcoholic beverages comprised approximately 16% of revenue. Call-Ahead Seating and Carside Carryout were available at every Carrabba's location.

OSI purchased half interest in Carrabba's Italian Grill, two somewhat upscale Italian-themed restaurants in Houston, Texas, in 1993 and, two years later, acquired sole rights to develop the concept. The company bought back 47 franchised units for $138 million in stock, closed several less successful locations, and began a major remodeling effort in 1998. In 2004, OSI operated 171 Carrabba's Italian Grill restaurants; all were company owned.

Fleming's Prime Steakhouse and Wine Bar

Acquired by OSI in 1999, Fleming's Prime Steakhouse and Wine Bar (31 company-owned units) offered a menu featuring aged USDA prime corn-fed beef, chops, fresh seafood, chicken, salads, sides, and desserts plus a creative wine list in an upscale casual setting. The average check was $55–$65 per person; 33% of the 2003 revenues at Fleming's came from alcohol. With wines categorized by grape variety and each section arranged from lighter to more full-flavored choices, the Fleming's wine list was anything but intimidating. Each of the Fleming's concept restaurants had dining rooms that could be configured in a variety of ways to accommodate large and small groups as well as private dining functions.

In addition to regular menu choices, Fleming's had created three unique four-course menus and wine pairings for parties of six or more. Each of these "Discovery Dinners" was offered at three different price levels—$75, $100, and $150 per person.

Bonefish Grill

Founded in St. Petersburg, Florida, by Tim Curci and Chris Parker in 2000, this "polished casual" concept based on fresh grilled fish and other uniquely prepared seafood was acquired by OSI in 2001. The Bonefish Grill menu offered a wide choice of fresh seafood with unique sauces (lemon butter, lime-tomato-garlic, warm mango salsa, pan-Asian) and toppings plus beef, pork, and chicken entrees at prices ranging from $14 to $25. At the end of January 2005, Bonefish Grill comprised 62 company-owned and 4 development joint venture or franchise units.

Roy's

Roy's featured Hawaiian fusion cuisine with sauces and Asian spices developed by Chef Roy Yamaguchi. Innovative entrees at the 18 company-owned restaurants ranged in price from $21 to $65; the average per person check was $50–$60. Liquor sales accounted for approximately 29% of revenue. In 2003, Roy's debuted a prix fixe menu that was an immediate hit with guests and was expected to build dining frequency at this more sophisticated concept. Chef Yamaguchi's "Hawaii Cooks" series, aired on PBS, together with its companion cookbook, had created positive buzz for Roy's.

Lee Roy Selmon's

Developed by OSI in 2000, Lee Roy Selmon's was a family sports restaurant—a new category of dining experience that reflected the evolving role of sports entertainment in the American family lifestyle. Selmon's offers generous portions of "soul-satisfying Southern comfort cooking," with entrees such as Twisted Southern Chicken, the House Filet, and Firecracker Shrimp, priced from $12.79 to $18.99. Both locations—Tampa-Westshore and New Tampa—were company-owned joint ventures.

Cheeseburger in Paradise

Developed as a partnership between OSI and Jimmy Buffet's Margaritaville Holdings, Inc., the 11-unit Key West–themed Cheeseburger in Paradise concept restaurants offered a wide selection of American and island favorites, from giant cheeseburgers, shrimp fritters, and authentic key lime pie to Caribbean-flavored jerk chicken wraps, onion six strings, and chocolate nachos. Nightly live music, "frozen concoctions" from the Tiki bar, and special events, including Full Moon Parties and Sunset Celebrations, attracted a multigenerational customer base.

Paul Lee's Chinese Kitchen

Paul Lee's Chinese Kitchen was a partnership between OSI and Paul Fleming, the innovator behind both Fleming's Prime Steakhouse and Wine Bar and the successful publicly held P.F. Chang's China Bistro. In addition to positioning itself as a neighborhood restaurant, Paul Lee's had made take-out a key priority. The strategy for Paul Lee's, which opened its second location in November 2004, was based on a few key elements: dual kitchens, each with its own chefs, equipment, and ingredients, to more efficiently serve both take-out and dine-in customers; a separate take-out entrance to improve traffic flow; and the use of woks and deep fryers to reduce cooking time and expense and speed up customer turnover.

The core of Paul Lee's menu was traditional Chinese food: There was almost nothing on the menu customers would not have seen in their neighborhood restaurants, from Hot & Sour Soup and Crab Rangoon to Sweet & Sour Pork and Moo Goo Gai Pan. The extensive menu featured soups and salads, chicken, seafood, meat and pork, and noodles, rice, and freshly prepared vegetables. Aside from the traditional tea, Paul Lee's beverage menu offered beer, wine, and what are billed as "far east spirit concoctions." The average per person check at Paul Lee's Chinese Kitchen was $14, with children's entrees at $3.99.

Some industry observers questioned whether Paul Lee's could deliver the 25%–30% return on investment that OSI demanded with the lower average menu prices required to compete as a neighborhood Chinese restaurant. They also questioned whether the concept could match the percentage of revenue derived from alcohol delivered by the company's other restaurants.

Operations

For a company its size, OSI was surprisingly decentralized. The company's lean corporate structure shifted responsibility for key personnel and operating decisions to unit-level managers who, because of OSI's unique ownership structure, had their own money on the line. For most restaurant managers, the dream was to own a restaurant, so OSI designed a creative compensation system that made the general manager or proprietor a limited entrepreneur, requiring him or her to make a $25,000 investment and sign a five-year contract in exchange for a base salary plus 10% of the restaurant's cash flow. OSI did, however, centralize such key functions as purchasing. With almost 1,200 restaurants across eight concepts, the company's centralized purchasing team could bargain for the best quality and prices for meats, vegetables, and non-food items.

OSI's "one-shift culture" (with few exceptions, OSI's themed restaurants served dinner only) had been a key element in attracting and retaining top employees while keeping labor costs reasonable. A lunch and dinner concept required at least one additional management person per restaurant and created competition among servers for desirable time slots. An added benefit of dinner-only was that it provided more of a chance for employees to work hard but still enjoy life.

Financial Performance/Position

OSI's overall sales (restaurant sales plus other revenue) increased by 16.2% in 2003 compared to 2002 (11% in 2002, 11.6% in 2001, and 15.8% in 2000), while gross margin as a percentage of restaurant sales continued to improve. A number of factors, including higher health insurance and other employee benefit costs, resulted in higher labor costs that were only partially overcome by productivity increases. Other restaurant operating expenses increased from 19.9% of restaurant revenues in 2001 to 20.4% in 2002 and 21% in 2003. Operating income as a percentage of sales declined from 9.8% in 2002 to 9.6% in 2003, still significantly ahead of the 8.8% reported for 2001.

Restaurant sales for the first nine months of 2004 increased by 20.9% over the same period in the prior year, while cost of sales showed a slight increase (from 36.2% to 36.5%). Labor and labor-related costs increased 0.2%, to 24.8%, while other restaurant operating expenses increased 0.5%, to 21.5%, for the first nine months of 2004.

OSI's principal source of cash was operations. Operating activities contributed positive cash flow of $269.08 million for fiscal year 2003, $294 million for 2002, and $192.9 million for 2001; however, increases in inventories, income taxes payable, and the current portion of long-term debt negatively impacted liquidity for fiscal 2003. Details of OSI's financial position and performance are available in the company's annual report and SEC filings (*www.outback.com*).

Key industry measures included average unit volume, store operating margin, systemwide sales, and same-store or comparable sales. Average unit volume was a per store calculated average sales amount. This measure was used to assess changes in consumer traffic, pricing, and brand development. Per store operating margin was calculated as store revenue less store-level operating costs that were controlled or significantly influenced by store managers (cost of sales, restaurant operating expenses, and labor and related costs). Systemwide sales was a non-GAAP revenue measure that included total sales volume for all stores, regardless of ownership structure (company owned, franchise, joint venture). Same-store or comparable sales was a measure used across retail concepts to eliminate the impact of new store openings and to allow year-over-year comparison of existing stores.

Competition

Outback's eight restaurant concepts faced stiff competition from both single-location casual and fine dining restaurants and from other casual dining chains. Key competitors in the latter category included Brinker International and Darden International Restaurants, Inc.

With over 1,325 locations in the United States and Canada, Florida-based Darden was the leading operator of casual dining restaurants, including Red Lobster, Olive Garden, Smoky Bones BBQ, Bahama Breeze, and Seasons 52. Red Lobster, with just over 680 units, was the number one seafood chain, while Olive Garden, with approximately 543 locations, led the Italian dining segment. Both chains catered to families with midpriced menu items, themed interiors, and primarily suburban locations. With growth at both Red Lobster and Olive Garden restaurants slowing, Darden appeared to be counting on a national rollout of Smoky Bones BBQ (69 locations at the end of 2004) to jump-start revenue growth. The Bahama Breeze concept had been a disappointment to Darden, which was attempting to reposition the concept and turn financial performance around. Seasons 52, Darden's latest venture, comprised a single-location casual wine bar and grill.

Brinker International, owner and operator of Chili's Grill and Bar, Romano's Macaroni Grill, On the Border Mexican Grill and Cantina, Maggiano's Little Italy, Rockfish Seafood Grill, and Corner Bakery Cafe, was the number two casual dining operator, behind Darden. Named for its founder, casual dining pioneer Norman Brinker, the company had been able to successfully capitalize on America's love of ethnic and regional foods with its Chili's and Romano's Macaroni Grill restaurants, but it continued to struggle with its other concepts: Rockfish Seafood Grill had underperformed against expectations, while On the Border development had slowed to a halt. In October 2004, the Executive Vice President with responsibility for emerging brands resigned; the company subsequently eliminated that position.

The Industry

The highly fragmented restaurant industry was characterized by high initial investment, high labor costs as a percentage of overall costs, and intense competition across segments. As a whole, the restaurant industry outperformed the S&P 500 for the first 11 months of 2004, posting an 11% 5-year annual growth rate versus a 7% rate for the broader index. Year-to-date through December 23, 2004, the S&P restaurants index was up 29.7% (versus a 9.7% increase for the S&P 500), after rising 41% in 2003 (versus 27.4%).

Cost pressures were a key concern for the industry, primarily from increased beef, poultry, and dairy costs; labor costs; and uncertain fuel costs. While many commodities were below recent highs, they remained above 2003 levels. An additional concern was the vulnerability of input prices to weather and export demand. Competition for the lower-cost "B" sites that were part of the location strategy for OSI and its key competitors, had intensified, leading to higher prices and a scarcity of good locations.

A growing awareness of the consequences of unhealthy lifestyles—the U.S. Centers for Disease Control and Prevention in its recently revised statistics, estimated that more than 300,000 obesity-related deaths occurred each year—had spurred consumer demand for high-protein, low-carb dining options and created opportunities as well as threats for industry competitors. In addition to adding menu choices to accommodate diners' health and nutrition concerns, more individual and chain restaurants had begun to move beyond the standby "plateful of steamed vegetables" to offer innovative and flavorful vegetarian options.

Other trends included "global tapas," or small plate, menus as a way of giving diners more latitude in terms of ordering. This strategy of serving several small dishes at appetizer prices instead of the more traditional appetizer–entree model, was picking up around the country.

For two decades, a growing percentage of U.S. food dollars had been spent away from home. Factors contributing to this growth included an increase in the number of dual-income households, positive demographic trends, strong economic growth, and low unemployment rates. The casual dining sector in the United States continued to gain share from fast-food chains as a more affluent and somewhat older population favored full-service restaurants; this trend was expected to accelerate as the population ages.

In 2004, the National Restaurant Association was backing several legislative measures to curb frivolous lawsuits, increase the business-meal tax deductibility, and help shift the responsibility for tip reporting back to the Internal Revenue Service.

The cases in *Strategic Management and Business Policy–10th Edition* (and international version of this book) and *Cases in Strategic Management and Business Policy–10th Edition* were edited by the publisher and the book authors.

CASE 43

Movie Gallery, Inc.

J. David Hunger

Movie Gallery, Inc., in August 2006 was the second largest North American video rental company with 4,763 stores located in all 50 states plus Canada and Mexico. The company specialized in the rental and sale of DVD and VHS movies and video games under its subsidiaries, Movie Gallery, USA and Hollywood Entertainment.

The renting of videos began in the 1980s shortly after motion picture studios began selling videotapes of their movies to play on home videocassette player/recorders (VCRs). Because a typical videotape of a recent motion picture cost at that time around $15 to $25 to purchase, renting a movie for a few days for $5 made economic sense—especially if a person only wanted to view the movie once or twice. This made renting a movie much cheaper than paying about $10 for a couple to view the same film in a movie theater. Video rental stores quickly spread throughout North America as people invited friends and family to join them in eating pizza and watching rented movies in their living rooms.

Growth and Success

Movie Gallery was founded in 1985 by Joe Malugen and Harrison Parrish in Dothan, Alabama. Through its wholly owned subsidiary, M.G.A., the company's founders began operating video specialty stores in southern Alabama and the Florida panhandle, and franchising the Movie Gallery concept. By June 1987, the company owned five stores and had a franchise operation of 45 stores. Between 1988 and 1992, management consolidated the franchisees into 37 company-owned stores with annual revenues of $6 million. Using the proceeds from an initial public offering (IPO) in August 1994 to fund an aggressive expansion strategy, Movie Gallery grew to more than 850 stores by 1996 through more than 100 separate acquisitions. It also grew internally by building new retail outlets. During 1999 and 2000, for example, the company built 100 new stores each year. Additional acquisitions, including Blowout Entertainment in 1999 and

Video Update in 2003, raised the total number of stores to 2,000. The purchase of Video Update launched the firm's international presence with 100 retail outlets in Canada.

Movie Gallery's video stores primarily targeted small towns and suburban areas. By focusing on rural and secondary markets, the company was able to compete very effectively against the independently owned stores and small regional chains in these areas through its purchasing economies. It was able to deliver first-run movies at cheaper prices to customers in towns with fewer than 20,000 people.

The company's profits increased 57% from 2001 to 2004, resulting in its being listed Number 61 on *Business Week*'s 2005 list of the fastest-growing small companies.

Movie Gallery's top management made a strategic decision in 2005 to expand out of the company's target market by purchasing rival Hollywood Video for $1.2 billion. At the time, Hollywood Video's management had been fighting a hostile takeover bid by industry-leader Blockbuster, Inc. This acquisition raised Movie Gallery's store total to 4,700 outlets with revenues in excess of $2.5 billion annually.

Operating under the Hollywood Video and Game Crazy brands, Hollywood Entertainment primarily targeted urban centers and surrounding suburban neighborhoods and was especially strong on the West Coast where Movie Gallery was weak. It competed head-to-head with Blockbuster through excellent customer service and innovative marketing and merchandising programs. At the time of its purchase, Hollywood Entertainment operated 2,031 video rental stores and 20 free-standing video game stores throughout the United States. Its acquisition propelled Movie Gallery into second-place in the U.S. video rental market behind Blockbuster and made it a major player in large U.S. cities, such as Atlanta and Los Angeles.

In June 2005, the company added 61 retail stores to its presence in Western Canada by purchasing VHQ Entertainment. Among VHQ Entertainment's businesses was VHQ Online, a flat-fee, direct-to-home movie delivery service (*http://www.VHQonline.ca*). Canadian subscribers were able to choose from 52,000 movie titles, which would then be shipped by first-class mail to the customer's home for a basic monthly fee.

Consequences of Growth

The acquisition of Hollywood Entertainment left Movie Gallery heavily in debt. At the same time, the recent rise of online video rental services, such as Netflix, was cutting into retail store revenues and reducing the company's cash flow. Overall in-store sales for video rental outlets throughout the industry shrank 13% in 2005 to $7.1 billion, according to Adams Media Research, Inc. Online sales, in contrast, more than doubled to $1.4 billion in that same year.

Movie Gallery's sales slid 5% to $2 billion in 2005. By the end of the year, Movie Gallery recorded a $553 million loss. Absent one-time charges, it earned $31 million—a 38% decline from the previous year's profit. With just $135 million in cash at the end of 2005, Movie Gallery's management found itself facing possible bankruptcy. Movie Gallery's stock, worth about $3 on April 24, 2006, had lost more than 90% of its value since April 2005. Investors in mid-2006 had short positions (betting that the stock would decline further) on 18.6 million of the company's 32 million shares.

Competition

Movie Gallery was not alone in its financial difficulty. Blockbuster, the largest U.S. competitor in video rental stores, also lost money in 2005—around $450 billion.

In contrast to the situation at Movie Gallery and Blockbuster, Netflix, Inc., earned $41 million in profits on $688 in revenue during 2005. The company's shares rose 157% in the 12-month period through April 2006. With 5 million subscribers, Netflix management expected revenues to reach $990 million in 2006. CEO Reed Hastings had set the objective of Netflix reaching 20 million subscribers (around 20% of U.S. households) between 2010 and 2012.

Netflix had a different business model from that used by Movie Gallery and Blockbuster. Once Netflix subscribers selected a movie from the web site (*http://www.netflix.com*), a DVD was mailed to them for $5.99 per movie. A flat rate subscription service was also available. After viewing the movie, subscribers would mail back the DVD in order to rent another movie. Pressure from Netflix, which didn't charge late fees, forced Blockbuster's management to drop most late fees, costing it approximately $400 million in 2005. Although 70% of Blockbuster's rentals were new releases, the reverse was true of Netflix. The company promoted lesser-known movies that often received little distribution in movie theaters. The average customer of Netflix was an over-35 woman with family income of $75,000 or less.

Netflix was not the only company using the movies-through-the-mail business model. Amazon had successfully copied the Netflix postal model in Britain and Germany and was thinking of launching a postal movie service in the United States. In response, Netflix management was exploring the option of delivering movies online. Apple had pioneered downloading digital music through its iTunes and was likely to expand into video. Microsoft entered the music-download business in 2006 with its Zune digital player. In August 2006, Nokia bought Loudeye, an American digital music distributor, to develop its own service for its music-enabled handsets.

Video downloads were already being offered by Movielink.com, which was owned by five large film studios. News Corp's web sites, including MySpace.com, were planning to sell films and shows from the group's Fox network. The main problem with video downloads was the large size of video files, leading to long download times. The increasing availability of broadband cable and DSL should shorten these download times and make video downloads more popular. Broadband-equipped televisions and personal video recorders should also make the process easier.

Current Situation

In 2006, Movie Gallery's founders were still very active in the company. Joe Malugen served as Chairman of the Board, President, and Chief Executive Officer of Movie Gallery. Harrison Parrish was Vice Chairman of the Board and Senior Vice President. Both had seats on the corporation's board of directors. They were very much aware that the industry was changing and that Movie Gallery's management needed to take action to stem the losses and to position the company for future success.

For the first six months of 2006 ending July 2, total revenues were $1.3 billion compared to $1.3 billion for the same period a year earlier (assuming revenues from Hollywood Entertainment had been included in the 2005 totals). Rental revenue was 82.1% of total revenues with the remaining 17.9% coming from product sales. During this six-month period, same-store revenues decreased 5.6% from the same period in 2005. Interestingly, same-store revenues decreased only 1.3% at Movie Gallery branded stores compared to a 7.5% drop at Hollywood Entertainment branded stores. Management felt that the better performance of the Movie Gallery brand was caused by the resiliency of its Eastern-focused rural and secondary market presence as well as the success of the company's efforts to sell previously viewed titles from Hollywood stores at Movie Gallery stores.

Although the company reported a net loss of $14.9 million in the second quarter of 2006 (compared to a $12.2 million loss during the same period in 2005), the company's year-to-date net income was $25.5 million (compared to $6.2 million during the same six-month period in 2005). According to management, the company had sufficient cash to operate the business, satisfy working capital and capital expenditure requirements, and meet the company's foreseeable liquidity requirements, including financial covenants for its debt service for the remainder of 2006. Although the company's cash and cash equivalents totaled only $21,151,000 as of July 2, 2006, compared to $51,122,000 on July 3, 2005, accounts payable had dropped from $194,000,000 on July 3, 2005, to $92,156,000 on July 2, 2006. Long-term debt (including current portion) declined slightly to $1,100,943,000 on July 2, 2006, from $1,143,359,000 on July 3, 2005.

According to Chairman, President, and CEO Malugen in Movie Gallery's *2006 Second Quarter Report:*

> Our business continues to be affected by a weak home video release schedule and other industry-wide challenges, but we are making great progress on a number of internal initiatives intended to improve Movie Gallery's financial and operational performance. We continue to expect a slow late summer, as is typical due to the seasonality of our industry, with gradually improving business conditions beginning in October when the first of several $100 million titles will be released to home video. In the meantime, Movie Gallery is aggressively pursuing opportunities to increase revenues and further improve operating efficiencies. We have engaged Merrill Lynch to advise us on ways to improve our capital structure as well as Alvarez & Marsal, a leading turnaround management, restructuring and corporate advisory firm.

Responding to the firm's financial problems, Movie Gallery's management twice renegotiated lending agreements with bankers to ease payment terms. Management planned to close 175 underperforming and overlapping stores and lay off 380 of its 1,800 workers by the end of 2006. Hoping to cut at least 20% from its $500 million in annual rental expenses, it was negotiating subleases in almost half of its stores. Most of the financial benefits associated with lease renegotiation were expected to begin in 2007 with the bulk of the financial benefits to be realized in 2008 and beyond. Although the company opened 30 new stores in 2006 (which were already in the pipeline), management planned to curtail new store openings over the next several years in order to maximize free cash flow. Management was also reviewing its asset portfolio to identify any non-core assets it could divest for cash. (Movie Gallery's annual and quarterly reports and SEC filings are available via the company's web site at *www.moviegallery.com.*)

What Next?

Movie Gallery's stock price began to rise to after the company's announcement of its first-quarter results on May 11, 2006, and by August 9, 2006 a share of its stock was selling for $6.47. Even though the financial results for the first six months of 2006 showed an improvement in the company's financial position compared to 2005, the company's stock price fell to $2.97 on August 10, 2006, with the announcement of Movie Gallery's second-quarter results.

Management's implementation of a turnaround strategy was showing some indications of success. The reduction of costs and expenses was certainly important, but what should management do to increase revenues and profits? How could Movie Gallery be positioned for future success?

Glossary

10-K form An SEC form containing income statements, balance sheets, cash flow statements, and information not usually available in an annual report. p. 355

10-Q form An SEC form containing quarterly financial reports. p. 355

360-degree performance appraisal An evaluation technique in which input is gathered from multiple sources. p. 197

Absorptive capacity A firm's ability to value, assimilate, and utilize new external knowledge. p. 303

Acquisition The purchase of a company that is completely absorbed by the acquiring corporation. p. 166

Action plan A plan that states what actions are going to be taken, by whom, during what time frame, and with what expected results. p. 253

Activity ratios Ratios that indicate how well a corporation is managing its operations. p. 356

Activity-based costing (ABC) An accounting method for allocating indirect and fixed costs to individual products or product lines based on the value-added activities going into that product. p. 266

Adaptive mode A decision-making mode characterized by reactive solutions to existing problems, rather than a proactive search for new opportunities. p. 21

Advisory board A group of external business people who voluntarily meet periodically with the owners/managers of the firm to discuss strategic and other issues. p. 324

Affiliated directors Directors who, though not really employed by the corporation, handle the legal or insurance work for the company or are important suppliers. p. 40

Agency theory A theory that states that problems arise in corporations because the agents (top management) are not willing to bear responsibility for their decisions unless they own a substantial amount of stock in the corporation. p. 39

Altman's Bankruptcy Formula A formula used to estimate how close a company is to declaring bankruptcy. p. 360

Analytical portfolio manager A type of general manager needed to execute a diversification strategy. p. 241

Annual report A document published each year by a company to show its financial condition and products. p. 355

Assessment centers An approach to evaluating the suitability of a person for a position. p. 244

Assimilation A strategy which involves the domination of one corporate culture over another. p. 252

Association of South East Asian Nations (ASEAN) A regional trade association composed of Asian countries of Brunei, Indonesia, Malaysia, the Philippines, Singapore, Thailand, and Vietnam. p. 7

Autonomous (self-managing) work teams A group of people who work together without a supervisor to plan, coordinate, and evaluate their own work. p. 125

Backward integration Assuming a function previously provided by a supplier. p. 167

Balanced scorecard Combines financial measures with operational measures on customer satisfaction, internal processes, and the corporation's innovation and improvement activities. p. 272

Bankruptcy A retrenchment strategy which forfeits management of the firm to the courts in return for some settlement of the corporation's obligations. p. 178

Basic R&D Research and development that is conducted by scientists in well-equipped laboratories where the focus is on theoretical problem areas. p. 121

BCG (Boston Consulting Group) Growth-Share Matrix A simple way to portray a corporation's portfolio of products or divisions. p. 179

Behavior control A control that specifies how something is to be done through policies, rules, standard operating procedures, and orders from a superior. p. 265

Behavior substitution A phenomenon that occurs when people substitute activities that do not lead to goal accomplishment for activities that do lead to goal accomplishment because the wrong activities are being rewarded. p. 281

Benchmarking The process of measuring products, services, and practices against those of competitors or companies recognized as industry leaders. p. 275

Best practice A procedure that is followed by successful companies. p. 311

Board of director responsibilities Commonly agreed obligations of directors include: setting corporate strategy, overall direction, mission or vision; hiring and firing the CEO and top management; controlling, monitoring, or supervising top management; reviewing and approving the use of resources; and caring for shareholder interest. p. 36

Board of directors continuum A range of the possible degree of involvement by the Board of Directors (from low to high) in the strategic management process. p. 37

BOT (build-operate-transfer) concept A type of international entry option for a company. After building a facility, the company operates the facility for a fixed period of time during which it earns back its investment, plus a profit. p. 174

Brainstorming The process of proposing ideas in a group without first mentally screening them. p. 96

Brand A name that identifies a particular company's product in the mind of the consumer. p. 118

Budget A statement of a corporation's programs in terms of money required. p. 17

Business model The mix of activities a company performs to earn a profit. p. 110

Business plan A written strategic plan for a new entrepreneurial venture. p. 322

Business policy A previous name for strategic management; it has a general management orientation and tends to look inward with concern for integrating the corporation's many functional activities. p. 3

Business strategy Competitive and cooperative strategies that emphasize improvement of the competitive position of a corporation's products or services in a specific industry or market segment. p. 15

Cannibalize To replace popular products before they reach the end of their life cycle. p. 90

Capability A corporation's ability to exploit its resources. p. 106

Capital budgeting The process of analyzing and ranking possible investments in terms of the additional outlays and additional receipts that will result from each investment. p. 120

Captive company strategy Dedicating a firm's productive capacity as primary supplier to another company in exchange for a long-term contract. p. 177
Cash cow A product that brings in far more money than is needed to maintain its market share. p. 180
Categorical imperatives Kant's two principles to guide actions: A person's action is ethical only if that person is willing for that same action to be taken by everyone who is in a similar situation and a person should never treat another human being simply as a means but always as an end. p. 67
Cautious profit planner The type of leader needed for a corporation choosing to follow a stability strategy. p. 241
Cellular organization A structure composed of cells (self-managing teams, autonomous business units, etc.) that can operate alone but can interact with other cells to produce a more potent and competent business mechanism. p. 229
Center of excellence A designated area in which a company has a capability or a core competence. p. 184
Center of gravity The part of the industry value chain that is most important to the company and the point where the company's greatest expertise and capabilities lay. p. 112
Central American Free Trade Agreement (CAFTA) A regional trade association composed of El Salvador, Guatemala, Nicaragua, Costa Rica, the United States, and the Dominican Republic. p. 7
Clusters Geographic concentrations of interconnected companies and industries. p. 107
Codes of ethics A code that specifies how an organization expects its employees to behave while on the job. p. 66
Codetermination The inclusion of a corporation's workers on its board of directors. p. 42
Collusion The active cooperation of firms within an industry to reduce output and raise prices in order to get around the normal economic law of supply and demand. This practice is usually illegal. p. 157
Commodity A product whose characteristics are the same regardless of who sells it. p. 84
Common-size statements Income statements and balance sheets in which the dollar figures have been converted into percentages. p. 359
Competency A cross-functional integration and coordination of capabilities. p. 106
Competitive intelligence A formal program of gathering information about a company's competitors. p. 92
Competitive scope The breadth of a company's or a business unit's target market. p. 147
Competitive strategy A strategy that states how a company or a business unit will compete in an industry. p. 145
Competitors The companies that offer the same products or services as the subject company. p. 94
Complementor A company or an industry whose product works well with another industry's or firm's product and without which a product would lose much of its value. p. 86
Complication to evaluation and control Constraints in not-for-profit organizations that make it difficult to properly evaluate and control performance. p. 346
Complication to strategy formulation Constraints in not-for-profit organizations that make it difficult to formulate a new strategy. p. 345
Complication to strategy implementation Constraints in not-for-profit organizations that make it difficult to implement a new strategy. p. 346
Concentration A corporate growth strategy which concentrates a corporation's resources on competing in one industry. p. 166
Concentric diversification A diversification growth strategy in which a firm uses its current strengths to diversify into related products in another industry. p. 170
Concurrent engineering A process in which specialists from various functional areas work side-by-side rather than sequentially in an effort to design new products. p. 125
Conglomerate diversification A diversification growth strategy that involves a move into another industry to provide products unrelated to its current products. p. 170
Conglomerate structure An assemblage of legally independent firms (subsidiaries) operating under one corporate umbrella but controlled through the subsidiaries' boards of directors. p. 115
Connected line batch flow A part of a corporation's manufacturing strategy in which components are standardized and each machine functions like a job shop but is positioned in the same order as the parts are processed. p. 194
Consensus A situation in which all parties agree to one alternative. p. 207
Consolidated industry An industry in which a few large companies dominate. p. 86
Consolidation The second phase of a turnaround strategy that implements a program to stabilize the corporation. p. 177
Constant dollar Dollars adjusted for inflation. p. 360
Constraint on strategic management A characteristic peculiar to a not-for-profit organization that constrains its behavior and affects its strategic management. p. 344
Continuous improvement A system developed by Japanese firms in which teams strive constantly to improve manufacturing processes. p. 195
Continuous systems Production organized in lines on which products can be continuously assembled or processed. p. 124
Continuum of sustainability A representation which indicates how durable and imitable an organization's resources and capabilities are. p. 109
Contraction The first phase of a turnaround strategy which includes a general across-the-board cutback in size and costs. p. 177
Cooperative strategies Strategies that involve working with other firms to gain competitive advantage within an industry. p. 157
Co-opetition A term used to describe simultaneous competition and cooperation among firms. p. 161
Core competency A collection of corporate capabilities that cross divisional borders and are wide spread within a corporation, and is something that a corporation can do exceedingly well. p. 106
Corporate brand A type of brand in which the company's name serves as the brand name. p. 119
Corporate capabilities See capability. p. 106
Corporate culture A collection of beliefs, expectations, and values learned and shared by a corporation's members and transmitted from one generation of employees to another. p. 116
Corporate culture pressure A force from existing corporate culture against the implementation of a new strategy. p. 206
Corporate entrepreneurship Also called intrapreneurship, the creation of a new business within an existing organization. p. 306
Corporate governance The relationship among the board of directors, top management, and shareholders in determining the direction and performance of a corporation. p. 36
Corporate parenting A view that considers the corporation in terms of resources and capabilities that can be used to build business unit value as well as generate synergies across business units. p. 183
Corporate reputation A widely held perception of a company by the general public. p. 119
Corporate scenario Pro forma balance sheets and income statements that forecast

the effect that each alternative strategy will likely have on return on investment. p. 202
Corporate stakeholders Groups that affect or are affected by the achievement of a firm's objectives. p. 59
Corporate strategy A strategy that states a company's overall direction in terms of its general attitude toward growth and the management of its various business and product lines. p. 164
Corporation A mechanism legally established to allow different parties to contribute capital, expertise, and labor for their mutual benefit. p. 36
Cost focus A low-cost competitive strategy that concentrates on a particular buyer group or geographic market and attempts to serve only that niche. p. 149
Cost leadership A low-cost competitive strategy that aims at the broad mass market. p. 148
Cost proximity A process that involves keeping the higher price a company charges for higher quality close enough to that of the competition so that customers will see the extra quality as being worth the extra cost. p. 149
Crisis of autonomy A time when people managing diversified product lines need more decision-making freedom than top management is willing to delegate to them. p. 222
Crisis of control A time when business units act to optimize their own sales and profits without regard to the overall corporation. p. 222 See also *suboptimization.*
Crisis of leadership A time when an entrepreneur is personally unable to manage a growing company. p. 222
Cross-functional work teams A work team composed of people from multiple functions. p. 214
Cultural integration The extent to which units throughout an organization share a common culture. p. 116
Cultural intensity The degree to which members of an organizational unit accept the norms, values, or other culture content associated with the unit. p. 116
Deculturation The disintegration of one company's culture resulting from unwanted and extreme pressure from another to impose its culture and practices. p. 252
Dedicated transfer line A highly automated assembly line making one mass-produced product using little human labor. p. 194
Defensive centralization A process in which top management of a not-for-profit retains all decision-making authority so that lower-level managers cannot take any actions to which the sponsors may object. p. 346
Defensive tactic A tactic in which a company defends its current market. p. 155
Delphi technique A forecasting technique in which experts independently assess the probabilities of specified events. These assessments are combined and sent back to each expert for fine-tuning until agreement is reached. p. 96
Devil's advocate An individual or a group assigned to identify the potential pitfalls and problems of a proposal. p. 207
Dialectical inquiry A decision-making technique that requires that two proposals using different assumptions be generated for consideration. p. 208
Differentiation A competitive strategy that is aimed at the broad mass market and that involves the creation of a product or service that is perceived throughout its industry as unique. p. 147
Differentiation focus A differentiation competitive strategy that concentrates on a particular buyer group, product line segment, or geographic market. p. 149
Differentiation strategy See differentiation. p. 147
Dimensions of national culture A set of five dimensions by which each nation's unique culture can be identified. p. 256
Directional strategy A strategy that is composed of three general orientations: growth, stability, and retrenchment. p. 165
Distinctive competencies A firm's core competencies which are superior to those of competitors. p. 106
Diversification A basic growth strategy that implements the expansion of product lines or expanding into another industry. p. 170
Divestment A sell-out strategy that refers to selling off a division of a corporation with low growth potential. p. 178
Divisional structure An organizational structure in which employees tend to be functional specialists organized according to product/market distinctions. p. 115
Downsizing Planned elimination of positions or jobs. p. 245
Due care The obligation of board members to closely monitor and evaluate top management. p. 37
Durability The rate at which a firm's underlying resources and capabilities depreciate or become obsolete. p. 109
Dynamic industry expert A leader with a great deal of experience in a particular industry appropriate for executing a concentration strategy. p. 241
Dynamic pricing A marketing practice in which different customers pay different prices for the same product or service. p. 191
Earnings per share (EPS) A calculation that is determined by dividing net earnings by the number of shares of common stock issued. p. 268
Economic value added (EVA) A shareholder value method of measuring corporate and divisional performance. Measures after-tax operating income minus the total annual cost of capital. p. 270
Economies of scale A process in which unit costs are reduced by making large numbers of the same product. p. 125
Economies of scope A process in which unit costs are reduced when the value chains of two separate products or services share activities, such as the same marketing channels or manufacturing facilities. p. 125
EFAS (External Factor Analysis Summary) Table A table that organizes external factors into opportunities and threats and how well management is responding to these specific factors. p. 97
80/20 rule Rule stating that one should monitor those 20% of the factors that determine 80% of the results. p. 282
Electronic commerce The use of the Internet to conduct business transactions. p. 7
Engineering (or process) R&D R&D concentrating on quality control and the development of design specifications and improved production equipment. p. 121
Enterprise resource planning (ERP) software Software that unites all of a company's major business activities, from order processing to production, within a single family of software modules. p. 278
Enterprise risk management (ERM) A corporate-wide, integrated process to manage the uncertainties that could negatively or positively influence the achievement of the corporation's objectives. p. 267
Entrepreneur A person who initiates and manages a business undertaking and who assumes risk for the sake of a profit. p. 319
Entrepreneurial characteristics Traits of an entrepreneur which lead to a new venture's success. p. 328
Entrepreneurial mode Strategic decision making by one powerful individual in which the focus is on opportunities; problems are secondary. p. 20
Entrepreneurial venture Any new business whose primary goals are profitability and growth and that can be characterized by innovative strategic practices. p. 318
Entry barriers An obstruction that makes it difficult for a company to enter an industry. p. 83
Environmental scanning The monitoring, evaluation, and dissemination of information from the external and internal environments to key people within the corporation. p. 73

Environmental uncertainty The degree of complexity plus the degree of change existing in an organization's external environment. p. 72
Ethics The consensually accepted standards of behavior for an occupation, trade, or profession. p. 66
European Union (EU) A regional trade association composed of 25 European countries. p. 7
Evaluation and control A process in which corporate activities and performance results are monitored so that actual performance can be compared with desired performance. p. 262
Evaluation and control information Information to use in the evaluation and control of performance. p. 263
Evaluation and control process A process in which corporate activities and performance results are monitored so that actual performance can be compared with desired performance. p. 262
Executive leadership The directing of activities toward the accomplishment of corporate objectives. p. 49
Executive succession The process of grooming and replacing a key top manager. p. 243
Executive type An individual with a particular mix of skills and experiences. p. 241
Exit barrier An obstruction that keeps a company from leaving an industry. p. 84
Expense center A business unit that uses money but contributes to revenues only indirectly. p. 274
Experience curve A conceptual framework which states that unit production costs decline by some fixed percentage each time the total accumulated volume of production in units doubles. p. 181
Expert opinion A nonquantitative forecasting technique in which authorities in a particular area attempt to forecast likely developments. p. 96
Explicit knowledge Knowledge that can be easily articulated and communicated. p. 109
Exporting Shipping goods produced in a company's home country to other countries for marketing. p. 171
External environment Forces outside an organization that are not typically within the short-run control of top management. p. 11
External strategic factor Environmental trend with both high probability of occurrence and high probability of impact on the corporation. p. 82
Extranet An information network within an organization that is available to key suppliers and customers. p. 128
Extrapolation A form of forecasting which extends present trends into the future. p. 96
Factor affecting new venture success An issue that has a substantial impact on a new venture's performance. p. 327
Family business A company that is either owned or dominated by relatives. p. 332
Family directors Board members who are relatives of the founder and own significant blocks of stock. p. 40
Financial leverage The ratio of total debt to total assets. p. 120
Financial strategy A functional strategy to make the best use of corporate monetary assets. p. 191
First mover The first company to manufacture and sell a new product or service. p. 154
Flexible manufacturing A type of manufacturing that permits the low-volume output of custom-tailored products at relatively low unit costs through economies of scope. p. 125
Forward integration Assuming a function previously provided by a distributor. p. 167
14-A form An SEC form containing proxy statements and information on a company's board of directors. p. 355
Fragmented industry An industry in which no firm has large market share and each firm serves only a small piece of the total market. p. 86
Franchising An international entry strategy in which a firm grants rights to another company/individual to open a retail store using the franchiser's name and operating system. p. 173
Free cash flow The amount of money a new owner can take out of a firm without harming the business. p. 269
Full vertical integration A growth strategy under which a firm makes 100% of its key supplies internally and completely controls its distributors. p. 167
Functional strategy An approach taken by a functional area to achieve corporate and business unit objectives and strategies by maximizing resource productivity. p. 189
Functional structure An organizational structure in which employees tend to be specialists in the business functions important to that industry, such as manufacturing, sales, or finance. p. 114
GE Business Screen A portfolio analysis matrix developed by General Electric, with the assistance of the Mc Kinsey and Company consulting firm. p. 181
Geographic-area structure A structure that allows a multinational corporation to tailor products to regional differences and to achieve regional coordination. p. 235
Global industry An industry in which a company manufactures and sells the same products, with only minor adjustments for individual countries around the world. p. 87
Globalization The internationalization of markets and corporations. p. 6
Goal displacement Confusion of means with ends, which occurs when activities originally intended to help managers attain corporate objectives become ends in themselves or are adapted to meet ends other than those for which they were intended. p. 280
Goals An open-ended statement of what one wants to accomplish, with no quantification of what is to be achieved and no time criteria for completion. p. 14
Green-field development An international entry option to build a company's manufacturing plant and distribution system in another country. p. 173
Gross domestic product (GDP) A measure of the total output of goods and services within a country's borders. p. 360
Growth strategies A directional strategy that expands a company's current activities p. 165
Hierarchy of strategy A nesting of strategies by level from corporate to business to functional, so that they complement and support one another. p. 15
Horizontal growth A corporate growth concentration strategy that involves expanding the firm's products into other geographic locations and/or increasing the range of products and services offered to current markets. p. 169
Horizontal integration The degree to which a firm operates in multiple geographic locations at the same point in an industry's value chain. p. 169
Horizontal strategy A corporate parenting strategy that cuts across business unit boundaries to build synergy across business units and to improve the competitive position of one or more business units. p. 185
House of quality A method of managing new product development to help project teams make important design decisions by getting them to think about what users want and how to get it to them most effectively. p. 310
Human resource management (HRM) strategy A functional strategy that makes the best use of corporate human assets. p. 197
Human diversity A mix of people from different races, cultures, and backgrounds in the workplace. p. 127

Hypercompetition An industry situation in which the frequency, boldness, and aggressiveness of dynamic movement by the players accelerates to create a condition of constant disequilibrium and change. p. 90
Idea A concept for a new product or service. p. 321
IFAS (Internal Factor Analysis Summary) Table A table that organizes internal factors into strengths and weaknesses and how well management is responding to these specific factors. p. 129
Imitability The rate at which a firm's underlying resources and capabilities can be duplicated by others. p. 108
Index of R&D effectiveness An index that is calculated by dividing the percentage of total revenue spent on research and development into new product profitability. p. 311
Index of sustainable growth A calculation that shows how much of the growth rate of sales can be sustained by internally generated funds. p. 360
Individual rights approach An ethics behavior guideline that proposes that human beings have certain fundamental rights that should be respected in all decisions. p. 67
Individualism-collectivism (IC) The extent to which a society values individual freedom and independence of action compared with a tight social framework and loyalty to the group. p. 256
Industry A group of firms producing a similar product or service. p. 11
Industry analysis An in-depth examination of key factors within a corporation's task environment. p. 73
Industry matrix A chart that summarizes the key success factors within a particular industry. p. 91
Industry scenario A forecasted description of an industry's likely future. p. 96
Information technology strategy A functional strategy that uses information systems technology to provide competitive advantage. p. 198
Input control A control that specifies resources, such as knowledge, skills, abilities, values, and motives of employees. p. 265
Inside directors An officer or executive employed by a corporation who serves on that company's board of directors; also called management directors. p. 39
Institution theory A concept of organizational adaptation that proposes that organizations can and do adapt to changing conditions by imitating other successful organizations. p. 9
Institutional advantage A benefit for a not-for-profit organization when it performs its tasks more effectively than other comparable organizations. p. 344
Integration A process that involves a relatively balanced give-and-take of cultural and managerial practices between merger partners, with no strong imposition of cultural change on either company. p. 251
Intellectual property Special knowledge used in a new product or process developed by a company for its own use and is usually protected by a patent, copyright, trademark, or trade secret. p. 301
Interlocking directorate A condition that occurs when two firms share a director or when an executive of one firm sits on the board of a second firm. p. 43
Intermittent system A method of manufacturing in which an item is normally processed sequentially, but the work and the sequence of the processes vary. p. 123
Internal environment Variables within the organization not usually within the short run control of top management. p. 11
Internal strategic factors Strengths (core competencies) and weaknesses that are likely to determine whether a firm will be able take advantage of opportunities while avoiding threats. p. 106
International transfer pricing A pricing method used to minimize the effect of taxes on the measurement of performance across international markets. p. 276
Intranet An information network within an organization that also has access to the Internet. p. 128
Investment center A unit in which performance is measured in terms of the difference between the units resources and its services or products. p. 275
ISO 9000 Standards Series An internationally accepted way of objectively documenting a company's high level of quality operations. p. 265
ISO 14000 Standards Series An internationally accepted way to document a company's impact on the environment. p. 265
Issues priority matrix A chart that ranks the probability of occurrence versus the probable impact on the corporation of developments in the external environment. p. 81
Job characteristics model An approach to job design that is based on the belief that tasks can be described in terms of certain objective characteristics and that those characteristics affect employee motivation. p. 231
Job design The design of individual tasks in an attempt to make them more relevant to the company and to the employee. p. 231
Job enlargement Combining tasks to give a worker more of the same type of duties to perform. p. 231
Job enrichment Altering jobs by giving the worker more autonomy and control over activities. p. 231
Job rotation Moving workers through several jobs to increase variety. p. 231
Job shop One-of-a-kind production using skilled labor. p. 194
Joint venture An independent business entity created by two or more companies in a strategic alliance. p. 159
Justice approach An ethical approach which proposes that decision makers be equitable, fair, and impartial in the distribution of costs and benefits. p. 67
Just-In-Time A purchasing concept in which parts arrive at the plant just when they are needed rather than being kept in inventories. p. 196
Key performance measures Essential measures for achieving a desired strategic option—used in the balanced scorecard. p. 272
Key success factors Variables that significantly affect the overall competitive position of a company within a particular industry. p. 91
Late movers Companies that enter a new market only after other companies have done so. p. 154
Law A formal code that permits or forbids certain behaviors. p. 66
Lead director An outside director who calls meetings of the outside board members and coordinates the annual evaluation of the CEO. p. 45
Lead user A customer who is ahead of market trends and has needs that go beyond those of the average user. p. 296
Leading Providing direction to employees to use their abilities and skills most effectively and efficiently to achieve organizational objectives. p. 240
Lean Six Sigma A program developed to identify and improve a poorly performing process. p. 231
Learning organization An organization that is skilled at creating, acquiring, and transferring knowledge and at modifying its behavior to reflect new knowledge and insights. p. 9
Levels of moral development Kohlberg proposed three levels of moral development: preconventional, conventional, and principled. p. 65
Leverage ratio An evaluation of how effectively a company utilizes its resources to generate revenues. p. 356
Leveraged buy-out An acquisition in which a company is acquired in a transaction financed largely by debt—usually obtained from a third party, such as an insurance company or an investment banker. p. 191

Licensing arrangement An agreement in which the licensing firm grants rights to another firm in another country or market to produce and/or sell a branded product. p. 159

Lifestyle company A small business in which the firm is purely an extension of the owner's lifestyle. p. 331

Line extension Using a successful brand name on additional products, such as Arm & Hammer's brand first on baking soda, then on laundry detergents, toothpaste, and deodorants. p. 189

Linkage The connection between the way one value activity (for example, marketing) is performed and the cost of performance of another activity (for example, quality control). p. 113

Liquidation The termination of a firm in which all its assets are sold. p. 178

Liquidity ratio The percentage showing to what degree a company can cover its current liabilities with its current assets. p. 356

Logical incrementalism A decision-making mode, that can be viewed as a synthesis of planning, adaptive, and entrepreneurial modes. p. 21

Logistics strategy A functional strategy that deals with the flow of products into and out of the manufacturing process. p. 196

Long-term contract Agreements between two separate firms to provide agreed-upon goods and services to each other for a specified period of time. p. 169

Long-term evaluation method A method in which managers are compensated for achieving objectives set over a multiyear period. p. 283

Long-term orientation (LT) The extent to which society is oriented toward the long term versus the short term. p. 257

Lower cost strategy A strategy in which a company or business unit designs, produces, and markets a comparable product more efficiently than its competitors. p. 147

Management audit A technique used to evaluate corporate activities. p. 273

Management By Objectives (MBO) An organization wide approach ensuring purposeful action toward desired objectives. p. 254

Management contract Agreements through which a corporation uses some of its personnel to assist a firm in another country for a specified fee and period of time. p. 174

Market development A marketing functional strategy in which a company or business unit captures a larger share of an existing market for current products through market penetration or develops new markets for current products. p. 190

Market location tactics Tactics that determine where a company or business unit will compete. p. 155

Market position Refers to the selection of specific areas for marketing concentration and can be expressed in terms of market, product, and geographical locations. p. 118

Market research A means of obtaining new product ideas by surveying current or potential users regarding what they would like in a new product. p. 297

Market segmentation The division of a market into segments to identify available niches. p. 118

Market value added (MVA) The difference between the market value of a corporation and the capital contributed by shareholders and lenders. p. 271

Marketing mix The particular combination of key variables (product, place, promotion, and price) that can be used to affect demand and to gain competitive advantage. p. 118

Marketing strategy A functional strategy that deals with pricing, selling, and distributing a product. p. 190

Masculinity-femininity (MF) The extent to which society is oriented toward money and things. p. 256

Mass customization The low-cost production of individually customized goods and services. p. 125

Mass production A system in which employees work on narrowly defined, repetitive tasks under close supervision in a bureaucratic and hierarchical structure to produce a large amount of low-cost, standard goods and services. p. 194

Matrix of change A chart that compares target practices (new programs) with existing practices (current activities). p. 216

Matrix structure A structure in which functional and product forms are combined simultaneously at the same level of the organization. p. 226

Mercosur/Mercosul South American free-trade area including Argentina, Brazil, Uruguay, and Paraguay. p. 7

Merger A transaction in which two or more corporations exchange stock, but from which only one corporation survives. p. 166

Mission The purpose or reason for an organization's existence. p. 12

Modular manufacturing A system in which pre-assembled subassemblies are delivered as they are needed to a company's assembly-line workers who quickly piece the modules together into finished products. p. 195

Moral relativism A theory which proposes that morality is relative to some personal, social, or cultural standard, and that there is no method for deciding whether one decision is better than another. p. 65

Morality Precepts of personal behavior that are based on religious or philosophical grounds. p. 66

Multidomestic industry An industry in which companies tailor their products to the specific needs of consumers in a particular country. p. 87

Multinational corporation (MNC) A company that has significant assets and activities in multiple countries. p. 78

Multiple sourcing A purchasing strategy in which a company orders a particular part from several vendors. p. 195

Multipoint competition A rivalry in which a large multi-business corporation competes against other large multi-business firms in a number of markets. p. 185

Mutual service consortium A partnership of similar companies in similar industries that pool their resources to gain a benefit that is too expensive to develop alone. p. 158

Net present value (NPV) A calculation of the value of a project that is made by predicting the project's payouts, adjusting them for risk, and subtracting the amount invested. p. 205

Network structure An organization (virtual organization)that outsources most of its business functions. p. 228

New entrants Businesses entering an industry that typically bring new capacity to an industry, a desire to gain market share, and substantial resources. p. 83

New product experimentation A method of test marketing the potential of innovative ideas by developing products, probing potential markets with early versions of the products, learning from the probes and probing again. p. 297

No-change strategy A decision to do nothing new; to continue current operations and policies for the foreseeable future. p. 176

North American Free Trade Agreement (NAFTA) Regional free trade agreement between Canada, the United States, and Mexico. p. 7

Not-for-profit organization Private nonprofit corporations and public governmental units or agencies. p. 340

Objectives The end result of planned activity stating what is to be accomplished by when and quantified if possible. p. 14

Offensive tactic A tactic that calls for competing in an established competitor's current market location. p. 155

Open innovation A new approach to R&D in which a firm uses alliances and connections with corporate, government, and academic labs to learn about new developments. p. 193

Operating budget A budget for a business unit that is approved by top management during strategy formulation and implementation. p. 274
Operating cash flow The amount of money generated by a company before the costs of financing and taxes are subtracted. p. 269
Operating leverage The impact of a specific change in sales volume on net operating income. p. 124
Operations strategy A functional strategy that determines how and where a product or service is to be manufactured, the level of vertical integration in the production process, and the deployment of physical resources. p. 193
Opportunity A strategic factor considered using the SWOT analysis. p. 321
Orchestrator A top manager who articulates the need for innovation, provides funding for innovating activities, creates incentives for middle managers to sponsor new ideas, and protects idea/product champions from suspicious or jealous executives. p. 306
Organization slack Unused resources within an organization. p. 166
Organizational analysis Internal scanning concerned with identifying an organization's strengths and weaknesses. p. 106
Organizational learning theory A theory proposing that an organization adjusts to changes in the environment through the learning of its employees. p. 9
Organizational life cycle How organizations grow, develop, and eventually decline. p. 224
Organizational structure The formal setup of a business corporation's value chain components in terms of work flow, communication channels, and hierarchy. p. 114
Output control A control that specifies what is to be accomplished by focusing on the end result of the behaviors through the use of objectives and performance targets. p. 265
Outside directors Members of a board of directors who are not employees of the board's corporation; also called non-management directors. p. 39
Outsourcing A process in which resources are purchased from others through long-term contracts instead of being made within the company. p. 169
Parallel sourcing A process in which two suppliers are the sole suppliers of two different parts, but they are also backup suppliers for each other's parts. p. 196
Pattern of influence A concept stating that influence in strategic management derives from a not-for-profit organization's sources of revenue. p. 343
Pause/proceed with caution strategy A corporate strategy in which nothing new is attempted; an opportunity to rest before continuing a growth or retrenchment strategy. p. 175
Penetration pricing A marketing pricing strategy to obtain dominant market share by using low price. p. 191
Performance The end result of activities, actual outcomes of a strategic management process. p. 18
Performance appraisal system A system to systematically evaluate employee performance and promotion potential. p. 244
Performance gap A performance gap exists when performance does not meet expectations. p. 19
Periodic statistical report Reports summarizing data on key factors such as the number of new customer contracts, volume of received orders, and productivity figures. p. 274
Phases of strategic management Four levels of development through which a firm generally evolves into strategic management. p. 4
Piracy The making and selling counterfeit copies of well-known name-brand products. p. 277
Planning mode A decision-making mode that involves the systematic gathering of appropriate information for situation analysis, the generation of feasible alternative strategies, and the rational selection of the most appropriate strategy. p. 21
Policy A broad guideline for decision making that links the formulation of strategy with its implementation. p. 15
Political strategy A strategy to influence a corporation's stakeholders. p. 205
Population ecology A theory which proposes that once an organization is successfully established in a particular environmental niche, it is unable to adapt to changing conditions. p. 8
Portfolio analysis An approach to corporate strategy in which top management views its product lines and business units as a series of investments from which it expects a profitable return. p. 179
Power distance (PD) The extent to which a society accepts an unequal distribution of influence in organizations. p. 256
Pressure-cooker crisis A situation that exists when employees in collaborative organizations eventually grow emotionally and physically exhausted from the intensity of teamwork and the heavy pressure for innovative solutions. p. 223
Primary activity A manufacturing firm's corporate value chain including inbound logistics, operations process, outbound logistics, marketing and sales, and service. p. 113
Primary stakeholders A high priority group which affects or is affected by the achievement of a firm's objectives. p. 60
Prime interest rate The rate of interest banks charge on their lowest-risk loans. p. 360
Private nonprofit corporation A non-governmental not-for-profit organization. p. 340
Privatization The selling of state-owned enterprises to private individuals. Also the hiring of a private business to provide services previously offered by a state agency. p. 341
Procedures A list of sequential steps that describe in detail how a particular task or job is to be done. p. 17
Process innovation Improvement to the making and selling of current products. p. 299
Product champion A person who generates a new idea and supports it through many organizational obstacles. p. 306
Product development A marketing strategy in which a company or unit develops new products for existing markets or develops new products for new markets. p. 189
Product innovation The development of a new product or the improvement of an existing product's performance. p. 299
Product life cycle A graph showing time plotted against sales of a product as it moves from introduction through growth and maturity to decline. p. 118
Product R&D Research and development concerned with product or product-packaging improvements. p. 121
Product/market evolution matrix A chart depicting products in terms of their competitive positions and their stages of product/market evolution. p. 305
Product-group structure A structure of a multinational corporation that enables the company to introduce and manage a similar line of products around the world. p. 235
Production sharing The process of combining the higher labor skills and technology available in developed countries with the lower-cost labor available in developing countries. p. 174
Professional liquidator An individual called on by a bankruptcy court to close a firm and sell off its assets. p. 242
Profit center A unit's performance, measured in terms of the difference between revenues and expenditures. p. 274
Profit strategy A strategy that artificially supports profits by reducing investment and short-term discretionary expenditures. p. 176
Profitability ratios Ratios evaluating a company over a period of time. p. 356

Profit-making firm A firm depending on revenues obtained from the sale of its goods and services to customers, who typically pay for the costs and expenses of providing the product or service plus a profit. p. 341
Program A statement of the activities or steps needed to accomplish a single-use plan in strategy implementation. p. 16
Propitious niche A portion of a market that is so well suited to a firm's internal and external environment that other corporations are not likely to challenge or dislodge it. p. 142
Public governmental unit or agency A kind of not-for-profit organization that is established by government or governmental agencies (such as welfare departments, prisons, and state universities). p. 340
Public or collective good Goods that are freely available to all in a society. p. 340
Pull strategy A marketing strategy in which advertising pulls the products through the distribution channels. p. 190
Punctuated equilibrium A point at which a corporation makes a major change in its strategy after evolving slowly through a long period of stability. p. 18
Purchasing power parity (PPP) A measure of the cost, in dollars, of the U.S.-produced equivalent volume of goods that another nation's economy produces. p. 79
Purchasing strategy A functional strategy that deals with obtaining the raw materials, parts and supplies needed to perform the operations functions. p. 195
Push strategy A marketing strategy in which a large amount of money is spent on trade promotion in order to gain or hold shelf space in retail outlets. p. 190
Quality of work life A concept that emphasizes improving the human dimension of work to improve employee satisfaction and union relations. p. 127
Quasi-integration A type of vertical growth/integration in which a company does not make any of its key supplies but purchases most of its requirements from outside suppliers that are under its partial control. p. 169
Question marks New products that have potential for success and need a lot of cash for development. p. 180
R&D intensity A company's spending on research and development as a percentage of sales revenue. p. 120
R&D mix The balance of basic, product, and process research and development. p. 121
R&D strategy A functional strategy that deals with product and process innovation. p. 192
Ratio analysis The calculation of ratios from data in financial statements to identify possible strengths or weaknesses. p. 356
Real options approach An approach to new project investment when the future is highly uncertain. p. 205
Red tape crisis A crisis that occurs when a corporation has grown too large and complex to be managed through formal programs. p. 223
Reengineering The radical redesign of business processes to achieve major gains in cost, service, or time. p. 229
Relationship-based governance A government system perceived to be less transparent and have a higher degree of corruption. p. 64
Repatriation of profits The transfer of profits from a foreign subsidiary to a corporation's headquarters. p. 74
Replicability The ability of competitors to duplicate resources and imitate another firm's success. p. 108
Resources A company's physical, human, and organizational assets that serve as the building blocks of a corporation. p. 106
Responsibility center A unit that is isolated so that it can be evaluated separately from the rest of the corporation. p. 274
Retired executive directors Past leaders of a company kept on the board of directors after leaving the company. p. 40
Retrenchment strategy Corporate strategy to reduce a company's level of activities and to return it to profitability. p. 176
Return on equity (ROE) A measure of performance that is calculated by dividing net income by total equity. p. 268
Return on investment (ROI) A measure of performance that is calculated by dividing net income before taxes by total assets.p. 268
Revenue center A responsibility center in which production, usually in terms of unit or dollar sales, is measured without consideration of resource costs. p. 274
Reverse engineering Taking apart a competitor's product in order to find out how it works. p. 108
Reverse stock split A stock split in which an investor's shares are reduced for the same total amount of money. p. 192
Risk A measure of the probability that one strategy will be effective, the amount of assets the corporation must allocate to that strategy, and the length of time the assets will be unavailable. p. 204
Role of the board of directors in strategic management Three basic tasks (monitor, evaluate and influence, initiate and determine) that are carried out by the board of directors. p. 37
Rule-based governance A governance system based on clearly-stated rules and procedures. p. 64
Sarbanes-Oxley Act Legislation passed by the U.S. Congress in 2002 to promote and formalize greater board independence and oversight. p. 46
Scenario writing A forecasting technique in which focused descriptions of different likely futures are presented in a narrative fashion. p. 96
Secondary stakeholders Lower priority groups which affect or are affected by the achievement of a firm's objectives. p. 60
Sell-out strategy A retrenchment option used when a company has a weak competitive position resulting in poor performance. p. 178
Separation A method of managing the culture of an acquired firm in which the two companies are structurally divided, without cultural exchange. p. 252
SFAS (Strategic Factors Analysis Summary) Matrix A chart that summarizes an organization's strategic factors by combining the external factors from an EFAS table with the internal factors from an IFAS table. p. 139
Shareholder value The present value of the anticipated future stream of cash flows from a business plus the value of the company if it were liquidated. p. 269
Short-term orientation The tendency of managers to consider only current tactical or operational issues and ignore strategic ones. p. 279
Simple structure A structure for new entrepreneurial firms in which the employees tend to be generalists and jacks-of-all-trades. p. 114
Six Sigma A program developed to identify and improve a poorly performing process. p. 230
Skim pricing A marketing strategy in which a company charges a high price while a product is novel and competitors are few. p. 191
Small-business firm An independently owned and operated business that is not dominant in its field and that does not engage in innovative practices. p. 312
SO, ST, WO, WT Strategies A series of possible business approaches based on combinations of opportunities, threats, strengths, and weaknesses. p. 145
Social capital The goodwill of key stakeholders, which can be used for competitive advantage. p. 59
Social entrepreneurship A business in which a not-for-profit organization starts a new venture to achieve social goals. p. 348

Social responsibility The ethical and discretionary responsibilities a corporation owes its stakeholders. p. 56
Societal environment Economic, technological, political-legal, and sociocultural environmental forces that do not directly touch on the short run activities of an organization but influence its long-run decisions. p. 73
Sole sourcing Relying on only one supplier for a particular part. p. 195
Sources of innovation Drucker's proposed seven sources of new ideas that should be monitored by those interested in starting entrepreneurial ventures. p. 326
Sponsor A department manager who recognizes the value of a new idea, helps obtain funding to develop the innovation, and facilitates the implementation of the innovation. p. 306
Stability strategy Corporate strategies to make no change to the company's current direction or activities. p. 175
Staffing Human resource management priorities and use of personnel. p. 240
Stages of corporate development A pattern of structural development that corporations follow as they grow and expand. p. 220
Stages of international development The stages through which international corporations evolve in their relationships with widely dispersed geographic markets and the manner in which they structure their operations and programs. p. 233
Stages of new product development The stages of getting a new innovation into the marketplace. p. 305
Stage-gate process A method of managing new product development to increase the likelihood of launching new products quickly and successfully. The process is a series of steps to move products through the six stages of new product development. p. 309
Staggered board A board on which directors serve terms of more than 1 year so that only a portion of the board of directors stands for election each year. p. 44
Stakeholder analysis The identification and evaluation of corporate stakeholders. p. 60
Stakeholder measure A method of keeping track of stakeholder concerns. p. 269
Stakeholder priority matrix A chart that categorizes stakeholders in terms of their interest in a corporation's activities and their relative power to influence the corporation's activities. p. 205
Standard cost center A responsibility center that is primarily used to evaluate the performance of manufacturing facilities. p. 274
Standard operating procedures Plans that detail the various activities that must be carried out to complete a corporation's programs. p. 218
Star Market leader that is able to generate enough cash to maintain its high market share. p. 180
Statistical modeling A quantitative technique that attempts to discover causal or explanatory factors that link two or more time series together. p. 96
Steering control Measures of variables that influence future profitability. p. 264
Stewardship theory A theory proposing that executives tend to be more motivated to act in the best interests of the corporation than in their own self-interests. p. 40
Strategic alliance A partnership of two or more corporations or business units to achieve strategically significant objectives that are mutually beneficial. p. 157
Strategic audit A checklist of questions by area or issue that enables a systematic analysis of various corporate functions and activities. p. 23
Strategic audit worksheet A tool used to analyze a case. p. 362
Strategic business unit (SBU) A division or group of divisions composed of independent product-market segments that are given primary authority for the management of their own functions. p. 115
Strategic choice The evaluation of strategies and selection of the best alternative. p. 207
Strategic choice perspective A theory which proposes that organizations adapt to a changing environment and have the opportunity and power to reshape their environment. p. 9
Strategic decision-making process An eight-step process that improves strategic decision making. p. 21
Strategic decision-making process for entrepreneurial venture A set of eight interrelated steps through which strategic decision making is applied to form entrepreneurial ventures. p. 321
Strategic decisions Decisions that deal with the long-run future of an entire organization and are rare, consequential, and directive. p. 20
Strategic factors External and internal factors that determine the future of a corporation. p. 10
Strategic group A set of business units or firms that pursue similar strategies and have similar resources. p. 88
Strategic management A set of managerial decisions and actions that determine the long-run performance of a corporation. p. 3
Strategic myopia The willingness to reject unfamiliar as well as negative information. p. 81
Strategic piggybacking The development of a new activity for a not-for-profit organization that would generate the funds needed to make up the difference between revenues and expenses. p. 348
Strategic planning staff A group of people charged with supporting both top management and business units in the strategic planning process. p. 52
Strategic R&D alliance A coalition through which a firm coordinates its research and development with another firm(s) to offset the huge costs of developing new technology. p. 301
Strategic rollup A means of consolidating a fragmented industry in which an entrepreneur acquires hundreds of owner-operated small businesses resulting in a large firm with economies of scale. p. 152
Strategic type A category of firms based on a common strategic orientation and a combination of structure, culture, and processes that are consistent with that strategy. p. 88
Strategic vision A description of what the company is capable of becoming. p. 49
Strategic window A unique market opportunity that is available only for a limited time. p. 142
Strategic-funds method An evaluation method that encourages executives to look at development expenses as being different from expenses required for current operations. p. 284
Strategies to avoid Strategies sometimes followed by managers who have made a poor analysis or lack creativity. p. 201
Strategy A comprehensive plan that states how a corporation will achieve its mission and objectives. p. 14
Strategy formulation Development of long-range plans for the effective management of environmental opportunities and threats in light of corporate strengths and weaknesses. p. 138
Strategy implementation A process by which strategies and policies are put into action through the development of programs, budgets, and procedures. p. 214
Strategy-culture compatibility The match between existing corporate culture and a new strategy to be implemented. p. 249
Structure follows strategy The process through which changes in corporate strategy normally lead to changes in organizational structure. p. 219
Stuck in the middle A situation in which a company or business unit has not achieved a generic competitive strategy and has no competitive advantage. p. 150

Suboptimization A phenomenon in which a unit optimizes its goal accomplishment to the detriment of the organization as a whole. p. 281

Sub-stages of small business development A set of five levels through which new ventures often develop. p. 330

Substitute products Products that appear to be different but can satisfy the same need as other products. p. 85

Supply-chain management The formation of networks for sourcing raw materials, manufacturing products or creating services, storing and distributing goods, and delivering goods or services to customers and consumers. p. 128

Support activity An activity which ensures that the primary value-chain activities operate effectively and efficiently. p. 113

SWOT analysis Identification of strengths, weaknesses, opportunities, and threats that may be strategic factors for a specific company. p. 138

Synergy A concept which states that the whole is greater than the sum of its parts; that two units will achieve more together than they could separately. p. 170

Tacit knowledge Knowledge that is not easily communicated because it is deeply rooted in employee experience or in a corporation's culture. p. 109

Tactic A short-term operating plan detailing how a strategy is to be implemented. p. 153

Taper integration A type of vertical integration in which a firm internally produces less than half of its own requirements and buys the rest from outside suppliers. p. 168

Task environment The part of the business environment that includes the elements or groups that directly affect the corporation and, in turn, are affected by it. p. 73

Technological competence A corporation's proficiency in managing research personnel and integrating their innovations into its day-to-day operations. p. 121

Technological discontinuity The displacement of one technology by another. p. 122

Technological follower A company that imitates the products of competitors. p. 192

Technological leader A company that pioneers an innovation. p. 192

Technology sourcing A make-or-buy decision that can be important in a firm's R&D strategy. p. 300

Technology transfer The process of taking a new technology from the laboratory to the marketplace. p. 121

Time to market The time from inception to profitability of a new product. p. 289

Timing tactics Tactics that determines when a business will enter a market with a new product. p. 154

Tipping point The point at which a slowly changing situation goes through a massive, rapid change. p. 335

Top management responsibilities Leadership tasks which involve getting things accomplished through and with others in order to meet the corporate objectives. p. 48

Total Quality Management (TQM) An operational philosophy that is committed to customer satisfaction and continuous improvement. p. 255

TOWS Matrix A chart that illustrates how the external opportunities and threats facing a particular corporation can be matched with that company's internal strengths and weaknesses to result in four sets of strategic alternatives. p. 144

Tracking stock A type of common stock that is tied to one portion of a corporation's business. p. 192

Transaction cost economics A theory which proposes that vertical integration is more efficient than contracting for goods and services in the marketplace when the transaction costs of buying goods on the open market become too great. p. 167

Transfer price A practice in which one unit can charge a transfer price for each product it sells to a different unit within a company. p. 275

Transferability The ability of competitors to gather the resources and capabilities necessary to support a competitive challenge. p. 108

Transformational leader A leader who causes change and movement in an organization by providing a strategic vision. p. 49

Transparent The speed with which other firms can understand the relationship of resources and capabilities supporting a successful firm's strategy. p. 108

Trends in governance Current developments in corporate governance. p. 47

Triad The three developed markets of Japan, North America, and Western Europe forming a single market with common needs. p. 79

Triggering event Something that acts as a stimulus for a change in strategy. p. 19

Turnaround specialist A manager who is brought into a weak company to salvage that company in a relatively attractive industry. p. 242

Turnaround strategy A plan that emphasizes the improvement of operational efficiency when a corporation's problems are pervasive but not yet critical. p. 176

Turnkey operation Contracts for the construction of operating facilities in exchange for a fee. p. 174

Uncertainty avoidance (UA) The extent to which a society feels threatened by uncertain and ambiguous situations. p. 256

Utilitarian approach A theory which proposes that actions and plans should be judged by their consequences. p. 67

Value chain A linked set of value-creating activities that begins with basic raw materials coming from suppliers and ends with distributors getting the final goods into the hands of the ultimate consumer. p. 111

Value-chain partnership A strategic alliance in which one company or unit forms a long-term arrangement with a key supplier or distributor for mutual advantage. p. 159

Vertical growth A corporate growth strategy in which a firm takes over a function previously provided by a supplier or distributor. p. 167

Vertical integration The degree to which a firm operates in multiple locations on an industry's value chain from extracting raw materials to retailing. p. 167

Virtual organization An organizational structure that is composed of a series of project groups or collaborations linked by changing nonhierarchical, cobweb-like networks. p. 228

Virtual team A group of geographically and/or organizationally dispersed coworkers that are assembled using a combination of telecommunications and information technologies to accomplish an organizational task. p. 126

VRIO framework Barney's proposed analysis to evaluate a firm's key resources in terms of value, rareness, imitability, and organization. p. 106

Weighted-factor method A method that is appropriate for measuring and rewarding the performance of top SBU managers and group-level executives when performance factors and their importance vary from one SBU to another. p. 283

Z-value A formula that combines five ratios by weighting them according to their importance to a corporation's financial strength to predict the likelihood of bankruptcy. p. 360

Name Index

A. C. Nielsen Co., 93
AB Electrolux, 41, 153, 247, 359
ABB Asea Brown Boyeri AG, 117
ABC network, 201
Abdelsamad, M. H., 358
Abraham, S., 376*n*, 384*n*
Abraham, S. C., 391*n*
Ace Hardware, 196
Acklesberg, R., 402*n*
Acohido, B., 376*n*
Adelphia Communications, 46
Adidas, 83
Adler, P. S., 381*n*
Admiral, 252
Adobe, 285
Aeppel, T., 398*n*
Aerospatiale, 158
Affrim, H., 398*n*
AFNOR, 277
Agle, B. R., 382*n*
Agrawal, V., 390*n*
Ahlstrom, D., 379*n*
Aibo, 305
Ainuddin, R., 398*n*
Airboard, 305
Airbus Industrie, 2, 83, 158, 205
Ajax Continental, 253, 254
Alamo, 148
Albertson, 149
Alcatel-Alsthom NV, 117
Alcoa, 158
Aldi, 148, 172
Aldrich, H., 377*n*
Alexander, J. A., 405*n*
Alexander, K., 399*n*
Alexander, L. D., 329*n*
Alexander, M., 183, 184, 388*n*, 389*n*
Aley, J., 401*n*
Ali, S., 402*n*
Allen, 164
Allen, J., 387*n*
Allen, R. S., 398*n*
Alley, J., 386*n*
Allied Corporation, 166
Allied Signal, 166, 243
Allio, M. K., 404*n*
Allport-Vernon-Lindzey Study of Values, 63
Almanac of Business and Industrial Financial Ratios, 366
Almeida, P., 399*n*
Alpert, M., 402*n*
Alta Vista, 355
Altman, R., 360
Amabile, T. M., 395*n*
Amana, 153
Amason, A. C., 392*n*
Amazon.com, 20, 159, 269
Amburgey, T. L., 392*n*
AMD, 155
AME, 15
American Airlines, 6, 15
American Can Company, 87
American Cancer Society, 348
American Cyanamid, 235
American Express, 252
American Hospital Supply (AHS), 128
American Management Association, 199, 266
American Productivity & Quality Center, 276
American Society for Industrial Security, 93
American Standards Institute, 277
Ames, 162
Amgen, 301
Amidon, D. M., 397*n*
Amoco, 112
Amoco Chemical, 196
AMR Research, 8
Amram, M., 391*n*
Anaheim Ducks, 51
Anchor Steam, 327
Andersen, T. J., 376*n*
Anderson, C., 206, 691*n*
Anderson, C. A., 388*n*
Anderson, S., 389*n*
Andrew, J. P., 399*n*
Andrews, K. Z., 387*n*, 397*n*
Andriessen, F., 403*n*
Angwin, D., 390*n*
Anheuser-Busch, 43, 111, 119, 156, 158, 159, 172, 173, 275
Annual Report Gallery, 366
Annual Statement Studies, 366
Anslinger, P., 387*n*
Ansoff, H. I., 383*n*
Ante, S. E., 391*n*
Anterasian, C., 389*n*
Aossey, B., 138
Apke, T. M., 400*n*
Apple Computer, 49, 84, 107, 121, 148, 155, 169, 223, 275, 279, 294
Applegate, J., 404*n*
Apria Healthcare, 38
Archer Daniels Midland (ADM), 157
Aristotle, 208
Arizona Iced Tea, 178
Arlow, P., 382*n*, 402*n*
Arm & Hammer, 142, 189–90, 390*n*
Armenakis, A. A., 395*n*
Armour, S., 395*n*
Armstrong, L., 397*n*
Arndt, M., 376*n*, 381*n*, 382*n*, 390*n*, 391*n*, 393*n*
Arner, F., 392*n*
Aronloff, C. F., 402*n*, 404*n*
Arthur D. Little, Inc., 87, 292, 298
Arthur, M. M., 381*n*
Ascarelli, S., 398*n*
Ascher, K., 404*n*
Asda Group, 172
Asea Brown Boveri (ABB), 235
Ashbaugh, H., 378*n*, 379*n*, 380*n*
Ashcroft, M., 35
Ashkenas, R. N., 394*n*
Ashman, D. P., 391*n*
Associated Consultants International, 87
Association of Southeast Asian Nations (ASEAN), 6, 7, 86
Astachan, J., 333
Aston, A., 390*n*, 392*n*
AT&T, 192, 244, 252, 270
AT&T Wireless, 192
Atkins, B., 378*n*
Atwater, H. B., 183
Audia, P. G., 383*n*
Augustine, N. R., 379*n*
Aupperle, K. E., 381*n*, 385*n*
Automotive Resources, 277
Avis, 239
Avnet, Inc., 95
Avon Company, 197
Avon Products, 23, 93, 106
Axelton, K., 329
Axion, 190

Baan, 128, 278
Bachman, J., 385*n*
Bachmann Industries, 225
Backover, A., 380*n*
Bacon, D. C., 405*n*
Badaracco, J. L., 68, 382*n*
Baden-Fuller, C. W. F., 383*n*, 393*n*
Badger, T. A., 392*n*
Bag, Borrow Or Steal, 329
Bagley, C., 327, 403*n*

Bain & Company, 5, 175, 243, 272, 276
Baker, S., 399*n*
Baker, W. H., 401*n*
Baldor Electric Company, 194
Baldwin Locomotive, 72
Baldwin, T. T., 377*n*, 394*n*
Baldwin-United, 225
Balfour, F., 277
Balkin, D. B., 398*n*
Ballow, J. J., 376*n*
Bamford, C. E., 403*n*
Banbury, C., 237
Band-Aids, 214
Bangs, D. H., 405*n*
Bank of Montreal, 38
Banker, R. D., 390*n*
Bankers Trust, 243, 246
Banking Act of 1933, 43
Baptist Health Systems, 349
Baptist Hospital of Nashville, 348
Barkema, H., 388*n*
Barker, R., 269, 396*n*
Barnes, F. C., 396*n*
Barnett, W. P., 392*n*
Barnevik, P., 117
Barney, J. B., 106, 157, 381*n*, 384*n*, 385*n*, 387*n*, 391*n*, 402*n*
Barrett, A., 392*n*, 394*n*, 404*n*
Barthelemy, J., 391*n*
Bartholomew, D., 385*n*
Bartlett, C. A., 393*n*
Barton, T. L., 397*n*
Baucus, D. A., 381*n*
Baucus, M. S., 381*n*
Bauerschmidt, A., 403*n*
Baum, J. A. C., 376*n*, 379*n*
Baum, J. R., 402*n*
Baumol, W. J., 401*n*
Beamish, P. W., 387*n*–388*n*
Bear, M. M., 387*n*
Beaver, G., 380*n*
Bechtel Group, Inc., 23
Beck, R., 387*n*
Beckstead, S. M., 401*n*
Bedejan, A. G., 395*n*
Begun, J. W., 405*n*
Behling, O. C., 396*n*
Bell Labs, 308
Bell South, 273
BellCore, 311
Belluzzo, R., 308
Ben & Jerry's Ice Cream, 59
Bend-Ems, 228
Benetton, 229
Benner, M. J., 400*n*
Bennett, C. J., 381*n*
Bennis, W., 380*n*
Bensoussan, B. E., 384*n*
Berenbeim, R. E., 381*n*
Berggen, E., 399*n*
Bergh, D. D., 388*n*
Berkshire, 170
Berkshire Hathaway, 286
Berle, A. A., 41
Berman, J., 35
Berner, R., 393*n*
Bernstein, A., 385*n*
Berry, J., 391*n*
Berry, M., 215, 383*n*, 402*n*
Bert, A., 392*n*
Best Buy, 91, 134, 212
Best Western, 38
Bestfoods Asia Ltd., 277
Bethune, Gordon, 3
Bettis, R. A., 383*n*, 389*n*
Beverland, M., 403*n*
Beyer, J. M., 383*n*
Bezos, Jeff, 20
Bhambri, A., 381*n*
Bianchi, A., 403*n*
Bianco, A., 382*n*, 394*n*
Bierly, P. E. III, 384*n*, 401*n*
Big Idea Group, 193
Biggs, E. L., 378*n*
Bigley, G. A., 394*n*
Bigness, J., 390*n*
Bilderbeek, J., 393*n*
Bill of Rights, 67
Birkinshaw, J. M., 184, 390*n*, 399*n*
Birley, S., 402*n*, 404*n*
Bisquick, 183
Biz, 190
Black & Decker, 159
Black Entertainment Television, 326
Black, J. S., 247, 395*n*
Blackberry, 336
Blackburn, R. S., 385*n*
Blackburn, V. L., 402*n*
Blackmore, J., 383*n*
Blackwell, C. W., 396*n*
Bleakley, F. R., 390*n*
Bleeke, J., 387*n*
Blenkhorn, D. L., 384*n*
Block, Z., 309
Blockbuster, 75, 169
Blodgett, L. L., 387*n*
Bloom, R., 126
Bloomberg, 366
BMW, 118, 286, 297, 332
Body Shop, 49, 359
Boeing, 8, 17, 83, 125, 198, 228
Boeker, W., 390*n*, 394*n*
Bombardier, 170
Bond, M. H., 258, 396*n*
Booksfree.com, 329
Borrus, A., 51, 378*n*, 380*n*
Bosch, R., 76
Bose Corporation, 196
Boston Consulting Group, 3, 179
Boston Pops Pops Orchestra, 349
Boston Symphony, 349
Boulding, W., 386*n*
Boulton, W. R., 401*n*
Bower, J. L., 388*n*, 399*n*
Bowman, E. H., 376*n*
Boyd, B. K., 379*n*, 383*n*
Boyle, M., 387*n*
BP Amoco, 112, 168
Braam, G. J. M., 397*n*
Bracker, J. S., 402*n*
Bradlees, 162
Bradley, D. B., III, 402*n*
Brady Bunch, 77
Brady, A., 400*n*
Brady, D., 384*n*–385*n*, 399*n*, 404*n*, 405*n*
Brancato, C. K., 397*n*
Brastemp, 194
Bray, H., 378*n*, 380*n*
Breed, A. G., 149
Breen, J., 402*n*
Bremner, B., 387*n*, 395*n*
Brenneman, G., 242
Bresser, R. F., 376*n*
Brewer, P. C., 397*n*
Brews, P. J., 377*n*
Bridge, J., 376*n*
Bristol Myers Squibb, 243
British Aerospace, 158
British Airways, 6, 15, 341
British Petroleum, 112, 286, 359
British Standards Institute, 277
Britannica.com, 21
Brockmann, E., 395*n*
Brodsky, N., 151, 386*n*
Bromiley, P., 376*n*
Brouthers, K. D., 388*n*, 403*n*
Brouthers, L. E., 388*n*
Brown, B. M., 402*n*
Brown, C., III, 389*n*
Brown, D., 212, 288
Brown, K. G., 385*n*
Brown, T., 386*n*
Brull, S. V., 395*n*
Bruner, R. F., 388*n*
Brunswick, 76
Brusger, J., 70, 134, 212, 288
Brush, T. H., 376*n*–377*n*
Bruton, G. D., 395*n*, 402*n*
Brynijolfsson, E., 217, 392*n*
Buchholtz, A. K., 378*n*, 391*n*
Buchko, A. A., 394*n*
Budweiser, 158–159, 172, 277
Buffet, W., 170
Buick, 115, 169, 220
BuildPoint, 8
Burgelman, R. A., 307, 401*n*
Burger King, 88, 242
Burgman, R., 376*n*
Burns, J., 380*n*
Burrows, P., 19, 302, 384*n*, 387*n*, 389*n*, 399*n*
Burton, T. M., 258, 387*n*
Busch Gardens, 76

Busenitz, L. W., 389*n*, 390*n*, 391*n*, 402*n*
Bushholtz, A. K., 379*n*
Busija, E. C., 389*n*
Business Cycle Development, 365
Business Environment Risk Index, 87
Business International, 87
Business Periodical Index, 366
Business Roundtable Institute for Corporate Ethics, 66
Business Week, 46, 366
Butler, R. J., 377*n*
Bygrave, W. D., 403*n*
Byme, J. A., 391*n*
Byrnes, N., 269, 378*n*
Byron, W. J., 57, 381*n*

Cadbury, A., 380*n*
Cadillac, 17, 115, 169
Calantone, R. J., 392*n*
Callahan, C. V., 376*n*
Callinicos, B., 267
Calori, R., 395*n*
Calpers, 51
Campbell, A., 13, 51, 183–84, 218, 377*n*, 388*n*, 389*n*, 392*n*–393*n*
Campbell-Hunt, C., 386*n*
Canadair, 170
Canadian National Railway, 173
Canavan, J., 379*n*
Cannella, A. A., Jr., 41, 394*n*
Cannon, 169, 286
Cantrell, R. S., 379*n*
Capell, K., 384*n*
Capital Cities/ABC, 51
Cardinal, L. B., 376*n*, 388*n*
Carey, D. C., 394*n*
Carey, J., 390*n*, 401*n*
Cargill, 332
Carland, J. A. C., 401*n*
Carland, J. C., 376*n*, 401*n*–402*n*
Carland, J. W., 376*n*, 401*n*–402*n*
Carnival Cruise Lines, 76
Carow, K., 388*n*
Carpenter, D., 376*n*, 382*n*
Carpenter, M. A., 379*n*–380*n*, 394*n*–395*n*, 398*n*
Carper, W. B., 388*n*
Carr, L. L., 378*n*
Carr, N. G., 391*n*
Carraher, S., 377*n*
Carrefour Group, 332
Carroll Food, 167, 169
Carroll, A. B., 57, 381*n*
Carroll, S. J., Jr., 396*n*
Carter, N. M., 386*n*
Carter, Rick, 253
Caruana, A., 403*n*
Cascade, 294
Cascio, W. F., 389*n*, 395*n*
Case, 75
Case Cutlery, 20
Casey's General Stores, 208
Cassidy, U., 329
Castro, A., 391*n*
Castro, J., 401*n*
Caterpillar, Inc., 119, 230
Catholic University of America, 57
Cavanagh, G. F., 67–68, 382*n*
Caves, R. E., 386*n*
CD/International, 355, 365
Celestial Seasonings, 25
Celta, 195
Center for Financial Research & Analysis, 354
Central American Free Trade Agreement (CAFTA), 6, 7
CEOExpress, 366
Cetron, M. J., 382*n*
Chadwick, C., 389*n*
Chae, M. S., 381*n*
Chakravarthy, B., 384*n*
Chan, P. S., 400*n*
Chandler, A. D., 10, 219, 223, 242, 377*n*, 392*n*
Chandra, G., 397*n*
Chang, S., 234
Charan, R., 273, 397*n*
Charmin, 149, 185
Chattopadhyay, P., 383*n*, 391*n*
Chawla, S. K., 397*n*
Checca, N., 391*n*
Checkers Restaurants, 354
Cheerios, 56, 83
Chen, M-J, 380*n*
Chesbrough, H. W., 390*n*
Chevrolet, 115, 220
Chevron, 205
Chi, P. C. K., 386*n*
Chiang, J., 400*n*
Children's Television Workshop, 349
Chinta, R., 400*n*
Cho, D. S., 386*n*
Cho, T. S., 380*n*
Choi, T. Y., 396*n*
Choudhury, N., 387*n*
Chow, D., 277
Chrisman, J. J., 386*n*, 403*n*
Christen, B., 386*n*
Christensen, C. M., 123, 312, 385*n*, 399*n*
Chrysler Corporation, 6, 42, 125, 193, 195, 209, 266, 297, 306
Chuanzhi, Liu, 18
Chung, S. Y., 386*n*
Chung, W., 6, 384*n*
Church & Dwight Company, Inc., 142, 189–90, 390*n*
Churchill, N. C., 333, 403*n*
Chussill, M. J., 400*n*
CIA World Fact Book, 367
CIGNA, 272
Cinacalcet, 301
Circuit City, 169
Cisco Systems, 15, 58, 94, 167, 175, 186, 298, 302
Cistercian Abbey of Our Lady of Spring Bank, 339, 348
Citicorp, 243
Clark, D., 391*n*, 398*n*
Clark, Martire & Bartolomeo, 286
Clark, S. M., 382*n*
Clausing, D., 401*n*
Clayton Act, 43
Clegg, S. R., 376*n*, 392*n*
Clorox Company, 156
Clorox Super Detergent, 156
CNN, 49
Coca-Cola Company, 118–19, 127, 144, 156, 178, 270–71, 279
Cockburn, I. M., 383*n*
Cohen, E., 319
Cohen, W. M., 400*n*
Colbert, A. E., 385*n*
Coleman, H. J. Jr., 393*n*
Coles, J. W., 379*n*
Colgate-Palmolive, 189, 190
Collier, N., 377*n*
Collingwood, H., 382*n*
Collins, D. W., 378*n*, 379*n*–380*n*
Collis, D. J., 389*n*
Colt Manufacturing, 225
Columbia-Presbyterian Medical Center, 349
Colvin, G., 63, 385*n*, 388*n*
Comcast, 47
Commandeur, H. R., 377*n*
Compact Disclosure, 355, 365
Compaq, 84, 105, 150, 175–6
CompUSA, 169
Compustat, 355, 365
ConAgra, 207
Conference Board, 40, 59
Conger, J. A., 391*n*
Conlin, M., 381*n*, 383*n*
Construcciones Aeronáuticas, 158
Contardo, I., 390*n*
Conti, R., 395*n*
Continental Airlines, 3
Conyon, M. J., 380*n*
Cook, M., 386*n*
Cooper and Lybrand, 157
Cooper, A. C., 386*n*–387*n*, 403*n*
Cooper, C., 63
Cooper, C. L., 395*n*
Copeland, T., 391*n*
Corkindale, D. R., 399*n*
Corning, Inc., 231, 240
Corporate Library, 44, 46
Corporate New Ventures (CNV), 312
CorporateInformation.com, 366
CorpTech, 367
Corriher, S. E., 382*n*
Cortese, A., 385*n*
Cosby Show, 77
Cosco, J., 377*n*

Cosier, R. A., 392*n*
COSMOS, 274
Council for Harmonization of Electrotechnical Standards of the Nations of the Americas, 277
Country Assessment Service, 87
CoverGirl, 166
Covin, J. G., 388*n*, 401*n*, 403*n*
Cowen, J. L., 225
Cox Family Enterprise Center, 333
Coy, P., 381*n*, 391*n*
Credit Suisse First Boston, 192
Crockett, R. O., 381*n*, 393*n*, 401*n*
Crosier, D., 196–7
CSA, 277
CSX Corporation, 171
Cullin, D., 326
Cummings, S., 377*n*
Cummings, T., 381*n*
Curran, J. J., 389*n*
Current Business Reports, 365
CVS Drugs, 162, 192
Cypher, 214

D'Aveni, R. A., 90, 377*n*, 383*n*, 386*n*
Dacin, M. T., 392*n*
Dacin, T., 392*n*
Daft, D., 127
Daily, C. M., 379*n*–380*n*, 388*n*
Daimler-Benz, 6
Daimler-Benz Aerospace, 158
DaimlerChrysler, 251
Daksh eServices Ltd., 199
Dale, K., 196
Dalsace, F., 388*n*
Dalsimer, J. P., 405*n*
Dalton, D. R., 379*n*–380*n*, 388*n*
Danhua, X., 302
Daniels, J. D., 398*n*
Danielson, C., 377*n*, 394*n*
Darragh, J., 393*n*
Dart Industries, 59
Das, T. K., 387*n*
Datta, D. K., 394*n*
Daum, J. H., 379*n*–380*n*
David, F., 403*n*
David, G., 393*n*
David, J. H., 380*n*
Davids, M., 64, 382*n*
Davidson, W. N., III, 379*n*
Davidsson, P., 402*n*
Davies, J., 377*n*
Davis, B., 402*n*
Davis, J. H., 41
Davis, R. H., 405*n*
Davis, S. M., 228, 393*n*
Dawley, D., 395*n*
Dawley, D. D., 389*n*
Dawson, C., 396*n*
Dayton Hudson, 59, 162
DBands, 319
de Kluyver, C. A., 384*n*
Dean Foods Company, 192
Dean, H., 192
Dean, J. W., Jr., 377*n*–378*n*
Dean, T. J., 403*n*
Debelak, D., 382*n*
DeCastro, J. O., 386*n*
Dechant, K., 382*n*, 391*n*
DeDee, J. K., 389*n*
Deener, B., 390*n*
Defining Moments, 68
Degeorge, 65
Dehaene, A., 378*n*
Delawder, 266
Delery, J. E., 398*n*
Delios, A., 388*n*
Dell Computer, 77, 83–4, 105, 109–110, 129, 148, 150, 176, 195, 199, 286, 312
Dell, M., 105, 109, 175
Delmar, F., 402*n*
Deloitte & Touche Consulting Group, 79
Deloitte Research, 209
Delphi, 195
deMan, A. P., 387*n*
DeMarie, S. M., 377*n*, 384*n*, 385*n*
Demb, A., 378*n*
Deming, W. E., 195, 196
Denis, J., 405*n*
DeNisi, A. S., 391*n*
Dennis, W. J., Jr., 402*n*
Desai, A., 379*n*
DeVuyst, V., 378*n*
Di Benedetto, C. A., 392*n*
Diamond Multimedia Systems, 224
Dickson, P. H., 396*n*, 403*n*
Diffusion of Innovations, 306
DIN, 277
Dino, R. N., 378*n*
Directory of Market Research Reports, 365
Directory of National Trade Associations, 366
Disney, R., 51
Disney, W., 111
DiStephano, J. J., 387*n*
DiVerde, D., 394*n*
Dixon, L., 196
Dobbin, F., 382*n*
Dockers, 210
Dodge Viper, 209
Dollar General, 17
Dollinger, M. J., 383*n*
Donaldson, G., 378*n*, 397*n*
Donaldson, L., 41, 392*n*
Donnely, F., 403*n*
Doritos, 292
Dougherty, D., 400*n*
Douglas, T. J., 396*n*
Douma, M. U., 393*n*
Douma, S., 388*n*
Dow Chemical, 231, 296
Dow, D., 398*n*
Dowd, T. J., 382*n*
Dowling, G. R., 385*n*
Dranikoff, L., 389*n*
Draulans, J., 387*n*
Drazin, R., 394*n*
Dreese, M., 70, 134, 212, 288
Dreux, D. R., 402*n*
Drew, S., 393*n*
Drew, S. A. W., 398*n*
Drucker, P. F., 174, 326, 339, 403*n*, 404*n*
Drury, C., 390*n*
Duchan, D., 391*n*
Due, T., 390*n*
Duening, T. N., 397*n*
Dugall, S. S., 400*n*
Dun & Bradstreet's Online, 366
Dun's Review, 366
Dunn, P., 397*n*
DuPont, 180, 198, 219–20, 223
Durant, W., 223
Dushnitsky, G., 390*n*
Dyer, J. H., 387*n*, 394*n*

EADS, 2
Eastern Airlines, 2, 225
Eastman Kodak, 72, 245
Eaton Corporation, 283
eBay, 19, 226, 279, 329
Eckerd College, 345
Eckerd Drugs, 162
Ecola, 366
Economic Espionage Act, 93
Economic Indicators, 365
Economic Report of the President to Congress, 365
Economist Intelligence Unit, 87
Economist, The, 366
Edmondson, G., 388*n*, 392*n*, 395*n*
Edvinsson, L., 389*n*
Egan, M., 398*n*
Ehrbar, A., 397*n*
Eikner, A. E., 404*n*
Einhorn, B., 302
Eisenhardt, K. M., 377*n*, 391*n*
Eisenmann, T. R., 381*n*
Eisner, M., 45, 51
Elango, E., 388*n*
Electrolux AB, 41, 153, 247, 359
Elenkov, D., 398*n*
Elgin, B., 389*n*
Eli Lilly, 270
Elliot, J. R., 76
Ellison, L., 105, 166, 222
Ellstrand, A. E., 378*n*–379*n*, 380*n*
El-Namacki, M. S. S., 401*n*
Elsass, P. M., 392*n*
Elstrom, P., 395*n*
Emerson Electric, 43, 185
Emerson, R. E., 404*n*
Encyclopaedia Britannica, 21
Encyclopedia of Associations, 366
Engardio, P., 277

England, G. W., 382*n*
Enhanced Tracker, 274
Enron, 36, 46, 62, 63, 65
Ensign, P. C., 184, 390*n*
Enterprise Rent-A-Car, 239
Entrepreneur's Guide to Business Law, The, 327
Epstein, L. D., 376*n*
Equal Employment Opportunity Commission, 248
Equitable Life, 37
Ericsson, 169, 186
Ernst & Young, 293
Ernst, D., 387*n*
Estée Lauder, 77
e-Steel, 8
European Aeronautic & Space Company (EADS), 2
European Union (EU), 6, 7, 78, 86
Excel, 83

Fahey, L., 103, 384*n*, 387*n*, 402*n*
Fairlamb, D., 392*n*
Falshaw, J. R., 386*n*
Fang, Y., 232
Fannin, R., 398*n*
Farrell, C., 403*n*
Federal Trade Commission, 131
FedEx, 128, 167, 198, 279, 286, 326
Feeser, H. R., 403*n*
Feldman, M. S., 392*n*
Felsenthal, E., 405*n*
Fennell, M. L., 405*n*
Ferlie, F., 404*n*
Fiat Group, 322
Fiegenbaum, A., 383*n*
Fiegener, M. K., 402*n*
Field, J. M., 390*n*
Fields, D., 319, 402*n*
Fiet, J. O., 402*n*
Financial Times, 286
Finkelstein, S., 379*n*
Finsbury Data Services, 93
Fiorina, C., 150, 180
Fishburne, R., 385*n*
Fisher, A. B., 397*n*
Fisher, S. R., 395*n*
Fishwick, F., 377*n*
Fitzgerald, A., 386*n*, 389*n*
Flanagan, D. J., 388*n*
Fleisher, C. S., 381*n*, 384*n*
Flora, B., 383*n*
Florida, R., 404*n*
Florin, J., 402*n*
Floyd, S. W., 377*n*
Flyer, F., 384*n*
Flynn, E. J., 380*n*, 400*n*
Focus Systems, 169
Fogarty, T. A., 377*n*
Fogg, C. D., 381*n*
Folgers, 159
Fombrun, C. J., 385*n*, 395*n*
Forbes, 293, 366
Ford Motor Company, 111–12, 127, 195, 223, 297, 332
Ford of Britain, 233
Ford, H. I., 111, 167, 223
Forrester Research, 209
Fort, J., 35
Fortune, 366
Foster, M. J., 401*n*
Foster, R., 122
Fouts, P. A., 381*n*
Fowler, J., 401*n*
Fowler, K. L., 398*n*
Fowler, V., 402*n*
Francis, S. C., 394*n*
Frank J. Zamboni & Company, 142
Frank, H., 403*n*
Frank, R., 258
Franko, L. G., 400*n*
Frantz, M., 400*n*
Fraser, D., 79
Fredrickson, J. W., 24, 378*n*, 380*n*
Freedman, D. H., 400*n*
Freeman, K., 259
Freeman, R. E., 270, 381*n*
Freundlich, N., 401*n*
Fridson, M. S., 405*n*
Fried, V. H., 388*n*, 402*n*
Friedman, M., 57, 381*n*
Friesen, P. H., 393*n*
Frito's Corn Chip, 292
Froelich, K. A., 404*n*–405*n*
Frost and Sullivan, 87
Frost, T. S., 184, 390*n*
Fujitsu Ltd., 201
Fuld, L., 383*n*
Fuld-Gilad, Herring Academy of Competitive Intelligence, 81
Fulk, J., 383*n*
Furst, S. A., 385*n*

Gable, M., 382*n*
Gadella, J. W., 392*n*
Gadiesh, O., 384*n*, 392*n*
Galante, S. P., 401*n*
Galbraith, C. S., 112, 391*n*, 398*n*
Galbraith, J. R., 111, 384*n*, 401*n*
GameChanger, 312
GameFly, 329
Garai, R., 387*n*
Garcia, F., 393*n*
Gard, L., 381*n*–382*n*
Garg, V. K., 382*n*
Garsombke, D. J., 402*n*
Garsombke, T. W., 402*n*
Garud, R., 399*n*
Garvin, D. A., 151, 377*n*
Gashurov, I., 393*n*
Gates, B., 49, 90
Gateway, 77, 84, 105
Gatorade Xtremo Thirst Quencher, 292
Gaumitz, B. R., 382*n*
GE Capital International Services, 199
Geberlein, C., 377*n*
Gee, E. P., 387*n*
Geitner, P., 172
Geletkanycz, M. A., 379*n*, 391*n*
Genentech, 285
General Electric Company (GE), 3, 6, 16–17, 23, 38, 72, 106, 117, 119, 125, 153, 157, 169–70, 181, 198–99, 208, 223, 231, 243, 244, 245, 270–1, 275, 284–6, 300
General Foods, 116
General Mills, 56, 83, 92, 183, 294
General Mills Foundation, 56
General Motors Corporation, 17, 49, 72, 110, 116, 169, 178, 195, 207, 219–20, 223, 226, 247, 271
Gentry, R. J., 380*n*
George, E., 383*n*
George, G., 400*n*
Georgia-Pacific, 196, 270
Geranios, N. K., 386*n*
Gerber, 294
Geringer, J. M., 387*n*
Gerlach, M. L., 379*n*
Gerstner, I. V., Jr., 380*n*
Gerstner, L., 21, 49, 177, 377*n*
Getz, G., 399*n*
Ghemawat, P., 386*n*
Ghobadian, A., 376*n*
Ghoshal, S., 393*n*
Ghosn, C., 251, 396*n*
Gibson, J. W., 396*n*
Gibson, L. L., 385*n*
Gilad, 95, 103
Gilbert, D. R., 381*n*
Gilbert, J. A., 397*n*
Gilbert, J. L., 384*n*, 392*n*
Gillette, 108–110, 154, 273, 294
Gilley, K. M., 377*n*, 395*n*
Gimeno, J., 390*n*
Gimeno-Gascon, F. J., 403*n*
Gincarlo, C., 302
Ginsberg, 306, 401*n*
Gioia, D. A., 382*n*
Girl Scouts, 348
Gladwell, M., 335, 404*n*
Gladwin, T. N., 383*n*
Glaister, K. W., 386*n*
Glass, H. E., 388*n*–389*n*, 391*n*, 403*n*, 404*n*
Glick, W. H., 383*n*, 391*n*
Global Crossing, 36, 46
Global Entrepreneurship Monitor, 317
Gluck, F. W., 376*n*
GM, 266
Godfrey, A., 404*n*
Gogoi, P., 388*n*
Gold, I., 377*n*
Gold, S., 51

Goldberg, D. I., 397*n*
Golden, B. R., 394*n*
Golden, T. D., 382*n*
Goldenberg, D. L., 397*n*
Golder, P. N., 386*n*
Gomes-Casseres, B., 160
Gomez-Mejia, L. R., 398*n*
Goodale, J. C., 401*n*
Gooding, R. Z., 392*n*
Goodrich, B. F., 308
Goodstein, J., 390*n*, 394*n*
Goodyear Tire & Rubber, 126, 195
Google, 47, 355
Goold, M., 183–4, 218, 388*n*, 389*n*, 392*n*, 404*n*
Gopalakrishnan, S., 401*n*
Gopinhath, C., 394*n*
Gordon, B., 387*n*
Gordon, G. G., 395*n*
Gordon, S. S., 377*n*
Governance Metrics International (GMI), 46
Govindarajan, V., 397*n*
Graham, J. L., 389*n*
Grant, R. M., 21, 107, 376*n*, 377*n* 384*n*, 391*n*
Grant's, 162
Graves, S. B., 381*n*, 400*n*
Gray, D., 377*n*
Greco, J., 391*n*, 394*n*
Green, H., 387*n*, 391*n*
Green, J., 393*n*
Greenberg, H., 397*n*
Greene, J., 390*n*
Greening, D. W., 381*n*
Greenpeace, 60
Gregersen, H. B., 257, 395*n*
Greiner, L. E., 222–3, 381*n*, 392*n*
Gretzky, W., 98
Greve, H. R., 383*n*
Grey-Wheelright, 259
Griffin, R. W., 232
Grim Reaper, 149
Grimm, C. M., 376*n*, 386*n*, 394*n*
Grint, K., 393*n*
Grossman, L. M., 384*n*
Grossman, W., 399*n*
Group Danone, 235
Grove, A. S., 19, 60, 86, 204, 381*n*, 388*n*
Grover, R., 51, 391*n*, 399*n*
Grow, B., 389*n*, 392*n*, 394*n*
Gruber, R., 397*n*
Grupo Transportacion Ferroviaria Mexicana (TFM), 173
Gulati, R., 400*n*
Gumpus, A., 397*n*
Gundry, L. K., 403*n*
Gupta, A. K., 392*n*
Gupta, N., 398*n*
Gupta, U., 403*n*
Guth, W. D., 306, 382*n*, 383*n*, 401*n*
Guthrie, J. P., 394*n*
Guyon, J., 117
Hackman, J. R., 232
Hagey, R., 386*n*
Hahn, S., 380*n*
Haines, V. Y., III, 390*n*
Halal, W. E., 382*n*
Hall, E. H., Jr., 397*n*, 400*n*
Hallmark, 294
Halpern, M. T., 405*n*
Hambrick, D. C., 24, 41, 378*n*, 379*n*, 381*n*, 387*n*, 391*n*
Hamel, G., 384*n*, 399*n*
Hamermesh, R. G., 389*n*
Hamilton, 265
Hamilton Beach, 159
Hamilton, R. D., III, 396*n*
Hamm, J., 393*n*
Hamm, S., 234, 391*n*, 399*n*
Hammer, M., 230, 393*n*
Handy, C., 376*n*
Hanoka, M., 395*n*
Hansen, B., 379*n*, 399*n*
Hansen, M. H., 381*n*
Harback, H. F., 395*n*
Harbin Brewery Group, 173
Hardee's, 88, 329
Harding, D., 389*n*
Hardy, C., 392*n*, 400*n*
Harley-Davidson, 231, 246
Harman, C. L., 381*n*
Harper, R. M., 404*n*
Harrigan, K. R., 168, 388*n*
Harrington, A., 399*n*
Harris Poll, 59
Harrison, D. A., 379*n*, 392*n*, 395*n*
Harrison, J. S., 400*n*
Hartman, R. I., 395*n*
Hasbro, 29, 226
Hatfield, J. D., 381*n*
Hathaway, 170
Hatten, K. J., 333, 383*n*, 404*n*
Hatten, M. L., 383*n*
Hauser, J. R., 401*n*
Havens, C., 389*n*
Hawthorne, 56
Hayashi, A. M., 392*n*
Hayes Corporation, 224
Hayes Microcomputer Products, 223–4, 226
Hayes, D., 223–4, 226
Hayward, M. L., 41
He, L., 380*n*
Head & Shoulders, 277
Headd, B., 401*n*
Health Midwest, 349
Healthy Choice, 207
Heaney, P. D., 397*n*
Heatherington, D., 224
Hedley, B., 180, 389*n*
Heeley, M. B., 400*n*
Heene, K. A., 384*n*
Heffron, F., 345, 405*n*
Hegarty, W. H., 393*n*
Hegel, 208
Heiens, R. A., 386*n*
Heimer, M., 405*n*
Heineken, 129
Heisz, A., 385*n*
Helfat, C. E., 376*n*, 379*n*, 384*n*
Helms, M. M., 398*n*
Hempel, J., 381*n*
Henderson, P., 327
Henderson, R. M., 383*n*
Hendrickson, A. R., 385*n*
Hendrickx, M., 376*n*
Henkoff, R., 387*n*, 394*n*
Hennart, J. F., 387*n*
Henricks, M., 396*n*, 404*n*
Henry, D., 398*n*
Herd, T., 215, 392*n*
Heron, R., 388*n*
Herron, L., 403*n*
Hershey Foods, 279
Hertz, 239
Hesterly, W. S., 379*n*
Hewitt Associates, 251
Hewlett-Packard Company (HP), 105, 116, 150, 158, 169, 175, 196, 243, 251, 308, 311
Hickman, C., 303, 400*n*
Hickson, D. J., 377*n*, 393*n*
Hill, C. W. L., 310, 398*n*, 399*n*, 400*n*, 401*n*
Hill, G. C., 399*n*
Hill, J. S., 381*n*
Hill, T., 386*n*
Hinterhuber, A., 393*n*
Hisich, R. D., 402*n*
Hitt, M. A., 299, 377*n*, 384*n*, 387*n*, 390*n*–392*n*, 395*n*, 400*n*
Hock, C. A., 397*n*
Hodgetts, R. M., 386*n*, 398*n*
Hoechst, 349
Hoerr, J., 393*n*–394*n*
Hof, R. D., 385*n*, 399*n*, 401*n*, 403*n*
Hofer, C. W., 304, 327, 330, 383*n*, 403*n*
Hoffman, J. J., 389*n*, 395*n*
Hoffman, W., 393*n*
Hofstede, G., 256–8, 396*n*
Holden, N., 117
Hollywood Entertainment, 169
Holmes, S., 376*n*, 377*n*, 385*n*, 391*n*
Holstein, W. J., 387*n*, 401*n*
Holt, K., 377*n*
Home Café, 160
Home Depot, 17, 162, 176, 191, 218, 226, 279
Honda Motor, 107, 150, 173, 237, 286
Honeywell, 196
Hoover, 93
Hoover Europe, 145
Hoover, R., 232, 241
Hoover, V. L., 386*n*–387*n*
Hoover's Online Corporate Directory, 94, 355, 365–6

Hopkins, H. D., 387*n*
Hopkins, J., 401*n*
Hopkins, K., 397*n*
Hopkins, S. W., 376*n*
Hopkins, W. E., 376*n*
Hormozi, A. M., 396*n*
Hornsby, J. S., 399*n*, 402*n*
Horovitz, B., 386*n*, 387*n*
Hoskisson, R. E., 378*n*, 390*n*, 400*n*
Hostess Cup Cakes, 178
House, R. J., 380*n*, 396*n*
Hovde, M. A., 388*n*
Hovis, J., 95
Howard, W., 391*n*
Hoy, F., 401*n*
Hoyde, M. A., 391*n*, 403*n*
Hrebiniak, L. G., 393*n*
Huawei Technologies, 302
Huber, G. P., 391*n*
Huellmantel, A. B., 376*n*
Huff, P. I., 404*n*
Huffman, T. R., 390*n*
Huggies, 155
Hunger, J. D., 26, 51, 53, 200, 342, 378*n*, 397*n*, 404*n*
Hunt, M. R., 377*n*
Hunter, L. W., 389*n*
Huse, M., 379*n*
Hussey, D. E., 388*n*, 404*n*
Huston, L., 399*n*
Hwang, P., 398*n*

I2 Technologies, 8
IBM, 21, 23, 49, 80, 84, 92, 103, 110, 119, 150, 158, 176–7, 193, 196, 198–201, 244, 285–6, 295
Ibrahim, N. A., 376*n*, 402*n*
IFI, 332
Ihlwan, M., 385*n*
Illinich, A. Y., 388*n*
Immelt, J., 245
Imrie, R., 404*n*
In Search of Excellence, 283
Inc., 366
Indenburg, P. J., 393*n*
Index of Corporations and Industries, 366
Industry Norms and Key Business Ratios, 366
Industry Survey, 366
Industry Week, 366
Infasource Services, 47
Infogrames, 318
Ingersoll-Rand, 196
Ingram, R. T., 405*n*
Inkpen, A. C., 160, 389*n*
Innovation and Entrepreneurship, 326
Innovator's Dilemma, The, 312
Insinga, R. C., 391*n*
Institute for Scientific Information, 311
Institutional Shareholder Services (ISS), 46
Integra, 308
Intel Corporation, 15, 60, 83, 85–6, 105, 108, 119, 153, 155, 185, 204, 271, 294
Interbrew, 173
Intercontinental Hotels, 201
Internal Revenue Service (IRS), 35
International Electrotechnical Commission (IEC), 277
International Harvester, 225, 278
International Organization for Standardization (ISO), 277
International Specialty Products, 306
International Standards Association, 265
Internet Explorer, 111
Interstate Bakeries, 77, 178
Intira Corporation, 186
Investment Survey, 365
Investor AB, 41
Investor Responsibility Research Center, 47
iPod, 155, 294
Ireland, R. D., 387*n*
Iron City Beer, 158
Irvin, N., II, 383*n*
Isdell, N., 144
Ito, M., 403*n*
Ittner, C. D., 397*n*, 398*n*
Ivancevich, J. M., 397*n*
Iverson, K. F., 262, 396*n*
Ivory, 118
Iwata, E., 383*n*, 399*n*
Izumi, H., 226

J&J, 228
J. D. Edwards, 278
J. P. Morgan Chase & Company, 200
J. Sainsbury, 172
J.D. Edwards, 128
Japanese Industrial Standards Committee (JISC), 277
Jassawalla, A. R., 384*n*, 385*n*
Java-Log, 72
Javidan, M., 384*n*, 396*n*
JCPenney, 161–2, 192
Jenk, J., 387*n*
Jennings, D. F., 392*n*
Jensen, B., 389*n*
Jensen, M. C., 398*n*
Jenster, P. V., 404*n*
Jeong, E., 395*n*
JetBlue Airlines, 3, 89
Jewel, 149
Jobs, S., 49, 121, 223, 294
Johannet, J., 70, 134
John Deere, 75, 191
Johns Hopkins University Institute for Policy Studies, 339
Johns, G., 232
Johns-Manville, 225
Johnson & Johnson, 61–2, 185, 209, 214, 219, 286
Johnson, J., 72
Johnson, J. L., 380*n*
Johnson, J. M., 277
Johnson, R. A., 378*n*, 389*n*, 398*n*, 400*n*
Jonash, R., 399*n*
Jone, P., 294
Jones Surplus, 254
Jones, B., 379*n*
Jones, D., 379*n*, 398*n*
Jones, M., 218
Jones, P., 378*n*
Jordan Industries Inc., 186
Joshi, S., 405*n*
Journal of Business Venturing, 403*n*
Joyce, T., 397*n*
Joyce, W., 377*n*
Joyce, W. F., 393*n*
Judge, T. A., 380*n*–381*n*
Judge, W. O., Jr., 378*n*, 396*n*
June, H., 376*n*
Jung, C., 259
Just Toys, 228

Juttner, U., 384*n*
Kahaner, L., 294, 378*n*
Kahn, J., 318
Kalafut, P. C., 403*n*
Kale, P., 387*n*
Kalnins, A., 384*n*
Kambil, A., 390*n*
Kansas City Southern (KCS), 173
Kant, I., 67–68, 382*n*
Kanter, R. M., 158, 387*n*, 389*n*, 405*n*
Kao, A., 381*n*
Kaplan, N. J., 171
Kaplan, R. S., 389*n*, 397*n*
Kargar, J., 402*n*
Kaske, K., 299
Kassinis, G., 379*n*
Katey, B., 391*n*
Katz, J. P., 378*n*, 398*n*
Katzenberg, J., 51
Kaufman, S. P., 376*n*
Kazanjian, R. K., 394*n*
Kearney, A. T., 172, 215
Keating, B. P., 404*n*
Keating, M. O., 404*n*
Keats, B. W., 377*n*, 384*n*, 395*n*, 402*n*
Keebler, 298
Keels, J. K., 395*n*
Keenan, F., 390*n*
Keirsey Temperament Sorter, 259
Kelleher, H., 49
Keller, J. J., 396*n*
Kelley, B., 391*n*
Kelley, D., 403*n*
Kellogg Company, 190
Kelly, K., 394*n*
Kendrick, T., 383*n*
Kennedy, R. J., 398*n*
Kentucky Fried Chicken, 131
Keogh, J., 382*n*

KeraVision, Inc., 273
Kerr, S., 398*n*
Kerstetter, J., 399*n*
Kerwin, K., 396*n*, 399*n*
Kessler, F. H., 401*n*
Ketchen, D. J. Jr., 383*n*, 386*n*, 387*n*
Kets de Vries, M., 403*n*
KFC, 131, 138, 250
Khan, Z. U., 397*n*
Khanna, P., 380*n*
Khanna, T., 387*n*
Kickul, J., 403*n*
Kids Kab, 327
Kilmann, R. H., 395*n*
Kim, D. J., 386*n*
Kim, H., 394*n*
Kim, L., 172
Kim, W. C., 398*n*
Kimberly-Clark, 155, 185
King, D. R., 388*n*
Kinko's, 167
Kirin, 158
Kirkman, B. L., 390*n*
Kirkpatrick, D., 392*n*
Kirsch, R. J., 398*n*
Kleenex, 118
Klein, H. E., 384*n*
Kleiner, A., 393*n*
Kline, D. M., 385*n*
KLM, 169, 171
Kluger, A. N., 391*n*
Kmart, 161, 176, 225
Knapp, E., 389*n*
Kochhar, R., 390*n*
Kocourek, P. F., 386*n*
Kohl's, 161–2
Kohlberg, L., 65, 68, 382*n*
Kohut, G. F., 382*n*
Koller, T., 389*n*
Kompass International, 366
Kono, T., 388*n*
Konopaske, R., 397*n*
Korbar, T., 395*n*
Korn, H. J., 390*n*
Korn/Ferry International, 38, 42, 47, 243, 378*n*
Korunka, C., 403*n*
Korvette's, 162
Koskisson, R. E., 399*n*
Kotler, P., 118
Kotulic, A. G., 377*n*
Kozlowski, D., 35–6, 45
Kraatz, M. S., 376*n*, 394*n*
Kraft Foods, 235, 354
Kramer, M. R., 59, 381*n*
Krause, A., 270
Krause, I., 311, 401*n*
Kremer, L., 194
Kripalani, M., 302, 392*n*
Krishman, R. A., 405*n*
Krishnan, H., 405*n*
Kroll, M., 378*n*–379*n*, 386*n*, 398*n*
Krug, J. A., 159, 393*n*
Kuczmarski & Associates, 294
Kulatilaka, N., 391*n*
Kumar, K., 382*n*, 405*n*
Kunii, I. M., 381*n*
Kunstler, B., 313
Kuperman, J., 386*n*
Kuratko, D. F., 399*n*, 402*n*
Kurlantzick, J., 381*n*
Kwon, S. W., 381*n*

L. Light, 378*n*
L'Oreal, 286
Labatt, 158
Labich, K., 391*n*
Lademan, J. M., 397*n*
Lafley, A., 193, 293
LaFond, R., 378*n*, 380*n*
Lamont, B. T., 388*n*–389*n*
Lampert, E., 162
Land, E., 223
Lane, H. W., 387*n*
Lane, P. J., 41, 400*n*
Langford, R., 389*n*
Langley, M., 405*n*
Langlley, A., 405*n*
Langowitz, N. S., 400*n*
Larcher, D. F., 379*n*, 397*n*, 398*n*
LaRochelle-Cote, S., 385*n*
Larsen, P. C., 403*n*
Larsen, R., 209
LaserMonks, 339
Lashinsky, A., 398*n*
Lasserre, P., 382*n*
Lau, R. S. M., 377*n*
Lavelle, L., 378*n*, 380*n*, 394*n*, 399*n*, 404*n*
Lavender, L., 404*n*
Lawler, E. E., 385*n*
Lawrence, P. R., 228, 393*n*
Lay's Potato Chips, 292
Leadership Development Center, 244
Lear, 195
Learjet, 170
Leavell, H., 378*n*
Lederman, L. L., 81
Ledford, G. E. Jr., 385*n*
Lee, H., 386*n*, 395*n*
Lee, J., 277, 385*n*, 397*n*
Lee, K. S., 404*n*
Lee, L., 392*n*
Legend, 18
Lehn, K., 397*n*
Lei, D. T., 377*n*, 388*n*, 390*n*, 391*n*, 398*n*
Leiblein, M. J., 388*n*, 391*n*
Lemire, C., 389*n*
Lemon Fresh Comet, 156
Lengnick-Hall, C. A., 400*n*
Lenovo, 18
Lenox, M. J., 390*n*
Leontiades, M., 384*n*
Lere, J. C., 382*n*
Lerner, L. D., 402*n*
Lestoil, 298
Leuchter, M., 395*n*
Leuz, C., 325
Levenson, P. N., 378*n*
Levi Strauss & Company, 259
Levin, I. B., 334, 401*n*
Levin, R. I., 404*n*
Levine, M., 308
Levinthal, D. A., 400*n*
Levy, D., 326
Lewin, A. Y., 377*n*
Lewis, J., 253–4
Lewis, M., 393*n*
Lewis, V. L., 403*n*
LexisNexis, 93
LG Group, 332
Li, K-Q, 160
Li, L., 387*n*, 403*n*
Li, M., 385*n*
Li, S., 64, 382*n*
Li, S. X., 393*n*
Lieberman, D., 51
Lieberman, M. B., 386*n*
Lim, G. H., 403*n*
Lincoln Electric, 88
Lind, B., 389*n*
Lindblad, C., 383*n*
Linn, A., 376*n*
Linneman, R. E., 384*n*
Lionel, 225
Lioukas, S., 376*n*
Lipton, 178
Little, D., 197, 390*n*
Liu, J., 311, 401*n*
Livingston, R., 198
Loarie, T., 273
Locke, E. A., 383*n*, 403*n*
Lockheed Martin, 8, 198
Loeb, W., 210
Loewen Group, 152
Loise, J. K., 393*n*
Lon, H., 402*n*
Long-Term Economic Growth, 365
Lorange, P., 160, 387*n*, 395*n*
Lorenzoni, G., 393*n*
Lorsch, J., 403*n*
Lotus, 295
Love, L. G., 384*n*, 395*n*
Low, J., 397*n*, 403*n*
Lowe's, 162
Lowry, T., 51, 404*n*
Lozeau, D., 405*n*
Lu, J. W., 387*n*
Lubatkin, M. H., 41, 378*n*, 393*n*–394*n*, 396*n*, 400*n*, 402*n*
Lublin, J. S., 395*n*
Lucent, 308
Lucent Technology, 260
Lucier, C., 394*n*

Lueger, M., 403*n*
Luk, D. M., 395*n*
Luke, R. D., 405*n*
Luker, W. A., 377*n*
Lumpkin, G. T., 395*n*
Lussier, R. N., 401*n*, 404*n*
Lutz, B., 209
Lynch, J. G., 389*n*
Lynch, R. P., 387*n*
Lynn, G. S., 399*n*
Lyons, B., 397*n*

MacAvoy, 379*n*
MacDonald, 215
MacDonald, T., 392*n*
MacMillan, I. C., 309
Macy, B., 226
Macy's Department Stores, 225
Maddox, R., 225
Magic Chef, 15
Magnusson, P., 277
Magretta, J., 404*n*
Maheraultl, L., 404*n*
Mahon, J. F., 387*n*
Mahoney, J. T., 388*n*
Maisco Capital Management, 269
Makadok, R., 386*n*
Makhija, A. K., 397*n*
Malekzadeh, A. R., 251, 395*n*
Mallory, G. R., 377*n*
Malmendier, U., 50, 381*n*
Malone, M. S., 385*n*, 399*n*
Manco, Inc., 276
Mandel, M. J., 63
Maney, K., 51, 385*n*
Manikutty, S., 404*n*
Mann, L., 398*n*
Mansfield, E., 400*n*
Manuals on Investment, 365
Maquire, J., 391*n*
March, J. G., 393*n*
Marcoux, A., 390*n*
Maremont, M., 403*n*
Margolis, J. D., 59, 381*n*
Marino, L., 396*n*
Market Research.com (Findex), 93
Markoczy, L., 392*n*
Marlboro, 119, 227
Marriott, 196
Martins, L. L., 385*n*
Mary Kay Corporation, 93
Mascarenhas, B., 386*n*
Massachusetts General Hospital, 349
Massarsky, C., 339
Masterson, S. S., 396*n*
Mathews, J. A., 393*n*
Matlack, C., 376*n*, 392*n*, 393*n*
Matsushita Electric Industrial Corporation, 117, 301
Mattel, 193, 198, 229
Matthews, C. H., 401*n*
MaxiShips software, 198
Maybelline, 77
Mayer, R., 380*n*
Maynard, M. T., 385*n*
Maytag Company, 16, 107, 193
Maytag Corporation, 13, 59, 60, 98, 118, 131, 141, 148, 153, 158, 174, 192, 252, 300, 363, 371, 397
Mazzarol, T., 402*n*
McAlary, S., 398*n*
McCann, J. E. III, 388*n*
McCarthy, M., 51
McCarthy, M., 383*n*
McCoy, Bernard, 339
McDermott, D., 224
McDonald, M. L., 383*n*
McDonald's Restaurants, 61, 77, 88, 119, 138, 197–8, 218, 243
McDonnell Douglas, 2
McDougal, P. P., 403*n*
McDowell, J., 401*n*
McEvily, S. K., 384*n*
McGee, J. E., 384*n*
McGill, M., 388*n*
McGill, R., 404*n*
MCI, 186
McKenna, M. G., 386*n*
McKesson, 259
McKinsey & Co., 47, 122, 179, 181, 243, 255
McLaughlin, C. P., 404*n*
McLeodUSA, 157
McNatt, D. B., 380*n*
McNealy, S., 19
McWhirter, W., 401*n*
McWilliams, A., 381*n*
Mead Corporation, 38
Means, G. C., 41
Medical Foods, 327
Medley, G. J., 404*n*
Medtronic, 38
Mendenhall, M., 395*n*
Menon, A., 383*n*
Menon, K., 394*n*
Mercedes-Benz, 148, 277
Mercer Delta Consulting, 46
Merck & Co., 294
Mercosur, 6, 7, 78, 86
Meredith, G. G., 391*n*
Merlyn, P., 401*n*
Merrill Lynch, 93, 279
Merrill, G. B., 391*n*
Merritt, J., 378*n*, 394*n*
Mesa Airlines, 170
MeshNetworks, Inc., 301
Messerli, A., 197
Metro, 172
Metropolitan Museum of Art, 348
Meyer, G. D., 392*n*
Meyer, H., 381*n*
Mezias, J. M., 387*n*
Michaels, C. E., Jr., 323
Michalisin, M. D., 385*n*
Microsoft Corporation, 15, 49–50, 84, 86, 90, 105, 119, 121, 142, 153–5, 193, 243, 267, 271, 279, 286, 295–98
Microsoft Office, 295
Midamar Corporation, 138, 149
Mike, B., 395*n*
Miles, G., 88, 229, 393*n*
Miles, R. E., 383*n*, 393*n*
Miller Brewing, 173
Miller, C. C., 376*n*, 388*n*, 391*n*
Miller, D., 385*n*, 393*n*, 394*n*
Miller, D. J., 388*n*, 391*n*
Miller, M. C., 402*n*
Miller, S. H., 383*n*, 393*n*
Millstein, 379*n*
Millstone, 159
Minnesota Mining & Manufacturing Company (3M), 197
Minow, N., 378*n*
Mintzberg, H., 18, 20, 209, 403*n*
Miramax Films, 51
Mirvis, P. H., 389*n*
Mishra, A. K., 395*n*
Mishra, K. E., 395*n*
MIT, 199
Mitchell, G., 51
Mitchell, R. K., 382*n*
Mitchell, W., 377*n*
Mitsubishi Motors, 251
Mitsubishi Trading Company, 87
Modelo, 158
Modem Express, 224
Moesel, D. D., 400*n*, 402*n*
Mohrman, S. A., 385*n*
Molnar, M. J., 376*n*
Money, R. B., 389*n*
Monks, R. A. G., 378*n*, 379*n*
Montagno, R. V., 399*n*
Montemazon, E. F., 398*n*
Montgomery Ward, 162, 225
Montgomery, D. B., 386*n*
Monthly Labor Review, 365
Moody's, 46, 94
Moore, G., 122
Moore, J. H., 394*n*
Morgan Motor Car Company, 149
Morone, J. G., 399*n*
Morris, J. R., 389*n*
Morris, M. H., 403*n*
Morrison, A., 402*n*
Morrow, J. L. Jr., 389*n*
Mosakowski, E., 168
Mossville Engine Center, 230
Motley Fool, 399*n*
Motorola, 11, 125, 169, 230, 236, 241, 295, 301, 307
Motorola's Personal Networks Group, 307
Mr. Clean, 294, 298
Mr. Clean AutoDry, 294

Mr. Coffee, 159
Mr. Donut, 190
Mroczkowski, T., 395*n*
Mrs. Fields Cookies, 319
Mugler, J., 403*n*
Muir, N. K., 392*n*
Muirhead, S. A., 381*n*
Mulford, C. L., 402*n*
Muller, J., 385*n*
Mulvey, P. W., 392*n*
Muralidharan, R., 265, 396*n*
Murmann, J. P., 390*n*
Murphy, D., 395*n*
Murray, E. A. Jr., 387*n*
Music Land, 134
My Idea, 312
Myers-Briggs, 259
Mystic, 178

Nacher, T., 399*n*
Nadler, D. A., 378*n*
Naffziger, D. W., 399*n*
NAFTA, 78, 86
Nahavandi, A., 251, 395*n*
Naisbitt, J., 383*n*, 388*n*
Nantucket Nectars, 178
Nardelli, R., 218
Nare, B., 404*n*
Nargundkar, R., 400*n*
NASDAQ, 40, 46–7
Nathan, M., 391*n*
National Association of Corporate Directors, 37
National Car Rental, 239
National Cash Register, 252
National Energy Associates, 319
National Federation of Independent Business, 329
National Organization for Women, 248
National Science Foundation, 317
Naunus, B., 380*n*
Nayak, P. R., 400*n*
Naylor, J., 393*n*
Nayyar, P. R., 399*n*
NCR Corporation, 125, 252
Neale, M. R., 399*n*
NECX, 8
Neff, T. J., 379*n*–380*n*
Nemec, C., 379*n*
Neptune, 307
Nerkar, A., 399*n*
Nestea, 178
Nestlé, 127, 235, 286
Netscape, 111, 154, 295, 297
Neubauer, F. F., 378*n*
Neubaum, D. O., 379*n*
New Balance, 83
New York and Presbyterian Hospitals Health Care System, 349
New York Hospital-Cornell Medical Center, 349
New York Stock Exchange, 40, 45, 46, 47
Newbury Comics, Inc., 70, 134, 212, 288
Newman, W. H., 344–5, 386*n*, 405*n*
Newport News Shipbuilding, 13
Ng, D., 404*n*
Nicholls-Nixon, C. L., 400*n*
Nickelodeon, 149
Nickerson, J. A., 376*n*
Nicolaes, J., 403*n*
Niehoff, B. P., 378*n*
Nielsen, R. P., 348, 405*n*
Nijssen, E. J., 379*n*, 397*n*
Nike, Inc., 6, 61, 83, 148, 164, 192, 229, 243
Nissan Motor Company, 173, 251
NiteBite, 327
Nixon, R. D., 395*n*
Nobel, R., 399*n*
Nohgria, N., 377*n*, 400*n*
Nokia, 119, 286
Noorda, R., 161
Nord, W. R., 376*n*, 392*n*
Nordstrom, 116, 208
Norr, H., 388*n*
Norris, D., 149
Nortel Networks, 312
North American Free Trade Agreement (NAFTA), 6, 7
Northwest Airlines, 42, 169, 171
Norton, D. P., 131, 389*n*, 397*n*
Novak, R. S., 390*n*
Novell, 161
Noxell Corporation, 166
Noxzema, 166
Nucor Corporation, 262
Nuemo, P., 400*n*
Nutrasweet, 85
Nutt, P. C., 386*n*

O'Boyle, T. F., 400*n*
O'Neill, H. M., 378*n*, 389*n*, 391*n*, 404*n*
O'Regan, N., 376*n*
O'Reilly, B., 385*n*, 393*n*, 395*n*
O'Reilly, C. A., III, 400*n*
Ocasio, W., 394*n*
Oddou, G., 395*n*
Oden, H. W., 305
Ogden, D., 394*n*
Oghe, H., 378*n*
Ohio Public Employees Retirement System, 51
Ohmae, K., 79, 297, 383*n*
Oil of Olay, 166
Oldham, G. R., 232
Oleck, J., 381*n*
Olive Garden, 88
Oliver, C., 379*n*
Olivetti, 181
Ollinger, M., 392*n*
Olson, B. J., 377*n*
Olson, E. M., 390*n*, 392*n*, 401*n*
Open Standards Benchmarking Collaborative, 276
Oracle Corporation, 105, 138, 166, 222, 278
Orbitz, 47
Orion Pictures, 225
Orlitzky, M. F. L., 381*n*
Osborne, J. D., 383*n*
Oster, S. M., 390*n*
Osterveld, J., 400*n*
Ouchi, W. G., 396*n*
Overseas Business Reports, 366
Overstreet, G. A., 404*n*
Owens, M., 348
Owens-Corning, 279

P. F. Chang's, 151
Paikeday, T., 326
Palich, L. E., 388*n*
Palm Pilot, 155
Palmer, T. B., 391*n*
Palo Alto Research Center (PARC), 121
Pampers, 155
Pan Am Building, 201
Pan American Airlines, 225
Pan, Y., 386*n*
Panasonic, 117
Panda Restaurant Group, 151
Paper, D., 393*n*
Paramount Pictures, 51
Pare, T. P., 397*n*
Parish, W., 319
Park, A., 384*n*
Park, D., 392*n*
Park, N. K., 387*n*
Park, S. H., 64, 382*n*, 387*n*
Parkinson, D., 76
Parnell, J. A., 377*n*, 394*n*, 402*n*
Pascarella, P., 122, 385*n*
Pasternack, B. A., 376*n*
Patel, 65
Patterson, M. L., 300
Paulson, A. S., 399*n*
Pearce, J. A. II, 378*n*, 384*n*, 389*n*, 402*n*
Pearson, J. N., 402*n*
Peel, M. J., 376*n*
Pegels, C. C., 383*n*
Pekar, P. Jr., 376*n*
Pelino, D., 244
Penenberg, A. L., 383*n*
Peng, M. W., 378*n*
Pennings, J. M., 389*n*
Pennington, A., 329
Pentium, 204
Pentland, B. T., 392*n*
Penttila, C., 404*n*–405*n*
PeopleSoft, 128, 166, 278
Pepper, J., 92
Pepsi Cola, 118, 178, 292
PepsiCo, 49, 243, 250, 276, 292, 359
Perkins, J., 388*n*

Perkins, K., 43
Perry, S. C., 402*n*
Peter Brabeck-Letmathe, 235
Peteraf, M. A., 384*n*
Peters, 283
Peters, T. J., 398*n*
Pettit, R. R., 388*n*
Petty, J. W., 403*n*
Petty, K., 404*n*
Peugeot Citroen, 332
Pfeffer, J., 404*n*
Pfeifer, S., 404*n*
Pfizer, 38, 243
Pharmacia AB, 258
Pharmacia Upjohn, 121
Phatak, A. V., 398*n*
Phelps, C., 386*n*
Philip Morris, 173
Philip's, 107
Phillips, S. J., 402*n*
Pine, B. J., 385*n*
Pineda, R. C., 402*n*
Pirates of Silicon Valley, 121
Pitcher, P., 380*n*
Pitt, D., 382*n*
Pittiglio Rabin Todd & McGrath, 311
Pitts, R. A., 377*n*
Pitts, R. A., 395*n*
Pittsburgh Brewing Company, 158
Pizza Hut, 138, 151, 250
Plato, 208
Pohang Iron & Steel Company, LTD. (POSCO), 42
Point, S., 385*n*
Pointer, D. D., 405*n*
Poirier, C. C., 386*n*
Poison, Inc., 139
Pojman, L. P., 382*n*
Polanyi, M., 384*n*
Polaroid Corporation, 201, 223, 270
Polek, D., 391*n*
Political Risk Forecasts, 87
Political System Stability Index, 87
Pollock, T. G., 398*n*
Pontiac, 115
Poole, D., 381*n*
Poon, J. M. L., 398*n*
Pope, J., 386*n*
Porac, J. R., 398*n*
Porrini, P., 175, 389*n*
Port, O., 390*n*, 401*n*
Porter, M. E., 59, 72, 82–5, 87, 95, 101, 107, 113, 145, 158, 153–4, 156, 193, 381*n*, 383*n*–384*n*, 386*n*, 388*n*, 390*n*
Post-It Notes, 196–7
Poterba, J. M., 385*n*
Potlach Corporation, 149
Potter, M. J., 379*n*
Pouder, R. W., 379*n*, 391*n*
Powell, T. C., 396*n*
Powell, W. W., 404*n*–405*n*
Power, C., 399*n*
PowerShip, 198
Prahalad, C. K., 234, 383*n*, 384*n*, 399*n*
Preece, S., 381*n*
PricewaterhouseCoopers, 93, 286
Priem, R. L., 382*n*, 392*n*, 395*n*
Probert, J., 382*n*
Procter & Gamble (P&G), 15, 59, 80, 83, 89, 92–3, 108, 112, 119, 129, 149, 155–6, 166, 185, 189–90, 193, 220, 338, 242, 249, 277, 292–3, 297–8, 312
Product and Development Management Association, 298
Project GLOBE, 257
Provan, K. G., 405*n*
Puffer, S. M., 377*n*
Pugliese, D., 383*n*
Puranam, P., 380*n*

Qian, G., 403*n*
Quaker Oats, 178, 270, 359
Quaker Soy Crisps, 292
Quinn, J. B., 20, 199, 377*n*, 391*n*, 403*n*
Qwest, 36, 46, 157

Rabello, K., 403*n*
Radebaugh, L. H., 398*n*
Radiata, Inc., 167
Rahim, A., 403*n*
Raia, C., 303, 400*n*
Rajagopalan, N., 394*n*
Rajan, M. V., 397*n*
Ramaprasad, A., 383*n*
Ramasswamy, K., 388*n*, 394*n*
Ramirez, G. G., 380*n*
Ranft, A. L., 378*n*
Rangan, V. K., 347, 405*n*
Rao, S. S., 397*n*
Rappaport, A., 390*n*, 399*n*
Rasheed, A. M. A., 377*n*
Raymond, L., 393*n*
Raynor, M., 79
Raytheon, 273
Rechner, P. L., 381*n*, 392*n*
Redmond, W., 390*n*
Reebok International, 6, 66, 83, 229, 237
Reed, S., 392*n*
Reeves, M., 385*n*
Register of American Manufacturers, 366
Register of Corporations, 365
Reichert, A., 389*n*
Reimann, B. C., 389*n*
Reinemund, S., 49, 292
Reinhardt, A., 385*n*, 392*n*
Renault, 251
Renshaw, A. A., 217, 392*n*
Reputation Institute, 286
Research Health Services, 349
Research In Motion, 336
Reuer, J. J., 388*n*
Reynolds, P. D., 386*n*, 403*n*
Rhee, D. K., 386*n*
Richard, O. C., 391*n*
Richardson, J., 390*n*
Richardson, S. A., 378*n*, 379*n*
Richardson-Vicks, 166
Ricklefs, R., 403*n*
Rigby, D., 376*n*
Ring, P. S., 168
Rite Aid, 162
Rivard, S., 393*n*
River Rouge plant, 167
Rivkin, J. W., 387*n*
RJR Nabisco, 271
Ro, Y., 42
Roadway Logistics, 196
Robbins, D. K., 389*n*
Robbins, S. M., 398*n*
Roberson, B., 377*n*
Robert Morris Associates, 358
Robert, M., 400*n*
Roberts, B., 47
Roberts, D., 277, 388*n*
Roberts, P. W., 385*n*
Roberts-Witt, S., 390*n*
Robinson, G., 391*n*
Robinson, K. C., 403*n*
Robinson, R. B., Jr., 402*n*–403*n*
Robinson, W. T., 400*n*
Robustion Products, Inc., 72
Rockwell Aerospace, 2
Roddick, A., 49
Rodriques, A. F., 398*n*
Rogas, E., 308
Rogers, E. M., 306, 400*n*
Rollins, K., 105
Rolm and Haas, 38
Roman Catholic Church, 207
Roman, M., 381*n*
Romanelli, E., 377*n*
Rosen, B., 385*n*, 390*n*
Rosenberger, J., 391*n*
Rosenblum, D., 389*n*
Rosenkopf, L., 399*n*
Rosenkrans, W. A. Jr., 103, 384*n*
Ross, D., 239
Ross, J., 392*n*
Roth, K., 381*n*, 395*n*
Rothaermel, F. T., 399*n*
Rothman, H., 397*n*
Rothschild, W. E., 394*n*
Rousseau, D. M., 385*n*
Rovitt, S., 389*n*
Rowe, D., 401*n*
Rowe, W. G., 396*n*
Rowley, I., 399*n*
Rowley, T. J., 393*n*
Roy, M. H., 400*n*
Royal Dutch Shell, 96, 168
RSD, 158
Rubbermaid, 89, 96, 276, 292

Ruckert, R. W., 401*n*
Rudney, G., 404*n*
Rue, L. W., 376*n*, 402*n*
Ruefli, T. W., 376*n*
Ruffles, 292
Rumelt, R. P., 382*n*, 387*n*
Rushlo, M., 386*n*
Russo, M. V., 381*n*
Rynes, S. L., 381*n*, 385*n*

S. S. Kresge, 162
SABMiller, 173
Sabritas, 292
Sabritones, 292
Safeguard, 277
Safeway, 149
Safieddine, A., 390*n*
Sager, I., 177, 379*n*, 380*n*, 381*n*
Salancik, G. R., 404*n*
Samson, D., 398*n*
Samsung, 332
Sanchez, C. M., 394*n*
Sanchez, J. I., 395*n*
Sanchez, R., 385*n*
Sandberg, W. R., 327, 330, 392*n*, 403*n*
Sanders, W. G., 398*n*
Sanford C. Bernstein & Company, 292
SAP AG, 128, 278
Sapet, C., 318
Sapienza, H. J., 392*n*
Sara Lee Corporation, 190
Sarason, Y., 237
Sarbanes-Oxley Act, 46, 324
Sargent, R., 14
Sashittall, H. C., 384*n*, 385*n*
Saturn, 115
Savage, R., 283
Sayles, L. R., 401*n*
Saxton, M. J., 395*n*
Saxton, T., 388*n*
SBC Communications, 43
Sbrollini, M., 72
Scamehorn, R. C., 376*n*
Scheim, E. H., 385*n*
Schelhardt, T. D., 397*n*
Schendel, D. E., 382*n*–383*n*, 387*n*
Scherreik, S., 390*n*
Schiller, Z., 387*n*
Schilling, M. A., 310, 393*n*, 399*n*, 401*n*
Schine, E., 398*n*
Schlange, L. E., 384*n*
Schlereth, J., 393*n*
Schlit, H., 354
Schlitz Brewing Company, 40
Schlosser, J., 383*n*
Schlosser, R., 393*n*
Schmidt, D. R., 398*n*
Schmidt, F. L., 381*n*
Schmidt, J. A., 264
Schneider, A., 389*n*
Schoenecker, T. S., 386*n*
Schomburg, A., 386*n*
Schonberger, R. J., 396*n*
Schonfeld, E., 269
Schoorman, F. D., 41, 380*n*
Schroeder, M., 401*n*
Schroeder, R. G., 390*n*
Schultze, W. S., 378*n*, 402*n*
Schwartz, K. B., 394*n*
Schwartz, M., 400*n*
Schweiger, D. M., 392*n*, 393*n*, 396*n*
Schwenk, C. R., 392*n*, 401*n*
Scotch tape, 196
Scott Paper, 185
Scott, L., 389*n*
Scott, S. G., 401*n*
Seaman, S. L., 392*n*
Sears Holdings Corporation, 162
Sears Roebuck, 77, 91, 151, 176, 219, 226, 244
Securities and Exchange Commission (SEC), 40, 46, 325, 366
Seeger, J. A., 402*n*
Segil, L., 160, 387*n*
Seidel, M. L., 379*n*
Seidenberg, Ivan, 50
Seiko, 298
Selden, L., 389*n*
Senge, P. M., 377*n*
Serer, A., 387*n*
Serpa, R., 395*n*
Service Corporation International, 38, 152
Serwer, A., 384*n*
Seth, A., 388*n*
Sexton, D. L., 318, 402*n*
Shaffer, M. A., 395*n*
Shamsie, J., 385*n*, 386*n*, 394*n*
Shane, S., 402*n*
Shank, J. K., 397*n*
Shapiro, D. L., 390*n*
Sharer, K., 301
Sharfman, M. P., 378*n*
Sharif, M. F., 397*n*
Sharma, A., 389*n*
Sharpe, R., 395*n*
Shaver, J. M., 377*n*, 384*n*
Shaw, J. D., 398*n*
Shea, C., 56
Shearson, 252
Sheehan, C., 387*n*
Shen, W., 380*n*, 394*n*
Shenkir, W. G., 397*n*
Shepherd, D., 403*n*
Sheppard, J. P., 379*n*
Sherman, H., 379*n*
Shiefer, A., 382*n*
Shook, C. L., 395*n*
Shrader, C. B., 402*n*
Shrader, R. C., 403*n*
Shuman, J. C., 329, 402*n*
Sidhu, J. S., 377*n*
Siegel, D., 381*n*
Siemens AG, 117, 159, 169, 299
Siesfeld, T., 397*n*
Signal Companies, 166
Silicon Valley, 107–8
Silva, M., 400*n*
Silverman, B. S., 376*n*
Simerly, R. L., 385*n*
Simmonds, P. G., 388*n*
Simon, H. A., 377*n*
Simon, J. G., 404*n*
Simon, M., 403*n*
Simpson Industries, 178
Singapore Airlines, 286
Singer-Loomis, 259
Singh, H., 387*n*
Singh, V., 385*n*
Sinha, D. K., 389*n*, 391*n*
Sinha, K. K., 390*n*
Sirkin, H. L., 399*n*
Sirower, M. L., 389*n*, 390*n*
Sjogren, B., 400*n*
60 Minutes, 277
Skaggs, B. C., 390*n*
Skloot, E., 349, 405*n*
Skyrme, D. J., 397*n*
Slater, R. W., 398*n*
Slater, S. F., 390*n*, 392*n*
Sloan, A. P. Jr., 207, 220, 392*n*
Slocum, J. W., Jr., 377*n*, 388*n*, 395*n*, 398*n*
Smart, T., 387*n*, 391*n*
Smircich, L., 385*n*
Smith, A. C., 380*n*, 405*n*
Smith, G., 383*n*, 388*n*, 398*n*
Smith, J. A., 377*n*, 382*n*
Smith, K. G., 376*n*, 383*n*, 386*n*, 394*n*, 403*n*
Smith, M., 394*n*
Smith, M. F., 397*n*
Smith, R. D., 385*n*
Smithfield Foods, 167–169
Snapple, 178
Snow, C. C., 88, 229, 383*n*, 386*n*–387*n*, 393*n*, 398*n*
SoBe Beverages, 292
Society of Competitive Intelligence Professionals, 366
Sommerlatte, T., 399*n*
Sonfield, M. C., 404*n*
Song, J., 387*n*
Song, K. P., 388*n*
Song, M., 392*n*
Song, Y. I., 383*n*
Sonnack, M., 399*n*
Sonnenfeld, J. A., 380*n*, 382*n*
Sony, 109–10, 155, 286, 297, 301
Sony Walkman, 295
Soper, B., 397*n*
Sorensen, J. B., 385*n*, 400*n*
Sorking, A. R., 405*n*
South African Breweries (SAB), 142, 144, 173
Southern California Edison, 319

Southwest Airlines, 3, 16, 49, 89, 105, 110, 148, 156, 286, 312
Spanos, Y. E., 376*n*
Spector, P. E., 395*n*
Spekman, R., 53
Spencer Stuart, 42
Sperlich, H., 297
Spreitzer, G. M., 395*n*
Springer, M., 390*n*
Sprint PCS, 192, 270
Sprules, R., 72
SSA, 278
St. Onge, S., 390*n*
Stafford, E. R., 381*n*
Stalk, G., Jr., 400*n*
Standard & Poor, 46, 94, 358
Standard Oil, 219, 244
Standifird, S. S., 385*n*
Stanley Works, 279
Staples, 14, 15, 192, 196–7
Starbucks, 286, 312
Statistical Abstract of the United States, 365
Staw, B. M., 376*n*, 392*n*
Stearns, T. M., 386*n*
Steele, F. L., 402*n*
Steensen, J., 186
Steensma, H. K., 391*n*, 393*n*, 396*n*
Steinway, 155
Stepanek, M., 401*n*
Stephan, J., 390*n*
Sterling, J., 393*n*
Stern Stewart & Company, 270
Stern, G., 395*n*
Stern, S., 383*n*
Stevens, S., 390*n*
Steward, M., 162
Stewart Enterprises, 152
Stewart, G. B., III, 397*n*
Stewart, K. J., 379*n*
Stewart, T. A., 398*n*, 401*n*
Stewart, W. H., Jr., 377*n*, 401*n*
Stipp, D., 403*n*
Stivers, B. P., 397*n*
Stobaugh, R. B., 398*n*
Stofford, J. M., 383*n*
Stonecifer, 2
Stoner, C. R., 395*n*
Stonich, P. J., 398*n*
Strauss, G., 381*n*
Stuart, T. E., 400*n*
Stubbart, C. I., 383*n*
Subramaniam, M., 395*n*
Subramanian, R., 394*n*, 405*n*
Sull, D. N., 377*n*
Sullivan, J., 127
Summers, L. H., 385*n*
Sun Microsystems, 19
Super Size Me, 62
Survey of Current Business, 365
Swartz, M., 35
SWD, Inc., 266
Sweo, R., 377*n*
Swiffer, 312
Symonds, W. C., 377*n*, 378*n*

Taco Bell, 250
Taggart, J. H., 393*n*
Tagiuri, R., 382*n*
Taisei Corporation, 23
Takeishi, A., 391*n*
Tan, H. H., 380*n*
Tan, S. J., 403*n*
Tancredi, J., 306
Tannenbaum, J. A., 386*n*
Tanzer, J., 381*n*
Target, 23, 38, 161–2, 273
Tate, G., 50, 381*n*
Tavakolian, H., 393*n*
Tayles, M., 390*n*
Taylor, A., 239
Taylor, M. S., 396*n*
Teagle Foundation, 349
Technic, 117
Techtronix, 308
Teece, D. J., 382*n*, 387*n*, 389*n*
Teledyne, 270
Tellis, G. J., 386*n*
Teng, B. S., 387*n*
Tenneco, 270
Tennessee Valley Authority, 205
Teradyne, 307
Tergesen, A., 397*n*
Tesco, 172
Tesone, D. V., 396*n*
Tetenbaum, T. J., 395*n*
Texas Gas Resources, 171
Texas Instruments, 38, 306
Textron, 285
Thain, D. H., 221
Thilgen, T., 388*n*
Thomas, A. S., 394*n*, 402*n*
Thomas, H., 383*n*
Thomas, J. B., 382*n*
Thomas, L. G., III, 392*n*
Thomke, S., 399*n*
Thompson, J. D., 404*n*
Thornton, E., 380*n*, 389*n*
Threat, H., 397*n*
3Com, 302
3M Corporation, 16, 38, 196, 231, 235, 292–3, 296, 306, 309
TIAA-CREF, 40
Tide, 83, 277
Tihanyi, L., 378*n*, 380*n*
Timex, 148
Titman, S., 390*n*
Toccacelli, J., 381*n*
Toegel, G., 391*n*
Tomkins, A., 383*n*
Tomlinson, D., 389*n*
Tonge, R., 403*n*
Toombs, L., 378*n*
Toro, 170
Torres, N. L., 329, 401*n*
Toshiba, 159, 169
Tosi, M. L., Jr., 380*n*, 396*n*, 398*n*
Tower Records, 75, 134
Towner, J., 399*n*
Townsend, A. M., 385*n*
Toyota Motor, 119, 129, 150, 173, 186
Toys 'R' Us, 162, 159, 173
TradeMatrix, 8
Trading Process Network, 198
Transmet Corporation, 326
Transportacion Maritma Mexicana, 173
Travis, V. R., 334, 404*n*
Treacy, M., 95, 384*n*
Treece, J. B., 389*n*
Trend Micro, 234
Trevino, L. K., 382*n*
Tricon Global Restaurants, 250
Trips, 302
TRW Systems, 228
Tsang, E. W. K., 318, 377*n*
Tsui, A. S., 387*n*
Tufano, P., 391*n*
Tully, S., 397*n*
Tuna, I., 378*n*
Tung, R. L., 395*n*
Tupperware, 95
Turner, D. B., 381*n*
Turner, L., 36
Turner, T., 49
Tushman, M. L., 377*n*, 400*n*
TWA, 201
Twinkies, 77, 178
Tyco International Ltd., 35–6, 45–6, 63
Tyler, B. B., 392*n*

Ullmann, A. A., 194
Ungson, G. R., 387*n*
UNICEF, 348
Unilever, 189–90, 235
Union Carbide, 196
United Airlines (UAL), 42, 170, 201
United Auto Workers Local 600, 127
United Express, 170
United Parcel Service, 127
U.S. Chamber of Commerce, 93
U.S. Congress, 40
U.S. Department of Defense, 8
U.S. General Accounting Office, 348
U.S. Industrial Outlook, 365
U.S. Internal Revenue Service (IRS), 276, 348
U.S. National Association of College and University Business Officers, 349
U.S. Navy, 281
U.S. Robotics, 224
U.S. Securities and Exchange Commission (SEC), 35, 39, 40, 46, 94, 366
U.S. Small Business Administration, 299, 317, 348
U.S. Steel, 42

United Steel Workers, 126
United Way, 341
University of Southern California, 46
Unterman, I., 404*n*
Upjohn Pharmaceuticals, 258
UPS, 15, 198, 326
Urschel Laboratories, 191
Useem, J., 399*n*, 403*n*
Useem, M., 377*n*
Uzumeri, M. V., 396*n*

Vafeas, N., 379*n*
Vaghefi, M. R., 376*n*
Vaidyanath, D., 387*n*
Valikangas, L., 401*n*
Value Line, 94
Van Alstyne, M., 217, 392*n*
van Brugge, R., 292
Van de Ven, A. H., 168
Van Der Linde, B., 266
van Oijen, A., 389*n*
Van Riel, C., 385*n*
Vanac, M., 405*n*
Varchaver, N., 378*n*
Varian, T., 396*n*
Vedder, R. G., 383*n*
Veiga, J. F., 382*n*, 388*n*, 395*n*
Vella, A. J., 403*n*
Venkatraman, N., 395*n*
Verdier, L., 404*n*
Verdin, P. J., 384*n*
Verizon Communications, 50
Vermeulen, F., 389*n*
Versteeg, A., 385*n*
VerticalNet, 8
Very, P., 395*n*
Veterinary Centers of America, 152
Vibert, C., 384*n*
Vidal Sassoon, 166, 277
Vidal, D. L., 381*n*
Viskny, R. W., 382*n*
Visual Insights, 308
Vogelstein, F., 377*n*
Volberda, H. W., 377*n*, 387*n*
Von Bergen, C. W., 397*n*
Von der Embse, T. J., 382*n*
Von Hippel, E., 296, 383*n*, 399*n*
Vorhies, D. W., 389*n*
Voss, B., 388*n*, 392*n*

W&T Offshore, 47
Waddock, S. A., 381*n*
Wade, J., 403*n*
Wade, J. B., 398*n*
Wagley, R. A., 382*n*
Wagner, J. A., III, 392*n*
Wagner, S., 400*n*
Wagner, T., 225
Wake Forest University, 259
Waldman, D. A., 380*n*, 395*n*
Walgreen Company, 76, 162
Walker, O. C., Jr., 401*n*
Walker, P. L., 397*n*
Walkman, 155, 305
Wall Street Journal Index, 366
Walleck, A. S., 376*n*
Wallender, H. W., III, 344–5, 405*n*
Wal-Mart, 105, 108–10, 129, 148, 151–2, 171–2, 175, 178, 193, 208, 210, 276, 278, 286, 332
Walsh, F., 35, 45, 59
Walsh, J. P., 381*n*
Walston, S. L., 389*n*
Walt Disney Productions, 45, 51, 111, 118, 148, 201, 224
Walters, B. A., 377*n*, 382*n*
Ward, J. L., 402*n*, 404*n*
Waring, G., 392*n*
Warner Brothers, 51
Warner, M., 379*n*
Warner-Lambert, 23
Waterman, R. H., 283, 398*n*
Watkins, S., 63, 65, 382*n*
Watson, W. E., 401*n*
Weaver, K. M., 396*n*, 403*n*
Webb, J., 307
Webber, A. M., 400*n*
Weber, H. R., 378*n*
Weber, J., 388*n*, 404*n*
Weber, Y., 393*n*, 396*n*
WebFountain, 80, 92
Weinstein, H., 51
Weisul, K., 379*n*
Welch, D., 377*n*, 388*n*, 396*n*
Welch, J., 208, 245
Weldon, W., 214
Wells, F., 51
Welsch, H. P., 403*n*
Werle, M. J., 391*n*
Werner, S., 398*n*
West, G. P., III, 392*n*
Westbrook, R., 386*n*
Westhead, P., 402*n*
Westinghouse, 157
Westly, S., 51
Westphal, J. D., 379*n*, 383*n*
Weyerhauser, 112
Wharton School of Business, 293
Wheaties, 56
Wheatley, J., 390*n*
Wheelen, T. L, 26, 51, 200, 319, 322, 323, 342, 378*n*, 379*n*, 404*n*
Wheeling-Pittsburgh Steel, 42, 225
Whirlpool, 38, 107, 153, 194, 198, 270, 279, 300
White, J. B., 398*n*
White, M. A., 395*n*
White, M. C., 394*n*
Whitford, D., 403*n*
Whitman, M., 119, 226, 279, 329
Who Wants to Be a Millionaire, 201
Whyte, G., 392*n*
Wiersema, F., 95, 384*n*
Wiersema, M., 52, 381*n*, 394*n*
Wiggenhorn, W., 377*n*, 394*n*
Wiggins, R. R., 376*n*
Wiklund, J., 403*n*
Wilcox, R. T., 385*n*
Willard, G. E., 401*n*, 403*n*
Williams, J. R., 109, 390*n*
Williams, M. L., 386*n*
Williamson, O. E., 168
Williamson, P. J., 384*n*
Wilson, D. C., 377*n*, 393*n*
Wilson, H. J., III, 390*n*
Wilson, I., 376*n*
Windows, 84, 121, 154
Windows 95, 295
Winfrey, O., 336
Winnebago (RVs), 76
Winter, S. G., 168
Wiseman, R. M., 391*n*
Wisersema, 95
Wissema, H., 383*n*
Wonder Bread, 72, 178
Wong, M., 377*n*
Woo, C. W., 403*n*
Woo, C. Y., 390*n*, 400*n*–401*n*, 403*n*
Woods, T., 164
Woodyard, C., 388*n*
Woolco, 162
Wooldridge, J. R., 398*n*
Word, 83
WordPerfect, 295
World Bank, 318
World Trade Annual, 366
World Trade Organization (WTO), 86, 302
WorldCom, 35, 36, 46, 62, 63
Worrell, D. L., 379*n*
Wortman, M. S., 398*n*
Wright, M., 390*n*
Wright, P. M., 378*n*–379*n*, 386*n*, 396*n*, 398*n*
Wyatt, J., 382*n*
Wymonds, W. C., 378*n*
Wynett, C., 312

Xerox Corporation, 107, 121, 231, 244, 245–6, 275, 308
Xie, J. L., 232
Xin, K., 387*n*

Yamada, K., 399*n*
Yamaha, 155, 277
Yang, B., 383*n*
Yang, D. J., 385*n*
Yankelovich Partners, 355
Yauger, C. C., 405*n*
Yen, H., 382*n*
Yeung, B., 377*n*
Yoder, S. K., 401*n*
Young, C. E., 389*n*
Young, L., 380*n*, 384*n*
Young, M. N., 379*n*

Forward integration, 167
Four-corner exercise, 101
Fragmented industry, 86, 151
Franchising, 173
Free cash flow, 269
Frontal assault, 155
Fuel cells, 75
Functional performance, 273
Functional strategy, 15, 189
Functional structure, 114, 222, 332
Fuzzy logic, 193

GE business screen, 181, 305
Generation Y, 77
Generations, 76
Genetically altered organisms, 75
Geographic-area structure, 235
Global industries, 87, 232
Global issue, 42
Global MNC, 278
Goal conflicts, 345
Goal displacement, 280, 345
Goal, 14
Golden rule, 67
Goods, public, 340
Governance, relation-based, 64
Governance, rule-based, 64
Green-field development, 173
Gross domestic product (GDP), 202, 360
Gross margins, 354
Group, strategic, 88
Growth strategies, 165
Growth, 225
Growth, horizontal, 169
Growth, vertical, 167
Guerrilla warfare, 155
Guidelines, control, 282
Gut feel, 209

Hierarchy of strategy, 15
Hit another home run, 201
Horizontal growth, 169
Horizontal integration, 169
Horizontal strategy, 185
House of quality, 310
Hubris, 50
Human assets, 106
Human diversity, 127
Human resource management (HRM) strategy, 31, 197
Hurdle rate, 17
Hypercompetition, 90, 152

Idea, 321, 335
IFAS (Internal Factor Analysis Summary) Table, 129, 369
Imitability, 108
Implementation, 33
Implicit strategies, 15
Incentives, strategic, 283
Income statements, 355–6, 359
Independent business units, 308
Index of R&D effectiveness, 311
Index of sustainable growth, 360
Individual rights approach, 67
Individualism-collectivism, 256
Industry analysis, 73, 343
Industry fragmented, 86
Industry matrix, 91
Industry scenario, 96
Industry structure, 151, 327
Industry value-chain, 112
Industry, 11
Industry, fragmented, 86, 151
Industry, global, 87, 232
Industry, multidomestic, 87, 232
Influence pattern, 343
Information systems (IS), 31
Information systems, strategic, 278
Information systems/technology, 127
Information technology strategy, 198
Innovation, 291
Innovation, open, 193
Innovation, sources, 326
Innovations, successful, 294
Innovations, unsuccessful, 294
Input controls, 265
Inputs, 347
Inside directors, 39
Institution theory, 9
Institutional advantage, 344
Integration, 251
Integration, backward, 167
Integration, forward, 167
Integration, full, 168
Integration, horizontal, 169
Integration, quasi-, 168
Integration, taper, 168
Integration, vertical, 167
Integration manager, 240
Integrator, 240
Intellectual property, 301
Intelligence, competitive, 92
Interest rate, prime, 360
Interlocking directorate, 43
Interlocking directors, direct, 43
Interlocking directors, indirect, 43
Intermittent systems, 123
Internal consistency, 208
Internal environment, 11, 28
Internal strategic factors, 106
International development, stages, 233
International entry options, 171
International strategic alliances, 233
International transfer pricing, 276
Intranet, 128
Intuition, 209
Investment centers, 275
Islamic law, 78
ISO 14000 Series, 265
ISO 9000 Series, 265
Issues priority matrix, 81
Job characteristics model, 231
Job design, 231
Job enlargement, 231, 346
Job enrichment, 231
Job rotation, 231, 245
Job shop, 194
Joint venture, 159, 173
Justice approach, 67
Just-in-time (JIT), 196

Keiretsu, 43
Key performance measures, 272
Key success factors, 91
Knowledge, explicit, 109
Knowledge, tacit, 109

Laissez-faire, 57
Late movers, 154
Law, 66
Lead director, 45
Lead users, 296
Leader, transformational, 49
Leadership, executive, 49
Leading, 240
Leading, international issues, 256
Lean six sigma, 216, 231
Learning organization, 9
Learning process, 18
Legal responsibilities, 57
Levels of moral development, 65
Leverage ratios, 356
Leverage, financial, 120
Leverage, operating, 124
Leveraged buyout, 191
Licensing, 172
Licensing arrangements, 159
Life cycle, organizational, 224
Life cycle, product, 118
Lifestyle company, 331
Line extensions, 189–90
Linkages, 113
Linking pins, 346
Liquidation, 178
Liquidity ratios, 356
Location tactic, 155
Locus of control, 328
Logical incrementalism, 21
Logistics strategy, 196
Logistics, 30
Long-term contracts, 169
Long-term evaluation method, 283
Long-term orientation, 257
Losing hand, 201
Lower cost strategy, 147

Management audits, 273
Management buy outs, 191
Management by objectives (MBO), 254, 257
Management contracts, 174
Management development, 243
Management, top, 27, 48

Managing technology and innovation, 291
Manufacturing resource planning (MRP II), 194
Manufacturing strategy, 194
Manufacturing, flexible, 125
Market development, 190
Market location tactic, 155
Market position, 118
Market research, 297
Market segmentation, 118
Market value added (MVA), 271
Marketing, 28, 117
Marketing mix, 118
Marketing strategy, 190
Masculinity-femininity, 256
Mass customization, 125, 195
Mass-production, 194
Matrix of change, 216
Matrix structure, phases, 228
Matrix structure, 226
Matrix, outsourcing, 200
Matrix, product/market evolution, 305
Matrix, TOWS, 144
Maturity, 225
Measures of performance, 268
Measures, key performance, 272
Measuring performance, 263
Measuring performance, problems, 279
Merger, 166, 349
Micro new ventures department, 308
Mindshare, 269
Mission statement, 13, 25, 294, 344
Mission, 12, 143, 347
MNC, global, 278
MNC, multidomestic, 278
Model, business, 110
Modem, 224
Modular manufacturing, 195
Moore's law, 122
Moral development levels, 65
Moral relativism, 65
Morality, 66
Multidomestic industries, 87, 232
Multinational corporation (MNC), 78, 232, 278, 359
Multiple sourcing, 195
Multipoint competition, 185
Mutual exclusivity, 208
Mutual service consortium, 158
MUUs (monthly unique users), 269

Need for achievement, 328
Need for control, 329
Net income, 354
Net present value (NPV), 205
Network structure, 228
New entrants, 83
New product business department, 307
New product experimentation, 297
New product development stages, 305
New venture division, 308
New venture, guidelines, 330
Niche, market, 142, 328
Niche, propitious, 142
No change strategy, 176
Not-for-profit organizations, 340
Not-for-profit strategies, 347

Objectives, 14, 143
Offensive tactic, 155
Open innovation, 193
Operating budgets, 274
Operating cash flow, 269
Operating leverage, 124
Operation, turnkey, 174
Operations, 30, 123
Operations strategy, 193
Opportunity, 321, 329, 335
Options, real, 205
Orchestrator, 306
Organization slack, 166
Organizational analysis, 106
Organizational assets, 106
Organizational learning, 9
Organizational learning theory, 9
Organizational life cycle, 224
Organizational routines, 218
Organizational structures, 114, 226
Other stakeholders, 86
Output controls, 265
Outputs, 347
Outside directors, 39
Outsourcing, 169, 198
Outsourcing, disadvantages, 199
Outsourcing, errors, 199
Outsourcing matrix, 200

Parallel sourcing, 196
Parenting, corporate, 165
Part-time workers, 127
Pattern of influence, 343
Pause/proceed-with-caution strategy, 175
Penalties, 346
Penetration pricing, 191
Performance, corporate, 267
Performance, divisional, 273
Performance, functional, 273
Performance, measuring, 263
Performance appraisal system, 244
Performance evaluations, 273
Performance gap, 19
Performance, 18, 263
Periodic statistical reports, 274
Phantom stock, 312
Phases of strategic management, 4
Physical assets, 106
Piggybacking, strategic, 339, 348
Pioneer, 154
Piracy, 277
Planning mode, 21, 320
Policies, 208
Policy, 15
Political strategy, 205
Political-legal forces, 73
Politics, 345
Population ecology, 8
Portable information devices, 75
Portfolio analysis, 165, 179, 305, 343
Portfolio analysis, advantages, 182
Portfolio analysis, limitations, 182
Portfolio matrixes, 305
Posture, strategic, 26
Power distance, 256
Precision farming, 75
Pressure-cooker crisis, 223
Pricing, dynamic, 191
Pricing, penetration, 191
Pricing, skim, 191
Pricing, transfer, 275
Primary activities, 113
Primary stakeholders, 60
Prime interest rate, 360
Private nonprofit corporations, 340
Privatization, 341
Problem children, 180
Procedures, 17, 218
Process innovations, 299
Process R&D, 299
Product champion, 306
Product development, 189–90
Product innovations, 299
Product life cycle, 118
Product R&D, 121, 299
Product/market evolution matrix, 305
Product-group structure, 235
Production sharing, 174
Professional liquidator, 242
Professionalization, 346
Profit centers, 274
Profit maximization, 57
Profit strategy, 176
Profitability ratios, 356
Profit-making firm, 341
Profits, repatriation, 274
Program, 16, 216
Project manager, 228
Property, intellectual, 301
Propitious niche, 142
Prospectors, 89
Public goods, 340
Public governmental units, 340
Pull strategy, 190
Punctuated equilibrium, 18
Purchasing power parity (PPP), 79, 99
Purchasing strategy, 195
Push strategy, 190

Quality of work life, 127
Quality, dimensions, 151
Quasi-integration, 169
Question marks, 180